One of the major transformations in world history during the twentieth century has been the slow shift in the balance of world economic and political power from the Atlantic to the Pacific Rim. Japan has played a key role in spurring this transformation. Once an isolated island society, little known to its neighbors and practically unknown to the West, Japan has emerged today as a leading economic power. The country's rise to a position of international prominence has not been a smooth process, however – it has come only after a period of turmoil and conflict.

This is the first volume to be published in *The Cambridge History of Japan*, the first major collaborative synthesis that presents the current state of knowledge of Japanese history for the English-reading world. Volume 6 provides a general introduction to Japan's history during the first three quarters of the twentieth century, with emphasis on political, economic, social, and intellectual trends. Leading historians have contributed essays, based on recent Western and Japanese scholarship, dealing with the development of domestic politics, particularly the politics of representative institutions, and Japan's relations with the outside world, including its prewar territorial expansion and aggrandizement on the Asian continent. The essays also survey Japan's economic development, describe the changes that took place in the working and farming classes (which until recently constituted the majority of the Japanese population), and assess the ways in which intellectuals viewed these and other long-term social and economic changes.

Although written by specialists, this volume will be an important reference work for general readers as well as scholars and students of modern Japanese history.

# THE CAMBRIDGE HISTORY OF JAPAN

*General editors*

JOHN W. HALL, MARIUS B. JANSEN, MADOKA KANAI, AND DENIS TWITCHETT

## Volume 6
## The Twentieth Century

# THE CAMBRIDGE HISTORY OF JAPAN

## Volume 6
## The Twentieth Century

Edited by
PETER DUUS

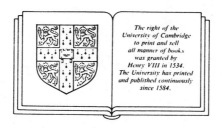

*The right of the University of Cambridge to print and sell all manner of books was granted by Henry VIII in 1534. The University has printed and published continuously since 1584.*

CAMBRIDGE UNIVERSITY PRESS
CAMBRIDGE
NEW YORK PORT CHESTER MELBOURNE SYDNEY

Published by the Press Syndicate of the University of Cambridge
The Pitt Building, Trumpington Street, Cambridge, CB2 1RP
40 West 20th Street, New York, NY 10011, USA
10 Stamford Road, Oakleigh, Melbourne 3166, Australia



First published 1988
Reprinted 1990

Printed in the United States of America

*Library of Congress Cataloging-in-Publication Data*
The Cambridge history of Japan.
Contents: v. 6. The twentieth century / edited by Peter Duus.
1. Japan – History. I. Hall, John Whitney, 1916 –
DS835.C36 1988 952 88-2877

*British Library Cataloguing in Publication Data*
The Cambridge history of Japan.
Vol. 6 : The twentieth century.
1. Japan, to 1987
I. Duus, Peter
952

ISBN 0 521 22357 1 (v. 6)

# GENERAL EDITORS' PREFACE

Since the beginning of this century the Cambridge histories have set a pattern in the English-reading world for multivolume series containing chapters written by specialists under the guidance of volume editors. Plans for a Cambridge history of Japan were begun in the 1970s and completed in 1978. The task was not to be easy. The details of Japanese history are not matters of common knowledge among Western historians. The cultural mode of Japan differs greatly from that of the West, and above all there are the daunting problems of terminology and language. In compensation, however, foreign scholars have been assisted by the remarkable achievements of the Japanese scholars during the last century in recasting their history in modern conceptual and methodological terms.

History has played a major role in Japanese culture and thought, and the Japanese record is long and full. Japan's rulers from ancient times have found legitimacy in tradition, both mythic and historic, and Japan's thinkers have probed for a national morality and system of values in their country's past. The importance of history was also emphasized in the continental cultural influences that entered Japan from early times. Its expression changed as the Japanese consciousness turned to questions of dynastic origin, as it came to reflect Buddhist views of time and reality, and as it sought justification for rule by the samurai estate. By the eighteenth century the successive need to explain the divinity of government, justify the ruler's place through his virtue and compassion, and interpret the flux of political change had resulted in the fashioning of a highly subjective fusion of Shinto, Buddhist, and Confucian norms.

In the nineteenth century the Japanese became familiar with Western forms of historical expression and felt the need to fit their national history into patterns of a larger world history. As the modern Japanese state took its place among other nations, Japanese history faced the task of reconciling a parochial past with a more catholic present. Historians familiarized themselves with European accounts of the course of civilization and described Japan's nineteenth century turn from military to civilian bureaucratic rule under monarchical guidance as part of a larger, worldwide pattern. Buckle, Guizot, Spencer, and then Marx successively provided interpretative schema.

The twentieth-century ideology of the imperial nation state, however, operated to inhibit full play of universalism in historical interpretation. The growth and ideology of the imperial realm required caution on the part of historians, particularly with reference to Japanese origins.

Japan's defeat in World War II brought release from these inhibitions and for a time replaced them with compulsive denunciation of the pretensions of the imperial state. Soon the expansion of higher education brought changes in the size and variety of the Japanese scholarly world. Historical inquiry was now free to range widely. A new opening to the West brought lively interest in historical expressions in the West, and a historical profession that had become cautiously and expertly positivist began to rethink its material in terms of larger patterns.

At just this juncture the serious study of Japanese history began in the West. Before World War II the only distinguished general survey of Japanese history in English was G. B. Sansom's *Japan: A Short Cultural History*, first published in 1931 and still in print. English and American students of Japan, many trained in wartime language programs, were soon able to travel to Japan for study and participation with Japanese scholars in cooperative projects. International conferences and symposia produced volumes of essays that served as benchmarks of intellectual focus and technical advance. Within Japan itself an outpouring of historical scholarship, popular publishing, and historical romance heightened the historical consciousness of a nation aware of the dramatic changes of which it was witness.

In 1978 plans were adopted to produce this series on Japanese history as a way of taking stock of what has been learned. The present generation of Western historians can draw upon the solid foundations of the modern Japanese historical profession. The decision to limit the enterprise to six volumes meant that topics such as the history of art and literature, aspects of economics and technology and science, and the riches of local history would have to be left out. They too have been the beneficiaries of vigorous study and publication in Japan and in the Western world.

Multivolume series have appeared many times in Japanese since the beginning of the century, but until the 1960s the number of professionally trained historians of Japan in the Western world was too small to sustain such an enterprise. Although that number has grown, the general editors have thought it best to draw on Japanese specialists for contributions in areas where they retain a clear authority. In such cases the act of translation itself involves a form of editorial cooperation that requires the skills of a trained historian whose name deserves acknowledgment.

The primary objective of the present series is to put before the English-reading audience as complete a record of Japanese history as possible. But the Japanese case attracts our attention for other reasons as well. To some it has seemed that the more we have come to know about Japan the more we are drawn to the apparent similarities with Western history. The long continuous course of Japan's historical record has tempted historians to look for resemblances between its patterns of political and social organization and those of the West. The rapid emergence of Japan's modern nation state has occupied the attention of comparative historians, both Japanese and Western. On the other hand, specialists are inclined to point out the dangers of being misled by seeming parallels.

The striking advances in our knowledge of Japan's past will continue and accelerate. Western historians of this great and complex subject will continue to grapple with it, and they must as Japan's world role becomes more prominent. The need for greater and deeper understanding of Japan will continue to be evident. Japanese history belongs to the world, not only as a right and necessity but also as a subject of compelling interest.

JOHN W. HALL
MARIUS B. JANSEN
MADOKA KANAI
DENIS TWITCHETT

# CONTENTS

# MAPS, FIGURES, AND TABLES

## MAPS



## FIGURES



## TABLES

# PREFACE TO VOLUME 6

The twentieth century poses a problem for the historian. The actors on the historical stage are in the midst of an ongoing drama, and our observation of this drama, to say nothing of our understanding of it, is also in flux. Research on the history of twentieth-century Japan, much of it in the social sciences, seems to be expanding at an almost exponential rate. The study of the Japanese economy alone has become a major academic cottage industry in the past decade, engaging specialists both inside and outside the field of Japanese studies. By its very nature, then, a volume of this sort, concentrating on the twentieth century, is an exercise in obsolescence. Like the later volumes of the first Lord Acton's *Cambridge Modern History,* this volume is the most likely among those of the *Cambridge History of Japan* to require early revision.

Given this reality, it seemed wiser to plan the volume as a discursive guide to twentieth-century Japan than as a complete Baedeker with each site and vista along the way properly noted and catalogued. For example, there is less space, and hence less detail of coverage, devoted to political and diplomatic history than there might have been. But as there are many excellent monographs in English on these subjects, readers will not have trouble filling in the obvious gaps in the record. It may be more difficult for them to find succinct accounts of other subjects, particularly in economic, social, and intellectual history, and hence the contents err in their favor.

The volume is divided into four main sections: The first provides a general guide to the development of domestic politics, particularly the politics of representative institutions; the second deals with external relations, with the most emphasis on Japan's territorial expansion and aggrandizement on the Asian continent, as well as the consequences that flowed therefrom; the third section provides an overview of economic development during the twentieth century; and the final section deals with changes in the working and farming classes, which constituted the majority of the Japanese population until recently, as well as the conceptual or theoretical lenses through which intellectuals viewed these and other long-term changes. Clearly, much has been left out of this volume, not the least of which is a comprehensive treatment of changes in education, higher culture, the fine arts, and literature. But time is short, history long, and such truncation inevitable.

This volume uses conventional romanization for Japanese and Korean terms, but it stands by the old Wade–Giles system of romanization for Chinese terms. Because many scholars in Chinese studies now prefer to use the pinyin system, this practice may appear retrograde, if not outright imperialistic. However, most Japan specialists have not yet caught on to the new system, and hence all six volumes of the *Cambridge History of Japan* will rely on the old one. An alternative would have been to provide both Wade–Giles and pinyin romanization, but that seemed unnecessarily cumbersome. Chinese studies scholars offended by reliance on the Wade–Giles system should remember that it is also being used in the *Cambridge History of China*. Throughout the text, values expressed in billions are in American billions.

References mentioned in the footnotes or in the source notes of tables and charts will be found in the list of Works Cited at the end of the volume. The list comprises most major works in English on modern Japanese history.

We wish to thank the Japan Foundation for grants that covered costs of manuscript fees, translation of chapters by Japanese contributors, editorial expenses, and meetings.

PETER DUUS

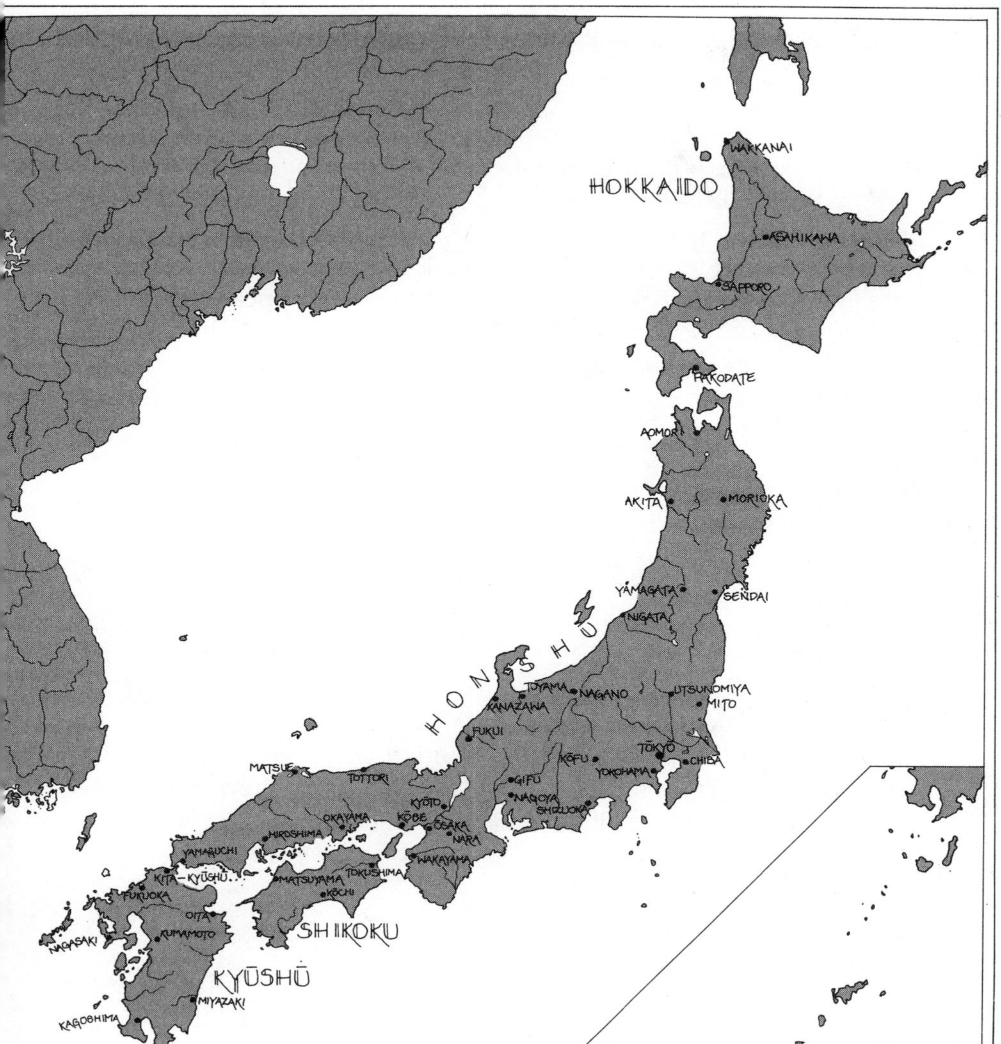


Map of modern Japan

# CHAPTER 1

# INTRODUCTION

Writers of contemporary history face a curious paradox. Because they have lived through the period they describe, they should have an easy time writing about it. But in fact, the contemporary historians' task is far more intractable than is that of the medievalists who have no direct experience of the world they study. The medievalists' task is made easy by the fact that moth and rust have destroyed much of the evidence for their period. By contrast, evidence at the contemporary historians' disposal is, for all practical purposes, limitless. For every volume of *Kamakura ibun,* for example, there are shelf miles of official papers, private papers, books, periodicals, photographs, and films documenting even a single year of the twentieth century. This embarrassment of riches provides contemporary historians with an amount of material that the medievalists cannot hope for even in their wildest dreams, yet this abundance limits what contemporary historians can confidently understand in a lifetime. Contemporary historians can explore a narrow problem definitively in a way that medievalists cannot, but they have more difficulty grasping the larger context of that problem.

In a sense, contemporary historians know too much but understand too little. Although the medievalists may never really be sure how Minamoto Yoritomo died, they can have few doubts about Yoritomo's place in history. On the other hand, even though the health and political problems of a contemporary politician like Tanaka Kakuei are chronicled in the daily press, the contemporary historians cannot be entirely confident about their assessment of Tanaka, if only because he is still alive and his biography not yet complete. The contemporary historians' difficulties in finding the proper purchase on the history they study were aptly summarized by Geoffrey Barraclough:

> The very notion of contemporary history, it has been maintained, is a contradiction in terms. Before we can adopt a historical point of view we must stand at a certain distance from the happenings we are investigating. It is hard enough at all times to "disengage" ourselves and look at the past dispassion-

ately and with the critical eye of the historian. Is it possible at all in the case of events which bear so closely upon our own lives?[1]

Contemporary historians, like physicians who treat themselves, are simultaneously subject and object. Even if they participated only as observers in the events they describe, they are still part of them. The immediate past is likely to have affected their lives in a way that the remote past has not, and the mood of their own time is intertwined with that of the period they are studying. Historians are likely to think about World War II quite differently in 1980 than they did in 1950 or will in 2010 if they live that long. And their change in view will be affected not simply by the discovery of new evidence or a more sophisticated synthesis of monographic studies, as it might be if they were thinking about the Gempei War. Rather, it will have been affected by the passage of time. What has happened since the end of the war will color their perceptions of why it happened and what it meant.

The difficulty of establishing perspectives on contemporary history complicates the problem of periodization. There are obvious historical punctuation points, but the shape of the whole text is not always clear. This volume, for example, deals with "twentieth-century Japan." Twenty-five years ago, historians of Japan might have questioned whether this constituted a coherent historical period at all. Although it probably would have made some sense to see the years from 1895 to 1945 as a chronological unit, unified by the rise and fall of the Japanese empire, what was to be done about the postwar period? How could it have been made to fit with the preceding half-century? Some would have answered: "It does not fit. The Japanese have made a clear break with their militarist and expansionist past. Postwar Japan is a new society, peaceful and democratic, and it is entirely different from prewar Japanese society." Others would have been quick to doubt whether Japan had really changed or whether many of the forces at work in prewar Japan were not still active and influential in the postwar period too. And such historical assessments would have reflected political judgments about the direction of Japan's future rather than a dispassionate attempt to chart the trajectory of Japan's development.

There is a strong and obvious case to be made that the twentieth century is not a coherent historical unit. The year 1945 constitutes a major dividing point in modern Japanese history, second in importance only to 1868. It is easy to see on one side of that divide a

1 Geoffrey Barraclough, *An Introduction to Contemporary History* (Harmondsworth, England: Penguin, 1967), pp. 14–15.

Japan ridden with internal conflict, plagued by economic fluctuations, feared and hated by its Asian neighbors, and locked in a confrontation with the advanced capitalist nations; and on the other side, a Japan unified by a national political and social consensus, enjoying sustained economic growth and affluence, and at harmony with both its Asian neighbors and other capitalist nations. In short, on the one side of that divide is Imperial Japan, and on the other is Japan Incorporated. The contrast, we are aware, is a caricature, but as someone once observed, a caricature often resembles its subject more than a photograph does, for it captures an essence, not a likeness. Certainly, many Japanese would testify to the importance of postwar change. The generation of Japanese alive in 1945 witnessed a dislocation in their own lives, and in that of their society, as radical as any before or since. In 1968, the centennial year of the Meiji Restoration, two out of three persons responding to an *Asahi shinbun* opinion survey considered the Pacific War the most important event in the preceding century – only 14 percent mentioned the Meiji Restoration. Clearly, 1945 will remain for many a decisive turning point in modern Japanese history.[2]

Yet as we enter the final decades of the twentieth century, the dimensions of that divide seem less and less formidable. The continuities between prewar and postwar Japan are clearer than they were in the immediate postwar period. Much contemporary history has been written not by historians but by social scientists, and the hegemonic historical paradigm in most social sciences is an evolutionary model, stressing long-term developmental trends. This model has indeed shaped our understanding of twentieth-century history. To be sure, the model comes in several varieties – that of the Marxists, of the "modernization" theorists, and of the developmental economists – each offering different interpretations of twentieth-century Japan. The Marxist view stresses the growth of a society dominated by monopoly capital, riven by class struggle, and propelled into territorial expansionism before the war, and characterized by neocolonialism and "managerial fascism" after the war. The more bland and less dramatic view of the modernization theorists has seen Japan developing steadily into a secular mass society, increasingly bureaucratic in character, and converging toward a pattern of impersonality and equality in social relations characteristic of Western society. Finally, the developmental economists – who can no longer

2 The survey was conducted in August 1968 and reported in the September 20, 1968, edition of the *Asahi shinbun*. Cited in Akio Watanabe, "Japanese Public Opinion and Foreign Policy, 1964–1973," in *The Foreign Policy of Modern Japan*, ed. Robert A. Scalapino (Berkeley and Los Angeles: University of California Press, 1977), p. 111.

be accused of practicing a "dismal science" – have charted basic continuity in Japan's modern economic growth, interrupted but not broken by the political and military upheavals of the mid-century. All these views, whether optimistic or pessimistic in their assessment of twentieth-century Japan, share the assumption that beneath the surface pattern of change, the historical process is a seamless web spun on an evolutionary loom.

Change and continuity are themes with which contemporary historians must deal more often than do other historians. In broad terms it is possible to see the social, economic, and political patterns that link the Japan of 1980 with that of 1900, yet what gives twentieth-century history its texture are the subtle variations, and the sometimes-not-so-subtle transformations, within those patterns. When to emphasize change – the variations and transformations – and when to emphasize continuity – the overall patterns – is to some degree an arbitrary choice for historians, depending on the scale, duration, and purpose of their project. As the several chapters of this volume indicate, social or economic historians are more likely to argue for continuities than are political or diplomatic historians. Yet the important thing to bear in mind is that either emphasis is likely to yield insight into the overall shape of twentieth-century history.

But where does the twentieth century begin, and where does it end? Collective human behavior, always unruly and unpredictable, is not easy to fit into the tidy compartments we use to mark the passage of time. Periodization is arbitrary, especially when historians are *in medias res*, as contemporary historians always are. Curiously, it is easier to set a terminal date than a beginning date for this volume's coverage. The two "shocks" of 1972–3, the sudden revaluation of the yen and the equally sudden leap of world oil prices, marked the end of the postwar era of rapid economic growth. Although in the long run the Japanese managed to overcome many of the economic and political problems created by these two shocks, it is convenient to set a boundary there.

The beginning is less easy to define. A strong case can be made that the "twentieth century" began well before the turn of the century, in that certain long-term problems and trends that have affected Japan well into the twentieth century were already visible then. Certainly many of the authors of this volume would agree. Professor Crawcour begins his discussion of economic change in the mid-1880s; Professor Peattie begins his discussion of the colonial empire in the mid-1890s;

and Professor Mitani begins his discussion of political parties in the late 1890s. Others have suggested that the 1890s saw a remarkable shift in the mood of Japan.[3]

We shall probably be not too wrong if we adopt 1895 as the beginning of the twentieth century. Whereas the victory over China was a "shock" different from those that Japan experienced in 1972–3, it had a decisive impact on the subsequent history of the country's relations with the outside world. In regard to the economy, the end of the war was also an important turning point. For the first time, many Japanese leaders began to think of Japan as an industrial and commercial nation, not as an agricultural one. The sudden inflow of Chinese indemnity money helped finance Japan's development of heavy industry, especially iron and steel; the indemnity also enabled Japan to shift to the gold standard; the opening of the China market provided an additional stimulus for Japan's textile industry; and the government began to promote more actively the export of Japanese manufactured goods. By 1895 there was no question that an industrial revolution was well under way.

In politics too, the year 1895 marks the beginning of a shift away from rule by the Meiji oligarchs to a new generation of political leaders. In December 1895 the Jiyūtō reached an entente with the Itō cabinet, the first of a series of temporary alliances between oligarchic prime ministers and political parties in the lower house of the Diet during the late 1890s. When Itō Hirobumi resigned from the premiership six years later, he was the last of the Meiji oligarchs to serve in that office. Even though the oligarchs continued to play an important role as *genrō* (elder statesmen), their influence gradually receded during the next two decades. Power passed into the hands of younger leaders drawn from the military, the civil bureaucracy, and the political parties. As we shall see, their authority was narrower and less stable than that of the oligarchs, and the shift that began in 1895 was therefore of considerable significance.

3 As Kenneth Pyle observed, "Somewhere in the terrain of the late 1880s and early 1890s lies a major watershed in modern Japanese history. On one side lies a Japan occupied with domestic reform; a curious, self-critical, uncertain Japan; a Japan still in the making, preparing for the future, impelled by a robust and often naive optimism; above all, an experimental Japan, open to the world, trying new institutions, testing new values, intent on reordering her society and government. On the other side lies a Japan with a renewed sense of order and discipline in her national life; a Japan less tractable, less hospitable to social reform, less tolerant of new values; a self-esteeming Japan, advertising her independence and destiny; above all, a Japan with a heightened sense of her own unity and exclusiveness." Kenneth B. Pyle, *The New Generation in Meiji Japan: Problems of Cultural Identity* (Stanford, Calif.: Stanford University Press, 1969), p. 188.

## JAPAN AND THE OUTSIDE WORLD: FROM AUTONOMY TO DEPENDENCE

Without doubt it is in Japan's relations with the outside world that the most striking historical discontinuities are to be found.[4] The end of World War II looms as a major historical marker. Before 1945 the leaders of Japan were consumed by an obsession with national defense and with preserving freedom of action in international affairs. Although they cooperated with other world powers through alliances or treaties, they did not wish to be subordinate to or dependent on any foreign nation. The drive for national autonomy began with the drive to end the "unequal treaties" in the 1890s and accelerated in the 1920s and 1930s. By contrast, after 1945, independent action in world politics nearly disappeared as an option for the national leadership, and until the early 1970s, the dependence of Japan on a foreign power, the United States, was palpable and undeniable. No prime minister was willing to take a foreign policy initiative considered contrary to the interests of the United States, and few leaders advocated the creation of a truly autonomous military force able to defend the country without outside support, such as Japan possessed before 1945.

This dramatic shift in Japan's relations with the outside world – from autonomy to dependence – was part of a broader change in that world. At the beginning of the twentieth century, European expansion was at its peak. European colonial domination had been extended over much of the non-Western world; balance-of-power politics in Europe affected the state of politics in the world; and decisions over the fate of hundreds of millions of non-European peoples were made in the European capitals. Just two generations later, the European colonial empires had been toppled and supplanted by complex networks of trade, foreign aid, and security agreements; an international market dominated by European capital, products, and technology had been replaced by one governed by several regional economic systems; and a world in which Europe was the cultural center had become one of enormous cultural diversity. The imperialist order dominated by the nations of the European peninsula had given way to a complex multipolar international system dominated by two great superpowers, the United States and the Soviet Union.

As the first non-Western nation to emerge as a world power, Japan

4 A survey of prewar Japanese foreign policy may be found in Ian Nish, *Japan's Foreign Policy, 1868–1942: Kasumigaseki to Miyakezaka* (London: Routledge & Kegan Paul, 1977).

played a significant but complicated role in bringing about these great changes in the international order.[5] Because it was the only world power to have experienced imperialist intrusion, however briefly, in the late nineteenth century, Japan's prewar foreign policy acquired a peculiar ambivalence. On the one hand, having successfully resisted Western political encroachments and negotiated its way out of the unequal treaty system imposed on the country in the 1850s, Japan served as a model and inspiration to anticolonialist movements in all parts of Asia, even as far away as India. On the other hand, as Japan acquired its own colonial territories in Taiwan, Korea, and southern Sakhalin, established a sphere of influence in southern Manchuria, and enjoyed the privileges of a treaty power in China proper, its leaders came to share the same anxieties, aspirations, and ambitions as those of the Western imperialist nations. (For example, the first international diplomatic gathering attended by Japanese representatives was the Peking Conference of 1900, convened to deal with the settlement of the Boxer Rebellion, an outburst of popular xenophobic antiimperialism.)

These conflicting aspects of Japan's peculiar international position at the turn of the century led its leaders to practice a curious form of antiimperialist imperialism. They could run with the hare or hunt with the hounds, as external circumstance and internal interests dictated. As the first Asian nation to modernize, Japan attracted the interest of anticolonial and antiimperialist political movements throughout Asia. Even before the turn of the century, a handful of would-be reformers in Korea and China looked to Japan for the secrets of national wealth and strength. The Japanese victory over Russia in 1905 made it clear to other non-Western peoples that the Europeans were neither omnipotent nor invincible. It is no accident that during the first decade of the twentieth century, Indochinese anticolonial nationalists like Phan Boi Chau and Chinese nationalist reformers like Liang Ch'i-ch'ao and Sun Yat-sen sought refuge or support in Tokyo, nor is it surprising that Japanese sympathizers tried to encourage them. The Pan-Asianist idea that Japan, as the first successful non-European modernizer, was obligated to assist the uplift of less fortunate neighboring peoples enjoyed wide currency from the beginning of the century onward.[6]

5 Richard Storry, *Japan and the Decline of the West in Asia, 1894–1943* (New York: St. Martin's Press, 1979).

6 For a pioneering work on Japanese Pan-Asianism, see Marius B. Jansen, *The Japanese and Sun Yat-sen* (Cambridge, Mass.: Harvard University Press, 1954). Another informative work is by Joshua A. Fogel, *Politics and Sinology: The Case of Naitō Kōnan (1866–1934)* (Cambridge, Mass.: Harvard University Press, 1984).

But if victory over Russia gave hope to anticolonialist movements around the world, it also intensified the Japanese quest for freedom of action. Japan's acquisition of colonies on the Asian mainland, especially on the Korean peninsula, was intended to reduce Japan's defense vulnerability, but ironically it had the opposite effect of increasing its concerns over national security. As its boundaries of empire expanded, so did its zone of vulnerability. After Japan's triumph over Russia in 1905, the army general staff demanded more manpower to defend the new colonial possessions, and the navy asked for a larger fleet. Far from allaying strategic anxieties, an imperialist foreign policy fed them, and military expenditures continued to grow.

The contradiction between imperialist foreign policy and antiimperialist Pan-Asianist rhetoric became all too apparent during World War I. The withdrawal of Western power prompted Japanese leaders to pursue the country's interests, unconstrained by concern over Western reaction. Japan's declaration of war against Germany licensed the Japanese seizure of the German concessions on the Shantung peninsula as well as its Pacific territories, and the absence of countervailing Western power emboldened new attempts to secure a hegemonic position in China, first through the Twenty-one Demands and then through the Nishihara loans. And at the Versailles conference, the Japanese delegation assiduously protected its newly acquired hold over its Shantung and German Pacific colonies. It thus became increasingly clear to many Asian nationalists that Japan was as much a threat as a model. In 1917 Phan Boi Chau, the Indochinese patriot who had based his anti-French movement in Japan shortly before the Russo-Japanese War, declared that Japan had superseded all the European powers as the most dangerous enemy of Asia and that Japanese policy toward its Asian neighbors – Korea and China – was cut from the same cloth as that of the European colonial powers.[7]

At the beginning of the century the Meiji leaders had accepted the imperialist order as normal, and they had dealt with the European colonial powers within a framework of international law and balance-of-power politics. But their successors in the 1920s and 1930s had to deal with a world in which imperialism was increasingly under attack. Wilsonian internationalism trumpeted the right of national self-determination; Leninist antiimperialism called for the oppressed peoples of the world to light the spark of world revolution; and indigenous

7 Cited in David G. Marr, *Vietnamese Tradition on Trial, 1920–1945* (Berkeley and Los Angeles: University of California Press, 1981), p. 16, n. 2.

nationalism throughout the non-Western world challenged colonial regimes. The post–World War I leadership faced a far different set of policy options than their Meiji predecessors had. It was no longer necessary to accept the old imperialist order and all that came with it.[8]

The first alternative was to follow the lead of the Western powers but to insist that Japan was the paramount regional power in East Asia, with needs and interests that required special recognition or concessions from the European powers. For example, Foreign Minister Shidehara Kijūrō, a pro-Western diplomat who advocated close cooperation with the Anglo-American powers, never lost sight of the fact that Japan needed an independent military capacity and that its interests, particularly in East Asia, did not always jibe with those of the Western powers. The second alternative was to assert that Japan, because of its proximity to East Asia and its growing political and economic interests there, should act with little concern for the attitudes or reactions of the European powers there. The foreign policy of Tanaka Giichi, described by Professor Hata, best represented this alternative. The third alternative was to assert that Japan had a vital historical mission to overturn the existing international status quo, dominated by the European imperialists, and to pave the way for the construction of a new international order based on a new set of moral and political principles. Kita Ikki, for example, called on Japan to raise the "virtuous banner of an Asian league and take the leadership in a world federation which must come."[9]

During the 1920s, Japanese foreign policy shifted back and forth between the first and second alternatives. Hoping to forestall renewed imperialist rivalry in East Asia and fearful of a naval arms race, the Japanese government cooperated with the attempt at the Washington Conference (1921–2) to establish regional collective security arrangements in East Asia. But during the rest of the decade, Japanese leaders periodically asserted their inclination to treat Japan as a regional power with interests in East Asia that overrode the imperative of internationalist cooperation. Covert dabbling in Chinese warlord politics in Peking and in the provinces, as well as Japan's independent position at the Peking Tariff Conference in 1925 and Japan's two Shantung expeditions in the late 1920s, gave notice that Japanese interests were not completely served by multilateral cooperation. The

8 A standard account of the period is by Akira Iriye, *After Imperialism: The Search for a New Order in the Far East, 1931–1941* (Cambridge, Mass.: Harvard University Press, 1965).
9 George M. Wilson, *Radical Nationalist in Japan: Kita Ikki, 1883–1937* (Cambridge, Mass.: Harvard University Press, 1969), chap. 4.

shifts in Japanese foreign policy between cooperation and independence prompted both domestic and foreign observers to characterize it as "dual diplomacy."[10]

After 1931, however, Japanese foreign policy turned toward the third alternative – the assertion of complete autonomy from the other imperialist powers.[11] The occupation of Manchuria by the Kwantung Army, Japan's withdrawal from the League of Nations, the difficulty of reaching an agreement on naval arms limitations at the London Conference, and the increasingly frequent assertion of slogans like "Asia for the Asians" reflected the Japanese leadership's desire to loosen its moorings to the European imperialist camp. Those moorings were finally and irrevocably cut by the unanticipated, though not unwelcome, outbreak of war with Nationalist China in 1937. The Pan-Asianist ideas that had enjoyed currency at the turn of the century acquired new vigor in the notions of a "New Order in East Asia" and the "Greater East Asia Co-Prosperity Sphere." Although both of these visionary conceptions of Japan's historic role in world politics were rationalizations for a policy of expansion already under way, they did reflect a widespread belief that the imperialist order established by the European powers in the nineteenth century had come to an end and that the world system would be reorganized into economically self-contained and politically autonomous supranational regional blocs.[12]

Even though the Japanese were not successful in establishing their Greater East Asia Co-Prosperity Sphere, they did manage to destroy the foundations of European colonial domination throughout East and Southeast Asia. If the European war represented the turning point in the transition from an old world order dominated by the

10 Cf. Akira Iriye, *After Imperialism*. See also Gavan McCormack, *Chang Tso-lin in Northwest China, 1911–1928: China, Japan and the Manchurian Idea* (Stanford, Calif.: Stanford University Press, 1977), pp. 119–26.

11 There are many excellent works on the foreign policy of Japan during this period: James B. Crowley, *Japan's Quest for Autonomy: National Security and Foreign Policy, 1930–1938* (Princeton, N.J.: Princeton University Press, 1966); James W. Morley, ed., *Japan Erupts: The London Naval Conference and the Manchurian Incident, 1928–1932* (New York: Columbia University Press, 1984); James W. Morley, ed., *The China Quagmire: Japan's Expansion on the Asian Continent* (New York: Columbia University Press, 1983); James W. Morley, ed., *Deterrent Diplomacy: Japan, Germany and the USSR, 1935–1940* (New York: Columbia University Press, 1976); and James W. Morley, ed., *The Fateful Choice: Japan's Advance into Southeast Asia, 1939–1941* (New York: Columbia University Press, 1980). The four works edited by Morley are translations from the multivolume series *Taiheiyō sensō e no michi: kaisen gaikōshi* published by the *Asahi shinbun* press in 1962–3.

12 See William Miles Fletcher III, *The Search for a New Order: Intellectuals and Fascism in Prewar Japan* (Chapel Hill: University of North Carolina Press, 1983), chap. 7; Gordon Mark Berger, *Parties Out of Power in Japan, 1931–1941* (Princeton, N.J.: Princeton University Press, 1977), chap. 4.

colonial powers to a new postwar order dominated by the superpowers, a parallel transition was taking place in East Asia under Japan's initiative. Japan's military expansion after 1941 toppled colonial regimes in the Dutch East Indies, Malaya, the Philippines, and eventually French Indochina. The Japanese occupying forces had no difficulty in finding collaborators who saw the Japanese, initially at least, as liberators, and Japan's encouragement of anticolonialist nationalists in Southeast Asia paved the way for the wave of antiimperialist revolutions, civil wars, and liberation movements, successful and unsuccessful, that swept the region after 1945. In China too, the Japanese invasion prompted the European powers to end the last vestiges of the "unequal treaty" system.

With the defeat in 1945, the leaders of Japan found themselves in a new world, under new circumstances that did not admit the possibility of autonomy in diplomatic action. The postwar "new order in East Asia" was quite different from what the prewar leaders had anticipated. First, the destruction of Japan's military capability and the surrender of its colonial empire severely reduced its international status and narrowed its range of action. Second, the prostration of China, which had spurred the development of a "continental policy" since the turn of the century, was at an end, and the country came under a unified regime established by the Chinese Communist Party. Third, the ruthless and brutal policies of Japanese military forces in China and Southeast Asia, to say nothing of its long colonial rule in Korea and Taiwan, left most of its Asian neighbors with hostile feelings toward Japan. Finally, the major Western European powers involved in prewar regional politics, most notably Great Britain, had lost or were losing their influence there, and a new triumvirate of non-European powers – the United States, the Soviet Union, and eventually the People's Republic of China – dominated regional politics. This new configuration radically altered the range of policy alternatives open to Japan and radically reduced its capacity to act as a free agent in international politics, even if its leaders had wanted to.

The postwar leaders, however, no longer conceived of Japan as a great power nor expected that it would play a central role in world politics.[13] Indeed, during the first decade or so following the war, Japan's leaders were at pains to live down the nation's reputation as a disruptive expansionist power. The new constitution ratified by the

13 Cf. John W. Dower, *Empire and Aftermath: Yoshida Shigeru and the Japanese Experience, 1878–1954* (Cambridge, Mass.: Harvard University Press, 1979); Shigeru Yoshida, *The Yoshida Memoirs* (New York: Houghton Mifflin, 1962).

Diet in 1946 renounced Japan's sovereign right to wage war or to maintain a war-making potential, and in the late 1940s some Japanese leaders proposed that Japan remain a weak but neutral power whose security would be protected by some sort of international guarantee by the major powers. Its national self-image had shrunk considerably since the prewar days when the majority of the Japanese public had actively or passively supported expansion, proud that Japan was ranked as a first-class power, with powerful armies and fleets, a prospering overseas empire, and no serious regional rivals. In 1951, toward the end of the American Occupation, a *Yomiuri shinbun* poll found that 47 percent of the respondents responded affirmatively when asked whether they thought Japan was inferior to "civilized countries" like the United States and Great Britain, the bitter enemies of a decade earlier.[14] It is no wonder that some foreign observers concluded the Japanese suffered from a national inferiority complex and that both its leaders and the public saw Japan powerless to choose any course of action in foreign policy that did not involve dependence.

During the immediate postwar years, Japan's first priority was to end the American Occupation and regain formal sovereign independence, and the second was to restore the country to international respectability. After the peace treaty with the United States had been signed in 1951, the debate reopened on the direction of Japan's foreign policy.[15] The range of alternatives, however, was much narrower than in the prewar period, and the assumptions behind the debate were quite different. The sense of threat from the outside, so palpable since the Meiji period, no longer obsessed Japanese leaders or the Japanese public as it once had. Neither was the quest for prestige as a military and diplomatic power a central consideration in foreign policy decisions. Recovery, prosperity, and stability at home were more important than were foreign adventures or high international visibility. At one end of the debate were those who proposed a policy of "true neutrality" of noninvolvement in the international struggle between the two superpowers and their satellites; at the other were conservative leaders who wished to reestablish a more or less independent military capability that would enable Japan to act once again as an international free agent; and in between were those who proposed to become a

14 See Watanabe, "Japanese Public Opinion," p. 119.
15 Donald C. Hellmann, *Japanese Domestic Politics and Foreign Policy: The Peace Agreement with the Soviet Union* (Berkeley and Los Angeles: University of California Press, 1969); George R. Packard III, *Protest in Tokyo: The Security Crisis of 1960* (Princeton, N.J.: Princeton University Press, 1966).

dependent or satellite of one of the superpowers, through either a military alliance with the United States to guarantee Japan's security or a "positive neutrality" that aligned Japan's foreign policy with that of the Soviet Union and its allies.

Given Japan's growing economic linkages with the United States and the presence of American military forces in Japan, the easiest (and most pragmatic) alternative was alignment with the United States. Although Japan's ability to build a first-class military and naval force, including nuclear weaponry, grew as its economy recovered in the 1950s and 1960s, leaders like Yoshida Shigeru, Kishi Nobusuke, and Ikeda Hayato continued to calculate that the best interests of Japan would be served by close ties with the United States. Neutrality held no advantage, and accelerated rearmament would divert resources from economic recovery and growth. During the 1950s and 1960s the Japanese government consciously adopted a "low posture" in relations with the outside world, making the pivot of its foreign policy its economic and security ties to the United States. Indeed, apart from its alignment with the United States, Japan really had no foreign policy except, perhaps, its opposition to nuclear weapons, as expressed in the three "nonnuclear principles" proclaimed by Prime Minister Satō Eisaku in 1968.

What concerned Japanese leaders was making subtle shifts in the relationship that would bring Japan into a less asymmetrical relationship with its superpower mentor. The creation of the National Self-Defense Force and limited rearmament in the 1950s, the revision of the Mutual Security Treaty in 1960, the initiation of regular cabinet-level meetings between representatives of both countries in the early 1960s, and the long drawn-out negotiations over the reversion of Okinawa and the Ryūkyū Islands to Japanese sovereignty in the late 1960s and early 1970s all were directed to this end. As the relative strength of the United States as a world power began to dwindle, an element of "partnership" was introduced into the United States–Japan relationship in the 1960s. Curiously, public support for the alliance, as reflected in public opinion polls, grew stronger, as if to show that the Japanese preferred to be dependent on a weaker than on a strong United States.

The transformation of Japan from a country seeking equality and acceptance by the imperialist powers into a country content under the patronage of a major superpower could not have been predicted at the turn of the century. The Meiji leaders had fought hard to escape the constraints of the unequal treaty system imposed in the 1850s and

1860s, but Yoshida Shigeru had little choice in 1951 but to accept a Mutual Security Treaty that seriously compromised Japan's sovereignty by requiring a kind of "extraterritorial" right for American military personnel to be stationed in Japan and by permitting the country to be used as a base for American military forces over which the Japanese government had no control. The treaty's more egregiously unequal elements were eliminated in 1960, but it was not until 1972 that Okinawa was returned to Japan's sovereign control.[16]

By the early 1970s, Japanese leaders were emboldened to begin asserting some independence in foreign policy. This was made possible by external events over which they had little control. The collapse of the Bretton Woods system of fixed foreign exchange rates cut the yen free from the dollar, and the oil crisis of 1973 brought home the reality that continued economic growth required greater freedom of action in dealing with the producers of essential raw materials and resources. By the mid-1970s, Japanese foreign ministers could speak of "cutting the umbilical cord" binding Japan to the United States or of pursuing an "omnidirectional diplomacy." Much of this new assertion of independence was rhetorical, and there appeared to be little change in the basic assumptions of Japanese foreign policy (let alone the emergence of a coherent global strategy). But in small ways – by independent overtures to the People's Republic of China, by increases in external investment in primary resource developments, by efforts to distance itself from American Middle Eastern policy – the Japanese government moved cautiously toward greater freedom of action. But in no sense did this represent the quest for great-power status that had moved the oligarchs at the turn of the century.

## DOMESTIC ECONOMIC CHANGE: FROM SUCCESS TO SUCCESS

If there has been change and discontinuity in Japan's external relations, the most striking continuity in contemporary Japanese history is its steady growth into one of the largest and most productive industrial economies in the world. In 1900, Japan's industrial revolution was just getting under way, but by 1973 its output of goods and services surpassed that of every advanced market economy except the United States, and its per-capita GNP was higher than that of the United

16 A useful summary of foreign policy discussion in the 1960s is provided in Donald C. Hellmann, *Japan and East Asia: The New International Order* (New York: Praeger, 1972).

Kingdom, the first industrialized nation. Although these facts may seem to argue more for change than for continuity, the phenomenon of change itself has been constant. The curve of growth, sloping more sharply upward as the century unrolled, was unbroken except during the war years, and the economists' statistical extrapolations chart it as a continuous line.

Only in recent decades, however, has the continuity of Japanese economic growth attracted much attention. Even in the mid-1950s, as Japan was about to begin its remarkable spurt of postwar growth, it was still widely regarded as a less developed country, far behind the world's other industrial powers. In 1955 its GNP was one-fifteenth that of the United States and only half that of Germany; its per-capita income ranked thirty-fifth among the capitalist bloc nations; nearly 40 percent of its work force was engaged in agriculture; and it was the second largest borrower from the World Bank. At best Japan appeared to be a third-rate economic power, far behind the Western nations and even weaker than its neighbor China, then undergoing a major push toward industrial growth and economic modernization. In 1957 Edwin O. Reischauer observed, "The economic situation in Japan may be so fundamentally unsound that no policies, no matter how wise, can save her from slow economic starvation and all the concomitant political and social ills that situation would produce."[17] Far from being idiosyncratic, this observation was a mainstream view, shared by foreign and Japanese observers alike.

The origins of such a view are not difficult to discover. It mirrored pessimistic images of the economy pervasive in the prewar period. Whereas the century had begun with a flush of optimism about Japan's economic future, more sober assessments had become commonplace by the 1920s. Orthodox economists, mindful of widespread symptoms of economic slowdown, emphasized Japan's backwardness and vulnerability, and foreign observers often echoed them. In 1930 John E. Orchard noted, "[Japan's] possibilities for industrialization are limited and there seems to be no prospect that Japan can attain a position of major importance as a manufacturing nation. . . . The past has been beset with difficulties; the prospect for the future none too brilliant."[18] The country was poorly endowed with industrial resources like iron ore and coal; its dense and rapidly growing popula-

17 Edwin O. Reischauer, *The United States and Japan*, rev. ed. (New York: Viking Press, 1957), p. 51.

18 John E. Orchard, *Japan's Economic Position: The Progress of Industrialization in Japan* (New York: McGraw-Hill, 1930), pp. 482, 489.

tion was pressing against limited arable-land resources; it faced serious shortages of capital; and it was a latecomer in the struggle for markets – its only assets were cheap labor and proximity to the Asian market. At best it could become a supplier of inexpensive light manufactures to its slightly more backward neighbors. Orchard thought that Japan might be the "forerunner of a new and saner industrial order" based on decentralized small-scale enterprises supplied with abundant electrical power rather than based on the highly concentrated industrial centers characteristic of the West, with all their attendant social evils. Other Western observers expressed alarm at the possibility of Japan's becoming a "yellow industrial peril." During the 1930s it was common for foreigners to view Japan as a vicious competitor, making its way into markets once dominated by the advanced industrial nations, especially Great Britain, by means of "cheap wages" and "social dumping."

Marxist economists and other critical observers in Japan took a more catastrophic view, seeing the economy teetering on the verge of a systemic crisis that would bring the collapse of capitalism in Japan. Japan's problem, they argued, sprang not from poor factor endowments but from basic structural weaknesses. Theorists like Yamada Seitarō pointed out that Japan's economic development had been deformed by the militaristic character of its industrial growth and the existence of a vast poor rural population laboring under semifeudal conditions. Other Marxists disputed the particulars of Yamada's arguments, but they agreed that the economy was fundamentally flawed. Such views also found a sympathetic Western audience. In her brilliantly polemic *Japan's Feet of Clay* (1937), Freda Utley portrayed the Japanese economy as on the verge of collapse:

> How precarious then is the Japanese national economy. Even in peace time she can only make ends meet by a feverish expansion of cheap manufactures. . . . All this . . . has only been made possible by means of inflation, reduced wages, a shrunken home market, and acute agrarian distress. Japan's export has been a hunger export, a desperate effort to make ends meet, to keep afloat her almost bankrupt national economy. . . . the whole top-heavy economic structure rests on the narrow foundation of a primitive small scale agriculture which is now too weak to bear the great burdens placed upon it and threatens at any moment to crack and bring the whole vast superstructure crashing to the ground.[19]

Despite this structural weakness, or perhaps because of it, Utley concluded, Japan was about to expand overseas.

19 Freda Utley, *Japan's Feet of Clay* (New York: Norton, 1937), pp. 53, 201.

To be sure, even before war broke out in 1941, some observers did not think Japan's economic future so dim, but the wartime destruction encouraged a return to pessimism. The economy's structural "backwardness" – its relatively low per-capita income, the large proportion of the population engaged in agriculture, and the peculiar "dual structure" in which large modern factories existed side by side with flimsy and unstable small workshops – still persisted. Growth during the 1950s was often regarded as anomalous, the product of a catching-up process of economic reconstruction rather than an indicator of stable long-term performance. The persistence of "backward" characteristics made it difficult for many foreign observers to grasp the "economic miracle" in the making.

Breathlessly optimistic assessments of Japan's economic future, and hence a positive evaluation of its economic past, emerged only in the 1960s. This new view was stimulated not only by the emergence of developmental economics as an academic subdiscipline but also by the increasingly impressive performance of the Japanese economy and the growing visibility of Japanese manufacturing exports in the world market. The admission of Japan into the Organization for Economic Cooperation and Development in 1964 marked an "official" recognition of Japan's new economic status, and new modes of comparative econometric analysis revealed that even in the prewar period the economy had neither stagnated nor verged on collapse but in fact had been one of the fastest growing in the world. Statistics were marshaled to show that Japan had enjoyed an extraordinarily high economic growth rate for several generations. Many structural features once labeled as "backward" came to be regarded as the foundation for the ongoing "economic miracle." By the early 1960s, scholars and public officials began to speak of a "Japanese model" of economic growth for "late developing countries" to follow, and by the early 1970s, Japan was being touted as an example for the advanced industrial economies as well. In 1970 Herman Kahn predicted that by the year 2000 Japan would achieve the world's largest GNP and surpass even the United States in industrial productivity and standards of living.[20]

Against this changing perception of Japan's economic development since the turn of the century, it has become easier to discern the long-run patterns of continuity in growth. The concept of "modern eco-

20 Herman Kahn, *The Emerging Japanese Superstate: Challenge and Response* (Englewood Cliffs, N.J.: Prentice-Hall, 1970).

nomic growth" – that is, internally generated development based on the assimilation of modern technology, a permanent and stable infrastructure, and continuing international contacts – has underlined the overall continuity in the economic history of contemporary Japan. The irregularities in this growth, once regarded as moments of crisis or near collapse, came to be interpreted as transient episodes. For example, Kazushi Ohkawa and Henry Rosovsky portrayed twentieth-century economic growth as a series of developmental "waves" characterized by a spurt of rapid growth followed by less rapid growth.[21] Although they identified "long swings" in the GNP growth rate, marked by "peaks" and "troughs," they emphasized "trend acceleration," the long-term tendency for the growth rate to rise. The overall pattern has been rapid development from the end of the Russo-Japanese War to the end of World War I, followed by a slowdown in the 1920s; another period of growth in the 1930s, abruptly terminated by the outbreak of World War II; and the period of spectacular postwar growth beginning with the end of the American Occupation and continuing until the slowdown of the early 1970s. As this periodization suggests, internal political change and relations with the outside world have played key roles in the economic history of twentieth-century Japan. Growth itself has to be explained by internal economic dynamics, but its timing or pacing has been much affected by noneconomic factors.

The main point, however, is that the new emphasis on the pattern of long-term economic growth in prewar Japan has pointed to a major continuity in contemporary Japanese history, one that can be demonstrated with an assuring array of statistical information. The argument for continuity in twentieth-century economic history rests on nonquantifiable evidence as well.[22] Certain features in the sociopolitical environment of growth have persisted from the prewar through the postwar periods: a tolerance of the government's flexible involvement in promoting economic growth; a disinclination to cling to pure market models for the economy; a predilection for oligopolistic organization; a tempering of market relationships by indigenous social traditions or

21 Kazushi Ohkawa and Henry Rosovsky, *Japanese Economic Growth: Trend Acceleration in the Twentieth Century* (Stanford, Calif.: Stanford University Press, 1973).

22 The following works stress continuity of the economy before and after 1945: Angus Maddison, *Economic Growth in Japan and the USSR* (London: Allen & Unwin, 1969); Kunio Yoshihara, *Japanese Economic Development: A Short Introduction* (Tokyo: Oxford University Press, 1979); Kazushi Ohkawa and Miyohei Shinohara, eds., *Patterns of Japanese Economic Development: A Quantitative Appraisal* (New Haven, Conn.: Yale University Press, 1979); Takafusa Nakamura, *The Postwar Japanese Economy: Its Development and Structure* (Tokyo: Tokyo University Press, 1981).

customs; and a continuing orientation toward external markets. Even though the postwar economy was much larger in scale, it inherited many features of the prewar economy.

## *Government and the economy*

As Professor Crawcour points out in his chapter, the government has actively intervened in the economy since the beginning of the Meiji period. Government officials, unconstrained by a commitment to laissez-faire ideas, have been willing to promote selected aspects of economic growth, and private business leaders have been willing to accept or tolerate such official intervention when it suited their needs or interests. The classic pure market model, in which the profit-maximizing private entrepreneur provides the main impetus to growth and the invisible hand works smoothly and infallibly, has not found an enthusiastic audience in twentieth-century Japan. Rather, the Japanese ideology of economic growth has emphasized collective or national interests, whether seen in terms of national strength and security or popular prosperity, and has assumed a central role for state involvement.[23]

Prewar policymakers, corporate leaders, and many intellectuals were attracted to the economic doctrines of the later developing European industrial countries, especially the ideas of the German historical school, introduced to Japan around the turn of the century.[24] The appeal of these ideas undoubtedly was reinforced by their resonance with traditional conceptions of the role of the state, appropriate social relations, and distributive justice, but they also suggested how Japan might exploit the "advantages of followership." Marxist economics was introduced into Japan in the 1920s but did not gain influence until the 1930s when the success of the Soviet Union's Five-Year Plans and the production crisis in the advanced Western economies enhanced its credence. As a result, even non-Marxist bureaucrats and intellectuals in the 1930s came to advocate increased state management and central planning.

Although the government's role in promoting economic growth has

23 For a useful discussion of the government's role in the economy, see William W. Lockwood, *The Economic Development of Japan: Growth and Structural Change* (Princeton, N.J.: Princeton University Press, 1954), chap. 10; William W. Lockwood, *The State and Economic Enterprise in Japan: Essays in the Political Economy of Growth* (Princeton, N.J.: Princeton University Press, 1965).

24 Kenneth B. Pyle, "Advantages of Followership: German Economics and Japanese Bureaucrats, 1890–1925," *Journal of Japanese Studies* 1 (Autumn 1974): 127–64.

rarely been questioned, its mode of intervention has altered subtly over time. The Meiji leaders assumed that once industrialization had begun, the government would move to the sidelines. Private initiative, private profit, and private property would provide the main incentives for growth. The state was expected to play a facilitative rather than a managerial or entrepreneurial role. During the early decades of the twentieth century, the hand of the government remained visible, tempering market conditions to promote specific industries, to expand overseas trade, and to induce investment in newly acquired colonial territories, but its involvement was limited largely to carefully selected large-scale capital-intensive enterprises deemed essential to national interests – iron and steel, shipbuilding, the national rail network, and arms production. Economic policy was sectoral rather than macroeconomic.

The government rarely intervened to promote growth in industries in which the private sector had comparative advantage. Until the 1930s the modern sector was governed largely by market forces and private initiative. Light industry (cotton textiles, ceramics, food products, soap, and other consumer goods) was largely on its own, and so were the heavy industries that grew up during Japan's "second industrial revolution" during World War I (chemicals, electrical goods, machine tools, and fertilizer). And when one looks at the "traditional" sector, the absence of government intervention is even more striking. The small factory owner, the shopkeeper, the self-cultivating farmer, and even the small landlord all were at the mercy of market forces – the ebb and flow of demand, prices, and interest rates. Although foreign observers continued to be struck by the extraordinary degree of collusion between the government and modern enterprises, those inside the economy often had a quite different perspective. The majority of the working population was operating in a pure market context, in which the government adopted a hands-off policy and did little to promote production except through diffusion of technical information or limited regulation. In other words, government intervention in the economy was skewed toward large-scale capital-intensive enterprise, whereas the majority of entrepreneurs, investors, and workers had to confront the vagaries of the marketplace.[25]

During the 1930s, reformist bureaucrats, intellectuals, and politicians called for an end to a "liberal economic structure" and the establishment of a "controlled economy." The worldwide post-1929 eco-

25 For post–World War I economic developments, see Takafusa Nakamura, *Economic Growth in Prewar Japan*, trans. Robert A. Feldman (New Haven, Conn.: Yale University Press, 1983), pt. 2.

nomic crisis revealed the weakness of laissez-faire capitalism. There was a concerted bureaucratic effort to expand the government's role in the economy from facilitative and regulatory activities toward more directive and managerial activities. As Professor Nakamura suggests in his chapter, when the country moved from a state of "semi-emergency" to "full emergency" during the middle of the decade, a whole new repertoire of techniques for government intervention developed – central planning, industrial targeting policy, wage and price controls, and rationing of both raw materials and consumer goods – in order to build up a "national defense state." Although a full-blown "controlled economy" was never imposed on the country, even during the war, the sphere of autonomous business decision making shrank considerably.[26]

During the postwar period, many of these same mechanisms were used to promote economic recovery and growth. In 1946 the Economic Stabilization Board was established to bring order to the postwar economic chaos created by the wartime destruction, and by 1955 it had evolved into the Economic Planning Agency responsible for economic forecasting and overall indicative economic planning. More important, two powerful agencies, the Ministry of Finance and the Ministry of International Trade and Industry (MITI), used a wide range of incentives and controls (for example, import restrictions, tax advantages, accelerated depreciation schedules, low-cost credit, and "administrative guidance") to channel investment into high-growth industries. As Professor Kōsai argues, when the rate of growth accelerated, economic controls were relaxed, especially in foreign trade and foreign exchange restrictions, but government ministries continued to work closely with large corporations, exchanging information and engaging in other kinds of informal cooperation.

The political economy of twentieth-century Japan has thus rested continuously on a shifting balance between reliance on market forces and resort to government intervention. As Ohkawa and Rosovsky put it, "Japan retained some advantages of capitalism, i.e. efficient producers, while reaping the benefits of socialism, i.e. considerable government control over the economic effort and direction."[27] Although the government's regulatory role has tended to increase, perhaps most dramatically in the labor market, its principal role has been developmental.

26 Jerome B. Cohen, *Japan's Economy in War and Reconstruction* (Minneapolis: University of Minnesota Press, 1949); Chalmers Johnson, *MITI and the Japanese Miracle: The Growth of Industrial Policy, 1925–1975* (Berkeley and Los Angeles: University of California Press, 1982), chaps. 4, 5. 27 Ohkawa and Rosovsky, *Japanese Economic Growth*, p. 225.

The reason, as Professor Crawcour points out, has been an acute awareness that as an industrial latecomer with a limited industrial raw material base, Japan could survive international competition only through the external economies provided by government policy.

### *The social organization of production*

Just as there was little resistance to government intervention in the economy, so too there has been a persistent belief in twentieth-century Japan that market relationships did not operate in quite the same way in Japan as in the Western economies. With the exception of socialists, Marxists, and other social reformers, most political or intellectual leaders have been reluctant to admit that exploitation or unfairness might exist in the social organization of Japan's economy. Whereas market relationships in the "individualistic" West were based purely on the cash nexus, it was argued, in Japan they were modified by a sense of cooperation and deference among economic actors. Mutual trust rather than binding legal obligation was the model for economic behavior; and the village, the household, the traditional workshop, and the patriarchal family provided templates for economic relationships.

These ideas first surfaced in the debate in the late 1890s over whether or not to institute factory legislation. Although business leaders were willing to entertain government intervention in other aspects of the economy, they wished to keep the conditions of employment and the wage contract outside its writ. Businessmen who opposed factory legislation were quick to point out that the natural bonds of affection, harmony, and loyalty that bound workers to their employers made it unnecessary. "In our country," the Tokyo Chamber of Commerce contended, "relations between employers and employees are just like those within a family. The young and old help one another and consult together in both good times and bad, and they are enveloped in a mist of affectionate feelings."[28] The workplace ethic in Japan, in other words, was entirely different from that of the advanced economies of the West.

At the turn of the century, social realities in the factories, mines, and workshops were at considerable variance from this conception. Muck-raking journalists like Yokoyama Gennosuke revealed the poverty and squalor of Japan's "lower classes," and later social exposés

28 Byron K. Marshall, *Capitalism and Nationalism in Prewar Japan: The Ideology of the Business Elite, 1868–1941* (Stanford, Calif.: Stanford University Press, 1967), p. 58.

revealed the exploitative character of employment in the textile industries, in which adolescent female factory operatives were often kept in prisonlike confinement. The "mists of affection" touted by the Tokyo Chamber of Commerce were belied by the behavior of employers who increased their profit margins by cutting labor costs and by the authoritarian employer–labor relationships to which Professor Taira alludes in his chapter.

Yet it would be wrong to dismiss the notion of a "familistic" workplace ethic as simple hypocrisy or pure ideology. By the 1920s many large corporate enterprises, particularly in the capital-intensive heavy industries, systematically pursued policies of company paternalism aimed at keeping workers docile and content. Workers were recruited young and trained in company-run schools; a system of "lifetime" employment was introduced; wage scales were increasingly linked to seniority; works councils or other consultative bodies were set up to resolve workshop disputes; and company welfare programs were established to provide health care and other nonwage benefits. These new employment practices were instrumental rather than ideological in intent, designed in part to retain the services of skilled workers in demand by competitors and in part to ward off pressure from the militant and activist labor movement that emerged in the post–World War I years. But the corporate managers, to explain and justify their paternalistic policies, returned to the idea that social relationships in Japan were unique, reflecting a deeply embedded cultural concern for harmony, cooperation, and mutual trust.[29]

At the same time, it should be remembered, the ideology of labor–employer harmony was accepted by many workers as well. In the 1920s a militant labor movement, distrustful of capitalism and committed to adversarial tactics, had emerged in Japan, and for the first time there were large-scale strikes in many key industries. But the movement remained limited in size and never managed to capture the allegiance of the majority of workers, even in the most developed industrial sectors. Although there are many reasons for the "failure" of the prewar labor movement, undoubtedly the most important had to do with the character of the work force itself. Leaving aside the female factory operatives in the textiles industries, who were inherently difficult to organize, most male industrial workers came from backgrounds

29 Ronald P. Dore, *British Factory–Japanese Factory: The Origins of National Diversity in Industrial Relations* (Berkeley and Los Angeles: University of California Press, 1973), pt. 3; Andrew Gordon, *The Evolution of Labor Relations in Japan: Heavy Industry, 1853–1955* (Cambridge, Mass.: Harvard University Press, 1985).

that militated against involvement in labor unions. Often they were recruited when quite young, still in their late adolescence fresh from an elementary education that drilled into them the familistic or communitarian values that were part and parcel of corporate management ideology. Moreover, as Gary Allinson noted, workers often came from a rural environment in which labor relationships were diffuse, production was undertaken for collective goals, and age hierarchy prevailed.[30] Given this background, they were likely to accept the idea that labor and capital were not adversaries but collaborators engaged in a common enterprise with common goals and interests.

Paternalistic ideology and employment practices, limited to a few large enterprises in the prewar period, became more widely diffused in the 1950s and 1960s. Some Western observers argued that the persistence of these practices indicated a lack of "rationality" in Japanese management. But the publication of James Abegglen's *The Japanese Factory*[31] in 1958 led to a wider appreciation outside Japan of their economic utility. Leading Japanese businessmen and officials often pointed out that the "Japanese employment system" – lifetime employment, seniority wage scales, and enterprise unionism – contributed substantially to high-speed economic growth by cutting worker time lost through labor disputes, by encouraging innovation from below, by facilitating quality control, and by generally enhancing worker productivity. Critics attacked the "Japanese employment system" as a social myth, as only a minority of workers – permanent workers in large enterprises – received its benefits. But it is true that the system has produced a peculiar sort of industrial proletariat, whose members are seemingly committed to an ideology of mutual obligation and who are not inclined to disrupt social harmony by unseemly protest. Indeed, aside from those in the early postwar years, there were no major labor disputes in the leading growth industries such as electronics, heavy machinery, or automobiles but only in the public-service sector such as national railroad workers or in declining industries such as coal mining.

## *Japan in the world economy*

The twentieth century has also witnessed Japan's deepening involvement in world markets, making its domestic economy sensitive and

30 Gary D. Allinson, *Japanese Urbanism: Industry and Politics in Kariya, 1872–1972* (Stanford, Calif.: Stanford University Press, 1975), chap. 5.

31 James C. Abegglen, *The Japanese Factory: Aspects of Its Social Organization* (Glencoe, Ill.: Free Press, 1958).

responsive to external changes. For example, the ratio of exports and imports to GNP, a simple and obvious measure of a country's economic dependence on the outside world, rose sharply from 1900 until World War II. Increased dependence on foreign trade has characterized industrialization in many countries, but the initial rate of increase was extremely high in Japan because of its limited resource base. The Meiji leaders were well aware that the country's power and prestige were hostage to its ability to promote foreign trade. Thus unless Japan could sell its goods in the world market, it could not acquire the armaments needed to protect its expanding empire or fulfill the needs of its growing manufacturing sector. Because the Japanese could not hope to export either agricultural products or mineral resources – the path taken by many non-Western economies – the only remaining avenue was to expand its trade through the export of manufactured goods.

By the turn of the century, political and business leaders had acquired a kind of "export-or-die" psychology. Determined to make the best of the country's disadvantages, the government actively encouraged trade expansion by establishing the Yokohama Specie Bank to facilitate foreign exchange transactions, by strengthening consular economic reporting, by subsidizing the construction of an ocean-going merchant marine, and by encouraging the formation of export associations or cartels. Private industry, initially led by the cotton textile manufacturers, engaged in an aggressive export-promotion drive that accelerated steadily. By the 1930s, for example, Japan had become the world's major exporter of cotton manufactures, making inroads into regional markets once dominated by the British.[32]

From the Japanese perspective, the world market was divided into two major spheres, each requiring a different trade strategy. In trade with the advanced Western economies, the Japanese sought imports of machinery, arms, semimanufactures like pig iron, chemicals, and other industrial goods. In return they exported primary goods (raw silk and tea), silk woven goods, and labor-intensive craft products. The pattern of Japanese trade with the less developed economies was rather different. Here Japan enjoyed certain advantages – cheaper labor, lower transportation costs, better commercial intelligence and knowledge of the culture, and more aggressive marketing – that enabled its manufactures to compete with those of the West. In Asian markets, and more generally in the less developed world, Japan sold

32 For the development of prewar foreign trade, see Lockwood, *The Economic Development of Japan*, chaps, 6, 7; Ohkawa and Shinohara, *Patterns of Japanese Economic Development*, chap. 7.

inexpensive light industry products like cotton yarns, cotton textiles, and other assorted manufactures such as soap and matches, and it bought raw materials (e.g., iron ore and other mineral ores) or foodstuffs (e.g., rice).

Although trade with the advanced Western economies took place in a multilateral free-trade structure, Japan dealt with the less advanced countries in a political framework characterized by bilateral and asymmetrical imperialist relationships. In China, the largest and most promising Asian market until the 1930s, Japan operated within the "unequal treaty" system. On the one hand, the treaty system impeded the growth of Chinese competition and, on the other, constrained the Japanese from acquiring special economic privileges not shared with the Western powers. The acquisition of the Kwantung (Liaotung) territories and the South Manchuria Railway Line in 1905, however, facilitated the commercial penetration of the three northeastern provinces, which supplied Japan with agricultural goods like soy beans and important industrial raw materials. The Japanese also enjoyed privileged markets in their colonial possession of Taiwan and Korea, where they had little difficulty squeezing out the foreign competition.

The China market loomed large in the eyes of Japanese political and business leaders, who saw a natural complementarity between its vast potential demand and Japan's burgeoning manufacturing capacity. Trade with China initially dwarfed trade with the colonies. In 1910 the total volume of commodity trade with China, including the Kwantung territories, was about five times that of Korea and Taiwan combined. Japanese exports made their strongest advance in north China rather than the Yangtze Valley or south China where Western business was well entrenched. But trade with the colonies increased until it absorbed nearly one-quarter of Japan's exports in 1935.

Japan's trade with the outside world, as well as its share of world trade, grew steadily during the first three decades of the century. During the 1930s, however, there were major disruptions in Japanese markets in both the advanced and less developed countries. In part, these disruptions had political causes. Japan's seizure of Manchukuo in 1931–2 had an immediate and dramatic impact on its trade with China, and its growing aggression on the continent alienated its major Western trading partner, the United States. But equally important was the rise of economic nationalism. Tariffs in the Western economies had already begun to rise in the 1920s, first in the United States and then in Europe, and the onset of the world depression accelerated this long-term movement as Western markets shrank and as Western governments adopted beggar-thy-neighbor economic policies. As the 1930s wore on, administrative controls over trade proliferated, and the multilateral patterns of trading characteristic of the pre-1929 period gave way to the emergence of economic blocs centering on the British Commonwealth, the United States, France and the Low Countries, and Germany. The rise of economic nationalism affected not only the European metropolitan countries but also their colonies.

Japan's reaction to this fundamental shift in the character of the world economy was conditioned by its desire to revive a lagging domestic economy and by a growing feeling that the world was moving away from the international free-trade system. In the early 1930s, as Professor Nakamura states in his chapter, the Japanese government adopted "proto-Keynesian" policies that enabled its economy to recover more quickly than could the industrialized countries in the West, but apprehension of the future of free-trade principles persisted among political, bureaucratic, and business leaders. While attempting to improve competitive advantages in the shrinking world market, these policies also moved toward creating a Japan-centered yen bloc that would reduce Japan's dependence on the advanced countries. Plans were launched for the rapid economic development of the puppet state of Manchukuo, and industrial investment shot upward in the older colonies, particularly in Korea. Efforts were also made to gain privileged access to the rich resources of north China. Strategic considerations played a large, perhaps dominant, role in this aspect of Japanese policy, whose initiative came from the army, but it ultimately rested on a consensus that Japan had to establish economic as well as political autonomy from the West. Autarkic thinking of this sort eventually led to the vision of a "new economic order in East Asia."

The attempt to create an exclusive autarkic economic sphere in East Asia to counteract Japan's dependency on the West was self-contradictory. Without the import of technology, critical raw materials, and producer durables from the advanced Western economies or their colonies, Japan could not hope to become economically independent. In no way was this contradiction more poignantly demonstrated than by the American economic sanctions imposed on Japan to dissuade it from expansionism. The petroleum embargo of July 1941 forced the Japanese to resolve the contradiction by military means. But Japan lacked the naval strength to protect the autonomous economic sphere it sought to carve out in East and Southeast Asia, and the collapse of the Greater East Asian Co-Prosperity Sphere underlined the impossibility of seceding from the world market.

After 1945 the degree of Japan's dependence on the world market, as measured by the ratio of exports and imports to GNP, declined. In part this change occurred because foreign trade came to a virtual standstill in the late 1940s and in part because the domestic market expanded at a much more rapid rate than did the external markets in the 1950s and 1960s. But qualitatively, Japan's dependence on access to raw materials and technology from abroad remained important, and the drive to promote exports to keep the economy going did not slacken. In contrast with the prewar period, however, Japan's economic relationships with the outside world were in far greater harmony with its political relations. As indicated earlier, the postwar political leaders accepted that Japan's economic dependence involved a degree of political dependence and indeed managed to turn that political dependence to economic advantage.

In the postwar period the shape of the world market was quite different from what it had been before the war, and so was Japan's relationship to it.[33] Gone were the privileged colonial markets in Korea and Taiwan, and the Chinese economy was closed off after the revolution in 1949 and the outbreak of the Korean War. Lingering hostility toward Japan in areas that had been under Japanese control during the war made it difficult to reenter these markets until the 1960s. On the other hand, the advanced countries of Western Europe and North America were committed to the reconstruction of a postwar international economy in which goods and services could flow freely across national boundaries and nations would not be tempted to promote their gain at the expense of others, as in the 1930s. With the onset of the cold war the Soviet Union and its satellite economies withdrew from participation in the system of relatively unrestricted free trade, and the institutions established to promote it, such as the International Monetary Fund (IMF) and the General Agreement on Trade and Tariffs (GATT), were used to shore up the weaker economies in the non-Communist bloc of developed countries. The new international economic order worked very much to the advantage of Japan.

During the 1950s the United States acted as a sponsor for Japan's reentry into the world market. Despite European distrust, based on memories of the prewar competitiveness of Japanese exports, the United States backed Japan's membership in the GATT and IMF.

33 Hugh Patrick and Henry Rosovsky, eds., *Asia's New Giant: How the Japanese Economy Works* (Washington, D.C.: Brookings Institution, 1976), chap. 6.

More important, the United States allowed Japan to maintain administrative controls on imports of American goods while giving unrestricted access to Japanese products in the American market. And it made no attempt to restrict the flow of American technology to Japan, even at bargain prices. The resulting transfer of technology played a key role in the subsequent recovery and growth of the Japanese economy. During the 1960s, when it became increasingly evident that the yen was seriously undervalued at the exchange rate set in 1949 (¥360 to $1.00), the United States put no pressure on Japan to revalue its currency. This favorable political context, coupled with the economy's basic strength and a carefully calibrated system of trade regulation, enabled Japan to continue its prewar policy of enhancing exports and limiting imports.

By the time Japan's economic growth moved into high gear in the early 1960s, foreign trade had risen dramatically. Between 1961 and 1971, imports increased eightfold and exports ninefold, and after 1964 the economy enjoyed regular positive trade balances for the first time in its modern history. During the 1960s the external environment continued to be favorable, with world trade and the world GNP on the rise and a trend toward the reduction of tariffs on manufactured goods exported by the developed nations. In most of Japan's principal markets, tariffs dropped by an average of 35 percent in the 1960s. Owing to a decline in raw materials costs, increased labor productivity, inflation abroad, and a fixed exchange rate for the yen, Japanese manufacturing prices fell relative to those of other economies, making Japanese exports increasingly competitive. Japanese firms invested aggressively in the development of new manufactured products to sell in the advanced countries. In 1970, in contrast with the prewar period, over 90 percent of Japan's exports were the products of its manufacturing sector (chemical products 6.4 percent; machine goods, 40.5 percent; and other manufactured goods, 46.8 percent).

The export drive of the 1950s and 1960s was marked by a reluctance to remove administrative controls on foreign imports and by a disinclination to borrow from abroad. Japanese business and political leaders continued to fear that the economy might be overwhelmed by foreign goods and capital. In 1960 a decision was finally taken to open up the economy more fully, but "liberalization" was phased in only gradually. Balanced budgets and a high domestic savings rate meant there was little need to import foreign capital. By the same token there was little Japanese overseas investment until 1969 when controls were eased in response to positive foreign exchange balances. Some overseas investment flowed into labor-intensive industries like textiles – as wages rose and plant sites became less available in Japan – but most went into the development of natural resources such as oil, coal, uranium, iron ore, and nonferrous ores consumed by Japanese industry. Indeed, nearly half of Japan's foreign investment in the early 1970s was in mining operations.

## DOMESTIC POLITICS: FROM INSTABILITY TO STABILITY

When we turn to the political history of the twentieth century, the question of change and continuity becomes more difficult to sort out. A strong case can be made for fundamental discontinuity. Constitutional change in 1947, for example, decisively reformulated the rules of the political game. Even more striking has been the rapid circulation of elites and the almost kaleidoscopic change in the governing regimes. The stability of political leadership that prevailed through the early Meiji period began to crumble at the turn of the century. The first generation of postoligarchic leaders – like Katsura Tarō, Saionji Kimmochi, Yamamoto Gonnohyoe, and Terauchi Masatake – had far less control over their cabinets than the oligarchs had had. In the 1920s they were replaced by the leaders of the major political parties in the Diet; and in the 1930s and 1940s, shifting coalitions of high civil bureaucrats, military and naval leaders, and party leaders came to power. It was only in the mid-1950s, with the consolidation of the conservative political parties into the Liberal Democratic Party, that stability of authority and consistency in policy returned to the political scene.

The structural instability of the prewar constitutional system resulted from a deep ambivalence in the oligarchic generation's political outlook. On the one hand, their conception of government was shaped by a powerful intellectual tradition – the notion of *keisei saimin* – which assumed that public officials, dedicated to maintaining morality and order, should govern the "people," who were inclined to follow petty, narrow, and selfish impulses rather than the public good. On the other hand, the oligarchs were aware that pure bureaucratic rule was neither possible nor desirable in the modern world. Even a strong bureaucratic-monarchical country like Imperial Germany tolerated some degree of popular political participation. Although probably not committed to notions of popular wisdom or power sharing, the oligarchs created a popularly elected House of Representatives in the Imperial Diet as a means of uniting society behind the government. The house's function was, in effect, plebiscitary, a mode of creating or testing the consensus behind national policy.[34]

The difficulty with this configuration of institutions, as Professor Mitani comments, was that it tended toward political fragmentation rather than bureaucratic integration. Ironically, in pre-1945 Japan there probably was more consensus on national goals – development as a world power, the maintenance of an overseas empire, promotion of economic growth – than there was on who should carry them out. At fault was the constitutional system itself. As R. P. G. Steven remarked, it was a "hybrid" system that frustrated the emergence of a strong cabinet because it placed veto power in the hands of so many other organs of state.[35] Not only did appointed officials have to contend with a House of Representatives whose check-and-balance functions overrode its integrative functions, but also the notion itself of a nonpartisan bureaucracy proved a sham. Far from presiding over affairs and staying aloof from petty politicking, high officials intrigued enthusiastically and shrewdly for sectional interests.

The constitutional changes initiated by the American Occupation after 1945 brought to an end the structural instability of this political system. The postwar reforms eliminated many autonomous prewar loci of power – the Privy Council, the independent naval and army high commands, and the House of Peers – that had checked (and even defied) the cabinets. The revised constitution also mandated clear rules for the transfer of power. The head of the government was to be elected by the lower house of the National Diet, thus eliminating the prewar system of institutionalized irresponsibility that placed this function in the hands of an agent – the emperor – who never exercised it. The choice of a cabinet no longer rested on the discretion of an inner circle of imperial advisers like the *genrō* and the *jūshin* who attempted to pull together coalitions of powerful veto groups. Rather, it rested on control of the House of Representatives and, beyond that, on a popular electoral base. By simplifying the constitutional structure, these reforms eliminated much of the prewar political volatility.

Nevertheless, for most of the twentieth century, political conflict

34 On the development of the Meiji constitutional system, see George M. Beckmann, *The Making of the Meiji Constitution: The Oligarchs and the Constitutional Development of Japan, 1868–1891* (Lawrence: University of Kansas Press, 1957); George Akita, *Foundations of Constitutional Government in Modern Japan, 1868–1900* (Cambridge, Mass.: Harvard University Press, 1967); Joseph Pittau, *Political Thought in Early Meiji Japan* (Cambridge, Mass.: Harvard University Press, 1967).

35 R. P. G. Steven, "Hybrid Constitution in Prewar Japan," *Journal of Japanese Studies* 3 (Winter 1977): 183–216.

among fractured elites, internally divided and competing among themselves, has shaped the pattern of Japanese domestic politics. Contemporary observers, and later scholars and historians, have often characterized this conflict as moral drama. Some, focusing primarily on the political elites, have seen change as a consequence of the clash of political principles – "liberalism versus authoritarianism," "democracy versus totalitarianism," or "civil-military conflict." Others have tried to analyze political change in terms of class struggle: a rising bourgeoisie pitted against an entrenched absolutist regime, landlords and capitalists against rising peasants and workers, finance capital and its bureaucratic minions against a burgeoning socialist movement, and so forth. And still others have reduced political conflict to a meaningless struggle for power, fueled by ambition and self-interest. The stress, as in all good drama, has been on conflict and confrontation.

The historiography of twentieth-century politics has also been colored by a tendency to see political conflict moving toward a "normal" or natural outcome. Contemporary observers and historians often tacitly assume that political change should move in a particular direction or toward a particular outcome. This has led them to ask such questions as Why did democracy fail in prewar Japan? Why was there no strong socialist or proletarian movement in prewar Japan? Why did the Communist Party remain weak? Why did the American Occupation abandon its attempts to "democratize" Japan and instead adopt a "backward course" later pursued by the conservative political parties? In other words, political history asked why something *did not* happen rather than why something else did.[36] This line of inquiry is perfectly legitimate, especially for those wishing to learn from experience, but it reverses the historians' usual quest, which is to understand what did happen and why.

As it has become possible to place Japan's modern political experience in a broader comparative perspective, cross-cultural as well as temporal, dramatic dichotomies and conflict paradigms have been supplanted by a more complex, less dramatic understanding of contemporary political history. Before the 1960s the Japanese political system was usually placed at one end of a spectrum that extended only a short distance to the older democracies in the advanced industrial societies

36 Representative of this approach are such works as Robert A. Scalapino, *Democracy and the Party Movement in Prewar Japan: The Failure of the First Attempt* (Berkeley and Los Angeles: University of California Press, 1962); George Oakley Totten III, *The Social Democratic Movement in Prewar Japan* (New Haven, Conn.: Yale University Press, 1966); Stephen S. Large, "Perspectives on the Failure of the Labour Movement in Prewar Japan," *Labour History* 37 (November 1979).

of Western Europe and North America at the other end. But as a tier of one-party states appeared on the periphery of the Soviet Union and as more and more independent postcolonial regimes emerged in the less developed world, the length of the comparative perspective altered radically. Lines of continuity between prewar and postwar Japanese politics became more obvious, and the Japanese political system began to resemble more closely the Western constitutional parliamentary states with which it had once been constrasted. As one American political scientist observed, "In contrast to many late modernizers, Japan . . . resembled far more a Madisonian-Montesquieuian state than a Leninist or a Rousseauian monolith."[37]

Alternative perspectives on the prewar Japanese political system stress its "pluralistic" character. As suggested earlier, much of the struggle and conflict of prewar politics was generated less by dramatic clashes over political principle or class interests than by a constitutional check-and-balance system that compartmentalized the power of various political elites but did not provide a strong mechanism to referee their struggles. In this sense, pluralism is identified with the fragmentation and circulation of elites struggling for control of the government. But attempts to apply the concept of pluralism in its more usual sense – the competition among social and economic interests for influence over the formation of national policy – have been less common, and studies of interest politics have usually focused on the postwar period. It is clear that prewar Japanese politics was pluralistic in this sense as well, though obviously not to the same degree as were more fragmented and less centralized constitutional states like the United States and Great Britain.

Insofar as the political history of twentieth-century Japan is defined by changes in regime and the instability of the political elite, its politics have been far more volatile than have those of older and more stable representative systems in North America, Western Europe, and the British Commonwealth. On the other hand, compared with the rest of the world, especially those societies like Japan that had no premodern representative tradition, Japanese politics looks fairly stable. The country has not been affected by the kinds of popular revolutions that shook Russia in 1917 or China in 1949, nor has it been subject to the anticolonial struggles and upheavals of decolonization that have troubled many of the less developed countries. In some

37 T. J. Pempel, "Political Parties and Social Change: The Japanese Experience," in *Political Parties: Development and Decay*, ed. Louis Maizel and Joseph Cooper (Beverly Hills, Calif.: Sage Publications, 1978), p. 314.

measure, this relative stability must be attributed to the timing of Japan's decision to modernize. Its modernizing revolution – the Meiji Restoration – had already resolved many of the issues that bedeviled other non-Western countries in the twentieth century. And although one can argue that the telescoped modernization that followed in the wake of the Restoration "distorted" Japan's political development before 1945, it is equally plausible to suggest that the post-Restoration reforms – the creation of a civil bureaucracy, the commitment to industrialize, and the promulgation of a constitution that included representative institutions – were less responsible for those distortions than was the ill-fated attempt at continental expansion. Such an argument becomes persuasive if one looks behind the volatility of prewar cabinets to the long-run continuities that have characterized Japan's political system.

## *Political parties*

The history of political parties offers plausible evidence for strong continuities in twentieth-century politics. Parties have attracted the attention of historians more than have other actors in the political process, with the possible exception of the military services. The prewar confrontations in Japan between its cabinets and the parties in the House of Representatives had dramatic appeal, and the fortunes of the parties provided a useful way of charting the changes among the various elements in the political elite. Then, too, Western historians have tended to identify politics with parliamentary politics and to ignore the less visible forms of political competition within bureaucracies. In any event, the development of party politics provides a means of tracing political change and continuity in the twentieth century.[38]

During roughly the first two decades of the century, as Tetsuo Najita and others found, the main focus of political conflict was the political parties' attempt to diminish and dislodge the influence of oligarchic-bureaucratic factions (the so-called *hanbatsu*), in particular that led by Yamagata Aritomo, who harbored a keen and enduring

38 The standard works on the development of political parties in Japan are by Tetsuo Najita, *Hara Kei in the Politics of Compromise, 1905–1915* (Cambridge, Mass.: Harvard University Press, 1967); Peter Duus, *Party Rivalry and Political Change in Taishō Japan* (Cambridge, Mass.: Harvard University Press, 1968); Berger, *Parties;* Robert A. Scalapino and Junnosuke Masumi, *Parties and Politics in Contemporary Japan* (Berkeley and Los Angeles: University of California Press, 1962); Haruhiro Fukui, *Party in Power: The Japanese Liberal Democrats and Policy-Making* (Canberra: Australia National University Press, 1970); Nathaniel B. Thayer, *How the Conservatives Rule Japan* (Princeton, N.J.: Princeton University Press, 1969).

distrust of political parties. But the politics of the period cannot be reduced to a simple confrontation between two well-defined sets of opponents. The struggle was complicated, first, by internal divisions among the oligarchs and the impatience of younger members of the *hanbatsu* factions to assume full control over the government. This led men like Itō and Katsura to cross the line of confrontation between party and *hanbatsu* by striking temporary alliances with party leaders or by forming their own political parties. There was also intense division and rivalry among party politicians. These had less to do with principles and platforms than with power and influence, access to ministerial positions in the cabinet, and the interests of local voters. The two major parties – the Seiyūkai (organized in 1900) and the Dōshikai (organized in 1913; later reorganized as the Kenseikai in 1916 and as the Minseitō in 1927) – probably diverged less on stated policy and principles than did parliamentary parties in any other advanced industrial society (including Imperial Germany where an active and vocal Social Democratic Party clashed ideologically with more centrist and conservative parties).

Party rivalry was often regarded by contemporary and later observers as a reason for party weakness, but it also made possible cabinet–Diet coalitions that paved the way to party rule. Indeed, between 1905 and 1918, with one exception, no cabinet took power that did not enjoy the support of the majority party or a majority coalition in the House of Representatives. Concomitantly, the number of political party leaders holding ministerial portfolios increased. By the 1910s it was so clear that the political parties would eventually assume full control over the government that a number of important high-ranking officials resigned their official posts to become party members, a practice familiar in postwar politics as well.

The emergence of party cabinets after 1918, then, did not mark a dramatic break in political practice, but a delicate shift in the balance of political power away from the oligarchic factions to the House of Representatives. The shift took place for several reasons: First, there were fewer and fewer members of the oligarchic factions willing or able to organize an effective government; second, oligarchic leaders like Yamagata, though preferring a weak and divided Diet, decided that the political party leaders were neither as radical nor as irresponsible as they had once seemed; and third, by 1924, all the Meiji oligarchs were dead, save for Saionji Kimmochi, a man disinclined by temperament or principle to resist the trends of the times. The accession of party cabinets represented neither a fundamental change in the institutional configuration nor the triumph of the principle of representative democracy. Rather, it resulted from a pragmatic decision that ratified political reality.

During the decade and a half following World War I, the political parties emerged as the hegemonic elite in the political system, dominating the cabinet, the formulation of national policy, and, to a lesser degree, the execution of policy. With the exception of three short-lived "transcendental cabinets" in 1922–4, party leaders served as premiers and cabinet ministers until 1932. By contrast, the civilian and military bureaucracies saw their political influence, though not their prestige and popular status, dwindle. A token of this shift was the increasing number of officials who allowed themselves to be co-opted by the political parties. The most dramatic defection was that of Tanaka Giichi, cultivated by Yamagata to assume leadership of the "Chōshū lineage" in the army, who agreed to become president of the Seiyūkai in 1925.

Control over the cabinet had an effect on the political parties that is often overlooked. Accession to power forced the parties' leaders to grapple with national problems and to shoulder responsibility for solving them. It was no longer sufficient for the party leaders simply to bargain for a place at the table; they had to prepare and serve the meal. Marked differences over a wide range of policies – the expansion of suffrage, the introduction of labor and social legislation, the budget and tax policy, military expenditures, and the China policy – deepened and sharpened party rivalry. Although both parties relied on rural constituencies for electoral support and turned to large business concerns for political funds, they differed on many issues. The Seiyūkai tended to adopt a free-spending fiscal policy, a conservative position on social issues, and a hawkish view of foreign policy. By contrast, the Kenseikai favored fiscal retrenchment, a constructive response to social problems, and an internationalist orientation in foreign policy. There has been far too little study of policy formation during the period of party hegemony, however, to speak with assurance about the significance of these policy differences.

Even during the years of their hegemony, however, the political parties remained suspect in the public eye. Even though the two major parties managed to capture the votes of the enfranchised electorate, they were not the objects of deeply felt political commitment. (A voter willing to die for the emperor would surely not have done the same for the Seiyūkai or the Minseitō.) The frequent revelation of public scandals in the press – the trading of political or economic favors for political funds – eroded the parties' moral authority, and within the parties as well, reform-minded members often harbored contempt for their colleagues. As crises began to shower down on the country after 1927, doubt spread not only among the public but also among the other elites about the suitability of party leaders as national leaders. The assassination in 1932 of Inukai Tsuyoshi, the last prewar party prime minister, was the immediate reason for the end of the political parties' hegemony. But given the overwhelming sense of internal disorder and external threat that spread in the early 1930s, the end might have come less dramatically, by the same kind of subtle shift in the balance of power that took place in 1918.

During the early 1930s, Saionji, assisted by a group of informal advisers known as the *jūshin* (senior ministers), decided to promote the organization of nonpartisan "national-unity cabinets" (*kyōkoku itchi naikaku*). These drew support from all the major political elites: the parties, the military services, the civilian bureaucracy, and even the House of Peers. This effort to achieve a balance of power among the major political elites collapsed after the February 26 incident in 1936, and the army leadership, divided though it was, assumed an even larger role in forming the cabinet. It used informal pressure as well as its power to prevent the nomination of a war minister, so as to thwart the formation of governments it opposed. But even after General Tōjō Hideki assumed power as prime minister in late 1941, the army high command was neither unified nor omnipotent, and the political parties, though formally dissolved in 1940, were never systematically suppressed, nor was the functioning of the Diet suspended.

It was not until postwar constitutional revision that the political parties once again moved to the center of the political stage. Even so, the stabilizing effects of the new constitution were not immediately evident. The prewar conservative parties were in disarray, deprived of key leaders by the Occupation purges and flooded with "new men" in the postwar elections. The parties on the left had developed considerable strength. In contrast with the last prewar election when the largest left-wing party, the Social Mass Party, won only 9.1 percent of the popular vote, in the 1947 election the Japan Socialist Party won 26.3 percent, and the Japan Communist Party 3.7 percent, of a much larger electorate. The parties of the left benefited from the people's disillusionment with the entrenched conservative leadership, widespread economic hardship and deprivation, and the sudden growth of an organized labor movement. Their appearance introduced the possibility of a new kind of conflict and a new kind of instability in Japanese politics, despite the reordering and simplification of the political structure. The intense and bitter disputes between the parties of the left and those of the right over the American alliance, rearmament, and the "reverse course" during the early 1950s foreshadowed a type of political polarization so far not experienced in Japan. The growth of the left-wing vote in the early 1950s seemed to mark a trend toward the eventual emergence of a left-dominated government, and many knowledgeable politicians and political observers assumed that the demographic change, the shift of more people into cities and more workers into industry, guaranteed the ultimate triumph of the socialists.

As is so often the case, the long-term extrapolation of current events was not an accurate guide to the future. In 1955 the fragmented and bickering conservative political parties united to form the Liberal Democratic Party (LDP), which dominated the House of Representatives and controlled the cabinet for the next three decades. At its inception the party was a coalition of factions, or small leader-oriented parties, often divided by intense personal rivalries and competition to secure control of the cabinet and ministerial posts. In a sense, the struggle over national leadership moved from the floor of the Diet to the Liberal Democratic Party headquarters. Even though it was divided by internal rivalry, the party always managed to stand behind the party president, whose selection for that office automatically assured him the office of prime minister. Party unity alone, however, cannot explain its continuity in power. Indeed, unity would have meant little if the party had lost control over the House of Representatives.

In defiance of what seemed to be inevitable trends in the 1960s, the left vote declined and the electorate continued to return Liberal Democratic majorities to the lower house of the Diet. This can be attributed to historical developments mentioned earlier. First, as Professor Fukui's chapter suggests, there was a broad-based consensus behind the LDP-supported goals of achieving a high growth rate and raising the country's standard of living. As long as the economy's overall performance was improving, the Liberal Democratic Party continued to gain or hold its own at the polls. Voters gave less weight to the issues of social justice or fair distribution of wealth raised by the left. Second, foreign policy issues also receded in importance after the renewal of the Mutual Security Treaty in 1960. The reduction of American forces and bases in Japan removed a visible source of popular hostility to the alliance with the United States, and the fragmentation of the so-called progressive bloc of countries during the Sino-Soviet split confused and fractured the left wing as well. The left wing's faltering grip on public support of domestic and foreign policy issues, coupled with the collapse of unity in the Communist bloc, led the moderate wing of the Japan Socialist Party to split and form the Democratic Socialist Party in 1960. This fragmentation of the principal opposition party was a final factor in the continued domination of the Liberal Democratic Party.

Although the political parties have consistently played a key role in twentieth-century politics, it is clear that their experience has been rather different from that of parties in the older and more stable parliamentary countries. It is only in the latter half of the century that they became the dominant force in control of government. The practice of party politics and the processes of voting, bargaining, and compromise that lie at the heart of any functioning parliamentary system had to acquire a legitimacy that they lacked at the turn of the century when the constitutional structure was only a decade old.

## *The civil bureaucracy*

By contrast, the professional bureaucracy, especially the higher civil service officials occupying the top positions in the government ministries, had little need to acquire legitimacy. Regarded by the Meiji oligarchs as their true heirs, bureaucrats constituted a privileged and protected elite. They were to provide the stability and continuity in government that the contentious and factious party politicians could not. The professional bureaucracy was a creation of the civil service examination system established in the late 1880s.[39] The educational system was designed to funnel the brightest and the best – as determined by academic performance – into its ranks. In 1900 an ambitious young man aimed not at becoming a lawyer or a businessman or a politician but at making his way through the "dragon gate." The pre-Meiji notion that the official was a gentleman and a scholar, possessed of superior intelligence and cultivation, afforded a respectability to bureaucratic service that other professions did not have. If there was much public resentment, and even ridicule, of bureaucratic arrogance, there was also deference to and respect for those in the higher reaches of the official hierarchy.

The intent of the civil service examination system was to create a

39 On the prewar bureaucracy, see Robert M. Spaulding, Jr., *Imperial Japan's Higher Civil Service Examinations* (Princeton, N.J.: Princeton University Press, 1967); Robert M. Spaulding, Jr., "The Bureaucracy As a Political Force, 1920–1945," in *Dilemmas of Growth in Prewar Japan*, ed. James W. Morley (Princeton, N.J.: Princeton University Press, 1971).

politically neutral administrative service dedicated to the national good rather than to sectarian or partisan interests. Officials, after all, were "servants of the emperor." The professional élan of the higher civil service rested on a sense that they were indeed better arbiters of the national interest than were elected officials or private citizens. When party leaders attempted to secure high ministerial posts for their followers in the late 1890s, Yamagata Aritomo did his best to insulate permanently the bureaucracy from partisan influence. Most civil service recruits remained aloof from politics, spending their careers in public administration and managerial roles. During the first decade of the century, especially after 1905, they made their way into the highest echelons of the ministerial bureaucracies, serving as vice-ministers and ministers.

Ambitious officials who reached the top of the career civil service looked for political careers beyond it. Anxious to use the technical skills and personal connections of high civil service officials, party leaders often actively recruited promising senior officials. As Tetsuo Najita showed, Hara Takashi attempted to bring younger members of the Home Ministry bureaucracy into the Seiyūkai, and prefectural governors used their offices as stepping-stones to electoral politics.[40] A number of leading officials from the Ministry of Finance, notably Wakatsuki Reijirō and Hamaguchi Osachi, also became top leaders of the Kenseikai-Minseitō. But even in the 1920s this "partisanization of the bureaucracy" affected only a tiny minority of the professional civil service.

Perhaps it is more important to emphasize other trends affecting the higher civil service during the prewar period. First, the bureaucracy was becoming more and more compartmentalized. Senior officials usually began and ended their careers within a single ministry. Lateral transfer from one ministry to another, though possible, was not the norm. As a result, officials developed strong loyalties to their ministries, or even the bureaus within the ministries to which they belonged. Although this had the advantage of encouraging specialization and familiarity with the ministry's functions – whether it was to draft budgets, operate the national railway system, or regulate religious institutions – it also encouraged sectional rivalries among and within the various ministerial bureaucracies, especially over a share of the national budget. Second, as society grew more complex and the functions of the government expanded, there were frequent jurisdictional

40 Najita, *Hara Kei*.

squabbles among the various ministries as they sought to co-opt new responsibilities. Sometimes these disputes were resolved through the creation of new ministries, such as the splitting of the Ministry of Commerce from the Ministry of Agriculture in 1925 or the elevation of the Social Affairs Bureau of the Home Ministry into the Welfare Ministry in 1938. Often interministerial disputes involved struggles over the formulation of policy. When a militant labor movement appeared in the 1920s, the Home Ministry and the Ministry of Commerce drafted competing labor law legislation and in the 1930s continued to struggle over how to deal with the labor question. In short, the higher civil service was neither monolithic nor above politics, and its members constantly tried to expand their spheres of administrative competence and control.

The collapse of party rule in the 1930s provided an opportunity for reformist or activist bureaucratic leaders to strengthen their political role. The decade saw the emergence of what the press called "the new bureaucrats" (*shinkanryō*), an elastic term that summarized a number of developments. On the one hand, there was a group of officials, mainly in the Home Ministry and the most "partisanized" of the ministerial bureaucracies, who worked to end the consequences of "party abuses" – the spread of electoral corruption, the erosion of bureaucratic control over the countryside, the penetration of party influence into the ministerial bureaucracies, and so forth. These men were behind the "election purification" campaigns of the early 1930s. At the same time, younger officials, mainly in the economic ministries – Commerce, Agriculture, and Transportation – aimed at increasing bureaucratic control over the economy and society in order to boost production while reducing social tension. Disillusioned with the market system as a result of the post-1927 collapse of the economy, and often under the influence of Marxist or national socialist ideas, these economic bureaucrats wanted to replace de facto laissez-faire policy with centralized economic decision making. They viewed bureaucratic rationality as preferable to market rationality. Interestingly, these technocratic reformers found ready allies among not only the military bureaucrats who wanted to create a new national mobilization structure in preparation for a major war but also the parties of the moderate left, who favored a basic restructuring of the economy.[41]

The emergence of reformist elements in the higher civil service represented a reaction against both party rule and the conservatism of

41 Cf. Berger, *Parties;* Johnson, *MITI and the Japanese Miracle.*

the regular ministerial bureaucracies. To circumvent the old-line ministries, new centralized coordinating bodies such as the Cabinet Research Bureau (Naikaku chōsakyoku), the Cabinet Planning Agency (Kikakuchō), the Cabinet Planning Board (Kikakuin) were organized to cut across normal boundaries of ministerial jurisdiction. But it was external crisis that accelerated the proliferation of bureaucratic controls and the creation of new extraministerial bureaucratic mechanisms. During the middle of the 1930s, but particularly after the outbreak of war with China in 1937, legislation placed sweeping administrative control over the economy in the hands of the civilian bureaucracy. With a greater or lesser degree of self-consciousness, many of these "new bureaucrats" attempted a managerial revolution that would end the "anarchy" of the market by substituting the bureaucratic manager for the corporate executive or the private entrepreneur in economic decision making.

The "new order movement" of 1940 offered the occasion for further expansion of bureaucratic controls. Although the movement itself was backed by a curious coalition of political forces – army leaders intent on building a home-front mobilization structure, politicians intent on reforming and strengthening the parties by consolidation, moderate left politicians and activists intent on social reform, and right-wing elements hoping for the establishment of a totalitarian structure – its ultimate beneficiaries were the civilian bureaucrats. The Home Ministry, whose power over the countryside had been diluted by the rise of party governments, used the structure of the Imperial Rule Assistance Association and its various adjunct organizations to place local communities under tighter supervision and control. Its powers for social management were far greater than they had ever been. Grandiose plans for an "economic new order" were also floated in 1940, and though never put into effect in their more radical form, bureaucratic control over the war economy increased. To be sure, the civilian bureaucracy was no more a monolith than it had been before, and jurisdictional infighting, complicated by the involvement of the military services and corporate business, continued, but the run of the bureaucracy's writ had expanded substantially by the end of the Pacific War.

Ironically, it was under the American Occupation, whose goal was the democratization of the political system, that the civilian bureaucracy enjoyed unprecedented influence. As Chalmers Johnson wrote, "From approximately 1948, the beginning of the occupation 'reverse course,' until the conservative merger of 1955, the answer to who governs Japan is clearly the bureaucracy."[42] The reasons for this upsurge in the power of civilian bureaucrats are in part structural and in part related to policy. Despite the frontal assault of the American Occupation on Japan's prewar political and constitutional structure, the civilian bureaucracy remained relatively intact.[43] The Home Ministry and certain other centralized agencies were abolished; the police and local government systems were decentralized; and efforts were made to reform the Ministry of Education; but for the most part the ministerial bureaucracies continued to function as before. Lacking the manpower to impose direct military government on a defeated Japan, the American Occupation chose to govern through this existing administrative structure. The Americans also imposed economic controls far more sweeping than even the Japanese wartime government had, and it shifted responsibility for their administration from the business-dominated wartime "control associations" to ministerial bureaucracies. Public corporations were set up to manage various key sectors of the economy. Business leaders, already conditioned by wartime controls, went along with these new arrangements, and the political parties, their leadership weakened by the Occupation's administrative purges and divided on policy questions, relinquished the initiative in many areas of policymaking.

Only with the consolidation of the conservative parties into the Liberal Democratic Party in 1955 did the power of the civilian bureaucracy begin to recede. The party's growing involvement in national policy decisions reduced the relative autonomy of high bureaucratic officials. The LDP Political Affairs Research Committee, made up of Diet members and organized into subcommittees corresponding to important ministries and administrative agencies, began to play a larger role in policy formulation. Ministerial bureaucracies, now routinely consulting with this body, had to respond to its members' concerns and interests. Masumi Junnosuke, an eminent political scientist, even went so far as to observe that central government agencies had become no more than "business offices for the Liberal Democratic Party's Political Affairs Research Bureau."[44] At the same time the durability of the LDP's control over the Diet and the cabinet, and

42 Chalmers Johnson, "Japan: Who Governs? An Essay on Official Bureaucracy," *Journal of Japanese Studies* 2 (Autumn 1975): 1–28.

43 A useful work on the postwar bureaucracy is by Akira Kubota, *High Civil Servants in Postwar Japan: Their Social Origins, Educational Background, and Career Patterns* (Princeton, N.J.: Princeton University Press, 1969).

44 Quoted in Itō Daikichi, "The Bureaucracy: Its Attitudes and Behavior," *The Developing Economies* 6 (December 1968): 447.

hence over the budgetary process, made the ministerial bureaucrats equally susceptible to informal pressure from Diet members acting on behalf of local or national interest groups. To a degree this represented a return to patterns prefigured if not established in the 1920s, and so too did the tendency for ambitious civil service officials to run for political office or to assume leadership positions in the Liberal Democratic Party after retiring from the bureaucracy. From 1957 until 1972 every Liberal Democratic Party president, and hence every prime minister, was a former official.

In contrast with the political parties' volatile fortunes, the civilian bureaucracy has endured in twentieth-century politics. Despite the postwar American-sponsored constitutional and structural reforms, the administrative structure has remained highly centralized. Even the concessions to the American notion of a more democratic decentralized or federal structure – that is, the establishment of popularly elected prefectural governors and increased powers for prefectural assemblies – foundered. These local bodies remained weak in contrast with either the national Diet or the central ministerial bureaucracies. The postwar political structure was as Tokyo centered as it had been since the Meiji period, and the central ministerial bureaucracies continued to devise the policy and legislative alternatives presented to governments as well as to implement policy decisions. The only major change, perhaps, was that the civil bureaucracy became more tightly integrated into the politics of interest articulation and interest representation than it had been before the war.

## *Interest politics*

Since the turn of the century the interstices between the political parties and the bureaucracy, on the one hand, and the general population, on the other, gradually have been filled by pressure- or interest-group activities. Pressure-group politics emerged in Japan for most of the same reasons that it arose in the other capitalist parliamentary countries. First, by its very nature, the parliamentary system legitimized the principle of representation of interests. If voters in a particular district were given the right to return a representative to the national Diet, then it was equally natural for particular economic or occupational groups to seek representation of their interests as well. (Already in the 1880s, prefectural assembly members had begun lobbying for particular local or economic interests.) Second, as society became more complex, the bureaucracy expanded its jurisdiction. State authority penetrated deeper and deeper into society, and new laws or official regulations dealt with activities heretofore free from governmental interference. In response, those affected often organized to influence the exercise of state authority. Third, accelerating economic development generated conflicts between new and old economic interests. Decisions made about the economy – concerning taxes, budget, tariffs, subsidies, or state investment – were bound to benefit some sectors of society and hurt others. Pressure groups thus provided a means of mediating or resolving such conflicts.

To be sure, a residual traditional distrust of "private" or sectional interests persisted. In his official commentary on the constitution, for example, Itō Hirobumi presented the view that even members of the lower house of the Diet were "representatives of the whole country" rather than delegates "commissioned merely to attend to matters entrusted to them by their own constituents."[45] The parts were expected to act on behalf of the whole. This self-contradictory notion of representation was not very different from contemporary views of representation in the West, but it was bolstered by the tradition of bureaucratic elitism. Although public attitudes remained influenced by such ideas, political practice quickly diverged from them. By the beginning of the century, even Itō had come to recognize the necessity of representing particular interests as well as the public good.

Local chambers of commerce, agricultural associations, and industrial associations had already come into being in the 1870s and 1880s in response to official prompting.[46] The government encouraged their formation to promote domestic solidarity in the face of Western economic competition. Such groups were more like semicorporatist agencies of the state than like the political voluntary associations that had emerged in Western Europe and North America. Generally they did not function as lobbying or pressure groups. For example, before 1890, business lobbying took the form of discrete compacts arrived at by business and political leaders out of the public view and without public debate.

After the Diet opened, however, organized interest groups representing a group of firms or a whole industry almost immediately made their

45 Itō Hirobumi, *Commentaries on the Constitution of Empire of Japan*, trans. Miyoji Itō (Tokyo: Chūō daigaku, 1906), pp. 73–4.
46 On the development of interest groups, see Ishida Takeshi, "The Development of Interest Groups and the Pattern of Political Modernization in Japan," in *Political Development in Modern Japan*, ed. Robert E. Ward (Princeton, N.J.: Princeton University Press, 1968).

debut. So did the competition of interests and pressure-group politics. Particular industries began to lobby for legislation or policy changes designed to protect or increase their profits. In the early 1890s, for example, the Greater Japan Cotton Spinners' Association mounted an aggressive campaign to end import duties on its raw material – raw cotton – and to end export duties on its main product – cotton yarn. Such a policy, however, conflicted with the desire of agrarian interests to protect the domestic cultivation of cotton and to keep land taxes low by keeping import and export duties high. The antitariff campaigns demonstrated to the cotton spinners, and to business leaders more generally, that business had a distinct and definable set of interests quite different from those of other economic groups and that considerable pressure and bargaining were required to protect them. It also made them aware of their political weakness.

By the late 1890s the business community became more militant in advancing its political claims vis-à-vis rural interests. There was to be no alliance of "rice and textiles" in the Japanese Diet like the alliance of "rye and iron" in the German Reichstag. As Professor Mitani states, business groups bombarded the cabinet, the Diet, and the political parties with resolutions calling for an increase in land taxes to finance the growing budget, and landowning interests fought hard against it. The movement to increase land taxes quickly turned into a movement to change the electoral law so as to increase urban (and therefore business) representation in the Diet. The two movements not only demonstrated the growing political self-consciousness of business leaders but also achieved a high degree of success. During the first two decades of the century, pressure-group and interest-group politics became routinized at several levels. The political parties in the Diet became the vehicle for the articulation of both local and national interests. As several scholars have demonstrated, the leadership of the Seiyūkai attempted to bring top business leaders into their parties and used Diet powers over the budget and ministerial power over the prefectural bureaucracy to engage in pork-barrel politics, particularly after the Russo-Japanese war. Local public works projects such as building branch railroad lines, roads and bridges, and irrigation systems and improving harbors were levers to raise local electoral support. Although rival parties often railed against such abuses, by the 1920s this kind of political logrolling had become routine.

As the relative importance of the modern sector grew and the cooperation of business leaders became crucial to the success of certain national policies, the central government systematically solicited the opinions of business leaders. At the turn of the century the need for business backing of an expansionist foreign policy was critical, but other policy issues also became important as time went on. In 1896, 1897, and 1898 the government convened three Higher Agriculture, Commerce, and Industry Commissions to discuss a wide range of postwar economic problems: the expansion of foreign trade, the shift to a gold standard, the introduction of foreign capital, the establishment of overseas banking facilities, the treatment of factory workers, and even immigration policy. These high-level conferences brought leading bankers, foreign traders, shipping company executives, and manufacturers together with representatives from the ministerial bureaucracies. Although the government's purpose was undoubtedly to create consensus rather than to debate policy, the business representatives were candid in expressing their views, often to the frustration of the bureaucratic participants. These conferences established precedents for official "investigative commissions" (*chōsakai*) or "deliberative councils" (*shingikai*) intended to give representatives of business a formal role in policymaking. Several key bodies were convened during the 1910s and 1920s: the Seisan chōsakai (1910–12), the Keizai chōsakai (1916–17), the Rinji kokumin keizai chōsakai (1918–19), the Shōkō shingikai (1927–30), and the Rinji sangyō shingikai (1930–5.) Even though their function may often have been ritualistic, these formal bodies implicitly recognized the practicality, if not the legitimacy, of securing behind the national policy the support of a powerful interest group.

As the economy grew more complex, interest-group organizations proliferated. Most were specialized associations representing specific business, trade, or occupational groups (for example, the Shipbuilders Association), geographical regions (for example, the Osaka Manufacturers' Association), or specific regional industries (for example, the Hokkaido Colliers' Association). Although their interests were often parochial, they often formed alliances or coalitions when a single issue affected a number of groups. During the 1920s, for example, the cotton spinners' association allied with local chambers of commerce at home and merchant associations abroad in order to protest anti-Japanese activities in China. There also emerged important "peak associations" representing the general interests of a particular occupation or economic group. Agricultural interests, particularly those of the landowning elements, for example, were represented by the Imperial Agricultural Association, established in 1910 with government encouragement, and local business was represented nationally by the

Japan Chamber of Commerce, organized in 1922. Particularly striking, however, was the rise of peak associations representing large modern manufacturing firms – the Japan Industrial Club (1916), the Japan Economic Federation (1922), and the National Federation of Industrial Associations (1931). Industrial leaders felt that the opinions of bankers and financiers, on whom the government relied heavily, did not necessarily represent the views of business as a whole.

During the 1920s there were also attempts to build interest organizations representing economically weaker and politically less powerful segments of the population, such as wage labor (Japan Federation of Labor, 1920) or tenant farmers (Japan Peasants Union, 1922). Although these organizations tried to advance the interests of their putative constituents, for example, through the legalization of trade unions or the reduction of rents, they developed in fundamental opposition to the sociopolitical status quo. Leaders were often drawn not from the ranks of ordinary workers or peasants but from the intelligentsia committed to a global transformation of society. As Professors Duus and Scheiner indicate, the post–World War I labor movement participated in both the universal manhood suffrage movement and the proletarian party movement, and its leaders often advocated socialism in one form or another. Given the overwhelmingly conservative character of public sentiment, nurtured as it was by the indoctrination of traditional values through the elementary education system, these pressure groups representing the less privileged strata remained small in size and politically weak. Their leaders were accused of advocating dangerously disruptive alien philosophies of class struggle, and their political activities were frequently the object of official suppression.

During the 1930s, "reformist bureaucrats" as well as many civilian politicians in both the established and the proletarian political parties proposed curbing the prevalence of pork barrel politics, pressure-group activities, and interest politics through the imposition of state controls over key economic or occupational groups. These corporatist proposals were part of a more general effort to replace the liberal economic structure with a controlled economic structure, but they also reflected a craving to return to a social harmony and national unity thought to have been shattered by class conflict and political partisanship in the 1920s. Bureaucratic attempts to impose restraints on interest-group activities ranged from plans to introduce central economic planning to the establishment of new official mechanisms to resolve labor disputes. Many outside the ministerial bureaucracies, including party politicians as well as right-wing activists, called for a totalitarian system to discipline the unruly interests and to subordinate private gain to public interest. In 1940 the "new order" movement tried to bring all interest associations into hierarchical structures dedicated to "national profit" (*kokueki*). The new order failed to materialize, but the pressure of war curbed overt pressure-group activities.

The rapidity with which interest groups were reconstituted after the war illustrates the degree to which they had become embedded in political practice. Although big business organizations were the first to revive, usually based on a framework provided by prewar associations, the American Occupation authorities actively encouraged the growth of labor unions and agricultural cooperatives. By the 1950s a whole new set of pressure groups – those representing particular occupations (e.g., physicians), those seeking assistance from the government (e.g., military veterans and pensioners, postwar repatriates, or war-bereaved families), or those advocating particular policy positions (e.g., opponents of nuclear weapons), became active players in the political process. Economic interest groups, powerful peak associations, and protest organizations clamored for government attention and public support on a far wider scale and on a far wider range of issues than the prewar groups had.

The most powerful voices, however, have been those of national peak associations with large and expert staffs, a smoothly functional organizational structure, and a high degree of representativeness. As Pempel and Tsunekawa asserted, the development of these organizations has not been even from one sector of society to another.[47] By the late 1960s virtually all major industries had been organized into powerful hierarchical associations, and about one hundred of these trade associations, together with several hundred large industrial firms, were organized into the Federation of Economic Organizations, whose leader was often as powerful and frequently more respected than was the prime minister. Nearly all farm families also belonged to branches of the National Association of Agricultural Cooperatives, a body able to present a powerful united front to politicians and ministerial bureaucrats. By contrast, despite a sudden burst of organization in the immediate postwar period, the labor force employed in secondary and tertiary industry has remained relatively unorganized. Only 34.5 percent of the labor force was unionized in 1970. The intrusion of deep ideological differences and disputes among national labor leaders also frag-

47 T. J. Pempel and K. Tsunekawa, "Corporatism Without Labor? The Japanese Anomaly," in *Trends Toward Corporatist Intermediation*, ed. P. C. Schmitter and G. Lehmbruch (Beverly Hills, Calif.: Sage Publications, 1979).

mented the labor leadership. In any case, labor pressure groups have had far less political bargaining power than have the interest groups representing either big business or the farm population.

To some extent, the weakness of the conservative political parties' organizations, with their limited party memberships and weak ties between national party headquarters and local constituencies, strengthened farm and business interest groups. Interest groups with large mass organizations, such as the National Federation of Agricultural Cooperatives, could mobilize crucial voter support for Diet candidates in a way that the national party headquarters could not, and in return they expected continuation of rice price supports and other legislation favorable to farming interests. In the upper house of the National Diet, national peak associations with large national constituencies often nominated and elected their own candidates without the mediation of party endorsement. The conspicuous efforts of the Liberal Democratic Party in the late 1950s to win the support of major national occupational associations illustrates the degree to which conservative leaders consciously cultivated interest-group support in an attempt to offset their organizational weaknesses. By the same token, large business enterprises and the national business peak associations supplied conservative party candidates and the national headquarters with political funds in return for greater access to policymakers and influence over public policy.

Ironically, the large national labor federations, by linking their political fortunes to the parties of the left – the Socialist Party, the Communist Party, and eventually the Democratic Socialist Party – cut themselves off from access to the inner circle of power. The choice was deliberate, reflecting ideological commitment as well as prewar political connections, but it had important tactical implications. Instead of trying to exercise pressure on national politics through petition or behind-the-scenes negotiation, the large labor federations took to the streets in overt campaigns to influence public opinion by mass demonstrations, sit-ins, and acts of civil disobedience. Intended to influence the government from the outside, these protest tactics were more symbolic than instrumental. During the 1950s when confrontational politics was at its postwar peak, mass demonstrations and public protest imposed significant psychological boundaries beyond which national policy could not stray (e.g., massive rearmament). But as the political fervor declined, public demonstrations became almost ritualistic, prompting complaints from intellectuals and pushing student radicals toward tactics of violent confrontation.

Successful interest groups realized that their efforts to change national policy or to gain access to state resources had to be focused on the Liberal Democratic Party. One political scientist characterized them as "beggar groups," parasitic and submissive to authority rather than forthright in their defense of principle. It is more usual, however, to liken the triangular relationship among pressure groups, the ministerial bureaucracies, and the Liberal Democratic Party to the children's game of *jan-ken-pon* (like the American game of "scissors-paper-stone"). This is a game in which no player has a preponderant advantage and any player can win and lose simultaneously. Pressure groups have tended to be submissive to bureaucracies but aggressive in putting pressure on the Liberal Democratic Party. The Liberal Democratic Party has been solicitous of pressure groups able to deliver votes or political funds, but it can exercise leverage over ministerial bureaucracies through control of the national budget. And the ministerial bureaucracies have been careful not to offend ruling party politicians while remaining aware of how their own discretionary administrative powers can affect the fortunes of particular interest groups. Although obviously this metaphor is more elegant than the reality, it does suggest the peculiarly close relationships among conservative party politicians, ministerial bureaucracies, and interest-group associations.

On the other hand, the *jan-ken-pon* metaphor understates the complexity of postwar interest politics. None of the main actors is monolithic in nature. As we have already seen, the Liberal Democratic Party is a coalition of factions, not all of them in full agreement. Although party factions did not often initiate policy, antimainstream factions sometimes vetoed or obstructed the policies of other factions. Powerful ministerial bureaucracies such as the Ministry of International Trade and Industry (MITI) and the Ministry of Finance were often at loggerheads on key policy issues, and sometimes ministerial bureaucracies were internally divided as well, with one bureau opposing the policies advocated by another. And most obviously, the claims of interest groups conflicted, particularly over economic policies such as industrial restructuring, in which declining industries had interests different from those of growing industries, or over competition for access to government funds and protection. On rare occasions, conventional boundaries between conservative and left broke down, as when Keidanren and Sōhyō joined against the Liberal Democratic Party and the Japan Medical Association in a dispute over increases in health insurance medical fees, which meant higher costs for both employers and employees. In sum, as one political scientist put it, there have been no "simple and permanent" coalitions among the major actors who dominated policymaking in postwar Japan.

It does, nevertheless, seem indisputable that a complex system of interest bargaining and interest representation has grown up in Japan since the turn of the century, as it has in most Western parliamentary systems. Whether interest politics has encouraged "structural corruption" or organized "interest articulation" in a manner highly beneficial to economic growth, it seems no different in kind from what goes on in other capitalist political economies. Concomitantly, the notion that party politicians or state bureaucrats work on behalf of the public interest has lost plausibility and has perhaps contributed to a structural malaise in politics. Indeed, from the mid-1950s to the early 1970s, public opinion polls showed a steady decline in the number of respondents who felt that the Diet represented the "will of the people."

# PART I

# DOMESTIC POLITICS

CHAPTER 2

# THE ESTABLISHMENT OF PARTY CABINETS, 1898–1932

The year 1924 marked a turning point in the history of Japanese domestic politics. In January, Kiyoura Keigo, the incumbent president of the Privy Council, was nominated as prime minister and chose all his cabinet except for the military service ministers from the membership of the House of Peers. The House of Representatives had been bypassed in the selection of cabinets since the fall of the Takahashi Korekiyo cabinet in June 1922. Angered by this, the leaders of the three major opposition parties in the lower house – Katō Takaaki (Kenseikai), Takahashi Korekiyo (Seiyūkai), and Inukai Tsuyoshi (Kakushin Club) – met in February 1924 to organize a united front to bring down Kiyoura's "cabinet of peers." Because the first Labour Party government had been organized in England just a few weeks before, the general public as well as many party politicians felt that the Kiyoura government was swimming against the tides of history.

In the general election of May 1924, the three-party coalition, brandishing the slogan of "protecting constitutional government," won a majority in the House of Representatives. Faced with the prospect of intransigent opposition in the lower house, Kiyoura chose to resign. In June the three opposition parties formed a coalition cabinet under the premiership of Katō Takaaki, president of the Kenseikai, the plurality party in the House of Representatives. The formation of this "cabinet to protect constitutional government" (*goken sanpa naikaku*) was of great significance. For the first time in modern Japanese history, the result of a general election, that is, a change in the majority in the House of Representatives, had brought about a change of cabinets in Japan.

From June 1924 until May 1933 the country was alternatively governed by six political party cabinets, a time known as the period of party cabinets or party governments. Only two of the five prime ministers (Hamaguchi Osachi and Inukai Tsuyoshi) held seats in the House of Representatives during this period, but all were presidents of political parties who assumed office while leading either the majority party or the next largest party in the lower house. In his *Kenpō satsuyō*

(Outline of constitutional law) written in 1926, Minobe Tatsukichi, professor of constitutional law at Tokyo Imperial University and the most important ideological spokesman for party government, suggested that Japan was following the model of responsible party cabinets provided by England:

> Since its promulgation, our constitution has developed in a manner completely contrary to the expectations of its authors. Institutionally the system of cabinets responsible to the Diet has no place in the constitution, but it has been firmly established as a customary practice. It is now recognized as a natural principle that when there is a loss of Diet confidence [in the cabinet], especially in the House of Representatives, [the cabinet] must dissolve the lower house and appeal to public opinion, or it must offer a general resignation.[1]

Thus, in both theory and fact, party cabinets had become politically orthodox (see Table 2.1).

The establishment of party cabinets is particularly significant given the antiparty biases of the Meiji leaders who drafted the constitution. One of their purposes was to ensure that there would be no connection between the establishment or duration of the cabinets and the will of the Diet, especially the lower house. It is well known that Itō Hirobumi, the principal author of the Meiji constitution, felt that party cabinets were not appropriate for Japan in the 1880s. As he observed in a speech after the promulgation of the constitution, "It is difficult to avoid the emergence of parties or factions in the Diet or in society," but it is "troublesome to have them influence the government."[2] Political parties might be inevitable, but it was not necessary to give them a share of the power (see Figure 2.1).

To be sure, even before the promulgation of the constitution or the opening of the Diet in 1890, some Meiji leaders wanted to form a powerful progovernment political party in the Diet. Inoue Kaoru, Itō's close political ally, together with Mutsu Munemitsu, Aoki Shūzō, and several other higher officials, hoped to organize a Jichitō (Self-Government Party), a national political party supported by provincial administrative officials and local landlords – in Inoue's words, the "provincial aristocracy." They wanted to ally this party of provincial aristocrats with the Kaishintō, whose leader, Ōkuma Shigenobu, was serving as foreign minister and negotiating a revision of the unequal treaties.[3]

The majority faction within the Meiji leadership opposed Inoue's

1 Minobe Tatsukichi, *Kenpō satsuyō* (Tokyo: Yuhikaku, 1926), pp. 129–30.
2 Sashihara Yasuzō, ed., *Meiji seishi*, vol. 8 (Tokyo: Fuzanbō shoten, 1893), pp. 1941–3.
3 Mikuriya Takashi, *Meiji kokka keisei to chihō keiei 1881–1890* (Tokyo: Tokyo daigaku shuppankai, 1980), pp. 195–8.

TABLE 2.1
*Japanese cabinets, 1885–1932*

| Prime minister | Cabinet number | Cabinet term |
|---|---|---|
| Itō Hirobumi | 1st | 22 December 1885 to 30 April 1888 |
| Kuroda Kiyotaka | | 30 April 1888 to 24 December 1889 |
| Yamagata Aritomo | 1st | 24 December 1889 to 6 May 1891 |
| Matsukata Masayoshi | 1st | 6 May 1891 to 8 August 1892 |
| Itō Hirobumi | 2nd | 8 August 1892 to 18 September 1896 |
| Matsukata Masayoshi | 2nd | 18 September 1896 to 12 January 1898 |
| Itō Hirobumi | 3rd | 12 January 1898 to 30 June 1898 |
| Ōkuma Shigenobu | 1st | 30 June 1898 to 8 November 1898 |
| Yamagata Aritomo | 2nd | 8 November 1898 to 19 October 1900 |
| Itō Hirobumi | 4th | 19 October 1900 to 2 June 1901 |
| Katsura Tarō | 1st | 2 June 1901 to 7 January 1906 |
| Saionji Kinmochi | 1st | 7 January 1906 to 14 July 1908 |
| Katsura Tarō | 2nd | 14 July 1908 to 30 August 1911 |
| Saionji Kinmochi | 2nd | 30 August 1911 to 21 December 1912 |
| Katsura Tarō | 3rd | 21 December 1912 to 20 February 1913 |
| Yamamoto Gonnohyōe | 1st | 20 February 1913 to 16 April 1914 |
| Ōkuma Shigenobu | 2nd | 16 April 1914 to 9 October 1916 |
| Terauchi Masatake | | 9 October 1916 to 29 September 1918 |
| Hara Takashi | | 29 September 1918 to 13 November 1921 |
| Takahashi Korekiyo | | 13 November 1921 to 12 June 1922 |
| Katō Tomosaburō | | 12 June 1922 to 2 September 1923 |
| Yamamoto Gonnohyōe | 2nd | 2 September 1923 to 7 January 1924 |
| Kiyoura Keigo | | 7 January 1924 to 11 June 1924 |
| Katō Takaaki | 1st | 11 June 1924 to 2 August 1925 |
| Katō Takaaki | 2nd | 2 August 1925 to 30 January 1926 |
| Wakatsuki Reijirō | 1st | 30 January 1926 to 20 April 1927 |
| Tanaka Giichi | | 20 April 1927 to 2 July 1929 |
| Hamaguchi Osachi | | 2 July 1929 to 14 April 1931 |
| Wakatsuki Reijirō | 2nd | 14 April 1931 to 13 December 1931 |
| Inukai Tsuyoshi | | 13 December 1931 to 16 May 1932 |

plan for a progovernment party. Prime Minister Kuroda Kiyotaka, Privy Council President Itō Hirobumi, and Home Minister Yamagata Aritomo did not want the cabinet to be dependent on a single party in the Imperial Diet. They also cautioned against linking the local government system to party politics. In 1889, after the promulgation of the constitution, Kuroda made his well-known pronouncement about "transcendental government" (*chōzenshugi*) to a conference of prefectural governors: "The government must always take a fixed course. It must stand above and outside the political parties [*chōzen to shite seitō no soto ni tate*] and cleave to the path of supreme fairness and supreme justice."[4] This was clearly a rejection of Jichitō or a Jichitō–Kaishintō

4 Sashihara, *Meiji seishi*, p. 1931.

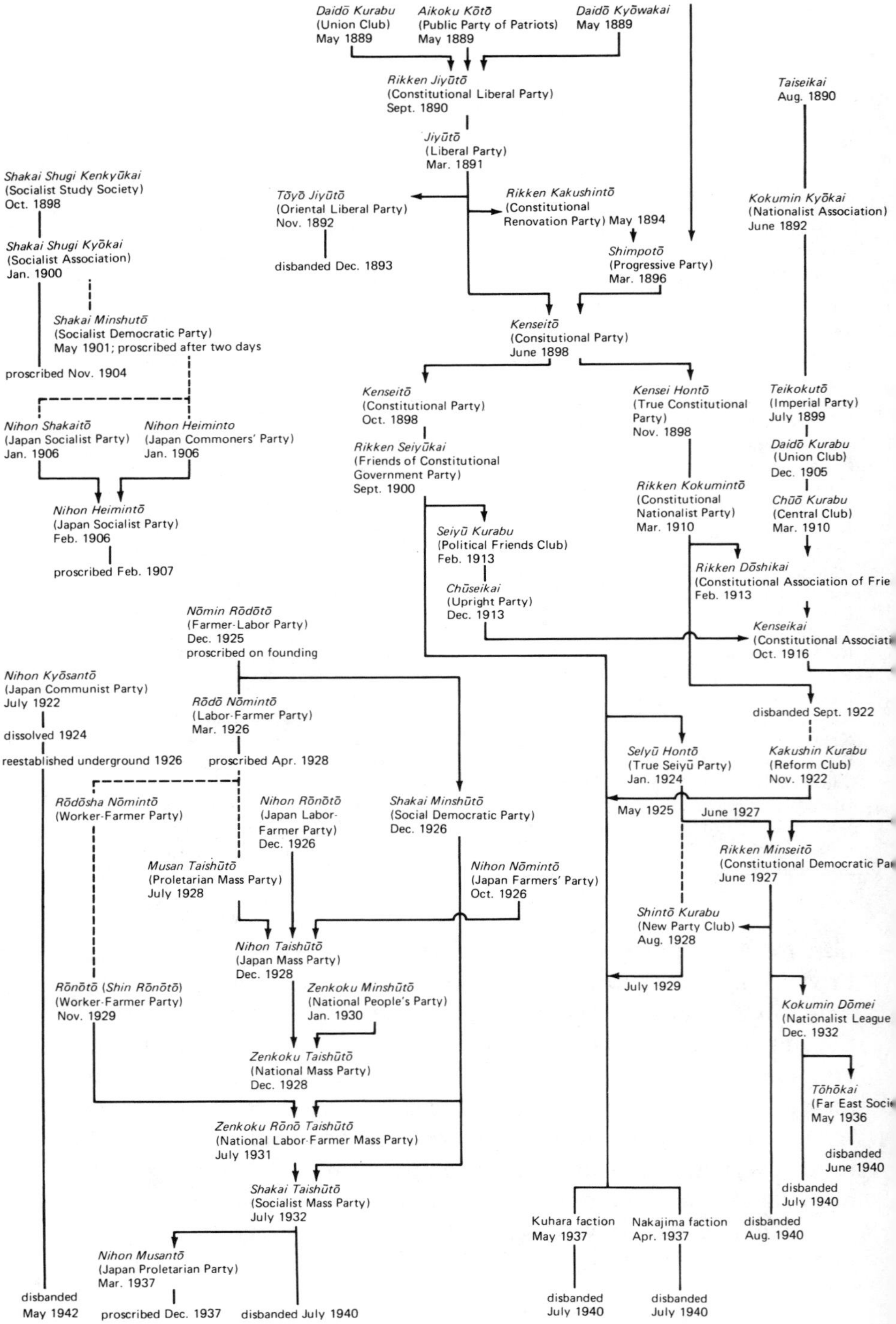


Figure 2.1. Political parties, 1889–1940. (Based on *Encyclopedia of Japan*, vol. 6. pp. 208–9.)

alliance, as was the Itō speech quoted earlier. Inoue, unhappy at his colleagues' reaction, criticized the majority faction in a letter to Mutsu Munemitsu: "I think that it is inept politics to make arrogant statements about the government's standing outside political parties."[5] The majority view nevertheless carried the day.

How was it then that political party cabinets finally emerged within a constitutional framework that embodied the antiparty sentiments of the majority faction of the Meiji leadership? How was it, as Minobe put it, that the "ideas of the drafters [of the Meiji constitution] were betrayed in reality"?[6]

## THE AMBIGUITY OF THE MEIJI CONSTITUTION

Let us first consider the ways in which the Meiji constitution hindered the formation of party cabinets.

The constitution contained two kinds of checks on the emergence of party government. First, there was the concept of the emperor's sovereign authority (*tennō taiken*). In Itō's view, the emperor's sovereign authority and the party cabinet system were fundamentally incompatible. In a letter he wrote from Germany during his investigation of European constitutional systems in 1882, he observed: "If one establishes parliamentary government, then one must reduce the authority of the emperor [*taiken*]. If one emphasizes the authority of the emperor, one cannot adopt parliamentary government."[7] Thus in his view, the two could not coexist. However, this does not mean that Itō favored direct imperial rule. In 1877–9 he had helped thwart the efforts of certain court officials to establish direct imperial rule; in 1885 he had supported the clear separation of the court (*kyūchū*) from the government (*fuchū*) by replacing the Dajōkan (Council of State) with a cabinet system; and above all, he had favored the establishment of the emperor as a constitutional monarch through the promulgation of a constitution that defined the emperor's authority.

Nevertheless, the emperor was more than a constitutional monarch; indeed Itō himself tried to make him so. For example, Itō stubbornly refused to equate the Japanese emperor with the English king. He argued that the Japanese monarch was different from other monarchs: "There is a great difference in our constitution compared with those of other countries. In no other country does a constitution specify as does

5 Mikuriya, *Meiji kokka keisei*, pp. 204–6. 6 Minobe, *Kempō satsuyō*, p. 130.
7 Hiratsuka Atsushi, ed., *Zoku Itō Hirobumi hiroku* (Tokyo: Shunjū, 1930), p. 48.

Chapter I [of our constitution] that the sovereign authority of the monarch [*kunshu no taiken*] is the [same as] the sovereign authority of the state [*shūken*]."[8] The idea of parliamentary sovereignty or popular sovereignty, one of the theoretical bases for party cabinets in liberal Western political systems, was specifically rejected in the letter of the Meiji constitution.

The Meiji constitution's other check on party government was its system of divided powers. Because the official interpretation of the constitution rejected the practice of direct imperial rule, the establishment of imperial sovereign authority did not mean that the emperor would directly exercise administrative authority. The real meaning of Article 3–"The emperor is sacred and inviolable"–was simply that the emperor did not have the capacity to assume political responsibility. He was placed beyond politics by being placed above it. The Meiji constitution, in somewhat ambivalent fashion, emphasized the emperor as the supreme constitutional monarch and granted him imperial sovereignty, yet at the same time it rejected the idea of direct imperial rule. The exercise of imperial sovereign power (*tennō taiken*) therefore had to be parceled out among the various organs of state. Itō explained this as a delegation of imperial sovereignty. But to the extent that all organs of state were premised on the absoluteness of imperial authority, they lacked the power either to oppose or to represent the emperor. Itō emphasized this point with respect to the Imperial Diet:

> The restoration of monarchical rule [*ōsei fukkō*] meant the restoration to the emperor of the right of sovereignty [*tōchi taiken*]. We believe that neither in their hearts nor in their minds do the subjects of Japan wish to create a body that would usurp the right of sovereignty and bestow it directly on the people so that the imperial house would lose its right to rule, as it did during the days of the usurpatious *bakufu*. Indeed, this would be contrary to our national polity [*kokutai*].[9]

Needless to say, the rejection of any "usurping power" (*hafu*) like the *bakufu* applied not just to the Diet but to all organs of state. The "restoration of monarchical rule" would permit no state organ to infringe on or usurp the absoluteness of imperial sovereignty.

In this sense, all organs of state sharing the exercise of imperial sovereignty in varying degrees existed relative to one another. Each organ existed independently of the others; each was directly answer-

8 Shunpōkō tsuishokai, *Itō Hirobumi den*, vol. 2 (Tokyo: Shunpoko tsuishokai, 1940), p. 652.
9 Hiratsuka Atsushi, ed., *Itō Hirobumi hiroku* (Tokyo: Shunjū, 1929), p. 227.

able only to the emperor; each had its own raison d'être for acting in the name of the emperor; and each had the function of checking the others. The court (*kyūchū*) and the government (*fuchū*) had their own special spheres; the cabinet, the Diet, and the judiciary were independent of one another, and each insisted on its equality with the others as independent separate organs; the Privy Council, maintaining its independence as an advisory organ to the emperor, could restrain the cabinet; and the military, reporting directly to the emperor, enjoyed an independence superior to that of all the other state organs.

Within the cabinet itself, each minister of state was directly and separately responsible to the emperor, giving each considerable independence vis-à-vis the prime minister and often making it difficult to maintain cabinet unity. Within the Imperial Diet too, the powers of the two chambers – the House of Representatives and the House of Peers – were balanced against each other in a way that promised conflict.

In sum, despite its emphasis on imperial sovereignty, or perhaps because of it, the Meiji constitutional structure embodied the separation of powers to a high degree; hence it also embodied a high degree of political pluralism. Behind the facade of a centralized and unitary imperial sovereignty worked a mechanism by which autonomous state organs mutually checked and balanced one another. Statecraft aiming at a pluralistic balance of power among the various organs of state shaped the actual operation of the Meiji constitutional structure. This system of divided powers, and the political pluralism that resulted, was grounded in the rejection of responsible parliamentary cabinets, or at least party cabinets, able to coordinate the government's legislative and administrative functions, as in the British system.

The system of divided powers reflected the basic character of eighteenth- and nineteenth-century Western constitutions on which the Meiji leaders modeled their own. For example, the drafters of the American Constitution had also tried to control the domination of the state by means of a parliamentary majority. This was why James Madison insisted so strongly on a bicameral system. The American Constitution's system of divided powers was intended above all to restrain tyranny by the majority. For the founding fathers of the United States, the highest purpose of the Constitution was the protection of liberty, especially religious liberty. They regarded party government, which implied control of the state by special interests, as incompatible with the claims of liberty. The highest purpose of the Meiji constitution, in contrast, was not the protection of liberty but the protection of imperial sovereignty. The system of division of powers could serve that goal, too. Just as the drafters of the American Constitution adopted the separation of powers and rejected party government in order to protect liberty, so too the drafters of the Meiji constitution insisted on the division of powers and rejected party cabinets in order to protect imperial sovereignty.

The concept of divided power sometimes was used ideologically in Japan to oppose the establishment of party cabinets. Hozumi Yatsuka, a professor of law at Tokyo Imperial University and well known as an ideological opponent of parliamentary rule, rejected English-style party cabinets as a kind of authoritarian political structure (*sensei seitai*), as they enabled one organ of state to dominate all the others. By contrast, he argued, constitutional government in Japan put into practice an American-style separation of powers to the highest degree. For Hozumi, the "national polity" (*kokutai*) embodied in the concept of imperial sovereignty was inseparable from the "political structure" (*seitai*) embodied in the practice of constitutional politics, that is, a divided-powers system.[10] In other words, the restraints on tyranny were as strong in the Japanese constitutional structure as they were in the American. Similarly, Uesugi Shinkichi, Hozumi's academic heir, emphasized that the basic principle of the Meiji constitution was the tripartite separation of powers. For example, in his interpretation of the constitution, Uesugi insisted that the judiciary was independent of the legislative power, and he argued for the right of judicial review (*hōritsu shinsaken*) by the Japanese courts.[11]

The prohibition of the publication of Minobe's *Kenpō satsuyō* (Outline of constitutional law) in 1935, as a result of the "organ theory" controversy, and the republication of Hozumi's long out-of-print textbook on constitutional theory reinforced the use of the separation-of-powers theory as an ideological weapon against the party cabinet system. During the Hirota Kōki cabinet, organized in 1936 under pressure from the army, members of the Army Military Affairs Section (Rikugunshō gunmuka) and the Cabinet Research Bureau spearheaded efforts to put into effect the cabinet's slogan: "renovation of all aspects of government (*shōsei isshin*)." One of their chief goals was to reform the Diet system.[12] In October 1936, Lieutenant Colonel Satō Kenryo, chief of the Internal Affairs Group (Gunmuka naiseihanchō) of the Military Affairs Section (Gunmuka naiseihan) in the War Ministry, was quoted

10 Hozumi Yatsuka, *Kempō teiyō* (Tokyo: Yūhikaku, 1935), pp. 67, 74–5.
11 Uesugi Shinkichi, *Teikoku kempō chikujō kōgi* (Tokyo: Nihon hyōronsha, 1935), pp. 164–5.
12 Hata Ikuhiko, *Gun fashizumu undōshi* (Tokyo: Kawade shobō shinsha, 1972), p. 177.

anonymously in the *Tōkyō asahi shinbun* as a representative of "influential reformist opinion" within the army:

Because the present-day Japanese Diet derives from the English-style parliamentary cabinet system, it devotes most of its energy to exercising its right to oversee the government rather than to legislate and to approve the budget. As a result, the Diet has been transformed into an arena of competition for political power, and important matters of legislation and budget approval are neglected. Hence, at the present moment, the Diet and the government, following American practice, should be considered as organs independent of each other, thereby establishing the principle of the tripartite division of power into executive, legislative, and judicial functions; the practice of organizing party cabinets based on a majority in the Diet should be abolished; and the party cabinet system should be completely rejected.[13]

Clearly, such views derived from Hozumi Yatsuka's theories regarding the Japanese political structure. The academic downfall of Minobe's theory, which had provided the most persuasive ideological support for party rule, marked the waning of party rule in practice.

The division of powers written into the Meiji constitution, and the political pluralism that resulted in practice, were, as we have seen, a product of the "restoration of monarchical rule" which rejected the notion of a "usurping power" (*hafu*) ruling in the place of the emperor, as the *bakufu* had. The existence of a political body resembling the *bakufu* remained consistently taboo under the constitution. Indeed, one of the reasons that the right wing later attacked the Imperial Rule Assistance Association in 1940–1 was that it resembled such a "*bakufu*-like body" (*bakufuteki sonzai*). The system of divided powers was intended to check the emergence of such a force and hence was consistent with the Restoration principle of returning sovereignty to the emperor.

The diffusion of power under the Meiji constitution meant that despite its superficially centralized framework, the political system lacked any institutional means of providing real unity. During his stay in Europe, Itō noted that the German emperor served this function: "Although the emperor constitutionally appears to be one of the parts of the [constitutional] machinery, he is not so in fact. He is the presiding agent who directs this machinery so that it is unimpeded in all things."[14] Itō tried to draw a parallel between the German emperor and the Japanese emperor. But because the Japanese emperor was supposed to be above politics, he could not become a "presiding agent" in the same way. Neither could the Japanese prime minister be

13 *Tōkyō asahi shinbun*, October 30, 1936. 14 Hiratsuka, *Itō*, p. 308.

likened to the German Reichskanzler. Under the system of joint ministerial responsibility, the Japanese prime minister's power to control members of the cabinet was weak, and in making policy, he had to work under the constraint of extracabinet bodies like the Privy Council and the military high commands. During the first ten years of constitutional government, the prime minister's position was even further weakened by the fact that – with the exception of the first Ōkuma cabinet in 1898 – no prime minister possessed a base of support in the Imperial Diet, especially in the lower house. Just as the emperor could not act like the Kaiser, Itō could not act like Bismarck.

If the formation of a balance of power among the fragmented organs of state making up the Meiji constitutional system were not to be left solely to chance, then some kind of extraconstitutional means had to be found to coordinate them so that the myth of imperial sovereignty (*kokutai*) could be reconciled with the constitutional reality of divided powers (*seitai*). The constitution had been drafted to prevent the emergence of a *bakufu*-like "usurping power" (*hafu*), but in order to make it run efficiently, there had to be an extraconstitutional force that would serve the function of such a power. The same, of course, was true of the American Constitution which also required an extraconstitutional element to make a highly fragmented constitutional system work. In the United States, this role was played by the two national political parties that controlled the national presidential elections. It is paradoxical but significant that these national political parties were organized by the drafters of the Constitution, men who had originally opposed the idea of political parties. According to the American historian Richard Hofstadter, ". . . we may say that it was the parties that rescued this Constitution against parties and made of it a working instrument of government."[15]

What emerged first in Japan as a "*bakufu*-like body" to coordinate the fragmented constitutional system was the *hanbatsu*, or "oligarchic clique." It was so called because most of its members came from either Chōshū or Satsuma, the two major domains (*han*) that had brought about the Meiji Restoration. The oligarchic clique could make the constitution work because its factional ties cut across the bureaucracy, the House of Peers, the Privy Council, the army, and the court. Its leaders were the *genrō*, elder statesmen, who in fact exercised many of

15 Richard Hofstadter, *The Idea of a Party System* (Berkeley and Los Angeles: University of California Press, 1969), p. 71.

the imperial prerogatives in the emperor's name. It was both historical irony and historical necessity that in order to run the constitutional system they had purposely created on the basis of a division of power, the very men who had attacked the legitimacy of the *bakufu* and overthrown it in 1868 should themselves become a *bakufu*-like body.

The leaders of the oligarchic clique, however, were unable to dominate one key organ of state, the House of Representatives. They had already rejected the idea of political parties and had neither the interest nor the organizational means to gather electoral support in the lower house of the Diet. This task was left to anti-*hanbatsu* leaders, many of them veterans of the antigovernment *jiyūminken* (popular rights) struggles of the 1870s and 1880s, who organized political parties to fight electoral battles and win Diet seats in the national elections. The two major political parties during the mid-1890s were the Jiyūtō (led by Itagaki Taisuke) and the Kaishintō, later renamed the Shinpotō (led by Ōkuma Shigenobu). It was they who controlled the majority of seats in the House of Representatives. Coming out of a tradition of opposition and resistance to oligarchic rule, the political parties acted as a fragmenting or decentralizing element in the constitutional structure. They threatened to use their constitutional power to block the passage of national budgets or national legislation. As long as the oligarchic leaders were committed to working within the Meiji constitutional structure, they could neither ignore nor reject the political parties if they wished to achieve internal political stability. On the contrary, they had to convert the parties into a tool for coordinating and centralizing power. To put it another way, the *hanbatsu* leaders had to develop links with the political parties.

It was also clear to the political parties that if they wanted to acquire more power, they had to cooperate or make political alliances with the *hanbatsu*. A majority in the lower house was not itself a guarantee of access to political power. In order to respond to the demands of provincial economic interests through the budgetary or legislative processes, it was necessary for the political parties to reach an understanding with the *hanbatsu* leaders who controlled the House of Peers. The *hanbatsu* leaders realized the limits to their ability to provide central direction within the constitutional structure, and the political parties realized the limits to their ability to expand their power. As a result, after the Sino-Japanese War of 1894–5 both political forces began to experiment with mutual alliances so as to overcome the limits under which each labored. This marked the first shift in the direction of party rule.

## THE ESTABLISHMENT OF THE SEIYŪKAI

Between 1895 and 1900, four *hanbatsu* cabinets attempted to make alliances with political parties, through either coalitions or cooperation. All but one (the third Itō Hirobumi cabinet) of these attempts succeeded. Except during the first Ōkuma cabinet of 1898, party politicians, whether affiliated with the Jiyutō or the Shinpotō, tried to cooperate with the *hanbatsu* leaders rather than to join against them. At first temporary in character, these party–*hanbatsu* alliances later turned into more stable long-term arrangements. The political parties not only cooperated in supporting *hanbatsu* cabinet policies, but they cooperated more directly by participating in the cabinets as well. None of this had characterized party–*hanbatsu* relationships before the Sino-Japanese War, especially during the first sessions of the Diet when both sides had been at loggerheads. The change shows how much of a transformation there had been in both the "transcendentalist" stance of the *hanbatsu* and the anti-*hanbatsu* stance of the "popular parties" (*mintō*).

The first step toward mutual rapprochement came at the end of the second Itō Hirobumi cabinet in November 1895 when the government struck an alliance with the Jiyūtō. The Jiyūtō's president, Itagaki Taisuke, became home minister in April 1896. Because this meant a major retreat from the principle of transcendentalism, its orthodox defenders reacted strongly. Most of the imperial appointees in the House of Peers, the Kokumin kyōkai (a lower-house faction led by Shinagawa Yajirō, who as home minister had directed government interference against the *mintō* opposition in the election of 1892), and some provincial governors serving directly under Itagaki responded to the Itō–Itagaki alliance with a sense of crisis. Looking to Yamagata Aritomo as a leader who could oppose Itō and the political party forces, they rallied to prepare for a Yamagata cabinet.

When the second Itō cabinet fell in September 1896, Matsukata Masayoshi was nominated prime minister in accordance with the custom of alternating that office between Chōshū and Satsuma men within the *hanbatsu* leadership. Since the inauguration of the cabinet system in 1885 when Itō Hirobumi, a Chōshū man, served as the first prime minister, the prime ministership had alternated between representatives from the Satsuma and Chōshū factions. In 1885 Itō was recommended for the office by Sanjō Sanetomi, the last imperial chancellor (*dajō daijin*), and the next three prime ministers – Kuroda Kiyotaka (Satsuma), Yamagata Aritomo (Chōshū), and Matsukata

Masayoshi (Satsuma) – each were nominated by their predecessors. After the formation of the second Itō cabinet in August 1892, a meeting of the *genrō* made up of representatives from both Satsuma and Chōshū nominated the incoming prime minister, but the principle of alternating between Satsuma and Chōshū men was followed until 1898.

The second Matsukata cabinet included not only representatives from Satsuma and Chōshū, but also Ōkuma Shigenobu, president of the Shinpotō, who served as foreign minister. The influence of the Shinpotō on the cabinet was substantial. The party supported the government in the lower house, and two Shinpotō-affiliated factions in the upper house (the Sanyokai and the Konwakai) did too. Dubbed the Matsukata–Ōkuma cabinet (*Showai naikaku*), this government was the second major party–*hanbatsu* alliance.

Itō returned to the prime ministership again in January 1898. Initially he proposed organizing a "national unity cabinet" (*kyōkoku itchi naikaku*) which would include the two major parties in the lower house, the Jiyūtō and the Shinpotō. Both parties favored cooperation, but the plan was ultimately frustrated by the breakdown of negotiations between them over the selection of cabinet ministers. In the end, the third Itō cabinet was organized on the principle of transcendentalism, much to the relief of the antiparty elements who had been maneuvering for a Yamagata cabinet. The cabinet lasted only six months, however. Both the major parties in the House of Representatives unfurled their banners as opposition parties when the cabinet introduced a bill to raise the land tax. The Kokumin kyōkai and the Yamagata wing of the *hanbatsu* gave their absolute support to Itō, but the Shinpotō and the Jiyūtō, in deference to provincial political interests, formed a coalition to defeat the bill. The antitax coalition in turn promoted a merger between the two parties to secure an absolute majority in the lower house. When Itō dissolved the House of Representatives because of opposition to the tax bill, the planned merger went forward. In June 1898 a new party, the Kenseitō, was organized from the ranks of the Shinpotō and the Jiyūtō, in effect reviving the tactics of "popular coalitions" that had characterized the first Diet sessions.

The prospect of a powerful new opposition party shocked and upset all the *hanbatsu* leaders. But they were divided in their views on how to deal with it. A group of hard-liners favoring noncooperation wanted to resist the new party by strengthening the solidarity of the Chōshū and Satsuma factions within the *hanbatsu*. They wanted to force through the Diet a fiscal policy that included both increased military expansion and increased taxes to finance it, even if a suspension of the constitution was required in addition to a dissolution of the Diet.

A second group, taking up an idea that had been proposed by Itō and abandoned many times before, wanted to organize a progovernment party to oppose the Kenseitō. The idea was that Itō, cooperating with Finance Minister Inoue Kaoru, would pull together a political organization made up of forces that directly or indirectly supported the land tax increase. As leader of the new party, Itō would fight the Kenseitō in the ensuing election. But Yamagata and his supporters opposed this plan. Yamagata realized the necessity of having a political party able to struggle against the Kenseitō, but he thought that it would violate the principle of transcendentalism for Itō to lead such a party while he was still both a prime minister and a *genrō*. He feared that such tactics would open the way to party cabinets.

A third group proposed a course of action that Itō finally chose, to hand over political power to the Kenseitō which was certain to control the House of Representatives after the coming general election. When an imperial conference (*gozen kaigi*) unanimously opposed the second proposal – the formation of a new party with Itō as its head – Itō offered his resignation. Because none of the other *genrō* wanted to fight the new party, Itō recommended that Ōkuma and Itagaki, the two principal leaders of the Kenseitō, be asked to form a cabinet. Inoue Kaoru argued that this alternative was preferable to forming a party under Itō's leadership. A Kenseitō cabinet with no base of power outside the Diet would have limited ability to centralize control over the government and would soon disintegrate. In other words, by a nice irony, a political party cabinet would bury by its own hand the practice of responsible government. Whether Itō agreed with Inoue's prediction is not clear, but there is no question that he took the initiative in proposing a Kenseitō cabinet. It was the best course of action for both himself and the antiparty elements in the *hanbatsu*.

As events turned out, Inoue's prognostication proved correct. The Ōkuma – Itagaki cabinet, formed in June 1898, probably should be called the first party cabinet in Japan. All its ministers, with the exception of the military service ministers, were members of the Kenseitō, and the party secured an absolute majority in the lower house in the 1898 election, capturing 244 seats out of 300. Despite this apparently strong position, however, the cabinet was beset by fatal weaknesses. The two military ministers, War Minister Katsura Tarō and Navy Minister Saigō Tsugumichi, both antiparty, made clear to

Ōkuma and Itagaki that they were entering the cabinet as "alien elements." Both intrigued with antiparty forces outside the cabinet to hasten its downfall. According to Katsura's later comment, the two service ministers were able to "paralyze the cabinet."[16] Beyond their intrigues, other factors generated by the internal politics of the Kenseitō worked against the longevity of the cabinet.

First, there was the internal dispute within the Kenseitō over the tax increase question. Although the Ōkuma–Itagaki cabinet, like all the cabinets after the Sino-Japanese War, was committed to plans for increased expeditures on military armaments and on expanded telegraph, railway and steel-making capacities, it could not do so without a tax rise to increase government revenues. Because the Kenseitō grew out of an alliance of two parties united against a land tax increase, the cabinet sought to raise other taxes. However, a powerful segment within the party reflecting urban industrial and commercial interests felt that the policy of increased expenditure should be pursued vigorously and effectively even if it meant higher land taxes. A representative of this view was Hoshi Tōru, leader of the Kantō faction of the old Jiyūtō and a powerful member of the Tokyo municipal assembly. Hoshi thought that party support should be broadened to include the urban mercantile and manufacturing classes as well as the well-to-do elements in the countryside. He also thought that a land tax increase was inevitable. But if he pressed these views, a rupture of the Kenseitō would be inevitable. The tax increase issue thus was a dispute over the future of the party.

There were also conflicts within the Kenseitō over the division of internal party authority. Former Jiyūtō members fought with former Shinpotō members over decisions about the establishment of branch offices, the selection of party officials, and the endorsement of official party electoral candidates. When the cabinet was organized, there also were conflicts over the distribution of ministerial posts and *chokunin*-rank official positions. Hoshi, taking advantage of the discontent generated by these disputes, worked with other former Jiyūtō members to bring down the cabinet in hopes of reviving the Jiyūtō as an independent party with an absolute majority in the lower house.

Opposed by powerful outside forces and riven by internal party conflict, the Ōkuma–Itagaki cabinet collapsed after a scant four months. The collapse of the cabinet demonstrated how weakened were

16 Katsura Tarō, "Katsura Tarō jiden," vol. 3 (unpublished material in the Kokuritsu kokkai toshokan, Kensei shiryō shitsu).

the bonds that had held together popular-party coalitions during the first Diet sessions. These coalitions had been brought together by the slogans "relief for the people" (*minryoku kyūyō*) and "reduction of the land tax" (*chiso keigen*). But as former Jiyūtō and Shinpotō politicians committed themselves to the postwar expansion of armaments and economic infrastructure and as they voiced their cooperation with a policy of "national wealth and power" (*fukoku kyōhei*), such slogans lost meaning. Opposition to the increase of land taxes had temporarily brought them together, but it would not have kept them together had either party succeeded in cooperating with the third Itō cabinet. Their relationship was not one of unity but of competition for hegemony in the Diet. Just as there were fragmentation and competition among the oligarchic forces, so too the fragmentation and competition grew more intense among the party politicians.

Hoshi Tōru moved most consistently toward an adversary relationship with rival party politicians. Indeed, he began to work actively for an alliance with the *hanbatsu* to increase the predominance of his party within the House of Representatives. After all, he was competing in the lower house not with the *hanbatsu* but with other party politicians. It was to position himself advantageously in this competition that he split the Kenseitō in October 1898 and prepared to ally with the second Yamagata cabinet, successor to the doomed Ōkuma–Itagaki government.

The orthodox transcendentalists, forced to the sidelines after the Sino-Japanese War, eagerly welcomed the formation of the second Yamagata cabinet in November 1898. It included members of the Yamagata faction as well as representatives of the Satsuma faction (Matsukata Masayoshi, Saigō Tsugumichi, and Kabayama Sukemori). It also excluded both party politicians and members of the Itō faction. But even such a cabinet had to secure cooperation from a majority in the lower house of the Diet to pass legislation and a budget to finance its industrialization and rearmament policies. Whatever its principles, in practice a transcendental cabinet like Yamagata's could not avoid cooperation with a political party. When Yamagata made overtures through Katsura Tarō to the Kenseitō, which now consisted mainly of former Jiyūtō men led by Hoshi Tōru, he was able to establish a working relationship. Confident of support in the lower house, Yamagata introduced a tax increase bill, including a land tax increase, in November 1898.

The Kenseihontō, which was composed of former Shimpotō members, naturally opposed the bill. But there were also divided counsels within the progovernment Kenseitō. Some members favored the bill, and others opposed it on hard practical grounds. "Reduction of land taxes" had been a slogan of the party in earlier sessions of the Diet. Opposition to land tax increases was a sine qua non for a party with a rural electoral base among the landowning classes. If the Kenseitō supported the land tax increase but the bill failed, then the House of Representatives would be dissolved, leaving the Kenseitō to face a hard battle in the following election. Hoshi built an internal party consensus in support of the tax bill by arguing that the future expansion of party power lay in building support among the urban mercantile and manufacturing classes, whose latent political power he had come to recognize. (Indeed, for that reason he had become a member of the Tokyo Municipal Assembly and the Tokyo Municipal Council.) Urban business interests, backed by provincial chambers of commerce, had organized the League to Increase Land Taxes (Chiso zōchō kisei dōmeikai) to lobby the government and the Diet membership. The Kenseitō had made the nationalization of the railroads, a demand of the railroad interests, as a condition for cooperation with Yamagata, and for this a tax increase was also needed. These were additional reasons that it was to the Kenseitō's advantage to support land tax increases and for Hoshi to win over opponents within his party. The final passage of the land tax increase bill in December 1898 marked a decisive stage in the rapprochement between the party politicians and the *hanbatsu:* It finally eliminated the land tax increase issue.

In 1900, during its next session, the Diet approved a bill proposed by the government to revise the House of Representatives Election Law. Once again the Yamagata government and the Kenseitō cooperated to meet the demands of the urban mercantile and manufacturing classes. The electoral revision had two key parts. First, the tax qualification on the right to vote in a lower-house election was lowered from ¥15 in direct national taxes to ¥10, a change that nearly doubled the number of eligible voters from 502,000 in 1898 to 982,000 in 1900; and the tax qualification on the right to stand for election was also eliminated. Second, the existing small electoral district (one member per district with a few districts returning two members) was replaced by a system of prefecture-sized rural electoral districts and independent urban electoral districts for cities with populations of over 30,000. The new system favored the urban districts, where as few as 30,000 could be represented by a Diet member, over the rural districts, where as many as 130,000 could be represented by one member.

The passage of the electoral law revision reflected the great importance that both the government and the Kenseitō attached to the demands of the urban merchants and manufacturers. In 1899 and 1900, city-based business groups had mounted a vigorous campaign to establish independent urban electoral districts. The League to Revise the House of Representatives Election Law (Shūgiin senkyohō kaisei kisei dōmeikai) formed in January 1899 proclaimed as its goal a revision of the election law "in order to expand the rights of our merchants and manufacturers and to achieve their full political enfranchisement." The president of the league was Shibusawa Eiichi, and its two chief secretaries were Ōkura Kihachirō and Yasuda Zenjirō, all powerful business leaders. The membership of the organization from the leadership down overlapped with that of the League to Increase Land Taxes, a clear indication that the tax revision movement was also a movement to increase business influence in politics. After late 1899, local chambers of commerce throughout the country also banded together to form the Joint Committee of the National Chambers of Commerce for the Revision of the House of Representatives Election Law (Senkyohō kaisei kisei zenkoku kakushi rengōkai). In the face of this movement, Hoshi Tōru and other Kenseitō leaders pursued the same logic as during the effort to raise the land tax. Backing election law revision gave the party an opportunity to gather support among the urban business class. In fact, the revised law increased the number of Diet members representing urban districts, from 17 (about 5.7 percent), out of a total of 300, to 61 (about 15.5 percent), out of 369 members.

The same session that passed the electoral law also approved the government-sponsored Police Peace Law (Chian keisatsuhō) which included regulations for the control of labor and tenancy disputes. In 1898 and 1899 there had been a number of large strikes, and the labor unions had made some headway among skilled workers in the railroad, shipbuilding, machinery, and printing industries. The government bill was a legal response to these alarming social trends. The Yamagata government is said to have modeled its draft on a bill that failed in the German Reichstag in May 1899 owing to the opposition of the German Social Democratic Party. There was hardly any debate at all on the bill in the Japanese Diet, in which the rural landlord and urban business classes were represented but the working class and the tenant class were not. The passage of the law made the leaders of the embryonic labor movement painfully aware of its limitations. In 1901 the Japanese Social Democratic Party was organized on the model of the German party, but the government immediately prohibited it.

There were limits to the 1898–1900 Kenseitō alliance with Yamagata. Whereas members of the Yamagata faction wanted party cooperation from outside the cabinet, they did not want party members to join the cabinet. When Hoshi saw that the reward for cooperation did not extend to the distribution of ministerial portfolios, he decided to end the alliance. Determined to participate in the cabinet that succeeded it, he visited Itō Hirobumi with a request that the elder statesman become president of the Kenseitō. This was in line with the strategy he had pursued consistently since the rupture of the Jiyūtō–Shinpotō coalition. His goal was to make his party the government party so as to secure hegemony in the lower house. His aim in approaching Itō was to win political advantage over the Kenseihontō, his rival in the competition for control of the House of Representatives.

Itō, on the other hand, wanted to form a new political party to remedy the long-standing weaknesses of the existing political parties, and so he turned down Hoshi's request to become the Kenseitō's president. The ever-resourceful Hoshi responded by offering to dissolve the Kenseitō and to merge its membership into Itō's new party. He thought that by hanging onto Itō's coattails, the Kenseitō could expand its influence and move closer to control over the cabinet.

The offer was attractive to Itō, whose consistent political goal since the end of the Sino-Japanese war had been the creation of a "national-unity" system that would include the political parties. From the spring of 1899, Itō had begun to think about organizing a party centering on his bureaucratic associates and drawing support from the urban mercantile and manufacturing classes. After negotiating with Hoshi, he also decided that it would be advantageous to his own political goals to absorb the Kenseitō membership with its provincial electoral bases into the new party. So he agreed to Hoshi's proposal. In September 1900 amid great fanfare, Itō announced the organization of the Rikken Seiyūkai, a new political party. It was to dominate Japanese party politics for the next two decades. More immediately, however, the organization of the party can be seen as the result of the logical conclusions reached out of political necessity by elements within both the *hanbatsu* and the political parties.[17] The *hanbatsu* leaders wanted stable support in the Diet, and the party politicians wanted greater access to control over the government.

17 Concerning the background of the Rikken Seiyūkai's establishment, see Mitani Taichirō, "Seiyūkai no seiritsu," in *Iwanami kōza Nihon rekishi* (Tokyo, Iwanami shoten, 1976), vol. 16 (*Kindai*, vol. 3), p. 16. In English the standard work on the Seiyūkai is by Tetsuo Najita, *Hara Kei in the Politics of Compromise, 1905–1915* (Cambridge, Mass.: Harvard University Press, 1967). See also George Akita, *The Foundations of Constitutional Government in Modern Japan* (Cambridge, Mass.: Harvard University Press, 1967).

Although conceived by Itō as the political core body that could coordinate the fragmented Meiji constitutional structure, the Seiyūkai did not completely absorb all the important actors in national politics. Within the *hanbatsu* it was opposed by the Yamagata faction, and within the Diet it was opposed by two smaller parties, the Kenseihontō and its offspring the Kokumintō. Of these two anti-Seiyūkai forces, the Yamagata faction was the more important, as it controlled a majority in the House of Peers to counterbalance the Seiyūkai's majority in the House of Representatives. This meant that cooperation between the *hanbatsu* and the parties, obviously needed to make the constitutional structure work as a coordinated instrument, took on a new form, especially after Itō's resignation as the Seiyūkai's president in July 1903.

Between the outbreak of the Russo-Japanese War in 1904 and the end of the Meiji period in 1912, power shifted back and forth between the two men who controlled the upper and lower houses of the Diet. Katsura Tarō, who as Yamagata's proxy manipulated a majority in the House of Peers, headed three cabinets during this period; and Saionji Kinmochi, who succeeded as the Seiyūkai's president, headed two.

Hara Takashi, the most influential Seiyūkai leader under Saionji, had concluded that political stability could be achieved only if two of the three major political elements – the Yamagata faction, the Seiyūkai, and the Kenseihontō – joined forces. He rejected the idea of a party coalition between the Seiyūkai and the Kenseihontō (later the Kokumintō) and chose instead to strike an alliance with the Yamagata faction through negotiations with Katsura. This opened the way to alternating control over the cabinet between the Seiyūkai and the Yamagata faction. Hara's strategy followed that of Hoshi, whom Hara had succeeded as leader of the Kantō faction within the Seiyūkai after Hoshi's assassination in 1901. The strategy contrasted with that of Inukai Tsuyoshi, one of the principal leaders of the Kenseihontō, who consistently called for a party coalition with the Seiyūkai.

Even though the Yamagata faction chose to strike bargains with the Seiyūkai, the largest party in the lower house, relations between the two were fraught with tension and conflict. The two political forces frequently fought over policy issues. From time to time Katsura urged the formation of an anti-Seiyūkai coalition (including the Kenseihontō) to curb the Seiyūkai's influence. The Yamagata faction, which controlled the House of Peers, wanted to free itself from the Seiyūkai's grasp, and the Seiyūkai, under Hara's initiative, sometimes challenged the dominance of the Yamagata faction in the upper house. Nevertheless, both the Seiyūkai and the Yamagata faction ultimately had to cooperate in carrying out important national policies, especially the management of the country's finances. It was easy for the Yamagata faction to deal with the Seiyūkai, as Hara and Matsuda Masahisa, the two main party leaders, could forge an internal party consensus. By working with them it was possible to achieve a stable and reliable give-and-take with the party. By contrast, even if the other Diet groups – the Kenseihontō and the various small factions linked to the Yamagata faction such as the Daidō Club, the Bōshin Club, or the Chūō Club into which the first two eventually merged – were to form an anti-Seiyūkai coalition, there would be substantial political differences among them. Furthermore, the Kenseihontō was split between those who wanted to ally with the Yamagata faction and those who wanted to ally with the Seiyūkai. Hence it was no easy matter to work out compromises on national policy with an anti-Seiyūkai coalition. The Yamagata faction had to rely on the Seiyūkai; and as long as Seiyūkai influence in the House of Peers was confined to a minority there, the party had to work with the Yamagata faction. This balance of power between the two houses in the Diet eventually fell apart as a result of the Taishō political crisis of 1912–13 when Katsura tried to break the hold of the Seiyūkai on the House of Representatives, by organizing his own political party, the Rikken Dōshikai.

In any case, it is clear that after the Sino-Japanese War, the *hanbatsu* leaders had learned that if they wished to overcome constraints on their ability to control the constitutional structure, they had to collaborate with the party politicians, form alliances with them, or organize political parties of their own. Ironically, by pursuing these tactics, the *hanbatsu* leaders did not bring the parties directly under their control. Rather, *hanbatsu* leaders were co-opted into the party system. The *hanbatsu* was a closed group whose original cohesion lay primarily in regional ties, and it was difficult to expand or reproduce through a process of self-regeneration. Ties within the *hanbatsu* rested on the shared experience of carrying out the Restoration and building a new state. These ties could not be transmitted to younger leaders, and neither could the enormous prestige acquired by the *genrō* in their service to the nation. The *hanbatsu* were used to being in the minority. When such a group attempted to transform itself into the majority because it needed the backing of numbers, it lost its rationale and its influence. In attempting to control a majority in the House of Representatives, the power of the *hanbatsu* leaders became attenuated, and in the end they were absorbed into the political party system.

With the passing of the *hanbatsu* leadership – that is, with the death of the *genrō* – one can ask whether there was any force but the political parties capable of acting as a political core body able to coordinate the fragmented constitutional structure. Was there any other potential "*bakufu*-like body" that could create linkages among the various organs of state, bringing cohesion to the operation of the state? The army, the Privy Council, and the administrative bureaucracy all had strong power as veto groups able to check the political parties, but all were based in one organ of state. Even though each group was highly independent, none could create the kind of linkages needed to make the government work smoothly, and hence none could become a *bakufu*-like body. If the stabilization of the constitutional structure was not to be haphazard and if there was to be a coordinating element that the constitution failed to provide, then there was nowhere to look but to the political parties. It was inevitable that they serve as a *bakufu*-like body.

To summarize, the party cabinets were paradoxically the inevitable product of a constitution shaped by antiparty sentiments. We can perhaps see this paradox as similar to the development in the American Constitution, likewise drafted by men of antiparty sentiment, of national political parties to provide cohesion in a separation-of-powers system, and of a presidential electoral system based on these national parties.

## CONDITIONS FOR PARTY CABINETS

Now let us consider the actual conditions that enabled the establishment of party cabinets between 1924 and 1933. What were the political realities that led to a general recognition that political party cabinets were superior to other alternatives?[18]

### *Relations between the House of Representatives and the House of Peers*

First there was the consolidation of the House of Representatives in a position superior to that of the House of Peers. As we have seen, the Seiyūkai was unable to absorb all the contending forces in the *hanbatsu* and the political parties. It had established itself as an absolute major-

18 Political developments between 1912 and 1927 are covered in Peter Duus, *Party Rivalry and Political Change in Taishō Japan* (Cambridge, Mass.: Harvard University Press, 1968).

ity party in the House of Representatives. But in the House of Peers the party had no more than unstable minority support. The upper house was dominated by the *hanbatsu* leadership, especially by Yamagata, who continued to be hostile toward the Seiyūkai. After Itō Hirobumi and his protégés left the party in 1903, the party's influence in the upper house declined even further.

Hara Takashi, the real power in the party and its chief strategist under Saionji, tried in various ways to reverse this situation. He began by making a direct approach to Katsura Tarō, Yamagata's chief lieutenant. Katsura, who became prime minister in June 1901, once boasted, "The House of Representatives may be Saionji's, but the House of Peers is mine."[19] In January 1906 Hara proposed to support Katsura in the House of Representatives if in return the pro-*hanbatsu* forces cooperated with Seiyūkai policy in the House of Peers. Katsura agreed. What was at stake, however, was not simply policy but control over the government itself. In effect Hara and Katsura had agreed to a give-and-take balance of power between the upper and lower houses of the Diet.

But Hara was not content with such a balance of power. He wanted to challenge the pro-*hanbatsu* hegemony in the House of Peers. When he became home minister under the first Saionji cabinet, he twice (in 1907 and 1908) introduced bills to abolish the *gun* (county).[20] The *gun* was an administrative unit that directly supervised the towns (*machi*) and villages (*mura*) at the lowest level of the local government system. It was established in 1890 by Home Minister Yamagata on the model of the Prussian *kreis*, the self-governing unit of the Junker class. Although the *gun* occupied an intermediate position between the local communities and the prefecture, it was not in fact a self-governing unit; rather, it was the lowest level of the Home Ministry bureaucracy. During the last years of the Meiji period, the county chief (*gunchō*) was appointed by the home minister. Politically the *gun* was the provincial base of the Yamagata faction which enjoyed enormous influence in the home ministry after the establishment of the local government system in the 1880s. By proposing to abolish the *gun* as an administrative unit, Hara was attempting to free the towns and villages, the provincial bases of political party power, from the influence of the home ministry

19 Hara Takashi, *Hara Takashi nikki*, vol. 2 (Tokyo: Fukumura shuppan, 1965), entry for April 18, 1909.

20 Concerning the political process in the dissolution of the *gun* system, see Mitani Taichirō, *Nihon seitō seiji no keisi–Hara Kei no seiji shidō tenkai* (Tokyo: Tokyo daigaku shuppankai, 1967).

and to increase the position and authority of the local officials, especially the local mayors. At the same time the abolition of the *gun* would also strike a severe blow to the influence of the Yamagata faction.

In order to win support for the *gun* abolition bill in the upper house, Hara arranged to bring two influential House of Peers members into the Saionji cabinet: One was Senke Takanori, member of the Mokuyōkai, an organization of hereditary baron-rank holders; and the other was Hotta Masayasu, member of the Kenkyūkai, the largest faction in the House of Peers, organized mainly of hereditary viscount-rank holders. Hara knew that there was no unanimity regarding the preservation of the *gun* system among Yamagata-linked imperial appointees in the House of Peers. He hoped that the debate over the *gun* abolition bill would split the majority factions in the House of Peers. Because he knew that there was support for the bill outside the Seiyūkai, he felt that the issue was a good one to challenge the *hanbatsu* forces. "Public opinion" was on his side.

The pro-*hanbatsu* majority in the House of Peers rested on cooperation between the Sawakai (the majority faction among the imperially appointed peers) and the Kenkyūkai (the majority faction among the hereditary peers). To maintain this power base, Yamagata and his lieutenants worked hard to turn the Kenkyūkai and other factions against the *gun* abolition bill. At the same time, they tried to outflank the Seiyūkai by creating an opposition majority in the lower house through the organization of an anti-Seiyūkai coalition made up of the Kenseihontō and the Daidō Kurabu, the second and third largest parties in the House. The clash between the Seiyūkai and the *hanbatsu* forces ended in a draw, however. The *gun* abolition bill passed in the House of Representatives but failed in the House of Peers. The balance of power remained unchanged. Nevertheless, the tactics that each side used were similar. Each tried to create a vertical linkage between the two houses by building majorities in both. These "vertical linkage" tactics were to be used again – in 1913 by the *hanbatsu* and in 1920 by the Seiyūkai.

Katsura was no more content with the existing balance of power between the two houses than Hara was. During his first two cabinets (1901–6, 1908–11), Katsura had secured for some policies solid Diet support through negotiations with Hara. As a result, both cabinets were relatively stable and long-lived. Once a cooperative relationship with Hara was established, Katsura had no difficulty in getting his budgets approved, and he had no need to discipline the House of Representatives by dissolving it. But Katsura was still not satisfied. In the final analysis, the Seiyūkai's support for his government rested on political horse trades. Hence it was neither permanent nor stable. If the Seiyūkai wanted to go its own way, it would do so.

For example, in 1911 during the second Katsura cabinet, when cooperation with the Seiyūkai was touted as "unity of understanding" (*jōi tōgō*), the party gave no support to Katsura's plan to convert to broad gauge the trunk railway line between Tokyo and Shimonoseki. The plan ran counter to the Seiyūkai policy of giving budget priority to the construction of new provincial railway lines, a policy the party used to build local electoral support.[21] From the end of the Russo-Japanese War into the 1910s, the Seiyūkai maintained its position as the majority party by pursuing a "positive policy" that promoted electoral support in the provinces. Through its bargains with the Yamagata faction, the party was able to manipulate priorities in the distribution of national expenditures. The core of the Seiyūkai's positive policy was increasing expenditures for the national transportation and communication network, by building railroads lines, improving harbors, damming and diking rivers, constructing roads, building bridges, and installing telephone and telegraph lines. Hara attached particular importance to railroad construction and harbor improvement. By acting as a conduit for requests from local communities for such nationally financed projects, the Seiyūkai managed to pick up support among the electorate. This "positive policy" was very much in contrast with the "negative policy" followed by the political parties before the Sino-Japanese War when they had called for "reductions in government expenditure" and a "reduction of the land tax."[22]

During the second Saionji cabinet (1911–12), the Seiyūkai resisted demands by Yamagata and Katsura to increase the army by two divisions. The Seiyūkai-supported cabinet naturally refused to go along with the army's request because it contradicted the cabinet's financial retrenchment policy aimed at dealing with import surpluses, increases in public indebtedness abroad, and the resulting large outflow of specie. There were political considerations as well. An increased military budget would threaten the expenditures for railroad construction and harbor improvement pushed by Home Minister Hara. Furthermore, in hopes of using the navy and the Satsuma faction to curb the power of the army and the Chōshū faction, Prime Minister Saionji and Justice Minister Matsuda had agreed to an increase in the naval budget at

21 For a discussion of the political struggle between the Seiyūkai and the second Katsura cabinet over plans to broaden the gauge of trunk-line tracks, see Mitani, *Nihon seitō*.
22 Banno Junji, *Taishō seihen* (Kyoto: Minerva shobō, 1982), pp. 68–115.

the expense of the army's plan for expansion. Yamagata and Katsura were very much on guard against the possibility that the Seiyūkai might join political forces with the Satsuma faction and the navy if both took the same position on the question of the military budget.

As long as the Seiyūkai controlled a majority in the House of Representatives, there were limits on the policy concessions that the Yamagata faction would negotiate with Hara. To be sure, Katsura did not once dissolve the lower house during his years in office after 1905, but he was well aware that his ability to do so was directly or indirectly restricted by the political bargains he had struck with the Seiyūkai. To maintain its majority in the House of Representatives, the Seiyūkai always wanted the advantage of facing the electorate as the progovernment party. For this reason, the party leaders made Katsura promise in return for their cooperation not to exercise his right to dissolve the Diet. When the first Saionji cabinet held a general election in May 1908 (the full term of the Diet had expired), the progovernment Seiyūkai won an absolute majority. Even so, the cabinet resigned only two months after the election. Many found it difficult to understand the reasons for this resignation, but probably it resulted from secret negotiations between Katsura and Saionji in which the Seiyūkai's president agreed to turn over power to Katsura on the understanding that he would not dissolve the Diet during his period as prime minister. In other words, a deal was struck whereby the Seiyūkai could maintain its majority position and the *hanbatsu* were given a smooth transfer of political power.

If it is true that Katsura could not exercise his constitutional power to dissolve the Diet because of bargains struck with Hara or Saionji, then the disadvantages of such bargains were considerable. If the lower house could not be dissolved, then the Seiyūkai majority remained unshakable, and the House of Representatives stayed under its control. The *hanbatsu* forces would continue to labor under this constraint. For this reason Katsura attempted, just as Hara had, to challenge the balance of power between the two houses.

When the second Saionji cabinet fell after the army refused to provide a war minister in retaliation for Saionji's refusal to increase the army by two divisions, Katsura was called back to office. In organizing his new cabinet, he decided to abandon the tactics of cooperation with the Seiyūkai he had followed since 1905. To secure hegemony in the House of Representatives, he organized a political party under his own leadership, the Rikken Dōshikai. His main effort was to gather together anti-Seiyūkai factions in the House of Representatives. These scattered minority parties had long discussed the possibility of an anti-Seiyūkai coalition to break its hold on the lower-house majority. Their interests meshed neatly with Katsura, who felt that the command of his own new political party would allow him to dissolve the lower house and preside over an election that would destroy the Seiyūkai majority.

A powerful segment of the political public thought that the organization of the third Katsura cabinet was a violation of the rules of constitutional government. Before his nomination as prime minister, Katsura had been serving as lord keeper of the privy seal and grand chamberlain, the two most powerful posts in the imperial court. His direct move into the cabinet made it appear that he was disregarding the clear political lines drawn between "court" (*kyūchū*) and "government" (*fuchū*) in order to serve the political interests of the Yamagata faction. A nationwide political movement to protest the "unconstitutionality" of the Katsura cabinet gathered momentum in late December 1912. Public rallies called for the "overthrow of *hanbatsu* government," and a vociferous press campaign was mounted against the new cabinet. In February 1913, bowing to the pressure of this first "movement to protect constitutional government" (*kensei yōgo undō*), Katsura resigned from office. His plan to overturn the balance of power between the two houses had been thwarted by political turmoil. A few months later he died of cancer. But the new political party he had organized remained intact under the leadership of Katō Takaaki, and so did his design for curbing the power of the Seiyūkai. Ironically, that design was carried out in 1915 under the second cabinet of Ōkuma Shigenobu, who was once regarded as the greatest enemy of the *hanbatsu*.

Ōkuma in 1915 was no longer the man he had been in 1898, for his own political career as leader of the Kenseihontō had been thwarted by the subsequent rise of the Seiyūkai. He had been nominated as prime minister by Inoue Kaoru, a *genrō* of the Chōshū faction. After the fall of the third Katsura cabinet in 1913, Inoue and Yamagata had become deeply concerned over the formation of the first Yamamoto Gonnohyōe cabinet, headed by an admiral of the Satsuma faction and supported by the Seiyūkai. They feared that the Satsuma faction (which had not produced a prime minister for fifteen years), supported by an alliance between the navy and the Seiyūkai, might seize a predominant position in the political world. When the Yamamoto cabinet fell in March 1914 as a result of a naval bribery scandal, the two *genrō* tried to reverse matters by organizing an Ōkuma cabinet supported by a coalition of the Dōshikai, the army, and the upper-house majority led by the Yamagata faction. In effect, this was a revival of the strategy Inoue had conceived in 1888–9 when he had proposed to build majority support for the government in the House of Representatives, by organizing the progovernment Jichitō and allying it with the Kaishintō led by Ōkuma. In 1914 Inoue did not command a party organization comparable to that of the Jichitō, but the army and the Yamagata faction could be used in its stead.

Although the *genrō* decision to back Ōkuma was certainly ingenious, it was neither unexpected nor accidental. A few years earlier, around 1911, Major General Tanaka Giichi, generally viewed as the rising star in the Chōshū faction, had hoped to recruit Kokumintō support for a Terauchi Masatake cabinet. He tried to cultivate ties with Ōkuma, who was invited to give a speech to one of the regiments under Tanaka's command as head of the Second Infantry Brigade. The invitation, extended by the putative heir of *hanbatsu* leadership to a man regarded as a symbol of the anti-*hanbatsu* forces, created quite a stir. But Ōkuma, who had withdrawn from the front lines of the political world after his ouster as president of the Kenseihontō in 1907, does not appear to have rebuffed Tanaka's approach. Indeed, Ōkuma was critical of the "movement to protect constitutional government" in 1912–13, and he had shown himself friendly to Katsura's new party, the Dōshikai. When the chance came to restore his political fortunes as prime minister in 1914, Ōkuma took it. Unlike Itagaki Taisuke, who had been forced out of political leadership with the formation of the Seiyūkai in 1900 and never recovered his political career, Ōkuma was finally able to return to the office he loved so much.

When nominated to form a cabinet in 1914, Ōkuma turned to the Dōshikai for support in the lower house. In the general election of 1915, his government worked assiduously to defeat the Seiyūkai. As a result of the election, the Seiyūkai fell to the position of second place in the Diet for the first time since its formation. It lost not only the absolute majority held in the House of Representatives since the Russo-Japanese War but also the stable base of power sustained by the inability of the *hanbatsu* forces to dissolve the Diet. With the collapse of an absolute majority in the lower house, the balance of power between the two houses was thrown out of kilter. The stable pro-*hanbatsu* elements in the House of Peers regained a position of political superiority over the divided parties in the House of Representatives.

In the lower house, where the Seiyūkai had lost its absolute majority, the smaller political parties that had suffered at the hands of the

Seiyūkai since 1900 regained their relative political importance. The Terauchi cabinet, which succeeded the second Ōkuma cabinet in 1917, therefore attempted to build Diet support by relying on neutral factions absorbed by neither the Seiyūkai nor the Dōshikai (renamed the Kenseikai in 1916). In other words, Terauchi tried to use the standoff between the two large parties in the House of Representatives to preserve his own political strength. This configuration in the lower house was very much to Yamagata's liking. In contrast with Katsura, he wanted no majority party in the House of Representatives, not even one under his own control. Instead, he preferred a multipolar balance among a number of weak minority factions. A fragmented lower house was a weak one, and to Yamagata that was desirable.

Hara Takashi, who had become the Seiyūkai's president in 1914, had not abandoned his goal of maintaining the Seiyūkai's position as the absolute majority party, and he was willing to curry favor with Terauchi in order to do so. The Seiyūkai leadership welcomed Terauchi's refusal to cooperate with Katō Takaaki of the Dōshikai, despite the urging of both Ōkuma and Yamagata. Publicly announcing an attitude of "benevolent neutrality" toward the Terauchi government, the Seiyūkai in reality acted informally as the progovernment party by supporting the prime minister, who had no lower-house majority of his own. When general elections were called in 1917, the Seiyūkai had the advantage of influence with the government, and as a result, it regained a plurality position in the lower house.[23] Once the election was over, the party leadership continued to pursue its public tactics of neutrality but privately sat waiting for the unpopular Terauchi's "self-destruction" and an opportunity to organize a successor cabinet based on the party's Diet plurality.[24]

The final emergence of a Seiyūkai cabinet in 1918 rested not so much on the party plurality as on the absence of anyone but Hara Takashi to succeed Terauchi. To be sure, the outbreak of world war and the changing social conditions brought about by the 1918 riots played a role in the *genrō* decision to nominate Hara. But more impor-

23 While maintaining contact with Terauchi cabinet members, Gotō Shinpei (home minister) and Den Kenjirō (communications minister), the Seiyūkai received both direct and indirect government support in the election battle. Gotō, as home minister, held the position of greatest responsibility in managing the election process. He accordingly instructed local governors to overturn the Kenseikai's "unnatural minority."

24 Toward the end of the Terauchi cabinet, Hara attempted to distance himself from the cabinet in order to avoid sharing Terauchi's fate. Hara was, however, able to avoid a showdown with Terauchi. With the rice riots, the government's existence was endangered, and Hara assumed a posture of watchful waiting, anticipating the opportunity afforded by the Terauchi cabinet's "self-destruction."

tant was the fact that no one else could organize a cabinet with firm support in both houses of the Diet. Certainly none of the junior members of the *hanbatsu* leadership were up to the task. Ōura Kanetake, Yamagata's chief political staff officer after Katsura's death, had been forced out of politics by involvement in an attempt to bribe Diet members.[25] Kiyoura Keigo or Hirata Tōsuke, two other Yamagata protégés, would have had difficulty in rallying majority support in the lower house. Indeed, if either had been nominated to succeed Terauchi, it was likely that the Seiyūkai and the Kenseikai would unite in an opposition movement.

By the time Hara came to power, the solidarity of the antiparty majority in the House of Peers led by Yamagata's followers had also been weakened, especially by the formation of the Dōshikai in 1913. Some of the imperially appointed peers linked to the Chōshū faction had joined the Dōshikai, and others had drifted toward a pro-Seiyūkai position. Katō Takaaki and Wakatsuki Reijirō, whose careers had been advanced by Katsura's patronage, became full-fledged party politicians, and Gotō Shinpei, whose ties were with Terauchi, was invited by Hara Takashi to join the Seiyūkai. In other words, lower-house partisanship had been introduced into the House of Peers.

Hara tried to take advantage of this "partisanization" (*seitōka*) of the House of Peers, especially among the imperially appointed members, to win over those hereditary peers who did not know where to turn for leadership. He succeeded in gaining support for the Seiyūkai from both the Hakushaku dōshikai, an organization of hereditary counts, and the Kenkyūkai, the largest faction of hereditary peers in the house. In May 1920, on the recommendation of the Kenkyūkai leadership, Ōki Enkichi (from the Hakushaku dōshikai) entered the Hara cabinet as minister of justice. This marked the final success of the "vertical linkage" tactics Hara had attempted but failed at in 1907–8. With this success came an even more pronounced division of the House of Peers into pro-Seiyūkai and pro-Kenseikai elements. In the anti-Seiyūkai camp were the Kōseikai (an organization of hereditary barons), the Sawakai (an organization of imperially appointed peers linked to Yamagata), and the Kenseikai-affiliated Dōseikai. The upper house, once a united citadel of antiparty forces, had undergone extreme partisanization.

While consolidating his alliances in the House of Peers, Hara also

25 For the significance of the Ōura incident from the perspective of political history, see Mitani Taichirō, *Kindai Nihon no shihōken to seitō: baishinsei seiritsu no seijishi* (Tokyo: Hanawa shobō, 1980), pp. 58–63.

engineered the passage in the lower house of a bill to replace the existing large election district system with a small district system. The revision of the House of Representatives Election Law in 1919 came as the movement for universal manhood suffrage was reaching its peak. We can assume that Hara's intention in introducing the small electoral district (one to three members per district) was to prepare for the rapid change in the political situation that could be expected to accompany the eventual passage of universal manhood suffrage. By making the electoral districts smaller, Hara sought to forestall and soften the impact of a sudden "massification" (*taishūka*) of the electorate. To him, the small district was an indispensable precondition for universal manhood suffrage. As home minister under the second Saionji cabinet, he had already tried to introduce the small district. At the time he had stressed to Yamagata, who feared universal suffrage, that the small district would be effective as a built-in stablilizer. The 1919 revised law also reduced the tax qualification on the right to vote, from ¥10 in direct national taxes to ¥3. The change doubled the size of the electorate, but it mainly benefited the small landlord class. Except for a few with very high incomes, urban residents who paid neither land taxes nor business taxes did not gain the right to vote. When an election was held under the new law in May 1920, the Seiyūkai regained its old position as the absolute majority party in the lower house.[26] The Hara cabinet thus became the first government in the history of modern Japan to enjoy a stable base of support in the Diet with pro-government majorities in both houses.

Although the creation of alliances in the upper house by both the major parties in the lower house was an essential precondition for a party cabinet system, it was not a sufficient condition. As the partisanization of the upper house accelerated, there emerged the possibility that a party-affiliated cabinet of peers might be organized with majority support in the House of Representatives or that a "neutral" (that is, nonparty) cabinet might be organized by taking advantage of the balance of power between the Seiyūkai and the Kenseikai. After the assassination of Hara in 1921 and the resignation of his successor Takahashi Korekiyo in 1922, both these possibilities became realities. The Katō Tomosaburō cabinet (1922–4), based on Kenkyūkai support, was an example of the former alternative, and the second Yamamoto Gonnohyōe cabinet (1923), based on an alliance of the Satsuma faction, the old Terauchi faction, and the Kakushin Club, was an

26 See Mitani, *Nihon seitō seiji*, pp. 184–204.

example of the latter. If the political parties wished to end nonparty cabinets, they had to carry Hara's vertical linkage tactics to their logical conclusion and to establish the political superiority of the majority in the lower house. In other words, the political parties had to establish the precedence of the House of Representatives over the House of Peers.

This goal animated the second "movement for constitutional government" which in 1924 unfurled its banner of opposition to the Kiyoura Keigo cabinet. To be sure, one faction of the Seiyūkai led by Tokonami Takejirō in an attempt to maintain Hara's former ties with the upper house split from the main party to support the Kenkyūkai-backed "cabinet of peers." But Takahashi Korekiyo, the Seiyūkai's president, gave up his own title as viscount, resigned from the House of Peers, and decided to stand for election to the lower house. His forthright opposition to the "peers' cabinet" epitomized the significance of the second movement to protect constitutional government. When the anti-Kiyoura parties – the Seiyūkai, the Kakushin Club, and the Kenseikai – collectively won a majority in the election, Kiyoura had no choice but to resign. His successor was Katō Takaaki, president of the Kenseikai, which held a plurality of seats in the lower house. This series of events in 1924 marked the clear precedence of the House of Representatives over the House of Peers. Until the collapse of the Inukai cabinet in 1932, the House of Representatives became the chief arena for contests over control of the cabinet. The process of political change, which began with a balance of power between the two houses at the time of the Russo-Japanese War and ended with the partisanization of the House of Peers, left the House of Representatives in a position superior to that of the House of Peers. This change was the most important precondition for the establishment of party cabinets.

## *Constitutional theory*

Parallel to this trend in practical politics were important changes in the dominant political ideology. By the mid-1920s the constitutional interpretations of Minobe Tatsukichi, who provided theoretical legitimization for party cabinets, came to dominate not only the academic community but also the highest levels of the bureaucracy. His *Kenpō satsuyō,* first published in 1923, carried his arguments to their logical conclusion. In contrast with Hozumi Yatsuka and Uesugi Shinkichi, who opposed the idea of party rule, Minobe claimed superiority under the Meiji constitution for the legislative branch:

> Our constitution, unlike the American Constitution, is not based on the principle that the legislative, the judicial, and the executive branches occupy positions equal to one another. The actions of the legislative branch express the highest will of the state, and the judicial and the administrative branch are not equal to it but stand below it.[27]

According to Minobe, the Imperial Diet was not an organ of state empowered by the emperor, but an "organ representative of the people" grounded directly in the constitution. This interpretation of the constitution necessarily legitimized responsible cabinets or party cabinets, as the House of Representatives where the political parties were dominant was more typical of the Diet's characterization as "representative of the people" than was the House of Peers.[28] In his *Chikajō kenpō seigi* published in 1927, Minobe wrote as follows:

> The Diet is made up of two houses. However, even if it is assumed that they are both equal in law, when it comes to the question of political power, the two houses ought not to occupy an equal position at all. Of the two houses in the Diet, the one possessed of the main political power must be the one that depends on public election by the people.[29]

After the Katō cabinet was established in 1924, Minobe called for a reform of the House of Peers. He advocated abolition or reduction in the number of peers whose membership depended on status or property qualification, and he proposed that imperially appointed members be nominated by appropriate electoral groups rather than by the incumbent prime minister. His goal was clearly to depoliticize the House of Peers.

The imperially appointed members of the House of Peers were unusually influential high officials who had risen to positions such as vice-minister, director of the Bureau of Legislation (Hōseikyoku), superintendent of metropolitan police (Keishichōsōkan), or director of the Police Bureau in the Home Ministry, in an outgoing cabinet. As a reward for their services, usually just before the end of the cabinet, they were recommended for peerages by the prime minister and appointed by the emperor. Businessmen and scholars were also appointed, but many of them also had close ties with the retiring government. Consequently, most imperial appointees had strong partisan connections. Minobe contended that the political coloring of the imperial appointees should be diluted by switching from a system of nomination by the government to nomination by appropriate organizations

27 Minobe, *Kenpō satsuyō*, p. 506. 28 Ibid., p. 317.
29 Minobe Tatsukichi, *Chikujō kenpō seigi* (Tokyo: Yuhikaku, 1927), p. 435.

other than the government. The selection of peers by election among the members of the Imperial Academy (Teikoku gakushiin), mandated by the revised House of Peers regulations in 1925, can be seen as a step toward modest peerage reform paralleling Minobe's position. According to Minobe's interpretation, political struggle should focus on the House of Representatives, and the House of Peers should simply assume the passive function of exercising a check on party politics.

Because Minobe's theories regarding the centrality of the Diet were used as the basis for questions on the official examinations for the higher civil service (*kōtōkan*) or for the judicial service (*shihōkan*), his ideas were diffused widely and deeply throughout the bureaucratic structure of power. By the mid-1920s Minobe's constitutional theory thus had become authoritative doctrine. Because it provided an ideology for party rule appropriate to Japan, its acceptance was an important precondition for the establishment of party cabinets.

### *The neutralization of the Privy Council*

The third condition for the establishment of party cabinets was the political neutralization of the Privy Council. As the highest formal body of advisers to the emperor, the council had had a strong voice in domestic politics since its establishment in 1888. By providing the emperor – really the cabinet – with opinions on the establishment or revision of major laws, the Privy Council came to have a considerable influence on the formation of national policy. Whenever the government presented major legislation to the Diet, it first had to seek the council's advice in the name of the emperor and receive its approval. In this sense the legislative process under the Meiji constitution was two tiered.

The Privy Council also had the right to provide opinions on the ratification of international treaties and agreements. When the Meiji constitution was drafted, care was taken to exclude the Diet from participating in the treaty-making process. The right to conclude or ratify treaties was lodged solely in the emperor's sovereignty (*taiken*). But because the Privy Council was the body that exercised this right in the emperor's stead, its influence on foreign policy was necessarily substantial.

The council's political importance in both domestic and diplomatic policy was clearly reflected in the choice of Privy Council presidents. From 1888 until 1924, during the entire period leading to the era of party rule, all but one of the presidents of the Privy Council were men who had served as prime minister. In the protocol of the imperial court, the president of the Privy Council ranked third behind the *genrō* (formally, those had been decorated with the Grand Order of the Chrysanthemum) and the incumbent prime minister. The selection of the council's members was usually decided by consultation between the *genrō* and the prime minister. Yamagata, whose tenure in the post lasted seventeen years, served continuously as the council's president from the death of Itō Hirobumi in 1909 until his own death in 1922. During that time he brought ex-bureaucrats from his own faction into the Privy Council, just as he had brought them into the House of Peers, and with the same intent – to make the council an antiparty bastion. After Yamagata's death, the position went to his political protégé, Kiyoura. But after Kiyoura became prime minister in 1924, the political importance of the office was deliberately diminished.

The last of the *genrō*, Saionji Kinmochi, tried to promote the council's political neutralization by advising governments to appoint to the presidency either scholars or former bureaucrats with few political ties. It is said that Saionji was more supportive of the reform of the Privy Council than of the reform of the House of Peers proposed by the Katō cabinet in 1925. According to Yokota Sennosuke, minister of justice in the Katō cabinet, Saionji told the government:

> The House of Peers is simple because it can be manipulated, but there is one thing that cannot be. That is the Privy Council. It is more important. The House of Peers can always be reformed, so dealing with it is easy. Instead of doing that, get to work on the Privy Council.[30]

Saionji advised the Katō government to appoint a scholar to the council's presidency. Hamao Arata, a former president of Tokyo Imperial University, was chosen to succeed Kiyoura; Hozumi Nobushige, a former professor in the law faculty of Tokyo Imperial University, succeeded him; and Kuratomi Yūzaburō, a former Ministry of Justice official, followed in office until 1934. This pattern of selection also applied to the vice-president. Between 1924 and 1926, the post was filled by Ichiki Kitokurō, Hozumi Nobushige, and Okano Keijirō, all former professors in the law faculty at Tokyo Imperial University. Hiranuma Kiichirō took the post in 1926. Although he was a former Ministry of Justice official and held a doctoral degree, he was clearly a bureaucrat with political connections, and so for the next eleven years he was not allowed to rise to the presidency of the council.

Why did Saionji, who succeeded to Yamagata Aritomo's role in the court, take the initiative in neutralizing the Privy Council as a political

30 Kojima Kazuo, *Ichi rō seijika no kaisō* (Tokyo: Chūō Kōronsha, 1951), p. 222.

entity? One can speculate that he was trying to cut the close tie between "court" and "government" (*kyūchū* and *fuchū*) that had developed as a result of Yamagata's maneuverings, especially the recruitment of his faction members into the Privy Council. Perhaps fearful that the influence of the Satsuma faction might likewise penetrate the court, Saionji tried in every way to quash its attempt to have Yamamoto Gonnohyōe appointed as council president. His motives, it can be imagined, were similar in his exclusion of Hiranuma, a man not only connected with the Satsuma faction but also a promoter of the Kokuhonsha, an organization regarded by Saionji as fascist. In short, Saionji used all his political strength to guard against the court's monopolization by any particular political faction. To that end he worked for the neutralization of the Privy Council, especially its dissociation from the *hanbatsu* factions. The ultimate benefit redounded to the advantage of the political parties, however.

### *Party penetration of the bureaucracy*

The fourth condition for party cabinets was a growing accommodation between the political parties and the higher reaches of the bureaucracy. This accommodation took many forms, but it was most evident in the recruitment of former officials into the ranks of the party leadership. By the mid-1920s both the major parties were led by ex-bureaucrats: Katō Takaaki was a former diplomat; Takahashi Korekiyo had been head of the Bank of Japan; and Tokonami Takejirō had served long in the Home Ministry bureaucracy. In the late 1920s the top leaders of the Kenseikai (reorganized as the Minseitō in 1927) were two former Finance Ministry officials, Wakatsuki Reijirō and Hamaguchi Osachi. The Seiyūkai recruited men like Tanaka Giichi (a general and former war minister) and Suzuki Kisaburō (former superintendent of metropolitan police). Many incumbent officials or ex-officials also advanced the interests of one or the other of the major political parties without formally joining them. It was a common practice for an incoming party cabinet to replace incumbent prefectural governors with officials sympathetic to the government party's interests and to furlough those who were not. The kind of partisanization that transformed the House of Peers also spread to the higher echelons of the local government bureaucracy.

This partisanization of the bureaucracy had been foreshadowed by the personnel policies of Hara Takashi. While serving as secretary to Commerce and Agriculture Minister Mutsu Munemitsu in 1890, Hara had tried to weaken the Satsuma faction's influence in the ministry by emphasizing ability over personal connections in the employment of new officials, giving special preference to graduates of the law faculty of Tokyo Imperial University. After the Russo-Japanese War he had followed the same goal as home minister, promoting high officials within the ministry under the rubric of "selection of the up-and-coming" and "retirement of the old hands." In effect, he substituted managerial personnel practice based on achievement for ascriptive criteria of promotion. The result, probably intentional, was to weaken the influence of the dominant Yamgata faction and to nurture neutral or anti-Yamagata forces within the ministry. It goes without saying that high officials whose accomplishments were highly regarded by Hara and given preferential treatment became more sympathetic to the Seiyūkai. The foremost example of such officials was Tokonami Takejirō, who later became home minister in the Hara cabinet.

It can be hypothesized that this party–bureaucracy accommodation worked in several ways to the advantage of the establishment of party cabinets. First, the executive and judicial branches were kept in touch with the legislative branch through high officials or ex-officials involved in the parties. By co-opting the bureaucrats, the parties could provide a unifying element in the centrifugal Meiji constitutional structure. Second, the parties were better able to establish their political superiority over the bureaucracy. By attracting bureaucratic specialists and introducing their knowledge and experience into the legislative branch, the parties could better coordinate the various specialized activities of the administrative branch. Minobe's constitutional interpretation of the superiority of the legislative function gave this practice theoretical legitimacy. Third, in a society in which officials recruited through the higher civilian service examination were given higher ranking in court protocol than were members of the House of Representatives, the accommodation between the parties and the bureaucracy, especially the partisanization of the bureaucrats, helped enhance the prestige of the political parties.

### *The establishment of the jury system*

The fifth condition for party cabinets was the accommodation between the political parties and the judicial bureaucracy achieved through the establishment of the jury system in 1923.[31] In a sense this was another

31 See Mitani, *Kindai Nihon no shihōken.*

example of accommodation between the parties and the bureaucracy. But the judiciary with its ideology of the "independence of the judicial power" regarded itself as separate from the rest of the bureaucracy, and its hostile posture toward the parties was not unlike that of the army, which insisted on the "independence of high command." Toward the end of the Meiji period (after 1907), the judiciary, especially the procuratorial authorities, emerged as an independent political force. Like the army high command at the time, they harbored a deeply rooted aversion toward the political parties. In the investigation of the so-called Sugar incident of 1909, when the Dai Nihon Sugar Refining Company attempted to bribe various members of the House of Representatives to extend a law that returned a portion of the import duties on raw sugar to the sugar companies, the antipathy of the judicial authorities toward the parties was especially marked.

The parties, especially the Seiyūkai, also tried to introduce the jury system, which had been under consideration in Japan since the beginning of the Meiji era, in order to restrain procuratorial attacks on party politicians. Popular participation in the trial process would diminish the impact of the judiciary's antiparty inclinations. In 1919, the Special Deliberative Council on the Legal System was set up as an advisory body directly under Prime Minister Hara. The government, following the council's recommendations, introduced legislation to set up a jury system. In the process, Hara succeeded in securing the cooperation of Hiranuma Kiichirō and Suzuki Kisaburō, two key officials who had contributed to the increased influence of the procuratorial authorities.

In order to control the judiciary from within and to win its cooperation on the introduction of the jury system, Hara extended strong political backing to both men. Hiranuma had distinguished himself as vice-minister and then as chief procurator, under Matsuda Masahisa, the justice minister in the second Saionji and the first Yamamoto cabinets. Hiranuma built for himself a powerful base of influence within the judiciary, and it was natural that of all the ministers he had served, he respected Matsuda the most. When Hara organized his government, he followed Matsuda's tactics regarding the judiciary, offering the post of justice minister first to Hiranuma and then to Suzuki. When both declined, he assumed the post concurrently himself and made it a practice to rely on the two men's advice. Using the retirement system to ease elderly judicial officials out of office, Hara also opened the way for the appointment of Hiranuma as chief justice of the Supreme Court, and Suzuki as chief procurator. Hiranuma–

who aspired to become an imperial court official, perhaps grand chamberlain or keeper of the Privy Seal – took the post of chief justice, which meant that he was an ex-officio member of the Imperial Household Council. Hara suggested that it would be the best way to achieve his ambition. Suzuki, then serving as vice-minister of justice, was also nominated by Hara as an imperial appointee to the House of Peers. Both men had initially opposed the jury system, but ultimately both went along with Hara's plan. Suzuki became a member of the Seiyūkai, and after the assassination of Inukai Tsuyoshi in 1932, he became president of the party. Although Hiranuma never entered the party, he supported it from the outside and played a role in pushing it to the right in the 1930s.

Before its introduction to the Diet, the jury system bill was discussed in the Privy Council, where antipolitical party forces strongly opposed it. But in 1922 after Hara's death, the council finally approved the bill, and in 1923 it became law after passing the Diet. The jury system, less through its operation (from 1928 to 1943) than through the process by which it came into being, served to build relationships between the parties and the judiciary (especially between the Seiyūkai and the judicial bureaucracy under Hiranuma and Suzuki). These relationships contributed to the stabilization of the party cabinet system.

### *Rapprochement between the parties and the military*

The final condition for the party cabinet system was the rapprochement between the parties and the military that accompanied the creation of the Washington system. As the result of arms limitations agreed upon by Japan at the Washington Conference in 1921–2, the political parties were able to increase their ability to shape the national budget. Because the conference committed Japan to military cutbacks, the army high command could no longer insist, as it had before, that the expansion of the military budget should not be questioned. In 1922–3 the cabinet of Admiral Katō Tomosaburō, who had headed the Japanese delegation to the conference, curtailed the navy's construction program and reduced naval and army personnel strength. Although accepting a cut in the number of divisions, the army embarked on a plan to modernize its tactics and weaponry. To maintain standards of national military strength during a period of retrenchment, however, its leaders had to cooperate with the political parties. Both War Ministers Yamanashi Hanzō (1921–3) and Ugaki Kazushige

(1924–7) worked with civilian politicians to create a leaner but technologically more advanced army.

Bonds between the military leadership and the political parties also became closer with the decline in *hanbatsu* influence over the army after the death of Terauchi Masatake in 1919 and Yamagata Aritomo in 1922. Both men had been opponents of party influence over the government, but in the early 1910s Tanaka Giichi, who inherited the mantle of army leadership from Terauchi, began to develop close ties with the Seiyūkai, especially with Hara. He first approached Hara in 1914 hoping to obtain the majority party's support for the two-division increase that the army had called for since the Russo-Japanese War. As a result of their negotiations, both men came to realize the utility of future cooperation. Hara discovered that it was possible to establish communications through Tanaka with the army, especially with Yamagata. For his part, Tanaka realized that in order to achieve his long-standing aim of "popularizing the national defense" (*kokubō no kokuminka*), it was essential not only to continue expanding and strengthening the Reservists Association (*zaigō gunjinkai*) but also to secure the support of the political parties, especially the majority party in the Diet. But relations between Hara and Tanaka cooled during the second Ōkuma cabinet when the Seiyūkai slipped from its position as the majority party in the Diet. The two-divisions bill passed the Diet without the Seiyūkai's help, voted through by a new majority made up of the Dōshikai and other progovernment parties.

During the second Ōkuma cabinet and the succeeding Terauchi cabinet, Tanaka served as vice-chief of staff under Chief of Staff Uehara Yūsaku. As the putative successor to the leadership of the army's Chōshū faction, Tanaka held the real reins of control in the general staff headquarters. He also played a key role in promoting military intervention in the internal politics of both China and the Soviet Union, first in supporting Japanese opposition to the Yuan Shih-k'ai regime and then in urging Japanese participation in the Siberian expedition. Unlike Tanaka, Chief of Staff Uehara was not a member of the Chōshū faction. Rather, he was leader of a group of officers who wanted to weaken Chōshū's control over the service. However, he took the same position as Tanaka did in promoting a "positive continental policy." Indeed, at the time of the second Saionji cabinet, when Uehara was war minister and Tanaka was chief of the military affairs bureau (*gunmukyokuchō*), both men had pushed for the two-division increase and cooperated in forcing the cabinet's resignation when it opposed the measure.

When Tanaka became war minister in the Hara cabinet on the recommendation of Yamagata Aritomo, he went along with Hara's policy of cooperation with the United States. This policy marked the beginning of a shift away from the imperialistic continental policy championed by the army. As a result, conflict deepened between Uehara and Tanaka, and Tanaka leaned more markedly toward the Seiyūkai. Both Hara and Takahashi Korekiyo, his successor as party president, had a high regard for Tanaka's cooperative attitude toward the Seiyūkai's diplomatic and defense policies. Tanaka, an astute opportunist, was also keenly aware that it was necessary for the army to respond positively to the spread of international cooperation abroad and the growth of the parties' political role at home. Finally in 1925 he accepted an invitation to become president of the Seiyūkai, an office in which he served until his death in 1929.

Tanaka was not the only general to make his peace with the parties. Yamanashi Hanzō, who presided over the first round of arms reduction in the 1920s, also joined the Seiyūkai. Ugaki Kazushige, who presided over the second round, cooperated closely with the Kenseikai (later the Minseitō), the Seiyūkai's main rival in the Diet. Fukuda Masatarō, a general belonging to the Uehara faction, leaned toward an anti-Seiyūkai position as Tanaka moved toward the Seiyūkai, and for a time he decided to join the Minseitō.[32] The willingness of these high-ranking military officers to work with the political parties signifies how much the influence of the old *hanbatsu* had declined by the 1920s. If a military man harbored ambitions to head a cabinet, he could no longer rely on the patronage of a *genrō* like Yamagata but had to have good relations with the party leaders.

To be sure, party ties with the military forces were far more tenuous than were those with the civil bureaucracy or the judiciary. At all levels the officer corps remained jealous of its traditional autonomy from civilian control. The Uehara faction, mindful that its rival Tanaka was not only a Chōshū general but also close to the Seiyūkai, continued to push for eliminating *hanbatsu* influence over the army and at the same time insisted the army be kept nonpartisan, free from ties to the political parties. Committed to putting into practice the idea of "the independence of the high command" (*tōshiken no dokuritsu*), the Uehara faction tried to expand the army's political influence by reaffirming the need for a positive continental policy toward China

32 Oka Yoshitake and Hayashi Shigeru, eds., *Taishō demokurashii ki no seiji, Matsumoto Gokichi seiji nisshi* (Tokyo: Iwanami shoten, 1959), p. 573.

and the Soviet Union and by building a system for national general mobilization. Consequently, the partisanization of the military did not go very far. By the early Shōwa period, the Uehara faction produced a new generation of staff officers led by Generals Araki Sadao, Mazaki Jinzaburō, and Hayashi Senjūrō, who eventually became the nucleus of antiparty factions in the army.

On the other hand, as long as leaders like Tanaka and Ugaki were involved in cabinet decisions on critical issues of military and foreign policy, military objection to the advance of party power was less likely. Therefore, until the controversy over the London Naval Treaty in 1930, both the military and the naval high command maintained a position of nonintervention in domestic political struggles.

## CONCLUSION

This chapter outlined the six conditions that facilitated the establishment of the party cabinet system between 1924 and 1932: (1) the establishment of the superiority of the House of Representatives over the House of Peers, (2) the emergence of Minobe's constitutional theory as orthodox, (3) the political neutralization of the Privy Council, (4) party penetration of the civil bureaucracy, (5) party accommodation with the judiciary accompanying the introduction of the jury system, and (6) party rapprochement with the military.

None of these conditions was irreversible, however. If any or all of them were altered, then the party cabinet system would be faced with a crisis. In other words, the system was a fragile one. Party domination of the government could be upset if it appeared that the parties could no longer coordinate the constitutional structure, if Minobe's theory was rejected as heterodox, if the Privy Council intervened in disputes between the parties, if strong antiparty feelings regained strength in the civil bureaucracy and the judiciary, or if increased international tension prompted the army to reassert its domestic power. It was precisely these changes in the political environment that accompanied the end of party cabinets in 1932.

CHAPTER 3

# POLITICS AND MOBILIZATION IN JAPAN, 1931–1945

## INTRODUCTION

As Taichirō Mitani showed in Chapter 2, Japan's conservative political parties (*kisei seitō*) surmounted the obstacles to parliamentary influence in the Meiji constitution and during the 1920s occupied a prominent position in both the lower house of the Diet and the cabinet. From 1924 to 1932, the two conservative parties monopolized the premiership and extended their influence among other political elite groups. Between 1932 and 1940, however, party influence declined swiftly and steeply. In its wake, the opinions of administrative specialists in the civilian and military bureaucracies, joined by the views of a newly emergent business elite, became paramount in the determination of Japan's foreign and domestic policies.

Ironically, both the successes and failures of party politicians in amassing political influence were predicated on the development of a political culture in late Tokugawa and Meiji Japan that supported the proposition that those with a demonstrated practical ability to govern should be given the reins of political power. This conviction was first manifested in the *bakumatsu* era, when the muffled ideological tensions erupted between the hereditary principle of power transfer and the Confucian concept of "rule by the talented." The leaders of the Meiji Restoration also believed in the principle of meritocracy. They recruited talented young followers into their personal political factions (*hanbatsu*) and established institutions of higher learning (Tokyo Imperial University, the Army and Navy war colleges) to teach future leaders the expertise requisite to Japan's survival in the modern world. By 1910, these institutions had become the primary sources for the nation's civilian and military administrative leaders.

The Meiji legacy regarding the question of meritocratic rule was ambivalent. Many court noble and prominent daimyo houses of the mid-nineteenth century were given new patents of nobility in the 1880s and thereafter enjoyed considerable political power through their families' hereditary rights to hold positions in the House of Peers and the court itself. The legitimacy of the entire Meiji political structure, moreover, rested on the emperor's inherited authority, and the political duty of the newly titled nobility was defined as insulating the throne from attack, by means of service in the House of Peers and mediation among other political elite groups. On the basis of this mission, Japan's hereditary nobles enjoyed a continuing role in twentieth-century politics and survived severe attacks during the Taishō era (1912–26) with only a minimal curtailment of their inherited prerogatives.

Apart from the meritocracy represented by the Meiji leadership and its carefully educated successors, the hereditary nobility shared power in the early twentieth century with new political forces centered in the lower house of the Diet. By 1914, these forces had crystallized into two major political parties and several smaller splinter groups. In 1918 Hara Takashi became the first Japanese prime minister to hold office solely on the basis of his power as party leader. Hara and succeeding party presidents received appointments as prime minister because they were able to develop important linkages between their parties and other important nonparty political elite groups who monopolized access to the state's several organs. Consequently, they could help consolidate the dispersed political power of the ruling groups and obtain agreements among them on government policy. This ability proved crucial to the party politicians' fortunes. As molders of elite coalitions, they stabilized the fragile cabinet system created by the Meiji oligarchy, and as dominating forces in the lower house, they ensured that the cabinet policy agreements to which they were a party would be approved by the lower house as well.

The parties also had other abilities deemed essential to stable elite rule. At a time when the Meiji oligarchs and hereditary nobles feared that the impact of Japan's rapid economic and social transformation would cause discontented rural taxpayers and the rapidly emerging new business elite to challenge the institutional foundations of their power, the parties demonstrated their capacity to absorb these groups' political energies without disturbing the structure of the Meiji political settlement. By the early twentieth century, the principal form of political participation by big business was financial contributions to party campaign coffers. Meanwhile, political participation in the countryside was carefully controlled by local alliances between party politicians and traditional local political leaders (*meibōka*, or village headmen, landlords, schoolteachers, priests, and other local luminaries).

In return for pork-barrel legislation and party representation of local interests in negotiations with the national government, local leaders controlled their communities' voting behavior, supported friendly party politicians in elections, and defused local political movements to revise the institutions of government.

The parties were thus increasingly able to fulfill the essential functions of elite mediation, harmonize cabinet–lower-house relations, and integrate the local energies into national politics. By the second decade of the twentieth century, the parties' political capabilities were further augmented by the recruitment of key figures from the nobility and the civilian and military bureaucracies into party membership or party alignment. Having obtained several important ministerial posts for their members in exchange for lower-house support of cabinet budget proposals, the parties were able to influence the appointments of career bureaucrats to senior positions in the ministries under their control. Bureaucrats who aligned themselves with one or another party to gain such appointments were often recruited as party members after their official retirements. Similarly, from their position of strength in the lower house and cabinet, the parties gained the allegiance of important groups of hereditary nobles and imperial appointees in the House of Peers in exchange for an agreement to abstain from any far-reaching reform of that body's procedures of selection. And although they never had great influence over personnel selections in the armed services, their growing power obliged politically ambitious generals and admirals to court party support and even seek party membership after their military retirement. The influx of nonparty elite group members into the party camp provided essential linkages between party and nonparty elites, as well as specialized expertise within the parties for the conceptualization of future national policy proposals. So important to party fortunes were members of nonparty elite origin that all but one of the party leaders appointed as prime minister in prewar Japan were men who had successful careers in the civilian or military bureaucracy before becoming party politicians (see Table 3.1).

However, even at the zenith of party government in the mid-1920s, the efforts of party elite groups to wrest political control from the hands of their well-entrenched competitors were far from totally successful. The terms of the Meiji political settlement hindered the extension of parliamentary influence. And even when the parties had penetrated the bureaucracy, it was restricted by official regulations that limited the choice of senior officials to those who had demonstrated their talents through a series of highly competitive examinations. The

TABLE 3.1
*Japanese cabinets, 1929–1945*

| Prime minister | Cabinet number | Cabinet term |
|---|---|---|
| Hamaguchi Osachi | | 2 July 1929 to 14 April 1931 |
| Wakatsuki Reijirō | 2nd | 14 April 1931 to 13 December 1931 |
| Inukai Tsuyoshi | | 13 December 1931 to 16 May 1932 |
| Saitō Makoto | | 16 May 1932 to 8 July 1934 |
| Okada Keisuke | | 8 July 1934 to 9 March 1936 |
| Hirota Kōki | | 9 March 1936 to 2 February 1937 |
| Hayashi Senjūrō | | 2 February 1937 to 4 June 1937 |
| Konoe Fumimaro | 1st | 4 June 1937 to 5 January 1939 |
| Hiranuma Kiichirō | | 5 January 1939 to 30 August 1939 |
| Abe Nobuyuki | | 30 August 1939 to 16 January 1940 |
| Yonai Mitsumasa | | 16 January 1940 to 22 July 1940 |
| Konoe Fumimaro | 2nd | 22 July 1940 to 18 July 1941 |
| Konoe Fumimaro | 3rd | 18 July 1941 to 18 October 1941 |
| Tōjō Hideki | | 18 October 1941 to 22 July 1944 |
| Koiso Kuniaki | | 22 July 1944 to 7 April 1945 |
| Suzuki Kantarō | | 7 April 1945 to 17 August 1945 |

military was similarly insulated from overt political patronage by constitutional provisions ensuring virtual independence from the civilian branches of government on personnel matters. The social and political prerogatives defined for the peers made it difficult for the parties to attack them.

In addition, the acceptance of parliamentary influence was tempered by an awareness that the extension of party power beyond the lower house meant a corresponding decrease in the autonomy of nonparty elites. For example, although senior civil servants came to realize that their future appointments rested substantially on alignment with one or another party, their subordinates decried the growth of party influence on administration as an intrusion into an arena that they, as specialists trained at Tokyo Imperial University and by experience, felt properly to be their own exclusive province. They also protested the administrative turmoil that accompanied a shift from one party in power to its rival, for such shifts invariably brought the wholesale replacement of one set of party-aligned senior officials by another. In the armed forces, the "political generals and admirals" who cooperated with the parties were frequently criticized by their subordinates for compromising the military's sacred mission of national defense, simply for the sake of political expediency. Within the House of Peers, nobles such as Prince Konoe Fumimaro argued that the peerage's traditional mission was to transcend partisan alliances and alignments as a buttress of objective political judgment for the emperor. Even locally, village elites remained wary of any party effort to bypass traditional routes of mobilizing local political energies, and so they hedged their dependency on party linkages with ties to the bureaucracy in order to satisfy local interests and reinforce their own prestige and authority in the community.

Nonparty attitudes toward the parties' role as channels for the political articulation of mass interests were also ambivalent. On the one hand, established nonparty elites preferred the parties to democrats, socialists, anarchists, and communists, who disapproved of the propriety of elite government altogether. On the other hand, the parties' alliance with traditional village leaders frustrated progressive journalists, intellectuals, and representatives of the nascent labor and tenant movements and spurred liberal and socialist "reformist" movements for an overhaul of the political system or the replacement of existing party forces by groups more representative of the body politic. From another ideological perspective, archly conservative "Japanists" saw the parties not as harmonizing agencies between the government and people but as Western-style, conflict-oriented organizations, which obstructed the unification of the public will with that of the emperor and corrupted the sacred bonds between ruler and subject through their pragmatic political compromises and preoccupation with pork-barrel interests.

While parliamentary strength was thus in ascendance throughout the 1920s, the parties were still obliged to share power with several potent nonparty elite groups and to defend themselves against a wide variety of attacks on their position. To be certain, judgments at the dawn of the 1930s about the future of party influence generally concurred with those of a distinguished Western student of Japanese politics, who wrote in 1932 that "party cabinets may fairly be assumed to have become the established rule."[1] Nevertheless, the parties' successes during the 1920s required them to fend off the challenges of new political aspirants, and their control of the cabinet remained subject to the efforts of nonparty elites to regain lost ground in the competition for power.

In fact, the parties' position was soon to be fatally weakened by cataclysmic changes in the international and domestic environment

1 Harold S. Quigley, *Japanese Government and Politics: An Introductory Study* (New York: Century, 1932), p. 233.

during the late 1920s and early 1930s. Rather than promoting the continued expansion of party power, events in the 1930s fostered a significant diminution of party influence in national affairs, culminating in the dissolution of all formal party organizations in 1940. In China, the revitalized nationalist movement under Chiang Kai-shek posed an increasingly severe threat to Japanese economic and strategic interests in China and particularly in Manchuria. By the end of the 1920s, the Japanese had also begun to perceive a renewed menace to their position in Manchuria, and potentially to their own security, in the form of a reinforced Far Eastern military presence by the Soviet Union. Nanking and Moscow seemed disinclined to adhere to the Washington system's principles of peacefully resolving differences through multilateral consultation, as neither was a party to the Washington treaties of 1921–2. The Washington powers themselves showed little willingness to support the Japanese government's request for an internationally coordinated response to the threats it perceived to Japan's continental interests.[2] Japan's faith in the "cooperative diplomacy" of the Washington order was further undermined by British and American threats of a bilateral naval alliance against Japan in 1930 if it did not abandon its insistence at the London Conference on maintaining 70 percent of their individual cruiser strengths. Finally, the economic underpinnings of "cooperative diplomacy" were snapped by the world depression and the growth of economic nationalism after 1929. Paralleling these changes in the international environment, confidence in the parties' ability to govern was undermined at the beginning of the 1930s by both a prolonged agricultural depression in the Japanese countryside and shifting economic policies that appeared to benefit big business and financial speculators at the expense of the rest of the nation.

Together these developments not only intensified earlier criticisms of party government but also generated a growing sense of national crisis in Japan. Impartial observers and antiparty spokesmen alike began insisting that parliamentary politicians lacked sufficient moral fortitude and intellectual expertise to guide Japan through this troubled period. Slowly at first and then with accelerating speed, public support for party government eroded. In May 1932, the parties lost control of the premiership, and thereafter they were steadily excluded from the ranks of key decision makers. By 1941, no party representa-

2 See Akira Iriye, *After Imperialism: The Search for a New Order in East Asia* (Cambridge, Mass.: Harvard University Press, 1965).

tive sat in the cabinet. Throughout this decade, power devolved on those presumably talented to deal with pressing national problems. The technocrats of the government's civilian and military agencies became increasingly influential as they demonstrated their expertise in areas deemed essential to Japan's survival. Business leaders who specialized in economic management also established an independent base of political influence as the nation struggled first to recover from the depression and subsequently to mobilize its resources for an ambitious foreign and defense policy of national autonomy.

During the 1930s, all these groups sought to capitalize on their enhanced strength to broaden still further their political power and prestige. Their emergence, however, signified the establishment of a national leadership that had been narrowly educated and trained and lacked the breadth of vision characteristic of its Meiji predecessors. In the 1930s, each specialist elite group repeatedly insisted that its own vision of the future be adopted as the officially designated road to national survival and greatness. In the military, fierce debates over national defense and national mobilization rent the army's solidarity and placed the two services at odds with each other. Similar conflicts grew within and among the civilian ministries of government and between the government and business elites. None of the specialist elite groups possessed institutional or informal means of mediating elite conflict, and the cabinet's ability to choose among conflicting elite priorities thus declined with the growth of the specialists' influence. Moreover, no specialist elite group had a foothold in the Diet that might ensure the passage of cabinet legislative proposals into law. And none of them could independently engender popular participation in the affairs of state or strengthen citizen identification with the government at a time when the state was increasing its demands on the populace.

As a consequence of these difficulties, the late 1930s and early 1940s were characterized by a series of political disputes over whether the Meiji political system remained appropriate in an era of national crisis. Both "reformists" in the political elites and outsiders seeking new means of penetrating the institutional barriers to their own political influence advocated a variety of sweeping reforms to restructure existing mechanisms of allocating political power and mediating policy differences. On the other hand, the "conservative" forces among the elites responded to the challenges of national crisis within the existing framework of political institutions and tried to mitigate the debilitating effects of intraelite power struggles on Japan's national strength.[3] The highpoint of conflict between the reformist and conservative views occurred in the debate over establishing a "new political order" for Japan in 1940–1, and the aftershocks of this clash reverberated throughout Japanese politics during the ensuing years of war in the Pacific. Ultimately, none of the elite groups entrenched in the various institutions of government proved willing to surrender the political prerogatives they each had acquired under the existing institutions of state. Therefore, the political system continued to promote a pluralistic distribution of power, as it had since the establishment of constitutional government.

There were unquestionably important and readily perceptible shifts in the locus of power among elites between 1931 and 1945, but no single elite group proved capable of monopolizing control of the state or manipulating the citizenry to its own purposes. Although the specialist elites, and particularly the army, gained influence in national affairs, the institutionalized pluralism of the Meiji state continued to provide reduced but vital political roles for even the hereditary nobility and party politicians as conflict managers. Thus, controversy and competition for power remained distinguishing characteristics of domestic politics during the early 1940s, and important decisions such as whether to go to war in 1941 and how to coordinate the military and home front responses to wartime conditions thereafter still called for a consensus among a multiplicity of elites, rather than the arbitrary decision of one or another group.

Even though it proved possible in 1932 to exaggerate the degree to which the parties had secured a preeminent position in the cabinet, students of Japan's recent past have often overstated the extent and character of the changes in Japanese politics between 1931 and 1945. Only in recent years have historians begun to refine earlier and overly simplistic notions that the interests of monopoly capitalism determined national policy during this era, that the bureaucracy established totalitarian control over the citizenry, and that the military "took over" the apparatus of state. It is now evident that although business leaders acquired a new and influential voice in setting national goals, they were unable to dictate what those goals should be. It is also clear

3 The conflict between reformists and conservatives is treated pointedly in the historical writing of Itō Takashi, Japan's leading authority on early Shōwa politics. In English, see Takashi Itō, "The Role of Right-Wing Organizations in Japan," in *Pearl Harbor As History: Japanese-American Relations 1931–1941*, ed. Dorothy Borg and Shumpei Okamoto (New York: Columbia University Press, 1973), pp. 487–509, esp. pp. 487–90.

that severe schisms within bureaucratic and military leadership groups prevented any individual or faction from achieving a dictatorship or degree of political control analogous to that of contemporaneous wartime regimes in Germany, Italy, and the Soviet Union. Conservative forces in parliament, business, the bureaucracy, the right wing, and traditional local elites in the countryside blunted the reformists' attempts to reorganize the state, enhance their own power, and establish a monolithic system of governmental controls over all political and economic activities.

To recapitulate briefly the political characteristics distinguishing the period from 1931 to 1945 from the previous era, the fortunes of the political parties and the nobility declined while crisis and war accelerated the growing influence of a meritocracy focused on the civilian and military bureaucracies and the new business elite. On the other hand, difficulties in shaping the competitive elite perspectives and ambitions into national policy at the cabinet level, harmonizing cabinet and parliamentary views on vital legislation, and stimulating popular identification with national goals persisted and, indeed, intensified. The final years of political conflict in imperial Japan were highlighted by the reaffirmation of elitist pluralism, continuing efforts to overcome weaknesses in the Meiji political settlement, and further acknowledgment of an earlier recognized need to integrate the citizenry fully into the political life of the state. The following survey of the period between 1931 and 1945 thus concludes that the apparently sharp break in political development between the 1920s and 1930s was less abrupt than many have insisted and that the "dark valley" of politics in the early Shōwa era (1926–45) in many ways laid the foundation for the transformation of the Japanese political system in the years following the destruction of the empire.

## CHALLENGES TO PARTY POWER, 1929–1936

Power began shifting from parliamentary elite groups to the specialist elites during the premiership of Hamaguchi Osachi, president of the Minseitō. The Hamaguchi cabinet, which governed from 1929 to late 1931, came under heavy criticism for Foreign Minister Shidehara Kijūrō's reliance on arms limitation agreements and "cooperative diplomacy" to defend Japan's home waters and continental interests. Despite public government pledges that Japan's negotiators at the London Conference would not accept any limit on the navy's heavy cruiser tonnage of less than 70 percent of the individual cruiser strengths of the American and British fleets, the London treaty was based on a compromise among the three powers that was perceived in Japan as violating this commitment.[4] Coupled with a growing army perception of threats to Japan's position in Manchuria from Chinese nationalism and a Soviet military buildup in Siberia, the London treaty controversy fueled an attack on the government's apparent willingness to risk the nation's security for the sake of a questionable fidelity to diplomatic harmony with the Anglo-American powers.

The government's economic and fiscal policies, designed by Finance Minister Inoue Junnosuke, focused on a return to the gold standard, deflation, tight money, and reduced national budgets. Although Japan was able thereby to return to the gold standard in 1930 (in the midst of world depression), the Minseitō's policies did little to mitigate the severity of prolonged agricultural distress and poverty, the tendency toward increasing concentrations of wealth and economic power among industrial and banking cartels, and the growing differential in wages paid in large and small industries.[5] To make matters worse, when Britain again abandoned the gold standard in September 1931, the Minseitō government continued its fiscal policies and allowed financial speculators to amass huge holdings of specie at fixed prices in anticipation of the inevitable moment when Japan would follow suit and allow the yen to sink to its actual value against gold and the dollar.

The problems confronted by the Minseitō cabinet were formidable and arose to a large extent from changes in the international environment over which Japan had little control. Nevertheless, the political consequences of dealing with these issues were felt domestically. For example, a preponderance of the nation's leaders came to insist in the wake of the London treaty controversy that the army and naval general staffs be given a larger voice in determining defense policy than heretofore.[6] This consensus greatly enhanced the voice of military specialists in the formulation of future national defense policies. The government's failure to deal effectively with national security and eco-

4 James B. Crowley, *Japan's Quest for Autonomy: National Security and Foreign Policy, 1930–1938* (Princeton, N.J.: Princeton University Press, 1966), chap. 1.

5 For details of these trends, see Takafusa Nakamura, *Economic Growth in Prewar Japan* (New Haven, Conn.: Yale University Press, 1983), pp. 194–233.

6 Crowley, *Japan's Quest*, p. 79. The most thorough Japanese study of the political ramifications of the London treaty issue is by Itō Takashi, *Shōwa shoki seiji shi kenkyū* (Tokyo: Tokyo daigaku shuppankai, 1969); for a brief English treatment, see Takashi Itō, "Conflicts and Coalitions in Japan, 1930: Political Groups [and] the London Naval Disarmament Conference," in *The Study of Coalition Behavior*, ed. Sven Groennings, W. W. Kelley, and Michael Leiserson (New York: Holt, Rinehart, and Winston, 1970), pp. 160–76.

nomic issues also spawned desperate attempts by right-wing "double-patriots" to rid Japan of its leadership through assassination.[7] Hamaguchi was shot late in 1930 and turned control of his cabinet and party over to Wakatsuki Reijirō before dying of his wounds in August 1931. In the meantime, young officers and civilian revolutionaries, convinced of the bankruptcy of the Minseitō's leadership, planned abortive coups d'état in March and October 1931, with clandestine support from a number of army leaders agitated by the failure of "cooperative diplomacy" to curb the Chinese and Soviet threats to Manchuria. Other officers, such as Colonel Itagaki Seishirō and Lieutenant Colonel Ishiwara Kanji, were equally convinced that the Minseitō's "weak-kneed" continental policy would prove fatal to Japan's interests in Manchuria and in September 1931 unilaterally mobilized the Kwantung Army to carry out the Manchurian incident.[8]

The terrorism and arbitrary military actions of the early 1930s were an extreme expression of the widespread public dissatisfaction with party influence. Though both of these forms of illegal defiance were censured publicly, their perpetrators were equally praised for their profound, if misguided, devotion to the nation's interests. The growing antiparty mood of late 1931 prevented the government from taking any severe punitive measures against the miscreants, and instead, the Wakatsuki cabinet resigned in December. Its replacement, a government led by Seiyūkai party president Inukai Tsuyoshi, quickly abandoned the gold standard and called new elections in which the Seiyūkai overwhelmingly defeated the Minseitō. But as the financial speculators cashed in on the government's new fiscal policy and the depression worsened, terrorism resumed in early 1932 with fatal attacks on ex-Finance Minister Inoue and industrialist Dan Takuma. Finally, on May 15, 1932, a group of naval cadets aided by civilians and young army officers struck down Inukai in his official residence.

Inukai's untimely death left the last *genrō*, Saionji Kinmochi, with the difficult task of recommending a new prime minister for imperial appointment. Clearly, Wakatsuki's Minseitō was far too unpopular and weak to be returned to power at that time, but Saionji was also

7 Richard Storry, *The Double Patriots: A Study of Japanese Nationalism* (Boston: Houghton Mifflin, 1957) is the standard survey of terrorist incidents in the 1930s.

8 For a dissenting view, holding that the perpetrators of the incident had at least the tacit approval of their superiors in Tokyo, see Crowley, *Japan's Quest*, pp. 114–24. On the Manchurian incident, see Sadako Ogata, *Defiance in Manchuria: The Making of Japanese Foreign Policy, 1931–1932* (Berkeley and Los Angeles: University of California Press, 1964); and Mark R. Peattie, *Ishiwara Kanji and Japan's Confrontation with the West* (Princeton, N.J.: Princeton University Press, 1975), chap. 4.

reluctant to assign the premiership to Inukai's successor as Seiyūkai president, Suzuki Kisaburō. The enmity between Saionji and Suzuki was an old one, dating back to the efforts of the *genrō* to foster party government as a means of mediating intraelite disputes without directly involving the emperor in national politics. Suzuki was known to be an outspoken advocate of involving the emperor more actively as a unifying force in politics, and he had also been a vehement critic of the Washington order that Saionji helped fashion early in the 1920s. Against the backdrop of numerous terrorist incidents and a new military assertiveness in Manchuria, Saionji's antipathy for Suzuki's ideas encouraged the conclusion that the moment was inopportune for continuing party government. To replace the fallen Inukai, therefore, Saionji recommended to the emperor the appointment of Admiral Saitō Makoto.

The Saitō government came to power amidst the widespread feeling that the nation had entered a "period of emergency" (*hijōji*). In light of Japan's pressing problems in foreign relations and the domestic economy, both conservative parties found it highly politic to support the new cabinet, even though the prime minister was not drawn from their ranks. Saitō's coalition "national unity government" (*kyokoku itchi naikaku*) included five ministers selected from the two parties, along with several advocates of greater military and bureaucratic roles in national policymaking. The Minseitō found its strength so shattered by the events of 1929–31 and its 1932 electoral defeat that it committed itself to supporting national-unity government until it could regain its position in the lower house through new elections. Suzuki's Seiyūkai, on the other hand, agreed to back Saitō in the hope that the party would soon regain control of the cabinet after the crisis of the moment had passed.

Contrary to Suzuki's hopes, however, the premiership passed to Admiral Okada Keisuke when Saitō resigned in July 1934. To appreciate fully the factors that denied the Seiyūkai the anticipated fruits of its cooperation with Saitō and more generally frustrated a revival of political party influence, it is useful to review a number of important changes in the international and domestic environments during the 1932–4 period. The establishment of the state of Manchukuo in 1932, though publicly supported by both conservative parties in the lower house, provoked a serious rift between Japan and the Western powers. This schism opened wider early in 1933, when Japan withdrew from the League of Nations in response to the League's disapproval of Japan's use of force on the continent. In the face of growing international criticism, Japan became increasingly isolated from the West and reacted by rejecting Anglo-American influences in its political, social, and cultural life. Because both parties were closely associated in the public mind with the "cooperative diplomacy" of the 1920s and because the "Japanist" right wing had repeatedly condemned them as nothing more than Japanese emulations of the conflict-oriented and interest-articulating parties of the West, the Seiyūkai and Minseitō found it difficult to regain the political offensive in the new domestic environment.

The government's attempts to cope with the crises besetting the country during this period likewise had adverse effects on party power. For instance, the Saitō cabinet's economic recovery program undermined party influence by promoting greater bureaucratic intrusion into the lives of the populace and by enlarging the role of civilian officials in the determination and implementation of national policy. First, the government adopted a "positive" economic policy, which focused on new and larger budgets to stimulate economic demand and pull the nation out of the throes of the depression. To resuscitate the shattered agrarian sector and generate larger tax revenues for the new budgets, it was necessary to restore the rural economy. Saitō initiated an extensive program of public works construction to occupy unemployed labor and provide off-season work for the impoverished peasants. The power to approve and fund public works projects was vested with the prefectural governors, who were local agents of the home ministry.[9] The government also implemented the "Plan for the Economic Resuscitation of Agrarian and Fishing Villages" (Nōson gyoson keizai kōsei keikaku), which was funded and supervised by the Ministry of Agriculture and Forestry. Whereas the public works projects served to strengthen Home Ministry ties with the traditional local leadership, the Ministry of Agriculture and Forestry sought to create a nationwide network of agricultural guilds (*sangyō kumiai*) as new foci for rural power linked tightly to *its* offices.[10]

Both of these programs placed the parties further on the defensive in

9 *Naimushō shi*, 4 vols., ed. Taikakai (Tokyo: Chihō zaimu kyōkai, 1970), vol. 1, p, 410; vol. 2, pp. 506–9.

10 *Naimushō shi*, vol. 1, pp. 410–11; vol. 2, pp. 509–16; Ari Bakuji, "Chihō seido (hōtaisei hōkaiki): Burakukai chōnaikai seido," in *Kōza: Nihon kindai-hō hattatsu shi–Shihon shugi to hō no hatten*, vol. 6, ed. Fukushima Masao, Kawashima Takeyoshi, Tsuji Kiyoaki, and Ukai Nobushige (Tokyo: Keisō shobō, 1959), pp. 168–73; Ishii Kin'ichirō, "Nihon fuashizumu to chihō seido: 1943-nen no hō-kaisei o chūshin ni," *Rekishigaku kenkyu* 307 (December 1965): 2; Takeshi Ishida, "Movements to Protect Constitutional Government – A Structural Functional Analysis," in *Democracy in Prewar Japan: Groundwork or Facade?* ed. George O. Totten (Lexington, Mass.: Heath, 1965), p. 89.

the struggle for political influence. The Home Ministry's plan bypassed its representatives' role as distributors of local economic benefices, whereas the Ministry of Agriculture and Forestry's approach to economic recovery threatened the local monopoly of political power held by the parties' chief electoral agents, the traditional village leadership. When party spokesmen complained about these programs' "bureaucratic despotism," they were put in the awkward position of seeming to resist national economic recovery in order to defend local interest groups and inhibiting national harmony in order to preserve their rural political machines. The burden of dispelling this impression and shedding their image as the protectors of big business while the agrarian economy foundered proved extremely onerous in the parties' effort to regain power.

Significantly, the cabinet's concurrent implication of both ministries' economic recovery plans highlighted the difficulty that national-unity governments could have in establishing priorities among various specialist-elite group policy proposals. Deprived of the extracabinet forum of a ruling political party, in which contending elite positions had been harmonized under the guidance of the party leadership and translated into policy under a party prime minister, national-unity governments faced heavy pressure to acquiesce simultaneously to divergent elite priorities or to face an impasse in cabinet decision making and consequent collapse.

Undaunted by this problem, the parties' bureaucratic opponents seized the opportunity to strike at parliamentary influence in several other ways during Saitō's tenure as prime minister. Late in 1932, the Commission on the Guarantee of Officials' Status (Kanri mibun hoshō iinkai) was created to review the retirement of officials, severely restricting the power of party members in the cabinet to cashier senior bureaucrats who were not politically aligned with them. In February 1933, an imperial ordinance (*junsa mibun hoshō rei*) extended similar protection to the police officials of the Home Ministry.[11] These two measures, designed to reduce personnel turnover in important administrative posts, strengthened bureaucratic autonomy vis-à-vis party influence and contributed measurably to the decline of parliamentary elites' power. The parties also suffered a severe attack on their moral credibility at the hands of Justice Ministry procurators, who attempted to demonstrate party and business corruption in a scandal

11 Shiraki Masayuki, *Nihon seitō shi: Shōwa hen* (Tokyo: Chūō kōronsha, 1949), p. 154; *Naimushō shi*, vol. 1, pp. 404–5.

involving a government-approved sale of stock in the Teikoku jinken company. Although the accused party leaders and businessmen were finally acquitted in 1937, the parties' public image greatly suffered during the three-year period of official inquiry and trial.[12] A fourth blow was struck at the parties by Gotō Fumio (minister of agriculture and forestry from 1932 to 1934 and home minister from 1934 to 1936) and a coterie of former Home Ministry officials, who launched a series of "election purification movements" in the countryside in 1934. These campaigns sought to curb several traditional, if morally questionable, techniques of voter mobilization, by prohibiting vote buying and strengthening punishments for other violations of the election law.[13]

The strength of the military grew in parallel with the extension of bureaucratic power. As noted earlier, many military officers were dissatisfied with the party governments' "weak-kneed" approach to the defense and expansion of Japan's continental interests early in the decade. Antiparty sentiment was also strong in the services because officers sympathized strongly with the plight of the agrarian population and believed that parliamentary groups were the servants of "plutocratic interests." As indicated, some impetuous officers in both services had already expressed their political views through violence at home and in Manchuria. Most, however, confined their actions to legal channels and focused on devising new political, economic, and strategic plans for enhancing Japan's military strength.

It was difficult for the army and navy to reach agreement through a national-unity government on the most appropriate means to this end. Moreover, strong differences of opinion over policy became entwined in both services with personal and factional rivalries throughout the period from 1931 to 1945.[14] For example, all senior army leaders acknowledged as a lesson of World War I that modern weaponry and a strong socioeconomic foundation had become essential to the prosecution of total war. However, the Imperial Way faction (Kōdōha) attempted to strengthen the nation's spiritual readiness for war by emphasizing the imminence of hostilities with the Soviet Union, but its

12 Ichihara Ryōhei, "Seitō rengō undō no hasan: Teijin jiken o shōten to shite," *Keizai ronsō* 72 (March 1955): 161–82; Arthur E. Tiedemann, "Big Business and Politics in Prewar Japan," in *Dilemmas of Growth in Prewar Japan*, ed. James W. Morley (Princeton, N.J.: Princeton University Press, 1971), pp. 267–316, esp. pp. 294–6.

13 *Naimushō shi*, vol. 1, pp. 419–20; vol. 2, pp. 359–61.

14 On army factionalism, see Crowley, *Japan's Quest*, pp. 244–79; Jacob Kovalio, "The Personnel Policy of Army Minister Araki Sadao: The Tosa–Saga Theory Re-examined," in *Tradition and Modern Japan*, ed. P. G. O'Neill (Tenterden, Kent, England: Paul Norbury Publications, 1981), pp. 102–5.

political rivals in the army (loosely grouped together as the Control faction, or Tōseiha) concentrated less on preparing Japan for an immediate crisis and more on developing the infrastructure for economic mobilization and the production of modern weaponry for use over the long run.

The knowledge in both factions that Japan's next war might well be decided on the basis of overall national strength led army planners to see a close relationship between military power and their country's political, social, economic, and spiritual condition. As Colonel Nagata Tetsuzan remarked in 1927, "National mobilization [*kokka sōdōin*] is the task of marshaling the entire society of the state in times of need, moving from a peacetime footing to a wartime footing. The state must then organize, unify and utilize all available resources, material and human, producing a maximum national strength as military power."[15] From the perspective of preparing for total war, therefore, almost all spheres of national life became relevant to defense planning. Total war planning became particularly important following Japan's withdrawal from the League of Nations in 1933. In response to the nation's growing isolation, the Saitō government turned away from the discredited "cooperative diplomacy" to a new strategy of "autonomous strength" to protect Japan's international interests. This commitment was predicated on neutralizing "the influence of the Soviet Union, the Nationalist government of China, and the Anglo-American nations by a diplomacy rooted in the efficacy of Japan's military force."[16] It implied a massive development of Japan's industrial and military strength, sufficient to deal with all of the empire's hypothetical adversaries on land and sea. Moreover, it provided the rationale for extending the military's political influence into areas of government previously reserved for civilian control, on the grounds that military participation in civilian administration was essential to the herculean task of mobilizing for total war.

As seen earlier in regard to the government's adoption of two different economic recovery plans, the new defense policy was a product of the national-unity government's difficulty in establishing priorities among the competing viewpoints and aspirations of its specialist-elite supporters. By attempting to provide Japan with sufficient strength to deal simultaneously with the world's most formidable land forces (in China and the Soviet Union) and strongest navies (the British and

15 Nagata Tetsuzan, *Kokka sōdōin* (Osaka: Osaka mainichi shinbunsha, 1928), p. 14.
16 Crowley, *Japan's Quest*, pp. 195–9, 231.

American fleets), the cabinet had endorsed the policy preferences of both the army and the navy, without establishing a sound sense of priorities between them.

Nevertheless, having made its commitments to economic recovery and "autonomous defense," the government proceeded to create a series of new superagencies that cut across existing ministerial jurisdictions to harmonize policy planning and implementation among the specialist elites. These agencies had two important characteristics. First, they provided new channels for military participation in administrative matters previously reserved for civilian supervision. For example, the army won the right to administer an important component of Japan's foreign policy when the Manchurian Affairs Bureau (Tai–Man jimukyoku) was created in 1934 to provide military supervision of Japan's relations with Manchukuo.[17]

Second, they reflected a growing appreciation of the deficiencies of the Meiji constitutional structure, which rigidly compartmentalized the jurisdiction of each ministry and insulated it from the pressures of other government institutions. Although most officials rejected the intrusion of outside influences into their areas of responsibility, the new superagencies generated a group of "revisionist" bureaucrats who advocated a higher degree of centralized direction, coordinated planning, and policy implementation across ministerial boundaries.[18] Because the revisionists generally urged that their superagencies enjoy a larger voice in the determination of national policy, they encountered strong opposition from career officials entrenched in the ministries. But the revisionists found common cause with military officials, who favored the growth of the superagencies to circumvent barriers to their own participation in civilian affairs and to better prepare the state for national mobilization. Nowhere was this concordance of viewpoints better illustrated than in the establishment of the Cabinet Research Bureau (Naikaku chōsakyoku) in 1935. This new agency, created by the Okada cabinet, brought together skilled technocrats for policy planning from both the civilian and military bureaucracies, furnishing another new channel for military participation in civilian administra-

17 For a detailed discussion, see Robert M. Spaulding, Jr., "The Bureaucracy As a Political Force, 1920–1945," in *Dilemmas of Growth*, pp. 33–80, esp. pp. 67–76.

18 On the revisionist bureaucrats, see Spaulding, "The Bureaucracy As a Political Force," pp. 60–80; Robert M. Spaulding, Jr., "Japan's 'New Bureaucrats,' 1932–45," in *Crisis Politics in Prewar Japan: Institutional and Ideological Problems of the 1930s*, ed. George M. Wilson (Tokyo: Sophia University Press, 1970), pp. 51–70; Hashikawa Bunzō, "Kakushin kanryō," in *Kenryoku no shisō*, ed. Kamishima Jirō, vol. 10 of *Gendai Nihon shisō taikei* (Tokyo: Chikuma shobō, 1965), pp. 251–73.

tion and a centralized forum for the administrative reform proposals of the revisionist bureaucrats.

The linkages formed between the army and the revisionist bureaucrats were an important aspect of the political strategy of total war planners such as Nagata Tetsuzan to create a new network of interinstitutional relationships for the articulation and reconciliation of elite group views, centering on the army rather than the political parties. Nagata also developed a cordial relationship with court nobles such as Harada Kumao, Kido Kōichi, and Konoe Fumimaro, whose political mediation could be a valuable asset in achieving the army's mobilization objectives. To build parliamentary support for his plans, Nagata won the backing of the Social Masses Party (Shakai taishūtō) in 1934 and sought to mold a coalition of conservative Diet members in favor of mobilization legislation.[19]

Nagata did not live long enough to bring his ambitious political efforts to fruition. On August 12, 1935, he was hacked to death by an officer of the Imperial Way faction, who favored an immediate mobilization of the nation's energies for war over Nagata's more gradual fashioning of a political coalition to support long-term military and industrial development. Although Nagata's death threw the army into turmoil for several months, his plan to institute national mobilization reforms through an army-centered web of elite relationships, rather than by scare tactics and terror, ultimately became central to the army's strategy of preparing for total war.

The growing importance of the civilian and military bureaucracies in dealing with Japan's economic and security problems thus impeded the parties' efforts to retain their pivotal position in harmonizing diverse elite viewpoints into coherent national policies. By 1936, assassination and attrition had robbed them of several key leaders, such as Hamaguchi, Inoue, Egi Tasuku, and Kawasaki Takukichi of the Minseitō and Inukai, Mori Kaku, Takahashi Korekiyo, and Tokonami Takejirō of the Seiyūkai. Moreover, the growing legal insulation of senior officials from party patronage reduced the parties' ability to replenish their ranks with ex-officials aligned with them. The parties' loss of the premiership in 1932 and the Minseitō's crippling defeat at the polls also made party membership a less attractive route to power for retiring officials and military leaders with political ambitions.

These tendencies were exacerbated by the voluntary withdrawal of the Seiyūkai from a meaningful role in Okada's national-unity govern-

19 Sugihara Masami, *Atarashii Shōwa shi* (Tokyo: Shin kigensha, 1958), p. 74.

ment. Disaffected by Admiral Saitō's unwillingness to turn the cabinet over to Seiyūkai president Suzuki, the majority party refused to cooperate with the new government and expelled renegade members who chose to accept appointments from Okada. In December 1935, the rebels organized an independent party, the Shōwakai, reducing further the attractiveness of membership in the isolated Seiyūkai as a means to power. The recruitment of nonparty talent into the ranks thus became increasingly difficult. As one Minseitō leader, Matsumura Kenzō, later recalled, the Minseitō had little success bringing bureaucrats and financiers into the party after 1932, as they preferred to negotiate directly with other elites rather than working through party channels.[20] Matsumura's observation is borne out by the declining number of ex-officials, ex-military officers, and ex-businessmen and financiers elected to the Diet as conservative party members between 1928 and 1936. Forty-one ex-officials were elected in 1928, but only twenty-seven in 1936. Four former military leaders were elected as party members in the 1928 election, none in 1936. Ninety-seven former businessmen and financiers joined the lower house as party members in 1928; only seventy-two were elected in 1936.

Moreover, membership in one or the other of the two conservative parties became less attractive even among members of the lower house, a trend of serious concern to the Seiyūkai and Minseitō because their leverage with nonparty elites depended in large part on their ability to deliver lower-house support for cabinet compromises negotiated by their leaders. The number of successful lower-house candidates who remained independent of party affiliation rose from nineteen (4 percent) in 1932 to eighty-seven (19 percent) in 1936 and 112 (24 percent) in 1937.

The parties' declining importance in intraelite relations was also reflected in criticisms by those earlier sympathetic to the parties' quest for power. For example, Minobe Tatsukichi, whose constitutional theories had provided the legal rationale for parliamentary ascendancy, wrote in 1934 that sophisticated economic and social policy planning required specialized knowledge sorely lacking among party politicians. The Diet, he concluded, was no longer qualified to serve as anything more than an agency of ratification for the policy proposals of more skilled servants of the state; and it was unwise to return to the practice of organizing cabinets based on lower-house majorities.[21]

20 Nagai Ryūtarō hensankai, *Nagai Ryūtarō*, ed. Matsumura Kenzō (Tokyo: Seikōsha, 1959), p. 310.
21 Minobe Tatsukichi, "Waga gikai seido no zento," *Chūō kōron* 553 (January 1934): 9ff.

Even in their capacity as mediators between the state and the citizenry, the parties' functions came under new attack in the changing international and domestic environment of the early 1930s. Even though they continued to insist that they played an important role in "assisting the imperial rule" by articulating local demands, the party representation of rural elite interests ran counter to the government's growing interest in industrial and military mobilization. Whereas nonparty leaders had grudgingly conceded earlier that the parties' approach to mass political integration was preferable to more radical alternatives posed in the 1920s, the specialist elites' new preoccupation with economic recovery and the new defense policy fostered a search for new means of mass mobilization and control for reallocating and concentrating limited national resources on urgent national tasks. From this perspective, the parties' role in the countryside was perceived as inhibiting the economic recovery programs of the Home Ministry and the Ministry of Agriculture and Forestry, whereas their advocacy of local pork-barrel legislation and tax relief of both rural and established business interests obstructed the enlargement of the military budget and the development of military industries.

Hence, in addition to being criticized by supporters of the bureaucracy, the parties were vilified by military spokesmen who asserted that the sacred bonds uniting the military with the people were being imperiled by the parties' resistance to national-defense budgets and taxation. Local chapters of the Imperial Military Reservists Association (Teikoku zaigō gunjinkai) took the lead in rural antiparty political agitation as one manifestation of the military's effort to reduce the parties' political importance. The reservists also spearheaded a virulent campaign in 1934 and 1935 against Minobe Tatsukichi, whose constitutional theories had for three decades provided a legal buttress for the growth of parliamentary elites' influence.[22]

The parties' response to the challenges posed to their influence between 1932 and 1936 may be summarized briefly. With the exception of Minseitō's politician Nagai Ryūtarō, no major party figure proposed revitalizing the parties' power by redefining their role in mediating between the state and the populace.[23] They continued to be

22 On the complexities of the Minobe affair, see Miyazawa Toshiyoshi, *Tennō kikansetsu jiken*, 2 vols. (Tokyo: Yūhikaku, 1970); Frank O. Miller, *Minobe Tatsukichi, Interpreter of Constitutionalism in Japan* (Berkeley and Los Angeles: University of California Press, 1965), pp. 196–253; Richard J. Smethurst, "The Military Reserve Association and the Minobe Crisis in 1935," in *Crisis Politics in Prewar Japan*, pp. 1–23.

23 Nagai Ryūtarō hensankai, *Nagai Ryūtarō*, pp. 304 ff; Gordon Mark Berger, *Parties Out of Power in Japan, 1931–1941* (Princeton, N.J.: Princeton University Press, 1977), pp. 219–20.

small elitist organizations, composed largely of members and former members of the lower house and aspirants for seats in the Diet, who relied for their political strength on linkages to local village elites rather than mass support-groups. The Minseitō's official political strategy continued to consist of providing patient support for national-unity government until new elections could restore its parliamentary credibility; however the Seiyūkai, as indicated earlier, shifted from a position of cooperation with the cabinet to outright confrontation following the establishment of the Okada government.

In 1933 and 1934, the dominant factions of both parties considered forming an alliance to counter attacks by their nonparty rivals on them and their supporters in the village and business elites. Likewise, minority factions in both parties proposed a similar coalition to support civil and military advocates of continental expansion, larger military budgets, and more extensive management of the economy by the government.[24] Neither coalition plan proved successful, but the formation of Admiral Okada's cabinet in July 1934 and the parties' loss of the important Finance and Home Ministry portfolios prompted renewed negotiations for a merger of the parties. Factions in both parties approached retired general Ugaki Kazushige and Prince Konoe with proposals to head a new party based on a merger of the Minseitō with disaffected members of the Seiyūkai, but Ugaki declined on the grounds that not *all* conservative party members would be included in the new organization, and Konoe later demurred on the grounds that any restoration of party influence required new parliamentary approaches to mass mobilization.[25]

Consequently, there were few concrete results from the parties' efforts to retrieve ground lost in the early 1930s. The parliamentary elites' rationale for sharing power remained what it had been for several decades. Seiyūkai leader Hatoyama Ichirō wrote early in 1936:

So long as the legitimacy of the parties' existence is undeniable, it is obvious that those who, through elections, represent the popular will – that is, Diet members – should be the central focus of politics. Bureaucrats and soldiers who have the slightest desire to become involved in politics should undergo

24 For these parliamentary movements, see Ichihara Ryōhei, "Seitō rengō undō no kiban: 'Zaibatsu no tenkō' o shōten to shite," *Keizai ronsō* 72 (February 1955): 106–22; and Ichihara, "Seitō rengō undō no hasan," pp. 161–82.

25 Itō Takashi, " 'Kyokoku itchi' naikaku-ki no seikai saihensei mondai: Shōwa jūsan-nen Konoe shintō mondai kenkyū no tame ni," *Shakai kagaku kenkyū* 24 (1972): 60–1; Kiya Ikusaburō, *Konoe-kō hibun* (Wakayama: Kōyasan shuppansha, 1950), p. 9; Harada Kumao, *Saionji-kō to seikyoku,* 9 vols. (Tokyo: Iwanami shoten, 1950–6), vol. 4, pp. 389, 392–3; Iwabuchi Tatsuo, *Yabururu hi made* (Tokyo: Nihon shūhōpsha, 1946), p. 74.

the baptism of elections and taste their bitterness before they are deemed spiritually qualified to be fused with the masses. . . . Politics should be left to the politicians, administrative matters to the bureaucrats, and national defense to the soldiers. We must once again establish our original system of divided responsibilities.[26]

Lamentably for the parties, their competitors no longer shared this vision. On February 20, 1936, in the first general election in four years, the Minseitō leadership was rewarded for its patience with a plurality of 205 seats in the lower house (a gain of 59 seats). The Seiyūkai strategy of confrontation with Okada backfired, as the party lost 126 seats and elected only 174 of its candidates. President Suzuki suffered the additional humiliation of defeat in his own bid for election. But despite the Minseitō victory, neither party by this time commanded sufficient nonparty elite support to warrant the revival of party government. Although national-unity governments had already demonstrated their inability to make critical choices between competing elite viewpoints and seemed incapable of establishing new mechanisms for strengthening citizen identification with their purposes, Prince Saionji as *genrō* had little alternative but to advise that they be continued.

## PRELUDE TO NATIONAL MOBILIZATION, 1936–1937

By the beginning of 1936, the crisis atmosphere created by international isolation and agrarian depression had intensified. As already indicated, one major consequence of the crisis mentality gripping the nation was a reallocation of power from the political parties to the civilian and military bureaucracies. A second major consequence was Japan's progressive withdrawal from the nexus of treaties and relationships with the Anglo-American powers known as the Washington order. The policy of autonomous defense initiated in 1933 was confirmed in cabinet decisions of July and December 1934 and again in October 1935. By 1936, both the Washington and London treaties on naval arms limitations had lapsed, and Japan showed little interest in renewing them.

The new defense policy carried with it heavy commitments to the development of military industry and weaponry, and government spending in these areas stimulated recovery in certain sectors of the economy. State intervention in the lives of the citizenry, which had

26 Cited in Kawasaki Hideji, *Yūki aru seijika-tachi* (Tokyo: Sengoku shuppansha, 1971), pp. 267–8.

begun to intensify with the government's agricultural relief programs, seemed certain to increase still further as the nation's resources were channeled toward national defense. The principal political issues of the late 1930s therefore focused on the extent of state controls over the economy, the most effective means of allocating scarce financial and material resources, and the most appropriate methods of reorganizing the state apparatus to coordinate national planning and mobilize popular support for the defense effort.

The issues emanating from the policy of autonomous defense were debated not simply on their merits but also in terms of how their resolution would affect each political elite group. We have seen, for example, that from 1932 to 1936 the military and civilian bureaucracies promoted and exploited a sense of crisis to nudge the parties from the cabinet's command. Between 1936 and 1941, these two groups pursued a similar strategy to strengthen their own positions in the councils of state. They portrayed the parties as stubborn adherents of an outmoded political order, and themselves as the instruments of necessary change. In fact, however, the conflict between the advocates of the status quo and the proponents of change was not synonymous with the cleavage between party and nonparty elite groups. In each group were reformists who sought to strengthen their political position by arguing that Japan's security required sweeping changes in its national institutions, and conservatives whose political interests led them to insist that radical reform would destabilize the state and weaken its defenses.

The eighteen months between February 1936 and July 1937 marked an intensification of reformist pressure within each elite group to revise the Meiji political settlement. The reform issue was also frequently invoked by rising forces in the civilian and military bureaucratic elites, to dominate their own respective bailiwicks and to overcome other elites in the competition for political power. In the absence of the intraelite mediation functions previously performed by the parties, conflict between the reformists and conservatives posed a serious threat to the political stability of elite government; and, in desperation, the elites turned to the imperial court and a group of hereditary nobles to reconcile their differences.

This turbulent interlude began with the mutiny of some fourteen hundred troops of the army's First Division on February 26, 1936. Led by young officers associated with the Imperial Way faction, rebel units occupied the Diet, the Army Ministry, and the Tokyo Metropolitan Police Headquarters. They assassinated the privy seal (ex-premier

Saitō), Finance Minister Takahashi Korekiyo, and the inspector general of army education (General Watanabe Jōtarō of the Control faction) and narrowly missed killing Prince Saionji, Admiral Suzuki Kantarō (the grand chamberlain), and Prime Minister Okada. At one level, the rebellion marked the culmination of factional rivalries within the army, which focused on how best to mobilize for war. More broadly, it constituted an assault on the advocates of the status quo (conservative court officials, the finance minister, and the prime minister).[27]

The outcome of the rebellion remained unclear until the emperor himself intervened with a forceful command that the young officers be brought to heel. By the afternoon of February 29, the uprising had been quelled, but Okada resigned immediately. Anxious to preserve the political inviolability of the throne, Saionji chose a successor who could weld the contending elite groups into a cohesive coalition without provoking further terrorism or rebellion. In the end, he concluded, "there is no one but Konoe."[28] Prince Konoe declined the premiership, but his nomination marked a recognition by Saionji and others that court nobles such as Konoe, Kido, and Harada, who transcended partisan affiliations, represented the best prospect for conciliating tensions within and among the elite groups.

Frustrated in his first choice, Saionji recommended career diplomat Hirota Kōki, who took office as prime minister on March 9, 1936. As Hirota was constituting his cabinet, the army leadership seized the opportunity to press for a reformist orientation in government by threatening to torpedo his efforts if the cabinet were too conservative. Although Hirota averted an early abortion of his cabinet by deft political compromise, he faced a vexing eleven months in office as a mediator between the reformist and conservative viewpoints.

In April 1936, revisionist bureaucrats in the Cabinet Research Bureau drafted an administrative reform proposal designed to reduce the importance of existing ministries and elevate the bureau to a position of preeminence in policy planning. By fall, the army and navy ministers had likewise proposed a series of drastic administrative reforms. Their plans called for the creation of an organ under the prime minister's jurisdiction to deal with the budget and policy research, a personnel agency subject only to the prime minister's control to centralize the power of official appointments, the merger of several government ministries, the transfer of offices from one ministry to another, and the

27 For a detailed analysis of the rebellion, see Ben-Ami Shillony, *Revolt in Japan* (Princeton, N.J.: Princeton University Press, 1973).

28 Yabe Teiji, *Konoe Fumimaro*, 2 vols. (Tokyo: Kōbundō, 1952), vol. 1, p. 326.

expansion of agencies concerned with the regulation of trade, fuel, electricity, and the civilian aircraft industry. Their plan also proposed sweeping reforms in local government to parallel the centralizing of national administration.[29]

In a word, this plan constituted the first effort by the services, particularly the army, to reorganize Japan's economic, political, and administrative structure into a "national defense state" (*kokubō kokka*) ready to mobilize for total war. Colonel Ishiwara Kanji, Nagata's heir as the principal architect of mobilization planning in the army, had already directed the preparation of a preliminary schedule of economic development to underwrite this effort, the "Five-Year Plan for the Empire's Income and Expenditures."[30] Finance Minister Baba Eiichi, a supporter of the reform program, prepared a gigantic budget proposal for ¥3.13 billion to underwrite the implementation of Ishiwara's plan.

Predictably, the reform package and budget met with an outraged reaction from business and the ministries, and Hirota gingerly consigned them to two cabinet subcommittees for further consideration. In December, the Diet convened for formal deliberation of the proposals. Though vanquished in the struggle for control of the cabinet, party politicians in the lower house found themselves supported against the military's plans by powerful conservative allies in the bureaucracy, business, and the local elites who felt threatened by the reforms. The army leadership publicly questioned the parties' patriotism and circulated rumors of another February 26 incident to intimidate the lower house, but the politicians held their ground. Hamada Kunimatsu of the Seiyūkai offered to commit ritual suicide (*harakiri*) if the army minister could substantiate the charges of disloyalty and dramatically advised the minister to follow a similar course of action to atone for the baseless blasphemy of the Diet.[31] The enraged army minister, knowing that the lower house was not prepared to approve the military's programs, resigned on January 23, 1937, bringing down the Hirota cabinet with him.

The army's confrontation tactics peaked during the next few days. When the emperor designated the retired general Ugaki as the new

29 Hirota Kōki denki kankōkai, ed., *Hirota Kōki* (Tokyo: Chūō kōron jigyō shuppan, 1966), pp. 241–2; Ko-Baba Eiich-shi kinenkai, *Baba Eiichi den* (Tokyo: Ko-Baba Eiich-shi kinenkai, 1945), pp. 262–3; Nakamura, *Economic Growth*, pp. 271–2.

30 Tsunoda Jun, ed., *Ishiwara Kanji shiryō: Kokubō ronsaku* (Tokyo: Hara shobō, 1967), pp. 139–47.

31 For the lower-house record of Hamada's exchange with the army minister, see *Kanpō gogai – Shōwa 12-nen 1-gatsu 22-nichi, Shūgiin giji sokkiroku dai-3-go*, pp. 35–45.

prime minister, the army leadership refused to appoint a new army minister because they thought him too conservative to carry forward the reform program. The imperial mandate then fell on General Hayashi Senjūrō, a former patron of Nagata Tetsuzan. In his efforts to form a new government, Hayashi was initially assisted by associates of the mercurial Colonel Ishiwara, who seemed determined to push through the implementation of their economic and administrative reforms even if a dictatorial party in the lower house had to be organized to overcome parliamentary resistance. Conservatives throughout the national leadership were appalled by the Ishiwara group's actions and boycotted the cabinet-formation process. Hayashi thus found himself unable to develop a sufficiently broad base of support to assemble a slate of ministers for his government.[32]

Having just forced the resignation of the Hirota cabinet and the abortion of an Ugaki government over the reform issue, the senior army leadership recognized that it did not yet have a sufficiently strong consensus of national reform. Once it became evident that the bureaucratic, party, and business elites would not cave in to Ishiwara's pressures, General Hayashi expelled Ishiwara's men from his cabinet-formation headquarters and signaled his readiness to proceed at a more moderate pace. To win business's support for the economic development program envisioned in mobilization planning, Hayashi asked Ikeda Seihin, the former managing director of the Mitsui Bank, to join the cabinet. Ikeda had taken an extremely dim view of the reform and budget proposals submitted to the Diet at the end of 1936. "The present plans," he had declared, "are simply the fruits of the program of the middle-echelon army officers and the Kwantung Army. We should be aware that they will have an extremely bad influence in financial circles."[33] However, once Hayashi had formally disassociated himself from Ishiwara, Ikeda's position shifted:

> The Ishiwara plans present some difficult problems; the army's demand for a replenishment of national defense must obviously be dealt with in accord with the dictates of international conditions. The basis of the present economic structure must remain intact. . . . If we do exactly as the most powerful of the middle-echelon elements in the army wish, that structure will collapse and lead to chaos. On the other hand, however, we cannot disregard national defense.[34]

Indicating his willingness to work out an accommodation between the interests of business and the proposed mobilization program, Ikeda

32 Berger, *Parties Out of Power*, p. 115. 33 Harada, *Saionji-kō to seikyoku*, vol. 5, p. 198.
34 Ibid., pp. 254–5 (entry for February 10, 1937).

recommended that Yūki Toyotarō (formerly governor of the Industrial Bank of Japan) be appointed finance minister, and in February he himself became governor of the Bank of Japan.

The entrance of Yūki and Ikeda into Hayashi's government initiated a brief era of greater cooperation between business and the armed forces. Contemporary journalists called the new accommodation "tie-up finance," as the viewpoints of business and the military were at least temporarily conjoined. As Ishiwara's influence receded, the reform offensive assumed a more moderate tone. After Yūki had assumed control of the Finance Ministry, he pruned the budget from ¥3.13 billion to ¥2.77 billion and brought skilled technocrats Kaya Okinori, Ishiwata Sōtarō, and Aoki Kazuo back into the ministry to maintain a liaison with the army leadership in formulating a new program of economic and military development. At the same time, Ikeda sent Izumiyama Sanroku of the Mitsui Bank to represent him in unofficial negotiations with the army over revisions of the "Five-Year Plan." By May 15, the negotiators had agreed on an overall plan for developing the military-supply industries of Japan and Manchukuo; and on May 29, the Army Ministry drew up to final revised program as "The Essentials of a Five-Year Plan for Key Industries." Most of the provocative administrative reform proposals of the previous year were scrapped in the first draft.[35]

The "tie-up finance" arrangements of early 1937 were significant in several ways. First, they established the buildup of Japan's military strength as the highest priority of national policy. Henceforth, all proposals requiring governmental approval were evaluated in terms of their contribution to military preparedness. Tie-up finance also offered the prospect of a compromise approach among the elites to economic and defense policymaking, replacing Ishiwara's strategy of sharp confrontation with the bureaucratic and business elites. At the same time, business leaders virtually abandoned their dependency on the conservative parties to represent their interests and instead began participating and negotiating directly through Ikeda, Yūki, Izumiyama, and others with the nonparty elites in government.

Not surprisingly, conservative politicians felt themselves increasingly vulnerable after the loss of business support. Their sense of aban-

35 Izumiyama Sanroku, *Tora daijin ni naru made* (Tokyo: Tōhō shoin, 1953), pp. 106–7; *Nichi-Man zaisei keizai kenkyūkai shiryō*, 3 vols. (Tokyo: Nihon kindai shiryō kenkyūkai, 1970); Nakamura, *Economic Growth*, pp. 268–85; Tsunoda, *Ishiwara Kanji shiryō*, pp. 148–50; International Military Tribunal for the Far East, "Proceedings," mimeograph, Tokyo, 1946–49, pp. 8260 ff.

donment was further provoked by General Hayashi, who excluded the parties from his cabinet. Although Hayashi invited three Diet politicians to serve as ministers, he made the appointments contingent on their resignations from party membership. Only Yamazaki Tatsunosuke of the small Shōwakai acceded to this stringent demand. The prime minister also refused to appoint parliamentary vice-ministers, thereby denying the Diet even a perfunctory and symbolic role in his administration. Hayashi evidently hoped that he could force the parties to merge into a single new organization to overcome parliamentary opposition to administrative reform, but his plans came to naught.[36] When the prime minister abruptly called new elections for the second time in fifteen months, the two major parties campaigned vigorously against his government and successfully retained their dominance of the lower house. Conceding defeat, Hayashi resigned shortly after the results of the election became known.

His successor as prime minister was Prince Konoe, now firmly established as a prominent behind-the-scenes mediator of conflicts among the elites. Known to be a supporter of the emerging consensus on limited reform represented by tie-up finance, the popular Konoe had already been sought out as a possible party president by several parliamentary groups in 1934 and 1935. He was therefore regarded as more likely than any other leader to win lower-house support for reform legislation.

Following the lead of the Hayashi government, Konoe's cabinet adopted a moderate tone in foreign policy. The government took the position that implementation of a new economic and military preparedness program would best be achieved by avoiding untimely conflicts with either the Anglo-American powers or the Chinese nationalist movement. In his domestic policy, Konoe was equally conciliatory. To mollify Ishiwara's reformist supporters, he invited Baba Eiichi back into the government as home minister, but to pacify Ikeda and Yūki, he gave the key Finance and Commerce ministry portfolios to career bureaucrats Kaya Okinori and Yoshino Shinji. Hayashi's service ministers retained their posts under Konoe, and Hirota was brought back into government as the foreign minister. Konoe also appointed two party members to ministerial positions and allowed them to retain their party affiliations.

Konoe's national-unity government came into power on the basis of an emerging consensus among the nonparty elites on the broad outline

36 See Berger, *Parties Out of Power*, pp. 108–20.

of a new policy of military and industrial development. As the government prepared to refine and implement its policies, however, it still confronted essentially the same political problems faced by preceding national-unity cabinets. That is, it still lacked any formal or informal mechanism for perpetuating the consensus it sought among the political elites; it still had no means of procuring lower-house support for the cabinet's program; and it had yet to devise any solution to the problem of mobilizing popular support and citizen identification with the goals and policies of the state.

It was clear that the government would soon impose major new financial burdens on the people, for the implementation of the development program required a concentration on and a rigorous regulation of the use of the nation's resources. Anticipating opposition from the rural population and its lower-house representatives, Agriculture and Forestry Minister Arima Yoriyasu urged that the government organize a new political party to mobilize the countryside, replace the ties between the rural elites and the conservative parties as a new vehicle for the articulation of local interests, and serve as a forum for the harmonization of those interests with the government's goals. If adopted, Arima's suggestion would have further undermined the traditional village elites as leaders of rural opinion, and the lower-house party representatives as the principal linkage between the populace and the cabinet. However, because the parties had demonstrated considerable residual strength during the Hirota and Hayashi governments, Arima's proposal was politically unfeasible, and so the Konoe cabinet ignored it.[37]

Instead, the government launched a nonpartisan popular campaign encouraging increased savings and reduced consumption to free capital for industrial development. Nevertheless, Arima's futile proposal had raised a fundamental issue: How could the government expect continuing popular support for a burdensome national defense policy when most of the population was still struggling with a depressed economy and looked to the village elites and parties to obtain government relief? The Konoe cabinet and its successors had three options. First, the government might attempt to reform the established mechanisms for controlling the citizenry and articulating its interests, as Arima was implicitly recommending in his call for a new government-run political party. Second, the government might simply appeal to

37 For an account of the cabinet meeting of June 15, 1937, see Yabe, *Konoe Fumimaro*, vol. 1, p. 392.

popular patriotism, emphasizing the overriding importance of subordinating citizens' individual welfare to the security of the state. And finally, if these two approaches failed, the government might stifle dissent by means of political repression, as it had in destroying the Japan Communist Party earlier.[38] All three options were pursued with varying success between 1937 and 1945, but the political struggles among the elites from mid-1937 to 1941 focused primarily on the wisdom of adopting the first option through the creation of a new mass-mobilization political party.

## THE CHALLENGE OF THE REFORMISTS, 1937–1939

As the Konoe government stood poised to draft specific legislation for the five-year industrial development plans, Japan unexpectedly found itself at war. A skirmish near Peking between Chinese and Japanese forces on July 7, 1937, escalated into full-scale hostilities within six weeks. Colonel Ishiwara and his supporters feared that a protracted engagement on the continent would stymie the five-year plan and frustrate the long-range goal of establishing a secure position of hegemony in East Asia.[39] But many military experts and civilian leaders saw the "China incident" as an opportunity to deal a swift and decisive blow to the Chinese nationalist movement. In the end, the latter view prevailed. Anticipating an early victory, the Konoe government sent Japan's forces racing through the cities of northern and central China in pursuit of the Nationalists' armies. By mid-December, the Nationalist capital of Nanking had been seized and raped by the Japanese; in early January 1938, Konoe pledged to eradicate Chiang's government. Apart from Ishiwara and several other knowledgeable military specialists, few national leaders believed that the prime minister's pledge would require many months to fulfill.

Between 1937 and 1940, the hostilities in China had several significant implications for Japanese politics. Initially, the war defused the issue of reform, as responsible national leaders declined to disrupt the home front with struggles over the nature of the political system. While troops were in the field, moreover, the lower house supported them enthusiastically and mitigated its confrontation with the cabinet.

38 On the suppression of Communism, see George M. Beckmann and Okubo Genji, *The Japanese Communist Party 1922–1945* (Stanford, Calif.: Stanford University Press, 1969), esp. chap. 9. Ideological suppression is more broadly discussed in Richard H. Mitchell, *Thought Control in Prewar Japan* (Ithaca, N.Y.: Cornell University Press, 1976).

39 On Ishiwara's concerns, see Peattie, *Ishiwara Kanji*, chap. 8; and Crowley, *Japan's Quest*, chap. 6.

The war also provided the government with a convenient issue on which to mobilize popular support and temporarily obviated the need to devise new organizations to strengthen mass identification with national goals and purposes. However, the cabinet soon decided to capitalize on its newfound strength by seeking legislative approval of the five-year plan; and by early 1938, it was purposefully patronizing the reform movement to pressure conservative legislators into sanctioning its programs.

Later, as the war dragged on beyond the government's original expectations, the military consumption of resources in the field began having an adverse effect on the nation's economy and threatened to impede the long-range program of military and industrial development, as Ishiwara had feared. In order to mobilize the resources and national determination to fight the war in China and still execute the five-year plan, reformists insisted on first establishing a dictatorial party in control of both the cabinet and the lower house and then restructuring the linkages of popular mobilization between the government and citizenry. Conservatives were able to blunt the reformists' challenge in late 1938 and throughout 1939. By 1940, however, with the war still draining away vital national resources and diminishing popular support of the government, the reformists appeared on the verge of establishing a new political order.

When Konoe convened an emergency session of the Diet in late July 1937, his primary interest was simply to set the stage for systematically implementing the five-year plan at a later date. Adopting a conciliatory position toward the lower house, he announced that he would disassociate himself from any effort to undermine conservative-party domination of the Diet and that he would reinstate the parliamentary vice-minister system which had lapsed under Hayashi. The prime minister also carefully limited his reform proposals to the least controversial prerequisites of the five-year plan. In response, the Diet passed thirty-four of the cabinet's thirty-five legislative proposals, including the "Iron and Steel Manufacturing Law" it had rejected previously. On September 9, another special Diet session patriotically approved a huge ¥2.2 billion supplementary authorization for military expenses in China.

The next regular Diet session was scheduled to begin at the end of December, at which time the cabinet judged that hostilities in China would soon end without interrupting its timetable for military and industrial development. Konoe thus saw the Seventy-third Diet as an excellent opportunity to exploit the war-generated patriotism in the parties and to overcome the parliamentary hurdles that had frustrated earlier reform measures. He gave instructions to the Cabinet Planning Board (Kikakuin) – which had evolved from the Cabinet Research Bureau to become the principal government agency for mobilization planning – to speed its preparation of key legislation related to the five-year plan. As Commerce and Industry Minister Yoshino wrote frankly,

> The Government takes the view that we should utilize the China Incident as an opportunity to make another decisive stride in Japan's industry and economy, and is desirous of obtaining some benefit for the future industrial and economic development of the country out of the measure[s] . . . adopted in connection with the Incident.[40]

Konoe's strategy also involved manipulating right-wing antiparty sentiment to weaken conservative resistance to the government's proposals in the Diet. Shortly before the Seventy-third Diet session opened, he gave the Home Ministry portfolio to Admiral Suetsugu Nobumasa, who was in the midst of a movement to unify the highly fragmented right wing into a cohesive political force against the parties. Many Japanist right-wing (*kannen uyoku*) groups rallied to Suetsugu's cause because they abhorred the concept of competitive elections among party candidates. Right-wing reformists (*kakushin uyoko*), on the other hand, hoped to use his movement to build electoral support for their efforts to seize control of the lower house from the conservative parties. Despite divergent attitudes toward the election system, both flanks of the right wing agreed that the Minseitō and Seiyūkai should be replaced in the lower house by a single party wedded to cabinet policies rather than the interests of local village elites or big business.[41] For Konoe, however, patronage of the right wing's antiparty campaign was largely a device for pressuring the lower house to pass his government's legislative program.[42]

The cornerstone of the government's legislative package was the general mobilization bill, which crystallized military and revisionist-bureaucratic thinking on how to maximize the development and mobilization of Japan's resources for military preparedness.[43] The bill

40 Shinji Yoshino, "Our Planned Economy," *Contemporary Japan* 6 (December 1937): 371.

41 See Kinoshita Hanji, "Kokumin shugiundō no gen-dankai," *Chūō Kōron* 615 (December 1938): 216–23; Itō, "The Role of Right-Wing Organizations," pp. 487–509; Imai Seiichi and Itō Takashi, eds., *Kokka sōdōin*, vol. 2 of *Gendai shi shiryō*, 44 vols. (Tokyo: Misuzu shobō, 1974), pp. 3–4.

42 As part of his tactics, Konoe supported the antiparty activities of Nakamizo Tamakichi. See Berger, *Parties Out of Power*, pp. 147–9.

43 Yabe, *Konoe Fumimaro*, vol. 1, pp. 473–4; Board of Planning, "On the National Mobilization Law," *Tokyo Gazette* 11 (May 1938): 1–9.

called for widespread official controls over the economy and political decision-making structure to ensure wartime military strength. In the event of war, the government was to be authorized to adjust the supply, demand, and allocation of labor to maximize production, to draft labor into military industries, to control wages, and to extend working hours when conditions warranted such measures.

The bill also empowered the government in wartime to control production, transportation, exports, imports, and the use of important buildings and land. It could also order private manufacturers to install new equipment to increase productive capabilities and could restrict such installations and expansion elsewhere when deemed detrimental to military production. Control associations and cartels were to be established to facilitate government control of industry and finance, and the government was to be given a voice in setting overall production and financing policies. The power to institute price and profit controls, register the professions and abilities of citizens, compel schools to train additional technicians to meet anticipated wartime requirements, and subsidize military production could be exercised at the government's discretion, even in peacetime. In short, the bill was intended to free the government from Diet restraints on massive intervention into all aspects of national economic life during wartime.

Konoe intimated that if the Diet rejected the bill, he would organize a new political party centered on the antiparty right-wing campaign.[44] However, he also opened the way to compromise. Because the cabinet's ultimate objective at this point was implementation of the five-year plan, rather than mobilization for a short-term conflict in China, Konoe indicated that the enabling legislation would not be used while fighting continued on the continent. He also agreed to appoint Diet members to a consultative mobilization council to be constituted whenever the mobilization statute was invoked.[45] Thus reassured, the Diet yielded to the pressures on it and approved the bill on March 24.

The government's second major legislative proposal during the Seventy-third Diet was a bill to establish state management over electric power generation and transmission facilities.[46] Debate over the bill

44 Yabe, *Konoe Fumimaro,* vol. 1, pp. 478–9; Arima Yoriyasu, *Seikai dōchūki* (Tokyo: Nihon shuppan kyōdō kabushiki kaisha, 1951), p. 141; Harada, *Saionji-kō to seikyoku,* vol. 6, pp. 245, 253. 45 Yabe, *Konoe Fumimaro,* vol. 1, pp. 476–8.

46 For details, see Yoshida Kei, *Denryoku kanrian no sokumen shi* (Tokyo: Kōtsū keizaisha shuppanbu, 1938); Nagai Ryūtarō hensankai, *Nagai Ryūtarō,* pp. 362–425; Hashikawa, "Kakushin kanryō," pp. 251–73; Okumura Kiwao, "Henkakuki Nippon no seiji keizai," in *Kenryoku no shisō,* pp. 274–90.

provoked a precedent-setting confrontation between its reformist adherents, who held that greater state control of the economy – approximating national socialism – was required to mobilize the empire in crisis, and the conservatives, who argued that Japan's economic strength could be maximized by adhering to the existing system of capitalist enterprise. On one side, military advocates of state economic controls insisted that the state assume the ownership and management rights over the electric power industry. Revisionist bureaucrats on the planning board, such as communications specialist Okumura Kiwao, likewise stressed the primacy of the state's interests over those of individual entrepreneurs, but they were willing to sanction continued private ownership as long as the state had management rights. The electric power companies' cartel disagreed vociferously, insisting that both ownership and management rights be left in private hands. The cartel position was supported by conservative bureaucrats, such as Vice-Minister of Communications Hirazawa Kaname, who opposed extensive state intervention and instead called for government production incentives to the private power companies.

Although Konoe's threats of alignment with the right wing underscored his determination to see the electric power bill passed, the legislation could not gain Diet approval without extensive emendation. In both the lower and upper houses, parliamentary supporters of conservative business interests secured revisions that allowed the existing power companies to continue managing their enterprises under state supervision, to participate through a new electric power commission in the management of the new public electric power generation company, and to receive handsome compensation for any facilities they transferred to the new public company.

By the time the Seventy-third Diet ended its deliberations, it had approved 86 measures proposed by the government, as well as more than 110 items related to the 1938–9 budget. As a result, the government had made significant inroads into the Diet's legislative prerogatives and had obtained new state authority over private capital. Moreover, because civilian and military technocrats staffed both the Cabinet Planning Board and the new state-run electric power company, the legislation opened new channels for their influence over the nation's economic and political affairs. Nevertheless, even though the political power of the business and parliamentary elites had been impaired by the new statutes, it was far from destroyed. The parties, for example, had forced the government to postpone implementation of the mobilization law until circumstances more serious than the conflict in China had arisen, and they had also assured themselves of at least an advisory role in setting policy on the new mobilization council. The electric power law enabled business to retain a significant role in setting policy for the state-run electric power company and compensated owners well for their losses. The new law set a pattern for redefining the relationship of the state to private enterprise. Official controls over business remained much lighter than those over other aspects of the wartime economy, and the business elite henceforth became a full partner with the military and civilian bureaucracy in the economic management of the nation.[47]

Consequently, the reformist camp was far from satisfied by the outcome of Konoe's encounter with the Diet. For example, Arima Yoriyasu complained that "while the Diet undoubtedly gave its careful consideration to the bills presented, and put on a show of affirming national unity and complete confidence in the government, its actual conduct represented a shocking departure from its words."[48] He then began organizing a new reformist party based on the agricultural guilds, aimed at overthrowing local elite dominance of the rural economy, increasing production, reducing land taxes, and implementing state controls over financing and rental incomes.[49] Some right-wing reformists pursued their own separate plan to create a new political party, to confront conservative party influence nationally and in the countryside.

By fall, they and Arima were prepared to merge their efforts in the Dai Nippontō (Greater Japan Party), intended to become a dictatorial organ working with the government and the military in the formulation, ratification, and implementation of national defense state policies. They were joined in this effort by the Social Masses Party, which by 1937 had abandoned its goal of social democracy in favor of supporting the army's program of state economic controls. They also found new support among a number of other Diet politicians, who either were linked politically with military industries that would flourish in a national defense state or were estranged from the Minseitō and Seiyūkai leaders and hoped to seize control of the lower house through the new party.[50]

The new-party forces also received encouragement from allies in the military and revisionist-bureaucratic ranks, who saw the possibility of using a mass-based political organization both to undermine conserva-

47 Tiedemann, "Big Business and Politics," p. 311.
48 Cited in Adachi Gan, *Kokumin undō no sai-shuppatsu* (Tokyo: Kasumigaseki shobō, 1940), pp. 14–16. 49 Ibid., pp. 92–3. 50 Berger, *Parties Out of Power*, pp. 164–73.

tive critics of economic controls and to spearhead widespread public participation in the mobilization of resources and national commitment to the war and five-year-plan efforts. At the outset of the China incident in 1937, the cabinet had converted its original plan for a citizens' savings campaign into the Movement for Mobilizing Popular Morale (Kokumin seishin sōdōin undō). The movement was directed by a nonpartisan federation of organizations, including the parties, under the joint supervision of the Cabinet Information Commission, the Home Ministry, and the Ministry of Education.[51] In response to a decided lack of public enthusiasm for the movement, the supervising government agencies began to study ways of strengthening the campaign in mid-1938.[52] Each agency attempted in the process to seize exclusive control of the movement from the others, and the Ministries of Agriculture and Forestry and Commerce and Industry also tried to insinuate themselves into its management. By late 1938, therefore, bureaucratic rivalries had been superimposed on the clash between reformists and conservatives over the creation of a new mobilization party.

The new-party movement reached a crescendo of activity in October and November, when Konoe was rumored to be on the verge of assuming the party presidency. However, the Japanist right wing and Admiral Suetsugu were suspicious that the new-party campaign was actually a covert effort to establish a left-wing socialist regime.[53] They joined conservatives in opposing the movement and consequently reduced the likelihood that a unified right-wing political force could be organized against the existing parties in the lower house. And although Prime Minister Konoe had patronized the reformists at the beginning of 1938, his enthusiasm for upsetting the balance of power among the elites waned progressively with each passing month. By May, Konoe realized that his government's short-term military commitment against Chiang Kai-shek had failed to achieve the expected results and that his cabinet's five-year plan, which was predicated on a sustained period of peace, faced serious problems.[54] Economic projections throughout the spring and summer confirmed the prime minister's worst fears about the effects of the China war on the industrial

51 Participating organizations are listed in Yokusan undō shi kankōkai, ed., *Yokusan kokumin undō shi* (Tokyo: Yokusan undō shi kankōkai, 1954), pp. 28–30.

52 See "Kokumin seishin sōdōin sai-soshiki no ken," in *Kokka sōdōin*, pp. 4–7.

53 Yabe, *Konoe Fumimaro*, vol. 1, pp. 568–9.

54 As he conceded to Harada, "Until recently, while I don't say I didn't appreciate the need for peace, I wasn't too wise, was I. . . . In fact, Hirota and I were much too emphatic in calling for the downfall of the Chiang regime." Harada, *Saionji-kō to seikyoku*, vol. 7, pp. 5–6.

development plans. In June, moreover, an American "moral" embargo on aircraft, armaments, engine parts, bombs, and torpedoes further impeded the task of adequately supplying the combat forces. The military demand for goods and services drew production away from the export market, denying Japan foreign currencies needed to pay for imports anticipated in the five-year plan. At length, the cabinet decided that sections of the new mobilization law must be invoked, despite Konoe's earlier promises to the contrary.[55]

Anxious to defuse the political consequences of these reversals, Konoe found it expedient to turn for support to conservatives who advocated mobilization within the existing political and economic framework. In May, he persuaded both the retired general Ugaki and Ikeda Seihin to join the government. Ugaki's difficult charge as foreign minister was to effect a termination of hostilities in China without making any significant concessions on Japan's war aims; he resigned in frustration after less than five months in office. Ikeda's association with the Konoe cabinet lasted longer. Serving concurrently as finance minister and minister of commerce and industry, he was given wide-ranging power to supervise the government's economic mobilization program. When the military and its reformist supporters insisted that Article XI of the mobilization law be invoked, allowing the government to severely limit corporate dividends and compel banks to make loans for defense production, Ikeda was able with Konoe's support to gain substantial concessions for business in return for a generous government limit of 10 percent on dividends.[56] He thus played a crucial role in the conservatives' defense of the existing allocation of power among the elites.

Thus Japan's involvement in the China war ultimately exacerbated political conflict among the nation's elite groups, rather than promoting the establishment of rigid totalitarian political controls. The political cleavages manifested in the 1938 struggles for control of the lower house and the popular mobilization movement presaged the battle lines that appeared two years later in the movement for a new political order (*seiji shintaisei*). But the influential Prince Konoe, who appeared committed to the reformist camp in 1940, was not prepared to subject the nation to disruptive political turmoil over reform during the waning months of 1938. From late October, Konoe frustrated every re-

55 International Military Tribunal, "Proceedings," p. 8492; Horiba Kazuo, *Shina jihen sensō shidōshi* (Tokyo: Jiji tsūshinsha, 1962), pp. 170–2; Fujiwara Akira, Imai Seiichi, and Tōyama Shigeki, *Shōwa shi*, rev. ed. (Tokyo: Iwanami shoten, 1959), p. 160.
56 Tiedemann, "Big Business and Politics," pp. 310–11.

formist effort to challenge the existing balance of power among the elites or to gain control over popular mobilization.

The prime minister also recognized that his cabinet's mission to implement the five-year plan remained severely jeopardized by the China war. Rather than moderate Japan's peace terms, however, the government chose to redefine the war as a struggle against "the old order of Western imperialism and its principal Chinese agent, Chiang Kai-shek." Hoping to create a new regional context in which the clash of Chinese and Japanese nationalism might be resolved, Konoe announced in November that his nation's noble purpose was the construction of a "new order in East Asia" (*Tōa shinchitsujo*) led by Japan. Because this ambitious undertaking would require a considerable period of persuasion and military pressure to obtain Chinese recognition and then peace on the continent, the prime minister had to acknowledge that his cabinet's original goals could not be attained in the near future. At the beginning of January 1939, he therefore stepped down from the premiership and became president of the Privy Council.

Konoe's successor was Hiranuma Kiichirō, long considered the doyen of the Japanese right wing. Although earlier in the decade he had been a vitriolic opponent of the political influence of the conservative parties and big business, Hiranuma now shared Konoe's view that the war in China required national harmony rather than elite conflict. He quickly let it be known that as premier he held little brief for the reformists' cause.[57] Hiranuma's position dealt a fatal blow to the movement to unite the right wing and placed the Japanists resolutely in the ranks of the conservatives on the reform issue. The new prime minister resisted pressures for sweeping institutional change as staunchly as his predecessor had. When his cabinet reorganized the Movement for Mobilizing Popular Morale in April 1939, the net effect was to strengthen the movement's nonpartisan nature rather than to create a new political force against the parties. When it became necessary to invoke additional portions of the mobilization law, the cabinet carefully obtained the approval of parliamentary representatives on the National General Mobilization Council and limited its mobilization policies to measures, such as the enhancement of worker productivity, that might benefit business interests as much as the state.[58]

57 See the interpellation of Ogawa Gōtarō in the lower-house record for January 22, 1939, *Kanpō gogai–Shōwa 14-nen 1-gatsu 22-nichi, Shūgiin giji sokkiroku dai-3-go*, pp. 32–3; *Yokusan kokumin undō-shi*, p. 25.

58 For a list of cases in which the mobilization law was actually invoked during this period, see Board of Planning, "Invocation of the National General Mobilization Law," *Tokyo Gazette* 2 (March 1939): 20–1.

After the domestic reform issue had been defused, Hiranuma's major difficulties centered on whether Japan should ally itself militarily with Germany and Italy. To mitigate Japan's international isolation after withdrawing from the League of Nations and abrogating the Washington and London treaties, the Hirota cabinet had concluded an anti-Comintern pact with the Axis powers in November 1936. Faced two years later with growing Anglo-American criticisms of Japan's aggression in China and the renewed specter of Soviet power in the north, the army and its civilian supporters encouraged expanding the 1936 accord into a full-scale military alliance. The navy, on the other hand, was still not prepared to meet the military responsibilities such an agreement might impose if the Anglo-American powers decided to confront the Axis on the seas. The Hiranuma cabinet agreed that a military pact with the Axis might neutralize Soviet power, but before the army and the prime minister could persuade the navy to accept the alliance, Germany abruptly concluded a nonaggression pact with the Soviet Union in September 1939. With the thrust of his foreign policy thereby undermined, Hiranuma immediately resigned in favor of General Abe Nobuyuki.

The Abe cabinet lasted less than five months. The new prime minister attempted to continue Hiranuma's working relationship with conservatives in the Diet leadership, business, and the senior civilian bureaucracy. But he also had to bear the brunt of widespread discontent over wartime economic dislocations. Severe drought and increased military demand created extensive food and power shortages at the end of 1939 and seriously eroded popular support for the government and its policies.[59] Military anxiety over economic conditions and public morale prompted army officials once again to consider creating a new political party as a mobilization organ in the national defense state. For the growing number of politicians in the Diet opposed to the leaders of the Minseitō and Seiyūkai, the antigovernment mood came as a renewed opportunity to press for the implementation of their plans for a new party as well. Because the senior leadership of the two conservative parties supported Prime Minister Abe, many junior members of the parties tried to form a lateral alliance with independents and reformist right-wing forces in the lower house. They began a campaign with the dual objective of creating a new party to promote economic reforms and overturning the coalition between Abe and the

59 Hayashi Shigeru, *Taiheiyō sensō*, vol. 25 of *Nihon no rekishi* (Tokyo: Chūō kōronsha, 1967), p. 131; Fujiwara et al., *Shōwa shi*, pp. 174–5.

senior parliamentary leadership. On January 7, 1940, the new-party forces gained majority support for a lower-house resolution of no confidence in the government. Abe's options were to resign or dissolve the lower house, and because the army leadership was reluctant to risk an election with public morale at such a low point, he chose to resign.[60]

Abe's withdrawal marked the third time in three years that the lower house had been instrumental in bringing down a cabinet. It was the second time that the victim of lower-house agitation had been a general. The message conveyed to the powerful army elite was that implementation of a national defense state would require a stronger and more stable base of support in the lower house than national-unity cabinets had hitherto been able to muster. Army leaders thus sought to ally with the dissidents in the lower house, who saw military patronage as an opportunity to regain a share of the power the parties had progressively surrendered since 1932.

The inability of senior parliamentary leaders to control the lower-house rank and file at the beginning of 1940 provided a stark warning that unless they reestablished themselves in a position of political patronage and provided their members with the power and prestige that had originally served to induce politicians to join the conservative parties, their membership would desert them and leave them without influence. At the same time, the loss of party discipline itself demonstrated that no party leader at that moment was strong enough to command serious consideration as Abe's successor. Irrespective of the lower house's capacity to break a cabinet's power, none of the existing parties had the internal cohesiveness or the following among nonparty elites to give birth to a new government. Conservatives in business, the bureaucracy, the navy, the court, and the parties therefore threw their support behind a nonparty figure, Admiral Yonai Mitsumasa, as the new prime minister.

Yonai's appointment again demonstrated the residual political strength of the forces who favored maintaining the status quo that had existed since the middle of the Konoe government's tenure in office. At the same time, however, it firmed the resolve of reformists to create a new political party to eclipse the conservative influence. Throughout the first half of 1940, reformist pressures on the government mounted steadily, and as a new war in Europe progressively

60 Shiraki, *Nihon seitō shi*, pp. 284–6; Sugihara, *Atarashii Shōwa shi*, pp. 173–6; Sugihara Masami, *Kokumin soshiki no seiji-ryoku* (Tokyo: Modan Nipponsha, 1940), pp. 23–4. The *Asahi shinbun* carried a complete list of those supporting the resolution of no confidence in its January 8, 1940, edition.

transformed the international environment, Prince Konoe agreed to assume the premiership again and create a new political order.

## JAPAN'S NEW POLITICAL ORDER, 1940–1945

When Admiral Yonai assumed office on January 16, 1940, international politics in East Asia and the world were in a highly volatile state of flux. In China, Japan was pursuing yet another approach to establishing its primacy on the continent, through the creation of a new Nationalist regime under Wang Ching-wei. Because it was widely conceded in Tokyo that this strategy would make it impossible for Chiang Kai-shek to sue for peace unless totally defeated on the battlefield, the Wang plan carried with it the strong likelihood of a long-term Japanese military presence in China. In the European conflict, which began in September 1939, Germany scored an impressive string of victories over Britain and its allies, and the United States soon began bolstering Britain's flagging strength with lend-lease assistance. In January, the Americans expanded their "moral embargo" on Japan into the abrogation of the United States–Japan Treaty of Commerce and Navigation. The possibility of a total American embargo on strategic materials became a vital factor affecting Japan's autonomous defense policy. Another variable was added to the equation of international politics when Nazi successes between April and June 1940 opened the strategically located and resource-rich European colonies in Southeast Asia to whichever power was bold enough to seize them.

Although Yonai's appointment represented a confirmation of conservative strength among the elites, the instability of the international environment led to a renewed focus on military preparedness, enlarged the influence of the military in policymaking, and reinforced reformist demands for institutional changes to permit the rapid domestic mobilization of national energies. While the two military services struggled with each other to reach agreement on foreign and military policies, the army ultimately took the lead in demanding new initiatives abroad and sweeping reforms at home to ensure the protection and expansion of Japan's international interests. The degree to which turmoil abroad strengthened the military's political position at home was amply reflected by its ability to win new policy commitments to alliance with the Axis powers, expansion into Southeast Asia, and new approaches to the management of Japan's human and material resources. These commitments threatened to embroil the nation in a military confrontation with the Anglo-American powers and alter fundamentally the allocation of wealth and power in Japan itself.

From the perspective of securing Japan's primacy in East Asia, the army's leaders saw in the rapidly changing world situation a number of new problems and opportunities. In China, they supported establishing the Wang regime while temporarily escalating military pressure on Chiang Kai-shek to end the thirty-month war. However, the army was equally prepared to delay recognition of Wang's government if that would facilitate a negotiated truce with Chiang. In the event that Chiang resisted both the Japanese offer of negotiations and the creation of a rival regime, the army argued that it must eventually abandon its all-out attacks on the Nationalists in favor of a long-term occupation of China.[61] Late in the spring, the collapse of Western Europe under the German onslaught opened the possibility for Japanese expansion into Southeast Asia, as a potential staging ground for the short-term strategy of new attacks on Chiang and as a source of strategic materials – including oil – to reduce economic dependency on the United States. In order to move south, the army felt it wise to neutralize Soviet pressures in the north and possible Anglo-American resistance in the south, by concluding a military alliance with the Axis. The navy, which had been deterred from southern expansion only by fears of combined Anglo-American resistance, shared the army's view that the situation in Europe represented a "golden opportunity" for Japan. Navy leaders thus grew more supportive of the army's advocacy of an Axis alliance to take advantage of the power vacuum in the south.[62]

In the military's view, a long-term occupation of China, expansion into Southeast Asia, and continued military preparedness against the Soviet Union required the creation of a "high-degree national defense state" at home. To accomplish simultaneously their ambitious military and foreign policy goals, all national resources had to be tightly controlled and coordinated by a streamlined but powerful centralized administration in which military leaders held key positions of leadership. To enact the legislation authorizing such a high-degree national defense state, the army's political experts knew that they needed a powerful support group in the lower house as well as a sympathetic cabinet in power.

The Yonai government hardly seemed an ideal vehicle for the real-

61 Bōeichō bōei kenshūsho senshishitsu, *Daihon'ei rikugunbu,* 2 vols. (Tokyo: Asagumo shimbunsha, 1967–8), vol. 2, p. 7.

62 See Sadao Asada, "The Japanese Navy and the United States," in *Pearl Harbor As History,* pp. 225–59, esp. pp. 248–50.

ization of these plans. Despite the navy's changing views on southern expansion and alliance with the Axis, Admiral Yonai had been a stubborn opponent of the campaign to align Japan with the Axis in 1939. His foreign minister, Arita Hachirō, also sought to minimize military inroads in the formulation of foreign policy and favored a China policy focused exclusively on recognizing Wang Ching-wei's regime. Yonai continued General Abe's attempts to accommodate business and the conservative senior leadership of the lower house by inviting four party politicians to serve in his cabinet.[63] As the new government assumed office, therefore, the army was already watching carefully for opportunities to drive it from power and create a new political party to endorse its own domestic programs.

One such opportunity arose two weeks after Yonai became premier. On February 2, Saitō Takao of the Minseitō delivered a sharp speech in the lower house, criticizing the moralistic hypocrisy of calling the China conflict a "holy war against Western imperialism."[64] In Saitō's view, the war constituted a simple struggle for power between the strong and the weak, and Japan's position was undermined by the army's simultaneous approach to Chiang and Wang. Saitō's cold-blooded analysis of the army's nuanced policy toward the Nationalists provoked enormous anger in the army, for it cast doubt on the military's mission of building a new order in East Asia, for which thousands of soldiers had already given their lives.[65] The army leadership pressed the lower house to have Saitō's criticisms stricken from the Diet record and to expel the veteran politician from its membership. The speaker of the lower house quickly had Saitō's remarks deleted, on the grounds that the Minseitō leader's comments might encourage the Chinese to doubt the firmness of Japan's resolve in the war. Within a month, the coalition of new-party advocates that had forced General Abe from office engineered Saitō's expulsion from the Diet as well. On March 9, the lower house passed a resolution supporting the prosecution of the "holy war" in China (Seisen kantetsu ketsugi an), and the new-party coalition organized itself formally as the "League of Diet Members Supporting the Prosecution of the Holy War" (Seisen kantetsu giin renmei).

63 Matsuno Tsuruhei, Shimada Toshio, Katsu Masanori, and Sakurauchi Yukio.

64 For the complete text of Saitō's speech, including segments expurgated from the official lower-house minutes, see Saitō Takao, *Saitō Takao seiji ronshū* (Izushi-machi, Izushi-gun, Hyōgo-ken: Saitō Takao sensei kenshōkai, 1961), pp. 19–41.

65 For the army's reaction, see Bōeichō bōei kenshūsho senshishitsu, *Daihon-ei rikugunbu Dai Tōa sensō kaisen keii* (Tokyo: Asagumo shimbunsha, 1973), vol. 1, pp. 270–6; Koiso Kuniaki jijoden kankōkai, ed., *Katsuzan kōsō* (Tokyo: Koiso Kuniaki jijoden kankōkai, 1963), p. 692.

The league was widely and correctly perceived as the prelude to a new political party backed by the army.[66] Senior lower-house leaders, who found themselves confronted by the potential disintegration of their party organizations, turned to Prince Konoe for their salvation. Their hope was that Konoe would again blunt the challenge of the reformists, while still proving sufficiently acceptable to the military to permit the preservation of the political status quo. By the late spring of 1940, a number of leading Minseitō and Seiyūkai figures had conveyed to Konoe their willingness to dissolve their own parties to join any new organization he would agree to create.[67]

However, Konoe's earlier opposition to reform was greatly affected by the recent changes in the international environment. If anything, he was rather pleased by the growth of reformist pressures on the Yonai cabinet and the lower-house leadership in early 1940. Yonai had been the first prime minister appointed over his opposition since the February 26 incident, and Konoe had less empathy with the government's policies than with the army's strategy of allying with the Axis, moving south, neutralizing the Soviet Union, and negotiating Chiang's surrender in China. Konoe's views on domestic political reform also seem to have become congruent with those of many reformists. After eight years' experience with national-unity governments, Konoe had come to the conclusion that the diffusion of political power institutionalized by the Meiji constitution no longer served Japan well.[68]

Konoe contended that neither the Diet nor elections dominated by party politicians and their local-elite allies were adequate to integrate the people into the life of the state, particularly when international crisis demanded extraordinary effort and sacrifice by the citizenry. Furthermore, bureaucratic squabbling over the prerogatives of formulating and implementing important national policies resulted, in his view, from the narrowly specialized viewpoints of officials protected in their ministries by the civil service codes and the additional protection afforded to bureaucratic appointees at the beginning of the decade. The infighting that had characterized reappraisals of the nation's popular mobilization campaigns in 1938, and the disputes between the army and navy over the Axis alliance in 1939 and 1940, were characteristic of flaws in the constitutional order that might become fatal at a moment when international turmoil required a high degree of administrative coordination for the formulation and implementation of Ja-

66 Bōeichō, *Daihon'ei rikugunbu Dai Tōa sensō kaisen keii*, vol. 1, pp. 276–77.
67 Berger, *Parties Out of Power*, pp. 250–1.
68 The following discussion is based on Berger, *Parties Out of Power*, pp. 263–7.

pan's foreign and domestic policies. Finally, Konoe argued that the institutional weakness of the premiership restricted the prime minister's ability to monitor and control the political activities of the military. The Meiji political settlement had deprived the cabinet of the leverage to force a choice between army and navy priorities or to coordinate military perspectives on national policy with those of other elite groups.

To deal with these problems, Konoe proposed in 1940 to establish a new political order in Japan. The keystone of the new system was to be a new political party, embracing all existing groups in the lower house but dominated by himself as president. Privately, Konoe calculated that the conservative parties would account for only 40 percent of the new party's membership; the majority of members would be "new" and "reform-minded" individuals. Popular energies would be integrated under the party's monolithic control through two hierarchically structured mass organizations: a nationwide network of guilds linking the party to the economic pursuits of the people and a second hierarchy of youth groups, educational bodies, and cultural groups tying the party to popular life.

By simultaneously holding the positions of party leader and prime minister, Konoe thought he could strengthen the prime minister's position in controlling the people, the lower house, the bureaucracy, and the military. Based on a mass organization, the new party would provide channels for mobilizing the people in the service of the cabinet's policies. Political support from the new-party membership would permit the cabinet to obtain Diet approval for its policies and legislation. The political leverage that a prime minister could derive from the support of the new party would enhance his position in negotiating with both the bureaucracy and the armed services. In short, the party would become a new extracabinet mechanism for welding the elites into a cohesive governing coalition and linking the people with the formulation and execution of national policies.

Konoe's plan rested on a shrewd appraisal of the deficiencies of the Meiji system as a framework in which to establish a national defense state, and it offered a radical prescription for solving the political problems inherent in national-unity government. Konoe recognized that his proposal for a strong premiership and new party represented a fundamental challenge to the institutional prerogatives of all elite groups. As the only political organization of the lower house, the new party would virtually eviscerate the functions of the lower house, by transferring them to the new party itself. The party's mass organizational base would bypass the established rural leadership for the formal articulation of local interests and thereby undermine the traditional village elites. The multiple bureaucratic linkages of central ministries to the countryside also would be supplanted by the new popular organization. Moreover, Konoe proposed establishing a centralized policymaking organ under the prime minister's jurisdiction that would further weaken the ministries' policy role, and he called for a reform of the civil service system that would permit the appointments of men from outside the bureaucracy to leading government positions. Finally, the new party would engulf the armed forces in its membership and mass organizations and thereby bring them under Konoe's control as party president. Combined with this approach to controlling the military elites, the prince's reform plans provided for the establishment of a supreme defense council that would permit the prime minister to influence the military planning of the two service ministries and the general staffs.

A proposal as sweeping as Konoe's new order was certain to evoke widespread opposition from all entrenched political forces. Konoe conceded privately that his plans would also require a fundamental reinterpretation of the Meiji constitution, which had been designed specifically to ensure a diffusion of power among several elite groups rather than a concentration of power in the hands of a single individual or political party. To avoid the instantaneous rejection of his ideas, Konoe presented them in muted and reassuring language. To the public, he promised that "we will faithfully respect our constitution."[69] To leaders in the lower house, he intimated that the new order would restore parliamentary influence and rescue them from losing power altogether with the disintegration of their party organizations. To the new-party activists in and out of the Diet, he presented his program as an opportunity to circumvent the domination of current parliamentary leaders and the exigencies of the existing electoral system, both of which had deprived them of a leading political role. To the military, he implied that the new order would provide the political framework for the ratification of the national defense state ideal, with strong centralized economic planning and tight political controls. The new order also seemed to open the way for military technocrats to assume important official positions denied them by the existing civil service code. To the revisionist bureaucrats, his institutional reforms offered positions of influence that far exceeded those of their current

69 Yabe, *Konoe Fumimaro*, vol. 2, pp. 106–7; Oda Toshiyo, *Yokusan undō to Konoe-kō* (Tokyo: Shunpei shobō, 1940), p. 10.

offices, and to more conservative officials, the new order was portrayed as a vehicle for overcoming local elite resistance to the extension of government administration into the village.

Impressed by the public presentation of Konoe's views and impelled by an increasing sense of urgency as the Nazi tide in Europe exposed the vulnerability of the colonies in Southeast Asia, in late spring, the army moved swiftly to replace Yonai with Konoe. On June 16, Army Minister Hata Shunroku resigned, and the army brought down the government by refusing to provide a successor. Prince Saionji, who had once regarded Konoe as his protégé in mediating political conflict, was now too infirm and appalled by the implications of Konoe's new-order plans to participate in recommending a new prime minister to the throne. Instead, the new privy seal, Kido Kōichi, canvassed the views of all former prime ministers as senior statesmen (*jūshin*). They agreed quickly that the army's position left no room for the appointment of anyone but Konoe.

Before formally accepting the premiership, Konoe held an extensive round of policy discussions at his residence with the men slated to hold key positions in his cabinet: Foreign Minister Matsuoka Yōsuke, Navy Minister Yoshida Zengo, and Army Minister Tōjō Hideki. These talks were designed to maximize Konoe's leverage over his cabinet. They took place under the implicit threat that Konoe would decline the emperor's offer to lead the government if his key ministers were unwilling to support his policy views. Satisfied that this maneuver had resulted in accord, Konoe swiftly organized his cabinet.

At the July 26 cabinet meeting, the government adopted an "Outline of Basic National Policies" (Kihon kokusaku yōkō) that laid out the framework for domestic reform. Predicated on the need to establish a national defense state for the implementation of Japan's international goals, the "Outline" was a blueprint for the new political order and the creation of a planned economy, with stringent controls over finance, production, and consumption. The "Outline" called as well for the cultivation of a national morality that put loyal service to the state ahead of private interests and individual welfare.[70] The following day, a joint meeting of the cabinet and the military command formalized the new regime's foreign policies. For the first time, the use of force was authorized in Japan's expansion into Southeast Asia, and the army's two-pronged strategy of intimidating Chiang while slowing

70 For a text of the "Outline," see Gaimushō, ed., *Nihon gaikō nenpyō narabi ni shuyō bunsho* (Tokyo: Hara shobō, 1966), vol. 2, pp. 436–7.

recognition of the Wang government in China was confirmed as national policy.[71] There was also a tacit understanding that the achievement of Japan's objectives overseas would require the conclusion of a military alliance with Germany and Italy and the neutralization of the Soviet menace by either force or diplomacy.

The political elites responded almost immediately to Konoe's plans for a new political and economic order. The Social Masses Party had already expressed commitment to the new order by dissolving on July 6. The conservative party organizations all followed suit by August 15. Although their motives differed, both the senior lower-house leadership and the new-party adherents in the Diet seemed anxious to identify themselves quickly with Konoe's new party. They hoped thereby to obtain party positions that would permit them to enlarge their own political influence and that of the Diet in the formulation and implementation of national policy. On the other hand, Home Ministry bureaucrats sought to gain control of the popular organization that Konoe had proposed, in order to extend the ministry's reach into every hamlet and municipality. But the Ministry of Agriculture and Forestry resisted this initiative, fearing that the Home Ministry would undermine its supervision over local economic guilds in the name of a streamlined administrative approach to mobilization. The political party forces recognized that the Home Ministry's plans could shatter their preeminent role in linking the countryside politically to Tokyo, and army leaders also opposed the creation of a Home Ministry monopoly over local mobilization because they preferred to launch a radical partisan movement to engender local support for the national defense state. Rather than placing party-allied village leaders or local government officials in charge of local mobilization, the army wanted Imperial Military Reservist Association members installed as local branch leaders of the popular organization. In other words, each political elite group hoped to use the new political order to expand its influence, without surrendering any of its existing power.[72]

Before the political struggle over the new order was formally joined, the Konoe government swiftly implemented the agreements reached in July on the nation's foreign policies. In China, the Japanese armed forces intensified bombing and political maneuvers in hopes of persuading Chiang to surrender. Plans for Japanese recognition of the

71 See the official foreign policy document "Sekai jōsei no suii ni tomonau jikyoku shori yōkō," in *Nihon gaikō nenpyō*, pp. 437–8. On the significance of this decision, see Robert J. C. Butow, *Tojo and the Coming of the War* (Princeton, N.J.: Princeton University Press, 1961), pp. 150–3.

72 Berger, *Parties Out of Power*, pp. 275–85, 320.

Wang regime were slowed to give Chiang time to come to the conference table. Following negotiations with Vichy France, the government dispatched troops into northern Indochina to establish a foothold for southern expansion. To counter the anticipated resistance from the United States and Britain, the Konoe government concluded the military alliance with Germany and Italy so ardently sought by the army earlier.

All of these steps were taken against the backdrop of a continuing military commitment in China and the heightened likelihood of economic embargo or possibly armed resistance from the Anglo-American powers. They carried with them a need for greater military preparedness, greater national commitment to the policy of autonomy and expansion, and a more highly supervised utilization of the limited human and material resources available for their implementation. Hence, they served to strengthen the army's case for the establishment of the national defense state and national mobilization.

On August 28, 1940, Konoe convened at his official residence the first meeting of the Preparatory Commission for Establishing the New Political Order.[73] The commission was composed of thirty-seven prominent national leaders, drawn from each political elite group, and its mission was to advise the prime minister on the contours of the new political order. Along with many enthusiastic reformists, however, the group included numerous conservatives who believed that major reforms would not only destroy their political and economic interests but also obstruct successful national mobilization. Many business leaders on the commission, for example, objected to the new economic order on the grounds that industrial management had to remain in private hands in order to maximize wartime production. Many senior bureaucrats, particularly those with careers in the Home Ministry, held that the state's existing administrative structure could accommodate the requirements of national mobilization without major institutional reforms and that a new mobilization would create local political chaos at a time when administrative order and efficiency were essential. Rural leaders sought to preserve their dominance of local affairs by insisting that the proposed reforms of political and administrative linkages to Tokyo would reduce their ability to mobilize communities and thus inhibit effective popular mobilization. The senior lower-house leadership, though obliged to explore the opportunities that

73 For a summary and analysis of the commission's deliberations, see Berger, *Parties Out of Power*, pp. 300–8, 311–13.

Konoe's new party might offer for resuscitating their national influence, remained staunch supporters of the interests of the business and local elites. They, too, were disinclined to tamper with the existing mechanisms of controlling national wealth, productive capacity, and local politics. And finally, spokesmen for the Japanist faction of the right wing contended that the sacred ties binding the divine emperor to his subjects were strong enough to ensure prompt citizen compliance with government commands, provided that strong efforts were made to educate the citizenry in the "way of the subject." In the Japanists' view, the reforms propounded by the army and Prince Konoe violated the imperial constitution and threatened to create a new *bakufu*-usurping governing power from the legitimately constituted organs of state.

The clash of elite interests in the Preparatory Commission and the delicacy of Japan's international position during the early fall led Konoe to defer a fundamental resolution of the controversies evoked by his new-order plans. On October 12, 1940, he created the Imperial Rule Assistance Association (IRAA) (Taisei yokusankai) as the institutional embodiment of the new political order, but he postponed a definitive explanation of how the IRAA would be integrated into the state or how it would serve to mobilize the population. However, the organization's reformist character had already been compromised in several respects. Konoe's choices of IRAA officers, for example, reflected his inclination to include representatives of all elite viewpoints, rather than simply those with reformist aspirations. Moreover, early plans to organize local IRAA branches and deliberative assemblies representing vocational and cultural group affiliation were abandoned in favor of the Home Ministry's recommendation that local branches be organized on the basis of existing prefectural, municipal, town, and village administrative units. The IRAA's capability to act independently as a local agency of political mobilization was further diminished by an agreement to appoint local officials as IRAA branch chiefs.[74]

Reformists attempted to counter these losses by packing local IRAA branch office staffs with their supporters. The army directed reservists to flood the membership of the branches as well. But late in 1940, Konoe conceded the struggle to the conservative camp. In December, he replaced two reformist cabinet members with two prominent Japanists dedicated to limiting the scope of IRAA activity. In order to

74 *Yokusan kokumin undō shi*, p. 136; Berger, *Parties Out of Power*, pp. 310, 322–3.

secure an operating budget for the organization, Konoe agreed in early 1941 to abolish the IRAA Diet bureau, eliminating a potential rivalry between that organ and the senior parliamentary leadership. Finally, in March, he purged the IRAA of all remaining reformist leaders and turned over the organization to the Home Ministry as an appendage of the state's existing administrative structure.

Although Konoe's personal motives for abandoning the reformist cause remain open to speculation, the results of his actions in early 1941 were decisive.[75] Until its dissolution in June 1945, the IRAA served largely as a mobilization agency of the government. The Home Ministry controlled both the national and local offices of the organization and used the IRAA hamlet branches to strengthen its controls over the population. Within each local government unit, citizens were organized into neighborhood associations (*tonarigumi* or *rinpohan*), in which traditional community pressures to conform evoked widespread, if sometimes superficial, compliance with directives from Tokyo. The neighborhood associations also allocated rationing coupons as wartime shortages developed during the later stages of the Pacific War. Apart from these practical functions, the IRAA served during its short period of existence as the primary government agency for mobilizing popular morale in support of the state, as the Japanists had insisted it should.

Reformist hopes for radically restructuring the nation's economy were also frustrated in late 1940. Throughout the fall, revisionist bureaucrats and army technocrats on the Cabinet Planning Board drew up new policies to establish a new economic order.[76] Their plans called for a dramatic increase of official intervention in the economy, including the transfer of management functions to the state from private owners of large industries. Spokesmen from the business community, the conservative parties, and the Japanist right wing charged that the nationalization of industrial management was tantamount to communism and violated constitutional guarantees of private property rights. On the other hand, the planning board's proposals were endorsed by

75 Konoe's somewhat disingenuous account of his intentions at the time is recorded in *Konoe Fumimaro-kō no shuki: Ushinawareshi seiji* (Tokyo: Asahi shimbunsha, 1946). The remarkable coincidence of the waxing and waning of prospects for a negotiated settlement of the war in China with Konoe's shifting attitude toward the new political order suggests that in 1940, as in 1938, the prince was unwilling to provoke domestic political turmoil over the reform issue if Japan's troops were still engaged in military operations. See Berger, *Parties Out of Power*, pp. 253–60, 274–5, 308–11, 317–18, 332.

76 For a detailed study of these politics, see Nakamura Takafusa and Hara Akira, "Keizai shintaisei," in "*Konoe shintaisei*" *no kenkyū* (*Nenpō seijigaku 1972*), ed. Nihon seiji gakkai (Tokyo: Iwanami shoten, 1973), pp. 71–133.

the military, the revisionist bureaucrats, anticapitalist right-wing reformists, socialists and national socialists in the IRAA, and men such as Arima Yoriyasu, who wanted to right imbalances of wealth and political influence between the industrialized cities and the agrarian countryside.

Konoe defused this controversy, which briefly threatened the life of his cabinet, by scrapping the most controversial features of the planning board's legislation while gearing the economy toward the support of the military's defense program. The new economic policy adopted by the cabinet on December 7, 1940, recognized the need for a planned economy but assured the nation's entrepreneurs a prominent position in the agencies of economic planning. No mention was made of state management or official control over private enterprise.[77]

Although the political parties remained dissolved, few other changes in the political landscape survived the reformist challenge of 1940 and 1941. All state institutions legitimized by the Meiji constitution remained intact and retained their original functions. If anything, the power of those who maintained that the nation could best be mobilized by preserving, rather than reforming, the existing political system was enhanced. The reformist right-wing and new-party coalition in the lower house, for example, was severely weakened by the IRAA's failure to become a new political party. Konoe's compromises strengthened the position of conservative party leaders and allowed them to regain control over their rank and file. The Cabinet Planning Board, staffed by revisionist bureaucrats and military officials, continued to serve as an important agency for policy coordination, but it never became the prime minister's brain trust. The old-line ministries continued to function during the war with little loss of power. Indeed, the Home Ministry strengthened and expanded its powers, as it assumed control of the IRAA's mobilization activities. Business, too, continued to play an independent role in determining how best to allocate national economic resources for wartime needs, and the army was unable to build stable support in the lower house or a large organized partisan following in the countryside.

Thus, although the Japanese government made decisions in 1940 and 1941 that led inexorably to war with the Anglo-American powers, pluralistic elite politics persisted as it had during the previous decade of policymaking. As the moment of decision for war in the Pacific approached, the cabinet's tendency to heed the views of experts contin-

77 Berger, *Parties Out of Power*, p. 331.

ued unaltered. The voice of the military, and of bureaucrats skilled in mass control and mass mobilization, grew larger in the councils of state. It would be wrong, however, to assert that the nation fell unwillingly under the control of these elite groups or was dragged into war by them. Less than two weeks before the Japanese attack on Pearl Harbor, the lower house was aflame with patriotic speeches against the pernicious Anglo-American powers, and Diet leaders appealed to the cabinet to issue a call to arms to rally the people. Such sentiments dramatically demonstrated the willingness of party and nonparty elites to entrust the empire's destiny to their experts on military affairs. Indeed, the major schism over whether or not to go to war in the Pacific was a difference of opinion between the army and navy over the likelihood of defeating the American Pacific Fleet. Ultimately, the army placed the burden of responsibility for making this important judgment on the navy, which would bear the brunt of the fighting. When the navy conceded that Japan had good prospects to win a short-term war (of eighteen months or less), representatives of the high command, the cabinet, the Privy Council, the Diet, and the court were sufficiently reassured to accept a policy of war.

Prince Konoe, whose foreign policies in 1937 and 1940 had contributed so much to the diplomatic impasse between Japan and the Anglo-American powers, was one of the few national leaders to disapprove of this line of action. Believing that war in the Pacific could not work to Japan's advantage, he attempted to avert conflict through a summit conference with American president Franklin Delano Roosevelt during the late summer of 1941. The Americans, however, insisted that all Japanese gains in China and Southeast Asia be renounced before coming to the conference table, and the British, embattled in Europe, worked assiduously to stiffen the American position in the Pacific. Konoe thus found himself with as little room to maneuver internationally as at home, where a growing consensus favoring war had begun to develop. Frustrated in his efforts to ward off the outcome that his own policies had made inevitable, Konoe resigned in October. His successor was General Tōjō, the army minister since 1940. Less than two months later, Japan was at war.

Apart from the problems of waging war, Tōjō faced the same political tasks as his predecessors had. He had to mold the ministries, business, and the Diet into a cohesive coalition to guarantee stable government and a coordinated national mobilization program. Initially, he attempted to resolve some of his political difficulties by retaining his position as army minister and taking over the post of home minister as well. In February 1942, he yielded the Home Ministry portfolio to career bureaucrat Yūzawa Michio but continued to serve concurrently as army minister until his cabinet resigned in July 1944. Ironically, as his power waned, Tōjō acquired more posts, taking over as minister of munitions in November 1943 and chief of the army general staff in February 1944. However, this strategy did not measurably enhance his ability to bend other elite groups to his will. Competition between the army and navy over strategic priorities and materials, for example, continued throughout the war, and civilian ministries competed intensely as well over budgets and raw materials. A special wartime administrative law (Senji gyōsei shokken tokureihō) in March 1943 authorized the prime minister to issue orders regarding production to ministries dealing with economic mobilization, but this measure failed to end the endemic struggles among the elites.[78]

The military continued to make significant inroads into administrative areas previously closed to their representatives. Military officers sat on the Cabinet Planning Board, the Cabinet Information Board, the Asian Development Board (later the Greater East Asia Ministry), the Ministry of Munitions (established in 1943 to replace the Ministry of Commerce and Industry), and the semigovernmental control associations that monitored business activity. Although civilian leaders resented military intrusions into their spheres of operation and strongly opposed them on occasion, they tolerated a limited military presence in their midst as a temporary wartime necessity. The presence of military officers helped synchronize the work of civilian offices with cabinet policy but was insufficient to institutionalize military control over civilian affairs even in wartime.

The lower house had for years been the object of army and reformist attack, and under Tōjō, opponents of the conservative party leadership renewed their attempts to undermine lower-house influence. Following the initial series of military victories in the Pacific, Tōjō called a parliamentary election in early 1942 to create a Diet membership loyal to the army. The general stressed that political participation through voting constituted a patriotic duty and hoped that the election would itself serve to mobilize popular morale. The army channeled its political campaign efforts through the Imperial Rule Assistance Young Adults' Corps (Yokusan sōnendan), a cluster of local groups under the joint supervision of the Home Ministry, the Ministry of Education,

78 Ben-Ami Shillony, *Politics and Culture in Wartime Japan* (Oxford, England: Clarendon Press, 1980), p. 31.

and the army. It sought first to establish a monopoly of control over the organizations and then to use them in the election campaign on behalf of reformist candidates. By relying on the *sōnendan*, the army hoped to bypass the conservative village elites and weaken the politicians' traditional power bases. Tōjō had a semigovernmental commission (Yokusan taisei seiji kyōgikai) designate officially sponsored candidates, and the *sōnendan* were instructed to campaign for them against conservative incumbents throughout the country.

There is little evidence to suggest that Tōjō's electoral objectives were attained. The voters do not appear to have regarded the exercise of the franchise as different from that of previous elections. The army was unable to strip the Home Ministry of a voice in controlling the *sōnendan*, and the nominating commission was led by General Abe Nobuyuki, who as prime minister had favored working with conservative party politicians. Predictably, the most active members of Abe's commission were the very parliamentary leaders that Tōjō had hoped to oust from the lower house. Through their influence, 234 incumbents received official nomination; 100 other incumbents ran without endorsement. In fact, only 85 incumbents failed to win either the commission's nomination or the voters' approval, and only 1 major party figure was defeated in the election. The total of 199 new Diet members was higher than in the elections of 1930 (127), 1932 (123), and 1936 (125) but was not significantly different from the 181 new members elected in 1928; and in part, the high number of new faces was attributable less to the reformists' successes than to the unique five-year lapse between the 1937 and 1942 elections. In the end, the army and its reformist allies were forced to acknowledge that the plan to create a pliant Diet had been a failure.[79]

In late 1942 and early 1943, the army attempted to establish yet another new political force based on the *sōnendan*. However, the lower house was able to block the formation of a central headquarters for the loose federation of local groups, and the Home Ministry prevented the army from allowing the *sōnendan* to disrupt its local apparatus. Ulti-

79 Figures compiled from Asahi shimbunsha, ed., *Yokusan senkyo taikan* (Tokyo: Asahi shimbunsha, 1942). On the army's disappointment, see Satō Kenryō, *Dai Tōa sensō kaikoroku* (Tokyo: Tokuma shoten, 1966), p. 287; for a reformist assessment, see Tsukui Tatsuo, ed., *Nippon seiji nenpō: Shōwa jūshichi-nen* (Tokyo: Shōwa shobō, 1942), vol. 1, pp. 235–6. See also Edward J. Drea, *The 1942 Japanese General Election: Political Mobilization in Wartime Japan* (International Studies, East Asian Series Research Publication 11) (Lawrence: Center for East Asian Studies, University of Kansas, 1979). For a different evaluation of the 1942 election, See Robert A. Scalapino, "Elections and Political Modernization in Prewar Japan," in *Political Development in Modern Japan*, ed. Robert E. Ward (Princeton, N.J.: Princeton University Press, 1968), p. 283.

mately, Tōjō was obliged to turn over control of the *sōnendan* to the Home Ministry, as Konoe had done with the IRAA in 1941.[80] Thereafter, the prime minister worked to conciliate, rather than challenge, the Diet leadership. In April 1943, two lower-house leaders were appointed to cabinet posts, and another party leader joined them in 1944. Five lower-house leaders held cabinet portfolios in the Koiso and Suzuki cabinets, which succeeded Tōjō's after 1944, and the parliamentary vice-minister system, which had again lapsed under Konoe in 1940, was reinstated. Although the wartime Diet appeared to do little more than rubber-stamp cabinet legislative and budget proposals, parliamentary unanimity was a product of the widespread desire to avoid any public appearance of discord in wartime and was achieved by the government only through extensive behind-the-scenes negotiations and compromises with the Diet leadership.

War therefore generated extraordinary pressures for popular and elite conformity to government policy goals, but it did not permit the reconstruction of the political order along the totalitarian lines advocated by reformist proponents of the national defense state. Beneath the veneer of national unity, political competition remained intense among and within the political elites, and the Meiji political order strained to confine conflicts within boundaries permitting stable government. When at last the nation faced the difficult decision of whether to surrender in the summer of 1945, the system designed to insulate the throne from political responsibility buckled and finally failed. Even though Tokyo and other Japanese cities lay in ashes, and Hiroshima and Nagasaki were destroyed by atomic explosions, the national political elites represented in the Supreme War Leadership Council were still divided on the question of surrender. It remained, finally, for the emperor to intervene directly into the political process and declare that the time to "endure the unendurable" had arrived, before the government could decide to surrender on August 15, 1945.

Hence, as Japan girded for the occupation of its territory by the victorious Allied forces, its leadership was acutely aware of deficiencies in the existing political system. Although vested political interests in the institutions of state and emotional attachment to them remained strong, the wartime experience paved the way for an acceptance of constitutional revision in the postwar years. Moreover, war and national mobilization had exacerbated the tensions arising originally from Japan's transformation from an agrarian to a highly industrial-

80 See "Dai Nippon yokusan sōnendan shi," in *Yokusan kokumin undō shi*, pp. 893–926.

ized urban nation, and the desire for reform by forces underrepresented in the allocation of power under the Meiji constitution continued to grow. Although the Japanese had not lost confidence in the ideal of rule by the meritocracy, they were prepared by their wartime experiences to examine and accept a new context for the insulation of the throne from political responsibility, the harmonization of party and nonparty elite groups' views and aspirations, and the integration of the political energies of the citizenry with the goals of the state. This readiness, along with the sobering experience of defeat in total war, had a decisive impact on shaping Japan's receptivity to the reforms of the Allied Occupation and to the creation of a new and democratic form of government in postwar Japan.

## CHAPTER 4

# POSTWAR POLITICS, 1945–1973

Politics in modern society is both a cause and an effect of socioeconomic change. Sometimes it is possible to discern and trace the causal link between the two; that is, a specific political action is seen to cause a specific socioeconomic change, and vice versa. More often, however, the direction of the link is fuzzy and difficult to determine. A political action is seen to result from a set of socioeconomic conditions and in turn to bring about a new set of socioeconomic conditions. The relationship between politics and socioeconomic change in postwar Japan is no exception.

During the twenty-eight years between the summer of 1945 and the summer of 1973, the Japanese society and economy underwent an obvious and far-reaching transformation. On the other hand, politics appear to have changed little, in fact so little that a casual observer might have missed it completely. Upon closer examination, however, it becomes evident that politics, too, underwent a significant change during the period, in a close and complex relationship with the change in the society's socioeconomic conditions. The unstable multiparty pattern that prevailed during the first postwar decade yielded to a short-lived quasi-two-party system in the second half of the 1950s and then to a stable one-party-dominated multiparty regime in the 1960s and 1970s.[1]

It is thus possible, in terms of both socioeconomic changes and shifts in the balance and alignment among the political parties, to divide these twenty-eight years into two distinctive periods. During the six and a half years of the Allied Occupation and the few years immediately following it, the nation was still economically fragile, socially confused, and politically unsettled. Only toward the end of this period did the government and people began to feel that the

1 These correspond to what Giovanni Sartori calls, respectively, limited pluralism, two-party, and predominant party systems. For this chapter, terms more descriptive than Sartori's are useful. For comparison, see Giovanni Sartori, *Parties and Party Systems: A Framework for Analysis* (Cambridge, England: Cambridge University Press, 1976), esp. chaps. 5, 6.

hardest part of postwar rehabilitation and reconstruction was over and that there was a future to look forward to. During the next eighteen years, however, Japan evolved into an altogether different kind of society. It became conspicuously and increasingly prosperous, confident, and stable.

Political change in postwar Japan was both a cause and an effect of socioeconomic changes. To be more precise, it was an aspect of a complex social dynamic unfolding under a set of unusual domestic and international circumstances, of which the nation's economic and social changes were important aspects.

## THE POLITICS OF ADJUSTMENT: THE OCCUPATION AND ITS IMMEDIATE AFTERMATH

On August 14, 1945, the Imperial Japanese government notified the Allied powers of its intent to accept the provisions of the Potsdam Declaration of July 26 and to sign the terms necessary for carrying out those provisions.[2] At noon the following day, the emperor's prerecorded message announcing the termination of hostilities was broadcast to the entire nation. Two weeks later, the Supreme Commander for the Allied Powers (SCAP), General Douglas MacArthur, arrived in Japan. His mission was to accomplish the Occupation's basic objectives as proclaimed in the Potsdam Declaration and spelled out in greater detail in the United States Initial Post-Surrender Policy for Japan issued on August 29, 1945. These objectives were (1) to ensure "that Japan will not again become a menace to the United States or to the peace and security of the world" and (2) to establish eventually "a peaceful and responsible government," preferably closely conforming to principles of democratic self-government, "which will respect the rights of other states and will support the objectives of the United States as reflected in the ideals and principles of the Charter of the United Nations."[3] In order to accomplish these objectives, SCAP would immediately disarm occupied Japan and permanently demilitarize and democratize it through a sweeping program of political, economic, and social reforms.

No sooner had SCAP moved into its new general headquarters

2 For the texts of the Potsdam Declaration, the Japanese note of final acceptance and related documents, see Government Section, Supreme Commander for the Allied Powers, *Political Reorientation of Japan, September 1945 to September 1948*, vol. 2: *Appendices*, republished ed. (Grosse Pointe, Mich.: Scholarly Press, 1968), app. A.

3 See "United States Initial Post-Surrender Policy for Japan," in SCAP, *Political Reorientation of Japan*, pp. 423–6.

(GHQ), in Yokohama for the first two weeks and then in Tokyo, than a stream of directives began to flow instructing the newly formed caretaker government of Japan to implement specific measures to achieve the Occupation's objectives. All the institutions and leaders held responsible for the crimes committed against humanity by the militarist Japanese empire were removed, and in their place, new and democratic institutions and personnel were to be installed. In fact, the ministries of Greater East Asian Affairs, Munitions, and Agriculture and Commerce were abolished a few days before SCAP's arrival. On September 2, 1945, SCAP Directive No. 1 ordered the Imperial General Headquarters to begin to demobilize all Japanese armed forces, and eleven days later the Imperial General Headquarters itself was abolished. The arrest of war criminal suspects also began. In the middle of October, the Special Political Police and the Public Peace Maintenance Law (Chian ijihō) went out of existence. In the next two and one-half years, some 5,700 war criminal suspects were tried by the International Military Tribunal for the Far East; 920 of them were found guilty; some 200,000 "ultranationalists" were purged from public office; Shinto was discontinued as the state religion; the largest holding and trading companies (zaibatsu) were dissolved; rural land reform was instituted; and the civil service was overhauled.[4]

The Imperial constitution of Japan was "amended" in theory, but it was replaced in reality by an entirely new constitution based on a set of fundamentally different principles. It was drafted by personnel of the GHQ's Government Section (GS) in early 1946. After debate in the Diet, it was promulgated in November 1946 by the Japanese government.[5] It transferred sovereignty from the emperor to the people, renounced war and the nation's right of belligerency, and guaranteed to all citizens a long and comprehensive list of civil liberties. The Diet was declared the "highest organ of state power" and "the sole lawmaking organ of the state." Its structure remained bicameral, but the nonelective House of Peers was replaced by an elected House of Councilors, and the House of Representatives became the larger and more powerful of the two chambers. Vested with executive power, the cabi-

4 For an overview of the Occupation policies and their outcomes, see Oka Yoshitake, ed., *Gendai Nihon no seiji katei* (Tokyo: Iwanami shoten, 1958), pt. 1; Robert E. Ward, "Reflections on the Allied Occupation and Planned Political Change in Japan," in *Political Development in Modern Japan*, ed. Robert E. Ward (Princeton, N.J.: Princeton University Press, 1958), chap. 13.

5 On the making of the 1947 constitution, see Satō Tatsuo, *Nihonkoku kenpō seiritsu shi*, 2 vols. (Tokyo: Yūhikaku, 1962, 1964); Kenpō chōsakai, *Kenpō seitei no keika ni kansuru shō-iinkai hōkokusho*, no. 2: *Kenpō chōsakai hōkokusho fuzoku bunsho* (Tokyo: Kenpō chōsakai, July 1964).

net was now collectively responsible to the Diet. The judiciary was constitutionally independent and coequal, if not superior, to the Diet and the cabinet, with the supreme court given the power of judicial review.[6] Finally, the new constitution explicitly established the principle of local autonomy.

Other laws followed to establish new rules and procedures for the operation and administration of the Diet, the cabinet, the imperial household, courts of justice, local government, the national and local public services, and the like. The once powerful Home Ministry was broken down into lesser and innocuous units: the ministries of Labor, Health and Welfare, Construction, and Local Autonomy.

With the departure of the Home Ministry also went the state police and its special service units under the ministry's tightly centralized control. Ordinary police functions were then divided into two categories, one composed of a unified force called the National Rural Police and the other made up of thousands of mutually autonomous municipal police forces.[7] The new Labor Union Law guaranteed to all workers the right to organize and engage in collective actions to improve their working and living conditions.[8] A sweeping land reform resulted in the wholesale redistribution of Japan's agricultural land, and of the wealth and power associated with landownership. The highly elitist education system directly controlled by the Ministry of Education was also thoroughly overhauled and democratized. A system of compulsory and free six-year primary and three-year secondary schools and voluntary three-year high schools and four-year universities modeled after the American public educational system was introduced, along with the principle of coeducation of male and female students.[9] Equally important, the administrative control of the primary through the high schools was decentralized by the creation of elected local boards of education. Under the new constitution and the revised civil code, the privileged status that the old system had accorded to the male head of a family was abolished, and the principle of legal equality between a husband and wife was established.[10]

6 On the theory and practice of judicial review under Japan's 1947 constitution, see Dan F. Henderson, ed., *The Constitution of Japan: Its First Twenty Years, 1947–67* (Seattle: University of Washington Press, 1968), pt. 2.

7 Hoshino Yasusaburō, "Keisatsu seido no kaikaku," in *Sengo kaikaku*, ed. Tōkyō daigaku shakaikagaku kenkyūjo, 8 vols. (Tokyo: Tōkyō daigaku shuppankai, 1974–5), vol. 3: *Seiji katei*, pp. 287–350.

8 See Tezuka Kazuaki, "Kyū-rōdōkumiaihō no keisei to tenkai: Shoki rōdō iinkai no kinō bunseki o chūshin to shite," in *Sengo kaikaku*, vol. 5: *Rōdō seisaku*, pp. 254–8.

9 Takemae Eiji, *Senryō sengo shi: Tai-nichi kanri seisaku no zenyō* (Tokyo: Keisō shobō, 1980), chap. 7.

10 Watanabe Yōzo, "Sengo kaikaku to Nihon gendaihō," in *Sengo kaikaku*, vol. 1: *Kadai to shikaku*, pp. 103, 105–6.

SCAP's reformist zeal, however, lasted for only a few years. By about 1950 many of the legislative and administrative measures previously undertaken to accomplish the Occupation's initial goals, namely, the demilitarization and democratization of Japan, had been or were about to be significantly modified or abandoned altogether. In response to rising cold war tensions, a "reverse course" intensified during the last months of the Occupation and continued under Japanese governments in the post-Occupation period.

When the Korean War broke out in the summer of 1950, SCAP ordered a purge of all members of the Japan Communist Party's Central Committee and then suspended the party's central newspaper, *Akahata* (Red Flag). This was followed by the suspension of news bulletins published by local party branches and a systematic and extensive purge of communists and communist suspects in the public services, mass media, and key industries.[11] Meanwhile, the reinstatement of those who had been purged earlier under the initial demilitarization and democratization policy began in the spring of 1947. As a result, virtually all of the 201,815 persons who had once been purged had regained their civil rights and political freedom by the end of 1951.[12]

The demilitarization policy was reversed when at SCAP's order the National Police Reserve was established in August 1950 as a first step in Japan's gradual rearmament. When the Japanese peace treaty was signed in San Francisco in September 1951, a bilateral mutual security treaty was also concluded between Japan and the United States to provide military protection for disarmed Japan, "in the expectation, however, that Japan will itself increasingly assume responsibility for its own defense against direct and indirect aggression. . . ."[13]

During the first few post-Occupation years, the Japanese government pushed the "reverse course" further by persuading the Diet to pass a series of bills either nullifying or seriously modifying the intent of the early Occupation's key reforms. These bills included laws tightening the control of subversive activities (passed in July 1952), estab-

11 See Shisō no kagaku kenkyūkai, ed., *Kyōdō kenkyū: Nihon senryō kenkyū jiten* (*Kyōdō kenkyū: Nihon senryōgun*, app.) (Tokyo: Tokuma shoten, 1978), p. 150.

12 Hans H. Baerwald, *The Purge of Japanese Leaders Under the Occupation*, vol. 8: *University of California Publications in Political Science* (Berkeley and Los Angeles: University of California Press, 1959), pp. 78–9.

13 For the text of the treaty, see George R. Packard III, *Protest in Tokyo: The Security Treaty Crisis of 1960* (Princeton, N.J.: Princeton University Press, 1966), pp. 355–7. On the circumstances surrounding the negotiations on the peace and security treaties, see Nishimura Kumao, *San Furanshisuko heiwa jōyaku*, vol. 27: *Nihon gaikōshi* (Tokyo: Kajima heiwa kenkyūjo, 1971); and Frederick S. Dunn, *Peace-Making and the Settlement with Japan* (Princeton, N.J.: Princeton University Press, 1963).

lishing an embryonic defense agency innocuously named the Safety Agency (August 1952), regulating more stringently strikes and other forms of worker actions (August 1953), softening antimonopoly regulations (July 1953), strengthening central control over the schools (May 1954) and over the police (June 1954), and finally, establishing the Defense Agency and the Self-Defense Forces (June 1954).[14] Critics regarded these and other similar measures as part of a concerted effort by the conservatives to subvert the postwar reforms and to revive the prewar authoritarian and militarist regime, an effort dubbed "reverse course" by the media.

None of the legislative and administrative measures undertaken after April 1952, when the peace treaty went into effect and the Occupation formally ended, could be directly attributed to SCAP's or Washington's policies. The entire reverse course was nonetheless often associated with and blamed on the shift of the Occupation policy in the late 1940s and, in the minds of many Japanese, tainted the accomplishments of the demilitarization and democratization programs that SCAP once vigorously encouraged. As a result, the reaction of the Japanese public to the Occupation and its policies was diverse and complex. Some either supported or opposed the Occupation regime because of its initial crusade against militarism and authoritarianism, whereas others did so because of its later crusade against communism.

## *Japanese government in the early Occupation period*

The first two postwar Japanese cabinets were not formed through electoral processes and therefore were technically not representative of the Japanese people at large. The first was led by a relative of the emperor and a general of the Imperial Japanese Army, Prince Higashikuni Naruhiko. He was ordered by the emperor, on the recommendation of the Lord Keeper of the Privy Seal, Kido Kōichi, to form a caretaker cabinet following the resignation of the last wartime cabinet led by General Suzuki Kantarō, on August 15, 1945.[15] Other members of the cabinet were selected mainly by former prime minister Prince Konoe Fumimaro and former Cabinet Information Bureau president

14 Seki Hiroharu, "Taigai kankei no kōzō to gaikō," in *Nenpō seijigaku,* 1977: *55-nen taisei no keisei to hōkai: Zoku gendai Nihon no seiji katei,* ed. Nihon seiji gakkai (Tokyo: Iwanami shoten, 1979). pp. 77, 85; Takabatake Michitoshi, "Taishū undō no tayōka to henshitsu," *Nenpō seijigaku,* 1977, p. 324.

15 Amakawa Akira, "Dai-43-dai: Higashikuni naikaku: Miyasama naikaku no shūsen shori," in *Nihon naikakushi roku,* ed. Hayashi Shigeru and Tsuji Kiyoaki, 6 vols. (Tokyo: Daiichi hōki, 1981), vol. 5, pp. 3–8.

TABLE 4.1
*Japanese cabinets, 1945–1974*

| Prime minister | Cabinet number | Cabinet term |
|---|---|---|
| Higashikuni Naruhiko | | 17 August 1945 to 9 October 1945 |
| Shidehara Kijūrō | | 9 October 1945 to 22 May 1946 |
| Yoshida Shigeru | 1st | 22 May 1946 to 24 May 1947 |
| Katayama Tetsu | | 24 May 1947 to 10 March 1948 |
| Ashida Hitoshi | | 10 March 1948 to 15 October 1948 |
| Yoshida Shigeru | 2nd | 15 October 1948 to 16 February 1949 |
| Yoshida Shigeru | 3rd | 16 February 1949 to 30 October 1952 |
| Yoshida Shigeru | 4th | 30 October 1952 to 21 May 1953 |
| Yoshida Shigeru | 5th | 21 May 1953 to 10 December 1954 |
| Hatoyama Ichirō | 1st | 10 December 1954 to 19 March 1955 |
| Hatoyama Ichirō | 2nd | 19 March 1955 to 22 November 1955 |
| Hatoyama Ichirō | 3rd | 22 November 1955 to 23 December 1956 |
| Ishibashi Tanzan | | 23 December 1956 to 25 February 1957 |
| Kishi Nobusuke | 1st | 25 February 1957 to 12 June 1958 |
| Kishi Nobusuke | 2nd | 12 June 1958 to 19 July 1960 |
| Ikeda Hayato | 1st | 19 July 1960 to 8 December 1960 |
| Ikeda Hayato | 2nd | 8 December 1960 to 9 December 1963 |
| Ikeda Hayato | 3rd | 9 December 1963 to 9 November 1964 |
| Satō Eisaku | 1st | 9 November 1964 to 17 February 1967 |
| Satō Eisaku | 2nd | 17 February 1967 to 14 January 1970 |
| Satō Eisaku | 3rd | 14 January 1970 to 7 July 1972 |
| Tanaka Kakuei | 1st | 7 July 1972 to 22 December 1972 |
| Tanaka Kakuei | 2nd | 22 December 1972 to 9 December 1974 |

Ogata Taketora, who served in the Higashikuni cabinet, respectively, as the de facto deputy prime minister and the chief cabinet secretary[16] (see Table 4.1).

The primary mission of the first postwar cabinet was to prevent and, if necessary, put down possible revolts by recalcitrant elements in the Japanese armed forces in the wake of Japan's surrender and during the critical initial phase of the Allied Occupation of the nation. Composed of largely conservative but loyal representatives of the prewar and wartime Japanese establishment, the cabinet succeeded in helping the nation make the unprecedented and painful transition from belligerency to peace without major mishap. During the fifty hectic days that it lasted, the cabinet dealt with the arrival of the Occupation forces, the installation of the SCAP GHQ, the signing of Japanese surrender, and the implementation of the first batch of SCAP directives and instructions. However, it was unable to cope as successfully with the SCAP memorandum of October 4, 1945, ordering the re-

16 Ibid., pp. 21–2.

moval of all forms of restriction on political, civil, and religious liberties, and it resigned the following day.[17]

Prince Higashikuni's immediate successor, Shidehara Kijūrō, was appointed by the emperor, again on Lord Keeper of the Privy Seal Kido's personal recommendation.[18] Kido consulted with the president of the Privy Council, Hiranuma Kiichirō, and used the former diplomat and foreign minister in the Higashikuni cabinet, Yoshida Shigeru, as his intermediary in negotiations with Shidehara on the one hand and with SCAP on the other. Shidehara, a former diplomat, reappointed his onetime subordinate, Yoshida, as foreign minister and a member of the House of Peers, Tsugita Daisaburō, as chief cabinet secretary. The three men then decided on other members of the cabinet, including five members of the House of Representatives associated with, but not representative of, the defunct prewar political parties.[19]

The Shidehara cabinet lasted about seven months. In that period, it presided over the implementation of the reforms stipulated in the aforementioned memorandum of October 4, 1945, and a series of other and equally revolutionary measures to demilitarize and democratize the nation. The latter included implementation of a five-point instruction that SCAP issued directly to Shidehara on October 11, 1945, ordering (1) the emancipation of women through their enfranchisement, (2) the encouragement of the unionization of labor, (3) the liberalization of education, (4) the abolition of systems that held the people in constant fear through secret inquisition and abuse, and (5) the democratization of economic institutions.[20] Under SCAP pressure, the cabinet also initiated a radical land reform, an equally sweeping purge of "ultranationalists," and, above all, efforts to amend the constitution.[21]

While Shidehara and his cabinet struggled to keep up with the succession of SCAP directives in the midst of a deepening economic crisis, the first postwar House of Representatives general election was held on April 10, 1946. No party won a clear majority, which resulted in a long delay in the appointment of Shidehara's successor. After complicated negotiations among the leaders of the major parties, Shidehara recommended to the emperor the appointment of Hatoyama Ichirō, the founder and president of the Japan Liberal Party, which had won a plurality in the general election. That same night,

17 Ibid., pp. 22–9. For the text of the memorandum, see SCAP, *Political Reorientation of Japan*, vol. 2, pp. 463–5.
18 Amakawa, "Dai-44-dai: Shidehara naikaku: 'Minshu' kaikaku no hajimari," in *Nihon naikakushi roku*, vol. 5, pp. 33–4. 19 Ibid., pp. 36–8.
20 For the text of the instruction, see SCAP, *Political Reorientation of Japan*, vol. 2, p. 741.
21 Amakawa, "Dai-44-dai: Shidehara naikaku," pp. 38–58.

however, SCAP announced Hatoyama's dismissal and after another round of negotiations among the parties, Yoshida was appointed first as a Liberal Party executive and then as the new prime minister.[22]

A well-known Anglophile among prewar Japanese diplomats and a prominent opponent of the military during World War II, Yoshida, unlike Hatoyama, proved acceptable, though hardly a boon, to SCAP and the reformists in the GHQ. The first postwar party cabinet of Liberal and Progressive Party politicians thus was born. During the next twelve months, the cabinet invested most of its time and energy in feeding the starving nation and coping with the specter of a general strike called by the newly organized labor unions. Yoshida and his cabinet, however, also oversaw, if often reluctantly, an extension of the purge program, the implementation of a substantially expanded land reform, a sweeping educational reform, and parliamentary debates on and the approval of a new SCAP-authored constitution.[23]

Before it resigned on May 20, 1947, the Yoshida cabinet also presided over the enactment of a newly drafted House of Councilors and a revised House of Representatives members election laws, the Local Self-Government Law and the National Diet Law. Having thus helped lay the basic rules of electoral and parliamentary politics under the new system, the Liberals and Progressives (by then renamed Democrats) campaigned in the first Diet elections under those very rules and, ironically, lost to the Socialists. The fall of the first Yoshida cabinet and the arrival of the first and, so far, the only postwar Socialist-led cabinet completed the transition from the wartime regime to the postwar system of representative government.

## *Parties and elections in occupied Japan*

At the outset of the Occupation period, all but one of the main political parties of postwar Japan made their appearance (see Figure 4.1). Two of them were prewar conservative parties regrouped and renamed the Japan Liberal Party (Nihon jiyūtō), composed of former Seiyūkai politicians, and the Japan Progressive Party (Nihon shimpotō), composed of former Minseitō members plus a few associated with one Seiyūkai fac-

22 Amakawa, "Dai-45-dai: Dai-l-ji Yoshida naikaku," in *Nihon naikakushi roku*, vol. 5, pp. 74–7; Inoki Masamichi, *Hyōden Yoshida Shigeru*, vol. 4: *Santen no maki* (Tokyo: Yomiuri shinbunsha, 1981), pp. 8–14; J. W. Dower, *Empire and Aftermath: Yoshida Shigeru and the Japanese Experience, 1878–1954* (Cambridge, Mass.: Harvard University Press, 1979), pp. 309–10. See also Yoshida Shigeru, *Kaisō jūnen*, 4 vols. (Tokyo: Shinchōsha, 1957), vol. 2, p. 90.

23 Amakawa, "Dai-45-dai: Dai-l-ji Yoshida naikaku," pp. 81–93; Inoki, *Hyōden*, vol. 4, chap. 23.

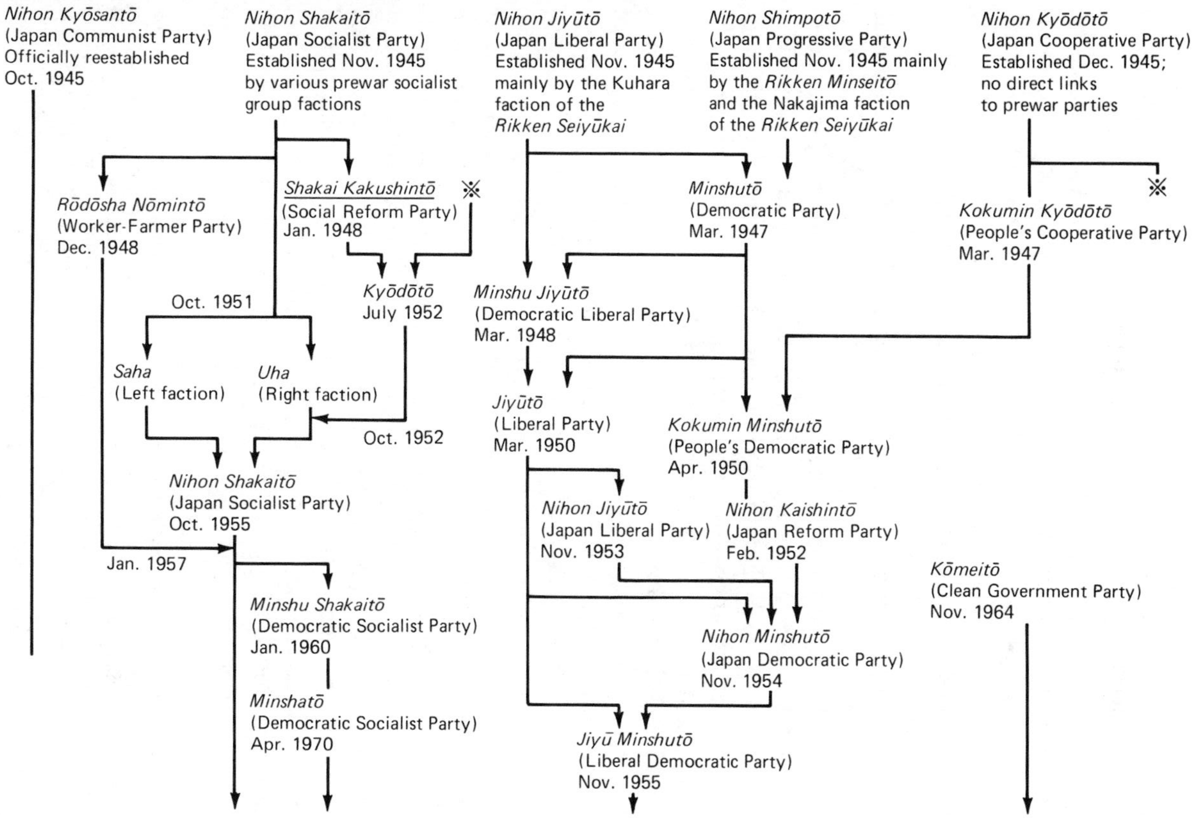


Figure 4.1. Political parties, 1945–1974. (Based on *Encyclopedia of Japan*, vol. 6., p. 209.)

tion.[24] Both parties came into being in November 1945. A third conservative party, the Japan Cooperative Party (Nihon kyōdōtō), followed a few days later. The Progressives changed their name to Democratic Party (Minshutō) in 1947 and then split in 1949, one half joining the Liberals and the other half the Cooperativists. The Democrat-Cooperative group was called the National Democratic Party (Kokumin minshutō) for a while but adopted a new name, the Reform Party (Kaishintō) in early 1952. When the Allied Occupation of the country ended, there were thus two rival conservative parties.

Developments on the left side of the ideological and partisan divide paralleled those on the right. Two rival parties, both with longstanding and tangled roots in the party politics of prewar Japan, reestablished themselves in late 1945. Of the two, the Japan Socialist Party (Nihon shakaitō: JSP) first appeared in early November. A coalition of several competing schools of the prewar socialist movement, the party split twice, in early 1950 and late 1951.[25] At the end of this period, right-wing and left-wing Socialist parties were fighting each other even while competing with the Japan Communist Party (Nihon kyōsantō: JCP), which had been reestablished in December 1945.[26]

The initial purge order of November 1945 cost the Progressives about 93 percent and the Liberals about 45 percent of their seats in the House of Representatives, only a few months before the first postwar general elections.[27] On the other hand, the Socialists suffered little from the purge, and the Communists not at all. The reestablishment of the JCP was in fact made possible by direct SCAP intervention: It was at SCAP's order, and in the face of considerable resistance by the Japanese government, especially by the justice and home ministers of the Higashikuni cabinet, that some three thousand political prisoners, including leaders of the prewar JCP, were set free in October 1945.[28]

The first postwar general elections of April 1946 were unusual in

24 For a concise description of the origins of the major parties of postwar Japan, see Itō Takashi, "Sengo seitō no keisei katei," in *Senryōki Nihon no keizai to seiji*, ed. Nakamura Takafusa (Tokyo: Tokyo daigaku shuppankai, 1979), pp. 339–82. See also Haruhiro Fukui, *Party in Power: The Japanese Liberal-Democrats and Policymaking* (Canberra: Australian National University Press; Berkeley and Los Angeles: University of California Press, 1970), chap. 2.

25 See Alan B. Cole, George O. Totten, and Cecil H. Uyehara, *Socialist Parties in Postwar Japan* (New Haven, Conn.: Yale University Press, 1966), chap. 1; J. A. A. Stockwin, *The Japanese Socialist Party and Neutralism: A Study of a Political Party and Its Foreign Policy* (Carlton, Victoria: Melbourne University Press, 1968), chap. 4.

26 On the evolution of the Communist movement in postwar Japan, see Robert A. Scalapino, *The Japanese Communist Movement, 1920–1966* (Berkeley and Los Angeles: University of California Press, 1967), especially chaps. 2, 3.

27 Itō, "Sengo seitō," in *Senryōki Nihon*, pp. 96, 99; Fukui, *Party in Power*, p. 38.

28 Takemae, *Senryō sengo shi*, pp. 99–156.

several ways. First, SCAP intended these elections to serve as a plebiscite on the issue of constitutional revision in general and on the SCAP draft of the revision in particular and so scheduled them to serve that purpose.[29] Second, for the first time since 1919, a "large" multimember electoral district system was adopted. Each prefecture constituted a unified electoral district and returned between four and fourteen members, each voter casting between one and three ballots, depending on the number of members to be elected in the district.[30] This was novel enough to ensure some unexpected results. The participation of women for the first time, the result of another SCAP policy, added to the uncertainty and confusion. The result was the emergence of a fragmented multiparty pattern and an unstable cabinet led by Yoshida.

The next general elections of 1947 also resulted in a surprise, even though the large district system was abandoned and replaced by the more familiar "medium-sized" multimember system – a system that had been in effect between 1925 and 1945. Under this system, a subdivision of a prefecture constituted an electoral district, each district returning between three and five members and each voter casting a single ballot.[31] For the first time in the country's history, the Socialists won a plurality, no doubt with the support of a substantial segment of the newly organized labor movement. The party became a senior partner in a coalition government formed by Democrats and National Cooperativists. The general elections of 1949, too, were different in that a single party – the Liberals – won majority-party status for the first time since 1945, and at the same time, the Communists won significant representation with thirty-five seats. The performance of the two parties reflected the economic impact of the Dodge line austerity policy, which was welcome from the establishment's point of view and devastating from labor's.

The 1949 general elections also were noteworthy in another respect. For the first time, a substantial number of senior civil servants ran for and won Diet seats, apparently lured by the vast decision-making power invested in the new Diet by the 1947 constitution.

The Liberals maintained their majority position in 1952 but won only a plurality in 1953 and 1955. The Communists, meanwhile, were virtually wiped out by the "Red purge" of 1950, winning no seats in 1952, one in 1953, and two in 1955. As the first phase of postwar Japanese politics drew to a close, the pattern of the balance of power

29 See Kenpō chōsakai, *Kenpō kaisei no keika*, pp. 350–1, 453–4.

30 Shūgiin and Sangiin, eds., *Gikai seido shichijū-nen shi*, 12 vols. (Tokyo: Ōkurashō insatsukyoku, 1960–2), *Shiryō-hen*, pp. 278–87.

31 Ibid., pp. 288–308.

among the main political parties was thus roughly the same as it had been at the beginning. The electorate remained uncertain and skittish. Many were unhappy with the state of both the economy and politics. Fifty-six percent of the respondents in a 1953 public opinion poll were dissatisfied with the performance of their representatives in the Diet, and 60 percent in a 1954 poll did not feel that government policies reflected their opinion.[32]

### *Japanese reaction to the Allied Occupation*

Despite the unprecedented scope and depth of SCAP's "democratic reforms," there was remarkably little overt opposition or resistance from the Japanese public to either the Occupation as such or its specific policies. There were several reasons for this rather surprising situation.

First, the majority of the Japanese were tired of the war, which had long ceased to be an inspiring experience and by the summer of 1945 had turned into an endless nightmare. They had probably not expected the war to end when and how it did, but neither did they have reason to object to the sudden outbreak of peace after the succession of air attacks against the major cities of the country, culminating in the destruction of Hiroshima and Nagasaki by atomic bombs.[33] Furthermore, many were inclined to blame the government, especially the military, for both the war and its consequences.[34]

Nonetheless, there was apparently a widespread initial fear among the Japanese public of the Occupation and its military personnel. Some communities in and around Tokyo were beset by rumors of assaults on Japanese women by American servicemen, rumors that may have been based on memories of the Japanese soldiers' conduct in China and Southeast Asia in earlier years.[35] The fear, however, did not last long, partly because it was not well founded. According to one incomplete estimate, 957 incidents involving members of the Occupa-

32 Shinohara Hajime, *Gendai nihon no bunka henyō: Sono seijigaku-teki kōsatsu* (Tokyo: Renga shobō, 1971), pp. 88–9.

33 For pertinent comments, see Fukawa Kiyoshi, "Nihonjin no hi-senryō kan," in *Kyōdō kenkyū: Nihon senryō*, ed. Shisō no kagaku kenkyūkai (Tokyo: Tokuma shoten, 1972), pp. 16–18; Watanuki Jōji, "Kōdo seichō to keizai taikoku ka no seiji katei," in *Nenpō seijigaku*, 1977, pp. 142.

34 See comments in Yanaihara Tadao, "Sōsetsu," in *Sengo nihon shōshi*, ed. Yanaihara Tadao, 2 vols. (Tokyo: Tōkyō daigaku shuppankai, 1958), vol. 1, pp. 13–14.

35 Fukawa, "Nihonjin no hisenryō kan," p. 21; Chihara Jun, "Gunju sangyō rōdōsha no haisen e no taiō," in *Kyōdō kenkyū: Nihon senryō*, p. 99; and Kata Kōji, "Gunsei jidai no fūzoku," *Kyōdō kenkyū: Nihon senryō*, p. 260.

tion forces were recorded in the first two months of their presence – from the beginning of September to the end of October 1945 – in Yokohama where, before the arrival of the Occupation units, the mayor had advised leaders of the neighborhood associations to evacuate the young women to safer places.[36] According to another record, throughout the country, 2,536 Japanese were killed and 3,012 were injured in incidents involving foreign troops between September 1945 and September 1958.[37] These numbers were by no means negligible, but they were not as large as many Japanese had anticipated. Some Japanese accepted them fatalistically, if resentfully, to be endured like earthquakes or floods.[38] For many others, however, this fear was rapidly replaced by a sense of relief and even trust.

Second, the mass media were under SCAP's tight control throughout the Occupation period. Whereas the country was ruled in most respects indirectly through the existing machinery of the Japanese government, the control of the information media was an exception. At the beginning of the Occupation, a system of direct control was established for both the press and radio through the enforcement of rigid rules known as the press and radio codes.[39] The strict adherence to these codes was ensured by informal guidance and direction provided by the Civil Information and Education Section (CIE) of the GHQ and the prepublication censorship of manuscripts and radio programs by the Civil Censorship Department (CCD) of the Civil Intelligence Section (CIS). Dissemination of information about the censorship system itself was strictly controlled, and there were no significant infractions of the rules by Japanese authors, publishers, or broadcasters. The Japanese public was thus kept almost totally uninformed and unaware of the practice.[40]

The ordinary Japanese reader or listener was treated instead to a flood of articles and programs depicting or symbolizing the virtues of American democracy. Alongside the hitherto suspended but once popular literary and current affairs magazines, such as *Shinchō, Bungei*

36 Tsukuda Jitsuo, "Yokohama kara no shōgen," in *Kyōdō kenkyū: Nihon senryō*, pp. 114–16, 121.

37 Tsukuda, "Yokohama kara no shōgen," pp. 114, 128. Unfortunately, no details are available regarding the specific circumstances surrounding any of these incidents.

38 Fukawa, "Nihonjin no hisenryō kan," p. 25. See also Shinohara Hajime and Miyazaki Ryūji, "Sengo kaikaku to seiji karuchā," in *Sengo kaikaku*, vol. 1, p. 246.

39 Okudaira Yasuhiro, "Hōsōhōsei no sai-hensei," in *Sengo kaikaku*, vol. 3: *Seiji katei*, p. 390, n. 17; Arai Naoyuki, "Senryō seisaku to jānarizumu," in *Kyōdō kenkyū: Nihon senryō*, pp. 177–9. See also Fukushima Jurō, "Senryōka ni okeru ken'etsu seisaku to sono jittai," *Senryōki Nihon*, pp. 339–82.

40 Arai, "Senryō seisaku to jānarizumu," p. 179; Fukushima, "Senryōka ni okeru ken'etsu seisaku," pp. 340–2, 370.

*shunjū*, *Chūō kōron*, and *Kaizō*, which reappeared one after another after the autumn of 1945, a beginners' reader in colloquial English came on the market in late 1945, followed the next year by the Japanese edition of the *Reader's Digest*.[41]

The traditionally austere repertory of the nation's broadcasting monopoly, the Japan Broadcasting Corporation, or NHK (Nihon hōsō kyōkai), became considerably more "democratic" and colorful with the addition of such novel programs as "Watashitachi no kotoba" (Our words), "Nodo jiman shirouto engeikai" (Amateur singers' contest), "Hōsō tōronkai" (Roundtable of the air), and "Senshū no kokkai kara" (The Diet last week).[42] The inspiration probably came from the staff of the CIE and CCD, both of which were headquartered in the NHK building in downtown Tokyo. An English conversation course, disarmingly entitled "Come, Come English Conversation," was broadcast for fifteen minutes every weekday evening at 6:00 P.M. and was taught by Hirakawa Tadaichi, a repatriated chief newscaster on the staff of NHK's international broadcasting department. The program enjoyed an unrivaled audience rating throughout the Occupation period and long afterwards, inspiring over one thousand fan clubs throughout the country. Hirakawa may well have been the most effective advertiser and popularizer of linguistic as well as cultural and political "Americanisms."[43]

Finally, the importation and distribution of foodstuffs donated by the United States government in response to persistent requests by the Yoshida government helped change many Japanese minds. On July 5, 1947, both houses of the Diet officially thanked the Americans in a nonpartisan resolution of gratitude.[44] More generally, the Japanese were profoundly impressed with both the affluence and the generosity of the Americans as they perceived them through the relief goods as well as the mass media.

The Japanese reaction to the Occupation and its policies was thus pragmatic rather than ideological. They accepted disarmament and democracy just as they accepted the arrival of SCAP and the foreign troops; they tried to make the best of a bad situation without fighting what they saw as a force beyond their control. It is highly doubtful that, if left alone, the Japanese on their own initiative would have undertaken

41 See Asahi shinbunsha, *Hyakka binran* (*Asahi nenkan*, 1969, app.), p. 54.
42 Okudaira, "Hōsōhōsei no sai-hensei," p. 399; Takemae, *Senryō sengoshi*, p. 322.
43 Takemae, *Senryō sengoshi*, pp. 315–44.
44 Fukawa, "Nihonjin no hisenryō kan," pp. 22–4; Iwamoto Sumiaki, "Senryōgun no tai-nichi nōgyō seisaku," in *Senryōki Nihon*, p. 188.

any of the most important reforms of the Occupation period. The Japanese press began to advocate amending the constitution only after SCAP ordered the Japanese government to do so, and though few newspapers actively opposed it, both the form and substance of the new constitution stunned even the most liberal among them.[45] Considering that an overwhelming majority of Japanese wanted the institution of the emperor to be preserved, the most important reason for the absence of public opposition to the new constitution may well have been that it provided for the retention of the throne, if only as the symbol, rather than the ruler, of the nation.[46]

In any event, the Japanese did not win but simply were given all the new rights and freedoms spelled out in the new constitution. Like the relief goods that arrived in the midst of the 1946 food crisis, democracy was delivered by the Occupation via the Japanese government and was accepted by the bewildered public without a burst of enthusiasm. The amendment of the constitution was not a significant issue in the April 1946 House of Representatives general elections; indeed, many opposition candidates campaigned with the slogan "Food Before a New Constitution."[47] As time passed, however, the significance of the reforms began to sink in, especially among those who either benefited or suffered from them most directly.

### *The masses and the Occupation*

The masses generally benefited from the Occupation's policies and reforms, although they did not profit equally. For some, the experience of the Occupation was not only confusing but even painful.

Women were one of the most obvious and important beneficiaries of the Occupation. After all, they represented one-half of the entire population and, in a system of universal adult suffrage, would control one-half of the vote. The emancipation and enfranchisement of women were not obviously or completely the handiwork of SCAP. The Japanese suffrage movement dated back to the 1910s. Some important officials in the Japanese government, including Home Minister Hori-

45 Kenpō chōsakai, *Kenpō seitei no keika,* pp. 7, 417–28. See also Matsushita Keiichi, "Sengo kenpōgaku no riron kōsei," in *Sengo kaikaku,* vol. 3, p. 29; Shimizu Mutsumi, "Kenpō 'kaisei' to gikai-seido kaikaku," in *Sengō kaikaku,* vol. 3, pp. 61–62, 89.

46 The results of public opinion polls in December 1945 and February 1946 showed that 95 percent and 91 percent, respectively, of the respondents supported the institution of the emperor. See Takemae, *Senryō sengo shi,* pp. 93–94; Tsuji Kiyoaki, "Sengo kaikaku to seiji katei," in *Sengo kaikaku,* vol. 3, p. 4; Shimizu, "Kenpō 'kaisei,' " in *Sengo kaikaku,* vol. 3, p. 62.

47 Shimizu, "Kenpō 'kaisei'," p. 62. See also Shimane Kiyoshi, "Tsuihō kaijo o yōsei suru ronri," in *Kyōdō kenkyū: Nihon senryō,* p. 236.

kiri Zenjirō, were favorably predisposed on the issue in the autumn of 1945 before SCAP officially referred to it for the first time in an October 11 statement on the five major reforms to be undertaken by the Japanese government.[48] Following the SCAP statement, both the Socialists and the Communists, as well as a group of scholars led by Takano Iwasaburō, proposed including in the new constitution provisions guaranteeing the equality of the sexes.[49]

In early February 1946, when the GS staff drafted its own revision of the Imperial constitution, the three-member Civil Rights Committee established in the GS's Public Administration Division (PAD) prepared a draft of detailed provisions on the status and rights of women. The draft, however, was rejected by the Steering Committee, on the grounds that it was too detailed to be included in a constitution.[50] The details were thus left to the revision of the Civil Code, which was undertaken in the following year by a group of Japanese academic specialists, with little direct involvement by SCAP personnel.[51]

The role of the Americans was nonetheless critical to the implementation of the principles established in the constitution and the revised civil code. The Labor Ministry's Women's and Minors' Bureau and its prefectural counterparts, all of which played a crucial watchdog role in the first few years following the laws' revisions, were largely the creations of interested SCAP personnel, notably those in the relevant divisions of the Government, Economic and Scientific (ESS), Civil Information and Education, and Public Health and Welfare (PHW) sections.[52]

As was true for most other reforms of the early Occupation period, the Japanese public was both uninvolved in and indifferent to the moves within the SCAP and the Japanese government toward the emancipation and enfranchisement of women. In a November 1945 survey of two hundred towns and villages, the majority of respondents were found to be uninterested, and only about 40 percent were even slightly interested in the issue.[53] Within a few years, however, Japanese women began to take advantage of their new legal status and rights to change not only their own personal lives but increasingly to influence large issues of national and local politics as well. SCAP's

48 Soma Masao, "Senkyo seido no kaikaku," in *Sengo kaikaku*, vol. 3, pp. 105, 112, n. 31.
49 Yoda Seiichi, "Senryō seisaku ni okeru fujin kaihō," in *Senryōki Nihon*, pp. 279, 284–5.
50 Yoda, "Senryō seisaku ni okeru fujin kaihō," pp. 279–82. See also SCAP, *Political Reorientation of Japan*, vol. 2, p. 104.
51 Yoda, "Senryō seisaku ni okeru fujin kaihō," p. 287. 52 Ibid., p. 292.
53 Yoda, "Sengo kazoku seido kaikaku to shin kazoku kan no seiritsu," in *Sengo kaikaku*, vol. 1, pp. 289–90.

direct and indirect support of the profeminist reform no doubt won the Occupation many appreciative friends, if not immediately, then in the long run.

Tenant farmers also directly benefited from an Occupation-sponsored reform. Like the grant of the vote to women, land reform had been an issue in the Japanese bureaucracy since the 1920s. In fact, the initiative for the first postwar legislative action came from a Japanese source rather than SCAP. A bill drafted by officials of the Agriculture and Forestry Ministry's Bureau of Agricultural Administration had been approved by a council of cabinet ministers and introduced to the House of Representatives by the time SCAP officially raised the issue in a December 9, 1945, memorandum to the Japanese government.[54] The SCAP action thus did not cause the first land reform bill to be drafted and debated in the Diet, but it did help it to be promptly passed by both houses by the end of the year.

Technically a revision of the Agricultural Land Adjustment Law of 1938, the new law required the redistribution within five years of land owned by absentee landlords and any portion of land owned by resident landlords that exceeded about five hectares.[55] This law, however, proved unsatisfactory to SCAP, and so a second land reform legislation, called the Owner–Farmer Establishment Special Measures Law, was enacted in October 1945. This latter law authorized the government to purchase at fixed prices and redistribute all agricultural land owned by absentee landlords and portions of such land owned by resident landlords that exceeded one hectare (three hectares in Hokkaido). It also imposed rigid ceilings on the rents that could be collected on tenanted land.[56]

The ensuing redistribution revolutionized Japan's rural society and, in the long run, its role in local and national politics. Some 80 percent of tenanted agricultural land was actually redistributed to boost the ranks of owner and owner–tenant farmers from 73.4 percent of the total farm households to 92.1 percent, leaving less than 8 percent still landless.[57] Despite the landlords' protests, the 1946 law was vigor-

54 Amakawa Akira, "Senryō seisaku to kanryō no taiō," in *Kyōdō kenkyū: Nihon senryōgun: Sono hikari to kage,* ed. Shisō no kagaku kenkyūkai, 2 vols. (Tokyo: Tokuma shoten, 1978), vol. 1, p. 223.

55 Uehara Nobuhiro, "Nōchi kaikaku katei to nōchi kaikaku ron," in *Sengo kaikaku,* vol. 6: *Nōchi kaikaku,* chap. 2; Yoshida Katsumi, "Nōchikaikakuhō no rippō katei: Nōgyō keiei kibo mondai o chūshin to shite," in *Sengo kaikaku,* vol. 6, chap. 4.

56 Uehara, "Nōchi kaikaku katei," p. 65; Yoshida, "Nōchi kaikakuhō," p. 176.

57 Ōuchi Tsutomu, "Nōchi kaikaku," in *Shōwa keizai shi,* ed. Arisawa Hiromi (Tokyo: Nihon keizai shinbunsha, 1976), p. 270. See also Ōishi Kaichirō, "Nōchi kaikaku no rekishiteki igi," in *Sengo kaikaku,* vol. 6, pp. 34–5.

ously enforced, and the momentous changes it brought about were ensured permanence by the Agricultural Land Law of 1952, which in effect perpetuated the provisions of the Owner–Farmer Establishment Special Measures Law and those of a 1950 cabinet ordinance regulating farmland prices.[58]

The land reform helped avert an imminent economic and political crisis in rural Japan and the radicalization of the rural poor. By the spring of 1946, Japan's rural population had swollen with demobilized soldiers returning from overseas as well as hordes of refugees from war-ravaged cities. Between April 1945 and April 1946, the rural population increased by more than one million, or by nearly a quarter-million households, about half of which had no land of their own.[59] The crowding was especially hard on the small farmers – the overwhelming majority of Japanese farmers at the time – many of whom barely survived on the crops they grew themselves and depended on nonagricultural jobs for any additional income. According to a Ministry of Agriculture and Forestry survey, about 70 percent of the approximately 5.7 million farmer households owned less than one hectare of land in 1946.[60] It was this large group of small and often impoverished farmers that benefited most from the land reform of 1946. As a result, many gave up, at least temporarily, their part-time nonagricultural employment and income.

The tendency of small farmers to supplement their income with either full-time or part-time nonagricultural jobs dates back to the late 1930s. Between July 1937 and February 1941, for example, about 1 million farmers were either drafted into or voluntarily found employment in war-related industries, and more than half of them emigrated from their native villages.[61] In 1941, nearly 60 percent of farmer households had some members, often heads of households, holding nonagricultural jobs, and on the average 60 percent of the income received by a farmer household was derived from nonagricultural sources. Although the land reform did not reverse the tendency in the long run, it did slow it down for a while. The number of farmer households relying primarily on farm income and only secondarily on income from other sources decreased from about 2.019 million in 1941 to 1.753 million in 1950.[62] Although the number of households whose income

58 For more details, see Watanabe Yōzō, "Nōchi kaikaku to sengo nōchihō," *Sengo kaikaku*, vol. 6, pp. 107–10.

59 See Eguchi Eiichi, *Gendai no "tei shotoku sō,"* 3 vols. (Tokyo: Miraisha, 1979–80), vol. 1, p. 272, Table 3-3. 60 Ibid., p. 278. 61 Ibid., p. 267.

62 Yano Tsuneta kinenkai, ed., *Nihon kokusei zue*, 1981 ed. (Tokyo: Kokuseisha, 1981), p. 209.

depended more on nonagricultural employment than on farming increased somewhat during the same period, the number of part-time farmer households as a whole decreased from about 58 percent of the total to about 50 percent.

The decline in the number of part-time farmer households did not indicate an immediate and significant improvement of living conditions for their members. Until the mid-1950s, the average income of farmer households consistently lagged behind that of nonfarmer households by nearly 10 percent in 1953 and 1954.[63] Rural Japan was, however, significantly stabilized by the land reform, both economically and politically.

Farmers became an increasingly cohesive and effective economic force, thanks largely to the development of agricultural cooperative unions established by the Agricultural Cooperative Union Law of 1947. These cooperatives were also a creation of the Occupation authorities, specifically the GHQ's National Resource Section (NRS). As such, they were in theory "autonomous, free, and democratic," although they were in practice virtual replications of the wartime agricultural associations (*nōgyōkai*).[64] Like the latter, they were semipublic entities financially supported and administratively controlled by the Agriculture Ministry bureaucracy, especially after the enactment in 1951 of the Agricultural Cooperative Union Reconstruction and Adjustment Law. Nonetheless, they enjoyed considerable influence not only in local communities but also with the political parties and politicians, mainly because of their all-inclusive membership.

From the beginning, but especially after the June 1954 revision of the Agricultural Cooperative Union Law, each local union consisted of virtually all practicing farmers in a given village. The organization functioned also as the sole collecting agent for rice – whose distribution remained under rigid government control until the end of the 1960s – as well as the central village store, warehouse, and banking facility.[65] Coordinated by prefectural federations and national headquarters, the several thousand local cooperatives collectively com-

63 Kokumin seikatsu sentā, ed., *Kokumin seikatsu tōkei nenpō '80* (Tokyo: Shiseidō, 1980), p. 57.
64 Iwamoto, "Senryōgun no tai-nichi nōgyō seisaku," pp. 190–1; Ishida Takeshi, "Sengo kaikaku to soshiki oyobi shōchō," in *Sengo kaikaku*, vol. 1, pp. 163–4.
65 See Takeshi Ishida and Aurelia D. George, "Nōkyō: The Japanese Farmers' Representative," in *Japan & Australia: Two Societies and Their Interaction*, ed. Peter Drysdale and Hironobu Kitaoji (Canberra: Australian National University Press, 1981), pp. 194–214; Michael W. Donnelly, "Setting the Price of Rice: A Study in Political Decisionmaking," in *Policymaking in Contemporary Japan*, ed. T. J. Pempel (Ithaca, N.Y.: Cornell University Press, 1977), pp. 143–200.

prised a formidable pressure group to defend and promote the farmers' expanding economic and political interests.[66]

Whereas women and tenant farmers were direct beneficiaries of the Occupation-sponsored reforms, the situation of employees in the industrial and service sectors was more complicated. The Occupation's initial policy was clearly prolabor. The SCAP memorandum of October 1945, which ordered the emancipation of women, also directed the Japanese government to encourage the organization of labor unions, so that they might have an influential voice in safeguarding the working people from exploitation and abuse and in raising their living standards.[67] Accordingly, a labor union bill was hastily drafted by Home Ministry officials, was perfunctorily debated and passed by the Imperial Diet, and became law in late December of the same year. Although it was far from radical, permitting both management and government considerable power to interfere with and control the unions' activities,[68] it nonetheless encouraged employees to organize at a pace and on a scale unprecedented in the history of the Japanese labor movement. By the end of the year, some 500 unions had been formed, with about 385,000 members; by the end of 1946, these numbers had grown, respectively, to over 17,000 and 4.849 million.[69] The last figure represents about 40 percent of those employed in the mining, manufacturing, and service industries in that year. Over a half of them were affiliated with the three major national federations formed in 1946: the left-wing National Congress of Industrial Unions (Zen Nihon sangyōbetsu rōdō kumiai kaigi: Sanbetsu), the right-wing Japan National Federation of Labor (Nihon rōdō kumiai sōdōmei: Sōdōmei), and the centrist Japan Labor Union Congress (Nihon rōdō kumiai kaigi: Nichirō kaigi).

Labor unions not only sprang into existence in great profusion but also displayed a great deal of militancy, often engaging in intense "production management" (*seisan kanri*) struggles aimed at wresting from management the power of decision making. In 1946 alone, nearly 845,000 unionists participated in approximately 1,260 industrial dis-

66 During the first few years of the Occupation, a radical peasant movement thrived under the direction of the Japan Peasant Union, originally founded in 1922 and reestablished in 1946. After 1947, however, it quickly lost popular support, partly because of internal conflict but mainly because of the growing conservatism among the newly liberated peasants. For a brief discussion of the subject, see Tanaka Manabu, "Nōchi kaikaku to nōmin undō," in *Sengo kaikaku*, vol. 6, chap. 7.

67 See SCAP, *Political Reorientation of Japan*, vol. 2, p. 741.

68 Takemae Eiji, "1949-nen rōdōhō kaisei zenshi: Senryō seisaku o chūshin to shite," in *Senryōki Nihon*, pp. 306, 316–17.

69 Ōkouchi Kazuo, *Sengo Nihon no rōdō undō*, rev. ed., *Iwanami shinsho*, no. 217 (Tokyo: Iwanami shoten, 1961), p. 37.

putes, roughly one-third of which involved demands for employee participation in production management.[70] At the national level, Nichirō kaigi negotiated with the major employer organization, the Federation of Economic Organizations (Keizai dantai rengōkai: Keidanren), for the establishment of a central forum for management–labor consultation and coordination called the Economic Reconstruction Conference.[71] Organized labor thus won and maintained a position of equality, if not superiority, vis-à-vis management during the first few years of the Occupation.

The popularity of the labor movement during this period reflected the severity of the economic hardships that the average worker suffered in the wake of the disastrous war as well as the union's apparent success in negotiating wage increases and employee participation in management. In 1947, private-sector wages in real terms were still as low as about 30 percent of the 1934–6 average[72] but made substantial gains in the following years, by as much as about 50 percent in 1948, 28 percent in 1949, and another 28 percent in 1950. By 1952, wages reached a level slightly higher than that of the prewar peak years.[73]

The sudden upsurge of radical unionism, however, was somewhat artificial. The majority of Japanese workers had never been radical, and the initial success of the postwar labor movement, particularly its left wing, depended largely on SCAP's approval and support. According to a February 1946 opinion poll, an overwhelming majority of the employees supported the institution of the emperor, the quintessential symbol of tradition and continuity in an era of revolutionary change and adjustment.[74] Moreover, employees of large zaibatsu-affiliated companies apparently remained bound by the mystique of corporate solidarity and loyalty to the owner and his family.[75] For a while, SCAP's well-publicized support and the impotence of management encouraged the rise of militant unionism, but after SCAP's support was withdrawn in the wake of the abortive general strike by public service unions in early 1947, the tide of radical unionism turned.

At the instigation of the Labor Division of the GHQ's ESS, and with the tacit support of the Japanese government and employers, dissidents in the secretariat of Sanbetsu spearheaded the "democratization" program in the months following the failure of the public service general

70 Ibid., p. 48. 71 Takemae, "1949-nen rōdōhō," pp. 302–3.
72 Fujinawa Masakatsu, *Nihon no saitei chingin* (Tokyo: Nikkan rōdō tsūshinsha, 1972), p. 317, Table 4-4. 73 Ibid., pp. 316–17. 74 Yoda, "Sengo kazoku seido," p. 291.
75 Chihara, "Gunju sangyō rōdōsha," pp. 88–9.

strike in February 1947.[76] In March 1948, they established the Democratization League which thereafter steadily expanded its membership and influence among both Sanbetsu affiliates and Nichirō unions. The league's anticommunist campaign was bolstered by a SCAP directive of July 22, 1948, instructing the Japanese government to deny public servants the right to engage in collective bargaining and strikes.[77] When the "Red purge" swept the public services and key private-sector industries following the outbreak of the Korean War, most unions had come under the control of anticommunist leadership. They put up little fight even against the dismissal of minor union officials whose affiliation with the Communist Party was not even proved.[78]

A few months before fighting broke out in Korea, the democratization movement evolved into a new national labor federation, the General Council of Japanese Trade Unions (Nihon rōdō kumiai sōhyōgikai: Sōhyō). By far the largest among the several competing labor federations, Sōhyō ironically became a militantly antiestablishment and moderately procommunist organization under the direction of its first secretary-general, Takano Minoru, and his supporters, who constituted the left-wing faction among the Democratization League leaders. Sōhyō did not entirely neglect bread-and-butter issues. In fact, it campaigned vigorously, if unsuccessfully, for the establishment of a minimum wage law.[79] More efforts, however, went into political and ideological campaigns – against Japanese rearmament, American bases, the U.S.–Japanese Mutual Security Treaty, and revision of the constitution. Wage and working conditions tended to be given short shrift in favor of socialism and world peace.

During the first half of the 1950s, Takano's political line dominated Sōhyō, and Sōhyō dominated the Japanese labor movement. Meanwhile, under heavy government and management pressure, the workers began to drop out of the ranks of organized labor. Many workers were disillusioned and alienated by the leadership's highly political and divisive platform and by the continuing internecine struggle between the left and right factions. The total union membership peaked in 1948, when about 34,000 unions boasted a combined membership of 6.677 million, representing 53 percent of the total work force in the secondary and tertiary sectors.[80] During the next three years it de-

76 On the role of the Labor Division, see Takemae Eiji, "Reddo pāji," in *Kyōdō kenkyū: Nihon senryōgun*, vol. 1, pp. 279–84.
77 See Kume Shigeru, "Kokutetsu rōso to Suzuki Ichizō ni miru senryōka rōdō undō," in *Kyōdō kenkyū: Nihon senryō*, pp. 55–7; Ishida, "Sengo kaikaku to soshiki," p. 185.
78 Takemae, *Senryō sengo shi*, pp. 201–9, 213. 79 Fujinawa, *Nihon no saitei chingin*, pp. 62–5.
80 Ōkouchi, *Sengo Nihon no rōdō undō*, pp. 75–6.

clined by almost 1 million, and the rate of unionization fell by about 10 percentage points. The deflationary program introduced in early 1949 to implement recommendations of a United States mission led by a Detroit banker, Joseph Dodge, and known as the "Dodge line" considerably aggravated the situation from labor's point of view. Not only did annual gains in real wages rapidly shrink after 1950, but over a quarter-million public service employees and almost as many in the private sector, especially in small businesses, lost their jobs in the wake of the "disinflation" caused by the enforcement of the program.[81]

Thus, to most of the employees in the industrial and service sectors, the Occupation and early post-Occupation period began with great promises and ended in confusion and disappointment. The benefits they received were far more ambiguous and elusive than were those that women and tenant farmers enjoyed.

### *The elite and the Occupation*

In contrast with the workers, members of the Japanese elite generally suffered more than benefited from the Occupation-sponsored reforms. As was the case with the workers, however, the impact of the Occupation and its specific policies varied a great deal among segments of the elite.

In December 1946, eleven of the fourteen imperial princes and their families lost their status as members of the imperial family and substantial parts of their wealth as well, because they were related to the emperor.[82] All the peers and their families lost their titles and privileges overnight in accordance with Article 14 of the new constitution. They and the approximately one million landlords, whose farmland was in effect confiscated and redistributed in the land reform of 1947–52, were victims of the Occupation policy.[83]

81 Fujinawa, *Nihon no saitei chingin*, p. 316, Table 4-2; Shimura Yoshikazu, "Antei kyōkō," in *Shōwa keizai shi*, pp. 308–11.

82 See Takahashi Hiroshi and Suzuki Kunihiko, *Tennōke no misshi tachi: Hiroku senryō to kōshitsu* (Tokyo: Tokuma shoten, 1981), pp. 167–8.

83 Most studies of the land reform give considerably higher estimates of the number of affected landlords. The authoritative report edited by the Land Reform Records Commission, for example, refers to 3,829,785 landlords involved. These estimates, however, are vastly exaggerated, for in many cases the same landlord was counted several times if his land was taken piecemeal in more than one of the twenty-four waves of assessment, designation, and transfer of title that took place during the nearly five-year period. The same landlord was frequently also classified as both a resident and an absentee if his property lay both inside and outside the locality where he resided. See Fukui Haruhiro, *Jiyū minshutō to seisaku kettei* (Tokyo: Fukumura shuppan, 1969), pp. 211–12, n. 2.

So too were the owners of the seventy-five holding and trading companies dissolved under the "deconcentration of economic power" program, as well as their families, notably those who belonged to the Mitsui, Mitsubishi, Sumitomo, and Yasuda zaibatsu.[84] Over 200,000 persons were purged, one-half of whom were military personnel. Although all those purged were eventually reinstated, most suffered enormously from the temporary, though sometimes permanent, loss of employment and income and the stigma of being purged, for many years after reinstatement.

On the other hand, the three houses headed by the emperor's brothers were permitted to retain their imperial status and much of the social prestige, if not the economic privileges, that went with that status.[85] The emperor himself was deprived by the new constitution of his status as the sovereign and was reduced to being a symbol of the state. The change in his constitutional status and role, however, was not as important as it might seem, considering the largely symbolic role that Japanese emperors had traditionally played.[86] Far more significant was the fact that the monarchy was not abolished. The monarch was neither forced to abdicate nor brought before the war crimes tribunal, despite considerable public pressure in most Allied nations, including the United States, for his prosecution for the role he had allegedly played in the initiation and execution of the war.[87] The emperor's remarkable fate, both as a person and as an institution, was based on a decision by SCAP, a decision that no doubt was shaped by the favorable impression the emperor himself made on General MacArthur, especially during their first face-to-face encounter on September 27, 1945.[88] But not to be underestimated, much less forgotten, in this regard are the energetic lobbying efforts made on the emperor's behalf by a dozen or so intermediaries, including MacArthur's trusted military secretary, Brigadier General Bonner Fellers; his Earlham Col-

84 On the dissolution of the zaibatsu and its consequences, see Eleanor M. Hadley, *Antitrust in Japan* (Princeton, N.J.: Princeton University Press, 1970); Shibagaki Kazuo, "Zaibatsu kaitai to shūchū haijo," in *Sengo kaikaku*, vol. 7: *Keizai kaikaku*, chap. 2.

85 Takahashi and Suzuki, *Tennōke no misshi tachi*, pp. 159–60; Frazier Hunt, *The Untold Story of Douglas MacArthur* (New York: Devin-Adair, 1954), p. 408.

86 See John Whitney Hall, "A Monarch for Modern Japan," in *Political Development in Modern Japan*, ed. Robert E. Ward (Princeton, N.J.: Princeton University Press, 1968), chap. 2.

87 Watanabe Hisamaru, "Shōchō tennōsei no seijiteki yakuwari," in *Tennōsei to minshū*, ed. Gotō Yasushi (Tokyo: Tōkyō daigaku shuppankai, 1976), pp. 234–5; Hunt, *The Untold Story*, pp. 408, 420–1.

88 See Courtney Whitney, *MacArthur: His Rendezvous with History* (New York: Knopf, 1956), pp. 420–1.

lege fellow alumna, Isshiki Yuriko; and her friend and Bryn Mawr–trained educator, Kawai Michi.[89]

The experience of the majority of big businessmen and higher civil servants was far more diverse and complex. On balance, they benefited more from SCAP and Japanese government policies of the period than they suffered from them.

The initial SCAP policy, and the various legislative and administrative measures taken by the Japanese government to implement it, were prolabor and antimanagement, at least implicitly. Employers were the most obvious and direct target of the Property Tax Law of November 1945 and the Wartime Compensation Special Measures Law of October 1946, both of which were enacted to increase the tax revenue of the financially beleaguered government.[90] However, employers did not suffer long, as they soon organized to fend off pressure from the reformers in the GHQ and the newly organized labor movements.

The major existing employer organizations, such as the Japanese Federation of Economic Organizations (Nihon keizai renmeikai), the Important Industries Council (Jūyō sangyō kyōgikai: Jūsankyō), the National Council of Commercial and Industrial Associations (Zenkoku shōkō keizaikai kyōgikai), and the Central Council of Commercial and Industrial Unions (Shōkō kumiai chūōkai) were all disbanded shortly after the end of the war. But before long new organizations bearing somewhat different names were formed. In April 1946, the Committee for Economic Development (Keizai dōyūkai) made its appearance, followed in August by Keidanren. The Japan Federation of Employer Associations (Nihon keieisha dantai renmei: Nikkeiren) was founded in April 1948, in order to combat the rising tide of left-wing labor unionism.[91] These employer organizations soon became powerful and effective political lobbies, with their influence reaching deep into the heart of the conservative establishment.

The shift in the Occupation policy, combined with the growing concern about the deepening economic crisis, led the Japanese government after the middle of 1946 to develop and implement a series of

89 One author has written of Fellers: "I am constantly startled to find the reflection of Fellers' ideas in the general's pronouncements. . . . 'Emperor Hirohito,' he told a correspondent, 'is no more a war criminal than Roosevelt. . . .' " See Mark Gayn, *Japan Diary* (Tokyo: Tuttle, 1981), p. 343. For the identities and activities of other intermediaries, see Takahashi and Suzuki, *Tennōke no misshi tachi*, passim.

90 Inoue Ichirō, "Senryō shoki no sozei gyōsei," in *Kyōdō kenkyū: Nihon senryōgun*, vol. 1, pp. 264–72.

91 Ishida, "Sengo kaikaku to soshiki," in *Sengo kaikaku*, vol. 1, pp. 184–5; Sakaguchi Akira, "Iki fukikaesu zaikai," in *Shōwa keizai shi*, pp. 292–5.

programs to assist businesses in key industries, through both the provision of public funds and special tax breaks. The main targets and beneficiaries of the early preferential funding programs under the so-called priority production (*keisha seisan*) system were the coal-mining, iron and steel, electric power generation, shipbuilding, and fertilizer industries.[92] The Reconstruction Finance Bank established by law in October 1946 provided in the next two years some ¥126 billion in special loans to the major producers in the target industries. At about the same time, the commercial banks were rapidly rehabilitated, with substantial government assistance provided under the Banking Institutions Reconstruction and Adjustment Law of October 1946.[93]

Tax breaks played an increasingly important role in the rehabilitation and development of the postwar Japanese economy in general and the growth of robust businesses in particular, especially after the 1950 tax reform based on the recommendations of the Shoup mission.[94] In 1951, for example, the manufacturers of certain types of machinery were allowed special accelerated depreciation. In 1952 the electric power companies were allowed tax-deductible reserves against future drought, and insurance companies were given tax-deductible premium payments on life insurance policies. In 1953 it became possible to separate interest from the rest of one's income when computing one's individual income tax, a device designed to encourage savings by individual depositors and also to help banks, and generous tax-free reserves were allowed against export trade–related losses. Finally, in 1954 the withholding rates for income from dividends were lowered, and dividends earned on newly issued stocks became entirely tax free.[95]

Except in the first year or so, the Occupation thus turned out to be quite benign to the majority of employers in the key manufacturing and service industries. Overall, they did far better than labor, not to mention former landlords and onetime leaders of the zaibatsu business empires.

The case of higher civil servants is even more complex. It was one of SCAP's principal initial policy objectives to overhaul and reform the civil service bureaucracy, the "key instrument in the totalitarian regimentation of the people's life."[96] But once GHQ decided to rule Japan

92 Watanuki, "Kōdo seichō," in *Nenpō seijigaku,* 1977, pp. 152–3, 155; Miyashita Buhei, "Keisha seisan hōshiki," in *Shōwa keizai shi,* pp. 286–9.

93 Hara Shirō, "Kinyū kikan tachinaoru," in *Shōwa keizai shi,* pp. 295–8.

94 On the work of the Shoup mission, see Hayashi Takehisa, "Shaupu kankoku to zeisei kaikaku," in *Sengo kaikaku,* vol. 7, chap. 5.

95 Satō Susumu, *Nihon no zeikin* (Tokyo: Tōkyō daigaku shuppankai, 1979), pp. 38–9.

96 SCAP, *Political Reorientation of Japan,* vol. 1, p. 246.

indirectly through the existing machinery of the Japanese government, the survival of at least a segment of the civil service personnel became a foregone conclusion. Therefore, most of the bureaucrats in the central government, including those at the highest ranks, not only survived the Occupation-sponsored reforms but even participated in their formulation and implementation, including measures designed to overhaul the civil service itself. This was particularly true for the middle- and senior-level Foreign Ministry officials who filled most of the key posts in the Central Liaison Office established on August 26, 1945, to help SCAP implement the initial Occupation policies.[97]

Although nearly 80 percent of military personnel down to the level of corporal and 16 percent of the members of the Imperial Diet were purged, less than 1 percent of civil servants were.[98] Once assured of their continuing employment in the various ministries and agencies of the central government, they began to participate, sometimes willingly and sometimes unwillingly, in the implementation of SCAP's initial policy objectives. The involvement of the Japanese bureaucrats significantly affected both the form and the substance of the most important legislation enacted during the Occupation. The Labor Union Law of 1945 and the first land reform are good examples. So are the amendments to the House of Representatives Members Election Law, which was approved by both houses of the Imperial Diet at about the same time, and the House of Councilors Members Election Law, which was passed a year later. In both cases the original bills were drafted by Home Ministry bureaucrats.[99] The new Diet law enacted in March 1947 resulted from negotiations between the SCAP staff, on one hand, and the House of Representatives Committee on Legislative Investigation and the Cabinet Bureau of Legislation, on the other.[100] In some cases, the interaction between SCAP personnel and Japanese bureaucrats was far more complex.

The reform of the police was first undertaken by the staff of the Home Ministry's Police Bureau in the spring of 1946 and then was studied by a public advisory group called the Police System Council appointed in November of the same year.[101] However, the Police Law

97 See Kazuo Kawai, *Japan's American Interlude* (Chicago: University of Chicago Press, 1960), pp. 19–20.
98 Ishida, "Sengo kaikaku to soshiki," in *Sengo kaikaku,* vol. 1, p. 185; Kume, "Kokutetsu rōso to Suzuki Ichizō," in *Kyōdō kenkyū: Nihon senryō,* pp. 55–7.
99 Soma, "Senkyo seisaku," in *Sengo kaikaku,* vol. 3, pp. 93, 119. See also Amakawa, "Senryō seisaku to kanryō," in *Kyōdō kenkyū: Nihon senryōgun,* vol. 1, p. 225.
100 Shimizu, "Kenpō kaisei," in *Sengo kaikaku,* vol. 3, pp. 82–5.
101 Hoshino Yasusaburō, "Keisatsu seido no kaikaku," in *Sengo kaikaku,* vol. 3, pp. 320–5.

that followed in December 1947 and that authorized the establishment of 95,000-member municipal police units and a 300,000-member national rural police force reflected SCAP's, especially the GS's, view, which favored maximum decentralization rather than the ascendancy of either Japanese group.[102]

The reform of the local government system was accomplished in two stages: In the first stage, four bills designed to increase the autonomy of, respectively, metropolitan Tokyo, other cities, towns and villages, and prefectures were drafted by Home Ministry officials and then were debated, amended, and passed in September 1946 by both houses of the Diet. In the second, an advisory group was appointed and, under Home Ministry bureaucrats' guidance, prepared a draft local self-government bill, which was then debated by the Diet and significantly amended in response to SCAP's, as well as several Japanese ministries', demands before it was passed in March 1947.[103]

Still more complex was the reform of the civil service itself. Here again, the initiative came from the Japanese government. The Cabinet Bureau of Legislation began to study the issue seriously in late September 1945 and by the middle of November submitted to the cabinet specific recommendations that followed those previously proposed by several groups, notably by the Imperial Rule Assistance Association (IRAA) in January 1941.[104] Most of these recommendations were implemented by a series of imperial ordinances in the spring of 1946. In July of the same year, however, an *ad hoc* advisory group was appointed to review the reforms, and in late October it submitted to the cabinet a report proposing additional changes in the civil service personnel system.[105] The *ad hoc* group's proposals also were partially implemented, but no sooner had its report been presented to the government than still another working group, somewhat ambiguously named the Administrative Research Bureau, was established in the secretariat of the cabinet to prepare for the expected visit of an advisory mission from the United States.

The American group arrived in Japan at the end of November 1946. Officially named the United States Personnel Advisory Mission to Japan and popularly known as the Hoover mission after its leader, Blaine Hoover, the group worked closely with the staff of the Administrative Research Bureau, especially in administering and processing an exten-

102 Ibid., pp. 328–35.
103 Amakawa Akira, "Chihō jichi hō no kōzō," in *Senryōki Nihon*, pp. 136–7, 146, 150–9.
104 Ide Yoshinori, "Sengo kaikaku to Nihon kanryōsei: Kōmuin seido no sōshutsu katei," in *Sengo kaikaku*, vol. 3, pp. 149–51, 159–60, 162–3. 105 Ibid., pp. 165–7.

sive survey of personnel practices in the main ministries, and then independently prepared a draft of a National Public Servants Law.[106] To the surprise and dismay of the Japanese, not only was the document drafted by the American advisers alone, but more importantly, it contained a set of recommendations that represented a radical departure from the existing Japanese system and practices, including the establishment of an independent National Personnel Authority.

However, the National Public Service Law, which was promulgated in October 1947, was a substantially revised version of the Hoover mission's original draft.[107] Hoover left Japan for the United States on July 1 of that year, and during his absence the Japanese managed to amend many of the original draft's key provisions. For example, the National Personnel Authority was renamed the Temporary National Personnel Commission, and the commissioners' powers and responsibilities were considerably more limited than the Hoover mission's draft had envisaged. The provision prohibiting public servants from engaging in strikes and other forms of concerted work stoppages was simply omitted, as was the key word *class* in the article providing for the classification of positions.

In November, Hoover returned to Japan, followed by those he had recruited in the United States to staff the GS's newly established Civil Service Division (CSD). Under Hoover's personal direction and SCAP's explicit endorsement, the division began a comprehensive review, and then extensive revisions, of the 1947 law. In the process, many of the provisions of the original Hoover mission draft, which had been either omitted or substantially amended by the Japanese, were restored, including the original name of the national personnel agency and the prohibition of strikes by public servants.[108] The revisions were ratified by the Diet with few significant modifications and the new National Public Service Law was promulgated on December 3, 1948. Some of the revisions, however, were hotly debated, not only between the staff of the CSD and that of the Temporary National Personnel Commission, but, to further complicate the matter, also within the GHQ itself between the CSD and the ESS's Labor Division (LD).

The final outcome of the civil service reform thus reflected the intent of the original Hoover mission draft more faithfully than the

106 Ibid., pp. 178–90. See also Blaine Hoover's own account in SCAP, *Political Reorientation of Japan*, vol. 1, pp. 246–59.

107 Ide, "Sengo kaikaku to Nihon kanryōsei," in *Sengo kaikaku*, vol. 3, pp. 196–9; SCAP, *Political Reorientation of Japan*, vol. 1, pp. 253–4.

108 Ide, "Sengo kaikaku to Nihon kanryōsei," pp. 210–23.

1947 law did. It was nonetheless a compromise reached by negotiation and bargaining both between the Americans and Japanese and among the Americans themselves. To an important extent, it also reflected the shift in the concerns of the Occupation policy, from Japan's demilitarization and democratization to its economic rehabilitation and political stabilization. SCAP's new objectives were basically agreeable to the upper echelon of the Japanese government bureaucracy, and so were many of the provisions of the 1948 National Public Service Law.[109] Of all the major prewar political institutions, the bureaucracy alone survived the Occupation with few visible changes. In fact, its overt political influence increased, rather than decreased, during the period.

## THE POLITICS OF DEVELOPMENTALISM: HIGH ECONOMIC GROWTH AND ITS CONSEQUENCES

Japanese politics between 1955 and 1973 was somewhat paradoxical. On the one hand, the period was characterized by recurrent and often violent confrontations between the conservative governments and the opposition parties, both inside and outside the halls of the Diet, and on the other hand, it was a period of stable and seemingly never-ending one-party dominance by the united conservatives.

Under the new constitutional structure adopted in 1947, a party's strength in the Diet determined its role in national politics. In theory, a party that controlled at least two-thirds of the seats in both the House of Representatives and the House of Councilors could become a *hegemonic party,* able to initiate amendments to the constitution and thus able to change the rules under which politics was conducted. In practice, however, no party ever attained such a position in the postwar period. On the other hand, if a party attained the position of *majority party,* controlling more than half of the seats in the House of Representatives, it could designate the candidate of its choice as prime minister. And if it controlled a majority in both houses, it could pass whatever legislation it wished to put before the Diet. Until the mid-1950s, only the Democratic Liberal Party (and its successor, the Liberal Party) ever attained a clear majority and only in the lower house (from 1949 to 1953).

The situation of the opposition was more complex. Under the new constitution and the 1947 Diet Law as amended in January 1955, there were four possible roles that an opposition party might play. First, a

109 Ibid., pp. 223–9.

party that controlled more than a third, but less than half, of the seats in either house could deny that house the right to transact business and could thwart the initiation of a constitutional amendment. This type of party could be called a *veto party*. Second, a party that could win at least fifty, but fewer than one-third, of the seats in the House of Representatives could present a bill affecting the budget or a motion to amend such a bill. This kind of party could be called a *significant opposition party,* but it could not hope to form a government by itself. Third, a party with fewer than fifty, but more than twenty, seats in the House of Representatives could present an ordinary bill not affecting the budget or a motion to amend such a bill, and it could be called a *minor opposition party*. Finally, a party with fewer than twenty seats in the lower house could be regarded as a *marginal opposition party*.

In early 1955 there was no majority party in the Diet. There were only a conservative veto party (the Democratic Party), one conservative and two left-wing minor opposition parties (the Liberals and the Right and Left Socialists), and a marginal group of conservative and left-wing members. This configuration of the Diet augured a period of potential political instability. The reunification of the Socialists in October 1955, and the merger of the two conservative parties into the Liberal Democratic Party the following month, radically transformed this situation. It created what many observers at first called a two-party system and later a one-and-a-half-party system.

By the time this period ended in the wake of the first "oil crisis" of the 1970s, six House of Representatives general elections had been called. In each of them the Liberal Democratic Party (Jiyū minshutō: LDP) won majority-party status, thus forming a reasonably stable government. On the opposition side, the Socialists split once more in late 1959, the right wing forming a separate party of its own, the Democratic Socialist Party (Minshu shakaitō, subsequently Minshatō: DSP). This was followed by the appearance of a new party associated with a Buddhist lay organization, Sōkagakkai. Originally called the Clean Government League (Kōmei seiji renmei), the party was renamed the Clean Government Party (Kōmeitō: CGP) in November 1964. The emergence of these two parties further fragmented and weakened the chronically divided opposition.

At the beginning of this period, the opposition consisted of only two parties of any significance: the united Japan Socialist Party (Nihon shakaitō: JSP) with veto-party status and the Communists with marginal-opposition strength. The split of the DSP reduced the parent JSP to the significant-opposition-party level, except in 1967 when it managed to regain a veto-party position. The addition of the CGP did not affect the JSP's relative position as directly as the defection of the DSP did, either vis-à-vis the LDP or among the opposition parties. It did, however, help keep the opposition's overall power divided among four different parties in a virtual stalemate and thus ineffectual against the party in power. The CGP held minor-opposition-party status in the last three general elections of the period in which it participated, whereas the DSP began in a marginal-opposition position in 1960, moved up to minor-opposition status in 1967, but fell back again to a marginal position in 1972. The JCP stayed in its customary marginal-opposition position throughout the period, except in 1972 when it exchanged that status with the DSP and rose to the minor-opposition level for the first time since 1949.

The first LDP government led by Hatoyama Ichirō lasted only a year, from November 1955 to December 1956. It provoked strong and persistent opposition to some of its principal foreign and domestic policies. For example, its efforts to conclude a peace treaty with the Soviet Union were opposed by many LDP politicians and senior Foreign Ministry officials. Negotiations ended in October 1956 in the issuance of a joint declaration normalizing diplomatic relations between the two nations, rather than a formal peace treaty.[110] Hatoyama's domestic legislative program met even more intense opposition from the Socialists and Communists. A bill to replace the existing multimember election districts with single-member districts was killed by the opposition. Several other bills, such as those amending the Defense Agency Establishment and the Self-Defense Forces laws, establishing the Committee on the Constitution to study possible revisions of the 1947 constitution, and making elected local boards of education appointive, survived the opposition and became law, but only after a bitter and protracted struggle with the opposition.

The confrontation between the LDP government and the opposition parties intensified during the administration of Hatoyama's successor, Kishi Nobusuke, a former Commerce and Industry Ministry bureaucrat and a member of the wartime Tōjō cabinet. Between 1957 and 1960, debates in the Diet were frequently interrupted by disorder and often accompanied by violence on the floor of the chambers. At issue was the handling of bills requiring periodical performance evalua-

110 On the process of Japanese-Soviet negotiations and decision making in the Japanese government, see Donald C. Hellmann, *Japanese Foreign Policy and Domestic Politics: The Peace Agreement with the Soviet Union* (Berkeley and Los Angeles: University of California Press, 1969).

tions of schoolteachers, increasing the duties and powers of police officers, and expanding the scope of competence of the Defense Agency and Self-Defense Forces. After the bitter battles over these issues, the focus of the controversy shifted to the proposed revision of the 1951 United States–Japan Mutual Security Treaty. The Kishi government won the ratification of the revised treaty in May 1960, but not until a succession of massive protest rallies and demonstrations claimed the life of a woman college student and led to the cancellation of a scheduled official visit by President Dwight D. Eisenhower.[111] Kishi and his cabinet resigned in the aftermath of the turmoil, and a leader of the JSP, Asanuma Inejiro, was assassinated a few months later.

Once the new security treaty was ratified and a new prime minister, Ikeda Hayato, was installed, calm and normalcy returned to both the halls of the Diet and Tokyo's streets, thanks largely to Ikeda's deliberate avoidance of controversial issues. The acquisition of surface-to-air missiles (SAMs) by the Self-Defense Forces in late 1962 and the announcement a few months later of a plan to bring a nuclear-powered U.S. submarine to a Japanese port threatened to, but did not, trigger another wave of violent protest.

The Ikeda government's domestic policy program was also noncontroversial. It was built around the much publicized "income-doubling" policy, which was to double the gross national product per person in ten years. This proved to be one of the most popular policies ever proposed by an LDP government. In 1963 and 1964, the threat of inflation caused widespread public concern; a chronic depression led to the closing of the nation's major coal mines; and the payment of compensation to former landlords for the losses caused by the Occupation's land reform provoked some opposition both inside and outside the Diet. None, however, led to a confrontation comparable to those during the Hatoyama and Kishi governments. The final report of the Commission on the Constitution was quietly submitted to and filed away by the cabinet in the middle of 1964.

The political lull was broken after Ikeda's retirement in November 1964. A new LDP government led by Kishi's younger brother, Satō Eisaku, remained in power for the next seven and a half years. His administration, however, was rocked by a series of legislative and ideological battles with the opposition. Particularly controversial were the ratification of the Eighty-seventh Convention of the International

111 See Packard, *Protest in Tokyo*.

Labor Organization (ILO), the normalization treaty with the Republic of Korea, the Tokyo–Washington negotiations on the return of Okinawa to Japanese administration and on the export of Japanese synthetic and woolen textiles to the United States, Japanese involvement in the Indochina war, strikes and occupation of campus buildings and premises by university students, and the spread of industrial pollution.[112] The government won virtually all of the major battles, but Satō's often high-handed, and sometimes underhanded, handling of the controversial issues eventually alienated and antagonized not only the opposition parties but also many in the LDP, the bureaucracy, and influential business groups.

With the exception of Ikeda's relatively brief rule, this period was characterized by political strife and tensions, during which the LDP governments and their policies were subjected to sustained and often virulent partisan and public attacks. Paradoxically, however, this was also a period of great stability in terms of the results of the Diet elections. The key to this paradox is the massive socioeconomic change during this eighteen-year period.

### *Costs and benefits of the "economic miracle"*

Ikeda's "income-doubling" plan was more a symbol and a consequence than a cause of Japan's "economic miracle." By the time it was announced, the nation's economy had entered the second of its three sustained booms in the 1950s and 1960s. The first, dubbed the "Jimmu boom" (*Jimmu keiki*), occurred in the 1950s, spanning a thirty-one-month period from the beginning of 1955 to the middle of 1957; the second, remembered as the "cave boom" (*iwato keiki*), began in the middle of 1958 and lasted for forty-two months until the end of 1961. During the first boom, the real GNP grew about 8 percent per year; during the second, the growth rate averaged over 10 percent. The last and longest in the series, the "Izanagi boom" (*Izanagi keiki*), began in late 1965 and lasted for fifty-six months until the middle of 1970, with an average growth rate of over 11 percent per year.[113]

112 On the politics in the period of the Satō government, see Watanabe Akio, "Dai 61-dai: Dai 1-ji Satō naikaku: 'Kanyō to nintai' kara 'kanyō to chōwa' e," "Dai 62-dai: Dai 2-ji Sato naikaku: Jūjitsu shita 3-nen kan," and "Dai 63-dai: Dai 3-ji Satō naikaku: Gekidō no 70-nendai e no hashi watashi," in *Nihon naikakushi roku*, vol. 6, pp. 101–211; Kusuda Minoru, *Shushō hishokan* (Tokyo: Bungei shunjūsha, 1975); Miyazaki Yoshimasa, *Saishō: Satō Eisaku* (Tokyo: Hara shobō, 1980).

113 See Kanamori Hisao, "Tenbō I: Kyōran dotō no naka no seichō," in *Shōwa keizai shi*, pp. 369–71; Kōsai Yutaka, "Iwato keiki," in *Shōwa keizaishi*, pp. 378–80; Iki Makoto, "Izanagi keiki," *Shōwa keizai shi*, pp. 474–7.

This succession of booms accelerated capital formation, induced massive plant and equipment investments, and vastly improved the competitive position of Japanese manufactures in international markets. By 1960 Japan's GNP had become the fifth largest among the world's market economies behind only those of the United States, West Germany, the United Kingdom, and France; by 1968, it had surpassed all but that of the United States. The economy's extraordinary growth and transformation had a far-reaching impact, not only on Japan's international status and image, but also on its domestic society and politics.

The rapid economic growth was an outcome of accelerated industrialization, which in turn was both a cause and an effect of the country's intensive urbanization. In the early 1960s a nationwide exodus of rural residents began. By the middle of the decade, numerous rural villages had been deserted, whereas urban areas, especially those around Tokyo, Osaka, and Nagoya, had begun to show signs of strain arising from overcrowding. By the end of the decade, the flow of migrants to the three largest cities had slowed down somewhat, but the flow to lesser urban centers, such as Sapporo, Sendai, Hiroshima, Fukuoka, and Kita-Kyūshū, had accelerated.[114]

Overcrowding caused an acute scarcity of space and housing in the major urban areas. This situation was exacerbated by the tendency, increasingly evident since the mid-1950s, for traditional extended families to break up into smaller nuclear families. As a result, nearly 45 percent of urban employee households were renters in the first years of the 1970s.[115] Meanwhile, the price of urban land rose rapidly. In the fifteen years between 1955 and 1970, the price index for urban residential land increased about fifteen times on the average, and in the six largest cities it increased more than twenty times.[116] To make the situation worse, the differential between the growth rate of land prices and the prevailing interest rates led the majority of urban landlords to hold on to their property as long as possible, thus adding to the already great pressure on the housing markets and pushing up the land prices still further.[117]

The effects of this rapid industrialization and urbanization affected not only the housing markets in the larger and older cities but also the

114 Nishio Masaru, "Kaso to kamitsu no seiji gyōsei," in *Nenpō seijigaku*, 1977, p. 231.

115 Keizai kikaku chō sōgō keikaku kyoku, ed., *Shotoku shisan bunpai no jittai to mondaiten: Shotoku bunpai ni kansuru kenkyūkai hōkoku* (Tokyo: Ōkurashō insatsukyoku, 1975), pp. 82–3.

116 *Kokumin seikatsu tōkei nenpō '80*, p. 135.

117 Itō Mitsuharu, *Hoshu to kakushin no Nihonteki kōzō* (Tokyo: Chikuma shobō, 1970), p. 165.

physical environments of lesser and younger urban centers. During the decade of "income doubling," the nation was gripped by a "regional development" fever as well; municipalities throughout the country competed to lure more and bigger industries with a view to balancing their chronically deficit-ridden budgets by expanding and diversifying the local sources of tax revenue. By the spring of 1969, about 90 percent of the prefectures, 60 percent of the cities, and 35 percent of the towns and villages had issued special ordinances designed to attract industries.[118] The percentage figures were considerably higher for municipalities in the least developed prefectures along the Japan Sea coast.

The industrialization of rural Japan in effect dispersed the costs, as well as the benefits, of rapid economic growth. By the middle of the decade, for most communities invaded by complexes of industrial plants and support facilities, the pollution of the air, water, and soil had become an affliction as serious and common as congestion and shrinking space.[119] The rapid spread of pollution, combined with delays in effective responses by the national and local governments, gave rise to public movements, first among those directly victimized by industry-based pollution and subsequently among growing numbers of other concerned citizens to demand compensation for damage done and to call for the closure of facilities or the halt of activities believed to be the main sources of pollution and other unwanted by-products of intensive industrialization.

Victims of organic mercury poisoning in Minamata City, Kumamoto Prefecture (Minamata disease) and their relatives were the first to organize in 1958 what became known as either a residents' movement (*jūmin undō*) or a citizens' movement (*shimin undō*). By the mid-1960s similar movements were begun by those affected by other major pollution-caused afflictions, notably asthma in Yokkaichi City, Mie Prefecture (Yokkaichi asthma), cadmium poisoning in communities along the Jintsū River in Toyama Prefecture (itai-itai disease), and mercury poisoning along the Agano River in Niigata Prefecture (Niigata Minamata disease).[120] By the early 1970s, citizens' movements had spread to many

118 Nishio, "Kaso to kamitsu," p. 209, n. 20. See also Mizuguchi Norito, "Kamitsuchi ni okeru seiji sanka: Osaka daitoshi ken o rei to shite," in *Nenpō seijigaku, 1974: Seiji sanka no riron to genjitsu*, ed. Nihon seiji gakkai (Tokyo: Iwanami shoten, 1975), p. 148.

119 While Japan's GNP grew at the average rate of 10.7 percent per year between 1960 and 1970, the quantities of sulfur dioxide and nitrogen dioxide in the air also increased at the estimated annual rate of 13.4 percent and 11.0 percent, respectively, the chemical oxygen demand (COD) loading at 12.7 percent, and the total volume of industrial waste at 13.8 percent. See Otoda Masami, "Kōgai mondai," in *Shōwa keizai shi*, p. 506.

120 For an overview of these and other cases, see Kankyō-chō, *Kankyō hakusho* (annual) (Tokyo: Ōkurashō insatsukyoku).

communities throughout the country, far beyond the circles of those directly affected by the particular pollution-related diseases. Of the approximately three thousand organizations of this type identified in 1973, most were concerned primarily with environmental issues, but about 40 percent were interested in much more general national and local policy issues, such as housing, education, public health, and inflation.[121]

The citizens' movements of the late 1960s and 1970s were as diverse in their origins and membership characteristics as in their concerns. According to a 1973 survey, about 45 percent of the citizens' movement organizations then in existence were traditional neighborhood associations of long standing, commonly called block or hamlet associations; about 15 percent were peer groups also of considerable vintage, such as women's and youth associations, parents' and teachers' associations, or artists' and writers' circles; nearly 12 percent were extensions of political parties or trade unions; and less than 30 percent were newly formed issue-oriented organizations.[122] The majority of these movements were politically conservative, concerned not with fundamental reform but with the protection or promotion of particular local interests within the limits of the existing political and economic order.[123]

Nonetheless, the growth of the citizens' movements helped focus media attention on local economic and social issues and on the role of local governments. In the areas particularly affected by the negative impact of the rapid industrialization and urbanization, citizens' movements tended to support antiestablishment candidates in prefectural and municipal elections, whether they were officially independent or endorsed by an opposition party. This support paved the way for the election of a substantial number of "progressive" governors, mayors, and city assemblypersons. When the National Association of Progressive Mayors (Zenkoku kakushin shichō kai) was formed in 1964, some 60 mayors joined it, and by 1971 the number had increased to 106.[124] Meanwhile, a "progressive," Minobe Ryōkichi, won the governorship of the Tokyo metropolitan prefecture in 1967, and another, Kuroda Ryōichi, was victorious in the second most populous prefecture,

121 *Asahi shimbun*, May 21, 1973. See also Nishio Masaru, "Gyōsei katei ni okeru taikō undō: Jūmin undō ni tsuite no ichi-kōsatsu," in *Nenpō seijigaku*, 1974, p. 75.
122 Ibid., p. 76. See also Margaret A, McKean, "Political Socialization Through Citizen's Movement," in *Political Opposition and Local Politics in Japan*, ed. Kurt Steiner, Ellis S. Krauss, and Scott C. Flanagan (Princeton, N.J.: Princeton University Press, 1980), chap. 7.
123 Nishio, "Gyōsei katei," in *Nenpō seijigaku*, 1974, pp. 80–1; Yokoyama Keiji, "Toshi saikaihatsu to shimin sanka no seidoka," *Nenpō seijigaku*, 1974, pp. 104–8.
124 Nishio, "Kaso to kamitsu," in *Nenpō seijigaku*, 1977, p. 243.

Osaka, in 1971. Ninagawa Torazō, the first elected governor of Kyoto in 1950, became the first six-term governor in the nation's history in 1970.[125]

Like the reforms of the Occupation, the "economic miracle" of the late 1950s and 1960s produced far more beneficiaries than victims. Despite the serious losses of both population and economic assets suffered by some farming communities, those who stayed on their farms managed not only to survive but also to benefit from the change. Despite the unforeseen and unwanted consequences that attended the intensive industrialization and population movements, most urban employees were economically far better off after the miracle than they had been before it. And finally, despite the recurrence of violent clashes between the LDP governments and the opposition, the nation's masses were mainly satisfied with the economic performance of the succession of conservative administrations.

### *Farmers in the era of rapid urbanization and industrialization*

During the decade and a half of intensive industrialization and urbanization, most of the nation's local communities lost population. The largest losers were those located in rural areas and heavily dependent on farming. As a result, the number of farmer households declined from 6.043 million in 1955 to 5.342 million in 1970, or by 11.6 percent over the fifteen-year period.[126] Second, the size of farmer households also declined from slightly more than 6 persons to slightly fewer than 4, reducing the total population of farmer household members by nearly 28 percent. Third, the proportion of farmer household members who actually engaged in farming, whether full time or part time, decreased from an average of 53 to 39 percent, thus reducing the total agricultural work force by about 47 percent.[127] Finally, the number of full-time farmer households, all of whose members engaged principally in farming, declined by about 60 percent. The average farmer household in 1955 had 2.7 members engaged full time in farming, but in 1970 it had only 1 such full-time

125 On Ninagawa's career and politics, see Ellis S. Krauss, "Opposition in Power: The Development and Maintenance of Leftist Government in Kyoto Prefecture," *Political Opposition*, chap. 11.

126 See Asahi shinbunsha, *Asahi nenkan*, 1966, p. 401; 1971, p. 384. See also Ōhashi Takanori, *Nihon no kaikyū kōsei* (*Iwanami shinsho*, no. 789) (Tokyo: Iwanami shoten, 1971), p. 115. In 1960, the typical Japanese rural hamlet consisted of sixty-four households, of which thirty-one, or 61 percent, were farmers'; ten years later, it consisted of eighty-one households, of which thirty-seven, or 46 percent, were farmers'. See Nishio, "Kaso to kamitsu," in *Nenpō seijigaku*, 1977, pp. 210–11.

127 *Asahi nenkan*, 1958, p. 569; 1966, p. 401; 1971, p. 384.

farmer, who was likely to be either an old man or a woman.[128] Young people, especially males, left in droves for nonfarming jobs. One out of every 4 farmers between thirty-five and thirty-nine years old in 1955 had quit farming by 1970, and 1 out of every 3 between twenty-five and twenty-nine years old did so.[129]

The rising ratio of rural households partly dependent on farming for their income to those completely dependent on such incomes predated World War II and, after a temporary halt following the Occupation's land reform, rose again after 1950. By 1955, there were already nearly twice as many households of the first type as of the second type. This trend accelerated during the next decade and a half, with the ratio changing to 3.6:1.0 in 1965 and 5.4:1.0 in 1970.[130] The average farmer household derived 71 percent of its income from farming in 1955, but only 48 percent in 1965 and 37 percent in 1970.[131] Economically as well as numerically, the typical household in the rural Japan of the early 1970s thus had two wage earners to one farmer.

The dramatic decline of agricultural population and the number of all-farmer households resulted from a combination of circumstances. The fragmentation of farmland, an unintended consequence of the postwar land reform, pushed people out of farming. According to a February 1960 survey, for example, 38 percent of the nation's farmer households owned less than 0.5 hectare of farmland, 32 percent between 0.5 and 1.0 hectare, and 25 percent between 1.0 and 2.0 hectares. In other words, about 70 percent owned less than 1.0 hectare and about 94 percent less than 2.0 hectares.[132] For the majority of farmer households, there was too little land available for farming to absorb even their own labor all year round, especially during slack seasons. The surplus of agricultural labor resulting from the fragmentation of farmland was considerably augmented in the 1960s by the rapid mechanization of farming methods. Small tractors, which had been in use since the early 1950s, became quite common by the early 1960s, and in 1962 about two-thirds of farmer households owned one.[133] At the same time, a variety of herbicides and insecticides were also introduced, further reducing the amount of human labor that could profitably be invested in farm work.

Although the small size of the farms owned by individual farmer

128 Uraki Shin'ichi, *Nihon nōmin no henkan katei* (Tokyo: Ochanomizu shobō, 1978), pp. 28–9.
129 Miyake Ichirō, "Yūkensha kōzō no hendō to senkyo," in *Nenpō seijigaku*, 1977, p. 265.
130 *Nihon kokusei zue*, 1981, p. 209.
131 Ibid., pp. 212–13; *Kokumin seikatsu tōkei nenpō '80*, p. 56.
132 *Nihon kokusei zue*, 1981, p. 208, Table 16-6.
133 Itō, *Hoshu to kakushin*, pp. 82–3.

households and the introduction of labor-saving devices acted as a powerful push behind the outflow of the agricultural work force, the expansion of industries provided an equally powerful pull. Employment opportunities in the major urban centers lured large numbers of young people away from the villages. More important, during the 1960s, numerous factories and offices were located, or relocated, in rural areas, attracted by the abundant, cheap, and pliant labor still available there and helped by the rail and highway networks that were vastly expanded during the decade.

This migration of population from rural to urban areas and the work force's shift from the agricultural to the industrial and service sectors affected the farmers' economic and social status in various ways. Many rural hamlets, particularly those in remote and hilly regions, lost most of their younger inhabitants and remained as poor as, or even poorer than, they were previously. One study shows that in 1970 the average farmer household of 4.4 members in a fairly typical agricultural prefecture, Mie, had an annual income of about ¥1.350 million and spent ¥1.055 million for living expenses and an additional ¥116,000 for taxes and other public levies. Comparable households in the more remote and hilly parts of the same prefecture, however, earned an average of only ¥948,000.[134] But the latter type of households were not typical in either Mie Prefecture or Japan as a whole. More farmer households substantially improved their standards of living in both absolute and relative terms.

In Mie Prefecture, the average farmer's real household income roughly quadrupled between 1955 and 1970.[135] At the same time, the nominal values of such a household's current assets and buildings increased twenty to twenty-five times and thirty-five to forty times, respectively. Nationwide, the change was even more dramatic: The average farmer household gained by an increase in the nominal value of its current assets from ¥282,000 in 1960 to ¥1,644,700 in 1970 and ¥3,103,000 in 1973.[136] This amounts to a 58 percent increase in ten years and a 110 percent increase in thirteen years.

Farmers' income improved as well. The average farmer household income was roughly equal to that of the average self-employed household throughout this period.[137] It was slightly less than three-quarters of the average employee household income in 1960, but it caught up

134 Uraki, *Nihon nōmin*, pp. 35, 41–2. 135 Ibid., p. 31.
136 Keizai kikaku chō, *Shotoku shisan bunpai*, p. 44.
137 See *Kokumin seikatsu tōkei nenpō '80*, p. 57.

by 1970.[138] In 1970, farmers owned per household as many amenities, such as color television sets, washing machines, and refrigerators, and more automobiles than did either white-collar or blue-collar workers.

One important cause of the farmers' growing affluence was the good prices of their staple product, rice, thanks largely to generous government subsidies. Rice distribution remained a government monopoly until 1969, but from the government's point of view, it was a consistently unprofitable operation after 1952 when the price at which the government bought rice from the farmers began to exceed the price at which the government sold it to registered rice dealers. In the early 1960s, the system became even more unprofitable, as the latter price fell below the consumer price.[139] From the rice farmers' point of view, however, this was a profitable arrangement that they naturally exploited as much and as long as they could.

Another factor contributing to the farmers' improved living standards was the dramatic increase in the market value of farmland. In Mie Prefecture, for example, the price of average-grade wet farmland doubled, and that of a comparable grade of dry farmland increased 2.2 times in the ten years between 1960 and 1970.[140] More significantly, nearly one-third of the prefecture's farmland was converted to residential and industrial use during the same period, and the value of this type of land rose three to twenty times as fast as did either wet or dry farmland. By either selling part of the farmland at the inflated price or simply holding on to it, the average farmer thus gained.

Much less obvious but no less important than the impact of the rising price of either rice or land was that of the increasing number of farmer household members who abandoned farming for off-farm jobs. The income of a typical Mie Prefecture farmer household derived from farming increased about three times in nominal terms and a little less than twice in real terms between 1955 and 1970.[141] Meanwhile, its income attributable to nonfarming employment increased eight times in nominal terms and about five times in real terms. In 1970 such a household thus earned ¥600,000 to ¥900,000 from farming and ¥1.200 million to ¥1.400 million from nonfarming employment. Interestingly, however, those households that divided their sources of income evenly between farming and nonfarming jobs, rather than

138 Nishio, "Kaso to kamitsu," in *Nenpō seijigaku,* 1977, pp. 210–11.
139 Ibid., p. 217. See also Ishida and George, "Nōkyō," in *Japan & Australia;* Donnelly, "Setting the Price of Rice," in *Policymaking in Contemporary Japan.*
140 Uraki, *Nihon nōmin,* pp. 140–1. 141 Ibid., pp. 29–30.

those that depended considerably more on one or the other type of employment, did best. To cite the Mie Prefecture study again, those households engaged exclusively in farming earned an average total of ¥1.113 million in 1970; those that depended more on nonfarming sources of income than on farming earned ¥1.236 million; and those that drew their income equally from both farming and nonfarming jobs earned ¥1.574 million.[142] In any event, how much a farmer household depended on off-farm employment income significantly affected its overall standard of living.

The diversification of employment among members of farmer households had another important, and subtle, socioeconomic impact. It tended to reduce income inequalities among the farmer households themselves. According to an Agriculture Ministry study, the farming income differential among farmer households increased nationwide between 1957 and 1973, but the differential of total farmer household income measured by the Gini coefficient slightly decreased during the same period, owing to the counterbalancing effects of income from nonfarming sources.[143] The sharp decline in the overall agricultural population and the even sharper increase in farmer households dependent on diversified sources of income which took place

142 Ibid., pp. 42–7.

143 Keizai kikaku chō, *Shotoku shisan bunpai,* pp. 28–30. The Gini coefficient is defined as the ratio of the area between the Lorenz curve and the diagonal to the total area under the diagonal. The ratio equals zero when the distribution of income is perfectly equal, that is, when the Lorenz curve overlaps the diagonal line (see diagram). Numerically, the Gini coefficient is defined as

$$G = \frac{ABC - ABCDE}{ABC} = 1 - \frac{\sum_{i=1}^{s} r_i(y_i + y_{i-1})}{10{,}000} \quad \left(s = \frac{100}{r_i}\right)$$

For explanations and discussions of the properties and limitations of the measure, see ibid., pp. 2–3; and also Richard Szal and Sherman Robinson, "Measuring Income Inequality," in *Income Distribution and Growth in the Less-Developed Countries,* ed. Charles R. Frank, Jr., and Richard C. Webb (Washington, D.C.: Brookings Institution, 1977), pp. 504–5.

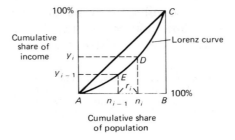

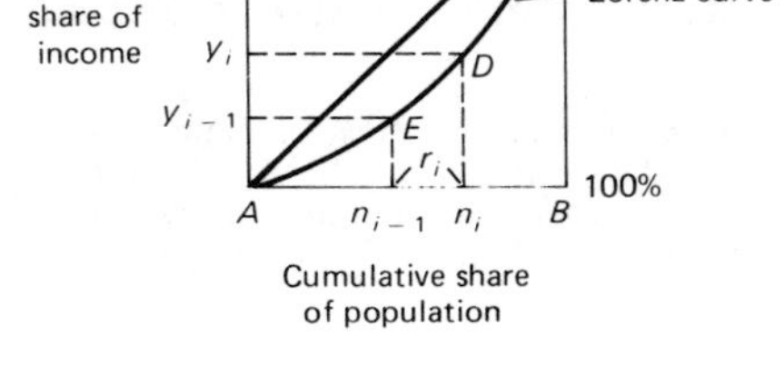

between 1957 and 1973 thus not only enriched the majority of the nation's farmers but also made its villages economically more, rather than less, homogeneous.

The farmers' growing affluence added to the financial health and political effectiveness of the agricultural cooperatives. The growing strength of cooperatives in turn helped individual farmers further improve their socioeconomic status. Agricultural cooperative unions had become the hubs of economic activity in most rural communities by the mid-1950s. During the first half of the decade, however, they were still vulnerable, for several reasons. The wartime system of government-controlled distribution of agricultural produce, under which the agricultural associations had acted as the sole authorized marketing agents, had been dismantled, except for rice, after the end of the war. This deprived postwar agricultural cooperatives of a potentially lucrative business. They also often suffered from imprudent credit sale practices, which left them with many unpaid bills and a slow inventory turnover.[144] The cooperatives' food-processing businesses, such as the production of sweet-potato starch, usually were not profitable, because of depressed market conditions. Finally, the cooperatives' generally impoverished members kept their collective assets too limited to permit much expansion or diversification of operations. But this situation changed dramatically in the early 1960s, partly because of a government-sponsored consolidation program and partly because of the increasing affluence of the cooperatives' members.

The Mie Prefecture study shows that between 1955 and 1965 the number of multifunctional cooperatives – as opposed to those specializing in the marketing of their members' produce, the bulk buying of merchandise on behalf of members and mutual funds and investment operations – declined from 400 to 145, whereas the membership of each increased from several hundred, on the average, to several thousand.[145] At the same time, virtually all the money received by members for rice sold to the government through a cooperative, as well as most of the money made by individual members selling vegetables, fruit, livestock or land, was routinely deposited in the cooperatives' accounts to be lent or invested at a profit for both the depositors and the cooperatives.[146] Until the growing criticism of the rice-price support system in the face of mounting stockpiles of unsold rice led the government in the late 1960s to curb production, the nation's farmers

144 Uraki, *Nihon nōmin*, pp. 197–206. 145 Ibid., pp. 205–6. 146 Ibid., p. 229.

and their agricultural cooperatives enjoyed unprecedented prosperity and security. And so they were bound to be a major pillar of the conservative rule during this period.

### *Urban workers and the "economic miracle"*

The majority of those who left farming during the decade and a half of extraordinary economic growth joined the swelling ranks of the urban working class. According to a 1965 survey, forty-six of every one hundred children of farmers deserted farming, and twenty-nine of them joined the blue-collar ranks.[147] Despite the increase in their numbers resulting from the massive shift in the work force, urban employees made substantial gains during this period, owing to the even faster rise in labor productivity and wages.

Real wages steadily rose at an accelerating rate, and by 1970 they were an average of 2.3 times what they were in 1955.[148] But these gains were by no means evenly distributed among all members of the working class. Day workers who depended on odd jobs found through either public or private employment agencies were, as a rule, paid the minimum wage, which was substantially lower than half of the average wage received by those regularly employed.[149] Although the number of registered day workers declined by about 45 percent during the 1960s, there were still some 300,000 of them in 1970.[150]

Numerically more important were those employed by small businesses hiring fewer than one thousand workers each, especially those hiring fewer than one hundred each. Employees of such businesses accounted for 83 and 53 percent, respectively, of the nation's wage earners in 1965.[151] With the possible exception of male workers thirty years old or younger, wages in these businesses consistently lagged behind those in larger establishments.[152] In the case of female workers fifty years of age or older, the prevailing regular monthly wages paid by businesses with eleven to one hundred employees were about 56

147 Naoi Masaru, "Sangyōka to kaisō kōzō no hendō," in *Hendōki no Nihon shakai,* ed. Akuto Hiroshi, Tominaga Ken'ichi, and Sobue Takao (Tokyo: Nihon hōsō kyōkai, 1972), p. 100.

148 Miyake, "Yūkensha kōzō," in *Nenpō seijigaku,* 1977, p. 270. See also Fujinawa, *Nihon no saitei chingin,* p. 316, Table 4-2.

149 Fujinawa, *Nihon no saitei chingin,* pp. 472–3.

150 Eguchi, *Gendai no "tei shotoku sō,"* vol. 1, p. 156.

151 *Asahi nenkan,* 1971, p. 416; Sōrifu tōkei kyoku, ed., *Nihon no tōkei,* 1976 (Tokyo: Ōkurashō insatsukyoku, 1976), p. 41.

152 The average wages paid to male employees by businesses hiring between 10 and 990 workers were slightly higher than those paid to their counterparts in businesses hiring 1,000 or more. See Fujinawa, *Nihon no saitei chingin,* p. 352.

percent of those paid by businesses hiring one thousand or more workers, and likewise, semiannual bonuses were generally about 26 percent. Low wages were thus associated with small businesses, which in the 1960s were typically found in the textile, lumber, leather- and food-processing industries, and wholesale and retail trades.[153]

As the rapid growth of the economy led to an acute labor shortage in the early 1960s, however, wages in small businesses began to rise faster than did those in larger businesses. As a result, the glaring gaps between them substantially narrowed. In 1960 in businesses hiring between 30 and 99 workers the mean wages were slightly less than 60 percent, and in those hiring between 100 and 499, the mean was slightly more than 70 percent of the mean in businesses hiring 500 or more persons. By 1970 the wages for the smaller businesses were slightly less than 70 percent and slightly more than 80 percent, respectively, of those for the larger businesses.[154]

There was another gap in wages among workers in different age groups, owing to the seniority-based pay system (*nenkō joretsu*). The average starting wage for a young secondary school graduate was a small fraction of what a veteran in his or her forties was paid after thirty years of service. This gap, too, considerably narrowed during the 1960s, for several reasons. First, the increasing shortage of labor, particularly young labor, substantially raised the younger workers' wages, as well as wage levels in small businesses in general.[155] Second, young workers tended to be hired in disproportionately larger numbers by large firms, as compared with small businesses. In 1968, for example, businesses hiring fewer than one hundred workers accounted for about 30 percent of workers in the fifteen-to-nineteen age bracket and 64 percent of those in the fifty-five-to-sixty-four age bracket, whereas businesses hiring one thousand or more workers accounted for 37 percent of the former, but only 12 percent of the latter.[156] Finally, the seniority system itself began to be modified under the pressure of increased labor costs resulting from the combination of the across-the-board rise in wages and the depletion of the once-abundant pool of young and cheap labor. As a result of these changes, the starting wages of secondary and high school graduates rose quite rapidly as the mean for all workers and seniority-based

153 Ibid., pp. 329–31.
154 *Nihon kokusei zue*, 1981, p. 423. See also Fujinawa, *Nihon no saitei chingin*, pp. 318–19; Itō, *Hoshu to kakushin*, pp. 74–5.
155 Tanaka Manabu, "Rōdōryoku chōtatsu kikō to rōshi kankei," in *Sengo kaikaku*, vol. 8: *Kaikaku go no Nihon keizai*, p. 180.
156 Ōhashi, *Nihon no kaikyū kōsei*, pp. 157–8.

differentials shrank. Between 1960 and 1970, the mean for those under twenty-five years old gained between 12 and 14 percentage points against the mean for those in their forties, who were collectively the highest paid group under the seniority system.[157]

Sex discrimination was a persistent source of wage differentials among older employees. In 1958, for example, female workers between twenty and twenty-four years of age were paid on the average about two-thirds of what their male counterparts earned, but those between forty and forty-nine years of age were paid less than one-third of what male workers in the same age bracket received.[158] During the next decade and a half, these gaps narrowed somewhat. The mean for all female workers rose from 41 percent of the mean for all male workers in 1958 to 47 percent in 1970. The proportion of female workers among the lowest paid 10 percent, however, substantially increased during the same period, from 77 percent to 87 percent.

Despite the glaring and in some respects greater inequality arising from sex discrimination, female workers staged no major revolts. One reason was custom and inertia; in most occupations, women had always been paid considerably less than men had, and they always had been discriminated against. Another reason was probably the tendency of younger and unmarried women workers to continue to live with their parents and to pay relatively little for housing and, in many cases, food; and of older and married women workers to regard their wages basically as supplements to their husbands' earnings. According to a 1971 Ministry of Labor survey, female workers consistently emphasized their life at home over their work on the job more than male workers did.[159]

In any event, the real income of worker households not only increased significantly but also became less unequal than previously, because of the reduction, though not the elimination, of the traditional sources of discrimination and inequalities. An Office of the Prime Minister study shows that the average worker household income rose from about ¥53,000 per month in 1963 to ¥113,000 in 1970, whereas the Gini coefficient fell from 0.2153 to 0.1787.[160] The trend toward greater equality was helped by the legislation of minimum wage standards. These standards were implemented initially through the mechanism of voluntary agreements among employers as provided for in the 1959 Minimum Wage Law and, after the 1968

157 See Fujinawa, *Nihon no saitei chingin*, pp. 324, 334–5. 158 Ibid., pp. 342–3.

159 Rōdō daijin kanbō tōkei jōhō bu, ed., *Nihonjin no kinrō kan* (Tokyo: Shiseidō, 1974), pp. 9, 47–51. 160 Keizai kikaku chō, *Shotoku shisan bunpai*, pp. 11–12, 19.

revision of the law, mainly through the intervention of the Central Minimum Wage Council. By the end of 1971, approximately 90 percent of the nation's industrial workers and 40 percent of employees in the wholesale and retail trades were covered by the law, which guaranteed minimum wages roughly equal to the high school graduates' starting wages.[161]

Consumer prices of key commodities and services remained remarkably stable throughout this period, despite the phenomenal rise in wages and incomes. Prices did rise sharply, however, in certain areas of the small-business sector, reflecting the growing labor costs. Between 1956 and 1970, movie tickets in Tokyo rose about 3.7 times on the average, the price of a haircut 2.7 times, admission to a public bath house 2.5 times, a newspaper subscription 2.3 times, and both rail and city bus fares doubled. On the other hand, telephone and telegraph charges remained the same; gas, water, and postage rates increased moderately by 7, 21, and 40 percent, respectively; and electricity costs actually decreased by 7.5 percent.[162]

Material comforts were made more available by means of a series of tax cuts, and income taxes were reduced in 1957, followed by cuts in inheritance and corporate taxes the next year.[163] In 1962, indirect taxes such as alcohol taxes and certain commodity taxes were substantially reduced. Sweeping across-the-board cuts were made in 1966, followed by more selective but nonetheless substantial cuts in income taxes in 1969. The combination of stable consumer prices and significant increases in disposable incomes contributed to the growing affluence among both white-collar and blue-collar workers.

Many workers experienced changes in other aspects of their lives as well. Between the two world wars, and especially since the end of World War II, the larger Japanese firms had depended heavily on the practice of guaranteeing lifetime employment (*shūshin koyō*). To retain skilled workers, these firms based their wages on length of service.[164] The lifetime employment practice largely survived the "economic miracle." First, the system applied to a relatively small number of

161 Fujinawa, *Nihon no saitei chingin*, pp. 472–3.
162 *Kokumin seikatsu tōkei nenpō '80*, p. 134. 163 Satō, *Nihon no zeikin*, pp. 24–8.
164 On the history and functions of the permanent employment and seniority-based wage systems, see Walter Galenson and Konosuke Odaka, "The Japanese Labor Market," in *Asia's New Giant: How the Japanese Economy Works*, ed. Hugh Patrick and Henry Rosovsky (Washington, D.C.: Brookings Institution, 1976), pp. 609–27. See also Yasukichi Yasuba, "The Evolution of Dualistic Wage Structure," in *Industrialization and Its Social Consequences*, ed. Hugh T. Patrick (Berkeley and Los Angeles: University of California Press, 1976), pp. 253–4; Robert E. Cole, *Japanese Blue Collar: The Changing Tradition* (Berkeley and Los Angeles: University of California Press, 1971), pp. 75–81, 113–17.

workers, perhaps no more than about 20 percent of the total in the early 1960s.[165] The generally tight labor market during the rapid economic growth also argued for the continuation, rather than the abandonment, of devices to lure and keep scarce skilled workers. The practice of basing wages principally on length of service, which roughly equaled age, however, came under increasing strain, as the diminishing supply of young workers began to push up the starting wages of secondary and high school graduates and thus indirectly the already high wages of the older employees.

In 1962 Nikkeiren called for a shift to a new system of wage determination based on skill and performance.[166] The ideas underlying the new system were imported from the United States and popularized through what was commonly called the quality control (QC) or zero defects (ZD) movement. A common practice associated with the movement was to divide workers into numerous self-regulating work teams, each with a leader appointed from among the workers themselves. The result was the emergence of a new class of workers charged with a variety of quasi-managerial duties, invested with appropriate titles, and rewarded by wage increments for their added service. According to a study made in the late 1960s, one in every five employees of Toyota Motor Company and one in every four of IBM Japan belonged to this emerging class of Japanese-style foremen.[167]

Combined with the effects of the rapidly rising worker-household incomes, this latest version of the Japanese system of management had a profound impact on the attitudes and behavior of individual workers and labor unions alike. Despite the moderate rise in worker mobility, resulting mainly from voluntary separation in an era still characterized by full employment, the system helped maintain, even strengthen in many cases, the employees' morale and loyalty to management.[168] A 1968 *Nihon keizai shinbun* survey of 1,200 male employees between twenty-five and thirty years of age, drawn from a national sample of 150 large firms, found three-quarters of the respondents generally satisfied with the current conditions of their lives.[169] A 1971 Ministry of Labor survey using a random sample of 26,058 workers found majorities in all age groups, except those in the below-twenty group, satisfied with their current jobs.[170]

165 Koji Taira, "Characteristics of Japanese Labor Markets," *Economic Development and Cultural Change* 10 (January 1962): 150–68.
166 Tanaka, "Rōdōryoku chōtatsu kikō," in *Sengo kaikaku*, vol. 8, p. 180.
167 Ōhashi, *Nihon no kaikyū kōsei*, pp. 141–5.
168 Watanuki, "Kōdo seichō," in *Nenpō seijigaku*, 1977, p. 171.
169 *Nihon keizai shinbun*, January 1, 1969.
170 Rōdō daijin kanbō, *Nihonjin no kinrō kan*, pp. 12, 54–5.

Few workers were entirely happy with their living conditions. Many were in fact unhappy with their wages or salaries. Two-thirds of those polled in the aforementioned 1971 government survey, for example, expressed dissatisfaction with their wages, and about the same number with the amount of their current savings.[171] In other words, most Japanese workers in the late 1960s and early 1970s were generally content with the improvement in their living conditions brought about by the rapid growth of the economy, but they nonetheless felt that their wages were lower than they should have been. As far as they were concerned, the primary task of a labor union was to win higher wages from management.[172]

Leaders of the major labor federations adapted, with varying degrees of success, to the increasingly evident bread-and-butter concerns of the rank and file. In the largest of the national federations, Sōhyō, the leadership passed in 1955 from the ideologue of the left, Takano, to a pair of pragmatists, Iwai Akira and Ōta Kaoru.[173] The latter introduced a wage negotiation strategy soon to be known as the "spring offensive" (*shuntō*). Annual wage negotiations between individual enterprise-based unions and employers were coordinated and directed by Sōhyō. In the 1960s the strategy became a standard operating procedure for Sōhyō and its affiliates, and it significantly contributed to the across-the-board rise in wage rates during that period.

An important reason for the success of the spring offensive strategy was the employers' generally conciliatory and cooperative attitudes. In the benign and optimistic atmosphere of the decade following the 1960 battles over the United States–Japan Mutual Security Treaty and the close of major coal mines in southern Fukuoka Prefecture, management–labor antagonisms were largely buried or papered over, and a pattern of relationships that some called "lovers' fights" (*abekku tōsō*) evolved.[174] The right-wing International Metal Federation–Japan Council, or IMF–JC, as it has been better known since its founding in 1964, advocated management–labor cooperation on the ground that labor's contribution to increased productivity, rather than strikes, would win higher wages for the workers.[175] After the mid-1960s, unions in the fastest-growing private-sector industries, such as those represented by the IMF–JC, replaced the public service employees' unions,

171 Ibid., pp. 18–19, 93–6.
172 Ibid., pp. 186, 200; Shinohara, *Gendai Nihon no bunka henyō*, p. 157.
173 Takemae, "1949-nen rōdōhō," in *Senryōki Nihon*, pp. 303–4; Tanaka, "Rōdōryoku chōtatsu kikō," in *Sengo kaikaku*, vol. 8, p. 170.
174 See Ishida, "Sengo kaikaku to soshiki," in *Sengo kaikaku*, vol. 1, p. 153.
175 Tanaka, "Rōdōryoku chōtatsu kikō," in *Sengo kaikaku*, vol. 8, p. 192.

such as those represented by Sōhyō, as the pacesetters in the spring offensive wage negotiations.

The shift of pocketbook power from public- to private-sector unions had immediate effects on the balance of power among the major labor federations. By 1973 the IMF–JC had grown into a 1.8-million-member federation of leading unions in the iron and steel and metal industries, in automobile and home appliance manufacturing, and in shipbuilding.[176] An even more formidable coalition of ideologically moderate unions was built around the All Japan Trade Union Congress (Zen Nihon rōdō kumiai kaigi: Zenrō) and its successor, the Japan Confederation of Labor (Zen Nihon rōdō sōdōmei: Dōmei), founded in 1954 and 1964, respectively. Between 1963 and 1973, Zenrō–Dōmei absorbed nearly 1 million private-sector workers, most of them defectors from the left-leaning Sōhyō, and became the nation's second-largest labor federation, with a membership of some 2.3 million, as compared with Sōhyō's 4.3 million.[177]

The "embourgeoisement" of labor and the peasantry brought about a revolution of values and attitudes among the Japanese electorate. The erosion of class consciousness and loyalty among those who had traditionally supported the opposition parties, especially the Socialists, greatly helped the LDP to dominate both national and local politics throughout this period. It was as if Japan were about to turn into a classless society of increasingly and uniformly affluent and conservative citizens.

### *The rise of a middle-class majority*

Between 1955 and 1970, the proportion of farmers in the nation's total work force declined from about 40 percent to 19 percent, and there was a corresponding rise in the proportion of the urban white-collar and blue-collar workers, from 42 to 60 percent.[178] The rapid improvement and equalization of living standards for farmers and workers thus meant similar changes for most Japanese.

But neither poverty nor inequality was entirely eliminated. As late as 1972, more than a third of the households in a Tokyo ward were found to have incomes below the poverty line established by the Livelihood Protection Law (¥771,000 for a household of four).[179] The inci-

176 Takabatake Michitoshi, "Taishū undō no tayōka to henshitsu," in *Nenpō seijigaku*, 1977, pp. 349–50.

177 Ibid., pp. 344, 349–50; Watanuki, "Kōdo seichō," in *Nenpō seijigaku*, 1977, pp. 170–1. See also Ōhara shakai mondai kenkyūjo, *Nihon rōdō nenkan*, vol. 50 (Tokyo: Rōdō junpōsha, 1979), p. 177.

178 Eguchi, *Gendai no "tei shotoku sō,"* vol. 3, pp. 488–9.

179 Ibid., vol. 1, pp. 55–7.

dence of poverty thus defined was particularly high among households either headed by those under twenty years old or over seventy years old, or consisting of single old men, women, or couples.[180] In fact, the number of households receiving public assistance increased somewhat between 1960 and 1970, as did the number of households without an employed member.[181] In the late 1960s and 1970s, however, the amounts of assistance provided under the Livelihood Protection Law increased faster than did consumer prices. The development of social security and tax-supported pension plans further helped alleviate the plight of the poor, especially single parents and the aged.[182] By the end of this period, absolute poverty, as opposed to relative poverty, had been largely eliminated.

Occupation-based income differentials remained significant but steadily diminished. An important reason was the increasing homogeneity in young job seekers' level of education, which was clearly a major determinant of their occupation.[183] Educational background as a determinant of occupational career and income gradually lost much of its importance as the number of those who went to high school and college rapidly increased. Whereas only slightly over half of the graduates of secondary schools entered high school in 1955, nearly 90 percent did so in 1973; the proportion of high school graduates who entered colleges and universities rose from less than 5 percent to over 30 percent in the same period.[184] The rapid rise in the wage rates of younger workers, noted in the preceding section, reduced education-based income differentials to the rather negligible levels of 1.0:1.6 between primary school and college graduates and 1.0:1.1 between high school and college graduates.[185]

In 1955, the highest incomes were earned by those holding managerial, sales, specialist, and clerical jobs, in that order, and the lowest incomes were earned by farmers and unskilled, skilled, and semi-skilled workers, also in that order.[186] The mean income of managerial

180 Ibid., no. 1, pp. 72–3, 77. 181 Keizai kikaku chō, *Shotoku shisan bunpai*, pp. 163–6.

182 Ibid., pp. 154, 157; Keizai kikaku chō, ed., *Kokumin seikatsu hakusho: Shōwa 54-nen ban* (Tokyo: Ōkurashō insatsu kyoku, 1979), p. 164.

183 According to a 1975 study, for example, 1 percent of primary and secondary school graduates, 7 percent of high school graduates, and 34 percent of college and university graduates held managerial or specialist jobs, whereas 54 percent, 41 percent, and 15 percent of each category of graduates were manual workers, and 33 percent, 11 percent, and 1 percent, respectively, were farmers. See Imada Takatoshi and Hara Junsuke, "Shakaiteki chii no ikkansei to hi-ikkansei," in *Nihon no kaisō kōzō*, ed. Tominaga Ken'ichi (Tokyo: Tōkyō daigaku shuppankai, 1979), pp. 184, 191–4.

184 Imada Sachiko, "Gakureki kōzō no suisei bunseki," in *Nihon no kaisō kōzō*, p. 133; *Asahi nenkan*, 1977, p. 598.

185 Tominaga Ken'ichi, "Shakai kaisō to shakai idō no suisei bunseki," in *Nihon no kaisō kōzō*, pp. 50–1. 186 Ibid., pp. 43–4; *Kokumin seikatsu hakusho*, 1977, pp. 124–37.

personnel was about four times higher than that of farmers. For the next twenty years, managers stayed at the top of the scale, and farmers exchanged their place at the bottom with unskilled workers. However, managers' mean income grew only 7.2 times during the decade, whereas farmers' and unskilled workers' incomes grew 13.8 and 12.0 times, respectively. As a result, the mean income of managers was only 2.3 times that of unskilled workers in 1975.[187] By the late 1960s, income distribution in Japan thus looked similar to that in the United Kingdom and somewhat more equal than that in West Germany.[188]

Along with incomes, household savings both increased and equalized during the 1960s. The relatively higher rate of savings among the poor reflected the perceived inadequacies in the social security and publicly supported welfare programs. According to a 1961 national survey, one-third of the respondents saved mainly in order to cope with such contingencies as family illnesses, another third to pay for their children's education, and nearly 10 percent to support themselves in their old age.[189] The sharp rise in the household incomes of the poor in the 1960s thus enabled them to save considerably more than could the poor of the 1940s and 1950s.

All the while, the distribution of fixed assets, as opposed to income and savings, remained wildly unequal. The deliberately low capital gains tax rate in effect between 1970 and 1975 for the sale of land owned by the seller for five or more years (the rate was set at 10 percent for 1970–1 and rose to 15 percent in 1972–3, and 20 percent in 1974–5) helped perpetuate, if not aggravate, the remaining inequalities in income distribution.[190]

These inequalities, however, were apparently not conspicuous enough to nurture class consciousness among the majority of the nation's farmers or workers. According to one estimate, those identifying themselves as middle class increased from 37 percent in 1958 to 61 percent in 1973. If one includes those who preferred to call themselves either lower-middle or upper-middle class, the percentage figure reached 90 percent by 1970.[191] Most, if not all, of the self-

187 The Gini coefficient for all households declined substantially during the 1960s and the first two years of the 1970s, from 0.3236 in 1961 to 0.2705 in 1972, although it rose to 0.2736 and even higher in the mid-1970s. See *Kokumin seikatsu hakusho*, 1979, p. 145.

188 Keizai kikaku chō, *Shotoku shisan bunpai*, pp. 33–6.

189 Shinohara, *Gendai nihon no bunka henyō*, pp. 54–5. See also Mita Munesuke's comments in *Asahi shimbun*, February 25, 1969.

190 Satō, *Nihon no zeikin*, p. 28.

191 Miyake, "Yūkensha kōzō," in *Nenpō seijigaku*, 1977, p. 270. See also Takabatake, "Taishū undō," in *Nenpō seijigaku*, 1977, p. 342; and Naoi Michiko, "Kaisō ishiki to kaikyū ishiki," in *Nihon no kaisō kōzō*, p. 376.

identified members of this expansive middle class were presumably satisfied with the present state of affairs.

### *Values, party identification, and electoral outcomes*

Satisfaction with the material conditions of life cut across party, generational, and occupational lines. At the end of this period, 80 percent of the LDP supporters, 75 percent of the JSP and DSP, 70 percent of the CGP, and 65 percent of the JCP supporters were satisfied with the current conditions of their lives.[192] Economic issues were thus less important to both the general electorate and the political parties. Prosperity and affluence, as represented by the rapid increases in household savings, made the Japanese considerably more conservative in the 1960s and early 1970s than they had been during the Occupation and early post-Occupation period.[193] Asked in a 1960 poll to name the nation's single most important goal, twice as many respondents in metropolitan Tokyo named peace as those who named the well-being of their own family, and the latter outnumbered by two to one those who named any other goal.[194] Of the respondents in rural Hitachiōta, only slightly fewer mentioned peace, whereas substantially more, but far fewer than the peace advocates, mentioned family well-being. In that same year, government efforts to persuade the Diet to ratify the revised United States–Japan Mutual Security Treaty touched off a series of protest rallies and demonstrations, not because the public had suddenly become revolutionary or anti-American, but because many thought that the government efforts threatened the peace or the democratic rules of government or both.[195]

The rise of middle-class conservatism, however, did not lead to an end of ideology. Throughout this period, conflicts over fundamental values and commitments continued to divide both the electorate and the parties. According to a 1973 survey, 27 and 20 percent of those who identified with the LDP and DSP unequivocally supported capitalism, whereas only 5 and 10 percent of those who identified with the JCP and CGP did so.[196] On the other hand, 69, 60, and 51 percent of

192 Kazama Daiji, "Chūnensō no shiji-seitō betsu seikatsu ishiki," in *Nihonjin kenkyū*, no. 2: *Tokushū: Shiji-seitō betsu nihonjin shūdan*, ed. Nihonjin kenkyūkai (Tokyo: Shiseidō, 1975), p. 146.
193 Mita Munesuke, *Gendai Nihon no shinjō to ronri* (Tokyo: Chikuma shobō, 1971), p. 139.
194 Shinohara, *Gendai Nihon no bunka henyō*, p. 72.
195 See Seki, "Taigai kankei," in *Nenpō seijigaku*, 1977, p. 105; Takabatake, "Taishū undō," in *Nenpō seijigaku*, 1977, pp. 335–6.
196 Hayashi Chikio, "Nihonjin no ishiki wa seitō-shiji betsu ni dō chigau ka," in *Nihonjin kenkyū*, no. 2, pp. 40–7.

the CGP, LDP, and DSP supporters opposed communism, but only 9 and 37 percent of the JCP and JSP supporters did so. Few supporters of any party opposed "democracy," but the term meant different things to the different groups. To the LDP and DSP supporters, it was incompatible with both socialism and communism; to CGP supporters, it was compatible with socialism but not with communism; to JCP supporters, it was compatible with both socialism and communism; and finally, to JSP supporters, it was neither clearly compatible nor clearly incompatible with either ideology. Similarly, in the late 1960s, LDP and DSP supporters preferred the United States to both the Soviet Union and the People's Republic of China by a wide margin, whereas JSP and JCP supporters preferred the Soviet Union and China to the United States by an equally wide margin.[197] Two-thirds of middle-aged LDP supporters and substantial majorities among CGP and DSP supporters had respect for and generally favorable feelings toward the emperor, whereas only about half of JSP and less than one-third of JCP supporters shared such feelings.[198]

Opinion was divided along party lines particularly on issues of equality, both among nations or within Japanese society. Among LDP supporters those who believed that absolute equality is unattainable, if not undesirable, far outnumbered those who did not believe this, but the opposite was true among JSP, CGP, and, especially, JCP supporters.[199] Those LDP and CGP supporters who held the view that the Japanese were racially superior to other peoples outnumbered those who rejected such a view, but among JSP and JCP supporters those who rejected the racist view outnumbered those who upheld it. CGP, LDP, DSP, and JSP supporters overwhelmingly approved, but JCP supporters opposed, the views that women should take their husbands' family names and that after children are born, they should mind the home rather than hold jobs.[200] Both LDP and DSP supporters supported the legalization of prostitution, whereas JSP, CGP, and JCP supporters opposed such a move.[201]

Values and party identification were related to such variables as age, sex, education, occupation, and place of residence. Throughout this period, substantially and consistently higher percentages of those in their fifties preferred the LDP than did those in their twenties,

197 Karube Kiyoshi, "Nihonjin wa donoyō ni shite shiji-seitō o kimeru ka," in *Nihonjin kenkyū*, no. 2, pp. 82–3. See also Hayashi, "Nihonjin no ishiki," in *Nihonjin kenkyū*, no. 2, pp. 14–27.
198 Kazama, "Chūnensō," in *Nihonjin kenkyū*, no. 2, p. 145.
199 Karube, "Nihonjin wa donoyō ni," in *Nihonjin kenkyū*, no. 2, pp. 82–3.
200 Kazama, "Chūnensō," in *Nihonjin kenkyū*, no. 2, p. 132.
201 Karube, "Nihonjin wa donoyō ni," in *Nihonjin kenkyū*, no. 2, pp. 82–3.

whereas substantially higher percentages of those in their twenties consistently preferred the opposition parties than did those in their fifties.[202] Each party was thus identified with particular segments of the electorate. The LDP was favored by older male employers, the self-employed, and farmers.[203] The JSP, on the other hand, was predominantly a party of urban employees under forty years old with either high school or college diplomas.[204] The DSP, CGP, and JCP all drew most of their electoral support from the major urban centers, but their popularity was most stable, respectively, among male white-collar, female blue-collar, and younger blue- and white-collar voters of both sexes.[205] CGP supporters were mainly primary and secondary school graduates, whereas JCP supporters were much better educated.

Between the late 1950s and early 1970s, the voter turnout in rural areas remained consistently higher than that in urban areas.[206] However, electoral behavior changed in other respects. At the beginning of this period, turnout was substantially higher among male voters than among female voters, and slightly higher among younger and better-educated voters than among older and less-educated voters. By the end of this period, the male–female difference had disappeared, and the turnout among older and less-educated voters had surpassed that among younger and better-educated voters. This trend benefited the LDP and hurt the opposition, especially the JSP.

Radio and especially television became important influences in the 1960 general elections, when the major private networks for the first time gave the candidates time for campaign commercials.[207] NHK followed suit a year later by starting a one-hour program called "Meeting the Prime Minister." TV commercials with candidates' pictures and brief summaries of their curricula vitae became a standard election-time program after 1963, and longer and more elaborate campaign speeches began to be telecast after 1969.[208] The influence of the audiovisual media on voters' decisions was hard to measure but was

202 Miyake, "Yūkensha kōzō," in *Nenpō seijigaku*, 1977, p. 280. See also Kazama, "Chūnensō," in *Nihonjin kenkyū*, no. 2, p. 130.

203 NHK hōsō yoron chōsajo, ed., *Gendai nihonjin no ishiki kōzō* (*NHK Books*, no. 344) (Tokyo: Nihon hōsō shuppan kyōkai, 1979), pp. 228–9. See also Miyake, "Yūkensha kōzō," in *Nenpō seijigaku*, 1977, pp. 266–9; Kazama, "Chūnensō," in *Nihonjin kenkyū*, no. 2, p. 130; Asahi shinbunsha yoron chōsa shitsu, ed., *Asahi shinbun yoron chōsa no 30-nen: Nihonjin no seiji ishiki* (Tokyo: Asahi shinbunsha, 1976), pp. 8–9, 76–8.

204 *Asahi shinbun yoron chōsa*, p. 83. 205 Ibid., p. 13.

206 Miyake, "Yūkensha kōzō," in *Nenpō seijingaku*, 1977, pp. 288–9. See also Shinohara, *Gendai Nihon no bunka henyō*, pp. 140–1.

207 Uchikawa Yoshimi, "Masukomi jidai no tenkai to seiji katei," in *Nenpō seijigaku*, 1977, pp. 313–14. 208 Ibid., p. 319; Miyake, "Yūkensha kōzō," in *Nenpō seijigaku*, 1977, p. 293.

probably significant, considering that television set ownership increased from less than 1 percent of the nation's households in 1955 to over 90 percent in 1973.[209]

Considerably more obvious was the effective mobilization of constituents through a network of local campaign machines. LDP politicians were the first to try to build personal campaign machines (*kōenkai* or support associations), soon after the party was founded in the mid-1950s. By the early 1960s, such groups had grown to constitute a shadow party of over 10 million members, whereas the membership of the LDP itself remained no more than a few hundred thousand.[210] In each election district, votes were garnered and delivered to particular LDP candidates by *kōenkai,* often led by local politicians, such as prefectural and city assemblymen, and supported by major interest groups in the area. Politicians in other parties began to emulate the LDP's example, but with less successful results.

The LDP was helped by its image as the main force behind the economic miracle, thanks to the consistently progrowth policies pursued by the succession of conservative cabinets. The party was helped also by the ineptitude and lack of credibility of the opposition parties, especially the JSP.

In a 1959 poll, only about 12 percent of the respondents expected the Socialists ever to come to power in the foreseeable future.[211] In the wake of the unsuccessful 1960 campaign against the ratification of the new United States–Japan Mutual Security Treaty, the JSP lost to the LDP substantial numbers of its supporters, particularly among the young.[212] For the first time, more voters in their twenties supported the LDP than the JSP. Moreover, the decline of the JSP's popularity was most conspicuous among organized labor. Between 1960 and 1969, the members of Sōhyō-affiliated unions who supported the party fell from 72 to 39 percent, whereas the percentage of those who did not support any party increased from 14 to 39 percent.[213] According to a 1967 study by Sōhyō's own research department, less than a quarter of its rank and file supported and looked forward to the arrival of socialism. The remain-

209 Ichikawa, "Masukomi jidai," in *Nenpō seijigaku,* 1977, p. 304; *Nihon no tōkei,* 1966, p. 304.

210 Miyake, "Yūkensha kōzō," in *Nenpō seijigaku,* 1977, p. 295. See also Gerald L. Curtis, *Election Campaigning Japanese Style* (New York: Columbia University Press, 1971), chap. 5; Nathaniel B. Thayer, *How the Conservatives Rule Japan* (Princeton, N.J.: Princeton University Press, 1969), chap. 4.

211 Shinohara, *Gendai Nihon no bunka henyō,* p. 33.

212 *Asahi shimbun yoron chōsa,* p. 18; Hayashi Chikio, "Sengo no seiji ishiki," in *Jiyū* (January 1964): 57–65.

213 Watanuki, "Kōdo seichō," in *Nenpō seijigaku,* 1977, p. 171. See also Miyake, "Yūkensha kōzō," in *Nenpō seijigaku,* 1977, p. 296; and Takabatake, "Taishū undō," in *Nenpō seijigaku,* 1977, p. 349.

ing three-quarters either preferred the existing system of capitalism or wanted to see only a partial and gradual reform of it.[214] Unsurprisingly, the JSP's membership stagnated at about 50,000 until the late 1960s and then began to slip until it was reduced to about 37,000 in 1973. The JSP's share of the vote and its number of seats in the House of Representatives general elections both steadily dropped from 33 percent and 166 seats in 1958 to 22 percent and 118 seats in 1972.[215]

Of the three lesser parties, the DSP did not make much headway in either formal membership or broader electoral support, despite the significant gains made by the party's main source of support, the Dōmei-affiliated unions. The party claimed to have 70,000 members after its split from the JSP at the end of 1959, but it apparently lost half of them by 1973.[216] The party won 7.7 percent of the vote and thirty-one seats in the 1969 House of Representatives elections, its best electoral performance of this period, but it suffered a disastrous defeat in the next general elections of 1972 when it won only nineteen seats with 6.9 percent of the vote. The party's ambiguous ideological and programmatic commitments appear to have been the main cause of its trouble. During the first decade of its existence, the party became increasingly indistinguishable from the LDP in its platform and legislative performance.[217]

The CGP and the JCP both did considerably better. The CGP advertised a membership of one-half million in 1964 when the party contested the House of Councilors election for the first time, but by 1973 the number had fallen to 160,000, mainly owing to the party's nominal "separation" and independence from the parent organization, the Sōkagakkai, in 1970.[218] Despite the dip in formal membership, however, the party retained its virtual monopoly of Sōkagakkai members' votes, which swelled to several million in the early 1970s.[219] As a result, the CGP managed to avoid falling to the bottom of the heap, and it was able to maintain its minor-opposition status, even after the 1970 public severance of its umbilical cord.

214 Takabatake, "Taishū undō," in *Nenpō seijigaku*, 1977, p. 340, n. 9.

215 *Naigai senkyo dēta ('78 Mainichi nenkan bessatsu)* (Tokyo: Mainichi shinbunsha, 1978), pp. 2–7; *Asahi nenkan*, 1974, p. 259; Jiji tsūshinsha, *Jiji nenkan*, 1958 (Tokyo: Jiji tsūshinsha, 1958), p. 149; Nakano Tatsuo and Iizuka Shigetarō, *Nihon o ugokasu soshiki: Shakaitō minshatō* (*Nihon o ugokasu soshiki series*) (Tokyo: Sekkasha, 1968), pp. 64–7.

216 *Jiji nenkan*, 1961, p. 58; *Asahi nenkan*, 1974, p. 263.

217 For relevant comments, see Taketsugu Tsurutani, *Political Change in Japan* (New York: McKay, 1977), pp. 164–8.

218 *Asahi nenkan*, 1966, p. 297; 1974, p. 262.

219 The Sōkagakkai itself claimed a membership of over 15 million. See Tsurutani, *Political Change*, p. 153. But precise figures are not available. For an excellent discussion of the problems in estimating the organization's membership, see James W. White, *The Sōkagakkai and Mass Society* (Stanford, Calif.: Stanford University Press, 1970), pp. 57–61.

The JCP was a marginal party in 1955, with two of its members sitting in the House of Representatives and polling about 2 percent of the vote in the general elections of that year. By 1973, however, it had established itself as a respectable minor-opposition party, with thirty-eight seats in the House of Representatives and about 10 percent of the vote among the nation's electorate under its control. The party's achievement was all the more impressive considering that alone among the several Japanese parties of this period, it relied for its electoral success more or less exclusively on the vote and work of its own membership. In 1955 the JCP had no more than about 20,000 members, but by 1973 that figure had grown to over 300,000.[220] In the early 1970s the JCP was an equal of the LDP rather than of any other opposition party in terms of both membership and campaign funds at its disposal. These remarkable gains resulted largely from the skillful and effective adaptation of the party's platform and policies to socioeconomic changes. The party transformed itself from an inveterate opponent into an outspoken defender of the existing constitutional order.

In the face of these developments, the "two-party" system of 1955 changed into a "quasi-multiparty" system. The LDP ceased to be a majority party in terms of its share of the vote in the 1967 House of Representatives elections, and it lost its majority position in the House of Councilors in 1971. The party nonetheless remained a majority party in the House of Representatives throughout this period, partly because of the retention of the outdated electoral boundaries originally drawn in 1947, which grossly overrepresented rural constituents at the expense of their urban counterparts, and partly because of the party's recruitment of successful independent candidates after each election.[221] More important, generalized public support for the LDP remained virtually unchanged from 1955 to 1973, probably because o the favorable socioeconomic climate and the increasing fragmentatior of the opposition. In a series of *Asahi shinbun* polls, support for th LDP hovered around 45 percent and for the opposition as a whole few percentage points lower.[222] Whenever the LDP's popularity tool

220 See Haruhiro Fukui, "The Japanese Communist Party: The Miyamoto Line and Its Prob lems," in *The Many Faces of Communism*, ed. Morton A. Kaplan (New York: Free Pres 1978), p. 284.

221 J. A. A. Stockwin, *Japan: Divided Politics in a Growth Economy* (New York: Norton, 1975 pp. 91–6. See also Scott C. Flanagan, "Electoral Change in Japan: An Overview," in *Politic Opposition*, ed. Steiner et al., pp. 45–7.

222 *Asahi shinbun yoron chōsa*, pp. 13–14.

a sharp dip, as it did in the spring of 1960 during the last days of Kishi's government and in late 1971 and early 1972 during the last months of Sato's, a change of prime ministers reversed the trend and restored the balance. In the early 1970s, the one-party-dominated multiparty system had yet to face a real crisis.

# PART II

# EXTERNAL RELATIONS

# CHAPTER 5

# THE JAPANESE COLONIAL EMPIRE, 1895–1945

## CIRCUMSTANCES AND MOTIVATIONS

Japan's rise as a colonial power stands as an anomaly in the history of modern imperialism, one that can be understood only in the context of Japan's historical and geographic circumstances and the world events in the latter half of the nineteenth century. Launched in the high noon of the "new imperialism," the Japanese colonial empire[1] was to a large extent formally patterned after the tropical empires of modern Europe. Yet, as the only non-Western imperium of modern times, Japan's overseas empire stood apart from its European counterparts, its circumstances scarcely duplicated elsewhere.[2]

The first and most arresting aspect of the Japanese empire is the fact that the metropolitan homeland itself only narrowly escaped colonial subjugation, surviving as one of the four Asian nations (along with China, Siam, and Korea) to escape obliteration in the flood of Western dominance in the nineteenth century. As it was, Japan's emergence as a colonial power in the late 1890s came just as the nation was extricating itself from the unequal treaty system imposed three decades earlier by the Western powers. The reasons for this remarkable phenomenon – the pull of other Asian opportunities on aggressive Western energies at mid-century and the revolutionary transformation of Japan from a weak, feudal, and agrarian country into a modern industrial power economically and militarily capable of resisting foreign domination – have been so extensively explored in this and other histories that they

1 I shall deal here with only the formal colonial empire, that is, with the territories acquired by Japan before 1931 through cession by treaties given the sanction of international recognition. I shall thus set aside the informal imperialism in China and Manchuria, including the Japanese settlements, concessions, and railway "zones" in those countries, as well as the Japanese conquests in China, Southeast Asia, and the southwest Pacific from 1937 to 1945. Yet, as I shall argue, these outer spheres of interest and unassimilated wartime conquests became the consequence, the justification, and the eventual undoing of the inner formal colonial empire.

2 To date, the best comprehensive treatment of the Japanese colonial empire in English is *The Japanese Colonial Empire, 1895–1945*, ed. Ramon H. Myers and Mark R. Peattie (Princeton: Princeton University Press, 1984).

need no repetition here. What does require reemphasis is that both historical timing and an overriding concern for national security were basic to the initial direction of Japanese expansion.

Sealed up during 250 years of self-imposed isolation, Japan had been a passive spectator to the advance of Western power in Asia and, by the time of its emergence as a colonial power, had lost the opportunity to preempt a dominant position on the Asian continent or in the Pacific. Moreover, the struggling nation's limited political, economic, and military resources did not permit it the luxury of staking a claim to more distant regions of the globe, even if the Meiji leadership had been so inclined. Thus, in establishing a colonial empire, Japan was obliged to assert claims over neighboring areas close to the home islands where it could maximize its political, military, and economic strength. In climate and geography the Japanese colonial empire – Karafuto (the Japanese-held southern half of the island of Sakhalin below the fiftieth parallel), the Kwantung Leased Territory (the Japanese leasehold on the Liaotung peninsula), Korea, Taiwan, and the Nan'yō (the Japanese designation of its mandate over the former islands of Micronesia) – stretched from pine to palm. Yet, except for its island possessions in the south Pacific, it was a fairly compact empire, composed of territories at no great distance from the mother country (see Map 5.1). Thus, even though Japan was an island nation and its colonial possessions lay literally overseas, the thrust, and ultimately the purpose, of its empire was both region and continent directed.

The overriding Meiji concern for Japan's insular security also served to circumscribe the empire's location and dimensions. No colonial empire of modern times was as clearly shaped by strategic considerations, a fact demonstrated by the processes through which the empire's individual components were acquired. Many of the overseas possessions of Western Europe had been acquired in response to the activities of traders, adventurers, missionaries, or soldiers acting far beyond the limits of European interest or authority. In contrast, Japan's colonial territories, (with the possible exception of Taiwan), were, in each instance, obtained as the result of a deliberate decision by responsible authorities in the central government to use force in securing a territory that would contribute to Japan's immediate strategic interests. Largely continental in dimension, these interests, directed initially toward Korea, China, and Manchuria, were more akin to the traditional link that Britain drew between its own security and that of the Lowlands across the English Channel than they were to the advantages sought and enjoyed by Europeans on more distant shores.

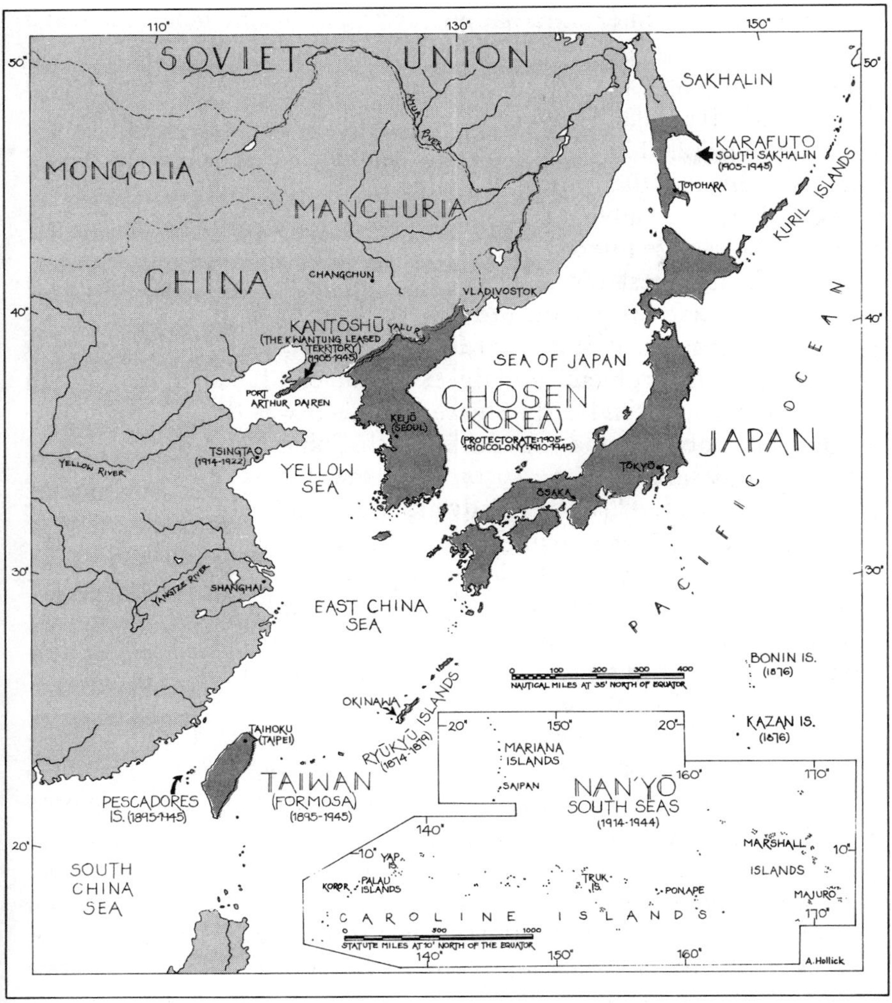


Map 5.1. The Japanese colonial empire, 1895–1945.

But if strategic security was the initial rationale for obtaining control over adjacent island territories and continental buffer zones on the way to creating a near-at-hand formal empire, the same rationale made it impossible to give finite limits to Japan's imperial ambitions even after it had assembled its formal empire. As early as the 1880s, even before Japan had launched a bid for empire, Yamagata Aritomo's famous dicta on the compass of Japan's strategic concerns spoke of concentric circles of national interest radiating outward from the home islands: a "cordon of sovereignty," encompassing territory related to the nation's survival and thus under direct and formal occupation, and a "cordon of advantage," seen as necessary to protect and guarantee the inner line.[3] Implied in this doctrine was the necessity of preserving the outer line through the control of buffer zones. Once those had become areas of Japanese "advantage," territories still farther distant became matters of Japanese interest.

Thus, in its quest for security, the empire became involved in a series of strategic "problems" that were to torment Japan's domestic politics and imperil its foreign relations: In the early Meiji period it was the "Korean problem" and the extension of a Japanese foothold in Asia; in the Taishō and early Shōwa periods it was the "Manchurian-Mongolian problem" and the conflict with Chinese and Russian interests in northeast Asia; in the 1930s it was the "China problem"; and in the 1940s it was the "southern advance problem" which involved the fatal extension of Japanese interests toward the Western colonial territories of Southeast Asia. The inner logic of Japan's strategic doctrine thus committed the empire to ever-expanding and ever-receding security goals, each colonial acquisition being seen as a "base" or "outpost" from which the empire could, in some way, control a sphere of influence over more distant areas.[4]

The regional dimensions of Japan's empire created its own singularities. Because of its Asian provenance, its largest, most populous, and most important territories, Taiwan and Korea, were not empty stretches settled thinly by ethnic groups profoundly different from the Japanese in racial origins or cultural traditions but were well-populated countries, whose peoples were racially related to their Japanese conquerors, with whom they also shared a common cultural heritage.

This sense of cultural affinity with its subject peoples, unique among the imperia of modern times, not only shaped the Japanese attitudes toward colonial governance once the empire was assembled but also played at least a peripheral role in the creation of the empire. Although Meiji Japan lacked a missionary spirit akin to Christian evangelism, a sense of idealism related to the "uplifting" of less fortu-

3 Marius B. Jansen, "Modernization and Foreign Policy in Meiji Japan," in *Political Development in Modern Japan*, ed. Robert Ward (Princeton, N.J.: Princeton University Press, 1968), p. 182.

4 Yamabe Kentarō, "Nihon teikokushugi to shokuminchi," in *Iwanami kōza Nihon rekishi*, vol. 19 (Tokyo: Iwanami shoten, 1963), pp. 207–8.

nate Asian neighbors was part of the imperial motivations of late nineteenth-century Japan. The political and social reformism of the Meiji liberal movement found an outlet for its energies and frustrations on the Asian continent and fired some Meiji activists with dreams of transforming corrupted and decaying Asian civilizations through reform, visions that they sought to realize through their own efforts. Individual propagandists for imperial expansion in late Meiji could speak of a Japanese "mission," as did the journalist Tokutomi Sohō when he declared in 1895 that it was Japan's obligation to "extend the blessings of political organization throughout the rest of East Asia and the South Pacific, just as the Romans had once done for Europe and the Mediterranean."[5] But an officially sponsored sense of national destiny to inspire reform from above and to guide backward Asian peoples along the path of modernity pioneered by Japan did not appear until the early twentieth century, when the formal empire was already in place.

There were lesser motivations for empire, of course. The elements of adventure and excitement inherent in the prospect of overseas activity after centuries of national isolation and inertia spurred individual Japanese like Fukushima Yasumasa, Hattori Toru, and Taguchi Ukichi to lone exploits on the Asian continent or peregrinations in the South Seas.[6] Accounts of such activities helped quicken the imagination of the reading public about Japanese courage and vigor on far frontiers. But the flag seldom followed the wanderings of these adventurers, and even their literary impact was muted, for Japan produced no Rudyard Kipling or George Henty to turn the romantic view of empire building into a national mystique.

Yet, if idealism and romanticism did not greatly promote the emergence of Japan as a colonial power, new perceptions of Japanese rank and status certainly did. In part this was due to the Japanese abandonment of the harmonies of the Sino-centric cultural order for the strident doctrines of inevitable international struggle trumpeted by the social Darwinism of the day. It was also due to a quick acceptance by Japan of the Western indicators of prowess and prestige that measured a nation's progress in a new and dangerous world. Among those,

5 Quoted in Kenneth Pyle, *The New Generation in Meiji Japan: Problems in Cultural Identity, 1885–1895* (Stanford, Calif.: Stanford University Press, 1969), p. 181.

6 See for example, Hanzawa Hiroshi, *Ajia e no yume* (Tokyo: San'ichi shobō, 1970); Kaneko Tamio, *Chūō Ajia ni haitta Nihonjin* (Tokyo: Shinjimbutsu ōraisha, 1973); and Yano Tōru, *Nihon no Nan'yō shikan* (Tokyo: Chūō shinsho, 1979).

colonial empires, along with constitutional government, industrialization, national bureaucracies, and modern armies and navies, were seen as hallmarks of national progress and vitality and, more important, international power.

Historical timing also set the Japanese empire apart from its European counterparts in the matter of economic interests. Economic explanations of the European "new imperialism" in the late nineteenth century emphasize the dominating financial interests of the capitalist class, the persistent congestion of capital in domestic manufacturing, and the consequent need to open up new markets and new investment opportunities in foreign lands. Japanese imperial expansion, however, began before the nation's industrial growth, and a shortage, not an excess, of capital was one of Japan's main economic problems in the 1890s. Moreover, it is not apparent that the acquisition of Japanese colonial territories derived from the schemes of bankers or merchants "manipulating" the Meiji leadership. Nor was any colonial territory acquired to protect an already flourishing economic interest there. Indeed, the Japanese government, like that of late nineteenth-century Germany, had difficulty in luring domestic capital into colonial investment at the outset of its imperial venture.[7]

Although the classic Leninist argument that imperialism is the full-blown and dying stage of the capitalist system thus seems unworkable in the Japanese case, much modern Japanese scholarship has attempted, with varying degrees of success, to qualify and refine that approach. In the process, related explanations have been offered to substitute for the workings of surplus private capital, including the development of "state capitalism," the politics of an "absolutist emperor system" controlled by an "imperialist bourgeoisie" and "parasitic landlords," as well as the aggressive designs of the military and bureaucracy in Japan that supposedly provided the impetus behind Japan's initial imperialist venture.[8] Whatever one may think of the logic of these various explanations, they do not buttress the idea that the profit motive was the central engine behind Japan's drive to extend its influence onto the Asian continent.

7 To date, the most persuasive critique in English of the primacy of economic interests in the initial stages of Japanese imperialism is the ninth chapter of Hilary Conroy's *The Japanese Seizure of Korea, 1868–1910* (Philadelphia: University of Pennsylvania Press, 1960), pp. 442–91.

8 See, for example, Shōichi Fujii, "Capitalism, International Politics, and the Emperor System," in *The Emergence of Imperial Japan: Self-Defense or Calculated Aggression?* ed. Marlene Mayo (Lexington, Mass.: Heath, 1970), pp. 75–82; and Inoue Kiyoshi, "Nihon teikokushugi no keisei," in *Kindai Nihon no keisei*, ed. Rekishigaku kenkyūkai (Tokyo: Iwanami shoten, 1953), pp. 51–130.

This is not to say that Japan's imperial ambitions lacked an economic dimension. Recent approaches to the study of economic interests in Japanese imperialism have highlighted the economic concerns of the Meiji leaders who directed the acquisition of the empire and have shown that the upper echelons of government and business shared a common belief in the economic promise of Asia.[9] But two facts must be kept in mind. First, these economic interests emerged most clearly after, not before, the initial steps were taken on the road to empire. Second, the ambitions of Japanese business in Asia were directed largely toward the mainland of China and toward Manchuria, and although they came to be a potent force in Japanese imperialism in its widest sense, they played little role in the assembling of the formal colonial empire and thus furnish inadequate evidence for arguments about its economic inevitability.

In any event, the origins of the Japanese imperium cannot be reduced to monocausal explanations. Writing over a quarter of a century ago, William Lockwood noted:

> As usual in the folklore of imperialism, so intertwined were considerations of military power, economic advantage, national prestige, and "moral obligation" that even the honest testimony of the makers of Japanese policy is an unreliable guide to the facts. The quest for empire in East Asia was impelled by no single motive except as most Japanese were indoctrinated with a mystical faith in the imperial destiny. It drew support from various interest groups and for differing reasons. Its momentum and direction reflected the political struggle at home, as well as the resistance it met abroad.[10]

Lockwood's last statement reintroduces the question of circumstance rather than motivation. Japan's precarious position in Asia in the late nineteenth century makes one hesitant to assert that Japan's rise as a colonial power was inevitable. Yet it is probable that given the energy and efficiency of its newly transformed institutions, Japan would have come to dominate adjacent portions of the decaying Chinese empire, regardless of the motivation. In this sense, Japanese imperialism was more situational than deliberate in origin. The aggressive movement of Japanese forces into Korea, China, and Micronesia was as much due to the absence of effective power to resist it as it was to specific Japanese policies and planning.

9 Peter Duus, "Economic Dimensions of Meiji Imperialism: The Case of Korea, 1895–1910," in Myers and Peattie, *Japanese Colonial Empire*, pp. 128–171.

10 William L. Lockwood, *The Economic Development of Japan: Growth and Structural Change, 1868–1938* (Princeton, N.J.: Princeton University Press, 1954), p. 534.

## THE EMPIRE ASSEMBLED, 1895–1922

The first overseas territories that Japan acquired were the "no man's islands" of the surrounding seas. In the 1870s and 1880s, Japan established effective sovereignty over the Bonin, Ryūkyū, and Kurile islands, as well as strengthening its grip on Hokkaido through an intensified program of colonization. But this effort was less the initial step toward colonial expansion than it was a reassertion of national authority over territories traditionally within the Japanese cultural sphere. It was in this sense, therefore, a clarification of national boundaries of the sort common to nation building in nineteenth- and twentieth-century Europe.[11]

It was Japan's turn toward the Korean peninsula that marked its first step outside the Japanese cultural area and its first effort in modern times to exert influence, if not direct control, over an alien people. Although in a formal sense Korea was to be the next-to-last addition to the colonial empire, it was the first to attract Japanese ambition.

Beginning in the 1880s, an increasingly aggressive Japanese involvement in Korea, whose course can only be touched on here, displayed a range of motivations – adventurism, idealism, and obsession with strategic security – already identified. The "conquer Korea" debate of the early 1870s split the new Japanese leadership over the issue of whether to divert the tensions and energies of early Meiji Japan toward a weaker and more backward neighbor. This led in turn to the ill-conducted expedition to Taiwan in 1874, momentarily releasing the energies of the frustrated ex-samurai elite but ending with no permanent territorial gains to show for it. Over the next two decades, as Japan gathered military and naval strength sufficient to confront China over primacy in Northeast Asia, Japanese diplomats, garrison commanders, traders, and adventurers worked sporadically with Korean reformers and agents provocateurs, to undermine both Chinese influence on the peninsula and the authority of the stubbornly traditional Korean government.

When the collision with China finally occurred in 1894, Japanese armies quickly drove the Chinese out of Korea, crossed the Yalu River, and occupied the strategic Liaotung peninsula. By February 1895 they had seized Weihaiwei on the Shantung peninsula. Everywhere triumphant, the Japanese Imperial General Headquarters pondered the best means to exploit these successes, in terms of both

11 Jansen, "Modernization and Foreign Policy," pp. 164–71.

offensive operations and territorial concessions to be sought from China. The outright annexation of Korea was neither planned nor necessary and, in any event, would have risked the active opposition of the foreign powers, especially Russia. Yet the Japanese public, exhilarated by a series of spectacular victories on land and sea, eagerly anticipated some sort of territorial rewards. The Meiji leadership, as well, viewed the acquisition of new territory as a means of enhancing imperial prestige.

For its part, the army favored holding on to the Liaotung peninsula and driving on toward Chihli Province and Beijing. But the civilian government, aware that major conquests on the Chinese mainland risked dangerous international repercussions, favored the "southern strategy" advocated by the navy. This approach called for the rapid occupation of Taiwan and the Pescadores as the operation least likely to provoke Western intervention and yet, at the same time, most likely to satisfy public demands for the fruits of victory.[12] During the negotiations at Shimonoseki in February 1895, with an expeditionary force already in possession of the Pescadores and another prepared to land on the north coast of Taiwan, Japan demanded and was ultimately awarded Taiwan, the Pescadores, and the Liaotung peninsula. All three were ceded to Japan by the subsequent peace treaty. Yet within three months, the "Triple Intervention" (by Russia, Germany, and France) forced Japan to retrocede Liaotung to China which, in turn, was soon forced to lease the peninsula to Russia, to the suppressed fury of Japan.

Thus, although the main thrust of Japan's expansionism had been directed toward Korea and although confrontation on the peninsula had furnished the immediate casus belli between Japan and China, immediate strategic and diplomatic circumstances determined that Taiwan would become the first outright possession of the Japanese colonial empire.

As a result of its victory over China and the diminution of Chinese influence in Korea, Japan had tightened its grip on that country. Japanese "advisers" forced a growing number of modernizing reforms on a weak but obdurate Korean government, efforts that made Japan and reformism ever more odious to the Korean upper classes. At the same time Japan increased its economic stake in Korea with the construction of railways and a rapid growth in commercial activ-

12 Edward I-te Chen, "Japan's Decision to Annex Taiwan: A Study of Mutsu–Itō Diplomacy," *Journal of Asian Studies* 37 (November 1977): 63–7.

ity throughout the peninsula. Then, between 1898 and 1904, Japanese ascendancy in Korea seemed temporarily checked by the counter-expansion of Russian influence there. Once again, the government saw its strategic interests threatened by a rival power. Once again it determined to confirm its primacy in Korea, peacefully if possible, by force of arms if necessary. Russia was offered an arrangement – the noted *Man–Kan kōkan* – that would recognize Russian primary in Manchuria in exchange for a completely free hand for Japan in Korea. When Russia, blinded by its own expansionist visions, brushed aside this proposal, the Japanese leadership saw no other course but open hostilities.

Japan's territorial conquests in the ensuing conflict with Russia from 1904 to 1905 formed the basis for its next colonial acquisitions. In frightful combat and at terrible cost Japanese armies reconquered the Liaotung peninsula and the strategic ports of Dairen and Port Arthur, which it had been forced to relinquish in 1895. To the north-east, Japanese units landed on the southern end of Sakhalin and rapidly extended their control, so that Japan might use the island as a bargaining chip in the subsequent peace negotiations. During the peace talks at Portsmouth in 1905, the Japanese representative was instructed to insist on the cession of the Liaotung peninsula and on Russian acknowledgment of Japan's complete freedom of action in Korea, but only to bargain for the cession of Sakhalin.[13]

In the subsequent treaty signed at Portsmouth, Japan gained its first two demands, in addition to acquiring all Russian rights and privileges in south Manchuria, but was forced to compromise on Sakhalin, obtaining only the southern half of the island below the fiftieth parallel, to which the Japanese gave the name Karafuto. In December 1905, according to the Manchurian Remedial Protocol, China was obliged to accept the treaty arrangements that had applied to Manchuria and specifically consented to transferring to Japan the Russian lease on Kwantung Province – the Liaotung peninsula – now designated the Kwantung Leased Territory. (In 1915, under Japanese pressure, the Chinese extended the lease for ninety-five years.) With Port Arthur and Dairen in its possession, Japan held the finest naval base and potentially one of the most important trading centers on the coast of northeast Asia.

This turn of events hardly lessened Japan's pressure on Korea. In-

13 Shumpei Okamoto, *The Japanese Oligarchy and the Russo-Japanese War* (New York: Columbia University Press, 1970), pp. 112–8, 124.

deed, Korea's last pretensions as an independent nation were now short-lived. With the end of hostilities and the elimination of Japan's last effective rival to the control of Korea, it was not long before that unfortunate country was totally absorbed into the Japanese colonial empire. The penultimate stage of this process was the creation of a Japanese protectorate over the country in November 1905, backed by overwhelming Japanese military force, which transformed Korea into a virtual Japanese satellite. Although the Korean monarch was permitted to keep his throne, all power was vested in the office of the resident general. Its occupant, the Meiji oligarch Itō Hirobumi, aimed at a modernizing, benevolent administration capable of gaining Korean co-operation while strengthening Japanese control. This "moderate" approach by an essentially civilian administration, governing Korea just short of outright Japanese annexation, soon met opposition in both Japan and Korea. Japanese hard-liners in the government and ultranationalist pressure groups outside it kept up an incessant criticism of the "weak-kneed" policy of the resident general and demanded the immediate annexation of Korea. In Korea itself, the bitter protest of Korean patriots of every class and calling swelled into open rebellion between 1908 and 1910 and was extinguished only by the most brutal military suppression and at the cost of nearly twelve thousand Korean lives. Although Itō himself strove to maintain a policy of paternalistic reform in Korea short of full Japanese control, his assassination in 1909 by a Korean patriot provided the more oppressive elements in Tokyo, the military in particular, with a pretext for ending the last fiction of Korean autonomy. In 1910, Korea was formally annexed into the Japanese empire, and an iron-fisted general, Terauchi Masatake, was officially installed as governor general.[14]

The final addition to the Japanese colonial empire was acquired four years later when Japan was once more able to use a sudden turn in international events to its own profit. With the outbreak of hostilities in Europe in 1914, Japan was quick to recognize the slight risk and considerable gain in joining the Allies as a belligerent. The immediate object of Japan's designs was Germany's colonial territories in Asia and the Pacific: Tsingtao on the Shantung peninsula and the German island possessions in Micronesia – the Marshalls, the Carolines, and the Marianas (excluding Guam) – all of which were isolated and weakly defended. A territorial foothold on the China coast had long been the ambition of Japanese expansionists in and out of government. The

14 Conroy, *The Japanese Seizure of Korea*, pp. 325–82.

South Pacific, though hardly a region of traditional concern to Tokyo, had held a singular fascination for a variety of Japanese travelers, traders, and colonization enthusiasts since the 1880s. With the emergence of American and Japanese naval rivalry in the Pacific, the Japanese navy suddenly saw the advantage of acquiring advance bases in those seas.

The first phase of Japan's efforts during World War I to extend and consolidate its interests in East Asia and the western Pacific was a series of military and naval operations to assault and capture the German colonies in the opening weeks of the war. Tsingtao fell after a stubborn but futile resistance by its German defenders, and the isolated island territories were seized without resistance by Japanese naval units.

The second diplomatic phase of this expansion was designed to secure international recognition of Japan's claims to the territories that it had summarily occupied, an undertaking considerably more difficult, as the speed and aggressiveness of Japanese moves in East Asia and the Pacific had aroused the suspicion and hostility of Britain, Australia, New Zealand, and the United States.[15] By the end of the war, however, Japan had collected secret agreements from most of the Allied powers confirming its expropriation of these territories and, using these, was later able to press its claims during the Paris peace negotiations.

Subsequent treaty arrangements, however, forced the Japanese to modify their territorial objectives. The German Micronesian islands were assigned to Japan as a Class C mandate under the League of Nations, subject to the proviso that Japan make no effort to fortify them. Although these arrangements were less than perfect from Tokyo's point of view, Japan willingly consented to them, offset as they were by similar nonfortification restrictions on American possessions in the Pacific.

In any event, from the outset of its administration, Japan regarded the Nan'yō, as its new Pacific territories were collectively called, as an integral part of the Japanese empire. Japan's acquisition of Tsingtao, which had raised a storm of protest in China and in the United States, proved to be of shorter duration. In 1922, at the Washington Conference, Japan was obliged to yield to American pressure and to retrocede the colony to China.

15 David Purcell, Jr., "Japanese Expansion in the South Pacific, 1890–1935," Ph.D. diss., University of Pennsylvania, 1967, pp. 69–100.

By 1922, therefore, Japan's formal colonial empire was complete. Its imperial ambitions, however, were not yet satisfied, nor was its economic, political, and military penetration of Northeast Asia substantially lessened. The consequent risk to the empire, which had won grudging acceptance from the West by World War I, was hardly recognized by those Japanese in and out of government who most aggressively pushed for its extension. Heedless of the end of the old imperialist world order that had tolerated the growth of Japanese imperialism, or of the tide of nationalism and anticolonialism abroad in Asia, Japan pressed ahead on the continent in an illusory quest for final security and economic autonomy. Fatally linked to these ever-receding goals, the formal empire became a base and an arsenal for the increasingly dangerous effort to dominate ever-expanding buffer zones and, as such, was finally overtaken by disaster in World War II.

## EVOLUTION OF THE EMPIRE, 1895–1941

The history of Japanese colonialism begins with a military pacification effort in Taiwan by Japanese military forces not unlike that undertaken by the United States Army against Filipino rebels after the conclusion of American hostilities against Spain. Directed against a resistance movement headed by local Taiwanese leaders unreconciled to the prospect of Japanese rule over the island, the five-month campaign (June–October, 1895) ravaged parts of the island and was costly to both the Japanese army (which suffered over seven thousand casualties, mostly from disease) and the indigenes (who suffered many thousands more). The Japanese operation left all but the island's inner mountain regions under firm Japanese control. In those forest strongholds the aboriginal tribesmen carried on a guerrilla warfare against Japanese security forces. Though it posed no real obstacle to the overall Japanese control and development of the island, this sporadic but bitter resistance smoldered in the interior for over thirty years.

Development of the empire's first colony was slow in coming. Lacking any experience or tradition as a colonial power, Japan had acquired Taiwan without long-range objectives for its management. The island was seen in some quarters as being as much a liability as an asset, a response provoked by an initial period of chaos, carpetbagging, and mismanagement under military rule, not uncommon to European colonial ventures in their early stages.

Yet within a few years, pride, purpose, and efficiency were manifested in the administration of General Kodama Gentarō, fourth governor general of the island, and his chief civil administrator, Gotō Shinpei. Doctor, bureaucrat, and later businessman and statesman, Gotō's accomplishments in restructuring the political, social, and economic order in Taiwan transformed the territory from an embarrassment into a colonial showcase and made him Japan's most distinguished colonial administrator in the empire's fifty-year history. Working with a brilliant and energetic cluster of subordinates, including Nitobe Inazō, who was to become a distinguished scholar and statesman in his own right, Gotō sought a "scientific" approach to colonial governance and development that emphasized thorough and extensive research as the basis of colonial policies. The result was a series of well-planned and coordinated efforts dealing with a wide range of colonial problems and creating an effective infrastructure of schools, public health facilities, agricultural improvements, transportation and communications, and urban and port development, which collectively transformed a backward, economically fragmented, and debt-ridden territory into a modern economically self-sufficient colonial possession. All this was accomplished with the passive acquiesence of a submissive population.[16]

In Korea, pacification was undertaken by a more openly authoritarian military administration, despite the vehement protest and occasionally active resistance of a fearful, obstinate, and antagonized colonial people. The period of the protectorate, 1905–10, had seen the Japanese Residency General devote its efforts to taking over the institutions of Korean government, including those of the police, military affairs, transportation, communications, and the courts, in order to establish Japanese control over the peninsula. During the subsequent decade the Government General had grown into a powerful machine of centralized bureaucratic control that undertook the wholesale transformation of Korea's political, educational, and social structures. It also created the institutions of a modern economy by building a transportation and communications network linking the entire country and creating new monetary and financial systems. In the process of these modernizing efforts, the Koreans were effectively deprived of freedom of assembly, association, press, and speech, and initial efforts were made to liquidate the very concept of a Korean identity. Under the draconian administration of Governor General Terauchi, Korea now entered that dark epoch of developmental shock known to its chroniclers

16 Chang Han-yu and Ramon H. Myers, "Japanese Colonial Development Policy in Taiwan, 1895–1906: A Case of Bureaucratic Entrepreneurship," *Journal of Asian Studies* 22 (August 1963): 433–49.

as the "period of military rule," a term that in English hardly conveys the crushing impact of the Japanese army and police on every aspect of Korean life. "Regulations of every kind poured forth wildly and were as harshly enforced," noted a Japanese journalist in Korea at the time, adding that "so completely were the people's liberties restricted that the entire peninsula could be said to have been militarized."[17]

On the Liaotung peninsula the early years of the Japanese military administration were fraught with difficulties. Financial problems, international complications over the exact status of the territory, poor administration of the lower echelons, and a flood of carpetbagging failures from the home islands made for unstable conditions in the colony. Troublesome, too, was the fact that Kwantung Government General, though headed by a military officer, was entangled in a web of relationships with various ministries and bureaus in matters of administration, external relations, and military command in Manchuria as well as in the Leased Territory.[18] By 1919, however, the administration of the territory had been reorganized into a Kwantung government – Kantōchō – headed by a civilian governor residing in Dairen. The influx of immigrants, both Japanese and Chinese, was more closely supervised, and the South Manchuria Railway Company, the driving force behind Japanese exploitation and development in both Manchuria and the Leased Territory, had begun a series of projects in the colony centered on the development of Dairen that, within fifteen years, emerged as one of the great ports of Asia and the Pacific.

Karafuto was the only Japanese dependency in which the Japanese did not have to be concerned with the administration of an alien people. An island where only a few scattered Ainu tribesmen and Russians had settled prior to the Japanese conquest, Karafuto came to be peopled almost exclusively by the Japanese who were its settlers. As Japan's only true settlement colony, Karafuto, in its colonization, exploitation, and development, was much more like Hokkaido of a quarter-century before. Indeed, despite its dependent status, remoteness, and harsh environment, to the Japanese, Karafuto always seemed to be a part of the home islands. The colony's homogenous racial composition thus made its history less troubled by tensions between ruler and ruled and helps explain why the initial period of military administration after the Japanese conquest quickly gave way to the establishment of a Karafuto government – Karafutochō – headed

17 Quoted in Yamabe Kentarō, *Nihon tōjika no Chōsen* (Tokyo: Iwanami shinsho, 1975), p. 13.
18 Shimada Toshihiko, *Kantōgun* (Tokyo: Chūō kōronsha, 1965), pp. 6–10, 10–12; Ōyama Azusa, *Nichi-Ro sensō no gunsei shiroku* (Tokyo: Fūyo shobō, 1973), pp. 19–25.

by a civilian governor. With the exception of a brief period of turmoil and mismanagement involved in the temporary occupation of the northern half of the island from 1920 to 1925, the history of the colony was uneventful, though the exploitation of its physical resources comprised one of the most rapacious episodes of both government and private capital in the history of the Japanese empire.[19]

In the South Pacific, international circumstance shaped the first years of Japanese rule. A docile Micronesian population offered no resistance to the Japanese naval garrison that controlled the islands from its headquarters at Truk during World War I. Yet the delay in obtaining an internationally confirmed basis for Japanese jurisdiction in Micronesia made it difficult to establish permanent institutions of civil administration and postponed an officially sponsored program of immigration. Nor did the first Japanese economic ventures in Micronesia, centered on a struggling and heavily subsidized sugar industry in the Marianas, seem to justify the increasing expense of managing and developing the islands. Indeed, not a few in the home government came to view the islands as an encumbrance and proposed that Japan abandon them. But such was the group's potentially strategic position, despite the limitations imposed by the nonfortification clause of the Washington Naval Treaty, that they were retained at the particular insistence of the naval high command.[20] The delay in establishing a permanent civil administration, moreover, did not postpone intensive Japanese activities in the islands designed to bring the native populations under Japanese influence and control. Although the South Seas government–Nan'yochō–headed by a civilian governor, was not established until 1922, the impact of the Japanese presence on the Micronesian population in terms of education, language, and manners was so immediate that an American visitor to the Marshalls in 1919 described it as a "Japanning" of the islands.

Throughout the empire, this initial stage of colonialism, once Japanese order had been established, was characterized by an effort to set up regimes that clearly resembled European colonial administrations in character and purpose. Japanese publicists in these decades spoke proudly of the nation's achievements as a new colonial power, and the

19 See, for example, John Stephan, *Sakhalin: A History* (Oxford, England: Clarendon Press, 1971), pp. 88–9.

20 For a detailed discussion of Japanese mandate rule in Micronesia, see Mark R. Peattie, *Nan'yō: The Rise and Fall of the Japanese in Micronesia, 1885–1945* (Honolulu: University of Hawaii Press, 1988).

Japanese in the colonies themselves constructed a life-style and physical environment built on privilege, money, and authority not unlike their counterparts in European tropical colonies. For this reason, and because Japanese efficiency gave success to these efforts, Western commentary on Japanese colonialism in this stage was overwhelmingly favorable. British and American visitors to Taiwan and Korea spoke glowingly of the "amazing progress" of Taiwan under Japanese administration, of the "courage, devotion, and insight" of the Japanese administration in Korea after centuries of "racial and political decay." Only a few foreign observers amended this lavish praise by noting that Japanese colonialism was harshly authoritarian and quite exploitive, that the Taiwanese had little affection for their colonial rulers, and that Korean attitudes toward Japanese rule were those of outrage and despair. Undoubtedly, this benign view from abroad was in large part shaped by the fact that, outwardly at least, Japanese colonialism at this stage closely resembled that of the European nations themselves.

Powerful currents of political change in the Japanese homeland and abroad from 1914 to 1920 began to push Japanese authorities toward a more liberal administration of the colonies. In Japan, these trends were marked by an erosion of the influence of both the *genrō* and the military and by a concomitant rise in political party power, more democratic in domestic policy and more accommodative to the interests of Japan's colonial populations. Abroad, the emergence of Wilsonian idealism, particularly the principle of the self-determination of peoples, gave heart to Taiwanese and Koreans who sought autonomy for their homelands and placed Japanese colonialism increasingly on the defensive.

In Taiwan by 1914, these ideas had already encouraged an "assimilation movement" designed to provide Taiwanese with certain basic civil rights under the Japanese constitution, while keeping Taiwan generally within the empire, an effort supported by a number of distinguished liberals in Japan, of whom Itagaki Taisuke was the most prominent. Vehemently opposed by Japanese colonials in Taiwan, the movement was soon banned by the Taiwan Government General. It was succeeded by moderate Taiwanese demands for home rule to be achieved through the election of a Taiwanese legislature and for restrictions on the authority of the Government General. The colonial government utterly rejected such notions and made no concessions whatsoever to the home-rule movement. Yet such was the docility and moderation of Taiwanese nationalism that Japanese authority on the island remained unchallenged by the advocates of either assimilation or home rule.[21]

In Korea, the rigor with which Japan's first proconsul on the peninsula, General Terauchi Masatake, had attempted to enforce Korean conformity to Japan's institutions and values had created violent antagonisms that could not be permanently contained. Nonetheless, the explosion of Korean national resentment on March 1, 1919, stunned all elements of informed opinion in Japan. The March First movement demonstrated the depth of Korean detestation of Japanese administration, as well as the influence of Wilsonian ideals on Korean national sentiment. It also showed the progress of Korea toward a sense of nationhood, bringing together over two million Koreans in a call for national liberation. The Japanese response, launched against an unarmed and generally unresisting popular movement, was instantaneous and bloody.[22] The brutal methods used by Japanese officialdom to stamp out the protest drove the remaining Korean resistance leaders to exile in foreign countries and left a legacy of Korean hatred of Japan.

The horrified protests around the world, as well as in Japan, against colonial reaction in Korea encouraged those political forces in Japan that sought to moderate Japanese colonial policy. To Prime Minister Hara Takashi, who believed that colonial administration should be guided by the same sort of bureaucratic reform that had recently evolved in Japan, the March 1919 crisis in Korea and the death of the incumbent military governor general in Taiwan provided opportunities to attempt administrative changes throughout the empire that would modify Japanese rule. The first step was to abolish or limit military administration in those colonies where it still existed, as it had proved both oppressive and unresponsive to civilian direction. In Taiwan, Hara was successful in attaining this objective, and his appointment of Den Kenjirō, a trusted political party colleague, ushered in a decade and a half of civilian administration for the colony. In Micronesia, too, the Japanese naval administration gave way to a civilian government, more appropriate to the islands' mandate status. But in Korea, strategic considerations and the adamant resistance by the Japanese military turned aside Hara's efforts to apply the principle of civilian rule. Although by law a civilian could have been appointed governor general at Keijō (Seoul), in practice, Japan's administration

21 Harry J. Lamley, "Assimilation in Colonial Taiwan: The Fate of the 1914 Movement," *Monumenta Serica* 29 (1970–1): 496–520; Yamabe, "Nihon teikokushugi to shokuminchi," pp. 236–7. 22 Yamabe, *Nihon tōjika no Chōsen*, pp. 58–101.

in Korea continued to be headed by an unbroken chain of military autocrats.

Nevertheless, a series of modest reforms pointed toward greater opportunities for Koreans in government, education, and industry and demonstrated greater Japanese respect for Korean culture. In part, these changes were wrought by an administration in Tokyo that believed in bringing the colony into closer relationship with an administratively liberalized and reformed Japan. In part, they were due to a belated recognition that the Korean problem, which had become for Japan as intractable as the Irish problem had been for Britain, required at least minimal concessions to reduce the explosive pressures of Korean nationalism. It was for this latter reason that during the decade of "cultural rule" (*bunka seiji*), Korea was granted a number of reforms of a kind never conceded to the more docile colonial population of Taiwan. In 1920, the Japanese government announced a number of social, political, and economic changes designed to permit greater self-expression for Koreans, to abolish abuses in the judicial system, to eliminate discrimination in the treatment of Japanese and Koreans in public service, to equalize educational and economic opportunity, to promote agriculture and industry, and generally to give Koreans greater voice in the management of their own affairs.[23]

Had not Prime Minister Hara been assassinated in office, it is possible that the transformation of these symbolic pronouncements into substantive advances for Korean aspirations might have been undertaken with greater vigor. As it was, the feeble administrative and social reforms of the ensuing decade hardly realized Hara's objective of extending Japanese liberties and rights to Korea, let alone satisfied Korean demands for political, social, and economic autonomy. Filtered as it was through a colonial administration that still held in contempt Korea's political capacities, the liberalization of Japanese rule quickly evaporated into empty slogans. Still, if neither the depth nor the tempo of colonial reform went far in meeting the Koreans' legitimate demands, the more overtly arbitrary and oppressive aspects of Japanese administration were at least muted throughout the empire during this decade, and the effort to construct modern economic facilities and institutions in the colonies continued apace.

For these reasons Japan continued to earn a favorable international rating as a respectable colonial power. It appeared to have brought peace and order to all the territories under its control, to be lessening

23 David Brudnoy, "Japan's Experiment in Korea," *Monumenta Nipponica* 25 (1970): 172–4.

the military cast of its colonial administrations, to be undertaking responsible reform in Korea, and to be meeting its material obligations as a mandatory power in the South Pacific. Its colonial ports were open to the trade of all nations, and the economies of all its colonial territories appeared to be developing rapidly. If Japanese colonial policy contained almost no accommodation to the concept of trusteeship – preparing its dependent peoples for self-rule – much the same could be said about the colonial policies of the Netherlands, Portugal, Belgium, Italy, or even France in this period.

In any event, the thin coating of liberal reform and modest accommodation to the interests of Japan's colonial peoples, initiated by Japan's civil government in the 1920s, was soon dissolved in the acids of aggressive nationalism and military necessity in the 1930s. The social and economic dislocations at home and the uncertainties and instabilities abroad – particularly in East Asia – are among the primary causes that many historians have assigned to the shift of Japan toward domestic authoritarianism, an accelerated tempo of nationalism, and the resurgent influence of the military in shaping national policy. Regardless of the relative emphasis that one may assign among such causes, their consequences remilitarized the Japanese colonial empire and transformed its dependencies into regimented and exploited bases for aggressive Japanese expansion into East and Southeast Asia. In the process these changes sharply altered both Western and Japanese perceptions of Japan as an accepted and acceptable colonial power.

In the overheated political atmosphere of the 1930s, the Japanese empire once more became expansive, though less through considered decisions at its metropolitan center than through the arbitrary initiatives of Japan's field armies abroad. Moving first from the Kwantung Leased Territory and Korea into Manchuria and from there into north China, Japanese garrisons on the continent, acting largely on their own, ushered in an era of military expansion outside the boundaries of the formal empire not unlike the forward sweep of late nineteenth-century French military imperialism in West Africa. By the latter half of the decade, these initiatives had drawn Japan into bloody encounters with the Soviet Union and a frightful war of attrition with China.

In 1940, as the drift of international events tempted Japan to move into Southeast Asia, Japan's southernmost dependencies, Taiwan and the Micronesian islands, became staging areas for such operations. Although there is scant evidence that Japan violated its mandatory obligations by fortifying the Nan'yō before its withdrawal from the League in 1933, by the end of the decade Japan was hurriedly preparing naval and air facilities in all of the Micronesian island groups.

Because Japan's colonial territories were increasingly thrust into a strategic role, it was inevitable that the empire's colonial administrations should have been remilitarized in the 1930s. Beginning in 1932, the commander of the Kwantung Army in Manchuria concurrently held the post of governor general of the Kwantung Leased Territory, and by mid-decade a general once more took over the colonial administration of Taiwan. Only in Karafuto and the Nan'yō did civilian officials still continue to head colonial governments. (In 1940, the latter was placed under de facto control of the Japanese navy which formally assumed responsibility for the Micronesian islands in 1943.)

Central to the concerns of Japanese colonial policy in the new decade were the economic consolidation of the empire and the integration of its colonial economies to meet the wartime requirements of the home islands. Perceiving a world trend toward the creation of autarkic units, Japan's leadership, both civilian and military, became convinced that Japan must build its own economic bloc to which the nation must look for its survival. In this perspective the colonies were chiefly seen as productive units of a central economic engine, geared to the creation of a self-sufficient garrison state. By 1939, therefore, the colonies' populations and resources had been rapidly and ruthlessly harnessed to Japan's growing needs for labor, foodstuffs, strategic raw materials, and military supplies. In Korea and Taiwan, particularly, forced-draft programs of military industrialization rapidly transformed these colonies into logistical bases to support aggressive war. In this final, militarized, exploited, and regimented condition, the empire was hurled into Japan's violent confrontation with the United States and was shattered in the process.

## JAPANESE COLONIAL POLICY: CONCEPTS AND CONTRADICTIONS

There was nothing in the way of national experience or tradition before 1895 that might have aided Japan in the development of a well-articulated colonial policy or doctrine, though various interests had impelled Japan along the course of empire. Yet as Japan assembled its overseas imperium, two basic approaches to Japanese colonial rule did indeed appear. Centered on conflicting notions of race that were themselves shaped by the historical timing and cultural circumstances of

Japan's entry onto the colonial stage, these conceptions of colonial policy were inherently contradictory. But it should not be supposed that their differences were so obviously antagonistic to one another that they divided those Japanese who acted on or wrote about colonial affairs into two mutually hostile groupings. On the contrary, both doctrines contributed to the formation of Japanese colonial policy, at least during the first quarter-century of the empire. Moreover, Japanese colonial policy in all its phases – conservative, liberal, and militarized – displayed two overriding continuities: first, the primacy of Japanese interests – largely strategic but to a lesser extent economic – over those of the dependent people and, second, the absence of any arrangements to prepare those peoples for self-rule, even in the distant future.

The first of the two Japanese conceptions of Japanese colonial policy was European in origin and orientation, and its adoption by Japanese administrators and publicists had much to do with the fact that Japan entered its colonial tasks at the zenith of European colonialism. Its characteristics thus stemmed from the assumptions and predilections common to the "New Imperialism" of late nineteenth-century Europe and derived largely from European colonial empires whose territories were geographically dispersed and racially diverse.

It was, first, a racially separatist approach to colonial rule, and as such, it reflected the prevailing social Darwinist predilections. It accepted without reservation the notion that not only did "biological laws" determine the course of human institutions but also that there were "biological" – that is, racial – differences in the political capacities of various peoples. It thus assumed, on the one hand, the separate evolution of races according to their inherent capacities or incapacities to modernize and, on the other hand, the moral right of "superior" races to dominate and guide the destinies of "lesser" peoples.[24]

This theory of colonial governance was, moreover, self-consciously "rational" in its application and mirrored the current European conviction that the techniques of modern science could be brought to the task of orderly social change. Thus, Gotō Shinpei's systematic, research-oriented approach to the development of Taiwan and his perception of the island as a laboratory, wherein experiments in social engineering could determine the course of change in the country, were manifestations of the pseudoscientific assumptions of nineteenth-century Europe about the administration of alien peoples, specifically the "scientific

24 See, for example, Yosaburo Takekoshi, "Japan's Colonial Policy," in *Japan to America*, ed. Naoichi Masaoka (New York: Putnam, 1915), pp. 96–9.

colonialism" of Wilhelmian Germany, where Gotō had been trained as a medical doctor.[25]

Like much of European colonial policy at the time, this Japanese conception of empire was also paternalistic and cautiously humanitarian in tone and rhetoric. It incorporated the assumption that along with their own self-interest in the acquisition of overseas territories, colonial powers must not neglect their colonial charges but should work earnestly for their welfare and eventual enlightenment. In the West this moralizing element was part of an obsessive sense of responsibility for the "improvement" of colonial peoples, as expressed in the French notion of *mission civilisatrice,* the Belgian concept of *moralisation,* the German *Eingeborenenfürsorge,* the Portuguese *politica da atraccao,* and of course the British "white man's burden." In the Japanese case this moral imperative stemmed not only from the assumption that the reforms already accomplished in Meiji Japan could be transferred to colonial peoples but also from the growing conviction that the nation had a "heavenly calling" (*tenshoku*) to enlighten other Asian peoples. "The highest and ultimate purpose of colonialism is the development of the human race," asserted Nitobe Inazō. "If we neglect humanitarianism then our great mission will have little success." The colonial publicist Mochiji Rokusaburō also spoke of the necessity of "humanitarian advances [in the colonies] through the diffusion of the culture of the mother country."[26]

Finally, this perspective on overseas administration was gradualist. It presumed, indeed insisted on, an infinite stretch of time for the benefits of colonial rule to work their good, unhurried by pressures from without or demands from within the colonies. In its most conservative form, this approach argued for the perpetuation of a colonial status quo in which colonial peoples would be kept in a permanently subordinate position to the colonizing race, without any political rights or responsibilities whatsoever. At its most accommodative level, it was not unlike the contemporary French doctrine of "association," which held that the colonies should retain a separate identity and be governed pragmatically, with due respect for the institutions of their individual peoples.

Between 1905 and 1920 this general approach to Japanese colonial policy was articulated by a growing body of informed opinion on

25 Ramon H. Myers, "Taiwan As an Imperial Colony of Japan, 1895–1945," *Journal of the Institute of Chinese Studies* 6 (Chinese University of Hong Kong, December 1973): 435.

26 Nitobe Inazō, *Zenshū,* vol. 4 (Tokyo: Kyōbunkan, 1969–70), pp. 371, 478; Mochiji Rokusaburō, *Taiwan shokumin seisaku* (Tokyo: Fuzanbō, 1912), pp. 431–2.

colonial matters in Japan. It was shaped in large part by a group of publicists – ex-administrators, scholars, politicians, and journalists – who were widely versed in modern European colonial theory but who also possessed a firsthand knowledge of colonial affairs from extensive service in the colonies, particularly Taiwan. Prominent in their own right, men like Nitobe Inazō, Tōgo Minoru, Mochiji Rokusaburō, Takekoshi Yosaburō, and Nagai Ryutarō produced a steady flow of commentary on the Japanese colonial empire in books, articles, and public lectures, as well as from chairs in colonial studies established at some of Japan's leading universities (at Tokyo Imperial University in 1908 and at Waseda University in 1909). Much of this commentary found its way into the official rhetoric of Japanese colonialism, particularly in Taiwan. In sum, it was rational, conservative, and paternalist. It perceived the colonies as separate territories, distinct from the homeland and not merely extensions of it; yet it took pride in Japan's participation in what was seen as a universal "civilizing mission."

The second Japanese conception of colonial rule contained a set of assumptions radically different from most of those underlying European colonial theory. It stemmed in large part from the general Asian provenance of the Japanese empire, specifically from the fact that there existed affinities of race and culture between Japan and its two largest and most populous colonies. It found expression in the doctrine of "assimilation" (*dōka*) that aimed at eliminating all differences between the colonies and the motherland. As a general concept, of course, assimilation was not uniquely Japanese, as it had found enthusiastic and articulate expression in French colonial theory. But there is scant evidence that French assimilationist doctrine had much influence in the formation of Japanese ideas on assimilation, which were distinctly Asian in origin and character.

At least four assumptions seem to have been central to the Japanese conception of assimilation. The first was a conviction that Japan had an indissoluble bond with other countries of the Chinese culture area – specifically Taiwan and Korea – as they shared a common system of writing as well as similarities of race and culture. To Japanese advocates of assimilation, these common cultural denominators offered the possibility of union between Japan and its Asian colonial subjects not conceivable in Europe's racially and culturally diverse tropical empires.

Second, Japanese ideas of assimilation contained a strongly moralistic element derived from Confucian tradition, an emphasis conveyed in an incessantly repeated phrase, "impartiality and equal favor" (*isshi dōjin*), which expressed the idea that all who came under the sovereign's sway shared equally in his benevolence. Because of its implied reference to the will of the Japanese emperor, it was a concept of powerful appeal to all Japanese. Yet, its vagueness meant that the concept could encompass a variety of interpretations to suit quite disparate political purposes. It could be given the most liberal construction, stressing the necessity to provide equal rights to colonizers and colonized, or the most authoritarian interpretation, concerned with the equality of all Japanese subjects, at home and in the colonies, in their obligations to the state.

The third distinguishing feature of the Japanese concept of assimilation was the mystical linkage drawn between the Japanese race and the Japanese imperial house, which together formed an imperial "family." This principle could be extended outward to include new populations brought under Japanese dominion, so that these too, could become "imperial peoples" (*kōmin*). Yet here again, the concept was so murky as to defy any precise application of rights and responsibilities to such "imperialized" nationalities, a vagueness that made it less a doctrine than a dogma. As a concept, assimilation came to have great appeal to a wide spectrum of Japanese, particularly because it implied a unidirectional change by colonized peoples toward the "higher" culture of their colonial masters. Thus, it meshed to a certain extent with the more Euro-centered concept of colonial rule, as it included the idea of "uplifting" and "civilizing" backward colonial peoples.[27]

Although much of Japanese assimilation theory contained lofty rhetoric about the necessity of a true merger of colonizers and colonized on the basis of familiarity and respect, the environment of Japanese colonialism rarely permitted the realization of such ideals. Assimilation of a quite limited, material sort was, however, actively promoted by Japanese colonial officialdom as a means of social control. By encouraging programs that Japanized the appearance and life-styles of Japan's colonial peoples, they sought to remold them outwardly into loyal, law-abiding Japanese. The colonial bureaucrat thus delighted in programs that induced Koreans, Chinese, and Micronesians to speak Japanese, to live in Japanese homes, to dress in modern Japanese clothing, and generally to reinforce their physical identity with the ruling elite. Ultimately, official policies supporting assimilation were reduced to this

27 Lamley, "Assimilation," pp. 496–9.

mechanical level and generally achieved results among those colonial populations that were similarly material and superficial.[28]

The most liberal and far-reaching interpretation of assimilation, however, centered on the idea of the direct application of the laws and institutions of metropolitan Japan to its territories overseas. Specifically, it implied an extension to the colonies of the same political rights and privileges enjoyed by Japanese in the home islands under the Meiji constitution. The idea of bringing the colonies into a closer relationship with a politically liberalized mother country had emerged early in the Taishō period, at the initiative of certain members of the Diet critical of the enormous power wielded by colonial governments in Korea and Taiwan and yet opposed to the idea of home rule for either country. It was essentially reflected in the colonial policies of Hara Takashi when he became prime minister. Hara and liberals in the Diet advocated the rapid and direct assimilation of the colonies into Japan's political structure, through advanced education, expanded civil liberties, and growing political responsibility for Japan's colonial populations, including colonial representation in the Diet as well as the elimination of restrictions hindering political union between Japan and its overseas possessions. "The desire of most Koreans is not for independence" insisted Hara in 1920, "but to be treated as the equals of the Japanese."[29] Whether or not Hara underestimated the force of Korean nationalism, however, the entrenched opposition by the Japanese military, by the colonial bureaucracies in Korea and Taiwan, and by the Japanese residents in those colonies blocked any opening toward the realization of his colonial objectives after his assassination and thus doomed any real extension of political equality to the colonies.

Despite this failure, the more liberal atmosphere of the 1920s ushered in by Hara did enable modest social and economic assimilationist reform in the colonies, particularly in Taiwan. That colony's first civilian governor general, Den Kenjirō, undertook a policy of "acculturation" (*kyōka*), a modest program designed to provide advanced education for the Taiwanese and equal employment opportunities for the Taiwanese and Japanese alike and to encourage the social and racial integration of the two peoples through the diffusion of the Japanese language and the encouragement of intermarriage between the

28 Ibid., pp. 503–4. The contradictions in Japan's assimilation policy are discussed in Hatada Takashi, "Nihonjin no Chōsenkan," in *Nihon to Chōsen*, vol. 3: *Ajia-Afurika Kōza* (Tokyo: Keiso shobō, 1965), pp. 5–10.

29 *Hara Kei nikki*, vol. 8 (Tokyo: Tōkyō Kengensha, 1950), p. 563.

races. But even the limited policy of "acculturation," initiated in Taiwan by Den and his immediate successors, was designed to proceed at only the most gradual pace. Indeed, at the decade's end the Taiwanese still occupied a distinctly second-class social and economic status in their own land.[30]

In any event, with the remilitarization, exploitation, and regimentation of the empire in the 1930s, this gradualist, modestly accommodative policy of assimilation gave way to one considerably more hurried, ideological, and coercive in nature. Japanese assimilationist theory had always had a hazy identification with the Pan-Asianist ideals of many Japanese, and now these themes of racial harmony, coprosperity, and union among Asian races came to be valued more highly than any universal "civilizing mission" of modern (Western) colonialism. Indeed, colonialism of the European variety came to be seen as an obstacle to Pan-Asian unity and was thus regarded by Japanese policymakers with increasing hostility. Japanese colonial policy also began to emphasize the mystical links between the emperor and his subjects at home and overseas. By the end of the decade, this concept had materialized into a strident, officially sponsored movement that aimed at the "imperialization" (*kōminka*) of Japan's dependent races but that, in its mystical rhetoric about equality, no longer spoke of the rights of Japanese subjects, only of obligations. The ideological regimentation that now began to grip all Japan's overseas territories reached its most severe limits in Korea, where the extreme efforts of the Government General to stamp out all forms of Korean identity, including the attempt to prevent any use of the Korean language, amounted to "colonial totalitarianism," in Gregory Henderson's words.[31]

Moreover, as the decade progressed, and as Japanese field armies began to overrun adjoining Asian regions, Japanese policymakers came to perceive both the territories of the formal empire and the newly occupied areas as one undifferentiated unit, Asian in composition and uncompromisingly Japanese in purpose and outlook. For this reason, all references to colonies were eliminated in favor of a distinction only between the "inner territory" – Japan – and the "outer territories" – the overseas possessions. The latter were now seen to be merely extensions of a single Japanese nation, without any separate colonial, let alone

30 E. Patricia Tsurumi, *Japanese Colonial Education in Taiwan, 1895–1945* (Cambridge, Mass.: Harvard University Press, 1977), pp. 146–56.

31 Gregory Henderson, *Korea: Politics of the Vortex* (Cambridge, Mass.: Harvard University Press, 1966), pp. 72–114.

national, identities of their own. The European colonial model was not only abandoned but also reviled as decadent and evil. Japan was to lead all Asian races (by force if necessary) in a national war of liberation to drive Western colonialism out of Asia.[32]

At the same time, official Japanese rhetoric about Japan's mission in Asia also began to display traces of overt racism. Despite incessant references to Asian racial harmony and coprosperity, the Japanese government increasingly spoke of Japan's dominant position within the Greater East Asian Co-Prosperity Sphere, and not a few among the Japanese military spoke openly of themselves as "master peoples."

Rent by these internal contradictions of imperial purpose, the final, "anticolonial" expression of Japanese colonialism could not garner the support of the peoples it increasingly oppressed and exploited in the name of equality, nor could it historically justify the empire after it collapsed in the rubble of the Pacific War.

## ADMINISTERING THE EMPIRE

At its outset, the empire was slow to establish administrative machinery for central colonial administration. During the empire's first several decades, successive administrative changes placed the separate colonies at different times under various ministries in Tokyo or under the prime minister's office. By the 1920s the expansion of the empire made it necessary that colonial administration be unified, but it was not until 1929 that a Ministry of Colonial Affairs (Takumushō), headed by an appointee of cabinet rank, was established to supervise all the component territories of the empire. Yet it must not be supposed that this office held powers anything like those of the British Colonial Office or the French Colonial Ministry, whose influence over their respective colonies was considerable. Rather, the effective central authority was exercised by individual ministries in Tokyo, particularly those of the army and navy, acting through their agents in the colonies. The Japanese Ministry of Colonial Affairs, while it existed, served largely as a coordinating and reporting instrument, and to the extent that it held any real authority at all, this power was exercised in the lesser colonies, not in Korea or Taiwan. With the outbreak of the Pacific War, the ministry was abolished, and in keeping with the empire's ideological and Pan-Asianist character, all its functions were taken over by the Greater East Asia Ministry (Dai Tōa-shō) which

32 Nagao Sakurō, *Nihon shokumin seisaku no dozō* (Tokyo: Yūhikaku, 1944), pp. 1–8, 29.

handled relations with all Japanese-occupied territory in Asia except for Taiwan, Korea, and Karafuto. In 1942 Korea was brought under control of the Home Ministry, and in 1944 Karafuto was absorbed into Japan as a mere prefecture.

The powerful influence of the military in Japanese colonial affairs also had much to do with the absence of an effective centralized colonial administration under the civil government in Tokyo. Because of the circumstances of the empire's formation, military government was the initial stage in the administrative evolution of all the colonies. Military men continued to play a predominant role in much of the rest of the empire's history. Given the general power and prestige of the Japanese military, as well as its independence from civil control, it is no wonder that the Japanese army and navy often had virtually free rein in Japan's territories overseas and thus helped isolate colonial governments from political developments in metropolitan Japan.

It was in Taiwan and Korea, however, where military authority was the most dominant, and in consequence, the colonial governments became the most autonomous and the most authoritarian. The governors general of those colonies – the only Japanese colonial officials to hold that title – held *shinnin* rank (which meant appointment in a ceremony personally attended by the emperor), the highest in Japanese officialdom. They possessed enormous executive, judicial, and even legislative powers, far greater indeed than those of any single office in the home government, that of the prime minister included. "Korea and Formosa," Edward Chen tells us, "were in effect empires within an empire, contrary to the goal of political integration repeatedly proclaimed by the Japanese."[33]

Nor was either the Government General, nor any other Japanese colonial government for that matter, troubled by having to deal with a colonial legislature or limited by an effective instrument for indigenous self-rule. Although it is true that in Korea, as a matter of appeasing Korean sentiment, there were far more indigenes in the colonial government than in Taiwan and that a Korean "central advisory council" existed in Seoul, an armory of legal restrictions by the Government General made these Korean "advantages" essentially meaningless.

Of these two colonial governments, that in Korea had far more awesome powers. Although appointments to the position of governor general in both colonies were in theory open to civilians after 1919,

33 Edward I-te Chen, "Japanese Colonialism in Korea and Formosa: A Comparison of the Systems of Political Control," *Harvard Journal of Asiatic Studies* 30 (1970): 155.

only in Taiwan was such a change actually made. In Korea, at the insistence of the Japanese army, the rule of military commanders continued unbroken. Because of the military's autonomy in the Japanese political system, the relationships of the governors general in Korea to the prime minister's office in Japan remained ambiguous. Although occasionally the former accepted the supervision of the latter as a matter of immediate convenience, almost to the end of Japanese rule, the governor general in Korea made his report directly to the emperor. Adding to the prestige of the office was the fact that the Japanese army nominated to it only officers of the highest rank and influence. Virtually invulnerable to interference from the civil government in Tokyo, the governors general of Korea functioned more as imperial proconsuls than as mere colonial officials.[34]

Nor were the governors general in Korea troubled by any need for deference to the Japanese Diet in Tokyo. In the empire's formative years the unresolved question of whether or not the constitution's provisions extended to the colonies provoked a challenge by the Diet to the authority of Japanese colonial governments. Specifically, the controversy centered on the question of whether the governors general of Taiwan or Korea could be given authority to issue *seirei*, legislative ordinances that in the colonies had the same effect as Japanese law, or whether, under the constitution, lawmaking power was reserved for the Diet. In Taiwan, this authority (granted under a highly controversial statute, Law 63) was eventually amended, so that every five years the Government General was forced to seek from the Diet an extension of these powers. In addition, the governor general in Taiwan was obliged to search for relevant Japanese law before issuing his own *seirei*. In Korea, however, the governor general's authority (under Law 30) remained undented by any such limitations.[35]

Thus, isolated from interference from either the home islands or the will of the Korean majority, the governor general in Korea was able to rule as a military autocrat. Beneath him the officials of the Government General comprised an enormous self-contained administrative elite in which most positions were reserved for the Japanese, who were too often arrogant in their omnipotence and contemptuous of Korean sentiment.

34 Kim Han-kyo, "The Japanese Colonial Administration in Korea: An Overview," in *Korea Under Japanese Colonial Rule: Studies of the Policy and Techniques of Japanese Colonialism*, ed. Andrew Nahm (Kalamazoo: Center for Korean Studies, Institute of International and Area Studies, Western Michigan University, 1973), pp. 41–53.

35 Chen, "Japanese Colonialism in Korea and Formosa," pp. 136–40.

In their local governments, Korea and Taiwan had virtually identical systems of administration. Provincial governments were headed by governors who in every case were Japanese who held *chokunin* rank (in which appointments were conferred by imperial order on the recommendation of appropriate officials, in this case by colonial governors general). Below these were county and municipal governments, and at the bottom of the administrative scale were the townships and villages. Koreans occupied most of the village headmen positions on the peninsula, some of the township magistrate offices, and even a few of the chief executive positions at the municipal and county levels, whereas the Japanese in Taiwan monopolized all three levels of local government. As a concession to elicit support of the indigenous peoples of both colonies, the colonial governments there provided the appearance of local autonomy in the form of consultative councils, which were supposed to inject Taiwanese and Korean opinion into the processes of local decision making. But in fact, they consisted largely of Japanese or pro-Japanese Taiwanese or Koreans, selected by the Governments General and not elected by the will of the colonial peoples. They were empowered, in any event, to offer only advice, which the governor general of either colony would accept or reject as he saw fit.[36]

The administrative structures of the three lesser colonies may be summarized briefly, for they did not greatly differ from those of Taiwan and Korea, except in the diminished prestige and restricted authority of their chief executives. Each was headed by a governor holding the *chokunin* rank, who was responsible, until World War II, to the prime minister through the minister for colonial affairs. All three colonies contained two levels of local government. The first of these, the district (or the municipality in the case of the Kwantung Leased Territory), was headed by a district governor who held *sonin* rank (that is, nominal appointment by the emperor but, in practice, appointment by the governor). Below this was the village government headed by a headman or chief. In Karafuto, the Japanese controlled all levels of administration. In the Kwantung Leased Territory and the Nan'yō, indigenous participation in government was restricted to the village level. Even on the remoter islands of the Nan'yō, moreover, the extension of Japanese colonial power undercut the authority of the original native elite: Although the Nan'yōchō did not replace the traditional village chiefs, it sometimes simply bypassed them by establishing a new hierarchy of native officials, appointed and paid by the district government.[37]

36 Ibid., pp. 141–6. 37 Yamabe, "Nihon teikokushugi to shokuminchi," pp. 217–19.

Whatever else may be said about Japanese administration in the overseas territories, one must give Japanese colonial administrators high marks as a group. Indeed, the competence and quality of the average Japanese colonial bureaucrat are remarkable when one considers that they had few of the professional advantages of their counterparts in the British or French colonial systems. Not only was there no Japanese colonial tradition, there also was no specialized colonial service or colonial school like those in Britain or France that might provide particular training in colonial administration. Neither was colonial service a time-honored profession, as it was in Britain, in which distinguished service in the colonies was an important ladder to social promotion and in which a far-flung "old boy" network kept alive the traditions of the colonial service and a steady supply of young talent flowing into it.

At the outset of Japan's colonial venture, certainly, Japan's first overseas officials, like those at the initial stage of German colonialism, were a mixed lot and included a number of adventurers, romantics, exploiters, and incompetents. But as Japan tightened its administrative grip on the colonies, these undesirables were shaken out of the system. By the second decade of Japanese colonial rule, foreign visitors to Taiwan and Korea were bringing back highly favorable impressions of the intelligence, dedication, and integrity of the Japanese bureaucracy they saw there.[38]

This general level of competence is largely explained by the fact that senior- and middle-level officials serving in the colonies were generally drawn from the graduates of Japan's imperial universities, particularly Tokyo Imperial University, who had passed the civil service examination. They were, therefore, not drawn from the public at large or even from among those Japanese who had considerable experience in the colonies, but from the various ministries and bureaus of civil government in metropolitan Japan. The thinking behind this arrangement seems to have been that it was better to have Japan represented overseas by individuals who had met the exacting and uniform standards of the Japanese bureaucracy than by brilliant innovators or those who had expertise in a particular colonial area. This is not to say that in making personnel assignments the Japanese government did not re-

38 See, for example, E. C. Semple, "Japanese Colonial Methods," *Bulletin of the American Geographical Society* (April 1913): 269; and A. J. Brown, *The Mastery of the Far East, the Story of Korea's Transformation and Japan's Rise to Supremacy in the Orient* (New York: Scribner, 1919), p. 361.

gard colonial experience as an asset, but many bureaucrats who served Japan overseas were transferred from colony to colony, their posting to any one colonial territory rarely being more than a few years. Undoubtedly, these arrangements also contributed to the aloofness and isolation of Japan's colonial officials from the indigenous peoples they administered. Yet because they were imbued with a sense of public service typical of Japanese civil government, they took their jobs seriously, and because they were openly given preferential treatment and reward (a point of bitter resentment by their Korean and Taiwanese co-workers similarly employed in colonial government), they were rarely tainted with corruption or malfeasance.

A key element in the general effectiveness of Japanese colonial administration was the availability of military and police power in such scale and pervasiveness as to ensure obedience to Japanese authority. In Korea the most sensitive and trouble-prone colony, Japan kept its greatest military strength at hand. Korea had been subdued and its army disbanded by one division and several infantry regiments; after 1920 the Japanese army permanently stationed two of its best divisions on the northern half of the peninsula. In addition, the Japanese maintained several air regiments and fortress garrisons in the country, along with a wide distribution of gendarmerie (*kenpeitai*) units throughout the colony. In Taiwan, considering its smaller size and smaller potential for civil unrest, the Japanese maintained a considerable military presence: a mixed brigade, an air regiment, an artillery regiment, detachments of the gendarmerie in all the main towns, and a garrison at the naval base at Mako in the Pescadores Islands. In the Kwantung Leased Territory, the Port Arthur Fortress Garrison and the nearby elements of the Kwantung Army were more than enough to handle any emergency. In Karafuto and the Nan'yō, however, Japanese military and naval forces were negligible until a year or so before the outbreak of the Pacific War.[39]

Significantly, Japan never augmented these overseas garrisons with colonial armies. Alone among the colonial nations, Japan was the only power never to raise any separate military contingents from among its colonial peoples, like the Indian Army of the British, the French Armée Coloniale, or the Force Publique of the Belgian Congo. In large part, this may have been because the Japanese could never contem-

39 Ōe Shinobu, "Shokuminchi ryōyū to gunbu," *Rekishigaku kenkyū* (September 1978): 10–41; Bōeicho bōei kenshūjō senshishitsu, eds., *Kantōgun*, vol. 1 (Tokyo: Asagumo shinbunsha, 1969), pp. 13–15.

plate the possibility of arming their colonial charges. Koreans and Taiwanese were recruited, indeed drafted, into the Japanese army in World War II, but only into labor battalions, not into separate colonial combat units.

Yet when one considers that Britain maintained only a few battalions to provide security for all its vast African territories, the military forces that Japan maintained in the colonies or had available nearby in the home islands seem indeed massive for the modest size of its empire. Undoubtedly, this preponderance of military power had an effect on the attitudes of Japanese colonial officials, who knew they could count on instant, loyal, and overwhelming military support and were therefore much less likely to temporize in dealing with their colonial populations.

Yet rarely did Japanese colonial governments have to call upon regular military forces to preserve order. The empire's first line of internal security was the double weave of two systems of law enforcement employed by the Japanese: modern and superbly efficient police forces supplemented by the clever exploitation of indigenous systems of community control.

As it was in so many other aspects, Taiwan became the model for Japan's system of law enforcement throughout the empire. The immediate problem after the acquisition of the island was the suppression of continuing anti-Japanese activities. The regular units of the Japanese army being too expensive to maintain as permanent local security forces, the Government General, at Gotō Shinpei's initiative, took steps to create a modern police force patterned after the police system in the home islands but adapted it to suit the conditions in Taiwan. Carefully recruited, rigorously trained, and distributed throughout the island, except in the wildest aboriginal areas of the interior (whose borders were patrolled by specially trained Japanese guard units), the Japanese police in Taiwan were placed in every village, ready to punish any resistance to Japanese authority quickly and efficiently.

What is more, the police became the backbone of local administration in Taiwan. Assigned a wide range of functions – tax collection, enforcement of sanitary regulations, public information, superintendence of local public works programs, and other supervisory tasks – the Japanese policeman became a colonial functionary whose responsibilities resembled those of the district officer in British Africa. During the next several decades the structure and function of this police system were perfected and extended to the other colonies, though they were adapted to regional circumstances.[40] In his omnipresent and seemingly omnipotent role, the Japanese policeman came to be the chief point of contact between the colonial government and local communities throughout the empire. Even the more remote atolls in the Nan'yō were each assigned a policeman to keep an eye on village government and to instruct the native population in modern agricultural techniques, in which he was often trained. To Japanese colonial authorities, the wide-ranging functions of the Japanese police were a source of continuing pride and an indication of the efficiency of the Japanese colonial government. In this perspective the predominant place of the policeman in colonial affairs gave evidence of the empire's law, order, and material progress.[41]

In his tasks the Japanese policeman was assisted, though never supplanted, by the indigenous police who always remained sharply subordinate in numbers, authority, and pay scale. Only in Korea, where the Japanese had taken over a national police force (which they had largely helped train) did indigenes occupy higher posts in the colonial police structure and comprise a substantial portion of the total colonial police force. But the Korean police was in no way independent of Japanese police authority.

Modern police forces were expensive and, by themselves, would not have been adequate to maintain both local order and bureaucratic control throughout the empire. To supplement and support the uniformed police in its various local functions, the Japanese were quick to exploit traditional systems of village security and leadership. Here again, Taiwan provided valuable precedents. Using his rapidly acquired knowledge of local customs, Gotō Shinpei was quick to adopt the ancient Chinese *pao chia* system of collective responsibility for maintaining law and order in the village. This mechanism for community control had, for centuries, contributed to the stability of rural China but had fallen into disuse in Taiwan. Under Gotō's direction, the *pao chia* (*hōkō* in Japanese) system became an effective mechanism for information gathering, militia mobilization, and the search and seizure of suspected dissidents. More than this, Gotō refurbished the

40 Ching-Chih Chen, "Police and Community Control Systems in the Empire," in Myers and Peattie, *Japanese Colonial Empire*, pp. 213–39.

41 To Western observers who visited the colonies, however, the ubiquitous and often inquisitorial presence of the Japanese colonial police became an increasingly onerous burden. Travel accounts by foreigners who passed through Japan's colonial territories almost always mentioned the official phobia about foreign spies and the police's constant surveillance and frequent questioning of foreign residents and visitors.

system so that it came to be used not only for local security but for general administrative purposes as well. Through it, the Government General was able to use local manpower to collect taxes, construct and maintain local public works, gather census data, and perform a myriad of other administrative tasks, all under the watchful eye of the Japanese police.[42]

The *pao chia* system, being a traditional Chinese institution, could not be used in Korea, Karafuto, or the Nan'yō with the same effectiveness as it was in Taiwan; being a rural control system, it was less appropriate to the metropolitan populace of the Kwantung Leased Territory. Nevertheless, building on their experience in community control, the Japanese learned how to manipulate traditional leadership mechanisms on the local level in all their territories (except in Karafuto, where the overwhelming portion of Japanese in the colonial population did not make it necessary to do so). In Korea, the Government General fostered a reemphasis on Confucian virtues, particularly those of loyalty to the sovereign (in this case the Japanese emperor) and appointed prominent local leaders who were willingly subservient to Japanese authority. In the Nan'yō, the Japanese police worked through village chieftains to reach into local Micronesian communities to ensure order and to guarantee compliance with Japanese directives.

Through these Japanese and indigenous mechanisms, the Japanese were able to extend tight bureaucratic control even to the empire's most remote parts. Unimpeded by any barriers to arbitrary and authoritarian rule and able to subject their colonial populations to constant police surveillance and to various systems of community control, the Japanese colonial governments thus ensured an unprecedented degree of law, order, and stability throughout the empire. In the process they created bureaucracies more centralized and more authoritarian than any that existed in Japan itself, a fact that accounts for the vigor and force with which Japan was able to carry out its colonial policies.

## THE JAPANESE COLONIAL ECONOMY: DEVELOPMENT AND EXPLOITATION

No aspect of Japanese colonial history is more complex and more subject to disagreement than the conduct of economic policy within the empire. Japan's capacity to create modern economic infrastruc-

42 Ching-chih Chen, "The Japanese Administration of the *Pao-chia* System in Taiwan, 1895–1945," *Journal of Asian Studies* 34 (February 1975): 391–446.

tures in the colonies, as well as to increase both agricultural and industrial production, was a source of great satisfaction to Japanese colonial authorities at the time and has been the focus of a significant amount of postwar scholarship on the economic dimensions of Japanese colonialism. Using these criteria it is legitimate to speak of the empire's economic "development." Yet in light of Japan's harsh demands on its colonial territories, the inequities it created between the Japanese and their colonial charges, and the distortions and imbalances it wrought in the colonies' economic structures, Japanese economic policy has been condemned in the postwar era by Japan's former colonial peoples and criticized by a majority of specialists in the field. In this perspective, Japan's economic activities in the colonies clearly merit the term *exploitation*. That the debate has come to include emotional recrimination, incomplete or disputed data, and highly specialized analytical methodology, in almost equal proportions, has made its resolution in the near future all the more unlikely.[43]

It is, however, possible to make certain generalizations regarding economic relations within the empire about which most might agree. Although these apply to some degree to the empire as a whole, they are drawn specifically from the cases of the two colonies that figured most largely in Japan's economic schemes, Taiwan and Korea.

No matter what the range of motives may have been for Japan's acquisition of an empire – and these appear to have been largely strategic rather than economic in nature – Japan was not slow in shaping its colonies to the homeland's economic advantage. In this sense, the economic structure of the Japanese empire was not dissimilar to the typical European colonial model, in which the colonial economies were developed to serve as docile producers of raw materials for the metropolitan power and as a market for its manufactures. What distinguishes the Japanese case was that although the European countries' attention to their colonial economies was sometimes desultory, Japan devoted continuous and assiduous planning and skill to its economic interests in the colonies. To paraphrase the words of one scholar, Japan's colonial economies suffered not from neglect but from overattention.

43 Examples of the "development" approach to Japanese colonialism can be found in Ramon H. Myers and Adrienne Ching, "Agricultural Development in Taiwan Under Japanese Colonial Rule," *Journal of Asian Studies* 33 (August 1964): 555–70; James I. Nakamura, "Incentives, Productivity Gaps, and Agricultural Growth Rates in Pre-War Japan, Taiwan, and Korea," in *Japan in Crisis: Essays in Taishō Democracy*, ed. Bernard Silberman and H. D. Harootunian (Princeton, N.J.: Princeton University Press, 1974), pp. 329–73. Examples of the "exploitation" approach are by Kwan Suk-kim, "An Analysis of Economic Change in Korea," in *Korea Under Japanese Colonial Rule*, pp. 100–7; and Asada Kyōji, *Nihon teikokushugi to kyū-shokuminchi jinushi sei* (Tokyo: Mizusu shobō, 1968).

It is obvious that only the power and resources of the Japanese state could account for the scale and direction of economic growth attained during the life of the empire. The transformation of the agrarian economies of Taiwan and Korea was wrought not so much by private venture capital as by energetic, enterprising colonial bureaucracies whose policies were designed to serve the needs of the central government in Tokyo and to create conditions in the colonies that would lead to economic growth and the eventual participation of private capital. To accomplish these objectives, Japan simply extended to the colonies the experiences and successes of the Meiji state in fostering prosperity in the home islands. Hard on the heels of the initial military and administrative measures that provided for a stable and secure colonial environment, therefore, the new colonial governments embarked on ambitious programs to create modern facilities and institutions that were essential to economic growth and that often were beneficial to the colonizers and colonized alike.

At the time that Japan acquired Taiwan, these efforts, unsupported as yet by colonial revenues and thus paid for by deficit financing, were an expensive burden for a central government that had so recently modernized its own domestic economy. It was therefore imperative for Japan to reduce this drain on its treasury and to make the colony financially independent as soon as possible and also to make it serve as a source of profit for the mother country. Like the Meiji state before it, the Taiwan Government General determined that the agricultural sector should bear the burden of the costs of modernization. To enable it to do so, the Government General exercised its massive authority to direct agricultural development, allocating the necessary expenditures, using special tax revenues to influence the behavior of agricultural producers, disseminating modern agricultural technology, and establishing monopolies in certain agriculturally based industries that were expected to provide substantial revenue. More importantly, the colonial government devoted the most intensive research and planning to developing those commodities that offered the best prospects for a quick return on investment and that at the same time would meet Japan's domestic needs. These efforts laid the foundations of a highly successful sugar industry between 1900 and 1910, which was heavily subsidized at first but which, within a decade, became the colony's leading industry and contributed to its eventual fiscal self-sufficiency. From sugar the Government General turned to the expansion and modernization of Taiwan's rice production, applying to it modern technologies and techniques, so that by the 1920s it became Taiwan's second major export to Japan.[44]

This pattern of massive government involvement in stimulating and commercializing agriculture, particularly through deficit financing, large-scale public investment, and the establishment of semigovernment monopolies, laid the foundation for the economies of all of Japan's overseas territories. Certainly, the pattern of agricultural development in the Kwantung Leased Territory and the Nan'yō was much the same, though from the beginning in Karafuto, the Japanese effort was much more exploitive, concentrating as it did on a rapacious use of the colony's timber reserves by private venture capital in the pulp-manufacturing industry.

Japan's colonial economic policies were in every case shaped to meet the needs of the metropolitan homeland, not those of the colonial populations themselves. For this reason, the evolution of Japanese colonial policies cannot be understood separately from the shifting economic circumstances of Japan's domestic economy during the empire's lifetime. Viewed chronologically, the evolution of this relationship between domestic need and colonial policy can be seen as having two distinct phases.

In the initial period, from approximately 1900 to 1930, the transformation of Japan from an essentially agrarian economy to an industrial base dictated a shift in the nation's economic needs. A booming industrial machine had begun to require markets abroad for its manufactures, markets to be found most easily in protected colonial territories from which foreign competition could most effectively be driven. During this phase, therefore, the trade of both Taiwan and Korea was made increasingly dependent on the metropole. Japan monopolized the principal colonial industries and established colonial customs systems that diverted the whole of their foreign trade to the home islands. At the same time the colonial governments vigorously prevented the development of industries that might challenge those in Japan.

Equally important was that Japan's domestic agricultural sector could no longer meet the demands of a growing domestic population. Having enjoyed surpluses in food grains at the end of the nineteenth

44 Samuel P. S. Ho, "The Economic Development Policy of the Japanese Colonial Government in Taiwan, 1895–1945," in *Government and Economic Development*, ed. Gustav Ranis (New Haven, Conn.: Yale University Press, 1971), pp. 289–99; Samuel P. S. Ho, "The Economic Development of Colonial Taiwan: Evidence and Interpretations," *Journal of Asian Studies* 34 (February 1975): 417–39.

century, because of the heroic efforts of the Japanese farmer in the early Meiji period, the nation now faced a shortage in those cereals. Importation of food from foreign countries was not a permanent solution, because of the drain on Japan's foreign exchange.

For these reasons Korea and Taiwan were developed as major food suppliers, Taiwan largely in sugar and Korea mostly in rice. Despite these efforts, however, and because of overheating in the Japanese economy provoked by rapid industrialization, food prices continued to rise in Japan, and food stocks, particularly rice, were insufficient to meet Japanese public demand. These conditions sparked the widespread rice riots of 1918, a wave of popular unrest that threatened to lead to a major upheaval. In response, the Japanese government directed the colonial authorities in Korea to undertake a massive effort to expand rice production on the peninsula. The resultant Rice Increase Plan involved intensive efforts to improve the technical aspects of Korean agriculture and to increase the acreage of arable land through the expansion of irrigation systems. These efforts did indeed substantially increase the peninsula's annual rice yield, so that Korea became the principal supplier of rice to the metropolitan power.[45]

Although the bulk of the populations of both Taiwan and Korea were agricultural, the impact of the Japanese programs to increase agricultural production was markedly different in the two colonies. In Taiwan, Japanese agricultural policies were mainly of direct benefit to the rural economy. Improved agricultural technology slowly spread throughout the island, raising not only production levels but also the yield per unit of land. Until the 1930s, moreover, shipments of Taiwanese rice had little effect on the consumption levels of the Taiwanese populace. Most importantly, the land registration program (1898–1903) conducted in order to obtain accurate data for agricultural planning and to provide for an enlarged and stable tax base did no great violence to the traditional landholding system and worked to the general advantage of the average farmer. In Korea, on the other hand, Japanese policy may be said to have worsened the quality of rural life, despite the gains in agricultural production. Although there appears to have been no Japanese plan to dispossess the Korean farmer of his land, the flood of land-hungry Japanese immigrants before the annexation, combined with a land registration program (1906–17) that ripped apart the complex fabric of Korean land tenure, threw numerous rural poor off the land

45 Suh Chang-chul, *Growth and Structural Changes in the Korean Economy, 1910–1940* (Cambridge, Mass.: Council on East Asian Studies, Harvard University, 1978), pp. 6–13.

and left them without title to it. Those tenant farmers who remained found themselves under the even tighter control of rapacious landlords, an increasing number of whom were Japanese farm managers and land speculators. Indeed, the inequities of the tenant–landlord relationship so minimized the incentives to the Korean farmer that his productivity per acre during this period hardly increased at all. Worse than this, the ruthless accomplishment of the original objectives of the Rice Increase Plan victimized the Korean consumer as well. All rice surpluses produced in Korea were shipped directly to Japan, and after the 1920s the consumption of rice by Koreans (half that of the much smaller population on Taiwan) actually dropped, the average Korean being obliged to eat lesser grains such as millet.[46]

In any event, by the end of the 1920s, both Taiwan and Korea had been molded into docile colonial economies, linked to the colonial power by a trade cycle of exported raw materials and foodstuffs and imported manufactured consumer goods. But at the outset of the 1930s, a dramatic shift in Japan's economic circumstances ushered in the second phase of its colonial economic policy and sharply redirected the colonial economies of Taiwan and Korea.

As Japan moved toward a semiwar economy and the consequent decision to create a self-sufficient industrial base, the two major colonies were seen as strategic contributors to this endeavor. During the first half of the decade, the colonial governments of Korea and Taiwan drew up plans for major industrialization programs and downgraded agricultural production as an economic priority. Other economic trends in Japan had already pointed to this shift. Foundering in the world crisis of 1929, Japan needed profitable investment opportunities to contend with these difficulties, and Korea, with its rich mineral resources, abundant hydroelectric power, and cheap labor, was suddenly perceived by the Japanese business community as an attractive market. There was, moreover, an agricultural depression in Japan, manifested particularly in the plummeting price of rice. In both Taiwan and Korea, therefore, agricultural expansion programs were curtailed, and industrial facilities were created to produce the raw materials – petrochemicals, ores, and metals – needed by Japanese heavy industry. These efforts were more successful in Korea than in Taiwan, owing to initial inadequacies of labor and transportation systems on the island, though by 1939 industry and agriculture occupied almost equal proportions of Taiwan's total

46 Myers and Ching, "Agricultural Development in Taiwan," pp. 560–5; Kwan, "An Analysis of Economic Change in Korea," pp. 100–7.

production. With the outbreak of Japan's war in China, Korea increasingly became a logistical base for Japanese military operations on the continent, and Korea's industrial plants turned to the task of keeping Japan's armies in China supplied. At the same time, rice shipments from Korea continued to flow toward the home islands, to the considerable hardship of the Korean populace.[47]

These industrialization programs, geared as they were to meet Japan's military needs, little benefited the peoples of Taiwan and Korea during those years, though they worked to the greater disadvantage of the latter. This is exemplified by the disparity in consumer services, wage differentials, and employment rates. For example, even though hydroelectric production in Korea nearly tripled that of Taiwan, less than 12 percent of Korean families enjoyed electric lighting, as compared with 36.3 percent of Taiwanese households (and over 90 percent of Japanese families in the home islands). Not only did the Taiwanese tend to receive higher wages than did their counterparts in Korea, but the wage differentials between Japanese and indigenes in the same jobs were also far greater in Korea than in Taiwan, where employment rates were also twice those of Korea.[48]

By the outbreak of the Pacific War, therefore, the economies of all of Japan's territories were harnessed to the needs of the embattled metropolitan power at the sacrifice of the welfare of Japan's colonial peoples. And yet the colonies collectively occupied only a moderately important position in the total economy of the home islands, particularly in terms of strategic imports. Although in the late 1920s, Korea and Taiwan supplied Japan with four-fifths of its rice imports, two-thirds of its sugar imports, and lesser amounts of minerals, lumber, and other items, Japan was never able to obtain from its colonies its chief requirements for a whole range of strategic products, including textile fibers, metals, petroleum, and fertilizers, which it was forced to seek abroad. During the empire's lifetime, moreover, the colonies provided Japan with no more than a modest export market for its manufactures (about 20 percent of Japan's industrial exports and about 10 percent of its textile exports in 1930). Japan's colonial trade, though it grew far more rapidly than did that with foreign countries, counted for only about one-quarter of the nation's total overseas trade.[49]

47 Yamabe, *Nihon tōjika no Chōsen*, pp. 188–95; Samuel P. S. Ho, "Agricultural Transformation Under Colonialism: The Case of Taiwan," *Journal of Economic History* 28 (September 1968): 324–6. 48 Kim, "The Japanese Colonial Administration," pp. 107–10.

49 Yamabe, "Nihon teikokushugi to shokuminchi," pp. 205–7.

Two questions are frequently raised about the significance of Japan's colonial economy. The first is the extent to which, in strictly economic terms, the empire was an asset or a liability to Japan. Obviously, a comprehensive and conclusive answer to this question is impossible, as there is no accounting system that can calculate the costs of maintaining a colonial establishment – military expenditures, government subsidies, administrative outlays, and the like – and match them logically against the returns – volume of trade, reductions in foreign exchange disbursements, repatriated capital, and so on. Although certain private Japanese groups undoubtedly found their colonial investments highly profitable, the net profit to the nation of its economic activities in the colonies is less certain, given the tariff preferences and subsidies that supported such enterprises.[50] At any given time, moreover, the economic benefits of empire accruing to Japan were very mixed, as the advantages of one group were often the costs of another. Because of imports from Korea, for example, city dwellers paid less for rice than they would have otherwise; on the other hand, Japanese rice farmers had less earning power. Overall, it appears that Japan's economic activities in the colonies were not cost effective (especially considering the tariff preferences and subsidies that supported them), though certain private Japanese groups found their colonial investments highly profitable. These points require considerably more data and study.

The second question pertains to the influence of Japan's economic policies on the postwar development of the former colonial territories, particularly Taiwan and Korea. At first glance, one would have to conclude that the Japanese contribution was real and indisputable. Whatever advantages the Japanese consumer may have gained at the time from the modernization and expansion of the agricultural sectors of Taiwan and Korea, it cannot be denied that both countries emerged from Japanese rule with efficient and productive agricultural systems. Nor is it disputable that the modern facilities and institutions – transportation and communications networks, modern banking and monetary systems, educational and administrative facilities, hospitals, and factories – that the Japanese created during the colonial period were of substantial importance in the economic advance of Taiwan and Korea.

Yet recent studies have come to cast doubt on the long-range economic contributions of Japanese colonialism to the former colonial

50 Lockwood, *The Economic Development of Japan*, pp. 50–2.

territories. Even though both Taiwan and Korea expanded their agriculture during their colonial periods, it does not appear that Japan provided the necessary elements of *sustained* nonagricultural growth in either colony. Because Japanese policies kept economic power out of the hands of the Taiwanese and Koreans, a modern entrepreneurial class failed to develop in Taiwan and grew only marginally in Korea. In both countries, because industrial and administrative positions requiring technical or managerial skills were so often filled by Japanese during the colonial period, few indigenous technicians or managers were available to either country, which resulted in massive dislocations in the economic machinery of Taiwan and Korea when the Japanese withdrew.[51]

## THE JAPANESE COLONIAL PRESENCE: EMIGRATION, SETTLEMENT, AND THE COLONIAL LIFE-STYLE

It was the great dream of many Japanese colonial theorists of the late Meiji and early Taishō periods that the colonies could become outlets for emigration, in which the nation's "surplus" population could find new living space under the Japanese flag and create overseas settlement colonies similar to those white settlements of the British Commonwealth. From faulty population statistics, an initial ignorance of physical conditions in the colonies, and much wishful thinking, Japanese colonial propagandists derived heady visions of mass emigration of energetic and resourceful Japanese agriculturalists who would create "new Japans" overseas, strengthening and increasing the Japanese race and furnishing foodstuffs for the health and vigor of the homeland.[52]

In fact, the circumstances and predisposition of those Japanese who did emigrate to the colonies undercut these rosy expectations. First, the initial conditions of health, climate, and civil unrest discouraged the settlement of certain colonies. In Taiwan many early immigrants fell victim to poor health conditions, an unfamiliar semitropical climate, and the sporadic attacks of rebellious Taiwanese. In Karafuto the bitter climate and psychological remoteness from the home islands also discouraged large-scale settlement. In Korea the problem was the population–land ratio. By the time of Korea's annexation, Japanese aspira-

51 Suh, *Growth and Structural Changes*, pp. 143–56; Ho, "The Economic Development Policy," p. 328.

52 See, for example, Tōgo Minoru, *Nihon shokumin ron* (Tokyo: Bunbudō, 1906), pp. 176–88, 243–6.

tions to colonize the peninsula had foundered on the fact that Korea was already filled – with Koreans. Although many Korean farmers had indeed been dispossessed by the new Japanese-directed system of land tenure, most of the cultivated land that was redistributed quickly found its way into the hands of a few landlords, Japanese and Korean.[53]

Nor did the Japanese who did emigrate to the colonies conform to the colonial theorists' cherished notions. Far from being pioneers willing to till the hillsides of Taiwan or Korea, most of the first wave of Japanese who rushed to the new territories were profit seekers, land speculators, opportunists, and carpetbaggers, who came seeking preferment and position in the new colonial administrations. So notorious was the conduct of many of these persons ("like dung flies following horses" complained one Japanese newspaper) that Japanese authorities had to repatriate a good number to Japan. Many came from the lowest social stratum of the Japanese countryside: tenant farmers, tinkers, peddlers, failed shopkeepers, and rural poor of every description. Geographic proximity meant that immigrants of this type washed into the peninsula in massive numbers and established an unusually extensive and abrasive occupation. From Kyushu, beginning some twenty years before Korea's annexation into the empire, these rural poor had entered the country in a growing tide, which has been likened to the influx of the European *pieds noirs* into North Africa in the same period. Spreading throughout the Korean countryside, they appropriated land, food, and farm animals from an increasingly outraged Korean populace. In the years immediately following the Russo-Japanese War, when this flood of impoverished interlopers reached its height, conditions in much of southern Korea were not unlike those of the post–Civil War American South. Indeed, the chaotic conditions in parts of rural Korea, where isolated Japanese settlements had to defend themselves against Korean counterviolence, have been likened to those of the native American frontier of the mid-nineteenth century.[54] By the 1920s this flood had receded. Many Japanese remained in the Korean countryside, a few buying or simply expropriating vast amounts of cultivated land, so that they became the new landlords of

53 Karl Moskowitz, "The Creation of the Oriental Development Company: Japanese Illusions Meet Korean Reality," *Occasional Papers on Korea*, no. 2: Joint Committee on Korean Studies, the American Council of Learned Societies and the Social Science Research Council, March 1974, pp. 73–109.

54 Gregory Henderson, "Japan's Chosen: Immigrants, Ruthlessness, and Development Shock," in *Korea Under Japanese Colonial Rule*, pp. 263–6. For the impressions of a Japanese immigrant in Korea during this turbulent period, see Muramatsu Takeji, "Shokuminsha no kaisō," pt. 6, *Chōsen kenkyū* (February 1968):52–3.

Korea. But most eventually gravitated to the cities where economic opportunity was greater.[55]

In the second, more stabilized phase of Japanese rule in the colonies, after most of the land had been legally apportioned, most of the government positions occupied, and the opportunities for quick profit nearly extinguished for those possessing little but their wits, the flow of Japanese immigrants to the colonies slowed to a trickle. Government plans to encourage agricultural immigration, as part of its program of "Japanizing" the colonies, were generally unavailing, despite generous inducements of free travel, low-cost loans, and handsome subsidies. The hardships, risks, and effort involved in clearing and cultivating land in the colonies discouraged most Japanese farmers. A few came and settled and farmed successfully, but in Korea, Taiwan, the Kwantung Leased Territory, and even Karafuto, Japanese agricultural communities remained small in size and number.[56]

These settlement patterns had profound consequences for the empire and for its racial, occupational, and geographical structure. First, the immigrationist objectives of Japanese colonial policy were never realized, and the colonies, insufficiently attractive to the average Japanese, never solved the nation's real or imagined demographic problems. For this reason and because of the natural increase of the indigenous majorities, the Japanese in the colonies, despite their gradual numerical increase, remained a tiny minority in the major colonies. (In 1905 the Japanese made up only 2 percent of the total population of Taiwan; nearly a quarter of a century later, that figure had grown to only 5.8 percent. Korea, despite the large numbers of Japanese immigrants before 1910, showed an even smaller minority: 1.3 percent in 1915 and 2.9 percent in 1939.) Because of their small numbers and despite their favored position among the indigenous majorities, the Japanese colonials were seldom influential in shaping colonial policy. Certainly, with the possible exception of the Japanese minority in Manchuria, overseas Japanese in Asia never attained the political importance of the French settlers in Algeria or the whites in Rhodesia.

The second consequence of the restricted Japanese immigration to the colonies was its effect on the social and occupational stratification in the empire. Although Japanese farmers were on the whole reluctant

55 Kajimura Hideki, "Shokuminchi Chōsen de no Nihonjin," in *Chihō demokurashii to sensō*, vol. 9: *Chihō bunka no Nihonshi* (Tokyo: Bun'inchi sokai shuppan, 1978), pp. 336–43.

56 Andrew Grajdanzev, *Modern Korea: Her Economic and Social Development Under the Japanese* (New York: Institute of Pacific Relations, 1944), pp. 79–80; Andrew Grajdanzev, *Formosa Today: An Analysis of the Economic Development and Strategic Importance of Japan's Tropical Colony* (New York: Institute of Pacific Relations, 1972), pp. 24–5.

to undertake the tasks of agricultural settlement in the colonies, a growing number of Japanese were able and eager to take advantage of opportunities in administration, commerce, and the white-collar professions. Thus, the Japanese who immigrated to the colonies in the second half of the empire did so chiefly as civil servants, managers, technicians, and merchants. "In all these towns," wrote a Western visitor to Taiwan in 1924, "one is struck . . . with the fact that the Japanese are not pioneers, that they are officials or merchants, government employees, or petty shopkeepers, exploiters or capitalists, but rarely tillers of the soil or clearers of virgin lands."[57] Thus the most comfortable and most lucrative occupations were essentially the preserve of Japanese colonials, and as a result, they occupied the highest social stratum in terms of prestige, salary, and life-style.

The Japanese monopoly of positions in government, commerce, and industry meant that urban concentration was a third characteristic of Japanese patterns of settlement in the colonies. By 1938, for example, 71 percent of all Japanese in Korea were concentrated in fifty urban centers on the peninsula, over half in ten cities, and 21 percent in Keijō (Seoul) alone. The largest cities in Taiwan held the greatest concentrations of Japanese on the island, and Japanese comprised 41 percent of the island's capital, Taihoku (Taipei). The Kwantung Leased Territory was largely urban, of course, and the Japanese comprised a substantial portion of the residents of Dairen and Port Arthur. Even in Karafuto, two-thirds of the overwhelmingly Japanese population were located in the largest towns and cities.

The exception to these general patterns of immigration and settlement was the Nan'yō, which differed from the other colonies in its racial and cultural composition and geographic situation. By disposition and cultural tradition, the Micronesian population was suited to neither rice farming nor agricultural labor. Thus, from the beginning the economic development of Japanese Micronesia was heavily dependent on Japanese labor. At the outset of Japanese rule, conforming to the general pattern of Japanese colonial settlement, immigrants from the home islands comprised only a small portion of the population of Micronesia (in 1920, slightly fewer than 4,000 out of a population of nearly 52,000). Then, at the beginning of the 1930s, spurred on by immigrationist propaganda and a program of generous government inducements to settle in the islands, the Japanese began to move into the Nan'yō in numbers that were massive in relation to its tiny

57 Harry A. Franck, *Glimpses of Japan and Formosa* (New York: Century Press, 1924), pp. 164–5.

landmass. Many came from Okinawa as contract laborers for the sizable sugar industry in the Mariana Islands (Saipan, Tinian, and Rota) and eventually stayed to open up small shops and stores. Others cultivated coffee, pineapples, or cassava. Still others, largely from the Ryūkyū Islands, came to fish the abundant tropical waters. By 1935, the number of Japanese coming into Micronesia had become what one American observer called a "rip tide" of immigration, and toward the end of the decade, Japanese substantially outnumbered the native Micronesians. The distribution of the Japanese in the Nan'yō was uneven, however. Far the largest number settled in the Marianas, the Palau Islands, and Ponape; very few went to the Marshall Islands.[58]

The Japanese in their colonies constructed for themselves a sunlit way of life common to colonials everywhere. One of the first tasks of the various colonial governments had been to create urban environments appropriate to the favored status of the colonizing race. The model, of course, was Taihoku (Taipei), the capital of Taiwan, which had been splendidly renovated at the beginning of the century under the direction of Gotō Shinpei, who was determined to demonstrate Japan's new status as a colonial power with the creation of a truly imperial city. Gotō's master plan, thoroughly Western in concept and design, transformed the dilapidated little city of Taipei, confined by its crumbling Chinese walls, into a modern colonial capital graced with broad, tree-shaded boulevards, parks, fountains, and impressive public buildings of brick and stone, of which the Government General Building, with its heavy Prussian mansard architecture, was the most magnificent. Within a few years Japanese colonial authorities had begun the expansion and modernization of all of Taiwan's provincial capitals along lines that were similar, though smaller in scale. Within a quarter of a century the empire could boast a number of handsome capitals – Keijō (Seoul), Dairen, Ryojun (Port Arthur), and Toyohara (in Karafuto) – which rivaled Western colonial cities in Asia and were better planned, more ordered, and more attractive than many cities in the home islands.

The physical arrangement of these capitals was often remarkably similar to their counterparts in the tropical empires of the West. Separated in each case from the older, more crowded commercial core of the original city and its indigenous majority was a Japanese residential section, quiet, orderly, and clean, with schools, hospitals, and recreational areas, all generally reserved for the Japanese, but open on a

58 Peattie, *Nan'yō*, chapter 6.

carefully restricted basis to selected members of the Taiwanese, Korean, or Chinese elite. Here, isolated from the crowding and noise of the "native quarter," the Japanese residents, surrounded only by their fellow nationals and by those indigenes who pulled the rickshas, swept the streets, collected the garbage, and hauled away the night soil, enjoyed a life of comfort and prestige not usually available to them in the less privileged surroundings of the metropolitan homeland. The amenities and pleasures available to Japanese colonials varied with the two colonies: In Taiwan, weary colonial officials or merchants could relax at the hot springs resorts in the hills behind Taihoku; in Korea and Taiwan there were numerous geisha and tea houses; in the Kwantung Leased Territory, fine beaches and parks eased life; and in Micronesia, the Japanese enjoyed the cool bougainvillea-covered verandas of their clubs and cottages. But everywhere, community separatism was the common pattern. Even in the smaller towns of rural Taiwan and Korea, the Japanese lived in tight, exclusive communities, out of contact with the populace around them.

The isolated existence of the colonial Japanese, in which they enjoyed homes, salaries, and public facilities and services far superior to anything available to the local populace, served to create attitudes of superiority and contempt toward the "natives," all too common to Western colonial systems. Over the years their own favored status and the demeaned position of the Korean, Taiwanese, and Chinese subjects of the empire came to be the natural order of colonial life, an outlook that made a mockery of Japanese rhetoric about the assimilation of colonizer and colonized.[59]

Ultimately, of course, these attitudes, in combination with the disasters that overtook and obliterated the empire and the homeland at the end of the Pacific War, foreclosed any future for the Japanese in the newly liberated colonial territories after 1945. Not only were Japanese colonials swept from their positions of privilege at the war's end; they also were herded together by the Occupation armies of the victorious allies and compelled to quit their colonial domiciles forever. In the Russian-occupied territories – Manchuria, the Liaotung peninsula, northern Korea, and southern Sakhalin – tens of thousands of Japanese soldiers and civilians were transported to Soviet labor camps, where many died and the rest faced long imprisonment before they again saw their homeland. Their compatriots in territories now under

59 Attitudes of one class of Japanese colonial elites toward indigenous peoples are discussed in Ozawa Yūsaku, "Kyū Nihon jinushi no Chosenkan," *Chōsen kenkyū* (December 1968):35–41.

American, British, or Chinese control – the Micronesian islands, Taiwan, and southern Korea – were repatriated more quickly, but their future was bleak. Stripped of all wealth, privilege, or function, this unhappy human wreckage was cast upon the shores of a ruined and defeated country whose once proud colonial reputation was now an object of universal hatred and disdain.

## THE INDIGENOUS RESPONSE TO JAPANESE COLONIALISM

Given the nature of the Japanese colonial presence, it was to be expected that all the colonial peoples welcomed the end of Japanese rule in 1945. What is remarkable, however, is the disparity in the depths of indigenous feeling toward Japanese overlordships within the various colonial territories.

In the case of Korea, the Japanese were faced with a virtual war of popular resistance in the years between the establishment of the protectorate and the annexation of the peninsula into the empire, after which the fires of national hatred continued to smolder until they burst out anew in 1919. The March First movement of that year was by any test a protest of national proportions. Only the most drastic Japanese measures, the massive presence of the Japanese army, and the imprisonment or exile of most of the leadership of the resistance brought the Korean people to a sullen obedience. Despite the belief by Japanese liberals, like Prime Minister Hara Takashi, that Koreans only wanted their just rights under the Constitution as subjects of an empire, few politically conscious Koreans in subsequent years would have been satisfied with anything less than complete independence from their colonial oppressor.[60]

In Taiwan, on the other hand, the indigenous majority tolerated, if it did not welcome, the Japanese presence. After an initial spasm of resistance by dissident elements during the first years of the Japanese occupation, the Taiwanese passively succumbed to the idea of colonial rule. Despite certain tremors of political and intellectual restiveness during and immediately after World War I, the public peace of the island was never seriously threatened.[61]

60 The March First movement and Japan's response to it are summarized in Yamabe, *Nihon tōjika no Chōsen*, pp. 58–100.

61 This assertion takes into account the Musha Rebellion of November 1930, a bloody uprising by aboriginal tribes in the mountains of central Taiwan that was provoked by Japanese abuse of the aborigines and by encroachment into their tribal territories. Both the origins of the rebellion and its merciless suppression by Japanese military forces using planes and artillery were subjects of heated debate in the Diet. But the violence, restricted to a remote interior of the island and involving a small ethnic minority, did not affect the Taiwanese majority.

The only Taiwanese political movements that ever operated with any degree of public support were those that either sought for Taiwanese the same rights and benefits guaranteed to Japanese under the Meiji constitution or sought home rule within the empire. It is a mark of the generally passive response of the Taiwanese to Japanese colonialism that these political initiatives were suppressed with little difficulty by the Japanese colonial authorities. Active but clandestine resistance to Japanese rule did not emerge again until the closing years of World War II.[62]

Japan's other colonial peoples were noticeably moderate in their response to Japanese rule. In Karafuto, of course, one cannot speak of an indigenous response, as the population of the colony was essentially Japanese. In the Kwantung Leased Territory, the Chinese majority seems to have undertaken little opposition to the Japanese presence, and indeed, during the turbulence of the warlord period in Manchuria and mainland China, many propertied Chinese refugees from those areas appear to have sought shelter in the colony's security and stability. In the Nan'yō, because of the vast dispersion of the islands themselves and the Japanese settlements on them, native attitudes toward Japan varied widely. The main impact of the colonial presence was felt in the Marianas, particularly Saipan, where the Japanese came to outnumber the Chamorro population by ten to one, and in the Palau islands, which contained the seat of colonial government in Micronesia. In those places, because of the loss of Micronesian land to the tidal wave of Japanese immigration, there was some resentment of the Japanese colonial presence. Indeed, in Palau this is said to have manifested itself in a semisecret anti-Japanese cult. At the same time, most Micronesians rapidly adopted Japanese customs, dietary habits, and language (though the islanders on Yap, disdainful of the Japanese, seem to have been the exception). In the eastern Carolines and the Marshalls the natives bore little enmity toward their Japanese masters until 1943–4, when they were subjected to the increasingly harsh demands of the besieged and isolated Japanese garrisons.[63]

Korea thus represented the single recalcitrant member of the empire. There were a number of reasons for the bitterly anti-Japanese sentiments of the Korean people, in contrast with the passive acceptance of Japanese colonialism by the other colonies, particularly Tai-

62 Yamabe, "Nihon teikokushugi to shokuminchi," pp. 236–7; Hyman Kublin, "Taiwan's Japanese Interlude, 1895–1945," in *Taiwan in Modern Times*, ed. Paul K. T. Sih (New York: St. John's University Press, 1973), pp. 331–6.

63 Peattie, *Nan'yō*, pp. 216–20.

wan.[64] There was, first, the historic animosity between the Korean and Japanese peoples dating back to Hideyoshi Toyotomi's invasion of the peninsula in the sixteenth century which had left a legacy of destruction and a tradition of Korean hatred nurtured by the Koreans down through the centuries. Reinforcing this heritage of enmity was the fact of Korea's cultural autonomy. Whereas Taiwan had never existed as more than a political subdivision and cultural appendage of China, Korea, despite its identification with the Chinese Confucian tradition, was a country with its own culturally rich traditions that went back at least as far as those of Japan. For these reasons, its people had no cause to feel any great sense of admiration or esteem for Japan. Korea was, moreover, a unified country in which, at the very time of its absorption into the Japanese empire, forces of modern national consciousness were beginning to break through the crust of moribund Confucian culturalism. To the Koreans, the expansion of Japanese power across the peninsula seemed to represent not an advance but an outrageous retreat in the country's history. The forcible suppression of this emergent national consciousness bears less similarity to situations in any of the Western tropical empires of the time than it does to the German occupation of Alsace-Lorraine from 1870 to 1918 or to the long British domination of Ireland. Moreover, the disruptive flow of Japanese immigration into the country at the outset of the Japanese colonial occupation served to fuel the indignation of the Korean people.

Moreover, when Japan annexed Taiwan, it became possible for the island's elite class either to stay in the colony and become Japanese citizens or to return to China, an arrangement that soon drained Taiwan of many of those persons who might have been most inclined to resist Japanese rule. On the other hand, when Japan took over Korea, it occupied an entire country, and so its elite classes had no "mainland" to which to return. More than this, the pathetic existence in Korea of the Korean royal family, virtual prisoners of the colonial government, served as a reminder of the nation's past and a rallying point for anti-Japanese national feeling.

One must also consider Japan's treatment of Korea, in contrast with that received by the other colonies. For example, that compared with the Taiwanese under Japanese rule, the Korean people fared worse in

64 For comparisons of Japanese rule in Korea and Taiwan, see Tsurumi, *Japanese Colonial Education*, pp. 172–6; and Edward I-te Chen, "Japan: Oppressor or Modernizer? A Comparison of the Effects of Colonial Control in Korea and Formosa," in *Korea Under Japanese Colonial Rule*, pp. 251–60.

nearly every economic category, and the Koreans, even more than Taiwanese, were subject to the most grinding ideological regimentation during the wartime years.

Last of all, one must recognize that all of these elements together tempered and intensified Korean national determination to succeed as a people. In this sense the Japanese colonial presence served as both a goad and a model. The Japanese contempt of Korean national aspirations and culture wounded Korean pride, and Japanese competition in industry, agriculture, and commerce provoked Korean antagonism. At the same time, Japanese technology, the effectiveness of the modern Japanese bureaucratic state, and the higher Japanese standard of living created a model that inspired both Korean envy and a determination to pursue such advances as an independent nation. The ultimate legacy of Japan to the Korean people was to endow them with national indignation. As the Korean scholar Lee Chong-sik noted, "Japan, through her conquest and rule of Korea, awakened and sustained Korean nationalism. Japan provided the negative and yet the most powerful symbol of Korean nationalism, a national enemy."[65]

Had Japan been content with the modest colonial empire it had acquired by the end of World War I and abjured the reckless military adventurism in Asia that spilled beyond its boundaries, Japanese colonialism might have made some effort to compromise, albeit belatedly, with the growing forces of nationalism that had begun to stir throughout the colonial world by 1939. It is true, of course, that the span of the Japanese colonial empire was too short, briefer, indeed, than the waxing and waning of Western imperialism, to have permitted the evolution of such policies. More to the point, speculation on the further liberalization in the empire, which seemed possible in the 1920s, cannot be separated from a recognition of the external forces and internal pressures that prompted Japan to embark on the path of aggression in the 1930s. What is certain is that the tightening demands on the energies, loyalties, and resources of Japan's colonial peoples by a nation at war with much of Asia and most of the West transmogrified an authoritarian but recognizably "Western" colonial system into an empire of the lash, a totalitarian imperium, that dragged along its peoples as it staggered toward defeat. Linked to the image of Asian conquest and to the horrors of the China and Pacific wars, stripped of any purpose beyond that of supplying Japan with the material necessi-

65 Lee Chong-sik, *The Politics of Korean Nationalism* (Berkeley and Los Angeles: University of California Press, 1973), p. 275.

ties for survival, this mutant colonialism shriveled in the holocaust of defeat in 1945. Without even a feeble commitment to the principle of trusteeship, without any sort of legitimization of rule over alien peoples beyond Japan's own interests, Japanese colonial policy, in its final phase, could not provide the nation with any pride of tutelary accomplishment when the empire was liquidated at the war's end. Unlike most Western decolonization in the postwar era, the transfer of power from colonizer to colonized came not as a gift, bestowed by a gracefully departing officialdom in an atmosphere of mutual confidence and respect, but as a decree by Japan's triumphant enemies, dispensed by their garrisons of occupation and received by peoples resentful of their colonial past.

Yet no former colonial power, save for America, has so successfully surmounted the loss of its former colonial territories as has Japan. For most European colonial nations, decolonization meant a shrinking of influence and prestige. According to David Fieldhouse,

> Above all, the end of the empire deprived the West of status. The countries of Europe were no poorer than they had been before, but they were infinitely smaller. They had been the center of vast empires; now they were petty states, occupied with parochial problems. Dominion had gone and with it the grandeur which was one of the rewards.[66]

To contemplate the postwar rebirth of the Japanese industrial phoenix, the fleets of Japanese-built tankers that swept the world's oceans, the global influence of decisions taken daily in Japanese corporate boardrooms, and Japan's economic domination of many of the Asian territories that it once occupied is to realize how unusual the Japanese experience in the postcolonial era has been. If Japan's success, reduced to the shoreline of its own islands, says much about the peripheral value of the old empire to the well-being of the Japanese people, it also demonstrates how persuasively Japan has redefined the nature of power and influence in a postcolonial world.

66 David Fieldhouse, *The Colonial Empires; a Comparative Survey from the Eighteenth Century* (New York: Delacorte, 1966), p. 394.

# CHAPTER 6

# CONTINENTAL EXPANSION, 1905–1941

## GREATER JAPAN OR LESSER JAPAN?

The world's attention turned toward Japan after its victory in the Russo-Japanese War. This small island nation in East Asia not only had escaped falling under the colonial control of the Western imperialist powers, but it also had emerged as an imperialistic nation in its own right, on its way toward hegemony in East Asia and the western Pacific. The advanced countries that opposed or supported Japan in the war against Russia, and other Asian countries that were the targets of Western expansion, contemplated Japan's future with a mixture of admiration and wariness.

In retrospect, it can be said that the Russo-Japanese War brought Japan to an important crossroads in the path of its national destiny. The basic issue was whether Japan should be satisfied with a limited success as a solid middle-sized nation or should drive toward becoming a great military power dominating the Asian continent. In the postwar years, journalists and intellectuals debated Japan's goals and direction during its next stage of development. The debate considered several issues: greater "Japanism" versus little "Japanism," northern advance versus southern advance, and army-first versus navy-first. Greater Japanism implied continued expansionism, whereas little Japanism implied satisfaction with the postbellum status quo. Northern advance and southern advance were somewhat more ambiguous terms. The first was generally understood to mean a policy of continental expansion from the Korean peninsula through Manchuria into China proper; the second was understood to mean expansion from Taiwan into south China and Southeast Asia. Army-first meant that the army would carry the main burden of expansion, whereas navy-first implied that the navy would. There was a tendency for greater Japanism to go hand in hand with northern advance, which in turn implied continental expansion and an army-first policy. Little Japanism tended to be associated with the southern advance and navy-first positions. The debate necessarily had strong politi-

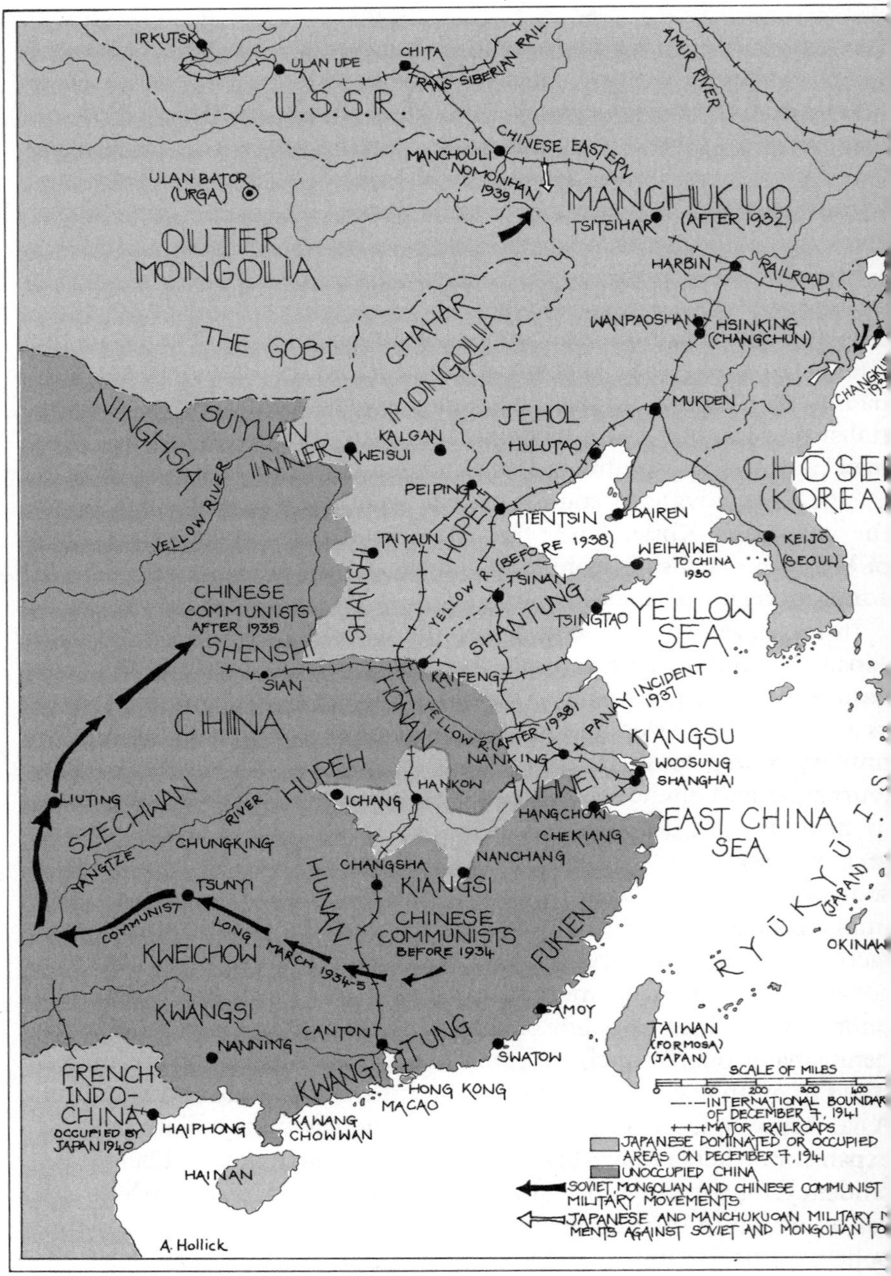


Map 6.1. Areas of China penetrated by Japan, 1941.

cal implications because it involved competition between the army and the navy over the expansion of military armaments.

One of the leading monthly journals, *Taiyō*, ran issues in 1910 and again in 1913 in which the contributors debated the pros and cons of the northern advance–southern advance strategies. It is apparent that the northern advance argument was not popular among the contributors, the majority of whom supported the southern advance argument that stressed the primacy of the navy over the army. Takekoshi Yosaburō, a leading journalist and critic who warmly supported the colonial development of Taiwan, argued that it was a "disadvantage for an island country to employ its strength on the continent" and that it was better to pursue economic advances to the south (by which he meant Southeast Asia). "Our future," he wrote, "lies not in the north but in the south."[1] Inukai Tsuyoshi, leader of the minority Kokumintō and a sympathizer of the Chinese revolutionary movement, argued that because there was "no danger of war in the North for the next ten years," Japan should assume a defensive posture in north Korea and instead turn toward the south, a task for which a "great navy" was necessary.[2] On the other hand, Major General Kusao Masatsune, a reserve general who saw the implications of a move south, wrote, "If Japan moved northward and northwestward beyond our present location, it would be aggression, but a war between Japan and the United States would be even more foolish."[3] Opposed to expansion of the navy, he proposed instead peaceful expansion into the South Seas.

A number of writers for the *Tōyō keizai shinpō* (The Oriental Economist) – Katayama Sen, Miura Tetsutarō, and Ishibashi Tanzan, among others – carried Kusao's argument to its logical conclusion. They opposed the ambitions of greater Japanism to expand in either direction, north or south. Instead they called for a lesser Japanism with the goal of building a compact "island welfare state" through the expansion of industry and trade.[4] Ishibashi wrote that Taiwan, China, and Korea were not "defensive palisades but highly flammable and dangerous dry brush." Japan, he said, should "abandon Manchuria, give independence to Korea and Taiwan, abandon economic rights in China, and live in peace with those weak nations."[5]

1 *Taiyō*, August 1911, pp. 81–92. 2 Ibid. 3 Ibid., November 1910.
4 Takayoshi Matsuo, "Katayama Sen, Miura Tetsutarō, Ishibashi Tanzan," in *Kindai Nihon to Chūgoku*, vol. 2, ed. Takeuchi Yoshimi and Hashikawa Bunsō (Tokyo: Asahi shinbunsha, 1974), pp. 68–83.
5 *Ishibashi Tanzan zenshū*, vols. 1–2 (Tōkyō: Toyo keizai shinpōsha, 1970).

Arguments in favor of the southern advance and lesser Japanism remained a minority opinion. The northern advance or continental policy not only had the overwhelming support of public opinion, but it also was the path chosen by the government. There were disagreements over timing and method, but the northern advance policy remained the mainstream position in Japanese foreign policy for the next several decades. As Tomizu Hiroto, a professor of law at Tokyo Imperial University, observed, "Northern advance is a historical reality."[6]

Komura Jutarō, foreign minister in the Katsura cabinet, was one of the chief architects of the continental policy. As the Japanese representative at the Portsmouth Peace Conference in 1905, Komura had crossed swords with Sergei Witte, the Russian delegate, but he had been unable to negotiate a peace settlement completely satisfactory to the Japanese public. Many Japanese, elated at their military victory over Russia, had expected Komura to bring home as prizes a huge indemnity and territorial cessions in Siberia. Professor Tomizu acquired his nickname "Professor Baikal" because he advocated cession of Siberia east of Lake Baikal to Japan. Such grand hopes did not materialize. Under the Portsmouth Treaty, Japan obtained only territorial control over southern Karafuto, a paramount position in Korea, a leasehold in the Liaotung peninsula, and the South Manchuria Railway concession. When the contents of the treaty became known, antitreaty demonstrations erupted into rioting – the so-called Hibiya incident – and an angry mob attacked Komura's residence.

Although Japan had failed to obtain either an indemnity or any territory apart from Karafuto, Komura hoped that Japan could maintain a foothold on the Asian continent as a springboard for further expansion. When he returned home from Portsmouth, he learned that the Katsura government had decided that because it would be difficult to operate the railway concessions in Manchuria because of postwar financial difficulties, it would give unofficial assent to the sale of the railroad line to E. H. Harriman, the American railroad magnate. Komura persuaded Katsura to cancel this decision, and despite poor health, Komura traveled to Peking, where he obtained the Ch'ing government's consent to Japan's new interests in Manchuria.

Yamagata Aritomo, the dominant senior figure in the army and another key figure in the shaping of the continental policy, insisted that Japan "should expand its national interests and sovereign rights"

6 *Taiyō*, August 1911, pp. 81–92.

toward the Ch'ing dynasty.[7] His protégé, Colonel Tanaka Giichi, a strong advocate of continental expansion and later war minister and prime minister in the 1920s, wrote in 1906 that Japan "should break free from its insular position, become a continental state, and confidently extend its national power."[8] These arguments, of course, were linked to an army-first and navy-second position and naturally invited resistance from the navy. Captain Satō Tetsutarō, known as the "Japanese Mahan," warned against pushing north, arguing that "an ocean state should not go too far into the continent."[9] He advanced a navy-first position, arguing that there was no danger of an island country like Japan being invaded by a foreign power and that Japan could defend its own trade routes if it had a powerful navy.

The views of army leaders like Yamagata and Tanaka were far more moderate than those of Colonel Matsuishi Yasuji, an army general staff officer who urged expansion first on the Asian continent, then into Southeast Asia and the South Seas, and finally into South and Central America.[10] His position combined the northern advance and southern advance views. It can also be seen as a harbinger of the concept of a Greater East Asia Co-Prosperity Sphere. Clearly, however, a grand scheme like Matsuishi's was a mere dream given Japan's real capabilities. By contrast, the views of Meiji leaders like Yamagata and Komura, who had worked hard to build a modern state, were fairly realistic and cautious.

The government's caution can be seen in the decision taken by the Katsura cabinet in July 1908 that "Japan should solidify the alliance with England, strive to maintain the entente with Russia, improve old friendships with Germany, Austria and Italy" and reaffirm cooperation with the United States.[11] The cabinet's view was that its continental expansion policy should be carried out within the limits permitted by the European powers and the United States and within a framework of international harmony. Such caution and realism diminished as time went on, eroded by the popular nationalism induced by two victorious wars in 1895 and 1905, by the displacement of older leaders by a younger generation, and by the army's increasing vociferousness and influence.

The government's commitment to a greater Japan orientation in

7 "Yamagata ikensho, October 1906," *Tanaka Giichi bunsho*, in possession of Yamaguchi Prefecture archives. 8 Tanaka Giichi, "Zuikan zatsuroku," *Tanaka Giichi bunsho*, 1906.
9 Satō Tetsutarō, *Teikoku kokubō shi ron shō* (Tokyo: Tōkyō insatsu, 1912), p. 547.
10 Matsuishi Yasuji, "Kokubō daihōshin ni kansuru iden" (December 26, 1906), in Bōeichō senshi shitsu, *Daihon'ei rikugunbu* (Tokyo: Asagumo shinbunsha, 1967), vol. 1, p. 153.
11 Ōtsu Jun'ichirō, *Dai Nippon kensei shi* (Tokyo: Hōbunkan, 1927–8), vol. 6.

foreign policy encouraged the military services to make plans for arms expansion. Military leaders ignored the postwar political clamor to "lift the tax burden from the people," and they had no qualms about intervening in politics to achieve their objectives. The army justified its call for a military buildup by citing the need to prepare for operations on the continent and the danger of a war of revenge by the Russians; the navy argued that it was necessary to counter the trend of the American navy toward expansion. These claims were not entirely convincing, as they raised suspicions that hypothetical crises were created in order to expand military armaments. Yamagata, concerned lest the differing policies of the two services cause discord between political goals and military strategy, promoted a unified policy. The resulting doctrine, "The Aims of Imperial National Defense" (Teikoku kokubō hōshin), sanctioned by the emperor in February 1907, listed Japan's hypothetical enemies as Russia, the United States, Germany, and France, in that order. It called for the buildup of the army to twenty-five divisions and the creation of a grand fleet with a core of eight battleships and eight battle cruisers (the so-called 8:8 plan). The document mainly promised both the army and the navy a substantial increase in strength.

The projected scale of arms expansion under the 1907 policy was 150 percent greater than the levels achieved at the end of the Russo-Japanese War. The expenditures required far exceeded what the government could afford to spend, as it had obtained no indemnity from Russia. The 1895 indemnity from China, of course, had been used to finance the arms buildup that enabled Japan's victory over Russia. When the emperor unofficially showed the national defense policy statement to Prime Minister Saionji Kinmochi, Saionji commented, "Our financial situation since the war does not allow the implementation of the whole military armament program at once. A little more time is desirable, so in reaching your decision please consider our national strength in light of these circumstances. . . ."[12]

The army and the navy, hiding behind the shield of national defense, continued to press the government for increased military expenditures. The situation was exacerbated by continuing army–navy rivalry for budget support. In 1910 the army requested that in addition to the existing nineteen divisions, two more be added to the Korea Army. Public sentiment favored naval expansion, and the Saionji gov-

12 Bōeichō senshi shitsu, *Daihon'ei kaigunbu: Rengō kantai* (Tokyo: Asagumo shinbunsha, 1970), vol. 1, p. 121.

ernment refused the request on the grounds of financial stringency. Frustrated and overzealous, the army leadership decided to bring down the Saionji cabinet in 1912 by arbitrarily ordering the war minister to withdraw from the cabinet. The ensuing political upheaval sidelined the two-division issue in the short run, but the increase was finally authorized by the Okuma cabinet in 1915 after the outbreak of World War I.

The navy continued to press its own demands for the implementation of the 8:8 fleet-building plan. After funds were appropriated for an 8:4 fleet and an 8:6 fleet, the Diet finally approved the 8:8 fleet plan in 1920. Because the size of capital ships had increased, it was predicted that naval expenditures would make up 30 percent of the national budget and that by the time the program was completed in 1927 that figure would reach 40 percent.[13] It was obvious that maintenance of such an immense navy was financially impossible for Japan. Thus, as a result of the Washington Conference in 1921–2, the 8:8 fleet plan was abandoned.

The emergence of both military services as powerful lobbying groups or veto groups within the state had great long-term significance for foreign policy. By taking advantage of regulations that required the service ministers to be generals or admirals on active duty, the military services could bring down cabinets they disliked or could manipulate them by hinting at such action. As the oligarchic generation died off, the ties that had united both the civilian and military sides of the *hanbatsu* weakened. The army began to function as an increasingly independent group, often moving away from government control. The army, of course, played the main role in the development of the continental policy, but the navy, which had originally been opposed to such a policy, did not neglect to exploit the opportunities when they arose.

## WORLD WAR I AND JAPAN

The basis of Japanese foreign policy immediately after the Russo-Japanese War was to advance on the continent within the framework of international cooperation. This policy reflected the domestic necessity of recovering from the Russo-Japanese War. The government concluded treaties and agreements, one after another, with the major powers in East Asia, laying the groundwork for a stable international environment. The postwar diplomatic network centered on the Anglo-

13 Ibid., p. 182.

Japanese alliance, regarded as the "marrow of imperial diplomacy."[14] It was woven together by the Russo-Japanese Entente (1907; later renewed in 1910, 1912, and 1916), the Franco-Japanese Entente (1907), and the U.S.-Japanese understanding known as the Root–Takahira Agreement (1908). Skillful diplomatic give-and-take was required to advance on the continent without threatening the interests and ambitions of the other advanced powers. In order to obtain Anglo-American assent to the Japanese position in Korea, the Japanese proposed trading the joint defense of India in its bargaining with Great Britain, and the security of the Philippines in its bargaining with the United States. In the Franco-Japanese Entente of 1907, the Japanese traded the recognition of French rule over Indochina in return for France's recognition of the results of the Russo-Japanese War. In short, if the Western powers agreed to Japan's new rights and interests in Korea, the Japanese in return would recognize their colonial possessions. Thus, despite the international appeals of the Korean emperor, no objection was heard from the Western powers when Japan announced its annexation of Korea in 1910.

In its entente with Russia, Japan reached a secret understanding that Manchuria would be divided into two equal spheres of influence, with both powers having the ultimate intention of annexation. But this arrangement was not to the liking of the United States which had expected the "Open Door" principle to apply to Manchuria. The Taft administration, inviting the backing of Great Britain, attempted to extend its own influence into the area. In 1909 Secretary of State P. C. Knox initiated the "dollar diplomacy" policy aimed at putting all Manchurian railway lines under the joint management of the powers in order to "smoke [Japan] out" of southern Manchuria.[15] But the Japanese and the Russians, erstwhile enemies, forged a joint front to stop the so-called Knox plan, and in March 1913 President Woodrow Wilson finally announced an end to the dollar-diplomacy offensive.[16]

In the meantime, revolutionary forces toppled the Ch'ing dynasty in late 1911. The internal political confusion in China intensified among the powers competing to grab the lion's share of the fragmenting polity. As a result, the "partition of China" proceeded even further. In Japan, Yamagata and the army leadership wanted to use the revolution

14 Cabinet council decision, "Tai-gai seisaku hōshin kettei no ken" (September 25, 1908), in *Nihon gaikō nenpyō narabini shuyō bunsho* (hereafter NGNSB), vol. 1, p. 309.

15 T. A. Bailey, *A Diplomatic History of the American People* (New York: Appleton–Century–Crofts, 1950), p. 580.

16 H. F. McNair and F. Lach, *Modern Far Eastern International Relations* (New York: Van Nostrand, 1950), p. 555.

as an opportunity to occupy southern Manchuria, but the Saionji government hesitated to go that far. Yamagata lamented, "We have missed a god-given opportunity, and I am truly and mightily indignant for the sake of our country."[17] The Russian government had considered taking over northern Manchuria but decided not to out of concern for opposition from the United States, Germany, and Great Britain. The Russians, however, did succeed in making Outer Mongolia independent and securing "freedom of movement" in western China in return for recognizing the same rights for the British in Tibet. Under the third Russo-Japanese entente in 1913, the Japanese obtained a sphere of influence in the eastern part of Inner Mongolia.[18]

Strong displeasure lingered in the Japanese army over the failure to seize control of southern Manchuria. Continental adventurers, in secret collusion with the army general staff, plotted military uprisings aimed at establishing independent regimes in Manchuria and Mongolia under the old Manchu and Mongolian ruling dynasties. The basic plan in 1912, and again in 1915, was to provoke a military clash that would involve Japanese forces. But both plots failed because the Japanese government remained aloof, allowing the local warlord, Chang Tso-lin, to put them down. The Japanese army simply lacked the prerequisites and the power to act independently, as it would in 1931. In the meantime, the real power in Manchuria remained in the hands of Chang Tso-lin, whom the Japanese government had to rely on in maintaining its vested interests there.

When World War I began in 1914, it would have been possible for Japan to stay out, but the Ōkuma cabinet almost immediately declared war on Germany. The government declared that "Japan must take the chance of a millennium" to "establish its rights and interests in Asia."[19] Clearly, the Japanese were less interested in what was going on in Europe than they were in the advantages that the war might bring in Asia. The war opened the way for the pursuit of a more vigorous continental policy unimpeded by the restraining influence of the Western powers. As a member of the allied coalition against Germany, Japan was able to obtain both "the gains of a participating country and the gains of a neutral country."

The main Japanese military operations were to seize German bases on the Shantung peninsula and in the Pacific. The German base at

17 Letter of Yamagata to Katsura, dated February 9, 1912, in Yoshimura Michio, *Nihon to Roshia* (Tokyo: Harashobō, 1968), p. 37.
18 Hata Ikuhiko, *Taiheiyō kokusai kankei shi* (Tokyo: Fukumura shuppan, 1972), p. 52.
19 Ibid., p. 114.

Tsingtao surrendered without much resistance after being surrounded by a single Japanese army division, and the defenseless Pacific islands were seized by the Japanese navy without bloodshed. The Allied powers wanted Japan to dispatch troops to Europe, but the Japanese government limited its military cooperation to sending convoy-escort destroyers to the Mediterranean and stalking German converted raiders operating in the Pacific and Indian oceans. Its main might was concentrated on expanding its sphere of influence in the Pacific.

In early 1915, six months after the beginning of the war, the Ōkuma cabinet presented China with the infamous Twenty-one Demands. Proposed as a draft treaty, the demands included provisions for Japanese to take over German interests in Shantung, for an extension of the leasehold in the Liaotung (Kwantung) peninsula, for an extension of commercial rights in Manchuria, for joint Sino-Japanese control over the Han-yeh-p'ing mines in central China, and for a limitation of China's right to cede control of coastal areas to third powers. The fifth and final group of demands, however, was really designed to turn China into a second Korea, by requiring the Chinese government to use Japanese advisers in its military, police, and financial administrations. Some Japanese diplomats had misgivings about the wisdom of the move. At the end of 1916, Foreign Minister Motono Ichirō wrote, "There are those who say that we should make China a protectorate or partition it, and there are those who advocate the extreme position that we should use the European war to make [China] completely our territory. . . . But even if we were able to do that temporarily, the empire lacks real power to hold on to it very long."[20] His reference to the lack of Japanese power to maintain a long-term hold on China recognized the resistance of the Chinese populace – through boycotts and demonstrations – to Japanese pressure. But had the United States not lodged strong and repeated protests, the Japanese government might well have begun the aggression in China that it delayed until 1931.

The Ōkuma cabinet issued an ultimatum that forced the regime in Peking to accept most of its demands, but Japan had to back off from the radical Group Five when Secretary of State William Jennings Bryan sent a strong note indicating that the United States could "not recognize" them. Although the United States, mindful of the balance of power, was flexible in its reaction, it also held fast to the principles of the Open Door doctrine and consistently expressed disapproval of

20 "Motono gaishō ikensho," in *NGNSB*, vol. 1, pp. 421–4.

Japanese actions that violated Chinese sovereignty. The doctrine of nonrecognition implied in the Bryan note was later taken up by Secretary of State Henry L. Stimson in 1931, and it reappeared yet again in the Hull note of 1941. It might even be said that the Bryan note laid down the "moral obligations" (*taigi meibun*) that led to the war between Japan and the United States.

As the war in Europe approached an end, the situation became ever more favorable to the advancement of Japan's continental policy. The United States entered the war in 1917, and the Russian Revolution erupted the same year. Given the likelihood that the Western powers would return to Asia after the war's end, many Japanese leaders were anxious to gain as much ground as possible beforehand. In the summer of 1918, a few months before the German surrender, the Terauchi government sent a force of seventy thousand to Siberia as part of the joint Allied intervention in the Russian Revolution. Significantly, Japan committed the most forces, and its forces stayed the longest, even after the other Allied powers had pulled out of Siberia. The Terauchi cabinet also concluded a joint-defense treaty with China under the pretext of preventing the spread of revolutionary currents from Russia to the Far East. Its provisions enabled the Japanese troops to move freely throughout almost all of China. By the time World War I ended in November 1918, Japanese military forces were able to operate in a zone that extended from Lake Baikal in the north, into the hinterland of Sinkiang Province to the west, and as far south as the former German-held island territories in Micronesia to the south. It was an area almost equivalent in extent to the regions occupied by the Japanese forces in 1942 in the Pacific War.

The question was whether the Western powers, especially the United States, would recognize these established facts. In November 1917 while on a visit to the United States, Ambassador Ishii Kikujirō succeeded in concluding a joint statement with Secretary of State Robert Lansing. Even though both countries recognized the principles of China's territorial integrity and equal opportunity for commerce and industry, the agreement also acknowledged that Japan had special interests in China. Ishii interpreted the agreement to mean that the United States recognized Japan's exclusive sphere of influence in all of China, and the emperor honored Ishii with a gracious message for his "diplomatic victory."[21] But just as many Japanese leaders had expected, once the war ended, the Western powers, led by the United

21 Hata, *Taiheiyō kokusai kankei shi*, pp. 127–8.

States, began a daring offensive to roll back Japan's position in Asia and to restore their prewar position.

## THE VERSAILLES–WASHINGTON SYSTEM

The new international order formed under the leadership of the victorious powers, especially Great Britain and the United States, after the smoke of war had cleared, is generally called the Versailles–Washington system. It originated in the Versailles Peace Conference of 1919 and was elaborated at the Washington Conference of 1921–2, where the Four Power Treaty and the Nine Power Pact attempted to freeze the status quo in the Pacific.

This international order had been organized to protect the interests of the two major victorious powers, Great Britain and the United States. The new system led to dissatisfaction among the countries that later turned fascist, such as Germany, which was suffering under the heavy burden of reparations, and Italy and Japan, which, although victorious, felt deprived of adequate rewards. The system also excluded the Soviet Union, which had survived the Allied intervention and was building the first socialist regime in history. The Soviet Union acted as a powerful outsider, seeking to expand the influence of the international Communist movement through the Comintern and making special efforts to support rising nationalist movements in colonial areas. The advanced capitalist countries scrambled to devise material and psychological countermeasures to defend their colonies abroad and to check subversive movements at home.

By the early 1920s, then, a balance of power had emerged among the three major world power blocs – the United States and Great Britain, leaders of the Washington system; the discontented powers of Germany, Japan, and Italy; and the Soviet Union, with its goal of creating an international socialist order. The equilibrium among these various blocs did not survive the buffeting of the Great Depression, a storm that struck the world economic system in 1929. International politics was swept on toward another great war in a series of crises brought about by attempts by the fascist countries to overturn the status quo. As it happened, it was Japan that led the way with the Manchurian incident.

Why did Japan eventually break away from the Versailles–Washington system? The main reason was that the rollback begun by the United States and Great Britain at the war's end forced Japan to give up most of the wartime gains it had made in the Asia–Pacific area. The rollback included the abolition of the Anglo-Japanese Alliance, the withdrawal of Japanese troops from Siberia, the 5:5:3 ratio in capital ships in a naval arms limitation treaty that left the Japanese fleet inferior in strength to those of the United States and Great Britain, the return of the Shantung concession to Chinese sovereignty, and the suspension of the Lansing–Ishii agreement. Many of these developments took place as a result of the Washington Conference. The most important agreement concluded at the conference was the Nine Power Pact of 1922, which liquidated all existing treaties between the powers and China and replaced them with the Open Door principles so long espoused by the United States. The pact was an indisputable victory for American diplomacy. According to A. Whitney Griswold, it was the "apotheosis of the traditional Far Eastern policy of the United States."[22]

The Japanese viewed these agreements with mixed feelings. There were those like Mochizuki Kotarō, a prominent journalist and Diet member, who complained, "Our empire has lost everything and gained nothing, and only the expense of building warships is spared."[23] Even stronger sentiments had been expressed in 1918 by Konoe Fumimaro, later to become prime minister, who argued that Japan "would be left forever a backward country" under the Versailles settlement.[24] The Japanese government, especially the diplomatic authorities, did not share these negative sentiments, however, nor did they regard the Versailles–Washington system as a total defeat for Japanese interests. In the early 1920s, many leaders, beginning with Prime Minister Hara Takashi, had enough self-confidence to accept the "world trends" and tried to extend Japan's national interests while adjusting to the new international framework centering on the League of Nations. To some extent, the same trends toward progressivism and pacificism expressed in Woodrow Wilson's idealism were at work in Japan.

From a practical point of view, the advantages of the new international system, especially those coming out of the Washington Conference, were by no means negligible. First, the treaties signed at Washington were the product of an ideology of the status quo, and they held out the possibility of a joint defensive front by the United States, Great Britain, and Japan to contain the expansion of Soviet international

22 A. W. Griswold, *The Far Eastern Policy of the United States* (New York: Harcourt, Brace, 1938), p. 331.

23 Kobayashi Yukio, "Tai-So seisaku no suii to Man–Mō mondai," in *Taiheiyō sensō e no michi* (hereafter TSENM), ed. Nihon kokusai seiji gakkai Taiheiyō sensō gen'in kenkyūbu (Tokyo: Asahi shinbunsha, 1962), vol. 1, p. 182.

24 *Nihon oyobi Nihonjin*, December 15, 1918; Yabe Teiji, *Konoe Fumimaro* (Tokyo: Kōbundō, 1952), vol. 1, p. 77.

communism and Chinese nationalism. Second, in regard to the mutual relations among the three powers, it was understood that in principle, the restrictions imposed on Japan were to be applied in the future and that they did not touch on those established special interests, especially in Manchuria and Mongolia, regarded by the Japanese as vital to their survival. Third, because the League of Nations lacked the ability to enforce any of its sanction provisions, it was clear that Japan could easily break away from the system whenever it felt advantageous to do so. As long as Japan remained able to expand through free competition and as long as Japan's special interests in Manchuria and Mongolia were not threatened by either China or the Soviet Union, the concessions Japan made in China – the return of the Shantung territory, for example – were not thought an undue price to pay for an end to international isolation.

Japan's commitment to the Washington naval arms limitation treaty created pressures to reconsider the army expenditures as well. First under War Minister Yamanashi Hanzō in 1922 and under War Minister Ugaki Kazushige in 1925, increases in military appropriations were checked. The resulting decline in the military's authority seemed to provide an opportunity to remove the ill effects of "dual diplomacy," which gave the military services as much voice in the making of foreign policy as the civilian diplomats had. It was an opportunity to restore real control over diplomacy to the civilian cabinets, now dominated by the political parties. Prime Minister Hara Takashi, and later Prime Minister Takahashi Korekiyo, both informally considered a plan to abolish the office of army chief of staff, though ultimately their scheme came to naught.[25]

The main exponent of working faithfully within the Washington–Versailles system without abandoning practical considerations in the Asia–Pacific area was Shidehara Kijūrō, the first career diplomat recruited by means of civil service examination to serve as foreign minister. Shidehara, who held that post under five Minseitō cabinets, had been vice-minister of foreign affairs, ambassador to the United States, and plenipotentiary at the Washington Conference. The interlinked components of his foreign policy were international collaboration, economic diplomacy, and nonintervention in China's domestic affairs.

1. International collaboration was generally accepted to mean diplomacy centering on the League of Nations, but basically it involved a policy of cooperation with the United States and Great Britain.

25 Hata Ikuhiko, *Gun fashizumu undō shi*, rev. ed. (Tokyo: Hara shobō, 1980), p. 275.

2. Economic diplomacy referred to emphasizing peaceful economic advance and shifting away from the policy of military pressure embodied in the Twenty-one Demands, the Siberian expedition, and military assistance to Chinese warlords, which had invited nationalistic resistance. This aspect of Shidehara's policy responded to the demands of Japanese industrial capitalists who had prospered greatly during World War I. It reflected an optimism and a confidence that Japan was strong enough economically to compete with the advanced Western economies without excessive political or military protection.[26] In fact, the volume of trade with China and other countries climbed under "Shidehara diplomacy." Shidehara himself was rather inflexible and intolerant of actions that violated economic rationality or infringed on economic interests as a result of "extraeconomic logic" or "noneconomic logic."

3. Nonintervention in China's domestic affairs, the most important element of Shidehara's policy, meant accepting the unification of China by the Kuomintang and sympathizing with China's demands for tariff autonomy and the abolition of extraterritorial rights. This was closely tied to the principle of economic diplomacy. It rested on the judgment that the establishment of a stable and unified government in China was desirable for the advance of Japanese economic interests and the expansion of its markets and that an imprudent policy of intervention would provoke nationalistic hostility and anti-Japanese boycotts.

These principles of Shidehara diplomacy dovetailed with the prevailing diplomatic environment. After the resumption of normal diplomatic relations between the Soviet Union and Japan in January 1925, Japan appeared to be moving away from international isolation, on the path to stable peaceful expansion. Yet this illusion of stability was soon demolished by the launching of a new Chinese Nationalist offensive. The resulting sudden shift toward Sino-Japanese confrontation brought the collapse of the entire Washington system.

## SHIDEHARA DIPLOMACY VERSUS TANAKA DIPLOMACY

At the time of the Washington Conference, the Kuomintang controlled only a small local regime in the region around Canton. But with the support of the Comintern and the Soviet Union, it launched the northern expedition against local warlord governments in 1926. By the

26 *Shidehara Kijūrō* (Tokyo: Shidehara heiwa zaidan, 1955), p. 256.

end of 1928 it had unified nearly all of China proper, excluding Manchuria. In the midst of this campaign, a coup d'état within the party shifted power from pro-Communist leftists to rightists under the leadership of Chiang Kai-shek. The influence of both the Soviet and Chinese Communists in the party vanished.

During this period of domestic turmoil, the Western imperialist powers competed to acquire the most advantageous position to guarantee their special interests. But they all agreed that the expansion of the Kuomintang's radical unification of the whole country was not desirable, and they all wanted to check the advance of Soviet influence. The most intransigent of the imperialist powers was Great Britain, which had the largest interests in the Yangtze River region. In 1927 the British tried to arrange a military intervention with American and Japanese help on the pretext of protecting foreign residents in China. In response, Chinese antiforeign nationalist movements were directed against Britain's gunboat policy, and trade between Britain and China was interrupted for nearly a year and a half.

In face of these developments, Foreign Minister Shidehara clung to his policy of nonintervention in Chinese domestic politics. In March 1927, during the so-called Nanking incident when revolutionary soldiers attacked consulates and foreign residences, Anglo-American gunboats responded with a bombardment, but the Japanese declined to join in. In negotiations with the Chinese to resolve the affair, Shidehara displeased the other powers by refusing to blame Chiang and by insisting that order must be restored on Chiang's initiative.[27] According to unofficial reports from the Japanese consul general in Shanghai, Shidehara had already learned of Chiang's plan to carry out an internal party coup against the left wing. Because Shidehara wanted to stabilize Japanese relations with a united China under Chiang, he thus avoided offending the Chinese leader.[28]

In April 1927, just a week after the antileft coup, the Minseitō cabinet led by Wakatsuki Reijirō fell from power. Shidehara was replaced by Tanaka Giichi, president of the Seiyūkai, who served as his own foreign minister. The immediate cause of the change in cabinets was a domestic matter, the Privy Council's rejection of the Wakatsuki government's plan for dealing with the bank panic. But the real reason was the conflict of opinion over Shidehara's China policy. Criticism of Shidehara's "weak diplomacy" grew stronger during the Nanking inci-

27 Usui Katsumi, *Nihon gaikō shi: hokubatsu no jidai* (Tokyo: Chūō kōron sha, 1971), pp. 32–9.
28 Ibid., pp. 37–9.

dent. A young navy officer attempted suicide, infuriated because he mistakenly thought that Shidehara was responsible for giving the order that forbade the bombardment of Nanking, and the naval landing force at Shanghai, acting in concert with the British and the Americans, requested the dispatch of army forces. The situation had even reached the point that the *Asahi shinbun*, supportive of Shidehara diplomacy in the past, urged the foreign minister to reconsider. Taking advantage of the anti-Shidehara mood, Mori Kaku, a key Seiyūkai leader, allied with hard-liners in the army and the Privy Council to unseat the cabinet. Even War Minister Ugaki Kazushige, a member of the Minseitō government, wrote that the fall of the cabinet "might well be good fortune for the empire."[29] It is not difficult to imagine how strong the dissatisfaction with the Shidehara policy had become.

The new Tanaka cabinet adopted an outwardly tougher policy toward the disorder brought about by the northern expedition. In May 1927 the government, following previous Seiyūkai demands that it "protect local residents," dispatched an army brigade to Shantung, where it forced the northern expeditionary forces back to the Yangtze River. This display of military force was known as the first Shantung intervention.

In June 1927 the Tanaka government brought local military and diplomatic officials to Tokyo for the Eastern Regions Conference, to enunciate the Tanaka cabinet's new foreign policy. The man who planned and chaired the meeting was Mori Kaku, parliamentary undersecretary for foreign affairs. He exercised real control over diplomacy, even though Tanaka formally held the post of foreign minister. The basic elements of Tanaka's diplomacy were (1) a policy of sending Japanese troops to protect local Japanese interests and residents whenever danger threatened and (2) a policy of "separating Manchuria and Mongolia" (*Man–Mō bunri seisaku*), intended to confirm Japan's special position in both areas and to prevent the Chinese revolution from spreading to Manchuria.[30] These policies were clearly the opposite of Shidehara's, which had respected China's sovereignty over Manchuria and had called for the evacuation of Japanese residents to safety if their lives were endangered.

The Eastern Regions Conference confirmed the principles of the Tanaka diplomacy, but it ended without agreement on specific plans. The general public impression was that Japan's China policy had been

29 Ugaki Kazushige, *Ugaki Kazushige nikki* (Tokyo: Mizusu shobō, 1970), vol. 2, entry for April 17, 1927.
30 Satō Motohide, "Tōhōkaigi to shoki Tanaka gaikō," *Kokusai seiji*, no. 66 (1980):89–90.

reversed 180 degrees. In China, an anti-Japanese economic boycott began, and it soon spread to Manchuria, where the first anti-Japanese demonstration took place at Mukden in September 1927. The Tanaka government adopted military countermeasures that were even stronger than before. When Chiang Kai-shek resumed the northern expedition in 1928, the Tanaka cabinet again dispatched two army divisions to Shantung. In May, Japanese and Chinese forces clashed at Tsinan. But Chiang's northern army bypassed Tsinan, moving toward Peking in pursuit of Chang Tso-lin's retreating forces. Anticipating certain victory by Chiang's forces, the Japanese advised Chang to abandon north China quickly, return to his old base in Manchuria, and try to rebuild his forces there under Japanese protection.

As a young officer during the Russo-Japanese war, Tanaka had saved Chang from execution as a Russian spy. He now aimed at expanding Japan's influence in Manchuria by supporting Chang's puppet regime while building new Japanese-controlled railway lines there. The Kwantung Army garrisoned in Manchuria, however, wanted to replace Chang – who had become too strong and difficult to deal with – with a more pliant figure. On April 18, 1928, Colonel Kōmoto Daisaku, a Kwantung staff officer, told a friend on the army general staff that he intended to assassinate Chang. "I will do it this time for sure," he said, " . . . with the determination to settle everything of twenty years' standing once and for all."[31] The return of Chang to Manchuria presented the Kwantung Army with a golden opportunity. On the morning of June 4, 1928, Kōmoto, in collusion with several of his colleagues, set an explosive charge under Chang's personal train as it passed through a suburb of Mukden. Chang died soon afterward from the injuries sustained in the blast. Kōmoto had hoped that the authorities in Tokyo would call out the Kwantung Army to occupy Mukden, but the order never came, and so the whole plot ended in failure.

The Kwantung Army announced that the Northern Expeditionary Forces were responsible for Chang's death, but rumors of a Japanese plot behind the incident spread quickly at home and abroad. The opposition parties in Japan questioned the government in the Diet, referring ominously to a "certain serious incident in Manchuria." Prince Seionji, the last *genrō*, reacted strongly. "I would never have let things get out of hand," he told a confidant.[32] Tanaka, who lamented

31 Letter from Kawamoto to Isogai, April 18, 1928, in Sagara Shunsuke, *Akai yūhi no masunogahara ni* (Tokyo: Kōjinsha, 1978), p. 149.

32 Harada Kumao, *Saionji kō to seikyoku* (Tokyo: Iwanami shoten, 1950), vol. 1, p. 10.

that "children never know their parents' mind," had originally intended to punish Kōmoto and his fellow conspirators. He had promised the emperor that he would do so. But because of strong army opposition, Tanaka was able to impose only light administrative punishment on the Kwantung army commander and on Kōmoto for having "committed a mistake in guarding the railroad." This leniency cost him his office. After the emperor reproached Tanaka for breaking his promise, his cabinet resigned in July 1929. Several months later, Tanaka died in despair.

Imperial ire over the handling of the Chang Tso-lin affair was the immediate cause of Tanaka's downfall, but his diplomatic policy had already reached a dead end in China. The two Shantung interventions, both intended to demonstrate a tough stance toward China, had not only failed to check the Kuomintang's effort to bring north China under control; they had also caused casualties among Japanese residents and provoked a growing popular anti-Japanese movement. To make matters worse, Tanaka's hope to resolve the Manchurian problem by gradually bringing Chang under control was thwarted by Chang's assassination. In December 1928, Chang Hsueh-liang, who had succeeded his father as the warlord of Manchuria, ignored strong warnings by the Japanese and merged his territory with the new Kuomintang government at Nanking. Just before his resignation the following July, Tanaka himself had been finally forced to recognize the Nanking government.

As Sino-Japanese relations deteriorated, Japan's ties with the Western powers, especially Britain and the United States, cooled as well. Both countries had made timely concessions to the Nanking government, including agreement to tariff autonomy, and both were trying to establish new and cordial bonds with the Chinese. Only Japan lagged behind.

Although the Tanaka and the Shidehara diplomacies have often been viewed as alternative policies, it is inappropriate to contrast them as completely opposite. Tanaka had no intention of blocking the Kuomintang's unification of China or abandoning traditional cooperation with the Anglo-American powers. He certainly did not envisage a plan for world conquest such as outlined in the counterfeit "Tanaka memorandum."[33] However, it is difficult to deny that in contrast with Shidehara, who maintained a consistent policy, Tanaka appeared vacillating and contradictory in his actions, swinging first one way and then

33 Morishima Morito, *Inbō, ansatsu, guntō* (Tokyo: Iwanami shoten, 1950), pp. 7–8.

another. For example, when Chiang visited Japan in the fall of 1927 while temporarily out of office, Tanaka indicated his intention not to interfere in the Kuomintang's unification of China. Despite that assurance, a few months later Tanaka dispatched the second Shantung expedition when Chiang reopened his northern campaign. Tanaka also revealed that he lacked the capacity to control the conflict over the direction of foreign policy between the foreign ministry and the army and its civilian allies such as Mori. Although Tanaka had succeeded Yamagata as head of the Chōshū lineage in the army, he was unable to budge it on the matter of punishing the Kwantung Army plotters like Kōmoto. In effect, that meant that he had abdicated to the army his initiative in continental policy. Tanaka was succeeded as prime minister by Hamaguchi Osachi, president of the Minseitō, and as foreign minister by Shidehara. Shidehara diplomacy took a new lease on life, but its failure was in sight.

## WAS MANCHURIA A LIFELINE?

Nothing better expresses the romantic view of Manchuria than one of the most popular military songs in Japan, written right after the Russo-Japanese War. It went as follows:

> Here in far-off Manchuria
> Hundreds of leagues from the homeland,
> Our comrades lie beneath the rocky plain
> Lit by the red setting sun.

During the Russo-Japanese War, Japan had spent ¥2 billion and shed the blood of nearly 100,000 soldiers. Its material rewards were the Kwantung Leased Territory, including Dairen and Port Arthur, and interests in southern Manchuria centering on the South Manchuria Railway Company. After the Chinese Revolution of 1911, Manchuria, the homeland of the Ch'ing rulers, slipped from the reach of the central authorities in China. It then came under the control of Chang Tso-lin, who enjoyed the backing of the Japanese army, and then of his son, Chang Hsueh-liang. Although the area was Chinese in name, it was thought of as a special zone to which Chinese sovereignty did not extend. Even the Lytton Commission of Enquiry dispatched by the League of Nations in 1932 to investigate the situation in Manchuria partially acknowledged this.

For those Japanese unable to satisfy their ambitions at home, Manchuria was a new frontier where they could fulfill their dreams of fame and fortune. Adventurers and merchants with a desire to get rich quick rushed to Manchuria. Some young men even joined mounted bandit gangs. When Japanese-American relations deteriorated as a result of the Japanese immigrant problem in California, Foreign Minister Komura urged a policy of concentrating Japanese immigration in Manchuria and Korea (*Man–Kan iminshūchūron*). In hopes of shifting the destination of immigrants to ease the population problem, he drew up a twenty-year plan to send 1 million immigrants to Manchuria.[34] The number of Japanese residents in Manchuria increased from 68,000 in 1909 to 219,000 in 1930. The majority were employees of the South Manchuria Railway Company and their families. About 1,000 were farmers, and the rest were adventurers, unscrupulous merchants, get-rich-quick artists, and other social undesirables. By contrast, each year 300,000 to 500,000 Chinese, mainly peasants, drifted into Manchuria, reaching a peak of 780,000 migrants in 1927.[35]

After the failure of the plot to take over Manchuria by assassinating Chang Tso-lin, a sense of crisis grew more intense within the Kwantung Army as the Chinese began to construct railway lines parallel to the South Manchuria Railway line and as Chang Hsueh-liang began to exert economic pressure on the Japanese settlers in Manchuria. It is usually argued that the Kwantung Army provoked the Manchuria incident because the diplomatic policies of Foreign Minister Shidehara were unable to cope with the extension to Manchuria of the Kuomintang regime's nationalistic "rights recovery" movement and its "anti-Japanese policy." Because diplomacy had reached an impasse, it is said, the Kwantung Army resorted to force to achieve its long-held ambition of bringing the region under Japanese control.

It remains doubtful, however, whether Japanese "rights in Manchuria" (*zai–Man ken'eki*) were of such enormous importance to Japan or so critically threatened as to justify a response by military action. For example, it was probably an exaggeration that the new parallel railway lines built by Chang Hsueh-liang brought about a decline in the profitability of the South Manchuria Railway line. At the time, Kimura Eiichi, a director of the company, argued: "The parallel lines are not the cause. The depression is. The public thinks the income earned in the good old days is normal, but the fall in income for the

34 Gaimushō, *Komura gaikō shi* 1953, vol. 2, p. 298; Manshūshi kenkyū kai, ed., *Nihon teikokushugika no Manshū* (Tokyo: Ochanomizu shobō, 1972), p. 15.
35 Rōyama Masamichi, *Nichi-Man kankei no kenkyū* (Tokyo: Shibun shoin, 1933), pp. 151, 205.

parallel Chinese lines is greater [than ours]."[36] Although the South Manchuria Railway admittedly made smaller profits because of the world economic slump, the competing parallel Chinese lines would have collapsed before the Japanese line did. Even Colonel Kōmoto, the plotter of Chang Tso-lin's assassination, admitted that the economic pressure felt by the Japanese residents in Manchuria was essentially due to their inability to compete with the Chinese immigrants' low standard of living, that it was not due to the Chiang government's anti-Japanese policy.[37]

Seen in this light, the Manchurian incident was really the product of a false "crisis in Manchuria and Mongolia" (*Man–Mō no kiki*). The Kwantung Army, as well as Japanese colonists favoring the use of force, worked hard to convince the Japanese government, the military high command, and the public at large that such a crisis existed. "Manchuria and Mongolia are not territories of China; they belong to the people of Manchuria and Mongolia," wrote Lieutenant Colonel Ishiwara Kanji. "It is a publicly acknowledged fact that our national situation has reached an impasse, that there is no way of solving the food, population, and other important problems, and that the only path left open to us is the development of Manchuria and Mongolia."[38] There were discrepancies, however, in Ishiwara's logic. Even if neither Manchuria nor Mongolia were Chinese territory, how did that justify Japan's claims to territorial rights? Would Japan's resource and population problems be solved even if Manchuria and Mongolia were seized? In the midst of hard times, would it be possible to raise the capital for their development? Ishiwara offered no concrete answers.

The Manchurian Youth League, organized by hard-liners in the Japanese resident community, also called for an end to Shidehara diplomacy. They sent a lobbying group to Japan to publicize the crisis of the South Manchuria Railway, but the public reception was cool.[39] This was only natural, considering the disastrous economic situation

36 "Explanation by Director Kimura at the Department of Overseas Affairs Meeting of December 7, 1930," *Kikan gendai shi*, November 1972, p. 162. According to statistics for 1937 found in *Minami Manshū tetsudō kabushiki kaisha sanjūnen ryakushi* (Dairen: Minami Manshū tetsudō kabushiki kaisha, 1937), profits were consistently made (although the curve was downward), and dividends were paid between 1927 and 1931; ibid., p. 724. Concerning the rumor of the South Manchuria Railway's loss of business, see Yamaguchi Jūji, *Manshū teikoku* (Tokyo: Gyōsei tsūshinsha, 1975), p. 52. 37 Sagara, *Akai yūhi no masunogahara ni*, p. 149.

38 Ishiwara, Kanji, "Genzai oyobi shōrai ni okeru Nihon no kokubō," in *Ishiwara Kanji shiryō*, vol. 2: *Sensō shiron*, ed. Tsunoda Jun (Tokyo: Hara shobō, 1967), pp. 422–32.

39 Hirano Ken'ichirō, "Manshū jihen zen ni okeru zaiman Nihonjin no dōkō," *Kokusai seiji*, "Manshū jihen," no. 43 (1970):66.

in Japan, where unemployment was mounting and popular hardship was widespread. There were crises enough at home without having to worry about Manchuria.

The central military authorities in Tokyo, though concerned about developments in Manchuria, took a more prudent position. A month before the Manchurian incident took place, the army prepared a document called "An Outline of Measures for the Solution of the Manchurian Problem."[40] It called for taking a year or so to consolidate the situation at home and abroad and to create a favorable public mood before resorting to a solution by force in Manchuria. Even though Ishiwara and his colleagues in the Kwantung Army were willing to defy the rest of the world, the central army authorities were concerned that the League of Nations would impose sanctions on Japan if force were used in Manchuria. Moreover, they thought that a local incident would be difficult to enlarge as long as Shidehara's foreign policy views prevailed. To overcome these obstacles, it would be necessary to administer a multiple shock by simultaneous coups at home and abroad.

In 1930 and 1931 the conditions for a military usurpation of political power at home continued to ripen. The Hamaguchi cabinet included three of the finest leaders produced by party politics – Prime Minister Hamaguchi Osachi, Finance Minister Inoue Junnosuke, and Foreign Minister Shidehara. But their policies produced distrust and dissatisfaction among all strata of the Japanese population. In fiscal policy, the Hamaguchi cabinet tried to strengthen Japan's economic capacity to compete in the international marketplace, in order to overcome the chronic slump. But Inoue's policies of tight finances, industrial rationalization, and a return to the gold standard coincided with the onset of world depression in 1929, and the economy sank to unprecedented depths. Many economic indicators fell to 50 to 70 percent of their normal levels.[41] Because all the sacrifices were borne by the farm communities and small- and medium-sized businesses, "Inoue financial policy" was interpreted as a policy to extend the political power of the parties who represented the interests of the zaibatsu. Successive revelations of political graft and corruption further diminished public confidence in party politics. In foreign policy, the compromise reached with the United States and England in 1930 at the London Naval Conference, where Japan agreed to an

40 Kitaoka Shin'ichi, "Rikugun habatsu tairitsu (1931–35) no saikentō," *Shōwaki no gunbu* (Tokyo: Yamakawa shuppansha, 1979), p. 54.
41 Sumiya Mikio, ed., *Shōwa kyōkō* (Tokyo: Yūhikaku, 1974), p. 236.

inferior ratio of auxiliary vessels, incurred the displeasure of the navy's "fleet faction." And criticism of Shidehara diplomacy continued to grow when the Kuomintang government called for "the rapid abolition of all unequal treaties and the recovery of all rights and interests." The "revolutionary diplomacy" of the Chinese overlapped the "crisis in Manchuria and Mongolia," widening fears that Japan might be forced to pull out of the continent completely.

The impasse at home and abroad provided the rationale for the sudden emergence of a "reform movement" (*kakushin undō*) in the army and the right wing. The movement hoped that the army would become a political force to replace the political parties, which had lost their purity and their ability to deal with the country's problems. There were disputes within the movement over which should come first, political reform at home through a "Shōwa restoration" (*Shōwa ishin*) or military action abroad to resolve the Manchurian problem, but efforts to accomplish both moved hand in hand. The Cherry Blossom Society (Sakurakai), organized by young army officers in the fall of 1929, plotted a military coup in March 1931 to place General Ugaki in control of the government. This so-called March incident failed when Ugaki refused to cooperate, but it was followed in the fall by another, even larger coup plan, the October incident, involving young naval officers and civilian right-wing activists.[42]

Meanwhile, in Manchuria a group of Kwantung Army officers led by Lieutenant Colonel Ishiwara and Colonel Itagaki Seishirō pushed forward preparations to deal with the Manchurian crisis by military force. Ishiwara, who blended his faith in Nichiren Buddhism with a knowledge of recent trends in military science to develop a unique theory of ultimate global war, was the theorist behind the plot; Itagaki, who as a military cadet had joined a secret society dedicated to continental expansion, was the practical manager. They maintained a liaison with the Cherry Blossom Society through Colonel Kōmoto, the assassin of Chang Tso-lin, now retired from active service. Their plans reached fruition in the fall of 1931.

On the night of September 18, Lieutenant Kawamoto Suemori of the Second Battalion of the Railroad Garrison set off an explosive charge on South Manchuria Railway tracks at Liutiaokou in the suburbs of Mukden. The conspirators had intended to stir up local confusion by derailing the Dairen Express, scheduled to arrive in Mukden

42 Karita Tōru, *Shōwa shoki seiji, gaikō shi kenkyū* (Tokyo: Ningen no kagakusha, 1978).

at 10:30 P.M. The train reached the blown-up section of track shortly after the explosion, swayed a bit, but passed over it safely.[43] Nonetheless, the Manchurian incident was set in motion.

Plans for military action in Manchuria had been hastened by leaks of the plot. Rumors had reached informed circles by mid-August, causing a drop in the stock of the South Manchuria Railway. The consul general at Mukden had sent reports of a plot to Foreign Minister Shidehara, who at a cabinet meeting asked War Minister Minami Jirō about their authenticity.[44] When Minami ordered Major General Tatekawa Yoshitsugu of the army general staff to Manchuria to stop the plot, Ishiwara and Itagaki stepped up their schedule by ten days. Even before his departure, Tatekawa had secretly informed the Kwantung Army that their plans were known. After conferring with Itagaki en route to Mukden, Tatekawa arrived several hours before the explosion went off, got drunk, and fell asleep in a Japanese restaurant. Later he excused the failure of his mission by commenting, "I didn't make it in time."[45] There were other general officers like Tatekawa who had committed themselves to the conspiracy or at least had guessed what was going on but pretended not to know. In this sense the Manchurian incident – as well as the March and October incidents – can be interpreted as a direct army challenge to political party rule.

## THE OCCUPATION OF MANCHURIA

The initial phase of the Manchurian incident ended with an almost bloodless victory, the overnight fall of Mukden. Chang Hsueh-liang, who was in Peking, ordered his subordinate officers to adopt a policy of nonresistance.[46] But if the Kwantung Army were to occupy all of Manchuria, as planned, Japanese troops had to advance outside the railway zone where Japan had treaty rights. On September 21, Ishiwara and his colleagues requested that the Kwantung Army commander Honjō Shigeru dispatch troops to Kirin to establish local order there. In fact, disturbances in the area had been provoked by the plotters. By this time, Honjō, who had not been privy to the plot, began to realize what his staff officers were up to. According to the

43 Hata Ikuhiko, "Ryojōkō jiken no saikentō," *Seiji keizai shigaku*, no. 183 (1981).
44 Seki Kanji, "Manshū jihen zen shi," *TSENM*, vol. 1, pp. 404–12.
45 Mori Katsumi, *Manshū jihen no rimen shi* (Tokyo: Kokusho kankōkai, 1976), pp. 19–80.
46 Usui Katsumi, *Manshū jihen* (Tokyo: Chūō kōronsha, 1974), p. 58.

army's military code, it was a capital offense for a local commander in a foreign country to move his troops without the emperor's consent. All through the night, the staff officers worked on Honjō, until at dawn he finally agreed to their request.[47] The dramatic effect of the troop dispatch was heightened when the Korea Army sent a division to relieve the Kwantung Army in Manchuria without first obtaining permission from the central army authorities.

The Wakatsuki cabinet, in which Shidehara remained foreign minister, adopted a policy of not expanding military operations. The central military authorities in Tokyo reluctantly followed suit. But the Kwantung Army completely ignored both their instructions and the cabinet's nonexpansion policy. A group of army general staff officers making preparations for the October incident to support the Kwantung Army's actions spread rumors that the Kwantung Army was planning to declare its independence from the homeland.[48] In December 1931 the Wakatsuki cabinet finally fell. The cabinet of Inukai Tsuyoshi, the Seiyūkai's president, reversed the direction of national policy by recognizing the occupation of Manchuria as an accomplished fact.

In response to the Japanese military action, Chang Hsueh-liang, who had concentrated his defeated soldiers in north China, continued guerrillalike attacks across the southwestern border of Manchuria. Chiang Kai-shek, whose plan was to appeal to the League of Nations and to recover Manchuria through pressure by the great powers, held back the central Kuomintang army as well.[49] Chiang, who wanted eventually to unify all of China, including Manchuria, was preoccupied with his domestic enemies, especially in the areas under the control of the Chinese Communist movement, and he was reluctant to commit his forces against the Japanese. If any force had been able to check the arbitrary actions of the Kwantung Army and its supporters in Tokyo, it would certainly have been international pressure by Great Britain, the United States, or the Soviet Union. But in fact, none of them decided to intervene. In the United States, Secretary of State Henry Stimson proclaimed the "nonrecognition doctrine," a refusal to accept the Japanese *fait accompli*, and the Hoover administration concentrated the Pacific Fleet at Hawaii under the pretext of

47 Katakura Tadashi, *Kaisō no Manshūkoku* (Tokyo: Keizai ōraisha, 1978), pp. 57–8; Ishii Itarō, *Gaikōkan no isshō* (Tokyo: Yomiuri shinbunsha, 1950), pp. 182–3.

48 Regarding this point, some say that the October incident was really a coup d'état planned by conspirators at higher levels in the military and aimed at provoking the Manchurian incident. See Fujimura Michio, "Iwayuru jūgatsu jiken no saikentō," *Nihon rekishi*, no. 393 (1981).

49 Chiang Kai-shek, *Shō Kai-seki hiroku: Manshū jihen* (Tokyo: Sankei shinbunsha, 1976), vol. 9, pp. 52–3.

maneuvers.[50] But the Americans were not able to take effective measures against the "Far Eastern crisis" because the country was foundering at the bottom of the depression. Great Britain was also in economic difficulty and was inclined toward appeasement, hoping to use Japan as a counterbalance to the Soviet Union. And the Soviet government was in the midst of economic reconstruction after the long period of factional strife between Stalin and Trotsky. Consequently, the Soviet leaders wanted to avoid international disputes for the moment. The Soviet government thus did not protest the Japanese advance into northern Manchuria, and in 1935 it sold the Soviet-owned Chinese Eastern Railway to Japan and withdrew to the Amur River line. If the Manchurian incident had been planned with the thought of avoiding foreign intervention, it can be said that its timing was perfect. The international circumstances served Japan well.

When fighting spread to Shanghai at the end of January 1932, international pressure against Japan's actions in Manchuria increased considerably. The Shanghai incident was touched off by a plot hatched by the Kwantung Army and Major Tanaka Ryūkichi, the Japanese military attaché stationed in Shanghai. Its purpose was to divert domestic and foreign attention away from Manchuria so that the Kwantung Army could complete its occupation of Harbin and the establishment of the new state of Manchukuo at a time when anti-Japanese sentiment reached its height overseas. But the incident soon expanded into a large military clash. Three army divisions had to be sent to rescue the beleaguered Japanese marine units. The army high command, however, was worried that a penetration of central China would provoke a joint intervention by the powers. Unlike Manchuria, where the Western powers had few substantial interests, central China had long been an area of Western economic and political activity. Just when the entire city of Shanghai had been occupied, the army clamped down on the hawkish elements and pulled out the Japanese troops.

In March 1932, having completed the occupation of all Manchuria, the Japanese created a puppet state there. The idea of establishing a new and independent nation in Manchuria had taken shape in the Kwantung Army immediately after the incident began. Their plans called for a new state free from the evils of domestic capitalism and unified under the slogan of a "paradise of benevolent government" (*ōdō rakudo*) and "harmonious cooperation among the five races" (*gozoku kyōwa*). Many government officials, economists, *rōnin*, and

50 Hata, *Taiheiyō kokusai kankei shi*, chap. 7, concerning Stimson's diplomacy.

farmer migrants rushed to Manchuria to become part of the ruling apparatus. As a result, Manchukuo literally became Japan's "lifeline colony." In 1934 Manchuria's original republican structure was changed to a monarchy. Henry Pu-yi, previously the head of state, was elevated to the position of emperor, with the authority of the Japanese emperor delegated to him. But the real power was kept in the hands of the commander of the Kwantung Army, who concurrently held the post of Japanese ambassador to Manchukuo.

The League of Nations' Lytton Commission, whose perceptive observers visited the scene in the spring of 1932, fully fathomed the situation inside Manchuria. The Japanese army, which expected the commission's report to be unfavorable to Japan, tried to stir up public opinion by promoting a movement to recognize Manchuria's independence. Foreign Minister Uchida Yasuya announced his "scorched earth diplomacy" (*shōdo gaikō*). "I will not yield one step in achieving this demand [the recognition of Manchuria]," he said, "even if our country is reduced to ashes." In September 1932 Japan formally recognized Manchuria. In March 1933, after having been defeated by a vote of forty-two to one on the acceptance of the Lytton Commission's report, Japan withdrew from the League of Nations. This meant that Japan had seceded from the Versailles system and had chosen "splendid isolation" instead. Italy and Germany, seeing the League's impotence, took a leaf from Japan's book and embarked on their own paths of expansionism.

One of the reasons that neither the League nor the powers were able to impose effective restraints on Japan was that its pattern of response defied expectation.[51] "Dual diplomacy" had been a problem since the time of the Siberian expedition, but there was no precedent for what occurred during the Manchurian incident, when local army forces ignored the nonexpansion policy that the Tokyo government had pledged to follow. Once the powers realized that Shidehara diplomacy was no longer effective, they stepped up the international pressure on Japan. But by that time it was too late to have any restraining effect. Japanese public opinion, which had stiffened overnight, backed the occupation of Manchuria as an accomplished fact. It was only ten years later on the eve of the Pacific War that the United States made effective use of the nonrecognition doctrine in the famous Hull note which called for a return to the pre-1931 status quo and demanded the liquidation of all *faits accomplis*.

51 Mitani Taichirō, "Kokusai kin'yū shihon to Ajia no sensō," *Kindai Nihon to higashi Ajia*, ed. Kindai Nihon kenkyūkai (Tokyo: Yamakawa shuppansha, 1980), pp. 117–27.

## THE QUEST FOR AUTONOMY

Was Japan's foreign expansion – from the Manchurian incident through the China conflict to the Pacific War – blind aggression whose objectives were military conquest and plunder like that of the Huns or the Mongols? Or was it a limited action aimed at achieving a "quest for autonomy"[52] as the world divided into economic blocs in the face of the Great Depression? Historians' interpretations have veered back and forth between these two extremes, but whichever position one takes, the period of transition from the Manchurian incident to the China war was clearly an epoch-making turning point.

The Manchurian incident played a role in Japan similar to that of the New Deal in the United States. The reflationary effects of increased military expenditure and increased war production revived the Japanese economy from stagnation.[53] The same thing happened in Germany when Adolf Hitler, after pulling the country out of the depression by building public works such as the *autobahn* and putting to work six million unemployed, embarked on a program of rearmament.[54] All three countries – the United States, Germany, and Japan – were unconsciously putting into practice the Keynesian methods of stimulating recovery and achieving full employment by means of military armaments expansion or public works projects.

Nevertheless, the worldwide spread of economic nationalism aimed at domestic economic recovery upset the self-regulating mechanisms of the international economy and promoted the formation of closed economic blocs. Japan and Germany, late-developing countries lacking self-sufficiency in natural resources, had to establish control over extensive economic zones in order to compete with the blocs controlled by the advanced nations. To justify such a policy, there emerged in Germany the notion of *Lebensraum* advocated by Nazi geopoliticians, and in Japan there emerged the notion of a "Japan–Manchukuo economic bloc." The reactionary folkish doctrines that permeated the fascist ideology in both countries can also be viewed as essential to their rejection of economic internationalism and their formation of closed economic blocs.[55]

52 James B. Crowley, *Japan's Quest for Autonomy* (Princeton, N.J.: Princeton University Press, 1966).

53 Nakamura Takafusa, ed., *Senkanki no Nihon keizai bunseki* (Tokyo: Yamakawa shuppan, 1981). See, in particular, the article by Blumenthal. General demand increased by 1.5 percent, as opposed to an increase in military expenditure of 2.2 percent from 1931 to 1936. The growth rate expanded from 0.5 percent in 1929 to 10.5 percent in 1933.

54 Sebastian Hafner, *Hitarā to wa nanika*, trans. Akabane Tatsuo (Tokyo: Sōhisha, 1979), p. 36.

55 See articles by Hatano Sumio, Takahashi Hisashi, and Gerhard Krebs, in *Nihon no 1930 nen dai*, ed. Miwa Kimitada (Tokyo: Sōryūsha, 1980).

For many years Japan's overpopulation and shortage of raw materials had been a cause of concern for the advanced countries. Although the population problem may simply have been (in Ishibashi Tanzan's phrase) an aggressor's "last excuse,"[56] there was a widespread international feeling that a social explosion in Japan could be prevented by providing Japan with an appropriate safety valve. Even in China there was a tacit acceptance that the occupation of Manchuria, where Chinese sovereignty was by no means completely clear, was a necessary evil. In any case, for the Kuomintang regime, the defeat of the Chinese Communist forces under Mao Tse-tung continued to be the most pressing objective.[57] Under these circumstances, between 1932 and 1935, harmony based on a tacit acceptance of the accomplished facts seemed to have been restored in Sino-Japanese relations.

In October 1935 Foreign Minister Hirota Kōki asked the Chinese to accept his "three principles": suspension of anti-Japanese activities, recognition of Manchukuo, and a joint defense against Communism. Hirota intended first to obtain China's agreement in principle and then to move on to specific and detailed arrangements. The real power over foreign policy, however, had shifted into the hands of the military. With the rise of a promilitary faction in the Foreign Ministry, the old "Kasumigaseki diplomacy" was on the wane, and some began to talk about the ministry as the "War Ministry's Foreign Affairs Bureau." As if to ignore Hirota's diplomacy, elements in the army, especially middle-ranking officers in the Kwantung Army whose appetite had been whetted further by the success in Manchuria, began to advance into north China, Inner Mongolia, and eventually mainland China in the latter part of 1935. Their pattern of action, relying on subversion, threats of force, and the establishment of puppet governments, was similar to that of the Kwantung Army at the time of the Manchurian incident. The rationale for their actions was to check the emergence of a strong and unified China.

After signing the Umezu–Ho Ying-chin and Doihara–Chin Te-chan agreements in June 1935, on the pretext of settling some trifling incidents, the Kwantung Army and the China Garrison Army drove the Chinese central armies from the provinces of Hopei and Chahar. Major

56 Ishibashi Tanzan, Editorial in *Tōyō keizai shinpō*, May 16, 1913, printed in *Ishibashi Tanzan zenshū* (Tokyo: Tóyō keizai shimpōsha, 1970–72).

57 Tung Hsien-kuang, *Shō Kai seki*, trans. Terashima Masashi and Okuno Masami (Tokyo: Nihon gaisei gakkai, 1956), p. 173. Tung stated: "On September 18, China was obliged to choose whether it should opt for a military counteroffensive or await the opportunity to drive the Japanese out of Manchuria through foreign intervention; China chose the latter. Japan however, continued its aggression, taking advantage of China's internal strife."

General Doihara Kenji was sent to north China where he tried to form an autonomous pro-Japanese regime by pulling together various warlords in the five northern China provinces. But these plans did not materialize because the Kuomintang central government successfully intervened politically. Although the Japanese created the East Hopei Autonomous Council, a pro-Japanese puppet regime in the northeastern part of Hopei, the Kuomintang countered it with the Hopei–Chahar Political Council headquartered at Peking. Using funds gained from smuggling operations through East Hopei, the Kwantung Army also formed a puppet government under Prince Te in Inner Mongolia and began to expand to the west.[58] Major General Ishiwara Kanji, now holding a key position in the army general staff, did not agree with such rapid and disorderly expansion. Rather, he stressed the immediate need to develop the resources of Manchuria and to build sufficient national strength for Japan to cope favorably with coming changes in the world situation. However, given his own previous record of defying central authority, Ishiwara had difficulty in controlling the adventurism flourishing among the junior officers.[59]

The result was that the Japanese, after seizing Manchuria's resources, lunged toward the main part of China in search of new and easy gains. In the meantime, a bloody factional struggle over leadership was raging within the army between the Control faction (Tōseiha) and the Imperial Way faction (Kōdōha). The struggle, culminating in the February 26 incident of 1936, ended with the victory of the Control faction and a shift in emphasis from internal reform to external aggression. It is clear that the aggressive actions of the Japanese military from the Manchurian incident onward were hardly so moderate as to be called a "quest for autonomy." Military action came first, and ideological justifications for *faits accomplis* were churned out afterward. By the time the "Japan–Manchukuo economic bloc" had broadened into the "Japan–Manchukuo–China economic bloc," Japanese forces had already invaded all parts of the Chinese mainland. Slogans extolling a "new order in East Asia" (*Tōa shinchitsujo*) and an "East Asian Gemeinschaft" (*Tōa kyōdōtai*) were soon supplanted by the "Greater East Asia Co-Prosperity Sphere" (*Daitōa kyōeiken*) when it became clear that the targets for further Japanese conquest were to be extended from East Asia to Southeast Asia and the western Pacific. As a result, the costs of acquiring a "self-sufficient economic sphere"

58 Hata Ikuhiko, *Nitchū sensō shi*, rev. ed. (Tokyo: Hara shobō, 1979), chap. 2, sec. 6.
59 Tsunoda Jum, ed., *Ishiwara Kanji shiryō*, vol. 1: *Kokubō ronsaku* (Tokyo: Hara shobō, 1971), p. 436.

exceeded the expected advantages. A paper prepared by the Research Bureau of the Foreign Ministry at the end of 1936 argued: "The practical advantages of an expansionist policy are slim. Ever since the Sino-Japanese War [of 1894–5], there has been a national deficit, and this deficit could not be paid off by ten or twenty years of colonial rule in the future." Instead, the paper explained, Japan should put aside considerations of profit or loss and pursue the ideal of "universal harmony" (*hakkō ichiu,* literally, "the eight corners of the world under one roof").[60]

Because Japan's limited national strength made it difficult to support the rapidly growing Co-Prosperity Sphere, Japan made up for its disadvantages by a ruthless policy of local plunder, reminiscent of early Spanish colonial policy. Land was seized for the settlement of Japanese immigrants in Manchuria; on the Chinese mainland business and enterprises were confiscated; and Japanese forces fighting in China and later in the Pacific lived off the land. The army purchased daily necessities with excessive issues of unbacked military scrip that inevitably brought local inflation. In modern history there has been no other instance of a foreign expeditionary force's adopting a policy of local self-sufficiency from the very outset. It was a glaring demonstration of the enormous disparities between slogans and realities. It was only natural that the Japanese army alienated the inhabitants of the occupied areas, who joked that the "Imperial Army" (*kōgun*) was an "army of locusts" (*kōgun*).

## THE CHINA CONFLICT

Recently it has become popular for Japanese historians to call the chain of aggression from the Manchurian incident onward "the fifteen-year war" (although strictly speaking, it lasted only thirteen years and eleven months). In this sense, the Manchurian incident, the war in China, and the war in the Pacific should not be viewed separately but as one continuous war.[61] The only occasion when war was formally declared in accordance with international law was in December 1941, but after 1931 not a day passed without gunfire (including guerrilla action) in the areas where Japanese forces operated.

It is questionable whether this war can be viewed as the conse

60 Gaimushō chōsabu, "Nihon koyū no gaikō shidō genri kōryō," December 1936, Gaik shiryōkan archives, File number A-1-0-0-6.

61 Ienaga Saburō, *Taiheiyō sensō* (Tokyo: Iwanami shoten, 1968), preface and pp. 1–4; Hat Ikuhiko, "Onnen shikan kara no dakkyaku," *Keizai ōrai,* February 1979.

quence of deliberate action based on a conspiracy by Class A war criminals, as Allied prosecutors insisted at the Tokyo war crimes trials. Although few in number, some Japanese did sense that the country's eventual downfall was inevitable if the war continued beyond the point of no return. At each crucial turning point during the 1930s, there were confrontations between "expansionist" and "nonexpansionist" factions, between those who wished to push forward and those who wished to restrain Japan's military advance to some extent. The distrust of Japan abroad, however, contributed to the failure of the nonexpansionist camp.

During the years between the Manchurian incident and the China war, the nonexpansionists foresaw that an invasion of China would prove fatal to Japan. They continued to insist that Japan concentrate on the development of Manchuria for the time being. As Finance Minister Takahashi Korekiyo observed to a group of ministry officials departing for Manchuria, "We opposed the Manchurian incident. Now that matters have come this far, I think that there is no more use talking about it. But we should not meddle in north China."[62] As we have already seen, during the latter half of 1935, the Kwantung Army had begun to advance into north China, even though order had not been established in Manchuria and investigation of its potential resources had not advanced very far. The military, disappointed at the rather unexpectedly low quality of iron ore and coal in Manchuria, could not resist the temptation of high-quality iron and coal in north China. Colonel Ishiwara, doubtful of the wisdom of penetrating north China, dispatched a trusted economic officer to Manchuria with a report that Manchuria alone could provide the resources necessary for the buildup of a national defense state, but it was difficult to dissuade the adventurers in the Kwantung Army.[63]

In July 1937 all-out war finally began between Japan and China. It began with a small military clash at the Marco Polo Bridge in the suburbs of Peking. The truth behind the incident, especially the question of who fired the first shot at the Japanese troops engaged in night maneuvers there, is one of the biggest remaining mysteries of the 1930s. In regard to who fired the first shot are the following hypotheses, in descending order of probability: (1) The "accidental shot" hypothesis is that a low-ranking Chinese soldier fired the shot out of fright at the Japanese night maneuvers; (2) the "Communist plot"

62 Nomura Masao, *Hōsō fūunroku* (Tokyo: Asahi shimbunsha, 1966), vol. 2, p. 70.
63 Hata, *Gun Fashizumu undō shi*, p. 234.

hypothesis attributes the incident to a conspiracy by the Chinese Communist Party's northern bureau, under the direction of Liu Shao-chi; (3) the "warlord plot" theory is that the clash was plotted by northern warlords such as Feng Yu-hsiang; and (4) the final hypothesis is that the first shot was fired as part of a private plot by special intelligence organs of the Japanese army or those connected with it.[64] To make matters more complicated, it is possible that those who committed the overt act were not those who instigated it. Whatever the truth of the matter, to the Japanese government, the Japanese military, and the Chiang government, the incident began as an accident.

There is also disagreement about why conditions had reached the point that a local clash could turn into a full-scale war. On the surface, Sino-Japanese relations had been in a lull after the end of 1936. There were no noteworthy points of contention between the two countries except for pending negotiations with Sung Che-yuan concerning the economic development of north China. In fact, during the six months before the Marco Polo Bridge incident, fewer newspaper articles appeared on the subject of Sino-Japanese relations than at any time since 1935. Should the period be viewed as a time of eased tension or as a calm before a brewing storm?

Before the incident, the Kuomintang government had been pursuing a compromise policy, resisting on the one hand and negotiating on the other. In 1935 with help from the British, the Nanking government had effected a currency reform that shifted the country from a silver standard to a managed currency, and strengthened the economic basis for national unification. In the summer of 1936 the government had suppressed the southwestern warlords and used the Suiyuan incident to pull together the various warlords in north China. After the Sian incident in December 1936, when Chiang Kai-shek was briefly confined by Chang Hsueh-liang, there was progress toward cooperation with the Chinese Communists. An anti-Japanese mood had been rising among the Chinese public, whose self-confidence had deepened as a result of these gains. But because the Nanking government still had not achieved its goal of complete unification, and because its military modernization was still in progress, it was premature to plunge into a war with Japan.

From the Japanese point of view, the Nanking government made a serious miscalculation when it adopted a confrontational stance and

64 Hata, *Nitchū sensō shi*, new ed., chap. 4, 1979; Hata Ikuhiko, "Rokōkyō dai-ippatsu no hannin," *Ichiokunin no Shōwa shi 3*, vol. 2: *Nitchū sensō* (Tokyo: Mainichi shinbunsha, 1979), p. 44.

directed its central army to move north the day after the Marco Polo Bridge incident.[65] Japanese army leaders thought that the crisis could be resolved by negotiations at the local level, just as other small disputes had in the past. At first the Japanese high command issued instructions calling for nonexpansion and local negotiations. Thus when it learned of the movement of the Chinese central army, it was perplexed. Within the Japanese army there emerged both expansionist and nonexpansionist factions.[66] The expansionists wanted to use the incident to strike a military blow at China to break the deadlock in north China. The nonexpansionists, on the other hand, opposed sending troops lest a clash with awakening Chinese nationalism drag Japan into the morass of a protracted war that, in Major General Ishiwara's words, would be like Napoleon's Spanish campaign. It was a reflection of this split in army circles that decisions to mobilize were made and canceled four times before a final decision was taken to send three divisions to north China on July 27. Neither Prime Minister Konoe nor Foreign Minister Hirota had clear views about what to do. In the final analysis, they simply followed the lead of the expansionist faction within the Japanese army. The decision was also much influenced by the press and public opinion which, stirred up by the army press, rashly called for the "punishment of a disorderly China" (*bōshi yōchō*).

All the while, fighting continued in north China. Peking fell after an exchange of fire lasting only one day and night. Sung Che-yuan's troops withdrew after offering almost no resistance. Japanese military forces then began to move south, heading toward the Yangtze River. On August 13 the situation in Shanghai worsened when fighting broke out between the Chinese army and Japanese naval landing units. The Japanese Navy, which had been passive until this point, called on the army for help. The cabinet decided to send a relief force of two divisions to Shanghai. On August 15 the Chinese general headquarters decreed a general mobilization, and with that the two countries plunged into a full-scale war that lasted for eight years.

In comparing the expansion of the China conflict with the Manchurian incident, there appear to be points of both similarity and difference. The occupation of Peking, like the earlier occupation of Muk-

65 Chiang Kai-shek, *Shō Kai seki hiroku 12, Nitchū zenmen sensō* (Tokyo: Sankei shinbunsha, 1976). In his diary on July 8, the day after the Marco Polo incident broke out, Chiang wrote that "the time has come now to make the decision to fight back as long as Japan has challenged us." On July 9, he ordered Military Bureau Chief Ho Ying-chin to start the reorganization of the army in preparation for all-out war and gave instructions to General Sun Lien-chung to move two divisions of the central army to North China. Ibid., pp. 21–2.

66 Hata, *Nitchū sensō shi*, chap. 5.

den, ended quickly without bloodshed. Japanese forces achieved their ostensible goals of "appropriate self-defense" and "chastisement." But whereas the expansion of military action was instigated by the Japanese forces during the Manchurian incident, Chinese forces were responsible in the case of the China war. In this sense, the dispatch of Japanese troops to Kirin in 1931 resembled the dispatch of Chinese troops to Shanghai in 1937. The Nanking government had taken no action to resist the Japanese in 1931 when Chang Hsueh-liang failed to do so, but in 1937 it opted for military resistance, even though Sung Che-yuan's forces initially offered almost no opposition. The final clash of the Chinese troops with a Japanese naval landing force at Shanghai, however, finally provoked the dispatch of a Japanese expeditionary army.

## THE ABORTED PEACE WITH CHINA

The Sino-Japanese War was the inevitable consequence of the precipitous continental policy that Japan had pursued since the Manchurian incident, but when the war began, not the Japanese government, nor the army, nor the military forces in China had the preliminary plans or the resolve to embark on a full-scale war. The Japanese army leadership, which had a low view of Chinese military strength and morale, optimistically believed that Japan could achieve a quick victory. Japanese forces seized Nanking in December 1937 and Hankow and Canton in October 1938, and in 1939 Japanese airplanes began bombing raids on Chungking. But Japanese expectations for quick victory remained unfulfilled.

The Chinese Communist Party wanted to engage in a total war of resistance against the Japanese. They restrained the peace view in the Kuomintang government which was inclining toward a compromise as Chinese military operations faltered. In March 1938 when the Suchow campaign ended with most of north China in Japanese hands and the prospects for China looked bad, Mao Tse-tung enunciated his famous "protracted war" theory, calling for final victory and inspiring a national fighting spirit. In military strategy as well, the Communists, who had acquired much experience in the civil war, advocated arming the populace and carrying on guerrilla warfare. Eventually these became standard tactics for the entire Chinese army and caused the Japanese forces much difficulty.

In the fall of 1938 after the completion of the Hankow campaign

Japanese forces abandoned their pursuit of the Chinese army. The Kuomintang government had evacuated from Nanking to Chungking in western China, where it assumed a defensive posture. Even with the commitment of 600,000 men, the Japanese could barely secure the "points and lines," the main cities and the railroad lines in the occupied territories. Except for a small number of officers in the nonexpansionist faction, neither the army nor the government had expected the hostilities in China to drag out into a long war of attrition.

Around the time of the fall of Nanking, in December 1937, some military leaders began to have second thoughts and urged an early end to the fighting. In modern warfare it was common sense that a country surrendered when its capital fell, but the Japanese military was upset when this common sense did not prevail in China. Impatient to make peace with China on appropriate terms and to end the war quickly, a host of peace movements came crowding onto the scene. In Shanghai, Hong Kong, Tientsin, and other cities with concessions under the control of neutral powers, self-proclaimed "China experts" of all sorts – military men, politicians, and *rōnin* adventurers – opened secret negotiations. All ended in failure.[67] On the Japanese side, there were disagreements over the severity or leniency of the terms as the war progressed; on the Chinese side there was distrust that the Japanese would not keep their promises even if the negotiations succeeded. A stalemate ensued. In the words of Bradford Lee, "Neither side wanted war, but neither adopted a conciliatory stance."[68] Even today there remain many unanswered questions about the debate within the Kuomintang between those who favored resistance and those who favored peace, and about which elements in the complex class structure supported resistance and which did not.

The Japanese government finally abandoned the idea of making peace. It turned instead to a policy of establishing a puppet government under the leadership of Chiang Kai-shek's political enemy, Wang Ching-wei, in hope that the Kuomintang regime at Chungking and its resistance by attrition eventually would wither away. However, the overextended Japanese lines were constantly exposed to guerrilla counterattacks launched by both Chiang's army and the Communist armies. It also became clear that the Wang Ching-wei government was a weak regime, unable to draw popular support and unlikely to survive

67 Hata, *Nitchū sensō shi*, chap. 3.
68 Bradford Lee, *Britain and the Sino-Japanese War 1937–39* (Stanford, Calif.: Stanford University Press, 1973), p. 15.

a day without the backing of the Japanese army. In its treaty with Japan, the Wang government accepted humiliating terms, including the recognition of Manchukuo, which John Boyle described as far more severe than the conditions of the cease-fire treaty in France between the Vichy government and the Nazis.[69]

Meanwhile, there were new anxieties for the Japanese in the north. The Japanese army had traditionally devised its operations plans and conducted maneuvers with the Russian (later Soviet) forces in East Asia as their principal hypothetical enemy. After the Manchurian incident, the Kwantung Army and the Soviet forces faced each other directly across the Amur River. Even though the danger of a clash between the two armies increased, the main force of the Japanese army was pinned down in the China theater. When two border incidents finally occurred – the Changkufeng incident (July–August 1938) and the Nomonhan incident (May–September 1939) – the Kwantung Army, which prided itself on the superior morale of its troops, met defeat at the hands of Soviet forces equipped with up-to-date military equipment. At a time when Europe was moving rapidly toward another great war, it seemed that Japan was on the verge of losing its valuable free hand in global politics.

The depth of Japan's frustration was revealed by the zeal with which it pursued various peace overtures toward China. The army was put in the awkward position of having to explain to the public why the continuous string of military victories and the huge dissipation of manpower in China did not end with the surrender of the Kuomintang. Out of this desperate quandary came the Konoe government's sudden and unprecedented announcement in January 1938 that Japan "would not negotiate with Chiang Kai-shek" (*aite ni sezu*). This opened the way to an endless war.

The government tried to shift to the powers the blame for the prolongation of the China war, by insisting that Chinese military resistance was kept alive by military and psychological assistance from the United States, Britain, the Soviet Union, and France. In fact, the Japanese army knew very well that the military value of "aid" from the United States, Britain, and France – entering China through the coast, over the border with French Indochina, or on the Burma Road – was negligible, that it amounted to little more than small-scale smuggling. Only the Soviet aid coming in through the northwest was at all substan-

69 John H. Boyle, *China and Japan at War 1937–45: The Politics of Collaboration* (Stanford Calif.: Stanford University Press, 1972).

tial.[70] Nevertheless, the Japanese government launched a strong anti-British movement on the grounds that Britain was a barrier to the solution of the war with China. It did so not only because Britain was the country with whom the Japanese had most friction over interests in China but also because Britain seemed to be a safer scapegoat than the United States, as Britain was tied down by pressure from Nazi Germany. False logic, however, often turns into real logic. Having abandoned any effort to resolve the conflict with China through negotiations between the principals, Japan moved toward a solution by a strange detour, namely, by arranging a military alliance with Germany and Italy to confront Great Britain and the United States, the two alleged interlopers. Had the same kind of psychology prompted Germany to abandon the war against Britain and strike against the Soviet Union? The war in the Pacific need not have been the logical consequence of the war in China, but the Japanese leadership, acting as if under self-hypnosis, chose the path toward certain self-destruction.

## TO THE PACIFIC WAR

At the beginning of this chapter was mentioned the grandiose scheme devised by Colonel Matsuishi Yasuji in 1906 for the conquest of the Asian continent, then Southeast Asia, and finally an invasion of the American continent. By 1940 this grand design, which seemed only fantasy a generation earlier, was on the verge of realization. The only difference between Matsuishi's scheme and the scope of the Greater East Asia Co-Prosperity Sphere enunciated by Foreign Minister Matsuoka Yosuke in the summer of 1940 was that Matsuoka substituted Australia for South America.[71]

The debate between the northern advance and the southern advance that had so enlivened late Meiji journalism also reappeared in a somewhat altered guise. By 1940 the original goals of the northern advance – the conquest of China south of the Great Wall by way of Korea and Manchuria – had already been achieved. The idea of a northern advance now literally meant moving into Siberia, that is, going to war with the Soviet Union. The southern advance meant using Hainan

70 With respect to Soviet assistance to China, see Hirai Tomoyoshi, "Soren no dōkō (1933 nen–1939 nen)" in *TSENM*, vol. 4. For U.S.–British help, see Nagaoka Shinjirō, "Nanpo shisaku no gaikōteki tenkai (1937 nen–1941 nen)" in *TSENM*, vol. 6. The amount of aid that flowed into China, including by way of the northwest route, was at its peak in June 1939 but amounted only to about 25,000 tons monthly, or merely two large cargo shiploads, according to NGS studies; Nagaoka, "Nanpo shisaku," *TSENM*, vol. 6, p. 27.

71 Hatano Sumio, "Tōa shin chitsujo to chiseigaku," in *Nihon no 1930–nen dai*, pp. 33–4.

Island as a springboard to solidify the Japanese position in northern Indochina, then heading into Southeast Asia, a treasure house of natural resources centering on the Dutch East Indies.

With outbreak of World War II in Europe in 1939, two of the major colonial powers in Southeast Asia, France and the Netherlands, had been overrun by the Germans, and a third, Great Britain, seemed on the verge of collapse. Faced with this golden opportunity, advocates of the southern advance coined the phrase "Don't miss the bus." But the American government, which had continued to remain a spectator to the Japanese conquest of China, showed a firm intent to prevent Japan's southern advance into Southeast Asia. The Japanese government, hesitant because it was assumed that Great Britain and the United States were inseparable, used its first chance to move south in the summer of 1940 to occupy the northern part of Indochina. When a second chance arrived a year later with the outbreak of war between Germany and the Soviet Union in the summer of 1941, after repeated internal debate on whether to invade Siberia or to resume a military advance to the south, the Japanese government made the fateful choice of occupying southern Indochina. The American government retaliated by announcing an embargo on petroleum, which assumed a resolve to go to war. From this point onward, war in the Pacific became inescapable.

Although historians have advanced various arguments about the immediate and more remote cause for the outbreak of war between Japan and the United States, no theory appears to have won universal acceptance. The Japanese government blamed the start of war in 1941 on the Hull note which demanded that Japan withdraw totally from China and return to the status quo before the Manchurian incident. From that standpoint, the prevailing view has been that the basic cause of the Pacific War was the problem of Japan's withdrawal from China[72] and that it "clearly and consistently lay in the problem of Sino-Japanese relations."[73] Hard-line Japanese navy leaders, who called for war in 1941, also thought that war with the United States had been made inevitable by confrontation with American attempts to "interfere" with Japan's continental policy under the slogans of maintaining the "Open Door" policy and the "territorial integrity of China." As Captain Ishikawa Shingo, a leader of the navy hawks, observed, "Ja-

72 Paul W. Schroeder, *The Axis Alliance and Japanese-American Relations* (Ithaca, N.Y.: Cornell University Press, 1971), p. 200.
73 Yoshii Hiroshi, *Shōwa gaikō shi* (Tokyo: Nansōsha, 1975), pp. 90–191.

pan and the United States are engaged in a struggle for the China mainland."[74] In fact, during the negotiations with the United States that began in the spring of 1941, the Japanese concentrated on the China problem, especially the withdrawal of Japanese troops. However, it is doubtful whether the United States, which consistently assigned first importance to the situation in Europe, placed as much importance on China as the Japanese thought it did. Stimson's "nonrecognition doctrine" in 1931 and Roosevelt's "quarantine speech" in 1938 were harsh in tone. But as Robert A. Divine observed, they actually represented nothing more than "hesitancy and indecision."[75] In fact, some American observers at the time thought the war in China might be to the United States' advantage. Stanley Hornbeck, adviser to the Far Eastern Division of the Department of State, pointed out that there might be some benefit if Japan continued to be bogged down in China, where it would fritter away its strength.[76]

If one looks closely at American reactions to Japan during this period, it becomes evident that the United States was extremely nervous about the Japanese move southward. Just before the outbreak of fighting, the United States suddenly withdrew a *modus vivendi* acceptable to Japan and offered instead the Hull note, which in the view of some amounted to a declaration of war. The American government did so because Washington had received intelligence that a Japanese convoy was moving south through the Taiwan Straits.[77] "The immediate cause of the war," Akira Iriye wrote, "was the Japanese policy of advancing to the south by force."[78] The Japanese leadership, preoccupied with the China problem, was not sufficiently cautious about the move south and did not understand the decisive impact that the action would have on the United States. This does not mean that the United States had special vital interests in Southeast Asia, including southern Indochina. To be sure, if Japanese air power were deployed to Saigon, the Philippines would be threatened by a flank attack, and so would Malaya, which produced rubber, the only major resource in which the United States was not self-sufficient.

Nevertheless, the cumulative weight of those factors was rather

74 Ishikawa Shingo, *Shinjuwan made no keii* (Tokyo: Tiji tsūshinsha, 1960), p. 6.
75 Robert A. Divine, *Roosevelt and World War II* (Baltimore: Johns Hopkins University Press, 1969), p. 19.
76 Hornbeck Memorandum, September 5, 1941, in Hornbeck Papers, Box 254, Hoover Institution, Stanford University, Stanford, Calif.
77 Sudō Shinji, "Tōjō naikaku to Nichi-Bei kōshō," *Kyōto Sangyō Daigaku ronshū* 10 (1980):33.
78 Iriye Akira, *Nichi-Bei sensō* (Tokyo: Chūō Kōronsha, 1978), p. 81.

small. The decisive factor is probably to be found in broad American strategic perspectives. Because wars usually occur as the result of a gradual intensification of crises, it is not inappropriate to seek the turning point toward war or peace in the general world situation immediately before the outbreak of war. In my view, the point of no return regarding war in the Pacific came with the conclusion of the Tripartite Pact in the fall of 1940. Of course, even after the point of no return had been passed, the possibility of avoiding war did not completely vanish. Rather, it should be understood that from the signing of the Tripartite Pact to the American embargo on petroleum, an already narrow range of choices narrowed even further until ultimately there was no way to avoid war. I stress the importance of the Tripartite Pact in particular because it determined finally the lines of allegiance and belligerence that governed World War II. After the outbreak of European hostilities in 1939, only two great powers remained neutral, the United States and the Soviet Union. It was clear that the entry of these two nations into the war would be the decisive key to victory or defeat. President Franklin D. Roosevelt assigned priority to the overthrow of Nazi Germany. He guided American world strategy by the simple but easily understood logic that Germany's friends were America's enemies and that Germany's enemies were America's friends. Leaders in Germany and Japan, on the other hand, seemed to have been under the influence of the fashionable Marxist view that confrontation between capitalism and socialism was inevitable, and they expected that by the end of the war the world situation would conform to this perception. In other words, because it was in the interest of the United States, Great Britain, Japan, and Germany to cooperate in the common goal of an anti-Communist crusade, a compromise among them should be possible under suitable conditions.

Events gradually undercut these expectations, but there remained another possible alignment of world powers, a joint front between fascism and socialism, as suggested by the Nazi-Soviet Non-Aggression Pact. But Foreign Minister Matsuoka Yōsuke, who had urged the signing of the Tripartite Pact, had an even grander dream. What he had in mind was to restore the world balance of power by bringing the Soviet Union into the Tripartite Pact so as to pit the Eurasian continent against the American continent.[79] Opponents as well as supporters of the Tripartite Pact placed considerable hopes on Matsuoka's conception, but the idea went no further than the signing of the Japanese-Soviet Neutral-

79 Miwa Kimitada, *Matsuoka Yōsuke* (Tokyo: Chūō Kōronsha, 1971), pp. 166–7.

ity Pact in 1941. Because the Soviet Union did not join the Tripartite Pact, its global strategic value was decisively reduced. Japan and Germany lay separated at the opposite ends of the Eurasian landmass with the Soviet Union in between.

On the eve of the Pacific War, when the alignments among the powers were changing rapidly, to misread the world situation was to invite fatal collapse. The worst possible misreading was for Japan to strike an alliance with Nazi Germany that had little direct advantage. The effort to use the Axis alliance to promote the resolution of the China war and to ease a move southward into Southeast Asia not only ended in disappointment, but it also decisively turned the Americans and the British into enemies of Japan. Perhaps it was only natural that Japan's strategic thinking, which focused exclusively on the Pacific and East Asia, could not adjust to strategic thinking on a global scale. From the vantage point of the Allied powers, however, Japan had become the enemy of the United States by befriending the "Nazi devils." Leaders in China, which had been on the verge of collapse, sensed this and regained the self-confidence needed to continue its resistance. On the day the Tripartite Pact was concluded in September 1940, Chiang Kai-shek wrote in his diary, "This is the best thing that could have happened to us. The trend toward victory in the war of resistance has been decided."[80]

Germany's inexplicable attack on the Soviet Union in June 1941 drove the Soviets into the Anglo-American camp, literally turning the war between the Axis powers and their opponents (or between the fascists and the antifascists) into a confrontation between the "have" and the "have-not" nations. In a total war, where matériel and technology were decisive factors, it was obvious from the outset who would win and who would lose under such an alignment. With the attack on Pearl Harbor on December 8, 1941, the China war was absorbed into the Pacific War. The Pacific Ocean became the main battlefield, and Japan shifted to a defensive stance on the Asian mainland.

For a time the United States considered using China as the shortest route to mount an attack on the Japanese home islands, but it became clear that the military capacity of China, the weakest ally of the United States, was not up to the task.[81] The Americans also hoped that China would replace Japan in assuming a leadership role in Asia once the war ended, but those expectations were also disappointed: It was not the

80 *Shō Kai-seki hiroku*, vol. 13: *Daitōa sensō* (Tokyo: Sankei shinbunsha, 1976), p. 61.
81 Michael Schaller, *The U.S. Crusade in China, 1938–1945* (New York: Columbia University Press, 1979), p. 39.

Kuomintang but the Chinese Communists who ultimately took control of China.[82]

The Japanese defeat in 1945 resulted in the complete withdrawal of Japan from the Asian continent, and it returned to the status of the small island state it had assumed before the Sino-Japanese war of 1894–5. However, not only the defeated but the victors as well found it difficult to maintain colonialism in the postwar period. The United States, which embarked on a continental policy in Japan's place after the war, was also unable to secure China, Korea, and Vietnam, and it was able to maintain a military presence only in the southern half of the Korean peninsula.

When one looks back at Japan's continental expansion from the 1890s to 1945, one can draw several conclusions. First, the pace of Japan's expansion was extraordinarily rapid. The extent of Japan's conquests, especially during the decade that followed the Manchurian incident, went even beyond what the Mongols had achieved under Genghis Khan. Second, Japan's mode of expansion, which began simply as the maintenance of colonies, turned into a policy of pillage and plunder. Third, despite that, the costs of Japan's conquest exceeded its profits, and it became clear that continental expansion was a losing proposition. Finally, it was difficult for Japan to establish *Lebensraum* as a world power on the Asian continent, which was relatively poor in resources. In this sense, a continental policy inevitably contained an impulse toward the next step, to press on toward a conquest of Southeast Asia. It was this in turn that led to war between Japan and the United States and brought catastrophe to the Japanese empire.

82 Christopher Thorne, *Allies of a Kind* (New York: Oxford University Press, 1978), p. 37.

# CHAPTER 7

# THE PACIFIC WAR

## HYPOTHETICAL ENEMIES

The general staffs of the Japanese armed forces, like those elsewhere in the world, devised contingency plans each year to cope with the possibility of hostilities against one or more powers. The Japanese army's war plans, reflecting emphases rather than strict numerical priorities, ascribed first importance to the Russians as the potential enemy from the time of the Russo-Japanese War until the birth of the Soviet Union. With the increase in American influence in the Far East attending a deterioration in U.S.-Japanese relations, the United States replaced Russia after 1918 as the main national enemy. The Japanese army was never as serious as the navy was concerning anti-American operations because hostilities did not appear imminent. Nevertheless, as early as 1918, Japanese war plans included an army–navy seizure of the Philippines to deny advanced bases to the United States Fleet in the western Pacific.

In the mid-1920s, civilian politicians pushed forward a program of reduction and budgetary retrenchment. Ugaki Kazushige, war minister between 1924 and 1927, feared that the lion's share of the limited national defense budget would go to the navy if the United States remained the prime national foe. To counteract this domestic pressure, the Japanese army began to draft new operational plans against the Soviet Union. In the late 1920s, however, the army general staff became more serious about the "northern threat." The first Soviet five-year plan was begun in 1928, and the Red Army's offensive against Chang Hsueh-liang's forces in Manchuria in 1929 was unexpectedly successful. A recrudescence of Soviet strength in the Siberian theater threatened Japan's own aspiration to a dominant position on the continent. Many army leaders came to believe more strongly than ever that Manchuria, and Siberia as far west as Lake Baikal, would become the ultimate battleground for the Japanese army and thus the front line of national defense. The reorientation of operational priorities was hastened by the Japanese Kwantung Army's swift conquest of

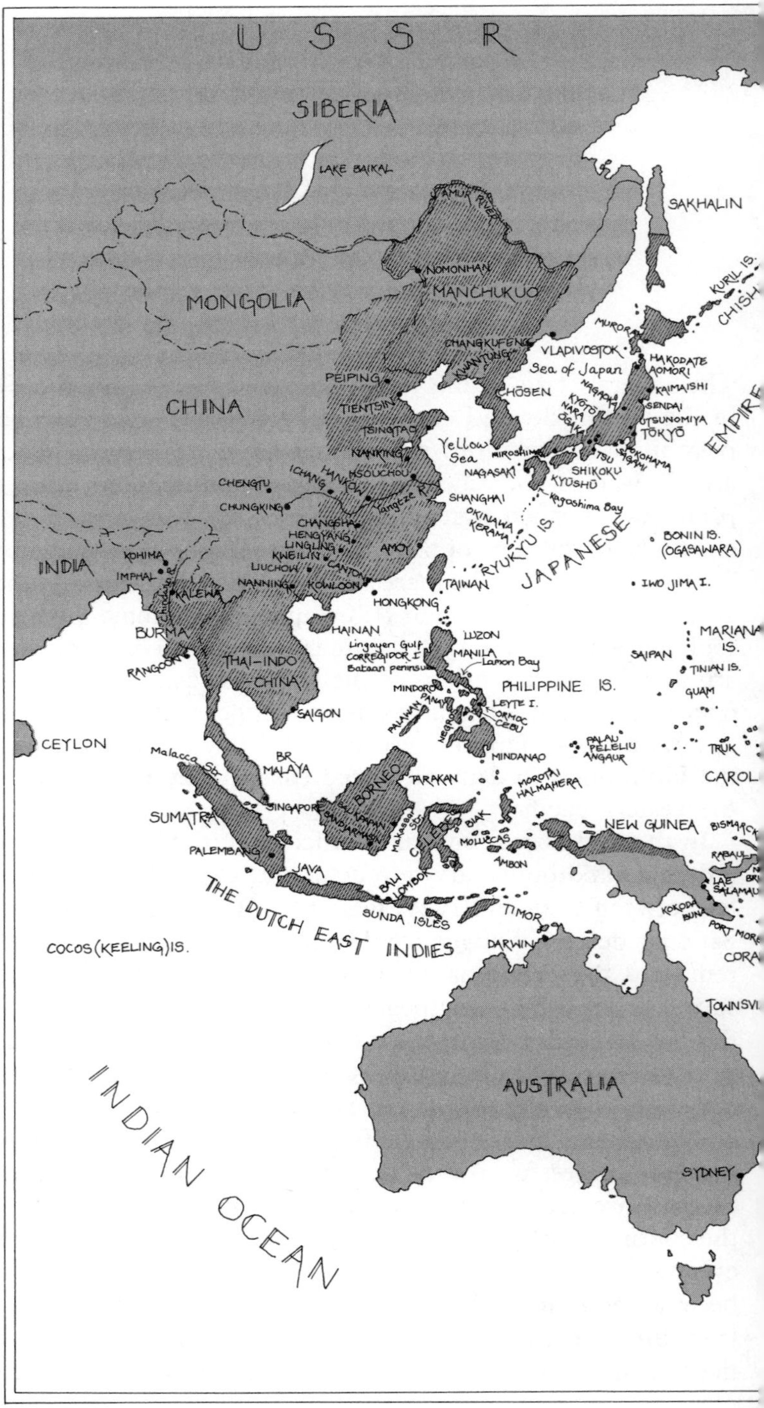
USSR
SIBERIA
LAKE BAIKAL
AMUR RIVER
SAKHALIN
KURIL IS.
NOMONHAN
MANCHUKUO
MONGOLIA
MURORAN
CHANGKUFENG
VLADIVOSTOK
HAKODATE
AOMORI
KWANTUNG
Sea of Japan
PEIPING
CHŌSEN
KAIMAISHI
SENDAI
CHINA
TIENTSIN
KYOTO
NARA
OSAKA
NAGAOKA
UTSUNOMIYA
TŌKYŌ
EMPIRE
TSINGTAO
Yellow Sea
HIROSHIMA
TSU
YOKOHAMA
SAGAMI
NANKING
NAGASAKI
SHIKOKU
HANKOW
HSOUCHOU
KYŪSHŪ
CHENGTU
ICHANG
Yangtze R.
CHUNGKING
SHANGHAI
Kagoshima Bay
CHANGSHA
OKINAWA
KERAMA
HENGYANG
LINGLING
KWEILIN
RYUKYU IS.
JAPANESE
BONIN IS.
(OGASAWARA)
INDIA
KOHIMA
IMPHAL
AMOY
LIUCHOW
CANTON
NANNING
KOWLOON
TAIWAN
IWO JIMA I.
KALEWA
HONGKONG
HAINAN
LUZON
MARIANA IS.
BURMA
Lingayen Gulf
CORREGIDOR I.
Bataan peninsula
MANILA
Lamon Bay
SAIPAN
TINIAN IS.
RANGOON
THAI-INDO-CHINA
PHILIPPINE IS.
MINDORO
PANAY
LEYTE I.
GUAM
PALAWAN
ORMOC
CEBU
SAIGON
NEGROS
CEYLON
PALAU
PELELIU
ANGAUR
TRUK
MINDANAO
Malacca Str.
BR. MALAYA
BORNEO
TARAKAN
CAROL
MOROTAI
HALMAHERA
SUMATRA
SINGAPORE
BALIKPAPAN
BANDJARMASIN
Makassar Str.
CELEBES
BIAK
NEW GUINEA
MOLUCCAS
PALEMBANG
AMBON
RABAUL
JAVA
LAE
SALAMAUA
BALI
LOMBOK
KOKODA
BUNA
THE DUTCH EAST INDIES
SUNDA ISLES
TIMOR
PORT MORE
COCOS (KEELING) IS.
DARWIN
CORA
TOWNSVI
AUSTRALIA
INDIAN OCEAN
SYDNEY

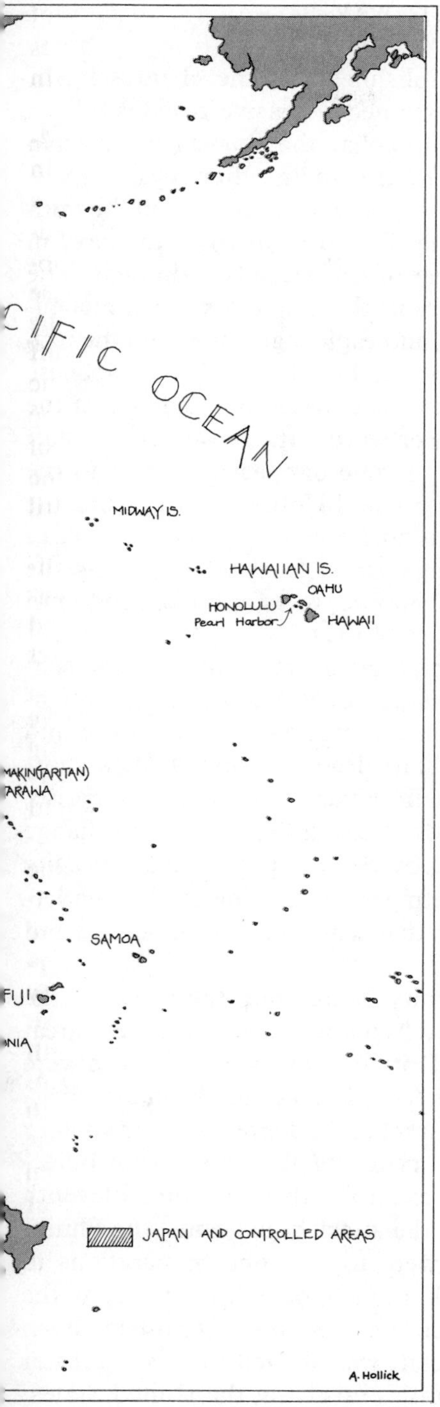


Map 7.1. Pacific theater in World War II.

Manchuria in 1931–2 and the establishment of the client state of Manchukuo. Because Japan's self-assigned defensive responsibilities now abutted Soviet Siberia and Mongolia, the Soviets were again named the primary national enemy in war planning after 1931.

The Japanese national defense policy was revised further in the mid-1930s. After the breakdown of the naval accords in 1935, the navy in particular stressed the growing danger of American containment. The giant American naval building program, the major American maneuvers conducted near Midway Island, and espionage reports on the top-secret Orange War Plan alarmed navy leaders. By 1936, the Japanese navy had drawn up new contingency plans based on "defense in the north, advance to the south." In other words, the naval general staff was looking toward Southeast Asia, a zone of special interest to the colonial powers there, especially Britain and Holland. As a result, the British were added to the list of national enemies in the revision of 1936. However, operational planning against England, involving the neutralization of Hong Kong and Singapore, was not introduced until 1939, and anti-Dutch operations not until 1941.

Japanese military leaders were thinking in terms of strategic self-defense, but the details of their envisaged operations remained offensive. Because Japan had a relatively underdeveloped industrial and technological infrastructure, its military leaders planned for a short war stressing opening moves and tactical execution, that is, surprise, provocation of early battle, and quick decision. There was no change in the fundamentals of this philosophy before 1941. Indeed, despite the operational refinements, the contingency planning of 1936 underwent no fundamental review and, in that sense, proved unhelpful and obsolete.

Part of the reason was the difficulty of meshing the views of the fighting services. After all, the navy's hypothetical enemies were great sea powers, the United States and Britain, and the army's foes were deployed mainly on the landmass of Asia. In an effort to adjust divergent priorities, the Japanese high command adopted a contradictory policy of simultaneous engagement – a concept abhorrent to any objective military planner. In 1937, for example, the Fifth and Eleventh Infantry Divisions were allocated to the attack plan against the Philippines at the same time that they were to continue preparations to engage the Soviets. Although each branch paid lip service to the other's central concern, the army kept its eyes on the continent. Even after 1939, when the army general staff was obliged to devote greater attention to the eventuality of hostilities involving the United States, operations planning did not progress beyond the visualization of attacks against the Philippines and Guam, basically designed to command the waters of the western Pacific against Plan Orange.[1]

## THE MORASS IN CHINA

It is ironic that the Japanese army, which had tended to worry about the Soviets and to ignore the Americans, played a vital role in bringing about the war against the United States. The single most important reason can be found in the China theater. Ever since the unplanned Marco Polo Bridge affair at Peking in July 1937, the army had found itself sinking into a quagmire that prescient staff officers likened to Napoleon's campaigns in Spain. When the first serious clashes erupted in north China, the entire Japanese garrison force amounted only to five thousand or six thousand men, built around one infantry brigade. At Shanghai, the navy had no more than four thousand bluejackets ashore. This modest scale of deployment reflected the fact that military plans did not envisage China as a principal national enemy. In 1936 the army general staff even ordered the China Garrison Army to train for operations against the Soviet army. The Japanese unit involved in the fateful fire fight at the Marco Polo Bridge in July 1937 was engaged in anti-Soviet, not anti-Chinese exercises. As fighting expanded between China and Japan in 1937, the original Japanese intention was to strike rapidly and capture a few key points. On the basis of fairly recent experience in Manchuria in 1931 and at Shanghai in 1932, it was widely thought that full-scale hostilities would be unnecessary, that local combat and threats of force could overwhelm the Chinese and cause the Nationalist government to sue for the cessation of hostilities on terms favorable to the Japanese.

The Chinese fought desperately, but they could not check the invaders, who soon overran Shantung, north China, and Shanghai. But contrary to Japanese expectations, the Chinese would not yield. Chiang Kai-shek ordered national mobilization. In response, Japanese troops, artillery, tanks, and aircraft were rushed to China from the homeland, Korea, and Manchuria, where the Kwantung Army was anxious to

1 *Gendaishi shiryō* (hereafter *GSS*), *Nitchū sensō* (1) (Tokyo: Misuzu shobō, 1964), vol. 8, pp. 686–90; Hayashi Saburō, *Taiheiyō sensō rikusen gaishi* (Tokyo: Iwanami shoten, 1951), pp. 2–3; Bōeichō bōeikenshūsho senshi shitsu (hereafter BBSS), *Senshi sōsho*, 102 vols. (Tokyo: Asagumo shinbunsha, 1966–80), *Daihon'ei kaigunbu rengō kantai* (1), pp. 173–9, 343–50, 466–78, 500–8; BBSS, *Daihon'ei rikugunbu* (1), pp. 151–93, 287–302; BBSS, *Hondo kessen junbi* (1), chap. 1; Takagi Sōkichi, *Taiheiyō sensō to riku-kaigun no kōsō* (Tokyo: Keizai ōraisha, 1967), pp. 191–6.

finish off the Nationalists and the Communists. Chinese resistance, it was hoped, would collapse if the capital at Nanking were seized. In December 1937 the city fell, Chiang Kai-shek fled, and the inflamed Japanese soldiery went on a rampage of killing, looting, and raping. The scale of the Shanghai–Nanking campaign is suggested by the casualties incurred in six weeks: There were over 70,000 Japanese killed and wounded and more than 367,000 Chinese casualties.

At the outset, the Japanese army general staff had not contemplated committing more than eleven to fifteen divisions to China or even drawing on reserves. Yet by the end of 1937, the Japanese already had had to dispatch sixteen divisions and 700,000 men, approximately the strength of the entire standing army. Although Tsingtao, Amoy, and Hsuchou fell by May 1938, victory was no nearer for the Japanese. A new offensive was launched to capture Hankow, Chiang's new capital. But neither the seizure of Hankow, nor that of Canton in October 1938, brought the desired end of hostilities. The Chinese established still another provisional capital westward through the gorges of the Yangtze at Chungking. It took the Japanese two more years to push even halfway closer. In June 1940 they reached Ichang, still about three hundred miles from Chungking. Japanese forces in China now numbered twenty-three divisions, twenty-eight brigades (the equivalent of another fourteen divisions), and an air division. The total of Japanese troops in China had risen to 850,000, a level maintained until 1943, when transfers to other theaters began.

Japanese forces in China suffered from or created a vicious circle of their own. The greater the area they managed to carve out, the more troop strength they needed. It was not unknown for local commanders to undertake new and expensive operations whenever the authorities in the homeland spoke of de-escalating the hostilities and limiting the forces in the field. Area commands called for a linkup of enclaves. By and large, the handling of the campaigns in China was of an *ad hoc* and piecemeal nature, although cumulatively the commitment came to represent a major proportion of total national strength.

Whereas the Japanese army was thinking in terms of Cannae, the Chinese were resorting to the less spectacular but calculated strategy of attrition to dissipate, overextend, and wear down the enemy. In Japan there were widening cleavages between the government and the high command, between the War Ministry and the General Staff, between the authorities in Tokyo and those in the field, and between the army and the navy. Staff meetings in Tokyo often were emotional. Officers were at loggerheads while civilian officials looked on impotently.

On the battlefront, the Japanese forces suffered from shortfalls in ammunition, tanks and equipment, shipping, and landing craft. Casualty tolls from disease and accidents exacerbated combat losses, and there was a shortage of officers as well as a lack of trained reinforcements.

Chinese counterattacks hurt the Japanese locally. From March to May 1938, the Japanese high command could no longer avoid diverting a portion of the troop strength previously reserved for hostilities against the Soviet Union. From this time, therefore, can be dated the Japanese army's abandonment of hope of localizing the conflict in China, and its loss of flexibility in dealing with the "northern problem." With the bulk of the Japanese army committed in China, the Kwantung Army in Manchuria had only six regular divisions to confront an estimated twenty Soviet rifle divisions, four or five cavalry divisions, fifteen hundred tanks, fifteen hundred planes, and 370,000 men deployed along the three thousand miles of Siberian and Outer Mongolian frontier. The Soviet air force included three hundred heavy bombers with a range of three thousand kilometers, twice the distance from Vladivostok to Tokyo. Soviet power in the Far East, economic as well as military, had been steadily building up. In a sense, the Kwantung Army was confronting the Soviets with a bluff.[2]

## COLLISIONS WITH THE SOVIET UNION

While the Japanese high command labored on mobilization matters necessary to raise and dispatch new divisions to China, senior planners shuddered privately about the danger of Soviet intervention and a "premature" two-front war. Just as the Soviet Union supported the Loyalist regime in the Spanish civil war, it provided the Nationalist regime in China with credits and sent war matériel, aircraft, and "volunteer" pilots. Meanwhile, between 1937 and 1939, three increasingly ominous military confrontations between the Soviet Union and Japan occurred on disputed Manchurian or Korean borders. In late June 1937, just before the Marco Polo Bridge affair, Japanese artillery batteries shot up Soviet gunboats plying the Amur River in north Manchuria. The Soviet government quickly backed down. A year later, in July–August 1938, the Japanese fought a short but severe battle with

2 *GSS*, *Nitchū sensō*, (2) vol. 9, passim; Hata Ikuhiko, *Nitchū sensō shi* (Tokyo: Kawade shobō, 1961), pp. 161–260, 273–343; Horiba Kazuo, *Shina jihen sensō shidō shi* (Tokyo: Jiji tsūshinsha, 1962), pp. 81–656; Nihon kokusai seiji gakkai, *Taiheiyō sensō e no michi* (hereafter *TSM*), 8 vols. (Tokyo: Asahi shinbunsha, 1962–3), vol. 3, pp. 342–63; *TSM*, vol. 4, chaps. 12; Usui Katsumi, *Nitchū sensō* (Tokyo: Chūō kōronsha, 1967), pp. 33–140; BBSS, *Daihon'ei rikugunbu* (2), pp. 11–39, 125–35; BBSS, *Honkon-Chōsa sakusen*, pt. 2.

the Soviets for possession of Changkufeng Hill, at a point where north Korea, Manchuria, and Siberia meet. This time, the Soviet side committed not only infantry but also long-range artillery, armor, and planes. Although the Japanese troops clung to the high ground until a cease-fire was arranged in Moscow in mid-August, the Korea Army voluntarily gave up the contested region afterward. If reconnaissance in force had been the intent of the Japanese army, it was soon learned that the Soviets in the Far East were no longer quiescent.

Displeased with the outcome of the Changkufeng episode and blaming the high command for timidity, the Kwantung Army responded with vigor to skirmishes at Nomonhan on the desolate west Manchurian frontier with Outer Mongolia in May 1939. The escalating but undeclared border war raged through the summer. Casualties were severe. The Japanese lost eighteen thousand men, the equivalent of a division and a half. Both sides used aircraft, armor, and artillery. Although Japanese infantrymen and pilots proved their courage and tenacity, General Georgy Zhukov's great offensive on August 20 smashed the Japanese Sixth Army. An armistice was agreed upon in the middle of September.[3]

Overwhelmed by Soviet material superiority and the skillful orchestration of combined arms, the Japanese army sought refuge in postmortem analyses stressing the power of the Japanese spirit and cold steel. Operational thinking remained essentially primitive, unscientific, complacent, narrow, and simplistic. Japanese commanders were little better than what Liddell Hart called "bow and arrow generals." The army's performance against the despised Chinese had contributed to the unshakable faith in spiritual inculcation (*seishin kyōiku*). Army leaders always argued that Japan's inferiority in raw materials, finances, and demographic base was counterbalanced by its moral and psychological superiority. In a new era of dive bombers, self-propelled artillery, and armored divisions, the Japanese continued to glorify a wasteful anachronism, an army of brave but unprotected foot soldiers.

Although the Kwantung Army leadership was purged after the setback at Nomonhan, basic war plans calling for an offensive against the Soviet Union were not modified. The new deputy chief of staff of the Kwantung Army, Major General Endō Saburō, urged the systematic buildup of Manchukuo and an immediate change in the Kwantung Army mission. He argued for a defensive strategy for the near future,

3 The definitive treatment of the Nomonhan incident is by Alvin D. Coox, *Nomonhan: Japan Against Russia, 1939*, 2 vols. (Stanford, Calif.: Stanford University Press, 1985).

entailing engagement of the Soviets on Manchurian soil if hostilities did occur. But his words fell on deaf ears. The army general staff's 1940 contingency plan retained the old offensive concept which remained on the books for another four years, until 1944.[4]

## THE ASCENT OF TŌJŌ

The emperor put his finger on Japan's fundamental dilemma when during a liaison conference in February 1938, he expressed doubts about the course of events in China. Was it feasible, the monarch asked the war minister, to be contemplating *three* national efforts at the same time: protracted hostilities with China, preparations against Soviet Russia, and expansion of the navy? General Sugiyama Shigemaru attempted to temporize, replying in effect that every effort would be made after consultations with the cabinet. Such waffling apparently left the emperor extremely dissatisfied, for this was the same Sugiyama who had assured the throne in 1937 that the China affair would be settled within a month or so.

Most of the dissonant themes seemed to find resolution in the person of Tōjō Hideki, who became vice-minister of war in 1938. A precise, well-connected, and self-righteous general known for his devotion to detail, Tōjō sought to squelch the more cautious elements in the army who were not dedicated to winning the conflict in China. In the autumn of 1938, Tōjō made a simplistic, fire-eating speech before the Veterans' Association claiming that the solution of the China problem had been delayed by Soviet, British, and American assistance to the Nationalists. Japan, he said, must make resolute preparations against the Reds in the north and the Anglo-Saxon powers in the south. Under banner headlines, the press reported that Tōjō advocated a two-front war.

After being transferred to the air force for a year and a half, Tōjō became war minister in the second Konoe cabinet in July 1940. As in 1938, a number of factors worked in his favor: his demonstrated administrative and executive skills in important assignments, his aggressive patriotism and political steadiness, his persuasiveness and sincerity, and his cultivation of important associates. At the beginning, Tōjō was impressed by Konoe's caution, by his exhortations to end the China war, and by his desire to improve the ties between the high command and the government and to harmonize interservice relations.

4 *GSS, Nitchū sensō* (3), vol. 10, pp. 3–68, 71–149; BBSS, *Kantōgun* (1), pt. 4, chap. 3, and pt. 5; Endō Saburō, *Nitchū jūgonen sensō to watakushi* (Tokyo: Nitchū shorin, 1974), pp. 180–4.

Apparently convinced that the best way to climb out of a hole was to widen it, the army leaders had decided that the impasse in China could be broken only by occupying Southeast Asia. The thrust of the Konoe cabinet's new policy was to transform the China conflict into a Greater East Asian War (*Dai Tōa sensō*). With the colonial powers distracted by German and Italian victories in Europe, Japan could turn toward the south, a region rich in vital resources. If Japan controlled the area, foreign assistance reaching Chiang Kai-shek from Indochina, Hong Kong, and Burma could be cut off. Bases in Vietnam would also prove useful as a springboard for further advances against objectives like Malaya and the Dutch East Indies. The southern advance was to depend on diplomacy, but force might be used if necessary. To both Tōjō and the experienced, voluble, and tough-minded foreign minister, Matsuoka Yōsuke, force was the servant of diplomacy, a deterrent or lever, not a bluff or provocation. Firmness, not conciliatory gestures, was needed to prevent encirclement.

Enthralled by the prowess of the German army and the rosy reports from Berlin, Tōjō and his associates favored closer ties with the Nazi regime. But important navy leaders were not enthusiastic. To persuade them, Tōjō argued that Japan ran the danger of "missing the bus." The defeat of France and Holland might presage German political control of their Asian colonies. The Germans assured the Japanese that the Tripartite Pact would restrain the United States from entering the war on Britain's behalf. Matsuoka parried questions by insisting that he intended to improve relations with the Soviet Union, that the Reich would assist Japan in obtaining oil, that a final decision about Japanese participation in the European War would not be automatic, that U.S.-Japanese ties would be improved when the opportunity arose, and that the chances of America's provoking a "critical situation" were only fifty-fifty.

The Tripartite Pact among Germany, Italy, and Japan, finally signed in September 1940, became one of the major stumbling blocks to good relations between the United States and Japan. Tōjō was glad to see pressure exerted on the Americans, who had been steadily hampering Japan's "necessary expansion." "World totalitarianism," he claimed, "will take the place of Anglo-Saxonism, which is bankrupt and will be wiped out." Japan had to ally itself with forces challenging the defunct status quo.[5]

5 *GSS*, *Nitchū sensō* (3), vol. 10, pp. 153–361; *TSM*, vol. 5, chap 1; *TSM*, vol. 6, chaps. 1, 2; BBSS, *Daitōa sensō kaisen keii* (2), chaps. 6, 7.

## FUMBLING FOR DIRECTION

Toward the end of 1940, the high command commenced a serious examination of potential military and naval operations against the Western powers; by the following spring, both the army and the navy general staffs were in agreement that if the Japanese used force in the south, this would mean war with the United States. There seemed to be good reason to downplay the Americans as a military adversary. Small, ill-equipped, and lacking trained reserves, the U.S. Army in 1941 has been compared with the Swedish army, a medium-sized military establishment. Japan's military and naval leaders selectively used reports that the American public was disunited, isolationist, decadent, and more interested in conducting business as usual than in waging desperate warfare. High-ranking Japanese officers who had studied in or been assigned to the United States or Britain began to be transferred out of important posts in the War Ministry or general staff, in favor of Germanophiles. The Japanese army willingly accepted the confident open predictions and estimates of the navy's hawkish elements, although a number of admirals entertained serious misgivings that they dared not voice.

Western opposition in Southeast Asia was deemed accurately to be disjointed and feeble. As late as 1940, however, when the Japanese moved into northern Indochina, the army – unlike the navy – still believed that even if the East Indies were occupied, Britain could be separated from the United States. The Americans could be expected to jettison British interests once the Germans had succeeded in bringing the "old and infirm" English to their knees, and hence there would be no need to fight. The Japanese army remained convinced that the navy would carry the main burden of operations against the Americans, and so they drafted only limited plans for ground offensives. They made no substantive preparations to defend the zones to be occupied or the resources to be exploited. Once Southeast Asia had been overrun, the army intended to withdraw its forces to the Manchurian theater to face the chief hypothetical enemy, the Soviet Union.

In early 1941, Foreign Minister Matsuoka decided on a grandiose diplomatic scheme designed to exert greater restraint on the United States while cutting off China from its last important source of external support. He would try to resolve the major tensions between Japan and the Soviet Union after the Nomonhan war, perhaps even bringing the Soviets into the Tripartite Pact – the so-called Continental Alliance idea. When Matsuoka traveled to Europe in the spring of 1941 he found that Russo-German ties were far more strained than he had expected, and so he settled for a five-year Soviet-Japanese Neutrality Pact, signed in Moscow in April. The following month, Matsuoka finally instructed the ambassador in Washington, Admiral Nomura Kichisaburō, to begin formal discussions with the Americans. German pressure compelled Matsuoka to adopt a bellicose stance from the outset, especially because he was losing hope that the United States would try to convince Chiang Kai-shek to negotiate a settlement with Japan from a position of weakness. In late May, Matsuoka estimated the prospect of success in the parleys with the United States at only 30 percent.

Since 1940 the American government had tried to restrain Japanese expansion through economic sanctions, a course of action no more successful than the Japanese policy of deterring counteraction and buildup by the United States by taking a tough stance. To little avail, the Americans had abrogated the Commercial Treaty of 1911, imposed embargoes on the export of scrap steel and iron, and reduced or threatened to cut off other vital raw materials. By 1941 the acquisition of oil from the East Indies was becoming crucial to the Japanese, but discussions with the Dutch, bolstered behind the scenes by the United States and Britain, were proceeding poorly. If the Japanese were to take military action against the Indies, they would also have to mount campaigns against Malaya and the Philippines. On May 3, Tōjō asserted that to conduct operations in Malaya, bases would be needed in Indochina and Thailand. Army Chief of Staff Sugiyama agreed on June 12 that troops should be sent into southern French Indochina to protect it from the Anglo-Saxons as well as to put pressure on China and the southwest Pacific region. When the topic arose again on June 16, Tōjō insisted that unless the task were undertaken by year's end, it would become necessary to abandon the whole idea of the Greater East Asia Co-Prosperity Sphere.[6]

## THE PERSIMMON THEORY

Despite many prior indications, the German invasion of the Soviet Union on June 22 took most Japanese civilian and military authorities by surprise. Complicated discussions ensued about policy vis-à-vis the

6 *GSS*, *Nitchū sensō* (3) vol. 10, pp. 365–88; Tanemura Sakō, *Daihon'ei kimitsu nisshi*, new ed. (Tokyo: Daiyamondosha, 1979), pp. 41–55; *TSM*, vol. 5, chap. 2; BBSS, *Daihon'ei rikugunbu* (2), pp. 235–41; Nobutaka Ike, *Japan's Decision for War* (Stanford, Calif.: Stanford University Press, 1967), pp. 53–6.

Russo-German War as well as the question of taking over south Indochina. The navy vigorously opposed a Japanese war against the Soviet Union, which was not its main hypothetical enemy. Matsuoka, however, predicted a swift German victory over both the Soviet Union and Britain in 1941 and led a personal campaign to get Japan immediately into the war against the Soviet Union. He was sure that the United States could not or would not assist Communist Russia if Japan attacked quickly. But Tōjō and the army resisted Matsuoka's arguments, as war with the Soviet Union would require giving up on China and the southern advance.

A series of liaison conferences eventuated in the climactic Imperial Conference of July 2. The conference endorsed the top-secret Outline of National Policies, which envisaged an advance south and, depending on the situation, a settlement of the northern question too. It reaffirmed specifically that the Japanese would apply pressure from the south to bring down the Chinese Nationalist regime. Primary attention was to be devoted to Indochina and Thailand. Significantly, Japan would not be deterred by the possibility of hostilities with the United States and Britain; that is, Japan would begin war preparations against both.

As for the Russo-German War, Japan would not intervene for the time being but would secretly improve military preparedness against the Soviet Union. This meant that the Kwantung Army would be increased from 400,000 to 700,000 men and provided with vast amounts of additional matériel, equipment, horses, and aircraft. The buildup in Manchuria was code-named *Kantokuen* (Kwantung Army special maneuvers). Units in Korea, Hokkaido, and southern Sakhalin would also be strengthened. Nevertheless, Japan would resort to force to settle the northern question only if the Russo-German War developed to Japan's own advantage.

Despite Tōjō's expressions of caution, anti-Soviet war fever seemed to be sweeping the War Ministry. A catchphrase of the time suggested Japan's proper stance toward the Russo-German War: One should wait until the persimmon ripened and fell. But there were varying interpretations of the idea. An impatient man might knock the persimmon off the tree with a pole when the fruit had only started to ripen. Others might believe that the persimmon was ripe only if it fell when the tree was shaken. Still others might argue that one should pick the persimmon off the ground only after it had dropped of its own weight. Tōjō was not immune to the hope of savoring the persimmon, although he remained careful about the method of obtaining it. On one occasion, he admitted that attention should be given to the possibility that the Germans could beat the Soviets if Japan cooperated; fighting alone, the Wehrmacht might bog down.

Meanwhile, Matsuoka's arbitrary activities and outbursts were impeding the progress of negotiations with the United States. For example, as soon as he learned of the German attack on Russia, he dared to tell the emperor, without first coordinating his views with those of the cabinet, that Japan should join the fray immediately. Prime Minister Konoe, discomfited, decided by mid-July that he might resign or else get rid of the foreign minister. On July 16, therefore, he adopted the latter course, organizing a new cabinet with Admiral Toyoda Teijirō as foreign minister. The main advocate of war with the Soviets was now out of power.

The Japanese intelligence service, noting the slowdown of the German invasion of western Russia, predicted in early August that a Nazi victory was impossible in 1941 and improbable thereafter. The Foreign Ministry also believed that the Russo-German War would be a protracted one. Tōjō and Sugiyama, however, remained surprisingly optimistic about Germany's chances and argued that the Soviets might be playing into the invaders' hands. In any case, the Japanese did not attack the Soviet Union; the persimmon was too green.[7]

## THE SOUTH BECKONS

At the end of July, the Japanese occupation of south Indochina took place on schedule, and as a result, Japan's relations with the United States, already poor, took a sharp turn for the worse. From Washington, Ambassador Nomura sent reports that the United States was drawing closer to the Soviet Union and would probably not stand by idly if Japan drove northward. Foreign Minister Toyoda felt that the Americans were overly excited and that efforts should be made to calm them down, but as he admitted to the U.S. ambassador in early September, he was having difficulty at home controlling opposing influences and dissident groups.

Seeking a path to break the impasse with the Americans, Konoe in early August proposed a summit conference between himself and President Franklin D. Roosevelt somewhere in the Pacific. To the relief of

7 Matsuoka Yōsuke denki kankōkai, ed., *Matsuoka Yōsuke* (Tokyo: Kōdansha, 1974), pp. 745–1080; Saitō Yoshie, *Azamukareta rekishi* (Tokyo: Yomiuri shinbunsha, 1955), chaps. 8–10; BBSS, *Daihon'ei rikugunbu* (2), pp. 340–53; BBSS, *Kantōgun* (2), chap. 1; Ike, *Japan's Decision*, pp. 77–90; Gomikawa Junpei, *Gozen kaigi* (Tokyo: Bungei shunjūsha, 1978), pp. 37–95.

the Germans and of hawkish elements inside Japan, the meeting never materialized. On September 6 the Imperial Conference approved a new policy paper developed by the high command. Although the emperor understood that the government intended to stress diplomacy instead of war, the policy paper placed the option for war ahead of the option for peace. The document asserted that Japan's own interests demanded that it complete war preparations against the south, tentatively by the last ten days of October, with full resolve to fight the United States, Britain, and the Netherlands if necessary. Limited by minimum desiderata and maximum concessions, the diplomats should try to achieve national objectives, but if the demands could not be met by the first ten days of October, the immediate decision should be made to commence hostilities against the three Western powers. An uneasy emperor expressed his earnest regret to the conferees that the army and navy chiefs of staff had not addressed the question of diplomacy's precedence over war.

Reference materials prepared for the meeting of September 6 reveal the high command's fundamental thinking. America in particular seemed determined to preserve the status quo in Asia: "To dominate the world and defend democracy, it aims to prevent our empire from rising and developing in East Asia." Under the circumstances, the policies of Japan and the United States were mutually incompatible. It was "inevitable historically that the conflict between the two nations, sometimes intense and sometimes mild, will eventually lead to war." A rationale and warning emerged: Unless the United States changed its policy, Japan was "put into a desperate situation, where it must resort to the ultimate step – war – to defend itself and assure its preservation." Even if Japan yielded and abandoned a portion of its national policy for the sake of a transient peace, America – its military posture reinforced – was bound to demand even more concessions. Eventually Japan would "lie prostrate at the feet of the United States."

The day after the Imperial Conference, Tōjō explained his thinking to Prince Higashikuni: The United States was putting pressure on Japan through an encirclement in concert with Britain, China, and the Netherlands. Peace on American terms doubtless would mean gradual impoverishment for Japan, whereas war offered a fifty-fifty possibility of victory. Tōjō admitted that there were risks in resorting to force but that that was better than "being ground down without doing anything."[8]

8 *GSS*, *Nitchū sensō* (3) vol. 10, pp. 531–47; *TSM*, vol. 6, pp. 245–71; BBSS, *Daihon'ei rikugunbu* (2), pp. 425–53; Ike, *Japan's Decision*, pp. 133–63.

## THE YAMAMOTO SCHEME

Victory over the United States, however, would depend mainly on victory at sea. The Japanese navy, dominated by battleship admirals, had long planned for decisive battles against the U.S. Pacific Fleet north of the Marshalls and east of the Marianas. But the outcome was not clear, and the war games degenerated into a war of attrition, which was unacceptable: The Japanese could not hope to defeat the United States by such indirect measures as the destruction of the American-Asiatic Flotilla, the conquest of U.S. possessions in the Far East, and the disruption of American maritime trade.

The first realistic plan for an unconventional attack against the U.S. battle fleet, redeployed to Hawaii in May 1940, was the idea of Admiral Yamamoto Isoroku, commander of the Combined Fleet. Whereas his colleagues could think only of submarine action and massive surface operations against targets in Hawaiian waters, Yamamoto drew lessons from the aerial torpedo assault tactics against battleships, revealed in the Japanese naval maneuvers of spring 1940. Major air operations against bases in the mainland United States were out of the question, but not against objectives farther west. Map maneuvers in November suggested to Yamamoto that the oil-rich Indies could not be subdued without provoking the United States as well as Britain into war, but the Japanese dared not risk inviting a counteroffensive by the U.S. Pacific Fleet while the main body of the Japanese navy was dispersed in the south. Consequently, by early January 1941, Yamamoto recommended to the navy minister that in the unhappy event of war against the United States, the Japanese should strive to cripple the Americans' main fleet in the Pacific by an air offensive concurrent with the initiation of the campaign into Southeast Asia. Enemy morale, civilian and military, would be damaged, perhaps to the point of helplessness; and the U.S. Navy would be prevented from harrying the exposed flank of the Japanese and unleashing psychologically disturbing air strikes against cities in the homeland.

Of course, many serious questions vexed Yamamoto. The Hawaii operation was spawned by desperation, and annihilation by the foe was a distinct possibility. On his own initiative, known only to a few trusted naval associates, Yamamoto ordered a top-secret feasibility study to be undertaken by Admiral Ōnishi Takijirō, an expert on naval aviation. Ōnishi was assisted by Commander Genda Minoru, who had studied the extremely successful November 1940 raid by British carrier-based planes against the Italian naval base at Taranto.

Genda concluded that a Japanese strike plan against Pearl Harbor was feasible, although dangerous, and that it would require all six of Japan's fleet carriers and its best pilots. Approximately four hundred aircraft of all types would be necessary. Armor-piercing bombs would be useful against the deck armor of battleships, the prime target, but torpedoes undoubtedly offered the best method of horizontal attack if launched at very low altitude and low speed. A small number of submarines should precede the task force.

After receiving Ōnishi's recommendations in early April, Yamamoto officially ordered the study of the Hawaii plan by his own Combined Fleet staff. As relations with the United States deteriorated, there was a gnawing sense in the Japanese navy that Japan's natural resources were being depleted while those of its antagonists were building up. In mid-September, after the annual map exercises at the Naval War College, Yamamoto tried out his Pearl Harbor scheme with a special study team of thirty high-ranking officers. Results were inconclusive. The first map play proved successful; the second, costly and far less promising. The participants questioned the possibility of maintaining secrecy and of refueling in the wintry north Pacific. When the chief of the naval general staff first learned of the Hawaii plan, he called it very risky. In the strategic sense, the naval general staff also questioned, not without reason, the wisdom of diverting the carriers' striking power from the Southeast Asia sector, particularly if the American Pacific Fleet did not launch an early offensive sortie. At the political level, too, the Japanese navy had not entirely abandoned hope for a diplomatic settlement, especially as cautious Admiral Nomura was ambassador in Washington.

Although a number of officers liked Yamamoto's plan, its opponents included many senior admirals: the designated task force commander, Admiral Nagumo Chūichi, a torpedo expert; his chief of staff, an air officer, Admiral Kusaka Ryūnosuke; Air Fleet Commander Tsukahara Nishizō; and even Admiral Ōnishi, whom Kusaka had influenced. The resistance was overcome by Yamamoto's reasoning, cajolery, and, ultimately, threat to resign unless the basic plan were adopted. Training for air operations was carried out in the shallow roadstead at Kagoshima Bay, which closely resembled Pearl Harbor.[9]

9 BBSS, *Daihon'ei rikugunbu* (2), pp. 416–17; BBSS, *Daihon'ei rikugunbu* (3), pp. 146–51; BBSS, *Hawai sakusen*, chaps. 1–3; Agawa Hiroyuki, *Yamamoto Isoroku*, new ed. (Tokyo: Shinchōsha, 1969), pp. 234–54; Hara Akinori, *Teikoku kaigun shireichōkan no nazo* (Tokyo: Tokuma shoten, 1972), pp. 11–48; Kusaka Ryūnosuke, *Rengō kantai sanbōchō no kaisō* (Tokyo: Kōwadō, 1979), pp. 24–45.

## JAPAN UNDER NEW MANAGEMENT

As the secret October deadline approached for successful consummation of negotiations in Washington, Tōjō took the position that Japan did not have time to make further adjustments in its final position on a draft understanding with the United States. "We are already behind schedule," the war minister reminded his colleagues on September 20, "and circumstances are pressing." Five days later, the armed forces' chiefs of staff shocked Prime Minister Konoe by insisting that October 15 be the very latest deadline for a peaceable settlement. The prime minister thought seriously of resigning. As the Japanese embassy admitted privately to the Americans, Nomura would have to show some results, or the Konoe cabinet might fall as the result of assassination, coup d'état, or sheer dissatisfaction with the impasse. Any new regime would undoubtedly be made up of hard-line military types in the grip of the Germans.

Sugiyama told the liaison conferees on October 4 that the high command was opposed to further delay, to which Admiral Nagano Osami added, "We want quick action." Clearly, the leadership of the armed forces had become convinced that the negotiations were hopeless and that the Americans were argumentative and uncompromising. The stumbling blocks to understanding were numerous and complex: the China problem, equitable access to the resources of Southeast Asia, reconciliation of the objectives of the Axis partners, and policies toward the Russo-German War.

At a liaison conference on October 9, Sugiyama reiterated the army's hard line. The high command, he insisted, would not extend the deadline beyond the fifteenth of the month. Pushed into a corner, Konoe tried desperately to win more time for negotiation from the service ministers, but Tōjō would not back down; risk taking, he told Konoe, was imperative on occasion. On the key question of withdrawing forces from China, Tōjō refused to consider compromise. Japan was at the point of no return. To change the decree of the Imperial Conference of September 6 was unthinkable.

At the liaison conference on October 14, Tōjō insisted that operational preparations for war be suspended only in case of diplomatic success; he was convinced that the talks were doomed. If Japan bowed to American demands regarding China, the protracted and expensive conflict on the mainland would have been rendered meaningless. Manchukuo and Korea would be endangered; north China would become Communist; and Japan would be entirely undone. Withdrawal from

China would mean dishonorable retreat. Compromise after compromise by one side was not diplomacy – it was unilateral capitulation. Tōjō wanted the parleys ended, preparations for early hostilities to continue, and the cabinet to resign.

Konoe's position was rendered untenable by Tōjō's obduracy, which presumably mirrored the stand of the senior military leadership. On October 16 his cabinet resigned. To the surprise of almost all observers, including the highest officers in the War Ministry, Tōjō was called on to form a new government. Undoubtedly a decisive consideration for the senior statesmen and imperial advisers was the expectation that Tōjō could best control the army if a reversal of the September decision provoked military opposition, political murders, or public right-wing disorders. The new premier, promoted to full general, was to remain on active duty and retain his post as war minister. His cabinet, announced on October 18, was made up mainly of army officers, navy officers, and top-ranking civilian bureaucrats. In short, the Japanese military was to have its turn taking full responsibility for governing the country, with no chance for excuses.[10]

## WEIGHING WAR VERSUS DIPLOMACY

Tōjō later denied vehemently that his new regime was determined from its inception to wage war. According to the chief cabinet secretary, Hoshino Naoki, time ran out because of the Japanese navy leaders' contention that if hostilities began after December 1941, Japan was sure to lose: "They said that they would certainly not be responsible for winning the war if it were to be started beyond the time limit after negotiations had failed." The balance-of-strength factor was very much on the mind of Tōjō and his associates. During the winter of 1940 the army asked the Economic Mobilization Bureau to evaluate Japan's economic position should it go to war against the United States and Britain as early as the following spring of 1941. The ensuing report pointed out the country's vulnerability in shipping and natural resources, especially liquid fuel. A new study undertaken in the summer of 1941, geared to a hypothetical deadline of November, found that beyond two years after the initiation of hostilities, Japan's industrial and economic capabilities could not be assured. If Japan launched full-fledged hostilities against America and Britain with stocks of fuel

10 BBSS, *Daihon'ei rikugunbu* (2), pp. 525–30; Ike, *Japan's Decision*, pp. 173–84; Shigenori Tōgō, *The Cause of Japan* (New York: Simon & Schuster, 1956), pp. 53–60.

available, air operations could last only a year or so, and decisive combat could be conducted at sea for only approximately six months.

Japanese critics have argued that the economic studies by the government and the armed forces were superficial, tardy, predetermined, and poorly coordinated. Nevertheless, the dire predictions fed the notion among military and naval chiefs that Japan should go to war quickly before its capacity to fight dwindled away. At the October 23 liaison conference, Navy Chief of Staff Nagano stated strongly that the situation was urgent and that concise deliberations were imperative, as the navy was consuming four hundred tons of oil per hour. General Sugiyama agreed that time was crucial, as matters had already been delayed a month. "Hurry up and go ahead," he urged. Although Tōjō insisted that the government preferred careful, responsible study, the psychological atmosphere limited his options. "It would have required enormous courage," observed Satō Kenryō, the military affairs section chief at the time, "to voice an anti-war view when pro-war fever was boiling." Publicly, Tōjō thundered, "There is no retreat." Privately, he admitted that the army could "manage somehow" in 1942 and 1943 but that he did not know what would happen after 1944.

The liaison conferences dragged on. On October 26 there was serious consideration of postponing hostilities until March 1942, but the service chiefs insisted that time was already working against Japan and that the navy in particular needed to get under way by the end of November 1941. Finance Minister Kaya Okinori tried to get at the heart of the problem of national strength by asking whether war or peace would be better to secure materials, but no clear-cut answer presented itself.

By October 30 the study of fundamental alternatives was completed at last. Essentially, the liaison conference concluded that although hostilities of course entailed risk, proceeding without war would be prohibitively costly to Japan's long-term power position. An early and successful resolution of the Japanese-American discussions could not be expected, and Tōjō believed that conditional agreement was not feasible. There was considerable discussion of the American insistence on a time limit for Japan's military withdrawal from China. The army naturally opposed any such limit, but Tōjō said he was willing to accept Japanese evacuation within twenty-five years, by 1966. The foreign minister argued against the general contention that acceptance of the American proposals would doom Japan to obscurity. When several other ministers, however, mentioned the need for further deliberations, Tōjō and the navy chief spoke at great length about the urgency of a prompt decision, even if the conferees had to meet all night on November 1.

The seventeen-hour marathon meeting of November 1 was marked by an unusual lack of consensus between the government and the high command. Both services resisted the notion of slicing thin the allowable time between the foreseen suspension of diplomatic negotiations and the initiation of hostilities, and both dismissed the "no war" alternative. Debate swirled around setting a date for a final deadline for ending talks with the Americans. After the army general staff finally accepted the deadline of November 30 for preparations, Tōjō asked for another day's delay, to which the army twice responded, "Absolutely not." Navy Minister Shimada Shigetarō finally wheedled an understanding from the army that negotiations might go on until at least midnight on November 30. Only if the diplomats had failed by that hour would there be war.

Much argument centered on the matter of guidelines for further parleys with the United States. The army's opposition to compromise was so violent that Foreign Minister Tōgō intimated that he might resign, an action that could bring down the government and force a new orientation in policy. Although each conferee privately nurtured varying degrees of pessimism regarding the prospects, the army's open vehemence had fostered consensus.

An Imperial Conference met on November 5 to provide formal sanction for the recommendations derived from the eight liaison conferences: Japan had decided to fight the United States and Britain as well as Holland; the armed forces would complete preparations targeted for hostilities at the beginning of December. Meanwhile, efforts would continue to be made to reach agreement with America, but a deadline of December 1 was set for the achievement of success. Close relations with Thailand would be developed immediately preceding hostilities, through pressure if possible, by force if necessary.

During the discussion that followed the formal presentations, Tōjō insisted that Japan's demands regarding China were not unreasonable, considering that a million men had gone to the continent at a cost of 100,000 casualties, bereavement of families, hardship for four years, and an expenditure of dozens of billions of yen. Premature military withdrawal would encourage the Chinese to "behave worse" than they had before 1937, even to the point of trying to take over Manchuria, Korea, and Taiwan. The foreign minister was obliged to confess however that given the short time for decisive talks – a mere two weeks – there was little hope for diplomatic success.

The chiefs of staff then provided a timetable of military and naval operations in the event that negotiations failed: a total of five months for the entire campaign against the Philippines, Malaya, and the Dutch East Indies. The president of the Privy Council praised the high command's estimates as realistic yet cautioned that predictions usually turned out badly. He understood the need for an early decision but identified several vital problems: the difficulty of engaging the powerful United States while the China conflict remained unresolved and the possibility that the Germans' war against Britain might turn into an anti-Japanese war, with the Americans joining the other white powers to encircle Japan because of a fancied Yellow Peril. In an unusually blunt comment, Hara Yoshimichi also reminded the conferees that Hitler had called the Japanese a second-class people.

Admitting that Hara's points were well taken, Tōjō argued that there was some hope for a breakthrough in the diplomatic deadlock, as the Americans were afflicted by various weaknesses of their own, centering on two-ocean operations, shortages of materials, and domestic problems. Through a vigorous deployment of armed forces, Japan would actually strengthen its negotiating hand. Anyhow, Tōjō confessed, he could think of no other method, given the present circumstances. His peroration summed up his fundamental outlook:

> How can we let the United States continue to do as it pleases, even though there is some uneasiness? Two years from now [1943] we will have no petroleum for military use; ships will stop moving. When I think about the strengthening of American defenses in the southwestern Pacific, the expansion of the U.S. fleet, the unfinished China Incident, and so on, I see no end of difficulties. We can talk about suffering and austerity but can our people endure such a life for long? . . . I fear that we would become a third-class nation after two or three years if we merely sat tight.

The recommended policy, Tōjō stressed, reflected an intensive study of problems and probabilities. On the larger question of the moral basis for Japan's entry into hostilities, the prime minister stated: "There is some merit in making it clear that Britain and the United States represent a powerful threat to Japan's self-preservation."

Neither Tōjō nor the other participants explored the fundamental question of how the war was to be ended. The prime minister simply remarked that if Japan were "fair in governing the occupied areas, attitudes toward us would probably relent." The Americans might be enraged for a while, but later they would come to "understand" Japan's motivations.

Although the decisions on November 5 laid down the long-range war aims of Japan's leaders, they were concluded in very general terms. A liaison conference on November 15 proposed more concretely that Japan strive quickly to destroy American, British, and Dutch bases in Asia and to ensure Japan's self-defense; every effort should be made to hasten the fall of the Kuomintang regime, to work for the capitulation of Britain in concert with the Germans and Italians, and to break the will of the United States; and early victories in the southwest Pacific would ensure a powerful strategic position with respect to raw materials and routes of transportation and would lay the groundwork for a protracted period of self-sufficiency. Views differed regarding the need to declare war before initiating hostilities.[11]

## DIPLOMACY FOUNDERS

As predicted in most quarters and feared in others, diplomatic conversations in Washington continued to sputter. Tōgō decided to reinforce the well-intentioned but inept Nomura with a professional diplomat, Kurusu Saburō. Instead of being dispatched to camouflage a Japanese decision for war, as many charged later, Kurusu left for Washington on November 5 – with Tōjō's blessing and the foreign minister's instructions – to impress Nomura with the urgency of the situation and to help break the impasse quickly. Soon it became apparent to the Tokyo government that the envoys in Washington were improvising desperately while the American position grew more unyielding. When Nomura and Kurusu proceeded to discuss the Japanese concept of the *modus vivendi*, which was largely designed to divert attention from the China problem, U.S. Secretary of State Cordell Hull's first reactions revealed that the Americans were incensed by any proposal to sever aid to Chiang Kai-shek. It was known that the secretary of state was already consulting with British, Australian, Chinese, and Dutch diplomats, which served only to confirm Japanese suspicions of an Allied cordon.

While the Japanese envoys in Washington tried to buy time for negotiations beyond November, the high command was hastening the state of operational readiness. On November 22, a liaison conference was already discussing the wording of a communiqué on the beginning of hostilities. Sugiyama warned that there was no time left from the standpoint of the military. Foreign Minister Tōgō realized, too, that

11 BBSS, *Daihon'ei rikugunbu* (2), pp. 574–87; ibid. (3), pp. 105–45, 152–72; Ike, *Japan's Decision*, pp. 184–249.

certain intransigent elements in the army and navy were actually trying to embarrass the negotiations by demanding that the American side agree to supply Japan with unreasonable amounts of oil.

The practical breakdown of U.S.-Japanese negotiations occurred even before the deadline allowed by the Japanese high command. Tōgō had hoped to allay American suspicions by promising to withdraw Japanese troops from Indochina when the China conflict was brought to an end or an "equitable peace" was established in the Pacific region. As a first step, Japan was prepared to transfer its troops from the southern to the northern part of Indochina as soon as the current negotiations with the United States produced agreement. But even though the Americans wanted Japanese troops out of Indochina entirely, a number of proposals transmitted by Tokyo stirred ire in Washington; for example, the United States should release "a required quantity" of petroleum to Japan and suspend assistance to Chiang Kai-shek. Secretary of State Cordell Hull thought the latest Japanese conditions, which were regarded as representing Tokyo's final position, to be uncompromising and intended virtually to force a surrender by the United States. The American government also knew about Japanese troop movements toward Indochina, presumably for use against Thailand.

Consequently, instead of addressing the Japanese suggestion of a *modus vivendi*, on November 26 Hull submitted to the envoys a strictly confidential, tentative, and uncommitted "outline of proposed basis for agreement," embracing four established principles of American foreign policy plus six brand-new points bearing on economic matters. This document is known as the Hull note, but the Japanese have called it the Hull ultimatum ever since. As a basis for Japanese-American agreement, it listed such terms as a complete withdrawal of Japanese military, naval, air, and police forces from China and Indochina; a mutual surrender of extraterritorial rights in China; and recognition of only the Nationalist government. Nomura and Kurusu told Hull that they found the note unacceptable. In Tokyo, the crestfallen Tōgō conferred immediately with the prime minister and his stupefied colleagues, who all agreed that there was nothing further to do. Many of the army and navy leaders were elated by the Americans' uncompromising attitude.

Once the top-secret Japanese deadline for a diplomatic settlement had passed, the Japanese navy released Admiral Nagumo's strike force. On November 26 the flotilla set sail from the mist-shrouded Kuril Islands, bound for Pearl Harbor. (After the war, Tōjō admitted that he was unacquainted with the operational details of the Hawaii assault, and the Foreign Ministry knew even less about the surprise nature of the impending attack.) On the same day, Tōjō advised the emperor of the distressing diplomatic developments. The monarch requested the further counsel of the senior ministers (*jūshin*). After briefings by Tōjō and Foreign Minister Tōgō, some agreed that there was no alternative to war, and others expressed concern about the prospects. Not one of the elder statesmen suggested that Japan accept the terms of the Hull note. Konoe did wonder whether it might still be possible "to persevere, to wait and see," but Tōjō asserted that discussions always reverted to the conclusion that war was unavoidable.

In preparation for the last Imperial Conference on December 1, a liaison meeting was convened on the preceding day. Tōgō secured agreement to alert the ambassadors in Berlin and Rome that U.S.–Japanese negotiations were on the verge of rupture and that the danger of hostilities was extremely high. Japan would want Germany and Italy to go to war against America immediately and to agree never to make a separate peace with the Anglo-Saxon countries. As for Japan's policy toward the United States during this last brief phase before war erupted, the conferees asked that diplomacy be used to prevent goading the Americans into accelerating their own state of preparedness. Foreign Minister Tōgō did not know the date when hostilities would commence until Admiral Nagano finally whispered to him, "December 8." Tōgō asked that the envoys in Washington be informed, but the conferees agreed that the diplomats would have to be sacrificed.

The Imperial Conference of December 1 met to review the failure of negotiations with the United States and to approve hostilities against the Western powers. There was no change in the arguments presented by the government or the high command, although efforts were made to balance a tone of optimism with ostensible attention to realities. In view of the lateness of the hour strategically, Privy Council President Hara's interpellations were not especially searching, but he stressed the need for psychological solidarity and suggested that early settlement of hostilities should be on the leaders' minds. Discerning no objections to the basic agenda before the conference, the prime minister concluded with a ringing declaration of loyalty and devotion to the throne at this moment when the empire was standing "at the threshold of glory or oblivion."

The rubber-stamp Imperial Conference was followed up by a liaison meeting on December 4. It was agreed that Japan's final diplomatic note to the United States, severing relations and in effect declaring war, should arrive in Washington neither too early nor too late in terms of the high command's operational needs. The most important thing now, observed one conferee, "is to win the war." While the foreign minister worked on the long final notification, Japanese army and navy attack forces moved into position in the southwestern and central Pacific. On December 2 the U.S. government asked for an explanation of the concentration of Japanese units in Indochina. The Japanese replied on December 5 that troop movements had been stimulated by Chinese Nationalist activity along the northern border of Indochina but that the reports were exaggerated. In receipt of sheaves of intelligence reports that Japanese forces were moving toward Malaya and Thailand, Roosevelt dispatched an urgent personal message to the emperor on December 6, urging Japan's withdrawal and restraint. The note was delayed by the army in Tokyo for ten hours, but it is improbable that prompt delivery would have made any difference, for no American guarantees or compromises were discerned, and Tōjō judged that the message could accomplish nothing.[12]

Despite the last-minute ineptitudes and misunderstandings, a certain sense of anticlimax characterized the Japanese side during the last week before the Pearl Harbor assault. Tōgō used the word *carefreeness* to describe the attitude of the high command after the decision for war had been reached. Under Tōjō's leadership, the government was about to leap from the veranda of Kiyomizu Temple. As Terasaki Hidenari, the first secretary in Washington, admitted privately at the end of November 1941: "Japan, like any other nation engaged in a protracted war, is psychologically 'abnormal' and a 'little off' in its thinking."[13]

## "TORA! TORA! TORA!"

After constant experimentation, by about November 11 the Japanese navy had resolved its final technical problems concerning aerial torpe-

12 In Washington, the Japanese embassy had bungled matters by delivering the final notification to Hull eighty minutes late on December 7 (local time) – an hour after the commencement of the raid against Oahu. That United States signal intelligence analysts had broken the Foreign Ministry's sensitive Purple cipher in 1940 and were thus able to intercept and decode all diplomatic message traffic does not absolve the Japanese staff in Washington from a charge of negligence that Tōgō himself admitted later. Learning from U.S. radio broadcasts about the alleged Japanese duplicity in striking militarily while peace talks were still under way, the foreign minister notified Tōjō. The latter was astonished, his first reaction being to wonder whether the Americans had not deliberately delayed delivery of the fateful telegram.

13 BBSS, *Daihon'ei rikugunbu* (2), pp. 655–76; Ike, *Japan's Decision*, pp. 249–85; Tōgō, *The Cause of Japan*, pp. 198, 210–13; Gwen Terasaki, *Bridge to the Sun* (Harmondsworth, England: Penguin, 1962), p. 71.

does. The staff's last major worry was whether the task force could get to the launching site, little more than two hundred miles from Oahu, without being detected. An approach by a great circle route, from the north instead of the west, was expected to bypass the usual merchantman lanes and to evade enemy reconnaissance. Various deceptive measures, for example, the creation of a phony signals network, were used to confuse U.S. intelligence and conceal the whereabouts of the fleet carriers, even briefly. On December 3, Admiral Yamamoto designated December 8 (Japan time) as Y Day. In Honolulu this would be December 7, a day chosen not merely because it was the Americans' sabbath but also because meteorological conditions would be good and the Pacific Fleet generally returned to port in full strength each weekend. The next combination of favorable factors would not occur until March 1942.

The Combined Fleet's headquarters ordered Admiral Nagumo to proceed for Hawaii with the signal "Climb Mount Niitaka!" By December 6, the thirty-one warships under Nagumo's command were speeding south southeast at twenty-four knots, blacked out, silent, and refueled for the last time. The two large carriers and the four light carriers each bore about seventy aircraft. The rest of the task force included two screening battleships, three cruisers, nine destroyers, and three submarines on patrol two hundred miles ahead. The fleet train of eight precious tankers had been released by December 7. Already en route to Hawaii were twenty-seven submarines, five of which carried midget submersibles, and eleven launch planes.

The waters were unexpectedly calm, and a light fog reduced visibility – "divine grace," in Commander Genda's words. Shortly before the launch, however, the anxious Nagumo received an intelligence report that eight U.S. battleships lay in the Pearl Harbor roadstead, not in open Lahaina anchorage. Unfortunately for the Japanese, every American carrier and heavy cruiser seemed to be absent. Nagumo had been given permission to abandon the operation if he encountered an enemy fleet as late as X minus two days, but by December 7 (Hawaii time), four hundred miles from the target, it was too late to change the plan. The American battleship flotilla was well worth the assault, and perhaps some of the carriers would be back in port by Sunday. No Japanese planes were diverted to look for the absent enemy warships.

At 6:00 A.M. on December 7, in rather heavy swells 230 miles north of Oahu, the initial waves of 183 aircraft began to take off, under the overall control of Commander Fuchida Mitsuo – bombers, torpedo planes, and Zero-*sen* fighters. Homing in on a Honolulu radio station, Fuchida was heartened to hear that visibility was excellent over the city. At 7:45 A.M. he ordered the plain code signal for the surprise attack. Four minutes later, convinced of victory, he exuberantly radioed Nagumo's carriers of impending success: "*Tora! Tora! Tora!*" (Tiger! Tiger! Tiger!). Astonishingly, the message was picked up by Japanese navy receivers in the homeland.

Only one of the ninety-four U.S. vessels in port was under way when, at 7:55 A.M., the dive bombers struck Hickam and Wheeler fields. Between 7:57 and 8:05, the torpedo planes hit Battleship Row; the Zeros strafed air bases; and the level bombers attacked the battleships. Observing the disaster from his warplane aloft, Commander Fuchida was amazed by the Americans' unpreparedness. Within approximately one hour, the first assault was over. At a trifling cost of nine planes, the attackers had turned Pearl Harbor into blazing chaos.[14] At 8:54 A.M. a second wave of 167 Japanese planes, under Commander Shimazaki, thundered in for another hour, concentrating on the less damaged warships. Because by then the Americans were putting up heavier resistance, Shimazaki's planes suffered somewhat more severely, losing 20 aircraft, but these losses were insignificant compared with those of the enemy.

Of the 231 U.S. Army aircraft on Oahu, 97 were written off as lost and 88 were considered repairable. U.S. Navy plane losses totaled 80, more than half of its inventory. The destruction was particularly severe because the aircraft were parked wingtip to wingtip for defense against saboteurs. Eight battleships were damaged or sunk; three destroyers were crippled; three light cruisers were damaged; and three auxiliaries were sunk or damaged. It took nearly three years to remove the fuel that spilled into the harbor. American personnel casualties numbered 4,575: U.S. Army, 226 killed and 396 wounded; and U.S. Navy and Marine Corps, 876 wounded and 3,077 killed, including 960 missing, mainly trapped aboard the capsized *Arizona*, from which the haunting tap-tap of the entombed men could long be heard. Japanese airmen lost in action amounted to 55.

14 Of the U.S. battleships, only the flagship *Pennsylvania*, in drydock, seemed unscathed. The *Arizona* was shattered and sinking; the *Maryland* and *Tennessee* were afire; the *West Virginia* was reportedly hit nine times; the *Oklahoma*, twelve times (a complete loss); and the *California*, three times. The only battleship under steam, the *Nevada*, had been struck at least once before beaching itself to keep the channel open. The *Utah*, a defenseless target ship, had already capsized. Moored next to a minelayer, the cruiser *Helena* took five torpedoes. Japanese accuracy had equaled practice performance: 55 percent of the torpedoes struck their targets, 25 percent of the high-level bombs, and nearly 50 percent of the dive-bombs.

At the Combined Fleet headquarters in Japan, staff officers were excited by the news of unexpected success. Although Nagumo's caution and reservations were well known, almost every officer wanted new orders rushed to the task force commander, directing him to complete the destruction of the Pacific Fleet either that night or the next morning. Admiral Yamamoto reportedly agreed that a new strike would be splendid, but because the details of Japanese losses were still not known, he felt that it would be best to leave matters to Nagumo. No follow-up orders were sent to the task force.[15]

## THE NAGUMO CONTROVERSY

Debate has raged for decades concerning Nagumo's decision to leave the Hawaiian waters in the early afternoon of December 7 after only two air strikes. Critics have always argued that despite Japan's obvious successes, the Pearl Harbor attack could not be termed decisive. As Fuchida told Nagumo at the time, many worthwhile targets remained: the American battleships mired in shallow water, dozens of other vessels, untouched hangars, shops, and oil tanks. A new air assault, launched even closer to Oahu, might conceivably have lured the U.S. carriers and heavy cruisers to their doom. Commander Genda and others have contended that the Japanese, beset by "medal fever," lost sight of unglamorous but important targets such as machine shops needed to repair the mauled American fleet and fuel storage facilities containing 4.5 million barrels of oil.

No one argues seriously that the Japanese should have landed an army on Oahu. Yamamoto knew that the Southeast Asia campaign took priority in amphibious and sealift resources and that a huge convoy of troop transports, moving for a month at eight knots, would have ruined the vital element of surprise. As Fuchida said, the Japanese had been thinking of little more than "pulling the eagle's tail feathers."

Apart from the fact that Nagumo, a battleship admiral, was unenthusiastic at best and timid at worst, he had good reasons for leaving the scene promptly: As many as five U.S. aircraft carriers might be lurking in the region, and the whereabouts of enemy heavy cruisers and submarines was unknown. Because the initial strikes had suc-

15 BBSS, *Daihon'ei rikugunbu* (2), pp. 174–5; BBSS, *Hawai sakusen*, chaps. 4–15; Agawa, *Yamamoto*, pp. 259–86; Toyoda Jō, *Namimakura ikutabizō* (Tokyo: Kōdansha, 1973), pp. 13–91; Matsushima Keizō, *Higeki no Nagumo chūjō* (Tokyo: Tokuma shoten, 1967), chaps. 3–4; Kusaka, *Rengō kantai*, pp. 45–87.

ceeded beyond expectations, little more could be anticipated from additional assaults against the same area. U.S. antiaircraft fire had been surprisingly strong, and Japanese losses could be expected to increase geometrically once the element of surprise was gone.

In addition, Japanese intelligence reported at least fifty large planes (presumably B-17s) still available to the defenders. It was dangerous for the Japanese attack force to hover within range of land-based enemy aircraft. The six aircraft carriers had to be brought home safely, for they represented the entire such force available to the Japanese navy. Meanwhile, the weather north of Hawaii had deteriorated, and the carriers were rolling at fifteen degrees. Attacks against ground targets would require refitting the ordnance loads, and any new strike would involve night flights and dangerous night landings. Illuminating the flight decks would invite retaliation, especially if the missing American carriers showed up. As for a follow-up air strike, some have argued that the turbid oil fires would only have obscured the bombers' aim.

Admiral Fukudome Shigeru, while deploring the insufficient Japanese reconnaissance efforts, suggested that Nagumo be credited with a wise decision to terminate the attacks. At the time, the naval general staff was not unhappy with Nagumo's safe and skillful disengagement. If the operation had turned out badly, Yamamoto would have been criticized for recklessness and Nagumo praised for caution.

The Pearl Harbor operation was no battle in the ordinary sense; it was a massacre. The overall evaluations may be grouped into three categories. Many commentators have called the raid a short-term masterpiece but a long-range blunder, which jolted the dozing American giant into revenge. As Admiral Hara Chūichi, a carrier division commander, put it, "President Roosevelt should have pinned medals on us."

A second school argues that the Japanese naval high command was foolish to think only of checking the U.S. Pacific Fleet as it proceeded with a campaign to seize control of the rich, invulnerable southern area, which would be developed during a protracted war. Certainly Yamamoto himself had wanted to shatter, not merely neutralize, the U.S. battle fleet at the onset of hostilities and to achieve decisive strategic results by retaining the initiative while the bloodied American Navy was in confusion.

The third school, represented by Fukudome, is convinced that the Pearl Harbor raid achieved superb results, nullifying the Rainbow Plan and preventing the Americans from retaking control of the sea until 1944. In the meantime, the Japanese were able to attain all of their initial strategic objectives without interruption. Fukudome argued that if Oahu had not been attacked and the Japanese had engaged the Americans in a conventional surface battle near the Marshalls and the western Carolines, "it would have been impossible for the Japanese to have inflicted greater damage than they did in the Pearl Harbor attack, however favorable our estimate."[16]

## FIRST-PHASE EUPHORIA

The Japanese high command envisaged an initial perimeter line extending from the Kuril Islands in the North Pacific to the Marshalls (including Wake) and the Bismarcks in the Central Pacific, on to Timor, Java, and Sumatra in the southwest, and thence through Malaya to Burma. Spearhead operations in Southeast Asia were assigned to the new Southern Army, whose commander, General Terauchi Hisaichi, arrived at his headquarters in Saigon on December 5. His prime objectives were Malaya and the Philippines, the British and American footholds in Asia. Operations proceeded like clockwork.

As the Japanese expected, on December 8 the Thai authorities yielded to diplomatic pressure and allowed immediate Japanese occupation of strategic points in the country. With their Thai flank secured, the Japanese invaded Malaya. On December 8, advance elements of General Yamashita Tomoyuki's Twenty-fifth army landed on the eastern side of the Malay Peninsula. Two days later, the main body of Yamashita's army came ashore without hesitation, as the naval air force based at Saigon had just destroyed the core of the British Fleet off Malaya: the new battleship HMS *Prince of Wales* and the old battle cruiser *Repulse*, operating without fighter cover.[17] The Japanese ground forces drove swiftly toward Singapore. By February 15, the entire "impregnable" city had been conquered, with a garrison of at least 85,000 (including 70,000 combatants) surrendered unconditionally by General Arthur E. Percival. With the loss of Singapore, the Allies were deprived of the western anchor of the Malay barrier and the home port of the British Far East Fleet. One foreign observer called the Malay campaign the most disastrous loss by England since Cornwallis capitulated at Yorktown.[18]

16 Toyoda, *Namimakura*, pp. 91–5; Hara, *Teikoku kaigun*, p. 19; Kusaka, *Rengō kantai*, pp. 50–1, 74–5.
17 BBSS, *Hitō Marei hōmen kaigun shinkō sakusen*, pt. 2, chap. 3.
18 BBSS, *Marei shinkō sakusen*, chaps. 1–8; BBSS, *Nansei hōmen kaigun sakusen*, pp. 161–6, 219–20, 281–7, 332–6; BBSS, *Hitō Marei hōmen kaigun shinkō sakusen*, pt. 2, chaps. 1, 2, 4–7.

The seizure of weakly defended Borneo, the third largest island in the world, was closely connected with the conquest of Malaya. On December 16 an expeditionary force of three battalions staged from Indochina landed on British Borneo. The official British surrender took place on January 19, 1942. Meanwhile, in early January, a detachment of three battalions moved against the southern part of the island, oil-rich Dutch Borneo. A stunning series of Japanese successes followed. Tarakan fell on January 11, Balikpapan on January 24, and Bandjarmasin on February 16. The small, retreating Dutch defense force was caught and forced to give up on March 8. By expeditiously overwhelming British and Dutch Borneo as well as Ambon and the Celebes, the Japanese acquired rich resources and important bases which enabled them to screen their sea and air lanes to Singapore.[19]

In the Philippines, the Japanese plan called for winning aerial supremacy and seizing air bases before the main ground forces made landings. The early operations proceeded precisely as scheduled. At midday on December 8, despite ample warning, half of the American air strength at Clark Field in Manila was destroyed by a one-hour air strike. Lead elements of General Honma Masaharu's Fourteenth Army began coming ashore on the island of Luzon. The main body was able to land at Lingayen Gulf on December 22 and at Lamon Bay on December 24. General Douglas MacArthur's hope of checking the invaders at the beaches ended in failure. Manila, declared an open city, was in Japanese hands by January 2, 1942.

The main objective of Imperial General Headquarters (IGHQ) had been attained well before the original deadline of forty-five or fifty days. Honma, however, paid scant heed to intelligence that the main American and Filipino forces were retreating toward the jungles, swamps, and mountains of the Bataan Peninsula and toward Corregidor Island. The Japanese, obsessed with the importance of Manila, wrote them off as enemy remnants. Although control of the harbor was still not assured, the high command felt sufficiently confident to withdraw Honma's best division (the Forty-eighth) and most of the Fifth Air Group for the Java campaign, one month ahead of schedule.

It soon became apparent to Honma that more than mopping up lay ahead, but requests for reinforcements earned him a reputation as a whiner. When the target date for decisive victory in the Philippines passed without result and Honma dared to suspend offensive operations because of alleged logistical, manpower, medical, and other weak-

19 BBSS, *Ran-in Bengaru wan hōmen kaigun sakusen*, pp. 17, 20.

nesses, Sugiyama and Tōjō thought of sacking him. Imperial General Headquarters assumed responsibility for operations in the south Philippines, leaving Honma free to concentrate against Bataan. His powerful offensive, finally begun on April 3, overran Bataan in less than a week, not the month that gloomy Honma had been fearing. Corregidor held out until May 7. Of the 53,000 combat prisoners taken during the fighting in the Philippines, about 9,500 were American. Many died during the infamous Bataan Death March. Honma was personally ignorant of the atrocities and certainly did not order or condone them.

Honma had taken four months more to accomplish his mission than Imperial General Headquarters had wanted, and he had committed excessive strength. Nonetheless, General Douglas MacArthur, the American commander, had managed to escape to Australia. Honma was also castigated by higher headquarters for leniency toward the Filipinos, who had resisted the Japanese and remained basically loyal to the Americans. After a scarcely decent interval, in August 1942 the general was relieved of his command and retired in semidisgrace.[20]

Hong Kong, the coveted conduit into China, had been taken in December. Even with reinforcements, the Commonwealth garrison numbered scarcely 12,000 men, ill equipped and almost devoid of air or naval support. Japanese forces detached from the Expeditionary Army in China attacked on December 8 and took Kowloon on the mainland on December 12. After severe preliminary artillery and aerial bombardment, amphibious troops landed on Hong Kong Island beginning on December 18. By the time the British command surrendered on Christmas Day, the defenders were worn down, short of water and ammunition, and depleted by about 4,400 casualties. Japanese losses were 2,754. Hong Kong – like Singapore and Manila, the symbol of Western preeminence in Asia – had fallen to the seemingly irresistible Japanese.[21]

## VICTORY FEVER CONTINUED

The war advanced into its next phase with the Japanese operations against Java and Burma. Toward the end of December 1941, Imperial General Headquarters moved up the date for the Java invasion by about a month. Ground forces assigned to occupy the Dutch East Indies came under General Imamura Hitoshi. On January 11 the Japa-

20 BBSS, *Hitō kōryaku sakusen*, chaps. 1–10; BBSS, *Nansei hōmen kaigun sakusen*, pp. 49–74, 224–5, 342–3; BBSS, *Hitō Marei hōmen kaigun shinkō sakusen*, pt. 1.
21 BBSS, *Honkon-Chōsa sakusen*, pt. 1.

nese landed in the northern Celebes where paratroopers saw action in combat for the first time. During the battle for Singapore, the Japanese conquered more key points on the road to Java. On February 14 and 15, Japanese paratroops and amphibious units attacked the air base and refineries around Palembang in South Sumatra. By February 17 the defenders had been driven to Java; the next day, Bali and Lombok fell. Timor was stormed on February 19 and 20.

The Japanese next hurled two invasion armies against Java in accordance with careful planning by IGHQ, which had reinforced Imamura with two infantry divisions. For air defense at the outset, there were only thirty operational Dutch fighters and some fifty other Allied aircraft. A last heterogeneous collection of old ABDA (American, British, Dutch, Australian) warships was shattered in the battle of the Java Sea on February 27, whereupon the Allied naval command collapsed. Japanese troops landed at both ends of Java on February 28 and March 1 in a great pincers maneuver. The defenders, confused by the energy and diffusion of the assaults, surrendered unconditionally on March 9. Only mopping-up actions remained for the Japanese forces in the Indies.

A garrison of 93,000 troops, of whom the Dutch numbered few more than 20,000, laid down their arms; the Japanese promptly announced the release of the Indonesian soldiers. Approximately 5,000 Australian, British, and American personnel were also captured. At a time when Allied strength and fortunes were at a perilously low ebb, the losses in men and equipment were enormous. The campaign had consumed only 90 instead of the anticipated 150 days. The defenders' attempts at sabotaging the rich oil fields proved pyrotechnical but not critical; the oil wells and large reserves of fuel were captured essentially intact. With the conquest of the Indies, the end of empire was at hand for the Europeans and Americans, and Japan's valued Greater East Asia Co-Prosperity Sphere had become a reality. As Winston Churchill said of the Singapore disaster, "The violence, fury, skill, and might of Japan far exceeded anything we had been led to expect."[22]

Because cutting off aid to Chiang Kai-shek had been one of the reasons for invading Southeast Asia, Imperial General Headquarters wanted to occupy Burma without delay. Reserve strength was unavailable for this operation, however, and it was necessary to defer it until the conclusion of the other thrusts. When the probable success of the

22 BBSS, *Ran-in kōryaku sakusen,* chaps. 3–8; BBSS, *Nansei hōmen kaigun sakusen,* pp. 1–30, 37–48; BBSS, *Ran-in Bengaru wan hōmen kaigun shinkō sakusen,* chaps. 1–5 (pp. 12, 14), 6–8.

Malay offensive became clear, on January 22, 1942, the high command ordered the Southern Army to proceed with the Burma campaign, although the end point of operations was not clarified. After the air bases in south Burma had been neutralized, the Fifteenth Army proceeded to defeat the Anglo-Indian forces near Rangoon on March 7; the Burmese capital fell next day. Further battles ensued in central Burma, culminating in an engagement on May 13 at which some twenty thousand British and Indian troops were crushed in the vicinity of Kalewa. The Fifteenth Army held up for the time being.[23]

Rounding out the Japanese conquests was the taking of objectives in the Central Pacific. The South Seas Detachment, three battalions under the direct control of Imperial General Headquarters, seized Guam on December 11, and navy forces subdued Wake on January 23. Landing parties invaded the Bismarcks also on January 23.

The keys to the Japanese victories during the first phase of operations included achievement of naval and air supremacy by neutralizing or destroying the American and British battle fleets, interservice coordination, and protection of troop convoys. The Allied defenders were spread thin, without prospects of reinforcement and usually unsupported by their colonial subjects. They thus were unable to stage set-piece battles or strong counterattacks.

The relative ease of the early Japanese operations led to undue optimism in both the field and the high command. The War Ministry suggested seriously that only twenty-one battalions be left in the south and that the rest of the forces be reapportioned to the homeland, China, and Manchuria. Although the army general staff felt that the garrison figure was too low, it accepted the basic concept of redeployment. Meanwhile, the Southern Army Headquarters, without bothering to obtain Tokyo's approval, abolished its Intelligence Section and combined it with Operations. This action, born out of contempt for the Allied armed forces, meant that the Japanese were unable to predict major enemy counteroffensive actions, even in the near future.[24]

## WHAT NEXT?

By the spring of 1942, the Japanese high command was pondering subsequent operations. The Soviet Union had "temporarily" survived

23 BBSS, *Biruma kōryaku sakusen*, chaps. 2, 3, 7–9; BBSS, *Ran-in Bengaru wan hōmen kaigun sakusen*, chap. 9.

24 BBSS, *Chūbu Taiheiyō rikugun sakusen* (1), pp. 17–47; BBSS, *Chūbu Taiheiyō hōmen kaigun sakusen* (1), pt. 2, chaps. 1–4; Hayashi Saburō, *Taiheiyō sensō*, pp. 70–1.

the German onslaught, but Britain seemed to be tottering. To bring down the English and discourage the Americans, thought was given to broadening the zone under occupation and to establishing an invincible structure for protracted warfare. War potential, especially air power, would be built up simultaneously. It was also judged relatively easy to defend occupied islands – as they were unsinkable aircraft carriers. The army did not expect Anglo-American counteroffensives until 1943: The United States was pursuing a Europe-first policy and could not spare much strength for the Pacific theater. In the navy's opinion, the Americans would need at least a year to recover from their debacle at Pearl Harbor.

The high command's deliberations over various alternative objectives convey an impression of opportunism and improvisation rather than workmanlike strategy. For example, the navy turned to ways of occupying Australia, a project beyond the army's capabilities but rendered tempting by the ease with which the Bismarcks had been taken. For its part, the army considered possible new operations, ranging from Cocos Island to Manchuria to Ceylon and eastern India. Eventually the two services were able to agree to establish an outer perimeter in the Pacific by occupying New Caledonia, Fiji, Samoa, eastern New Guinea, and the Aleutians.[25]

Although none of these objectives was beyond the capability of the Japanese, the fundamental fragility of the outer perimeter concept was exposed remarkably and unexpectedly by the Doolittle raid of April 18, 1942. Flying from the carrier *Hornet,* which was only about 650 miles from Japan before it was detected, thirteen U.S. Army B-25 bombers struck at Tokyo without serious opposition, and three additional planes hit targets in Nagoya, Osaka, and Kobe. Although the number of aircraft was small and the damage trifling, not one American plane was shot down over Japan by the befuddled air defense command. Humiliated by the violation of airspace over the imperial capital, the high command decreed an immediate acceleration of the planning for further offensive operations.[26]

An operation was launched to seize Port Moresby on the southwestern tip of New Guinea and, secondarily, Tulagi on the South Solomons' flank. Seven groups of troop transports and warships were staged from Rabaul at the end of April and beginning of May 1942.

25 BBSS, *Chūbu Taiheiyō rikugun sakusen* (1), p. 49.
26 BBSS, *Daihon'ei rikugunbu* (4), pp. 8–19; BBSS, *Hokutō hōmen kaigun sakusen,* pt. 1, chap. 4.

American intelligence, thanks to its breaking the Japanese codes, enabled Admiral Chester Nimitz to concentrate his forces at optimal locations, whereas the Japanese, despite far greater regional strength at this stage of the war, knew little about enemy dispositions and assets. The Japanese headquarters in Rabaul suspended plans to land directly at Port Moresby when a major naval clash developed on May 7 and 8. During the battle of the Coral Sea, the first naval engagement in history to pit carriers against carriers, aircraft conducted all of the combat. No surface ship even sighted an enemy vessel. Few warships were hit: the Americans lost their precious fleet carrier *Lexington* and two small vessels; the Japanese lost one light carrier (*Shōhō*) and sustained damage to one heavy carrier (*Shōkaku*).

Far greater were the strategic and psychological consequences. The twelve Japanese transports heading for Port Moresby, vulnerable to the prowling Allied task forces, turned back meekly, a decision for which Admiral Inouye Shigeyoshi has been criticized roundly. Second, two Japanese heavy carriers, the *Shōkaku* and the *Zuikaku*, which had lost a considerable number of planes and pilots, were put out of action just as the gigantic confrontation between navies loomed at Midway. Third, the destruction of the first Japanese carrier of any type in the Pacific War boosted Allied morale, which was at a nadir after the catastrophe at Corregidor.[27]

## THE MIDWAY AND ALEUTIANS OPERATIONS

Admiral Yamamoto, shaken by the implications of the Doolittle raid, forged ahead with offensive planning against the Midway sector. It was agreed that this operation should precede the envisioned attacks against Fiji and Samoa. In a closely related compromise between the army and the navy, a simultaneous diversionary invasion of the Aleutian Islands was projected. Nagumo's powerful carrier task force, which had scoured the Indian Ocean and raided Ceylon in early April 1942, was called back to the Pacific for the Midway operation. On May 5 the jittery Imperial General Headquarters ordered Yamamoto to move ahead in conjunction with the army.

The Midway plan called for the Combined Fleet to move eastward in force to seize Midway Atoll, located one thousand miles west of

27 BBSS, *Nantō hōmen kaigun sakusen* (1), pt. 1, chap. 5. Also see Tendō Akira, *Sangokai daikaisen: kantai jūgun hiroku* (Tokyo: Masu shobō, 1956).

Pearl Harbor, as an advance base and potential threat to Hawaii. More importantly, it was expected that the remnants of the U.S. Pacific Fleet would be lured into a decisive battle and defeated. For the main attack against Midway, Yamamoto amassed 6 aircraft carriers, 234 planes, 7 battleships, 14 cruisers, 43 destroyers, 13 submarines, 5 seaplane tenders, a fleet train of 15 ships, and 15 transports carrying five thousand troops. Yamamoto's grandiose scheme required superb timing and the orchestration of dispersed forces. Unfortunately for the Japanese, U.S. intelligence was able to read enemy signals traffic, again providing Admiral Nimitz with a considerable advantage in deploying his overextended forces.

The battle of Midway commenced on June 4. The Japanese carrier strike force commanded by Nagumo was able to overwhelm the outnumbered air defense and to smash ground installations on the island. Nimitz, however, had concentrated far larger naval forces (including carriers) than expected. Although Japanese fighters and antiaircraft fire inflicted fearful damage on the American carrier planes attacking the Japanese force bravely but in disconnected squadrons, Nagumo had to decide whether to rearm his torpedo aircraft with bombs for a follow-up strike against Midway and whether to recover returning planes or to launch bomber strikes immediately. Unexpected waves of American dive bombers from the *Yorktown* and *Enterprise* caught the Japanese betwixt and between. Aerial torpedoes were still lying on the hangar decks of the Japanese carriers instead of being stowed below, and aircraft were parked – fueled and armed – before they could take off. Nagumo's four carriers were lost in the ensuing action: the *Kaga* and *Sōryū* went down that night, and the *Akagi* and *Hiryū* had to be finished off by Japanese destroyers next morning. The Japanese also lost one heavy cruiser sunk and a second badly damaged; the Americans lost only the carrier *Yorktown* and one destroyer.

Yamamoto, aboard the giant battleship *Yamato,* had hoped to engage a crippled enemy fleet during classic night action, but as the enormity of Japanese losses became clear, he intelligently withdrew his flotilla early on June 5 without major action. Just as the battle of the Coral Sea had caused cancellation of the landing at Port Moresby, the battle of Midway necessitated the withdrawal of the ground forces earmarked to occupy the atoll. Yamamoto had lost not only the four fleet carriers but also approximately 2,200 crewmen and most of the seasoned pilots of the 234 planes destroyed. Japanese scouting and communication had been poor; intelligence, foolishly rosy. The defeat at Midway, although kept from the Japanese public at the time, must be termed the decisive battle of the Pacific War, for it ended Japanese supremacy on the high seas.[28]

The Aleutians sideshow proceeded as planned. Imperial General Headquarters had opted for a diversionary occupation of the islands instead of a protracted campaign of destruction. Assigned to the Aleutians task force were two light carriers, five cruisers, a seaplane tender, twelve destroyers, and eight transports with 1,550 men. American bases at Dutch Harbor in the eastern chain and Attu, Kiska, and Adak in the westernmost portion along the Great Circle route (the shortest approach to the Japanese homeland from North America) were to be nullified. (The minor Adak phase was eventually scrapped.) The operational plan resembled the *modus operandi* employed in Southeast Asia, entailing the preliminary neutralization of defenses, broad distribution of objectives, and multidirectional angles of assault. Considerations of weather and terrain precluded large-scale mobile action in the Aleutians. Although American intelligence possessed considerable detail concerning the Midway plan, far less was known about Japanese operations in the Aleutians.

Japanese carrier-based planes neutralized Dutch Harbor in raids between June 3 and 5, and troops went ashore unopposed at Attu on June 5 and at Kiska on June 7. Not until June 10 did the American command learn of the landings. Nimitz resisted the temptation to divert carriers to the North Pacific after the victory at Midway. During the next stage, the Japanese tried to maintain bases on the two bleak islands while the Americans tried to neutralize them. In August and September Imperial General Headquarters first opted to give up Attu and concentrate on Kiska, but after actually withdrawing the Attu garrison, the high command reversed itself and reoccupied the island in October. On February 5, 1943, Imperial General Headquarters decided to cling to the western Aleutians "at all costs," according higher priority to Attu as the Americans were building up their installations at Adak and Amchitka.

On May 11 the Americans landed a division at Attu. The Japanese garrison of about 2,600 men fought desperately but was overwhelmed by May 29. The body count totaled 2,351, but only 28 prisoners were taken, a ratio repeated throughout the Pacific War. Of the 11,000 U.S. assault troops, approximately 600 were killed, 1,200 wounded, and

28 BBSS, *Middouē kaisen*, chaps. 1–15; BBSS, *Chūbu Taiheiyō hōmen kaigun sakusen* (2), pt. 3, chap. 2; Agawa, *Yamamoto*, vol. 1, pp. 310–36; Toyoda, *Namimakura*, pp. 223–68; Matsushima, *Higeki no Nagumo chūjō*, pp. 150–73; Hara, *Teikoku kaigun*, pp. 8–9; Kusaka, *Rengō kantai*, pp. 120–56.

1,500 incapacitated by illness. At the last minute, the high command had prepared to evacuate the remnants of the Attu garrison, but events overtook them.

On May 20, Imperial General Headquarters reexamined the deteriorating situation in the Aleutians. Admitting that island operations lacking air and sea supremacy were doomed, the conferees reached the embarrassing decision to evacuate Kiska, whose garrison was twice as large as the one on Attu. Submarines began the slow process in late May; a destroyer squadron completed the task, speedily and efficaciously, on July 28. The Americans failed to detect the evacuation for more than two weeks after the last Japanese had departed. On August 15 an American-Canadian army of 34,000 men, in a flotilla of nearly one hundred ships, stormed the island only to find it empty.

Many have argued that the Japanese never should have bothered with the desolate Aleutians. At the time, however, the high command regarded the islands as a threat to the Kurils and even to the homeland, particularly if the Americans teamed up militarily with the Soviets. With a force of only 10,000 troops, complemented by indifferent naval and air assistance, the Japanese managed to divert as many as 100,000 Allied troops supported by sizable naval and air forces. Nevertheless, the Japanese squandered the entire Attu garrison, lost eighteen vessels and precious logistical and ordnance stores. Combined Fleet warships were deployed as backup at times when they were far more needed to block enemy operations at Guadalcanal. Additionally, the Kurils and even Hokkaido had to be reinforced after the Japanese were ousted from the Aleutians. Although the Japanese revealed great skill in evacuating endangered island garrisons, Imperial General Headquarters earned no luster for its vacillating and unproductive conduct during the Aleutian operation. Despite the costs, the campaign exerted scant influence on the Pacific theater as a whole, from either the Japanese or the Allied point of view.[29]

## RETAINING THE INITIATIVE

Because fifteen of the sixteen Doolittle aircraft landed in China (the sixteenth came down in Siberia) after bombing Japan, the Japanese high command accelerated the campaign to deny Chinese bases to the Americans. Three days after the raid, on April 21, 1942, Imperial

29 BBSS, *Hokutō hōmen rikugun sakusen* (1), chaps. 1–3; BBSS, *Hokutō hōmen kaigun sakusen*, pt. 1, chaps. 1, 2 and pt. 2.

General Headquarters directed the China Expeditionary Army under General Hata Shunroku to knock out Nationalist air bases on the central front, mainly in Chekiang and Kiangsi provinces, secondarily in Hunan. On May 15, Japanese forces advanced and soon routed the enemy in East Chekiang. An offensive by a second field army at the end of May and beginning of June had equal success. The two Japanese armies then launched a pincers operation that cleared the Chekiang Railway by July 1.

After their successes in China during the summer of 1942, the Japanese prepared a "last offensive" designed to seize Chungking sometime after spring 1943. The intensification of the battles for Guadalcanal, however, caused suspension of the operation on December 10. It was becoming clear that the Pacific War was not solving the China incident and that victory in the Pacific could not be found in the China theater. Indeed, China was becoming of secondary importance to the high command, which had begun to realize that, after all, one could not climb out of a hole by widening it.[30]

Still another consequence of the Japanese setback at Midway was the high command's decision on July 11, 1942, to suspend any operations against New Caledonia, Fiji, and Samoa. Not only had it learned the difficulty of taking a well-defended island, but there was also growing opinion that it would be more advisable to step up action in the western Indian Ocean, in conjunction with the German campaign against Suez. Imperial General Headquarters, however, remained convinced that severing the route between the United States and Australia was necessary to nip the Allied counteroffensive in the bud. The Seventeenth Army under General Hyakutake Haruyoshi was instructed to seize Port Moresby and nearby air bases in eastern New Guinea by pushing overland from Kokoda and Buna.

Without waiting for information from a long-range ground reconnaissance force, Hyakutake sent his South Seas Detachment ashore near Buna in the middle of July 1942. Pushing toward Port Moresby, the soldiers struggled across the wretched Owen Stanley Range, where they suffered from the tortuous terrain, disease, and hunger. Australian resistance was overcome, but supply proved impossible, and after approaching Port Moresby, the Japanese units were ordered to hold up on August 28. A month later, the detachment began the retreat

30 Horiba, *Shina jihen*, pp. 666–706; Usui, *Nitchū sensō*, pp. 141–62; BBSS, *Daihon'ei rikugunbu* (4), pp. 19–27.

toward Buna, harried by Australian troops all the way. It took them until the end of November to get back to Buna. Because the Seventeenth Army had become preoccupied with the fighting on Guadalcanal, Imperial General Headquarters formed an Eighteenth Army under General Adachi Hatazō to concentrate on eastern New Guinea. The axis of operations now shifted away from Port Moresby, toward Buna, Lae, and Salamaua.[31]

Over six hundred miles east of New Guinea, between Rabaul and the New Hebrides–New Caledonia sector to the southeast, lie the Solomon Islands. Several hundred Japanese Naval Landing Force personnel and two thousand construction men were at work on an airstrip on Guadalcanal in mid-1942, an operation so secret or at least so uncoordinated with higher headquarters that the Japanese army general staff did not learn about the project until U.S. troops came ashore in August. In the first American ground counteroffensive, the First Marine Division landed without opposition on August 7 at Guadalcanal, Gavutu, and Tulagi. The incomplete but critical air base (later known as Henderson Field) was taken on August 8. Although the American toehold was never retaken, months of fierce warfare ensued. In all, each side eventually lost twenty-four warships in the battles off Guadalcanal.

Imperial General Headquarters, underestimating the difficulty of recapturing Guadalcanal, ordered Hyakutake to regain the Solomons while continuing with his primary mission of conquering Port Moresby. By August 29, after enormous casualties were incurred on Guadalcanal and Henderson Field was being used by American planes, the high command reversed the operational emphasis from New Guinea to the Solomons and transferred an infantry division to the Seventeenth Army for this purpose.

In mid-September the Japanese army general staff modified its tactical practice on Guadalcanal. Instead of charging blindly forward, piecemeal and without much preparation, Japanese assault units were ordered to wait until reinforcements had been assembled and careful planning had been conducted in conjunction with the navy. Hyakutake himself left Rabaul for Guadalcanal on October 8. Lacking full control of the sea and air, the Japanese lost heavily in men, supplies, and ordnance. Japanese ground commanders estimated the American superiority in machine guns at six or seven times; in ammunition,

31 BBSS, *Minami Taiheiyō rikugun sakusen* (1), pp. 76–109, 167–230, 335–60; BBSS, *Chūbu Taiheiyō rikugun sakusen*, pp. 194–218, 324–95, 557–604; BBSS, *Nansei hōmen kaigun sakusen*, pp. 31–6, 373–96; BBSS, *Nantō hōmen kaigun sakusen* (1), pt. 1, chaps. 3, 4, and pt. 2, chap. 4.

beyond comparison. Front-line troops began to perish from hunger as well as disease. Transport ships carrying in fresh divisions were being sunk in increasing numbers.

On November 16, 1942, the high command had formed the Eighth Army under General Imamura Hitoshi to coordinate the two field armies operating in the Solomons and New Guinea. The army general staff struggled with the War Ministry to requisition more shipping for operational requirements, insisting that Guadalcanal must be retained to the last. If the Solomons were ordered to be evacuated, American counterattacks would prove too severe to allow a pullout. No less than 300,000 tons of shipping were imperative. Viewing matters from a broader national standpoint, the War Ministry opposed the army general staff's desires. It favored withdrawal from Guadalcanal and redeployment of forces along a strategic inner perimeter zone. Arguments raged, and staff officers even came to blows.

By December 12 the navy had lost heart in the Guadalcanal operation and proposed evacuation. After stubborn army general staff opposition was overcome, on December 31 an Imperial General Headquarters conference of army and navy leaders decided to abandon efforts to recapture Guadalcanal and to evacuate the islands by the beginning of February. Although forces at Buna were to fall back toward Salamaua, the hope of seizing Port Moresby had still not been given up. In other words, the Japanese were planning to pull in their horns in the forward districts and go over to the defensive in the Solomons. But neither Rabaul nor eastern New Guinea was to be abandoned.

No one was sure of the numbers of Japanese troops on Guadalcanal, but it was thought that from a force that might total 20,000, as many as 15,000 might be lost to enemy action during an evacuation. In fact, destroyers managed to bring out between 11,000 and 13,000 soldiers and sailors without interference in early February. For the first time in the Pacific War, the Japanese army had been forced to go on the defensive. During the six-month Guadalcanal campaign, it had lost about 25,000 men and 600 planes. American ground casualties were approximately 1,500 dead and 4,800 wounded.

Both Japanese services have been castigated for the reckless handling of a campaign beyond their capabilities. There had been no clear-cut decision as to the cutoff point after the success of the first-stage operations in the south in 1941–2. The navy had unrealistically considered thrusts as far afield as Australia and Hawaii, and the army found itself engaged heavily at Guadalcanal before any joint policy could be worked out with the navy. No amount of bravery could compensate for logistical impotence. Japanese military critics remain convinced that given the country's overall strength, the Guadalcanal operation was not at all feasible.[32]

## TIGHTENING THE PERIMETER

The capitulation of Italy in September 1943, presaging the release of Allied forces to the Far East, caused Imperial General Headquarters to reconsider its estimates of the enemy's counteroffensive capabilities. An Imperial Conference decided on new operational guidelines on September 30. The most noteworthy change was apparent in the high command's delimitation, for the first time, of an "absolute national defense sphere." It encompassed the Kurils, the Bonins, the Inner South Sea islands, western New Guinea, the Sunda Islands, and Burma. Clearly, the strategic perimeter was being constricted. The most pressing problems in the South Pacific were considered to be the reinforcement of the zone of absolute national defense, holding operations around the northern Solomons and New Guinea, and preparations for counteraction north of Australia in the Timor region. The Americans were designated the primary national enemy.[33]

The shift to a more realistic strategic posture cannot obscure the overconfidence that continued to affect the Japanese leadership. They continued to assume that the hostilities could be resolved by military action, not by diplomatic negotiations. It was not until the end of August 1943 that Prime Minister Tōjō even considered putting out feelers toward Chungking or making efforts to mediate the German–Soviet war. The government and military leaders were losing sight of the fact that Admiral Yamamoto's scheme of 1941 had been designed to buy time for Japan – time to construct a defensible perimeter and to negotiate a settlement of hostilities favorable to Japan, not time to fight a long drawn-out war. The prime minister's response to the Japanese reverses was to redouble his efforts, tighten his control, promote optimism, and suppress dissent. As General Honma later observed, "Tōjō believed that he could win such a complicated modern war simply by intensifying the people's spirit or by enhancing morale."

For the most part, the final two years of the Pacific War were

32 BBSS, *Chūbu Taiheiyō rikugun sakusen* (1), pp. 68–73, 86–94, 99; BBSS, *Minami Taiheiyō rikugun sakusen* (1), pp. 231–314, 385–534; BBSS, *Chūbu Taiheiyō rikugun sakusen* (2), pp. 7–23, 419–576; BBSS, *Nantō hōmen kaigun sakusen* (1), pp. 201, 227, and pt. 2, chaps. 1–3; ibid. (2), pts. 1–2; ibid. (3), chaps. 1–7; BBSS, *Chūbu Taiheiyō hōmen kaigun sakusen* (2), pt. 3, chaps. 3, 7.

33 BBSS, *Chūbu Taiheiyō hōmen kaigun sakusen* (2), pt. 4, chaps. 1, 4 (2); BBSS, *Mariana oki kaisen*, chaps. 1 (p. 2), 2–3.

characterized by Japan's strategic passivity. The military initiative had shifted to the Allies. Enemy counteroffensives were developing sooner and were far better articulated than Imperial General Headquarters had anticipated. America's enormous economic and industrial resources began to have an overpowering impact on the fighting. Whereas the Japanese were unable to replace the four fleet carriers lost at Midway, American shipyards were turning out innumerable escort carriers that became the core of task forces assaulting Japanese strongholds across the Pacific. The American strategy also surprised the Japanese high command by choosing to bypass certain well-defended islands, to leapfrog across the Central and Southwest Pacific, and to let isolated Japanese garrisons like those at Truk and Rabaul wither on the vine.

The Japanese outer perimeter in the South Pacific began to collapse in the summer of 1943 after their disengagement from Guadalcanal and the Aleutians. In the Central Pacific, the islands of Makin and Tarawa in the Gilberts, though fiercely contested, were lost in November 1943. Kwajalein and Roi in the Marshall Islands fell in February 1944. The high command was particularly unnerved by the powerful American air and naval bombardment of Truk that month, for it proved that Japanese naval aviation was no longer a match for the enemy. For the first time in the Pacific War, Imperial General Headquarters ordered divisions pulled out of the Kwantung Army in Manchuria and transferred to the south. Japanese army leaders blamed the tardy defensive preparation in the central and western Carolines, Marianas, and Bonins on the navy's lack of concern with ground warfare and narrow outlook on jurisdiction in the Pacific, whose defense was a naval responsibility. Three days after the Truk raid, Prime Minister Tōjō took the unprecedented step of assuming the concurrent post of chief of army staff.[34]

Symbolic of the enfeebled Japanese control of Pacific areas was the ambush of Admiral Yamamoto's aircraft during an inspection tour of Bougainville on April 18, 1943. Guided by intercepted intelligence, American P-38 fighter planes shot down and killed Japan's most brilliant strategist.[35]

If the defense of isolated atolls and islands posed insuperable logistical difficulties and precluded maneuver, the land operations offered

34 BBSS, *Chūbu Taiheiyō hōmen kaigun sakusen* (2), pt. 3, chaps. 4, 5 (p. 2), 6 (p. 4), and pt. 4, chaps. 2, 4 (p. 5).

35 BBSS, *Chūbu Taiheiyō hōmen kaigun sakusen* (2), pt. 3, chap. 8 (p. 4); Agawa, *Yamamoto,* pp. 306–27.

some hope of success. In 1944 the high command focused new attention on the China theater, where the Nationalist regime remained isolated but American air power was becoming more active, even posing a threat to the Japanese homeland. A Japanese offensive, launched in mid-April 1944, opened up the entire southern portion of the Peking–Hankow Railroad; by early May the northern and central fronts in China were linked. Between the end of June and early August, Japanese armies took Changsha and Hengyang (the Americans' advance air base). By November a new offensive overran other U.S. air installations at Lingling, Kweilin, Liuchow, and Nanning. But it proved impossible for the army to neutralize the B-29 long-range bomber bases at Chengtu in Szechwan Province, against which the Japanese could mount air strikes of only limited strength. The B-29 bombers continued to hit targets in northern Kyushu, south Manchuria, and Korea. When the Americans set up bases on islands in the western Pacific in 1945, the B-29s were transferred from China.[36]

Some Imperial General Headquarters staff officers saw prospects for success in the Burma theater. The Japanese planners were thinking of seizing a corner of India, in the Imphal area, to establish a puppet government and undercut British authority. Considerable efforts had already been made to create collaborationist regimes in Burma under Ba Maw and a provisional Indian government under Chandra Bose. In March 1943 the Burma Area Army Headquarters under General Kawabe Masakazu was formed. The political nature of the envisaged Imphal operation became so apparent that some officers were rightly convinced that higher headquarters regarded the launching of the campaign a foregone conclusion rather than a carefully considered option. Whatever reservations Imperial General Headquarters entertained were assuaged by the self-confidence and enthusiasm of General Mutaguchi Renya, commander of the Fifteenth Army on the Burmese central front. The notion of a successful campaign in South Asia also undoubtedly appealed to the increasingly harried Tōjō.

Allied counteractions had already begun on several Burmese fronts in early 1944. Chinese forces attacked in the north and northeast; Anglo-Indian troops, in central Burma and on the southern coast. The Thirty-third Army was established in April to deal with the Chinese, leaving Mutaguchi free for his offensive. His forces had already jumped off in early March. Making light of the enemy and almost ignoring logistics, Mutaguchi had been thinking in terms of a two-

36 Horiba, *Shina jihen*, pp. 707–40; Usui, *Nitchū sensō*, pp. 162–200.

week advance, but after initial progress, by early April the Japanese bogged down within sight of Imphal. Soon afterward, heavy monsoon rains began. Having lost half of its personnel en route to the front, the Fifteenth Army ran short of ammunition, supplies, and food. Demanding that the advance resume, Mutaguchi ordered the troops to devour their pack oxen and eat grass. His anger mounting, the general sacked two of his three division commanders, alleging that they lacked fighting spirit.

While the Anglo-Indian forces, excellently led by General William Slim, received aerial resupply and reinforcements, the Japanese units continued to disintegrate from sickness, hunger, lack of ammunition and antitank weapons, and inadequate air support. By late June the Allies had retaken Kohima and had cleared the road from Imphal. Mutaguchi, still dreaming of a decisive offensive, relieved the third of his division commanders, who defiantly broke off communications and retreated in order to save the last remnants of his division from destruction.

Japanese forces in Burma were smashed on every front. The Fifteenth Army lost over half of its 60,000 men in the disastrous retreat from the Chindwin River. Kawabe and Mutaguchi have been blamed for their inflexibility and unwillingness to withdraw and their reckless, emotional, and sophomoric conduct of operations. Imperial General Headquarters has also been censured for lack of resolution. Not until July 4 did it authorize suspension of the Imphal offensive, even though there had been no hope of success since May, when the rainy season had begun. Similarly, not until September 25 did the high command change the mission of the Burma Area Army from capture to interception of communications between China and India, a distinction that by then was academic. The Japanese were routed in Burma by the time they lost Rangoon in early May 1945. The entire Burma campaign of 1944–5, one of the worst debacles of the Pacific War, cost Kawabe more than 100,000 men.[37]

## EXIT TŌJŌ

If euphoria described the mood of Japan during Tōjō's early days as prime minister, then disillusionment bordering on despair described it by 1944. The Americans continued to land at will on Japanese-held

37 BBSS, *Biruma kōryaku sakusen,* pp. 271–4; BBSS, *Inpāru sakusen,* pts. 1–3; BBSS, *Irawaji kaisen,* pts. 1, 2; BBSS, *Shittan Mei-gō sakusen,* pt. 1; *SSNT,* vol. 9, passim.

islands in the Pacific. By the beginning of 1944, the bastion at Rabaul had been isolated. In April, U.S. forces came ashore in northern New Guinea, seizing the best air bases on the island. Trying to shuffle its forces, the Japanese high command appeared to lack an overall plan and meddled in operational details. On May 9 the Second Area army commander, General Anami Korechika, wrote in his diary: "The IGHQ's command is in a whirl." Soon afterward, U.S. troops stormed Biak Island, enabling the Americans to dominate the skies over Halmahera, the Strait of Malacca, and the Makassar Channel.

At the time, the army and navy high commands had been giving serious thought to checking the Allied advance by means of a decisive battle in the zone of the Marianas, the western Carolines, and New Guinea. As soon as Biak Island was invaded, the navy shifted sizable air strength to that sector, much to the army's annoyance. With Biak under U.S. control, Saipan and Tinian in the northern Marianas suffered an American preparatory bombardment on June 13, followed by troop landings on Saipan on June 15. Waging one of the toughest battles of the Central Pacific campaign, the defending Japanese forces of about one and one-half divisions were overwhelmed by month's end. On July 1, their commander reported to Tokyo that his men had not eaten for three days but were fighting on, devouring tree roots and snails. The last organized defense ended on July 9.

The defeat of the Japanese navy in the battle of the Philippine Sea, also known as the battle of the Marianas, contributed to the isolation and destruction of the Japanese garrison on Saipan. On June 19 and 20, the Japanese fleet was outfought and outmatched by Admiral Raymond Spruance's task force. Although five American warships were damaged, the Japanese lost two heavy carriers at the outset (leaving only one surviving carrier from the Pearl Harbor raid) and a light carrier as the battle progressed. Three more Japanese carriers, a battleship, a heavy cruiser, and a destroyer were damaged by aircraft and submarines. In two days of battle, 395 of the Japanese carrier planes were destroyed – 92 percent of their original strength. The Americans lost only 130 planes.

Once the Saipan garrison was destroyed and the naval forces were beaten in decisive battle for the second time, the Marianas island chain was doomed. Tinian, defended by one Japanese regiment, was invaded on July 24 and lost by August 1. Meanwhile, U.S. operations against Guam had begun on July 8. After thirteen days of bombardment by air and sea, American forces came ashore, linked up their beachheads by the end of the month after severe fighting, and drove the last main defenders to the northern shore by August 10. Another Japanese division and a half had been lost in the southern Marianas.

Japanese leaders well understood the significance of the Marianas campaign. On June 25, the emperor convened the first wartime meeting of field marshals and fleet admirals to review operations. It was agreed that the retention of Saipan was imperative but would be difficult to accomplish. If the island could not be secured, the enemy's use of its air bases should be impeded to the utmost. The defense of the inner perimeter had to be strengthened quickly. It was crucial to combine army and navy air power and to conduct unified operations.

Tōjō, however, had staked his reputation on the successful defense of Saipan. In May 1944, he had made the astonishing statement to the navy that the island was impregnable. Even the junior officers wondered whether the army's operational planners had misinformed the prime minister or whether he had spoken irresponsibly. A senior navy officer never forgot his misleading sense of relief when he learned that Tōjō had assured an Imperial Conference that ground preparations in the Marianas and Carolines were completed and that the Combined Fleet could operate at will.

After the devastating loss of Saipan, army war direction officers reached the conclusion that the war was lost and that hostilities must quickly be ended, particularly because Germany's days seemed numbered. Despite his reputation as a human dynamo, the narrow-minded and overconfident Tōjō could not cope with the pressures of supreme commandship and of fundamental national weakness. As defeat followed defeat, his star waned rapidly. Plans to unify the army and the navy air forces came to naught, as did plans to consolidate the two services under a single Imperial General Headquarters leader. When Tōjō sought to placate serious opposition by proposing that General Ushiroku Jun replace him as army chief of staff, he had to back down and accept Umezu Yoshijirō, the Kwantung Army commander. On July 14, 1944, despite Tōjō's opposition, his loyal associate Admiral Shimada Shigetarō was obliged to resign as navy minister, keeping only his post as navy chief of staff. Although Tōjō struggled cunningly to retain power, he had lost the confidence of the elder statesmen and imperial intimates who had installed him in 1941. In the midst of rumors of a coup d'état and perhaps even an assassination attempt against him, Tōjō resigned as prime minister on July 18, 1944.[38]

38 BBSS, *Chūbu Taiheiyō rikugun sakusen* (1), pt. 3: BBSS, *Chūbu Taiheiyō hōmen kaigun sakusen* (2), pt. 4, chap. 3 (p. 3); BBSS, *Mariana oki kaisen,* chaps. 4–6.

## THE KOISO–YONAI PHASE: PHILIPPINES TO IWŌ

On July 22, 1944, a new government was organized under two distinguished officers representing both services: General Koiso Kuniaki (most recently governor general of Korea) as prime minister, and Admiral Yonai Mitsumasa (a premier in 1940) as his deputy and also navy minister. During this stage of the war, Imperial General Headquarters concentrated its attention on four objectives: strengthening sea defenses on the front from the Philippines to Taiwan, the Ryūkyūs, the homeland, and the Kuril Islands; combining army, navy, and aerial strength to engage an enemy offensive against any of these districts; continuing the attacks against objectives in Hunan and Kwangsi provinces in China and offsetting the uncertain maritime routes by using transportation facilities on the Asian continent; and selecting offshore sea routes to ensure protection of shipping. Battle plans were prepared to fend off enemy attacks against the Philippines, the Taiwan–Ryūkyū area, the three main home islands, and the northern island of Hokkaido. Plans for the defense of the home islands projected potential invasion points in south and southwest Kyushu, southern Shikoku, and a number of sites in Honshu, such as Ise, Toyohashi, Sagami, Chiba-Ibaragi, Sendai, and Aomori.

When American forces overwhelmed the garrisons at Morotai and Peleliu–Angaur in mid-September, the high command concluded that the next enemy objective would be the Philippines. New army commands were established to meet the threat, and on September 22 Imperial General Headquarters directed the army commanders in Singapore, China, and Taiwan to complete operational preparations by late October.

In a fierce air war, U.S. navy planes whittled down the aerial strength that the Japanese were feeding southward into the Philippines theater. General MacArthur's main landings began at Leyte on October 20. A series of naval and air clashes ensued between October 23 and 26 – the battle of Leyte Gulf, the biggest naval engagement in history. In the course of daring but expensive maneuvers, the Japanese almost intercepted the American amphibious forces, but when the combat had ended, the Japanese carrier fleet had been destroyed, and other major elements had been crippled. The once-mighty Japanese navy would never again play an important role in the Pacific War.[39]

39 Gaimushō, ed., *Shūsen shiroku* (Tokyo: Shinbun gekkansha, 1952), chap. 9; BBSS, *Kaigun Shō-gō sakusen* (1), pt. 3; ibid. (2), pts. 1, 2; Hara, *Teikoku kaigun*, pp. 180–228; Kusaka, *Rengō kantai*, pp. 288–347.

Japanese ground defenses were weakened by insufficient troop training, lack of airpower and antitank weapons, and muddled planning. Logistics were complicated by the fact that 80 percent of Japanese shipping bound for the Philippines had been sunk since the summer of 1944. In addition, the command structure was brand-new and largely unacquainted with local realities. General Yamashita Tomoyuki, the recently appointed Fourteenth Area army commander, reached Manila only on October 6, and his chief of staff, General Mutō Akira, arrived on the day that the enemy landed on Leyte. Yamashita had been unenthusiastic about the plan to defend Leyte but was forced to follow the Southern Army's orders. By mid-November he recommended that the Southern Army reconsider the operation but was turned down. On December 11 the loss of Ormoc and its stores, on the west side of the island, virtually sealed the fate of Leyte, and Yamashita abandoned the idea of waging a decisive campaign there. The defense of the Philippines was continuously complicated by disagreements among the Imperial General Headquarters, the Southern Army, and Yamashita's Area Army.

U.S. forces landed on Mindoro Island, northwest of Leyte, on December 15. Nevertheless, Yamashita's defense of Leyte delayed the American invasion of Luzon at Lingayen by about three weeks, from December 20 until January 9, 1945. By February 3 the U.S. troops were outside Manila. Japanese navy units, not directly commanded by Yamashita, waged a vicious one-month battle for the capital, much of which was left in ruins. Corregidor fell to the Americans by February 26. Manila Harbor was open to Allied shipping by mid-March.

Yamashita's mauled units fell back into the mountains. The Americans were basically in control of Luzon by mid-June. Separated into three ill-supplied sectors, Yamashita's hungry and sick men resisted until the end of the war, but they were unable to mount any serious counteraction and did not destroy themselves in suicidal charges as Japanese troops had in other operations. Meanwhile, other U.S. forces had cleared the southern Philippines, invading Palawan, Panay, Cebu, and Negros, south and north Mindanao, and the Sulu archipelago. In the entire campaign for the Philippines in 1944–5, the Japanese lost much of their air strength and most of their navy and also incurred at least 317,000 casualties, including 7,200 prisoners.[40]

By early 1945, the high command began to subordinate all strategic considerations to the defense of the homeland. Once the Americans

40 BBSS, *Shō-gō rikugun sakusen* (1), pts. 1–3; ibid. (2), chaps. 1–10.

had retaken the Philippines, it was thought that they would proceed to Okinawa or would occupy the Bonin Islands and strike at Okinawa or Taiwan. The nearness of the island of Iwo to Japan – 660 miles from Tokyo – suggested that it would become an early objective of Nimitz's counteroffensive, a surmise strengthened by the U.S. naval and air bombardments that had begun in June 1944. The well-fortified garrison numbered approximately 17,500 soldiers and 5,500 navy personnel. Despite the isolation of his bastion and the shortage of drinking water, General Kuribayashi Tadamichi had managed to amass rice and other rations sufficient for sixty to seventy days.

Beginning in December 1944, the Americans subjected Iwo to the most severe preparatory air and naval bombardment ever hurled against any Pacific target. After a three-day barrage in the middle of February, an American corps began landing. The landmark of Mount Suribachi was seized on February 23, but the Japanese took full advantage of the terrain and the interlocking fire network to delay the penetration inland. The Japanese attempted counteroffensive actions, but by March 26 the remnants of the garrison, penned in the north of the island, were annihilated, many dying sealed into their caves by flamethrowers. The U.S. Marine units sacrificed about the same number of killed and wounded (23,000) as the Japanese lost in killed. The three airstrips on the island were promptly used by the Americans as bases for fighter aircraft escorting B-29s from Tinian and as emergency landing sites for crippled bombers returning from sorties against Japan.[41]

## THE STRUGGLE FOR OKINAWA

Unsure where the Americans would strike next, the Imperial General Headquarters decided to build up the garrison on Taiwan to eight ground divisions. The transfer of the first-class Ninth Division to Taiwan left the Okinawa zone with only two and a half divisions. Nothing came of a plan to send a replacement division from Japan to Okinawa, largely because the army general staff preferred to focus its efforts on defending the homeland. New emphasis was given to the use of special attack (*Tokkō*) units, suicidal aerial attack forces that first saw service in the Philippines campaign and were known popularly as *kamikaze*.

41 BBSS, *Chūbu Taiheiyō rikugun sakusen* (2), pts. 1–3; BBSS, *Hondo hōmen kaigun sakusen*, pt. 3, chap. 3.

From the tempo and direction of U.S. Navy task force activity in March 1945, the Japanese high command concluded that an invasion of Okinawa was imminent. American troops began to land in the Kerama chain west of Okinawa on March 26 and occupied their objectives in five days. Japanese army air squadrons were launched against U.S. transports in Okinawa waters, and navy aerial units attacked the enemy armada of more than one thousand vessels.

On April 1 the U.S. Tenth Army invaded the west coast of Okinawa and quickly overran two important air bases at Yontan and Kadena. Weakened by the transfer of the Ninth Division, the defending commander, General Ushijima Mitsuru, had decided not to fight on the beaches but to fall back with his main body to a line based on Shuri in the south, while secondary forces fought in the central and northern portions of the sixty-mile-long island. Two miles at its narrowest, Okinawa's defenses were severed at the waist by April 4. The Japanese launched major counteroffensives on April 8 and May 3 but were checked by firepower each time. By May 18 the Americans had broken the Shuri line; on May 23 they were outside Naha. Japanese strongpoints were reduced steadily. In effect, the Imperial General Headquarters gave up the island on May 26 when it transferred air strength to the defense of the homeland.

When U.S. troops reached the southern end of Okinawa on June 21, General Ushijima sent off a last, poignant message to Tokyo and then committed suicide with his chief of staff. Japanese dead exceeded 107,000; another 24,000 to 28,000 were sealed in caves. Prisoners numbered about 11,000, including many Okinawans. In fact, the high casualty toll suggests that perhaps 42,000 civilians fell victim to combat action. American ground and naval battle casualties totaled over 49,000 – the highest U.S. toll in the Pacific War.[42]

The Japanese high command had made desperate efforts to help the garrison on Okinawa. *Kamikaze* air attacks were spectacular and massive; the Americans counted 896 raids against Okinawa and another 1,000 against the fleet, especially destroyer and escort pickets and anchored aircraft carriers. In all, the U.S. Navy lost 36 ships sunk and 386 damaged, as well as 763 planes knocked out by all causes, but the grand total of Japanese aircraft downed is estimated at 7,830.

Despite the loss of aerial supremacy, on April 6 the Japanese navy dispatched the remnants of the Combined Fleet toward Okinawa in a

42 BBSS, *Okinawa hōmen rikugun sakusen*, chaps. 1–7, 9–14; BBSS, *Okinawa hōmen kaigun sakusen*, chaps. 1–3, 5–13.

sacrificial operation designed to draw off U.S. carrier squadrons and thus leave Allied surface forces vulnerable to a giant *kamikaze* assault. The force included the 72,000-ton superbattleship *Yamato* supported by only one light cruiser and eight destroyers. The *Yamato* lacked oil to return from Okinawa; if it had reached the island, it would have been beached and its eighteen-inch cannon employed to support the ground forces. On April 7, hundreds of U.S. planes caught the pathetic little Japanese flotilla only 175 miles from Kyushu. Bombs and torpedoes tore apart the *Yamato,* the cruiser, and four of the destroyers, with a total loss of about 3,700 men. The sacrifice was in vain. Only about one hundred *kamikaze* planes were able to sortie that day, damaging merely three American warships. Although psychologically understandable, the operation spelled the end of the Japanese navy.[43]

## THE SUZUKI CABINET AND INTENSIFICATION OF THE AIR WAR

Almost three and a half years after the outbreak of the Pacific War, none of Japan's enemies (the United States, Britain, and China) or its potential enemy (the Soviet Union) was remotely near capitulation. Instead, one of its allies, Italy, had surrendered, and the other, Germany, was all but defeated by April 1945. With Iwo Jima in enemy hands in March and the "last battle" being waged on Okinawa, the ineffective General Koiso, after stumbling along since July 1944, stepped down as prime minister on April 5, with a recommendation to the throne that he be succeeded by a powerful "IGHQ cabinet." None of the service chiefs favored Koiso's idea, and so the choice fell to Admiral Suzuki Kantarō, president of the Privy Council, who was seventy-nine years old, hard of hearing, and nonpolitical. No one could be sure whether Suzuki intended to wage a decisive struggle to the death or to make peace. He gave reassurances to the high command that the war would continue, but he also convinced his foreign minister, Tōgō Shigenori, that diplomacy would have a free hand.[44]

The Supreme War Direction Council agreed formally on April 30 to

43 BBSS, *Okinawa hōmen rikugun sakusen,* chap. 8; BBSS, *Hondo hōmen kaigun sakusen,* pt. 4, chap. 1 (p. 4); BBSS, *Okinawa hōmen kaigun sakusen,* chap. 4; BBSS, *Hondo kessen junbi* (1), pp. 286–90.

44 Gaimushō, *Shūsen shiroku,* chaps. 17, 19; Shimomura Kainan, *Shūsenki* (Tokyo: Kamakura bunko, 1948), pp. 3–13; Tōgō, *The Cause of Japan,* pp. 268–71; *Shōwa shi no tennō* (hereafter *SSNT*), 30 vols. (Tokyo: Yomiuri shinbunsha, 1967–75), vol. 1, pp. 292–336.

continue the hostilities.[45] If reason had played a part, the collapse of the Third Reich in May should have provided the rationale for a decision to end the war. Doom stalked from the skies as the Americans mounted air attacks on the home islands using the B-29 Superfortress, a powerful land-based bomber with a range exceeding 3,000 miles, a speed of 350 miles per hour, and a bomb load of more than eight tons. Japanese fighter planes encountered difficulty in climbing to the 30,000 feet of the bombers' daylight raids; only a few interceptors were able to make more than one pass at the B-29 formations. Night fighter units, ineffectually equipped and trained, could not cope with the medium-altitude night raids that the Americans mounted with overwhelming fury from February 1945. The Japanese warning system and ground control of interceptor operations were notoriously poor; there was a lack of early warning radar of effective quality or adequate quantity. The army and the navy failed to cooperate in the air defense. According to U.S. Twentieth Air Force records, only seventy-four B-29s were lost in 31,387 sorties between June 1944 and August 1945, a loss percentage of 0.24. It must be admitted, however, that after April 1945 the Japanese high command ordered the conservation of aircraft for defense against invasion of the homeland.

A total of sixty-six Japanese cities, congested and flammable, were devastated by B-29 incendiary raids. With the introduction of low-level night raids, blind bombing began to supplant attacks against strictly military targets. The scale of the B-29 assaults, which often lasted more than two hours, was staggering to the Japanese: May 23 – Tokyo, 520 bombers; May 25 – Tokyo, 564; May 29 – Yokohama, 450; July 8–10 – Sendai, and so forth, 497; July 12–13 – Utsunomiya, and so forth, 506; July 24 – Osaka–Nagoya, 599; July 28 – Tsu, and so forth, 562; August 1–2 – Nagaoka, and so forth, 766. The capital was leveled by particularly catastrophic bomber raids on February 25 and March 10, which took tens of thousands of civilian lives. "Tokyo has finally become scorched earth," the emperor lamented.

It has been calculated that the B-29s destroyed 40 percent of Osaka and Nagoya; 50 percent of Tokyo, Kobe, and Yokohama; and 90 percent of Aomori. At least 241,000 persons died, and 313,000 were injured in the raids against the homeland. Conventional bombing killed almost as many people as did the two atomic bombs in August. The evacuation of the major urban centers, begun in 1944, was intensi-

45 This body (*Saikō sensō shidō kaigi*), made up of the highest civilian, military, and naval leaders, was established in August 1944. It met in the presence of the emperor on crucial occasions.

fied the next year. Absenteeism at war factories grew to 70 or 80 percent. Those who survived the raids recall the tension, exhaustion, and lassitude brought on by the incessant alarms and alerts.[46]

## TOWARD A DECISIVE BATTLE

By the spring of 1945, Imperial General Headquarters expected enemy offensives against Taiwan, central and perhaps south China, Hainan, south Korea, and the Kuril Islands. Japan itself was being isolated from the Asian continent and the southwest Pacific, and attrition of production resources had begun. The main naval, air, and field forces were being engaged and destroyed, and the homeland was being brought within range of land-based fighter planes. If the situation continued to deteriorate rapidly, an invasion of Japan might be anticipated as early as the summer of 1945.

In fact, defensive preparations in the homeland were deplorable. There were labor shortages, and difficulties with mobilization and billeting, food and ordnance, jurisdiction and duties. Civilian war weariness was deepening. Coastal defenses were behind schedule, and secondary sectors were still in the planning stage. Because the high command had drafted no definitive guidelines for the Kantō region, most of the defense works there were inadequate or worthless. Weapons were poor; manpower quality was deteriorating; ammunition was short; and training levels were primitive. The transfer of troops and munitions from the continent grew extremely difficult in the face of Allied surface, air, submarine, and sea mining actions. By July, enemy warships dared to penetrate Hokkaido waters and bombarded land targets at Muroran Bay, Kamaishi, and Hakodate. Interservice controversies complicated the situation, particularly concerning homeland air defense operations.

Imperial General Headquarters labored throughout the spring and summer of 1945 to activate new ground and air units, to bring some forces home from the Kwantung Army, to transfer others from China to Korea and Manchuria, to husband precious fuel and aircraft, and to improve fortified belts. Although the China Expeditionary Army had been advocating a "last push" against Chungking, the central authorities in Japan demurred and ordered the redeployment of troops against possible enemy landings along the China coast. The high command

46 BBSS, *Hondo bōkū sakusen*, pts. 1–5; BBSS, *Hondo hōmen kaigun sakusen*, pt. 4, chap. 2; Hayashi Shigeru, *Nihon shūsenshi*, 3 vols. (Tokyo: Yomiuri shinbunsha, 1962), vol. 3, pp. 66–78.

expected that sometime after the fall of 1945 the Americans' main invasion effort would come against the Kantō Plain in Japan or against Kyushu and then the Kantō district. Although some expected the Soviets to intervene militarily in Manchuria when the Japanese homeland was in danger, others guessed that the Soviet Union would not be able to undertake a new war so soon after surviving the hostilities against Nazi Germany. At least, it was hoped, there was still some breathing space if the Soviet Union gave one year's notice to abrogate the Neutrality Pact of 1941, which was not scheduled to expire until April 1946.

Unable to shore up the tattered inner perimeter, military leaders called for a decisive battle in the homeland. The navy had been destroyed, but its support was no longer needed. The army still had about 5.5 million men, 169 infantry divisions, 4 tank divisions, and 15 air divisions, including scraped-together training units. Of the total of nine thousand operational aircraft, six thousand were held in reserve for the final battle. The way to certain victory, stressed Army Chief of Staff Umezu in mid-1945, lay in making everything on imperial soil contribute to the war effort and in combining the nation's total fighting strength, both material and spiritual, to annihilate the invaders. The fostering of a metaphysical will was the first rule; above all, a vigorous spirit of attack was required.

In keeping with the "bamboo spear psychology," the Diet passed the Volunteer Military Service Law mobilizing all males between 15 and 60 and all females between 17 and 40. The public was exhorted to pit flesh against iron, spirit against matériel, in the Japanese tradition of despising surrender. Defense plans centered on the mass use of special-attack tactics by regulars and guerrillas, and aggressive beach-line defense and death-defying combat. If by welding together the entire population, the Japanese could force the Americans to comprehend the tremendous manpower costs of an invasion, it might be possible to end the war on terms far better than unconditional surrender. The home islands, after all, were not the little atolls that had already cost the enemy dearly, nor was there any prospect that Japanese shipping could be destroyed or that all air bases could be eliminated. The Japanese army knew every cranny in the homeland and could prepare in depth beforehand against a foe of questionable stamina whose supply lines would be stretched to the maximum.

Imperial General Headquarters strategists sought a silver lining in the darkening clouds. Although the end of the war in Europe had given the United States a comfortable reserve of national war potential, they argued that a desire to "grab postwar profits" had already led to industrial demobilization. American fighting morale was being weakened by the fear of huge casualties. There had been an increase in labor strife, criticism of the military, and agitation from the ranks to engage in a precipitous demobilization. Should the United States be defeated in the assault on Japan itself, public confidence in the president and military leaders would decline abruptly; its fighting spirit would deteriorate in a flurry of recriminations; and Japan would find itself in a much more favorable strategic position.

Public pessimism was taboo, but privately Japanese military leaders were far from sanguine. Despite boasts about chances for a successful defense of the home islands, they had no real confidence of defeating second and third waves launched continuously, even if the American initial landing could be frustrated. When they appraised conditions objectively and concretely, the high command staff officers sensed that it would be impossible to defeat the invasion because Japan lacked weapons, ammunition, and foodstuffs. Increasingly, they realized that only one battle, the struggle for Kyushu, could ever be waged in practice. Lieutenant Colonel Fujiwara Iwaichi summed up the army's outlook in the summer of 1945:

> Relying for the most part on the suicidal bravery, ardent patriotism and fierce loyalty of the people, Japan prepared to wage the final decisive battle against an enemy far superior in both technical resources and manpower. In spite of the odds building against them, the Japanese people well knew that if their leaders were determined to carry out decisive combat on the sacred soil of the homeland, there was no alternative but to fight to the bitter end.

Added an Imperial General Headquarters staff officer: "We merely prepared for the final operations with the philosophy that we must fight in order to glorify our national and military traditions, that it was an engagement which transcended victory or defeat."[47]

## JAPAN IN EXTREMIS

By the summer of 1945, Allied pressure on Japan, from air and sea, grew so severe that it amounted to near-strangulation of the economy. In June, at a cabinet advisers' briefing at Premier Suzuki's residence, one elder statesman asked, "What if the enemy does not invade this year or next but instead pursues a policy of wiping out Japan by bombardment alone?" The Army's briefing officer was obliged to

47 BBSS, *Hondo kessen junbi* (1), chaps. 2–11; ibid. (2), chaps. 2–7; BBSS, *Hondo hōmen kaigun sakusen*, pt. 4, chap. 3; Hayashi Saburō, *Taiheiyō sensō*, chaps. 19, 21 (p. 3).

admit, with painful candor, that "that would pose the most troublesome course which could be adopted against us."

There was fear that the Americans might attempt to deepen Japan's worsening food crisis by razing its rice fields with a massive incendiary bombardment just before harvest time. The ineffectiveness of the air defense system also meant that portions of the homeland might soon be isolated from one another as unrelenting enemy air raids crippled the overtaxed and vulnerable transportation network. Aviation fuel reserves had dwindled to a point that there was not enough for all available planes to mount a final sortie. Oil had become more precious than blood.[48]

As an army general staff planner admitted at a secret conference on July 25, national strength and combat effectiveness had been decreasing day by day; the conduct of the war had become hopeless. Nevertheless, when the United States, Britain, and China issued the Potsdam Declaration calling for Japan's unconditional surrender on July 26, the authorities in Tokyo dared not move rapidly to terminate hostilities. The Allied leaders had warned that they would brook no delay, but the official response was to ignore the terms publicly while covertly requesting clarification and revision. Although the emperor had asserted unhesitatingly that the text of the Potsdam Declaration, as explained by Tōgō, was acceptable in principle, the government still attempted to conduct routine diplomacy at the eleventh hour. Hope was nurtured, for example, that the Soviet Union, which had not coauthored the Potsdam document, might serve as honest broker and intermediary.[49]

The consequences of the decision not to accept the Potsdam Declaration were calamitous for the Japanese. Whether from misunderstanding or a search for a pretext, both the Americans and the Soviets seized upon the presumable "rejection" of the terms to justify unlimited violence unleashed against tottering Japan. At 8:15 A.M. on August 6, after the all-clear had been sounded from an earlier reconnaissance alert, a single B-29 dropped the world's first atomic combat weapon on the city of Hiroshima. Between 130,000 and 200,000 people perished in agony or suffered horrible injury. The city ceased to exist.

With all communications severed, military authorities in the Hiroshima district could not notify Tokyo until the afternoon of August 6

48 Hayashi Shigeru, *Nihon shūsenshi*, vol. 3, pp. 52–65; Hayashi Saburō, *Taiheiyō sensō*, p. 242; *SSNT*, vol. 2, pp. 19–22.

49 Gaimusho, *Shūsen shiroku*, chaps. 35–36, 44, 46, 50; Tōgō, *The Cause of Japan*, pp. 304–14; *SSNT*, vol. 3, pp. 247–412; Shimomura, *Shūsenki*, pp. 87–94.

that a bomb of unprecedented destructive power had been employed by the enemy. The next day President Harry S Truman confirmed publicly that the weapon was atomic and warned that worse was in store unless the war was ended. The central government leaders were torn between skepticism and fear of revealing the possible truth to the populace. The newspapers of August 8 carried only a simple Imperial General Headquarters communiqué that Hiroshima had suffered considerably from a "new type of bomb." Meanwhile, investigations were conducted by intelligence, ordnance, medical, and scientific experts. On August 9 the high command received a report that a special kind of bomb had indeed been used but that burns could be prevented if one's body were covered. The local army headquarters indicated that people wearing white clothing and those hiding in air raid shelters had been burned only slightly, and that the huge fires were attributable to the fact that the bomb was dropped while the inhabitants were preparing breakfast. The army was not only trying to prevent panic but was also hoping to play down the effects of atomic weapons on existing plans for the decisive campaign in the homeland.[50]

Even before the field team's report arrived from Hiroshima, Foreign Minister Tōgō decided to recommend to the throne that the Potsdam Declaration be accepted immediately. When the emperor received him on the afternoon of August 8, the foreign minister conveyed everything that was known about the disaster, from both Japanese and enemy sources, and recommended that peace be sought right away. The monarch agreed that continuation of the war was hopeless and warned that precious time would be lost if attempts at bargaining were continued. Inconceivably, an emergency meeting of the Supreme War Direction Council was delayed because some members were reportedly unable to attend.

Troubles came not singly to Japan. Early on August 9, Foreign Ministry radio monitors picked up a Soviet broadcast announcing that the Soviet Union had declared war on Japan and that the Red Army was invading Manchuria. A cable from the Japanese ambassador in Moscow never reached Tokyo. Official word was not conveyed to the Foreign Ministry by the Soviet ambassador until August 10, two days after Soviet forces launched attacks not only on Manchuria but also on south Sakhalin, the Kurils, and Korea.

50 BBSS, *Hondo bōkū sakusen*, pp. 626–43; *SSNT*, vol. 4, pp. 77–316; Hayashi Shigeru, *Nihon shūsenshi*, vol. 3, pp. 80–95; Tōgō, *The Cause of Japan*, pp. 314–16; Shimomura, *Shūsenki*, pp. 94–9; Matsumura Shūitsu, *Sensen kara shūsen made*, new ed. (Tokyo: Shinchōsha, 1969), pp. 15–66; Gaimushō, *Shūsen shiroku*, chap. 37.

Many Japanese sources assert that the shock of the Soviet Union's "betrayal" – the violation of the remaining term of the Neutrality Pact of 1941 – caused greater consternation than did the news of the obliteration of Hiroshima by a single bomb. On learning of the Soviet invasion, War Minister Anami Korchika observed that "the inevitable has come at last." When Premier Suzuki asked Ikeda Sumihisa, the chief of the Cabinet Planning Board, whether the Kwantung Army was capable of repulsing the Soviets, Ikeda replied that the situation was hopeless. "Is the Kwantung Army that weak?" the prime minister sighed. "Then the jig is up."

While the Supreme War Direction Council was arguing about conditions for accepting the Potsdam Declaration in principle, a B-29 dropped the second atomic weapon, often called "the unnecessary bomb," on the city of Nagasaki at 11:30 A.M. on August 9. Approximately 80,000 to 100,000 were killed, injured, or left missing. The Japanese army announced that the Nagasaki bomb was not formidable and that the military had "countermeasures." The high command, Anami assured the cabinet on the same day, did not believe the war was lost. Together with Army Chief of Staff Umezu and Navy Chief of Staff Toyoda Teijirō, he spoke vigorously in favor of fighting on or at least of obtaining better conditions. Although victory was not certain, total defeat was by no means inevitable. Meanwhile, Japanese intelligence learned from imaginative Allied prisoners of war that the Americans possessed a hundred of the fantastic new bombs and that Tokyo was marked for final erasure.

The decision to surrender was made, in essence, by the emperor in the early hours of August 10. Unexpectedly asked by Prime Minister Suzuki to render his decision and thus break a deadlock in the cabinet, the monarch stated that he accepted Tōgō's recommendation to accept the Potsdam terms. The planning of the army and the navy had been "erroneous and untimely," despite the avowed intention to wage a decisive campaign on homeland soil, and the air raids were increasing in severity. "To subject the people to further suffering, to witness the destruction of civilization, and to invite the misfortune of mankind, are entirely contrary to my wishes." Disarmament of the loyal armed forces and indictment of citizens as war criminals were indeed painful to contemplate, but it was inevitable for the salvation of the country. Japan must bear the unbearable.

Nevertheless, the military and the government remained in conflict. As late as August 12, Umezu and Toyoda (without consulting Navy Minister Yonai) had recommended to the emperor that the government resolutely reject the enemy's clarification of terms, which called for the emperor's subordination to the authority of a Supreme Commander, Allied Powers. The high command judged that the foe intended to make Japan a tributary state and to debase the dignity of the throne, the apex of the national polity (*kokutai*). Despite these complications, the policy of seeking peace proceeded. On the morning of August 14, the emperor demanded and received military and naval compliance from the highest officers on active duty available. Shortly afterward, in an emotional Imperial Conference, the last of the war, the monarch bravely reiterated his decision for peace, in order to preserve the country's national polity and to save the population from annihilation. If necessary, he would personally appeal to the armed forces to maintain order.

On the night of August 14, the emperor signed and affixed his seal to the rescript ending the war. The cabinet then countersigned the document. Diehard army opponents of surrender in Tokyo tried to reverse the decision by force that same night but were foiled by elements loyal to the government. At noon on August 15, in an unprecedented radio broadcast, the voice of the emperor conveyed to the public in elliptical language the word of the decision to lay down arms instead of defending the homeland to the death.

Prime Minister Suzuki resigned on August 15 and was replaced by Prince Higashikuni Naruhiko on August 17. The surrender of Japan, attested to by the new foreign minister, Shigemitsu Mamoru, on behalf of the emperor and government and by General Umezu for the armed forces, took place formally aboard the American battleship *Missouri* in Tokyo Bay on September 2, 1945.[51]

## OVERVIEW

By any standard of measurement, Japan paid an enormous price in human and material terms for its part in the Pacific War.[52] The main

51 Gaimushō, *Shūsen shiroku*, chaps. 43, 54; Shimomura, *Shūsenki*, pp. 113–68; BBSS, *Hokutō hōmen rikugun sakusen* (2), pts. 1–2; BBSS, *Hondo bōkū sakusen*, pp. 646–50; BBSS, *Kantōgun* (2), chaps. 7, 8; Tōgō, *The Cause of Japan*, pp. 316–39; *Man-Mō shūsenshi* (Tokyo: Kawade shobō shinsha, 1962), pt. 1, chaps. 1, 2.

52 Japanese army wartime casualties have been estimated at 1.525 million to 1.675 million. The higher figure includes 1.140 million killed, 295,000 wounded, and 240,000 whose fate is unknown. Japanese navy records list 420,000 dead or missing and 9,000 disabled, for a total of 429,000. In addition, 31,000 merchant sailors were killed in action, an estimated casualty rate of 43 percent.

Civilian casualties have been placed at 300,000 dead and 24,000 missing in the homeland. Over 99 percent of these losses were caused by air bombing. Estimates of the injured range as proximate causes of that war have long been understood, although unevenly assessed: the China conflict, dependence on external sources of energy, and ties with the Axis powers. Nevertheless, once the war began, the exuberance of the early phase tended to obscure fundamental Japanese disadvantages that ultimately proved fatal against a superpower like the United States.

Half of the population, for example, was engaged in feeding the country, but 20 percent of the annual rice demand still had to be imported. In 1941, a relatively benign year, the total food level could support an average caloric intake, which was little more than 6 percent above the accepted minimum for subsistence. Yet between 1930 and 1940, the population of the home islands had increased by about 10 million, to more than 73 million, including the armed forces. By 1944 the total population exceeded 77 million. The standard of living, already in decline since the outset of the China conflict in 1937, fell catastrophically afterward. As a fraction of the gross national product, consumer expenditures were reduced by 37 percent in 1944. By the end of the Pacific War, Japan was isolated and on the brink of starvation.[53]

To cope with its huge civil and military requirements, the Japanese possessed what can best be termed a pygmy economy. Steel and coal production, at most, amounted to only one-thirteenth that of the United States; munitions production was never more than 10 percent. Productive capacity, vulnerable and essentially unenlarged, was insufficient to support the wartime demand. The military services never obtained their main production targets. Gross national product and real output rose unimpressively during the war years, although military expenditures consumed about 85 percent of national income by 1945.

To make up for deficiencies in raw materials by drawing on the resources of the conquered colonies of Southeast Asia, it was imperative that import-oriented Japan maintain a giant merchant fleet and keep the sea lanes open. Neither prerequisite was met as the wartime years went

high as 625,000. In Manchuria and China, after the war ended, 170,000 civilians are thought to have died; in Okinawa, 165,000.

In major naval categories, the loss-to-survival numbers were as follows: battleships – 8/4; aircraft carriers – 19/6; cruisers – 36/11; destroyers – 133/41; submarines – 131/59.

Aircraft wastage of all types amounted to about 20,000 in combat, 10,000 in training accidents, 20,000 attributable to other noncombat causes, and 4,000 planes to miscellaneous reasons. Gaimushō, *Shūsen shiroku*, app. 18; BBSS, *Hondo bōkū sakusen*, pp. 659–66; Shimomura, *Shūsenki*, p. 19; Hayashi Shigeru, *Nihon shūsenshi*, vol. 3, pp. 70, 72–3; *GSS, Taiheiyō sensō* (5) (1975), vol. 39, pp. 803, 820–3.

53 Gaimushō, *Shūsen shiroku*, app., pp. 41–2; Jerome B. Cohen, *Japan's Economy in War and Reconstruction* (Minneapolis: University of Minnesota Press, 1949), pp. 52, 56, 287–8. Also see Thomas R. H. Havens, *Valley of Darkness: The Japanese People and World War Two* (New York: Norton, 1978), chap. 7.

by. Because Japan had 6.35 million tons of available merchant shipping in 1941 – double the minimum amount deemed necessary – new construction remained relatively low. By the end of 1942, about 1.25 million tons had already been lost to enemy action, a scale of decrease that grew steadily worse: 2.56 million tons were lost in 1943, 3.48 million tons in 1944. By the war's end in 1945, Japan had only 2.6 million tons of shipping left, of which one-third was unserviceable. Premier Higashikuni told the Imperial Diet in September 1945 that "the basic cause of defeat was the loss of transport shipping."[54]

Japan's military and naval failures in the Pacific War inevitably exacerbated the underlying national weaknesses. Obsessed by the notion of surface engagements between grand fleets as in 1905 and 1916, the battleship admirals neglected the protection of merchantmen and downplayed the role of the submarine. Although the Japanese "Long Lance" torpedo far surpassed the capabilities of U.S. torpedoes in the initial stages of the war, Japanese submarine operations in general proved to be a dismal failure. In addition, both the army and navy underestimated the Allied ability to conduct air operations against Japanese industry and urban centers. The B-29 bomber was never countered successfully. That Japan was wide open to aerial bombardment, remarked Foreign Minister Shigemitsu, "came as a thunderbolt to the whole nation."

The Japanese themselves did not develop a strategic air command capable of sustained and heavy raids at long range against economic targets or rear zones. Apart from the attack on Pearl Harbor, the best that could be done was to dispatch carrier-borne planes against Darwin and Townsville in Australia and Colombo and Trincomalee in Ceylon; submarines against Sydney Harbor in Australia and Santa Barbara in California; and, strangest of all, thousands of ineffective little balloon bombs against North America. There was hope of perfecting "miracle weapons" such as atomic or bacteriological devices, but the comparatively low state of Japanese science and technology could not turn out weapons that were realistic or timely. The desperation of Japanese tacticians is demonstrated by the wasteful and indecisive commitment of thousands of *kamikaze* pilots in the Philippines and Okinawa campaigns.

54 BBSS, *Kaijō goeisen* (1971), charts 1–2, 6–8; Gaimushō, *Shūsen shiroku*, app., p. 27; Hayashi Shigeru, *Nihon shūsenshi*, vol. 3, p. 186; *GSS*, *Taiheiyō sensō* (5) (1975), vol. 39, pp. 803–26; Cohen, *Japan's Economy*, pp. 51 ("pygmy economy"), 52–8; Toyama Saburō, "Lessons from the Past," U.S. Naval Institute *Proceedings* (September 1982): 68; Shōda Tatsuo, *Jūshintachi no Shōwa shi*, 2 vols. (Tokyo: Bungei shunjūsha, 1981), pp. 335–6.

The Japanese also did not devise a joint-command system. After 1941–2, interservice cooperation and coordination were largely nominal. Rivalry and hostility were worsened by the customary contempt for and neglect of logistical considerations, despite the demands of a fast-moving war. Although the soldiers, sailors, and airmen fought with great tenacity, courage, and devotion, the quality of Japanese commanders was undistinguished. The Imperial General Headquarters seemed to excel only at shuffling forces and devising evacuations. Certainly the configuration of the atolls in the Pacific militated against maneuver and set-piece engagements, but when sizable forces were committed on landmasses, disaster also ensued in the face of superior firepower, mobility, and air cover, as at Imphal and Leyte.[55]

On the geostrategic level, Japanese thinking was characterized by wishful thinking, preconceptions, and insufficient attention to material factors. Less than helpful guidance, for example, was provided by the vague directives governing crucial phase-three operations: to intercept and destroy any attacking force that might threaten the strategic defense perimeter and to activate plans to destroy the American will to fight. Their early successes lulled the Japanese into a false sense of security. For far too long, they tended to think in terms of the outclassed Allied forces originally encountered in Southeast Asia and China. When Imperial General Headquarters bestirred itself to rethink strategy toward the end of 1943, it was too late. In addition, coalition planning and operations, concerted with the Germans, were nearly nonexistent.[56]

The Japanese had had no intention of conquering the United States. Compromise terms were the most that could ever have been expected, especially after the Allies called for unconditional surrender in 1943. From the objective point of view, as early as mid-1942 the more

55 Umihara Osamu, *Senshi ni manabu* (Tokyo: Asagumo shinbunsha, 1970), pp. 73–139; Mamoru Shigemitsu, *Japan and Her Destiny*, ed. F. S. G. Piggott, trans. Oswald White (London: Hutchinson, 1958), pp. 324–5; Toyama, "Lessons," pp. 68–9; Paul S. Dull, *A Battle History of the Imperial Japanese Navy (1941–1945)* (Annapolis, Md.: U.S. Naval Institute, 1978), pp. 103–11; Hayashi Saburō, *Taiheiyō sensō*, pp. 189–92.

56 BBSS, *Nantō hōmen kaigun sakusen* (1), pt. 1, chap. 6; BBSS, *Nansei hōmen kaigun sakusen*, pp. 85–9, 171, 176–7, 227; BBSS, *Ran-in Bengaru wan hōmen kaigun shinkō sakusen*, chap. 5 (p. 13); Hara, *Teikoku kaigun*, p. 7; Imai Takeo in Nihon gaikō gakkai, ed., *Taiheiyō sensō shūketsuron* (Tokyo: Tokyo daigaku shuppankai, 1958), chap. 2; Takagi, *Taiheiyō sensō*, pp. 139–43; Hayashi Saburō, *Taiheiyō sensō*, pp. 109–14. Also see Toyama Saburō, *Daitōa sensō to senshi no kyōkun* (Tokyo: Hara shobō, 1979); Hata Ikuhiko, *Taiheiyō sensō: roku dai kessen: naze Nihon wa yaburetaka* (Tokyo: Yomiuri shinbunsha, 1976); Fukudome Shigeru, *Kaigun no hansei* (Tokyo: Nihon shuppan kyōdō, 1951); Takayama Shinobu, *Sanbō honbū sakusenka: Sakusen ronsō no jissō to hansei* (Tokyo: Fuyō shobō, 1978), chap. 6; Umihara, *Senshi ni manabu*, pp. 5–42.

sensitive Japanese leaders knew that the only long-range hope for the country's salvation lay in a quick settlement of the war, on as favorable terms as possible. The emperor, for one, told the Privy Seal that after he learned of the results of the battle of Midway, prospects were "not bright." But as long as Tōjō remained premier, until 1944, nothing came of the monarch's hope for an early peace, although dealing from a position of strength was not to Japan's advantage beyond the first phase of hostilities, as Admiral Yamamoto had warned.

The rising Allied preponderance of tridimensional strength in the Pacific, already visible in the counteroffensives of 1942–3, became overwhelming as the defeat of Germany drew near. Allied forces were becoming available for transfer to the Far East, and the Soviets' entry into the Pacific War became more probable. In April 1944 Prince Mikasa suggested that the military leaders consider declaring Kyoto and Nara open cities. With the loss of Saipan in July 1944, the chief of naval staff later stated, "Hell was upon us." Upon hearing of the defeat in the Marianas, Imperial Guard Division Commander Mutō Akira told his aide, "Japan is defeated." When Iwo Jima was about to fall in March 1945, the deputy chief of staff warned that "Tokyo will become a battleground in a month."[57]

Although there was thus no dearth of realism in appraising Japan's chances for "victory" in the Pacific War, there was the problem of "being defeated gracefully." Japan as a nation had had no experience with invasion, capitulation, or foreign occupation. According to Colonel Obata Kazuyoshi, an Eighteenth Army staff officer, "It was thought that the struggle for the homeland would be difficult and would require years but, with the help of [the Kwantung Army in] Manchuria, would be fought to a draw." When Marquis Kido learned of the high command's high-sounding but impractical talk of a "decisive battle," he wondered whether Japan's chances were even "fifty-fifty": The army and navy seemed to be resisting out of "sheer obstinacy." It was well known to the leaders that the Kwantung Army had been enfeebled by the withdrawal of forces and equipment to various locations in the Pacific theater and Japan, leaving Manchuria helpless when the Soviet invasion came.[58]

In short, the Japanese leadership's decisions for war in 1941 and for capitulation in 1945 were colored by emotionalism. It was far easier to start the war than to end it, given the ascendancy of the short-sighted

57 Shōda, *Jūshintachi*, pp. 319–21; Alvin D. Coox, *Japan: The Final Agony* (New York: Ballantine, 1970), pp. 8, 10. 58 Coox, *Japan*, pp. 86–87, 100, 153.

hawks and the timidity of the doves. Japanese conduct of hostilities was characterized by calculated risk, gambles, intuition, inflexibility, and poorly defined objectives. In view of the pigheadedness to the last by many members of the high command, it is remarkable that the country somehow escaped the complete catastrophe promised by U.S. Air Force General Curtis LeMay in 1945: "We had two or three weeks of work left on the cities, a bit more to do on precision targets, and were just getting started on transportation. Another six months and Japan would have been beaten back into the Dark Ages."[59]

LeMay's tough language was typical of Western wartime propagandists and postwar prosecutors. The Allied Occupation authorities and the International Military Tribunal for the Far East (IMTFE) charged the Japanese with cunning, bestiality, and conspiracy in waging an illegal war of aggression. The alleged criminality was traced back to the Manchurian incident of 1931 by the Americans and to the Russo-Japanese War of 1904–5 by the Soviets. Indeed, use of the old terminology of "Greater East Asia War" (*Dai Tōa sensō*) was prohibited, and "Pacific War" (*Taiheiyō sensō*) replaced it officially.

Since Japan's recovery of sovereignty in 1952, a new outlook on the war has evolved in Japanese historians', journalists', and veterans' circles. A large number of widely read books and articles have resurrected the term "Greater East Asia War," on the grounds that "Pacific War" unduly emphasized the fighting against America and seemed to exclude the long war against China. Among the more famous works employing Greater East Asia War in their title were ex-Colonel Hattori Takushirō's early four-volume history (1953) and Hayashi Fusao's controversial two-volume study (1964–6). The newer literature revealed various strands of thinking about the war of 1941–5: "Greater East Asia War" implied that Japan had a *mission civilisatrice* in Asia; "Pacific War," that it was an aggressor; "imperialistic war," that it became embroiled in capitalistic bandits' struggles for world resources; and "war of liberation," that it nobly freed colonial peoples from Western oppressors.

Hayashi Fusao saw the war of 1941–5 as the culmination of a century of struggle against Western imperialism which began with Commodore Matthew Perry's arrival off Japan in 1853–4. To Ishikawa Tatsuzō, the war was the product of fifty years of "brainwashing" or militaristic education by the Japanese authorities. Others spoke of a fifteen-year

59 Coox, *Japan*, p. 154; Curtis E. LeMay with MacKinlay Kantor, *Mission with LeMay: My Story* (Garden City, N.Y.: Doubleday, 1965), pp. 368–84.

war going back to the Manchurian incident, as the IMTFE prosecutors had charged for other reasons. Usui Katsumi, however, called the idea of a fifteen-year war "monochromatic." He preferred to consider 1937 as the start of the wartime period and to extend the point of termination beyond 1945 in include the entire Occupation period through 1951 or 1952.[60]

In recent times, a bitter controversy arose concerning textbook revision in Japan. Residents of countries that had been invaded and occupied by the Imperial Army were incensed by reports of the softening of language regarding the war, whereby the Ministry of Education certified the "sanitizing" of certain passages in high school texts. Particularly offensive was the playing down of atrocities such as the Rape of Nanking, and the frequent suppression of the harsh wording formerly used to describe "invasion," "aggression," and "thrust." Critics in Japan and abroad feared that governmental attempts to control textbooks represented "part of a well-orchestrated, systematic plan to push the country to the Right." The critics had another profound concern: that survivors of the war would view it with nostalgia and that new generations would glamorize it out of ignorance.[61] In short, the matter of attitudes toward the war of 1941–5 remains vivid in Japan and those countries that it fought, whether the hostilities are termed the Greater East Asia or the Pacific War.

60 Cited works include Hattori Takushirō, *Daitōa sensō zenshi*, 4 vols. (Tokyo: Masu shobō, 1953); Hayashi Fusao, *Daitōa sensō kōteiron*, 2 vols. (Tokyo: Banchō shobō, 1964–6); Ishikawa Tatsuzō, "Kokoro no naka no sensō," *Chūō Kōron*, March 1963; Usui Katsumi, "On the Duration of the Pacific War," *Japan Quarterly*, October–December 1981, pp. 479–88. Also see Tamura Yoshio, ed., *Hiroku daitōa senshi* (Tokyo: Fuji shoen, 1952–5); Ueyama Shunpei, *Daitōa sensō no imi* (Tokyo: Chūō kōronsha, 1964); and the powerful critique by Ienaga Saburō, *Taiheiyō sensō* (Tokyo: Iwanami shoten, 1968).

61 For excellent summaries, see Yamazumi Masami, "Textbook Revision: The Swing to the Right," *Japan Quarterly*, October–December 1981, pp. 472–8; Murata Kiyoaki, "Emotion in Disputes," *Japan Times Weekly*, August 28, 1982; Taro Yayama, "The Newspapers Conduct a Mad Rhapsody over the Textbook Issue," *Journal of Japanese Studies* 9 (Summer 1983): 301–16.

# PART III

# ECONOMIC DEVELOPMENT

CHAPTER 8

# INDUSTRIALIZATION AND TECHNOLOGICAL CHANGE, 1885–1920

## ECONOMIC GROWTH, 1885–1920

The stabilization of the economy following the Matsukata deflation of the early 1880s marks the end of a transitional period in Japan's economic development and the beginning of the initial phase of modern economic growth that continued to the end of World War I. By the mid-1880s the costs of the Restoration and its aftermath had largely been met, and a start had been made on building an economic infrastructure. Although economic activity and life-styles were still scarcely touched by modern technology and organization, the seeds of a modern economic sector in industry, trade, and finance, on which Japan's future was to depend, were being sown.

It is from the 1880s that a reasonably reliable and comprehensive set of quantitative estimates (the LTES series) is available.[1] Prepared in the 1960s and subsequently adjusted in some details, these estimates have provided the material for some sophisticated analyses of Japan's experience.[2] The importance of quantitative data for the description and understanding of economic growth scarcely needs emphasizing. There are, however, caveats regarding these estimates. Although based on the consideration and evaluation of all available data, these estimates have been made into a consistent system by reference to an overall model that makes assumptions about the relationships of the various individual series to one another. Gaps in the data for the period before the late 1880s, moreover, can be filled only on the basis of some preconceptions about the speed and direction of growth. If

1 Ohkawa Kazushi, Shinohara Miyohei, and Umemura Mataji, eds., *Chōki keizai tōkei-suikei to bunseki* (hereafter LTES), 14 vols. (Tokyo: Tōyō keizai shinpōsha, 1965–); Kazushi Ohkawa and Miyohei Shinohara with Larry Meissner, eds., *Patterns of Japanese Economic Development: A Quantitative Appraisal* (New Haven, Conn.: Yale University Press, 1979).

2 Good examples are by Ohkawa and Shinohara, eds., *Patterns of Japanese Economic Development;* Kazushi Ohkawa and Henry Rosovsky, *Japanese Economic Growth: Trend Acceleration in the Twentieth Century* (Stanford, Calif.: Stanford University Press, 1973); and Allen C. Kelley and Jeffrey G. Williamson, *Lessons from Japanese Economic Development. An Analytical Economic History* (Chicago: University of Chicago Press, 1974).

these have resulted in inaccurate estimates for the 1880s, the impression they give of growth rates through the first phase of economic growth will be distorted. In fact, it is likely that as James Nakamura suggested,[3] production in traditional sectors for which information is hard to collect, such as agriculture and handicraft industry, has been seriously underestimated for these years. Despite these reservations, the figures become more reliable for later years and, for most of our period, may be accepted as reliable enough to indicate at least the main outlines of production, expenditure, and employment.[4]

International comparisons of output per capita in the early stages of Japan's economic development are impressionistic at best. Simon Kuznets estimated Japan's output per capita for the late 1870s at $74 in 1965 prices, which is between one-quarter and one-third of the levels in advanced countries at a similar initial stage.[5] Ohkawa thought this figure implausibly low and doubled it. The LTES estimates indicate a figure of $172 for 1887, still very low in comparison with initial levels elsewhere. Those who view the process of economic development in Japan as similar to that in other countries may feel that it should have been higher. Ohkawa and Shinohara believe that it could have been as high as $251 but concede that even in 1887, the Japanese economy was at a relatively low level.

By 1920, the end of the period covered in this chapter, gross domestic product in real terms (1934–6 average prices) had risen 2.8 times since 1885. Output of agriculture, forestry, and fisheries grew by 67 percent; commerce, services, and other by 180 percent; mining and manufacturing by 580 percent; transport, communications, and public utilities by over 1,700 percent; and construction by 170 percent. As a result of these differential rates of growth, the share of agriculture, forestry, and fisheries in total output fell from 42 percent to 25 percent; mining and manufacturing rose from 8 percent to 19 percent; and transport, communications, and public utilities rose from 1.5 percent to almost 10 percent, whereas the shares of other sectors changed little. Within these sectors the composition of output and the technical and organizational features of production changed consider-

3 James I. Nakamura, *Agricultural Production and the Economic Development of Japan* (Princeton, N.J.: Princeton University Press, 1966).

4 For critiques of the early years of the *LTES* series, see Nakamura Takafusa, "Chōki tōkei no seido ni tsuite – 19-seiki Nihon no jakkan no sūji o megutte," *Keizai kenkyū* 30 (January 1979): 1–9; Yasuba Yasukichi, "Senzen no Nihon ni okeru kōgyō tōkei no shinpyōsei ni tsuite," *Ōsaka daigaku keizaigaku* 17 (1977–8). and Nishikawa Shunsaku, " 'Chōki keizai tōkei' no keiryō keizaigaku – Ōkawa hoka *Kokumin shotoku* no tenbō rombun," *Kikan riron keizaigaku* 27 (August 1976):126–34.

5 Simon Kuznets, *Economic Growth of Nations: Total Output and Production Structure* (Cambridge, Mass.: Harvard University Press, 1971), p. 24.

ably. We shall examine these changes in later sections of this chapter, but we note here that although the greatest absolute increases in output came from the large food and textile sections, which were largely traditional in organization and technique, growth was fastest in modern transport and communications and in the metals and machinery industries in which technical change was most rapid.

Over the same period, the uses to which this growing production was put also changed. Personal consumption, which absorbed 85 percent of the rather low output in 1887, increased 2.4 times by 1920, but because total national expenditure had meanwhile increased 2.6 times, the share of personal consumption fell to 76 percent. Gross domestic fixed-capital formation, a major growth-promoting factor, increased over 6 times, and its share of total national expenditure rose from 9 percent to 21 percent. Japan's involvement with the world economy deepened dramatically, with its exports of goods and services and other foreign earnings rising 9.4 times and its payments for imports of goods and services and other current payments abroad rising nearly 12 times.

From 1885 to 1920, the population increased by 45 percent, and so the per-capita rates of increase were not as high as the total growth rates. Thus, although the total output of the Japanese economy (gross domestic product) rose 2.6 times, output per capita of population rose only 1.8 times. The rise in real personal consumption per capita, a rough measure of the rise in average standards of living, was a relatively modest 67 percent. The gainfully employed population rose by some 22 percent. Whereas the number of workers engaged in agriculture and forestry actually fell by about 1 million, the nonagricultural work force doubled from about 6.5 million to about 13 million, with the biggest increase in manufacturing, followed by commerce, transport and communications, and the service industries.

The Japanese government is widely credited with having played a large part in Japan's economic growth. Except during the Sino-Japanese and Russo-Japanese wars, the government's current and capital expenditures, including military expenditures, was between 7 and 11 percent of gross national expenditures, a rather modest proportion by today's standards. The government's role in capital formation, however, was much larger. From 1897 until the private investment boom during World War I, the government was responsible for 30 to 40 percent of all capital investment. Government investment was, moreover, heavily concentrated in the strategic heavy and engineering industries and in facilities such as railways which contributed in a number of crucial ways to the development of modern industry in Japan.

The economy did not grow at a constant speed between 1885 and

1920. Over the whole span of Japan's modern history the rate of growth has tended to accelerate. Along the way, however, there have been marked variations, often described as cycles, which suggests that they are associated with patterns inherent in the growth process itself. These variations were, however, associated also with specific events. For example, the depressing, though salutary, effects of the Matsukata deflation lasted through the mid-1880s. Recovery was then fairly rapid, based mainly on the development of the textile and traditional handicraft industries, railway building, and the stimulus of the Sino-Japanese War. Establishment of the gold standard in 1897 put a brake on expansion, and growth was much slower until about 1903. The Russo-Japanese War then boosted the heavy and engineering industries, and after a short postwar recession, growth picked up again. World War I effectively removed most of the advanced industrialized nations from competition in world markets as well as in the Japanese market, thus providing Japan with the opportunity to substitute domestically produced goods for imports and to increase exports of manufactures despite the relative backwardness of its manufacturing sector. The result was an unprecedented boom in which all sectors of the economy participated, but those industries in the forefront of modern developments, like engineering, shipbuilding, machine tools, and electrical engineering, grew the fastest. Despite a postwar slump and a succession of economic difficulties throughout the 1920s, the World War I boom firmly established the viability of modern industry in Japan. Although the traditional sectors of agriculture and small business were still responsible for the bulk of output and employment, by 1920 the economy's future growth clearly lay with the modern sector.

In the Meiji era, the traditional and modern sectors had grown concurrently. Although the still-small modern industrial system interacted with the existing economy, the relationship had been complementary rather than competitive. By World War I, however, the demands of the rapidly expanding modern sector increasingly conflicted with the needs of the traditional sector which supplied most of the consumers' needs. Thus there came into being a dual or differential economic structure that included a wide range of technology, productivity, wages, scales of production, profit rates, management practices, and forms of industrial organization. There were also characteristic differences in the nature of the markets in which products were sold and from which capital, labor, technology, intermediate goods, and managerial talent were acquired. Governments after the early Meiji era systematically used all the powers at their disposal to promote the growth of modern industry in what they saw as the national interest, even, if necessary, at the expense of the traditional sector. In the long run this policy made Japan into the advanced industrial country that it is today, but by favoring armaments, investment goods, and exports over consumption goods, for a long time government policy kept the living standards of most Japanese lower than they might have been and contributed to the social and political strains of the turbulent 1930s and 1940s and even later.

The availability of quantitative estimates of many aspects of Japan's economic activity tempts observers to explain its growth solely in terms of those quantitative aggregates and the relationships among them. Economic growth is not, however, a natural phenomenon subject to the operation of mindless natural laws but is the result of purposeful human behavior. What were the motives for economic growth and development in Japan? In one sense there were as many motives as there were individual economic decisions. Japan's leaders did not, however, believe that the sum of decisions about what was best for each individual would achieve the national objectives of promoting industrial development, catching up with the West, and becoming a world power. On the contrary, the importance of national policy and its implementation in shaping the course of Japan's economic development were stressed by the government, accepted by the average Japanese, and increasingly acknowledged in the public utterances of businessmen. As Takahashi Korekiyo said in his 1889 farewell to the students of Tokyo Agricultural College, "Gentlemen, it is your duty to advance the status of Japan, bring her to a position of equality with the civilized powers and then carry on to build a foundation from which we shall surpass them all."[6]

Depending on the relative importance ascribed to public and private motives, Japan's experience has been described as either "growth from above" or "growth from below." These two views should not be regarded as mutually exclusive. The production of goods for domestic consumption, for example, was in general the result of individual decisions and market behavior, but it was also influenced by public decisions about the rate of investment relative to consumption and official encouragement to retain traditional Japanese ways of life. Government decisions on defense and defense-related industries, foreign trade and payments, and education affected both the pace and the

6 Reproduced in Takekazu Ogura, *Can Japanese Agriculture Survive?* 2nd ed. (Tokyo: Agricultural Policy Research Institute, 1980), p. 14. Ironically, Takahashi was assassinated by ultranationalists in 1936 for trying to put a brake on government expenditures.

direction of industrial development. Leading entrepreneurs like Iwasaki Yatarō may have been as devoted to personal profit as were their counterparts elsewhere, but that profit depended heavily on the goodwill of the government. Entrepreneurs were constrained by public opinion, sometimes forcibly expressed, to conform to the image of the nationally minded businessman. In general, the state seems to have played an important role in countries like Japan that began their economic development relatively late. Irrespective of judgments about the motives, methods, and outcomes of public policy in Japan, to explain its economic development without referring to these factors would be to tell only part, and probably a misleading part, of the story.

Before World War I, growth from above and growth from below proceeded together. In any case, the modern sector was so small that its growth did not conflict with the expansion and development of the existing traditional economy. On the contrary, each complemented the other. Agriculture and the handicraft industry produced food and consumption goods for a growing population, as well as most of the exports that helped pay for imports of equipment and raw materials needed by modern industry. After the 1890s, modern industry provided inputs such as fertilizers for agriculture and cotton yarn and dyes for cottage weaving. Productivity rose in both traditional and modern occupations. The expansion and improvement of traditional activities still contributed most of Japan's economic growth, if only because of their overwhelming weight in the economy. The modern sectors of industry and commerce were still small, but it was in these that productivity was the highest and was rising the fastest and expansion was the most rapid. By 1920 the further growth of these modern sectors required some sacrifice of the interests of traditional producers. As the modern sectors expanded, their further growth increasingly required resources to be transferred from less productive traditional employments to new and more productive activities. The further this transfer proceeded, the faster was the growth of total output. This "trend acceleration"[7] became particularly noticeable after the Pacific War, but before World War I the modern sector was still an infant nurtured by the traditional economy rather than the engine of growth that it later became.

This chapter divides at 1913 the period between 1885 and 1920. Before World War I, the building of infrastructure was a large and productive field of investment. Economic growth came mainly from the expansion of existing activities, without any radical innovations in

7 See Ohkawa and Rosovsky, *Japanese Economic Growth*, pp. 39–42.

technology or organization. Most of the developments in the heavy and engineering industries were directly or indirectly related to defense and included government involvement. World War I is treated as a separate phase because it was then that the modern sector, although still small in terms of share of total output, became self-sustaining and began to provide the momentum for further growth. It was also in this period that problems associated with the dual, or differential, structure of the economy began to surface as the interests of new developments began to conflict at some points with those of existing activities.

## BUILDING INFRASTRUCTURE, 1885–1913

From 1885 to 1913, Japan's gross national product grew at an average annual rate of somewhere between 2.6 and 3.6 percent.[8] This growth was mainly achieved not by radical technological change but by the diffusion of existing techniques, a series of small technical improvements, increasing specialization, and an economic climate that rewarded producers better than the pre-Meiji system had done. A substantial contribution to economic growth both at this time and later, however, was made by the heavy investment in infrastructure such as ancillary services like banking, transport and communications, public utilities, education, and economic institutions. With the experience of the advanced industrial countries in front of them, Japan's leaders anticipated and provided for future needs for such infrastructure.

### *Banking*

The early decision, embodied in the National Banking Act of 1872 and its amendment in 1876, to base the Japanese banking system on the American model resulted in the establishment of nearly 150 national banks. Organized as joint stock companies, they were the first modern business enterprises in Japan. Along with a large number of small local quasi banks, the new national banks replaced the traditional system of financing productive industry, commerce, land development, and mining.[9]

8 This rather wide range reflects a corresponding degree of doubt about the estimates' accuracy. Ohkawa and Shinohara's *Patterns of Japanese Economic Development*, based on *LTES*, indicates about 2.7 percent whereas Nakamura Takafusa, *Senzenki Nihon keizai seichō no bunseki* (Tokyo: Iwanami shoten, 1971), pp. 5ff, prefers 3.6 percent.

9 For the development of banking in this period see Hugh T. Patrick, "Japan 1868–1914," in *Banking in the Early Stages of Industrialization*, ed. Rondo Cameron et al. (London: Oxford University Press, 1967), pp. 239–89.

The banks' large issues of inconvertible bank notes, however, contributed to the inflation of 1878–81. Consequently, this privilege was withdrawn as part of the Matsukata deflationary policies of the early 1880s, and a new central bank, the Bank of Japan founded in 1882, was granted the sole right to issue paper currency. Ordinary banking functions were gradually taken over by private commercial banks.

A few private banks were large city banks, such as the Mitsui and Konoike banks, which were part of the premodern financial system, or the Sumitomo and Mitsubishi banks, which originated in the financial operations of the large industrial combines (zaibatsu) and became central to their subsequent expansion. Most private banks, however, were relatively small local banks, of which there were about eighteen hundred by the turn of the century. Much of their capital came from local landowners and businessmen, and they did much to foster local production and development as well as to integrate local activity into the national economy and channel local finance into national projects. Recessions in the early 1900s forced consolidations and takeovers of some small banks, but unit correspondent banking on the United States pattern, rather than branch banking of the British type, was still the rule in Japan up to World War I.[10]

The Japanese banking system was nearly complete around 1900, with the establishment of several special-purpose banks that, although their capital was raised by public subscription, operated under government direction and mobilized longer-term finance for enterprises considered to be in the national interest. These special banks, based on German and French models, included the Hypothec Bank of Japan, the Industrial Bank of Japan, the Hokkaido Colonial Bank, and the Bank of Taiwan. The Industrial Bank in particular raised funds at home and abroad for long-term investment, including direct investment in the promotion of Japanese interests on the Asian mainland. In the absence of a developed bond market, the activity of these special banks was an important source of investment funds, even though political influence over the direction of their investment sometimes led to heavy losses.

A postal savings system, introduced as early as 1875, grew rap-

10 Unit banking is a system in which a large number of banks operate only from their head offices or from a small number of local offices. It is sometimes known as *correspondent banking* because the small unit banks are linked to wider financial markets through correspondent banks that act as their agents and hold their deposits. Branch banking is a system in which a few large banks provide banking services over a wide area through a large number of branches. The Japanese banking system of today, like that of France, is best described as a hybrid of these two types in which branch banking by the major city banks predominates.

idly, especially during and after the Russo-Japanese War, because although interest rates were low, it provided a convenient service to small savers. The government used these substantial funds to finance war expenditures and projects of national importance. Following the Savings Bank Act of 1893, many private savings banks were established, and as they paid a somewhat higher rate of interest than did the postal savings system, they attracted a large amount of deposits.

By World War I the banking system had developed, with the government's encouragement, to a point that it could act as an intermediary between savers and investors. Even before the Meiji era, Japan had a well-developed financial system serving trade and commerce and providing circulating capital for handicraft production as well as loans to domains on the security of their tax revenues. These loans were often for quite long terms and were sometimes employed in land reclamation, public works, or industrial development within the domain.[11] This stock of experience doubtlessly facilitated the establishment of a modern banking system at such a relatively early stage of Japan's economic development, but the new system went far beyond the old one. Banks were the first institutions in Japan to be organized on modern joint stock company lines and to use Western business methods. The early banks acted as promoters of commercial and industrial enterprises and were often the agents through which Western business technology was transferred. By the early twentieth century, moreover, the development of a unified national financial system had greatly reduced regional variation in interest rates. Most loans still went to finance trade, commerce, land improvements, agriculture, and local handicraft production, but the larger city banks, the zaibatsu banks, and the special banks played an increasingly important part in developing new factory industries, raising funds abroad, and financing government deficits. As Hugh Patrick pointed out, Japan's modern banking system did not simply develop in response to the needs of economic growth but was created in advance of demand and played a positive part in facilitating economic development.

## *Railways*

Almost from the start, the Meiji government gave high priority to transport and communications, partly for their commercial value, but

11 See E. S. Crawcour and Kozo Yamamura, "The Tokugawa Monetary System: 1787–1868," *Economic Development and Cultural Change* 18 (July 1970):pt 1, pp. 489–518.

also for their value for administration and internal security. Before World War I this sector absorbed more public and private investment than did any other single industry. The development of railways and shipping services provides good examples of how government and private groups combined in various ways to perform tasks of national importance.

Japan's first railway line, linking Tokyo with the port of Yokohama, was built by the government with funds, materials, and technical services provided by Great Britain through the good offices of the British minister, Harry Parkes. The construction of this line was followed by one linking Ōtsu on Lake Biwa with the port of Kobe via Kyoto and Osaka, and another across Honshū from Tsuruga on the Japan Sea to Handa on Ise Bay via the northern shore of Lake Biwa, Gifu, and Nagoya. When Matsukata Masayoshi became minister of finance in October 1881, however, Japan still had less than two hundred miles of railway in operation. As the result of his sharply deflationary fiscal policy, funds to finance further government railway building were scarce despite a clear national need. In 1880 Iwakura Tomomi persuaded a group of peers to invest their commutation bonds in a company to build a trunk railway from Ueno (Tokyo) north to Aomori. Railways, he told them, were a project of national importance, and as the inner bastion of the Imperial House, they should feel bound to invest in them. Summoning the governors of the prefectures along the proposed route, Iwakura directed them to raise subscriptions from suitable people under their administration, but Matsukata's tight money policy was beginning to bite, and so the response was disappointing.[12] The peers themselves asked for a government guarantee of a 10 percent return on their capital but eventually settled for 8 percent. In 1881 they obtained a railway license providing for nationalization after fifty years. When interest rates fell soon afterwards, the guarantee looked generous. With the announcement of profits of 10 percent on the first section of the line, shares were at a premium and further capital was raised without difficulty. The Ueno–Aomori line was completed in 1892, some three years behind schedule but virtually without foreign technical assistance.

12 See speeches by Itō Hirobumi, Ōkuma Shigenobu, and many others involved in railway projects in the late nineteenth century that appeared in *Tetsudō jihō* between 1899 and 1909 and were reprinted in Tetsudō Jihō Kyoku, ed., *10-nen kinen Nihon no tetsudō ron*. This work is included in Noda Masaho, Harada Katsumasa, and Aoki Eiichi, eds., *Meiji-ki tetsudōshi shiryō*, suppl. vol. 1 (Tokyo: Nihon keizai hyōronsha, 1981).

The government guidelines for private railways issued in 1887 provided for nationalization after twenty-five years. By this time railways were such an attractive investment that over the following decade some twenty railway companies were formed, with capital ranging from ¥40,000 to over ¥13 million, much of it raised from local businessmen. Private lines were built where traffic was the densest, and in the absence of competition, charges could be set high. Interest rates and construction costs fell, and operating costs were well below those of the national railways, as indeed they have been ever since. By licensing private railway companies, the government hoped to get lines built quickly. In this it was not disappointed, but most lines were built to serve local needs or in anticipation of immediate profits, and without a coherent overall plan. The Railway Construction Act of 1892 provided for a coordinated national network of trunk lines financed by issues of railway bonds totaling ¥36 million. From 1883 to 1903, operating track rose from a mere 245 miles, most of it built and operated by the state, to 4,500 miles, of which 70 percent was built and operated by private railway companies.[13]

In the late 1890s the government prepared to acquire the major private railways. When Prime Minister Saionji Kinmochi introduced the Railways Nationalization Bill in 1906, he claimed that the government had always favored state operation of the railways because of their national economic and strategic importance and had licensed private companies only because of fiscal exigencies. Although in the early 1870s there had been some support for private enterprise in principle, by the end of the century the importance of the state's role in national development had become widely accepted. By then, moreover, railways were no longer as profitable as they had once been, and most private companies were happy to accept the rather generous takeover terms. After 1906 the government acquired the assets of seventeen companies, including 2,800 miles of trunk line, for a total of ¥476 million.[14] By 1914 the capital investment of the Imperial Japanese Railways amounted to ¥1.007 million, more than the paid-up capital of all industrial companies combined. Through the World War boom, track in operation increased by about 25 percent, but traffic

13 See Tōyō keizai shinpōsha, ed., *Meiji Taishō kokusei sōran* (Tokyo: Tōyō keizai shinpōsha, 1927), pp. 615–19.

14 For details, see Teishin shō, ed., *Tetsudō kokuyū shimatsu ippan* (1909), reprinted in Takimoto Seiichi and Mukai Shikamatsu, eds., *Nihon sangyō shiryō taikei* (Tokyo: Chūgai shōgyō shinpōsha, 1927), pp. 11, 543–617.

increased much more,[15] and some 90 percent of this traffic was carried by the Imperial Japanese Railways.

The contribution of the railways to Japan's economic development, both then and later, was enormous.[16] They greatly reduced transport costs, thus promoting geographical specialization and mobility of labor and benefiting all sections of the population in the areas they served. They also increased the reach and efficiency of government administration and trained large numbers of engineers and skilled workers.

### *Shipping*

The development of Japan's shipping services is another example of collaboration between the state and private enterprise. During and after the Formosa expedition of 1874, Iwasaki Yatarō's Mitsubishi Company, with the official support of Ōkuma Shigenobu, obtained large subsidies from the government and, with every conceivable form of state aid and protection, used ruthless price cutting to overcome competition from the Imperial Japanese Steamship Mail Company (Nippon teikoku yūbin jōkisen kaisha), itself a recipient of government subsidies. After absorbing this rival, continued subsidies enabled Mitsubishi to eliminate the American Pacific Mail Steamship Company and the British Peninsular and Oriental Steamship Company from coastal steamer traffic, thus obtaining a virtual monopoly. In the climate of the 1881 budget cuts, Ōkuma's opponents in the

15 Table showing traffic increase, 1913–18:

| | 1913 | 1918 |
|---|---|---|
| Freight (million tons/miles) | | |
| National | 3,054 | 5,609 |
| Local | 115 | 334 |
| Total | 3,169 | 5,943 |
| Passengers (million pass./miles) | | |
| National | 3,691 | 6,569 |
| Local | 309 | 687 |
| Total | 4,000 | 7,256 |

*Source:* Tōyō keizai shinpōsha, ed., *Meiji Taishō kokusei sōran* (Tokyo: Tōyō keizai shinpōsha, 1927), pp. 617, 618. Local traffic was calculated from revenue figures on the assumption that local railway charges were the same as those of the national railways.

16 For details, see Tetsudōin, ed., *Honpō tetsudō no shakai oyobi keizai ni oyoboseru eikyō* (Tokyo: Tetsudōin, 1930).

government thought that Iwasaki was overcharging for his well-publicized services to the state and that a good part of the government subsidies granted for specific shipping services were being channeled into other projects of his own choosing and for his own enrichment. In the course of a government-orchestrated public outcry, Iwasaki was pilloried for being a self-centered capitalist entrepreneur when he should have realized that he had been granted the subsidies as an agent of the state. In 1882 the government promoted a new state-subsidized shipping concern, the Kyōdō unyu kaisha. With a capital of ¥6 million subscribed largely by shipowners in the Kansai and Echigo regions, the new company was intended to break the monopoly of the Iwasaki "sea monster," but after two years of wasteful competition that almost broke both companies, a government offer of a guaranteed 8 percent return induced them to merge into the Nippon yūsen kaisha (NYK), with Mitsubishi holding just over half the shares.[17] In 1884, Osaka shipowners led by Sumitomo founded the Ōsaka shōsen kaisha (OSK), which also received an annual subsidy of ¥50,000 to operate routes in and around the Inland Sea.

When NYK began operations in 1885 with 58 steamships totaling some 68,700 tons and 13 sailing ships totaling some 4,700 tons, it was clearly understood that the company was to operate as a semigovernment agency and that its ships were to be at the state's disposal in time of war or emergency. The government also stipulated the routes it was to service among Japan's main ports, as well as to the outer islands, Shanghai, Vladivostok, Inchon, and Tientsin. By 1893 Japan's merchant steamer fleet had grown to 642 vessels, with a total tonnage of 102,352 tons. Meanwhile, NYK had considerably raised its fleet's efficiency and began services to Manila, Hong Kong, Southeast Asian ports, and Australia, with a liner service to Bombay to carry Japanese imports of Indian cotton. Before 1900 many NYK masters and chief engineers were foreigners, but by 1920 all officers were Japanese.

Despite these developments, only 14 percent of the steam tonnage entering Japanese ports in 1893 was Japanese. National flag ships carried only 7 percent of exports and less than 9 percent of imports. After the Sino-Japanese War the Diet passed government-initiated bills for further subsidies. Between the Sino-Japanese War and the

17 For details and an assessment of Iwasaki Yatarō, see Yamamura Kozo, "The Founding of Mitsubishi: A Case Study in Japanese Business History," *Business History Review* 41 (1967): 141–60. For monographic treatment of the NYK line, see William D. Wray, *Mitsubishi and the N.Y.K., 1870–1914: Business Strategy in the Japanese Shipping Industry* (Cambridge, Mass.: Harvard University Press, 1985).

Russo-Japanese War, Japan's merchant steamship tonnage doubled with the help of massive subsidies. Although NYK incurred an operating loss of ¥1.8 million in 1903, it was able to pay a 12 percent dividend, owing to government subsidies amounting to 24.3 percent of its paid-up capital. During the Russo-Japanese War, subsidies fell briefly when partly replaced by generous government charters. In 1909, general subsidies were replaced by subsidies for particular overseas routes specified by the government, which controlled services and freight rates.

Between 1883 and 1913, massive government shipping subsidies expanded the merchant steam fleet from 45,000 tons to 1.577 million tons and raised its share of the tonnage entering Japanese ports to just over 50 percent. The cost to the taxpayer was high, partly because the fleets of established mercantile nations with which Japan was competing were also heavily subsidized. Yet the expenditure was considered justified on grounds of national prestige and security. At the same time the benefits were considerable. Construction and maintenance of the merchant fleet provided a stimulus to the heavy engineering industries at a stage when there was otherwise little demand for their products. The early introduction of shipbuilding technology and skills promoted the development of other branches of engineering and, indeed, modern industry in general, enabling Japanese industry to take full advantage of the opportunities presented by World War I.

### *Posts and telegraphs*

Even before the Meiji Restoration, the effectiveness with which government communicated with the population right down to the individual household and the volume of information so communicated seem to have been exceptional for a society at such a comparatively low level of per capita income. These means of communication, designed primarily to serve the government's needs, were energetically developed over the next three decades.

The number of post offices in Japan roughly doubled from about 3,500 in 1883 to over 7,000 in 1913; the number of postal articles handled increased from just over 100 million in 1882 to 551 million in 1897 and 1,664 million (plus 24 million parcels) in 1912.[18] Over this thirty-year period the number of postal articles (excluding parcels) per

18 The statistical information on posts and telecommunications in this section comes from Tōyō keizai shinpōsha, ed., *Meiji Taishō kokusei sōran*, pp. 672–3.

capita rose from about three a year to thirty-two a year, reflecting both the spread of literacy and the growing need for communication beyond the range of word of mouth. By the eve of World War I, mail usage was comparable to that of European nations.

Japan's first telegraph line was built from Tokyo to Yokohama in 1869, and telegraph services were expanded rapidly after 1890, largely for strategic and administrative purposes. The use of this service also grew quickly. From 2.7 million telegrams sent in 1882, the number rose through the Sino-Japanese War to reach 14 million in 1897 and again through the Russo-Japanese War to 27 million by 1907. By 1913 it had risen again to 40 million.

Telephones were introduced in 1890, with just under 400 subscribers connected to 2 exchanges. Here, too, expansion was rapid, and by 1913 there were over 200,000 subscribers connected to 1,046 exchanges. Over this period the average number of calls per subscriber per day rose from seven to twelve, a rather high figure suggesting that many of the telephones were installed in government or business offices.

By 1912, post offices and telecommunications as a whole employed some 84,000 people. The development of these services and the high circulation of newspapers and magazines indicate that Japan was even then becoming an information-based society. Thus the state acquired in this period the means of effective intervention and control in ways that only forty years earlier would have been beyond the capacity of the most advanced nations of Europe. At the same time these developments speeded the movement of goods and services and facilitated the spread and exchange of ideas.

### *Electric power*

Until the 1880s the main alternative to human effort in Japan was water power, which indeed remained well into the twentieth century an important source of power for food processing, silk reeling, and various handicraft industries. Large modern industrial plants for textiles, metals, machinery, ceramics and food processing, however, were steam-powered from the outset, and by 1887, steam had outstripped water as a source of industrial power. Yet it was not widespread and was so soon replaced by electricity that Japan never experienced a "steam age" like that of Western Europe from the mid-nineteenth century to World War I. The generation and distribution of electric power provided large economies external to individual enterprises and made possible changes in technology, scale, and organization in many industries and even in domestic life, substantially affecting the course of industrialization as a whole.

The first supplies of electric power were for lighting and were provided by private companies that proved extremely profitable from the start. The electric power industry required no state aid or encouragement and was subject to little regulation. The first electric company, the Tokyo Electric Light Company, was formed by Hachisuka Mochiaki and other peers, Shibusawa Eiichi, some of Shibusawa's business associates, and a number of rural businessmen – a group not unlike the backers of early railway development. The company began supplying electricity in 1887 and had installed 21,000 lamps by 1890. With falling charges and more efficient bulbs, electric lighting became increasingly popular. The number of lamps rose from 464,000 in 1905 to over 3 million in 1911 and about 5 million in 1913. Even so, over half of Japanese households were still without electric light. In 1903, electric power companies had a total generating capacity of 25,000 kilowatts. Generators attached to government or private industrial plants and electric railways provided another 25,000 kilowatts, most of which was for power rather than light. By 1913, electric companies produced 80 percent of all electricity. Although two-thirds of their sales were still for lighting, the demand for electricity as a source of power was rising sharply. Between 1911 and 1915, the number of electric motors quadrupled to nearly 43,000, and their total capacity rose from 44,000 horsepower to 182,700 horsepower.

Between the Russo-Japanese War and World War I, electrification was promoted by two technological developments, hydroelectric generation and high-tension transmission. The first hydroelectric generator for public supply had been built in 1892 in connection with a project to provide Kyoto with water by aqueduct from Lake Biwa. By 1910, electric power companies were producing more from hydroelectric than from thermal power, and by World War I, the ratio was two to one. Long-distance transmission technology, introduced into Japan soon after its first use overseas, made possible the development of large hydroelectric sites at a distance from consumption centers. When the Inawashiro Hydroelectric Plant in Fukushima Prefecture was linked to Tokyo in 1914, power was transmitted at 37,500 volts over a distance of 228 kilometers, one of the longest transmission lines in the world at the time.[19]

19 See Minami Ryōshin, *Dōryoku kakumei to gijutsu shinpo: Senzen-ki seizōgyō no bunseki* (Tokyo: Tōyō keizai shinpōsha, 1976), p. 213. Quantitative information on the electric power industry is taken from this work and Minami Ryōshin, *Tetsudō to denryoku*, LTES, vol. 12, 1965

These technological advances, combined with competition among the power companies, kept charges low, especially for lighting, and thus promoted the use of electricity. By buying power from electric companies and replacing cumbersome shaft-and-belt transmission by motors attached to individual machines, manufacturers raised mechanical efficiency and cut direct power costs. Labor and capital costs were sharply reduced as well. The low capital cost of electric motors compared with that of steam engines or generating plants put the use of electric power within the reach of small plants and even many cottage industries. This change led to new relationships between small plants originating in the traditional sector and larger firms based on imported technology and organization. In some cases smaller firms became suppliers or subcontractors to larger modern establishments. In others the market was divided so that the larger plants concentrated on standardized products and long runs that maximized the economies of scale, leaving other products to small plants using much less capital-intensive methods. The cotton textile industry, for example, was divided between large-scale producers of standard yard goods like sheeting and drill, and small-scale producers of kimono fabrics that differed from the traditional cottage industries only in their use of power looms.

By 1913 the capital stock employed in electricity generation was almost one-third of that employed in the railways. It was the high-technology industry of its time, but before World War I, almost all generating plants were imported and installed under the supervision of foreign engineers and technicians sent out by the manufacturers. The technological transfer effect was therefore slight until the spurt in electrical engineering that took place during the war.

## *Education*

The advantages of an educated, or at least a literate, population for the nation's economic and political development now seem obvious, but they were not widely appreciated in Europe before the mid-nineteenth century. Although traditional Japanese society was relatively literate for its economic level, the early Meiji government devoted few of its

Summaries of this work are available in Ryōshin Minami, "The Introduction of Electric Power and Its Impact on the Manufacturing Industries: With Special Reference to Smaller Scale Plants," in *Japanese Industrialization and Its Social Consequences*, ed. Hugh Patrick (Berkeley and Los Angeles: University of California Press, 1976), pp. 299–325; and Ryōshin Minami, "Mechanical Power in the Industrialization of Japan," *Journal of Economic History* 37 (December 1977): 935–58.

own limited resources to education, placing responsibility for elementary education on local authorities with little more than exhortation from the center. But in the new cabinet system of 1885, the Ministry of Education was given responsibility for the central direction and control of formal education at all levels. As the Imperial Rescript on Education of 1891 proclaimed, the aim of elementary education was to prepare young Japanese to perform their duties as imperial subjects, as laid down in the constitution of the previous year. The purpose of education was not only to impart literacy, numeracy, and basic skills but also to inculcate those virtues of discipline, obedience, harmony, and loyalty that have since been widely represented as traditionally, or even uniquely, Japanese.

From the start, the official emphasis was heavily on elementary education, four years of which became compulsory in 1890. Although financed by local authorities, public education was not yet free, but even so compliance was virtually universal by 1900.[20] Secondary education developed more slowly and on a limited scale. In 1903 only 4 percent (8 percent if miscellaneous semiofficial institutions are included) of the fifteen-to-nineteen age group were receiving education beyond the elementary level. This figure rose to 19.8 percent (27.7 percent) by 1908, but even in 1920 between one-half to three-quarters of young Japanese got no formal education beyond the compulsory elementary level, by then extended to six years. From 1890, secondary education was offered in a multitrack system designed to channel young people into broad occupational categories.

Vocational training was systematized under an ordinance in 1899 but remained patchy. Most training in industrial skills was provided outside the formal education system, at first in schools attached to government industrial establishments or by apprenticeship to craftsmen or associated with "patrons" (*oyabun* or *oyakata*). Despite the proliferation of technical schools, vocational colleges, and institutes after the Russo-Japanese War, as the demand for modern industrial skills expanded during World War I, vocational training tended to become internalized within the larger firms, as it has remained to this day. This development fragmented and internalized the market for

20 Of the ¥41.4 million of public funds spent on education in 1900, 55 percent was allocated to elementary education from village or town ward finances. If we add to this the fees paid by the villagers, it is clear that most of the cost of education was borne by the users. By 1920, total public expenditure on education had risen to ¥313 million, but half was still raised and allocated at the village level. For information on the role of education in Japan's economic development, see Solomon B. Levine and Hisashi Kawada, *Human Resources in Japanese Industrial Development* (Princeton, N.J.: Princeton University Press, 1980).

skilled labor, placing an unusually high value on those "traditional" virtues of loyalty and a sense of obligation to the employer. Concentrating training within the larger firms also reinforced their advantage vis-à-vis the small businesses.

Tertiary education was provided by a small number of national "imperial" universities (Tokyo, 1877; Kyoto, 1897; Kyushu, 1909) that trained personnel primarily for the higher administrative levels of the civil service and secondarily for big business. Then, as since, graduation from Tokyo University's law faculty was the entrée to a distinguished civil service career. After the 1890s, the larger companies followed the government's lead in recruiting university graduates as managerial staff. By 1900 the first generation of self-educated men or managers who had come up through the ranks was being replaced by graduates of Tokyo Imperial and Keio universities or the Tokyo Higher Commercial School (now Hitotsubashi University). Graduates of tertiary institutions were a very small elite who tended to be generalists and administrators rather than scientists or engineers. This shared university background created a sense of solidarity among the top echelons of both government and business.

Japan's education system took shape in the climate of reaction to early uncritical enthusiasm for Western culture, and it was characterized increasingly by nationalist ideology. Its aim, like that of conscription, was to create loyal subjects and docile workers, and it was effective in producing Japanese who not only did what they were told but even believed and felt what they were told to believe and feel. Perhaps a different kind of education might have avoided later political and military disasters, but there can be no doubt that the Japanese education system had positive effects on the nature of the industrial labor force, industrial relations, and the government's ability to manipulate economic life and economic growth. At the relatively liberal tertiary level, this type of education was not calculated to produce innovative scientists or thinkers. But at a time when Japan could draw on and adapt a large international pool of scientific knowledge and when technical competence was more valuable than innovative brilliance, the advantages of its system of education outweighed its disadvantages if judged solely from the standpoint of economic growth.

## THE TRADITIONAL SECTOR, 1885–1913

The introduction and growth of industries using technologies and methods of organization developed in the advanced industrial countries were central to Japan's economic development. To understand this development, therefore, we need to distinguish these "modern" activities from the indigenous or "traditional" economy. Conceptually this is not difficult. The modern sector includes manufacturing in factories using inanimate power and equipped with machinery imported from abroad or based on overseas models, whether the output be a new product like soap or a traditional one like cotton yarn or steel produced by new methods. Mining by engineering methods introduced from abroad is "modern," as are railways, merchant shipping, banking and insurance, and utilities like gas and electricity. Government services provided by central and local bureaucracies, education, the police, and the armed services are also part of the modern sector.

The traditional sector consists of agriculture, traditional industry, and traditional commerce and services. Agriculture is classed as traditional, as the techniques and organization of farming and the farmer's way of life have changed very little, despite the greater use of new items like chemical fertilizers. Cottage industries or very small workshops, even though they may use modern materials like chemical dyes and machine-spun yarn or produce new products like pencils or matches, are classed as traditional because here, too, their technology and organization of production did not require a sharp break with traditional practice. Retail trade, the construction industry, and transport by packhorses and riverboats all are traditional. (Transport by rickshaw, a mid-nineteenth-century innovation, may be a borderline case.)

When we try to quantify modern and traditional economic activity, however, two serious problems arise. The first is separating modern from traditional industry. Before 1914, quantitative information was collected and classified by industry – by what was produced rather than how it was produced – and so the statistical information for this period does not generally distinguish between production in a large modern factory and handicraft production by farmers as a side occupation. From time to time, information was collected and classified by size of workplace as measured by the number of workers. This information has been used to distinguish between traditional and modern industry on the assumption that production in plants with five or more (sometimes ten or more) workers could be regarded as modern industry.[21] The results of this procedure must be regarded as impression-

21 Estimates of the occupational distribution of the work force between 1872 and 1920 were made by Hijikata Seibi, "Shokugyō betsu jinkō no hensen o tsūjite mitaru shitsugyō mondai," *Shakai seisaku jihō* no. 108 (September 1929). His estimates are reproduced in Yamada Yūzō, *Nihon kokumin shotoku suikei shiryō,* rev. ed. (Tokyo: Tōyō keizai shinpōsha, 1957), pp. 152–3. Umemura Mataji prepared revised estimates for occupational distribution

istic. Nevertheless, because modern economic development is the growth of modern, as opposed to traditional, industry, any attempt to analyze that process without differentiating between them will miss the point; econometric analysis that treats Japanese industry as homogeneous can scarcely be taken seriously.

The second problem is separating traditional industry from agriculture, particularly for the early years of our period when a large part of industrial output was produced in rural villages by people classified as farmers. Even in the late 1880s well over half of Japan's cotton yarn and raw silk, for example, is estimated to have been produced in this way. Farming, however, carried greater social prestige than did other rural occupations, and so shopkeepers, pedlars, industrial workers, or entrepreneurs with traditional family links with the land tended to give their occupation as "farmer," even though their own or their families' involvement in agriculture might have been minimal. As manufacturing gradually became more clearly separated from agriculture, fewer nonfarmers were classified as farmers. This statistical anomaly accounts for part of the apparent reduction in the agricultural labor force. Although the transfer of labor and other resources from agriculture to traditional industry was important to the growth of the Japanese economy during this period, the extent of that transfer was less than the official statistics imply.

Although we must acknowledge and emphasize the data's shortcomings, changes in the relative size of the agricultural, traditional nonagricultural, and modern sectors are so central to Japan's economic growth that we must make some attempt to quantify them.

In the early 1880s most – 98 percent – of Japan's 22 million gainfully employed persons were engaged in economic activities that had changed little since the Meiji Restoration. Although just over 70 per-

between agriculture and nonagriculture for 1872 to 1905 and in the industrial sector between 1880 and 1883 and between 1906 and 1920. See Umemura Mataji, "Sangyō betsu koyō no hendō: 1880–1940-nen," *Keizai kenkyū* 24 (April 1973): 107–16. Umemura's revisions of Hijikata's figures indicate a larger nonagricultural work force in the 1880s, a smaller agricultural work force between 1885 and 1905, and a more pronounced movement of labor out of agriculture during World War I. A revised version of Umemura's estimates appears in Okhawa and Shinohara, eds., *Patterns of Japanese Economic Development*, pp. 392–4; while retaining his estimate of the total labor force, Umemura increased the numbers in agriculture and reduced those in nonagriculture and also raised the numbers in service industries at the expense of manufacturing.

If estimates of occupational distribution by industrial sector, especially for the early years, are still tentative, classification of the labor force into traditional and modern occupations should be regarded as impressionistic. The best are by Nakamura Takafusa, *Senzen-ki Nihon keizai seichō no bunseki*, pp. 338–9, and, for 1920 only, Nakamura Takafusa, "Zairai sangyō no kibo to kōsei – Taishō 9-nen kokusei chōsa o chūshin ni," in *Sūryō keizaishi ronshū*, vol. 1: *Nihon keizai no hatten*, ed. Umemura Mataji et al. (Tokyo: Nihon keizai shinbunsha, 1976), pp. 195–219.

cent were officially classified as farmers, agriculture probably absorbed closer to 60 percent of Japan's labor supply in actual work hours. On the same labor input basis, fishing and the construction industry each employed about 2 percent of the work force, traditional mining and manufacturing roughly one-sixth, and commerce and services a slightly smaller proportion. Only about 400,000 people worked in the modern sector. Of these, more than half were employed by central or local government as bureaucrats, police, servicemen, teachers, or workers in government arsenals and factories. Modern private enterprise employed fewer than 200,000 people. In the early 1880s, over 90 percent of Japan's net domestic product was produced by traditional activities. Agriculture, forestry, and fisheries with just over 70 percent of the labor supply produced just under half of the net domestic product. Traditional production of goods and services other than agricultural accounted for another 45 percent or so, and the modern sector contributed only about 5 percent of output. As Nakamura Takafusa observed, modern industry was like sparsely scattered islands in a sea of traditional industry.[22]

Between 1883 and 1913, Japan's labor force increased from 22 million to 26 million, and its sectoral distribution changed. The official statistics show the number of people engaged in agriculture falling slightly, whereas the nonagricultural labor force almost doubled, but in actual labor input the change was considerably smaller than these figures indicate. Within the nonagricultural sector, modern employment increased four times, whereas employment in traditional occupations rose by only 60 percent. Nevertheless, because of the overwhelming weight of traditional commerce and industry, those sectors absorbed most – over three-quarters – of the increase in the work force. Over these three decades the output of the Japanese economy increased by almost three times. Of this increase, the growth of agricultural output contributed about 20 percent, and other traditional-style production added 40 percent or more. Although the modern sector expanded two or three times as fast as did the traditional sector, it was so relatively small initially that it contributed less than a third of the growth of the national output. These figures are admittedly impressionistic, but the picture they give of the Japanese economy before World War I is not unrealistic. In particular, they highlight the importance of traditional activities and their contribution to economic growth.

22 Nakamura Takafusa, "Shijō kōzō to sangyō soshiki," in *Nihon keizai ron – Keizai seichō 100-nen no bunseki*, ed. Emi Kōichi and Shionoya Yūichi (Tokyo: Yūhikaku, 1973), p. 301.

### *Agriculture*

Because agriculture was such a large part of the Japanese economy at the start of its modern growth, its performance had an important bearing on the growth process. There have been various estimates of what that performance was. Using government statistics, Ohkawa and others estimated the rate of growth of real income produced in agriculture from around 1880 to World War I (1913–17 average) at just over 2.4 percent a year, with a rate of 3.3 percent to the turn of the century and just over 1 percent thereafter.[23] However, government statistics were very inaccurate for the early years. James Nakamura claimed that concealment of output and underreporting of yields had resulted in government figures for the period from 1875 to 1882 that showed only about half the actual output. Correcting for this, he derived an annual rate of growth of agricultural output from 1880 to World War I of between 0.8 and 1.2 percent, with the rate rising rather than falling after the turn of the century.[24] Ohkawa's estimate must be regarded as high because it implies for the early years a per capita caloric intake too low to be credible, but Nakamura's estimate must be regarded as low because it does not allow for any rise in per capita caloric intake as incomes rose. A more recent reworking of the statistics has produced results halfway between the two, indicating the gross farm value of production as growing at an average annual rate of 1.7 percent in constant 1934–36 prices, with the rate rising from 1.5 percent before 1900 to 1.8 percent after the turn of the century.[25] Although this estimate cannot be regarded as final, it is probably accurate enough for our purposes. Although the estimate scarcely indicates the kind of agricultural spurt once thought to be a major element in the initial phase of Japan's economic growth, it suggests a significant acceleration, as compared with the pace of agricultural progress in the century before the Restoration.

The expansion of agricultural output, both before and after 1900, was associated with the increasing use of conventional inputs like land, labor, machinery, and fertilizer, as well as with changes in organization and technology. Changes in composition also affected the value of the total output. From 1880 to 1900, agricultural inputs grew rela-

23 Kazushi Ohkawa et al., *The Growth Rate of the Japanese Economy Since 1878* (Tokyo: Kinokuniya, 1957), p. 17. 24 Nakamura, *Agricultural Production*, p. 115.

25 Umemura Mataji et al., LTES, vol. 9. Their estimates have not been significantly altered by subsequent minor adjustments. See Saburō Yamada and Yujirō Hayami, "Agriculture," in *Patterns of Japanese Economic Development*, pp. 85–103; and Yamada Saburō, "Nōgyō," in *Nihon keizai ron*, pp. 109–10.

tively slowly. The agricultural population appears to have been almost constant, even though actual labor input may well have risen when those who had devoted relatively little of their time to agriculture moved into other sectors. Reported rice paddy area was almost unchanged. Although the area of upland or dry fields increased, because of underreporting in the early years, this increase may have been more apparent than real. In any case, the average annual increase in arable land area was less than 0.5 percent. Fixed capital rose by less than 1 percent a year, and although current inputs rose somewhat faster, even in 1900 the use of commercial fertilizers and pesticides was quite limited.

After 1900 the farming population fell slightly, but the arable land area expanded faster than before; the use of implements, simple machinery, fertilizer, and other current inputs increased rapidly. This more widespread use of implements and fertilizers is consistent with the faster growth of output after the turn of the century, but over the whole period, agricultural output increased much more than did the resources devoted to agriculture. This disparity has sometimes been attributed to the more effective use of resources made possible by improvements in technology or organization. But the pace of such change in agriculture is typically slow, and before World War I, Japan seems to have been no exception.

In fact, the organization of Japanese farming changed little, and the scale of farming remained small. Average arable land per farm household was under one hectare in 1880, rose slowly to about one hectare in 1900, and then remained stable, but the median, or typical, farm was much smaller and changed only marginally in size. The only major organizational change during this period was in the structure of land ownership. With the removal of legal obstacles to land transfer, ownership tended to become more concentrated, and the relative supply of land and labor was such that those with more land than they could cultivate themselves found it advantageous to lease the surplus to tenants rather than to hire workers. Thus the proportion of land farmed by tenants increased gradually throughout the period, from about 35 percent in the early 1880s to about 45 percent by World War I, with the rate of increase highest in periods of economic depression. Between 1884 and 1886, in the aftermath of the Matsukata deflation, foreclosures – many for the nonpayment of taxes – transferred almost one-eighth of the country's cultivated land into the hands of creditors. By the end of the century, landlords, who had not been a particularly influential group at the beginning of the Meiji era, annually collected rents equivalent to almost a quarter of Japan's rice crop. With land taxes falling in real terms, the revenue lost by the government accrued mainly to landlords, who by 1900 had become a major source of local investment and enterprise as well as a powerful force in both local affairs and national politics.

Another significant organizational change was the establishment of village cooperatives under the industrial cooperatives (*sangyō kumiai*) legislation of 1900. Although these were voluntary organizations, they had become almost universal in rural villages by 1914. Together with the landlords, they acted as intermediaries between the farmers and the markets for materials and products, as vehicles for the introduction of new technology and equipment and as channels of communication with the government in a wide range of matters. These cooperatives were intended to strengthen the competitiveness of the small farmers, to help them survive in an increasingly capitalist environment, and to forestall the widening inequality and social unrest that might result from the unfettered operation of free competition. Although the lot of most farmers, especially tenants, was seldom happy and sometimes desperate, the cooperatives did improve productivity and reduce social tension.

Technological innovation in agriculture before the 1900s was limited. Early attempts to introduce European farming methods were not successful and were abandoned in the 1880s in favor of measures to promote and improve traditional small-scale farming through the combined efforts of the Ministry of Agriculture and Commerce, landowners, and expert farmers. Rather than introducing new technology, these measures encouraged the dissemination of existing expertise by pooling local knowledge and transferring it from the more advanced regions of Kinki and north Kyushu to the relatively backward regions in the east and north. Rising rice yields and narrowing variations within and among districts may indicate some diffusion of improved plant varieties, better seed selection, and more productive cultivation practices.[26] Nevertheless, change seems to have been marginal except in sericulture, in which an important technological development made possible a silkworm hatch in the late summer–autumn season as well as in the spring, thus increasing the output of cocoons by utilizing labor from farming families during what had been a slack season. By 1900 this "second crop" contributed over one-third of all Japan's co-

26 See Yujirō Hayami with Masakatsu Akino, Masahiko Shintani, and Saburō Yamada, *A Century of Agricultural Growth in Japan, Its Relevance to Asian Development* (Minneapolis: University of Minnesota Press, and Tokyo: Tokyo University Press, 1965), pp. 113–31.

coons. From 1880 to 1900 the growth of sericulture accounted for 20 percent of the growth of the gross value of agricultural production. If sericulture is excluded, the growth rate of agricultural output over this period is reduced to about 1.3 percent, but even this seems high compared with a 0.4 percent rate of growth of total inputs. What we know of technical progress seems scarcely sufficient to account for such a difference. It may well be that the growth of conventional inputs, especially labor, has been underestimated.

Between 1900 and 1920 the average growth rate of agricultural production (gross value) rose to 1.8 percent a year. Although the farm population fell, all other inputs increased considerably: arable land by 0.7 percent a year, farm implements and machinery by 2.0 percent, and current inputs by 4.7 percent, including a massive increase in the use of commercial fertilizers. Technological change, too, speeded up after the turn of the century. With government supervision and support, landowners realigned plots and improved drainage to raise fertility. A fourfold increase in the application of fertilizers would have been largely wasted without new plant strains and deep plowing. New varieties such as Shinriki, which were highly responsive to fertilizers, were propagated rapidly in the 1900s, and the development of the reversible short-bottomed plow in 1900 made deep plowing practicable. Soon after, the introduction of a rotary weeder, which was used between straight equidistant row of plants, greatly increased efficiency.

Apparently these changes were not greeted with universal enthusiasm, however, for some fourteen improvements were made compulsory under instructions issued in 1903 to the agricultural associations by the Ministry of Agriculture and Commerce. These included use of the brine flotation method of seed selection, oblong seed beds, and their conversion to paddy fields when the seedlings were planted out, improved seeds and implements, plowing with animals, and rice planting in equidistant checkrows. Similar regulations to improve agriculture were issued by prefectural governments and enforced by fines and an occasional jail sentence. Even so, the program achieved only limited results.[27] During the Russo-Japanese War, seed selection by the brine method was extended from one-half to two-thirds of all rice seed; plowing with draft animals became more common; and the planting out of rice in checkrows to facilitate tillage and weeding rose from one-third to almost half of the planted acreage.[28] It is surprising that a

27 See Takekazu Ogura, ed., *Agricultural Development in Modern Japan* (Tokyo: Fuji, 1963), pp. 159–71. 28 Ibid., p. 305.

practice now so firmly entrenched is of such recent origin. That inefficient or negligent farmers should be punished was generally accepted during the Tokugawa period, but attempts to apply this concept in the twentieth century met with widespread resistance. By 1910, punishments were generally abandoned in favor of encouragement by a system of subsidies and other financial incentives, although the government retained control over a wide range of agricultural matters.

Taken singly, these changes were small, but they were mutually reinforcing. New early-maturing strains of rice and other grains extended the area capable of double cropping, and more responsive varieties made profitable heavier applications of fertilizers and deep plowing. The greater use of commercial fertilizer, mainly Manchurian soybean cake, made possible some reduction in the area of grassland needed for green manure and fallow, thus releasing land for forestry and other direct production. All these changes were further reinforced by the emergence of greater opportunities for profitable farming. For pre-Meiji villagers, farming had been a duty rather than a profitable activity, and the burden of taxes fell so heavily on agriculture that villagers tried to maximize the time that they could devote to more profitable industrial and commercial pursuits. After the Restoration the incidence of direct taxation was still much heavier on agriculture than on industry, but the percentage of agricultural income taken by direct taxes fell from over 20 percent between 1883 and 1887 to just under 10 percent between 1918 and 1922.[29] Although traditional attitudes changed slowly, by World War I, farming had become more professional as developments in technology and marketing created new opportunities and incentives for the use of labor in agriculture at a time when other sources of rural income were beginning to decline.[30]

Agricultural progress in the initial phase of Japan's modern economic growth may not have been as fast as was once thought, nor was it by any means the only source of inputs for economic growth. As we shall see, industrial growth during this phase was mainly the growth of traditional production financed by the traditional industrial sector itself. Nevertheless, Japan did not suffer from the sort of agricultural lag that seems to have restricted economic growth in countries like the Soviet Union or China. Food production kept up with demand until 1900 and thereafter did not lag far behind. In 1880 an agricultural

29 See Tōbata Seiichi and Ōkawa Kazushi, eds., *Nihon no keizai to nōgyō* (Tokyo: Iwanami shoten, 1956), vol. 1, p. 381.

30 See E. S. Crawcour, "Japan, 1868–1920," in *Agricultural Development in Asia*, ed. R. T. Shand (Canberra: Australian National University Press, 1969), pp. 1–24.

labor force of 17 million fed a total population of 36 million at a rather low average level of nutrition. In 1920, with an agricultural labor force of just over 14 million, a population of 55 million or more enjoyed modest increases in food consumption per capita, with food imports, mainly from Korea and Manchuria, at no more than 8 percent of total consumption. This balance or near-balance was not achieved solely by improvements in agricultural output; to an important extent it depended on the fact that population growth was moderate and that the per-capita demand for food rose remarkably little.

The experience of other developing countries suggests that as per capita incomes rise from a fairly low level, more than half of the increase is spent on more or better food. In Japan, however, the proportion was much smaller, even though the average levels of nutrition were clearly well below the optimum. Traditional eating habits changed very little, and caloric intake per capita rose only slowly.[31] The reasons for this are not obvious. Estimates of the change in per capita food consumption and national income are not very reliable, and although it seems unlikely that they underestimate the change in food consumption, the rise in national income may be somewhat exaggerated by increasing statistical coverage. It may well be that cultural attitudes encouraged frugality in food consumption, especially by women, and that with increasing urbanization, the need to buy industrial products once produced in the household may have reduced the income that could be spent on food. Most important, however, increasing demands from other sources, especially investment and exports, kept the rise in personal consumption below that of national income per capita, so that its share of gross domestic expenditure fell from about 85 percent in 1880 to 70 percent in 1920. In addition, the greater inequality of personal incomes tended to raise average savings and reduce average consumption as the richer saved while the poorer went short.

The role of agriculture as a source of capital for industrial investment may have been exaggerated in the past by the difficulty of distinguishing agriculture from rural industry and commerce, but the land tax was certainly a vital source of revenue without which the Meiji government could not have survived, let alone have played such a central role in capital formation, the introduction of technology, and

31 See Hiromitsu Kaneda, "Long-Term Changes in Food Consumption Patterns in Japan," in *Agriculture and Economic Growth, Japan's Experience*, ed. Kazushi Ohkawa et al. (Princeton, N.J.: Princeton University Press, 1969), pp. 406–9.

the coordination of economic enterprise. In 1880, taxes on land and rural households provided about 70 percent of all national and local tax revenue. By the eve of the Russo-Japanese War, their share had fallen to one-third as revenues from income, business, and consumption taxes, especially the liquor tax, rose; and by World War I it was below 30 percent.[32] As the government's share of agricultural production fell, however, the share accruing to landlords rose in almost the same proportion, and landlords, as we have seen, had a high propensity to save and invest in both local and national enterprises.

The growth of foreign trade was a key factor in the initial phase of Japan's economic development. In the mid-1880s, total transactions with the outside world represented only 6 percent of all economic activity, but by the Russo-Japanese War they had risen to 20 percent, and by World War I, to 28 percent. In the 1880s over two-thirds of Japan's exports consisted of agricultural products, principally raw silk. By the Russo-Japanese War this proportion had fallen to one-third, whereas homegrown cotton, unable to compete in cost or quality, had been replaced by imports, greatly reducing agriculture's contribution to the balance of payments. Over the whole period, however, agricultural exports played a very valuable role in foreign trade and even during World War I provided a quarter of commodity exports.

In summary, the performance of agriculture during this period, if perhaps not so outstanding as once thought, was adequate. The introduction, dissemination, and sometimes enforcement of better methods of farming and the increasing operation of economic incentives, particularly via landlords, enabled a more efficient use of land and labor with a consequent expansion of output. On the other hand, the adequacy of supply depended also on limited rises in demand and the persistence of traditional patterns of consumption. The broad structural outlines of small-scale farming scarcely changed. Tenancy increased, and landlords and agricultural associations took over some of the functions of the *daikan* and village headmen of earlier times. Eco-

32 Estimates vary. See Kazushi Ohkawa and Henry Rosovsky, "The Role of Agriculture in Modern Japanese Economic Development," *Economic Development and Cultural Change* 9 (October 1960): pt 2, p. 61, where Table 14 shows land tax as a percentage of revenue from four "main taxes" (income tax, land tax, business tax, and customs duty) falling from 85.6 percent in the five years centered on 1890 to 55.8 percent for the five years centered on 1905 and 37.6 percent for the five years centered on 1915. By 1915, however, the four main taxes accounted for only 54.6 percent of the national tax revenue. I have calculated the sum of national, prefectural, and local (*chōson*) land taxes and local household tax as a percentage of all national and local tax revenue. Note that 90 percent of *chōson* were rural villages.

nomic horizons and opportunities may have widened in theory, but for the average farmer it was still a hard life with worse to come in the depressed conditions of the 1920s.

## *Traditional industry*

The policy of the early Meiji leaders was to catch up with the advanced countries of the West by "enriching the country and strengthening the armed forces," and they believed that the way to achieve this was to replace as quickly as possible the "backward" Japanese methods of production with the latest Western technology. Consequently, little thought was given to supporting or improving the existing industrial structure. In the 1870s, attempts to transplant Western production methods were generally unsuccessful, partly because a supporting infrastructure had not yet been built, but perhaps more importantly because methods developed in the Western nations proved unprofitable in Japan where capital equipment was much more expensive relative to labor. The initial policy response to this problem was either to establish modern industries as government enterprises or to reduce the cost of industrial plants to selected firms – broadly speaking the "political merchants" who developed into the zaibatsu – by making it possible for them to raise capital on favorable terms, while assisting with the selection, purchase, and import of machinery and providing technical assistance. The cost of this policy was substantial at a time when other demands were straining fiscal resources to the limit. In the course of Matsukata's fiscal reforms, government enterprises were sold to selected buyers at prices low enough to bring the cost of capital equipment more into line with Japanese conditions.

The recession that followed the Matsukata deflation, however, brought severe hardship to Japan's traditional industry. In 1884 Maeda Masana, a senior official of the Ministry of Agriculture and Commerce who had recently returned from a study tour of Europe, suggested after a thorough survey of Japan's economic grass roots that traditional industry was an indispensable resource; that with support and improvement it was capable not only of providing for rising consumption needs and exports to earn badly needed foreign exchange but also of being gradually developed to a level of productivity comparable to that of Western industry. Industrial modernization along these lines, he submitted, would result in methods suited to Japanese conditions of scarce capital and abundant labor, would involve far less cost than would the direct transplantation of Western factories, and would relieve the economic distress that constantly threatened rural Japan and was particularly acute in the postdeflation recession.[33]

Although not fully convinced by Maeda's arguments, the government did recognize the important role of traditional industry in the economy. Japanese consumer goods were produced in ways that had not changed since the country's opening. The kinds of housing, clothing, processed foods, and household utensils that made up the distinctive Japanese way of life retained their traditional patterns, and traditional industry continued to supply them. In this respect Japan differed from territories such as the Dutch East Indies, where a colonial system producing staple exports and importing many consumer goods had brought about the decline of the indigenous industrial system.

Personal consumption represented 80 percent of Japan's gross national expenditure in the 1880s but fell to 75 percent by the Russo-Japanese War and 72 percent by 1915. Consumption of nonagricultural goods and services,[34] however, was 35 percent of gross national expenditure in the 1880s and actually rose to 38 percent during the Russo-Japanese War and to 43 percent at the start of World War I. These figures show that it was a lag in consumption of agricultural products that kept total personal consumption relatively low. The consumption of nonagricultural goods and services expanded faster than did the economy as a whole. Because there were virtually no imports of these traditional goods, their production expanded as fast as consumption did.

As well as supplying consumer goods, traditional industry contributed to capital formation and exports. A large part of construction, road building, and other public works was carried out using traditional methods by workers employed and organized in traditional ways. Until the 1890s as much as half of Japan's major export item, raw silk, was produced by hand reelers. Handicraft products such as lacquerware, cloisonné, and damascene were prominent among Japanese exports after the opening of foreign trade in 1859. After 1900, Japan exported increasing quantities of pencils and other products that, though new to Japan, were produced by traditional cottage industry methods.

33 Maeda's findings and recommendations were presented in *Kōgyō iken* in 1885. This work with related materials and commentary is published as Andō Yoshio and Yamamoto Hirofumi, eds., *Kōgyō iken hoka Maeda Masana kankei shiryō* (Tokyo: Kōseikan, 1971). See also Soda Osamu, *Maeda Masana* (Tokyo: Yoshikawa kōbunkan, 1973).

34 Calculated as personal consumption less nonprocessed food. For this purpose, rice is regarded as an unprocessed food, even though rice milling was quite a large industry. This is partly balanced by the inclusion of the full cost of processed foods.

Traditional industry was important also as an employer of labor. During Japan's modern economic growth, its agricultural labor force declined, but the total gainfully occupied population rose. Until the 1930s the difference was absorbed almost entirely by the traditional sectors of secondary and tertiary industry. In the process the proportion of the work force in traditional nonagricultural occupations rose from 22 percent between 1882 and 1885 to 30 percent by the Russo-Japanese War, 32 percent by the eve of World War I, and 37 percent by 1920. These figures are conservative, as they assume that all workshops in which more than five persons were employed represented modern industry, whereas in fact many had continued virtually unchanged since before the Meiji Restoration.

In output of manufactures, the importance of traditional industry is hard to quantify because output data do not distinguish between traditional and modern production. According to a rough estimate, the proportion of manufactures produced by traditional means fell from nearly three-quarters in the 1880s to about one-half around the Russo-Japanese War and about one-third by World War I. This estimate of the importance of traditional industry as a producer of manufactures is probably conservative and may well exaggerate the speed with which production methods changed.

Apart from some brewing, oil-pressing, and metallurgical industries using water power and employing twenty or more workers, and city-based decorative craft industries, most traditional industries began as rural, largely part-time cottage industries. Circulating capital, often in the form of materials and sometimes equipment, was provided by merchants (*ton'ya*) who controlled the production process and marketed the output in the major cities. In the post-Restoration transition, "orderly marketing," once supervised by licensed merchant guilds or official marketing boards, largely broke down because of adverse effects on quality, prices, and credit arrangements. Food processing, the cotton industry from ginning to weaving, silk reeling, and some silk weaving were typical of this type of industry.

During the initial phase of Japan's economic growth there were a number of changes. First, some production moved from rural villages to nearby towns or larger cities where household workers or small workshops clustered in areas specializing in a particular trade. During the economic depression that followed the Sino-Japanese War and continued almost uninterrupted until the eve of the Russo-Japanese War, many people moved from villages to towns in search of work. When available, such work was usually of a kind to which these people had been accustomed in the villages and at wages similar to rural rates. Between 1898 and 1918 the urban population almost trebled. Although much of the increase was in tertiary occupations, the growth of urban manufacturing was considerable.

Second, traditional industries were reorganized into trade associations or cooperatives. Early attempts by the Meiji government to coordinate and control the production, financing, and marketing of traditional products through national agencies (*shōhōshi, tsūshōshi*) were soon abandoned in favor of policies that promoted new industries based on the latest technology from abroad. In 1879 the Osaka Chamber of Commerce began to reestablish order in the traditional trades, and at the end of 1880 it reported the formation of 189 trade associations, broadly similar to the pre-Restoration guilds (*nakama*). The following year the Osaka municipal government responded by issuing official regulations for the formation and management of trade associations. These regulations included provisions for registering members, electing officials, and maintaining product quality and commercial ethics, with penalties for offenders under the general supervision of the Osaka Chamber of Commerce. Similar moves were made in Tokyo and Kyoto. In 1884 the Ministry of Agriculture and Commerce issued national guidelines for the formation and management of trade associations. These provided for persons in agricultural, commercial, or industrial occupations to form local nonprofit organizations ostensibly for the members' mutual benefit. Registration and reporting provisions were similar to those of the Osaka municipal ordinance. Once an association had been approved and registered by the prescribed authority on the application of three-quarters or more of those eligible to join, membership by the remainder became compulsory. In Osaka at least, many trade associations so formed were actually the direct successors of guilds or associations that had continued in one form or another since before the Restoration.

In 1897 a new law enforced membership in the Major Export Trade Associations (Jūyō yushutsuhin dōgyō kumiai); and three years later all trades, whether export or otherwise, were required to organize into Major Product Trade Associations (Jūyō bussan dōgyō kumiai). These associations, which embraced the production and marketing of virtually all traditional manufactures, replaced the associations formed under the 1884 guidelines. The new trade associations were intended to maintain product standards, raise productivity, and control excessive competition (although price rigging was expressly forbidden), improve managerial skills, and achieve certain economies of scale. At the same time, like their premodern predecessors, they were a vehicle for the exercise of official control to ensure that free enterprise did not work to the disadvantage of the trade as a whole and that traditional industry developed in a way consistent with the national interest.[35]

Third, although Maeda Masana's gradualist proposals for industrial development based on progressive upgrading of existing industry were not accepted – largely because although they might "enrich the country," they would not immediately "strengthen the armed forces" – they alerted the government to the gains attainable at relatively little cost by improving technical standards and raising productivity in traditional industries.[36] With official encouragement some traditional industries achieved technological advances that enabled them to survive and compete alongside new enterprises based on imported technology. In the silk-reeling industry, for example, attempts to operate the most modern imported machine filatures proved unprofitable in conditions in which cheap experienced labor was plentiful and capital scarce and expensive. Under such conditions hand (*zakuri*) reelers were well able to compete. Hand-reeled silk was inferior in quality to machine-reeled silk, but a series of improvements raised both quality and productivity. Meanwhile, machine filatures were modified to suit Japanese conditions, and their cost fell rapidly. From an astonishingly high ¥1,500 per basin for the filatures imported from France in 1871 to equip the pioneer Tomioka mill, the cost per basin fell to ¥13.5 within a few years. Output per operative also almost doubled in the decade following the installation of the Tomioka plant and almost doubled again by the end of the century. Even so, hand reeling remained competitive, and its output continued to rise until the turn of the century, even though by 1894 filature silk exceeded hand-reeled silk in quantity and had captured the bulk of the export market because of its higher, more even quality. Hand-reeled output showed no tendency to fall until the 1920s when machine production expanded rapidly. In this industry, as in others, imported technology became successful only after it had been adapted to local conditions. In the process, the gap between "acclimatized," largely water-powered machine filatures and improved indigenous hand-reeling technology was narrow enough for each industry to learn from the other. In the absence of great economies of scale and with

35 See Miyamoto Mataji, "Shōkō kumiai," in *Nihon keizaishi jiten*, ed. Keizaishi kenkyūkai (Tokyo: Nihon hyōronsha, 1940), vol. 1, pp. 801–4, which clearly shows the continuity between Japan's modern trade associations and those of the pre-Meiji period. See also Watanabe Shin'ichi, *Nihon no keiei kōzō – Senzen hen* (Tokyo: Yūshōdō, 1971), pp. 53–79.

36 See Soda Osamu, *Chihō sangyō no shisō to undō* (Kyoto: Minerva shobō, 1980).

an abundance of cheap labor, the indigenous technology was thus able to remain viable for over fifty years.[37]

Even in the cotton textile industry, one of the first to be successfully modernized, the indigenous industry survived and developed. Despite imports of cotton yarn and cloth in the early Meiji era, the domestic production of raw cotton and its traditional processing industries continued to flourish until the 1890s, when hand ginning and spinning became unable to compete in either quality or cost with the modern mills by then established in Japan. The traditional cotton-weaving industry, on the other hand, flourished, and the output of narrow-width cloth for Japanese clothing increased fourfold between 1885 and 1910, making this one of the period's high-growth industries. Growth was achieved by improvements in equipment and materials and by greater specialization. Nevertheless the predominantly semirural cottage-industry nature of the trade remained practically unchanged. Even in 1910, 87 percent of looms were hand powered, and of these well over half were in cottages and another third in "factories" with not more than ten weavers.[38] By the 1930s the narrow-width cotton-weaving industry was converting to electric-powered looms but retained its traditional organization and character. The continued viablility of this industry owed much to the survival of the cotton kimono as everyday dress until the Pacific War and to the demand for a great variety of woven and dyed patterns that made long runs and mass production uneconomic.

This same demand for variety aided the survival and expansion of other traditional consumer goods industries such as ceramics, lacquerware, bamboo products, and handmade paper.[39] In addition, new products including matches, straw hats, brushes, Western-style umbrellas, and buttons were also produced by traditional methods, largely for export. Matches, for example, were made by a very labor-intensive putting-out system. The "maker," who financed the industry, often with funds from a local bank, provided the materials and sometimes simple equipment. One or more households shaped pinewood into billets; others split and cut the billets into matchsticks; and still others dipped them to make the heads, while other teams were making matchboxes and pasting labels on them. Finally, yet more

37 See Ōtsuka Katsuo, "Seishigyō ni okeru gijutsu dōnyu" in *Nihon keizai no hatten*, pp. 159–78, and Nakamura, *Senzen-ki Nihon keizai seichō no bunseki*, p. 64.

38 See Nakamura Takafusa, "Zairai men orimonogyō no hatten to suitai – Oboegaki" in *Sūryō keizaishi ronshū*, vol. 2: *Kindai ikō-ki no Nihon keizai – Bakumatsu kara Meiji e*, ed. Shinbo Hiroshi and Yasuba Yasukichi (Tokyo: Nihon keizai shinbunsha, 1979), pp. 219–33.

39 For further examples, see Chihōshi kenkyū kyōgikai, ed., *Nihon sangyōshi taikei*, 7 vols. (Tokyo: Tōkyō daigaku shuppankai, 1960).

teams of household workers packed the matches in the boxes and wrapped them in packets for shipment. The whole process took place within an area small enough for the goods and materials to be transferred from one stage to the next by handcart. One "maker" might employ several hundred people working in their own homes at rates of pay so low that often the whole family needed to work long hours to make a living.

From the 1880s to World War I, the growth of the traditional sector was a vital part of the whole economy's development. Not only was it responsible for the bulk of output growth, but it also nurtured the infant modern sector by providing and maintaining labor, contributing capital, and earning foreign exchange. Several factors account for its growth.[40] First, as we have already noticed, the persistence of traditional patterns of consumption provided a growing demand for traditional products as the population increased and incomes rose. Second, until World War I, traditional industry was the principal beneficiary of the new infrastructure, especially cheaper transport and a modern financial system. Third, the development of modern industry provided cheaper and better materials, like machine-spun cotton yarn, dyes and other chemicals, cardboard, and glass, which lowered costs in traditional industries. Investment in modern infrastructure, industry, and defense, moreover, raised incomes and thus demand for traditional goods and services. Finally, the export markets and the official encouragement of the traditional labor-intensive industries as export producers also stimulated growth. Because of the low labor costs, these industries were able to compete successfully with more highly mechanized producers in the relatively capital-rich advanced industrialized countries, much to their irritation.

Ohkawa and others have credited Japan with being able to maintain growth in both agriculture and industry.[41] It is now clear, however, that Japan's industrial growth before World War I was largely the growth of traditional industry. What appears as the concurrent growth of agriculture and industry was in fact the growth of the traditional sector as a whole. When the modern sector became self-sustaining and established itself as the leader in economic growth around World War I, the growth of the traditional sector, including both agriculture and the traditional industries, slackened as modern

40 See Nakamura Takafusa, "Zairai sangyō no hatten kikō – Meiji Taishō-ki no Nihon ni oite," *Keizai hyōron*, new series, 16 (January 1967): 134–56.

41 See, for example, Kazushi Ohkawa, *Differential Structure and Agriculture: Essays on Dualistic Growth* (Tokyo: Kinokuniya, 1972), pp. 165–81.

technology drew ahead, the sphere in which simple hand production was competitive narrowed, export prices declined, and consumer taste began to change. With the wartime surge in modern industrial development, the complementary relationship between the traditional and modern sectors changed to one of competition for resources, in which all the advantages were on the side of the modern sector. In the postwar recessions, as more and more people were unable to find employment elsewhere, incomes and living standards in the traditional sector fell markedly below those of the modern sector, creating in the 1920s a dual or differential economic structure that was characteristic of the interwar period and persisted well into the high-growth era of the 1960s. The problems of this differential structure were of great significance for both Japan's economic development and its social and political development but are outside the scope of this chapter.

## THE MODERN SECTOR, 1885–1913

In late nineteenth-century Japan, manufacturing was a very small part of a modern sector which was itself very small in relation to the whole economy. The new bureaucracy, the army and navy, the education system, modern railways, shipping, and finance provided the bulk of modern employment in the 1880s and even in 1913 employed over half of this sector's labor force. All contributed directly or indirectly to Japan's economic growth. But in the long run it was the development of the modern secondary industries that made it possible to employ a steadily increasing proportion of the work force at levels of productivity far higher than could be achieved with traditional organization and technology, thereby producing a sustained and in fact accelerating increase in overall output. In the late nineteenth century, however, the modern sector, including most modern manufacturing industries, still depended for its existence and growth on resources from the traditional economy and to some extent from abroad.

The order in which modern industries developed in Japan has interested economic theorists. Experience in the older industrial countries of the West suggested a progression from light industries, especially textiles, through mining and metallurgical industries, railways, and the age of steam to heavy engineering, chemicals, and the mass production of motor cars and other appliances. This was thought to be a natural progression, as capital accumulation and technological progress reduced the cost of capital, encouraging the introduction of increasingly capital-intensive methods of production. In Japan, too, this sequence, although compressed into a shorter span of time, was generally similar but had some important differences. We have seen how the development of railways and the merchant marine was able to precede the emergence of the iron and steel industry by relying on imports of rails, girders, rolling stock, ships, and other equipment. Mining developed early largely to supply export markets. Although cotton spinning and some other branches of the textile industry were the first modern manufacturing industries to be profitably established, modern iron and steel mills, shipbuilding, and some other branches of heavy engineering followed so closely as to overlap with them. In the few years that separated the beginnings of light and heavy industry, changes in the relative costs and availability of labor and capital were certainly not great enough to make relatively capital-intensive heavy industries profitable or competitive with imports. On the contrary, those heavy and engineering industries were established at great cost either as state enterprises or with government subsidies, guarantees, and protection. Most did not become economically viable until the World War I boom.

Here we see a major difference between the modern Japanese textile industry and, for example, the iron and steel industry. Both received government encouragement and assistance in one form or another – the textile industry to replace imports and reduce the drain on foreign exchange, and heavy industry to produce in the interests of national security. The former soon adapted to Japan's relative abundance of labor and thereafter became an attractively profitable investment. In the latter, however, the proportions of labor and capital were fixed within narrow limits by the technology, and so their establishment was justified on grounds of national security rather than economic viability.

Enterprises established in the national interest rather than in response to business opportunities tended to be promoted and managed by people with administrative experience and good government contacts rather than by those with sound business backgrounds. This has prompted the view that the typical entrepreneur of the Meiji era was of samurai rather than merchant background and that Japan's traditional business class was conservative and unable to adapt to the competitive world of free enterprise.[42] Whenever the criteria of the marketplace indicated genuine business opportunities, however, businessmen were

42 See, for example, Tsuchiya Takao, *Zaibatsu o kizuita hitobito* (Tokyo: Kōbundō, 1955); and Tsuchiya Takao, *Nihon no keieisha seishin* (Tokyo: Keizai ōraisha, 1959). For a more recent discussion, see Johannes Hirschmeier and Tsunehiko Yui, *The Development of Japanese Business, 1600–1973* (London: Allen & Unwin, 1975).

not slow to exploit them, as they did in the textile industry in the 1890s.

However, investment decisions based on grounds other than free-market considerations are not necessarily less effective or desirable in promoting modern economic growth. Neither economic theory nor experience suggests that the unhampered operation of free-market forces in a situation such as Japan's in the late nineteenth century allocates resources over time in a way that optimizes economic development. The Japanese authorities had no compunction about channeling resources into import-replacement projects designed to conserve foreign exchange, to enhance national security, or otherwise to promote what they saw as the national interest. The development of industries established for such reasons often itself helped create the conditions under which they could eventually be justified in terms of normal business calculations. The relationship between market forces and the pursuit of national objectives is woven into Japan's modern economic development in intricate patterns that need more detailed study.[43]

## *Light industry*

The textile industry was the only light industry to be firmly established on the basis of modern technology and organization before World War I. It consisted overwhelmingly of silk reeling and cotton spinning. Of the two, raw silk was superior in value of output and was far more important as an export commodity.

The modern silk-reeling industry began in the 1870s with the importation of filatures from Europe by the government and a few others. The cost of these filatures was high; the government's three-hundred-basin model plant at Tomioka, for example, was completed in 1872 at a cost of ¥198,000. But because of their high capital cost, poor management, and inexperienced labor, these early filatures could not compete successfully with traditional hand reeling. Not until the development of modified equipment at much less cost did machine reeling become profitable. After the late 1880s this "acclimatized" modern technology spread rapidly, especially in Nagano, Yamanashi, and Gumma prefectures, and by 1894 it produced more and better-quality

43 The many suggestive insights on this topic in the final chapter of William W. Lockwood, *The Economic Development of Japan: Growth and Structural Change 1868–1938* (Princeton, N.J.: Princeton University Press, 1954), have only recently begun to be followed up with as much enthusiasm as they deserve. See Sydney Crawcour, "Japanese Economic Studies in Foreign Countries in the Postwar Period," *Keizai kenkyū* 30 (January 1979): 49–64.

silk than did the traditional hand-reeling industry. The output per basin rose markedly and the production of filature silk continued to expand. After the 1890s the growth of the industry was firmly based on the new technology. Raw silk was already Japan's leading export before the introduction of modern technology, but with the improved quality of filature silk, promoted by producers' associations and checked by a government-sponsored system of inspection, the value of raw silk exports rose from an annual average of ¥17.7 million between 1883 and 1887 to ¥50 million between 1893 and 1897, ¥92.5 million between 1903 and 1907, and ¥206.8 million between 1913 and 1917.[44]

The success of the modern silk-reeling industry can be attributed only indirectly to government initiative. The technology as first introduced by the government was too capital intensive for the indigenous conditions of plentiful labor and scarce capital, but it did inspire local mechanics to produce modified capital-saving equipment. Although the scale increased over time, the optimum remained fairly small so that filatures could enjoy the advantages of being located close to sources of raw materials and local labor. As the industry became concentrated in Nagano Prefecture, however, it increasingly drew its workers from Toyama and other neighboring prefectures. Modern silk reeling was, moreover, well served by financial institutions that had grown up with the traditional hand-reeling industry, and it benefited from the buoyant export demand and elastic supplies of cocoons.[45]

Whereas Japan's raw silk was competitive from the start in international markets, Japan's indigenous cotton yarn could not compete with imports in either price or quality. Cotton yarn and fabric had been Japan's biggest imports throughout the 1870s, amounting in 1880 to ¥13.2 million, or 36 percent of the value of all imports. Faced with a shortage of foreign exchange, the government hoped that a more efficient domestic spinning industry could replace the imported product. At first officials believed, by analogy with silk reeling, that this could be achieved by using Western spinning machinery in small water-powered mills located in the cotton-growing areas and employing hand spinners then being made redundant by competition from imports. The government therefore imported ten, two-thousand-spindle-sets of spinning machinery and sold them on credit to entrepreneurs in various parts of the country. The importation of three more

44 With the growth of other export industries, raw silk's share of total export value fell over this period from 42 percent to 22 percent.

45 See Katsuo Otsuka, "Technological Choice in the Japanese Silk Industry: Implications for Development in LDCs," Working Paper Series no. A-05, mimeographed (Tokyo: International Development Center of Japan, March 1977).

sets was financed with public funds. The Akabane workshops of the Ministry of Industry, commissioned to make another set on a trial basis, eventually produced a copy of imported Platt Brothers equipment, but at twice the landed cost of the original and of such inferior quality as to be unusable. The whole program of introducing two-thousand-spindle mills proved a costly failure involving the expenditure of over ¥1.6 million of public funds between 1880 and 1884, from which virtually nothing was recovered.

Meanwhile, with the encouragement and support of the ubiquitous promotor Shibusawa Eiichi, a group of Kansai businessmen and others, including some outstanding managers with close government connections, raised ¥240,000 to found the Osaka Spinning Company, which began operation with 10,500 mule spindles in 1884. Learning from the earlier mills' mistakes, the new company used imported raw cotton (initially from China) which was cheaper and of somewhat more suitable quality than the domestic was. The mill was therefore located near the port and used steam in place of less reliable water power. No attempt was made to modify the equipment, as the silk-reeling industry had done, but operations were brought into line with indigenous conditions of plentiful labor and scarce capital by the simple but crucial capital-saving device of working two shifts around the clock. Because labor was already used very intensively, the Osaka mill employed roughly four times as many workers per unit of capital as its English or American counterparts did. The company was an immediate success. Within four years of coming into operation, it was paying dividends of 30 percent on a paid-up capital which had by then been increased fivefold to ¥1.2 million. Other businessmen were quick to follow suit. In 1888 the Japan Cotton Spinners' Association was reorganized to exchange information and experience, promote the development of the industry, and coordinate employment policies, with the members agreeing not to hire away one another's workers. Nevertheless, in the boom conditions of the time there were incessant disputes over the poaching of skilled workers.[46]

In the recession of 1890 the association worked to obtain subsidies and other incentives to penetrate overseas markets. The 5 percent export duty on cotton yarn was abolished in 1894, and the import duty on raw cotton was lifted in 1896. Meanwhile, the industry was converting from mules to ring-frame spindles, which were 50 percent more produc-

46 By contrast, in the early days, skilled hands were lent freely to act as instructors in new mills. The change is no doubt connected with the transition of the cotton-spinning industry from a "national interest" to a "profit motive" basis.

tive and could spin finer counts of yarn. The new spindles, however, required finer and longer staple cotton than was available from China, so in 1892 the association entered into an agreement to purchase Indian cotton in Bombay through its trading organ (Nichimen), and the following year negotiated favorable terms with NYK for cotton shipments from Bombay. After 1895 the domestic consumption of cotton yarn began to level off, and exports became the main avenue for further growth. Export growth was retarded by disruption of the Chinese market during the Sino-Japanese War, but in 1897 exports exceeded imports for the first time. The following year, however, a slump in domestic demand, rising costs, and a shortage of finance sharply reduced profits. To some extent the spinning companies had themselves contributed to these difficulties by their practice of paying high dividends while failing to make adequate provision for reserves, but the association prevailed on Minister of Finance Inoue Kaoru to bail them out by arranging export credits on favorable terms and low-interest loans totaling ¥2.371 million (8 percent of the total paid-up capital of all spinning mills at that time). This enabled the cotton spinners to repay loans and finance further expansion at a cost of capital well below the Japanese market rate. Although the recession continued, accompanied by short-time work and concentration through a series of takeovers by the top six firms, with government assistance, exports continued to rise.[47]

The weaving of cotton fabric was largely a cottage industry before World War I. Japanese-made power looms for weaving standard-width piece goods appeared around the turn of the century and increased in number after the Russo-Japanese War. By 1913 about 25,000 such looms, nearly 80 percent of them in weaving sheds operated by the largest spinning mills, produced 345 million yards valued at ¥215 million.

Cheap labor has often been cited as a reason for the success of the Japanese cotton-spinning industry. A high and rising proportion of the mill hands were female – over 80 percent in 1913 compared with about two-thirds in the United Kingdom and less than half in the United States. Most were uneducated teenaged girls recruited from rural areas where the decline of the cottage textile industry was reducing farmers' cash incomes. Although the girls lived under poor conditions virtually unregulated by legislation and worked twelve-hour shifts for cash wages

47 On development of the modern Japanese cotton-spinning industry, see Fujino Shozaburō et al., eds., LTES, vol. 11 (Textiles); Sanpei Takako, *Nihon mengyō hattatsu shi* (Tokyo: Keiō shobō, 1941). On government assistance to the industry, see Tsūshō Sangyōshō, ed., *Shōkō seisaku shi*, vol. 15: *Sen'i kōgyō* (1) (Tokyo: Shōkō seisaku shi kankōkai, 1968), pp. 158–208.

lower than the earnings of a cottage weaver or silk reeler and lower still than those of an Indian cotton mill worker, rural conditions were such that they could be readily recruited by smooth-talking agents prepared to pay a lump sum to the head of the household.[48] Once hired, however, few worked long enough to acquire a useful degree of skill. Despite the efforts of the Japan Cotton Spinners Association and although most of them lived in closely supervised company dormitories, about half absconded within a few months, and only about one in ten stayed for three or more years. The Kanebō Company tried to improve its labor supply by remaining outside the cotton spinners association and offering somewhat better pay and conditions. Although this does not seem to have reduced labor turnover, the association was worried enough to put heavy pressure on Kanebō to join.[49]

Compared with the United Kingdom or the United States, Japanese labor was cheap relative to capital, and the expansion of the cotton-spinning industry depended on using large numbers of workers in round-the-clock operations. It depended also on coordinating production through the cotton spinners association, promoting exports, and offering government assistance, including official warnings to mill owners against paying themselves more generous dividends than sound long-term management warranted. Nevertheless, by international standards, the industry was still small in 1913 when Japan had a total capacity of 2.34 million spindles, as compared with 55.5 million in the United Kingdom and 30.6 million in the United States. Even in the China market, where Japanese exports were heavily concentrated, the value of Lancashire's share was two and a half times that of Japan.[50]

Although cotton and silk were by far the biggest modern light industries, others had begun before World War I. The woolen textile industry began as a government enterprise because demand was overwhelmingly for military or official use and because production costs were too high to make it commercially profitable in the face of competition from imports. Early government policy was no more successful here than in the other examples already described. The first official move

48 A good source of detailed information, though rather questionable in regard to analysis, is by Takamura Naosuke, *Nihon bōsekigyō shi josetsu* (Tokyo: Hanawa shobō, 1971).

49 See Gary R. Saxonhouse, "Country Girls and Communication Among Competitors in the Japanese Cotton-Spinning Industry," in *Japanese Industrialization and Its Social Consequences*, ed. Hugh Patrick (Berkeley and Los Angeles: University of California Press, 1976), pp. 97–125; and Morita Yoshio, *Nihon keiesha dantai hatten shi* (Tokyo: Nikkan rōdō tsūshin, 1958), pp. 37–43.

50 See David S. Landes, "Technological Change and Development in Western Europe, 1750–1914" in *Cambridge Economic History of Europe*, ed. H. J. Habakkuk and M. Postan, vol. 6, pt. 1 (Cambridge, England: Cambridge University Press, 1965), pp. 443, 467–8.

was an unsuccessful attempt to introduce merino sheep as a domestic source of raw material, and in 1877 a government woolen mill was established at Senju to weave imported yarn into serge for uniforms. Not until the 1900s when wool muslin began to be used for everyday Japanese dress was the private woolen industry, with the aid of a 25 percent *ad valorem* import duty, able to compete with imports.[51] Other modern light industries established before World War I include sugar refining, brewing, printing, papermaking, and glassmaking, but in the overall development of Japanese industry in this period, they were of minor importance compared with textiles.

### *Heavy and engineering industries*

Heavy industries like iron and steel, shipbuilding, and engineering emerged at a relatively early stage in Japan's modern industrial development, not because they presented attractive opportunities to investors, but because the government was convinced that national military and economic security required a fair degree of self-sufficiency in those fields. The Japanese government was well aware that the world powers' strength and influence depended on their capacity to produce iron and steel, ships, and munitions, and it was convinced that catching up with the West implied a commitment to the development of these industries.

Iron and high-quality steel had been made in Japan for centuries; indeed, Japanese swords were prized in China and Southeast Asia as early as the sixteenth century. Excellent though it was, however, Japanese steel was produced by small-scale labor-intensive methods totally inadequate for military requirements in the late nineteenth century. Small experimental blast furnaces built by various domains in the 1850s and 1860s used a smelted iron ore with charcoal and produced wrought iron by puddling, a technology already out of date. Neither the Meiji government nor private firms were able to operate these plants profitably, and so their output was negligible.[52] For railways

51 See Keiichirō Nakagawa and Henry Rosovsky, "The Case of the Dying Kimono: The Influence of Changing Fashions on the Development of the Japanese Woollen Industry," *Business History Review* 37 (Spring–Summer 1963):64.

52 See Thomas C. Smith, *Political Change and Industrial Development in Japan: Government Enterprise 1868–1880* (Stanford, Calif.: Stanford University Press, 1955). Smith stresses the contribution to Japan's economic development made by the government's industrial undertakings in this period. Their contribution to output, however, was small. Most embodied technology inappropriate to Japan and were not, on the whole, the direct progenitors of modern Japanese industry. They did provide important opportunities for learning by doing but in most cases the knowledge and experience so gained could have been acquired more easily and at less cost in other ways.

bridges, ships, and munitions, Meiji Japan relied on imported iron and steel. From 1888 to 1893 those imports averaged some 35,000 tons a year, valued at about ¥2 million. Military expenditures increased fourfold during the Sino-Japanese War and, under the ten-year armament plan initiated in 1896, remained high at around 5.3 percent of gross national expenditure, or nearly two and a half times the prewar ratio. With the additional demands of a railway-building boom, steel imports rose between 1898 and 1900 to an annual average of 182,000 tons, valued at over ¥10 million, compared with home production of less than 2,000 tons.

With little prospect of any growth in its steel industry, the Japanese government, itself the largest consumer of steel, had been considering establishing a government steel works since 1880. In 1891 the government put such a bill before the Diet, with an explanatory statement that included the following:

> Steel is the mother of industries and the foundation of national defence. Without a steel industry other industries cannot flourish and the armed services cannot be properly equipped. We all know that a country's prospects can be gauged by the state of its steel industry. If we want to make this country rich and strong we ought to set up a steelworks.

The statement went on to make a case for state intervention on the grounds of substantial external economies. To the private investor, selling imported steel was more profitable and required much less capital than establishing a steelworks in Japan. Nevertheless, because Japan was not short of iron ore, a Japanese steel industry would be able to compete profitably with imports if pig iron were available in sufficient quantities.

> If we put enough effort into exploration, discovery of iron ore is certain. The reason we have not made any discoveries to date is simply that, not having a steelworks, there was no demand for large quantities of pig iron. Thus, while the establishment of a steelworks would promote the development of the iron industry, there is no hope of a steelworks starting unless an iron industry develops. In these circumstances we shall never get a private enterprise steel mill so there is really no alternative but that the state should establish a mill.[53]

Prime Minister Matsukata Masayoshi, better known for selling off government industrial undertakings than for creating them, supported the bill in a speech stressing the defense need for steel and warning of the strategic dangers of relying on imports. He further claimed that

53 Tsūshō sangyōshō, ed., *Shōkō seisaku shi*, vol. 17: *Tekkō* (Tokyo: Shōkō seisaku shi kankōkai, 1970), pp. 70–1.

home-produced steel would be cheaper in the long run and pointed to the drain on foreign exchange reserves associated with the rapidly rising demand for steel.

An uncooperative House of Representatives rejected the bill by a large majority. In the following year a second attempt failed to obtain an appropriation of ¥2.250 million to establish a steel mill under the Ministry of the Navy. A third attempt, this time under the auspices of the Ministry of Agriculture and Commerce, passed the House of Peers but was rejected by the House of Representatives which also slashed naval construction. Not until the Sino-Japanese War had been in progress for six months did the government finally obtain the Diet's approval for an integrated steel mill, at a cost of ¥4.095 million. In 1901 the Yawata Ironworks began operation with a designed capacity of 210,000 tons of steel and planned to rise to 300,000 tons in 1906 and 380,000 tons in 1911.[54] By 1911 the total capital cost had risen to over ¥50 million, and another ¥27 million in state-backed loans had been invested to develop the Hanyenping iron mines in central China.[55] In its first ten years, Yawata accumulated operating losses of ¥9.7 million, but with experience and tariff protection after 1911, the enterprise began to operate at a profit, producing rolled steel competitive with imports. Rolled steel output was, however, far below expectations at 5,000 tons in 1901, 64,000 tons in 1906, and 181,000 tons in 1911. By 1913 it had risen to 216,000 tons, but Japan's total production still met only one-third of its domestic requirements.

The private iron and steel industry produced less than 10 percent of Japan's steel output before the Russo-Japanese War. During that war, however, it made some headway and by 1913 was responsible for about a quarter of the domestic production of pig iron and rolled steel. Whereas a private enterprise steel mill had been unthinkable twenty years earlier, several now emerged without overt subsidies. What made this possible was the assurance of government orders at profitable prices. With the huge increase in money available for defense – the Russo-Japanese War cost ten times as much as did the Sino-Japanese War – costs seemed unimportant to the government compared with the urgent needs of national security.

In an instructive example of state–private cooperation in "national interest" heavy industry, Hokkaidō tankō (Hokkaido Coal Mining)

54 Yawata seitetsusho, ed., *Yawata seitetsusho 50-nen shi* (Tokyo: Yawata seitetsusho, 1950), pp. 62–3.

55 These loans to the Hanyeping (Han-yeh-p'ing) company were the subject of some of the Twenty-one Demands served on the Chinese government in January 1915.

joined with Vickers Armstrong in forming Nippon seikōsho (Nippon Steelworks) to supply ordnance and other equipment to the navy. After the nationalization of their railway lines in 1906, the directors of Hokkaidō tankō found themselves with funds to invest, whereas the navy, frustrated by its experience of intransigent Diets, was looking for ways to satisfy its steel requirements and enhance Japan's self-sufficiency in armaments, by promoting private investment. Through the good offices of successive navy ministers, Admirals Yamamoto Gonnohyōe and Saitō Minoru, the Hokkaidō men came to an arrangement with the commander of the Kure naval base, which in turn interested Vickers Armstrong in the project. By 1913 Nippon seikōsho, with fixed capital of ¥22 million and rated annual capacity of 157,500 tons of steel, was second only to Yawata.

Several mills to make finished steel from ingot and scrap were founded during this period. Some, like Nippon Steel Pipe, Fuji Steel, and Kobe Steel, eventually became major steel manufacturers. All received technical assistance and profitable orders from government agencies. Kobe Steel (originally Kobayashi Steel) owed its success to Kosugi Tatsuzō, a senior engineer of the Kure Naval Arsenal who moved to the firm in 1904, bringing eight of his most promising colleagues with him. The whole group received a year's training at the Vickers steelworks in the United Kingdom before setting up an open-hearth furnace and ancillary plant at Kobe. With assurances of orders from the Kure Naval Arsenal at prices five to six times the prime cost, the project could scarcely fail. Under the navy's policy of raising the Japanese content of its hardware, this and other plants became virtual auxiliaries of the naval arsenals. Sooner or later most came under the aegis of one or another of the major zaibatsu. Coordination of private and public interests was then handled through channels of institutional communication between zaibatsu and government rather than through personal connections.

In 1913, Japan produced 255,000 tons of rolled steel, of which Yawata produced 85 percent, but relied on imports for over half of its pig iron and two-thirds of its rolled steel. Japanese steel production was only one-hundredth that of the United States, and U.S. Steel's Gary, Indiana, mill alone produced five times as much as did the whole Japanese industry. On the eve of World War I, Japan's steel output may have been, in G. C. Allen's words, "of very slight importance,"[56] but it was more than any country in the world had produced

56 G. C. Allen, *A Short Economic History of Modern Japan* (London: Allen & Unwin, 1946), p. 74.

in 1870, a measure of the industry's novelty and of the relative shortness of Japan's lag behind the Western powers.

Shipbuilding, like the steel industry, was closely linked to national security and consisted of state and private enterprises. Of the dockyards inherited by the Meiji government, Yokosuka became a naval dockyard, and Nagasaki passed to Mitsubishi, Hyōgo to Kawasaki, and Ishikawajima, after being closed by the government, to a company promoted by Shibusawa. By World War I, dozens of shipyards had sprung up, but only the naval dockyards at Yokosuka, Kure, and Sasebo and the private yards of Mitsubishi at Nagasaki and Kawasaki at Kobe, were capable of building large modern steamers. Until the Sino-Japanese War, Japanese shipyards were mainly used for repairs and refits. Equipment and technical competence were limited, and materials had to be imported at high prices. The then small domestic fleet of steamships consisted almost entirely of foreign-built vessels of which seventy-three (a total tonnage of 100,000 tons) were imported between 1880 and 1893. Under the major naval expansion plan initiated in 1883, only one naval vessel, the *Hashidate,* was built at the Yokosuka Naval Dockyard. All the rest were ordered from the United Kingdom or France. The Sino-Japanese War clearly showed the inadequacy of Japan's shipbuilding capacity. During the war years, all of the merchant marine's suitable vessels were pressed into service; more than eighty ships (a total tonnage of 160,000 tons) were bought from abroad; and many more were chartered. Most of these ships were steel-hulled steamers of two thousand or more tons. The only civilian shipyard capable of handling even repairs to vessels of this size was Mitsubishi's Nagasaki dockyard.

With a coming confrontation with Russia in mind, the government made strenuous efforts after 1895 to expand the naval fleet, but again all of the larger ships had to be ordered from foreign yards, and only seven torpedo boats were built or assembled in Japan. The Shipbuilding Encouragement Act of 1896 was designed to promote the domestic construction of merchant ships. Under its provisions, steel steamships built by wholly Japanese-owned private shipyards attracted a subsidy of ¥12 per ton for ships of between seven hundred and one thousand tons and ¥20 per ton for those of one thousand or more tons. A further subsidy of ¥5 per horsepower would be paid if the engines were made in Japan. These subsidies, however, scarcely made up for the higher cost of steel plate and other materials. Japanese shipping companies still found foreign shipyards cheaper, far better technically and more prompt in delivery than were the domestic yards. The Mitsubishi dockyard build the six-thousand-ton *Hitachi Maru* in 1898 with much help from the navy's experts, but it was not until the Navigation Subsidy Act was amended in 1899 to reduce subsidies payable for foreign-built ships to half that for domestically built vessels that Japanese shipyards received enough orders to warrant upgrading their facilities. Between 1899 and 1904, Mitsubishi and Kawasaki built twenty-six steamers of one thousand or more tons, including six of over five thousand tons.

Despite this modest progress, the Russo-Japanese War again found the industry wanting.[57] Once more, nearly the whole Japanese merchant marine was requisitioned for the duration, and imports of merchant ships soared to 314,000 tons. Deliveries of warships from foreign sources were cut off by suppliers anxious to maintain neutrality. Light though Japanese losses were compared with those of the Russian fleet, they included two battleships, two cruisers, and fourteen smaller ships. Under wartime pressure and regardless of cost, the naval dockyards succeeded in building a battleship, an armored cruiser, and two second-class cruisers, and the Mitsubishi and Kawasaki yards, which in 1904 could build nothing bigger than a torpedo boat, built destroyers. Even the naval dockyards, then much better equipped than the private yards were, used very labor-intensive methods. The battle cruisers *Tsukuba* and *Ikoma*, for example, were built by workers operating like waves of shock troops without the aid of large gantry cranes or pneumatic riveters.

As a result of this wartime progress, however, Japan became practically self-sufficient in naval construction. Of the seventy-eight naval vessels totaling 360,000 tons commissioned between 1905 and 1915, all but seven were built in Japan, a quarter of them by private industry. Merchant shipbuilding also advanced. With tariff increases on imported ships from 5 percent *ad valorem* in 1897 to 10 percent in 1906 and 15 percent in 1910, the subsidies, though still of great benefit to the major shipping companies, became a relatively less important source of encouragement to shipbuilders.[58]

Because of both the official recognition of shipbuilding as essential to national defense and naval influence and technical assistance, by

57 The Russo-Japanese War cost ten times as much as did the Sino-Japanese War and stretched the Japanese economy to the limit. Casualties, too, were heavy.

58 Mitsubishi zōsen KK, sōmuka, ed., "Honpō kindai zōsen hogoseisaku no enkaku," reprinted in *Nihon sangyō shiryō taikei*, vol. 5, pp. 729–822.

1914 the industry had, with the aid of subsidies and tariff protection, reached a position from which it could profit from the exceptional opportunities presented by World War I.

The development of the engineering industries generally belongs to the post–World War I period, but their origins date back to the 1880s when military arsenals and the Miyata Small Arms Company began to manufacture rifles in some quantity. We have already described the early progress in the manufacture of marine engines. This was followed by the manufacture of rolling stock, and by the 1890s Japan was producing a growing proportion of the goods wagons and passenger carriages required by its expanding railway network. The first Japanese-built locomotive was assembled in the government's Kobe railway workshops in 1893 under the direction of an English engineer,[59] but this was hardly more than an advanced exercise in technical training. Even in 1912, of Japan's stock of 2,636 locomotives, only 162 were of Japanese manufacture.[60] In textile machinery, the Toyoda Automatic Loom Company produced powered looms in quantity by 1913 in what may have been Japan's first mass-production engineering plant, but almost all spinning machinery was imported before World War I.

The manufacture of electrical equipment began with telegraphic and telephonic equipment. Although government workshops played an important role in introducing the technology, most of the development was by private enterprise. One of the leading firms, Oki Kibatarō's Meikōsha (now Oki denki kōgyō), used profits accumulated during the Sino-Japanese and Russo-Japanese wars to become a competitive producer of telephones, whose price was brought down from ¥55 to ¥10 or even less within fifteen years.[61] The production of electric generators and motors was in the experimental stage and involved a good deal of tinkering until Tokyo Electric in 1905, and then the Shibaura (now Toshiba) works, obtained access to General Electric capital, patents, and technology in return for a share in their companies. Other firms like Nippon Electric (NEC), Mitsubishi Electric, and Fuji Electric later made similar arrangements with major foreign electrical concerns, but for a decade or more after the Russo-Japanese War, General Electric technology dominated the industry. Other

59 Richard Francis Trevithick, brother of Francis Henry, also a locomotive expert with the Japanese railways and a grandson of Richard (1771–1833), whose inventions entitle him to be considered the inventor of the locomotive steam engine.

60 Arisawa Hiromi, ed., *Gendai Nihon sangyō kōza*, vol. 5: *Kikai kōgyō (1)* (Tokyo: Iwanami shoten, 1960), p. 50.

61 Oki Kibatarō denki hensan gakari, ed., *Oki Kibatarō* (Tokyo: Oki Kibatarō denki hensan gakari, 1932), p. 105.

branches of engineering were of little significance before World War I. The value of Japan's machine tool output, a good indicator of the state of its engineering industries, was a mere ¥30,000 in 1914. To put the matter in better perspective, even in 1930 "the entire complex of mining, metallurgy and machinery industries furnished no more than 8% of Japan's national product."[62]

The development of heavy industry and engineering clearly depended on state support, most of which was linked to considerations of national security and defense. The effect of war and preparations for war on Japan's modern economic development has been the subject of some debate. Until World War I the growth of the modern sector was strongly correlated with military expenditure. When military expenditure rose sharply during the Sino-Japanese and Russo-Japanese wars, the modern sector grew rapidly. After each of those wars both the share of military expenditure in gross national expenditure and the share of the modern sector's output in GNP fell somewhat but remained above prewar levels. According to Harry Oshima, "the most important lesson of Meiji public finance is that rapid economic growth and rapid militarization of the economy are fundamentally incompatible."[63] William Lockwood stressed "the continual drain of armaments on Japan's limited capital resources, on her advanced machine skills; and especially on the government budget itself" and suggested that "a small fraction of these sums spent on reducing disease and accident rates in urban industry, for example, would have increased productive efficiency as well as human well-being."[64] In the 1930s and 1940s the heavy and engineering industries were indeed so closely geared to defense that their contribution to the civilian population's living standards was far from obvious. On the other hand, as Kozo Yamamura pointed out, military preparedness was "the principal motivation behind creating and expanding the arsenals and other publicly-financed shipyards and modern factories which acted as highly effective centers for the absorption and dissemination of Western technologies and skills" and provided "at critical junctures" the demand for private firms.[65] Whether in the long run the game was worth the candle is a matter for individual judgment rather than eco-

62 Lockwood, *The Economic Development of Japan*, p. 575.
63 Harry T. Oshima, "Meiji Fiscal Policy and Agricultural Progress" in *The State and Economic Enterprise in Japan: Essays in the Political Economy of Growth*, ed. William W. Lockwood (Princeton, N.J.: Princeton University Press, 1965), p. 381.
64 Lockwood, *The Economic Development of Japan*, p. 577.
65 Kozo Yamamura, "Success Illgotten? The Role of Meiji Militarism in Japan's Technical Progress," *Journal of Economic History* 37 (March 1977): 113.

nomic calculation. Attempts to assess what the effect on national income would have been if military had been replaced by civil investment must fail, if only because military investment was not simply a component of national income but an inseparable part of a whole economic, political, social, and ideological system.

## WORLD WAR I

World War I rescued Japan from fiscal and balance-of-payments problems that might otherwise have retarded its economic growth. Victory over Russia cost, along with appallingly high casualties, a direct expenditure of ¥2 billion. The strains of the war affected Japan's economy for nearly a decade. A large part of the war's cost was financed by overseas borrowing that raised foreign indebtedness from less than ¥100 million in 1903 to ¥1.4 billion in 1907. Between 1909 and 1913, deficits in current international payments continued to run at around ¥80 million to ¥90 million annually, precluding an expansionary fiscal policy and prolonging the postwar recession. During this same five years the tax burden per capita, although almost double the pre-1904 level in real terms, did little more than cover military expenditures and service the national debt. But despite these difficulties, output grew at a respectable 3 percent a year, well above the prewar average.

The outbreak of war in 1914 did not bring immediate benefits to Japan. Indeed, the dislocation of the world economy initially added to its difficulties. After 1915, however, the war transformed the economic climate. Although formally engaged on the Allied side, Japan took virtually no part in the hostilities, and so its economy benefited not only from Allied orders for munitions and manufactures but also from the removal of Western competition in both domestic and Asian mainland markets. Between 1914 and 1918, Japan's real gross national product rose by 40 percent, an average annual rate of nearly 9 percent. This growth was accompanied by a massive turnaround in international trade and payments and a spurt in private industrial investment. Because such a high proportion of output went into exports and investment and because productivity in consumption goods industries lagged, gains in personal consumption and average standards of living were much more modest. The distribution of income, too, became more unequal as some investors and speculators made large profits from the boom, whereas those on relatively fixed incomes found their living standards reduced by inflation. As private enterprise in modern industry and commerce, hitherto heavily dependent on government support, suddenly became highly profitable, the modern business establishment (*zaikai*) acquired a new degree of confidence and political influence. The foundation of the Industrial Club of Japan in 1917 by leaders of modern industry headed by representatives of the zaibatsu was symbolic of their new status. When economic conditions returned to normal early in 1920, much of the optimism and confidence of the war years was shown to have been misplaced, but modern industry had made real progress, and the foundations had been laid for self-sustaining industrial growth. This growth continued even in the difficult conditions of the 1920s, whereas change in traditional industries producing consumer goods for the home market was much slower, and the gap between these and modern large-scale industry began to widen.

## *Foreign trade*

In 1913 Japan paid around ¥70 million a year in interest abroad, and partly for this reason, current international payments were running a deficit of about ¥90 million a year. Had this situation continued under the gold standard system in operation at the time, it would have necessitated a fairly severe retrenchment that would have further hampered recovery and led to a period of slower growth. But the export opportunities provided by the war removed this balance-of-payments restraint and permitted an investment boom of unprecedented proportions.

The initial disruption of trade at the outbreak of war caused both exports and imports to fall, but in 1915 receipts from exports and shipping services rose sharply, though imports continued to decline, producing a record current surplus of over ¥200 million. This surplus reached a peak of ¥1 billion in 1917 and totaled ¥3 billion between 1915–1919. Over the same period Japan was a net exporter of long-term capital to the extent of ¥1.5 billion, changing from a debtor nation to a substantial international creditor. Although merchandise exports increased by only a third in volume, world prices rose so high that their value rose over threefold and the value of manufactured exports, mainly textiles, rose sixfold. Asian markets absorbed about half of these exports. There was little change in the geographical distribution of exports until 1919 when European demand collapsed and was replaced by increased sales to the United States. The war years also brought a huge increase in foreign exchange earnings from shipping services. With the Allied merchant fleets suffering heavy losses, freight and charter rates soared to ten or twenty times their 1914 level. Japan's merchant marine expanded from 1.58 million gross registered tons in 1914 to 2.8 million in 1919. Net annual foreign earnings from shipping rose from ¥41 million to a peak of over ¥450 million in 1918.

The financial system could not cope with so large and so sudden a change in international payments at a time when international gold movements were suspended because of the war. The inflationary effects of foreign payments surpluses therefore went unchecked, and the subsequent failure to bring down prices far enough in the postwar years was the main reason that the foreign balances accumulated during the war were run down. Nevertheless, the gains of the war boom were not entirely wasted. Most of the postwar increase in imports went for raw materials, semifinished goods (mainly iron and steel), and machinery to support an expanded manufacturing sector.

Although the output of all sectors increased between 1914 and 1919, the greatest percentage gains (valued at constant 1934–6 prices) were in manufacturing (72 percent) and transport, communications, and power (60 percent). Increases in mining (26 percent) and agriculture (11.5 percent) were much lower.[66] The farm-labor force fell by 1.8 million, but there was a rise of 2.6 million in nonagricultural employment. The mining and manufacturing share of net domestic product in current prices rose from 20 percent to 30 percent but fell back after the war and did not again regain the wartime peak until 1935.[67] Thus, in both output and employment, the share of primary industry fell, but that of the secondary and tertiary industries, especially the modern manufacturing sector, rose during the war.

## *Agriculture*

Improved agricultural productivity, due partly to the diffusion of technical advances introduced in the decade before 1914, was stimulated by increased domestic and export demand for agricultural products that resulted in more than a trebling of prices. Much of the wartime increase in agricultural output was, in fact, due to a 60 percent increase in the output of cocoons to supply the strong United States demand for raw silk. But the steep rise in food prices ultimately proved disadvantageous to farmers when widespread discontent among urban consumers, cul-

66 Ohkawa and Shinohara, eds., *Patterns of Japanese Economic Development*, pp. 289 (agriculture), p. 305 (manufactures), and p. 313 (commerce and services). The figure for mining is from LTES, vol. 10, p. 265. 67 LTES, vol. 1, p. 240.

minating in the rice riots of 1918, and political pressure from manufacturers to keep down wage costs forced the government to abandon agricultural protection in favor of increasing imports of cheaper rice and other staple foods from the colonial territories of Korea and Taiwan.

### *Heavy industry and machinery*

It was in industry that change was fastest and most far-reaching. Between 1914 and 1919, manufacturing output increased by 72 percent, with only 42 percent more labor, representing a substantial productivity gain per worker. This was achieved by a large increase in capital investment. Paid-up capital of manufacturing companies increased five- or sixfold, but business was so good that for the leading companies, the rate of profit on paid-up capital rose from around 15 percent to over 50 percent. The highest output growth was in machinery (29 percent per annum), with slower growth in textiles (11 percent), iron and steel (9 percent), and food products (5 percent) and other consumer goods. In the machinery industry, including shipbuilding, vehicles, and machine tools, expansion and technical progress was mainly the work of private industry, whose capacity increased greatly relative to that of government establishments.

Shipbuilding, which had made considerable advances in scale and technology during the Russo-Japanese War, was stimulated by a rise in the price of new ships from ¥120 to a 1918 peak of ¥800 per gross registered ton. The industry increased its work force from 26,000 to 95,000 and its output from eight vessels totaling 40,500 gross registered tons in 1915 to 174 totaling 600,000 gross registered tons in 1918. With prices soaring, the value of output increased from ¥7 million to ¥405 million, but the cost of materials rose sharply too. By 1918, steel plate was fifteen times its 1914 price and in such short supply in April of that year that the major shipbuilders contracted to receive 128,000 tons of American steel in return for an equal deadweight tonnage of ships, and the following month they contracted for a further 123,000 tons of steel in exchange for twice that weight of ships.[68] Demand was so buoyant and profits so large – ships under construction were frequently sold and resold at a huge profit – that even the small, ill-equipped yards that had proliferated during the war yielded good returns. The leading builders greatly raised productivity

68 The United States' embargo on steel exports was one reason for the shortage. These swap deals were exempted from the embargo.

by standardization and improved programming, almost halving construction times. Mitsubishi installed a model-testing tank and other research facilities, and several yards upgraded their technical standards to meet the navy orders' requirements. When demand collapsed at the end of the war, most of the small yards failed, but Mitsubishi, Kawasaki, and three or four other advanced yards were kept going by orders from the navy, which was anxious for these builders to maintain their technical staff and facilities as a national defense resource.[69]

In the manufacture of rolling stock as well, the role of private enterprise increased under the patronage of the Ministry of Railways, which adopted a policy of placing orders with private firms and providing technical assistance where necessary. Confidence in these firms' technical standards was apparently limited, as the ministry's own workshops produced and supplied wheels, axles, bogies, and other parts crucial to safe operation and entrusted little more than coach building and assembly to the private contractors. Locomotives and tenders, however, were fully built by larger specialist firms with technical standards comparable to those of the ministry's own workshops.[70]

During the war, the leading shipbuilding firms, like Mitsubishi and Kawasaki, also expanded their general engineering capacity, building large steam and water turbines for the rapidly growing electric power industry. The output of steam engines, turbines, pumps, and internal combustion engines rose sharply as the major makers expanded their work forces tenfold. By the end of the war Japan was close to self-sufficient in these products. Stimulated by rapid electrification and with technical and managerial assistance from the major firms' American partners, the manufacture of electric motors and equipment was the most advanced branch of the engineering industry, boasting modern machinery, capital-intensive methods, and high standards of quality. As in other branches of engineering, few of the small firms that mushroomed during the war survived the return of overseas competition, but the larger firms that had greatly improved their capacity during the war remained competitive in medium-to-small generators, motors, transformers, and switching gear and even made some headway in the Chinese market.

With so many manufacturers eager to expand during the war, the demand for machine tools was extremely strong, and with imports

69 "Honpō kindai zōsen hogosaku no enkaku," pp. 778–821.
70 "Kikai kōgyō," in *Nihon sangyō shiryō taikei*, vol. 7, p. 33.

reduced to a trickle, domestic producers did their best to fill the gap. Output rose from a very low prewar level to a 1918 peak of nearly seventeen thousand tons, mainly general-purpose lathes but including as well a few turret lathes; planing, milling, and boring machines; radial drills; and gear hobbers. Although the Ikegai Ironworks, one of the oldest and most advanced tool makers, produced good, well-designed precision machinery, much of the domestically produced equipment was of inferior quality. This in turn affected the quality of the goods the equipment was used to produce. Because products of better quality could not be obtained, even indifferent machinery found a ready market, but when imports resumed (with the United States replacing the United Kingdom as the main supplier), the machinery could not be sold. Only the best makers, like Ikegai, were able to survive, owing to orders from the army and navy, which regarded a domestic machine tool industry like shipbuilding as essential to defense purposes.

The most severe wartime shortages were in iron and steel. Private steel-making capacity was still very small in 1914. Even with the expansion of the state steelworks at Yawata after the Russo-Japanese War, Japan produced only one-third of its rolled steel requirements. The price of pig iron skyrocketed from the 1913 average of ¥49 per ton to a maximum of ¥541, steel rod from ¥75 to ¥559, and steel plate from ¥85 to as much as ¥1,285.[71] In January 1916 the government obtained the Diet's approval to double Yawata's output by 1922, at a cost of ¥35 million, but escalating costs and difficulties in obtaining equipment abroad delayed the plan's implementation. By 1919 the plant's output had risen by only about 20 percent. In the wartime sellers' market, however, its operations were highly profitable. In contrast with losses of over ¥11 million accumulated during its first decade of operation, Yawata's wartime profits totaled ¥151 million, more than enough to cover the accumulated losses and the whole capital investment. Leaders of private enterprise, who had long believed that too much of the taxpayers' money had been invested in the state's steel industry, now resented the profits it was making. With the backing of the newly formed Industrial Club of Japan, private iron and steel makers obtained a substantial quid pro quo for dropping their opposition to the state-operated Yawata works, in the form of the Iron and Steel Promotion Act of 1917. Under its provisions, companies with an annual capacity of 35,000 or more tons were eligible to

71 "Honpō kindai zōsen hogoseisaku no enkaku," pp. 809–10.

acquire land on very favorable terms and to import plants and materials free of duty, and individual plants with a capacity of 5,250 or more tons were exempted from business and income taxes. With this encouragement, several small steel mills were set up, many using pig iron from Manchuria and Korea, but the greatest gains were made by large producers such as Nippon Steel's integrated mill in Hokkaido, Mitsubishi's mill in Korea and the Ōkura group and the South Manchurian Railway Company using Manchuria's rich mineral deposits. By 1919, the private enterprise output of pig iron had risen from 80,000 tons to over 500,000 tons, and the output of rolled steel from 52,000 tons to 277,000 tons. This was twice as much pig iron and almost as much steel as Yawata produced at the time, but in the postwar recession, private output fell, whereas that of Yawata continued to rise.[72] Although Japan still produced only half of its rolled steel requirements, with new capacity coming on stream, this proportion was rising, and imports came increasingly from Manchurian and other mainland sources under Japanese control.

### *Textiles*

The demand for textiles, though not as strong as for the products of heavy industry and engineering, was buoyant during the war. Cotton spinners were able to raise their dividends from an average of 13 percent between 1910 and 1913 to an average of 46 percent between 1918 and 1920 on a paid-up capital that had trebled in the interval. Financial expansion was not matched by the expansion of productive capacity. Between 1914 and 1919 the number of spindles in operation rose by about one-third, but output increased by only one-sixth, mainly because high-quality imported equipment and parts were not available. The output per worker, however, rose significantly, as a fourfold wage rise stimulated spinning companies to use their workers more economically.[73] With output barely able to supply strong domestic demand, Japanese spinners were unable to exploit opportunities in the Chinese market and instead invested some of their profits to acquire cotton-spinning capacity in China itself. On the other hand, the spinning companies increased their weaving capacity by 75 percent and their output of cotton cloth by 50 percent. Exports of cotton cloth also rose greatly in value, though much less in quantity.

72 "Honpō seitekkōgyō gaikyō," in *Nihon sangyō shiryō taikei*, vol. 7, pp. 620–1.
73 *Meiji Taishō kokusei sōran*, pp. 610–11.

The silk industry, after suffering from the disruption of its overseas markets at the outbreak of war, enjoyed an unprecedented boom as domestic and United States markets expanded. From a low of ¥700 per one hundred catties in November 1914, the price of raw silk rose to a peak of almost ¥4,000 in January 1920 before plummeting to ¥1,195 in August. Production and exports rose by 60 percent in volume and by far more in value, bringing comparative prosperity to hundreds of thousands of sericulturalists and cottage silk weavers.

### *From "traditional industry" to "small-scale industry"*

In contrast with the industries producing for military or investment demand, those producing for domestic or foreign consumption remained mainly labor-intensive, small in scale, and slower to accept technological innovation. The main change was the application of electric power to traditional production processes. By 1919, 26 percent of plants with five to fourteen workers used electric power, compared with only 7.8 percent in 1914.[74] In organization and style of production, these industries changed little, but their role in the economy, especially their relationship with large modern businesses, was undergoing a transformation. Whereas the traditional industry of the Meiji era had been the mainstay of the economy and its growth had been the necessary complement to the growth of the modern sector, in the post–World War I recession, small-scale industry became very much the poor relation or even the servant of modern business. By that time, small-scale industry included not only traditional consumption-goods industries but also small engineering workshops that had emerged to meet wartime shortages, often as suppliers to larger firms. Those that survived the postwar slump received cast-off equipment and even workers from the larger firms and acted as a reserve of capacity to meet temporary or peak demand.

Although small-scale industries continued to employ the majority of industrial workers, their labor productivity fell far below that of the capital-intensive modern enterprises that responded to the postwar recession by drastically reducing their work forces and more efficiently using those they retained. It was at this time that gaps began to open in wage and profit rates, as between small businesses and leading modern firms. The postwar recession also saw the emergence of differences in the structure of markets for products and factors of produc-

74 LTES, vol. 12, pp. 228–45.

tion that later characterized what has been called the "dual" or "differential" economic structure.[75]

## THE ROLE OF THE STATE

No explanation of industrialization and technological change in Japan between 1885 and 1920 would be complete or satisfying without considering the role of the state. Its part in creating the infrastructure of administration, transport and communications, financial institutions, and education was of major importance in providing the environment in which industry and commerce could expand and develop. All sectors of the economy benefited, but throughout the Meiji era, traditional sectors were the greatest beneficiaries, if only because of their aggregate size. We have already discussed the part played by official subsidies, protection (after tariff autonomy was gained), technical assistance, and government demand in the establishment of modern industries like shipping, shipbuilding, and engineering. Let us turn to a consideration of the general impact of the state on the economy.

### *Fiscal and monetary policy*

The Meiji government inherited a taxing power that had put at the disposal of central and local authorities about 20 percent of the national output, a high proportion for a preindustrial country.[76] In the twenty years after the Restoration, the fiscal system was renovated, and the tax base altered and enlarged. Between 1880 and 1920, central and local government income averaged 14 percent of Japan's gross national product, giving the government the power to allocate substantial resources without increasing customary levels of taxation.

Fiscal policy, that is, influencing the economy through the level and structure of central and local budgets, has generally been regarded as important to Japan's economic development in this period. In the 1880s, about half of the government's revenue was raised from agriculture. Although this proportion fell steadily as taxes on consumption, income, and property rose, taxation on the whole before World War I fell more heavily on agriculture and traditional businesses than on the modern sector. Its regressive nature tended to restrict consumption and to promote saving, with positive effects on the rate of growth.

75 Ohkawa, *Differential Structure and Agriculture*, p. 61.
76 Cf. E. Sydney Crawcour, "The Tokugawa Heritage," in *The State and Economic Enterprise in Japan*, p. 31. The figure of 25 to 27 percent given there now seems on the high side.

Military expenditures absorbed the greatest percentage of total government outlays (including capital expenditures), rising from 15 percent in the late 1880s to an average of 34 percent between 1890 and 1900 and 48 percent between 1901 and 1910, before falling back to 41 percent between 1911 and 1920. Whatever its other implications, these expenditures stimulated the growth of the modern sector. Transfer payments,[77] mainly interest on public debt, the second largest budget item, were as high as 15 percent of all government expenditures in the late 1890s and averaged 9 or 10 percent for the remainder of the period. On the whole, these transfers were from lower to higher income groups and so tended to promote income inequality and therefore saving. Over the period as a whole, about 10 percent of all expenditures was for transport and communications.[78] Direct subsidies to industry, though a relatively small budget item, could be quite crucial to particular industries like shipbuilding.

Through monetary policy, governments affected price trends and general business conditions. About half of the period between 1888 and World War I was characterized by the sort of mildly inflationary climate in which business is said to thrive. Budget deficits during the Sino-Japanese War raised the inflation rate to about 10 percent, but with the introduction of the gold standard, prices steadied. The move from silver- to gold-based yen facilitated overseas borrowing, but at the sacrifice of the stimulus to exports that had until then been provided by the steady depreciation of silver. Partly for reasons connected with the move to the gold standard, business conditions were only fair until the Russo-Japanese War, when budget deficits again raised prices, especially of manufactures, despite large foreign borrowings. The war was followed by a period of contractionary fiscal policy designed to maintain the external value of the yen and to facilitate service of the foreign debt. Prices stabilized until the rapid World War I inflation which reflected wartime shortages and the financial system's inability to cope with the surge in foreign exchange holdings. For the period as a whole, fiscal and monetary policy might best be described as moderately benign rather than as a major positive factor in eco-

77 Transfer payments are government expenditures that are not spent on goods and services supplied in the year of payment. Other examples are welfare payments and government pensions. Transfer payments are not included in the national accounts as part of the gross national product.

78 These figures are from Ohkawa and Shinohara, eds., *Patterns of Japanese Economic Development*, pp. 370–4. The figure for transport and communications is derived from Harry T. Oshima, "Meiji Fiscal Policy and Agricultural Progress," in *The State and Economic Enterprise in Japan*, pp. 370–1.

nomic growth. Considering the strains with which policy had to cope, however, this was a creditable performance.

### *The polity and the market*

Did the Japanese government simply provide an infrastructure and a business climate favorable to economic enterprise, leaving investment and production decisions to be determined by market forces? Or were there important areas in which the government effectively preempted those decisions, overriding such considerations as relative factor prices and demand conditions? Is it possible, in other words, that state intervention brought about more growth than would otherwise have occurred?[79]

Some economists oppose state intervention on the grounds that it cannot raise total output above the level that would be produced by the operation of competitive markets. Free competitive markets are not, however, necessarily the best strategy for long-run dynamic growth. Specifically, market forces do not maximize long-run growth when the returns from an investment depend on other developments outside the investor's control. We have already seen that in the 1890s neither an ironworks nor a steel mill in isolation was a profitable investment on market grounds, though both together were profitable. A coal mine might not be profitable without a railway to carry its product to the market, but a railway might not be economical without the development of both the coal mine and other industries along its route. Yet all of these might be highly productive investments as parts of a state-supported development program.

In the advanced industrial countries with which economists were most familiar, these facts were thought to be minor exceptions to the general proposition, and in any case the state could not be expected to see far enough into the future to identify them.[80] Such situations are, however, typical of a backward economy whose development requires introducing many new activities. In a late-developing economy, moreover, they can readily be identified by reference to advanced econo-

79 This question was raised in Chalmers Johnson, *MITI and the Japanese Miracle: The Growth of Industrial Policy, 1925–1975* (Stanford, Calif.: Stanford University Press, 1982), pp. 3–34. See also David E. Williams, "Beyond Political Economy: A Critique of Issues Raised in Chalmers Johnson's *MITI and the Japanese Miracle*," Social and Economic Research on Modern Japan, Occasional Paper no. 35 (Berlin: East Asian Institute, Free University of Berlin, 1983).

80 Those who oppose government intervention in the economy on economic or ideological grounds attribute Japan's economic success to the triumph of free enterprise rather than to effective government policy. See R. P. Sinha, "Unresolved Issues in Japan's Early Economic Development," *Scottish Journal of Political Economy* 16 (June 1969): 141–8.

mies in which a more productive industrial system is already operating. In those circumstances, a government with the will and the means to carry out or coordinate investment in new industries can play an important role. This may, in fact, be the greatest advantage of economic backwardness.[81]

Japan's leaders had the knowledge, the will, and the means to play such a role, and they had no ideological inhibitions about doing so. They had before them a working model, as it were, of an industrial economy acquired by observing Britain, France, Germany, and the United States. This is not, of course, to suggest that the Japanese government's economic measures were systematically designed according to a long-term master plan. Even though the bureaucracy had access to detailed economic information, it made mistakes, such as the early uncritical introduction of Western technology without sufficient regard for Japanese conditions. Much government intervention was piecemeal or opportunistic. After 1890, disbursements were often more influenced by electoral tactics than by development strategy, and government leaders were often at cross-purposes. Nevertheless, the extent of Japan's success seems to indicate the existence of such a wealth of possibilities for constructive intervention that many were realized, despite the less-than-optimal government strategy.

The Japanese government's will to promote economic growth is clear from the political history of the period and needs no elaboration here. Its power to do so derived from its considerable fiscal resources, amplified through control of the Bank of Japan, the Hypothec Bank, the Industrial Bank of Japan, other special banks, and the postal savings funds. By selectively guaranteeing loans and dividends, moreover, the government could influence the investment of private funds. The active role of government in economic life derived also from a tradition of state intervention in pre-Restoration times, when the primacy of the administrative power and the detailed regulation of economic life were taken for granted.[82]

In the older industrial countries of the West, classical economic doctrines postulated the universal pursuit of profit as the "invisible hand" that maximized total outputs. This theory both justified busi-

81 Cf. the title piece in Alexander Gerschenkron, *Economic Backwardness in Historical Perspective: A Book of Essays* (Cambridge, Mass.: Harvard University Press, 1962); and Ronald Dore, *British Factory–Japanese Factory: The Origins of National Diversity in Industrial Relations* (London: Allen & Unwin, 1973), pp. 404–20.

82 Tokugawa political theory assumed that the labor and ingenuity of the people was at the disposal of the administrative power. This view, though greatly modified during the Meiji era, never entirely disappeared and enjoyed a spectacular revival in the 1930s and 1940s.

ness activity and limited the economic role of the state. Although the libertarian ideas of John Stuart Mill and others were introduced to Japan soon after the Restoration, they did not take root. After the 1880s it was the German Historical school, especially Wagner, Stein, and List, that formed the mainstream of academic economic thought and set the tone of the Nihon Shakai Seisaku Gakkai, the professional association to which almost all Japanese economists belonged from the late 1890s until it disbanded in 1924.[83] The German Historical school not only provided a rationale for the state's role in economic development but was more in tune with Japanese nationalist feeling than were the English Classical economists.[84]

In Japan, the concept of the "invisible hand" was never widely accepted; profit beyond what was necessary for a decent livelihood required some other ethical basis, usually a claim of service to the state, a justification that was fully consistent with Confucian thought.[85] Even Shibusawa Eiichi, the champion of private enterprise, said that his aim was "to build modern enterprise with the abacus and the Analects of Confucius."[86] The more successful the entrepreneur was, therefore, the more dependent he would be on the government, not only for material protection and subsidies, but also for validation of his claim to be working for the good of the nation. Failure to obtain this validation could be both socially and financially disastrous, a situation that gave the government great power vis-à-vis the top ranks of modern business leadership.

Early attempts at the direct state operation of modern industries were on the whole unsuccessful and were later dismissed as experimental or for demonstration purposes, although there is little evidence to suggest that this was the original intention. Much more successful were arrangements that gave private concerns, conspicuously the zaibatsu, the responsibility for establishing elements of a modern industrial system with government backing and the assurance that comple-

83 See Sumiya Etsuji, *Nihon keizaigaku shi*, rev. ed. (Kyoto: Minerva shōbō, 1967).

84 "The Germans are fond of saying that the Physiocrats and the school of Adam Smith underrated the importance of national life; that they tended to sacrifice it on the one hand to a selfish individualism and on the other to a limp philanthropic cosmopolitanism. They urge that List did great service in stimulating a feeling of patriotism, which is more generous than that of individualism, and more sturdy and definite than that of cosmopolitanism." [Alfred Marshall, *Principles of Economics*, 8th ed. (London: Macmillan, 1949), p. 634.]

85 Note the contrast with nineteenth-century China where there was a much sharper separation between business and the state. Successful Chinese entrepreneurs could maintain a claim to be serving the state only by investing their profits in enrolling their families in the ranks of the scholar–gentry class from which they could then enter the bureaucracy.

86 Quoted in Johannes Hirschmeier, "Shibusawa Eiichi: Industrial Pioneer," in *The State and Economic Enterprise in Japan*, p. 243.

mentary elements would materialize. While operating in the context of a basically capitalist economy, these private concerns acted in part as agents of a government committed to the success of their enterprise. The relationship was reminiscent of that between Tokugawa domain administrations and merchants who ran industrial and commercial enterprises on the domains' behalf for the profit of both parties. Because the zaibatsu were ready to use their financial strength, ties with government, and managerial resources to adopt new technology in various industries, they were well placed to realize gains from externalities not available to a single firm in a single industry. The zaibatsu's advantage was cumulative and accounts in large measure for their dominance of the modern sector in the interwar period.

State intervention in traditional economic activity was quite different. Traditional handicraft and cottage industries were not, as a rule, critical to national security or prestige. Observation of European industrial economies suggested that except for corner stores, custom-made luxury trades, and other enterprises in which small scale was an advantage, the fate of traditional industries was to decline and eventually disappear. In these areas, government policy was to intervene only to alleviate the social stresses expected to accompany this inevitable decline or to prevent excessive competition from lowering product quality or reducing export prices. In the former policy category fell encouragement of agricultural and industrial cooperatives, credit unions, and trade associations; in the latter, agricultural extension work, inspection stations, and research establishments. The advocacy of cottage industry employment as a source of supplementary cash income for marginal farmers was a premodern legacy persisting well into the twentieth century.[87] Otherwise, the traditional economy was left to the operation of market competition and the effort and initiative of millions of those ordinary men and women for whom William Lockwood had such respect.[88]

The sphere of the free-market economy was quantitatively large, but it would be misleading to infer that free-market competition was therefore the paramount force in Japan's economic development or that the role of administrative action was marginal. Insofar as free-market forces tended to maximize the output of the traditional economy in a static or short-run sense, they increased the resources available for investment in economic development. The more dynamic features of that develop-

87 For details, see Dai Nihon fukugyō shōreikai, ed., *Nihon no fukugyō* (Tokyo: Dai Nihon fukugyō shōreikai, 1911). 88 Lockwood, *The Economic Development of Japan, passim.*

ment, however, were shaped by decisions emerging from consultation and cooperation between government and modern business leaders. The government's policies certainly do not merit unqualified approval. Some resulted in massive waste and unnecessary suffering for both Japanese and the victims of Japanese aggression overseas. If, nevertheless, government intervention and manipulation were an important positive factor in Japan's economic development up to 1920, it is because they did not on the whole counteract the underlying economic conditions and in fact enabled a fuller realization of the economy's development potential than would have been achieved without them.

# CHAPTER 9

# DEPRESSION, RECOVERY, AND WAR, 1920–1945

## INTRODUCTION

The Japanese economy experienced great changes as a result of World War I. With the disappearance of European and American products from Asian and African trade, these extensive markets suddenly became wide open to Japanese products. Export volume and prices shot up, and Japan's industries reveled in an unprecedented boom. A spate of new firms appeared in rapid succession; stock prices soared; and the whole country rang with the sound of hammers at work on new-factory construction. Products like steel, machinery, and chemicals, for which Japan had been dependent on imports, began to be produced domestically. From its status as a debtor nation to the tune of ¥1.1 billion on the eve of the war in 1913, Japan had, by the end of 1920, transformed itself into a creditor nation with a surplus exceeding ¥2 billion. Despite social unrest such as the 1918 rice riots and the intensification of the labor and peasant movements that accompanied the galloping inflation produced by the war boom, the Japanese economy expanded as a result of the war.

When the war ended, however, so did the boom. Because of the renewed export competition and the resumption of imports that had long been suspended while Europe was at war, the international payments balance reverted to a deficit, and holdings of gold and foreign exchange began to diminish. This chapter will trace the path of the Japanese economy from the 1920s to the end of the Pacific War.[1] This period may be divided into three parts: the deflation and depression from the 1920s to 1931, recovery and chemical and heavy industrialization from 1932 to 1937, and the era of war and collapse through 1945.

Table 9.1 indicates the growth rates of real gross national expendi-

1 An excellent study in English is Hugh Patrick's "The Economic Muddle of the 1920s," in *Dilemmas of Growth in Prewar Japan*, ed. James W. Morley (Princeton, N.J.: Princeton University Press, 1971).

TABLE 9.1

*Growth rates of real spending and income, 1900–1944*

| | GNE | Gross domestic fixed capital formation | Private consumption spending | Exports and income from abroad | Imports and income going abroad | Primary industries | Secondary industries | Tertiary industries | GNE deflator |
|---|---|---|---|---|---|---|---|---|---|
| 1900–13 | 1.9 | 4.8 | 1.8 | 8.4 | 7.2 | 1.4 | 6.2 | 2.2 | 3.8 |
| 1913–19 | 6.2 | 8.4 | 4.7 | 6.5 | 5.1 | 3.3 | 6.2 | 7.4 | 13.6 |
| 1919–31 | 1.6 | −0.7 | 2.2 | 5.8 | 5.8 | −0.7 | 4.7 | 0.7 | −2.8 |
| 1931–37 | 6.2 | 8.3 | 3.2 | 12.3 | 5.2 | 3.3 | 7.7 | 4.9 | 1.2 |
| 1937–44 | −1.3 | 6.2 | −6.9 | −11.4 | −8.5 | | | | 18.9 |

*Source:* Calculated from Ohkawa Kazushi et al., *Kokumin shotoku: Chōki keizai tōkei*, vol. 1 (Tokyo: Tōyō keizai shinpōsha), 1974, pp. 213, 214, 217.

TABLE 9.2
*International comparison of real growth rates*

| | 1870–1913 (%) | 1913–1938 (%) |
|---|---|---|
| United States | 4.6[a] | 1.1 |
| Great Britain | 2.1 | 0.7 |
| Germany | 2.7 | 1.8 |
| Italy | 1.5 | 1.7 |
| Denmark | 3.2 | 1.9 |
| Norway | 2.2 | 3.0 |
| Sweden | 3.0 | 2.4 |
| Japan | 2.4[b] | 3.9 |

[a] From the average for the years from 1869 to 1878 and then to 1913.
[b] From 1887 to 1913.
*Source:* United States: U.S. Department of Commerce, *Historical Statistics of the United States* (Washington D.C.: U.S. Government Printing Office, 1975). European countries: B. R. Mitchell, *European Historical Statistics* (New York: Macmillan, 1975). Japan: Ohkawa Kazushi et al., *Kokumin shotoku: Chōki keizai tōkei*, vol. 1 (Tokyo: Tōyō keizai shinpōsha, 1974), pp. 213, 214, 217.

tures (GNE) for these periods and the growth rates of real gross output by type of industry. This table shows that during each period there were large differences in the growth rates of GNE and its components and of gross output by type of industry. The rate of price increase varied as well. The principal features of these three periods can be seen in these variations. Table 9.2 presents an international comparison of real GNE growth rates. Japan's rapid growth from the 1950s onward is well known, but its growth rate following World War I was also outstanding by international standards and may be viewed as the prelude to the rapid growth following World War II. It is also possible to regard such growth as the material basis for the policies of military expansionism that led to the Pacific War.[2] Both these contradictory perspectives contain some truth. Hence emerges an additional theme of this chapter: How was rapid growth achieved in this period, and what did Japan obtain as a result?

2 Yamamura Kōzō, "Kikai kōgyō ni okeru seiō gijutsu no dōnyu," in *Washinton taisei to Nichibei kankei*, ed. Hosoya Chihirō and Saito Makoto (Tokyo: Tōkyō daigaku shuppankai, 1978). Yamamura contends that technological progress in the machine tool industry during the 1920s provided the material foundation for the military adventures of the 1930s.

## THE ERA OF RECESSIONS

Although prices in the United States and Britain soared to more than twice their prewar levels after World War I, both countries returned to the gold standard without devaluing their currencies against the price of gold. It was thought that reinstituting the gold standard at prewar parity would constitute a "return to normalcy" (in the words of President Warren G. Harding). However, this amounted to adopting a severely deflationary policy that would cut back postwar prices to prewar levels, about half of the current prices. World prices did in fact fall in the 1920s. John Maynard Keynes, author of *Monetary Reform* and *The Economic Consequences of Mr. Churchill,* publicly criticized these policies, but his warnings went unheeded. As is well known, Keynes was also critical of the harsh reparations demands imposed on Germany, but this, too, was ignored. As it turned out, international finance during the 1920s was sustained by the international capital flow, whereby Germany used the capital it received from America to make reparations to England and France, which used the same money to redeem their war debts in the United States. But after the New York stock market crisis in 1929, American capital was withdrawn from Europe, causing a financial strain in Germany that eventually provoked a crisis that brought on world depression.

These events had immediate repercussions in Japan as well. The goal of Japan's economic policy, like that of Britain and the United States, was to return to the gold standard at the prewar price of gold. The Japanese government did not do so until the advent of the world depression in 1929, but during the 1920s the economy was constantly constrained by the worldwide deflation and by the government's goal of returning to the gold standard. Accordingly, the Japanese economy showed a mild deflationary trend after World War I. Moreover, the balance-of-trade deficit persisted. The gold and foreign exchange (specie) holdings that had accumulated during the war declined steadily. For these reasons, Japan's domestic financial policy also shifted toward austerity. This was a period of unprecedented testing for the Japanese economy, which had developed under the influence of inflationary trends since the Meiji period. It was particularly difficult for the new heavy and chemical industries and for capital-weak new firms that had emerged during and after the war. It was also difficult for

3 Ōkurashō zaiseishi hensanshitsu, *Shōwa zaiseishi–Dai 10-kan: kin'yū (I)* (Tokyo: Tōyō keizai shinpōsha, 1955), pp. 155–80.

agriculture, which was troubled by competition from cheap rice imported from Korea and Taiwan and highly susceptible to trends in the New York silk market.

Chronologies of the Japanese economy of the 1920s often refer to this period as one of recurring panics of greater or lesser magnitude.[4] The post–World War I boom turned into a panic with the stock market crash of 1920. The death knell of wartime prosperity had sounded. Domestic funds dried up as monetary austerity was imposed in order to suppress inflation and the mounting outlays for imports that accompanied the shift toward deficit in 1919 in the international payments account. Despite this, the business community continued to expand and speculate boldly. The result was ruin. In only a few months, stock market prices and commodity market prices for rice, raw silk, and cotton yarn collapsed to less than half their former values. There was a stream of trading company, bank, and factory bankruptcies, and economic conditions became chaotic.

The government and the Bank of Japan did their utmost to provide relief. For example, purchasing companies (*kaitorigaisha*) were organized to handle inventory backlogs of raw silk, and a policy of bold lending to depressed industries was established. Losses suffered by smaller zaibatsu like Furukawa, Suzuki, Kuhara, and Masuda, especially hard hit by failures of speculative enterprises during the financial panic, provided new opportunities for the four leading zaibatsu: Mitsui, Mitsubishi, Sumitomo, and Yasuda. Because they maintained sound management policies and did not depend on speculative profits, even during the war boom, the large zaibatsu suffered few losses in the panic. In addition, the leading spinning companies like Kanebō and Tōyōbō had built up large secret reserves during the war, and so they were able to cover the declining prices of their inventories, which were caused by the panic and losses due to customer bankruptcies, thereby maintaining their position unshaken. The dominant position of the four great prewar zaibatsu and the large spinning companies remained firm.

In April 1922, when it appeared that the financial crisis had at last been resolved, a small panic was touched off when a trader (Ishii Sadashichi) went bankrupt after losing heavily on daring rice speculations. At the end of 1922, eleven small banks in western Japan failed in rapid succession. Then, on September 1, 1923, the Tokyo–Yokohama

4 Nihon ginkō chōsakyoku, "Sekai taisen shuryogo ni okeru honpō zaikai dóyōshi," and "Kantō shinsai yori Shōwa 2-nen kin'yū kyōkōni itaru waga zaikai," in *Nihon kin'yūshi shiryō: Meiji Taishō hen*, vol. 22 (Tokyo: Okurasho insatsu kyoku, 1959–60).

region was dealt a crushing blow by a powerful earthquake and the devastating fires that spread in its wake. This crisis was weathered with the help of a government-implemented month-long moratorium on payments in the Kantō area. The Bank of Japan also averted a panic by rediscounting commercial bills that were to have been paid in the area ("earthquake bills.") The Bank of Japan's rediscounts totaled ¥430 million.[5] The devastation wrought by the great earthquake was enormous. According to estimates made at the time, in seventeen prefectures, but primarily in Tokyo, 554,000 out of 2.288 million households lost their homes; 105,000 people lost their lives; 30,000 were injured; and 250,000 lost their jobs. The gross national wealth in 1909 was estimated at ¥86 billion, and losses due to the earthquake were put at between ¥5.5 billion and ¥10 billion.[6] These blows made impossible a return to the gold standard. Exports declined sharply, albeit temporarily, and supplies for reconstruction increased imports. Consequently, the balance of payments went deeply into the red, and the exchange rate fell sharply. Early in 1924 the government raised some foreign exchange by issuing ¥600 million in foreign bonds in Britain and the United States. However, the extraordinarily high interest rate, reflecting Japan's international credit standing at the time, became the target of criticism at home. The reconstruction of the Tokyo–Yokohama area firms that had sustained losses because of the disaster was of course not simple, and the balance sheets of many deteriorated. In 1925, as the postwar business slump continued, Takada shōkai, a large trading company, failed.

A "financial crisis" occurred in March and April of 1927.[7] A large Kobe trading company, Suzuki shōten, which was hard hit by the panic of 1920, had just barely managed to stay in business by borrowing huge sums from the Bank of Taiwan, a colonial bank of issue. In March 1927 the firm found itself unable to settle its loans of ¥67 million. At the time there was a proposal before the Diet calling for the government to dispose of a total of ¥207 million in outstanding earthquake bills and to indemnify the Bank of Japan for losses amounting to ¥100 million. The Bank of Japan was to extend long-term loans to banks holding earthquake bills, and each bank in turn was to have its holders of earthquake bill liabilities redeem their obligations over a period of ten years. While this proposal was being debated, Suzuki shōten's internal condition was revealed, including its relationship with the Bank of Taiwan, and the unsound manage-

5 Tōyō keizai shinpōsha, ed., *Meiji Taishō kokusei sōran* (Tokyo: Tōyō keizai shinpōsha, 1927), pp. 759–60. 6 Nihon ginkō chōsakyoku, "Sekai taisen," p. 876. 7 Ibid., p. 866.

ment of some other banks as well. This set off a run on several banks, resulting in the suspension of operations for many. The earthquake bill proposal was ultimately voted down. In April 1927 when the Privy Council rejected a proposal for an urgent imperial order for the relief of the Bank of Taiwan, the bank temporarily closed down; Suzuki shōten went bankrupt; and the Wakatsuki cabinet collapsed. The bank run had nationwide repercussions. Banks throughout the country were closed on both April 22 and 23. In the meantime, the government announced a twenty-day nationwide payments moratorium. It then decided on a policy for reorganizing the Bank of Taiwan and providing general relief measures for the banks through the Bank of Japan. Calm was thus at last restored. Eleven percent of all bank deposits nationwide were withdrawn during this bank run, and as many as thirty-two banks suspended operations.[8] Among the latter were such presumed bastions of financial soundness as the Fifteenth Bank, a depository for the Imperial Household Ministry (Kunaishō), and the Bank of Ōmi, which had provided extensive credit to the textile industry.

Owing to continuing deflationary declines in commodity prices and in the value of real estate and other financial assets, many business firms continued to operate in the red and to depend on borrowed funds. But the banks supplying these firms with capital were unable to collect on their loans. The deterioration of economic conditions turned into a quickly spreading financial panic.[9] The smaller panics earlier in the decade had occurred for virtually the same reasons as this one, but the failures of such nationally known Japanese firms as the Bank of Taiwan, Suzuki shōten, and the Fifteenth Bank touched off a nationwide crisis. To cope with the situation, the Bank of Japan distributed large quantities of capital. The crisis was resolved, but the return to the gold standard was thereby once again postponed.

One reason that the business conditions of companies and banks deteriorated during this period was that the executives of many small regional banks often were managing other firms as well. After their banks had invested in these companies, their operations stagnated. Finally, these companies went bankrupt and, with them, their creditor banks as well. Concerned about this, the Ministry of Finance amended the Banking Law in March 1927 to prohibit bank managers from simultaneously managing other businesses and stipulated that

8 Ibid., pp. 927–9.
9 Nakamura Takafusa, *Showa kyōkō to keizai seisaku* (Tokyo: Nihon keizai shinbunsha, 1978), pp. 47–51.

any bank with capital of under ¥1 million (¥2 million or less in the large cities) should increase its capital to ¥1 million or merge with another bank within five years. For this reason, the number of banks, which had stood at 1,575 at the end of 1926, fell to 651 by the end of 1932.[10] The banks' business conditions markedly improved as a result of these measures, but at the same time local industries and small businesses also felt the financial pinch.

Because of the prolonged slump that lasted from the postwar crisis of 1920 until the financial panic of 1927, bankruptcies occurred in rapid succession, particularly in the secondary industries that had expanded during the war. Firms that managed to survive were forced to scale down their operations, and many workers lost their jobs. New hires were held down, too. On the other hand, however, the number of small- and medium-sized factories increased. Many workers who lost their jobs set up small factories in order to earn a livelihood. However, these firms were low-income, small urban commercial and service enterprises that absorbed people who could not choose their working conditions and who sought employment simply in order to survive. For this reason, the populations of the large cities continued to increase.[11] The farm villages were in a continuous recession from 1925 onward owing to the worldwide surplus of agricultural commodities and the fall in prices. Farmers were forced to increase their production of silk cocoons in order to maintain their incomes. But this resulted only in a further drop in international prices, and so the farmers were caught in a vicious circle whereby their redoubled efforts to increase production only pushed prices lower.

Again, the only firms that continued stable operations in the midst of this turmoil were the leading textile companies and companies belonging to the big zaibatsu groups such as Mitsui, Mitsubishi, Sumitomo, and Yasuda, which had abundant funds and sound management policies. Some zaibatsu banks were even hard pressed to find ways to use the large influx of deposits from the smaller and weaker banks after the financial panic.[12] The zaibatsu extended their network of influence in the economy by taking over, through stock transfers, the sounder firms owned by companies such as Suzuki shōten or by founding new firms in fields such as rayon and chemicals. Each of the zaibatsu amassed for itself tremendous power in every field of indus-

10 Ōkurashō zaiseishi hensanshitsu, *Shōwa zaiseishi*, pp. 79–117.
11 Takafusa Nakamura, *Economic Growth in Prewar Japan*, trans. Robert A. Feldman (New Haven, Conn.: Yale University Press, 1983), pp. 218, 220.
12 Ikeda Shigeake, *Zaikai kaikō* (Tokyo: Konnichi no mondaisha, 1949), pp. 116–17.

ry, from finance and insurance to mining, foreign trade, warehous-ng, chemicals, paper, metals, and textiles. As a group they reigned upreme over the Japanese industrial world.[13] The power of the aibatsu at this time probably attained its highest peak since the end of he Meiji period. However, with this notable exception, the outlook or the Japanese economy did not appear bright. Nevertheless, as Table 9.3 shows, the economy, mainly secondary industry, continued o grow in this troubled period. Why?

The fundamental condition for this growth likely resulted from the act that the economy adjusted the balance of social demand and sup-ly not by quantitative controls but by price fluctuations.[14] As in the xample of the vicious circle of expanding cocoon production volume nd the falling price of cocoons, it was impossible to regulate the olume of production in agriculture. The core of the manufacturing ndustry at this time was the production of consumer goods such as aw silk, cotton cloth, sugar, and flour. Competition among the firms n these fields was fierce. Even though temporary cartels were formed, was difficult to limit production volume and stabilize prices, as the nterests of the individual firms did not coincide. Intense competition mong the three large firms in the paper industry shows that even in n oligopolistic industry, it was not possible to support prices by estricting production. There were additional examples, too, such as he impact of international dumping of products like ammonium ulphate and matches, or the heavy blow suffered by domestic coal as a esult of imports from Manchuria.

Oligopolistic tendencies became conspicuous in a number of indus-ies such as electric power in which firms continued to merge. Cartels ere formed autonomously in every industry as a way of dealing with hronic slumps. Thus, during this period, monopolistic economic ower rapidly strengthened and the domination of "monopoly capital" ecame conspicuous. But although it is clear that large firms occupied high position in Japan's economic world, it cannot be said that they sed their power to maintain price supports or price rigidity in the arkets. Monopoly prices emerged after the passage of the Important ndustries Control Law in 1931 as a means of dealing with the world epression. The law required outsiders to keep cartel agreements and

See Takahashi Kamekichi, *Nihon zaibatsu no kaibō* (Tokyo: Chūō kōronsha, 1930).

Satō Kazuo, "Senkanki Nihon no makuro keizai to mikuro keizai" in *Senkanki Nihon keizai no kenkyū*, ed. Nakamura Takafusa (Tokyo: Yamakawa shuppansha, 1980), pp. 3–30. Satō's clarification of the function of price fluctuations is applicable to the Japanese economy of this period.

TABLE 9.3

*Employed population by industry (thousands of persons)*

| | 1920(A) | 1925(A) | 1930(A) | 1935(A) | 1940(A) | 1940(B) | Feb. 1944(B) | Dec. 1945(B) |
|---|---|---|---|---|---|---|---|---|
| Primary industries | 14.388 | 14.056 | 14.648 | 14.450 | 14.523 | 14.192 | 14.028 | 18.053 |
| Agriculture and forestry | 13.855 | 13.540 | 14.084 | 13.871 | 13.974 | 13.363 | 13.155 | 17.520 |
| Secondary industries | 6.274 | 6.324 | 6.151 | 6.811 | 8.212 | 8.419 | 9.951 | 5.670 |
| Manufacturing | 5.071 | 5.109 | 4.848 | 5.498 | 6.565 | 6.845 | 8.089 | 4.314 |
| Tertiary industries | 5.355 | 6.432 | 7.331 | 8.410 | 7.728 | 9.403 | 7.575 | 6.346 |
| Commerce | 3.398 | 4.260 | 4.902 | 5.482 | 5.000 | 4.083 | 1.555 | 1.794 |
| Totals | 27.260 | 28.105 | 29.619 | 31.211 | 32.500 | 32.231 | 32.695 | 30.069 |

*Source:* Figures in columns marked A are annual averages from Umemura Mataji, "Sangyō-betsu koyo no hendō 1880–1940-nen" in Hitotsubashi University Economic Research Institute, *Keizai kenkyū*, April 1973. Figures in columns marked B are estimates from Cabinet Statistics Office, *Kokusei chōsa*, October 1 (for 1940 data); Cabinet Statistics Office, *Shōwa 19-nen jinkō chosa* (for 1944 data); and *Rinji kokumin tōroku* (for 1945 data). Presented in Arai Kurotake, *Taiheiyō sensōki ni okeru yūgyō jinkō no suitei*, report of the Japan Statistical Association.

reinforced their powers of control. The foregoing shows that economic growth was achieved in conjunction with the expansion of industries, but at the same time, it also indicates why business profits accompanying growth did not necessarily increase as well.

The second main factor in Japan's economic growth was the supply of capital and the protectionist policies toward industry. For example, in 1920 when the silk-reeling industry formed the Imperial Silk Filature Company (Teikoku sanshi kabushiki kaisha) as a cartel to buy up and freeze surplus raw silk in order to support silk prices, the government provided assistance in the form of huge loans.[15] Many large firms borrowed low-interest funds indirectly from the Bank of Japan when facing crises. There were also instances in which the government assisted companies by leasing plants and equipment.[16] In agriculture, a rice law was passed in 1921. The government began buying and selling operations to stabilize rice prices, and it paid out subsidies under a variety of guises.[17] The tariff revision of 1926 substantially raised duties on steel machinery and gave liberal protection to the heavy and chemical industries.[18]

The third main factor was an increase in the government's public investment. Under the slogan of a "positive policy," the Seiyūkai party, in power from 1918 to 1922, vigorously spent public funds on the construction and expansion of railroads, harbors, highways and bridges, riparian improvements, new and expanded educational facilities, and subsidies for the improvement and reclamation of arable land.[19] These policies were an expression of the personal views of Prime Minister Hara Takashi and Finance Minister Takahashi Korekiyo regarding the promotion of regional industries. At the same time they were a means of expanding party power at the regional level. The party's main rival, the Kenseikai (renamed the Minseitō in 1928), stressed fiscal balance and strove to reduce public investment, but when the party came to power in the mid-1920s, public investment spending remained at prior levels owing to the need for post-1923 earthquake reconstruction. Large provincial cities also actively invested in order to modernize. As a result of the impact of public investment, a large drop in the growth rate was avoided.

The fourth factor behind growth was the development of the elec-

15 Nihon ginkō chōsakyoku, "Sekai taisen," pp. 585–8, 598. 16 Ibid., pp. 591–620.
17 Ōuchi Tsutomu, *Nihon nōgyō no zaiseigaku* (Tokyo: Tōkyō daigaku shuppankai, 1950), pp. 116–59.
18 Discussed in detail in Miwa Ryoichi, "1926-nen kanzei kaisei no rekishiteki ichi," in *Nihon shihonshugi: Tenkai to ronri*, ed. Sakasai Takahito et al. (Tokyo: Tōkyō daigaku shuppankai, 1978). 19 Nakamura, *Economic Growth in Prewar Japan*, pp. 157–73.

tric power industry and the effects of its spread.[20] Investment in electric power generation in the mountainous areas and its transmission to regions around Tokyo and Osaka, where demand was great, flourished during this period. Electrochemical industries using this electric power (ammonium sulfate, electric hearth furnace industries, and the like) sprang up, and small factories using electric power expanded. The production of electric machinery, electric cables, light bulbs, and radios naturally increased as well. The development of streetcar networks in the suburbs of the major cities, the opening up of new residential areas, and the attendant stimulus to residential construction also encouraged growth.

In addition, those industries built up during World War I, such as machinery, steel, and chemicals, acquired foreign technology during this decade and eventually moved into full-scale production. Japan, which had once depended on imports for virtually all its machinery, was at last able to achieve self-sufficiency in this area. Second, as the heavy and chemical industries were taking root, heavy industrial belts grew up between Tokyo and Yokohama and between Osaka and Kobe, and a pool of skilled male workers formed in these areas. In order to retain the skills and know-how of these workers within their own organizations and to thwart the budding labor movement, many firms gradually adopted policies such as the lifetime employment system and the seniority pay system, later considered to be the distinguishing features of "Japanese management." The joint labor–management conference system, which was the prototype of the "company labor union," was also a product of this era.

The Japanese economy, which had continued to grow despite these difficulties, was stricken by a severe crisis when the Great Depression suddenly hit in 1929 and the Minseitō cabinet simultaneously lifted the embargo on gold exports at the old parity.[21] Since 1897 the Japanese yen had been valued at 0.75 grams of gold. The rate of exchange against the dollar during this period was ¥100 to $49⅞. In 1916, Japan and the other world powers placed an embargo on gold exports. Although the European powers and the United States lifted their gold embargoes by 1928, Japan alone kept its intact. The nation had an excess of imports over exports (see Figure 9.1); the exchange rate was considerably lower than it had been at the old parity; and gold and foreign exchange reserves steadily decreased. Even in 1929, the yen reached a minimum rate against the dollar in the range of ¥100 to $43.

20 Minami Ryoshin, *Dōryoku kakumei to gijutsu shimpō* (Tokyo; Tōyō keizai shinpōsha, 1976), provides a full-scale study of this question.

21 Nakamura Takafusa, *Shōwa kyōkō to keizai seisaku* (Tokyo: Nihon keizai shinbunsha, 1978).

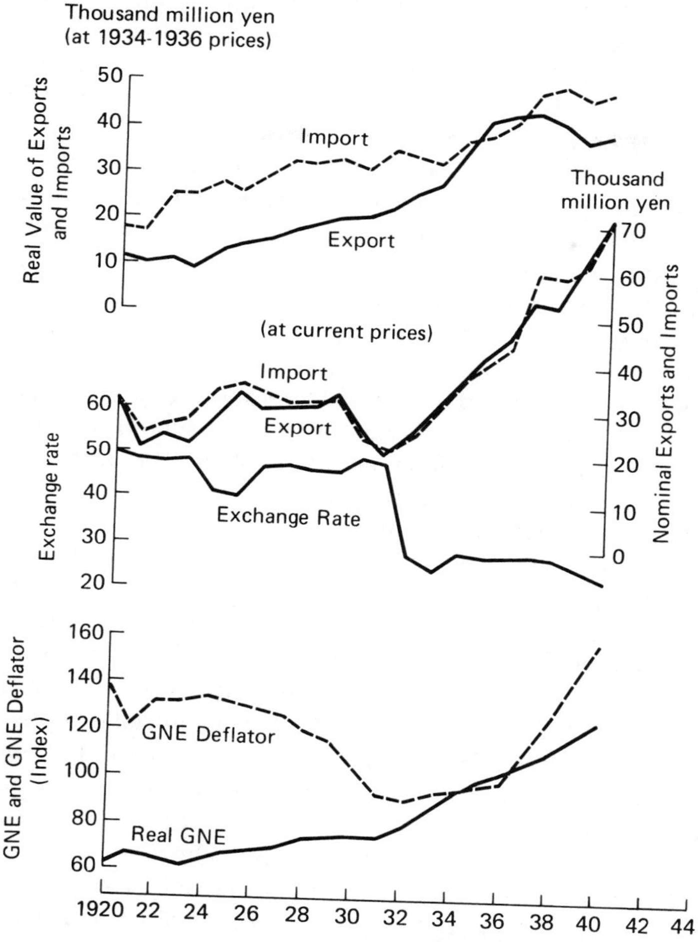


Figure 9.1. Fluctuations in foreign trade, the exchange rate, GNE, and prices. [From Yamazawa Ippei and Yamamoto Yūzō, *Chōki keizai tōkei–14: Bōeki to kokusai shūshi* (Tokyo: Tōyō keizai shinpōsha, 1974).]

Removal of the gold embargo at the old parity would mean a rise in the exchange rate, causing a further increase in the already excessive imports. In order to prevent this, domestic demand would have to fall, and deflationary policies would have to be adopted to pull prices downward. This meant forcing still further hardships on industry. Nevertheless, Inoue Junnosuke, the Finance Minister in the Hamaguchi cabinet, resolutely lifted the gold embargo at the old parity.

Theoretically it would also have been possible to lift the embargo at the so-called new parity, under which the yen's value in gold would have declined in accordance with the market rate of foreign exchange, without damaging business and economic interests.[22] Removal of the embargo at a new parity was hinted at the conclusion of the Genoa Conference of 1922. Ishibashi Tanzan, Takahashi Kamekichi, and other economic journalists, following Keynes's criticism of Winston Churchill, advocated lifting the embargo at this new parity. But there were at least two reasons that Finance Minister Inoue did not choose to do so. The first was his political judgment that a currency devaluation would adversely affect the national prestige. The second reason was his doctrine of "consolidating the business world," according to which deflationary policies should be adopted to promote exports and improve the balance of payments, noncompetitive firms should be eliminated, and the economy's international competitiveness should be strengthened. The Minseitō government took the same course that Churchill had chosen for Great Britain in 1925. Both academic and financial circles supported Inoue's policy and applauded its resoluteness.

While the impact of the American panic of October 1929 was still reverberating throughout the world, the Japanese government lifted the gold embargo at the old parity in January 1930. These two blows struck the Japanese economy simultaneously, and the country was plunged into a severe depression. As the advanced nations began dumping and domestic demand declined, the chemical and heavy industries, which were uncompetitive by international standards, sank and were forced to reduce their work forces. The mining industry, too, confronted with competition from Manchurian coal, dismissed nearly 40 percent of its workers. Although Japan's world-class textile industry was highly competitive, many firms nevertheless chalked up losses. Osaka godōbō, one of the five leading spinning companies, was forced to merge with Tōyō Spinning (Tōyōbō). Even at Kanebō, reputed to be the top firm, a fifty-four-day strike occurred when management proposed a 40 percent wage cut. Every industry formed cartels, striving to reduce output and maintain prices. The government enacted the Important Industries Control Law, which empowered it to compel firms to follow the cartel agreements, and it worked to strengthen the "self-regulation" of industry.[23] Hardest hit, however,

22 Takahashi Kamekichi, *Taishō Shōwa zaikai hendōshi*, vol. 2 (Tokyo: Tōyō keizai shinpōsha, 1954), consistently criticizes Inoue's financial policies from this position.
23 Maeda Yasuyuki, *Shōkō seisakushi Dai 11-kan: Sangyō tōsei* (Tokyo: Tsūshō sangyō kenkyūsha, 1964), pp. 47–76.

were the farm villages, already having been battered by economic slumps throughout the 1920s. The countryside reeled under the sudden drop in the prices of key commodities such as rice and silk cocoons.[24] There were many instances reported of salary payments for village primary schoolteachers being postponed for half a year due to shortfalls in local tax revenues, and of increases in the number of homes that had their electricity cut off. In metropolitan areas the number of unemployed grew, and the majority of recent university graduates were unable to find work.

To cope with this crisis, the Minseitō government did not change its policies. Instead, it continued fiscal and monetary austerity, waited for a recovery from the depression, and attempted to maintain the gold standard. Figure 9.1 shows that even between 1929 and 1931, imports and exports increased steadily in real terms, as did real GNE. In nominal terms, however, there was a marked decline in all three. This demonstrates that the depression was concentrated in a decline in prices, reflecting the special characteristic of the Japanese economy. In 1931, export prices had fallen to 40 percent, and the GNE deflator to 73 percent of their respective 1929 levels. As a result, both firms and farm households went into the red, and unemployment grew. Although this pattern was typical of depressions since the nineteenth century, this one was the most severe in Japan's history. Amid the growing social unrest, Prime Minister Hamaguchi Osachi was wounded by a right-wing youth's bullet that claimed his life after he retired from office. Nevertheless, the Minseitō cabinet did not depart from its original policies.

On September 18, 1931, the Manchurian incident occurred. Despite Tokyo's policy of nonexpansion, the Kwantung Army produced a succession of military *faits accomplis* and expanded the battlefront. This put the government in a difficult position. On September 23, immediately after the incident, Great Britain went off the gold standard. Because of the financial crisis in Germany, it had become impossible to recover British funds there. As orders to reclaim funds invested in Britain came pouring in from continental investors threatened by this situation, it had finally become impossible to cope with the volume. From the perspective of the world economy as a whole, the abandonment of the gold standard by Great Britain, the home of the world's gold standard system, marked a shift toward the international managed currency system of the 1930s and afterward. In Japan, speculators, who had already recognized that maintaining the gold standard was impossi-

24 Nakamura, *Shōwa kyōkō to keizai seisaku*, pp. 107–12.

ble, began both to sell yen and to buy dollars in hopes of realizing profits on the forthcoming decline of the yen. The major speculators were actually foreign banks in Japan and wealthy individuals, but the zaibatsu banks, especially the Mitsui and Mitsubishi banks, were considered to be the principal actors at the time. The Mitsui Bank, for example, had been investing in British government securities via the United States because it was difficult to make stable investments in Japan during the depression. When those funds were frozen, the bank bought dollars to cover them, but this was erroneously reported as "dollar buying" speculation.[25]

In the face of these trends, the Minseitō cabinet continued to support the gold standard in accordance with its established policy. The matter turned into an issue that affected the political fate of the Minseitō cabinet. Finance Minister Inoue harshly criticized those purchasing dollars. Mitsui and Mitsubishi, regarded as the main speculators in dollars, thus became the targets of social opprobrium. Because the government and the Bank of Japan tightened monetary conditions by raising the discount rate in order to absorb the speculators' funds, the depression became even more severe. Dollar speculators, particularly the foreign banks, could not readily reverse their course and cancel their dollar buy-orders. As the end-of-December delivery date rapidly approached for the bulk of the foreign-exchange dollars sold, their expected hope of realizing speculative gains grew steadily dimmer. On December 11, the Minseitō cabinet finally collapsed, disagreeing over Home Minister Adachi Kenzō's insistence on a coalition with the Seiyūkai. It is said that a speculator's plot lay behind Adachi's actions, but even today the facts are not clear.

Succeeding to power, the Seiyūkai cabinet of Inukai Tsuyoshi brought Takahashi Korekiyo to the office of finance minister. On December 13, 1931, gold was reembargoed, and payments of specie were suspended. This act proclaimed the end of the gold standard in Japan forever. The relationship of trust and cooperation between Japan's financial circles and those in Britain and the United States gradually cooled afterward. This relationship, cultivated by Japanese financial circles since the Russo-Japanese War of 1905, had made it possible for Japan to raise foreign capital after the Kantō earthquake and to float local bond issues and electric power company bonds repeatedly during the 1920s. But with the Manchurian incident, the founding of Manchukuo and the outbreak of the Shanghai incident, Thomas La-

25 Ikeda, *Zaikai kaikō*, pp. 135–53.

nont of the Morgan Bank began to take an unfriendly view of Japan.[26] This cooling of international financial relationships meant that when apan faced a balance-of-payments crisis, it could no longer look broad for help. However, for several years after Japan's departure rom the gold standard, the Japanese economy followed a course of apid revival and development, and so the balance-of-payments prob-em became a severe constraint for Japan only after war began with hina in 1937.

## RECOVERY

Vith the exception of a six-month interim out of office, Takahashi Korekiyo was at the fiscal and monetary helm as minister of finance rom the time Japan left the gold standard in December 1931 until he vas felled by an assassin's bullet in February 1936.[27] This was the era of ne so-called Takahashi finance. While avoiding abrupt changes, Taka-ashi gradually relaxed the monetary conditions and promoted industry nd foreign trade. In order to do so, he began lowering the discount rate om 1932 onward, reducing it from 6.6 percent to 3.7 percent by July 933. He took a laissez-faire position on the falling exchange rate. llowed to settle to its natural equilibrium level, the rate of exchange gainst the U.S. dollar had dropped from ¥100 to $49⅞ to around $26 y mid-1932 and, after falling below $20 at the end of that year, settled t about $30.80. This was a devaluation of more than 40 percent. Fiscal pending for the military and for rural village relief increased, growing n 1932 by 32 percent over 1931 levels. Central government expendi-ures declined from ¥1.74 billion in 1929 to ¥1.48 billion in 1931 and nen increased to ¥1.95 billion in 1932 and ¥2.25 billion in 1933, after hich they were fixed at a level of about ¥2.2 billion. Spending in-eases were financed with government bonds, but in order not to phon private funds off the market with a huge government debt issue, "Bank of Japan acceptance issues" formula was adopted.[28] The Bank Japan underwrote the bonds when issued, and whenever there was a rplus of funds on the market as fiscal spending proceeded, the Bank Japan would sell bonds to financial institutions.

Mitani Taichirō, "Kokusai kinyū shihon to Ajia no sensō," in *Kindai Nihon Kenkyū*, vol. 2: *Kindai Nihon to Higashi Ajia*, ed. Kindai Nihon kenkyūkai (Tokyo: Yamakawa shuppansha, 1980), pp. 126–7. This study is an outstanding piece of research on the Morgan Trading Company's Thomas W. Lamont.

An excellent summary of Takahashi's ideas and policies from the point of view of his contemporaries may be found in Fukai Eigo, *Kaikō 70-nen* (Tokyo: Iwanami shoten, 1941), chap. 21.

Ibid., pp. 268–70.

At the heart of the early phase of "Takahashi finance," which lasted until 1933, was a triad of policies consisting of low interest rates, a low exchange rate, and increased fiscal spending. Under these policies the Japanese economy began to recover rapidly. In 1929, at the time the gold embargo was lifted, Takahashi had argued publicly that there was a difference between a nation's economy and that of an individual.[29] Saving and economizing produced increases in individual assets, but for the nation as a whole, they caused a decline in demand and depressed production. Even the money spent at geisha houses became income for the geisha and cooks, and this in turn was respent, increasing demand for the nation as a whole. If gold were disembargoed fiscal spending squeezed, and public works investment suspended Takahashi argued, contractors and their employees would lose their jobs first; then as their expenditures declined, the effects would spread to other fields, and both incomes and employment in general would fall, thereby inviting a business slump. Takahashi intuitively understood the "theory of effective demand" subsequently advanced by Keynes, and from that point of view, he criticized lifting the gold embargo at the old parity. As finance minister, Takahashi's policies were based on the concept of promoting effective demand.

These policies were successful. The economy expanded first as result of the revival of exports and then under the stimulation of increased fiscal spending. According to a survey of the data in Table 9. for the years 1932 to 1936, the largest contribution to growth was made by exports. Chiefly responsible for the export increase were textile products such as cotton and rayon fabrics, industries in which depression-induced rationalization – that is, efforts to increase productivity – meshed with the low exchange rate to produce remarkable advances. The rapid increase in Japanese exports during the depression provoked boycotts of Japanese goods in countries such as Britain, India, and the United States. Discriminatory tariffs and import quotas were imposed on Japanese goods, and there were numerous trade disputes.[30] The second-fastest-growing sector after exports was private investment with both production facilities and residential construction growing at about the same rate. Purchases in government spending were lower than expected. From 1933 onward, Takahashi strove to hold down

29 Takahashi Korekiyo, "Kinshuku seisaku to kinkaikin," in *Zuisōroku,* ed. Takahashi Korekiyo (Tokyo: Chikura shobō, 1936).

30 For the recollections of Inoue Kiyoshi, Okada Gentarō, Tawa Yasuo, and others, see Ando Yoshio, ed., *Shōwa seijikeizashi e no shōgen,* 3 vols. (Tokyo: Mainichi shinbunsha, 1972), vol. 1, pp. 283–306.

TABLE 9.4

*Increases in real gross national expenditure (¥ billions)*

| | GNE | Personal consumption expenditure | Government operating expenditures | Gross government fixed-capital formation | Gross private fixed-capital formation | Exports and income from abroad | (Less) Imports and income going abroad |
|---|---|---|---|---|---|---|---|
| 1931 | 13.323 | 9.754 | 1.685 | 0.902 | 1.058 | 2.029 | 2.105 |
| 1936 | 19.338 | 13.328 | 2.183 | 1.427 | 2.209 | 4.580 | 4.389 |
| Amount of increase during this period | 6.013 | 3.574 | 0.498 | 0.525 | 1.151 | 2.551 | 2.284 |
| Rate of increase during this period (%) | 45.1 | 36.6 | 29.6 | 58.2 | 108.8 | 125.7 | 108.5 |
| | | | 39.5 | | | | |

*Source:* Calculated from Ohkawa Kazushi et al., *Kokumin shotoku: Chōki keizai tōkei*, vol. 1 (Tokyo: Tōyō keizai shinpōsha, 1974), pp. 214, 218–21.

fiscal spending increases, including military spending, and to reduce the issuing of public bonds. It was once widely believed that the revival of prosperity in the early 1930s was due to increased military spending, but this is incorrect. According to Miwa Ryoichi, the rate of dependence of heavy and chemical industrial output on military demand was at its maximum in 1933 at 9.8 percent and then declined to 7 percent in 1936. For the machinery industry, this rate peaked in 1932 at 28 percent but fell to 18 percent in 1936.[31] Even though the political clout of the military grew stronger, the influence of military spending on the economy was not all that great.

Along with military spending, an important item of fiscal expenditure during this period was the outlay for public works projects for rural village relief ("expenditures to meet the national emergency" – *jikyoku kyōkyūhi*).[32] At the beginning of 1932, rural village relief became a major issue. The assassins of former Finance Minister Inoue Junnosuke, Dan Takuma of the Mitsui zaibatsu, and Prime Minister Inukai Tsuyoshi in the May 15 incident, were farm village youths from Ibaraki Prefecture. In the wake of the bloody May 15 incident, representatives from the peasantry and the provinces submitted a stream of petitions to the Diet. The political parties aligned themselves with their demands. In the summer of 1932 they settled on a plan that called for joint expenditure by the central and regional governments of a total of ¥800 million on rural public works projects creating opportunities for peasants to obtain cash incomes during the three-year period from 1932 to 1934. The plan also provided for low-interest loans of ¥800 million to farm villages over the same period and for the amortization of high-interest obligations. The level of government expenditure on rural relief compares favorably with the increases in military spending during the same period. If the supply of low-interest funds is included as well, the implementation of the plan may even be considered to have had a stimulating effect on the economy, surpassing even that of military spending. The situation of the rural villages gradually improved as the Ministry of Agriculture encouraged the industrial associations movement and the self-reliance movement (*jiriki kōsei undō*).

Policies protecting infant industries were also reinforced. In 1932 tariffs were raised on most chemical and heavy industrial products, particularly pig iron. Considering the roughly 80 percent increase in

31 Miwa Ryoichi, "Takahashi zaiseiki no keizai seisaku," in *Senji Nihon keizai*, ed. Tokyo daigaku shakai kagaku kenkyūjo (Tokyo: Tokyo daigaku shuppankai, 1979), pp. 165, 167.
32 Ibid., pp. 120–2.

TABLE 9.5
*The progress of chemical and heavy industrialization*

| | Index of gross output for manufacturing industries | Share of gross output produced by the steel, nonferrous metals, machinery, and chemical industries (%) |
|---|---|---|
| 1920 | 61.4 | 32.3 |
| 1930 | 100.0 | 35.0 |
| 1936 | 175.8 | 45.0 |
| 1940 | 218.2 | 59.2 |

*Source:* Calculated from Shinohara Miyohei, *Kōkōgyō* (Tokyo: Tōyō keizai shinpōsha, 1972), vol. 10, pp. 142, 143.

import prices from 1931 to 1933, caused by the declining exchange rate, it may well be that the chemical and heavy industries found it substantially easier to secure domestic markets for themselves. The shipbuilding and marine transport industries benefited when the government began to pay subsidies in 1932 for the dismantling of old ships and the construction of new ones.[33] Incentives had been granted to the automobile industry since the beginning of the depression, and after 1936 still more substantial protection was added in connection with munitions production. In this way various industries made a steady recovery, seizing on new opportunities for development.

The rapid growth of the rayon industry attracted much attention in industrial circles. By improving their technology, leading firms like Tōyō Rayon, Teijin, and Asahi Bemberg became the world's largest producers of artificial fibers, establishing themselves as a major export industry in the latter half of the 1930s. The technology of such industries as electrical machinery and machine tools, represented by Toshiba and Hitachi, also began to approach world standards and at last became capable of meeting domestic demand. With support from the military, the aircraft industry also raised its level of technology. As Table 9.5 shows, the expansion of chemical and heavy industrial output was remarkable. Its share in the value of the output of manufacturing industries rose by 10 percent from 1931 to 1936 to constitute 45 percent of the total.

Another feature of this period was the emergence of the "new zaibatsu" such as Ayukawa Yoshisuke's Nissan (Japan Industrial Company), Noguchi Shitagau's Nitchitsu (Japan Nitrogen Company), Mori Nobuteru's Shōwa hiryō (Shōwa Fertilizer, later known as Shōwa

33 Ibid., pp. 123–5.

denkō), Nakano Tomonori's Nisso (Japan Soda), Ōkochi Masatoshi's Riken, Inc., and Nakajima Chikuhei's Nakajima hikkōki (Nakajima Aircraft).[34] Nissan controlled firms in mining, automobiles, chemicals, fisheries, records, marine transport, and civil engineering through its holding company. This new zaibatsu grew rapidly by progressively buying up at low prices the stocks of firms whose operations were foundering, improving their performance, and channeling the profits into Nippon sangyō, Nissan's holding company. When Nippon sangyō's stock rose as a result, its capital increased, and these funds were used to expand still further Nissan's sphere of activities. Nippon chisso (Japan Nitrogen Corporation), using electric power obtained from its own hydroelectric generating operations to enter the chemical industry, built a large hydroelectric generating plant in north Korea in the 1920s and produced ammonium sulphate, gunpowder, and methanol with the abundant and cheap electrical power generated there. The cost of Nippon chisso's ammonium sulphate was especially low, making this company one of the strongest firms in Japan at the time. Noguchi Shitagau, the firm's founder, also achieved great success in the rayon industry. Shōwa Fertilizer, which started out as a tiny provincial company, expanded by adopting the process that the Tokyo Industrial Laboratory had developed for manufacturing ammonium sulphate and by linking this process to the development of hydroelectric stations. Nakano Tomonori attained success in the soda industry by presiding over Japan Soda and branching out into related fields. As a Tokyo Imperial University professor, Ōkochi headed up the Institute of Physical and Chemical Research. Devoting his attention to industrial applications of the technology and products developed there, he engaged in a broad range of projects, from piston rings to synthetic sake. Nakajima, a navy officer promoting a domestic airplane industry, turned his hand to producing military aircraft. Toyota had produced automobiles since the 1920s building on the technology it had developed to manufacture automatic looms.

These new zaibatsu grew by taking advantage of technology that had been accumulating since the 1920s, the economic development that followed the reimposition of the gold embargo, and the stagnation of monetary conditions. The managers of these new zaibatsu had several things in common: They were technical and military men, not management specialists; they developed their firms on the basis of new

34 See Miyake Seiki, *Shinkokontserun tokuhon* (Tokyo: Shunjusha, 1937); and Wada Hidekichi, *Nissan kontserun tokuhon* (Tokyo: Shunjusha, 1937).

technology; they had few links with the existing zaibatsu and financial institutions; and they had little capital. All of them also started up new industries using state capital. Whereas they were engaged mainly in the chemical and heavy industries and had the capability to produce munitions in wartime, their technology was also useful in peacetime. As such, their firms could easily adapt to postwar economic growth. Because the economy of the 1930s had already produced pioneers like Toyota and Nissan, it also had clear links with the post-1950s economic growth.

Special laws to promote the development of the chemical and heavy industries passed the Diet in rapid succession.[35] Beginning with the Oil Industry Law passed in 1934 and the Automobile Manufacturers' Law in 1936, special laws covering the synthetic oil, iron, machine tools, aircraft-manufacturing, shipbuilding, aluminum and light metals, organic chemicals, and heavy machinery industries had been passed by 1941. Their provisions were generally similar. Government approval was required for the firms' yearly plans via a government licensing system; unified standards and control over manufacturing and distribution were imposed; firms were directed to respond to the requirements of the military and the public interest; and the government could order the expansion and improvement of plants and equipment as well as changes in methods of operation and production plans. These special laws ruled that enterprises incurring losses be compensated according to government decree. The laws also provided other forms of protection, such as exemption from land expropriation, income taxes, and corporate taxes; the granting of bounties and subsidies, special privileges for debenture flotations; and the compulsory amortization of plant and equipment. The protectionist policy embodied in these special laws contributed greatly to the development of the chemical and heavy industries during the war and may be regarded as the genesis of the postwar policy of promoting these industries.

In the meantime, the older established zaibatsu, which had become the targets of social opprobrium, did their best in the early 1930s to avert criticism. The Mitsui zaibatsu, partly because it was the most severely criticized, set up a foundation called the Mitsui hōonkai (Mitsui Repayment of Kindness Association) to perform social work services and forced the resignation of Mitsui bussan's managing director, Yasukawa Shunosuke, who had been criticized for his "aggressive" activities. Mitsubishi and Sumitomo made similar efforts. Frequently

35 Maeda Yasuyuki, *Shōkō seisakushi Dai 11-kan*, pp. 238–50.

likened to the "conversion" (*tenkō*) of Communist Party members, suc behavior was called "zaibatsu conversion." The activities of the olde zaibatsu were generally conservative in this period, and their influenc in the economy as a whole declined. Because fiscal spending increase went to farm villages or to small- and medium-sized enterprises, th expansion of deposits in zaibatsu banks was also slow. After 1933 th Sanwa Bank of Osaka, which had many provincial branches, led i volume of deposits.

But as a consequence of the Shōwa financial crisis, oligopolistic con trol in individual industries advanced. During the recovery period huge trusts were formed in the iron and paper industries. In 1933 seve private iron–steel manufacturing firms merged with the government operated Yawata Iron and Steel Works to form the Nippon seitetsu KK (Japan Steel Company), which controlled 97.5 percent of domestic pi iron production and 51.5 percent of domestic steel ingot production Before the Shōwa financial crisis, the market had been controlled b means of a cartel centered on the Yawata Iron Works, but as a result o the merger it became possible to control the market through a singl giant firm. The same year, Mitsui's Ōji Paper Company, Ōkaw Heizaburō's Fuji Paper Company, and Sakhalin Industries merged t form the Ōji Paper Company, a large trust that controlled 90 percent o newsprint production. Because imports of steel products and machine made paper were depressed by the low exchange rate, these monopolie ended up dominating their respective domestic markets, and after th war they were broken up by the economic deconcentration policy During 1932 and 1933, large-scale business mergers were also carrie out in rapid succession in banking, beer, and machinery. The function of cartels were also strengthened. The large electric power companies hard-pressed during the depression and plagued by the pressure of thei loans from financial institutions, acceded to the demands of the zaibats banks to form an electric power federation. When prices for good produced in industries dominated by trusts and cartels increased as result of these trends, the criticism of these monopolies grew stronge In 1936 the Important Industries Control Law was amended so as t suppress the activities of the cartels.[36]

In the 1930s, Japan also focused on the economic development o the puppet state Manchukuo and the economic penetration of nort China. With support from the government in Tokyo the Kwantun Army, in de facto control of Manchuria, collaborated with the Sout

36 Ibid., pp. 68–72.

Manchurian Railway Company (Mantetsu) to set up the Mantetsu Economic Research Bureau and the First Economic Construction Plan for Manchukuo. The plan's essential goals, which rested on an ideology critical of a free economy and domestic capitalism, were to prevent "capitalists" from monopolizing profits, to "promote the good of all the people," "to place key economic sectors" under state control, and to develop economic interdependence between Manchuria and Japan.

With regard to currency, the Manchukuo Central Bank was established, and a managed currency (the *yuan*) linked to the Japanese yen at parity was issued.[37] Japan and Manchukuo thus had a shared currency, and the "Japan–Manchukuo Economic Bloc" came into being.[38] This measure was in line with general worldwide trends after the abandonment of the gold standard, that is, the creation of a "sterling bloc" centered on Great Britain and the Commonwealth, and a "dollar bloc" centered on the United States. In industrial development, key industries such as steel, gold mining, coal mining, oil, ammonium sulphate, soda, coal liquefaction, electric power, automobile transport, and air transport were placed under state control. Following the principle of establishing one company per industry, special corporations were created by the Manchukuo government and the South Manchurian Railway, each putting up 30 percent of the capital and the remainder being raised from the general public.[39] The Manchukuo government supervised the personnel and accounting of these special companies, but it also granted them special privileges such as profit subsidies and tax exemptions. Because Manchukuo was originally founded under the slogans of "Denounce capitalism" and "Keep out the zaibatsu," direct investment from metropolitan Japan was excluded. The capital for industrial development was raised through the issue of South Manchurian Railway debentures. Domestic capital was permitted to be used in industries not considered key, but a policy was adopted to discourage the development of industries that competed with domestic Japanese production, such as rice cultivation and cotton spinning.

Because this conception of Manchurian development was based on the anticapitalist ideology of the Kwantung Army and the South Manchurian Railway, the domestic economic community was hostile. The

37 Kobayashi Hideo, "Manshū kinyū kōzō no saihensei katei–1930 nendai zenhanki o chūshin to shite," in *Nihon teikokushugika no Manshū,* ed. Manshūshi kenkyūkai (Tokyo: Ochanomizu shobō, 1972), pp. 151–74. 38 Ibid., pp. 196–206.

39 Hara Akira, "1930 nendai no Manshū keizai tōsei seisaku," in *Nihon teikokushugika no Manshū,* pp. 44–9.

flotation of South Manchurian Railway debentures thus fared poorly. Furthermore, it was impossible for the South Manchurian Railway, whose personnel came mainly from railroad or military backgrounds, to provide the workers necessary for extensive industrial development. This was the Achilles' heel of the South Manchurian Railway Company, which, on the pretext of cooperating in building the new country, was attempting to control the Manchukuo economy. It was also the reason that the company gradually became estranged from the army. After 1933 the Kwantung Army drew up a plan to split the South Manchuria Railway Company into a group of independent affiliates (*kogaisha*), one for each sector. The South Manchurian Railway Company's functions were limited to managing the railroad and acting as a holding company for the affiliate companies. The Kwantung Army also devised a plan to strengthen its control over the affiliate companies. The plan came to naught, but rather than abandon it, the army continued to look for an opportunity to put it into effect.[40]

Driven by a sense of crisis and aware that it might be necessary to comply with the army's plan, the South Manchurian Railway planned to move south of the Great Wall into north China. After 1934 the Kwantung Army cooperated with the North China Garrison army to establish a de facto sphere of influence in north China by cutting it off from Kuomintang control and setting up pro-Japanese political regimes. It also developed plans for obtaining from the area raw materials such as iron ore, coal, and salt, which were in short supply in Manchukuo. The South Manchurian Railway did the research for this project.[41] In 1935 the railway established the Hsingchong ("Revive China") Company as its affiliate. The North China Garrison Army succeeded in establishing a pro-Japanese regime in eastern Hopei and a regime with a certain degree of autonomy from Nanking in Hopei-Chahar. After 1936 the Japanese negotiated with both these regimes for rights to develop their raw material resources, but the effort did not make much progress, owing to opposition from the Chinese. But these practical maneuvers did enable the advance by Japan's big spinning companies into the Tientsin area, particularly after 1936.

The domestic situation in Japan changed radically with the increased power of the military after 1936. On February 26, 1936,

40 Hara Akira, " 'Manshū' ni okeru keizai seijisaku no tenkai–Mantetsu kaisō to Mangyō sōritsū o megutte" in *Nihon keizai seisakushi ron,* ed. Andō Yoshio (Tokyo: Tokyo daigaku shuppankai, 1976), vol. 2, pp. 211–13, 296.

41 Nakamura Takafusa, "Nihon no kahoku keizai kosaku," in *Kindai Nihon kenkyūkai,* vol. 2, pp. 159–204.

Takahashi Korekiyo was killed by a military assassination squad. Under the newly formed Hirota cabinet, which was dominated by the demands of the military, the economy strayed from the path of economic rationality. Since 1934 Takahashi had consolidated the level of fiscal spending, had done his utmost to curb the expansion of military spending, and had tried to reduce the size of government bond issues. These policies seem to have reflected the views of Fukai Eigo, governor of the Bank of Japan and a close partner of Takahashi, who agreed with Keynes's theory of true inflation. According to this theory, if there is a surplus of capital plants and equipment, raw materials, or labor, an expansion of demand will not induce inflation, but if that margin of surplus is lost, inflation will occur. Fukai appears to have believed that Japan had achieved virtual full employment in the latter half of 1935.[42] Takahashi's opposition to an expanded scale of military and fiscal spending was thus based on such thinking.

Finding it impossible to oppose the demands of the military, Finance Minister Baba Eiichi of the Hirota cabinet attempted to cooperate with them. He approved a five-year large-scale armament expansion plan for the army and a six-year plan for the navy.[43] The national budget for fiscal year 1937 was almost 40 percent larger than that of FY 1936. This budget expansion was to be covered by a large tax increase and national bond issues. To facilitate the issue of public bonds, Baba lowered the discount rate and revived a low-interest-rate policy. Business leaders resisted the proposed tax increase, but at the same time they moved to increase imports in anticipation of inflation and a stronger demand for imported raw materials accompanying the expansion in military demand. As a result, the balance of payments was heavily in the red at the end of 1936. At the beginning of the year, the country had to begin shipping gold abroad. Price increases also became noticeable. Baba's policies failed immediately, and after a clash with the Diet in January 1937, the Hirota cabinet was replaced by the Hayashi cabinet. The new finance minister, Yūki Toyotarō, reduced Baba's budget, curtailed the tax increases, and mended relations with business leaders. When the first Konoe cabinet was organized in June 1937, Kaya Okinori and Yoshino Shinji, two leading bureaucrats, took office as minister of finance and minister of commerce and industry.

In the army, Ishiwara Kanji, the planner and executor of the Man-

42 Fukai, *Kaikō 70-nen*, pp. 322–331. See also Yoshino Toshihiko, *Rekidai Nihon ginkō sōsai ron* (Tokyo: Mainichi shinbunsha, 1976), pp. 186–8.
43 Aoki Nobumitsu, *Baba Eiichi den* (Tokyo: Ko Baba Eiichi-shi kinenkai, 1945), pp. 263–4.

churian incident, took the lead in formulating a plan to expand direct military preparations for the expected outbreak of war with the Soviet Union, to expand the chemical and heavy industries, and to establish a firm base for munitions production. This plan's objective was to expand the productive capacity of the Japan–Manchukuo economic bloc, swiftly drawing on the resources of Japan, Manchukuo, and north China. Table 9.6 shows that ¥6.1 billion of the needed capital was to come from domestic Japan and ¥2.4 billion from Manchuria.[44] The army plan, which took approximately one year to draft, was presented to the Konoe cabinet, which was organized with the mission of implementing it. In the summer of 1936, Ishiwara, seeking a review of the plan, had shown the newly completed first draft to a few politicians, including Konoe, and to members of financial circles such as Ikeda Shigeaki, Ayukawa Yoshisuke, and Yūki Toyotarō. He obtained their informal consent to cooperate in implementing the plan. Yūki's appointment as finance minister, Ikeda's appointment as governor of the Bank of Japan during the Hayashi cabinet, and Konoe's subsequent appointment as prime minister all were intended to encourage the realization of this plan.

The Konoe cabinet was unable to use such methods as fiscal and monetary stringency, suppression of domestic demand, reduction of imports, and promotion of exports to eliminate the balance-of-payments deficit. Immediately after taking office, Finance Minister Kaya and Commerce and Industry Minister Yoshino announced three economic principles: "expansion of productive capacity, balance of payments equilibrium, and regulation of the supply and demand for goods." This announcement indicated that their attention would be turned to establishing priorities for commodity imports and expanding productive capacity within the constraints imposed by preserving the balance-of-payments equilibrium. It implied the necessity of implementing direct national controls over commodity imports and capital. Economic controls were thus invoked across the board after the outbreak of the Sino-Japanese War in July 1937, but even if the war had not occurred, it is highly likely that sooner or later controls would have become unavoidable.

In Manchuria, the Manchuria Five-Year Development Plan, based on Ishiwara's first draft, was drawn up and immediately put into effect in 1937. It was thought that to carry out this plan, skilled specialists should manage industrial production. In November 1937 Nissan's

44 Nakamura, *Economic Growth in Prewar Japan*, pp. 268–85.

TABLE 9.6

*Production targets in the five-year plan for key industries*

| | (A) Production targets | | | (B) Present capacity | | | (A) as a proportion of (B) | | |
|---|---|---|---|---|---|---|---|---|---|
| | Total | Japan | Manchuria | Total | Japan | Manchuria | Total | Japan | Manchuria |
| Ordinary automobiles (1,000s) | 100 | 90 | 10 | 37 | 37 | — | 2.7 | 2.4 | — |
| Machine tools (1,000s) | 50 | 45 | 5 | 13 | 13 | — | 3.8 | 3.5 | — |
| Rolled steel (1,000s of tons) | 13,000 | 9,000 | 4,000 | 4,850 | 4,400 | 45 | 2.7 | 2.0 | 8.9 |
| Oil (1,000s kl) | 5,650 | 3,250 | 2,400 | 364 | 210 | 154 | 15.6 | 15.5 | 15.6 |
| Coal (1,000s tons) | 110,000 | 72,000 | 38,000 | 55,560 | 42,000 | 13,560 | 2.0 | 1.7 | 28.0 |
| Aluminum (1,000s tons) | 100 | 70 | 30 | 21 | 21 | — | 4.8 | 3.3 | — |
| Magnesium (1,000s tons) | 9 | 9 | 3 | 0.5 | 0.5 | — | 4.8 | 3.3 | — |
| Electric power (1,000s kw) | 12,750 | 11,170 | 1,400 | 7,210 | 6,750 | 460 | 1.7 | 1.7 | 3.0 |
| Shipbuilding (1,000s tons) | 930 | 860 | 70 | 500 | 500 | — | 1.9 | 1.7 | — |

*Note:* Other than these, the production target for weapons was ¥960 million, a 2.1-fold increase over current capacity, and the target for airplanes was 10,000 (Japan, 7,000; Manchuria, 3,000).

*Source:* "Jūyō sangyō go-ka-nen keikaku jisshi ni kansuru seisaku taikō (an)," Ministry of the Army, May 29, 1937. Shimada Toshihiko and Inaba Masao, eds., *Gendaishi shiryo*, vol. 8. *Nitchū sensō* (1) (Tokyo: Misuzu shobō, 1964), pp. 730, 746.

Ayukawa Yoshisuke founded Manchurian Heavy Industries (Mangyō). Using Nissan's capital and technology, he gathered all the Manchurian companies in the heavy and chemical industries under its control.[45] The South Manchurian Railway become a holding company concentrating on operating the railroad, and its reorganization was accomplished only after many setbacks.

## WAR

In July 1937 Japan plunged into an undeclared war with China. Contrary to expectations that it would be decided quickly, the war stretched on. The nation's economic strength was strained by shortages of key raw materials, particularly oil, and the tightening of economic controls. Economically, the outbreak of the China war was but a continuation of the trajectory along which the country had already been hurled. The Japanese economy was administered with the sole object of meeting the military demand. Ordinary industry and popular livelihood were sacrificed to that end. Although several factors linked to postwar economic growth were developed during this period, the process as a whole was a march to destruction.

The most persistent feature of the war economy was the continual strengthening of economic controls. War with China broke out just after the government accepted the army's plan for heavy and chemical industrialization. There was no alternative but to administer the economy by strengthening controls and by giving priority in allocating limited materials and capital to meet military demand. The necessity for economic controls had been urged by young bureaucrats, military personnel, and even economists since the 1920s.[46] The worldwide depression made clear that the capitalist free economies had come to a standstill. The need to control the economy and to institute planning could be seen from the success of the Soviet Union's five-year plans. The military also contended that World War I had demonstrated that the next war would be a total war requiring the mobilization of the economy as well as the polity. Research on the development of a mobilization structure had in fact been conducted at the Natural Re-

45 See Hara, " 'Manshū' ni okeru keizai seijisaku no tenkai," in *Nihon keizai seisakushi ron*, vol. 2, pp. 209–96.

46 Nagata Tetsuzan, "Kokka sōdōin junbi shisetsu to seishōnen kunren" in *Kokka sōdōin no igi*, ed. Tsujimura Kusuzō (Tokyo: Aoyama shoin, 1925), is a good example of early ideas on mobilization. An outstanding summary of the mobilization scheme focusing on the military may be found in Mikuriya Takashi, "Kokusaku tōgō kikan setchi mondai no shiteki tenkai," in *Kindai Nihon kenkyū*, vol. 1: *Shōwa-ki no gunbu* (Tokyo: Yamakawa shuppansha, 1979), sec. 1.

sources Agency since 1927. Ideological demands for a system of economic control had been tried in Manchukuo after 1932, but at home their realization was limited to the unification of the electric power generation and transmission industry in 1938. Full-scale economic controls in Japan proper were instituted only when other alternatives were discounted.

During the first three months of the China war in 1937, military expenditures came to ¥2.5 billion, an amount virtually equal to the national budget for the year. Faced with a pressing need to check increases in imports and currency expansion, the government passed the Temporary Capital Adjustment Law and the Temporary Export and Import Commodities Law. In March 1938, the Diet enacted the National General Mobilization Law. Under these laws, the government acquired sweeping powers: (1) The establishment of firms, capital increases, bond flotations, and long-term loans came under a licensing system; (2) the government was empowered to issue directives concerning the manufacture, distribution, transfer, use, and consumption of materials connected with imports and exports, particularly their restriction or prohibition; and (3) the government was also empowered to issue directives on the conscription of labor power, the setting of working conditions, the disposition of firms' profits, the use of funds by financial institutions, the administration, use, and expropriation of factories and mines, and the formation of cartels.[47] These measures were invoked one after another as the war situation became more grave.

In October 1937 the Cabinet Planning Board (Kikakuin), charged with comprehensive planning, began operations.[48] Its major responsibilities were to regulate the supply and demand for major commodities necessary for economic activity and to draw up a materials mobilization plan. The required volume of key raw materials imports on which Japan depended – for example, iron and steel, oil, copper, aluminum, raw cotton, wool, and rubber – was calculated as the difference between the combined military, government, and industrial demand and the domestic supply. Within the constraints set by the amount of available foreign exchange, an import plan was drawn up for each commodity, and the commodities were allocated among the army, the navy, and the private sector. These plans were initially made for October to December 1937. From then until the defeat, plans were first prepared every year and then subsequently every quarter. To imple-

47 Maeda, *Shōkō seisakushi Dai 11-kan*, chaps. 2, 3.
48 Mikuriya, "Kokusaku tōgō kikan setchi."

ment the Five-Year Plan for Key Industries, the planning board also prepared the Industrial Capacity Expansion Plan, which it put into effect in 1939.[49]

Japan thus quickly entered a wartime controlled economy. Economic control policies were unavoidable because of the political necessity of raising funds for huge military outlays, ensuring raw materials for the import-dependent chemical and heavy industries, and producing munitions. Japan's foreign trade situation at this time is shown in Table 9.7. After 1938 the aggregate foreign trade balance was in the black. A breakdown of these figures, however, shows that an export surplus was maintained in the yen bloc, in which settlements were made in yen, but in other areas, in which convertible foreign exchange was required, there was a continuous import surplus. For key raw materials such as coal, iron ore, and salt, Japan could be self-sufficient in the yen bloc; but for oil, bauxite, scrap iron, rare metals such as nickel and cobalt, crude rubber, raw cotton, and wool, Japan was compelled to depend on imports from dollar and sterling areas. Efforts to promote further its chemical and heavy industries increased Japan's dependence on the British and American currency areas. The materials mobilization plan, launched at a time of large import surpluses in 1937, was drawn up on the assumption that an estimated ¥3 billion in foreign exchange revenues from 1938 exports would be available, but owing to a slump in the United States and the slack production of cotton textiles for export, the figure was slashed to ¥2.5 billion by midyear. Because priority in the allocation of imported goods was for munitions and for use in expanding productive capacity, the import of materials used for consumer production, such as raw cotton and wool, was cut back. Because of the increasing squeeze on consumer goods as well as poor rice harvests, a rationing system for rice, matches, and sugar was adopted in 1940. Fearing soaring prices, the government fixed prices and initiated price controls. But these new controls only stimulated black market dealings. In order to crack down on such activity, the economic police was established. Allocations of munitions goods were made on the basis of a coupon system, but it was not always easy to obtain the actual goods. Everywhere, complicated controls proliferated.

The Japanese continued to do their utmost to develop the resources of Manchuria and China. The North China Development Corporation

49 See commentary in Nakamura Takafusa and Hara Akira, eds., *Kokka sōdōin*, vol. 1: *Keizai (Gendaishi shiryō 31)* (Tokyo: Misuzu shobō, 1970).

TABLE 9.7

*The balance of international trade in the 1930s (¥ millions)*

| | Totals | | | Trade with the yen bloc (China, Manchuria, and Kwantung) | | | Trade with the world outside the yen bloc | | |
|---|---|---|---|---|---|---|---|---|---|
| | Exports | Imports | Settlement balance | Exports | Imports | Settlement balance | Exports | Imports | Settlement balance |
| 1931 | 1.147 | 1.235 | −89 | 0.221 | 236 | −15 | 0.926 | 1.000 | −74 |
| 1932 | 1.410 | 1.431 | −21 | 0.276 | 206 | 70 | 1.134 | 1.226 | −72 |
| 1933 | 1.861 | 1.919 | −56 | 0.411 | 281 | 130 | 1.450 | 1.636 | −186 |
| 1934 | 2.171 | 2.283 | −111 | 0.520 | 311 | 209 | 1.652 | 1.972 | −320 |
| 1935 | 2.499 | 2.472 | 27 | 0.575 | 350 | 225 | 1.924 | 2.122 | −198 |
| 1936 | 2.693 | 2.764 | −71 | 0.658 | 394 | 264 | 2.035 | 2.370 | −335 |
| 1937 | 3.175 | 3.783 | −608 | 0.791 | 437 | 354 | 2.384 | 3.346 | −962 |
| 1938 | 2.690 | 2.663 | 27 | 1.166 | 564 | 602 | 1.524 | 2.099 | −575 |
| 1939 | 3.576 | 2.918 | 658 | 1.747 | 683 | 1.064 | 1.829 | 2.235 | −406 |
| 1940 | 3.656 | 3.453 | 203 | 1.867 | 756 | 1.111 | 1.789 | 2.697 | −908 |
| 1941 | 2.651 | 2.899 | −248 | 1.659 | 855 | 804 | 992 | 2.044 | −1.052 |

*Source:* Japan Ministry of Finance, Customs clearance statistics, 1931–41.

and the Central China Promotion Corporation set up affiliates in their respective regions to develop natural resources. Coal and iron ore development were given top priority in China, and the Japanese army went as far as to reduce the number of trains transporting local food supplies in order to send coal to Japan. In Manchuria, Manchurian Heavy Industries, headed by Ayukawa Yoshisuke, worked to establish every kind of industry in the region, including automobile production. However, Ayukawa's plan to try to introduce American capital and technology into Manchuria proved overly optimistic. It ignored America's nonrecognition of Manchukuo and the Open Door principle. When his plan finally failed, Ayukawa had to resign.[50]

In July 1939 the United States announced the abrogation of its Treaty of Commerce and Navigation with Japan. In January 1940 the United States became free to restrict exports to Japan as a form of economic sanction. The outbreak of the European war in September 1939 led to expectations that strategic goods imports would become more difficult. From 1939 to 1940, Japan mobilized all the gold and foreign exchange it could and boosted its imports of petroleum products, rare metals, and other strategic goods. The Bank of Japan's gold reserves were nearly depleted.[51] In July 1940, observing Nazi Germany's successful invasion of France and expecting the imminent defeat of Britain, Japan's military drew up plans to invade Singapore and the Dutch East Indies (now Indonesia) to gain access to their abundant supplies of raw materials such as oil, rubber, and tin. Support was growing for the reckless view that the war in China remained unresolved because Britain and the United States were backing the Kuomintang government and that Japan should act in concert with Germany to defeat Britain and force the United States to withdraw from Asia. In September 1940, Japan advanced into northern French Indochina (present-day North Vietnam) and signed a treaty of alliance with Germany and Italy. The United States responded by tightening its export restrictions against Japan and then steadily turned the screws to reduce Japanese economic power.

In 1939, Japan instituted general wage and price controls and established a unified nationwide wage system. The workers in the commerce and service industries were conscripted for compulsory work in munitions production. The companies' dividend rates were restricted, and finance was placed under comprehensive controls as well. Intend-

50 Hara, " 'Manshū' ni okeru keizai seijisaku no tenkai," pp. 248–95.
51 See the explanatory comments in Nakamura and Hara, eds., *Kokka sōdōin*, vol. 1, pp. lxix–lxxii. See also in the same volume, "Ōkyū butsudo keikaku shian" and "Setsumei shiryō."

ing to increase munitions production, the government in the fall of 1940 put forth plans for a New Economic Order parallel to the New Political Structure being organized at the same time.[52] The intent of this plan was to shift firms from a profit basis to a production basis; to separate the owners of capital from the managers of the firms; to designate government officials as managers; to make firms increase their production in accordance with government directives; and to organize cartels called industrial control associations to implement government economic controls such as production quotas and materials allocations. The business community opposed this plan, on the ground that it was a "communist" idea that threatened the fundamental principles of a capitalist economy. A compromise was finally reached, but just barely.

In early 1941 Japanese-American negotiations began. During their stormy course Germany invaded the Soviet Union. In July, Japan advanced into southern French Indochina. In response, the United States froze Japanese assets in America and imposed a total embargo on petroleum exports. The embargo on petroleum, Japan's most critical war matériel, was the biggest trump card the United States held. Japan's army and navy had reserves of 8.4 million kiloliters of petroleum products, an amount that could meet its military demand for no more than two years of fighting. Opinion within the army and navy was dominated by the belligerent view that Japan should go to war with Britain and the United States to obtain raw materials from Southeast Asia rather than give in to external pressure. This mood propelled the country into the Pacific War.[53]

Six months after the beginning of hostilities, Japan occupied a vast area demarcated by a boundary running through Burma, Thailand, the Malay Peninsula, Singapore, Sumatra, Java, Borneo, the Celebes, and the Solomon Islands. Some observers thought that with petroleum supplies safely in hand, the dream of the Greater East Asia Co-Prosperity Sphere had been realized. Many firms moved to invest in the development of mines, rubber, and raw cotton in the region, and some even laid plans for hydroelectric power and aluminum refining. The government drew up the optimistic Plan for the Expansion of Productivity, using "Greater East Asia" as its arena. The plan projected that within fifteen years, production would be expanded from three to five times the cur-

52 See Nakamura Takafusa and Hara Akira, "Keizai shin taisei" in *Nihon seiji gakkai nenpō 1972-nen* (Tokyo: Iwanami shoten, 1972).
53 Nakamura Takafusa, "Sensō keizai to sono hōkai," in *Iwanami kōza, Nihon rekishi,* vol. 21: *Kindai 8* (Tokyo: Iwanami Shoten, 1977), pp. 115–16.

TABLE 9.8
*Figures on the Pacific War and ocean-going transport*

| | 1941 (December only) | 1942 | 1943 | 1944 | 1945 |
|---|---|---|---|---|---|
| *Losses of ship tonnage* | | | | | |
| No. of ships | 12 | 202 | 437 | 969 | 639 (271 |
| No. of tons (1,000s) | 56 | 948 | 1,793 | 2,058 | 1,503 (756 |
| *Ship construction* | | | | | |
| No. of ships | 4 | 77 | 254 | 699 | 188 |
| No. of tons (1,000s) | 6 | 265 | 769 | 1,700 | 560 |
| *Volume of oceangoing transport* | | | | | |
| Planned (A) (1,000s tons) | 41,408[a] | 40,368 | 33,397 | 27,820 | 9,400 |
| Achieved (B) (1,000s tons) | 39,601[a] | 39,486 | 33,047 | 20,720 | 7,279 |
| Rate of plan achievement (B/A %) | 95.6 | 97.8 | 99.0 | 74.5 | 77.4 |
| Of amount achieved: | | | | | |
| Japan, Manchuria, and China (1,000s tons) | | 21,914[b] | 29,624 | 18,151 | 2,003[c] |
| Southeast Asia and others (1,000s tons) | | 862[b] | 3,605 | 2,627 | 137[c] |
| *Volume of Southeast Asian raw material shipments to Japan* | | | | | |
| Oil (1,000s kl) | – | 1,428 | 2,623 | 1,500 | – |
| Bauxite (1,000s tons) | – | 323 | 792 | 565[d] | – |
| Crude rubber (1,000s tons) | – | 65 | 78 | 68[d] | – |
| Manganese ore (1,000s tons) | – | 71 | 89 | 67[d] | – |
| Totals, including other items (1,000s of tons, except for oil) | – | 1,514 | 1,581 | 909[d] | – |

[a] Totals for Apr. to Dec. 1941.
[b] Jul. to Dec. 1942. [c] Jan. to Mar. 1945.
[d] Figures for 1944 are forecasts.
*Source:* Nakamura Takafusa, "Sensō keizai to sono hōkai," in *Iwanami kōza, Nihon rekishi, vol. 21: Kindai 8* (Tokyo: Iwanami shoten, 1977), Tables 5, 8, 9.

rent level. The immediate problem, however, was how to fight a war with the raw materials Japan now controlled.

There were no longer any foreign exchange restrictions for raw material imports from the Greater East Asia Co-Prosperity Sphere. Payment was made with Japanese military scrip or with Southeast Asia Development Bank vouchers. Marine transport capacity rather than foreign exchange became the critical bottleneck. The tonnage of Japan's ocean-going capacity at the beginning of the Pacific War was 6.5 million gross tons, of which about 5.5 million gross tons, excluding tankers and repair vessels, could be mobilized (see Table 9.8). It was thought that even if 2.9 million gross tons of army and navy warships were used for combat or military service, 3 million gross tons, including tankers, would be kept in service for freight transport to provide the transport capacity necessary to keep production going at the level called for by the 1941 Materials Mobilization Plan. At the beginning of

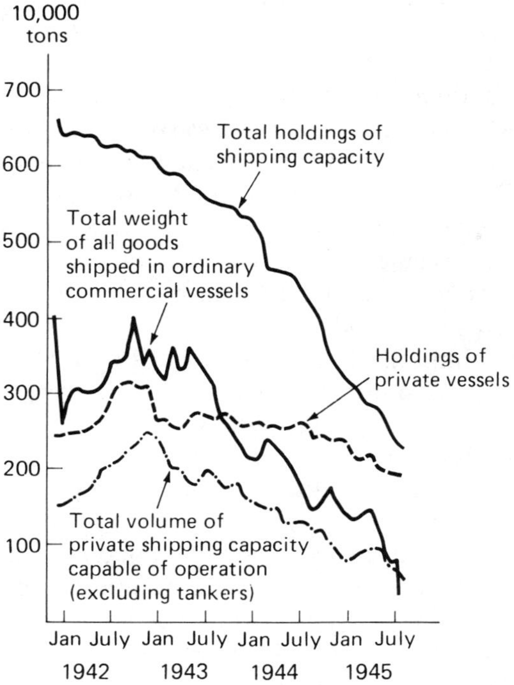


Figure 9.2. Shipping capacity and shipment of goods during World War II. [From Oi Atsushi, *Kaijō goeisen* (Tokyo: Nihon shuppan kyōdō, 1952), appended tables.]

the war, based on estimated annual losses of 800,000 to 1 million tons and estimated annual production of 600,000 tons of new ships, it was forecast that Japan could maintain 3 million gross tons of capacity. This forecast proved excessively optimistic.[54]

In reality, the army and navy vessels were not replaced easily, and losses exceeded expectations. Realizing the importance of shipping, the Japanese government tried to increase shipbuilding output, but marine transport tonnage continued to decline. As Table 9.8 indicates, shipments of Southeast Asian raw materials, in particular, failed to meet expectations. Figure 9.2 shows the decline in shipping capacity as a barometer of fighting strength. Japan's ship tonnage (civilian vessels) for transporting general commodities reached a peak in October 1942 as a result of the cancellation of military vessel requisitioning, but after the battle of the Solomon Islands, its ship tonnage shifted

54 Ibid., pp. 116–17.

into decline. After the latter half of 1943, in particular, it fell steadily because of the all-out American sea and air offensive. Especially notable was the decline of volume shipped, which dropped in conjunction with the ships' falling rate of operation. After the fall of the Marianas in July 1944, the sea lanes to Southeast Asia were blocked, and so it became impossible to procure raw materials anywhere but Japan, Manchuria, and China. In 1945, when food shortages in the homeland reached crisis proportions, the transport of grains and salt from China and Manchukuo became the ultimate mission for shipping, but even that was brought to a standstill by air attacks. In regard to marine transport, Japan had already lost the war in the summer of 1944.[55] Jerome Cohen summarized this situation: "It may be said that in large measure Japan's economy was destroyed twice over, once by cutting off of imports and secondly by air attack."[56]

Domestic production trends until defeat are shown in Table 9.9. Wartime controls clearly expanded Japan's chemical and heavy industrial production and reduced the output for private demand in such industries as textiles. For this reason, production in industries catering to private demand, including agriculture, continued to decline after the latter half of the 1930s. The Japanese were forced to endure extreme hardship. Even within the heavy and chemical industries, the outputs in various sectors achieved maximum levels in different years. Because production priorities focused on aircraft and ships during the Pacific War, the production of materials such as steel and chemicals fell from 1943 onward. Production efforts were concentrated solely on final products such as weaponry, military aircraft, and ships. As a result of extraordinary effort, aircraft production increased from 6,174 planes in 1941 to 26,507 in 1944, and the production of warships grew from 201,000 to 408,000 tons, both peak levels of output.[57] However, the eleventh-hour production effort was unable to turn around the deteriorating war situation.

At the beginning of the Pacific War, the Japanese government was behind in its efforts to organize a wartime economic mobilization, and began only in the fall of 1942. Because Japan's early military successes exceeded expectations, government leaders overlooked the necessity of all-out economic mobilization efforts. When the American counter-

55 See ibid., pp. 123–36.

56 Jerome B. Cohen, *Japan's Economy in War and Reconstruction* (Minneapolis: University of Minnesota Press, 1949), p. 107.

57 According to Okazaki Ayakoto, *Kihon kokuryoku dōtai sōran* (Tokyo: Kokumin keizai kenkyū kyōkai, 1953).

TABLE 9.9

*Wartime production indexes (1937 = 100)*

| | Agriculture production index | Rice | Mining production index | Coal | Manufacturing production index | Steel | Machinery | Chemicals | Textiles | Foods |
|---|---|---|---|---|---|---|---|---|---|---|
| 1936 | 98 | 102 | 92 | 92 | 85 | 87 | 75 | 87 | 88 | 91 |
| 1937 | 100 | 100 | 100 | 100 | 100 | 100 | 100 | 100 | *100* | 100 |
| 1938 | 98 | 99 | 106 | 108 | 103 | 115 | 110 | 114 | 83 | 101 |
| 1939 | *105* | *104* | 112 | 113 | 114 | 123 | 135 | *122* | 83 | *104* |
| 1940 | 99 | 92 | *120* | 125 | 119 | 128 | 163 | 120 | 75 | 90 |
| 1941 | 95 | 83 | *120* | 125 | 123 | 132 | 188 | 120 | 60 | 78 |
| 1942 | 100 | 101 | 118 | 121 | 120 | 140 | 195 | 100 | 48 | 69 |
| 1943 | 96 | 95 | 119 | *127* | 121 | *156* | 214 | 87 | 31 | 58 |
| 1944 | 76 | 88 | 108 | 120 | *124* | 146 | *252* | 80 | 17 | 47 |
| 1945 | 59 | 59 | 51 | 74 | 53 | 52 | 107 | 33 | 6 | 32 |

*Source:* Agriculture: Production indexes compiled by Ministry of Agriculture and Forestry using 1933–5 as the base period (*Dai 30-ji Nōrinshō tōkeihyō*). Mining and manufacturing: Ministry of International Trade and Industry, *Shōwa 35-nen ki jun kōkōgyō shisū sōran*. (Italicized figures are the maximum values reached by each index during this period.)

attack began, the failure to mobilize adequately became an irretrievable handicap. In any case, once the need for the mass production of aircraft and ships became clear, the Japanese government attempted to "make the impossible possible." For example, in order to increase steel production, the government set up a large number of simple twenty-to-one-hundred-ton-capacity small blast furnaces in Korea, Manchukuo, and China. Their performance was extremely poor, however, and they did not produce the expected results. In order to cope with shortages of metal materials, including scrap iron, the government collected city streetcar rails, the handrails of bridges, and even the bells in Buddhist temples. The textile industry's spinning machinery was scrapped and turned into raw materials for shells. In the wake of shutdowns and cutbacks, many factories in the consumer goods industry were converted into munitions factories. Good results were produced in the shipbuilding industry in 1943 by using a "snowball" method. Shipbuilding volume was expanded by importing iron ore only in the amount needed to build ships, and the ships thus built were then used to import more iron ore. In order to cut down on the volume of ocean shipping, various kinds of production facilities, including blast furnaces, were transferred to China and Manchuria, and the practice of on-the-spot production was adopted, but this effort disappointed expectations.

In the fall of 1943, in order to increase munitions production, especially aircraft, a Ministry of Munitions was established by merging the Cabinet Planning Board and the relevant departments in the Ministry of Commerce and Industry. At the same time a Munitions Companies System was inaugurated. Key firms were designated as "munitions companies"; those in charge of production were given titles as government officials; employees were treated as impressed labor and not allowed to quit their jobs; and the companies were responsible for increasing production in accordance with government instructions.[58] But the government also compensated these firms for losses. In each industry designated, financial institutions took responsibility for supplying the necessary capital.

The labor force presented a difficult problem during the war. Out of a population of slightly under 80 million, 2.4 million had been conscripted into military service by the end of 1941. In August 1945 this number had swelled to 7.2 million. To compensate for the resulting

58 Jūyō sangyō kyōgikai, *Gunjukaishahō kaisetsu* (Tokyo: Teikoku shuppan, 1944). No coherent study of the munitions companies exists.

labor shortage, young men in consumer goods or tertiary industries were conscripted and mobilized to work in factories and mines. After 1944, students from the middle-school level up were employed in munitions production and forced to suspend studies of any kind almost entirely. In the consumer goods industries, especially textiles, and in the tertiary industries, firms either converted to wartime production or went out of business as raw materials and merchandise disappeared. Their machinery and equipment were scrapped for munitions production, and their workers were put to work in factories and mines. The government promoted the forced reorganization of business, and it compelled small- and medium-sized enterprises to convert to munitions production or go out of business, mainly in order to mobilize their workers.[59] The 1944 bulge in the secondary industry work force and the deterioration of the tertiary industry work force, as seen in Table 9.3, were the consequences of such policies.

The quality of daily life suffered. After 1938 it became impossible to obtain cotton and woolen goods. In 1940 necessities such as rice, *miso* (bean paste), and soy sauce were rationed, but these, too, gradually ran short, and food shortages for the urban population became severe in 1943. The standard daily Japanese caloric intake was 2,200 calories, including 70 grams of protein, but the actual daily intake in 1941 was 2,105 calories and 64.7 grams of protein. By January 1944, rations provided a mere 1,405 calories.[60] People tried to stave off starvation by foraging in the farm villages or buying on the black market outside official distribution channels. The government had put limited price controls into effect after the start of the China war for fear of inflation. In 1940 the government began setting official prices for everything, but it was impossible to eradicate illegal transactions. From a 1937 base-year value of 100, the consumer price index rose to 149 in 1940, 208 in 1944, and 254 in May 1945. If black market prices are included, these indexes must be calculated as 161 for 1940 and 358 for 1944.[61] The latter figures are most likely closer to the actual situation.

After 1940 the government officially set wage levels on the basis of type of employment, educational background, age, and number of years of experience. This was done because it was feared that wage–cost increases would cause price increases. Because wage rates were calculated on the basis of official prices, they could never catch up

59 Yui Tsunehiko, *Chūshō kigyō seisaku no shiteki tenkai* (Tokyo: Tōyō keizai shinpōsha, 1964), pp. 342ff.

60 Hōsei daigaku Ōhara shakai mondai kenkyūjo, *Taiheiyō sensōka no rōdōsha jōtai* (Tokyo: Tōyō keizai shinpōsha, 1964), p. 149.

61 Cohen, *Japan's Economy*, p. 356.

with actual consumer price increases. Real wages sank to almost half their prewar level.[62]

By the time of defeat in August 1945, Japan had lost approximately three million lives (more than half were military personnel) and a quarter of its national wealth. The remaining total value of its national wealth was virtually the equivalent of what it had been in 1935. The war reduced the accumulation of the intervening decade to charred and smoldering ruins.[63] It is also true, however, that the conditions for sustaining postwar economic growth were already sprouting among those ruins. The wartime munitions industry provided the prototype for the chemical and heavy industrial sector, which was at the heart of postwar growth. Machine gun factories began to produce sewing machines, and range finder plants began making cameras. Linkages between big factories and small business subcontractors that developed in the munitions industry also became the basis for the postwar subcontracting system. So too the designation of specific financial institutions to finance munitions companies created close relations in which can be found the origins of the postwar "financial groupings" (*kinyū keiretsu*). Administrative guidance by government ministries and the Bank of Japan, often pointed to as a special characteristic of postwar Japan, was also a legacy of the wartime controls. The seniority wage system spread throughout the economy when wage controls were instituted, and enterprise unions were the successors of the Patriotic Industrial Associations (Sangyō hōkōku kai) organized in each firm after the labor unions were broken up. During the war the government purchased rice on a dual-price system, buying cheaply from landlords but paying a higher price when buying directly from producers in order to accelerate increased rice production. This practice had the effect of lowering rental rates, thus clearing the way for the postwar land reform. Even though the recollection of the wartime period is repugnant to those Japanese who lived through it, it was a stage preliminary to rapid postwar growth.

## CONCLUSION

Both for the world and for Japan, the period from 1920 to 1945 was an unusually stormy and convulsive era. Looking back on the course that

62 Yamada Junzō, "Senjichū no rōdōsha" in *Gendai Nihon shihonshugi taikei:* vol. 4, *Rōdō*, ed. Aihara Shigeru (Tokyo: Kōbundō, 1958), p. 97.

63 Keizai antei honbu, *Taiheiyō sensō ni yoru wagakuni no higai sōgō hōkokusho* (Tokyo: Keizai antei honbu, 1948).

the Japanese economy pursued during those years, one may point out the following special features relevant to the postwar experience. First, the trend toward chemical and heavy industrialization that began during World War I constantly accelerated. Second, precedents for economic policies aimed at economic growth and full employment had already achieved success in the 1930s. Third, the prototype of postwar Japan's distinctive economic system was molded during the war years, although not necessarily intentionally. These circumstances also explain why Japan was able to achieve remarkably high growth, even by world standards, in the 1920s and 1930s.

However, even from a strictly economic standpoint, the economy of the 1920s and 1930s differed in several respects from that of the post–World War II era. First, politics were in absolute ascendancy over the economy. Examples of this are the removal of the gold embargo at the old parity for reasons of national prestige; the imposition of economic controls in conjunction with the military invasion of China and plans for war with the Soviet Union; and the plunge into the Pacific War without a dispassionate assessment of the nation's economic strength. Second, after the breakdown of the classical principle of laissez-faire, many policies were experimented with on a trial-and-error basis, but no general principle clearly emerged in its place. The failure of Inoue's fiscal policies and the success of Takahashi's are conspicuous examples of this. Third, the economy's extraordinary experience under wartime controls, when all was concentrated on winning the war, reduced the lives of the people to ruins.

# CHAPTER 10

# THE POSTWAR JAPANESE ECONOMY, 1945–1973

From 1945 to 1973, the Japanese economy maintained an annual growth rate of nearly 10 percent. Because the standards for measuring national income changed during this period, there is no continuous statistical series. However, when the existing data are linked and recalculated, Japan's real GNP shows an annual growth rate of 9.6 percent from 1946 to 1973.[1]

The first decade of this high economic growth was a period of recovery from the economic dislocations brought about by Japan's defeat in World War II. During the war, Japan's maritime transport was cut off by the Allied powers, and it had been difficult to obtain raw materials. In effect, this blockade was continued by postwar restrictions that the American occupying forces imposed on foreign trade, and it was exacerbated by social and economic disorder. Real GNP per capita in 1946 declined to 55 percent of the 1934–6 level as a result, and it did not recover that level until 1953.

The tempo of Japan's postwar recovery from the wartime destruction appears rapid in comparison with that of the countries of Western Europe, because the postwar collapse in Japan was so great, but it actually took the prewar per capita GNP longer to recover in Japan than it did in Europe. In 1951 the per capita national income, based on the prevailing exchange rates, was one-twelfth that of the United States and two-fifths that of West Germany.[2] But once the postwar recovery was complete, Japan maintained an extremely high rate of growth for more than fifteen years. Indeed, the performance of Japan's economy was outstanding compared with that of the other industrial economies.

1 Because of the confusion accompanying Japan's defeat in the war, there was no official estimate of its GNP in 1945. Figures for 1946 to 1955 can be found in Keizai kikakuchō, *Gendai Nihon keizai no tenkai* (Tokyo: Keizai kikakuchō, 1976), p. 578; and for 1955 to 1965 (old SNA) and 1965 to 1973 (new SNA), Tōyō keizai shinpōsha, *Shōwa kokusei sōran* (Tokyo: Tōyō keizai shinpōsha, 1980), p. 99.

2 Keizai kikakuchō chōsakyoku, ed., *Shiryō: Keizai hakusho 25 nen* (Tokyo: Keizai kikakuchō, 1972), p. 9 (chart 2), pp. 11–12.

During this period of rapid economic growth (*kōdō seichō jidai*) (1955 to 1972), Japan was in the process of introducing technological innovations and catching up economically with the West. This period can be divided into two subperiods: from 1955 to 1965 when the economy experienced three major booms (the "Jimmu boom," the "iwato boom," and the "boom that did not feel like one" [*kōkyokan naki keiki*]); and from 1966 to 1972 when the economy grew steadily until the "oil shock" and the onset of "crazy inflation" (*kyōran infure*).

Even after the period of high growth ended in 1973, however, the momentum of the economy continued. By 1975, for example, per capita GNP had reached 62 percent of the United States' and 65.9 percent of West Germany's and had outstripped the levels of Great Britain and Italy.[3] The gap between Japan and the other advanced countries continued to narrow. As a result of its rapid growth, Japan had risen to become one of the world's economic superpowers (*keizai taikoku*).

## POSTWAR ECONOMIC REFORM AND RECOVERY

### *Postwar economic reforms*

The transformation of Japan's postwar economy took place against the background of a democratization reform program promoted by the American Occupation forces. These reforms, of course, were not solely the result of the Americans' initiatives but were also shaped by the efforts of Japanese who either cooperated with the Americans or fought with them, in pursuit of their own ideals or agendas. Three economic reforms of particular importance were land reform, dissolution of the zaibatsu, and labor reform.

*Land reform.* Before land reform, 45.9 percent of Japan's agricultural land was tenanted. Before the war, tenant rent amounted to 5 percent of the national income, and tenancy disputes reached a peak of six thousand in 1935. It had been the policy of the prewar Ministry of Agriculture and Forestry to promote owner-cultivatorship in order to solve the tenancy problem. In the fall of 1945, as an extension of that policy, the Agricultural Land Adjustment Law was revised, limiting landholding to five *chōbu* and requiring that rent be paid in cash.

3 Based on OECD National Accounts (1986); Keizai kikakuchō kokumin shotokuka, *Kokumin shotoku dōkō* (Tokyo: Keizai kikakuchō, 1986).

The American Occupation forces, feeling that this legislation did not go far enough, sent a memorandum on land reform to the Japanese government on December 9, 1945, urging a more extensive change. The so-called second land reform was carried out by the promulgation of the Law for the Special Establishment of Independent Cultivators on October 21, 1946. The law provided for all the land owned by absentee landlords to be purchased by the government; for the land of noncultivating resident landlords to be limited to less than one *chōbu;* for the land of owner-cultivators to be limited to three *chōbu;* and for land purchased by the government to be resold to tenant farmers. Because the real price of the land dropped drastically as the result of inflation, land reform was almost equivalent to confiscation.

During land reform, 1,916 million hectares, or 37.5 percent of the agricultural acreage, changed hands. The land of over 3.7 million landlords was purchased by the government.[4] As a result of the reform, tenanted land was reduced to only 10 percent of agricultural land; the tenants' rent became negotiable; and tenant disputes disappeared. The farmers became more willing to work; the farming villages became more politically stable; and agriculture developed with the help of government price supports and investment in infrastructure. Opportunities for urban employment grew with the rapid growth and reduced the fragmentation of landholdings and agricultural underemployment created by the outflow of people to the countryside immediately after the war.

As a result of land reform, Japanese agriculture after the war became the province of independent farmers. On the other hand, even after the economy moved into its rapid growth phase, the number of farmers with part-time jobs increased, and landholdings remained fragmented. This impeded the improvement of agricultural productivity. In order to solve this problem, many urged increasing the scale of cultivation and encouraging the rental of land. There was a growing demand for a change in the policy of making owner-cultivators central to agriculture (*jisakunō chūshin shugi*), a policy based on the goals of both the Occupation forces and the prewar agrarian reformers in Japan.

*Dissolution of the zaibatsu.* From the outset the American Occupation intended to dissolve the zaibatsu, which some American officials felt had been complicit in waging Japan's war of territorial conquest. In

4 The basic materials on land reform may be found in Nōsei chōsakai nōchi kaikaku kiroku iinkai, ed., *Nōchi kaikaku tenmatsu gaiyō* (Tokyo, 1951). The standard work in English is by R. P. Dore, *Land Reform in Japan* (London: Oxford University Press, 1959).

October 1945 the Occupation decided to dissolve the head offices (*honsha*) of the zaibatsu holding companies and in April 1946 established a committee to reorganize the holding companies. By June 1947, eighty-three companies had been designated as holding companies. Of these, twenty-eight were reorganized as family holding companies, and the rest were allowed to continue as production enterprises after their stockholdings had been transferred. In the meantime, on July 3, 1947, the Occupation authorities ordered the dissolution of the Mitsui Trading Company and the Mitsubishi Trading Company.[5]

In April 1947 the enactment of the Anti-Monopoly Law, based on American antitrust laws, established Japan's Fair Trade Commission. The following December, the Diet passed the Law for the Elimination of Excessive Economic Concentration, which provided for the dissolution of any company deemed monopolistic. Under these laws, eighteen large firms were dissolved, and their factories were redistributed. The Japan Steel Corporation was split into two firms (Yawata Steel and Fuji Steel); Mitsui Mining was divided into two firms (Mitsui Mining and Kamioka Industries); Mitsubishi Industries was divided into two (Mitsubishi Mining and Taihei Mining); Mitsubishi Heavy Industries was divided into three firms (Eastern Japan Heavy Industries, Central Japan Heavy Industries, and Western Japan Heavy Industries); Tokyo Shibaura Electric divested itself of twenty-seven out of forty-three plants; and Hitachi Manufacturing divested itself of nineteen out of thirty-five plants. As a result of these and other dissolutions, the degree of concentration in the iron and steel, shipbuilding, beer-brewing, papermaking, and other industries was substantially reduced.

Some large enterprises that had dissolved or divided under the economic deconcentration reemerged after the end of the Occupation. The Mitsubishi Trading Company was revived in 1954, the Mitsui Trading Company in 1959, Mitsubishi Heavy Industries in 1964, and the New Japan Steel Corporation in 1970. The zaibatsu's head offices may have disappeared, but the enterprises were reconcentrated into "enterprise groups" (*keiretsu*), centering on banks, through mutual stockholding and financing. Critics often referred to this as the "revival of the zaibatsu."

The dissolution of the zaibatsu and the abolition of concentration permanently affected the economy. The concentration of production, which had been reduced by the antizaibatsu legislation, was further

5 The basic material on dissolving the zaibatsu can be found in Tokushu kaisha seiri iinkai, ed., *Nihon zaibatsu to sono kaitai* (Tokyo, 1951). The standard work in English is by Eleanor M. Hadley, *Antitrust in Japan* (Princeton, N.J.: Princeton University Press, 1959).

diluted as a result of high growth. The competition among enterprises became livelier. Industrial firms not affiliated with the prewar zaibatsu expanded into large enterprises because of opportunities for new entry and enlargement of scale. Among the large postwar firms are many, such as Toyota, Hitachi, and New Japan Steel, that had no relationship to the prewar zaibatsu. The emergence of Kawasaki Steel and Sumitomo Metals as steel makers, the entry of Honda into the passenger car industry, and the rapid growth of Sony and Matsushita suggest that the Japanese industrial organization, on the whole, continued to be competitive. It can be said that this competitive industrial structure developed as a result of the postwar dissolution of the zaibatsu and the abolition of concentration.

*Labor reform.* At the core of labor reform was the enactment of three labor laws: the Labor Union Law, modeled on the American Wagner Act and promulgated in December 1945, established the right of workers to organize and bargain collectively, exempted labor union activity from civil law, and defined unfair labor practices. The Labor Relations Adjustment Law, promulgated in September 1946, defined the limits of strike behavior and established procedures for the settlement of labor disputes. The Labor Standards Law of April 1947 legislated improved working conditions, such as the prohibition of forced labor, the establishment of an eight-hour working day, the limitation of female and minor employment, and the provision of compensation for work-related injuries. These three laws, but especially the Labor Union Law, stimulated labor union activity.

The labor union movement grew rapidly in the immediate postwar years. Because of the runaway inflation and the general impoverishment of the population, labor disputes were frequent. In 1948 the rate of unionization of the industrial work force (including workers in transport, construction, mining, and manufacturing) was over 50 percent, and the number of enrollees was 6.677 million. In some of the industrial disputes, the labor unions adopted aggressive tactics such as "production control," whereby the workers actually took over the management and control of production.

A general strike organized by the public labor unions was planned for February 1, 1947, but the Occupation authorities prohibited the strike immediately before it was to begin. The confrontation between Occupation Policy and the labor movement became more pronounced in July 1948 when the government, in response to a letter from General Douglas MacArthur, promulgated an ordinance that abolished the right of public employees to strike. For a long period thereafter, a struggle for control of the labor union movement ensued between those who considered political issues as primary and those who considered economic issues as primary. As the union movement consolidated on the basis of "enterprise unions" that incorporated all the workers of a firm into a single union, "the principles of Japanese-style unionism," stressing the primacy of economic issues, predominated. In 1955 so-called spring offensives (*shuntō*) began, thereby routinizing the negotiations for wage hikes.

The Occupation and its policies also had an indirect effect on the economy. First, the defeat ended Japan's attempts to increase its economic advantage through war and military means. On the contrary, under the protection of the American "nuclear umbrella," Japan did not need to spend much on defense, and so capital, human resources, and human energy could flow into more efficient activities. Second, under the American Occupation, the Japanese had sustained contact with a foreign country for the first time, and many more Japanese than ever before were able to observe firsthand the high American standard of living and the efficient organizational methods supporting it. Finally, the Occupation brought a change in Japan's elites. New leaders in politics, business, and the bureaucracy turned their energies toward the restoration of a vigorous economy in the midst of postwar confusion.

## *Postwar economic policy*

The postwar leaders were faced with creating a new framework of economic policy responsive to the conditions created by defeat. In part this meant restoring the economy devastated by war; in part it meant bringing postwar inflation under control; and in part it meant establishing the policy principles to be followed in promoting further economic development.

Like all defeated countries in modern times, postwar Japan was beset by deep inflation. Prices had begun to rise during the war even under wartime price controls, and once the war ended, the inflationary pressures grew. Production stagnated but demand, suppressed during wartime, was ready to ignite. Public bonds and other kinds of financial assets had accumulated during the war, and if converted into currency, they could fuel an explosive inflation. To deal with this situation, the government in February 1946 adopted an emergency policy of restricting bank accounts, levying taxes on property, and controlling prices. But these measures merely arrested inflation temporarily,

TABLE 10.1
*Price trends (1934–6 average = 1.00)*

| | Wholesale price index | Annual rate of increase (%) | Consumer price index | Annual rate of increase (%) |
|---|---|---|---|---|
| 1946 | 16.27 | – | 50.6 | – |
| 1950 | 246.8 | 97.3 | 219.9 | 44.3 |
| 1955 | 343.0 | 6.8 | 297.4 | 6.2 |
| 1960 | 352.1 | 0.5 | 328.0 | 1.9 |
| 1965 | 359.4 | 0.4 | 443.2 | 6.2 |
| 1970 | 399.9 | 2.2 | 577.9 | 5.5 |
| 1973 | 463.3 | 5.0 | 719.5 | 7.5 |

*Source:* Keizai kikakuchō, *Gendai Nihon keizai no tenkai* (Tokyo: Keizai kikakuchō, 1976), pp. 616–18.

and from 1946 to 1947, inflation took off. In 1946, wholesale prices were 16.3 times the 1934–6 levels, and by 1950 they were 246.8 times as high (see Table 10.1).

Restoring industrial production was also a major task. The immediate postwar economy was in a state of collapse. The resumption of production was hindered by the disrupted inflow of raw materials from abroad. Until limited private trade was established in August 1947, foreign trade was controlled by the Occupation authorities, and even after that date, the system of public management of trade remained basically unchanged. On the other hand, there was a positive legacy from the wartime economy, that is, capital stock in the heavy and chemical industries and an abundant supply of workers with experience in modern industrial activity. Because it was not possible to rely on imported raw materials, the production bottleneck could be broken only by using domestic coal resources.

Professor Arisawa Hiromi of Tokyo University proposed the so-called priority production method to stimulate industrial production. His plan envisaged first increasing the production of coal by concentrating materials and capital in the coal-mining industry, then using the greater coal output to produce steel, and finally investing the increased steel output in the further increase of coal production. This method of lifting domestic production by its own bootstraps was the government's central policy in 1947–8. In order to implement the priority production method, the Yoshida cabinet established the Reconstruction Finance Bank (Fukkō kin'yū ginkō), lent a large amount of capital to the coal industry, gave substantial price subsidies to the iron and steel industry, and set priorities for materials to key industries.[6] Consequently, in 1947 the output target for coal, 30 million tons, was just barely achieved.

The priority production method is often regarded as a successful example of Japan's interventionist policy in the heavy and chemical industries and it is seen as leading later in the direction of "industrial policy" (*sangyō seisaku*). It certainly was an important stimulus to the resumption of production. Japan had no other way of bringing about the recovery of its economy than using the heavy and chemical industry base it had acquired by the end of the war. As U.S. Secretary of the Army Kenneth Royall noted in January 1948, "It is clear that Japan can not support itself as a nation of shopkeepers and craftsmen and small artisans any more than it can exist as a purely agricultural nation."[7] But it would be a mistake to overestimate the significance of the priority production method. Japan used its existing plant capacity in its chemical and heavy industries but did not intend to expand its scale. Steel production was just 740,000 tons in 1947, no comparison with the 100 million tons produced in the 1970s. The priority production method was in effect a policy of "forced import substitution" developed during a period when the economy was closed to the outside world and raw material imports were curtailed. When the conditions that created it changed, it was abandoned.

Even this degree of industrial recovery would not have been possible if Japan had not been able to retain its chemical and heavy industry base. The initial postwar reparations policy recommended in the Pauley Report of December 1945 was to remove all equipment from Japan's war industry and to reduce drastically its capacity in such defense-related industries as steel, machine tool production, and merchant shipping. As the international situation changed and American economic policy toward Japan shifted away from punitive measures toward economic rehabilitation, these goals were modified.[8] As Secretary of the Army Royall pointed out in his January 1948 speech, if Japan were to achieve political stability and retain its free government, it had to have a healthy independent economy; and furthermore, the United States could not continue to provide indefinitely hundreds of millions of dollars in aid to Japan.

In response to the need to curtail inflation as well as to promote

6 Noted in Kōsai Yutaka, "Fukkōki," *Nihon no sangyō seisaku,* ed. Komiya Ryūtarō (Tokyo: Tōkyō daigaku shuppankai, 1984), pp. 30–4; Kōsai Yutaka, *Kōdō seichō no jidai,* ed. Komiya Ryūtanō et al. (Tokyo: Nihon hyōronsha, 1981), pp. 44–58.
7 Ōkurashō, ed., *Shōwa zaiseishi* (Tokyo: Tōyō keizai shinpōsha, 1982), vol. 20. p. 185.
8 Ibid., p. 440.

Japan's economic recovery and self-sufficiency, the United States dispatched Joseph M. Dodge, a Detroit banker who had planned currency reforms in occupied Germany, to recommend changes in the Japanese government's economic policies. A believer in classic economic liberalism, Dodge recommended a series of policies that he regarded as necessary to establish economic stability that would enable recovery. The major points of the policy that Dodge set forth in March 1949 were (1) balancing a consolidated national budget in order to reduce inflationary pressures; (2) terminating the activities of the Reconstruction Finance Bank, whose loans were uneconomical; (3) decreasing the scope of government intervention in the economy, especially in the form of subsidies and price controls; (4) establishing an exchange rate of ¥360 to $1.00; and (5) returning to international trade through private channels instead of through government trading agencies. These policies continued in force for the next two and a half years, though with decreasing emphasis as the Korean War promoted growth. In the long run, the so-called Dodge line established the principles of balanced budgets, orthodox finance, stabilized prices, and a fixed exchange rate that constituted one side of government policy during the period of high growth.

## MACROECONOMIC PERFORMANCE

The period of rapid economic growth was conditioned by macroeconomic conditions such as labor supply, capital accumulation, price trends, income distribution, and the growth of demand. All of these were interrelated in complex ways.

### *The increase in the labor force*

One of the conditions that enabled Japan's rapid economic growth was a smooth and abundant supply of labor. Japan had been overpopulated before the war, and there was a substantial population increase in the immediate postwar years as demobilized soldiers and repatriated inhabitants of Japan's overseas possessions returned home. According to a special census in 1947, the total population was 78.101 million, a marked increase over the 1940 census population (71.933 million) and the 1944 estimated population (74.433 million) (see Table 10.2). In 1947, however, the country was in a state of economic dislocation, and employment was difficult to find. The number of employed had increased by only 846,000 compared with that of 1940, and the total

TABLE 10.2
*Changes in population (in thousands)*

| | Total population | Employed population | Employed in agriculture | Employed in manufacturing | Employed in wholesale and retailing |
|---|---|---|---|---|---|
| 1940 | 71,933 | 32,482 | 13,557 | 6,863 | 4,097 |
| 1947 | 78,101 | 33,328 | 16,622 | 5,439 | 2,477 |
| 1950 | 83,200 | 35,625 | 16,102 | 5,689 | 3,963 |
| 1955 | 89,276 | 39,621 | 14,890 | 6,902 | 5,472 |
| 1960 | 93,419 | 43,719 | 13,127 | 9,544 | 6,909 |
| 1965 | 98,275 | 47,633 | 10,857 | 11,507 | 8,563 |
| 1970 | 103,720 | 52,110 | 9,333 | 13,540 | 10,059 |
| 1975 | 111,940 | 53,015 | 6,699 | 13,158 | 11,364 |

*Source:* Tōyō keizai shinpōsha, *Shōwa kokusei sōran* (Tokyo: Tōyō keizai shinpōsha, 1980), vol. 1, p. 29.

TABLE 10.3
*Changes in the labor force*

| | Worker population (in thousands) | Labor force as percentage of population | Unemployment rate (%) |
|---|---|---|---|
| 1948 | 3,484 | 64.6 | 0.7 |
| 1950 | 3,616 | 65.5 | 1.2 |
| 1955 | 4,194 | 70.8 | 1.8 |
| 1960 | 4,511 | 69.2 | 1.1 |
| 1965 | 4,787 | 65.7 | 0.8 |
| 1970 | 5,153 | 65.4 | 1.2 |
| 1973 | 5,326 | 64.7 | 1.3 |

*Source:* Tōyō keizai shinpōsha, *Shōwa kokusei sōran* (Tokyo: Tōyō keizai shinpōsha, 1980), vol. 1, p. 58. Statistics are not continuous, and so accurate comparison is difficult.

employment rate (that is, the number of employed divided by the total population) had declined from 45.2 percent to 42.7 percent. The distribution of employment had also changed radically. Whereas the number of workers in manufacturing had declined by 1.400 million and in service industries by 600,000, the number of workers in agriculture had increased by 3 million. As these figures demonstrate, Japan in the immediate postwar period had a surplus of labor and a dearth of employment.

Between 1948 and 1955, however, the working population increased at the high annual rate of 2.6 percent (see Table 10.3). There were two reasons: first, those born in the first half of the 1930s, when the birthrate was high, had reached working age; second, there was an increase in the labor force as a proportion of the population. Although the number of workers had grown substantially, the rate of fully unemployed had also increased. The fact that there was much discussion of a "dual structure" in the labor market (that is, that wage differentials were related to the scale of enterprise) suggests that even in this period there was latitude in the demand for labor.

The annual growth rate of the labor force decreased to 1.3 percent from the period 1955–1965 to the period 1965–1973. By international standards, this was not low. Even though the postwar baby boom increased the size of the working age population, the rate slowed down because (1) the wartime decrease in the birthrate resulted in a decline in the number of new entrants into the labor force between 1955 and 1960; and (2) from 1960 to 1965 many young people continued their education instead of entering the work force. The continuing slowdown in the expansion of the working population in the late 1960s reflected a decline in the birthrate after the end of the baby boom. Meanwhile, because the economy's growth rate continued to be high, the unemployment rate began to drop in the late 1950s. By the early 1960s, wage differentials based on scale of enterprise had narrowed, and for the first time the number of jobs exceeded the number of new graduates. By 1967 the number of job openings exceeded the number of job seekers in the general labor market. The Japanese economy had reached a state of full employment.

As the labor market moved from a surplus of labor to a shortage of labor, economic growth was sustained by a shift of workers among industrial sectors and the substitution of capital inputs for labor inputs. The number of agricultural workers decreased by 1.7 million between 1945 and 1955, by 4 million between 1955 and 1965, and by 4.2 million between 1965 and 1975. By contrast, the number of manufacturing industry workers increased by 4.6 million between 1965 and 1975 (see Table 10.3).

The qualitative changes in the labor supply were as important as the quantitative changes. In prewar Japan, textile industry workers were the heart of the industrial work force, accounting for one-third of the industrial workers. Most typical were the female workers in the cotton-spinning industry who started working in their late teens after graduating from higher elementary school, to augment the family budget, and who quit their jobs in their twenties, to get married. Their working life was short; changes in the work force were frequent; and wages were low. The workers who played the leading role in industrial development from the wartime expansion of the chemical and heavy industries through the period of postwar growth were skilled male workers in the iron and steel and machine industries. They were lifetime employees; they acquired specific skills through on-the-job training; and they contributed positively to small-group production units within the enterprise. They expected improvements in wages and working conditions through seniority and economic growth. Compulsory education was extended from six to nine years, and the rate of those continuing their education increased so that the intellectual quality of the work force also improved.

### *Savings and capital accumulation*

The Pacific War inflicted enormous material damage on Japan, amounting to one-fourth of the national wealth (see Table 10.4). By the end of the war, the national wealth had declined to its 1935 level. In effect, the war nullified any capital accumulation between 1935 and 1945. If we compare productive activities, however, it is clear that there was still some leeway in the economy. Real GNP fell to only half the prewar level. If we look at industries by sector, we can see that although the rate of capacity in the consumer goods industries was damaged because many factories had been converted to war production, by contrast, the damage rate was relatively low in the heavy and chemical industries. The steel and electric power generation industries even emerged from the war with plant capacity above prewar levels (see Table 10.5).

As we have already seen, the first postwar attempt to stimulate industrial production – the priority production method – tried to combine this abundant capital stock with surplus labor. The bottleneck was the difficulty of obtaining raw material imports. After Japan was allowed access to foreign markets, its economic recovery proceeded rapidly. During the recovery period, investment in plant concentrated on repair and renewal. The marginal capital coefficient (i.e., the amount of investment necessary to increase the GNP by 1 percent) remained low.

By 1955, when the level of economic activity had returned to prewar levels, investment in new facilities became necessary, as there had not been much investment during the recovery period. Japan's capital stock was becoming obsolete, weakening the international competitiveness of Japanese industry. After the Korean War rationalization investment began in a number of industries. By the latter half of the 1950s, Japanese industry was moving toward investment in modern produc-

TABLE 10.4

*Wartime damage to national wealth (¥1 million at time of defeat)*

| | Amount of damage | National wealth before damage | Damage rate (%) | National wealth remaining at end of war | National wealth in 1935 | Rate of increase (%)[a] |
|---|---|---|---|---|---|---|
| Buildings | 22,220 | 90,435 | 24.5 | 68,215 | 76,275 | Δ10.6 |
| Industrial machinery and equipment | 7,994 | 23,346 | 34.2 | 15,352 | 8,501 | 80.6 |
| Shipping | 7,359 | 9,125 | 80.6 | 1,796 | 3,111 | Δ42.3 |
| Electrical and gas equipment | 1,618 | 14,933 | 10.8 | 13,313 | 8,987 | 48.1 |
| Railroad and rolling stock | 1,523 | 15,415 | 9.8 | 13,892 | 13,364 | 4.0 |
| Telegraph, telephone, and water supply | 659 | 4,156 | 15.8 | 3,497 | 3,229 | 8.2 |
| Producer goods | 7,864 | 32,953 | 23.8 | 25,089 | 23,541 | 6.6 |
| Household property goods | 9,558 | 46,427 | 20.5 | 36,869 | 39,354 | Δ6.6 |
| Other | 5,483 | 16,340 | 33.5 | 10,857 | 10,839 | 4.5 |
| Total | 64,278 | 253,130 | 25.3 | 188,852 | 186,751 | 1.1 |

[a]Delta (Δ) indicates decrease.

*Source:* Keizai antei honbu, *Taiheiyō sensō ni yoru wagakuni higai sōgō hōkukusho* (Tokyo, 1949); Nakayama Ichirō, ed., *Nihon no kokufu kōzō* (Tokyo: Toyō keizai shinpōsha, 1959).

TABLE 10.5
*Productive capacity at time of defeat (¥1 million at time of defeat)*

| | Peak capacity before 1944 | Capacity as of August 15, 1945 | Percentage remaining | Capacity at end 1941 | Rate of increase (%) |
|---|---|---|---|---|---|
| Hydroelectric power (1,000s kw) | 6,074 | 6,233 | 102.6 | 5,368 | 116.1 |
| Ordinary iron and steel materials (1,000s tons) | 7,998 | 8,040 | 100.5 | 7,506 | 107.1 |
| Aluminum (tons per month) | 11,100 | 8,350 | 75.2 | 7,240 | 115.3 |
| Machine tools (tons) | 190 | 120 | 63.1 | 110 | 109.1 |
| Petroleum refining (1,000s kl) | 3,739 | 1,443 | 38.5 | 2,359 | 61.2 |
| Soap (1,000s tons) | 278 | 99 | 35.9 | 278 | 54.5 |
| Cotton and staple fiber spinning (million bolts) | 13.8 | 2.8 | 20.2 | 13.8 | 20.2 |
| Cotton textile weaving (1,000s looms) | 393 | 123 | 31.4 | 393 | 31.4 |
| Bicycles (1,000s) | 3,600 | 720 | 20.0 | 2,880 | 25.0 |

*Source:* Keizai antei honbu, *Taiheiyō sensō ni yoru wagakuni higai sōgō hōkukusho* (Tokyo, 1949); Nakayama Ichirō, ed., *Nihon no kokufu kōzō* (Tokyo: Tōyō keizai shinpōsha, 1959).

tive facilities. New technologies were introduced, and the face of Japanese industry changed. This was known as the process whereby "investment induced investment" (*tōshi ga tōshi o yobu*). During the latter half of the 1960s, in response to labor shortages, investment in labor-saving technology began, and in the 1970s, investment in antipollution facilities started.

The rate of increase in capital stock was 1 percent to 2 percent higher than the growth rate of the economy as a whole. The reason was that the expansion of plant investment was comparatively low from 1945 to 1955 but rose rapidly after 1955. This high rate of capital formation was financed not from foreign capital but from the increase in domestic savings, particularly individual savings.

The consumption expenditures of the average urban worker household in 1946–7 amounted to more than 100 percent of his or her income. By 1955 that had dropped to 90.8 percent, a level similar to that of the prewar period (the 1934–6 average was 88.3 percent). As economic growth advanced, the propensity to consume continued to decline, and the savings rate increased to twice the prewar rate. After 1955 the Japanese economy was characterized by high savings and high investment.

There are various hypotheses explaining the high rate of household savings. Some argue that because income grew more rapidly than expected, consumption did not keep pace, with the result that savings increased; others point to the population's relative youth; and still others say that because housing and social welfare facilities lagged behind the rest of the economy, people accumulated savings for the future. But the period of high growth was also one in which more people considered themselves as reaching middle-class status, and the high savings rate may be connected to this change in social consciousness.

Personal savings were not invested directly in business but were deposited in bank accounts. In turn, business enterprises financed their investment by borrowing from the banks. Under this system of "indirect finance," there emerged the low rate of self-capitalization among businesses that is so characteristic of the period of rapid growth.

### *The balance-of-payments ceiling*

The most direct limitation on economic growth between 1945 and 1973 was the international balance of payments. From the end of the war until 1955, it was feared that Japan would not be able even to finance basic imports of food and raw materials. Without aid from the United States or the special procurements program during the Korean War, when the American military bought supplies and repaired equipment in Japan, it would not have been possible to achieve balance-of-payments equilibrium during this period (see Table 10.6).

After 1955 the balance-of-payments current account approached equilibrium. However, Japan had adopted a policy of vigorous domestic growth without dependence on foreign capital. Its foreign currency reserves were kept as low as possible, and any reserves that could be spared were used for the growth-oriented expansion of income and imports. At the same time the government also pursued a policy of maintaining the foreign exchange rate at ¥360 to $1.00, set in 1949. As a result, whenever there was a deficit in the balance-of-payments current account, the government had no choice but to decrease the tempo of economic expansion and to reduce imports in order to bring the international balance of payments back into equilibrium. When there were balance-of-payments deficits in 1954, 1957, 1961, and

TABLE 10.6
*International balance of payments (in thousands of $)*

| | Current transactions | Trade balance | Nontrade balance | Transfer balance | Long-term capital balance | Total balance | Foreign exchange reserve |
|---|---|---|---|---|---|---|---|
| 1946–50 | 726 | −958 | −340 | 2,005[a] | −79 | 726 | – |
| 1951–55 | 525 | −1,964 | 2,211[b] | 277 | −110 | 464 | 738 |
| 1956–60 | 114 | 466 | −103 | −248 | 1 | 139 | 1,824 |
| 1961–65 | −1,358 | 1,955 | −3,038 | −275 | 321 | −1,037 | 2,107 |
| 1966–70 | 6,201 | 13,626 | −6,548 | −877 | −3,605 | 4,525 | 4,399 |
| 1971–73 | 12,285 | 20,466 | −7,131 | −1,030 | −15,319 | 2,344 | 12,246 |

[a]Including aid. [b]Including special demand.
*Source:* Tōyō keizai shinpōsha, *Shōwa kokusei sōran* (Tokyo: Tōyō keizai shinpōsha, 1980), vol. 2, pp. 652, 660.

1963, the government adopted a tight money policy, helping the balance of payments to recover relatively quickly.

As the international competitiveness of Japanese industries improved between 1955 and 1965, the balance of the current account came into equilibrium. After 1965, a surplus in the current account grew gradually, and Japan built up its foreign currency reserves. The reason for this was that the price of Japanese export goods remained comparatively stable while inflation was spreading from the United States, then engaged in the Vietnam War, to other advanced industrial nations. This made Japanese products relatively cheap in the world market. In 1970, with a surplus in the current account, the Bank of Japan adopted a defensive tight money policy, and the result was a dramatic increase in Japan's balance-of-payments surplus. In order to cope with this surplus, the yen was revalued in 1971, and in 1973 it was moved to a floating rate.

### *Price trends*

Even after the Dodge stabilization plan had braked the postwar runaway rise in prices, Japan continued to have to contend with inflation. When the Korean War broke out, inflationary trends resumed in 1951 and halted only in 1954 with the adoption of a tight money policy. The immediate postwar inflation had been led by a rise in consumer prices, but the Korean War's inflation was led by an increase in the price of producer goods. As a result of this inflation, the foreign exchange rate, which had been set low in 1949 at the time of the Dodge stabilization, became relatively high. The international balance of payments went out of equilibrium, and the international competitiveness of Japanese industry weakened. In order to deal with these problems within the framework of a fixed exchange rate, Japan thought it necessary to curtail costs in its heavy and chemical industries, and many industries began to invest in rationalizing and modernizing their facilities.

Between 1955 and 1960, prices were relatively stable, but after 1960, a new pattern of inflation appeared – wholesale prices remained stable but consumer prices rose. This pattern occurred as the result of the following mechanism:[9] First, under the system of fixed exchange rates, the economy was managed in such a way that if there were no worldwide inflation, export and wholesale prices would remain stable. Second, even though the wage gap between large and small enterprises was decreasing, owing to the shift from labor oversupply to labor shortage, there was still a gap between them in terms of productivity increases. Productivity rose in the large mass-production enterprises, but labor costs – and hence production costs – rose in labor-intensive small and medium manufacturing and service enterprises. Third, a rise in consumer prices was tolerated as long as it had no impact on wage increases, and hence on the price of export goods.

In other words, although prices were stable in a sector in which the increase in productivity rate was high, prices and costs rose in those in which productivity was low. Increases in consumer prices were usually held down by low wages in sectors in which labor productivity was low, but when full employment eliminated those workers willing to work for low wages, "productivity gap" inflation of the kind described emerged.

In the late 1960s there was a worldwide trend toward inflation. Under these circumstances, as long as a fixed exchange rate prevailed and an attempt was made to avoid an increase in balance-of-payments surpluses, the only way to accelerate the expansion of domestic demand was through fiscal means. In 1969 a tight money policy was adopted to avoid a rise in prices. As we have seen, this only expanded the surplus in the international balance of payments. Consequently, in the early 1970s the government tried to increase the money supply and to expand fiscal expenditures. As a result of these measures, as well as foreign inflation, by the fall of 1973 the wholesale price level in Japan had risen 20 percent

9 The basic work on this subject is by Takasuka Yoshihiro, *Gendai Nihon no bukka mondai*, rev. ed. (Tokyo: Shinhyōron, 1975).

TABLE 10.7
*Distribution of national income (as a percentage of national income)*

| | Employees' income (%) | Self-employed income (%) | Individual property income (%) | Corporation income (%) | Ratio of employer income per capita to employee income per capita (%) |
|---|---|---|---|---|---|
| 1935 | 38.0 | 31.1 | 23.4 | 8.7 | – |
| 1946 | 30.7 | 65.4 | 3.6 | 1.1 | |
| 1950 | 41.8 | 45.6 | 3.1 | 9.9 | 59.4 |
| 1955 | 49.6 | 37.1 | 6.8 | 7.9 | 57.6 |
| 1960 | 50.2 | 26.5 | 9.8 | 14.3 | 60.5 |
| 1965 | 56.0 | 23.4 | 11.6 | 10.6 | 64.8 |
| 1970 | 54.3 | 20.0 | 11.7 | 15.8 | 68.5 |

*Source:* Tōyō keizai shinpōsha, *Shōwa kokusei sōran* (Tokyo: Tōyō keizai shinpōsha, 1980), vol. 1, p. 91. The number of self-employed persons, family employees, and self-employed income per person versus employee income per person is based on Keizai kikakuchō, *Gendai Nihon keizai no tenkai* (Tokyo: Keizai kikakuchō, 1976), p. 599.

higher than it had been a year before. At this point the Organization of Petroleum Exporting Countries (OPEC) raised its prices, plunging Japan into a surge of hyperinflation, or "crazy prices" (*kyōran bukka*). The policy of maintaining a fixed exchange rate helped prevent the development of inflation until the middle 1960s, but it had the opposite effect in the 1970s when there was worldwide inflation and Japanese industry had grown more competitive.

### *Income distribution*

In regard to the distribution of national income (see Table 10.7) immediately after World War II, the income going to individual business owners expanded abnormally, but the shares of national income going to employee income, property income, and corporation income substantially declined. This was because modern industrial production was paralyzed, and many people had become farmers or merchants in order to survive economically. As the postwar economy recovered, the shares of national income going to employee income and corporate income were rapidly restored, but the share of income from property remained low. The reason that property income stayed low was that income from tenant rents had virtually disappeared owing to land reform, and interest, land prices, and housing rents were controlled by the government to check inflation.

In the period of rapid economic growth, employee and corporate income shares steadily increased, and the share of individual business owners dropped below even prewar levels. The increase in corporate income reflected increases in business profit due to high investment and high economic growth. Changes in the occupational structure accounted for the greater income share of employees, who were growing in number, and the decrease in the share for individual business owners, who along with family employees, were declining in number. But the per capita income of employees, as compared with the per capita income of individual business owners or family employees, shows the gap between them as narrowing.

The distribution of individual income moved toward greater equality. The postwar reforms – land reform, zaibatsu dissolution, and labor reform – all worked toward equality in income distribution. Postwar inflation and impoverishment, together with the 1946 levy of property tax, promoted an "equality of poverty." As the economic recovery progressed, income distribution showed signs of becoming less equal, but by about 1960, with the reduction of wage differentials accompanying full employment, the trend toward equalization of income resumed, especially with respect to wages. During the period of rapid growth, Japan, among all the advanced industrial nations, became the country with the most equal income distribution.[10]

Equality of income distribution was a precondition for the spread of middle-class consciousness among the population. By the 1960s nearly 90 percent of the Japanese people felt that they enjoyed a middle-class standard of living (see Table 10.8). This middle-class consciousness spurred the rapid diffusion of durable consumer goods, a rising rate of children entering universities, a strong desire for home ownership, and a high savings rate, all of which stimulated economic growth. The development of mass-production industries supplying materials needed to make consumer durables increased the demand for labor, accelerated the achievement of full employment, facilitated the movement of the labor force, and stimulated the more equal distribution of income. In turn, these fostered a Japanese-style mass-consumption market economy in which an expanding demand for consumer durables coexisted with a high savings rate. This dynamic logic of industrial society sustained the high growth rate.

10 M. Sawyer, *Income Distribution in OECD Countries* (Paris: OECD, 1976). Tachibanaki Yoshiaki, "Shūnyū bunpai to shotoku bunpu no fubyōdō," *Kikan gendai keizai*, no. 28 (1977): 160–75. Using Sawyer's work, Tachibanaki calculated the Gini coefficient for the distribution of gross (pretax) income as follows: Japan 0.335, Sweden 0.356, West Germany 0.396, American 0.404, and OECD average 0.366.

TABLE 10.8
*Increase in middle-class consciousness*

| | 1958 (%) | 1964 (%) | *1967* (%) |
|---|---|---|---|
| Upper | 0 | 1 | 1 |
| Upper middle | 3 | 1 | 8 |
| Middle | 37 | 50 | 51 |
| Lower middle | 32 | 31 | 28 |
| (Subtotal) | (72) | (87) | (87) |
| Lower | 17 | 9 | 8 |
| Not clear | 11 | 3 | 4 |
| Total | 100 | 100 | 100 |

*Source:* Keizai kikakuchō, *Gendai Nihon keizai no tenkai* (Tokyo: Keizai kikakuchō, 1976), p. 207.

TABLE 10.9
*Increases in demand items (annual percentage rate)*

| | 1946–50 (%) | 1950–55 (%) | 1955–60 (%) | 1960–65 (%) | 1965–70 (%) | 1970–75 (%) |
|---|---|---|---|---|---|---|
| Final private consumption | 10.2 | 9.9 | 7.8 | 9.0 | 9.7 | 6.2 |
| Private housing | 1.9 | 10.2 | 14.4 | 17.4 | 14.0 | 5.3 |
| Private enterprise plant facilities | | | 22.2 | 10.8 | 22.2 | 1.1 |
| Final government consumption | 13.4 | 2.4 | 2.6 | 7.1 | 5.1 | 5.6 |
| Public capital formation | Δ 9.2 | 23.3 | 12.2 | 16.2 | 10.8 | 6.8 |
| Exports | 99.5 | 13.9 | 13.0 | 14.7 | 15.4 | 11.8 |
| Imports | 25.1 | 18.1 | 16.9 | 13.2 | 17.1 | 6.7 |
| Gross national expenditure | 9.4 | 8.9 | 8.5 | 10.0 | 12.3 | 5.0 |

*Source: Kokumin shotoku tōkei:* 1946–55: Keizai kikakuchō, *Gendai Nihon keizai no tenkai* (Tokyo: Keizai kikakuchō, 1976), pp. 578–9. 1955–65, 1965–75: Tōyō keizai shinpōsha, *Shōwa kokusei sōran* (Tokyo: Tōyō keizai shinpōsha, 1980), vol. 1, pp. 99–100. Figures based on old SNA.

### *The growth of demand*

The postwar Japanese economy maintained a rapid growth within the limits imposed by its balance of payments and without relying on foreign capital. Substantial savings, an abundant supply of labor, domestic investment, and consumption demand made this possible. If we look at the GNP from 1946 to 1955 as classified by demand items, the increase in individual consumption is remarkable. Since 1955 the expansion of investment in public facilities has also been striking, and until 1970 exports showed a tendency to rise as well (see Table 10.9).

TABLE 10.10
*Household expenses of urban workers*

| | Engels coefficient | Average propensity to consume (%) |
|---|---|---|
| 1935 | 36.4 | 88.4 |
| 1946 | 66.4 | 125.9 |
| 1950 | 57.4 | 98.1 |
| 1955 | 44.5 | 90.8 |
| 1960 | 38.8 | 85.1 |
| 1965 | 36.3 | 83.2 |
| 1970 | 32.4 | 80.1 |
| 1973 | 30.4 | 77.8 |

*Source:* Tōyō keizai shinpōsha, *Shōwa kokusei sōran* (Tokyo: Tōyō keizai shinpōsha, 1980), vol. 2, p. 358.

The reason for the expansion of consumer demand in the postwar reconstruction was that during the war, Japan's living standards had dropped dramatically, almost to subsistence levels. This stimulated the pressure toward recovery. Once recovery was accomplished, investment in the modernization of plant became more active, and the expansion of consumption was sustained by the diffusion of consumer durables. The process by which mass production developed in Japan was also the process by which it became a mass-consumer society.

In response to industrial development, people changed both their jobs and their residences. From 1955 to 1970 the number of employees increased 15.22 million, from 18.17 to 33.39 million; the cities' population increased from 50 to 75 million, and their percentage of the total population increased from 56.3 to 72.1 percent. The shift toward employment (excluding self-employment) and urbanization went hand in hand.

Consumption levels also doubled during this period. If we look at the consumption content of an urban worker's household budget, we can see that the Engels coefficient dropped from 44.5 percent in 1955 to 32.4 percent in 1970 (see Table 10.10). By contrast, the amount spent on acquiring appliances increased 8.5 times, and cultural and entertainment expenses rose 5.1 times.

In 1957, 7.8 percent of nonagricultural households owned black-and-white television sets, but by 1965 the rate had increased to 95 percent. During the same period, the number of households owning electric or gas refrigerators changed from 2.8 to 68.7 percent, and that for washing machines from 20.1 to 78.1 percent (see Table 10.11).

TABLE 10.11
*Diffusion of consumer durable goods (percentage of nonfarming households)*

| | 1957 (%) | 1960 (%) | 1965 (%) | 1970 (%) | 1975 (%) |
|---|---|---|---|---|---|
| Black-and-white television sets | 7.8 | 44.7 | 95.0 | 90.1 | 49.7 |
| Color television sets | – | – | – | 30.4 | 90.9 |
| Sewing machines | 61.9 | 69.5 | 83.9 | 84.5 | 84.8 |
| Stereo sets | 4.0 | – | 20.1 | 36.6 | 55.6 |
| Tape recorders | – | – | 20.2 | 35.3 | 54.9 |
| Cameras | 35.7 | 45.8 | 64.8 | 72.1 | 82.4 |
| Cars | – | – | 10.5[a] | 22.6 | 37.4 |
| Electric or gas refrigerators | 2.8 | 10.1 | 68.7 | 92.5 | 97.3 |
| Washing machines | 20.2 | 40.6 | 78.1 | 92.1 | 97.7 |
| Vacuum cleaners | – | 7.7 | 48.6 | 75.4 | 93.7 |
| Air conditioners | – | – | 2.6 | 8.4 | 21.5 |

[a]Including light vans.
*Source:* Tōyō keizai shinpōsha, *Shōwa kokusei sōran* (Tokyo: Tōyō keizai shinpōsha, 1980), vol. 2, pp. 603–4.

The ownership of durable consumer goods continued to rise in the latter half of the 1960s, though consumer preferences shifted toward expensive goods. In 1967, only 2.2 percent of nonagricultural households owned color televisions, but by 1975, 90.9 percent did. The ownership of automobiles also increased from 11 percent in 1967 to 37.4 percent in 1975 and that of air conditioners from 2.6 to 21.5 percent. These durable consumer goods, called by such names as the "three household sacred items" or "three C's," were proof of Japan's emergence as a mass-consumption society. Because most of the Japanese people considered themselves as belonging to the middle class, it was easy for their life-styles to become homogeneous. This encouraged the rapid diffusion of consumer durables, as people tried to keep up with their neighbors.

The major increase in employment that accompanied Japan's industrial development reduced the number of lower-income employees and equalized income distribution. If wages in companies with more than 500 workers are given an index of 100, wages of enterprises with 30 to 99 workers were at an index of only 58.8 in 1955, but by 1965 this had risen to 71. Within enterprises, wage differentials by job category were comparatively low.

As noted earlier, by 1970, among all the advanced countries, Japan enjoyed the most equitable distribution of individual income. Japan's rate of home ownership was lower than in the United States but higher than that in Western Europe. The rate of students continuing their education beyond the compulsory level increased from 47.4 percent in 1955 to 79.4 percent in 1970, and the rate of students entering colleges and universities increased from 17.2 to 24.2 percent (these rates increased by 1975, to 91.9 percent and to 38.4 percent).

## THE CHANGING INDUSTRIAL STRUCTURE

The most significant development in the Japanese economy from the end of the war until 1973 was its emergence as one of the world's most advanced industrial powers.

### *Industrial rationalization plans*

Beginning in the early 1950s the government coordinated a series of rationalization plans in Japan's key industries. Whereas the major goal of "priority production" had been to resuscitate the coal and steel industries, the main aim of industrial rationalization was to reduce the costs in these industries. The Korean War stimulated demand in Japan and vitalized Japanese industry, but prices rose sharply, making Japanese goods expensive. The increase in coal and steel prices reduced the international competitiveness of machinery and other industries. Rationalization plans aimed at modernizing plant facilities were undertaken in order to bring down these production costs.

During the first steel rationalization plan, it was anticipated that ¥63 billion would be invested between 1951 and 1954. In fact, actual investment reached ¥120 billion by 1953. Old-style pull-over plants were replaced by strip mills which made the rolling process more efficient. The government launched the development of a major industrial park in Chiba Prefecture on land reclaimed from Tokyo Bay. In 1953 the Kawasaki Steel Company, a new entrant into the industry, opened in the park the most modern integrated steel facility in the world. Located on the waterfront, the production line was a continuous process from the delivery of raw materials to the blast furnace to steel production to rolling. Other, better-established steel-producing firms soon followed suit with the construction of similar facilities. The first rationalization plan substantially modernized the Japanese steel industry.

By contrast, in the coal industry, which realized great profits during the Korean War when excess demand produced coal shortages everywhere, plans to rationalize production through investment in the introduction of advanced mining technology from West Germany and the digging of deep shafts never materialized. Because the quality of Japan's coal deposits was poor, it was not possible to achieve the cost reductions needed to make the industry competitive internationally. In addition, when a lengthy coal strike occurred in the fall of 1952, key industries reduced their reliance on coal as an energy source and shifted to oil and electric power.

Apart from attempts at rationalization in the steel and coal industries, rationalization through technological innovation took place in other industries in the early 1950s. In the electric power industry, hydroelectric power was developed on a large scale, and thermal model plants were imported; in the shipbuilding industry, new methods for the construction of ocean ships were introduced; in the ammonium sulfate industry, production shifted from electrolysis to the gas method; and efforts were made to nurture the synthetic fiber industry.

Just as the priority production method had attempted to restore postwar production by using existing prewar and wartime plants in isolation from the world market, the industrial rationalization plans of the early 1950s tried to lower costs by renewing and modernizing its production facilities and by improving Japan's international competitiveness under a fixed exchange rate. These plans assumed an open world market. Investment in rationalization also helped reduce production costs.

Whereas priority production had been carried out by means of direct government controls, industrial rationalization plans were generally implemented as independent plans carried out by private business enterprises. To be sure, the government intervened in the process, making it a kind of joint venture between the government and key private enterprises, but the government did not use price controls (price subsidies) or commodity controls to achieve its ends. Instead, it relied on other methods. In March 1951 the Japan Development Bank (Nihon kaihatsu ginkō) was established to promote capital accumulation and rapid economic growth. In March 1952 the Enterprises Rationalization Act was passed and the Special Tax Measures Law was amended to assist developing industries. The government had an arsenal of new methods to promote the development of industries specially targeted for rationalization – special tax treatment, subsidy of interest on shipbuilding, loan of government funds through institutions like the development bank, the establishment of the Electrical Power Source Development Company (Dengen kaihatsu KK), the use of import quotas, controls over the import of foreign capital, and "administrative guidance." The popular notion in the 1970s that there was a so-called Japan Incorporated, a close alliance between government and business, with the government directly guiding the activities of private firms, rested largely on impressions of how the Japanese economy operated during this period. But it would be a mistake to regard Japan as a "planned economy" or the government as an "economic general staff" even in this period. Government and business did share information with each other and made their views known to each other, but the final investment decisions were in the hands of the business firms.

### *The development of technical innovation*

Between 1955 and 1965, investment for modernization was in full swing. In the steel industry, the second rationalization plan followed the success of the first rationalization plan. Most noticeably it provided for substantial construction of shoreline mills for pig iron production and the widespread diffusion of strip mills and pure oxygen converters. The first rationalization plan, devised when the industry's base was weak, attempted to reduce production costs and relied on government loans. By contrast, the second plan modernized facilities in order to increase capacity in anticipation of increased demand. Because the industry also expected high profits, it relied less on government funding. Whereas the first rationalization plan required an investment of ¥120 billion, the second plan used an investment of over ¥500 billion. When the second rationalization plan ended, Japan's iron and steel output exceeded that of France, Germany, and Britain, rising to second place behind the United States. In number of hot strip mills, Japan was second only to the United States, and it achieved first place in the efficiency of its pure oxygen converters and in the ratio of coke used to steel ingots produced. In other words, both quantitatively and qualitatively, Japan had become a first-class producer of iron and steel.

Under both priority production and the industrial rationalization plans of the early 1950s, coal had ranked in importance with the iron and steel industry as a key industry. The coal industry, however, failed to overcome its natural disadvantages through rationalization investment. Moreover, labor–management relations within the industry deteriorated, and the supply of coal became less stable. For that reason, energy demand continued to shift from coal to electric power and oil. Japanese industry could develop even faster if it shifted from a high-cost domestic resource to a cheaper foreign resource, namely, petroleum. At this time, new oil fields were being discovered in the Middle East, and the price of crude oil was dropping dramatically. Further savings in energy costs were achieved through the use of high-speed supertankers, which reduced the cost of transporting oil to Japan.

The electric power industry was also changing. Before 1955 the industry had relied primarily on hydroelectric power and only secondarily on thermal power, but then the relationship was reversed, with the primary reliance shifting to thermal power generation. In 1955 when the construction of thermal plants using heavy oil began, hydroelectric power plants produced 7.48 million kilowatts, and the thermal plants produced only 4.1 million, but by 1961, hydroelectric power and thermal power accounted for approximately the same amount, 9.444 million kilowatts and 9.75 million kilowatts, respectively. The scale of thermal plant capacity increased from 58,000 in 1958 to 2.2 million in 1960 and 3.75 million in 1965. The reasons that hydroelectric power declined as the principal source of electrical power were, first, that the number of sites suitable for the construction of hydroelectric plants decreased and, second, that the importation of energy resources was a way of overcoming the limitation of domestic resources.

The shift to new sources of energy also affected the chemical industry. A flourishing carbide industry, relying on hydroelectric power, had supplied carbide for the domestic production of vinyl chloride, acetate, and other chemical products. But in the late 1950s a new petrochemical industry producing polyethylene and polystyrene developed, relying on imported naptha and the introduction of new naptha-cracking technology.

Parallel to the technical innovation in producer goods industries, there was also a technical innovation in the production of consumer durables. Mass-production methods were introduced to meet the domestic demand for automobiles and home electric appliances such as television sets and refrigerators, as well as the export of sewing machines, transistor radios, and cameras.[11]

Around 1950 there had been debates about whether Japan should rely for its supply of automobiles on imports or whether it should try to develop a domestic automobile industry under protection. The outcome was the goal of developing a protected domestic automobile industry, and many automobile companies tried to acquire technology through technical tie-ups with foreign automobile manufacturers. In 1955, Toyota, the top producer of automobiles, had a five-year mod-

11 The 1960 *Nenji keizai hōkoku* analyzed the period as "a period in which the machine tools industry led the development of industry." Keizai kikakuchō chōsakyoku, *Shiryō: keizai hakusho 25 nen* (Tokyo: Keizai kikakuchō, 1972), pp. 214–15.

ernization plan with a monthly production target of only three thousand vehicles. But the modernization of its production facilities accelerated, and the scale of production greatly expanded. By around 1960, when Toyota built a compact car plant at Motomachi and Nissan built one at Oppama, each new plant projected a monthly production of ten thousand vehicles. New mass-production equipment such as transfer machines and automatic braces were also introduced.

The mass production of motor vehicles had a major impact on related industries. First, in the iron and steel industry, thin-plate production progressed rapidly. Investment in plant modernization, such as the installation of strip mills, supported the mass production of automobiles. Second, a specialty steel and machine tool industry, whose production volume earlier had been limited by a small market was presented with new opportunities as the mass production of automobiles grew. The value of the output of machine tools in 1955 was ¥5 billion, but by 1962 it had reached ¥100 billion, twenty times as much, and its international competitiveness was also strong. In 1956 Toyota and related industries began using the now-famous *kanban* method (also known as the "zero inventory method" or "just-in-time production"). Subcontracting firms bought secondhand machinery from parent companies, enabling them to begin mechanization and rationalization, leading to an expansion of the machine tool market.

In the electrical machine industry, conditions were about the same. The improvement in the quality of steel silicon plate provided the basis for mass production. Small- to medium-sized enterprises related to radio and television production also were rationalized and developed into an export industry.

The modernization of Japanese industry relied on the introduction of foreign technology. During the war, Japan had been technologically isolated from the rest of the world, and by the war's end a major technological gap existed. But this gap was soon closed by the massive introduction of technologies from foreign companies. In the early 1950s, technologies were introduced through technical tie-ups with foreign firms in the automobile industry (Nissan and Austin, Isuzu and Hillman), television production (NEC and RCA), and nylon (Tōyō Rayon and DuPont). From the late 1950s and during the 1960s both the number of technologies imported and the payments for them increased, further improving Japan's technological standards (see Table 10.12).

Because Japan did not encourage direct foreign investment after

TABLE 10.12
*Technological imports*

| | Items imported | Price paid (U.S. dollars) |
|---|---|---|
| 1949–55 | 1,141 | 69 million |
| 1956–60 | 1,773 | 281 million |
| 1961–65 | 4,494 | 684 million |
| 1966–70 | 7,589 | 1.536 billion |
| 1971–75 | 10,789 | 3.205 billion |

*Source:* Tōyō keizai shinpōsha, *Shōwa kokusei sōran* (Tokyo: Tōyō keizai shinpōsha, 1980), vol. 1, p. 662.

World War II, this introduction of foreign technology was achieved through technical cooperation without capital tie-ups. The "commercialization of technology" was the only possible way to achieve technological innovation while avoiding foreign control of Japanese business. Many foreign firms were willing to sell their technology because the Japanese market was regarded as too small to be worth developing. The cost of acquiring foreign technology was often quite expensive for individual Japanese firms, but technical innovations enormously increased the productivity of Japanese industry. The Japanese also tried to improve upon the technology that they imported. Often such improvements were made as a new technology was applied to the production process, thereby enhancing Japan's international competitiveness.

The government expanded its policies of nurturing new growth industries such as petrochemicals and machine tools as well as such established basic industries as steel, coal, and shipbuilding. In 1955 the government adopted the Petrochemical Industry Development Policy and in 1956 passed the Temporary Measure for the Promotion of the Machine Tool Industry. The heart of industrial development policy lay in special tax measures and loans from the Japan Development Bank, but other measures were used as well, such as foreign currency allotments, the licensing of foreign capital imports through technical tie-ups, and other forms of administrative guidance.[12] The role played by active competition among enterprises and an energetic entrepreneurial spirit in economic growth was large, and so the effect of government protection and development policies should not be overestimated. Nevertheless, the 1956 law promoting the machine tool industry, for exam-

12 Kōsai, "Fukkōki," pp. 38–42.

ple, was successful in promoting or rationalizing and modernizing the small- and medium-sized machinery producers.

### *Liberalization of trade, foreign exchange, and capital*

Until the 1960s, foreign trade, foreign exchange, and capital movements were under government control, as they had been during wartime. Major resources were scarce, and it was felt that a free market would not achieve an optimal allocation of resources for economic reconstruction. But once the economy had recovered from its postwar dislocation and its involvement in the world market had increased, there was strong foreign pressure on the Japanese, especially from the United States, to liberalize these controls. Foreigners saw import liberalization as a means of increasing their imports, and some Japanese argued that import competition would improve the efficiency of Japanese enterprises.

In June 1960 the government adopted the outline Plan for the Liberalization of Foreign Trade and Foreign Exchange which aimed at raising the liberalization rates from 40 percent (as of March 1960) to 80 percent within three years. The plan was subsequently revised, and by October 1962 the liberalization rate had reached 88 percent (see Table 10.13). In 1963 Japan became an International Monetary Fund (IMF) Article 8 country, which meant that it could no longer place restrictions on foreign exchange, and in 1964 it joined the Organization for Economic Cooperation and Development (OECD), an international consultative body founded in 1961 to promote the liberalization of trade and capital movements. By the beginning of the 1970s, in order to deal with growing surpluses in the international balance of payments, Japan renewed its efforts to liberalize trade.

Japan's participation in the OECD brought the liberalization of capital. In June 1967 the government adopted the Fundamental Plan for Capital Liberalization. The first stage of liberalization took place in July 1967, permitting a 50 percent liberalization in 33 industries and 100 percent in 17 others (including shipbuilding and steel). The second liberalization stage took place in February 1969, when 50 percent liberalization was permitted in 160 categories and 100 percent in 44. The third stage took place in September 1970, and a fourth in August 1971. In April 1971 capital liberalization was applied to the automobile industry, and in 1974, 50 percent liberalization was permitted in electronic computers and 100 percent in real estate.

Japan's adoption of liberalization measures was regarded by foreign

TABLE 10.13
*Rate of liberalization (percentages)*

| | | | |
|---|---|---|---|
| 1959 (end of Aug.) | 26 | 1961 (end of Dec.) | 70 |
| 1959 (end of Sept.) | 33 | 1962 (end of Apr.) | 33 |
| 1960 (end of Apr.) | 40 | 1962 (end of Oct.) | 88 |
| 1960 (end of July) | 42 | 1963 (end of Apr.) | 89 |
| 1960 (end of Oct.) | 44 | 1963 (end of Aug.) | 92 |
| 1961 (end of Apr.) | 62 | 1965 (end of Feb.) | 94 |
| 1961 (end of July) | 65 | 1966 (end of Oct.) | 95 |
| 1961 (end of Oct.) | 68 | 1967 (end of Apr.) | 97 |

*Iote:* Months are indicated in which there were changes in the liberalization rate.
*ource:* Keizai kikakuchō, *Gendai Nihon keizai no tenkai* (Tokyo: keizai kikakuchō, 1976), p. 46.

ritics as being tardy in comparison with liberalization among the Western European countries. In Japan many took the view that the nternational competitiveness of Japanese industries and enterprises vas weak and that liberalization would have an adverse impact on hem. Controls on imports and capital were needed to protect infant ndustries or noncompetitive industries and also employment in the ndustries affected. When it became clear that liberalization was inevitable, many argued that Japanese industry had to be made more competitive in order to cope with its effects.

The announcement of plans to liberalize foreign trade and foreign xchange in 1960 stimulated investment in new plant facilities, as did he announcement of Prime Minister Ikeda Hayato's Income Doubling Plan, which proposed doubling the national income in the next en years. The result was an acceleration of the modernization investment boom of the early 1960s. By contrast, the capital liberalization olicies of the late 1960s provided one of the main reasons for a rise in he number of company mergers and amalgamations. The most imporant of these were the amalgamation of Mitsubishi Heavy Industries in 964, the amalgamation of the Nissan and Prince automobile companies in 1965, the amalgamation of the Nisshō and Iwai trading companies in 1968, the merger of the Yawata and Fuji steel companies in 970, and the merger of the Daiichi and Nihon Kangyō banks in 1971. lthough these mergers may not have promoted modernization in the ame way that plant investment did, they did not necessarily harm apan's international competitive position.

Liberalization, as it turned out, did not hinder high economic rowth but, on the contrary, was one of main factors stimulating and ccelerating it. As a result of liberalization, the Japanese economy also

TABLE 10.14
*Production and exports, classified by heavy and light industries (in ¥1 billion)*

| | Production | Exports |
|---|---|---|
| *1951* | | |
| Heavy industries | 2,570 | 199 |
| Light industries | 2,293 | 274 |
| *1955* | | |
| Heavy industries | 4,053 | 330 |
| Light industries | 2,956 | 360 |
| *1960* | | |
| Heavy industries | 11,786 | 741 |
| Light industries | 4,905 | 572 |
| *1965* | | |
| Heavy industries | 21,624 | 2,029 |
| Light industries | 8,757 | 756 |
| *1970* | | |
| Heavy industries | 55,772 | 5,180 |
| Light industries | 17,718 | 1,182 |
| *1975* | | |
| Heavy industries | 98,543 | 14,059 |
| Light industries | 29,372 | 1,549 |

*Source:* Uno Kimio, Input–Output Table in Japan 1951–80, Tsukuba University Department of Social Engineering–Multiple Statistic Data Bank Report no. 14 R2 (November 1983). Industrial numbers: Heavy industry (11 to 22); light industry (4 to 10, 23).

became more closely linked with the world economy. At the same time, the elimination of controls on foreign exchange, foreign trade and capital movements reduced the intervention of government in domestic industry and promoted the market economy in Japan.

## *The expansion of exports*

In the mid-1960s many people thought that the period of high growth was coming to an end. The economy was heading toward a recession There was a wave of large-scale bankruptcies, the most dramatic being the management crisis of the Yamaichi Securities Company, and the Bank of Japan made special loans in order to avoid a financial crisis But despite this, the economy continued to grow even faster than before, sustained not only by investment in industrial plant and growing consumer demand but also by exports.

Traditionally, textiles had been Japan's principal export industry whereas its chemical and heavy industries depended on domestic demand. According to Table 10.14, production in heavy industry (met

TABLE 10.15
*Major export items*

| | 1930 ¥1,000 | 1950 ¥100 million | 1960 ¥100 million | 1970 ¥100 million | 1975 ¥100 million |
|---|---|---|---|---|---|
| Synthetic textiles | – | – | 116 | 2,252 | 3,863 |
| Organic pharmaceuticals | | 3 | 45 | 1,436 | 3,653 |
| Plastics | – | 6 | 115 | 1,536 | 2,958 |
| Iron and steel | 8,579 | 260 | 1,397 | 10,237 | 30,165 |
| Metal products | 22,428 | 93 | 532 | 2,569 | 5,346 |
| Office machines | – | 0.4 | 6 | 1,186 | 2,307 |
| Metal-processing machinery | – | 5 | 28 | 417 | 1,342 |
| Textile machinery[a] | 3,852 | 68 | 371 | 1,172 | 2,323 |
| Television sets[b] | – | | 10 | 1,382 | 2,326 |
| Radios[b] | – | 0.3 | 521 | 2,502 | 3,933 |
| Tape recorders | – | – | 34 | 1,623 | 1,879 |
| Automobiles[b] | – | 2 | 281 | 4,815 | 18,392 |
| Motorbikes[b] | – | 0.3[c] | 29 | 1,381 | 3,430 |
| Ships | 5,452 | 94 | 1,037 | 5,075 | 17,803 |
| Precision instruments | 2,727 | 28 | 346 | 2,261 | 5,420 |
| Watches[d] | 1,463 | 4 | 13 | 466 | 1,360 |

[a]Including sewing machines. [b]Except parts.
[c]Including three-wheel motor vehicles.
[d]Table clocks and wall clocks.
*Source:* Ōkurashō, *Nihon bōeki geppyō* (Tokyo: Nihon kanzei kyokai, 1966–76) and *Gaikoku bōeki geppyō* (Tokyo: 1928–30). Sōrifu tōkeikyoku, *Nihon tōkei nenkan* (Tokyo: Mainichi shinbunsha 1950–60).

als, chemicals, machinery, etc.) had overtaken production in light industry (textiles, etc.) by 1955, but light industry exported not only more of its production but also a higher proportion of its production. This reflected the traditional pattern. But after 1960, even though light industry still exported a high percentage of its production, heavy industry exported even more. By 1965 exports as a percentage of total production was the same; by 1965 heavy industry exported a higher proportion of its production than did light industry; and by 1975 heavy industry had far outdistanced light industry. Although heavy industry's dependence on foreign markets increased, light industry withdrew from the export market and relied primarily on domestic demand.

The extraordinary expansion of passenger automobile exports after 1965 was a typical example of this shift. In 1971, Japan exported 1.78 million automobiles, or 63.7 percent more than in the previous year. The export of television sets, tape recorders, and other electronic goods also became more important (see Table 10.15). According to business surveys at the time, many firms entered the 1970s intending

TABLE 10.16
*Major import items*

| | 1930 ¥1,000 | 1950 ¥100 million | 1960 ¥100 million | 1970 ¥100 million | 1975 ¥100 million |
|---|---|---|---|---|---|
| Meat[a] | 8,871 | 0.5 | 51 | 523 | 1,96[illegible] |
| Seafood | 19,023 | 1.6 | 15 | 942 | 3,55[illegible] |
| Wheat | 41,509 | 530 | 637 | 1,146 | 3,31[illegible] |
| Corn | 3,749 | 5 | 292 | 1,465 | 3,37[illegible] |
| Soy beans | 36,664 | 86 | 387 | 1,317 | 2,79[illegible] |
| Sugar | 25,972 | 166 | 400 | 1,022 | 4,99[illegible] |
| Wool | 73,609 | 214 | 955 | 1,254 | 1,52[illegible] |
| Cotton | 362,046 | 989 | 1,553 | 1,695 | 2,51[illegible] |
| Iron ore | 18,955 | 51 | 769 | 4,350 | 6,51[illegible] |
| Copper ore | – | 0.8 | 254 | 1,809 | 2,39[illegible] |
| Raw rubber | 17,930 | 145 | 638 | 542 | 55[illegible] |
| Timber | 53,078 | 10 | 613 | 5,659 | 7,76[illegible] |
| Coal[b] | 34,203 | 38 | 508 | 3,636 | 10,24[illegible] |
| Crude petroleum | 89,565 | 88 | 1,674 | 8,048 | 58,31[illegible] |
| Petroleum products | | 64 | 487 | 1,980 | 4,01[illegible] |
| Liquefied petroleum gas | – | – | 0.00004 | 293 | 2,30[illegible] |
| Liquefied natural gas | – | – | | 83 | 1,17[illegible] |
| Organic pharmaceuticals | – | 2.9 | 182 | 816 | 1,43[illegible] |

[a]Including whale. [b]Mostly raw coal.
*Source:* Ōkurashō, *Nihon bōeki geppyō* (Tokyo: Nihon kanzei kyokai, 1966–76) and *Gaikoku bōeki geppyō* (Tokyo: 1928–30). Sōrifu tōkeikyoku: *Nihon tōkei nenkan* (Tokyo: Mainichi Shinbunsha 1950–60).

to increase their dependence on the export market. Behind this tendency for Japanese industry to increase its exports was the strengthening of its industrial competitiveness caused by the inflation in the United States created by the expansion of the Vietnam War while the exchange rate remained fixed at ¥360 to $1.00. The rapid rise in exports, however, caused economic friction between the two countries, with the result that Japan placed voluntary restrictions on the export of iron and steel in 1968 and textiles in 1971.

Fuel resources continued to be Japan's major imports. According to Table 10.16, the dependence on imported energy sources increased after the 1950s. In 1955 domestic energy sources accounted for 7[illegible] percent of the energy supply, and imports accounted for 24 percent; in 1965 domestic sources accounted for only 33.8 percent, and imports made up 66.2 percent; and in 1970 domestic sources had fallen to 16.[illegible] percent, and imports had risen to 83.5 percent.[13] Apart from fuels, the other main import items were food products and mineral resources.

The structure of its foreign trade, then, was one in which Japan

13 Tōyō keizai shinpōsha, *Shōwa kokusei sōran*, p. 391.

exported the products of heavy industry and imported the raw materials to make up for domestic insufficiency. The increase in Japanese exports exceeded that of world trade, and the expansion of imports paralleled the growth rate of the domestic economy. In order to maintain this balance, the Japanese economy had to maintain a growth rate higher than the world average. However, even though in 1970 inflation was spreading worldwide, domestic prices remained relatively stable. Hence, despite Japan's high growth, its surpluses in current account were rising.

In August 1971 President Richard Nixon sought a revaluation of the world's major currencies by ending fixed exchange rates, and by the end of the year the yen was revalued to a rate of ¥308 to $1.00. But this revalued rate did not last for long. In February 1973 Japan shifted to a floating exchange rate, and in the fall of 1973, the Organization of Petroleum Exporting Countries (OPEC) increased the price of crude oil fourfold. These successive shocks had a major impact on the Japanese economy, which depended on the export of heavy industry goods and the import of energy. These shocks marked the end of Japan's period of high growth, but nonetheless, Japanese industry continued to be oriented toward exports, with the result that these problems persisted into the 1980s.

## CHARACTERISTICS OF JAPANESE ENTERPRISES

While adjusting to postwar reform, economic rehabilitation, and the onset of high growth, the Japanese economy developed certain characteristics at the microeconomic level that were quite different from those of either the prewar Japanese economy or the Western economies. To be sure, many of these characteristics originated in the prewar period, but they acquired a more definite shape with the postwar reforms and the onset of rapid growth. In regard to management, the raising of capital, labor–management practices, or subcontracting, Japanese firms emphasized long-term relationships. Market and organization influenced each other in complex ways, and a balance was maintained between adaptability and stability in business practices.

### *Enterprise organization and management*

Most Japanese enterprises were joint stock companies, but large enterprises were usually part of an enterprise group (*keiretsu*) whose affiliated enterprises and financial institutions held one another's stocks, thereby avoiding the risk of unfriendly takeover bids by other firms. It was customary for a firm's managers to be chosen from among its long-time employees, who acted in accordance with what they saw as the long-term interests of the enterprise, which they viewed as a group of employees. Japanese enterprises were therefore likely to aim at long-term growth rather than short-term profits, and managers were extremely concerned with market share.

Before the war, the zaibatsu holding companies controlled extensive networks of firms by controlling dominant shares of stock. After the postwar dissolution of the zaibatsu, many former client or affiliate firms and financial institutions organized themselves into enterprise groups (*keiretsu*). Within the *keiretsu*, firms held one another's stock in order to avoid outside takeovers. The amount of stock for sale on the stock market was small, and its value rose remarkably. According to Miyazaki Giichi, in 1970, 57.1 percent of all limited stock companies were controlled by corporations, 20.7 percent by managers, and only 20.5 percent by stockholders.[14] One of the reasons that Japanese business leaders opposed the introduction of foreign capital and were anxious about the liberalization of capital in the late 1960s was that they wished to retain control of their enterprises.

Although this pattern of ownership and management was common in large firms, there were some exceptions. First, many small- and medium-sized enterprises were individually owned. Second, the large enterprises were often controlled by their founder and his family. This was true of the growth industries' leading firms such as Matsushita, Sony, Honda, Toyota, Tōyō kōgyō, Suntory, Kyoto Ceramics (Kyocera), and Daiei. Third, the stock market played an important role in evaluating the firms, as increases in capital investment were influenced by current stock prices. After 1965 in particular, the ratio of equity capital to total assets rose. Even though Japanese enterprises were heavily dependent on borrowing, they had to increase their capitalization as they grew in order to secure loans. Thus in high-growth industries, the possibility of securing loans was enhanced by increased capitalization.

### *The primacy of indirect financing*

During the period of high growth, firms invested more capital than they accumulated internally. But the rate of individual savings was

14 Miyazaki Giichi, *Gendai Nihon no kigyō shūdan* (Tokyo: Nihon keizai shinbunsha, 1976), p. 290.

TABLE 10.17
*Flow of funds during rapid economic growth – 1965 (in ¥1 trillion)*

| | Savings in excess of investment | Deposits | Loans | Securities |
|---|---|---|---|---|
| Individuals | 2.6 | 2.7 | 1.1 | 0.3 |
| Enterprises | 1.1 | 2.1 | 4.0 | 0.5[a] |
| Central government | 0.1 | – | – | 0.2[b] |
| Public corporations and local governments | 1.1 | – | 0.5 | 0.8[a] |

[a]Issued. [b]Flotation of long-term national bonds.
*Source:* Tōyō keizai shinpōsha, *Shōwa kokusei sōran* (Tokyo: Tōyō keizai shinpōsha, 1980), vol. 2, p. 116.

high, and the major portion of individual savings were concentrated in bank deposits. Bank loans to individual enterprises served the function of mediating between individual savings and loans to or investment in business enterprises. This type of indirect financing is one of the principal characteristics of this period. Table 10.17 outlines this money flow in 1965.

Obviously, the banks were important to this system of indirect financing. It is sometimes said that the large "city banks" (as commercial banks are called in Japan) stood at the pinnacle of the enterprise groups in the same way that headquarters companies (*honsha*) stood at the pinnacle of the prewar zaibatsu, as they both exercised similar economic power. According to Miyazaki Giichi's "one set hypothesis," because enterprise groups led by banks tried to acquire affiliated enterprises in all industries and to cover the whole range of industries and financial institutions, there was intense investment competition. Others take the view that the banks carried out a profitable "credit rationing" to the firms in the heavy and chemical industries while cooperating with the government's policy of keeping interest rates artificially low.

But even though the city banks were vital to the transfer of savings into investment, that did not mean that they could disregard market forces in distributing capital or that they had discretionary powers in deciding to whom they would lend. First, because there were many city banks, they had to compete to acquire high-quality customers for loans. Second, there were many other financial institutions to which firms could turn for loans besides city banks, for example, long-term credit banks and life insurance companies. Third, as Japan's economic growth accelerated, high-growth enterprises, in particular, built up their own capital reserves through which they could finance themselves. Fourth, after 1965 as the government began to float public bonds, the movement of interest rates was liberalized.

Although the banks cultivated long-term relationships with firms under the system of indirect financing, that does not mean that the banks distributed capital or set interest rates unilaterally as they wished. The mechanisms of a competitive market were still at work and so the image of the city banks as omnipotent in the business world is misleading.

### *Labor–management practices*

During this period of high growth, labor–management relations were characterized by lifetime employment, seniority-based wages, and company unions. As a rule, enterprises hired new school graduates and gave them on-the-job training. Because enterprises valued personnel skills, workers were hired for a very long term (until retirement age), and wages were based on seniority. Because both labor and management tried to achieve stability in employment, both approached wage settlements with flexibility. The bonus system also helped stabilize employment, by transferring some of the firm's risk to the workers.

The existence of such labor–management practices helped develop the workers' skills and improve productivity by increasing their desire to participate in the production process, thus making high growth possible. This also made labor–management relations relatively stable (see Table 10.18).

Although these labor–management practices prevailed in large enterprises, they were not always followed by medium and small enterprises. Generally, these practices applied to only about 30 percent of all employees, but among the rest of the employed population, job changes were frequent, and the rate of labor organization was low.

According to Table 10.19, by about 1965, as the labor market became tight, medium and small enterprises paid higher wages to younger employees. If they had not, they would not have been able to obtain as many workers as they needed. This meant that the wages for younger workers were determined in a homogeneous external labor market. In the case of older workers, the wage differential grew more pronounced. The reason was that wages in larger enterprises rose because workers had been employed longer and their wages were

TABLE 10.18
*Labor unions and labor disputes*

| Year | Number of unions[a,b] | Number of union members (thousands)[c] | Estimated organization rate (%)[a,d] | Number of disputes[e,f] | Number of participants in disputes (thousands)[e,g] | Number of workdays lost (thousand days)[e,h] |
|---|---|---|---|---|---|---|
| 1955 | 32,012[i] | 6,166[i] | 37.2 | 1,345 | 3,748 | 3,467 |
| 1956 | 34,073[i] | 6,350[i] | 34.8 | 1,330 | 3,372 | 4,562 |
| 1957 | 36,084[i] | 6,606[i] | 34.7 | 1,680 | 8,464 | 5,652 |
| 1958 | 37,823[i] | 6,882[i] | 33.9 | 1,864 | 6,362 | 6,052 |
| 1959 | 39,303[i] | 7,078[i] | 31.5 | 1,709 | 4,682 | 6,020 |
| 1960 | 41,561 | 7,652 | 32.2 | 2,222 | 6,953 | 4,912 |
| 1961 | 45,096 | 8,360 | 34.5 | 2,483 | 9,044 | 6,150 |
| 1962 | 47,812 | 8,971 | 34.7 | 2,287 | 7,129 | 5,400 |
| 1963 | 49,796 | 9,357 | 34.7 | 2,016 | 9,035 | 2,770 |
| 1964 | 51,457 | 9,800 | 35.0 | 2,422 | 7,974 | 3,165 |
| 1965 | 52,879 | 10,147 | 34.8 | 3,051 | 8,975 | 5,669 |
| 1966 | 53,985 | 10,404 | 34.2 | 3,687 | 10,947 | 2,742 |
| 1967 | 55,321 | 10,566 | 34.1 | 3,024 | 10,914 | 1,830 |
| 1968 | 56,535 | 10,863 | 34.4 | 3,882 | 11,758 | 2,841 |
| 1969 | 58,812 | 11,249 | 35.2 | 5,283 | 14,483 | 3,634 |
| 1970 | 60,954 | 11,605 | 35.4 | 4,551 | 9,137 | 3,915 |
| 1971 | 62,428 | 11,798 | 34.8 | 6,861 | 10,829 | 6,029 |
| 1972 | 63,718 | 11,889 | 34.3 | 5,808 | 9,630 | 5,147 |
| 1973 | 65,448 | 12,098 | 33.1 | 9,459 | 14,549 | 4,604 |

[a]As of end of May. [b]Number of separate labor unions.
[c]Number of labor union members in individual unions.
[d]Number of labor union members as a percentage of number of employees.
[e]Annual statistics.
[f]Including disputes accompanied by strikes.
[g]Number of members in organizations involved in disputes.
[h]Number of working days against the total number of workers participating in strikes and number of workers when plant was closed.
[i]Number of members of separate labor unions.
*Source:* Rōdōshō, *Rōdō tōkei yōran* (Tokyo: Ōkurashō insatsukyoku, 1965–73).

based on seniority, whereas in small and medium enterprises there was a great deal of labor mobility and no seniority-based scale, and so older workers were more affected by the labor supply.

The large enterprises, of course, did not employ only long-term workers. Around 1960 when the economy grew faster than expected, large enterprises hired a large number of temporary workers, whom they eventually made regular employees. In the 1970s the number of temporary, daily, or part-time employees increased. Subcontractors were also used as a source of labor. Although the labor markets were becoming more and more internalized in large enterprises, the internal and external labor markets still influenced each other.

TABLE 10.19

*Wage differentials between large enterprises and small and medium enterprises (enterprises with over 1,000 employees = 100.0)*

<table>
<tr><th rowspan="2">Age of employees (years)</th><th colspan="5">Enterprises with 100 to 999 employees</th></tr>
<tr><th>1954[a]</th><th>1961</th><th>1965</th><th>1970</th><th>1975</th></tr>
<tr><td>20 to 24</td><td>83.8</td><td>93.1</td><td>107.3</td><td>100.7</td><td>98.2</td></tr>
<tr><td>25 to 29</td><td>81.1</td><td>90.4</td><td>107.4</td><td>101.7</td><td>98.9</td></tr>
<tr><td>30 to 34</td><td>76.3</td><td>81.6</td><td>101.2</td><td>98.9</td><td>97.7</td></tr>
<tr><td>35 to 39</td><td>72.1</td><td>74.0</td><td>94.3</td><td>95.0</td><td>94.6</td></tr>
<tr><td>40 to 44</td><td rowspan="2">69.5</td><td rowspan="2">67.4</td><td rowspan="2">85.9</td><td rowspan="2">88.7</td><td>90.2</td></tr>
<tr><td>45 to 49</td><td>85.6</td></tr>
<tr><td>50 to 54</td><td rowspan="2">66.8</td><td rowspan="2">65.5</td><td rowspan="2">78.2</td><td rowspan="2">79.0</td><td>81.7</td></tr>
<tr><td>55 to 59</td><td>76.6</td></tr>
<tr><td>over 60</td><td>88.6</td><td>87.7</td><td>80.9</td><td>85.3</td><td>80.3</td></tr>
<tr><th rowspan="2"></th><th colspan="5">Enterprises with 10 to 99 employees</th></tr>
<tr><th>1954[b]</th><th>1961</th><th>1965</th><th>1970</th><th>1975</th></tr>
<tr><td>20 to 24</td><td>77.5</td><td>89.7</td><td>114.1</td><td>104.9</td><td>98.7</td></tr>
<tr><td>25 to 29</td><td>70.5</td><td>80.2</td><td>109.6</td><td>103.8</td><td>97.4</td></tr>
<tr><td>30 to 34</td><td>65.8</td><td>64.3</td><td>96.5</td><td>96.3</td><td>92.9</td></tr>
<tr><td>35 to 39</td><td>59.6</td><td>54.7</td><td>86.2</td><td>88.5</td><td>85.5</td></tr>
<tr><td>40 to 44</td><td rowspan="2">55.0</td><td rowspan="2">45.7</td><td rowspan="2">74.7</td><td rowspan="2">78.5</td><td>78.3</td></tr>
<tr><td>45 to 49</td><td>73.5</td></tr>
<tr><td>50 to 54</td><td rowspan="2">52.4</td><td rowspan="2">43.9</td><td rowspan="2">65.8</td><td rowspan="2">68.2</td><td>67.5</td></tr>
<tr><td>55 to 59</td><td>65.1</td></tr>
<tr><td>over 60</td><td>72.2</td><td>65.9</td><td>73.2</td><td>82.2</td><td>72.6</td></tr>
</table>

*Note:* For 1954 and 1961, the differential between "cash salary amount regularly provided" for manufacture workers; after 1965, the differential between "fixed salary amount" for male workers of all industries investigated. In 1965 and 1970, total number of industries except service industries. In 1961 and 1965, wages in April; after 1970, wages in June.

[a]Enterprises with 100 to 499 employees. [b]Enterprises with 30 to 99 employees.

*Source:* Rōdōshō, *1954 nen kojinbetsu chingin chōsa; 1961 nen chingin jittai sōgō chōsa. Chingin kōzō kihon tōkei chōsa hōkoku,* 1965, 1970, 1975.

## *The development of subcontractor enterprises*

Another characteristic of this period was the degree to which large enterprises relied on small and medium enterprises as subcontractors. According to a survey in 1976, 82.2 percent of the large manufacturing enterprises relied on outside suppliers, and 58.1 percent of all small and medium manufacturing enterprises had subcontracting relationships with large firms.

It is often said that large firms used subcontractors as a way of adjusting to changes in general business conditions. When business was brisk they used the subcontractors, but when business slowed, the large firms stopped their orders or offered only below-cost prices. In other words, the large firms made their subcontractors completely subservient and exploited their cheap labor and production costs for their own profit. If this were the case, however, it would be difficult to understand why the number of subcontractors increased as the economy grew. According to a survey of subcontractors asked why they had gone into the business, many gave reasons such as "I can concentrate on production without having to worry about making sales efforts" or "The flow of work is stable." Among firms using subcontractors, the principal consideration in selecting a subcontractor was whether or not it possessed special technology or plant facilities.[15]

Subcontracting firms tried to use the technical and managerial skills of the owner continuously and over the long term. They stood between the market and the internal organization of the contracting firm, combining the adaptability of the market with the ability of the large firm to make long-term plans. This created a particularly efficient way of organizing production. In the automobile industry, for example, Toyota's "just-in-time" supply system depended heavily on subcontractors to improve productivity.

## ECONOMIC POLICY

Most discussions of government policy focus on "industrial policy" or "industrial targeting," and many maintain that Japan's economy is tightly managed, but such a monolithic picture is not correct. Economic policy is shaped by the interaction of the government bureaucracy, business interests, pressure groups, and the ruling Liberal Democratic Party. It is a mixture of certain basic macroeconomic policies and sectoral or microeconomic policies. Moreover, economic policy is neither fixed nor unchanging over time but has adjusted to changing economic conditions, though not always successfully.

### *The assumptions of postwar economic policy*

In 1955, even after Japan had recovered economically from the war, it still was small and relatively weak economically. National income was low; the international balance of payments was unstable; and overpopulation prevented full employment. The goal of Japan's economic policy was to overcome its status as a small economy and to join the

15 Yutaka Kōsai and Yoshitarō Ogino, *The Contemporary Japanese Economy* (New York: Macmillan, 1984), p. 72.

ranks of the advanced industrial powers; the limitation on its economic policy was that as a small economy, Japan faced a ceiling on its balance of payments. To achieve its goal, Japan had to maximize its growth, enhance its international competitiveness, and achieve full employment. But because Japan was still a minor economy, it had to consider first its balance of payments.

Given its limitations with respect to its balance of payments, the Japanese government sought to avoid changing the existing exchange rate and the inflow of foreign capital. A balance in the current account under fixed prices thus became an important policy target. With respect to financial policy, whenever the balance of payments worsened (in 1954, 1957, 1961, and 1963), finances were tightened. With respect to fiscal policy, the 1949 Fiscal Law mandated sound finance, and public bonds were not issued to raise government funds. With respect to taxation, in 1960 a tax investigation commission recommended that the ratio of tax revenue to national income not exceed 20 percent.[16] "Small government" and a financial policy sensitive to the international balance of payments were the characteristic rules of classical capitalism. Except for the prohibitions on capital movement, the framework of Japan's postwar economic policy was typical of that under the gold standard.

On the other hand, because Japan wanted to catch up with the advanced countries, its economic policy had another side. In 1952, Japan's foreign currency reserves stood at $900 million, rising to $1.8 billion in 1960, but after that they hardly increased at all, reaching only $2 billion in 1967. Meanwhile, Japan's imports had risen threefold, and its money supply had increased by two and a half times. The government adopted a policy of increasing the money supply and expanding the economy as far as the international balance of payments allowed. Because the domestic money supply was not related to foreign exchange reserves, this policy differed from that under the gold standard. Because Japan's foreign exchange reserves were small, it had to pursue a tight money policy in order to manage its foreign exchange funds whenever the international balance of payments moved into a deficit.

In fiscal policy, the national budget was balanced, and every effort was made to maintain "small government" by using part of the natural increase in tax revenues resulting from economic growth to reduce

16 See the 1960 report of the Tax System Investigation Commission (Zaisei chōsakai). For a comment on this, see Komiya Ryūtarō, *Gendai Nihon keizai kenkyū* (Tokyo: Tōkyō daigaku shuppankai, 1975), pp. 107–8.

taxes. At the same time, however, special tax measures, direct government financing, and other sorts of government intervention were used as tools of industrial policy to promote Japan's international competitiveness.[17] In its macroeconomic policy the government followed the principle of balanced budgets, but at the same time in its microeconomic or sectoral policy, it followed government interventionist principles, by providing special tax measures for and fiscal investment in particular industries.

Japan's economic policy during this period, therefore, used two contrasting approaches: a sectoral or microeconomic interventionist policy that assumed Japan was a small economy aimed at catching up with the advanced industrial countries; and orthodox macroeconomic financial and fiscal policies that assumed Japan was a small economy heeding the limitations on its international balance of payments.

### *Changes in economic policy*

By achieving economic growth through industrial modernization, Japan gradually became free of the limitations imposed by its international balance of payments. It was well on the way to changing from a minor into a major economic power. As a result, its microeconomic interventionist policy (at least the protecting and nurturing of particular industries) became more difficult.

Japan's participation in the OECD in the 1960s required that it liberalize its controls over foreign exchange, foreign trade, and capital movements. At the same time, there were not only those who argued that liberalization would improve economic growth, but there were also foreign pressures at work. Liberalization deprived the government of the means to intervene in private enterprise, and interest rates also moved freely in the domestic financial market as the government continued to float government bond issues.

The government naturally hesitated to reduce taxes or give financial assistance to enterprises that were able to compete in international markets. The diversification of the industrial structure, moreover, made it difficult to identify the needy industries. Government finance turned from industry to the improvement of housing facilities and the

17 Scholars do not agree on how to evaluate this industrial policy. For example, see the relevant chapters of Komiya Ryūtarō, *Nihon no sangyō seisaku* (Tokyo: Todai shuppankai, 1984); Komiya Ryūtarō, *Gendai Nihon keizai kenkyū;* Tsuruta Toshimasa, *Sengo Nihon no sangyō seisaku* (Tokyo Nihon keizai shinbunsha, 1982); Ueno Hiroya, *Nihon no keizai seido* (Tokyo: Nihon keizai shinbunsha, 1978); Chalmers Johnson, *MITI and the Japanese Miracle, The Growth of Industrial Policy 1925–1975* (Stanford, Calif.: Stanford University Press, 1982).

TABLE 10.20
*Fiscal investment and loan program (¥100 million)*

| | 1955 | 1960 | 1965 | 1970 | 1975 |
|---|---|---|---|---|---|
| Housing | 415 | 789 | 2,259 | 6,896 | 19,966 |
| Living environment facilities | 230 | 569 | 2,010 | 4,168 | 15,573 |
| Public welfare facilities | 64 | 109 | 585 | 1,017 | 3,133 |
| Educational facilities | 136 | 214 | 493 | 790 | 2,752 |
| Small and medium enterprises | 244 | 784 | 2,045 | 5,523 | 14,505 |
| Agriculture, forestries, and fisheries | 266 | 439 | 1,169 | 1,785 | 3,795 |
| Subtotal | 1,355 | 2,904 | 8,561 | 20,179 | 59,724 |
| Preservation of national land and restoration after disasters | 231 | 401 | 506 | 560 | 1,100 |
| Roads | 110 | 272 | 1,284 | 3,078 | 7,444 |
| Transportation and communications | 366 | 915 | 2,250 | 4,723 | 11,849 |
| Regional development | 255 | 436 | 1,124 | 1,431 | 3,059 |
| Subtotal | 962 | 2,024 | 5,164 | 9,792 | 23,452 |
| Key industries | 471 | 838 | 1,262 | 2,028 | 2,764 |
| Promotion of exports | 210 | 485 | 1,219 | 3,800 | 7,160 |
| Total | 2,998 | 6,251 | 16,206 | 35,799 | 93,100 |

*Source:* Ōkurashō, *Zaisei tōkei* (Tokyo: Ōkurashō insatsukyoku, 1962– )

environment (see Table 10.20), and government intervention in private enterprise became stronger in environmental pollution and labor regulation. In addition, public opinion turned against large mergers or amalgamations.

At the same time, macroeconomic policy, finally freed from the balance-of-payments ceiling, became more flexible. Using the 1965 recession as an opportunity, the government began to raise revenues by issuing public bonds, abandoning in practice the principle of balanced budgets. Under the slogan of "increasing welfare through increasing the tax burden," the government made plans to increase the taxation rate. In 1967 and 1968 efforts were made to return to a balanced budget (i.e., limiting the issue of public bonds and increasing public debt). But the liberation of macroeconomic policy from balance-of-payments restraints reached a peak with the announcement of Prime Minister Tanaka Kakuei's Plan to Reconstruct the Japanese Archipelago in 1972 and with plans to broaden the coverage of social insurance policies in 1973.

After 1968, as Japanese industry became more competitive and world inflation spread, Japan's foreign exchange reserves increased rapidly, climbing from $2 billion in 1967 to $18.3 billion in 1972. Even though Japan enjoyed a positive balance of payments, the Bank of Japan, contrary to previous practice, adopted a tight money policy to keep the domestic economy from overheating, but the positive balance of payments continued to climb, and foreign exchange reserves accumulated. The Bank of Japan then shifted to a looser policy, and between 1970 and 1973 the money supply increased 20 percent a year. In other words, the government returned to the policy it followed in the 1960s of easing the money supply when the balance of payments was in the black. But in the midst of world inflation, increasing the domestic money supply while maintaining fixed exchange rates was bound to create inflation. With the announcement of the Plan for the Reconstruction of the Japanese Archipelago, first land prices and then commodity prices rose. Just before the "oil shock" of 1973, Japan's wholesale prices had increased by more than 20 percent over the previous year, even without an oil price hike.

Even with the adoption of a policy of financial and fiscal expansion, the balance of payments did not stop expanding. Indeed, it was strengthened by the revaluation of the yen in 1971 and the shift to a floating exchange rate in 1973. Had Japan earlier revalued the yen on its own initiative, instead of increasing the money supply, inflation might have been eased, if not avoided. But Japan realized too late that the significance of the balance of payments had changed and so made the wrong policy choice. Instead of revaluing the yen, the government tried to maintain its parity. The freedom of action that the government had acquired with the end of its balance-of-payment constraints was misused, thereby incurring inflation and bringing to an end the period of high growth.

# PART IV

# SOCIAL AND INTELLECTUAL CHANGE

CHAPTER 11

# THE TRANSFORMATION OF RURAL SOCIETY, 1900–1950

It is not difficult to find continuities in the Japanese countryside. Small-scale family farming on holdings averaging less than three acres prevails today as in 1900. Despite almost a century of modern economic growth, the number of farm families has remained fairly constant, declining only slightly from five and one-half million at the turn of the century to five million in the late 1970s. There has been continuity not only in the number of farm families but also in the families themselves: The overwhelming majority of Japanese farmers today are the descendants of farmers in the Meiji era (1868–1912). As in the past they reside in small hamlets, clusters of an average of fifty to sixty farmhouses surrounded by rice paddies and upland fields. Rice remains their principal field crop, accounting for 59 percent by value of total field crop production in 1900 and 53 percent in 1970.

Yet contrasts with the past abound, and collectively they make the countryside vastly different from what it was eighty years ago. Japanese agriculture is no longer the highly labor-intensive undertaking it used to be. At the turn of the century it took roughly one hundred days of labor to grow an acre of rice. Today, owing primarily to the diffusion of capital-intensive farming methods, thirty to thirty-five days will suffice, and output per acre is almost 70 percent higher than before. The dependence of farm families on agricultural income has also declined markedly. In 1920, the year of Japan's first modern census, 70 percent of farm families were classified as full-time farmers who derived 90 percent or more of their income from agriculture. In 1972, only 14 percent of farm families were classified as full-time farmers; 86 percent were classified as part-time farm families; and 70 percent of the latter earned less from agriculture than from nonagricultural sources.

Less susceptible to measurement but no less significant is the contrast between rural communities past and present. To be sure, continuities still exist. Owing to, among other factors, their spatial separation from neighboring communities and the exigencies of rice culture (especially the need to coordinate the flooding and draining of adjacent rice paddies), hamlets retain a fairly high degree of social cohesion. Resident households are expected, as they were generations ago, to contribute to the well-being of the hamlet as a whole by taking part in the upkeep of communal property and by voting for a mutually agreed-upon candidate to represent local interests in the larger village of which their hamlet is a part. A number of formal and informal ceremonies designed to promote communal solidarity still take place. Yet despite the persistence of these and other features of communal life, the hamlet today differs in important ways from the hamlet of the past. Probably the greatest difference stems from a sharp reduction in status distinctions among hamlet residents. Once hierarchically structured, with local power securely in the hands of the wealthiest households, the hamlet is now essentially a community of equals.

This latter social transformation is usually portrayed in the Western literature on Japan as a fairly recent phenomenon, the product primarily of the land reform carried out during the post–World War II Occupation. In fact, the land reform, though certainly important, was the culmination of slow, evolutionary processes that date from the late nineteenth century. These processes and the tensions and social changes they generated are the subject of this chapter.

Four policies implemented by the Meiji government in the late 1870s and 1880s set these processes in motion. The one with the most immediate impact was the land tax reform. Designed primarily to secure a stable source of government revenue, the tax reform involved far more than taxes. The principle of seignorial control of arable land, by either the Tokugawa *bakufu* or the daimyo, was abandoned and private property rights established. Title deeds were issued to those farmers customarily recognized as landholders, and long-standing prohibitions on land transfers were eliminated. A new tax system was then established on the basis of private property rights. Instead of taxes in kind levied on the official output of each rural community, taxes in cash, pegged initially at 3 percent of the assessed value of land, were levied on each individual landowner. (This reform had no impact on rural rents. As in the past, rents were levied in kind, generally in rice, at a fixed volume per unit area.)

In both its implementation and its operation, the new tax system contributed to greater economic differentiation among the rural population. At a stroke, the assignment of title deeds replaced with a single, standard, full ownership the welter of rights to arable land that had proliferated during the Tokugawa period. Many farmers who had pawned or mortgaged their land to wealthier neighbors were reduced to the status of landless tenants when title deeds were awarded to their creditors. Others who possessed permanent tenancy rights that amounted to shared ownership of the land in question were unable to press their claims successfully and so became ordinary tenants of the newly recognized owners.

Nor were the recipients of title deeds immune to changes in their economic status. According to one estimate, the average landowning farmer had to market 30 percent of his produce in the 1870s to meet his tax obligations. When agricultural prices fell, as they did during the government-induced deflation of 1881–4, the burden of taxation increased, and many farmers had to borrow money to make ends meet. For some, that marked the first step in the slow and painful loss of their land; first one field and then another would be sold to cover debts, until none was left. Their misfortunes were gains for others, of course. Although its dimensions cannot be measured precisely, landownership became concentrated in the decades following the tax reform.[1] Those landowners who had cash in reserve during the deflationary years or at other times when their neighbors needed loans were able to expand their holdings. When they had acquired as much land as they were willing or able to farm themselves, they became landlords, renting their newly acquired fields to the former owners. As a result, tenancy, which had accounted for roughly 27 percent of arable land at the time of the Meiji Restoration, increased to 45 percent in 1908.

While the land tax reform was creating greater inequality among farmers, the government's reforms of local administration were creating greater distance between the communities in which those farmers lived and the Japanese state. During the Tokugawa period, the villages had functioned simultaneously as the basic unit of domainal administration and as the primary locus of farmers' economic and social activity. The same community that paid taxes to the warrior elite allocated water, access to communal land, and other essentials of farming to its resident households and organized their roof repairs, weddings, and funerals. By the 1880s this was no longer the case. A massive reorganization of the countryside had occurred in which the 79,000 villages of the Tokugawa period had been combined into some

1 Data on landownership were not collected systematically until 1908. Thereafter, statistics were compiled and published annually by the Ministry of Agriculture. Even the latter record does not permit precise measurement of the concentration of landownership, however, for only the total number of owners of specified ranges of land area (e.g., one to three hectares, ten to fifty hectares), not the amount of land falling within each range, was reported. For a detailed discussion of the shortcomings of these landownership statistics, see Tōbata Seiichi, "Jinushi no shohanchū," *Kokka gakkai zasshi* 55 (June 1941): 37–56.

14,000 larger villages. The latter, regarded by government officials as fiscally sound and hence capable of sustaining a variety of old and new tasks, became the basic units of administration in the local government system established, after years of experimentation, in 1889.

The old villages did not merge completely into the new, however, contrary to the wishes of bureaucrats in the Home Ministry who regarded them as inefficient remnants of feudalism. Relegated to the status of hamlets – or, in the official nomenclature, sections (*aza*) – and given no formal role in local government, they continued to function as the primary sphere of the farmers' lives and the focus of their loyalties.[2] To its residents, the community was still a village (*mura*) as in the past, forced by the government into association with adjacent communities. The new village to which they nominally belonged was regarded as an artificial and threatening institution. Safety lay in continued, if not greater, solidarity among the hamlet's residents.

Two additional policies that the government implemented at this time, compulsory elementary education and universal military conscription, also brought change to the countryside, though much more slowly. One of the new tasks assigned to Meiji villages was the construction of primary schools, which local children of both sexes were required to attend. The period of schooling, initially set at sixteen months, soon was extended to four years and in 1907 was extended once more to six years. Another new task was the preliminary medical examinations for conscription. After 1873, all young men became eligible for three years of active military service, followed by four years in the reserves.[3]

Education and conscription had far-reaching consequences for rural society. On the one hand, both provided farmers with new skills and attitudes, which in turn helped generate dissatisfaction with existing forms of inequality. On the other hand, both exposed farmers to their new nation, inculcating patriotism and creating a new willingness among them to see themselves and their communities as part of a larger whole. Not until the early 1900s, however, when significant numbers of rural schoolchildren reached adulthood and the soldiers in Japan's second foreign war returned home did these consequences become apparent. What then ensued was a forty-year period of fer-

2 For a discussion of the Meiji local government system, see Kurt Steiner, *Local Government in Japan* (Stanford, Calif.: Stanford University Press, 1965), chaps. 2, 3; Tadashi Fukutake, *Japanese Rural Society*, trans. Ronald Dore (New York: Oxford University Press, 1967), chaps. 8, 10; Shima Yasuhiko et al., *Chōson gappei to nōson no henbō* (Tokyo: Yūhikaku, 1958).

3 The period of active service was reduced to two years in 1905.

ment that left virtually no aspect of rural society untouched and created a basis, in attitudes and aspirations if not always in formal institutions, for further change in the postwar era.

## RURAL SOCIETY IN THE LATE NINETEENTH CENTURY

At the turn of the century, despite having been consigned to oblivion by the architects of the new local government system, Japan's hamlets continued to exist as relatively autonomous communities and to constitute the basic territorial units of rural society. Although each community was considered unique by its inhabitants, they actually had many features in common. Chief among them was their corporate character. The hamlet was not a gesellschaft consisting of individuals in voluntary association with one another but a gemeinschaft consisting of interdependent households joined in a common purpose. That purpose was, as it had been for centuries, survival in a world of scarcity.[4]

How potently scarcity operated as an underpinning of community life depended to an extent on the hamlet's location. Where climatic conditions and prevailing agricultural technology permitted double cropping – at the turn of the century, roughly that portion of the Japanese archipelago to the southwest of Tokyo – there was less risk of shortfalls in the food supply than there was in the single-crop regions to the northeast. Where proximity to cities or transportation routes facilitated cash cropping, there was greater opportunity to profit from farming than there was in isolated hamlets. But these were relative, not absolute, advantages, and each generated new risks while moderating old ones: To farmers who depended heavily on the marketplace, for example, a sharp decline in prices could be as disastrous as a poor harvest could be. Throughout the country, then, farming remained a highly vulnerable undertaking. From time to time there might be several good years in succession, when crops were bountiful or prices high, but more than that was required to erase memories of hardship during lean years or to weaken long-established forms of cooperation within the hamlet.

These forms were comprehensive in scope, involving all aspects of the hamlet residents' economic, social, and political lives. Indeed, there was considerable overlap among these putatively separate spheres of

4 The following discussion is based primarily on Ushiomi Toshitaka et al., *Nihon no nōson* (Tokyo: Iwanami shoten, 1957), pt. 1; Kawashima Takeyoshi, "Nōson no mibun kaisō sei," in *Nihon shihonshugi kōza* (Tokyo: Iwanami shoten, 1954), vol. 8, pp. 405–33; Fukutake, *Japanese Rural Society*, pt. 3.

activity. What distinguished one form of cooperation from another was less its character than the level at which it occurred, the hamlet as a whole or one of its neighborhood subdivisions.

Most hamlets at the turn of the century still retained the political structure under which they had operated as villages in the past. Each had a headman who represented the community in its dealings with the outside world (formerly the warrior class, now the administrative village and beyond that the Meiji state), supervised the day-to-day affairs of the community itself, and presided at hamlet meetings (*yoriai*). The latter were held at least once a year, and the heads of all households belonging to the hamlet were expected to be present.

That did not necessarily mean the heads of all households living in the hamlet, for mere residence did not confer membership in the collectivity. New arrivals, which might mean people who had resided in the hamlet for only ten or fifteen years, had to qualify for membership by demonstrating their willingness to contribute to the welfare of the community as a whole and, in some cases, by paying an "entrance fee." Moreover, what had once been granted by the community could be taken away. If hamlet members violated established norms of behavior, they were subject to fines and other punishments; and if their behavior was deemed sufficiently flagrant, they were subject to ostracism (*murahachibu*).

What made community membership desirable and ostracism terrifying was the hamlet's ownership of two essential means of agricultural production, water for irrigation and forests for fuel, fodder, and green manure. The Meiji government originally had planned to transfer control of these communal resources to its newly created administrative villages, but widespread local opposition had forced a retreat: In exchange for allowing themselves to be consolidated into villages, the hamlets retained control of much of their property. Formal membership in the hamlet provided rights of access to it and at the same time created obligations to share in its upkeep.

These rights and obligations constituted one of the main items on the agenda of the hamlet's meetings. When each paddy field in the community would be flooded, how many days each household could collect wood and cut grasses in the communal forest – such were the rights that required attention. The obligations consisted of paying dues and performing labor services – so many days of work each year on hamlet roads, bridges, and forest trails or a fixed amount of money, saké, or food as a substitute.

In some cases, labor services were assigned to individual households, but more often they were assigned to the hamlet's neighborhood subdivisions (*kumi*), which in turn allocated tasks to their members. Descended from the five-family groups of the Tokugawa period, *kumi* generally had expanded in size to ten or twenty adjacent households. Their activities were by no means confined to the maintenance of hamlet property but extended to every facet of rural life. It was the *kumi* that mobilized labor for rice planting and other farming tasks that required cooperation, that sent housewives to help out at weddings and funerals, and that supplied aid and comfort to the victims of a fire or serious illness.

All these forms of cooperation, even those involving the most onerous tasks, provided opportunities for social contact among community residents. It was customary to drink large quantities of saké after hamlet meetings and to celebrate with feasting the completion of hamlet work assignments. There were special songs that were sung while the rice seedlings were being planted and special feasts prepared for when the task was done. The women who came to help at weddings and funerals had a chance to exchange gossip in the kitchen. These moments of pleasure and relaxation with one's neighbors served not only to moderate the drudgery of everyday life but also to reinforce feelings of communal solidarity.

If a hamlet consisted of households of roughly equal economic and social status, the maintenance of solidarity, although by no means automatic, was relatively simple. Having the same means, the families in the hamlet tended to have the same needs and interests. Any disagreements among them that could not be resolved by informal discussion or forgotten by getting drunk together at a communal feast could be presented to the hamlet *yoriai* and some sort of compromise worked out. But at the turn of the century, such communities were the exception, not the rule. In most hamlets, economic and social inequality prevailed among the households and so made the maintenance of solidarity considerably more complex.

At a conceptual level, one can divide the households in these latter communities into three separate categories on the basis of differences in landownership and lineage, or pedigree (*iegara*). At the top were the wealthy households (*gōnō*) who owned more land than they needed to cultivate in order to sustain themselves by farming. Typically they owned forestlands as well, which gave them direct access to wood and grasses. They could trace their ancestry to the community's original settlers, perhaps even to warriors who had combined farming with fighting during the wars of the fifteenth and sixteenth centuries. Their

TABLE 11.1
*Farm households by status and scale of cultivation (excluding Hokkaido and Okinawa)*

| | 1908 | 1937 |
|---|---|---|
| Total number of households | 5,261,328 (100%) | 5,283,703 (100%) |
| a. Status | | |
| Owner-cultivators | 1,729,415 (32.9%) | 1,602,140 (30.3%) |
| Tenants | 1,434,224 (27.2%) | 1,399,122 (26.5%) |
| Owner-tenants | 2,097,689 (39.9%) | 2,282,451 (43.2%) |
| b. Scale of cultivation[a] | | |
| Less than 5 *tan* | 2,003,298 (38.1%) | 1,799,886 (34.1%) |
| 5 *tan* to 1 *chō* | 1,754,060 (33.3%) | 1,867,001 (35.3%) |
| 1 to 2 *chō* | 1,031,122 (19.6%) | 1,236,009 (23.4%) |
| 2 to 3 *chō* | 306,421 (5.8%) | 291,581 (5.5%) |
| 3 to 5 *chō* | 124,785 (2.4%) | 78,369 (1.5%) |
| 5 *chō* or more | 41,642 (0.8%) | 10,857 (0.2%) |

[a]One *chō* (10 *tan*) equals 2.45 acres, or 0.992 hectare. According to the distinctions made in this chapter, those households cultivating less than 1 *chō* can be considered "small farmers"; those cultivating 1–3 *chō*, "middling farmers"; and those cultivating 3 *chō* or more, "wealthy farmers."
*Source:* Data from Chūō bukka tōsei kyōryoku kaigi, *Nihon ni okeru nōgyō keiei narabi ni tochi shoyū no hensen ni kansuru sankō shiryō* (Tokyo: Chūō bukka tōsei kyōryoku kaigi, 1943).

more immediate ancestors had served as village headmen during the Tokugawa period. Next were the households that owned only enough land to support themselves by farming. Lacking claims to elite ancestry, they nonetheless had deep roots in the community, their families having lived there for perhaps a century or more. Both economically and socially they constituted a respectable but not imposing stratum of middling farmers (*chūnō*). Third were the small, or poor, farmers (*shōnō, hinnō*) who owned no land of their own and who, as tenants, rented all the land they cultivated from their wealthier neighbors. Either immigrants from elsewhere or the branch households (*bunke*) of older households, they occupied the bottom rung of a social hierarchy in which the venerability of community membership conferred prestige, just as they occupied the bottom rung of an economic hierarchy based on the ownership of land (see Table 11.1).

In reality, however, the status distinctions among households were rarely this clear-cut. Not only was there considerable differentiation within each category of households, but the lines between categories were blurred as well. In economic terms, wealthy farmers could range from the owners of over 2,500 acres of land, of whom there were fewer than a dozen nationwide in 1900, to those owning slightly more than two and one-half acres, the norm for family farming at the time. Some

TABLE 11.2
*Landowning households by size of holding (excluding Hokkaido and Okinawa)*

| | 1908 | 1937 |
|---|---|---|
| Total number of households | 4,802,891 (100%) | 4,873,429 (100%) |
| a. Number owning | | |
| Less than 5 *tan* | 2,267,093 (47.2%) | 2,463,250 (50.5%) |
| 5 *tan* to 1 *chō* | 1,277,702 (26.6%) | 1,267,521 (26.0%) |
| 1 to 3 *chō* | 899,986 (18.7%) | 864,050 (17.7%) |
| 3 to 5 *chō* | 227,496 (4.7%) | 181,143 (3.7%) |
| 5 to 10 *chō* | 94,049 (2.0%) | 71,390 (1.5%) |
| 10 to 50 *chō* | 34,348 (0.7%) | 24,269 (0.5%) |
| 50 *chō* or more | 2,217 (0.05%) | 1,806 (0.04%) |
| b. Estimated number of landowning households not engaged in farming (noncultivating landlords) | 975,787 | 988,838 |

*Source:* Chūō bukka tōsei kyōryoku kaigi, *Nihon ni okeru nōgyō keiei narabi ni tochi shoyū no hensen ni kansuru sankō shiryō* (Tokyo: Chūō bukka tōsei kyoryoku kaigi, 1943). In the absence of survey data on landlords, one can only estimate their number. The standard way of doing so is to subtract the number of landowning farmers (that is, owner-cultivators and owner-tenants) from the total number of landowners.

cultivated little or no land themselves, deriving most of their income from tenant rents, whereas others farmed most of the land they owned and rented out only a few parcels to tenants. Among the latter, those with modest holdings for a *gōnō* differed only slightly from their prosperous *chūnō* neighbors (see Table 11.2).

Nor did the *chūnō* households actually constitute a homogeneous group. Some might own all the land they could farm, but others combined owner-farming with tenancy, typically because they had encountered hard times and had been forced to sell a portion of their land, which they now leased from its new owner.[5] Those whose misfortunes had multiplied and who tenanted most of the land they once had owned differed little in economic terms from the landless tenants. Indeed, a landless tenant who cultivated a substantial holding might be better off than his declining *chūnō* neighbor and was certainly better off than other landless tenants in his community who cultivated smaller holdings or than day laborers who possessed no cultivating rights at all.

5 Not all owner-tenants had previously owned all the land they cultivated. Some were former tenants who had been able to purchase land. As Morris D. Morris argued in "The Problem of the Peasant Agriculturalist in Meiji Japan," *Far Eastern Quarterly* 15 (1956): 357–70, increases in the number of owner-tenant households after 1908 should not necessarily be construed as evidence of the farm households' increasing poverty.

Changes in economic status were not confined to the *chūnō* households. *Gōnō* could become wealthier, or they could decline to *chūnō* or even *shōnō* status. Tenants might purchase land and rise into *chūnō* or, albeit rarely, into *gōnō* ranks. Whether these changes occurred gradually over long periods of time or more suddenly, as in the aftermath of a particularly good or bad year for farming, they upset the correspondence between wealth and lineage that had existed in most communities in the past: The oldest families were not necessarily the most affluent any longer, nor were socially inferior immigrant or branch households necessarily poor.

Hamlets differed markedly from one another in both the extent of differentiation among their constituent households and the degree of divergence between the economic and social hierarchies those households formed. Some hamlets contained only *gōnō* and *shōnō* households. Others, probably the majority, contained all three categories of households but in varying combinations: one or several wealthy households, a majority or minority of owner-farmers, a greater or smaller proportion of landless tenants than of tenants who also owned some land. When and by whom the hamlet had been founded, how much change there had been in the fortunes of resident households, and how recently those changes had occurred and for what reasons were other variables that distinguished one hamlet from another and that combined with peculiarities of topography and soil conditions to sustain the impression among hamlet residents that their community had a character all its own.

Status differences among households were manifested not only in contrasting standards of living but in numerous other ways as well. In communities where status lines were clearly drawn, two Buddhist temples might exist, one for upper-status families and one for low-status families, and families of differing status might not arrange marriages or adoptions with each other. More commonly, low-status farmers were expected to use polite forms of address toward their superiors and to step aside and let them pass on roads and footpaths. The seating order at hamlet meetings and social gatherings also followed status lines.

Probably the most common manifestation of status distinctions was in the realm of politics. Just as the seating order at hamlet meetings replicated the community's hierarchy, so too did officeholding and decision making. Almost without exception, upper-status households continued to supply hamlet headmen, as they had in the past, and the only hamlet offices open to low-status farmers were night watchman or grave digger. Nor did all members of the community participate equally in the hamlet *yoriai*. Those seated at the front of the room in recognition of their superior status dominated the proceedings. Those in the middle spoke up rarely, and those at the back remained silent even when issues of pressing concern to them were discussed. Indeed, in many communities, a small group of men from upper-status households met before the *yoriai* to decide all the issues on the agenda. Their recommendations were then presented to the entire membership for *pro forma* ratification.

Hamlet leaders were supposed to think of the well-being of the community as a whole in all the decisions they made, but this noble standard was not always attained. The headman and his advisers might skim off a portion of the proceeds from the sale of timber in the hamlet forest or plan improvements in the community's irrigation system that benefited their own lands first and foremost. Some of the food and drink served at their meetings and charged to hamlet funds might find its way into their pantries. To the extent that such abuses were known or suspected, they provoked resentment among other residents of the community, but given the etiquette and institutions of status inequality, the open expression of complaints was virtually impossible.

Even communities with scrupulously honest leaders – and such communities did exist – were not immune to potentially disruptive tensions. The very heterogeneity of the hamlet's members created conflicting needs and interests that were difficult to reconcile. Temporarily reducing cutting rights in the hamlet's forest might make sense from the standpoint of conservation, for example, but those farmers without woodlands of their own would have to purchase firewood to make up the difference. Similarly, those with cash on hand could pay their way out of hamlet work assignments if they found it more convenient than supplying labor, but others had no choice. Even if it meant falling behind in chores on their own holdings or losing the wages they might earn by working for someone else, they had to turn out. Because the most affluent residents made hamlet policy, their concerns tended to take precedence. The community's poorer members were left to complain in private about their lot or to exact a degree of rough justice by stealing a few choice vegetables from their wealthy neighbors' fields.

More than the inertia of tradition or the compensations of petty theft were needed to sustain community solidarity in these conditions. Occasions such as communal feasts, at which the status quo was celebrated to the accompaniment of plentiful food and drink, played a part, as did controversies with neighboring hamlets over the water supply or some other external threat around which residents could close ranks. Equally, if not more, important were the relationships among households of differing status, which served to mute the hardships of subordination and, for the time being at least, to prevent conflict within the hamlet over the distribution of wealth and power.

These relationships were of three types: those between the main and branch houses of the same family, those between landlord and tenant, and those between patron and client.[6] All three relationships might exist in a given community, and any two households might be linked simultaneously by more than one tie. In general, however, one relationship predominated within the community and among its households. Which one it was depended to a great extent on the community's location and the prevailing level of economic development.

During the seventeenth century, as one means of protecting the small peasant proprietors on which its tax revenues were based, the warrior class had imposed its own system of primogeniture on the countryside. Thereafter, as a general rule, the eldest son of a farm family inherited both the family headship and all the family lands. Only holdings above a certain minimal area could be divided and a portion given to a younger son. When such divisions, which were confined by definition to *gōnō* families, occurred, the main line (*honke*) of the family retained the larger share of property. The younger son, who now headed a branch family (*bunke*), received very little land and remained economically dependent on the *honke*. He and his successors were expected to continue in perpetuity paying homage to the main line, commemorating its ancestors as their own and deferring to the leadership of its current head.

Although found throughout the country at the turn of the century (and not unheard of today), *honke–bunke* ties appear to have been particularly important in isolated mountain hamlets and hamlets scattered throughout northeastern Japan – in short, in regions where commercial farming remained relatively undeveloped. In some of these communities, one main house and its numerous branches, some of remote origin and some recently formed, might constitute the entire

6 A fourth relationship, between *shinrui*, or relatives (whether by blood or marriage), has been omitted from this discussion, owing to the lack of data for the turn of the century. The impression one gains from the literature is that in the early 1900s, ties of this type generally were structured along main/branch household or patron/client lines. They have gained in importance since then and, in particular, since 1945.

population. Elsewhere, several different and competing lineage organizations (*dōzoku*) existed, the main houses of each one forming a hierarchy based on the number of dependent houses they possessed.[7]

In contrast, landlord–tenant ties prevailed in regions where commercial agriculture was relatively well developed, in particular, in hamlets throughout the Kinki and Chūgoku districts of southwestern Japan and elsewhere in hamlets located in fertile river valleys or near large cities.[8] Some landlords headed families with illustrious pedigrees and rented their fields to tenants whose forebears had been their forebears' household servants. Others had acquired their landholdings more recently, by means of moneylending and mortgage foreclosures, and had as their tenants farmers who had once been owner-cultivators. Still others had financed land reclamation projects and had as their tenants those who had done the actual labor required. Whether of old or recent origin, landlord–tenant ties were in principle less permanent than *honke–bunke* ties. The core of the relationship was business – the exchange of land for a portion of its fruits – not blood, and either party was free to take his business elsewhere. Given the virtually untrammeled property rights granted to landowners by the Meiji civil code and the brisk demand for tenancies that existed throughout the country at the time, this situation worked to the disadvantage of the tenant farmers, who generally sought to minimize the risk of eviction from all the land they cultivated by renting small parcels of land from as many landlords as possible.

Patron–client ties occupied a kind of functional and geographical swing position between the other two relationships. A form of fictive kinship in which one party assumed for his lifetime a "parent role" (*oyabun*) and the other a "child role" (*kobun*), patron–client ties could be used to buttress *honke–bunke* relationships that had grown weaker and more impersonal over the generations or to smooth the "rough edges" of landlord–tenant relationships by adding an explicitly affective dimension. They could also exist independently, linking individuals and households that had no connection other than residence in the same community. Although found throughout the countryside (and indeed throughout Japanese society), patron–client ties appear to have been particularly numerous and important in the mountainous dis-

7 For a detailed discussion of *dōzoku*, see Chie Nakane, *Kinship and Economic Organization in Rural Japan* (London: University of London, Athlone Press, 1967), pp. 82–123.
8 More information on landlords may be found in Ann Waswo, *Japanese Landlords: The Decline of a Rural Elite* (Berkeley and Los Angeles: University of California Press, 1977).

tricts of central Japan, where *dōzoku* lineage organizations and large landlords were both relatively rare.[9]

Despite the differences among them, all three relationships shared certain key characteristics. Each was vertically structured, linking a superior and inferior household, and each imposed a wide-ranging set of obligations on the parties to it. Whether tenant, *kobun* or *bunke*, the inferior party owed loyal service to the superior. He and the members of his household were expected to pay their respects at the master's house and perform any necessary chores during the New Year's and midsummer Obon celebrations and whenever a wedding, birth, or funeral took place. They also helped with the annual cleanup of the master's house and storerooms and with the planting and harvesting of his crops. Superiors, in turn, were obligated by custom to extend benevolent protection to their dependents: to lend them food, money, or tools as necessary, to intercede on their behalf whenever they had difficulties with other hamlet residents or with the government, and to find employment and marriage partners for their children.[10]

A final similarity, which stemmed from the other two, was the impact of these relationships on the community. By functioning as a kind of insurance policy for low-status households, all three relationships helped make tolerable their poverty and political impotence. At the same time, opportunities for contact among low-status households were minimized. Dependent households knew and probably cared more about their masters' affairs than about those of other households like their own; their peers were, at best, competitors for the benefits that the elite dispensed. Instead of leading to class consciousness, then, potentially disruptive tensions within the hamlet were defused, and the gemeinschaft was maintained.

This was, of course, a net result. Solidarity did not occur spontaneously or endure on its own. It was achieved by human agency and needed constantly to be renewed by the same means. That proved possible, by and large, in the late nineteenth century. Disputes of one sort or another erupted, to be sure, but almost none of them challenged the rural social order. Perceived imperfections in the system, not the system itself, were at issue. Harmony appears to have been regarded as a necessary and therefore desirable state, requiring a de-

9 See John W. Bennett and Iwao Ishino, *Paternalism in the Japanese Economy: Anthropological Studies in Oyabun–Kobun Patterns* (Minneapolis: University of Minnesota Press, 1963), esp. chap. 9; also Nakane, *Kinship and Economic Organization*, pp. 123–32.

10 For a brief discussion of these reciprocal obligations, as reported by Ariga Kizaemon and Tsuchiya Takao in the 1930s, see Bennett and Ishino, *Paternalism*, pp. 214–21.

gree of self-restraint and compromise to attain. Nor was inequality seriously questioned by rural residents. That some should be rich and some poor, some powerful and some powerless was considered natural, if indeed it was consciously considered at all. Although the farmers continued to believe in the desirability of harmony, the assumption that inequality was natural did not survive the turn of the century.

## THE ROOTS OF PROTEST

It will come as no surprise to those who study rural societies elsewhere in the world that scholars have disagreed about rural social change in early twentieth-century Japan. As is usually the case, it is not the events themselves that are at issue but, rather, what caused them and what they signified. Because these disagreements continue today and because my own views lie more or less squarely in the revisionist camp, some attention to the main lines of controversy is in order.

Scholars generally agree that farmers became increasingly restive after the turn of the century and that their restiveness was manifested during the Taishō and early Shōwa eras in two streams of protest. One was the tenant farmer movement, which led to the creation of tenant unions and a marked increase in tenancy disputes after World War I. The other was *nōhonshugi,* literally "agriculture-is-the-base-ism," a loosely defined set of ideas extolling farming as a way of life and the rural community as a model for the nation as a whole. Institutionally more amorphous than the tenant movement, *nōhonshugi* nonetheless spawned a variety of organizations, ranging from community-based farm cooperatives to a few blood brotherhoods plotting acts of political terror.

Until the early 1960s, scholars treated these two streams of protest separately, itself an act of interpretation. The tenant movement represented the kindling of revolutionary energy at the rice-roots level of Japanese society. Impoverished by high rents in kind, tenant farmers spontaneously turned against their landlords and began demanding both rent reductions and more secure cultivating rights. Because the landlords were the rural elite, their position buttressed by the civil code and their interests protected by government officials, tenant protests at the local level constituted the beginnings of an assault on the Japanese state itself. But proper guidance from the organized left was required for that assault to develop. When labor union leaders and Marxist intellectuals began providing that guidance in the 1920s, the government became alarmed. By means of outright repression and various social and economic policies designed to divert the tenant farmers' attention from the true causes of their plight, the government succeeded in ending the threat that the tenant movement posed.[11]

If the tenant movement represented to these scholars what might have been, *nōhonshugi* represented reality: the emergence of emperor-centered ultranationalism and Japanese fascism. Using the school system, the military reservist associations, and the organs of local government, the state sought in the early 1900s to shore up the status quo in the countryside and to prevent the development of class consciousness that had accompanied industrialization in the West. Its efforts met with an enthusiastic response from the rural elite. Landlords found themselves threatened by the development of capitalism in the nation as a whole and by tenant militancy in the countryside. Eagerly they championed frugality, hard work, and communal solidarity as a means of defending themselves against both developments. The economic problems facing farmers as industrialization progressed and the tensions within rural communities heightened were to be resolved by reaffirming the importance of agriculture and the time-honored conventions of rural life.

Mobilized initially by the state itself and functioning as agents of state policy, these local *nōhonshugi* advocates began to pursue an independent course in the mid-1920s as economic conditions in the countryside worsened. From a profarming position they veered steadily toward antiurbanism and anticapitalism. By the early 1930s they were providing both funding and manpower to the right-wing secret societies whose plans for a Shōwa restoration represented "fascism from below" and whose activities provided the Japanese military with the opportunity to intervene in politics and establish "fascism from above."[12]

Since the early 1960s this portrayal of developments in the Japanese countryside has been challenged by a younger generation of scholars. Proceeding chronologically in their reappraisal of this view and only recently grappling with the 1930s, these scholars have yet to produce a comprehensive new paradigm for rural Japanese history from 1900 to 1945 and have indeed found much to disagree about among themselves. Nonetheless, their research to date has yielded a significantly different interpretation of the roots of rural protest movements than

11 A representative example of this interpretation of the tenant movement is Nōmin undōshi kenkyūkai, ed., *Nihon nōmin undōshi* (Tokyo: Tōyō keizai shinpōsha, 1961).

12 For examples of this interpretation, see Barrington Moore, Jr., *Social Origins of Dictatorship and Democracy: Lord and Peasant in the Making of the Modern World* (Boston: Beacon Press, 1967), chap. 5, pp. 291–313; Maruyama Masao, *Thought and Behaviour in Modern Japanese Politics*, expanded ed., ed. Ivan Morris (London: Oxford University Press, 1969), chap. 2.

that set forth in the older literature and contains the outlines, albeit still shadowy at best, of a substantially different view of the relationship between the countryside and the Japanese government in the 1930s.[13]

Instead of a clear-cut distinction between the tenant movement and *nōhonshugi*, revisionist scholars stress the similarities between the two. In their initial phases, both reflected the interests and aspirations of the middling stratum of rural society. It was the more affluent among the tenant farmers, those who cultivated larger than average holdings and/or owned land of their own, who organized rent strikes and unions in the 1910s and 1920s. Similarly, it was the owner-cultivators and substantial owner-tenants who most enthusiastically supported pro-farming *nōhonshugi* during the same period. Both were essentially petty-bourgeois movements, and both sought political representation as well as economic betterment for their members.

In addition to relocating the personnel involved in both streams of protest at the center rather than at the two extremes of rural society, the revisionists have also redefined the role of the state and presented a much more complex portrayal of the relationship between the rural population and the central government than appears in the earlier literature. Although concerned about the development of class consciousness in Japan, government officials did not see shoring up the status quo in the countryside as the solution. Rather than relying solely on the rural elite as intermediaries between ordinary farmers and the state as in the past, they sought in the early 1900s to establish direct influence over all rural residents.[14] At the same time they renewed their assault on the vestiges of hamlet autonomy. These two initiatives produced contradictory effects that were to bedevil government policymakers for the next three decades and generate a marked degree of rivalry among the government ministries concerned with rural affairs.

On the one hand, efforts to establish direct influence over the rural population encouraged centrifugal forces within rural communities. New, centrally administered organizations such as the youth groups

13 Far too diverse in their methods and emphases to be termed a *school*, these scholars include Kano Masanao, Kinbara Samon, Mori Takemaro, Nakamura Masanori, Nishida Yoshiaki, Suzuki Masazuki, Yasuda Tsuneo, and Yui Masaomi.

14 The timing of this shift is one of the points on which revisionist scholars disagree, with some arguing for the years immediately after the Russo-Japanese War of 1904–5 and others for the 1920s or 1930s. Their disagreement arises in large part from the differing criteria they apply: Although the former want to elucidate the beginnings of what was actually a gradual process, the latter seek its culmination.

and reservist associations that were established after the Russo-Japanese War provided opportunities for local leadership to farmers of no more than modest wealth and lineage. Far from opposing the state, these newly mobilized farmers identified with its goals, and that identification emboldened them to challenge the economic and political prerogatives of the local elites.

On the other hand, and more or less simultaneously, the government's efforts to eliminate the vestiges of hamlet autonomy encouraged centripetal forces in rural communities. Faced with an external threat, hamlet residents from all strata rallied in defense of their communities and sought means to protect themselves from the administrative villages into which they were being more fully absorbed and ultimately from the state that demanded that absorption. These centripetal forces did not overwhelm the centrifugal forces producing local conflict but coexisted with them in a complicated and highly volatile mix. The same farmers who identified with the state when seeking internal reform of their communities were suspicious of the state when considering their communities in relation to Japanese society as a whole. Nationalism became firmly rooted in the countryside, but the desire for communal autonomy persisted.

What about the 1930s? It is difficult to generalize about an ongoing scholarly process, but what seems to concern revisionist scholars most is not political terrorism, which they regard as a minor facet of *nōhonshugi*, but the impact of the Shōwa depression on all Japanese farmers. Another and related characteristic is these scholars' concern with local history. Unlike their predecessors who emphasized the ideas and policies of government officials, agricultural experts, and intellectuals of both the right and left, revisionist scholars focus on ordinary farmers and rural communities and seek to define what happened from the inside out. In their research, they emphasize how farmers perceived their problems and the actual implementation and impact of government policies.

In accounting for the demise of the tenant movement in the early Shōwa period, revisionist scholars, though not ignoring the role of government countermeasures, stress the errors of the movement's leftist leaders, in particular their insistence on the need to protest Japanese imperialism. However crucial such protests may have been to the Comintern and the revolutionary cause in Japan, they did not appeal to significant numbers of Japanese tenant farmers or seem relevant to the economic problems foremost in their lives. In contrast with the left, local advocates of *nōhonshugi* won increasing support among farmers of all strata precisely because they offered solutions to those economic problems. It was their practical program of cooperatives and credit associations, not their ideology, that accounted for their growing popularity and local influence.

That influence, in turn, alarmed the central government which, on both military and political grounds, could not tolerate the existence of popular movements that it did not control. From the early 1930s onward, and especially after the outbreak of war with China in 1937, government officials sought with renewed determination to achieve command of the countryside. To what extent they succeeded is a question on which no consensus has yet emerged – hence my earlier reference to the "shadowy outlines" of a new view of the relationship between the countryside and the government during these crucial years. I suspect, however, that one prominent feature of that view will be the extent to which officials had to compromise with popular sentiment in order to achieve a modicum of the spiritual and material mobilization they sought. Far from imposing controls as they saw fit, they found it necessary to build on aspirations for economic equality and hamlet autonomy in designing a new social order for the countryside. If the results had anything to do with fascism, a term revisionists employ with considerable wariness,[15] it was fascism from within, not that from above.

Assuming, as I am inclined to do, that the revisionist model of rural social change is the more accurate, what then were the common roots of tenant militancy and *nōhonshugi?* What caused restiveness among middling farmers in the early 1900s and motivated them to question the existing distribution of wealth and power? Two factors appear to have been of crucial importance: (1) the acquisition by middling farmers of skills and experiences that formerly had been monopolized by the rural elite and (2) the accumulation among those same farmers of new and newly perceived economic grievances to which the rural elite seemed reluctant to attend.

## *The impact of education and conscription*

Not all *gōnō* had been literate during the Tokugawa period, but virtually all literate farmers had been *gōnō*. Their ability to read and write, which in some cases extended to mastery of the Confucian classics and the formal epistolary style favored by the warrior class, had served as

15 The term almost always appears in quotation marks and often only at the beginning and end of their published work.

one of the bases of their local political power: Only they could comprehend the regulations issued by the domain officials and keep the records that the officials demanded. With the institution of compulsory elementary education in the 1870s as part of a projected nationwide system of primary, secondary, and university education, what had earlier been a perquisite of wealth became a universal obligation. The *gōnō* monopoly on literacy began to erode.

One must be careful not to exaggerate the speed with which literacy spread among the rural population or, for that matter, the degree of literacy that was achieved by products of the new educational system. As Koji Taira observed, elementary education was compulsory but not free in Meiji Japan. In addition to the indirect burden of local taxes, parents who sent their children to school had to bear a direct burden of tuition payments and miscellaneous fees for books and other school supplies. They also had to do without whatever labor their children supplied to the household economy. As a result, access to education remained sensitive to prevailing economic conditions and to levels of family income. Although enrollment figures rose from 27 percent of all school-age boys and girls in 1873 to 98 percent in 1910, the actual school attendance rate did not reach 50 percent until 1900. In 1910 it stood at 85 percent. That was a national average. The available data indicate that adult literacy rates, and hence school attendance rates half a generation earlier, were lower in the countryside than in the cities of Japan throughout the late nineteenth and early twentieth centuries. For the majority of both urban and rural Japanese, moreover, completion of the required four years of elementary schooling (six years after 1907) marked the end of formal education. In that length of time they had mastered *kana*, the phonetic symbols that could be used to "spell" Japanese words, but at best they had learned only a few hundred of the thousands of Chinese characters used in the written language. Their ability to read and write was thus seriously constrained.[16]

Despite these caveats, and in some respects because of them, the impact of education on rural society cannot be ignored. Merely by setting foot in Meiji classrooms, youngsters found themselves in an achievement-oriented setting in which performance, not wealth or lineage, counted. As Ronald Dore pointed out, "bows and respect language did not come too easily to the tenant who had been top of his class at the primary school while the landlord occupied only a mid-

16 Koji Taira, "Education and Literacy in Meiji Japan: An Interpretation," *Explorations in Economic History* 8 (July 1971): 371–94.

dling place."[17] Nor was the level of literacy that could be achieved in four years of schooling totally without utility, even though it fell far short of that required for full command of the written language. Owing to the widespread use during the Meiji period of *furigana* (*kana* symbols attached to characters to indicate their reading) in newspapers, magazines, and all but the most esoteric books, mastery of *kana* was a far more useful skill than it is today and provided access to a wide range of reading matter.

The available evidence suggests that ordinary farmers began putting that skill to use around the turn of the century. Newspapers, formerly confined to cities and towns, penetrated the countryside in increasing numbers. In their wake came magazines and journals tailored to the interests and abilities of the rural population.[18] Farmers also used writing more in their daily lives: in keeping accounts, in codifying hamlet rules, and in drafting bylaws for local agricultural societies.[19] Of particular significance was the drafting of bylaws for the tenant unions that were organized at this time. Only a few examples of these bylaws were uncovered in the 1920s when the government began to monitor tenant unrest: Whether or not more had been written, we do not know. Those extant are impressive documents, containing as many as thirty-six articles and specifying detailed rules and procedures.[20] Some of the terminology and general provisions may have been borrowed from the bylaws of agricultural societies or the landlord associations that had come into being in the 1880s and 1890s, but it was borrowing with a purpose and indicative of the drafters' more-than-marginal literacy. The latter, it appears, were relatively prosperous owner-tenants, that is, individuals from the middling, not the poorest, stratum of rural society.

That middling farmers generally had more years of schooling and hence higher levels of literacy than poor farmers did seems a reasonable conclusion. Precisely because elementary education imposed a direct financial burden on households, the children of middling farmers had greater access to it than did the children of poor farmers. Data from Okayama Prefecture in the early 1920s indicate what in all proba-

17 Ronald Dore, *Land Reform in Japan* (London: Oxford University Press, 1959), p. 54.

18 Suzuki Masayuki, "Taishōki nōmin seiji shisō no ichi sokumen – jō," *Nihonshi kenkyū*, no. 173 (January 1977): 7.

19 For the text of a set of hamlet rules drafted in 1897, see Kawamura Nozomu, "Kosaku sōgi ki ni okeru sonraku taisei," *Sonraku shakai kenkyū nenpō*, no. 7 (1960): 119–20.

20 Two examples of tenant union bylaws, one dated 1896 and the other 1902, may be found in Shimaneken nōrinbu, nōchi kaitakuka, ed., *Shimane ken nōchi kaikakushi* (Hirata: Shimane ken, 1959), pp. 118–20.

bility was true earlier in the century as well. For 5,583 members of the farm households surveyed, exposure to education varied directly with economic status: 70 percent of the roughly 950 individuals over the age of eight and under the age of forty who had no schooling whatsoever came from landless tenant households; 25 percent of those who had no schooling came from tenant households that also owned land; and only 5 percent came from owner-cultivator households that also leased land.[21]

Nor was the education of middling farmers confined to primary schools. Although they were much less likely than were their more affluent neighbors to prepare for university, they appear to have composed the majority of enrollees in second-class agricultural schools. Unlike first-class agricultural schools, which required five years beyond the compulsory level to complete and qualified their graduates for work in agricultural experiment stations and prefectural farm bureaus, these schools offered a three-year course of study in practical farming methods, and most graduates returned to their communities to farm the family land. Tuition was beyond the reach of poor farm households, but not excessive for substantial owner-tenants or typical owner-cultivators. When the number of such vocational schools increased after the Russo-Japanese War, even more sons of middling farm families gained access to the training they provided.[22] In the course of that training they learned how to read agricultural handbooks and technical journals as well as how to raise more or better crops.

Like education, military service provided rural Japanese with new skills and experiences. Many conscripts caught their first glimpses of city life when they reported to their prefectural capitals for final physical examinations. Once enrolled in basic training, they found themselves living in Western-style barracks equipped with such newfangled items as heating stoves, indoor plumbing, beds, and, after the turn of the century, electricity. They wore trousers, tunics, and sturdy boots for the first time in their lives and learned to use and maintain a variety of weapons and machinery. In the classroom they learned the rudiments of battle tactics, surveying, and map reading. Those whose ability to read and write was found deficient took supplementary literacy courses.[23]

21 Ōta Toshie, "Kosakunō kaikyū no keizaiteki shakaiteki jōtai," *Sangyō kumiai,* no. 261 (1927): pp. 84, 102–3. 22 Suzuki, "Taishō ki nōmin seiji shisō," p. 21.

23 Nobutaka Ike, "War and Modernization," in *Political Development in Modern Japan,* ed. Robert Ward (Princeton, N.J.: Princeton University Press, 1968), pp. 194–204; Keizō Shibusawa, comp. and ed., *Japanese Life and Culture in the Meiji Era,* trans. Charles S. Terry, vol. 5 of *Japanese Culture in the Meiji Era* (Tokyo: Ōbunsha, 1958), pp. 303–9.

Of even more significance in the long run were the ideological training that the conscripts received and the opportunities that they discovered to acquire a status honor different from that prevailing in the countryside. Both contributed to the restiveness among ordinary farmers when they returned to their communities and found themselves once again in a milieu demanding subordination and deference to the local elite.

Since the conservative, or Japanist, reaction of the 1880s,[24] lessons in traditional Japanese ethics had become a fundamental part of the curriculum in primary schools. From the 1890s onward a copy of the Imperial Rescript on Education was kept as a treasured possession in every school and read to the student body each year at a formal assembly. That these and related efforts to promote loyalty to the emperor and to his government had an impact on the hearts and minds of young children cannot be denied. But just as the level of literacy that youngsters could achieve during their basic schooling was limited, so too was the level, and the intensity, of the national consciousness they could acquire. The indoctrination that conscripts received in the army and navy brought into sharper focus the passive identification with the state and the vague conception of themselves as the emperor's subjects that they had acquired in school. An imperial rescript they were required to memorize told them that their first and foremost duty as soldiers and sailors was loyalty to the emperor.[25] They must be physically strong, morally pure, and willing to sacrifice their lives to fulfill that duty. If they were loyal, the army and navy would be strong, and the nation would be protected from evil. The reiteration of these and other themes in the camp lecture hall and on the parade ground induced a strong emotional response from the conscripts and instilled in them a much more active sense of nationalism than they had possessed previously.

At the same time, military service gave the conscripts opportunities for personal advancement. To an even greater extent than students in primary school, conscripts in the military were evaluated on the basis of their own ability and achievement. Those who excelled at soldiering tasks were rewarded with additional training and promotions. Those who could not pass muster languished as ordinary privates. Actual

24 For a brief discussion of the impact of this conservative reaction on educational policy, see Herbert Passin, *Society and Education in Japan* (New York: Columbia University Press, 1965), chap. 4, esp. pp. 62–91.

25 An English translation of "The Rescript to Soldiers and Sailors" may be found in Hillis Lory, *Japan's Military Masters: The Army in Japanese Life* (Westport, Conn.: Greenwood Press, 1943), pp. 239–45.

warfare added a new dimension to this process, for under the harsh and life-threatening conditions of the battlefield, one had the chance not only to win a promotion but also to become a hero.

We know relatively little about the heroes and ordinary soldiers of the Sino-Japanese War. Nor do we know much about the reception given those from rural backgrounds when they returned home.[26] Because the conflict was relatively small and victory for Japan was relatively easy, the impact of the war on rural society probably was fleeting at most. But that was not the case with the Russo-Japanese War a decade later. More than one million men were mobilized for combat, and even those in the inactive reserves were called up for some form of war service. Casualties totaled eighty thousand dead and roughly thirty thousand wounded in some twenty months of fighting. Port Arthur, which the Japanese had taken in a single day in 1894, withstood almost six months of full-scale attack.

Virtually every rural community in the country was affected by the war. Land taxes and excise taxes on such daily necessities as sugar and soy sauce were raised temporarily to help finance the war effort. Thousands of horses were requisitioned. Severe labor shortages were created as young and middle-aged men left the fields to report for duty. In many hamlets at least one family learned that a father or a son would not be coming back. Because of the immediacy of the conflict to their own lives, people were anxious for news from the front, and the government, anxious to maintain popular acceptance of what was becoming a costly venture, saw to it that news was supplied in as palatable a form as possible.[27] For the first time in Japanese history and with a wrenching abruptness, rural residents throughout the country followed developments abroad with the same intense concern that they had always lavished on their crops.

It was during the Russo-Japanese War that the custom of sending off newly conscripted soldiers with a feast and a parade through the hamlet first became widespread. Returning soldiers were welcomed with joy, relief, and copious amounts of saké. Those who returned with decorations for valor were especially well received, for in being honored by the emperor, they brought particular honor to their communities. For example, to have received the Order of the Golden Kite,

26 For a discussion of the heroes of the Sino-Japanese War, at least one of whom may have been fictitious, see Donald Keene, "The Sino-Japanese War of 1894–95 and Its Cultural Effects on Japan," in *Tradition and Modernization in Japanese Culture*, ed. Donald H. Shively (Princeton, N.J.: Princeton University Press, 1971), pp. 143–54.

27 Shunpei Okamoto, *The Japanese Oligarchy and the Russo-Japanese War* (New York: Columbia University Press, 1970), chap. 5.

in recognition of his exceptional bravery during the assault on Hill 203, brought immediate fame to a soldier from Saitama Prefecture named Yanagishita Iyasaburō. Significantly he came from a family of owner-tenants, and his military exploits provided him with a degree of prestige within his community that no one of his background had possessed before. Suddenly he was a man whose opinions counted. He merited a place of honor at hamlet gatherings and respectful treatment from one and all.[28]

Yanagishita's bravery may have been exceptional, but the hero's welcome he received was not. As a conflict that proved the importance of small, mobile infantry units, the Russo-Japanese War made heroes out of many ordinary soldiers and noncommissioned officers. Here and there throughout the country, farmers from middling and poor families returned home as celebrities and with ranks and decorations superior to those of their more affluent and powerful neighbors. Owners of less than an acre were corporals, whereas owners of ten acres were privates first-class. A day laborer held a seventh-class medal, but his hamlet chief, a substantial landowner, had only an eighth-class medal.[29]

Once the victory celebrations ended, tensions began to surface. Except at occasional ceremonies and drill exercises for those in the active reserves, these war heroes were expected to behave in ways befitting their inferior economic status. The available evidence suggests that they, and indeed many veterans of more ordinary rank and merit, found this difficult. Having developed a sense of their own competence and experienced the giving as well as the taking of orders, they did not like being told what to do by men whose authority was based on an accident of birth. Having seen something of the world beyond the hamlet and served the imperial cause in a foreign war, they found many aspects of rural life stultifying and much of the labor involved in farming demeaning. Some younger sons who returned from the war surveyed the menial jobs that were available to them at home and promptly reenlisted in the army. Their older brothers, lacking that option because they had to help cultivate the family land, had to deal with their discontent at home. Reports of veterans' "rowdy behavior" began to reach officials in country and prefectural governments within a few months of the war's end. Many veterans were "squandering" their separation bonuses on drinking parties and "fancy" clothing; a few even physically assaulted local officials.[30]

28 Suzuki Masayuki, "Nichi-Rō sengo no nōson mondai no tenkai," *Rekishigaku kenkyū*, 1974 special issue, p. 156. 29 Ibid., pp. 155–6. 30 Ibid., pp. 152, 155–6.

The antisocial behavior that regional authorities perceived among the war veterans was a major reason that in 1906 and 1907 they began urging the village mayors to establish local veterans' clubs (*gun'yūkai*). These clubs in turn served as the basis for the military reservist associations that were established after 1910, and as we shall shortly see, what had begun as efforts under the direction of the local elite to reintegrate soldiers into civilian life became, under the auspices of the Imperial Japanese Army, a means by which nonelite farmers could acquire local status and influence.

### *Economic grievances*

Unfortunately we lack a clear and unambiguous picture of macroeconomic trends in the agricultural sector between 1880 and 1920. Economists now agree that Japanese government data for the late nineteenth century underreport both acreages under cultivation and crop yields. They do not agree on what if anything should be done about that underreporting, and so the result is a lively and continuing controversy about estimates of subsequent growth rates in output, which must use as their basis those nineteenth-century data – as they exist or are corrected in one of a number of ways. Unless one is a party to this controversy, it is impossible to state with conviction whether (1) Japan began the Meiji era with high levels of agricultural output and thereafter its growth rates averaged only 1 percent annually, barely keeping pace with increases in population; (2) output was fairly low in early Meiji, increased at an annual rate of 2.8 percent between 1880 and 1905, and then slowed to 2.1 percent, for an average annual increase of 2.4 percent for the entire period, more than twice the rate of population growth; or (3) output increased at an average annual rate of only 2 percent for the entire period, with the rate accelerating, not declining, after 1905.

During the 1960s these rather different estimates of agricultural growth rates generated two radically different models of overall economic development in Japan in the Meiji and early Taishō eras: the prerequisite growth model, derived from the first estimate, in which increases in agricultural output preceded industrialization, and the concurrent growth model, derived from the second and third estimates, in which increases in agricultural output at a level substantially above increases in population accompanied industrialization. More recently, a third model, in which agricultural output expanded both before and during industrialization, has been put forward.[31]

The general mood observable in the Japanese countryside during the first three decades of the Meiji period lends support to the second and third models, but not to the first. Farmers did not behave as if their best years were behind them. On the contrary, they appeared to believe that the future held brighter prospects than the past did. There was a better circulation of information about seeds and pest control, mounting enthusiasm for new crops and improved tools, and a myriad of small-scale projects undertaken to improve irrigation and drainage. Government officials encouraged all this activity, but it seems unlikely that the farmers were merely responding to their exhortations. In addition to being skeptical of the government's motives, the farmers were intensely pragmatic. They needed tangible evidence that their productivity could be increased, and if the scattered examples we have of individuals who achieved significantly greater yields on the same plots of land are at all indicative of a more widespread phenomenon, then that evidence must have been available to them.[32]

To say that there was a mood of vitality rather than stasis in the Meiji countryside is not to say that the agricultural sector bore without strain its appointed role as a source of capital for industrialization. As Harry Oshima noted,[33] the land tax imposed a heavy burden on farmers, and very little of the revenues generated by the countryside was returned to it in the form of public spending. Because the taxes were also regressive, only the large landowners were likely to be left with resources over and above consumption needs to invest in farm improvements. As a result, agricultural growth was lower than it could have been and less uniformly diffused throughout the country than if

31 For an exposition of the prerequisite growth model, see James I. Nakamura, *Agricultural Production and the Economic Development of Japan 1873–1922* (Princeton, N.J.: Princeton University Press, 1966). For the concurrent growth model, see Bruce F. Johnston, "The Japanese 'Model' of Agricultural Development: Its Relevance to Developing Nations," in *Agriculture and Economic Growth: Japan's Experience*, ed. Kazushi Ohkawa et al. (Tokyo and Princeton, N.J.: Tokyo University Press and Princeton University Press, 1969), pp. 58–102; and Yujirō Hayami and Saburō Yamada, "Agricultural Productivity and the Beginning of Industrialization," in *Agriculture and Economic Growth*, pp. 105–29. For the third model, see Minami Ryōshin, *Nihon no keizai hatten* (Tokyo: Tōyō keizai shinpōsha, 1981), pp. 59–63.

32 For one example, see Nishida Yoshiaki, "Reisai nōkōsei to jinushiteki tochi shoyū: Niigata ken ichi tezukuri jinushi no bunseki," *Hitotsubashi ronsō* 63 (1970): 631–47; also Ronald Dore, "Agricultural Improvement in Japan, 1870–1890," *Economic Development and Cultural Change* 9 (October 1960): 69–91.

33 Harry T. Oshima, "Meiji Fiscal Policy and Economic Progress," in *The State and Economic Enterprise in Japan*, ed. William W. Lockwood (Princeton, N.J.: Princeton University Press, 1965), pp. 353–89.

public funds had been more readily available to finance improvements. Nor were the gains evenly distributed among the farmers. Although some prospered, others became enmeshed in poverty, losing their land because of tax arrears and, in some cases, selling their daughters into prostitution and pawning even their cooking utensils and bedding.

Although there were impoverished victims of change in almost every community, they were not the focal point of restiveness among the farmers after the turn of the century or the instigators of early assaults on the country's economic and political inequality. In Japan as elsewhere, it was those who had benefited in some measure from change and whose expectations of what was possible in life had risen who first challenged the status quo.

Throughout the late nineteenth century, increases in agricultural output had been brought about primarily by labor-intensive means. When modest investments of capital were required, the local elite generally was willing and able to supply the needed funds: noblesse oblige, self-interest, and affluence combined to make them champions of agricultural improvement.[34] Eventually, however, what Gustav Ranis termed the "slack" in the agricultural sector was used up, and inexpensive measures no longer yielded significant increases in productivity. Large-scale land and irrigation projects that transcended individual holdings and the boundaries of individual hamlets were now required.[35]

This situation did not develop at the same time everywhere, but in regions where incentives had been strong and "slack recovery" pursued vigorously, an impasse was apparent by the early 1900s. On the one hand, both the willingness and the ability of the local elite to sponsor agricultural improvements had declined. Only the very few "giant" landowners in the country had the wherewithal to fund improvements on the larger scale that now was necessary, and many of them, newly aware of the more attractive investment opportunities that existed in commerce and manufacturing, were reluctant to do so. Typical members of the elite, although wealthier than ordinary farmers, did not control adequate land or capital on their own; nor did

34 Waswo, *Japanese Landlords*, chap. 3; see also Ronald Dore, "The Meiji Landlord: Good or Bad?" *Journal of Asian Studies* 18 (May 1959): 434–55.

35 Gustav Ranis, "The Financing of Japanese Economic Development," in *Agriculture and Economic Growth*, pp. 37–57. "Slack" in the Japanese case consisted of excess workers on the land and reserves of productivity in the land. The former could be withdrawn and applied elsewhere without reducing agricultural output; the latter could be tapped by means of improved techniques of farming and small injections of capital.

mechanisms exist for planning improvements that involved more than a single community or for pooling local resources to finance them.[36] On the other hand, the ordinary farmers' interest in agricultural improvement had intensified. Unable to afford the risks of experimentation a few decades earlier, they had watched their more affluent neighbors try out new techniques and seen them reap impressive gains. Having followed suit on their own holdings, they too had achieved higher yields and become determined to discover yet other ways of increasing output. Soon after their determination crystallized, however, gains became more difficult to achieve.

Even if the concept had existed at the time, "slack" would have meant nothing to these farmers. As they diagnosed the situation, the key obstacle they faced was in gaining more control over their own time and labor. Every day they donated to the community – and as many as thirty days a year might be required of every able-bodied male and female – was a day during which they had to neglect their own livelihoods. If the number of days could have been reduced to the minimum or if wages could have been paid for the services performed, they would have been better off. Similarly, they began to calculate the costs of performing services for their superiors. Were the meals and simple gifts they received adequate compensation for the hours they spent working at the master's house? Did not the custom of planting the master's rice paddies first mean that their own harvests would be delayed and subject to greater risk from an early frost?

No matter how cogent their reasoning, ordinary farmers found it exceedingly difficult to change the prevailing customs. As underlings they could petition for reforms, but the elite still controlled decision making in the community. Ordinary farmers lacked the leverage to compel a discussion of, much less action on, the issues that concerned them. It was at this point that the central government became more concerned about rural affairs. One consequence of that concern and the policies that flowed from it was that ordinary farmers began to acquire the leverage they needed to press for the changes they desired.

### *Government intervention in rural affairs*

After the turn of the century and especially in the years immediately following the Russo-Japanese War, government policy toward the

36 See Waswo, *Japanese Landlords*, chap. 4, for a discussion of changes in the attitudes and behavior of the landed elite around 1900.

countryside shifted markedly. In place of the laissez-faire that had characterized policy since the Restoration, officials in both the civil and military bureaucracies now championed an active "social policy" and sought to link rural communities and rural residents more closely to the state. They did so for various reasons, chief among them being their recognition that national unity was imperative if Japan was to maintain its newly achieved status as a first-class country and their awareness that the economic burdens that that status imposed on the population made social and political conflict more likely. Though not ignoring Japan's cities, these officials concluded that the countryside merited attention first and foremost, for it was there that 80 percent of the population was located, inhabiting an environment as yet relatively untouched by "the baneful influences of civilization."[37] By promoting the countryside's material and spiritual health, they believed that a bulwark against social disruption could be maintained.

The new policies emanating from Tokyo at this time can be divided into three general categories: those concerned with agricultural improvement, those concerned with strengthening the villages' fiscal and administrative capabilities, and those concerned with organizing – or, more accurately, reorganizing – rural residents into a series of local associations under bureaucratic control.

## *Agricultural improvement*

Throughout the early Meiji period, government officials remained relatively untroubled by reports of distress sales of arable land or increasing tenancy. These were seen as the natural consequences of granting private property rights to the people. Good farmers would survive, and inspired by the ownership of the land they cultivated, they would produce more and better crops.

But by the late 1890s few officials retained such a sanguine view of laissez-faire. Japan was on the verge of becoming a net importer of food; urban brokers were complaining vociferously about the deteriorating quality of the rice they handled; and a few groups such as Ōi Kentarō's Debtors' Party had enjoyed brief successes in organizing the rural poor. There was discussion, but nothing more, about the need

37 Tokonami Takejirō, chief of the Home Ministry's Local Affairs Bureau, quoted in Kenneth Pyle, "The Technology of Japanese Nationalism," *Journal of Asian Studies* 33 (November 1973): 58. For a discussion of the evolution of an active social policy in Japan, see Kenneth Pyle, "Advantages of Followership: German Economics and Japanese Bureaucrats, 1890–1925," *Journal of Japanese Studies* 1 (Autumn 1974): 127–64.

for a law to regulate landlord–tenant relations and to slow the concentration of land ownership. Instead, officials focused on measures to raise the volume and quality of agricultural output.

The Land Adjustment Law of 1899 provided guidelines and modest subsidies for large-scale projects to regularize the contours of paddy fields and improve irrigation. The Agricultural Association Law enacted in the same year established a nationwide organization for the dissemination of information about farming, and in 1905 all farm households were required to join its local branches. The Industrial Cooperatives Law of 1900 encouraged the formation of rural credit, marketing, and consumer cooperatives.

A substantial restructuring of the vocational education system in agriculture was begun in 1903. In that year some 1,000 agricultural continuation schools were established throughout the country, each offering to young farmers a few months of practical training. In 1905 the number of first-class agricultural schools, whose curricula emphasized agricultural economics and law, was cut in half, and some fifty second-class agricultural schools with curricula emphasizing farming methods were established in their place. By 1912 the number of agricultural continuation schools had risen to over 5,500, and the number of second-class agricultural schools to 164. Finally, by the same year, some thirty prefectures had established quality standards and inspection programs for locally grown rice.[38]

## *Policy toward the villages*

Although various officials in the Ministry of Agriculture and Commerce had recommended tapping the farmers' hamlet-based loyalties to help promote agricultural development, their suggestions were ignored by the more powerful Home Ministry.[39] To the latter, the continued importance of rural hamlets to their residents hindered economic progress and threatened national unity. One of the primary goals of what became known as the Local Improvement Movement (*Chihō kairyō undō*), in which the Home Ministry played a leading role, was the destruction of hamlet "parochialism." Administrative villages were to be transformed from unruly combinations of hamlets

38 A detailed discussion of the evolution of agricultural policy may be found in Ogura Takekazu, *Tochi rippō no shiteki kōsatsu* (Tokyo: Nōrinshō nōgyō sōgō kenkyūjo, 1951).

39 Numerous writers refer to the rivalry between the Home Ministry and the Ministry of Agriculture and Commerce (after 1924, the Ministry of Agriculture and Forestry) over both jurisdiction and policy, but as yet no thorough study of that rivalry has been published.

into meaningful centers of local life. At the same time the inward-focused spirit of hamlet solidarity was to be replaced by a new ethos of "community in service to the nation" (*kokka no tame no kyōdōtai*).[40]

Of the steps taken in the early 1900s to achieve these ends, four were significant. First, a renewed effort was begun in 1906 to transfer the hamlets' communal property to village control. The hamlets owned three times the acreage owned by villages and four-fifths of all public forestland, which was seen both as a source of fiscal weakness in village government, which forced local officials to delegate many of their assigned tasks to the hamlets, and as a barrier to the efficient exploitation of resources in developing local farming and side employment. Second, a campaign was launched to eliminate as many independent hamlet shrines as possible, on the grounds that they embodied purely local concerns, and to replace them with one central shrine in each village. The latter would not only serve as a symbol of the corporate life of the village as a whole but would also represent, by means of ceremonial and administrative linkages with national shrines in the emerging system of state Shinto, the ideal relationship between local communities and the state.

Third, in conjunction with the decision made in 1907 to increase the number of years of compulsory education from four to six, a program of local school construction was initiated, which required consolidating the elementary schools in some villages into a single communitywide school and expanding the existing village schools to accommodate additional students. Fourth, a series of programs were established between 1900 and 1911 to acquaint such village-level officials as mayors, vice-mayors, and village assembly members with national goals and the critical role of the villages in achieving them.

### *Policy toward the rural population*

Equally vital to the Home Ministry's vision of local improvement were extending government control over a variety of autonomous local organizations and nurturing in them activities that served the national interest. With the importance of the home front demonstrated by the Russo-Japanese War, the Imperial Army joined in the effort, and the result by 1915 was a system of dovetailing rural associations that left only infants and old people free from bureaucratic guidance.

The agricultural associations mentioned earlier were one example.

40 Hirata Tōsuke, then home minister, quoted in Pyle, "Technology," pp. 61–2.

The local farming societies that had been formed under private auspices in numerous communities in the 1880s and 1890s were coopted into the Imperial Agricultural Association. Given legal recognition by the government and provided with a measure of financial support, what had once been voluntary associations became channels for the implementation of state economic policy. The Hōtoku movement (Hōtokukai), based on the teachings of Ninomiya Sontoku (1787–1856) and advocating diligence, thrift, and mutual aid among farmers, was another example. Seeing a useful basis for promoting rural harmony in the Hōtoku societies that were scattered throughout the Kantō region, the Home Ministry established the Central Hōtokukai in 1906 and began encouraging the formation of local branches throughout the country.

A third example was the extension of government supervision over local youth organizations. According to Kano Masanao, the young men's groups (*wakamonogumi*) that had existed in most rural communities during the Tokugawa period began to be revived in the mid-1890s. As in the past, their geographical basis was the "natural village," now the hamlet of a larger administrative village, and their functions related to everyday life – patrol duty to protect the community from fire or theft, labor services on communal land, and participation in festivals at the local shrine. Encouraged by community leaders as a means of combating the adolescents' "city fever" – the desire unleashed by the Restoration to rise in the world that proved harder to fulfill as time went by – these groups struck the Home Ministry as both threatening in their present form and potentially useful. On the one hand, they were manifestations of hamlet parochialism and hence to be combated. On the other hand, they encouraged the traditional virtues of hard work and service and therefore might function as a basis for a new nation-centered collective spirit.

From 1905 onward, the Home Ministry, working in concert with the Ministry of Education, sought to tame these organizations and mobilize them in the local improvement cause. They were given a new, more modern name – the *seinendan,* or youth corps. Hamlet-based groups were combined into villagewide associations, their headquarters in the village school and their adult leadership provided by the village mayor and school principal. The focus of their activities shifted from service as an end in itself to the study of ethics and physical conditioning. Finally an effort was made to eliminate regional diversity in the ages of the youth corps members. Until 1915 the youths in one village might belong between the ages of fifteen and twenty-five, whereas those in another village were eligible from fourteen to thirty. Thereafter membership was to begin when a young man finished elementary school and to end when he reached the age of twenty.[41]

Significantly, twenty was the age at which young men became eligible for conscription. After completing active duty, they were then expected to join their local reservist association (*zaigō gunjinkai*) and participate in its activities until they reached the age of forty. In part to provide continued military training for former conscripts but more to nurture among the people the patriotism and unity deemed essential to victory in total war, army leaders organized the Imperial Military Reservist Association in 1910, and by incorporating the veterans' clubs established after the Russo-Japanese War, they quickly created a nationwide network of local branches. The latter soon developed a close relationship with local youth groups and schoolchildren, organizing calisthenics and basic drill exercises for the one and patriotic ceremonies for the other. The disaster relief they provided and other services they performed made them increasingly important groups within their communities.[42]

In evaluating the impact of these government initiatives, one must be careful to distinguish between intention and effect. Clearly, the bureaucrats sought to mobilize the countryside in ways that served the national interest, but their success was neither immediate nor complete. Some of their policies – the transfer of hamlet property to the villages, for example – aroused such intense local opposition that a retreat from full implementation became necessary.[43] Others, such as rice inspection, solved one problem while at the same time creating another, in this case, discord between landlords and tenants over the extent of rent payments in approved grades of rice.[44]

Just as the Home Ministry was forced to moderate its campaign

41 Kano Masanao, "Meiji kōki ni okeru kokumin soshikika no katei," *Shikan* no. 69 (March 1964): pp. 38–42. By 1913 over 29,000 *seinendan* had been established, with a total membership of roughly 3 million.

42 For discussion of the activities of these local reservist associations, see Richard J. Smethurst, *A Social Basis for Prewar Japanese Militarism: The Army and the Rural Community* (Berkeley and Los Angeles: University of California Press, 1974), chaps. 2, 5. Smethurst also describes the mobilization of rural women.

43 For examples of direct and indirect resistance to shrine mergers, see Wilbur M. Fridell, *Japanese Shrine Mergers 1906–12: State Shinto Moves to the Grassroots* (Tokyo: Sophia University Press, 1973), chap. 4.

44 For an example of the discord caused by rice inspection, see Ann Waswo, "In Search of Equity: Japanese Tenant Unions in the 1920s," in *Conflict in Modern Japanese History: The Neglected Tradition*, ed. Tetsuo Najita and J. Victor Koschmann (Princeton, N.J.: Princeton University Press, 1982), pp. 381–2.

against hamlet property or risk alienating the very people whose allegiance it sought to gain, so too it had to stop short of the full absorption of hamlet-based associations into village units. Although all the organizations that the ministry encouraged were headquartered locally in the administrative village, each was further divided into hamlet branches, for only in that way could virtually universal participation be ensured. Formal leadership might be provided by the mayor or another member of the local elite, but a large share of the organization's day-to-day business was conducted within the hamlets by hamlet representatives.

Logical though it might have been for members of the elite to serve as the hamlets' representatives, such was not always the case – or so it appears from what is admittedly sketchy evidence. First, the elite had already been drawn into village and regional politics and had less time for purely local affairs. Second, there were other, nonelite residents of the hamlet who might well be better qualified to serve in what were, after all, functionally specific posts: graduates of agricultural schools who could explain land improvement projects to other farmers, for example, or former soldiers who could teach hamlet youths the elements of drill. Opportunities existed, in short, for ordinary farmers to assume leadership positions, however modest, within their communities.

The policy of the army toward leadership of local reservist associations – implemented, one suspects, in defiance of the Home Ministry – brought those opportunities even more within the reach of ordinary farmers. Until the formation of the Imperial Military Reservist Association in 1910, the army generally had followed the Home Ministry's "line" and recognized local veterans' clubs that were headed by village mayors and other elite individuals. After 1910, however, a radically new line was pursued. Membership in local reservist associations was confined to former soldiers (automatically excluding a number of prominent men who had managed to avoid conscription earlier in their careers), and leadership became tied to service rank: The senior local reservists were to run the organization and be responsible not to village officials but to their regional military commander and beyond him to the Army Ministry in Tokyo.

At a stroke a new, rigorously achievement-based standard for local influence was established that, in principle, was independent of the Home Ministry's local government system. Sons of the local elite might still qualify for leadership posts in the reservist associations, of course: With the middle-school educations that their familial wealth permitted them, they could enroll in reserve officers' training programs and return home with ranks superior to those of ordinary conscripts. The significant point was that wealth and lineage in themselves no longer guaranteed local power. Here and there throughout the country, farmers of inferior socioeconomic status found themselves thrust into leadership positions, acquiring in the process a visibility and a voice in local affairs that formerly had been denied them.[45]

## THE TENANT MOVEMENT

Farmers of middling and lower status became most visible and vocal through their participation in the tenant movement that began in the late 1910s. Until then their situation was very much as Mori Giichi described it in his *The Strategy and Tactics of Tenancy Disputes:*

> Back when tenant rents were called "tribute rice" and demands for rent reductions were called "requests for relief" all dealings with landlords were carried out on an individual basis. And the "relief" that was granted was meagre at best. When crops were poor owing to storms or drought or insect damage, tenant farmers would meet in secret just before the harvest and discuss how much relief to request. On the basis of the amount they agreed to, each tenant would then go off separately to negotiate with his landlords. To put it more accurately, he would set out to appeal to them.[46]

Mori's detailed but simply written handbook, published in 1928 as the fruit of his years of experience as a union organizer in Gifu Prefecture, appeared too late to be of much practical use – for reasons to be discussed later, the tenant movement was already on the wane by then – but it serves nonetheless as eloquent testimony to the changes in behavior and attitudes among tenant farmers that had occurred during the previous decade.

Until roughly 1917–18, conditions had indeed been as Mori described them. If tenant farmers met with one another at all, they did so furtively, late on moonless nights in the hamlet forest or some other secluded place. To be seen together was considered illicit, an offense against their community as well as against their landlords. With the latter they behaved with the utmost deference, appearing alone at the side entrances to their houses whenever they had an appeal to make and using humble language. Only a dire emergency justified such a visit, and tenants counted on their landlords' benevolence to rescue them from it. When rebuffed consistently by any one landlord, they

45 Suzuki, "Nichi-Ro sengo no nōson mondai," pp. 152–4, 156.
46 Mori Giichi, *Kosaku sōgi senjutsu* (Tokyo: Hakuyōsha, 1928), pp. 4–5.

were likely to conclude that he lacked "humanity" and so would join in such emotionally charged acts of revenge against him as not participating in the parade to send his son off to the conscription physical or behaving "unpleasantly" at weddings or funerals in his family.[47] By the mid-1920s, however, both the form and the underlying ideology of collective action among tenant farmers had been dramatically transformed. Tenant farmers met openly as members of formally constituted tenant unions. They insisted on collective bargaining with local landlords and presented demands, not appeals. Instead of expressive acts of revenge, they engaged in a wide range of goal-oriented activities designed to improve their lives and livelihoods.

Mori had much to say about how tenant farmers should pursue their interests, and both the illustrations he provided and the evidence available from other sources indicate that he was generalizing from current practices, not indulging in speculation. Violent behavior of any sort was to be avoided, not only because it might provoke intervention by the police, but also, and more importantly, because it was bound to create bitterness among people who had to go on living as neighbors. Of far greater utility in both the short and long term were an invincible united front among local tenants and well-orchestrated, even-tempered pressure on their adversaries.

The former required clearly defined regulations governing membership in (and resignation from) the union, a strike fund to enable members to survive a protracted dispute, and a variety of activities ranging from study groups to parades to bolster morale. The latter required knowledge and careful planning. Tenant farmers needed to be familiar with the laws affecting landlord–tenant relations and with those provisions they could exploit to their own advantage. Among them were that landlords had to deal with the bargaining agents to whom tenants had given duly executed powers of attorney and that once landlords had agreed to formal mediation of a dispute, they could not seek an injunction to keep tenants from harvesting standing crops. In addition, tenants needed accurate data on yields and farming costs to back up the case they would make, and so they had to wait for the right moment to present their demands. Immediately after the harvest was an ideal time, as tenants then were in possession of the crop and could use the leverage that gave them to negotiate with the more moderate or financially hard-pressed among local landlords for a

47 For examples of such behavior, see Nōmin undōshi Kenkyū-kai, ed., *Nihon nōmin undōshi*, pp. 663, 667, 818.

precedent-setting agreement. (Or, as a tenant union in Yamanashi Prefecture demonstrated, they could sell the crop, deposit the proceeds in the bank, and use the interest to finance a protracted dispute.) If the harvest were poor, so much the better, for at such a time, tenants enjoyed both a customary and a legal right to rent reductions. As long as they could prove that yields were significantly below normal – hence the need for accurate data – they could delay their rent payments with impunity until they won concessions on rent levels or some other matter of concern to them. As a newly coined saying put it: "In tenancy one profits more in lean years."[48]

That saying was but one manifestation of the new attitudes among tenant farmers. Poverty was no longer their fate, but the product of circumstances that they had the power to change. Nor was the economics of tenancy their sole concern. Unions pressed for the extension of voting and officeholding rights in hamlet governments to all hamlet residents regardless of property ownership, for less regressive local taxes, for the payment of wages at prevailing rates for communal labor, and for greater input by ordinary farmers in local agricultural associations and cooperatives. To reduce their reliance on the local elite, some unions bought their own funeral supplies and banquet dishes and established their own funds for aid in the event of natural disasters. Although they employed some of the old language of deference – using, for example, the word *petition* (*tangan*) which retained connotations of "a plea for mercy" – the unions devised a new, affectively neutral vocabulary for describing rents and landlord–tenant relations.[49]

### *The proximate causes of the tenant movement*

Although the impact of such programs as universal education and conscription is clearly discernible in the tenant movement – in the unions' reliance on the written word, for example, and in the tenants' ability to carry out detailed "battle plans" – one still must account for the timing of the movement's appearance. Why did tenant militancy materialize precisely when it did? In that connection, where tenant militancy materialized provides some useful clues.

Like peasant movements elsewhere in the world, the tenant move-

48 "*Kosaku ni wa fusaku no ho ga toku datta*," quoted in Takahashi Iichiro and Shirakawa Kiyoshi, eds., *Nōchi kaikaku to jinushi sei* (Tokyo: Ochanomizu shobō, 1955), p. 97.

49 Mori Giichi, *Kosaku sōgi*, esp. chaps. 2, 3; Waswo, "In Search of Equity," pp. 368–406 passim.

ment in Japan had a definite regional character. According to the most widely accepted statistics, 173 tenant unions had existed in 1917.[50] By 1923 their number had increased to 1,530 and membership totaled 163,931. In that year 64 percent of all unions and 55 percent of all union members were to be found in the sixteen prefectures of the Kinki and Chūbu regions of Honshu, which contained only 35 percent of the nation's tenant farmers. Four years later in 1927 when the number of unions had increased to 4,582 and membership had reached a peak of 365,322, a similar degree of regional concentration remained: 55 percent of all unions and 50 percent of all union members were to be found in the Kinki and Chūbu. What was true of the unions was true of the disputes as well. Of the 24,988 disputes recorded between 1917 and 1931, 14,494, or 58 percent of the total number, took place in the Kinki and Chūbu.[51]

The crucial distinction between these two regions and the rest of the country was economic. It was in the Kinki and Chūbu that "slack recovery" had been most vigorously pursued during the Meiji era. High yields per acre (for rice, roughly 40 percent greater than in northeastern Japan) had been achieved by 1907, and thereafter additional increases were slight. It was not simply that a relatively stable "pie" induced conflict among those claiming portions of it, however.

50 One might expect that a phenomenon occurring a few decades ago in a "first-rate" country whose leaders were sensitive to social conflict would be enumerated, but that is not the case. One encounters not a paucity of quantitative data but a profusion of mutually incompatible and apparently irreconcilable tallies, each prepared by a different government agency. By rough count there are four sets of statistics regarding tenant unions and tenancy disputes for every part of the country: (1) those compiled by the Home Ministry, whose police and social affairs bureaus were responsible for reporting to the government on rural unrest only until 1924 but who continued to do so on their own thereafter; (2) those compiled by the Agricultural Affairs Bureau of the newly reorganized Ministry of Agriculture and Forestry, formerly the Ministry of Agriculture and Commerce, which became the statistics of record after 1924 and which consistently reported more unions and more disputes than did the Home Ministry; (3) those issued retrospectively by the Labor Administration Bureau of the Ministry of Public Welfare, newly established in 1936, which differed somewhat less from the Home Ministry's tabulations than from those of the Ministry of Agriculture and Forestry; and (4) those compiled by various officials in each of the country's forty-seven prefectures, which concerned developments within their jurisdictions alone and which, on the basis of the scattered examples that have been uncovered to date, were almost always greater than those figures reported to and/or accepted by the central government bureaus to which they reported. (Gifu police reported to the Home Ministry in 1922 that 22 tenancy disputes had occurred in the prefecture the previous year; in 1932, the same agency acknowledged that 475 disputes had occurred in 1921. Similarly, prefectural records show that 120 disputes occurred in Saitama Prefecture in 1922, although the Ministry of Agriculture and Forestry statistics list only 57.) In this discussion I use the Ministry of Agriculture and Forestry data.

51 The Kinki region consists of Osaka, Kyoto, Shiga, Hyōgo, Nara, Wakayama, and Mie prefectures. The Chūbu region consists of Niigata, Ishikawa, Fukui, Nagano, Yamanashi, Shizuoka, Gifu, and Aichi prefectures. For a more detailed discussion of the regional character of tenant unrest, see Waswo, *Japanese Landlords*, chap. 5.

Of greater importance was the commercialization of all aspects of farming that accompanied the increased output. By the Taishō era, farmers throughout the Kinki and Chūbu led the nation in their use of fertilizer (roughly half of it purchased, not "home grown") and of draft animals for plowing and other farming tasks. Although landlords had supplied most of the rice sold commercially during earlier decades and continued to do so elsewhere in the country, by 1920 farm operators in the Kinki and Chūbu were heavily involved in the rice market, delivering roughly 50 percent by value of all the rice traded.[52]

Tenant farmers in the two regions were not excluded from these developments or from the risks they entailed. Because rents generally did not keep pace with increases in yields, they found themselves with more of the crop at their disposal. For some, especially those with small holdings, the increment was not substantial. If they sold any rice at all, it was out of an urgent need for cash at year's end when prices generally were lowest; the little they had sold of necessity they then usually had to buy back the next summer, when prices were higher, for their own food supply. For a significant minority of tenant farmers, however, involvement in commercial production was both quantitatively and qualitatively different. Those whose holdings had been (or gradually became) larger than average might well possess a substantial marketable surplus – in some cases on the order of sixty to seventy bales of rice – after deducting rents and basic food supply from their harvest. Unlike small-scale tenants whose involvement in the marketplace was marginal at best, these tenants deliberately and systematically engaged in commercial farming. They grew rice and other crops with the intention of selling as much of their output as possible, regarded outlays for fertilizer as investments in future profits, and timed their deliveries to market to take advantage of seasonal price increases.[53]

By mid-Taishō and to a degree not evident elsewhere in the country, there was a marked polarization of the tenant farming population in the Kinki and Chūbu areas. At one extreme was a shrinking but still large group of tenants who cultivated no more than an acre of land and struggled to wrest a hand-to-mouth existence from farming. At the

52 Nishida Yoshiaki, "Nōmin undō no hatten to jinushi sei," in *Iwanami kōza Nihon rekishi* (Tokyo: Iwanami shoten, 1975), vol. 18, p. 163.

53 The best account of these two classes of tenant farmers is found in Nishida Yoshiaki, "Shonō keiei no hatten to kosaku sōgi," *Tochi seido shigaku*, no. 38 (1968): pp. 24–41. For a detailed account of the difficulties that even substantial landlords faced in maximizing profits from rice sales, see Matsumoto Hiroshi, "Meiji Taishō ki ni okeru jinushi no beikoku hanbai ni tsuite," *Hitotsubashi ronsō* 60 (November 1968): 547–65.

other was a small but expanding group of tenants and owner-tenants who cultivated at least two acres of land and viewed farming as a profit-making enterprise. The tenant movement was the joint product of these two disparate groups, each supplying an essential ingredient. The initiative to establish local unions and the leadership of those unions came almost without exception from the ranks of upwardly mobile, profit-oriented tenants. But the sheer numbers that made the unions effective were supplied by small, economically distressed tenants.

The question then is, what brought together these two groups of tenants in the years after 1917? The Russian Revolution figures prominently in some of the literature on the subject, as does the Allied victory in World War I, the proclamation of the right of farmers to organize by the newly established International Labor Organization, and the rise of the Labour Party in Britain, but in my opinion one need hardly look so far afield. Of much greater immediacy and relevance were three successive economic "shocks" occurring in the Taishō era that created a shared, although differently motivated, desire for changes in rent policy among both groups of tenants. A contributing factor, which was related at least vaguely to contemporary events abroad, was the encouragement of the tenants by disaffected urban intellectuals.

The first economic shock was rice inspection. Because the central government had contented itself in the late Meiji with promoting rice inspection but had not specified what the approach to it should be, prefectures came up with a variety of programs, each shaped by the economic conditions and political forces prevailing within that prefecture. In general the earliest programs had focused on "export" rice, that is, on rice destined for sale outside the region of its production. In their formal operation, these programs had made local rice dealers who wished to participate in the export trade responsible for meeting quality standards and precisely for that reason had generated considerable protest from their ranks. At the same time these dealers were able to transfer some of this responsibility to their local clients. If, as was often the case, those clients were landlords, they in turn were able to transfer some of their responsibility to their tenants, principally by requiring them to supply rent rice in the smaller, sturdier bales that the major urban rice merchants preferred. This requirement in turn led to a relatively small number of disputes in the early 1900s in which the tenants demanded, usually but not always successfully, that they receive some sort of compensation for the additional labor and cost of meeting the new baling standards.

In the years following the Russo-Japanese War, however, a new form of rice inspection emerged that generated even more protest from tenant farmers. Some prefectures that had formerly operated export programs began to switch to programs in which all locally produced rice was subject to inspection. Others that had operated no inspection programs to date imposed similarly comprehensive "output" programs from the start. By 1915, sixteen prefectures in central and southwestern Honshū, most of them in the Kinki and Chūbu, had established output inspection, compared with only nine prefectures in the northeast.

Wherever output inspection was established, it was accompanied by efforts by local landlords to impose quality standards on rent rice. A minimally acceptable grade (e.g., third-class rice) would be specified for rents, with penalty payments demanded for rents that did not measure up. This posed problems for both small-scale and larger-scale tenants. For the former, the key difficulty was in producing an adequate volume of acceptable rice. Rice quality varied directly with the inherent quality of the paddy in which it was grown – to cite one obvious factor, a mostly sunny paddy yielded better rice than did a mostly shady paddy – and with the amount of green manure and fertilizer that the cultivator added to enrich the soil and encourage the healthy growth of seedlings. On both scores small-scale tenants were at a disadvantage, as they tended to farm inferior land and were able to afford few if any investments other than labor in improving it or their crops. As a result a high percentage of their yield in any given year was likely to be of inferior, low-grade rice.

For the larger-scale tenants, the key difficulty was quite different. They farmed better land as a rule, produced more than enough good-quality rice to pay their rents, but wanted to sell that rice themselves, as they knew it was worth more in the marketplace. Despite the differences in perceived difficulty, both groups could and did agree that they should resist the landlord's demands. In some communities, tenants objected to the very imposition of quality standards for rent rice. Elsewhere they demanded that the minimally acceptable grade be set lower than the landlords had proposed or that bonuses in either cash or kind be paid when the quality standards were met. Whatever the response, tenants with divergent interests had discovered a common ground for action.[54]

The second shock was delivered by the dramatic increase in rice

54 Nishida, "Nōmin undō," pp. 143–67 passim.

prices during the economic boom induced by World War I. This increase, which had led to the predominantly urban rice riots of 1918 and the fall of the Terauchi government, had also impinged on both groups of tenant farmers and created yet another basis for concerted action. For the majority of small-scale tenants who had to purchase rice for their own consumption during the year, the surge in prices threatened their survival: They could no longer afford to buy even small quantities of rice. For large-scale tenants, the surge in rice prices meant deprivation of another sort. Although they could and did reap greater profits from their own rice sales, they were prevented by the necessity of paying rents in kind from reaping all the profits that they might. They resented that. Accustomed to calculating as rent the cash value of the rice they delivered, they were acutely aware that their landlords, who had contributed little or nothing in the way of "inputs," were about to enjoy a windfall. Both groups of tenants could agree that rent reductions were essential, in the one case to make rice purchases less necessary and in the other to make greater rice sales possible.[55]

The third and final shock was delivered by the sudden end in 1920 to the wartime boom. Crop prices fell sharply and tended to fluctuate unpredictably at lower levels for the next several years. Because the prices of such essential items as salt and soy sauce declined less severely and local tax burdens continued to increase, small-scale tenants experienced little relief. Larger-scale tenants saw their hard-won prosperity threatened. Because raising output to compensate for lower prices was becoming increasingly difficult, their attention focused even more on reducing costs. Both groups could still agree that if rents were lower, their respective problems would be eased.

Of course, agreement between these two groups of tenants had to be hammered out and a strategy for achieving collective goals devised. What is striking about the forging of the tenant movement in Japan is the degree to which the necessary leadership – the engineering of a consensus among people with differing interests – came from within the tenant population. Individuals like Yanagishita Iyasaburō, the hero of Hill 203, had the time and the talent to devote to union leadership as well as the status within his community to be heard by tenants and landlords alike. Yamasaki Toyosada, another owner-tenant who as a youth had memorized much of the legal code, started

55 Nishida, "Shonō keiei," pp. 32–4. The wholesale price of rice in Tokyo increased from ¥ 13 per *koku* (150 kg) in 1915 to roughly ¥ 40 per *koku* in 1917–18.

out by organizing tenants in his own hamlet and eventually established a regional tenant federation in his native Shimane Prefecture. Other dissatisfied tenants observed what was happening in neighboring communities or read about union activities in the newspapers and were inspired to organize unions on their own.[56] It remains true, however, that valuable aid was provided by outsiders.

Some of this aid was relatively casual. A factory worker who had lost his job in the post–World War I depression might return to his native village and talk about his experiences in a labor union or in strikes. Or a lawyer in a nearby city might offer his services to a newly organized tenant union.[57] Other forms of aid were more systematic. From early 1919, inspired by "the trend of the times" abroad and the evidence of popular unrest at home, groups of urban intellectuals and political activists began touring the countryside giving lectures about the need for universal manhood suffrage, the industrial labor movement, and the defects of the tenancy system. In 1922 a number of these reformers met in Kobe to establish the Japan Farmers' Union (Nihon nōmin kumiai, abbreviated Nichinō). By 1925, 957 local tenant unions had affiliated with Nichinō, and the organization claimed a total membership of 72,794 (see Table 11.3). Beset thereafter by disagreements over policy among its urban leaders and a series of schisms and tenuous reunifications, Nichinō never came to direct the course of tenant protest in Japan, as its founders had hoped it would. On a day-to-day basis, however, its field agents gave practical advice to many tenant farmers on managing union affairs and helped them develop effective protest methods. Even nonaffiliated unions used the sample rent agreements and petitions that Nichinō distributed and from time to time requested legal aid from its various regional offices.[58]

### *The waning of the tenant movement*

Tenant militancy did not vanish in Japan, but from the late 1920s onward it began to subside. Some unions disbanded, and those that

56 According to a survey of 215 tenant union leaders in the early 1920s, 196 were local farmers. For more information on Yamasaki Toyosada, see Waswo, "In Search of Equity," pp. 379–406.

57 The lawyer referred to was Tamai Junjirō, second son of one of the largest landlords in Niigata Prefecture. When he offered his services to a tenant union, its leader advised him to "try being a farmer for a while first." Tamai saw the point of that, and for the next three years he farmed some family land in Fukushima. He later missed his father's funeral to help union members fend off efforts to evict them from their land, which made him a revered figure among local farmers. Nōmin undōshi kenkyūkai, ed., *Nihon nōmin undōshi*, pp. 1162–3.

58 More information about Nichinō may be found in George Oakley Totten, III, *The Social Democratic Movement in Prewar Japan* (New Haven, Conn.: Yale University Press, 1966), chap. 13.

TABLE 11.3
*Tenant unions and tenancy disputes, 1920–1941*

| Year | No. of tenant unions | Total no. of members | No. of tenancy disputes | Tenants: Total no. | Tenants: No. per dispute | Landlords: Total no. | Landlords: No. per dispute |
|---|---|---|---|---|---|---|---|
| 1920 | – | – | 408 | 34,605 | 84.8 | 5,236 | 12.8 |
| 1921 | 681 | – | 1,680 | 145,898 | 86.8 | 33,985 | 20.2 |
| 1922 | 1,114 | – | 1,578 | 125,750 | 79.7 | 29,077 | 18.4 |
| 1923 | 1,530 | 163,931 | 1,917 | 134,503 | 70.2 | 31,712 | 16.5 |
| 1924 | 2,337 | 232,125 | 1,532 | 110,920 | 72.4 | 27,223 | 17.8 |
| 1925 | 3,496 | 307,106 | 2,206 | 134,646 | 61.0 | 33,001 | 15.0 |
| 1926 | 3,926 | 346,693 | 2,751 | 151,061 | 54.9 | 39,705 | 14.4 |
| 1927 | 4,582 | 365,332 | 2,052 | 91,336 | 44.5 | 24,136 | 11.8 |
| 1928 | 4,353 | 330,406 | 1,866 | 75,136 | 40.3 | 19,474 | 10.4 |
| 1929 | 4,156 | 315,771 | 2,434 | 81,998 | 33.7 | 23,505 | 9.7 |
| 1930 | 4,208 | 301,436 | 2,478 | 58,565 | 23.6 | 14,159 | 5.7 |
| 1931 | 4,414 | 306,301 | 3,419 | 81,135 | 23.7 | 23,768 | 6.9 |
| 1932 | 4,650 | 296,839 | 3,414 | 61,499 | 18.0 | 16,706 | 4.9 |
| 1933 | 4,810 | 302,736 | 4,000 | 48,073 | 12.0 | 14,312 | 3.6 |
| 1934 | 4,390 | 276,246 | 5,828 | 121,031 | 20.8 | 34,035 | 5.8 |
| 1935 | 4,011 | 242,422 | 6,824 | 113,164 | 16.6 | 28,574 | 4.2 |
| 1936 | 3,915 | 229,209 | 6,804 | 77,187 | 11.3 | 23,293 | 3.4 |
| 1937 | 3,879 | 226,919 | 6,170 | 63,246 | 10.3 | 20,230 | 3.3 |
| 1938 | 3,643 | 217,883 | 4,615 | 52,817 | 11.4 | 15,422 | 3.3 |
| 1939 | 3,509 | 210,208 | 3,578 | 25,904 | 7.2 | 9,065 | 2.5 |
| 1940 | 1,029 | 75,930 | 3,165 | 38,614 | 12.2 | 11,082 | 3.5 |
| 1941 | 294 | 23,595 | 3,308 | 32,289 | 9.8 | 11,037 | 3.3 |

*Source:* Data from Nōmin undōshi kenkyūkai, ed., *Nihon nōmin undōshi* (Tokyo: Tōyō keizai shinpōsha, 1961), pp. 123, 127.

survived lost members fairly steadily. Few new unions were formed.[59] In theory this might have been because the tenants' demands had been fully satisfied, but in actuality that was not the case. Nor had the movement simply been repressed from above. What transpired can best be described as arrested development.

59 Although the number of unions did increase somewhat in the early 1930s (as shown in Table 11.3), in many cases this was the result of the existing county- or villagewide unions being combined into smaller units. In the same years, tenants steadily lost the initiative in disputes. During the 1920s they had usually been able to choose the demands they would make and the moment they would make them. Thereafter, they found themselves increasingly on the defensive. Although disputes increased in number, to a reported total of 47,704 for 1932 to 1941, they declined markedly in scale: from an average of 50 tenants, 13 landlords, and 34 *chō* of land per dispute in the 1920s to an average of 13 tenants, 4 landlords, and 9 *chō* of land in the 1930s. Most disputes in the 1930s were triggered by landlords who sought to evict tenants from their holdings or to obtain payment of rent arrears. This trend was pronounced in the Tōhoku and other outlying regions of the country, where the greatest increases in disputes were reported. Nationwide, the tenants' principal demand in disputes shifted from temporary or permanent rent reductions, the hallmark of disputes launched by tenant unions, to the continuation of tenancy rights or some form of compensation if tenancy were terminated. See Waswo, *Japanese Landlords*, chap. 5. The Tōhoku region consists of Aomori, Iwate, Miyagi, Akita, Yamagata, and Fukushima prefectures.

I do not share the view held by many scholars that the tenant movement had been flawed from its inception by the petty bourgeois character of its local leadership or by its stress on rent reductions. Both strike me as normal attributes for a movement emerging where and when it did. It has generally been the better-off sectors of the peasantry that have provided most of the leaders and activists in peasant movements: the Peasants' Revolt in late fourteenth-century England was no exception, and neither was the tenant movement in Japan. Unlike the former, however, the latter occurred in a modernizing nation-state in which there had been a considerable degree of institutional differentiation and specialization. Had landlords dispensed justice as well as land, or had the government dispensed land as well as justice, tenant concerns might well have been broader – perhaps even revolutionary – from the start. But such was not the case. Like the demands made by the early labor unions, those made by the early tenant unions reflected the specificity of economic and political relationships within the country.[60]

The problem as I see it was that unions did not subsequently develop a rationale for their existence that could survive cyclical changes in economic conditions and sustain broad participation over time. They did not primarily because of the ambivalence of all tenant farmers toward conflict; the inability of the movement's urban allies to comprehend, much less counteract, that ambivalence; and the ability of the government to avoid radicalizing tenant farmers while dealing with rural unrest.

As noted previously, unions were not concerned exclusively with the economics of tenancy, although that was indeed a major focus of their activities. Nor should the unions' demands, whether for rent reductions or local tax reform or voting rights within the hamlet, be construed merely as *ad hoc* reactions to the status quo. Tenants were clearly and in many cases consciously in revolt against the institutions and etiquette of status inequality. They had not, however, rejected communal harmony as an ideal. To justify their disruption of that harmony – to themselves as much as to others – they sought to portray landlords as the "traitors" to the community and themselves as its loyal defenders. As one union activist expressed it, "[W]e have organised unions . . . out of duty and love toward our villages and toward our ancestors who settled those villages originally and brought

60 For criticisms of the petty bourgeois character of the tenant movement, see Kawamura, "Kosaku sōgi ki," p. 132; Takahashi and Shirakawa, *Nōchi kaikaku*, pp. 102–3.

the land under cultivation." Confrontation and conflict were, at most, necessary evils, required to bring landlords to their senses and persuade them "to vow to strive for the benefit and happiness of the entire community."[61]

The very familiarity of the premise on which this justification was based was itself reassuring and helped in the short run overcome many tenants' reluctance to join an organization as alien to the community as a union. Yet recourse to that premise hindered the development of tenant militancy in at least two ways: first, by making it difficult to establish unions that transcended communal boundaries and, second, by leaving union members vulnerable to the equally familiar argument that when the community was threatened from without, as appeared to be the case during the Shōwa depression, everyone must close ranks and work together to protect it.[62]

Some of the local tenant leaders sensed these difficulties and worked to instill a broader sense of class identity among the union members. At first they were aided, indeed inspired, by Nichinō, whose founding proclamation stressed the important role of tenant farmers in feeding the nation, the shared problems that all tenant farmers faced, and the need for gradual but determined efforts to reform the tenancy system. As early as 1923, however, some Nichinō officials were stressing the similarities between tenant farmers and factory workers and urging a political alliance between the two. Within a short time, reflecting the rapidity with which Marxist-Leninist ideas spread among the Japanese intelligentsia, tenant farmers were being portrayed as manual laborers whose interests and aspirations were, or should be, identical to those of the industrial proletariat. Just as workers should be engaged in class struggle, so too should peasants. Conflict was not a necessary evil but a historical necessity.

To tenant farmers who were still cautiously exploring cooperation with their counterparts in adjacent hamlets, the idea that they had anything in common with urban factory workers appeared strange indeed. The idea of prolonged and deadly conflict to the finish, which is what the term "class struggle" meant to them, was frightening. Rather than moderating their rhetoric and embarking on a lower-key educational strategy – admittedly difficult for committed leftists anywhere in the world in the 1920s – Nichinō radicals became even more doctri-

61 The quotation is from an editorial in *Kosakunin,* a newspaper published by a regional tenant union in Shimane Prefecture. See Waswo, "In Search of Equity," pp. 379–406.

62 Throughout the 1920s most of the unions were organized at the hamlet level. Creating viable villagewide unions, much less supravillage unions, proved difficult.

naire. But they seemed not to notice that the poorest tenant farmers – especially those who owned no land of their own and, in that respect, most closely resembled a proletariat – were the most alarmed by their statements and among the first to withdraw from local unions.[63]

Harsh repression, which has inflamed popular passions and invigorated other protest movements, was also lacking in the Japanese case. It is true that a variety of subtle and not-so-subtle steps were taken to impede union activities. Landlords in some communities offered additional land on favorable terms to tenants who quit the local union. Some textile factories refused to hire young girls from districts where tenancy disputes were numerous, depriving their families of an accustomed and much-needed source of income. Prefectural officials dispatched auditors to the countryside to look for misuses of union dues and plainclothes police to gain advance knowledge of union plans. In some prefectures, newspapers were forbidden to publish items about unions and disputes – presumably to keep quiescent tenants from getting ideas – and new public peace regulations were issued making it illegal to boycott funerals or other communal events.[64] But in general both the volume and the intensity of repressive measures directed against tenant farmers appear to have been rather low.

Instead, after a brief period of near panic at signs that the Russian Revolution might be spreading to Japan, the government implemented a series of countermeasures designed to defuse tenant militancy on the one hand and eliminate leftist influence in the countryside on the other. Truly harsh measures were reserved for the leftists, who were arrested in mass roundups of "dangerous elements" in 1928, 1929, and 1931, thereby "sanitizing" the countryside. The tenant farmers themselves had various alternatives to overt protest, some of which tacitly recognized the legitimacy of their grievances. Among the key measures they implemented were (1) the Tenancy Conciliation Law of 1924, which established formal machinery for mediating disputes, (2) the Regulations for the Establishment of Owner-Cultivators, enacted in 1926, which provided low-interest loans to qualified tenant farmers to buy land, and (3) the revision of the Industrial Cooperatives Law of 1900 to encourage communities to cooperate in activities of the sort many unions had advocated.[65]

63 Nōmin undōshi kenkyūkai, ed., *Nihon nōmin undōshi*, p. 109.

64 For examples from Gifu Prefecture, see ibid., pp. 679–70, 689, 692–3; see also Waswo, "In Search of Equity," pp. 407–9.

65 A detailed case study of the ways in which the Regulations for the Establishment of Owner-Cultivators were used to defuse tenant militancy may be found in Nishida Yoshiaki, "Kosaku sōgi no tenkai to jisakunō sōsetsu iji seisaku," *Hitotsubashi ronsō* 60 (November 1968): 524–46.

Less tangibly but no less significantly, government officials spoke out whenever possible on the virtues of harmony and on the unique qualities of the Japanese polity that made class conflict inconceivable. In addition, they quietly urged landlords to grant rent reductions voluntarily before tenants formed unions and began demanding them and encouraged the organization of landlord–tenant conciliation associations to promote mutual understanding and goodwill.[66] Skillful conflict management curtailed the tenant movement.

## NŌHONSHUGI

Basic to the older paradigm of rural social change was the notion of virtually total discontinuity between the "progressive" 1920s and the "fascist" 1930s. Tenant militancy, like the universal manhood suffrage movement and leftist politics, belonged to and helped define the first decade. *Nōhonshugi* belonged to and helped define the second. Its earlier history received relatively little attention. What counted was its role during the 1930s as a direct and indirect instrument of fascist transformation.

In contrast, revisionist scholars assume that "Taishō democracy" and "Shōwa fascism" were related; in their emerging paradigm, the 1920s and 1930s form a continuum that must be considered historically. By starting in early Taishō and working forward, these scholars have shown that at least two distinct varieties of *nōhonshugi* developed among the rural population, one stressing the spiritual revitalization of the countryside and the other stressing both spiritual and economic regeneration. The former, referred to in the literature as traditional *nōhonshugi,* was advanced primarily by large landlords and prevailed in northeastern Japan where those landlords were concentrated. The latter, referred to as petty bourgeois *nōhonshugi,* was advanced by middling farmers elsewhere in the country – that is, by owner-cultivators, some of whom leased out a portion of their land, and substantial owner-tenants. Like the militant tenants, these middling farmers sought to improve their economic, political, and social status.[67] Although less

66 In 1921, there were 85 landlord–tenant conciliation associations; by 1929 they had increased to 1,986, with a total membership (including both landlords and tenants) of 244,943.

67 See, for example, Nakamura Masanori, "Keizai kōsei undō to nōson tōgō," in *Fuashizumu ki no kokka to shakai*, vol. 1: *Shōwa kyōko,* ed. Tokyo daigaku shakai kagaku kenkyūjo (Tokyo: Tokyo daigaku shuppankai, 1978), pp. 197–263. A slightly different version of this essay appears in Nakamura Masanori, *Kindai Nihon jinushi sei shi kenkyū* (Tokyo: Tokyo daigaku shuppankai, 1979), pp. 321–83. Other recent studies include Nishida Yoshiaki, ed., *Shōwa kyōkō ka no nōson shakai undō* (Tokyo: Ochanomizu shobō, 1978); and Yasuda Tsuneo, *Nihon fuashizumu to minshū undō* (Tokyo: Renga shobō shinsha, 1979).

alarming to the government than the tenant movement, petty bourgeois *nōhonshugi* nonetheless did require "management" before its challenge to the Japanese state was successfully defused.

### *The evolution of popular agrarianism*

The roots of petty bourgeois *nōhonshugi,* which for convenience I shall call popular agrarianism, can be traced to the frustrated ambitions of the sons of middling farm families in the years following the Russo-Japanese War. Having learned in elementary school about the achievements of the new Japan, they felt themselves trapped in the old. Civilization and enlightenment belonged to the cities; fame was reserved for statesmen, generals, and captains of industry. A generation earlier – or so it seemed in retrospect – it had been easy for rural youths to go off to the cities and make a career for themselves. Ambition and ability were all that they required. Now the obstacles were great. Only the sons of wealthy farmers could continue as full-time students after completing elementary school and qualifying for university, the new gateway to careers in government and business. The city jobs available to those with only a basic education were menial and poorly paid. One might save enough money to cover tuition at night school, but after working all day delivering newspapers or milk, it was hard to concentrate on studies, and one's health was likely to falter long before one advanced. Yet to stay in the countryside – or to return to it after an unsuccessful attempt at city life – was to consign oneself to an occupation without a future and a life without purpose.

The solution seized by many of these youths was to dedicate themselves to raising the economic and cultural level of the rural communities in which they lived: Unable to escape to the new Japan, they would recreate it at home. This was, to be sure, precisely the kind of dedication officials had hoped to mobilize in the local improvement movement, and for a time, government initiatives and youthful aspirations meshed. Youths from middling farm families attended agricultural continuation schools to learn new farming techniques that would help them solve the economic problems of agriculture. Participation in local youth groups heightened their sense of purpose and gave them an organizational base from which to act while satisfying their desire for cultural enrichment.

Imbued with missionary zeal, these youths were now highly critical of anyone in their age group who was still afflicted with "city fever." Rather than stemming from a negative evaluation of cities, however, their criticisms stemmed from a positive evaluation of agriculture. Once scorned as an occupation without a future, farming was portrayed by youths in early Taishō as "the great foundation of the country" and farmers, as the "mainstays of the people." The countryside did have serious problems, but they were considered to be of local origin: Too much talent had been lost to the cities in the past; the older generation did not understand modern approaches to farming; and most adults were too troubled by the difficulties of earning a living to devote sufficient attention to community affairs. Precisely because they had time, energy, and knowledge, rural youths considered themselves qualified to solve the rural crisis.[68]

By the mid-1920s a new phase in the evolution of popular agrarianism was apparent. Youthful reformers no longer held the countryside at fault for its problems. On the contrary, Japan's cities and industrialists were now blamed for the rural crisis. To solve it, more than rural improvement (*kairyō*) was required; rural reconstruction (*kaizō*) was essential, and that was something farmers had to accomplish for themselves, by their own efforts. Little help could be expected from the government.

A key factor in bringing about this shift in attitudes was the post–World War I depression. It was not simply that general agricultural conditions worsened after 1920. What mattered most was the impact of the depression on the middling farmers who had become more involved in commercial production in recent years and who now, as agricultural prices fell, faced hardship if not ruin. It seemed to them (and to their sons) that they were bearing a greater share of the burden imposed by the depression than were the middlemen with whom they dealt and the merchants who ultimately sold their rice or silk to consumers. Whether this was actually the case is not important. What counted was that farmers believed it. As one indignant youth wrote in 1923:

> We're told that the reason commodity prices are up and foreign trade is slack is that wages are too high, and that's because rice still costs too much. What nerve they have, shifting the blame onto poor workers and farmers while they sit back and rake in all those profits. . . . While farmers struggle to get by, city capitalists live in luxury. . . . There's a lot of talk these days about the dangers of socialism, but no one seems to recognize that capitalism is dangerous too. . . . We must overcome [its] tyranny, which is disrupting the peace of society.[69]

68 Suzuki, "Taishō ki nōmin seiji shisō," pp. 3–6; see also Nakamura, "Keizai kōsei undō," pp. 202–19. 69 Quoted in Suzuki, "Taishō ki nōmin seiji shisō," p. 12.

The government's response to the depression was also found wanting by the middling farmers. When Hara Takashi became prime minister in 1918, he did not do anything to maintain rice prices or to aid rural communities, despite heading a political party, the Seiyūkai, that was widely regarded as a "farmers' party." Instead, his policies appeared to favor industry and commerce. Similarly, the forty-sixth session of the Diet, in 1922–3, although heralded as "the session on rural problems," merely collected petitions from farmers but took no action on the issues – the need for reductions in the land tax, tenancy legislation, aid to small farmers – that those petitions raised.

The belief that Hara and the Diet had "played political games" with farmers' problems brought to the surface the resentment toward the central government that had been brewing for some time among rural youths. In planning the local improvement movement, government officials spoke of the importance of reciprocity in developing national unity and promoting prosperity. Not only did the people need to learn more about their country, but officials also needed to learn more about the people; they had to rely on popular initiatives, not merely on laws and regulations, to bring about the desired change. Quite soon, however, laws and regulations came to dominate the movement, and regional diversity became something to eliminate rather than exploit. From the outset, some preexisting youth groups simply ignored official efforts to recast them in a more uniform mold. Elsewhere, youths who took part in official *seinendan* activities also formed their own clubs to pursue their particular "civilian" interests, whether composing haiku or discussing politics. What had been a ripple in the 1910s became a torrent in the early 1920s, as youths came to believe that no one else really cared about the countryside. Autonomy became their watchword, and the number of independent youth groups and independently organized youth activities multiplied.[70]

A powerful focus for the resentments triggered by the depression and an impulse toward a new vision of the needs of rural society was provided by the Kantō earthquake of 1923. Tokyo – the country's political, economic, and cultural capital, the very embodiment of the new Japan – was devastated by violent tremors and raging fires. It was, a young farmer from Ibaraki Prefecture observed, a fate the city and its wealthy residents deserved:

> Of late the vainglorious striving of [those] city people had reached extremes that caused poor, simple farmers no end of anxiety. With their elegant clothes

70 Ibid., pp. 11–15.

> and their gold teeth, gold rings and gold watch chains, they flitted from one lavish social affair to another. They would go off on trips to the seashore or the mountains to escape the heat . . . and tour the famous sites. But now all that has vanished as if in a dream, consumed by fire, and suddenly they find themselves reduced to misery. It seems that Heaven found it necessary to chastise them with a natural disaster in order to protect the nation.[71]

It also seemed that there was a lesson in the earthquake for the rural youth. As a young man from Nagano Prefecture wrote in November 1923, all the features of modern civilization that youths had long admired flourished in the cities, but what had that civilization wrought but fleeting wealth and power? Did it not depend on the exploitation of others, especially farmers? It made no sense to import urban civilization to the countryside or to yearn for what was basically "deformed and unsound." Farmers needed instead their own "sturdy, popular, regional culture."[72]

That idea seems to have aroused considerable interest, but for the remainder of the 1920s no consensus emerged as to what a proper farmers' culture would be. Some advocated nature as a guiding principle; others toyed with Buddhism; and still others stressed such traditional values as sincerity and frugality. At the same time, despite their bold assertions about the decadence of city life, most youths remained intrigued by urban phenomena. They played baseball with enthusiasm and pooled their resources (or allocated youth group funds) to subscribe to such urban journals as *Chūō kōron* and *Gendai*. The very concept of *kaizō,* which served to distinguish their new, autonomous efforts at rural reform from those directed by the government, appears to have been inspired by a popular urban journal of that name and to have resonated with one of the main currents of contemporary urban liberalism.[73]

By the early 1930s the culminating phase in the evolution of popular agrarianism had been reached. What had begun as the special concern of rural youth was now advanced by middling farmers of riper years. Typically the veterans of earlier efforts to solve the rural crisis, they still blamed urban capitalism for the problems afflicting the countryside, and they still expected little help from the government. As in the

71 Quoted in ibid., p. 13.

72 "*Idainaru kokuminteki chihōteki bunka*"; quoted in Nakamura, "Keizai kōsei undō," pp. 211–12.

73 For a discussion of the popular dimensions of Taishō democracy, see Kano Masanao, *Taishō demokurashii no teiryū* (Tokyo: Nihon hōsō shuppan kyōkai, 1973). The early history of baseball in Japan is discussed in Donald Roden, "Baseball and the Quest for National Dignity in Meiji Japan," *American Historical Review* 85 (June 1980): 511–34.

past they stressed the importance of local efforts by the farmers themselves. But in contrast with the past, they now had a clear idea of the farmers' culture they sought to promote. It would be based on mutual aid, on the revitalization of communal solidarity. That revitalization was the prerequisite of rural economic recovery, the first step in what was now termed *rural regeneration* (*kōsei*).

As Masanori Nakamura demonstrated in his case study of one such advocate of popular agrarianism, Miyashita Itaru, it was not simple nostalgia for the past or desperate groping for a panacea to rural crisis that led to the focus on communal solidarity. On the contrary, some rather shrewd and practical reasoning was involved.

Reiterating an opinion he had held since the early 1920s, Miyashita declared in 1931 that "the suffering of farmers today arises primarily from the expropriation of their [rightful] profits for the benefit of businessmen and industrialists." This occurred directly, when farmers sold their produce to middlemen at prices over which they exercised no control, and indirectly when the tax payments or the postal savings deposits they made were used for urban development. Although a return to total rural self-sufficiency was out of the question, the farmers desperately needed to combat the existing "economic structure of capitalism" and find ways of guaranteeing that the wealth they produced would benefit the countryside.[74]

To think that this could be accomplished by individual action was ridiculous in Miyashita's opinion. A farmer on his own was too vulnerable to bargain successfully with the commercial interests with whom he dealt and impotent to circumvent them. Indeed, the farmers had come to believe in such individualism, which was evidence of the capitalist system's hold over the countryside; it was part of the problem, not part of the solution. Nor was further tinkering by the government with the industrial cooperatives law or the further development of regional marketing facilities the answer, although improvements in both spheres were certainly in order. The essential need was for farmers to organize thoroughly and systematically among themselves to assert their own collective interests in production, credit, and marketing.

The basic unit of that organization, Miyashita asserted, must be the hamlet, the embodiment of the "beautiful rural custom of mutual aid." No other newly created and therefore alien basis would do as well. With the households in each hamlet forming farming associa-

74 Nakamura, "Keizai kōsei undō," pp. 233–4.

tions (*nōji jikkō kumiai*) and all those hamlet associations participating in the village cooperative, the benefits of collective action would be secured. Those benefits, Miyoshita observed on other occasions, were not confined to economic recovery. Not only would farmers be freed from domination by urban capitalists, they also would be freed from the urban idea of the dichotomy of work and pleasure. They would rediscover a truly communal life based on "love and service" in which work provided opportunities for recreation and in which "securing a livelihood was itself a source of contentment."[75]

Like other advocates of popular agrarianism, Miyashita was concerned about an additional urban heresy, the idea of class conflict. While warning against unrealistic expectations that government aid would solve the rural crisis, he also took note of the "fantasy of social revolution." Rural distress had nothing to do with a confrontation between capital and labor, as some misguided people claimed. Rather, it stemmed from the confrontation between capitalists and farmers, "the opposition of city and countryside." To assert the existence of class conflict and encourage revolutionary struggle was "to ignore human nature . . . and rural ways." It was shortsighted and unrealistic to encourage internal squabbling when only harmony and cooperation could "protect the community from capitalism and [free it] from individualism." In national affairs, change had to be effected by political means, but in the villages it could be achieved only by unity.[76]

Like the tenant movement, popular agrarianism had allies and would-be allies outside the countryside. Since early Taishō, for example, journalists who reported on agricultural affairs for urban newspapers and magazines had been urging farmers to pay greater attention to national politics, especially to electing Diet members who were knowledgeable about farming and willing to defend rural interests. In 1922 a group of these journalists organized the Greater Japan Agricultural Policy Association, whose aim was "to study all aspects of agricultural policy in order to promote rural autonomy, the stability of agriculture and the creation of an agrarian culture." In 1923 the association began publishing a monthly journal, *Studies in Agricultural Policy*, and by 1924 it had fifteen thousand members throughout the country, a significant portion of whom, it appears, were middling farmers. One of the association's chief, but ultimately unsuccessful, goals was to establish a nationwide farmers' political party that would represent the country's five and

75 Ibid., pp. 235–7. 76 Ibid., pp. 238–9.

one-half million farm households when universal manhood suffrage went into effect.[77]

There were, in addition, individual champions of *nōhonshugi* who published books and tracts throughout the 1920s and early 1930s, upholding the superiority of rural values and criticizing the politics, economy, and culture of the urban-centered Japanese state. The best known of these advocates of "renovationist agrarianism" were Gondō Seikyō, whose writings supposedly provided the ideological inspiration for the Ketsumeidan incidents of February and March 1932 in which Inoue Junnosuke and Dan Takuma were assassinated, and Tachibana Kōsaburō, who ran an "academy of local patriotism" in Ibaraki Prefecture and who joined with junior officers in the army and navy in the attempted coup d'état of May 15, 1932.[78]

The writings of these groups and individuals certainly helped shape the thought and arguments of the popular agrarianists. It is also likely that acts of right-wing terrorism gave disgruntled farmers the same kind of satisfaction as had the Kantō earthquake earlier.[79] But the fact remains that the taproot of popular agrarianism lay deep in rural soil. Support among farmers for programs of rural regeneration increased in the early 1930s, owing far more to the impact of the Shōwa depression than to external guidance or exhortation.

### *Popular agrarianism and government policy in the 1930s*

The world depression hit Japan early in 1930, a few months after the stock market crash in New York City, and it hit the countryside hardest. The price of silk cocoons, which had been declining since the mid-1920s, dropped by 47 percent between September 1929 and September 1930, leaving in distress the roughly two million farm households who engaged in sericulture. Owing to both a drop in domestic demand and a bumper harvest, rice prices fell sharply in 1930, in some regions to a level below production costs. In 1931, a year of punishing crop failure in northern Honshu and Hokkaido, rice prices were still only slightly higher than they had been in 1916. The prices that farmers received for fruits and vegetables fell precipitously as well. Overall, rural cash incomes fell from an index of 100 in 1926 to 33 in 1931; they

77 Suzuki, "Taishō ki nōmin seiji shisō," pp. 15–18.

78 For a detailed discussion of the thought of Gondō and Tachibana, see Thomas R. H. Havens, *Farm and Nation in Modern Japan: Agrarian Nationalism, 1870–1940* (Princeton, N.J.: Princeton University Press, 1974), chaps. 7–11.

79 For an interesting account of the politicization of reservist and youth groups in late Taishō and early Shōwa, see Yui Masaomi, "Gunbu to kokumin tōgō," in *Shōwa kyōkō*, pp. 149–95.

had recovered only to 44 by 1934. The indebtedness of farm households increased markedly. Making matters worse, thousands of unemployed workers returned to the countryside, their train fare paid by the government in many cases, to wait out the depression with their already hard-pressed relatives.

One consequence of the depression was a surge in the number of tenancy disputes, especially in the Tōhoku region where relatively few disputes had occurred earlier. Not only had the locus of disputes changed, however; so too had their nature. Rather than being the product of a united front among local tenants and aimed at improving the terms of tenancy, most disputes now were triggered by small, cultivating landlords who sought to increase their incomes by evicting a few of their tenants and expanding the acreage they themselves farmed. On the defensive and in most cases lacking allies, tenants resisted as best they could, demanding that their cultivating rights be maintained or that they be compensated in some way for surrendering them.[80]

It was to defuse this conflict and the threat it posed to the communal solidarity on which their influence was based that the large landlords in the Tōhoku called for the spiritual revitalization of the countryside, by which they meant the reemphasis on hard work, frugality, and selfless dedication to duty and the renewal of bonds of interdependence among households of differing status. At the same time, they and landlords elsewhere in the country sent petitions to the Diet calling for price supports for rice, a reduction in the land tax, protection for creditors against defaulted loans, and other measures that reflected their interests as property owners and rentiers.

Another consequence of the depression was a surge in the middling farmers' support of popular agrarianism. During the early months of 1932, in a campaign organized by Gondō Seikyō and Tachibana Kōsaburō, 32,000 farmers in sixteen prefectures signed petitions to the Diet calling for a three-year moratorium on the repayment of farmers' debts, a one-yen-per-*tan* subsidy for the purchase of fertilizer, and substantial appropriations to promote emigration to Manchuria and Mongolia. In a number of communities, farmers turned for local leadership to men like Miyashita Itaru, who was elected mayor of his village at the unusually young age of thirty-five. Anticipating little meaningful assistance from the state and convinced that bold measures were required to solve their problems, the farmers began organizing their own relief efforts.

80 Waswo, *Japanese Landlords*, pp. 127–34.

According to the older paradigm of rural social change, the Japanese government's response to these developments was essentially regressive. What the countryside needed, the literature asserts, was a basic reform of the semifeudal system of land ownership; what it got instead was a series of measures designed to buttress the position of landlords and wealthy farmers and to promote adherence to traditional values among the rural population as a whole. Popular attention was diverted from the injustices of the status quo by an aggressive foreign policy and, ultimately, by war.

A radically different and in many ways more persuasive interpretation of the government's response was offered by Mori Takemaro in a brief essay published in 1971.[81] Though acknowledging that some of the legislation enacted by the Diet in 1932 and 1933 – in particular, laws relating to public works projects and compensation for defaulted loans – did indeed favor the rural elite, Mori sees this as a relatively minor element in what took place during the depression years. In his analysis, the driving force in shaping policy was not the Diet but a group of "new," or "renovationist," bureaucrats who came to dominate the Ministry of Agriculture and Forestry in 1932, following the May 15 incident and the demise of party cabinets. Seizing the initiative from the Home Ministry, they strove not only to stabilize the countryside but also to promote economic rationality in agriculture. One result of the measures they implemented as part of the rural economic rehabilitation program that the ministry launched in 1932 was the restructuring and strengthening of government controls over the rural population. Another was the enhancement of the status and local influence of middling farmers at the expense of the rural elite.

The first step in restructuring and strengthening controls over the rural population was absorbing into the village agricultural cooperatives the mutual aid societies, study groups, and other voluntary associations of farm households that existed at the hamlet or subhamlet level. In what amounted to the abandonment of the Home Ministry's long-standing, albeit unsuccessful, campaign against hamlet "parochialism," the Industrial Cooperatives Law was amended in 1932 to permit these local organizations to reconstitute themselves as legal entities (to be known as agricultural practice associations) and become formal members of cooperatives. In 1933 a five-year campaign was launched

81 Mori Takemaro, "Nihon fuashizumu no keisei to nōson keizai kōsei undō," *Rekishigaku kenkyū*, 1971 special supplement, pp. 135–52.

to encourage the formation of cooperatives in villages where none yet existed; expand the cooperatives' activities to include not only credit and marketing, the focus of most existing cooperatives, but also the purchase of essential producer and consumer goods and the joint use of tools, machinery, and livestock; and promote the membership of all farm households in village cooperatives and the membership of all village cooperatives into higher-level federations to form a comprehensive, nationwide system. To encourage compliance, villages that established cooperatives or expanded the scope of existing cooperatives became eligible for designation as "economic rehabilitation villages" and the receipt of government financial aid.[82]

From its inception, the rural economic rehabilitation program had also aimed at nurturing "mainstay elements" (*nōson chūken jinbutsu*) in the rural population. Rather vaguely defined at first as those endowed with "energetic and enterprising spirits," these mainstay elements subsequently were described as individuals who earned their livelihoods from farming and whose lives and values were rooted in the communities in which they lived. Beginning in 1934, each designated economic rehabilitation village was directed to select twenty or thirty such mainstay farmers as "leaders in the improvement of farm management." Those selected were then sent at government expense to a two-day training course run by the prefectural agricultural association. In addition to instruction in bookkeeping methods, each trainee was required to draft his own personal farm management improvement plan. After returning to their villages, the trainees formed a local society to study farm management, and they were expected to work to disseminate among other farmers in the community what they had learned about modern accounting methods and systematic planning.

Using Haga Village in Gumma Prefecture as a case study, Mori was able to demonstrate that these and related measures led to the creation of a new local power structure based on middle-status farmers. This happened not because the village landlords were weak. On the contrary, there were five landlords who each owned more than 10 *chō*, including two owning more than 50 *chō* each; collectively, they and numerous small landlords owned some 48 percent of the village land. The larger landlords dominated the village politics and, either directly or indirectly, controlled all but one or two of the eight hamlets of which the village was composed. They had played a leading role in the decision reached in 1936 to draft a rehabilitation plan and to apply for

82 By 1940, 81 percent of Japanese villages had been so designated. Ibid., p. 140.

designation as an economic rehabilitation village, and they had expected to control the efforts that resulted. Indeed, when Kobayashi Jirō, the second largest landlord in the village, became managing director of the village cooperative established a short time later, it seemed that their expectations were justified. What they had not realized, however, was that the bureaucrats heading the Ministry of Agriculture and Forestry had inserted a new guiding principle into its agricultural policy: Farm operators, not landowners, were the key to rural recovery. And because that principle was applied over the next few years, landlords found themselves shunted aside.

Although most of the landlords in the village, including the largest among them, farmed a small portion of their land, they did not qualify for nurturing as mainstay elements. Instead, most of those so nurtured in 1937 – the year after Haga achieved designated village status – who subsequently formed its society for the study of farm management, were middling farmers, each cultivating an average of 1.37 *chō* of land. Most numerous, constituting 65 percent of the total, were the owner-tenants, whose ranks included two men who had previously been active in the local tenant movement. They were followed by owner-cultivators, who constituted 27 percent of the total.[83]

Having nurtured these elements, the bureaucrats were not content to let them languish as members of a study group, nor were the farmers themselves content to do so. Instead, they and others of similar status organized agricultural practice associations throughout the village. As Mori demonstrated, considerably more than the reconstitution of existing voluntary associations into legally recognized corporate bodies resulted: The revision of the Industrial Cooperatives Law, which provided that reconstitution, also created an opening for the restructuring of collective activity that middling farmers were able to exploit to their advantage.

At the onset of the depression, most of the existing voluntary associations in Haga were dominated by landlords, and despite nominal concern with the promotion of agricultural improvements, they functioned primarily as mechanisms for regulating tenant rents and resolving landlord–tenant conflicts. Organized by hamletwide units, they replicated the political structure of the village, which landlords also dominated. By 1939 these hamletwide associations had been broken down into nineteen agricultural practice associations whose primary concern

83 The use of rural economic rehabilitation programs to defuse tenant militancy is an issue meriting further exploration.

was production and whose leadership came mostly from the ranks of owner-cultivators and owner-tenants.[84] As formal members of the village cooperative, these associations pressed for and secured the resignation of Kobayashi Jirō as its managing director and the appointment of an individual – as it turned out, a small cultivating landlord – more responsive to the farm operators' needs and interests.

Nor did the restructuring of collective activity, and its concomitant displacement of landlords, consist only in the establishment of agricultural practice associations. Early in 1937, at the behest of the Home Ministry, Haga established new hamlet associations (*burakukai*) throughout the village. As envisioned by the Home Ministry, which since 1935 had been seeking to regain the initiative it had lost to the Ministry of Agriculture and Forestry at the onset of the depression, these associations were to form the lowest link in a revitalized local government system and enable it to strengthen its own controls over the rural population. In addition to tax collection and other administrative tasks, hamlet associations were to concern themselves with local economic development, improvements in sanitation and health, encouragement of frugality, and promotion of patriotism, filial piety, and the spirit of mutual aid among hamlet residents.

In this undertaking, too, an opening existed that the middling farmers were able to use to their advantage. The committee charged with establishing hamlet associations first redrew Haga's administrative map, carving out a total of twenty-nine hamlets in place of the previous eight hamlets. In a few cases, old hamlet boundaries were crossed, for the committee felt no obligation to preserve the village's established administrative divisions. On the contrary, as its report to the prefectural governor observed, the committee's aim had been to delineate communities whose constituent households could cooperate in agricultural production. As was true of agricultural practice associations, the leaders of these new associations generally came from the ranks of owner-cultivators and owner-tenants.[85]

As Mori noted, there was a marked absence of coordination in this period between the Home Ministry and the Ministry of Agriculture and Forestry. The result of their competing initiatives in Haga – and, one assumes, in other villages as well – was a dual structure of hamlet associations on the one hand and agricultural practice associations on

84 According to Mori, 60 percent of the leaders of these agricultural practice associations in 1940 were owner-cultivators, and 30 percent were owner-tenants. Ibid., pp. 146–7.

85 According to Mori, 54 percent were owner-cultivators, and 23 percent were owner-tenants. Ibid., p. 148.

the other, only some of which coincided. (In Haga only twelve of the twenty-nine hamlet associations and nineteen agricultural practice associations had the same territorial base.) At the same time, a dual set of linkages to the state was created, one leading through the village assemblies under the jurisdiction of the Home Ministry and the other through the agricultural cooperatives under the jurisdiction of the Ministry of Agriculture and Forestry. Although we need to know more about why this competition existed and what its consequences were in later years at both the local and national levels, we cannot ignore the significance of what occurred, however untidy and inefficient it may have been. The old order in the countryside was not being shored up; it was being dismantled, and a new order based on middling farmers and smaller-scale collectivities was being created in its place.

For Mori, writing in 1971, it was this dismantling of the old order and the economic rationality on which the new was based that made rural economic rehabilitation part of "the formation of Japanese fascism." Criticizing earlier scholars for their portrayal of fascism as an expression of the unrelievedly "premodern," "feudal," and "irrational" character of Japanese society, he asserted that in Japan, as elsewhere, fascism was the product of modern development and embodied the principles and power of monopoly capitalism.

He also made it clear that he regarded the middling farmers as relatively minor actors in the fascist transformation, as he defined it. The government was both the architect and the engineer of what transpired. Despite sectional squabbling among key ministries, the government was united in its determination to prepare the nation for the total war that monopoly capitalism required. That meant, in regard to the countryside, achieving direct control over agricultural producers. Reeling from the blows delivered by the Shōwa depression, the middling farmers were seduced by the new emphasis on farm operation, as opposed to land ownership, in state agricultural policy. It occurred to them that by relying on the state and demonstrating their loyalty to it, they could expand their own farming operations and elevate themselves within their communities. In the new, smaller collectivities that came into being during the 1930s, which bypassed the older, landlord-dominated collectivities of the Meiji local government system, they rose to the status of petty bosses. In this way they were caught in the net of bureaucratic control.[86]

86 Ibid., p. 151.

Mori's formulation of the broader historical meaning of the rural economic rehabilitation movement persuaded other scholars to reexamine the politics of and the relationship between state and society during the early Shōwa period that continues to this day. Thus far, several lines of inquiry have been pursued: studies of Germany, Italy, France, Britain, and the United States during the 1930s that seek, either explicitly or implicitly, to place developments in Japan in comparative perspective; studies of policymaking within the Japanense government, which seek to identify those designing the solutions to the nation's problems at home and abroad; and studies of specific popular movements and local communities.[87]

At this writing, one can only speculate about what the outcome of these diverse – and, to date, cautious – studies will be. Substantial modifications of Mori's generalizations about the dynamics of Japan's fascist transformation seem to be in the offing. Although subsequent research has confirmed his basic finding that rural regeneration benefited the middling farmers, not the local elite, it has also shown that the trade-off he noted between the interests of those farmers and the government was not as sudden or as lopsided as he construed it. Efforts by the bureaucracy to control the countryside antedated the depression by some two decades, as did the desire among middling farmers for improvement in their economic, political, and social status. Nor do government bureaucrats appear any longer to have been the instigators of attempts at rural regeneration. On the contrary, both the idea and the specific policies to achieve it developed among the middling farmers themselves. What bureaucrats did during the depression years was to ratify, not form, popular aspirations for change.

They did so, I suspect, out of recognition of the challenge of those aspirations to the state, if left to mature on their own. By the early 1930s, popular agrarianism was becoming a secessionist movement that denied not only the legitimacy of urbanism and industrialism but also the utility of relying on the government for help. To bring the middling farmers back to the fold, bureaucrats had to offer them more than petty political roles within their communities. They had to permit the middling farmers to define those communities as they themselves saw fit, that is, to grant them a degree of the autonomy they sought.

87 See, for example, Tokyo daigaku shakaikagaku kenkyūjo, eds., *Fuashizumu ki no kokka to shakai*, 8 vols., esp. vol. 3, *Nachisu keizai to nyuu deiiru;* vol. 4, *Senji Nihon no hōtaisei;* and vol. 5, *Yōroppa no hōtaisei*.

## EPILOGUE

The wartime measures to control inflation, to allocate diminished supplies of fertilizer, and to maximize food production eroded even more rapidly the position of the rural elite than the depression years had done. The Rent Control Order of 1939 froze tenant rents at their current levels and empowered local officials to order rent reductions if necessary. The Staple Food Management Law of 1942 required that all rice be delivered to government warehouses, where it would be purchased at officially determined prices and distributed by government agencies. In addition, bonuses were paid to the actual producers of the rice delivered, to encourage greater output and maximum deliveries to the official market. At first, these bonuses were relatively modest, but they subsequently were raised at a rate far exceeding the increases in official rice prices. In 1945, noncultivating landlords received only ¥ 55 per *koku* for the rice they sold, whereas their tenants, as its producers, received ¥ 245; owner-cultivators received both the official price and the bonus, or ¥ 300 per *koku*. In short, the principle of direct attention to farm operators, including tenant farmers, was now applied openly and comprehensively throughout the nation. Although conscription, and death or injury in Japan's increasingly desperate military campaigns abroad, imposed a heavy burden on the rural population, in purely economic terms and in terms of local political influence, ordinary farmers made significant gains.[88]

Those gains were elaborated and institutionalized by the land reform carried out during the postwar occupation of Japan. Intended primarily as a social and political measure to promote "the revival and strengthening of democratic tendencies, establish respect for the dignity of man, and destroy the economic bondage which has enslaved the Japanese farmer to centuries of feudal oppression,"[89] the land reform imposed greater equity in land ownership on the rural population and greatly reduced income differences among farmers. By 1950 one-third of the total area of arable land in Japan had been transferred from the landlords to the actual cultivators. Absentee landlords, defined as those who lived outside the villages in which their fields were located, lost all their land. Resident landlords were permitted to retain no more than an average of one *chō* of tenanted land (four *chō* in

88 Ogura, *Tochi rippō*, pp. 720–32; Waswo, *Japanese Landlords*, pp. 135–6.

89 As stated in a memorandum dated December 9, 1945, from General Headquarters, Supreme Commander for the Allied Powers. The best account of the land reform in English remains Dore, *Land Reform in Japan*.

Hokkaido), and owner-cultivators were allowed an average upper limit of three *chō* (twelve *chō* in Hokkaido). The latter, who had constituted 31 percent of farm households in 1945, constituted 65 percent in 1950. Tenant farmers who owned no land themselves declined from 28 percent to 5 percent of all farm households. Rent in kind was prohibited; written tenancy contracts were required; and both cash rents and land transfers were rigorously controlled.

Although the land reform did not solve the problems of Japanese agriculture, and indeed may have exacerbated such problems as the diseconomies of small-scale farming, it completed the transformation of rural society that had begun in earnest some five decades earlier. This is not to say that rural social change ceased – far from it – but the changes since 1950 have been fundamentally different.[90] The long struggle of ordinary farmers against the unequal distribution of wealth and power was now over, and the hamlets in which they lived had become, in comparison with the past, communities of economic, social, and political equals. And that these communities remained important to their residents was now a matter more of choice than of necessity.

90 These changes are discussed in Ronald Dore, *Shinohata: A Portrait of a Japanese Village* (London: Lane, 1978); Gail Lee Bernstein, "Women in Rural Japan," in *Women in Changing Japan*, ed. Joyce Lebra et al. (Boulder, Colo.: Westview Press, 1976), pp. 25–49; Robert J. Smith, *Kurusu: The Price of Progress in a Japanese Village, 1951–1975* (Folkestone, Kent: Dawson and Sons, 1978).

CHAPTER 12

# ECONOMIC DEVELOPMENT, LABOR MARKETS, AND INDUSTRIAL RELATIONS IN JAPAN, 1905–1955

## INTRODUCTION

Japan's "first industrial revolution," led by the textile industries (cotton spinning, silk reeling, and fabrics), had lost momentum by about 1910. The outbreak of World War I, however, thrust Japan into the position of supplying the warring nations of Europe with war matériel and supplying the markets of Asia with consumer manufactures. As a result, the Japanese economy began to move toward a "second industrial revolution" with the sudden growth in heavy industries such as metal working, machines and equipment, and shipbuilding. But the economy could not absorb the output of this sector once the overseas demand decreased. When peace was restored and production resumed in Europe, the Japanese economy was forced into a period of retrenchment and reorganization. During a series of adjustments in the 1920s, the economy slowed down its development toward an advanced industrial structure. When this second industrial revolution finally arrived in the 1930s, the leading industries were those heavy industries geared to the requirements of war and imperial expansion overseas.[1] With Japan's defeat in World War II, it was forced back to its prewar economic level, from which it recovered by about 1952 to the "normal" level of the 1930s. By 1955, economic forces and institutional arrangements were well in place to launch a new era in Japanese economic history.

During this half-century of steady but uneven growth, manufacturing plants employing a large number of workers played a central role.

1 In modern Japanese economic history, war appears to have been a conscious endogenous variable in Japan's efforts for modernization. Although it is somewhat disagreeable to think of war in this light, the unprecedented peace for more than thirty years after World War II disposes scholars to be more objective about the role of war in Japan's prewar history. War then can be treated as "an investment" and worked into the economic system on an equal footing in other types of investment. See, for example, Kenneth E. Boulding and Alan H. Gleason, "War As an Investment: The Strange Case of Japan," in *Economic Imperialism*, ed. Kenneth E. Boulding and Tapan Mukerjee (Ann Arbor: The University of Michigan Press, 1972), pp. 240–61.

Employment management in these large enterprises evolved in many directions different from those of other advanced modern capitalist economies. Observers often refer to a "Japanese employment system" characterized by lifetime employment security coupled with pay scales based on length of service and jealously guarded by a labor union that limits its membership to the firm's regular employees. The origin, rationale, and mechanism of the Japanese employment system have created considerable controversy, because the management practices in large firms are not followed in other parts of the labor market in which workers are not guaranteed lifetime employment, in which wages and benefits are not determined strictly by seniority, in which labor is highly mobile, and in which because of the work force's mobility and small scale, unions are difficult to organize. The Japanese employment system thus refers only to practices in large firms; that is, the Japanese labor market is dualistic, with different labor relations styles prevailing in firms of different sizes.

This complex pattern of labor practices is derived from a process of economic differentiation affecting the whole economic system. First came the differentiation between the modern (or capitalist) and premodern (or traditionalist) sectors, and then came differentiation between large and small firms in the modern sector. But this pattern of employment management was also the result of noneconomic factors such as the rise of an indigenous labor movement, the outbreak of industrial conflict, and the intervention of the state in relations between employers and employees. The development of the Japanese employment system, moreover, was neither smooth nor continuous but, rather, was shaped by the ebb and flow of economic growth as well as by the noneconomic accidents of political change, war, expansion, and military defeat in World War II.

## THE DEVELOPMENT OF A WAGE LABOR MARKET

One of the few generally accepted empirical laws of economics is that the agricultural share of the labor force systematically declines in a developing economy and that an increasing proportion of the labor force is allocated to paid employment through a labor market.[2] At the outset of Japan's economic development, much of its labor force was engaged in small-scale agriculture. But by the time the economy had advanced, much of the labor force was employed for pay in occupa-

2 Colin Clark, *The Condition of Economic Progress*, 2nd ed. (London: Macmillan, 1951).

tions other than agriculture. But it is clear that in this transition, there is a rich history of quantitative growth, intersectoral reallocation, and occupational differentiation.

In Japan the small farms persisted. Despite changes in the distribution of landownership, as indicated by the rise of cultivated land under tenancy relative to total arable land, the number of farm households remained roughly constant from the 1870s through the 1930s. Because farm households followed the practice of primogeniture, their first priority was either to produce a son or to find an heir.[3] With the farm's future thus secured, the other (younger) sons were free to find occupations other than agriculture. It was this migration from agriculture that caused the decline in the proportion of Japan's labor force engaged in agriculture.

One way of assessing how extensively Japan's labor market developed is to look at the proportion of the labor force engaged in paid work. In 1872, paid employment is estimated to have been 1.7 percent in the primary sector (agriculture, fishing, and forestry), 33.7 percent in the secondary sector (mining, manufacturing, and construction), and 36.8 percent in the tertiary sector (all other activities). For the economy as a whole, the proportion of the labor force in paid employment was only 8.6 percent, reflecting the preponderance of self-employed farmers.[4] Industrialization had barely begun, and so most nonagricultural employers were owner-operators of small household enterprises employing only a few paid workers. The principal exceptions were government-owned factories and shipyards employing hundreds of workers. In 1872, most wage earners (one-third of the secondary-sector labor force) were not yet part of the modern industrial enterprise represented by the factory system. Rather, they were "premodern" wage labor.

During most of the Meiji period, the nonagricultural labor markets were composed of small unstable businesses, owner-operated busi-

3 The priority of farm households' claims on their own labor force was emphasized by Namiki Masayoshi in a number of controversial articles during the 1950s. One of the earliest of these articles is Namiki Masayoshi, "Nōka jinkō no idō keitai to shūgyō kōzō," in *Nōgyō ni okeru senzai shitsugyō,* ed. Tōbata Seiichi (Tokyo: Nihon Hyōronsha, 1956). Also see Namiki Masayoshi, "Chingin kōzō to nōka rōdōryoku," in *Nihongata chingin kōzō no kenkyū,* ed. Shinohara Miyohei and Funahashi Naomichi (Tokyo: Rōdō hōgaku kenkyūjo, 1961). Best known among Namiki's critics are Ono Akira and Minami Ryoshin. For a review of the controversy between Namiki and Ono and Minami, see Hatai Yoshitaka, "Nōka jinkō idō to keiki hendō," originally published in 1963 and translated as "Business Cycles and the Outflow of Labor from the Agricultural Sector" in *The Labor Market in Japan,* ed. Shunsaku Nishikawa and trans. Ross Mouer (Tokyo: Tokyo University Press, 1980), pp. 5–18.

4 Ishizaki Tadao, "Sangyō kōzō to shūgyō kōzō," in *Wagakuni kanzen koyō no igi to taisaku,* ed. Shōwa dōjinkai (Tokyo: Shōwa dōjinkai, 1957).

nesses, and mobile, low-wage enterprises. Such markets were transient, and the main participants were unspecialized but versatile all-purpose workers. These workers frequently moved in and out of many jobs, working either for themselves or for others. Earlier Japanese writers referred to this social stratum as "lower-class society" (*kasō shakai*).[5] Lower-class workers were not necessarily unskilled, however; a better way of describing them is to say that they were multiskilled.[6] In the language of current development economics, the Meiji labor market was like the "informal sector" of a less developed economy.[7]

It was only after considerable industrialization that sectoral or occupational differences in labor types and management styles became noticeable. The first major attempt at understanding Japan's occupational structure came in 1920 with the first population census. The implementation of the Factory Law of 1911 required the government to know which firms were large enough to be covered by the law and which were small enough to be exempted. The firms covered by the Factory Law had to conform to government standards by which privileges were granted and penalties were imposed. These industries became part of a "formal sector." Because the government was intervening in the labor market in order to protect the workers against employer abuses, occupational hazards, unemployment, and other detriments, this formal sector became a "protected sector." Once this formal, protected sector was established, many new labor market developments differentiated it from the informal, unprotected remainder of the urban labor market.

Qualitative changes in worker types can be discussed from aggregative and semiaggregative labor force data. Table 12.1 shows employment by sector, industry, and status. By 1920, agriculture's share in Japan's total employment had dropped to 54 percent from more than 70 percent during the early Meiji years. In the nonagriculture sector, which had grown to claim 46 percent of total employment, 73 percent of the workers were paid employees, up from about 35 percent in

5 Yokoyama Gen'nosuke, *Nihon no kasō shakai* (Tokyo: Kyobunkan, 1899). For an analytical use of *Kasō shakai,* much like today's informal sector in historical studies of Japanese labor markets, see Sumiya Mikio, *Nihon chinrōdō shiron* (Tokyo: Tokyo daigaku shuppankai, 1955) and *Social Impact of Industrialization in Japan* (Tokyo: UNESCO Japan, 1963).

6 The versatility and mobility of the working poor continue to this day and present a fascinating contrast with the lifetime commitment of the regular workers to their employers under the "Japanese employment system." The implication is that the poor are "un-Japanese." See Masayoshi Chubachi and Koji Taira, "Poverty in Modern Japan: Perceptions and Realities," in *Japanese Industrialization and Its Social Consequences,* ed. Hugh Patrick with the assistance of Larry Meissner (Berkeley and Los Angeles: University of California Press, 1976).

7 Subbiah Kannappan, ed., *Studies of Urban Labour Market Behaviour in Developing Areas* (Geneva: International Institute for Labour Studies, 1977).

TABLE 12.1
*Employment by sector, industry, and status, for selected years (in thousands and percentages)*

| | 1920 | 1930 | 1940 | 1950 |
|---|---|---|---|---|
| *Gainfully employed (in thousands)*[a] | | | | |
| All sectors | *27,260* | *29,619* | *34,177* | *36,160* |
| Primary sector[b] | *14,717* | *14,700* | *14,384* | *18,100* |
| Agriculture and forestry | 14,181 | 14,131 | 13,841 | 17,410 |
| Secondary sector[c] | *6,990* | *7,359* | *10,066* | *9,630* |
| Manufacturing | 4,604 | 4,754 | 6,955 | 6,230 |
| Public utilities | 1,170 | 1,294 | 1,523 | 1,710 |
| Tertiary sector[d] | *5,553* | *7,560* | *9,727* | *8,430* |
| Trade | 3,380 | 4,930 | 4,898 | 3,740 |
| Services | 2,174 | 2,630 | 4,818 | 4,050 |
| *Employees as percentage of gainfully employed*[e] | | | | |
| All sectors | *29.5* | *32.3* | *41.9* | *39.6* |
| Primary sector | *4.5* | *4.9* | *4.9* | *6.2* |
| Agriculture | 2.9 | 3.2 | 2.5 | 3.5 |
| Secondary sector | *67.4* | *64.5* | *80.9* | *79.8* |
| Manufacturing | 62.7 | 60.4 | 78.7 | 78.2 |
| Public utilities | 70.3 | 83.6 | 91.9 | 94.4 |
| Tertiary sector | *44.6* | *40.4* | *56.0* | *60.3* |
| Trade | 24.0 | 31.2 | 36.4 | 36.0 |
| Finance | 76.1 | 89.6 | 95.2 | 93.6 |
| Services | 67.8 | 75.1 | 79.1 | 65.1 |
| Ohkawa–Takamatsu estimates for "services"[f] | 16.9 | 17.1 | 38.7 | n.a. |
| *Modern-sector employees as percentage of gainfully employed* | | | | |
| Factory employment as percentage of manufacturing employment[g] | 39.6 | 39.9 | 65.5 | 59.8 |
| Modern-sector employment as percentage of total employment in finance[h] | 38.8[i] | 46.0[j] | n.a. | n.a. |
| Same adjusted for unpaid family workers[k] | 25.5 | 31.7 | n.a. | n.a. |

[a]Mataji Umemura's estimates in *Patterns of Japanese Economic Development: A Quantitative Appraisal,* ed. Kazushi Ohkawa and Miyohei Shinohara (New Haven, Conn.: Yale University Press, 1979), pp. 392–5.
[b]Includes agriculture, forestry, and fishing.
[c]Includes mining, construction, manufacturing, and "support and utilities" (transportation, communication, electricity, gas, and water).
[d]All sectors less primary less secondary.
[e]Tadao Ishizaki, "Sangyō kōzō to shūgyō kōzō," in *Wagakuni kanzen koyō no igi to taisaku,* ed. Shōwa dōjinkai (Tokyo: Shōwa dōjinkai 1957), pp. 665, 690–1.
[f]*Estimates of Long-Term Economic Statistics of Japan Since 1868* [LTES], vol. 1, ed. Kazushi Ohkawa, Nobukiyo Takamatsu, and Yūzō Yamamoto (Tokyo: Tōyō keizai shinpōsha, 1974), p. 131. This LTES series ends in 1940 and has no figure applicable to 1950; hence, "n. a." for 1950. "Services" here includes trade, finance, and personal services.
[g]Based on Table 12.2
[h]Ohkawa and Shinohara, eds., *Patterns of Japanese Economic Development,* p. 124. "Modern" finance refers to banking and insurance. "Traditional" finance refers to *mujin* (mutual loan association), money lending, and real estate lending.
[i]1915. [j]1926.
[k]Employment in finance appearing in the preceding row does not include "unpaid family workers" which should have been an important factor in "traditional" finance. But data on this category of workers are not available for finance. Adjustment is therefore made using the ratio of unpaid family workers to total employment for all "services" obtained from LTES, vol. 1.

earlier years. Not all of these nonagricultural wage and salary earners were employed in the formal sector (mines, factories, utilities, incorporated businesses, and government). Because an economy's degree of modernization is often determined from the proportion of employment in the formal (or modern) sector, it is useful to estimate the proportion of employment in that sector at different historical stages of the Japanese economy. According to Table 12.1, in 1920, paid workers represented 63 percent of Japan's total manufacturing employment. But factory employees, defined as those in manufacturing establishments with five or more workers were only 40 percent of this total. The other 60 percent were self-employed proprietors, working family members, and wage earners in workshops with fewer than five employees. If the formal sector is considered as modern, it is clear that more than fifty years after the Meiji Restoration of 1868, Japanese manufacturing in 1920 was not yet even half-modern.[8] And even this must be discounted further owing to a nonmodern bias in the sex composition of factory employment.

If the manufacturing industry was 40 percent formal and 60 percent informal, how representative was this proportion for all nonagricultural employment? In construction, wholesale and retail trade, and services, the proportion of the formal sector must have been much lower than in manufacturing. On the other hand, utilities and government must have been almost entirely formal, although they employed only a small proportion of the industrial labor force. There were also many casual workers with no industrial attachment. Thus the factories' share of manufacturing employment may well have marked the upper limit of nonagriculture's relative importance in the formal sector. Thus, as in manufacturing, Japan's entire nonagricultural work force was also less than 40 percent "modern" in 1920. By this calculation, the "modern wage and salary earners" would have been less than 15 percent of Japan's total employment (40 percent of paid workers in nonagriculture divided by all employed persons on the basis of the 1920 figures in Table 12.1).

The relative size of modern-sector employment hardly changed for a decade after 1920, but during the 1930s there was a substantial expansion of heavy industries, thereby drawing labor into the factories on an unprecedented scale. Factory employment increased nearly two and a

8 There has been much controversy over the nature and quality of Japan's industrial technology and organization. The issues concern the relative importance of factories, manufactures (or manufactories), and cottage industry within the manufacturing sector. For comments on the issues and abstracts of major Japanese works in this area, see Mikio Sumiya and Koji Taira, eds., *An Outline of Japanese Economic History, 1603–1940* (Tokyo: Tokyo University Press, 1979), chaps. 7, 15.

half times between 1930 and 1940. According to Table 12.1, in 1940, factory employment stood at 66 percent of manufacturing employment, indicating that manufacturing had finally become predominantly modern. Because the proportion of factory employment in manufacturing indicates the relative size of the modern sector in the entire nonagricultural sector, we can say that on the eve of World War II, Japan's nonagricultural employment had become predominantly modern.

Wartime destruction and disruption of the economy brought enormous setbacks in production, productivity, and employment structure, perhaps starting in the last two years of the war (1944 and 1945) and lasting well into the 1950s. The level of national output did not return to the prewar "normal" level of 1934–6 until 1952, and the employment structure reflected the impact of these setbacks. Compared with 1940, manufacturing employment in its major aspects was lower in 1950, and factory employment had shrunk by more than 30 percent. When the Allied Occupation ended in 1952, the Japanese economy had to begin where it was in the mid-1930s.[9]

### *The role of labor in modern-sector development*

In 1920, roughly half of the economy was agricultural, and less than 40 percent of the other half was modern. A small island of modern-sector employment was surrounded by the much larger sea of traditional employment, an image reminiscent of W. Arthur Lewis's celebrated model of "economic development with unlimited supplies of labor."[10] This model assumes that surplus labor outside the "capitalist" or modern sector drives down the compensation for labor to a minimum subsistence level and that until surplus labor is fully absorbed into capitalist-sector employment, wages will stay at the subsistence level of the traditional sector. The Lewis model does not distinguish between agriculture and the nonagricultural informal sector but lumps both together as traditional. Development economists have suggested an independent role for the nonagricultural informal sector and have postulated three basic sectors in a developing economy: the modern sector, the informal sector, and agriculture.[11] Informal-sector employ-

9 For a scrutiny and analysis of wartime and postwar data, see Umemura Mataji, *Sengo Nihon no rōdōyoku* (Tokyo: Iwanami shoten, 1964), esp. chap. 2, sec. 2.

10 W. Arthur Lewis, "Economic Development with Unlimited Supplies of Labour," *Manchester School of Economic and Social Studies* 22 (May 1954):134–91.

11 Lloyd G. Reynolds and Peter Gregory, *Wages, Productivity and Industrialization in Puerto Rico* (Homewood, Ill.: Irwin, 1965); John R. Harris and Michael P. Todaro, "Migration, Unemployment and Development: A Two-Sector Analysis," *American Economic Review* 60 (March 1970): 126–42.

ment serves as a labor reserve waiting to be absorbed into the modern sector as job opportunities expand there. If we assume that the cost or inconvenience of mobility is less when moving from the informal to the modern sector than from agriculture, it seems reasonable that workers should first move from agriculture to the informal sector and then wait for job openings in the modern sector. In effect, part of informal-sector employment becomes disguised unemployment.

Many economists have argued that the Lewis model only partially explains Japan's development. Gustav Ranis and John C. H. Fei suggested that the Lewis model, appropriately refined in their hands, fits Japan up to World War I.[12] Minami Ryoshin believes that conditions similar to "unlimited supplies of labor" lasted until about 1960.[13] At the same time, there have been "long swings" in Japanese development, each lasting twenty to thirty years from trough to trough in the time series of several key economic variables, including wages and employment.[14] If there were such long swings, it is difficult to understand how unlimited supplies of labor could be sustained for periods extending beyond the slack phase of long swings when labor redundancy increased. During the upswing phase, though with some lag in response, labor supplies tended to become scarce enough to drive up the labor costs at the expense of profits, thereby setting the stage for the next economic downturn.[15]

Employment is said to be elastic with respect to wages – in short, wage elastic – if it greatly increases in response to a small increase or no increase in wages. Conversely, employment is said to be wage inelastic if it increases very little or not at all in response to a large increase in wages. Figure 12.1 relates the index of factory employment to the index of real wages (both calculated from data in the prewar *Factory Statistics* and the postwar *Census of Manufactures*), suggesting that in Japan the elasticity of employment varied over time. There were four phases after 1909: (1) elastic employment, 1909 to 1920; (2) inelastic employment, 1920 to 1933; (3) elastic employment, 1933 to 1940; and (4) inelastic employment, 1940 to 1956. The crucial question is to what extent or in what ways these changing wage elasticities of factory employment can be related to changes in labor supply or demand.

12 John C. H. Fei and Gustav Ranis, *Development of the Labor-Surplus Economy* (Homewood, Ill.: Irwin, 1964).
13 Ryoshin Minami, *The Turning Point in Economic Development* (Tokyo: Kinokuniya, 1973).
14 Miyohei Shinohara, *Growth and Cycles in the Japanese Economy* (Tokyo: Kinokuniya, 1962); Kazushi Ohkawa and Henry Rosovsky, *Japanese Economic Growth* (Stanford, Calif.: Stanford University Press, 1973); Kazushi Ohkawa and Miyohei Shinohara, eds., with Larry Meissner, *Patterns of Japanese Economic Development* (New Haven, Conn.: Yale University Press, 1979).
15 Ohkawa and Rosovsky, *Japanese Economic Growth*, pp. 200–4.

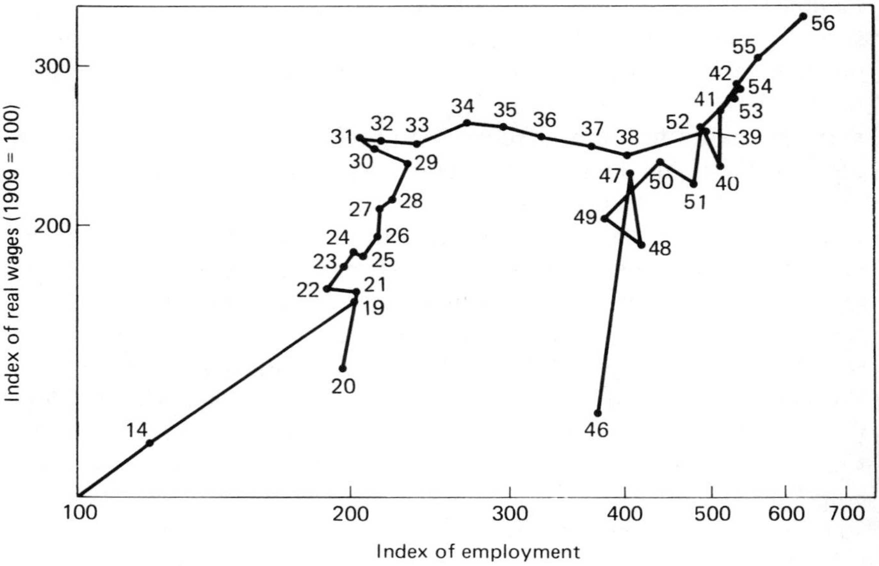


Figure 12.1. The relationship between real wages and employment in Japanese factories, 1909–1956 (1909 = 100); data for 1943–5 are not included. (From Shōwa dōjinkai, ed., *Wagakuni chingin kōzō no shiteki kōsatsu* (Tokyo: Shiseido, 1960), pp. 463–4.

On the whole, the wage–employment relationship between 1909 and 1919 suggests a fairly high wage elasticity of labor supply: Factory employment increased by 102 percent and real wages by 64 percent. During the boom years of World War I, the pressure of expanding market demand encouraged Japanese employers to increase their work forces as fast as possible. It is an indication of an elastic labor supply that when there is a rapidly increasing demand for labor, employment will expand faster than will the increase in real wages.

Then after 1919 there was a surprising turnaround in the wage elasticity of factory employment. Between 1920 and the early 1930s, factory employment hardly increased, but real wages rose by more than 70 percent. The questions here are whether the substantial increases in real wages during the 1920s were due to the relative scarcity of labor, and if so, why the elastic labor supply of the preceding decade changed so suddenly into an inelastic supply. One answer is that the continued absorption of a large number of workers in modern-sector employment year after year during the 1910s eventually exhausted the labor supply for this sector and that a lagging response to the developing labor scarcity brought about sudden upward adjustment of real wages during the early 1920s. But this does not account for the continued rise in real wages for several more years, even though there was no corresponding increase in employment. One suspects that the sustained rise in real wages during the 1920s may have been caused by new, nonmarket factors influencing the demand side of the labor market. Indeed, Japanese employers were changing their employment strategy under the pressure of new forces such as official regulation of industrial working conditions, labor unions, industrial conflict, public criticism of business behavior, and a new democratic social climate.

At the same time, the Japanese labor force was increasing more rapidly during the 1920s than in previous decades. A greater proportion of the rapidly increasing labor force was also better educated and more skilled. During the 1920s there was an accumulation of highly skilled workers outside the modern sector. In other words, the labor supply for the modern sector became more elastic every year during the 1920s. When Japan's "second industrial revolution" arrived during the 1930s, this accumulated labor reserve was drawn into modern-sector employment without the inducement of further increases in real wages. Thus there was another turnaround in the wage elasticity of factory employment in the 1930s.

As the result of employment expansion and the conscription of males for military service, labor became scarce in the late 1930s and even more so during World War II. Another round of low wage elasticity of factory employment therefore began and continued into the 1950s. This continuity is remarkable, as the postwar economy differed in many respects from the wartime economy, especially in the labor supply's sharp shift from wartime scarcity to the sudden and increasing surplus after the war.[16] Yet the wage–employment relationship has characteristics common to both periods. Data on wages and employment are not available for 1943 through 1945. But we could suppose that real wages and factory employment decreased during these years. Both wages and employment reached a new low point in 1946, the first full year after the war. When both bounced back, they tended to follow the upward path marked by the wage–employment relationship of 1939 to 1942. Thus, an awkward question arises: Despite underlying changes in the labor supply from wartime scarcity to postwar surplus, the actual wage–

16 Especially relevant here are the data presented in Umemura, *Sengo Nihon no rōdōryoku*, chap. 2, sec. 2.

employment relationship in Japanese factories was apparently subject to the same elasticity during the whole period. How can the wage elasticity of employment be the same under labor surplus as under labor scarcity? One explanation is that real wages, which determined the standard of living, were probably under greater pressure to recover their prewar level than the level of employment was. The role of nonmarket factors was also considerably greater in postwar than in prewar Japan. After 1945, trade unions and collective bargaining were legalized and encouraged for the first time in Japanese history. Legal labor standards were upgraded and expanded. Fluctuations in the wage elasticity of employment and in the role of institutional factors reduce the Lewis model's applicability to the Japanese experience. At best, the model fits the experience of the 1930s, when modern-sector employment was extremely elastic with respect to wages.

### *Agriculture as a source of labor for the modern sector*

The Japanese labor force after 1920 was composed of three segments: the modern sector, the urban informal sector, and agriculture. According to Mataji Umemura's latest estimates, prewar Japan's "outflow of agricultural working force" reached an all-time high during the decade of 1910–20.[17] During this period, this outflow from agriculture accounted for more than 80 percent of the increase in nonagricultural employment, also an all-time high. The labor force outflow from agriculture sank to less than a half as much between 1920 and 1930 and then rose again between 1930 and 1940. This labor force outflow from agriculture is almost perfectly correlated with the changes in factory employment, as illustrated in Figure 12.1.

No systematic data or estimates are available to show how much of the labor force migration from agriculture was to the modern sector and how much was to the urban informal sector. A study by the Ministry of Agriculture and Commerce of the previous occupations of factory workers indicates that as of October 1917, new factories established after the outbreak of World War I employed a total of 253,598 workers. About 90,000 moved to new factories from older, established ones, but the remaining 160,000 were new recruits. Of these, 103,430 or about 65 percent, had previously been agricultural workers.[18] Thus

17 Mataji Umemura, "Population and Labor Force," in *Patterns of Japanese Economic Development: A Quantitative Appraisal*, ed. Kazushi Ohkawa and Miyohei Shinohara with Larry Meissner (New Haven, Conn.: Yale University Press, 1979), p. 246.

18 Rōdō undō shiryō iinkai, ed., *Nihon rōdō undō shiryō*, vol. 3 (Tokyo: Rōdō undō shiryō iinkai, 1968), pp. 51–4.

during World War I, about two-thirds of the net increase in factory employment (or modern-sector employment in general) seems to have come from agriculture and one-third from the urban informal sector. The informal sector in turn was filled by an inflow of labor from agriculture as well as by an increase in the population. Probably over 80 percent of the net increase in this sector came from agriculture.

By the late 1930s this pattern had changed. Several partial surveys in 1938 concluded that 43 percent of the net increase in manufacturing employment was accounted for by recent school graduates (about one-half of them would have originated in farm households) and that from 37 to 45 percent of the remainder was accounted for by those coming from agriculture.[19] From these data, it appears that in 1938, manufacturing depended on agriculture for 42 to 47 percent of the net increase in its work force, considerably lower than the two-thirds of twenty years earlier. After several decades of modernization, Japan's modern-sector labor force was finally losing its traditional peasant background.

It is clear that the transfer of labor from agriculture to the nonagricultural sectors did not result simply from the expanding modern sector's absorption of the traditional sector's surplus labor. The existence of an independent urban informal sector complicated the labor migration out of agriculture. It is assumed that the modern-sector workers came from agriculture and returned to it whenever the modern sector contracted. But clearly this is an oversimplification.

Why did people move from agricultural to nonagricultural employment? Whenever workers leave their jobs and familiar environment for employment elsewhere, they probably are looking for higher wages.

A comparison of Minami's and Ono's estimates of agricultural wages and of manufacturing wages contains one major and one minor surprise.[20] The major surprise is that between 1880 and 1940, wages for women were generally higher in agriculture than in manufacturing. The wage differential for female workers was larger in the earlier years, when agricultural wages rose more than 50 percent above manufacturing wages, a situation that lasted until World War I. Under these circumstances, those women who moved from agriculture to industry were probably those who would not have earned the average agricultural wages. And these were the girls, often only ten or eleven years old, hired by textile factories. Their wages statistically lowered the

19 Nichi-Man nōsei kenkyūkai, *Saikin ni okeru jinkō idō no seikaku to nōgyō* (Tokyo: Nichi-Man nōsei kenkyūkai, 1940), pp. 54–8.
20 Minami and Ono, "Wages," in *Patterns of Japanese Economic Development*, chap. 13.

average female wages in manufacturing. However, their earnings in the textile factories were probably higher than whatever they could earn at home, and even though their wages were low, these children were at least earning their keep and relieving their parents of extra mouths to feed (*kuchi berashi*).

The minor surprise is the rough parity of wages for agriculture and manufacturing until World War I. Those men who left agriculture were not heirs or firstborn sons, and so if they stayed home, they would become wage-earning hired hands for their brothers, neighbors, relatives, or strangers. Unless they could acquire their own farms – and this opportunity was uncommon – they would be second-class members of their local communities. They were, in a sense, "disinherited" because of the institution of primogeniture. These nonheirs, not tied to the land, were able to compare the advantages of farm and nonfarm employment and to decide where they should work. However, the modern industries needing a large number of male workers were not developing fast enough to absorb these disinherited rural males. Table 12.1 shows that the proportion of the nonfactory labor force to the total manufacturing labor force was 60 percent even in 1920 or that many of the male migrants from agriculture went to the urban informal sector.

Furthermore, before the 1920s, the modern factories' management techniques were not yet sophisticated enough to make factory employment competitive. The factories hired the workers from the streets when job openings arose and sent them back to the streets when there was no more need for them. Thus, the workers shuttled steadily between the modern and informal sectors, producing a parity of male wages in all sectors of the economy. There was essentially one set of labor markets that allocated labor to the three sectors with a minimum of friction among them. This was probably the best approximation of the theoretical, competitive labor market that the real market's labor allocation could have created anywhere.

During the 1920s, however, the gap between manufacturing and agricultural wages widened. Labor transfers from agriculture to nonagriculture decreased concurrently, and the modern sector expanded at the same rate as or more slowly than the informal sector did. This was extraordinary in the light of the intersectoral labor market relationships that had prevailed before 1920. What was new about the Japanese economy of the 1920s was the segmentation of the labor market. The inordinate increases in modern-sector wages were caused by the rise of powerful noneconomic forces on the demand side of the labor market.

The high labor costs in turn limited this sector's capacity to absorb labor and deprived the urban informal sector and agriculture of their labor supply. Thus, wages in both agriculture and the urban informal sector fell relative to modern-sector wages. When the intersectoral wage differential was widest in the mid-1930s, agricultural wages stood at about 50 percent of manufacturing wages.[21] At about the same time, urban informal-sector wages, insofar as these can be inferred from the wages of the smallest firms of the modern sector available for 1932–3, would have been no more than 60 percent of the average modern-sector wages.[22] However, the expansion of the modern-sector employment during the rest of the 1930s and World War II, together with the withdrawal from the labor force of millions of able-bodied males who were sent to the front, depleted the Japanese labor force to the point that all wage differentials disappeared by the end of the war.

### *The role of women in Japanese wage labor markets*

In Japanese manufacturing up to the 1930s, the factory hands were predominantly female, whereas the workers in nonfactory manufacturing were predominantly male. Table 12.2 shows employment by sex and occupation between 1920 and 1950.

Women accounted for 35 to 50 percent of Japan's total employment in all industries. The male–female ratio was higher in manufacturing than in total employment. In 1940, men accounted for more than 70 percent of manufacturing employment and women for less than 30 percent. But factory employment, a subset of manufacturing employment, was different. Between 1920 and 1930, more than half of all factory workers were women. Between 1930 and 1940, however, this male–female ratio was reversed, making the image of the factory more congruous with that of modernization. If we consider the factory system a crucial component of economic modernization and recall that women rarely played a pioneering modernizing role before men did in any society, it is surprising that the Japanese factory system, supposedly the vanguard of modernization, was "manned by women" during a substantial period of Japan's modernization. For a long time, Japan's economic and technological advances were supported by the backwardness of the industrial labor force numerically dominated by women and girls.

21 Ibid., p. 234.
22 Yasuba, "The Evolution of Dualistic Wage Structure," in *Japanese Industrialization and Its Social Consequences*, p. 256.

TABLE 12.2
*Japanese employment by sex and occupational status, for selected years, 1920–1950 (thousands of persons)*

| | 1920 | 1930 | 1940 | 1950 |
|---|---|---|---|---|
| All industries, total | 29,966 | 29,341 | 32,231 | 35,575 |
| Male | 16,820 | 18,888 | 19,599 | 21,811 |
| Female | 10,146 | 10,463 | 12,632 | 13,763 |
| Manufacturing, total | 4,438 | 4,702 | 6,845 | 6,460 |
| Male | 2,892 | 3,276 | 4,959 | 4,510 |
| Female | 1,547 | 1,425 | 1,887 | 1,950 |
| Paid employment | 2,781 | 2,842 | 5,385 | 4,413 |
| Self-employment, including family labor | 1,702 | 1,860 | 1,460 | 1,243 |
| Factory employment | 1,758 | 1,875 | 4,486 | 3,861 |
| Operatives, total | 1,555 | 1,684 | 3,843 | 3,117 |
| Male | 730 | 796 | 2,545 | 2,034 |
| Female | 824 | 887 | 1,298 | 1,083 |
| Nonfactory manufacturing, total[a] | 2,680 | 2,827 | 2,359 | 2,599 |
| Nonoperative manufacturing, total[b] | 2,883 | 3,018 | 3,002 | 3,343 |
| Male | 2,162 | 2,480 | 2,314 | 2,476 |
| Female | 723 | 538 | 589 | 867 |

[a]Equals manufacturing total less factory employment.
[b]Equals manufacturing total less operatives.
*Source:* Ishizaki Tadao, "Sangyō kōzō to shūgyō kōzō," in *Wagakuni Kanzen koyō no igi to taisaku,* ed. Shōwa dōjinkai (Tokyo: Shōwa dōjinkai, 1957), revised and supplemented where appropriate by data from Rōdō undō shinyō iinkai, ed., *Nihon rōdō undō shiryō,* vol. 10 (Tokyo: Rōdō undō shiryō iinkai, 1968), and *Nihon rōdō nenkan,* no. 27 (Tokyo: Ohara Institute for Social Research, Hōsei University).

Table 12.2 also contrasts factory workers and nonfactory manufacturing workers by sex. In all the years shown in the table, female factory workers outnumbered female nonfactory manufacturing workers, and except in 1940, male workers were largely nonfactory workers. Especially in 1920 and 1930, male nonfactory manufacturing workers outnumbered male factory workers by a ratio of two and a half to one. These male nonfactory workers were mostly self-employed owner-operators, working members of their families, or wage-earners that they employed. But their workshops were too small to be considered factories, and their production methods were not sophisticated enough to be considered modern. These were the "cottage industries."

In today's less developed countries, factory workers, a minority in manufacturing employment, are a relatively privileged group compared with nonfactory workers. Likewise, in the 1930s, Japanese factory workers also were relatively privileged. This suggests that the prestige of factory employment was tied to the sex composition of the work force. Full modernization probably involves several simultaneous requirements: An economy cannot be modern without productive manufacturing; manufacturing cannot be modern without heavy industries and a factory system; and a factory system cannot be modern without being run by men. In Japan these requirements were fulfilled for the first time only in the late 1930s.

It is ironic that a male-dominated traditional society like Japan's was industrialized by drawing women and girls into industrial labor. But these female industrial workers did not enjoy any special advantages by participating in industrialization. Indeed, the abuses (like long hours of work without rest, few holidays, low wages, and accidents and health hazards) suffered by female industrial workers during Japan's industrial revolution, 1890 to 1910, led to the Factory Law of 1911. This law stipulated the minimum standards for employment, covering manufacturing establishments with fifteen or more workers. It prohibited firms from employing workers under the age of twelve and minors and women from working more than twelve hours a day or between 10 P.M. and 4 A.M. The law required at least two rest days per month for minors and women, at least four rest days per month for night-shift workers, and at least a thirty minute rest period per day when a day's work exceeded ten hours. The law also prevented firms from hiring minors for certain dangerous or disagreeable jobs and required firms to support disabled workers and their families.

Implementation of the Factory Law in and after 1916 offered some protection to female workers and minors against the worst abuses. But by the time Japanese employers had learned to live with the law, Japanese industrialization was moving to a new stage in which male labor was in greater demand than was female labor. Consequently, in the 1920s and 1930s, male wages increased faster than did female wages. Also during this period new employment practices were instituted, which foreshadowed the "Japanese employment system" and which stabilized employment relationships with male workers. The women and girls thus retreated into the shadows during Japan's second industrial revolution in the 1930s.[23]

## THE EMERGENCE OF DUALISM IN THE LABOR MARKET

As the links between the labor markets for industry and agriculture loosened between the two world wars, the nonagricultural labor market became more segmented; that is, some firms paid much higher

23 Hosoi Wakizo, *Jokō aishi* (Tokyo: Kaizōsha, 1925). See also Ōkōchi Kazuo, *Reimeiki no Nihon rōdō undō* (Tokyo: Iwanami shoten, 1952).

wages than those prevailing in the labor market. When the firms behaving in this fashion constitute a significant sector in terms of output, resources, employment, and market power, labor market segmentation becomes significant with respect to the entire economic system's equity.

The statistical evidence for the emergence of a dualistic labor market in prewar Japan is somewhat ambiguous. On the one hand, research by Odaka Konosuke suggests that certain large firms were beginning to pay much higher wages than their workers would have received if the market forces had been freer. In comparing the wages of twelve major firms with the wages paid in their regional labor markets, Odaka found that without exception, the firms' wages in the 1920s and 1930s increased relative to those of the markets.[24]

In research on the wartime and postwar periods, Odaka found that wage differentials may have disappeared during and immediately after the war, only to reappear in the 1950s. Data from plants owned by Mitsubishi Heavy Industries during this period indicate that the wages paid to workers in these plants were almost equal to market wages for equivalent trades (within a range of 1.0 to 1.2) between 1939 and 1950, but that they subsequently rose as high as 1.8 in 1958.[25]

The fact that some large firms pay higher wages than those prevailing in the labor market does not mean that most firms do. Such a generalization requires data on the wages and sizes of all firms in the economy. Unfortunately, there are no such data for Japan's prewar period. More plentiful postwar data like the annual census of manufacturing clearly show that during the 1950s, there were large wage differentials by size of plant. Thus, in the postwar period, large firms usually paid much higher wages than smaller firms did. But such generalizations about the prewar period are less certain.

Yasuba Yasukuchi's work on prewar wage differentials used data from 1909, 1914, and 1932–3. The 1909 and 1914 data, compiled from *Factory Statistics*, show that when wage payments are averaged over all workers, regardless of sex and age, there are no wage differentials by size of factory. But when wages are calculated separately for male and female workers, there are differentials of 20 to 30 percent between the smallest factories employing five to nine workers and the largest employing one thousand or more. With the average male wages at factories

24 Konosuke Odaka, "Historical Development in the Wage-Differential Structure," paper presented at the Japan Economic Seminar, New York City, April 14, 1973.

25 Odaka Konosuke, "Dainiji taisen zengo no kyū-Mitsubishi Jūkō rōdō tōkei ni tsuite," *Hitotsubashi ronsō* 74 (1975):1–16.

employing one thousand or more workers set at 100, for example, the average male wages at factories of five to nine were 80 in 1909 and 72 in 1914. Similar indices for female wages at the smallest factories were 76 in 1909 and 72 in 1914. Yasuba further refined the calculation of average wages by standardizing intersize differences in the work force's sex, age, working days, and white-collar–blue-collar mix.[26] This resulted in the smallest size–class wages amounting to 80.7 percent in 1909 and 71.3 percent in 1914 of the largest size–class wages.

The 1909 and 1914 data can be interpreted in various ways. Compared with random interfirm wage differentials in 1885, the 1909 and 1914 data suggest some consistency in the relation between wages and factory size. The data of 1932–3, although not directly comparable to the earlier data, after some adjustment show that the wages at the smallest factories were 82.3 percent of the wages at the largest factories in 1909, 78.5 percent in 1914, and 61.2 percent in 1932–3. Thus the wage differentials by size of factory were much greater in 1932–3 than in 1909 or 1914.[27]

On the basis of Odaka's and Yasuba's findings, it seems reasonable to conclude that significant wage differentials by size of firm or establishment first appeared in the 1920s. At this time some of the larger firms began to hire different kinds of workers or to establish different kinds of relationships with their employees. This can be described as the rise of "labor market dualism," a phenomenon intriguing to economists accustomed to rationalistic theories of efficient labor markets. Labor market dualism does not arise simply because some firms are large and some are small. As Odaka's research shows, the enterprises he examined had been operating in a competitive labor market for a long time before 1920, and the workers did not consider them especially desirable employers. There thus was considerable interfirm labor mobility, regardless of the firms' sizes. Then why did the dualistic wage structure arise? Why did major enterprises begin to treat their workers more generously than smaller firms did? Why did workers find the large firms more attractive as employers than the smaller firms during the 1920s?

26 Yasuba, "The Evolution of Dualistic Wage Structure," in *Japanese Industrialization and Its Social Consequences*, p. 259.

27 Ibid., pp. 258–9. This is not the same as saying that wage differentials by size of factory increased between 1914 and 1932–3. These differentials increased between 1909 and 1914 according to the available data. But they may have decreased during the World War I boom, as may be inferred from other data. This therefore may not be a consistently rising trend in these differentials from the data for 1909, 1914, and 1932–3. For a review of related data on wage differentials, see Koji Taira, *Economic Development and the Labor Market in Japan* (New York: Columbia University Press, 1970), pt. 1.

Yasuba's explanation attributes the rise of a dualistic labor market to the emergence of corporate paternalism in a few large firms. In contrast with the small firm or plant, where the employer knows his employees personally and takes care of all aspects of their work and life, the large organization is impersonal and remote. Therefore, in order to attract workers and to offset this impersonality, large firms must provide benefits that small firms cannot. They must provide a kind of institutionalized paternalism in the form of higher wages based on seniority, as well as better fringe benefits. Much of the differential between the large and small firms' wages, then, is the monetary equivalent of the personal attention and care that the small employer can give to his employees. In other words, higher wages compensate for the lack of personal paternalism.[28] Thus, according to Yasuba, wage differentials have a cultural cause; that is, employers in large organizations are forced to model themselves on traditional small enterprises in order to attract and hold workers. Though difficult to understand in terms of economic rationality, this corporate paternalism makes sense in terms of historical and cultural tradition.

But it seems equally compelling to argue that wage differentials might be determined by rational economic calculations and market efficiency. The reasons that large employers offer higher wages, periodic pay raises, and fringe benefits – especially severance pay, retirement allowances, and paid leave – all have one common denominator, that they are designed to encourage workers to stay in their employment as long as possible. In short, wages and benefits are based on the length of service that a firm wants from its employees. Why is length of service such an important variable, for which the firm is willing to pay an increasing amount of money? More generally, is more money the only means of achieving this objective? Are there no nonmonetary means? Penalties, including physical violence, have also been used in many countries, including Japan, as a means of discouraging workers from leaving jobs. Indeed, monetary inducements for longer service often were instituted after the negative sanctions failed.

Based on recent developments in labor market theory, we may now hypothesize that one of the most important institutional aspects of economic dualism is the large firms' need for "internal labor markets." Internal labor markets refer to job changes within a firm involving formal and informal training, assignment and reassignment, transfer, promotion, and the like. Internal job changes take place because the

28 Taira, *Economic Development*, pp. 285–6.

firm's technology changes, and employees learn new skills and acquire experience over time. These phenomena look much like job mobility in the labor market. But because they are confined to one firm, they are said to occur in the internal labor market. Internal labor markets generally exist in heavy industries (metals, metal products, machinery, equipment, appliances, precision instruments, and the like) in which firm-specific skills are most efficiently learned and maintained through continuous on-the-job training or experience. In interwar Japan, some major firms attempted to institute and improve the internal labor markets and retain workers as long as possible by a variety of inducements, penalties, and guarantees. A major publication of the Harmonization Society (Kyōchōkai) of 1929 contains an extensive review of conditions in the major industries, especially employment contracts and conditions.[29] Different firms used different instruments to increase worker retention rates. Among these are careful recruitment, company schools, periodic pay increases, occasional bonuses, allowances recognizing longer service, posting of bonds, oaths of loyalty and long service countersigned by workers' guarantors, and the setting of retirement and dismissal allowances based on length of service.

Two examples contrast employers' efforts to acquire a committed work force. One is the success of the principal paper producers, and the other is the failure of the major ceramics firms. Both groups of firms adopted elaborate recruitment policies, but the ceramics firms appeared less skilled in their use of economic incentives (wages and benefits tied to length of service). The paper firms made it a rule not to hire anyone with experience in another paper firm. In considering a worker for employment, the paper firms required physical and "mental" examinations, investigations of the worker's home life, and affidavits of two guarantors. When the worker appeared to offer a reasonable chance for long service as a result of these checks and guarantees, he was hired on probation for one to three months. When proven satisfactory, the worker then was given an employment contract for three to five years, which could be renewed if the worker so desired. The firms also made it known that they would not dismiss workers or deny contract renewals except under extreme circumstances. In addition, periodic pay increases, regardless of economic conditions, encouraged longer service. Severance benefits and bonuses were also tied to

29 Nakamura Hideo, ed., *Saikin no shakai undō* (Tokyo: Kyochokai, 1929), esp. chap. 2. See also S. B. Levine and H. Kawada, *Human Resources in Japanese Industrial Development* (Princeton, N.J.: Princeton University Press, 1980).

length of service. The Kyōchōkai's judgment was that the paper firms achieved a high degree of employment stability.[30]

The ceramics firms were equally careful in their recruitment but did not object to hiring experienced workers. After investigating the worker's education, ideological background, and physical fitness, the firm would then admit the worker on probation. During the next ten to fourteen days, the worker was required to submit his household registers, other instruments of identity, personal history, an oath of loyalty, and a pledge of long service jointly signed by guarantors. When the dossier was completed and proved satisfactory, the worker was considered a regular employee. The ceramics firms also adopted severance allowances tied to length of service. But they also extensively used piecework and offered no periodic pay increases, no or little bonuses, and no other inducements for long service. Not surprisingly, when Japan's general economic condition improved, workers left in droves for employment in smaller, more flexible firms in which overtime work was made available when the workers wanted it and in which there were fewer requirements for personal documents.[31] Besides differing in wage determination and administration, the paper firms emphasized internal training, whereas the ceramics firms relied on the workers' independently acquired skills and experience. The rejection by paper firms of experience acquired in other firms was the key to their success in building up and retaining their work forces. This discrimination against experienced workers became widespread in postwar Japan.

A closed internal market (open only at the entry level, with all higher levels staffed by internally trained and promoted personnel) is difficult to install quickly. First, it requires an efficient management that understands, measures, and organizes numerous jobs required for the operation of a major firm. Nothing short of a thorough job evaluation and work study can provide a technologically rational structure of jobs and positions. In addition, the firm also has to be sociologically rational by looking after individual workers from recruitment to retirement and following fair rules in recruiting, training, rewarding, and promoting employees. A simultaneous solution of the technological and sociological equations is theoretically possible, but its implementation runs into the constraints of time and resources. A new firm may have a blueprint of an ideal internal labor market, but it cannot wait

30 Levine and Kawada, *Human Resources*, pp. 75–7. For a detailed study of management history in the paper industry, see Hazama Hiroshi, *Nihon rōmu kanrishi kenkyū* (Tokyo: Diamondosha, 1964), chap. 2.

31 Nakamura, *Saikin no shakai undō*, pp. 83–6.

until its whole work force is staffed by workers internally trained and promoted. Instead, the firm must begin by recruiting workers with many levels of skills and experience, while simultaneously training at the entry level for future promotions. Different dropout rates at various levels further delay the synchronization of vacancies, promotions, and training.

From this point of view, the Japanese firms' practical solutions for the internalization of labor markets before the war were questionable. These included arbitrary discrimination against certain workers, the abuse of workers' dignity by excessive probing into personal and family backgrounds, and the manipulation of a firm's market power to shift costs and problems to weaker, smaller firms. Some of these discriminatory practices, however, were acceptable in terms of customary values and principles surviving from premodern days. The use of female workers in "women's jobs" was one such practice, and the enormous gap in status between manual and nonmanual workers was another. Manual workers were paid by the hour, day, or results, and they were generally considered interchangeable with factory hands. People with only a primary school education could not hope for anything higher than manual work unless they succeeded on their own. People with a middle-school education staffed lower- and middle-rank office jobs. People with a higher education moved directly into the managerial ranks.[32]

If management, conditioned by this nonegalitarian social climate, noticed the effects of the workers' different personal qualities on the firm's productivity and profitability, it is unlikely that it adopted a policy that produced the internal labor market out of concern for the workers' welfare. Although Japanese labor history has dubbed as paternalistic any individual attention that management paid to its workers, the essence of prewar Japanese paternalism was clearly a variant of Taylorism. And there is evidence that the Japanese studied Frederick Taylor's scientific management.[33] Instead of letting the worker decide what skills to learn and what career to pursue, Japanese management wanted to design the skills and career for him. As Taylor would have

32 Sakamoto Fijiyoshi, *Nihon koyōshi*, vol. 2 (Tokyo: Chūō keizaisha, 1977), esp. chap. 4.

33 Robert E. Cole, *Work, Mobility and Participation* (Berkeley and Los Angeles: University of California, 1979), pp. 108–10. Cole draws heavily on Kenji Okuda, "Managerial Evolution in Japan," a series of three articles in *Management Japan*, vol. 5, nos. 3, 4 (1971–2), vol. 6, no. 1 (1972). Another significant contribution is by Toshikazu Nakase, "The Introduction of Scientific Management in Japan and Its Characteristics – Case Studies of Companies in the Sumitomo Zaibatsu," in *Labor and Management: Proceedings of the Fourth Fuji Conference*, ed. Keiichiro Nakagawa (Tokyo: Tokyo University Press, 1979), pp. 171–202.

put it, the worker did not have to do the thinking for himself; management did all the thinking. This dovetailed well with Japanese concepts of authority and obedience in an organization. However, what made Japanese management practices different from American Taylorism was that instead of "task" management, Japanese managers directed their attention to "work force" management. American management at best captured the worker's thinking about a job, but Japanese management captured the worker's thinking about how to live – potentially a far more complete domination of the worker by management than Taylor probably imagined. Japanese scholars often characterize factory workers in large firms as "captive children reared into workers" (*kogaki shokkō*).[34] Because a full internal labor market was difficult to produce at short notice, Japanese management started with a manageable core of permanent workers, supplemented by temporary workers hired and fired at will and by contract workers brought in by subcontractors of certain production processes.

All these workers – causal, temporary, or contract – were physically inside the firm, so that a full internal labor market would have included them with the permanent workers. But they were not part of this market. Attempts to build an internal labor market thus involved a status differentiation and stratification of the work force. We might call this an "internal labor market dualism" and note that this internal dualism developed along with the external (interfirm) labor market dualism discussed earlier. In addition, the firm's production processes tended to be limited to the manufacture of finished goods, whereas parts and components were produced by numerous subcontractors under the major firm's financial and monopsonistic control. The underprivileged temporary workers, exploited subcontractors, and, in turn, their doubly disadvantaged workers were by-products of the privileges of permanent workers in the major firms' internal labor markets.

Building an internal labor market was a series of trial and error. One complicating factor was the cyclical fluctuation of general economic conditions that necessitated a similar expansion and contraction of the firm's work force. If too large relative to the level of production at the trough of a cycle, the size of a permanent work force would betray the workers' expectations of employment security. Japanese managers were competent strategists, however. They tended to choose depressed periods to structure their work forces, after having laid off

34 Okōchi Kazuo, *Kurai tanima no rōdō undō* (Tokyo: Iwanami shoten, 1970), pp. 163–71.

surplus workers during the preceding booms. The expansion during World War I was no time to institute permanent employment. The workers first were discharged en masse when the boom ended shortly after the end of the war. Then the "rationalization" of the work force structure began. Another opportunity arose toward the end of the 1920s with the Great Depression when the major factories cut back their forces, as may be seen from Figure 12.2.[35] This contraction was in a sense a cleansing process, enabling the firms to eliminate workers with characteristics that they considered unsuitable for the firms' interests. Foremost among such characteristics was trade union membership or sympathy, which was antithetical to the concept of "captive children." The cutback in employment during the depression drove the unions out of the major firms, and when economic expansion began after the depression in the 1930s, these firms started with lean, but select work forces of permanent workers. During the employment expansion in the 1930s, the firms acquired more experience in operating stratified work forces of permanent, temporary, and contract workers as well as commanding conglomerates of subsidiaries and affiliates. In the mid-1930s, many firms alarmed the public with their discriminatory employment practices and caused the government to investigate the problems of temporary employment. Official investigation revealed an extensive use of temporary workers.[36] Employment kept increasing, creating labor shortage and reactivating labor mobility. Labor turnover increased and helped reduce some of the permanent work force. But the times were no longer "business as usual," as the war required different ways of managing the work forces together with different social relations among the industries' different strata.

## LABOR CONFLICT AND INDUSTRIAL RELATIONS, 1920–1945

The labor market in the interwar period was also affected by the workers' organized and spontaneous challenges to their employers' authority and competence, particularly in the formal urban sector. Indeed, these challenges may have helped accelerate the improvement of wages and subsidiary benefits in large enterprises and forced em-

35 Because of the relatively sharper decline in large-factory employment, the weight of large factories in Japan's manufacturing can be said to have decreased. Some even jumped to a hypothesis that the monopolistic power of big business declined during this period.

36 For a review and critique of views of this kind, see Kazuo Sato, *Interwar Japan: Economic Changes and Consequences* (forthcoming), especially the chapter "Changes in Employment Concentration in Interwar Japanese Manufacturing."

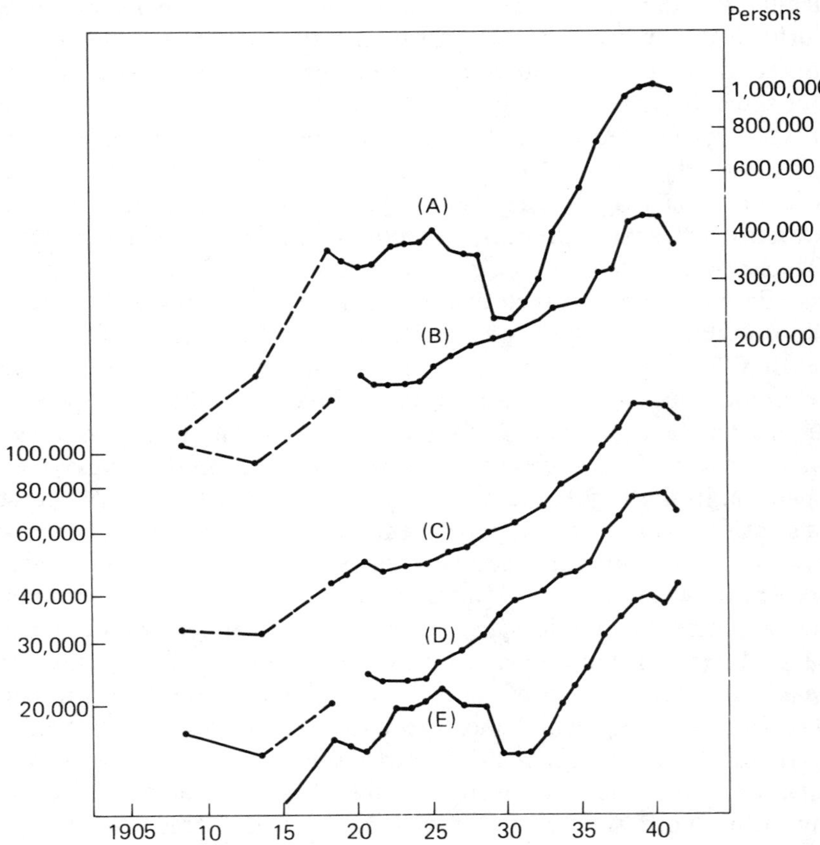


Figure 12.2. The number of operatives and the number of factories by size of factory. (A) Employment of operatives in factories employing one thousand or more operatives; (B) employment of operatives in factories employing five to ten operatives; (C) total number of factories; (D) number of factories employing five to ten operatives; and (E) number of factories employing one thousand or more operatives.

ployers to find new ways to manage their work forces. They also drew the government and state apparatus into the relationship between employer and employee and led to the development of mechanisms for outside parties to resolve labor conflicts.

In prewar Japan, employer–employee relations were generally authoritarian. Communication was poor and empathy shallow. Given the status difference and the social distance between them, the employee approached the employer with trepidation, which resulted in an incomplete articulation of issues or events. In most cases, the avoidance of direct communication was the least embarrassing kind of relationship in the workplace. The employer assumed that the relevant customs and traditions governing the employer–employee relationship were clear and that the unstated customary rules of behavior enabled the employee to understand and deliver what the employer wanted. Indeed, work-related communication was consciously minimized in prewar employment relations. Both sides depended on what they observed about each other and assumed that such observations would generate a mutual understanding of each other's roles and needs without explaining them in so many words. This type of relationship gave all of the authority and initiative to the employer, leaving the employee with nothing but obedience and performance. Thus, work required only a one-way communication, the employer giving orders with a minimum of instructions as to how they should be carried out and the employee silently fulfilling them to the best of his understanding. The determination of rules, techniques, procedures, rewards, and other conditions of employment was an unquestioned prerogative of the employer.

The great social distance between employers and workers was perceived by progressive workers and their leaders as one of the basic problems of Japanese industry. The Yūaikai (the Friendly Society, organized in 1912), which later became the most durable labor organization of prewar Japan, was an outspoken proponent of the need for workers and employers to develop mutual respect for each other. The monthly, later twice-monthly, organ of this society, *Yūai shinpō*, frequently pleaded for this. The tone and imagery of the Yūaikai's pleas, however, illustrate how powerful and arrogant the employers were and, in contrast, how powerless and pitiful the workers were. In its earlier years, the most that the Yuaikai thought it could get from employers was *oyagokoro* (hearts of parents), a far cry from anything that even remotely resembled social democracy. The *Yūai shinpō* of May 15, 1914, had this to say:

> At the risk of discourtesy, we note that among you employers there are people who limit the relationship between factory and worker to a purely economic one. They say, "We are doing you a favor by paying you wages for your work; so don't fuss, get going, work! . . . Can anyone consider such employers endowed with human feelings [*jōgi*]? . . . We workers are powerless souls born and raised under pitiful circumstances. We crave powerful protectors

with warm human feelings. We beg you to show hearts of parents. If you do, we too will show you hearts of children by working hard for you.[37]

The workers were not entirely helpless, however. Even in imperial Japan, they enjoyed a variety of freedoms, including the freedom to choose their employer. When the employment relationship became unsatisfactory, they had the right to quit and go elsewhere. The employers' authoritarianism was real, but its jurisdiction covered only the workplace. From the interplay of the unequal relationship in the workplace and the equal opportunity in the labor market emerged various worker strategies (though hampered by the employers' counterstrategies) for better jobs and higher wages.

Even though bargaining with employees on an equal footing was repugnant to authoritarian employers, they could not avoid adjusting to the consequences of an employee's decision to exercise his freedom to leave. An employee's resignation resulted in an economic loss to the employer, as work was interrupted until a replacement was found and trained enough to attain his predecessor's efficiency. But by raising wages and improving working conditions, employers could respond to excessive labor turnover with no loss of their customary authority vis-à-vis their employees. They did not yield to direct pressure; they were only adapting to the constraints of the labor market. Prewar Japanese employers seemed intent on preserving their authority, prerogatives, and superiority vis-à-vis their employees, while making unilateral concessions to their employees as required by the changing labor market conditions. But this type of employer behavior became indistinguishable from employer paternalism, in that both types of behavior resulted in changes favorable to employees. If being paternalistic is commendable, employers were likely to rationalize their offer of better conditions of employment as based on their regard for their employees' well-being, even though the truth may well have been that they had no other choice under the prevailing labor market conditions and the imperative of profit maximization.

The freedom to quit also affected the workers in an unexpected way; they acquired power over their employers because of their willingness to use it.[38] Once a worker made up his mind to quit, he could break out of the spell of his employer's authority. He could make a nuisance of himself to the employer with no fear of retaliation. The

37 *Nihon rōdō undō shiryō*, vol. 7 (1964), pp. 137–8.

38 The discussion here is to some extent inspired by Hirschman's analysis of the choice between *exit* and *voice*. See Albert O. Hirschman, *Exit, Voice, and Loyalty* (Cambridge, Mass.: Harvard University Press, 1970).

worst that could happen was that he would be fired, a course of action that he had already planned for himself. The power implicit in the decision to quit could also be used strategically even if the worker did not intend to leave.

When many workers shared this notion of a "quit weapon," they could forge a collective weapon – the "strike weapon." When several workers cooperated for common gains, they acquired a capability for collective action. When these common gains were perceived to be improved conditions of employment, the workers were ready for collective bargaining.

Workers in prewar Japan had no legally guaranteed rights to organize, to bargain with employers, or to act collectively. The imperial constitution permitted "freedom of association" within the limits of the law. The Public Peace Police Law, enacted in 1900, ruled it criminal for anyone to persuade others to join him in a labor union. The law was probably inspired by the apparent success of a modern labor movement that began after the Sino-Japanese War (1894–5). The first trade union in Japanese labor history, Tekkō kumiai (Metalworkers' Union), was organized in 1897 and quickly grew to a membership of more than five thousand in more than forty locals. After the passage of the Public Peace Police Law of 1900, the union disintegrated. Although the law did not ban unions as such nor outlaw strikes and other forms of collective action, it sought to prevent certain acts that a person might commit while persuading others to organize a union. The law's most crucial antiunion stipulation was Article 17 which prohibited coercion, violence, blackmail, slander, and instigation by an individual urging fellow workers to join a collective action or asking an employer to do things that he would otherwise not do. However, the police had unchallenged power to enforce the law at their discretion, which was usually weighted by the suspicion of any collective action as a criminal violation of Article 17. Despite generally strict enforcement, however, the law did not completely stamp out labor unions or labor disputes. Especially during World War I and the early 1920s, the scale and frequency of labor disputes increased considerably and undermined the police's effectiveness.

Figure 12.3 presents statistical data on work stoppages (strikes and lockouts, though predominantly strikes) between 1914 and 1945. The whole series and two subseries are shown, the latter pertaining to work stoppages due to workers' demands for higher wages and to workers' resistance to employers' attempts to reduce their wages. Accompanying the work-stoppage series in Figure 12.3 is an index of real daily

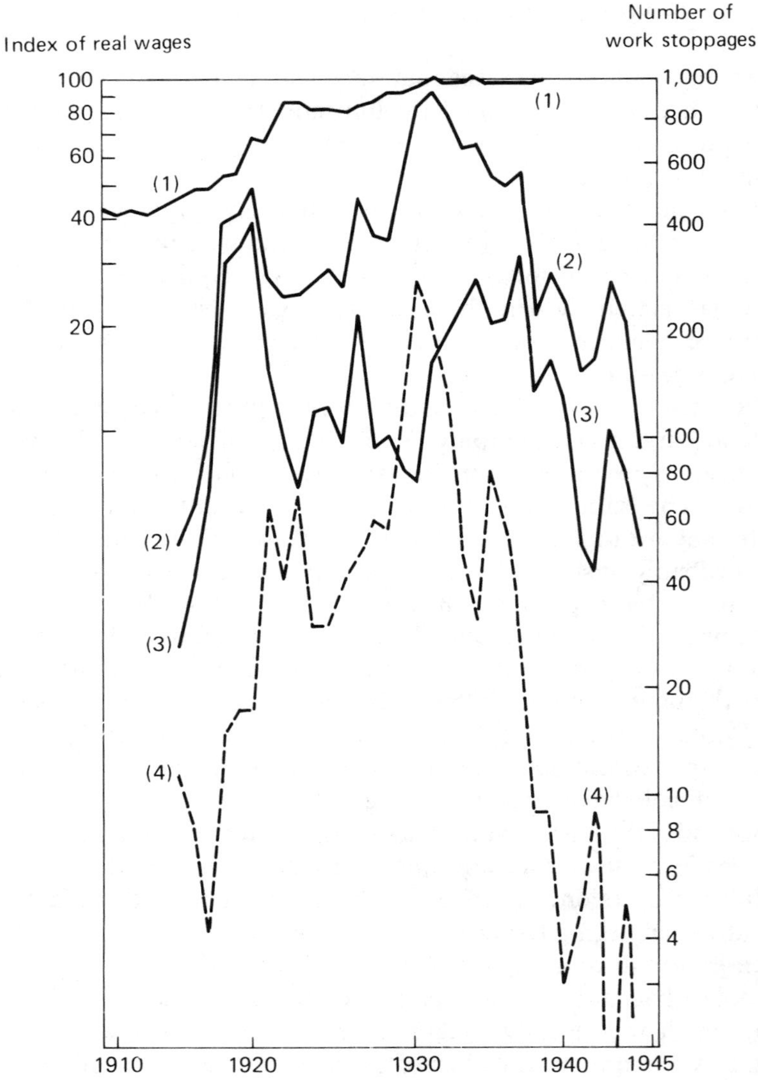


Figure 12.3. Index of real wages and number of work stoppages, 1910–1945. (1) The index of average daily wage earnings (1934–6 = 100) deflated by the consumer price index, all items (likewise). *Estimates of Long-Term Economic Statistics of Japan Since 1868*, vol. 8: *Prices*, p. 247 for wages, and pp. 135–6 for prices. Scale on the left. (2) The number of strikes and lockouts. Scale on the right. Rōdō undō shiryō iinkai, ed., *Nihon rōdō undō shiryō*, vol. 10 (Tokyo: Rōdō undō shiryō iinkai, 1968), pp. 468–9. (3) Work stoppages due to demand for higher wages. Rōdō undō shoiyō iinkai, ed., *Nihon undō shiryō*, vol. 10, pp. 468–9. (4) Work stoppages due to protest against wage reductions. Rōdō undō shiryō iinkai, ed., *Nihon undō shiryō*, vol. 10, pp. 468–9.

wage earnings (1934 to 1936 = 100). The index shows a remarkable correlation between real wages and patterns of labor disputes (with wages lagging behind labor disputes by two or three years). The flare-up of disputes between 1917 and 1919 was due mainly to workers' demands for higher wages in view of the rapid inflation accompanying the economic boom during World War I. When strikes for higher wages ran their course, strikes against wage cuts occurred in reaction to a sharp postwar recession between 1920 and 1922. The surge of industrial unrest during World War I was unprecedented in both quantity and quality, as seen in worker militancy, police brutality, and the general shock to society at large. Work stoppages peaked in 1931 and subsequently receded.

Surprisingly, Figure 12.3 shows a high level of work stoppages during the war years of 1941 to 1944. The wartime ethos emphasizing total dedication to national unity and harmony made squabbles over wages and working conditions at workplaces seem either petty or unpatriotic. Yet the record shows that such squabbles persisted in defiance of public imperatives for winning the war. This suggests the pluralism of values, the strength of the spirit of protest, and the diversity of interests despite the wartime thought controls. Some labor scholars interpret these wartime labor disputes as evidence of the Japanese worker's aspirations to individual autonomy, dignity, and respectability.

On the whole, prewar Japanese labor disputes were spontaneous and independent of the labor unions. The percentage of disputes involving unions rose in the latter part of the 1920s, but even at its peak in 1931, it was only a bit over 70 percent. Before 1925 or after 1932, unions were involved in less than 50 percent of labor disputes. In most strikes, a union was one of several external factors that the strikers used to strengthen their cause or improve their strategy. Often strikers hurriedly organized themselves into a union, and so some unions saw in strikes opportunities for extending their organization. Many strikes fell prey to such opportunistic union maneuvers. But some prudent unions refused to use strikes lightly or to allow themselves to be easily drawn into disputes outside their jurisdictions.

In the antiunion climate of prewar Japan, unions interested in their own organizational continuity had every reason to be cautious and proper in dealing with employers. Unions were hard to organize or expand. At the peak of unionization in 1931, only about 8 percent of nonagricultural wage and salary earners belonged to unions. Sōdōmei (Japanese Federation of Labor), reorganized from the Yūaikai in

1919, was the largest and hardiest national trade union and avowedly followed the philosophy of the American Federation of Labor. During the 1920s, Sōdōmei continually lost its radical union constituents. In 1925, some of these left-wing unions formed their own national center, the Nihon rōdō kumiai hyōgikai (Japanese Council of Trade Unions). Hyōgikai was strike happy, calling for work stoppages regardless of the consequences. In 1928 the Japanese government dissolved it as a Communist-dominated antistate organization. The Hyōgikai's leaders went underground and for a few more years continued to direct the organizational drive and industrial disputes. The aforementioned statistical increase in the rate of union involvement in industrial disputes between 1925 and 1931 coincided with the period of Hyōgikai activity. During the 1930s, left-wing unions merged and split, were born and died, and reorganized. Under the pressure of the war emergency, all unions, including Sōdōmei, disbanded in the summer of 1940.

## *Methods of resolving conflicts*

Through strikes and unionization, workers demonstrated the new social reality requiring legitimization by legislation. However, the political elite failed to respond constructively. In 1925 the Diet outlawed revolutionary (antistate or antiprivate property) ideologies by the notorious Chian ijihō (Public Peace Maintenance Law) and in 1926 legalized procedures for resolving industrial disputes, through the Rōdō sōgi chōteihō (Labor Dispute Conciliation Law).[39] But the Diet did not legalize trade unions, even though the need for a union law was widely recognized after World War I. A number of proposals were made by government officials, political parties such as the Kenseikai, and labor unions. In 1925, the Ministry of Home Affairs announced a draft bill, which was strongly opposed by employer organizations such as the Japan Industrial Club. After revisions, the bill was formally presented to the Diet in 1926 but died on the Lower House floor owing to lack of time. Efforts to enact a trade union law continued without success until the law was officially abandoned in 1930.

39 The title of this law is usually translated as indicated in the parentheses. But the crucial term, *chōtei*, which is translated as "conciliation" here, is translated as "mediation" in the English-language discussions of the postwar Labor Relations Adjustment Law enacted in September 1946. "Conciliation" is used for *assen* in the framework of the new law. The 1926 law uses only one term, *chōtei*, for all types of third-party interventions in labor disputes. The 1946 law, however, stipulates three kinds of such interventions: *assen*, *chōtei*, and *chūsai*, which are, respectively, "conciliation," "mediation," and "arbitration." In this law, "conciliation" is by an individual conciliator, and "mediation" is by a committee.

The Labor Dispute Conciliation Law enacted in 1926 in exchange for the elimination of Article 17 from the Public Peace Police Law at first looked like a step in the right direction. But it proved deceptive in the end. Neither unionization nor collective bargaining was legalized, but one kind of collective action, that is, a collective demand by a group of workers for improved employment conditions, received preferential legislative attention. It appears, however, that the law's intent was prejudicial from the beginning, for workers' collective action came into the purview of law only as the source of a potential labor dispute.

In prewar Japan, a strike was usually an outburst of accumulated frustrations and disappointments over the employer's failure to meet the employees' expectations regarding wages and working conditions. Despite the strikes' spontaneous nature, the striking workers displayed considerable discipline as a collectivity under an elected committee of leaders. (Long before they won the right to vote at national elections, workers were practicing democracy in everyday life.) They also showed an understanding of basic bargaining strategy by presenting their grievances and demands to the employer before striking. Many strikes had ominous beginnings, in which employers responded with anger, contempt, abusive language, refusal to see workers or acknowledge their petition, or threats to call in the police. Many accounts of strikes indicate that an outstanding feature of the relationship between employers and workers during a strike was the enormous difficulty for both parties to have a constructive dialogue to resolve their differences.[40]

But Japan is known for its skillful intermediation in many social and interpersonal relationships, and a strike stalemate is another opportunity for this talent to demonstrate its strength. The intermediary could

40 Obviously there is no such thing as a typical strike. It is only for efficiency that we resort here to a general description of how strikes occurred and how they were settled. However, one strike was analyzed for its general implications by George O. Totten, "Japanese Industrial Relations at the Crossroads: The Great Noda Strike of 1927–1928," in *Japan in Crisis: Essays on Taishō Democracy*, ed. Bernard Silberman and H. D. Harootunian (Princeton, N.J.: Princeton University Press, 1974). More can be learned about the patterns of labor disputes through descriptions and analyses of individual cases in the following sources: Aoki Kōji, *Nihon rōdō undōshi nenpyō*, vol. 1 (Tokyo: Shinseisha, 1968); Naitō Norikuni, "Rikugan no rōso hinin to danketsuken yōgo undō," in *Rōdō Keizai to rōdō undō* (Tokyo: Yuhikaku, 1966), pp. 209–33; Nakamura Hideo, ed., *Saikin no shakai undō* (Tokyo: Kyochokai, 1929); *Nihon rōdō undō shiryō*, vols. 6, 9; Okochi Kazuo, *Kurai tanima no rōdō undō* (Tokyo: Iwanami shoten, 1970); Ōmae Sakiro and Ikeda Shin, *Nihon rōdō undō shiron* (Tokyo: Nihon hyōronsha, 1966); Shiota Shōbei, *Sutoraiki no rekishi* (Tokyo: Shin Nihon shuppansha, 1966); Sumiya Mikio, ed., *Nihon rōshi kankei shiron* (Tokyo: Tokyo daigaku shuppankai, 1977); Tanaka Sogorō, ed., *Shiryō Taishō shakai undōshi* (Tokyo: San-ichi shobō, 1970); Yatsugi Kazuo, *Rōdō sōgi hiroku* (Tokyo: Nihon kōgyō shinbunsha, 1979).

be anyone with good reputation that would favorably impress the parties to a dispute. In prewar Japan, when no one dared disregard their authority, police officers were effective mediators in many labor disputes. Well-known labor leaders were also good mediators whose services were sought after by workers and employers alike. There were also unwelcome mediators – gangsters who blackmailed the employer with a promise to subdue his striking workers and accomplished the objective by threatening or even carrying out physical assaults on the workers. Politicians and officials at all levels – mayors, governors, legislators, and ministers of state – volunteered to mediate, depending on their own calculations of political advantage. Genuine as well as dubious intermediaries all flourished in prewar strikes in proportion to the primary parties' inability to handle their own relations and negotiations.

Statistics on the resolution of labor disputes indicate a larger role by the primary parties. Between 1897 and 1909, about 30 percent of strikes were settled by the primary parties themselves. About 13 percent were brought to an end because of dismissals of leaders or of some or all the strikers. More than half the strikes were called off when workers accepted terms of arbitration or yielded to pressures from public officials. Between 1922 and 1925, an average of only 16 percent of labor disputes were settled by conciliation with the help of third-party interventions.[41] Most disputes were settled by the primary parties themselves. But there was a reversal in the relative importance of primary and third parties after 1926 under the new Labor Dispute Conciliation Law.

At the time of legislation, the Labor Dispute Conciliation Law appeared to liberalize labor–management relations because it recognized labor disputes as an unavoidable social reality. The Labor Dispute Conciliation Law provided for a nationwide bureaucracy operating from the Home Ministry to handle matters related to the procedure of conciliation stipulated in the law. According to this stipulation, conciliation was to be effected only by an *ad hoc* tripartite committee organized for each dispute and composed of three representatives each for the primary parties (employer and employees) and a neutral party.

This otherwise splendid idea of a tripartite conciliation committee turned out to be too unwieldy to be practical. Throughout the prewar period, there were only six cases of conciliation that used this

41 *Nihon rōdō undō shiryō*, vol. 10 (1959), pp. 518–19. Also see Nakamura, *Saikin no shakai undō*, p. 812.

method.[42] The bureaucratic machinery deployed throughout the nation to service tripartite conciliation committees (expected to be formed in large numbers) found itself underutilized. Able bureaucrats lost no time in creating work for themselves, however, becoming unofficial conciliators for labor disputes. In other words, the officials adopted the traditional concept of intermediation. But because they were officials appointed by the national government, their conciliation carried greater authority than did that of private citizens. There also were the ubiquitous police eager to continue and expand their usual involvement in labor disputes. In addition, there were prefectural and local officials waiting in the wings for their share of service. One benefit of these officials' concerns was to crowd out the dubious private intermediaries previously mentioned.[43]

Conciliations accounted for less than 30 percent of all labor disputes during the first five or six years that the Labor Dispute Conciliation Law was in force. The percentage rose to nearly 50 percent by the end of the 1930s.[44] But this should not be interpreted as a decline in the employers' and employees' ability to manage their disputes by themselves. Most conciliated disputes were mediated by officials (national, police, prefectural, local, and other), rising from 62 percent in 1927 to 87 percent in 1937. Conciliations not based on applications from either or both of the primary parties accounted for 67 percent of total in 1929, which increased to 82 percent in 1937. Thus, in effect, the Labor Dispute Conciliation Law was just another form of governmental control over labor disputes.

"Conciliation" (*chōtei*) became less and less adequate as a description of what was really happening. The role of the police eventually bared the law's true nature. In 1927, the national conciliation officials handled 40 percent of the conciliations, and the police 13 percent. The national officials' share subsequently declined, and the police's in-

42 *Nihon rōdō undō shiryō*, vol. 10 (1959), p. 519. For the identities of these six cases, see Kazahaya Yasoji, *Nihon shakai seisakushi* (Tokyo: Nihon hyōronsha, 1937; republished in two volumes by Aoki shoten, 1951), vol. 2, p. 496.

43 Nakamura, *Saikin no shakai undō*, p. 813. This source (published in 1929 when the Labor Dispute Conciliation Law had been in effect for three years) considers the officials' conciliations rather fair. It suggests that because of the officials' fairness, workers often began disputes in order to take them to conciliation. Based on short period data, from the latter half of 1926 through March 1929, and showing the number of conciliated disputes by origin of application, Nakamura points out that the number of workers' applications was larger than that of the employers'. But this does not seem to support the hypothesized rise of this new strategy among workers. The tendency of workers' applications to outnumber employers' persisted throughout the 1930s, according to *Nihon rōdō undō shiryō*, vol. 10 (1959), p. 519. But their proportion to total conciliations was smaller during the 1930s. The proportion of official interventions rose and labor disputes decreased during the same period, as will be discussed presently.

44 *Nihon rōdō undō shiryō*, vol. 10 (1959), pp. 518–19.

creased. In 1937, 64 percent of conciliations were by the police and 16 percent by the national officials. After the outbreak of the Sino-Japanese War in the summer of 1937, the country increasingly moved onto a war footing. The police once again became preeminent in controlling labor disputes, forcing most to police conciliations, or "conciliations by saber" (*sāberu chōtei*), as they were called. The official subversion of conciliation during the 1930s was associated with a decrease in labor disputes, as earlier observed, as well as a deterioration of wages and working conditions. In 1937, Yasoji Kazahaya made the following observations about the system of "compulsory conciliation":

> [I]n giant armament factories, not only is there a *de facto* ban on labor disputes, but direct contacts and negotiations between management and worker representatives are prohibited. The government always enters between them as a compulsory conciliator. The resolution of a conflict is worked out between management and police and handed down by police to worker representatives. There is no bilateral economic transaction between management and labor on an equal footing. A third party, higher and more powerful than the primary parties, resolves the conflict by offering non-negotiable terms.[45]

### *From works councils to Sanpō*

Other methods of resolving conflicts were also attempted with varying success and unexpected results. In the wake of the unprecedented surge of labor disputes during and immediately after Word War I, employers flirted with the notion of works councils.[46] The type of council they favored most was a purely consultative type limited to agreeing with the employer on whatever he saw fit to consult the workers on. Of course, the machinery of the works councils provided a wide latitude for the distribution of power between employer and employee. Militant and organizationally experienced workers could turn a works council into the cell of a revolutionary movement, and a dominant employer could reduce it to complete obedience. Between 1919 and 1922, many private firms attempted to set up works councils and organized seventy-four. In 1927 there were ninety-six works councils set up in private firms. But the survival rate of these councils was rather low; only fifty-nine out of the ninety-six were still in operation in 1927, of which forty-four were begun between 1919 and 1922.[47] Obviously, playing with the works council idea was only a tactical

45 Kazahaya, *Nihon shakai seisakushi*, vol. 2, p. 495.

46 George O. Totten, "Collective Bargaining and Works Councils As Innovations in Industrial Relations in Japan during the 1920s," in *Aspects of Social Change in Modern Japan*, ed. R. P. Dore (Princeton, N.J.: Princeton University Press, 1967), pp. 203–43. The case of the maritime industry is analyzed on pp. 233–39.

47 Nakamura, ed., *Saikin no shakai undō*.

retreat for the employers under the impact of unprecedented worker militancy. When the employers were no longer frightened of labor disputes, they scrapped the idea entirely. Naturally, when the workers demanded works councils, the employers refused to go along. Any bid from the workers thought to be a permanent dent in the employers' authority was resisted at any cost. Employers were increasingly willing to make financial settlements through temporary payments as if paying ransom, but they were never reconciled to the idea of a dialogue with the workers on an equal footing.

The employers always wanted to destroy the labor unions in their enterprises or prevent them from being organized. They discriminated against or harassed workers suspected of leaning toward union activity, let alone becoming members. The best that the workers could expect (that is, the worst that the employers could be forced to accept) was tolerance of the idea that joining a union could be a matter of individual choice, without any implication that the employers should recognize the union that some of their employees actually joined. The great Noda strike discussed by George Totten was almost a "holy war" waged by the employer to purge his work force of any trace of union influence after several years of making humiliating concessions to the union.

Once the objective of destroying unions or keeping them out was attained, however, most employers could even affect a degree of benevolence. Thus, in the Noda case, after victory was assured, the employer exhibited his concern over the hardships of 435 dismissed workers by granting them severance pay, cost-of-living assistance, and lump-sum payments, which are said to have averaged ¥200 per worker, surely more than one hundred days of wages. Similar settlements were made in many other cases. But all this amounts only to a rise in the cost of maintaining the employers' authority. The price of authority to the employers rose even further when the workers learned the rules of the game; that is, workers already dissatisfied enough to quit could extract larger ransoms by creating disturbances before they left. One should not underestimate Japanese workers' practical ability to simultaneously submit to and manipulate their circumstances.

The turnover of trade unions (some unions newly formed and some older ones dismantled) was high, indicating the unions' basic insecurity in the antiunion climate of the interwar period. But high turnover also meant that many workers were involved in the labor movement and learned the art and problems of unionization. The prewar labor movement was characterized by ideological shifts, jurisdictional rivalries, pragmatic adjustments, tactical advances and retreats, militancy alternating with docility, and many other kinds of intractable maneuvers. A sequence of plant-level organizational dynamics often was as follows: first, a national union like Sōdōmei would secretly organize a small fraction of the work force of a plant that in due course would grow large enough to ask for recognition and negotiation; second, the initial test of power by a strike would result in the union's defeat and demise; third, some workers would form a second union or an employee association stressing moderation to placate the employer; and fourth, some time later, this second union would surprise the employer and the public by professing a true class-oriented unionism, starting the employer–union struggles all over again. The organizational history of prewar unionism is full of such drifts and shifts, births and rebirths of unions.[48]

Under these circumstances, collective bargaining between employer and employees as a means to adjust mutual claims and expectations was difficult to institutionalize. There was one exception, however. The Shipowners' Association and the Seamen's Union succeeded in instituting and maintaining a collective bargaining relationship. This relationship did not ensure perfect industrial peace, but it appears to have prevented occasional disagreements from bogging down in prolonged, irreconcilable disputes. Its conflict-minimizing function was demonstrated in 1928 when the Seamen's Union demanded a uniform minimum wage scale. To this demand, the Shipowners' Association responded by suggesting a labor–management committee of six members (three from each side) to study the issue and recommend a solution. The committee was formed but failed to produce a solution owing to its failure to manage its own internal dissensions. The seamen then sporadically resorted to work stoppages at various ports of Japan. In search for a way out of the impasse, the seamen and the shipowners agreed on a committee of seven arbitrators, promising each other that the results of the arbitration would be honored. The arbitration committee speedily (within four days) recommended a scale of minimum wages by rank of worker and ship size, which both sides accepted.

The first obstacle in the interwar pattern of employer–employee relations was the employer's inability to recognize as legitimate an employee's request to discuss matters related to wages and working conditions. The difference between this pattern and industrial relations in the shipping industry, in which both sides were organized and

48 For the organizational history of unionism in Japan from this perspective, see Nishioka Takao, *Nihon no rōdō kumiai soshiki* (Tokyo: Japan Institute of Labor, 1960); and Komatsu Ryuji, *Kigyōbetsu kumiai no seisei* (Tokyo: Ochanomizu shobō, 1971).

dealt with each other through representatives, was surely too vast to measure. And yet the maritime industrial relations of the interwar period were by no means extraordinary by standards of modern collective bargaining. If anything, they were immature, inexperienced, and fraught with the danger that good sense and discipline on either side might break down in ways typical of the primitive prewar pattern of employment relationships. In fact, localized work stoppages were frequent in the Japanese maritime industry and the Seamen's Union had trouble disciplining many of its local groups. Even so, the centralized collective bargaining machinery survived and functioned until the Seamen's Union disbanded in 1940, when the war economy demanded a reorganization of industrial relations under different principles.

In the 1920s and 1930s, the Seamen's Union survived in great part because of its right-wing nationalist ideology. When unionization was a movement often inspired by socialist or communist ideologies and regarded with suspicion and distrust by the public, employers, and the authorities, the preferred commitment of the Seaman's Union to the national interest ensured its safety and credibility in Japanese society. Although like other right-wing unions, it eventually failed to produce a viable reconciliation of unionism and nationalism when the role of unions was questioned during wartime, at least until then the Seaman's Union proved that nationalism and partiotism could offer ideological protection to the essentially insecure labor movement. This lesson did not pass unnoticed by other workers. Thus in the 1930s there was an unusual twist in the workers' strategy. Workers and unions brandishing their commitment to the national interest became increasingly right wing and, under the impact of deteriorating international circumstances, pushed capitalist employers into an awkward corner where they were made to appear selfish and unpatriotic.

Because of such strategy shifts, many labor unions were able to establish good relations with the police and especially the Special Superior Police (Tokkō keisatsu). Unions and workers learned to get along well with these once-feared agents of the state and often obtained their approval of industrial action before undertaking it. Indeed, even some regular police and special police officers were critical of some private firms' labor practices and working conditions. Although strategic concessions to the state later undermined the raison d'être of trade unionism, in the meantime unions used the police acquiescence to advance the standing of workers vis-à-vis their employers. Out of this twist in the triangular relationships of labor, management, and the state came a renewed interest in works councils. It was now the workers who, with the acquiescence and even the support of the police, promoted works councils or similar kinds of consultative machinery in which worker representatives and employers served on an equal footing and which ensured industrial peace or uninterrupted production for the good of society at large.

The case of Aichi Clock Company (Aichi tokei), a manufacturer of clocks and watches, which six thousand employees struck twice in 1937, illustrates how workers took advantage of the changing times. The conciliation by the police produced a settlement highly advantageous to the workers. Among other things, the settlement included an agreement to set up a labor-management consultative council. This experience at Aichi Clock and similar experiences at other firms in the same region prompted the Aichi Prefectural Police Department to devise machinery and procedures to promote industrial peace. The so-called Arakawa Plan, published in February 1938, is generally considered the genesis of the nationwide Sanpō movement. The Arakawa Plan envisaged a plant council (*kōjō kondankai*) made up of several representatives from the employers' and the employees' sides. The council's primary objective was preventing labor disputes. As soon as signs of conflict appeared, the council was to take charge of the problem and prevent it from developing into a dispute. If the council failed to resolve the conflict, a workshop committee for its resolution was to be organized with the participation of public authorities. If the objective was not attained at this "second level," the conflict was referred to a "third level," which was another, more authoritative, special committee. In this way, Japanese employers and employees began to move into a stage of industrial relations that reduced the employers' authority and raised the employees' status so that both could sit down together to discuss and agree or disagree on matters related to production, technology, and employment as well as roles and rewards for the members of the enterprise. Managerial authoritarianism, too, came to an end. Though incomplete when compared with fascist labor unions in Europe, enterprise corporatism in a corporatist state was born in Japan under the aegis of the Sanpō movement, 1938 to 1945.[49]

49 A serialized article by Hagiwara Susumu on wartime wage controls contains illuminating historical observations on the relationships between the Aichi Tokei incident and the Arakawa Plan on the one hand and the Sanpō system on the other. Hagiwara Susumu, "Senji chingin tōsei no isan," *Chingin Fōramu*, nos. 11–20 (1977), esp. nos. 17, 18. For the wartime labor economy, see J. B. Cohen, *Japan's Economy in War and Reconstruction* (Minneapolis: University of Minnesota Press, 1949), chap. 5; Takenaka Emiko, "Kyōkō to sensōka ni okeru rōdō shijo no henbō," *Kōza Nihon shihonshugi hattatsu shiron:* vol. 3: *Kyōkō kara sensō e*, ed. Kawai Ichirō et al. (Tokyo: Nihon hyōronsha, 1968), chap. 5.

Sanpō is the abbreviation of Sangyō hōkokukai (Society for Service to the State through Industry). As illustrated by the pioneer example of Aichi Clock Company, it emphasized the importance of harmony in capital–labor relations and promoted a new strategy for preventing labor disputes. In 1938 the Kyōchōkai (Harmonization Society), co-opting the aforementioned Arakawa Plan, organized the Sangyō hōkoku renmei (League for Service to the State through Industry). The idea was to organize a Sangyō hōkokukai (Sanpō) unit in each plant. The Kyōchōkai activity was given official approval by the ministries of Welfare and Home Affairs. Soon an overseeing organization, Dai Nippon sangyō hōkokukai (Greater Japan Association for Service to the State through Industry), was formed with the help of official subsidies to provide a national center for all the plant-level Sanpō units. Under the slogan of *jigyō ikka* (enterprise as a family), the Sanpō unit was conceptually likened to a "family" (*ie*). The Sanpō ideologues hoped to do away with the capitalist concept of enterprise and to transform the adversary relations between capital and labor into harmonious relations such as existed ideally between the family head and family members. According to Jerome B. Cohen, by 1940, Sanpō membership in manufacturing was 2.9 million persons, or about 41 percent of all gainfully employed persons in manufacturing, as shown in Table 12.1. The total Sanpō membership in all industries in 1940 stood at 3.5 million, and the total in 1945 was estimated to be about 6.4 million.[50]

Under the Sanpō system, a peculiar type of social democracy emerged in each firm. The Sanpō organization destroyed the traditional social distances and status differences between managers and workers, office employees and factory hands, more educated and less educated, males and females, and young and old. Despite their differences in function, position, and ability, all persons had equal dignity and importance as "members of the enterprise" working for the collective objective – maximal output for the country. Private life and family needs became subordinate to the enterprise's requirements, and the Sanpō enterprise was an organ of the state. Functionally, the firm's work force was structured like a military unit, and many elements of military-style organizational behavior were introduced. For example, every morning, workers would assemble to form squads, companies, and divisions in the factory's front yard and march to their respective jobs in the factory under the command of their unit leaders, who were

50 Cohen, *Japan's Economy in War and Reconstruction*, p. 285.

in turn commanded by the next layer of leaders. The military-style organization brought everyone face to face, or at least within sight in appropriate positions. The personal visibility of everyone and the application of the same basic rules of conduct to everyone created a sense of belonging and a shared understanding of the nature and problems of the entire enterprise. The regularization of the rhythm of work and life improved discipline and performance on the job.

The Sanpō enterprise unit became a comprehensive community concerned with all aspects of work and life. The enterprise organized recreational and educational activities. The workers were drilled in firefighting techniques in anticipation of air raids. They frequently participated in inspirational meetings studying books exalting the virtues of the emperor and the glory of the Japanese state. Sanpō made the enterprise a basic unit of national community, thus "nationalizing" not only production but also the souls and beliefs of the workers. Sanpō obviously promoted a greater homogenization of the Japanese throughout Japan. In a sense it brought about a remarkable social revolution. Because Japan surrendered before the homeland was invaded, Japanese workers made their transition to the postwar period maintaining a high degree of organization and morale in their workplaces. This meant that the enterprise as a community remained roughly intact at the beginning of the postwar period. This legacy of Sanpō helps explain why the most effective way to organize a union in the postwar period was by a mass conversion of the entire work force to the new principle of work-related organization, or unionism. Organized and orderly mass meetings within the enterprise were commonplace during the war. When circumstances changed, the social democracy that had grown up under Sanpō produced a sort of "town hall democracy" for collective action within the enterprise.[51]

## POSTWAR LABOR RELATIONS, 1945–1955

With the end of the war in 1945, the history of Japanese employment relations entered a new phase. A major aspect of this phase was the

51 Okochi Kazuo calls the enterprise labor union "Sanpō turned inside out" (*uragaeshini shita Sanpō*). Just as the state organized the Sanpō unit from above, the postwar labor union, which included all the former members of the Sanpō unit, was encouraged by the Occupation authorities from above. But the Occupation's encouragement worked upward and out from the rank and file (turned inside out). See Okochi Kazuo, *Rōdō kumiai undō no saishuppatsu* (Tokyo: Nihon hyōronshinsha, 1956), esp. pp. 72–4. For the effects of Sanpō on postwar union organization, see also Magota Ryohei, "Kigyōbetsu kumiai no keisei," *Journal of Humanities and Social Sciences* (Waseda University), no. 12, May 1975, pp. 21–38.

legitimation and development of the labor union as a permanent feature of the Japanese employment system.[52] Japan's postwar labor movement rose at a curious time.[53] No unions were organized in August 1945. There were only two labor unions at the end of September, a month and a half after the surrender, and only seven unions at the end of October. This timid beginning is puzzling because the disastrous end of a prolonged war might well have prompted large-scale uprisings against the regime by angry people. But nothing of the sort took place in Japan. The workers were quiet, and the wartime regime remained intact until the Allied Occupation began to dismantle it in October. The duration and effectiveness of wartime law and order for nearly two months after the surrender are surprising. Even during a period potentially ideal for successful internal rebellions, that is, between the surrender on August 15 and the arrival of an advance party of the Occupation forces on August 30, no one stirred to demand a rectification of past wrongs or a radical change in the ways to govern the nation. Japan showed no signs of revolutionary upheavals.

But once Japanese workers awoke to the opportunities for the labor movement created by American plans to democratize Japan, their efforts were intense and far-reaching. In early October 1945, General Douglas MacArthur issued a directive to remove prewar and wartime restrictions on civil, political, and religious liberties. In December 1945, the Trade Union Law was enacted, modeled on the United States' Wagner Act. For the first time in Japanese history, a law guaranteed the workers' right to organize and to bargain collectively, a right that was later enshrined in the 1947 constitution. In September 1946, the Labor Relations Adjustment Law was passed, superseding the prewar Labor Dispute Conciliation Law and related statutes. In September 1947, the Labor Standards Law came into being, supplanting the prewar Factory Law and other similar laws. It is significant that in the legislative program concerning labor, the Trade Union Law was the first to be enacted, establishing the primacy of collective bargaining as a means of determining wages and working conditions and resolving conflict between employers and workers. This meant that the market forces were no longer unbridled but had to yield to the

52 For an introduction to postwar Japanese industrial relations, see Suehiro Izutarō, *Nihon rōdō kumiai undōshi* (Tokyo: Chūō kōronsha, 1954). See also Solomon B. Levine, *Industrial Relations in Postwar Japan* (Urbana: University of Illinois Press, 1958). An interesting recent work is Andrew Gordon, *The Evolution of Labor Relations in Japan: Heavy Industry, 1853–1955* (Cambridge, Mass.: Harvard University Press, 1985).

53 Yamamoto Kyoshi, "Sengo rōdō kumiai no shuppatsuten," in *Nihon rōshi kankei shiron*, ed. Sumiya Mikio (Tokyo: Tokyo daigaku shuppankai, 1977), chap. 5.

pressures of organized forces on wages, working conditions, and conflict resolution.

Trade union membership rose from about five thousand workers in October 1945 to nearly seven million on the eve of the Dodge Plan in early 1949. The increase during 1946 alone accounted for nearly five million. Like the calm that preceded it, this explosive growth of trade unionism also challenges our comprehension of Japanese social phenomena. After the situation was stabilized, the enterprise union, a new and durable feature of postwar industrial relations, became visible. "Enterprise unionism" was a type of unionism under which, as a rule, all regular nonsupervisory workers of an enterprise were organized into one independent union. An enterprise union would not expand beyond the work force of a single enterprise or that of a single plant of a multiplant enterprise, although federations at the enterprise, industry, or national levels were possible and were often formed by enterprise unions.

The emergence of a trade union instantly absorbing a firm's entire work force is an extraordinary feat in the creation of solidarity and unanimity. That all the workers in a firm readily agreed to form and stay in one union was an extension of the organizational behavior and habits that Sanpō had cultivated. But Sanpō's organizational unit was not a bargaining unit. Nor was there any concept of bargaining in the Sanpō ideology. Thus, although the Sanpō form of enterprise offered an organizational basis for enterprise unionism, the question remains as to why Japanese workers after the war chose to remold their organization as a trade union. Did they know what a union was and how it differed from the Sanpō unit in which they worked? Who among them knew anything about trade unionism? Unfortunately, these simple questions have no simple answers. In fact, research into the roots of the postwar unionism has begun only recently.

It can be assumed that during the Sanpō years, especially between 1940 and 1945, there was little chance for workers to learn anything about the principles of trade unionism. Therefore when the war was over, a working knowledge of trade unionism was limited to those who were exposed to trade unionism before 1940. Then the crucial question is how many postwar workers had prewar trade union experience and were willing to become active again in the labor movement. A prevailing view suggests that postwar trade unions somehow spontaneously mushroomed among workers who learned about trade unionism for the first time in their lives and, with the encouragement of the Occupation authorities, were eager to put their newly acquired knowledge into practice. Most research on Japanese industrial relations emphasizes a break in the personal identities of trade union leaders between the prewar and postwar years. No one has claimed that all the prewar trade unionists were dead and buried before the rise of the postwar labor movement. But curiously, the orthodox view implies that the surviving prewar trade unionists contributed little or nothing to the rise of the postwar labor movement. Yamamoto Kiyoshi challenged this orthodoxy and, after examining the relevant data, concluded that the prewar trade unionists' involvement in the postwar trade union leadership was considerable.[54] Indeed, one of the earliest unions to rise again after the war was the large prewar Seamen's Union, reconstructed on October 5, 1945.

However, the prewar labor movement was diverse in ideological orientation, organizational strategies, and professed objectives. It was unable to form a united national center. Therefore, if the prewar trade unionists played a significant role in the postwar labor movement, this implied that the prewar type of internal division would surface again. Indeed, ideological wrangling, opportunism, and adventurism were at a new high in the Japanese labor movement after the war.

In regard to basic human rights and civil liberties, the postwar social climate was entirely new in Japanese history, and there was a tendency to identify the enjoyment of rights and liberties with radical shifts toward the left in outlook, attitude, and action in all aspects of life and work. Under these circumstances, it was natural that communists and socialists should enjoy an unprecedented degree of popularity among the Japanese at the enterprise level. Radical or militant trade unionism proved more attractive to workers than did a more moderate variety. Moreover, ideological biases also affected the organizing strategies of union leaders and made them respond to the Sanpō legacy in varying ways. For example, organizers from Sōdōmei (Japanese Federation of Labor, revived in the fall of 1945) used the traditional method of recruiting trade union members: They would go to factory gates and urge workers to join their unions ("leafleting at the plant gate"). While Sōdōmei organizers pursued this tactic, the unions were forming inside the enterprises, and many of them later affiliated with the leftist Sanbetsu kaigi (Japanese Congress of Industrial Unions).

After failing at first, Sōdōmei changed its organizing strategy and adopted new techniques. As a first step, it recruited potential leaders from among workers in an enterprise and helped them organize the

54 Ibid., pp. 267–73.

entire work force into a union, which was then taken into an appropriate industrial or geographical federation under the umbrella of Sōdōmei. But the setbacks in tactical adjustment and its own moderate ideological preferences cost Sōdōmei its rightful place as the preeminent national trade union center. It was outorganized by Sanbetsu. The two labor centers together claimed about a half of Japan's entire labor movement. The other half stayed in a variety of independent or neutral arrangements, mostly pure enterprise unions. Sōdōmei and Sanbetsu waged fierce "jurisdictional struggles" to capture these independents. Occasional gestures for truce and unity were made from both sides, and a few short-lived liaison councils were formed. However, Sanbetsu's strength suddenly began to crumble in the fall of 1947, and its subsequent disintegration was as spectacular as its prior rise.

During the most volatile postwar years, 1945 to 1948, workers were brutalized by inflation, lagging wages, unemployment, a scarcity of life's necessities, and production bottlenecks. With or without unions, industrial disputes broke out everywhere. Unions often came into being as by-products of spontaneous strikes. One memorable response to an employer's inadequate response to the workers' demands was the workers' seizure of the enterprise. In these cases, the workers managed the enterprise on their own after expelling the employer and continued production to ensure uninterrupted, often enlarged, earnings. Whether this was a movement of any ideological importance pointing toward a noncapitalist economic system composed of worker-directed firms or whether it was only an expedient like any other dispute tactics that workers have devised from time to time in the capitalist system has since been a subject of controversy among students of Japanese industrial relations. One thing is clear, however: Circumstances permitting, even the Japanese workers, who are generally not susceptible to ideological excesses, can launch an industrial action that, whether ideological or not, attacks the most "sacred" foundation of the capitalist economic system – private property in the means of production. In the historical context of early postwar Japan, the possibility of a socialist revolution was real in the minds of many Japanese. Every new instance of production control was hailed by radicals or feared by conservatives as another step toward revolution. The first example of production control took place at the *Yomiuri* newspaper in October 1945.[55] Incidents of production control peaked in the spring and summer of 1946.

55 Yamamoto Kiyoshi, *Sengo rōdō undō shiron*, vol. 1 (Tokyo: Ochanomizu shobō, 1977).

The Japanese government responded swiftly. On February 1, 1946, the four ministers of Home Affairs, Justice, Commerce and Industry, and Welfare jointly declared as unlawful any infringements on property rights. Although "production control" as such was not mentioned specifically, the intent of the announcement was clear.[56] But this did not deter the workers. Although the government finally cracked down on offending workers, it also conceded the merit of their argument that the demoralized employers in postwar confusion lacked the will to expand production and that some of them were even engaged in a speculative sabotage of production so as to profit from the rising prices of inventories under rapid postwar inflation. The workers also learned a few lessons about the difficulty of running a business. Society at large was on the whole negative toward production control, making it difficult for workers engaged in it to secure supplies or sell products.

Nevertheless, production control demonstrated how far worker militancy could go, even at the risk of breaking the law, toward modifying the distribution of decision-making power between management and labor in the operation of the firm. After production control, power relations between management and labor could never be the same again. The takeover of a firm by workers, legal or not, remains to this day a standing warning against employer incompetence. The threat of this possibility was no idle talk during the heyday of production control. It was clear that major concessions to the labor movement were in order.

Indeed, even the conservative Yoshida cabinet (May 1946 to May 1947) was compelled to heed the lesson by taking two major "socialist" steps. One was the adoption in December 1946 of an industrial priority plan formulated by a well-known Marixst economist, Arizawa Hiromi. The plan proposed concentrating on scarce resources in the expansion of coal, electricity, and steel production. These priorities reflected the Marxists and socialists' "heavy industry bias." The second major step was the inauguration in February 1947 of the Economic Reconstruction Conference, in which representatives of organized labor were given a major role. The national conference stood at the apex of industry-level and enterprise-level labor–management councils. Unfortunately, ideological differences among the labor leaders severely reduced the conference's effectiveness as a policymaking

56 The four ministers apparently failed to clear the declaration with the Occupation authorities in advance, which undermined its effects. See the comments on the event by Theodore Cohen, then head of the Labor Division of the General Headquarters, in *The Occupation of Japan*, ed. Lawrence H. Redford (Norfolk, Va.: MacArthur Memorial, 1980), pp. 197–8.

body, and it was dissolved in July 1948 after having done little more than provide educational and informational services. Signs of decline in the labor movement's power and influence surfaced during the life of this conference. In 1948 the rapid rise of Japanese labor from the shadow of Sanpō to partnership in governing Japan was suddenly reversed. Labor's fall was due in part to the "reverse course" of the Occupation policy.

Labor's militancy first tested the limits of the Occupation's tolerance in January 1947, when the public-sector unions planned a nationwide general strike.[57] On January 31, on the eve of the planned strike of February 1, General MacArthur ruled against it, although he made it clear at the same time that the ban of this particular strike implied no general restriction on workers' rights to collective industrial action. Nevertheless, this was the first major official action to tighten the perimeter of the labor movement. Fourteen months later, in March 1948, the Occupation authorities banned regional strikes by the postal workers. Then in July 1948, General MacArthur directed the Japanese government to deprive civil servants and other public-sector workers of their right to strike. In December 1948, an injunction was issued against a coal miners' strike. In 1949, the prolabor Trade Union Law, promulgated in December 1945, was revised, and the qualifications for legal strikes in the private sector were tightened. While the perimeter of the labor movement was tightened year after year in this way, the machinery and procedure of collective bargaining within the framework of capitalist industrial relations was encouraged at the same time, often with government guidance and supervision. Labor disputes diminished as a consequence.

In addition to the greater discipline imposed on the labor movement from above, there came a demand for greater union democracy from below among the rank and file of the trade unions. One of their objectives was to eliminate the influence of the Communist Party. Anti-Communist movements arose even within Sanbetsu, as well as the traditionally anti-Communist Sōdōmei. The first showdown occurred in October 1947 when independents and Sōdōmei-affiliated miners' unions pulled out of the National Council of Miners' Unions. The rift between pro-Communist and anti-Communist forces widened, and in January 1948 Sōdōmei openly proclaimed its determination to fight to oust the Communists from the labor movement. The

57 The importance of the abortive general strike planned for February 1, 1947, in the Occupation's labor history is emphasized by Theodore Cohen, "Labor Democratization in Japan: The First Years," in *The Occupation of Japan*, pp. 162–73.

forces in favor of union democratization within Sanbetsu organized an action league, Mindō (Alliance for Democratization), and after many inhouse quarrels with the Communists, left the parent body. In July 1950, Mindō and Sōdōmei organized a new national center, Sōhyō (General Council of Trade Unions). A few years later, a leftward swing of the Sōhyō leadership alienated Sōdōmei, which after its departure from Sōhyō, evolved into today's Dōmei, the second largest national labor center after Sōhyō. There also developed a much smaller labor center called Chūritsu rōren (Federation of Independent Unions). By 1955, the postwar period was definitely over for Japan's labor movement. A new era dawned about this time: the age of the *shuntō* (spring labor offensive). The structure of compromises and accommodations that had taken shape by 1955 continues to this day.

In the industrial relations system that emerged from the social selection during the Occupation period, the basic unit of the labor movement was the enterprise-based and enterprise-confined labor union, with collective bargaining as a main instrument of influence over management. Although temporary workers and women were still excluded from full entitlements to the benefits of the Japanese employment system, a high degree of social democracy prevailed between regular employees and managers of an enterprise. They all were equal "enterprise citizens" and equally enjoyed a long-term tenure often dubbed "lifetime commitment." The pricing of labor, that is, wage determination, required frequent bargaining, whereas other aspects of employment were locked in more durable collective agreements – work rules and related provisions. Management prerogatives were generally respected by workers but were exercised prudently and subject to intensive communications throughout the firm. Joint labor–management consultative committees were also active, ensuring that no decisions affecting workers were made or enforced unilaterally by management. Within the union, a high degree of union democracy and a scrupulous observance of democratic rules of decision making were firmly planted. Although industrial disputes were frequent and widespread in Japanese industry, they were resolved quickly, making long-term impasses or stalemates rare. Japan's capitalist economy, middle-class society, and conservative polity seem to be in a long-run equilibrium. Obviously it was during the Occupation period that this equilibrium solution was worked out, by reconciling a number of seemingly intractable equations of conflicting claims and counterclaims. With social problems in the workplace set aside by this solution, Japan after 1955 concentrated on economic activities leading to the economic "miracle" of the 1960s.

CHAPTER 13

# SOCIALISM, LIBERALISM, AND MARXISM, 1901–1931

In the 1890s many observers at home and abroad discovered that Japan had finally entered the mainstream of world history and had indeed become a principal actor in that history. As Ōkuma Shigenobu remarked at the end of the Sino-Japanese War, "Japan is no longer a Japan for Japan, but a Japan for the world." Although some Japanese viewed the end of their cultural and political isolation as cause for unrestrained self-congratulation, others were ambivalent about its implication for the future. If Japan became more like other modern nations, its material and political development might continue, but only at the expense of social harmony or cultural integrity. As the country moved into a new century, there was uncertainty over the shape of Japan's future.

One vision of the future saw Japan as eternally unique, able to maintain its traditional culture and values even in the midst of rapid economic and political change. This point of view, which we might call the particularist or exceptionalist perspective, found champions in the Seikyōsha writers of the early 1890s, who urged that the nation's cultural essence (*kokusui*) be preserved in the march toward modernity.[1] Given the polychromatic character of Japan's cultural past, however, it was difficult to identify this cultural essence. Unlike China, which boasted of an easily identifiable great tradition, Japan had none. Where, then, were the Seikyōsha writers to find the *kokusui* – in the myths and legends of the Shinto tradition, in the sensibilities of Heian culture, in the harsh ethos of the warrior class, in the boisterous arts of the Tokugawa townsmen, or in the austere puritanism of Tokugawa Confucianism?

Although the Seikyōsha writers were conspicuously vague about what made Japan unique, neotraditionalist scholars like Hozumi Yatsuka and Inoue Tetsujirō found it in a blend of Confucian morality

1 On the Seikyōsha writers, see Kenneth B. Pyle, *The New Generation in Meiji Japan: Problems of Cultural Identity, 1885–1895* (Stanford, Calif.: Stanford University Press, 1969).

and nativist myth that they shaped into a civil religion for the state. They converted the familiar idea of the *kokutai*, long employed in the Edo period to sanctify a hierarchical sociopolitical order with the emperor at its apex, into an explanation for the durability, uniqueness, and superiority of Japanese social and political mores. Simultaneously sacralizing the emperor as the descendant of Amaterasu and secularizing him as the source of worldly political values, they likened his role to that of the benevolent father, concerned for his subject/children but requiring their undivided allegiance. The family-state (*kazoku kokka*) concept, an ingenious ideological construct influenced by an organic conception of the state imported from the West, was powerful and pervasive: It informed the drafting of textbooks, the education of schoolteachers, and the training of lesser functionaries in the police, the military, and the judicial service. Although never formally adopted as a state creed, it became the basis of a highly particularistic nationalism that displaced critical political thought in the minds of its true believers.[2]

Even though the particularist/exceptionalist perspective on Japanese society enjoyed official respectability, many intellectuals found it difficult to accept. Products of a system of higher education whose curriculum depended on the "new knowledge" (*shinchishiki*) from the West, they were more inclined to a cosmopolitan conception of Japan's future, one that placed Japan fully in the mainstream of world history, subject to the same developmental laws and heading for the same future as were the more advanced nations of the West. Intellectuals of the late Meiji and Taishō periods frequently referred to the *jisei* (trends of the times) or *sekai no taisei* (trends in the world) to validate their proposals for political or social change. These words, which seem almost empty of meaning to the outsider, implied that there were discernible regularities or patterns of change in society, often unilinear in character. When linked with the concepts of social progress (*shakai shinpo*) or social evolution (*shakai shinka*), they conveyed the idea that the new was better than the old and that society improved over time. If the exceptionalist perspective chose to focus on timeless essences, cosmopolitan intellectuals looked at patterns of flux and often found in them historical inevitability.

Like the theorists of the family state, these intellectuals drew much of their vocabulary, conceptual and semantic, from Western thought.

2 For an excellent study of the origins of state ideology, see Carol Gluck, *Japan's Modern Myths: Ideology in the Making in the Late Meiji Period* (Princeton, N.J.: Princeton University Press, 1985).

The notion that there were fixed norms governing all societies was a familiar one, embodied in the Confucian concept of "principle" (*ri*), but it could not account for the dynamics of history, except in cyclical patterns of decline and restoration. The discovery that society could move to ever-higher levels of prosperity, rationality, or efficiency was perhaps the central intellectual revolution of the Meiji period. The notion of progress was to be found in nearly every tome and tract on social thought translated into Japanese, whether it came from a radical Rousseau or a conservative Bluntschli. To some degree, the concept of progress was complicated by the less optimistic social Darwinist ideas so influential in the 1880s, yet more often than not, social Darwinism, when applied to domestic rather than external developments, was construed in a positive sense, with the stress on the fittest who survived rather than on their struggle for existence.

The idea that there were regular patterns of social progress implied the basic commonality of humankind and the existence of a universal human psychology transcending the peculiarities of social, geographical, and historical context. Whereas the exceptionalist perspective extolled a unique "Japanese spirit" that was inaccessible to the alien mind, the cosmopolitan perspective often saw identical impulses at work in all persons and in all societies. This led to a simplified, even conventionalized, description of human behavior, but it also suggested that Japan was not a psychological lost continent inhabited by a separate species. The idea of social progress was also easy to associate with programs of social and political reform: If the future were always better than the past, then it could be used to rebuke the present as well.

In the early 1890s the cosmopolitan viewpoint found its most undiluted expression in the writing of Tokutomi Sohō and his circle.[3] In *Shōrai no Nihon*, Tokutomi described Japan as being in a transitional stage of development, moving like the advanced Western societies from a militaristic-aristocratic to an industrial-democratic society. Drawing on the writings of mid-Victorian liberalism, from John Stuart Mill to Herbert Spencer, Tokutomi argued that the tendency of human history was toward freedom, equality, prosperity, and peace. At times Tokutomi hovered on the edge of a rigid historical determinism, giving scant heed to the vagaries of historical accident or the impact of human will on history. But by the mid-1890s he had somewhat modified his conception of the future from a simplistic model of a laissez-faire society to one

3 On the development of Tokutomi's thought, see Kenneth B. Pyle, *New Generation*, and John D. Pierson, *Tokutomo Sohō, 1863–1957: A Journalist for Modern Japan* (Princeton, N.J.: Princeton University Press, 1980).

in which individualism was tempered by collectivism or state interventionism, even though he remained committed to a unilinear concept of historical development.

Even those most closely attached to a theory of universal human development, like Tokutomi, had only to look around to realize that social laws did not work in a vacuum but in a concrete time and place. When applied to Japan, laws of universal development often had to be bent to fit. For example, Tokutomi described the Meiji Restoration as an incomplete or unfulfilled revolution. Although he saw it as the culmination of long-term trends toward liberty that had brought down the old order, paradoxically and perhaps illogically, he saw these trends thwarted, stymied, or aborted in the post-Restoration era. Later, Marxist debates on the character of the Restoration and the development of capitalism in Japan wrestled with the same problem. "Trends of the times" often seemed to have a different velocity and follow a different trajectory in Japan. Though traveling toward the same destination as were the advanced nations of the West, Japan appeared to move on a bypath rather than the main highway.

Then, too, the model of the future presented by the advanced societies of the West was itself in a continuous process of transformation. Japan might have the "advantage of followership," but it had to follow a constantly moving target. Cosmopolitan perspectives on the future in the early twentieth century therefore kept shifting, and so this chapter will discuss several of its varied exponents – the late Meiji socialists, the democratic liberals of Taishō, and the Marxists and other left radicals of the 1920s. Often in contention with one another, they still shared a common discourse that made Japanese history part of universal history, and they agreed in rejecting the idea that Japan was unique in its structure and development.

## THE EMERGENCE OF SOCIALISM

If Tokutomi Sohō was one of the first Japanese intellectuals to apply a scheme of universal historical change to the history of Japan, he was also one of the first to discern lines of fracture in Japanese society. In contrasting the "commoners" (*heimin*) and the "aristocrats" (*kizoku*), however, Tokutomi was referring not so much to structural as to historical and generational divisions. The aristocrats were representatives of the "Old Japan," the parvenu Meiji leaders and a handful of holdovers from the ancien regime, who wished to turn the clock back to an era of privilege and caste. The commoners were everyone else, the ordinary workers and peasants as well as the well-to-do landed farmers, whose interests were tied to the present and future "New Japan." It was they who would benefit from the expansion of market freedom, equality of opportunity, and political enfranchisement promised by the laws of social development. Tokutomi saw the commoners and the privileged few as being at odds, but he did not suggest that one segment of society should be set against another or that there were exploiters and exploited in Japanese society. In short, he did not suggest the possibility of class conflict.

By the late 1890s, however, a number of observers feared that as the process of industrialization quickened, the gap between rich and poor would widen, and social harmony would weaken. In 1898 a group of law professors at Tokyo Imperial University led by Kuwada Kumazō (1869–1932) and Kanai En (1865–1933) organized the Social Policy Association (Shakai seisaku gakkai) to discuss the social problems associated with industrialization. Influenced by the successful social reforms of Bismarck and the ideas of conservative social reformers such as Lujo Brentano, Gustav Schmoller, and Adolf Wagner, members of the association argued that the pursuit of profit and unbridled competition that accompanied industrial growth under a laissez-faire policy would erode social stability and encourage social conflict. Basically procapitalist in their views, they attacked neither private property nor the market mechanism per se. Rather, they contended that the harshness of a laissez-faire system should be tempered by the introduction of factory legislation, workers' insurance programs, relief for poor people, and other measures of social policy. Socialism, however, was anathema to them, as it would impede national progress, pulling society back to a more primitive collectivist stage. In any case, these politically conservative professors saw no reason to think that socialism would be necessary in Japan. "The fact that the Japanese people established a constitutional system without shedding a drop of blood is a matter of great distinction in modern history," observed Kuwada in 1896. "In the coming economic revolution, too, why should it be impossible to solve this great problem peacefully?"[4]

If these conservative scholars hoped to save capitalism from its worst instincts by allaying class conflict through a timely adoption of social policy, the socialist movement, which emerged at about the same time, had no qualms about attacking capitalism itself from a radical perspec-

4 Kenneth B. Pyle, "Advantages of Followership: German Economics and Japanese Bureaucrats, 1890–1925," *Journal of Japanese Studies* 1 (Autumn 1974): 147.

tive. The manifesto of the Social Democratic Party published on May 20, 1901, proclaimed, "Our party, in response to the general trend at work within the world, and understanding the tendency of the economy, wishes to abolish the gap between rich and poor and secure a victory for pacificism in the world by means of genuine socialism and democracy." To achieve these ends, the socialists offered the standard fare of the Second International: public ownership of land and capital, nationalization of the means of communication and transportation, universal brotherhood, disarmament, and international peace. They also called for the abolition of the House of Peers and a reduction in the Japanese army and navy, sources of political and social inequity specific to Japan. Unlike the members of the Social Policy Association, the socialists were clearly at odds with their society.[5]

The socialist movement had its origins in a group that began meeting in 1898 at the Unitarian Society in Tokyo to study the writings of European socialist pioneers such as Saint-Simon, Proudhon, Fourier, and Marx, as well as American social reformers such as Henry George, William Bliss, and Richard Ely. Forty members of this group formed the Socialist Society in 1900, and it was from their ranks that the Social Democratic Party was organized in 1901. The party's founding members represented a social profile of the study group. All but one (Kōtoku Shūsui) were Christians; two had participated in the *jiyūminken* (popular rights) movement and later became journalists (Kōtoku Shūsui and Kinoshita Naoe); one was a university professor (Abe Isoo); and two were professional labor organizers or political activists (Katayama Sen and Nishikawa Kōjirō).[6]

During their first decade as a self-conscious movement, the Meiji socialists passionately indicted the moral failings and cultural decadence of their society. Whether materialists or Christians, the socialists depicted late Meiji Japan as corrupt and degenerate, dominated by special interests. In 1899, on the eve of declaring his calling as a socialist, the journalist Kōtoku Shūsui (1871–1911) lamented that since the Restoration, "national virtues had been supplanted by a vicious struggle for monetary gain." Seven years later, the editors of *Shin kigen* (New era), a Christian socialist journal, inveighed against a Japan "owned by the nobility and the rich classes who are degenerate and marked by corruption." And Katayama Sen, writing in the labor

5 Hyman Kublin, *Asian Revolutionary: The Life of Sen Katayama* (Princeton, N.J.: Princeton University Press, 1964), pp. 129–56.

6 Yamaji Aizan, "Genji no shakai mondai oyobi shakaishugisha," in *Shakaishugi shiron*, ed. Kishimoto Eitarō (Tokyo: Aoki shoten, 1955), pp. 95–115; Kublin, *Asian Revolutionary*, pp. 129–56.

newspaper *Rōdō sekai* (Labor World), deplored the selfishness of national politicians and described the Meiji government as incompetent and irresponsible. In short, socialists of all stripes saw the political and economic leadership of Japan as morally bankrupt.[7]

The late Meiji socialists did not distinguish moral criticism from social analysis, nor did they feel the need to do so. The Christian socialists, perceiving themselves as servants of the social gospel of Jesus, believed that socialism was the secular instrumentality to bring social and economic justice to Japan. Non-Christian leaders of the movement, often political journalists disillusioned with the Jiyūtō (Liberal Party) and the other political parties because of their accommodation with the Meiji government, identified themselves with the *bakumatsu* revolutionaries who had assailed the *bakufu* for its corruption. Christian or non-Christian, these men conceived of socialism as a means of social and moral regeneration, and they argued that government activity and economic organization had to be judged by their ethical effect on society. Their writings deliberately blended value judgment with factual statement. Even while following Marx's analysis of capitalism, they could not accept his moral agnosticism. If Marx had deliberately limited himself to an analysis of the structural and historical causes of capitalist development, or claimed to do so, the Japanese socialists elaborated on its injustices and amorality.[8]

To be sure, the socialists generally followed the conventions of Western Marxist analysis. Consider the criticism of capitalism in Kōtoku's *Shakaishugi shinzui* (The quintessence of socialism) and Katayama's "Waga shakaishugi" (My socialism), believed by most scholars to be the two finest pieces of Marxist writing in Meiji Japan.[9] Like Marx they praised the contributions of capitalism to the progress of modern society, and they marveled at its material production. Kōtoku and Katayama also concerned themselves with the paradoxes of capitalist development. With grotesque inconsistency, the greater part of humanity grew progressively poorer and more miserable under

7 Sharon Lee Sievers, "Kōtoku Shūsui, The Essence of Socialism: A Translation and Biographical Essay," Ph.D. diss., Stanford University, 1969, pp. 129–31; *Shin kigen* (Tokyo: Shinkigensha, September 10, 1906), no. 11; Kishimoto Eitarō and Koyama Hirotake, *Nihon kindai shakai shisōshi* (Tokyo: Aoki shoten, 1959), pp. 81–5.

8 Kōtoku Shūsui, *Teikokushugi: Nijūseiki no kaibutsu* (Tokyo: Iwanami shoten, 1954), conclusion; see Sievers's translation in "Kōtoku Shūsui," of Kōtoku's *Shakaishugi shinzui,* chap. 6; Katayama Sen, "Waga shakaishugi," in *Katayama Sen, Tazoe Tetsuji shū,* ed. Kishimotō Eitarō (Tokyo: Aoki shoten, 1955), pp. 112–16.

9 However much or little they read of Marx – a question often debated in recent studies – much of Kōtoku's and Katayama's terminology was Marxist, and with some exceptions it was accurately used. See Kōtoku, *Shakaishugi,* preface.

capitalism even as production grew by leaps and bounds. "Concurrent with the displacement of more and more workers by improved machinery," wrote Kōtoku, "there is a daily increase in the labor supply." Following Engels he argued that capitalism created an "industrial reserve army," an extraordinary surplus of workers who fought with one another over a decreasing number of jobs. Even the fully employed suffered. Under capitalism, workers lost all control of the "means of production." As Katayama observed, the wealth produced by workers was expropriated by the capitalists, and the workers became a dependent class, losing their freedom. In part, both men asserted, this was a consequence of the anarchy spawned by free competition and its ideology of the "survival of the fittest, the strong devouring the weak." In their view, class conflict was inevitable, a systematic consequence of the sharp divide between "a class called capitalists who monopolize the productive machinery and possess its products and a class of workers who possess nothing but their own labor."[10]

Kōtoku and Katayama touched on all the basic precepts of Marxism: the "labor theory of value," the theory of "surplus value," the "industrial reserve army," and the contradictions that inevitably "exist between socialized production and capitalist ownership." But both men parted from Marxist theory on a crucial point. Marx and his European followers insisted that theory had to be embedded in a historical perspective. Change, class, and class conflict each must be understood historically. "For the time being," Marx wrote, "class antagonisms are the motor of historical (social) development. Progress depends upon them." The internal contradictions of bourgeois society, Marx argued, were in fact both its propellant and essential to its functioning. For the Marxist, as George Lichtheim wrote, contradictions "cannot be legislated out of existence though they can be overcome 'at a higher level,' i.e., after history has reached the stage of the classless society." To the Meiji socialists, however, contradictions were seen not as the motor of history but as paradoxes to be deplored as the source of social injustice. Influenced by the ideas of social Darwinism as well as Marxism, they conceived of history as driven by ineluctable and impersonal evolutionary forces and often suggested that large historical changes were somehow inevitable. Yet they did not analyze the causes of historical dynamics or offer any systematic explanation of historical inevitability. There was almost an element of

10 See Katayama, "Waga," pp. 23–4, 32, 34, 36, 39–41, 49–50, 56, 60, 80–2, 91–3, 98–9; Kōtoku, *Shakaishugi*, pp. 142–5, 164, 178.

fatalism in this view of history. As Kōtoku wrote, "Revolution depends on Heaven, not on the strength of man."[11]

The Meiji socialists also conceived of the bourgeoisie differently than Marx did. For Marx the bourgeoisie had once been a "national class," a progressive class representing the interest of the whole society against its retrograde members, but as the pauperization of the masses accelerated, the class had lost its progressive role. In the *Communist Manifesto,* translated by Kōtoku and Sakai Toshihiko in 1904, Marx and Engels described the demise of the bourgeoisie as "unfit any longer to be the ruling class in society." The Meiji socialists, on the other hand, were curiously ambivalent about the historical role of the European bourgeoisie, whom they often referred to as "the middle class." The Japanese socialists understood the bourgeoisie normatively, abstractly rather than historically, and never structurally. Nothing better expressed their view than Kōtoku's statement: "The purpose of socialism is simply to create a middle class out of all society."[12]

In contrast with Marx, the Meiji socialists continued to stress the still progressive role of the bourgeoisie. In the West, said Kōtoku, it was the middle class that embodied the revolutionary spirit and became a force for action. In searching for a middle class in Japan's immediate past, both Kōtoku and Sakai found their analogue in the *shishi jinjin,* the "righteous patriots" who created the Meiji Restoration. They characterized the bourgeoisie, like the *shishi,* as moral exemplars, men who had "ideals" (*risō*), and men who (borrowing a Western concept) had "character" (*jinkaku*). Like the samurai class, the European bourgeoisie was neither indolent like the aristocracy nor economically deprived like the lower classes. By identifying the Meiji Restoration with the bourgeois revolutions of Europe, Kōtoku was suggesting that only a similar moral elite free of the constraints of status and economic deprivation could lead a socialist revolution. In fact, as we shall see, the socialists directly identified with both *shishi* and bourgeoisie by describing themselves as heirs of the Meiji Restoration.[13]

11 Katayama, "Waga," pp. 32–3, 41–2, 69–70, 86–7; Kōtoku, *Shakaishugi,* pp. 153–8, 182, 200; George Lichtheim, *Marxism: An Historical and Critical Study* (London: Routledge & Kegan Paul, 1961), pp. 46, 382–5; Hayashi Shigeru, ed., *Heimin shinbun ronsetsushū* (Tokyo: Iwanami shoten, 1961), pp. 188–97; Kōtoku Shūsui, *Hyōron to zuisō* (Tokyo: Jiyūhyōronsha, 1950), p. 27.

12 Lichtheim, *Marxism,* pp. 86–8, 142–54, 387–90; Kōtoku, *Shakaishugi,* pp. 183–4; Matsuzawa Hiroaki, "Meiji shakaishugi no shisō," in *Nihon no shakaishugi,* ed. Nihon seiji gakkai (Tokyo: Iwanami shoten, 1968), pp. 26–7.

13 Sievers, "Kōtoku Shusui," pp. 34–7, 94; Kōtoku, *Shakaishugi,* pp. 183–4; Matsuzawa, "Meiji shakaishugi no shisō," p. 45; John Crump, *The Origins of Socialist Thought in Japan* (New York: St. Martin's Press, 1983), p. 133; Saigusa Hiroto, *Nihon no yuibutsuronsha* (Tokyo: Eihōsha, 1956), p. 17; Nakamura Katsunori, *Meiji shakaishugi kenkyū* (Tokyo: Sekaishoin, 1966), p. 60.

Like the European Marxists, the Meiji socialists began with a critique of capitalist society, but it was the moral insensitivity of capitalism and its cruel social consequences that drew their most severe criticism. Both Kōtoku and Katayama called the inequity of economic distribution under capitalism a great crime. Under capitalism, Kōtoku wrote, not only did the workers face eleven hours of unremittingly harsh labor every day, but through expropriation, the product of their labor was "enjoyed by the indolent and the pleasure-seekers." Above all, what enraged both Kōtoku and Katayama, as well as their fellow socialists, was the corrupting effect of capitalism on civilization. Capitalism was a "curse on humanity," said Katayama; free competition created "an amoral and animalistic outlook on life." There was "nothing in life so cruel as the persistence of unemployment, endemic to the capitalistic world," wrote Kōtoku, because it turned men to thievery, women to prostitution, and plunged the "great majority of the world's humanity . . . into oblivion." "What," he added, "was to become of truth, justice and humanity?"[14]

Like socialists everywhere, Katayama, Kōtoku, Abe, and their fellow activists argued that reform and protest were only stopgap measures, not capable of correcting the basic evils that permeated the social organization of Japan. Also like many socialists, they had no quarrel with the material progress that industrial development had brought, and indeed they often praised it. What horrified the socialists, provoked their criticism of Meiji society, and animated their advocacy of socialism was the ascendancy of economic values and the disappearance of a moral center. They deplored the acquisitive ethic of the uncontrolled marketplace, the greed and the competitiveness that eroded moral relationships among the members of society. Although industrialization brought the benefits of prosperity, the cash nexus eroded the moral bonds of society.[15]

The socialists aspired to combine material progress with a social order suffused by compassion and impelled by morality. As Kōtoku wrote in 1901, the function of socialism was to bring harmony to society by removing the economic cause of strife; social harmony was its objective, and it was to be achieved not by laws or government discipline but by giving morals primacy over economics. Katayama once described socialism as "the *civilized society of our grandparents but*

14 Katayama, "Waga," pp. 33–5, 84–6, 104, 112–16; Kōtoku, *Shakaishugi*, pp. 78, 136–7; Matsuzawa, "Meiji shakaishugi no shisō," pp. 25–6.

15 *Shin kigen*, no. 5, March 10, 1906; Kōtoku, *Teikokushugi*, foreword, chap. 1; Kōtoku, *Shakaishugi*, pp. 145, 181–3; Katayama, *Waga*, pp. 24–5, 41–9, 59–62; 100–2.

*with production carried out by steam, electricity and compressed air* [his emphasis], that is, a society where a working man can obtain the greatest power and pleasure." Kōtoku spoke of the eradication of the "base desires" impelled by the atmosphere of free competition and called for their replacement by "competition for ideals, justice and the like . . . competition among good men." Sakai Toshihiko argued that if it were possible to achieve a unity of private and public interest, "the hateful thing called *economic relationships* [his emphasis] in society disappears and a relationship of love, warm and pure, spreads its wings freely." Abe more specifically asserted that "if the present social organization is reformed and each man is relieved of money worries, then we may look for a great change in morality." Sex crimes, crime itself, and in fact all problems arising from social relationships would disappear.[16]

For the socialists, social conflict, political venality, and a return to outmoded behavior were merely symptoms of the gross structural inequities in their society. Current evils, according to a writer in the *Yorozu chōhō,* a newspaper employing a number of socialist reporters, "may be ascribed not so much to the fault of those who are corrupt and degraded but to the system and organization of present society that caused them to fall into such a condition." At the same time, these evils demonstrated the Meiji government's responsibility for the spiritual and intellectual corruption of the individual and of society. "Our politicians," Kōtoku wrote, "have forgotten the original purpose of the revolution [the Meiji Restoration] and its original spirit [which was] based on freedom, equality and fraternity." As a result, further progress had been brought to a standstill. As Kōtoku wrote in yet another essay, the once-radical party movement had lost its spirit of opposition, and its leaders had become no more than government sycophants. By 1904 Sakai, as well as Kinoshita and Kōtoku, had given up hope that an independent and morally upright middle class would make its appearance in Japan; instead there was only a corrupted bourgeoisie, a hedonistic "gentlemen's gang" (*shinshibatsu*), besotted by extravagant indulgence in geishas and other luxuries.[17]

16 Kōtoku, *Shakaishugi,* pp. 164–201; Katayama, "Waga," pp. 104–5, 116, 126; Kōtoku, *Hyōron to zuisō,* pp. 25–6; Matsuzawa, "Meiji shakaishugi no shisō," pp. 22, 36–7.

17 Matsuzawa, "Meiji shakaishugi no shisō," pp. 24, 38–9; Kōtoku, *Teikokushugi, passim;* Hayashi, *Heimin shinbun ronsetsushū,* pp. 153–4; 161–5, 192; Nakamura, *Meiji shakaishugi kenkyū,* pp. 59–60; Mitani Taichirō, "Taishō shakaishugi no 'seiji' kan – 'seiji no hitei' kara 'seijiteki taikō' e," in *Nihon no shakai shugi,* ed. Nihon seiji gakkai (Tokyo: Iwanami shoten, 1968), p. 69; *Shin kigen,* no. 1, November 10, 1905.

Increasingly, socialism became a moral creed to which its adherents bore witness. The socialists conceived of themselves as a moral elite, true heirs to the spirit of the Meiji Restoration. Kōtoku described himself and his colleagues as "righteous patriots" (*shishi jinjin*) who would carry out a "great cleansing of society." All socialists, whether Christian or materialist, described socialism as an "ideal" or a "way," whose achievement, so it seems, was to be accomplished by religious acolytes. Acceptance of socialism and its goals was for its followers an act of self-abnegation and self-transcendence. In his prison letters, Kōtoku later wrote disparagingly of his past pride; he spoke of the need to rid himself of "what was unclean and ugly wherein I sought profit and name." He added, "Those who sacrifice their natural instincts most are truly those most advanced in morality."[18]

Socialists also took as their goal the creation of "men of character" (*jinkakusha*). Overcoming false individualism was a significant part of the socialists' task, argued Abe Isoo, and their ultimate objective was the creation of "cosmopolitan men" with universalistic ideals and goals.[19]

Yamaji Aizan (1864–1917), a contemporary social commentator and popular historian, observed that the socialists attracted young supporters because of their "seemingly religious devotion" to moral goals and reform in the face of government persecution. University students, like the socialists, thought of themselves as potential political and social leaders. But as Taoka Reiun (1870–1912), another social commentator and socialist sympathizer, wrote, these young men were "uncompromising, rough-mannered people with spirit" who either found government positions "inaccessible" or lost out to "clever sycophants." Socialism therefore was attractive not only because it attempted to solve social problems but also because it offered moral sustenance to those who felt themselves wrongly barred from office. Socialism gained their attention, as Kōtoku contended, because it took as its objective "the cooperation of all the people of society." It spoke to the frustrations of these restless (and as some argued) morally uprooted young people, by promising a society "completely based on the human feeling of brotherly love and humanity." It attracted their sympathy by suggesting that "men of character"

18 Matsuzawa, "Meiji shakaishugi no shisō," pp. 41, 57; Saguisa, *Nihon no yuibutsuronsha*, p. 17; Sievers, "Kōtoku Shūsui," p. 37; *Chokugen*, April 16, 1905.

19 *Chokugen*, April 16, 1905; *Rikugo zasshi*, no. 177, September 1895.

must ultimately triumph in a society in which leaders and led had lost their moral focus.[20]

## THE COLLAPSE OF THE SOCIALIST MOVEMENT

The Meiji government feared that the appearance of socialist doctrine in Japan portended social upheaval. The movement questioned the legitimacy of class divisions, propagated the idea of class warfare, and criticized fundamental institutions such as the military forces of a strong administrative state. In 1900 the Yamagata government promulgated the Public Peace Police Law intended to check the activities of labor and socialist organizations. Under the provisions of these regulations, in 1901 the Social Democratic Party was disbanded within twelve hours of the publication of its manifesto, and editions of newspapers that had published its manifesto were confiscated. According to Abe Isoo, the authorities offered not to close down the organization if the socialists agreed to strike from their manifesto two items: the abolition of the House of Peers and the reduction of arms expenditures. And although the authorities objected to the manifesto's references to destruction of the class system, interestingly they offered no objections to socialist principles such as the public ownership of land and capital or to political reforms such as universal manhood suffrage or the secret ballot. This clearly reflected an implicit official recognition that most of the manifesto presented no clear and present danger to the Meiji state and that its authors were not revolutionaries.[21]

The socialists objected to the state as an instrument of political oppression and to the corruption of officials, but none of them (with the possible exception of Kinoshita) objected to the state per se before the Russo-Japanese War. As Abe Isoo argued, the state could in fact be an instrument for the establishment of a socialist economy: "There are two sides to the nature of the state these days, namely, the state as a political entity and the state as an industrial entity. . . . The path to socialist politics is the gradual decline of the *authoritative* [his emphasis] agencies in politics and the development of economic agencies." In short, the state was acceptable as an agent of material progress but not as an agent of social or political control. It was even possible, Kata-

20 Yamaji, "Genji no shakai mondai oyobi shakaishugisha"; Matsuzawa, "Meiji shakaishugi no shisō," pp. 9, 36.

21 Gluck, *Japan's Modern Myths*, pp. 174–7; F. G. Notehelfer, *Kōtoku Shūsui: Portrait of a Japanese Radical* (Cambridge, England: Cambridge University Press, 1971), pp. 66–8; Abe Isoo, "Meiji sanjū nen no Shakai Minshutō," *Nihon shakai undōshi* (special issue) *Shakai kagaku* 4 (Tokyo: Kaizōsha, 1928), p. 77.

yama wrote, to contemplate the realization of socialism under the Meiji constitution. In fact, with the exception of Kinoshita, who openly called for rejection of the *kokutai* myth, Meiji socialists criticized neither the Meiji constitution nor the role of the emperor.[22]

Central to the socialist program was the idea of public ownership of the means of production – variously referred to as *seisan kikan, shakaiteki kyōyū,* and *kokuyū.* But for the most part, the Meiji socialists focused narrowly on the social welfare and managerial aspects of the socialization of the means of production. In their discussion of public ownership, they disregarded any analysis of the state as the political instrument of the ruling class and ignored the revolutionary role of the working class. More socialist than democratic, they took immediate aim only at the creation of a social-welfare state or some sort of state socialism. They conceived of the state as basically administrative and tried to depoliticize it by emphasizing its managerial functions. (Abe in fact thought of the ideal socialist state as being "one big insurance company.") By making the state managerial rather than political, they hoped to reduce political corruption, with the aim of achieving distributive justice.[23]

The socialists were less concerned with the revolutionary takeover of government than with ensuring that the material and economic needs of the people were fulfilled. Unless poverty and deprivation were ended, it would not be possible to bring about the moral regeneration of society. As Kōtoku said in 1899, "According to Confucius, the people should be made rich before teaching them." This view was shared by Sakai Toshihiko, who wrote, "If we desire to advance the general population beyond the desires of food, clothing, and shelter, we must carry out a fundamental reform of society; we must form a

22 It is interesting to note that Kōtoku wrote in 1902 that historically emperors in Japan had sought the well-being of the people and hence "were in complete accord with the principles of socialism" (Crump, *Origins of Socialist Thought*, pp. 126–7). Similar sorts of arguments were advanced by Abe as well, clearly in an attempt to establish the compatibility of socialism and the emperor system. For quotation from Abe, see Matsuzawa, "Meiji shakaishugi no shisō," p. 58; and for details, see Abe Isoo's articles in *Shin kigen*, nos. 1–8, 11, 12; Kōtoku, *Shakaishugi*, p. 68; Kōtoku, *Hyōron*, pp. 11–17; Hayashi, *Heimin shinbun ronsetsushū*, pp. 162–5; for quotation from Katayama, see Kishimoto Eitarō and Koyama Hirotake, *Nihon no hikyōsantō marukusushugisha* (Tokyo: San'ichi shobō, 1962), p. 10; for quotation from Kinoshita, see Nakamura, *Meiji shakashugi kenkyū*, pp. 38–42; and Yanagida Izumi, *Kinoshita Naoe* (Tokyo: Rironsha, 1955), p. 126.

23 Meiji socialists read both Richard Ely, who praised the social welfare state, and Albert Schaeffle, who set forth state socialism as the ultimate form of socialism. For a bibliography of readings, see Kōtoku, *Shakaishugi*, introduction; and Yamaji, "Genji no shakai mondai oyobi shakai-shugisha." For a discussion of terms used by socialists, see Matsuzawa, "Meiji shakaishugi no shisō," pp. 31–2. For a discussion of the state, see Kōtoku, *Shakaishugi*, conclusion; and Abe Isoo, *Shakaishugi ron* (Tokyo: Wabei kyokai, 1907), pp. 14–20.

society that guarantees the general population food, clothing, and shelter. In other words, we must make socialism a reality."[24]

For most of the decade after 1901, all socialists agreed on the efficacy of a parliamentary policy. The electoral success of the German Social Democratic Party, which they regarded as a mentor and model, gave them heart. Although Abe Isoo knew that socialist victory in Japan lay decades in the future, he confidently predicted in 1903 that "the final victory will be ours." Commitment to parliamentarism assumed that the achievement of socialism would not require political violence. As the editors of the *Heimin shinbun,* the principal socialist newspaper, argued in 1904, "The only way to achieve socialism is to seize power, and to seize power the majority of the Diet seats must be taken. To seize the majority in the Diet, public opinion in favor of socialism must be created." The socialists therefore not only committed themselves, as we have seen, to agitating, spreading propaganda, and publicizing their position, they also allied themselves with Diet politicians who called for the establishment of universal manhood suffrage.[25]

The socialists had no doubt that Japan would some day become a socialist state. Even before the founding of the Social Democratic Party, Kōtoku wrote, "Socialism is manifestly the great ideology and idealism of the twentieth century. . . . Socialism is the great principle that is to save the world; it is not a fantasy; it is a realistic proposition." But even though they looked forward to revolutionary change, the socialists did not think that it had to be achieved through violence or direct action. The function of the socialist movement, as Kōtoku saw it, was to act as the "midwife" of revolutionary change. "Revolution is destined; it is not brought about by human efforts. It must be led, but it cannot be manufactured. It is not something one can bring on, nor is it something one can escape." The role of the "revolutionist" therefore was to "judge what the conditions of society are and to guide the general trend of its progress so that we may hope to create a peaceful revolution." As a means to this end, Kōtoku supported universal manhood suffrage which he saw leading to socialist control over the Diet and local government. But he did not expect the people to seize control by themselves. He saw them instead as the beneficiaries of the moral elite who would be brought to power by their votes. His assump-

24 Quotations are from Matsuzawa, "Meiji shakaishugi no shisō," pp. 39–40.

25 Kōtoku, *Shakaishugi,* pp. 198–200; Kōtoku, *Hyōron,* pp. 20–3; Hayashi, *Heimin shinbun ronsetsushū,* pp. 156–61; Kishimoto and Koyama, *Nihon no hikyōsantō,* pp. 90–1; Matsuzawa, "Meiji shakaishugi no shisō," pp. 32–3, 40; Abe Isoo's article in *Rōdō sekai,* August 1, 1898.

tion, like that of the other socialists, was that "men of character" like themselves would guide the country peacefully toward its socialist transformation. In fact, the socialist movement drew on the burgeoning educated elite rather than on mass organizations or the masses.[26]

It was not until February 1906, after the establishment of the first Saionji cabinet, that the socialists were permitted to organize a legally recognized party able to run candidates for office, openly solicit members, and hold conventions. Though the names of several ironworkers, a few printers, a *jinrikisha* puller or two, and some miners from the Ashio copper mine appeared on its membership list, the Japanese Socialist Party (Nihon shakaitō) founded in February 1906 was essentially composed of middle-class intellectuals; its leaders were writers, reporters, and scholars, many of whom had been socialist activists early on. Legal restrictions, particularly the Public Peace Police Law, inhibited recruitment. No schoolteacher, Shinto or Buddhist priest, woman, nonadult male, or student could join a party. The latter exclusion particularly hurt the Socialist Party, as it was the students more than any other part of the population who read the socialists' publications and flocked to their meetings. Neither was there a labor movement to offer its support, as the Public Peace Police Law made unions practically impossible; and socialist organizers never really did try to rally workers to their ranks. As a result, the Japanese Socialist Party, as Arahata Kanson put it, had "plenty of commanding generals without troops to move."[27]

In any case, the Japanese Socialist Party survived only a year, largely because its members were accused of engaging in subversive political disturbances. During the spring and summer of 1906, the Japanese Socialist Party, along with the National Socialist Party (Kokka shakaitō) led by Yamaji Aizan, led a popular protest against a proposed increase in Tokyo's city tram fares. The campaign achieved its purpose, and the proposed fare increase was canceled. Katayama

26 Matsuzawa, "Meiji shakaishugi no shisō," pp. 32, 59–63; Kōtoku, *Shakaishugi*, pp. 195–200; Sievers, "Kōtoku Shūsui," p. 59; Yamaji, "Genji no shakai mondai oyobi shakaishugisha," *passim*. In 1907 the Metropolitan Police Bureau in Tokyo announced that there were a total of 25,000 socialists in the country, with 14,000 of them residing in Tokyo. The police acknowledged that this was a "rough figure" and did not explain the criteria by which they determined who was a socialist, but the report confidently categorized with exceptional (if suspect) precision the social status of many socialists: 3,200 workers, 7,500 students, 50 politicians, 180 soldiers, 60 priests or ministers, 10 judicial officials, 45 doctors, and 200 "unknown." A less optimistic tally by the Japanese Socialist Party itself that included the name of every person who appeared on the party rolls during its years of existence indicates a membership of only 200. Nakamura Katsunori, "Nihon Shakaitō no soshiki to undō," *Hōgaku kenkyō* 33 (October 1960): 28–31.

27 Nakamura, "Nihon Shakaitō no soshiki to undō," pp. 29–34; Kishimoto and Koyama, *Nihon no hikyōsantō*, pp. 37–62.

Sen declared it "the first victory of the red flag in Japan," but it proved to be a Pyrrhic one. The police arrested and jailed ten socialists active in the campaign, including Nishikawa and Ōsugi Sakae (1885–1923), and the cabinet agreed to keep a close eye on the Socialist Party, waiting for an opportunity to crack down on it.[28]

The opportunity came the following February when Sakai Toshihiko opened the party convention with a strong protest against the government's use of army troops to suppress a riot of some 3,600 miners and other workers who had bombed, burned, and virtually destroyed the facilities at the Ashio copper mine in Tochigi Prefecture. Government officials had quickly blamed the riot on the socialists, especially on their party journal, *Heimin shinbun,* even though there was little proof of their involvement. At the party convention Sakai called the government's use of military forces against the rioters "a grave blunder." Most of the resolution he proposed on behalf of the party's executive committee was more programmatic, a reiteration of the ideas and demands made by socialists throughout the decade. It proclaimed that the party sought "fundamentally to reorganize the existing social structure" so that the means of production would be owned in common by society, and it stated that the party should "arouse the workers' class consciousness," seeking to develop their "solidarity and discipline." The executive committee also expressed its "deep sympathy with all types of revolutionary movements struggling throughout the world." Five days after the convention opened, the government disbanded the party because of the subversive content of speeches and debates carried on at the convention.

The 1907 convention was also marked by a tactical rupture in the ranks of the socialist movement. Missing from the executive committee's resolution, conspicuously so as it had been an integral part of the socialist credo since 1901, was a declaration of the party's commitment to legal or constitutional tactics. A year earlier the party had promised "to advocate socialism within the limits of the law of the land," and for years the socialists had worked to broaden the electoral franchise. But now the executive committee avoided any discussion of the party's parliamentary role and merely suggested that party members were free to follow their own inclinations about involvement in the universal manhood suffrage movement. Neither Sakai nor the executive committee sought to repudiate parliamentary or legal tactics but merely

28 Nakamura, "Nihon Shakaitō no soshiki to undō," pp. 38–45; Kishimoto and Koyama, *Nihon no hikyosantō.*

wanted to mend the growing rift within the party. Kōtoku Shūsui had demanded that the party adopt the tactics of "direct action" and asserted that the general strike was the "means for future revolution." Tazoe Tetsuji (1875–1908), on the other hand, had demanded that the party reassert its commitment to the universal suffrage movement and the primacy of parliamentary tactics. The executive committee sought to find a compromise middle ground.[29]

During 1906 Kōtoku had discerned a shift in the "tide of the world revolutionary movement" away from parliamentary tactics toward more radical tactics of anarchosyndicalism. His discovery came in part as the result of his reading of Peter Kropotkin's anarchist tracts while in prison and in part as a result of his association with the International Workers of the World in California in 1905–6. Moreover, he was impressed by the successful tactics of the Russian revolutionary uprising during and after the Russo-Japanese war. If the Russian revolutionaries could act with such boldness and determination in a society that appeared much more backward than Japan's, how much more appropriate for Japanese revolutionaries to do so. Kōtoku had come to think that parliamentary action, instead of advancing the cause of socialism, seemed instead to be emasculating it. The European socialist parties stood in danger of becoming nothing more than "alternative bourgeois [*shinshi*] parties" incapable of functioning as revolutionary parties of the working class. In an appeal to Japanese youth Kōtoku wrote, "*The revolution* [his emphasis] to come is not the revolution of politics, not the revolution of the electoral law, nor that of parliament. . . . [T]he revolution of the future, it goes without saying, is the socialist, the anarchist revolution."[30]

For Kōtoku the meaning of revolution had changed, and so had the role of the socialist activist. He now advocated the use of "direct action" specifically a general strike, to paralyze society. "[I]f the [upper classes] had their food and clothing cut off, they would truly know the power of the workers. . . . [I]f the police know the truth of the socialist system can they really shoot their brothers and parents?" A general strike would not only make the ruling class aware of the workers' collective power but would raise the consciousness of the workers as well. "To achieve our objectives, which is a fundamental revolution

29 Nakamura, "Nihon Shakaitō no soshiki to undō," p. 28; Crump, *Origins of Socialist Thought*, pp. 250–2; Kishimoto and Koyama, *Nihon no hikyosantō*.

30 Hayashi, *Heimin shinbun ronsetsushū*, pp. 135–44. For a good translation of Kōtoku's "The Change in My Thought," see Crump, *Origins of Socialist Thought*, pp. 341–51; Mitani Taichirō, *Taishō demokurashiiron* (Tokyo: Chūō kōronsha, 1974), pp. 71–3; Nakamura, *Meiji*, p. 73; Matsuzawa, "Meiji shakaishugi no shisō," p. 34.

in the economic system, and the abolition of the wage system, it is more urgent to awaken the consciousness of ten workers than to get a thousand signatures on a petition for universal suffrage."[31]

In opposition to Kōtoku, Tazoe argued for the parliamentary tactics on the grounds that strikes and other extraparliamentary tactics would not ultimately improve the economic position of the workers. The locus of the capitalists' power was in the Diet, and if the workers were to challenge that power, they had to resort to parliamentary methods. He criticized the faddishness of Kōtoku, who urged that the Japanese radical movement keep pace with the latest shift in trends abroad; he himself thought that the socialist movement had to develop doctrines appropriate to the social and political situation in Japan. Within the party, only Katayama supported Tazoe, whereas Kōtoku's view appealed to younger members of the movement such as Ōsugi Sakae and Yamakawa Hitoshi.[32]

The debate between Kōtoku and Tazoe reflected a deepening awareness of the need for an appropriate way to raise the consciousness of the working class in order to accomplish the overthrow of capitalist society. The issue at stake between them was not the moral corruption of their society, on which they were agreed, but the way in which that corruption should be rooted out. Kōtoku wanted to raise the consciousness of the workers through the drama of "direct action," Tazoe through reliance on organization and votes. Kōtoku thought Tazoe's method was self-defeating, as any compromise with the political institutions of capitalism was corrupting. He feared that a parliamentary socialist party would ultimately come to terms with the ruling class, as the Jiyūtō had. If as Yamakawa suggested, Kotoku "denied politics," then Tazoe affirmed it. This divergence in views over whether to work within the given political structure or to overthrow it from without foreshadowed the tactical dilemma later to be debated in the 1920s by intellectuals and activists with a firmer grasp of Marxism. Both Kōtoku and Tazoe, though aware of the need to raise the workers' consciousness, still regarded the workers as tools or instruments for change rather than as men aware of their own needs and interests, and both still saw themselves as members of an enlightened moral minority.[33]

The socialist movement suffered an enormous setback in 1911 when the government hanged Kōtoku Shūsui and eleven others, including his

31 Sievers, "Kōtoku Shūsui," p. 108; Nakamura, *Meiji*, pp. 74–5; Kishimoto and Koyama, *Nihon kindai shakai*, pp. 100–3.
32 Kishimoto and Koyama, *Nihon kindai shakai;* Kishimoto and Koyama, *Nihon no hikyōsantō.*
33 Kishimoto and Koyama, *Nihon no hikyōsantō;* Mitani, *Taishō demokurashiiron*, p. 75.

lover Kannō Sugako, for the crime of conspiring to assassinate the emperor. The "Great Treason incident" (*daigyaku jiken*) was the culmination of a prolonged campaign to suppress the socialist movement. Although the socialists and their publications had been subjected to official harassment before 1907, the powerful elder statesman Yamagata Aritomo had increased his pressure on the first Saionji and second Katsura cabinets to suppress all social movements. Frightened by the Ashio incident, the first large-scale strike in Japan, as well as by other incidents of social protest, Yamagata felt that a period of "social destructionism" (*shakaihakaishugi*) had begun. Police agents stepped up their harassment of socialist newspapers: banned individual issues, arrested editors, and interfered with their distribution. Even the journals published by Katayama's parliamentary faction, which clearly asserted their belief that socialism could be achieved by legal means, were dealt with as harshly as were those associated with the anarchists.[34]

The arrest and execution of Kōtoku, leader of the anarchist wing, was intended to damn the entire socialist movement as subversive and a threat to the emperor and nation. But in fact, the government prosecutors were never able to prove that Kōtoku had more than an early and temporary interest in the conspiracy to assassinate the emperor. At the trial they focused on his "intent," not on any overt acts he committed. In any case, the trial ushered in what has been called the "winter years" (*fuyu no jidai*) of socialism. Nothing, or nearly nothing, could be published, and obviously no one dared to organize a political party or any other kind of political group. In his autobiography, Arahata even recalls that the government banned an entomological work entitled *Konchū shakai* (Insect society) because it contained the dreaded word *shakai* (society).[35]

## *MINPONSHUGI*

Although the "winter years" were bleak for the socialist movement, they were years of thaw for more moderate and cautious intellectuals – most of them contemporaries of younger socialists like Yamakawa Hitoshi, Ōsugi Sakae, and Sakai Toshihiko – who advocated greater democratization of the political process. Like the Meiji socialists, these young democratic liberals lamented the ethical poverty of poli-

34 Gluck, *Japan's Modern Myths*, pp. 170–6, 188, 219, 227; Crump, *Origins of Socialist Thought*, p. 304; Oka Yoshitake, "Generational Conflict After the Russo-Japanese War," in *Conflict in Modern Japanese History*, ed. Tetsuo Najita and Victor Koschmann (Princeton, N.J.: Princeton University Press, 1982), p. 217. 35 Notehelfer, *Kōtoku Shusui*, pp. 185–6.

tics and the meaningless struggles for power among the country's self-serving leaders, but they were more optimistic that the political system would soon change from within as the result of long-term evolutionary processes. The transition to a new imperial reign, from Meiji to Taishō, symbolized for them the passing of the old and a coming of the new, a break in political time. "The trend of the times demands a new politics, and they demand new men," wrote Maruyama Kanji in 1914. "To resist is like trying to make water run up hill. By new politics, I mean a politics that does not exclude Japan from the rest of the world; by new men I mean those who will move with the currents in the world. The road the Taishō era must travel cannot veer from the trend toward democracy."[36] Japan, like the rest of the world, was being swept along in a great democratic tide, and the "era of the popularization of politics" lay ahead. Visible everywhere were signs of an "awakening of the people" (*jinmin no jikaku*) or an "awakening of the nation" (*kokumin no jikaku*).

What initially gave the democratic liberals grounds for optimism was the steady escalation of popular demonstrations and street movements during the years following the Russo-Japanese War. Beginning with the anti–Portsmouth Treaty movement of 1905, these popular outbursts had culminated in the first "movement to protect constitutional government" (*kensei yōgo undō*) of 1912–13 and the protests over the Siemens affair in 1914. Their political meaning, however, was ambiguous. Although public demonstrations were solid evidence of the new "trend of the times" about which Maruyama spoke, they were also symptomatic of the failure of the constitutional process. "The reason we see these mob explosions today," observed Ukita Kazutami, "is that there is no public opinion adequate to check the government's use of its authority."[37] Denied other legal and constitutional means of making their views known, crowds had taken to the streets, rallying in public to denounce the nation's leaders, their policies, their selfish hold on power. Often demonstrators fell prey to the agitation of rabble-rousers and turned violent. The upsurge of popular political unruliness marked a breakdown in the national consensus and social harmony, a growing rift between the goals of the government and the goals of the people.

The liberal democratic intellectuals had no doubts about where to place the blame for this breakdown in national consensus. The fault

36 Maruyama Kanji, "Minshuteki keikō to seitō," *Nihon oyobi Nihonjin,* January 1913.
37 Peter Duus, "Liberal Intellectuals and Social Conflict in Taishō Japan," in *Conflict in Modern Japanese History,* p. 46.

lay not in capitalism or capitalist morality but in the backwardness of Japanese political development. The persistence of "bureaucratic government" (*kanryō seiji*) or "clique government" (*hanbatsu seiji*) perpetuated authoritarian politics and obsolete national priorities. In 1912–13, protestors had called for the "overthrow of clique government" and the "protection of constitutional government." Control over the government lay in the hands of a "privileged class" (*tokken kaikyū*) which selfishly arrogated to itself the right to decide the nation's destiny. With the same vehemence that the Meiji socialists had attacked the "gentlemen's gang," and for many of the same reasons, the Taishō democrats assailed the "aristocratic cliques" (*monbatsu*), "bureaucratic cliques" (*hanbatsu*), and "militarist cliques" (*gunbatsu*) who dominated politics. Unlike the socialists, however, they did not attack "capitalists," nor did they express any interest in restructuring the political economy along the lines suggested by the Second International.

The democratic liberals' overriding concern was with the political process. Reform of that process was the key to ending political conflict and strengthening the nation. Unlike the socialists, the liberals did not debate whether to pursue "parliamentary action" or "direct action." Their model was the liberal bourgeois representative democracies of the West, and commitment to the parliamentary process basically defined their political position. The democratic liberals had no quarrel with the state, or the idea of loyalty to the state, but only with the way that "bureaucratic government" commanded that loyalty – by docile obedience. They envisaged a political society made up of involved citizens, not passive subjects. Only if the parliamentary process were democratized, only if it were made more responsive to public opinion, and only if the people assumed greater control over the government, they argued, could the nation be held together.

Given their focus on the political process, the Taishō liberals did not concern themselves much with the "locus of sovereignty," an issue that had bedeviled constitutional theorists since the 1880s. In 1912 the journalistic debates between Uesugi Shinkichi, the heir of Hozumi Yatsuka, and Minobe Tatsukichi, author of the "organ theory" (*tennō kikan setsu*), had again brought that issue to public attention. Uesugi argued that sovereignty lay in the emperor, whereas Minobe argued that it lay in the state, of which the emperor was merely an "organ" or "mechanism" (*kikan*). For the democratic liberals this question seemed unrelated to the realities of politics. Yoshino Sakuzō, while a law student at Tokyo Imperial University, had come under the influence of Onozuka Kiheiji, who encouraged his students to investigate governmental policy and political practice. Onozuka contended that "political science" (*seijigaku*), that is, the study of political systems as they functioned historically, was as important as "juridical science" (*kokkagaku*), that is, the abstract analysis of the state as a legal concept. What counted for Yoshino, as well the other democratic liberals, was not where sovereignty lay but how it was to be exercised.

The publication of Yoshino Sakuzō's lengthy essay on constitutional government in 1916 (*Kensei no hongi o toite sono yūshū no bi o nasu michi o ronzu*) brought the democratic liberals' position into sharp focus.[38] The purpose of his essay was to describe the essential features of a democratic constitutional structure – the protection of individual rights, the separation of powers, the role of a representative assembly, and responsible cabinets – and to suggest why this model was appropriate for Japan. Like other liberals Yoshino deliberately avoided issues of juridical theory, that is, how to interpret the letter of the constitution, and concentrated instead on its "spirit," the values that gave it life. (As Ōyama Ikuo later observed, it was not possible to "interpret a system of law apart from the national spirit [*Volksgeist*].")[39]

The "spirit of constitutional government," Yoshino implicitly argued, could be discovered only if one searched for its historical roots. Like most advocates of democratic reform, Yoshino read modern history as the history of expanding liberty, the collapse of authoritarianism in the face of rising popular power. This "whig interpretation" of history, a legacy from the Meiji era, had first surfaced in the 1880s and 1890s among the advocates of constitutional government and a national assembly.[40] It tacitly assumed that yearning for freedom was a universal instinct and that the spread of constitutional government was its product.[41] Hence, Yoshino asserted, although constitutions might differ from country to country in their particulars, all constitutions were the "inevitable product of modern civilization," and all shared a "common spiritual root."

38 The essay appeared in the January 1916 issue of *Chūō kōron* and has been reprinted in Ōta Masao, ed., *Taishō demokurashii ronshū* (Tokyo: Shinsuisha, 1971), vol. 1, pp. 244–312. For an interesting treatment of Yoshino's thought, see Tetsuo Najita, "Some Reflections on the Political Thought of Yoshino Sakuzō," in *Japan in Crisis: Essay on Taishō Democracy*, ed. Bernard S. Silberman and H. D. Harootunian (Princeton, N.J.: Princeton University Press, 1974). Also useful is Peter Duus, "Yoshino Sakuzō: The Christian As Political Critic," *Journal of Japanese Studies* 4 (Spring 1978): 301–26. 39 Ōta, *Taishō*, vol. 1, p. 412.

40 Cf. Peter Duus, "Whig History, Japanese Style: The Min'yūsha Historians and the Meiji Restoration," *Journal of Asian Studies* 33 (May 1974): 415–36.

41 Cf. the following statement by Nagai Ryūtarō: "There is a law that the trend of civilization moves from autocracy to freedom. That human beings crave freedom and require equality is a natural desire, just as feathered creatures crave flight in the sky, and beasts of the field seek water from mountain streams when they thirst. . . ." *Shin Nihon*, March 1915, pp. 73–4.

It should not surprise us that Yoshino found the "common spiritual root" of all constitutions to be *minponshugi,* a term that became central to the political lexicon of the 1910s. *Minponshugi* was Yoshino's translation of the word *democracy,* but as his essay pointed out, the Western term conflated two seperate meanings: the idea that "legally, state sovereignty lay in the people" and the idea that "politically, the fundamental goal of the exercise of state sovereignty lay in the people." Democracy in the first sense, popular sovereignty, was better called *minshushugi.* It was clearly not applicable to Japan, whose constitution unambiguously lodged sovereignty in the emperor. Rather, it was democracy in the second sense that Yoshino meant by *minponshugi.* The concept was political, not legal or juridical. On the one hand, it meant that "the exercise of political power, that is, the 'purpose of government,' is in the welfare [*rifuku*] of the general populace [*ippan minshū*]"; on the other hand it also meant that "the determination of the goals of the exercise of political power, that is, 'policymaking,' depends on the will [*ikō*] of the general populace."[42]

Interestingly and ironically, Yoshino had borrowed the word *minponshugi* from Uesugi Shinkichi, his conservative colleague in the law faculty of Tokyo Imperial University, who argued that Japan had always been a country with a "monarchical sovereign [*kunshu*]" but never been a "monarch-centered [*kunpon*] polity" like the France of Louis XIV. Rather, it had been a "people-centered [*minpon*] polity" responsive to the needs and welfare of all the people, and the basic moral imperative of the imperial family had always been *minponshugi* ("the principle of people centeredness"). Uesugi was clearly stating that the Japanese monarchy was benevolent and that imperial sovereignty was compatible with popular welfare. But Yoshino used *minponshugi* not to defend the imperial institution or the *kokutai* but, rather, to show that "democracy" (= *minponshugi*) posed no threat to the imperial institution or the *kokutai.* He wanted to refute the view that democracy was a form of "dangerous thought." Danger lay not in *minponshugi,* said Yoshino, but in *minshushugi* – popular sovereignty – an idea that could lead to sedition in the hands of a radical like Kōtoku Shūsui. One of the reasons that Yoshino's essay had such an impact was that it brilliantly reconciled the democratic political process with the peculiarities of the Japanese constitutional structure, demonstrating that it was possible for Japan to participate in the "world trend" toward democracy without sacrificing its national essence.

42 Ōta, *Taishō,* vol. 1, p. 266.

In practical terms, Yoshino, like the other democratic liberals, asserted that *minponshugi* meant following the practices of modern representative parliamentary democracy. Even though representative institutions were a less-than-perfect embodiment of *minponshugi*, they did rest on the principle that the "people" (*jinmin*) should select their own leaders, and they did guarantee that policy would reflect the will of the people. Like other democratic liberals such as Minobe Tatsukichi or Nagai Ryūtarō, Yoshino also argued that a commitment to representative government, and hence to *minponshugi*, had been national policy since the Charter Oath of 1868 had called for the convening of assemblies and broad public discussion. Representative government was compatible not only with the ancient tradition of imperial sovereignty but also with the goals of the Restoration.[43]

Yoshino's essay immediately provoked debate. "*Minponshugi! Minponshugi!*" remarked one ironic observer. "These days night does not fall nor the sun rise without *minponshugi*. Anyone who does not talk about *minponshugi* is regarded as an eccentric badly out of touch with things."[44] Despite Yoshino's attempt to reconcile democracy with the *kokutai*, conservatives like Uesugi attacked the idea of representative democracy as incompatible with the Japanese monarchical order. Some liberals criticized Yoshino for making vague and simplistic distinctions or presenting a model of representative government already out of date, and still others offered their own pet neologisms – *minshūshugi, minseishugi, minjūshugi*, and *minjishugi* – as alternatives to *minponshugi*. But nearly all the leading liberal intellectuals – Kimura Kyūichi, Minobe Tatsukichi, Sasaki Sōichi, Ōyama Ikuo, and Kawakami Hajime – immediately accepted Yoshino's dichotomy between *minshūshugi* and *minponshugi* (if not always his terms) as well as his implication that democracy was compatible with the *kokutai*. There was also a solid consensus behind his programmatic proposals: an end to "bureaucratic government," the establishment of responsible cabinets, the subordination of the upper house to the lower house in the Diet, and, most important of all, the broadening of suffrage. "The expansion of the suffrage, together with strict enforcement of [election] control laws, is the most urgent task facing our nation," Yoshino wrote in 1916.[45]

The advocates of *minponshugi* were no more populist than were the Meiji socialists, however, and they too expected the representative process to produce a moral elite (or a meritocratic elite) not unlike

43 Ōta, *Taishō*, vol. 1, p. 275. 44 Ōta, *Taishō*, vol. 2, p. 101. 45 Ōta, *Taishō*, vol. 1, p. 298.

themselves. Before 1918 when Yoshino, Ōyama Ikuo, Nagai Ryūtarō, and other democratic liberals called for an expanded suffrage, it was the enfranchisement of all educated middle-class males that they had in mind. They wanted to substitute educational qualifications (or other tokens of social responsibility such as completion of military service or assumption of household headship) for the tax-paying qualifications on the right to vote. The lower orders – "those below the middle class" – were not yet ready for full political participation, nor were women. To be sure, the democratic liberals saw no intrinsic reason that the general populace should not be enfranchised in the long run, but they felt that the constitutional system was only a generation old and that it was difficult for the people to absorb the idea of self-rule or political representation after centuries under autocratic regimes. At the beginning of his *minponshugi* essay, Yoshino had lamented that even many members of the educated classes, who should be the "leaders of a nation's culture," did not fully understand the working and spirit of constitutional government; how much more difficult it would be then for the lower classes. The democratic liberals covered their ambivalence toward the masses, however, by contending that the people had to be prepared for full political enfranchisement through "political education" and a "transformation of their knowledge and morality." Raising their political consciousness was the first step in bringing them into the political process.

The democratic liberals also seem to have assumed that suffrage reform would take care of the problem of leadership. If the suffrage were broadened to include the educated middle classes, vote buying, bribery, and other forms of electoral corruption would decline, and "men of character" (*jinkakusha*) would stand for election. There was less agreement on just how the elected should represent those who elected them. On the one hand, it was obvious that representatives should reflect the will of the people, or at least public opinion. But the people did not always know what was best for them. As Yoshino often put it, the relations between the people and their representatives was like that between patients and physicians: The patients know that they are ill, but the doctors know how to cure them. "True *minponshugi* politicians make public opinion and lead it, but afterwards carry on government in accordance with public opinion," suggested Kawakami Hajime.[46] Like the Meiji socialists, the democratic liberals yearned for the emergence of knowledgeable and moral leaders, and they often

46 Kawakami Hajime, "Minponshugi to wa nanizoya," *Tōhō jiron*, October 1917.

pointed out that democratic countries in the West produced men like Wilson, Poincaré, and Lloyd George – eloquent, literate, and even scholarly intellectual aristocrats who were nonetheless able to respond to the popular will.

As we have already suggested, it was the growing rift between the government and the people that concerned the democratic liberals. The ultimate practical justification of their program was that democratization of the political process created national harmony and consensus. Representative government, the democratic liberals believed, would intensify commitment to the nation. The flaw of despotic or authoritarian government – such as the domination of government by "privileged classes" in Japan – was that it did not encourage voluntary commitment to national goals. Yoshino, Ōyama, Kawakami, and others used terms like *kanmin dōkyō* (cooperation of people and officials), *kunmin dōchi* (joint rule by sovereign and people), *kunmin dōsei* (joint government by people and sovereign), or *banmin dōchi* (joint rule of all the people) to describe the essence of constitutional government. These faintly traditionalistic terms were intended to suggest that democratic politics was an integrative process, creating solidarity within society by creating a sense of jointness or commonality.

Ōyama Ikuo developed these ideas into a theory of democratic nationalism. Drawing on the sociological theories of politics he had studied in the United States, he argued that the state rested on both the individual's instinct toward community ("associative consciousness" [*dōrui ishiki*]) and a "sense of common interest" (*kyōdō rigai kannen*). If the state suppressed the demands of the individual, then the whole society would be weakened. But if "associative consciousness" were strengthened and a "sense of common interest" were clarified, then the individual would spontaneously contribute to the welfare of the whole society. "We believe that true national unity [*kyōkoku itchi*] springs from an intense consciousness of the people's common interests [*kokumin kyōdō no rigai*]," wrote Ōyama Ikuo in 1917, "and this intense consciousness of common interest will come once the people have assumed joint responsibility for the management of the state as a result of the spread of the right to vote."[47] Democracy, in other words, was the "end point" (*shūten*) of nationalism. "Nationalism," he wrote, "must ultimately end in democracy." This argument rested on the assumption, which Oyama shared with the other democratic liberals,

47 Ōyama Ikuo, "Kokka seikatsu to kyōdō rigai kannen," *Shin shosetsu*, February 1917.

that the state was not only legitimate but neutral, standing above partisan, sectional, or class interests.

It was in their nationalism that the *minponshugi* liberals set themselves farthest from the Meiji socialists. Whereas the socialists had been strongly opposed to the Russo-Japanese War and had proclaimed the international solidarity of the working class when Katayama shook hands with Georgy Plekhanov at the Second International meeting in 1904, the democratic liberals took pains to point out that *minponshugi* was compatible not only with imperialism but also with militarism. Only anarchists believed in cosmopolitan liberty, observed Ōyama, whereas imperialism was expressive of the national spirit. In the midst of World War I it was difficult for the *minponshugi* liberals to be pacifist when the forces of democracy were pitted against the forces of autocracy, and militarism in the narrow sense of using military force was seen as compatible with democracy. At the end of the war many liberals began to speak of internationalism as well, but they construed that to mean not a supranational cosmopolitanism transcending national boundaries but an attempt to create harmonious relationships among nation-states by peaceful diplomatic means.

## TOWARD RADICALISM

The outbreak of the rice riots in 1918 confirmed the democratic liberals' claim that dire consequences would result if government were not more responsive to popular needs. As the *Tōyō keizai shinpō* editorialized shortly after the disturbances, "Unfortunately the political process in our country works effectively only for the property-owning minority, whereas the classes without property are hardly given any security at all. In one sense it is possible to say that those without property have no government at all. Herein lies the true cause of the riots."[48] Such disturbances occurred, said Yoshino, because governments do not bend an ear to the demands of the people. Nagai Ryūtarō pointed out that the riots revealed not only that the bureaucratic authorities were out of touch with the people but also that the Diet "neither possessed the will to understand the economic hardships of the people nor made efforts to eliminate them."[49]

To the liberals the rice riots indicated that the "awakening of the people" seen dimly on the horizon in 1914 had arrived and that events in Japan echoed the broader "trend of the times." The triumph of the

48 Quoted in Inoue Kiyoshi and Watanabe Tōru, eds., *Kome sōdō no kenkyū* (Tokyo: Yūhikaku, 1962), vol. 5, p. 240. 49 Nagai Ryūtarō, *Kaizō no risō* (Tokyo, 1920), pp. 9–10.

democratic powers in World War I, the collapse of autocratic regimes in Germany and Austria-Hungary, and the explosion of popular democratic and nationalist movements in central Europe confirmed the "world trend" toward democracy. On the other hand, the triumph of the "extremist" (that is, Bolshevik) government in Russia gave practical significance to the idea that democratization was essential to preserving social solidarity. The new Bolshevik government, wrote Ōyama Ikuo, was a "decadent form of democracy."[50] If a similar sort of upheaval were to be avoided in Japan, it was essential to forestall the growth of class consciousness and class conflict foreshadowed by the rice riots, and that could best be done by the passage of a universal manhood suffrage law.

In the wake of the rice riots, many leading *minponshugi* intellectuals moved toward greater political activism, but because many were academics or journalists, they saw their task as raising political consciousness rather than seizing political power. At the end of 1918, Yoshino brought together a group of his students to begin a systematic study of universal suffrage and electoral reform, and he joined with Fukuda Tokuzō, Ōyama Ikuo, and other liberal academics to found the Reimeikai, a society aimed at "enlightening" the Japanese public by discussing new political ideas. Other small organizations of young intellectuals, journalists, and politicians such as the Kaizō dōmeikai came together to discuss democratic reforms.[51] With the support of liberal professors like Yoshino and Ōyama, reform-minded students at the major national and private universities began to organize political societies of their own, such as the Shinjinkai at Tokyo Imperial University and the Minjin dōmei at Waseda University. To the extent that most of these groups or their members engaged in overt political activities, it was through support of, or participation in, the universal suffrage movement of 1919–20.[52]

But if the rice riots confirmed the position of the *minponshugi* liberals, it also revealed the limitations of their position. The advocates of democratic reform, although they repeatedly stressed the importance of "social policy" as a part of *minponshugi,* had been less attentive to the distribution of wealth within Japanese society than to the distribu-

50 Ōyama Ikuo, "Rōkoku kagekiha no jisseiryoku ni taisuru kashohi to sono seiji shisō no kachi ni taisuru kaidaishi," *Chūō kōron* 33 (May 1917).

51 For an informative discussion of several of these organizations, see Itō Takashi, *Taishōki "kakushin" ha no seiritsu* (Tokyo: Hanawa shoten, 1978).

52 On the universal suffrage movement, see Matsuo Takayoshi, *Taishō demokurashii no kenkyū* (Tokyo: Aoki shoten, 1966); Matsuo Takayoshi, "Dai-ichi taisengo no fūsen undō," in *Taishōki no seiji to shakai,* ed. Inone Kiyoshi (Tokyo: Iwanami shoten, 1969). The best Western-language treatment of the student movement in the 1920s is by Henry D. Smith II, *Japan's First Student Radicals* (Cambridge, Mass.: Harvard University Press, 1972).

tion of power. The rice riots – as well as the wave of strikes and other labor disputes that broke out at the end of World War I – made clear that most of the population lacked economic security as well as political rights. Ōyama Ikuo characterized the riots as a kind of "retaliatory confiscation," and Fukuda Tokuzō said the riots had occurred because the people had been pushed to a "point of extreme need" at which their right to survive overrode property rights. Still others pointed out that the basic cause of the riots was popular resentment at the great gap between rich and poor. Unlike the Hibiya riots and other post-1905 popular demonstrations, the rice riots had little to do with questions of governmental control or foreign policy. At stake, rather, were issues such as the existence of social division, unequal distribution of wealth, pervasive economic hardship, and the unresponsiveness of the propertied class to any of these problems.[53]

What made the resolution of these issues particularly urgent was the spread of labor unrest. Before World War I the police, invoking Article 17 of the Public Peace Police Law, had been able to contain the growth of working-class organizations, but wartime economic dislocations had provoked labor–management friction. In many factories, disgruntled workers began to organize strikes and unions. In 1914 there had been only 49 labor unions in Japan, but by 1919 there were 187, with a total membership of 100,000. The most important of these, the Yūaikai, founded by Suzuki Bunji as a "friendly society" in 1914, commanded a following of 30,000. The issues of social and economic justice raised by the rice riots were not a passing phenomenon but a cause for continuing concern.[54]

By the end of 1918, neologisms like *minponshugi* were gradually abandoned in favor of more straightforward terms like *minshushugi* or simply *demokurashii*. More important, the idea of democracy was construed more broadly to embrace not only the political process and political institutions but also the social structure itself. It came to imply the elimination of social privilege, the guarantee of economic equality of opportunity, and a fairer distribution of wealth. "True democracy," wrote Hasegawa Nyozekan in 1919, meant increasing the equality of opportunity not only politically but socially and economically as well; and Ōyama Ikuo argued that the purpose of "true democracy" was to construct a society in which all members could "live like

53 A collection of comments on the rice riots by important political and intellectual figures can be found in Inoue and Watanabe, eds., *Kome sōdō no kenkyū*, vol. 5.

54 The standard treatment of the Yūaikai in English is by Stephen S. Large, *The Rise of Labor in Japan: The Yūaikai, 1912–1919* (Tokyo: Sophia University Press, 1972).

human beings" and in which there was an "increase in opportunities for each individual to act in a positive way politically, socially, and economically." Now everything was game for democratization, even education and the arts.[55]

It was clear as the supporters of *minponshugi* began to debate the meaning of "true democracy" that lines of fracture were appearing in their ranks. In 1919 Fukuda Tokuzō, who joined with Yoshino Sakuzō to found the Reimeikai, distinguished between "capitalist political democracy" (*shihonteki seiji minshushugi*) and "social democracy" (*shakai minshushugi*), by which he really meant "socialist democracy." Neither, he said, represented "true democracy," as they favored the interests of one segment of society over another. The holistic conception of democracy central to the *minponshugi* argument was denied by a class-based definition of democracy.[56] Yoshino Sakuzō agreed with Fukuda that he opposed "social democracy" if that meant siding solely with the position of the workers' interests. The notion of a society divided against itself was repellent to democratic liberals of his stripe, and so was the political violence associated with socialist revolution. A true democrat could never become an "extremist," said Yoshino, because he saw the democratic political process not as a means to an end but as valuable in itself. One wing of the democratic movement was therefore turning its face firmly against any theory of class conflict or social conflict.

Curiously, however, Yoshino did not object to a socialist program of reform so long as it could be achieved through the constitutional process. Socialism stood for social policy. "A democrat [*minponshugisha*] does not necessarily have to be a socialist," he wrote in 1919, "but there is nothing to prevent him from being a socialist."[57] While continuing to advocate political reform – universal manhood suffrage, an end to the political autonomy of the military, abolition of the Privy Council, reform of the House of Peers, and so forth – Yoshino supported the legalization of labor union activities and social welfare policy after 1918. In short, Yoshino and other moderates like Fukuda, Abe Isoo, and Nagai Ryūtarō adopted a nondoctrinaire, non-Marxist kind of social democracy or social meliorism that linked democratic political reform to social welfare policy. Significantly, many of them were eventually involved in the organization of the moderate right wing of the "proletarian party movement" in the mid-1920s.

55 Ōta, *Taishō*, vol. 2, pp. 347–50, 475–82. 56 Ōta, *Taishō*, vol. 2, pp. 460–75.
57 Yoshino Sakuzō, "Minponshugi, shakaishugi, kagekishugi," *Chūō kōron*, June 1919.

But there were other advocates of *minponshugi* who wanted to move beyond political democratization to more sweeping and radical schemes of social reorganization. "Reconstruction" (*kaizō*) or "liberation" (*kaihō*) became their new catchwords. In 1919 a spate of new journals appeared, focusing on labor problems, social problems, social reform, and socialism, many of them started by former advocates of *minponshugi*. In January Kawakami Hajime began publication of *Shakai mondai kenkyū* (Studies in social problems); Hasegawa Nyozekan and Ōyama Ikuo founded *Warera* (We ourselves); in April *Kaizō* (Reconstruction), a new general interest magazine appeared, and in June so did *Kaihō* (Liberation). Some former liberals, most notably Kawakami Hajime, declared themselves Marxists, but others, like Ōyama Ikuo, were moving toward a vaguer (and perhaps romantic) identification with the working classes. And still others, like Hasegawa Nyozekan, were drawn to new models of social and political organization emerging in the West. Articles began to appear on alternative forms of political representation, including guild socialism or the Soviet system, in which economic interests rather than territorial interests were represented. The era when parliamentarism could be equated with democracy was at an end, and the issue had become not whether the "people" were represented in the political process but whether the emerging "fourth estate" (*daiyon kaikyū*) (that is, the working-class proletariat) was.[58]

The shift toward a more radical political position sprang from growing doubt about whether political democratization could guarantee social harmony and national unity, or indeed whether it was anything more than a political sham. The issue had been raised by Yamakawa Hitoshi, one of the younger members of the Meiji socialist movement, who wrote a series of penetrating critiques of both Yoshino and Ōyama. He dismissed Yoshino's distinction between *minshushugi* and *minponshugi* as a sophistry equivalent to saying that pork consisted of "two unrelated concepts – meat and fat."[59] (Perhaps, he added, Yoshino thought that fat was not suited to weak Japanese stomachs and so denied that it was pork.) But more to the point, in attacking Ōyama, Yamakawa denied the possibility that the state or the representative process could create social unity. Far from being neutral, states, governments, and parliaments were the instruments by which one class dominated others to its own material advantage. What dominated men was not their "associative consciousness" but their material interests. The usual

58 Ōta, *Taishō*, vol. 2, *passim*. 59 Ōta, *Taishō*, vol. 2, pp. 20–8.

state of all societies was not unity but conflict and the collision of material class interests. Only in primitive societies, in which people shared their goods and made decisions in common, was conflict absent – and only in primitive societies could one find democracy. Viewed through Yamakawa's Marxist perspective, history was not the history of liberty, nor did it find its culmination in the rise of parliamentary democracy. Rather, it was the history of the rise and fall of classes struggling for domination.

The impact of this conflictual view of history and social dynamics can perhaps best be seen in the defection of Ōyama Ikuo from his earlier defense of *minponshugi*. After he and Hasegawa Nyozekan founded their journal *Warera,* he spoke less and less of "class harmony," a national "sense of common interest," or "national unity." As the struggle between labor and capital seemed to intensify in 1920–1, Ōyama began to doubt that the intellectual could be a neutral or disinterested observer of the conflict, and eventually he concluded that the intelligentsia had to stand with the workers against their exploiters. Gradually he shed his commitment to a theory of democratic nationalism as well; he denied the possibility of reconciliation between labor and capital; he branded constitutional government in Japan as "crippled"; he attacked the social organization as flawed and unfair, giving all the advantages to the capitalists and none to the workers; and he expressed doubts about how representative the Diet was and whether the existing system of representation was effective at all.

With the publication in 1923 of his major theoretical work *Seiji no shakaiteki kiso* (The social foundation of politics), the transition was complete.[60] Ōyama now looked at political phenomena as the expression of a power struggle among social groups. He argued that human social life was dominated by interest relationships, especially economic interests, and that "the motor of social evolution" and the "origin of political and social inequality" lay in the struggle among social groups (including classes) which regarded all other social groups as enemies and ruthlessly pursued their own interests. The state therefore was not a neutral instrument for the common good but a means of domination by the triumphant group or class. Concepts like "people" (*kokumin*), "public interest" (*kōri kōeki*), "national morality" (*kokka dōtoku*), and "national spirit" (*kokumin seishin*), which had been so much a part of Ōyama's analytical vocabulary in the 1910s, he now regarded as inven-

60 The text may be found in *Ōyama Ikuo zenshū* (Tokyo: Chūō kōronsha, 1947), vol. 1.

tions of the dominant bourgeoisie to deflect resistance by the working class.

In adopting a theory of conflict to explain politics, Ōyama saw himself as trading a sentimental or idealistic position for one that was "empirical" and "scientific." As Kawai Eijirō later pointed out, one of the weaknesses of Taishō liberalism was its lack of an explicit philosophical or theoretical base. The *minponshugi* arguments for democratization did not grow out of a comprehensive understanding of how societies were organized, nor did it link political analysis to an understanding of basic human drives. Instead, it relied on an implicit optimistic faith in the inevitability of progress, in the triumph of morality over interest, and in the possibility of social harmony. Even the "whig view" of history crumbled when it was discovered that there was a history of human oppression as well as a history of human liberty. The theoretical poverty of democratic liberalism left it vulnerable to competition from "social science" theories of the sort that Ōyama embraced, but even more so from the social and historical theories of Marxism that took on new life in the 1920s.

## THE REVIVAL OF SOCIALISM

The "winter years" of socialism ended when the main survivors of the radical wing of Meiji socialism – Yamakawa Hitoshi, Ōsugi Sakae, Arahata Kanson, and others – broke their long silence on political and social issues. What emboldened them in part was the Russian Revolution of 1917. The mere news of the overthrow of the despotic czarist regime, Yamakawa often observed, had a profound effect on the radical socialists and anarchists. In May 1917 a resolution prepared by Yamakawa and Takabatake Motoyuki, and approved by thirty other socialists, expressed hope that the Russian Social Democrats would take the lead in ending the European war and launch an international struggle of workers against capitalism in all belligerent nations. Yamakawa and Takabatake enthusiastically greeted the seizure of power by the Bolsheviks in October as well. Aleksandr Kerensky's overthrow was right and proper, argued Takabatake, as he had attempted to use the soviets of workers and soldiers as a springboard to conciliation with the "gentlemen's gang." The Bolshevik victory confirmed their belief in the efficacy of direct action. The success of the Russian Revolution was assured, said Yamakawa, when Lenin and his proletarian followers refused to come to the aid of Kerensky's bourgeois democracy, and just as certainly the failure of the German revolution was assured by the German proletariat's support of bourgeois state capitalism.[61]

Yamakawa's theoretical analysis of the Bolshevik revolution – which he described as a "socialist revolution," in contrast with the "bourgeois revolution" in France – would probably have been acceptable to the Bolsheviks themselves. It also set the terms for a future analysis of the political status of the Japanese bourgeoisie and the revolutionary potential of the Japanese masses. "Russia," said Yamakawa,

> had begun its second revolution. Its first was a dual revolution, both a political revolution by the new bourgeoisie against the despotic bureaucratic state and a social revolution by the working masses against capitalism. These two revolutionary forces became one for the purpose of overthrowing the despotic state. . . . Up to that stage the Russian Revolution followed the course set by the great French Revolution. The divergence comes in the fate of the mass armies of each revolution. In the French case, the masses were conquered by the bourgeois forces, while in Russia, although the bourgeois political revolution was accomplished in the same manner, the masses were equipped, both intellectually and in matters of organization, to push toward socialist revolution.[62]

Few Japanese socialists, however, including Yamakawa, had heard of Lenin before, and none showed any understanding of Leninist theory. (In this, the Japanese were little different from the Europeans, as it was not until 1921 that translations of Lenin's work revealed that he had a systematic theory.) In 1917 Sakai Toshihiko described Lenin as an "anarchist." At first Yamakawa called him a "syndicalist" who used "direct action" to make a revolution, and in 1921 he characterized him as an "orthodox Marxist," to be contrasted with a figure like Karl Kautsky, the German social democratic leader, who had turned from revolutionary Marxism to bourgeois liberalism. Only gradually, as more and more of Lenin's work made its way into Japanese, were the implications of his ideas fully understood. For the time being, he was mainly admired as a revolutionary hero who succeeded in establishing a radical popular government in Russia.[63]

61 Ōsawa Masamichi, *Ōsugi Sakae kenkyū* (Tokyo: Dōseishi, 1968), pp. 274–7; Koyama Hirotake and Koyama Hitoshi, "Taishō shakaishugi no shisōteki bunka," *Shisō* 466 (April 1966): 121; George Beckmann and Okubo Genji, *The Japanese Communist Party, 1922–1945* (Stanford, Calif.: Stanford University Press, 1969), pp. 15–16; Mitani, *Taishō demokurashiiron*, pp. 93–100; Kishimoto and Koyama, *Nihon no hikyōsantō*, pp. 80–1; Watanabe Haruo, *Nihon marukusushugi undō no reimei* (Tokyo: Aoki shoten, 1957), pp. 42–3, 46, 143–9, 186–7; Thomas A. Stanley, *Ōsugi Sakae: Anarchist in Taishō Japan* (Cambridge, Mass.: Harvard University Press, 1982), pp. 128–9; Watanabe Toru, "Nihon no marukusushugi undō ron," in *Marukusushugi*, vol. 12: *Nihon* (Tokyo: Nihon hyōronsha, 1974), pp. 187–92.

62 Watanabe, *Nihon marukusushugi undō no reimei*, pp. 47–8.

63 Watanabe, "Nihon no marukusushugi undō ron," pp. 43–4, 175–86; Kishimoto and Koyama, *Nihon no hikyōsantō*, pp. 66, 73–5, 85; Beckmann and Okubo, *The Japanese Communist Party*, p. 13; Koyama and Koyama, "Taishō shakaishugi no shisōteki bunka," p. 121.

The veterans of Meiji socialism were also heartened by new stirrings of unrest among the people. Although the *minponshugi* liberals had viewed the rice riots with apprehension, the socialists saw them entirely in positive terms, as evidence of a growing class consciousness among the people. The socialists were also pleased by the growing militance of the labor movement. In 1919, at its national convention, the Yūaikai adopted a new name – the Greater Japan Federation of Labor and Friendly Association (Dai Nihon rōdō sōdōmei yūaikai) – and promulgated a new and more militant program that included demands for the legalization of trade unions, the establishment of a minimum wage, the passage of universal manhood suffrage, an eight-hour workday and a six-day workweek. During the war years, the Yūaikai had concentrated on resolving labor conflicts, but the Japan Federation of Labor took to the streets, organizing rallies to oppose the Peace Police Law and to support the universal manhood suffrage movement.[64]

On May 1, 1919, Sakai Toshihiko's journal *Shin shakai* publicly announced that it would fly the "flag of Marxism." Although Sakai and Yamakawa, who had joined his staff, announced that they would eschew politics for the moment, it was clear that they thought the country was on the verge of massive change. In the fall of 1919 Sakai wrote, "There is a strong sense that the end of the year marks the end of an age. The new year will be upon us soon. . . . I have a sense that we will for the first time step into a world of our own." A "socialist craze" seemed to be sweeping the country.[65]

The main participants in this "craze" were not only erstwhile liberals like Ōyama Ikuo and Kawakami Hajime, who rejected a commitment to parliamentary (that is, bourgeois) democracy for more radical social and political critiques, but also a new generation of university students and recent graduates who ultimately were to dominate the political and theoretical leadership of both the Communist and the non-Communist Marxist left in the 1920s. Students, of course, had been involved in the Meiji socialist movement; they probably accounted for a majority of the ten thousand subscribers to the *Heimin shinbun* and provided the readership for other socialist periodicals as well. But during the late Meiji period, few students joined in the socialist activities or agitation for social reform. They were, in the phrase of the political scientist Maruyama Masao, "merely admirers of

64 Beckmann and Okubo, *The Japanese Communist Party*, pp. 22–3, 102; Watanabe, "Nihon no marukusushugi undō ron," p. 152.

65 Watanabe, "Nihon no marukusushugi undō ron," pp. 44–5, 149–50; Beckmann and Okubo, *The Japanese Communist Party*, p. 12; Arahata Kanson, "*Kindai shisō* to *Shinshakai*," *Shisō* 460 (October 1962): 115–25; Koyama and Koyama, "Taishō shakaishugi no shisōteki bunka," p. 119.

a liberty which involved neither self-control nor responsibility." In his memoirs Yamakawa disparaged many of the student followers of Meiji socialism as "rucks, misanthropic cynics, and malcontents – in short, those who had dropped behind in the competition of capitalist society." By contrast, young men like Yamakawa, Arahata, and Ōsugi who became active in the movement as journalists or agitators did not graduate from college or university but deliberately chose lives of moral and political commitment instead of clambering up the conventional educational ladder of success.[66]

The students who became radicalized in the 1920s and 1930s, however, were "exemplary" students, confident of promising careers in academia, business, or the bureaucracy if they wanted them. Students who joined leftist movements, a Ministry of Education report observed, were "modest," "decent," "sober," and "diligent" young men. Investigations of the family backgrounds and personalities of arrested leftist students showed that 65.9 percent of those questioned fell into these categories and were classified as "good"; only 4.6 percent were typified as "hypochondriacal," "weakwilled," or "unrestrained" and classified as "bad." A report published by the ministry in 1933 refuted the prevailing assumption that only people who were unhealthy could become susceptible to "dangerous thoughts." "[T]he greatest number of leftist students under investigation," the report lamented, "were modest and sound in character."[67]

Not only did "exemplary" higher school and university graduates enter left-wing movements, but a number who became Marxist theoreticians returned to their alma maters as professors. Fukumoto Kazuo, Miki Kiyoshi, Kushida Tamizō, Sano Manabu, Hattori Shisō, and Hani Gorō became leading academic economists, philosophers, historians, and critics. As members of the academic establishment, they gave Marxism social cachet, moral respectability, and intellectual influence. Members of this intellectually accomplished group, many of whom received government grants for postgraduate study in Europe, transformed the relatively simple and often vulgar Marxism of the Meiji socialists, who had virtually ignored the dialectical dynamics of social change, into sophisticated and sometimes antagonistic theories of political action and social revolution.

66 Matsuzawa Hiroaki, *Nihon shakaishugi no shisō* (Tokyo: Chikuma shobō, 1973), pp. 65–7; Masao Maruyama, "Patterns of Individuation and the Case of Japan: A Conceptual Scheme," in *Changing Japanese Attitudes Toward Modernization,* ed. Marius Jansen (Princeton, N.J.: Princeton University Press, 1965), pp. 489–531, pages cited are 508–9, 514.

67 Maruyama, "Patterns," pp. 520–1.

What the new generation of student converts to the left shared with the older generation of socialists, to whom they first turned for leadership, was a belief that capitalism and the bourgeois state were on the brink of collapse. The "world trend" was toward social and political liberation, and the final stage of capitalism was well on the way. But the anarchist and Marxist leaders and their student followers did not think that revolution would drop like a ripe plum from a tree. The accomplishment of a Japanese social and political revolution lay in the hands of a self-conscious, class-conscious, and well-organized proletariat. Some older socialists who had been associated with the proparliamentary wing of the Meiji movement – Sakai Toshihiko, for example – at first cooperated with the liberal intellectuals in the organization of the universal suffrage movement, but by 1921 even Sakai had quit the movement and criticized it as "foolish." The more radical Marxists and anarchosyndicalists argued from the beginning that only through workers and their unions, not through Diet politics, universal suffrage, or even a socialist party, could they bring down the capitalist state.[68]

Undoubtedly, faith in the revolutionary potential of the Japanese workers and the Japanese labor movement was encouraged by the fact that activists in the Japan Federation of Labor in the spring of 1920 began to advocate the tactics of "direct action," opposing the universal suffrage movement and parliamentary tactics. The failure of a universal manhood suffrage bill to pass the Seiyūkai-controlled Diet in 1919 and 1920 probably deepened their disillusionment with parliamentary politics. Even Suzuki Bunji, who had begun his career as a moderate Christian social meliorist, called for the "thorough reform of present society" and described the Japanese industrial system as "violent and despotic." "We must first topple this despot," he said. "The inevitable consequence of the awakening of the workers will be the making of a new industrial system and organization."[69]

The awakening of the Japanese working class became the most significant and immediate project of the radical left. Only the proletariat, the Marxists and anarchosyndicalists argued, could be the active subject of a socialist revolution, and only the liberation of the working class could lead to the emancipation of the whole society. In contrast with their Meiji predecessors, the new generation of leftists also insisted that the workers' class consciousness could never be taken for

68 Watanabe, "Nihon no marukusushugi undō ron," pp. 154–5, 168–70.
69 Ibid., pp. 149–50, 70. Ōsawa, *Ōsugi Sakae kenkyū*, p. 184.

granted; it had to be cultivated. In the imagination of both radical ideologists and student activists the worker became simultaneously the potential hero of liberation as well as the object of tutelage, a child whose mind and will had to be nurtured and guided.[70]

Even though Meiji socialists had condemned the horrendous conditions under which workers labored and lived, few had become involved in working-class movements, and most had been indifferent to the workers' potential as conscious revolutionaries. At best, as in the writings of Kōtoku, the workers were conceived of as a mass whose participation in a general strike might trigger revolution. In part, this attitude of the Meiji socialists resulted from the weakness of the labor movement and the legal restrictions on unionization, but as Yamakawa later pointed out, it also derived from the socialists' obsession with pure theory. By contrast, in the 1920s, in order to capture worker support for their own movements, radical leaders and their student followers brought their theories and theoretical conflicts directly to the workers themselves, taking part in their organizations and their debates over tactics.

### ŌSUGI SAKAE AND ANARCHOSYNDICALISM

One of the most attractive and influential radical leaders in the early 1920s was Ōsugi Sakae, a former disciple of Kōtoku and the main theorist of the anarchosyndicalist position. What made him so appealing to young university students and graduates is clear from his writings, which overflow with feelings of boredom, oppression, and idealism that fostered a diffuse rebelliousness and a sense of affinity with the workers. But above all, Ōsugi appealed to the young because of his conception of revolution as personal emancipation. "It is only when we have developed a personal philosophy," he wrote in 1917, "that we become free. . . . No matter what happens then, we cannot become slaves."[71]

Students and graduates vividly expressed the mix of sentiments and impulses that attracted them into later agitation. At once altruistic and self-absorbed, they identified their own search for autonomy and their desire for relief from feelings of "suffocation" (*ikizumari*) with the emancipation of the workers. As one wrote, commitment to the cause of the workers allowed them to break the fetters of "trivial knowledge . . . formality and convention." They spoke of their desire to

70 Ōsawa, *Ōsugi Sakae kenkyū*, pp. 183–5.
71 Arahata, "*Kindai shisō* to *Shinshakai*," pp. 117–19; Ōsawa, *Ōsugi Sakae kenkyū*, p. 148.

express "true feelings"; they sought "a life that would be lived sincerely"; they wanted to fulfill themselves; and they dreamed of "an overflowing self" (*jiga no jūitsu*). Only as rebels and only as servants of "the multitude in their own country," wrote one, could they live life sincerely. At times this relationship with workers was described as a romance, a near physical infatuation, even a self-seduction. "I search for a lover," Kataoka Takeo wrote in the journal *Demokurashi* in 1919. "The laborer is my lover. I cannot wait until that pale face becomes cheerful. To bring a smile is the first step of love." Identification with the worker and his cause allowed young members of the elite to transcend themselves by becoming a "vanguard."[72]

Students and graduates in the early 1920s often wrote that the "discovery of social problems" made them rebels, even though no single idea or clear ideology inspired their actions. As Asō Hisashi (1891–1940) wrote, students felt they "knew the trend of the times." Their vocabulary was eclectic, neither specifically anarchosyndicalist nor Marxist. "To the people," the slogan used to exhort their fellows to join the worker's cause, had been borrowed from the nineteenth-century Russian populist cry, *v narodni*, but the Russian *narodniki* (populists) believed that a postrevolutionary social order would be constructed on the basis of the village community, an idea derided by Marxists and never a part of the Leninist canon. Although some graduates described themselves as "heralds" of revolution, as Asō suggested, they sought "to clothe the workers in all the books that they themselves had read." They would give workers "freedom (*jiyū*), justice (*seigi*), humanism, socialism, anarchism, revolution, syndicalism, and the IWW (Industrial Workers of the World)."[73]

The workers, however, were not attracted to the students by socialism or any other ideology but by their anarchistic attitude. What workers understood about students, one labor activist wrote, was "that they [students] burned with the same spirit. [To them also] capitalism was an unpardonable system." In a memoir written decades later, one worker recalled: "Ideas of Marxism, syndicalism, labor unionism all entered my head at one time. I didn't understand the distinctions very well."[74] But one simple thought was quite clear: "If workers organize, if we stop the factory smoke, we come into our own world. When we stop the smoke of the chimney, it will chasten the powerful. This would be the means of correcting the social evil."[75]

72 Matsuzawa Hiroaki, *Nihon shakaishugi*, pp. 65–9, 156.
73 Ibid., pp. 62–3, 148–52, 156–9. 74 Ibid., pp. 158–9. 75 Ibid., pp. 160–1.

Workers shared with students a feeling that resistance had to be total. As one worker wrote, "we would prefer an honorable defeat, even a miserable defeat . . . [never] cooperation or moderation." And still another said: "We will lose our families . . . we will lose human pleasure. We will live only by a revolutionary resistance toward capitalism." It was these ideals that brought students and workers to Ōsugi Sakae and anarchosyndicalism.[76]

It was inevitable that Ōsugi and other anarchosyndicalists would turn against Bolshevik policies in Russia, reject the suppositions of Marxist-Leninism, and become bitter antagonists of all Marxists in the Japanese social and labor movements. Ōsugi initially had hailed the coming of the Russian Revolution because he believed it had been achieved by "direct action," in which the masses had risen spontaneously and driven out Kerensky's bourgeois regime. In Japan, as elsewhere in the world, anarchosyndicalists found gratifying this image of the revolution. They had long argued that revolution could be accomplished by a spontaneous uprising of all of the oppressed classes, which, in the course of widespread insurrection, would topple the state and replace it by some sort of autonomous community. In the early 1920s, the anarchosyndicalist strategists believed that the overthrow of capitalism could be accomplished by purely industrial organization and struggle, and they rejected any kind of political activity or participation in bourgeois institutions. At the inaugural convention of the Japan Federation of Labor in 1919, for example, anarchosyndicalist militants objected to the organization's support for universal suffrage, and they rejected all proposals that implied the compatibility of unions with the imperial values of capitalism. And in a debate over direct action (*chokusetsu kōdō*) versus parliamentarianism at a 1920 meeting of the federation, the cry of a Kyoto anarchist delegate, "We reject the Diet," was greeted with applause from anarchists at the convention. If led by a militant rank and file, the anarchosyndicalists believed, the labor union alone could become the instrument of the proletariat in its struggle against the bourgeoisie and its state.

The anarchosyndicalists also refused to subordinate the economic struggle of the proletariat to the coming revolution. Characteristically then, labor unions led by anarchosyndicalists favored confrontation rather than conciliation, preferring to sabotage a factory rather than to seek a contract. As one militant Japanese anarchosyndicalist put it, "We do not say unions are useless. But they are effective only in

76 Ibid., p. 146, n. 43, 93, 167.

building, not in the work of destruction – destruction must come before building." In the brief period from 1920 to 1923 when the anarchosyndicalists commanded a prominent position in the labor movement, they tried to incite the workers to carry out massive strikes that would paralyze the entire economy and to incite the workers' hostility against the existing order. Tokyo celluloid workers, watchmakers, and printers and Yawata steel workers, influenced by anarchosyndicalist organizers and other direct-action militants, carried out violent strikes, smashed machines, and sabotaged workplaces. Inspired by the anarchosyndicalists, workers in 1920 at the Fuji Gas Spinning Company resolved "even to die" for the cause.[77]

By late 1922, anarchosyndicalist influence in the union movement had begun to weaken. Because of their insistence on spontaneity rather than organization and coordination, their demand for individual union autonomy rather than the acceptance of the federation's centralized authority, and their failure to achieve much by direct confrontation, the anarchosyndicalists lost influence to reformists and Communists. The news that the Soviet Union had begun to persecute anarchists such as Emma Goldman and to disregard the will of local soviets while centralizing all power in the party and central committee impelled Ōsugi to announce his disgust with Bolshevism and to break off all contact with Japanese Marxist-Leninists. For Ōsugi the establishment of the New Economic Plan, or NEP (which he believed was little more than a disguised attempt to establish state capitalism), and the reinstitution of national industrial discipline represented the end of the revolutionary era in Russia.[78]

Anarchosyndicalists had a vision of a secular millennium; they sought a future in which workers autonomously united to govern themselves in small communities. Workers needed neither a party nor an ideology, the French anarchosyndicalist George Sorel had argued; in fact, they should reject both as part of the bourgeois game in which workers were subject to the tyranny of bourgeois rule. For Ōsugi the encouragement of worker resistance, the necessity of unceasing conflict, and the call for disorder had the function of not merely disrupting contemporary society but of also liberating the workers (and those

77 Stephen S. Large, *Organized Workers and Socialist Politics in Interwar Japan* (Cambridge, England: Cambridge University Press, 1981), chaps, 1, 2; Ōsawa, *Ōsugi Sakae kenkyū*, pp. 263–9, 277–8, 311–12; Watanabe, "Nihon no marukusushugi undō ron," pp. 175–92, 206–16.

78 Large, *Organized Workers;* Ōsawa, *Ōsugi Sakae kenkyū*, p. 317; Watanabe, "Nihon no marukusushugi undō ron," p. 192.

who sought to aid them) from history and hierarchy. Men must begin anew, with a "clean slate" (*hakushi*), Ōsugi believed. But "clean slatism" did not imply a belief in the natural spontaneity of the masses: self-emancipation, the self-recovery of the masses, demanded an effort and a transformation of the consciousness of the workers by the workers themselves.[79]

In an essay entitled *Chitsujo binran* (The breakdown of law and order), Ōsugi wrote that the majority, bound by the thought and actions of their rulers, had been sacrificed to the "rules" of the few. By "disorder," a breakdown of law and order that he equated with "rebellion," workers could overcome "old values." Without rebellion, the individual could not attain "true existence" (*shin no sei*). Thus the breakdown of rules, in effect, the alienation of the workers from their past, became the only means by which the potential of both the masses and the individual could be achieved. "Living" in the modern world, for Ōsugi, meant "rebelling." Life without rebellion was not life but nonlife, death itself.[80]

Ōsugi exemplified in his life and thought the full sum of militant student ambivalence and aspiration. He doubted his ability to lead the workers because he believed he was crippled by his bourgeois or even petty bourgeois attitudes. Nonetheless, he offered the workers his leadership and the gift of his ideas, advising them that only by a life of constant rebellion could they overcome the tyranny of contemporary society. He summoned intellectuals to the cause of the workers, at times describing them as something like a vanguard. However, he questioned their revolutionary trustworthiness, identifying them as members of the bourgeoisie and hence no better than "passing friends among the enemy" (*teki no naka no yūjin*). But he also suggested that intellectuals could be useful to themselves and to the workers if they understood the workings of modern society, subsumed themselves to and "become one" (*ittaika*) with the workers, and used the agency of workers to "practice rebellion."[81]

Even more consistently than his anarchosyndicalist predecessor Kōtoku, Ōsugi lived a life of dramatic resistance. He had a flair for confrontation. At one time or another he repudiated all the conventions of his society, including the orthodoxies of his radical allies as

79 For Sorel, see Leszek Kolakowski, *Main Currents of Marxism*, vol. 2: *The Golden Age* (New York: Oxford University Press, 1978), p. 163; Ōsawa, *Ōsugi Sakae kenkyū*, pp. 171, 259.

80 Ōsawa, *Ōsugi Sakae kenkyū*, pp. 171–2, 184.

81 Stanley, *Ōsugi Sakae*, pp. 115–19; Ōsawa, *Ōsugi Sakae kenkyū*, pp. 115–19, 130, 183–4, 260; Mitani, *Taishō demokurashiiron*, p. 85.

well as those of his opponents. Although he liked the spirit of democracy, he hated what "the legal and political scientists call democracy and humanism." "Socialism," too, "I hate," he said, finding that orthodox socialism put too much emphasis on material determinism in the evolution of society and not enough on individual freedom. It is only a part of the truth, he asserted in criticism of socialism, that "new economics creates a new morality." No creed, no ism, no theory seemed wholly satisfactory. "For some reason," he wrote in February 1918, "I hate anarchism a bit."[82]

Underlying the ambivalence expressed in all of Ōsugi's arguments and attitudes was a belief, somewhat like that of his hero Nietzsche, that no fact was independent of interpretation and no vision of reality untainted by prejudice and perspective. Hence life became at its best a heroic act of interpretation in which the individual and the masses could transcend their society. Intellectuals, for example, had throughout history been thoroughly implicated in the ideological defense "of the ruling class and the deception of the oppressed classes." But if intellectuals abandoned their hegemonic role, desisted from imposing their ideology on the workers (an attitude, Ōsugi observed, prevalent among even socialist intellectuals), and resolved to be one "with the essence of the labor movement," they could overcome their class attitudes. In fact, Ōsugi's concern with individual freedom and his recommendation that individuals abandon their egos in order to find themselves (*jibun o torimodosu tame ni, jiga o kidatsu suru*) place him among the ranks of radical libertarians and in clear opposition to the Marxist socialists.[83]

Not surprisingly, then, in an essay published in 1919, Ōsugi quoted from Nietzche to the effect that the "perfection of individuality" is the ideal, and even if only a vision, it is one with the direction of life. "The essence of life," he wrote, "is always to find a way out of an impasse." As an anarchosyndicalist, Ōsugi turned this vision of self-transcendence outward toward society and sought social revolution. He rejected Marxism (as he also questioned nineteenth-century notions of rationalism and mechanical inevitability) not only because of its emphasis on necessity but also because he found its proposition that "new economics creates a new morality" only a part of the truth. A new morality, he insisted, must be created within the old order so that it can become the basis of the new. Ōsugi thus believed that all men, not merely one

82 Stanley, *Osugi Sakae;* Ōsawa, *Ōsugi Sakae kenkyū,* pp. 117–18, 174.
83 Ōsawa, *Ōsugi Sakae kenkyū,* pp. 168, 183.

special being, had the will to power of the "superman" (*chōjin*). Workers could therefore transcend their society collectively and autonomously; alienated from the present and their consciousness transformed, they could become the pacesetters of the future. And like the workers, the alienated radical student activists could share in the achievement of a new world.[84]

## YAMAKAWA HITOSHI AND THE "CHANGE IN DIRECTION"

The murder of Ōsugi by a military police captain in September 1923 robbed the anarchosyndicalist movement of its only charismatic leader. The movement, however, had been devastated a year earlier when the Comintern became more interested in Japan and Japanese leftists acquired a better understanding of Leninist theories of revolution. Some leftist factions began to call themselves Bolsheviks, and many Marxists acquired a new understanding of Lenin's ideas about the dictatorship of the proletariat and the proper role of a socialist or communist party vis-à-vis the masses. With the formation of the secret Japanese Communist Party in July 1922, these issues became the focal point of controversy between the Marxists and the anarchosyndicalists in the labor movement.

At the 1922 annual meeting of the Japan Federation of Labor, an alliance of Communists and labor reformers had engineered the adoption of a resolution favoring a highly centralized organization based on national industrial unions. Rejecting the anarchosyndicalist principles of union decentralization, autonomy, and self-government, in which any union had the right to join or withdraw from any association at any time, the convention called for political as well as standard union economic tactics – all anathema to Ōsugi. Despite Ōsugi's growing distaste for the Soviet Union, the convention also passed a resolution supporting the communist regime in Soviet Russia.[85]

Ōsugi had not only been defeated by Japanese Bolsheviks, but his longtime ally, Yamakawa Hitoshi, emerged as the ideological leader of the Bolshevik faction and the hero of the meeting. Yamakawa's July–August 1922 essay, "A Change in Course for the Proletarian Movement" (Musan kaikyū undō no hōkō tenkan), provided the slogan for the conference, "into the Masses" (*taishū no naka e*); and his denuncia-

84 Ibid., pp. 163–6.
85 See Large, *Organized Workers*, chaps. 1, 2; Beckmann and Okubo, *The Japanese Communist Party*, pp. 46–47; Ōsawa, *Ōsugi Sakae kenkyū*, pp. 267–9; Watanabe, "Nihon no marukusushugi undō ron," pp. 174–5, 205–11, 229–30; Matsuzawa, *Nihon*, pp. 101–2.

tion of the anarchosyndicalist "idealization of revolution" (*kannenteki kakumei*) received the approbation of Communists and labor reformers alike. Present at the convention as an auditor, as was Yamakawa, Ōsugi bitterly described the whole of the "Bolshevik gang" – Yamakawa, Sakai, and Arahata – as a "bunch of crooks."[86]

Just as the Bolshevik-Reformist defeat of the anarchosyndicalists represents a decisive shift in the prevailing tactics and dominant ideologies of the labor movement, Yamakawa's essay marks a critical juncture in the intellectual history of Japanese radicalism and particularly its theories of revolution. Rejecting the creed of millenarianism, which had dominated the thought of radicals since Kōtoku, Yamakawa also expressed his objections to the radicals' misdirected expressions of moral indignation and criticized the tactical stupidity of radical spontaneity. "Ten or twenty enthusiasts," he wrote,

> get together, dream about the next day of revolution and make big talk. . . . At best they would satisfy their "rebellious spirit" by taking "revolutionary action" against a policeman and spending a night under police detention. Although they reject the capitalist system, they actually do not lay a finger upon it.[87]

Yamakawa described the Japanese proletarian movement as having two aspects, a socialist movement and a labor movement. He castigated the former, including himself, for being overly concerned with the clarification of principles and the purification of ideology. As a result, socialists had isolated themselves from the proletariat as a whole, "[drawing] apart from the ordinary union members around them and even more so from the masses of the working class." They thus failed in their duty to raise the masses toward a maximum standard of class consciousness, instead allowing them to fall under the spiritual influence of the capitalists. Although Yamakawa praised the union movement, he found it lamentable that the advanced members, the organized workers, found themselves "separated from the ordinary worker." And finally, he criticized both for their "passive attitude" toward bourgeois government. Workers little realized, he wrote, that victories won on the economic front can be jeopardized by politics.

> On any front where capitalism expresses authority and control, we must move on . . . to an attitude of positive struggle. The political front is the place

86 Kishimoto and Koyama, *Nihon hikyōsantō*, pp. 95, 143–7. For quotation from Ōsugi, see Stanley, *Ōsugi Sakae*, p. 140. For Yamakawa's essay discussed in the next paragraphs, see Yamakawa Hitoshi, "Musan kaikyū undō no hōko tenkan," in *Yamakawa Hitoshi zenshū*, vol. 4, ed. Yamakawa Kikue and Yamakawa Shinsaku (Tokyo: Keisō shobō, 1967), pp. 336–45.
87 Beckmann and Okubo, *The Japanese Communist Party*, p. 51.

where the authority and control of the bourgeoisie find their most naked and direct expression. . . . Simply to reject the existing system of bourgeois politics ideologically cannot bring the slightest injury to it.[88]

"Change of Course" offered a tactical solution to both the isolation of the vanguard from the masses and the political passivity and fecklessness of both. Ultimately, Yamakawa explained, "Our goal is the destruction of capitalism. . . . Any reform short of that can never liberate us." But if the mass of workers do not demand the abolition of capitalism and instead "demand the improvement of their immediate daily life, our present movement must be based on this popular demand." Even though the "movement must become more practical" in order to bring vanguard and mass together through their mutual struggle, he hoped that the vanguard could raise the demands of the workers and persuade them to expand their goals. "Change of Course" did not signal, Yamakawa insisted, "a fall from the principle of revolution to reformism" but, rather, an accommodation to worker demands in order to build a "concrete" movement for the achievement of the final goal. The vanguard must therefore take its ideology to the masses, retain its revolutionary consciousness, and, he insisted, never dissolve within the masses. Thus the second charge of the essay, "advance toward a political struggle," urged upon the vanguard the need to lead the proletariat toward recognizing that their call for "rights of livelihood" and for the settlement of the unemployment problem were demands aimed at the state. Hence the practical economic struggle could not be separated from the political one. Although in this essay Yamakawa did not discuss political parties or indicate a change in his attitude toward universal suffrage, he urged upon the proletarian movement a new sort of political action. "If the proletariat truly rejects bourgeois politics, it must not be simply passive. . . . It must put up proletarian politics against bourgeois politics."[89]

Quite clearly, then, Yamakawa had repudiated both his own past position (and Ōsugi's continuing position) that standard union economic demands were politically ineffectual. Instead, he offered a near Leninist interpretation of the indispensable role of the vanguard in creating a revolutionary and social democratic consciousness among the proletariat. But in Yamakawa's discussions of the vanguard, and ultimately in his evaluation of the roles of trade unions and the secret vanguard party (that is, the Japan Communist Party [JCP]), he parted from Leninism. Lenin argued, and so would the JCP, that only the

88 Ibid., p. 52. 89 Ibid., pp. 46–7.

vanguard and organizers could guide the workers beyond the horizons of bourgeois society to revolution. Left to their own devices, workers could never, autonomously, become conscious revolutionaries. "Since," Lenin wrote, "there can be no question of an independent ideology formulated by the working masses themselves in the process of their movement, the only choice is either bourgeois or socialist ideology." For Lenin, no working class, however powerful the trade unions it created, was capable of attaining consciousness of the fundamental opposition between their class as a whole and the existing social system. "We have said," he wrote, "that there could not have been social democratic consciousness among the workers. It would have to be brought to them from without."[90]

Yamakawa, however, had long been ambivalent about the Bolsheviks' domination of the Russian workers. In a February 1922 essay, he was unwilling to testify fully to the "desirability" of the "leadership" or "dictatorship of the party"; he had merely accepted it as necessary, given the yet undeveloped class consciousness of the common people. Even earlier, in his criticism of *minponshugi* theories, Yamakawa had berated Yoshino and Ōyama for feigning a belief in majority rule but in reality calling for the rule of an "enlightened few." Democracy, he wrote, demands rule by the people, who are never ignorant of the real needs of society. And several months after the publication of his "Change of Course" article, he roundly denied the charges by an anarchosyndicalist that he had sold out the working class to an intellectual vanguard. By a vanguard, Yamakawa insisted, he meant only the organized and hence more class-conscious members of the working class.[91]

Yamakawa, in fact, never completely accepted Lenin's belief in the indisputable need of a vanguard to lead the workers to a revolutionary consciousness. He may or may not have been a Kautskyian, as the theoretician Fukumoto Kazuo later argued, but his insistence after 1919 that the workers' class consciousness was bound to develop through their struggle with capitalism and that labor organizations served both as organs of struggle for the workers' demands and as nuclei in the creation of new social styles was certainly closer to the thought of Kautsky than to Lenin. Even in his "Change of Course" article, which members of the JCP contended had been written under party orders (Yama-

90 This discussion of Lenin uses Leszek Kolakowski, *Main Currents of Marxism*, vol. 2, chap. 16; for quotations, see pp. 386, 387.

91 Yamakawa Hitoshi, "Rōdō undō ni taisuru chishiki kaikyū no chii," in *Yamakawa Hitoshi zenshū*, vol. 3, ed. Yamakawa Kikue and Yamakawa Shinsaku (Tokyo: Keisō shobō, 1967), pp. 26–39; *Yamakawa zenshū*, vol. 2 (Tokyo: Keisō shobō, 1966), pp. 82–91, 106–8; *Yamakawa zenshū*, vol. 5 (Tokyo: Keisō shobō, 1968), pp. 191–9.

kawa's denial was supported by Arahata), he wrote that class consciousness is comprehensible not simply for the few with enough erudition to discern it; it inevitably grows in the mind of every member of the working class, though not always at the same rate or to the same degree.[92]

By 1924 Yamakawa's differences with the JCP had become clear. Arguments over proper revolutionary theory and tactics led to an extensive struggle that took several forms. In the labor unions, reformists (or pragmatists, as they are sometimes called) and Marxists clashed over the role of unions in a bourgeois state. Inside and outside the unions there was a sharp split over revolutionary theory between the independent Marxists, led by Yamakawa, and those associated with the JCP. Throughout, it was Yamakawa who dominated: his perception of the proper tactics of the Japanese working class toward a united front with the bourgeoisie, his analysis of the character of the Japanese bourgeoisie and the workers' class consciousness, and his interpretation of the revolutionary potential of organized workers and the nature of the Japanese state. Yamakawa defined the policies and practices of a non-Communist Japanese Marxist and provoked a theoretical debate among all Japanese Marxists. Ultimately, Yamakawa and the JCP, particularly the theoretician Fukumoto Kazuo, confronted each other over issues of theory and practice expressed in Comintern doctrine. As a result, Japanese Marxists began a debate on the origins and development of the modern Japanese state that stimulated the social scientific analysis of modern Japanese history and thoroughly embedded Marxism in the intellectual life of Japan. But for Yamakawa or Fukumoto and all their fellows, the function of historical analysis, like that of social theory, was never merely academic. It provided the "scientific" basis for their criticism of the Japanese state, an intellectual perspective from which to criticize liberal formulas, and conceptual guidelines for a revolutionary movement.[93]

## Whose revolution is it?: Fukumoto versus Yamakawa

Within three years of the publication of "Change of Course," Yamakawa's strategic assumptions and theoretical conceptions were challenged by Fukumoto Kazuo (1894–1983). A graduate of the law faculty of Tokyo Imperial University who became a lecturer in eco-

92 Watanabe, "Nihon no marukusushugi undō ron," pp. 182, 198–200.

93 Ibid., pp. 184–5, 230–5; Koyama Hirotake and Sugimori Yasuji, "Rōnōha marukusushugi," in *Shōwa no hantaisei shisō*, vol. 3, ed. Sumiya Etsuji (Tokyo: Haga shobō, 1967), pp. 278–334.

nomics and law at Matsue Higher School, Fukumoto had recently returned from several years of government-sponsored study in Germany. While there he had steeped himself in the Marx–Engels classics and the works of Lenin, Rosa Luxemburg, and Karl Liebknecht. Using his encyclopedic knowledge of theory, a quality that particularly impressed young radical university students, Fukumoto by 1926 had revived the JCP and taken over its leadership.[94] As Hayashi Fusao, a leader of the *Shinjinkai*, wrote:

> The one thing that could not be doubted was his extreme erudition. The passages he quoted were all crucial lines that I had never read. Neither Yamakawa, nor Sakai . . . had once quoted these for us. These fresh contents forced me to realize the ignorance of Japanese Marxists – or at least so I, as a student theorist, thought.[95]

Fukumoto had also learned the skills of sectarian vituperation. Shortly after his return in 1924, in a public address at Kyoto Imperial University, he neatly undercut the arguments of the prestigious Marxist professor of economics, Kawakami Hajime, caricaturing him in front of his students as an "empiriocritic" (*keikenhihan*), a man who espoused a philosophy that Lenin had written a whole pamphlet to vilify. But in his first essays in *Marxism* (Marukusushugi), the major theoretical journal of the proletarian movement, Fukumoto confined himself to denouncing Yamakawa's "Change of Course" as a "vulgarization of Marxism." He slandered Yamakawa as an "economist," a Leninist term of opprobrium to describe those who believed that economic struggle alone can lead to political transformation without the direct intervention of a party devoted to political struggle. He accused Yamakawa of failing to understand the "underlying principles" of a "change of course." In essence, Fukumoto was merely providing theoretical documentation to demonstrate what already should have been clear: Yamakawa was not a Leninist.[96]

Fukumoto was a Leninist, however; or at least he believed that he had preserved the essence of Lenin's doctrine in his maxims for a purified proletarian movement. Fukumoto accepted as axiomatic that "our true change of course" depended on "raising proletarian consciousness through . . . theoretical struggle." As described by Lenin,

94 Koyama Hirotake, "Nihon marukusushugi no keisei," in *Shōwa no hantaisei shisō*, pp. 106–9.

95 Jeffrey Paul Wagner, "Sano Manabu and the Japanese Adaptation of Socialism," Ph.D. diss., University of Arizona, 1978, p. 58.

96 Iwasaki Chikatsugu, *Nihon marukusushugi tetsugakushi* (Tokyo: Miraisha, 1971), pp. 31–3; Furuta Hikaru, *Kawakami Hajime* (Tokyo: Tōkyō daigaku shuppankai, 1959), pp. 138–49; Kishimoto and Koyama, *Nihon no hikyōsantō*, p. 112; Koyama, "Nihon marukusushugi no keisei," p. 110.

he wrote, a correct "change of course" for the proletarian movement "is a qualitative process of change within a dialectic process." In tactical terms this meant that the proletarian movement must shift from trade union struggles to socialist political struggle. Like Lenin, Fukumoto did not believe that the proletariat could comprehend on its own the aptness or necessity of such a strategy. Rather than rely on changes in objective conditions, the proletariat must, by a subjective leap, gain a "genuine class consciousness" (a consciousness that Fukumoto equated with the possession of Marxist "knowledge" [*ninshiki*]). Only a "true vanguard party," a Communist party, would be a veritable source of socialist consciousness; only such a party "could use, direct, promote, or transform all political opposition, thereby making the proletarian movement a genuine class movement."[97]

After his return to Japan, Fukumoto decided that the broader tasks of the political struggle had to be set aside temporarily in order to deal with the corrupting influence of Yamakawa's "change of course" and his conception of a united front party. Yamakawa had envisaged and helped create, as he himself wrote in 1924, "a proletarian political movement uniting the largest possible part of the workers' movement in an organization that was as free as possible from bourgeois influence." Yamakawa believed that the leadership of this "united front" should fall to the organized proletariat in urban factories and the organized tenants in rural districts. The creation of such a party disturbed Fukumoto: Neither a vanguard party nor an illegal revolutionary corps, such an organization could never promote the revolutionary consciousness of the masses. In fact, Yamakawa had urged that it not be solely a proletarian vehicle. Rather, he believed, it should serve the broad democratic interest of the *lumpen,* all the unorganized, the colonial masses, the outcast *burakumin,* and even the lower elements of the petty bourgeoisie. Yamakawa also recommended that the vanguard elements dissolve themselves within the united front and "allow every fraction to express its views fully at the party congress and to be recognized fully within the party." Fukumoto felt that such a view, which ran counter to Lenin's conception of a party composed of professional revolutionaries dictating policy, would be disastrous. Lenin had found "fractionalism," the organized activity of groups of members who were free to express minority views, to be destructive to the ultimate aims of a revolutionary party. Fukumoto believed, moreover,

97 Iwasaki, *Nihon marukusushugi tetsugakushi,* pp. 32–5; Koyama, "Nihon marukusushugi no keisei," pp. 110–16; Kishimoto and Koyama, *Nihon no hikyōsantō,* pp. 129–37; Matsuzawa, *Nihon,* pp. 194–200.

that his own desire to create a Marxist consciousness among the proletariat would come to naught in a united front party: The vanguard would be dissolved in the mass. He argued that Yamakawa's conception of the natural growth of proletarian consciousness was, at best, mere "opportunism." Worse yet, Fukumoto wrote, Yamakawa had led the movement toward a belief in "spontaneity" and "infantile leftism," both thoroughly condemned by Lenin.[98]

Fukumoto therefore set as the immediate task of the Marxist left the establishment of a correct and unified theoretical program for the proletarian movement: "to give life to, deepen, and spread Marxism and Marxist influence." Following Lenin, he called for the creation of a Marxist vanguard that would follow a policy of "unity through separation" (*bunri-ketsugō*), a process by which genuine Marxists would be separated from false Marxists and reformists. This became the absolute prerequisite for the achievement of unity. In later years this glorification of ideological purity, the insistence on the priority of intellectual struggle over political praxis, and the worship of dogma would be denounced by both the Comintern and JCP. But for the moment (and some believe that it permanently damaged the movement), it turned the JCP into a confederation of mandarins and quite possibly made the Marxist movement of Japan the most theoretically sophisticated in the world.[99]

Obviously, Yamakawa could not accept Fukumoto's propositions. A proletarian party, he wrote, "should represent the highest expression of the revolutionary demands of the proletariat, not simply an abstraction based on strategies for the establishment of a new society; it should incorporate all elements of the proletariat and reflect its current interests and demands."[100] Yamakawa quickly reconfirmed his belief in a "united front party": It, and neither a secret nor a vanguard party, should take the lead of the Japanese proletarian movement.

Yamakawa opposed the reconstitution of the JCP and refused to join it. He also explained later that he believed that the "existence of the party in 1922–3 had been to the detriment of the overall movement." He opposed the reorganization of the party on empirical and

98 Matsuzawa, *Nihon*, pp. 199–200. For a discussion of united front strategies in Japan and the West, see Inumaru Yoshikazu, *Nihon no marukusushugi sono*, vol. 2: *Kōza gendai no ideorogii* (Tokyo: San'ichi shobō, 1961), pp. 39–40, 57–8; Koyama, "Nihon marukusushugi no keisei," pp. 89–92, 110–26; Koyama and Sugimori, "Rōnōha marukusushugi," pp. 283–8, 311–25; Iwasaki, *Nihon marukusushugi tetsugakushi*, pp. 34–5; Kishimoto and Koyama, *Nihon no hikyōsantō*, pp. 110, 125.

99 Kishimoto and Koyama, *Nihon no hikyōsantō*, p. 137; Koyama, "Nihon marukusushugi no keisei," pp. 112–14; Iwasaki, *Nihon marukusushugi tetsugakushi*, pp. 32–4.

100 Koyama, "Nihon marukusushugi no keisei," pp. 91, 94–7.

historical, not theoretical, grounds. "I felt that conditions being what they were in Japan, another Communist party at this time [1926] would not be any better. What suited Russia would not necessarily fit Japan." Yamakawa argued that only through an analysis of Japanese capitalism, an examination of the specific political structure of the Japanese ruling class, and an understanding of the historical peculiarity of the development of the modern Japanese state and society could a proper strategy for the proletarian movement be developed.[101]

Yamakawa took as the basis for his analysis Marx's typology of the capitalist stages of development, which described how the bourgeoisie in Europe had constituted itself as a class in opposition to the rule of feudalism and absolutism. But with a conceptual flexibility similar to Marx's social analysis in *The Eighteenth Brumaire of Louis Napoleon*, Yamakawa observed certain historical anomalies in the way that the Japanese bourgeois had acquired political rule. Thus he suggested an analysis at odds on critical points with that offered by the Comintern and JCP.

In 1922 the draft platform of the JCP (*koryō sōan*) had defined Japan as "semifeudal." Although, the draft pointed out, the state was controlled by a definite part of the commercial and industrial capitalists, "remnants of feudal relationships" were manifest in its structure. This semifeudal character was most clearly shown "in the important and leading role of the peers and in the basic features of the constitution." Moreover, Japanese capitalism "still demonstrates characteristics of former feudal relationships. . . . And the greatest part of the land is today in the hands of semifeudal landlords." The draft continued, "The emperor, who heads the Japanese government, [is] the biggest landlord of all." Members of the JCP at that time, particularly Sakai Toshihiko, chose to suppress this part. Given the semifeudal character of the Japanese state, the party recommended a joint struggle of proletariat and bourgeoisie to overthrow the imperial government as the correct political strategy, that is, a bourgeois revolution.[102]

Yamakawa accepted neither this strategy nor the historical interpretation on which it was based. "The center of power in our society," he insisted, "has decisively shifted from the bureaucracy to the bourgeoisie." When the Seiyūkai party rose to power and its leader, Hara Takashi, became prime minister, Yamakawa argued, "the political power of the bourgeoisie existent today was thus consolidated." But

101 Ibid.

102 For a full translation of the draft platform, see Beckmann and Okubo, *The Japanese Communist Party*, pp. 279–82; Inumaru, *Nihon no marukusushugi sono*, vol. 2, p. 45.

paradoxically, this transfer of power "explains the withering of democracy in Japan." Yamakawa explained this paradox by contrasting Japan's capitalist development with that of Britain. "Britain took fifty or seventy years to pass peacefully through the gradual establishment of bourgeois democracy, and under the most favorable circumstances." But Japanese bourgeois capitalism had grown up under the "tutelage of bureaucratic politics." Whereas British capitalism grew quickly in a period of free trade, Japanese capitalism was "warped" and the "political development of the country perverted . . . because it took place under the wing of medieval bureaucratic politics." In contrast with the European bourgeoisie, Yamakawa continued, the Japanese bourgeoisie "had no revolutionary period. What succeeded feudal aristocratic politics [in Japan] was not bourgeois democracy but, rather, bureaucratic militarist politics." Nor did the Japanese bourgeoisie ever "directly attack the bureaucracy in order to take state power." When the Japanese bourgeoisie consolidated their political power, they did so without any sense of a distinctly bourgeois class consciousness: They acted "almost without conscious purpose, in a fit of absence of mind." In fact, the Seiyūkai became the "representative bourgeois party . . . because it joined with and identified with the bureaucracy." Given these circumstances and the fact that Japanese capitalism had appeared during the imperialist stage in the development of world capitalism, Yamakawa concluded that "Japan had no leeway to elaborate a bourgeois democracy, or at least very little. Our age of bourgeois democracy, if it appears at all, will be very brief."[103]

As a result of his analysis of Japanese history, Yamakawa believed that the proletarian movement had simultaneously to seek the abolition of feudal institutions in society and to complete the democratization of Japan's political institutions. But given the rapidity of Japanese development, the proletariat – like the bourgeoisie – had not had enough time to constitute itself as a singular and conscious class. It thus faced the danger of "being absorbed by bourgeois and petty bourgeois political movements." It was on these grounds that Yamakawa believed it necessary for the proletarian movement to take the lead (and to do so immediately) in "uniting the largest possible part of the workers' movement in an organization that is as autonomous as possible from bourgeois influence."[104]

103 *Yamakawa zenshū,* vol. 5, pp. 77–82; Koyama, "Nihon marukusushugi no keisei," pp. 81–7; Koyama and Sugimori, "Rōnōha marukusushugi," pp. 282–4.
104 Koyama, "Nihon marukusushugi no keisei"; Koyama and Sugimori, "Rōnōha marukusushugi," pp. 281–2.

By contrast, Fukumoto did not ignore historical circumstances, but he saw historical changes in abstract global terms. Following Lenin and Luxemburg, he insisted that contemporary capitalism had reached its final and moribund stage of imperialism. Its collapse was imminent. Like Europe, Japan faced revolution, and its proletariat needed the guidance of a Leninist vanguard to accomplish its revolution.[105]

Ultimately, neither Yamakawa nor Fukumoto, neither the JCP nor Yamakawa's "united front" of laborers and farmers was victorious. All fell victim to government suppression. Fukumoto and Yamakawa also faced attack from the Comintern and many fellow leftists. The JCP expelled Fukumoto from the central committee in 1927, accusing him of Trotskyism, among other things. The Comintern described Fukumoto's insistence on "unity through separation" as an error "that will isolate the party from the mass organizations of the proletariat." Yamakawa, his opponents wrote, encouraged "passivity." By ignoring the role of the vanguard, they charged, he left the proletarian movement powerless to transcend events and so reduced both to following them. Nonetheless, through their debates, Yamakawa and Fukumoto made the entire left aware that a conceptual understanding of history was important to the analysis of contemporary affairs. As Yamakawa had made clear, the strategic concerns of the present were predicated on a correct understanding of the past. If nothing else, this insight raised the level of the historiography of the Meiji Restoration.[106]

## IDEOLOGICAL DIALECTICS: THE PARADOX OF JAPANESE MARXISM

No simple dichotomy between Leninists and non-Leninists or between Communist and non-Communist Marxists can do justice to the ideological complexity of Japanese Marxism in the 1920s and early 1930s. To be sure, Leninist theory and Comintern theses usually set the terms of discourse about proper political praxis for Marxists inside and outside the Japanese Communist Party alike. But throughout this period, a flood of translations and commentaries on the work of Marx, Kautsky, Rosa Luxemburg, and others kept the Japanese abreast of developments in European non-Leninist Marxism. (For example, a translation of Kautsky's *Karl Marx' Ökonomische Lehren*, a gloss on

105 Koyama, "Nihon marukusushugi no keisei," pp. 114–16.
106 Koyama, "Nihon marukusushugi no keisei," pp. 99–100, 134; Takeuchi Yoshitomo and Suzuki Tadashi, "*Shinkō kagaku no hata no moto ni* to *Yuibutsuron kenkyū*," *Shisō* 465 (March 1963): 108–10.

the first volume of *Capital*, became a best seller, as did Marx's work itself.) Radical students like Fukumoto, Miki, and Hani who went to study in Weimar Germany also brought back what Alvin Gouldner called "critical Marxism" – a Marxism infiltrated by neo-Hegelian, neo-Kantian, and Heideggerian ideas. The Japanese socialists might not have heard of Lenin in 1917, but ten years later Japanese Marxists were well aware of the main currents of Marxist thought in both Western Europe and the Soviet Union.[107]

Paradoxically, Marxism gained intellectual force and influence in the late 1920s and early 1930s even as the government intensified its crackdown on the Communist Party and defections from the movement increased. The intellectual significance that Marxism attained as a principium can be explained in part by the totality with which its theory of dialectical and historical materialism explained human social, economic, and political behavior. In Fukumoto's words, "Everything must be understood as forms in motion, in contradictory development and as part of a totality, that is, must be grasped dialectically." It is also true that Leninist ideas regarding the importance of theoretical purity and the hegemonic role of the rational intellectual appealed to the traditional bias of the Japanese mandarinate, as did the more general tendency of Western Marxism in the 1920s to give priority to theory over praxis and to emphasize cognitive clarity and consciousness. Although many academic Marxists like Miki, Fukumoto, and Hani were later attacked for their abstractness and their overemphasis on theory, a fault that some say has plagued Japanese Marxism ever since, it may have been precisely these qualities that made their writings so widely read.[108]

But Japanese Marxism also attracted the attention of intellectuals because of the apparent catholicity with which its chief ideologues integrated contemporary Western ideas into their theories. The extent of this can only be suggested. For example, Fukumoto was expelled from the JCP not merely because he insisted on the priority of theory but also because he emphasized the humanist element in Marx and asserted the priority of the transformation of consciousness in revolu-

107 Kishimoto and Koyama, *Nihon no hikyosantō*, p. 79. For a good discussion of these problems, see Iwasaki, *Nihon marukusushugi tetsugakushi*, chap. 1; Alvin Gouldner, *The Two Marxisms* (New York: Oxford University Press, 1980). For comparable Western Marxist developments, see Martin Jay, *The Dialectical Imagination* (Boston: Little, Brown, 1973), esp. pp. 76–80, 121–4, 272. A recent study of the Marxist debates in Japan is Germaine A. Hoston, *Marxism and the Crisis of Development in Prewar Japan* (Princeton, N.J.: Princeton University Press, 1986).

108 Takeuchi and Suzuki, "*Shinkō kagaku*"; Iwasaki, *Nihon marukusushugi tetsugakushi*, pp. 39–41; Matsuzawa, *Nihon*, pp. 199–200.

tionary practice. These ideas he had borrowed from Karl Korsch, a neo-Hegelian Marxist, and from Georg Lukacs, who had introduced Weberian ideas to Marxism. In contending that Japan was on the verge of revolution, a position totally at odds with the Comintern and the JCP, Fukumoto followed Rosa Luxemburg, who had argued in a pre–World War I debate with Lenin that in the imperialist stage of world history, crisis was universal throughout the capitalist world.[109]

For some Japanese Marxists, the humanist side of Marx's thought was tremendously appealing. In his interpretation of Marx's concept of commodity fetishism – usually explained by most Marxists as the simplest and most universal example of how the economic forms of capitalism conceal underlying social relationships – Kawakami Hajime found evidence that Marx had been concerned not with material things but with human relationships. In most of his work after 1927 Kawakami explored this humanistic relationship through a study of the Marxist classics, having found in neo-Kantian Marxism a way to integrate dialectical materialism and humanism. The younger Miki Kiyoshi, just at this time, infused his Marxism with theories of knowledge borrowed in part from Heideggerian existentialism. In his analysis of the dialectic between productivity and the relations of production, Miki introduced a primary *logos* of "existence," arguing in highly un-Marxian language that "man, in the process of life, is forced to advance an interpretation, in some manner, of his own quintessence."[110]

What Fukumoto, Kawakami, Miki, and many of their peers brought into Marxism was a belief in the significance of the human actor and the role of human self-consciousness in carrying out revolutionary praxis. The theory of revolution and social praxis that intellectuals found in Marxism offered a positive philosophical alternative to the ahistoricity and passivity of the prevailing academic philosophy of "self-cultivation," *kyōyōshugi*. Whereas self-cultivation encouraged individuals to indulge themselves in a world of individuality, Marxism offered a philosophy of action.[111] And it linked that philosophy of action with a universalistic or cosmopolitan conception of how human society developed, in Japan as elsewhere.

109 Yamanouchi Yasushi, "Iwayuru shakai ishiki keitai ni tsuite," *Shisō* 568, 569 (October 1971, November 1971): 23–37; 87–100.

110 Iwasaki, *Nihon marukusushugi tesugakushi*, pp. 102–8, 116–20, 128–32, 178–9; Yamanouchi, "Iwayuru shakai"; Ōuchi Hyōe, ed., *Miki Kiyoshi zenshū*, vol. 3 (Tokyo: Iwanami shoten, 1966–8), pp. 8–9.

111 Iwasaki, *Nihon marukusushugi tetsugakushi*, pp. 178–9; Takeuchi and Suzuki, "*Shinkō kagaku*," pp. 110–11.

# CHAPTER 14

# JAPANESE REVOLT AGAINST THE WEST: POLITICAL AND CULTURAL CRITICISM IN THE TWENTIETH CENTURY

## INTRODUCTION

Throughout much of Japan's modern history, the West has contributed to its formulation of theories of culture and action. At one level the image of a monolithic West replaced an earlier interpretation of China as the "other." In the twentieth century and especially after World War I, Japan's conceptualization of the West affirmed a theory of militant and articulate revolt against the "other," usually imagined as a collective threat to Japan's national independence and cultural autonomy. The construction of the "other" required that it be portrayed as the mirror image of the indigenous culture. It was this representation of the "other" that clarified for the Japanese the essence of their own culture. This reversing of images was no less true in the Tokugawa period, when an idealized China had constituted the "other," than in the twentieth century, when a monolithic West did. If the "other" defined what was exceptional in Japanese culture, it also offered a model of excellence against which such distinctiveness could be measured. Just as Tokugawa writers focused on the world of the ancient sages, changing it into an unhistorical abstraction whose values existed only in pure form in Japan, so twentieth-century thinkers imagined a Japan destined to reach new levels of achievements realized by no single Western nation. Through this doubling of images, they shaped a theory of action aimed at maintaining a pure, indigenous cultural synthesis protected from outside elements that might disturb the perceived equilibrium. It was precisely because Japanese saw the urgency of keeping their culture uncontaminated and hence preserving its essence against the threatened external pollution that many felt justified using militant forms of political and cultural action.

Although desperate and even violent resistance against the West spread among nationalistic groups in the 1920s, reaching a climax in the mid-1930s, the concern for keeping Japan's culture pure prompted others to try more moderate ways of preventing Japan from assimilating too closely with the West. The impulse behind these efforts can be traced to the cosmopolitanism in the 1920s and the general conviction that Japan had contributed its own unique voice to a global civilization whose diversity was unified by a broad conception of humanity. Yet the emphasis on Japan's special contribution to world civilization narrowed easily in the political environment of the late 1920s and early 1930s to a preoccupation with the status of Japan's uniqueness. Many believed that by realizing the best of East and West, Japan had achieved a new cosmopolitan culture. The recognition of having achieved this unprecedented synthesis validated the subsequent belief that Japan was uniquely qualified to assume leadership in Asia, although much of the rhetoric that the writers used referred to the world at large. Whereas an earlier cosmopolitanism promoted the ideal of cultural diversity and equivalence based on the principle of a common humanity, which served also to restrain excessive claims to exceptionalism, the new culturalism of the 1930s proposed that Japan was appointed to lead the world to a higher level of cultural synthesis that surpassed Western modernism itself.

The ambiguity between the capacity of an indigenous culture to withstand change and the claims of new knowledge demanding transformation was at the heart of the Meiji Restoration of 1868. On the one hand, the Meiji restorers announced, in the opening decree proclaiming the Restoration, that the aim of the new policy was to return to the "events of antiquity and Jimmu Tennō's state foundation." This meant returning to origins, a mythical time before Japan had been corrupted by Buddhism and Chinese civilization, and to the unalloyed practices of native experience. Yet at the same time, the new government declared in the Charter Oath its determination to "search for new knowledge throughout the world" and to "eliminate old customs" "based on the universal way." The former intention led to a belief in cultural exceptionalism and even to presumptions of superiority in Japan's relations with foreigners. It also emphasized the basic similarity of all Japanese before the differentiating and alienating influence of foreign cultures and called attention to the real separation between demands of similitude (Japan) and difference (the "other"). The latter inspired the creation of the modern state and the transformation of Japanese society, classically expressed in the 1870s and 1880s as the establishment of "civilization and enlightenment" (*bunmei kaika*). Hence the call to origins authenticated all those proposals directed toward what was essential and spiritual and what was irreducibly Japanese, even though society had changed visibly and materially. The search for new knowledge, on the other hand, was identified with progressive development, modernity, and the West. The terms of cultural uniqueness increasingly stressed ends and essence, and the pursuit of rational knowledge privileged means and instrumentality. In the end the conflict was expressed in a struggle between culture – or the nation's distinctive spirit – and modern civilization – especially as expressed as functional political structure – and desperate efforts to overcome this polarization. Only Japan's defeat in the Pacific War and its dazzling economic recovery offered the occasion to complete the unfinished business of realigning these opposite claims and concealing their inherent contradiction in an improbable synthesis of Japan and the West.

## RESTORATIONIST REVOLT

The particular militancy of the Japanese revolt against the West stems from the historical model of the loyalist samurai who overthrew the Tokugawa *bakufu* in the 1860s and established the Meiji state. In this model there were two related but distinct orientations in the theory of a restorationist action. One emphasized the necessity of resolving the question of domestic politics by ridding the country of incompetent leaders and ineffective institutions. It was believed that unless domestic problems first were solved, the nation would be left defenseless against the hostile ambitions of Western colonial powers. The other orientation focused on the foreign problem and sought to solve it through frontal military strategies. Whereas the theories of Kita Ikki and their ultimate incorporation in the mutiny of radical young officers on February 26, 1936, exemplify the first orientation, the calculated attack on Pearl Harbor in 1941 – after a decade of trying to resolve the foreign problem – represents the second orientation.

Beginning in the 1920s, with the assassination of Prime Minister Hara Takashi in Tokyo Station in 1921 and continuing thereafter in single acts of terror, the radical restorationists shunned public debate and conciliation as a way of resolving domestic political problems and instead used strategies of direct and violent action in order to shock and even shatter the confidence of political and industrial leaders. Drawing on the historical analogy of the sixteenth century when the "lower overthrew the upper" (*gekokujō*), activists reminded their contemporaries that the idea of loyalty did not always mean compliance with the commands of superiors, that it could also mean righteous rebellion against incompetent and insensitive leaders. Indeed, this idea of loyalty functioned as a double-edged sword to cut down the constitutional leadership and to remove all obstacles from achieving the goal of expelling the Western presence in Japan and Asia.

Although it would be difficult to reduce all aspects of the Japanese revolt to a single doctrine or mode of action – as the ramifications were complex and branched over diverse areas of the culture – there are, nonetheless, some general characteristics that most of the groups and thinkers shared. Western conceptions of legal reason and rational cultural norms, often conveyed in the idiom of progress, rationalism, modernization, or simply Westernization, all came under scrutiny and were invariably modified but more often rejected as extensions of structures of power aimed at expanding Western interests. Moreover, such Western notions were seen as manipulating the indigenous cultural values in ways that were inimical to the legacies of a distinct history, particularly the aesthetic impulse of an elegant inheritance, and contrary to the communitarian experience vivified by the collective memory of the folk. Often these aesthetic and communitarian values were signified by the vague yet provocative phrase calling attention to the "national political essence" (*kokutai*), a concept that conjured up mythical associations of a mystical union of spirit and body and that evoked a distinctive past and the creative potential for a unique future. The conception of *kokutai* captured in a single verbal compound the entire range of ideological virtues that defined what it meant to be Japanese, as opposed to the "other."

The Japanese revolt also tended to link the resolution of Japan's problems with the revival of Asia as a world area, to emphasize the commonality of Asian peoples in their struggle to eliminate Western colonialism. Here, Japanese attitudes corresponded to the shift noted earlier from the Meiji enlightenment and its faith in rational progress to a preoccupation with an indigenous cultural spirit free from the constraints of alien logic and science. Thus, during the industrial and social revolutions that followed the Meiji Restoration, Japanese leaders spoke confidently of "leaving Asia" – *datsu-A* – meaning principally the zone of Chinese civilization, and "entering Europe" – *nyū-Ō* – but this pattern was reversed in the twentieth century. Now leaders urged a "reentry into Asia" and an "abandonment of Europe," *nyū-A, datsu-Ō*. This reversal in phraseology was significant both politically and culturally. Politically, it referred to a growing expectation that Japan, as a newly industrialized nation in Asia, should rightfully assume responsibility for developing that area. But a closer reading of the slogan suggested Japanese hegemony in Asia and the removal of outside interference. Culturally, the call to reenter Asia heralded the reidentification of Japan with its continental roots, a return to its original sphere of civilization and the maintenance of Japan's unique place in it.

This was early and powerfully articulated by the art historian Okakura Tenshin (1862–1913), who in a series of books (*The Ideals of the East*, 1902, and *The Book of Tea*, 1903), sought to establish Asia's cultural equivalence to the claims of Western hegemony. Okakura first formulated the principles that all Asians shared: "Asia is one," he wrote in *The Ideals of the East*, "The Himalayas divide, only to accentuate, two mighty civilizations, the Chinese with its communism of Confucius, and the Indian with its individualism of the Vedas." But, he added, this geographical divide has not "interrupted" a common inheritance marked by a "love for the Ultimate and Universal." It was precisely this shared disposition for the ultimate and universal that had enabled Asians everywhere to produce the great religions of the world and to emphasize the ends, not the means, of life that Okakura believed distinguished the maritime civilizations of the West. Although Asians had a mutual view of the world, Japan, he proposed, represented this cultural consensus through its aesthetic values. Indeed, Japan functioned as the key to this great cultural code, attesting to "the historic wealth of Asiatic culture" and therefore illuminating "its treasured specimens." Japan, Okakura announced, "is the museum of Asiatic civilization." What he meant by this strategy of substituting the part for the whole is that the artistic accomplishments of the Japanese had encapsulated the "history of Asiatic ideals" to form "sand-ripples" on the national consciousness with "each successive wave of Eastern thought." Long before writers like Watsuji Tetsurō identified the elements of the two different cultural styles, Okakura proposed that Japan alone assimilated two different ideals in an enduring tension: the Asian love for grand visions of "universal sweep" grounded in the concrete and particular and the Western propensity for science and "organized culture" "armed in all its array of undifferentiated knowledge, and keen with the edge of competitive energy." But Okakura was certain that the Japanese example would withstand the challenge of science and industry, to preserve the Asian "spirit" and to lead to a higher synthesis of both.[1]

The twentieth century witnessed a powerful cultural and political

1 Kakuzo Okakura, *Ideals of the East, with Special Reference to the Art of Japan* (Rutland, Vt.: Tuttle, 1970), pp. 1–9, 206–7, 236–44.

ground swell of resistance and revolt against the domination of Asia by Western powers, in which Japan assumed the role of leading this Asian renaissance. Yet before Japan could undertake this leadership role, it felt it necessary to cleanse its own society in a great "spiritual" restoration aimed at lowering the nation's reliance on Western modes of political and economic thought and organization. The various attempted coups and assassinations of the early 1930s – often under the authorizing banner of "restoration" (*ishin*) or "reconstruction" (*kaizō*) – all shared the conceptual assumption that the times demanded direct action promising the establishment of a new order in Japan, unified and freed from the corrosive influence of the West. Indeed, thinkers and activists such as Okawa Shūmei, Inoue Nisshō, Tachibana Kosaburō, Kita Ikki, Gondō Seikei, and others represent nothing less than a program to "expel the barbarians" in the name of culture and spirit, or *jōiron,* as this sentiment was defined in the 1860s before the Meiji Restoration.

Another dimension of these theories of action prompted various evaluations relating to the performance of the modern Japanese state. It was widely believed that the Japanese state had been created in response to the threat to the nation's independence posed by the encircling Western powers. But underlying this conviction was the deeper fear of the structure of law enabling the formation of the modern state. This siege mentality in Japan led to the paradoxical conclusion that the best defense against the Western nation-states was the construction of a modern, legal state of its own. In other words, from the beginning, distrust of the West accompanied the act of state building in Japan, as the following quotation from Kido Takayoshi, one of the early leaders of the Meiji Restoration, illustrates:

> There is an urgent need for Japan to become strong enough militarily to take a stand against the Western powers. As long as our country is lacking in military power, the law of nations is not to be trusted. When dealing with those who are weak, the strong nations often invoke public law but really calculate their own gain. Thus it seems to me that the law of nations is merely a tool for the conquest of the weak.[2]

The magnitude of the challenge suggested here reveals the urgency requiring the revolutionary samurai to construct the Meiji state. Yet a principal consideration of these Meiji state builders was to make sure that the Japanese state, as they envisaged it, would minimize and

2 Masao Miyoshi, *As We Saw Them* (Berkeley and Los Angeles: University of California Press, 1979), p. 143.

eventually obliterate the perceived disparity between Japan and the superior Western powers. Such a mission required continuous demonstration that Japanese achievements were equal to Western accomplishments. But ironically, it was precisely the need for demonstration that escalated the conflict that Japan hoped to avoid. For although Japan underwent with breathtaking speed a political and industrial transformation in order to establish a new relationship with the Western countries, the real and perceived challenge of a permanent condition of national peril never disappeared. Rather, this sense of continuing siege led to the belief that the challenge should be speedily resolved once and for all, in what many came to call the "war to end all wars" (*saishū sensō*). Many were convinced that such a war would definitively expel the West from Asia, would make the continent free for Asians, and thus would complete Japan's own "spiritual" revolution. Simultaneously, movements of dissent were unleashed against the modern state itself for its failure to realize the original vision of the Meiji Restoration, owing to the diverting influence of excessive Westernization, hence the "bureaucratization" of the constitutional system.

Among such proponents of revolt against domestic politics, one group dramatized the inadequacy of the state's constitutional structure and sought to alter it through violent confrontation. The other group rejected the primacy of structure altogether as a Western aberration and instead invoked the power of the spirit to bind all Japanese together in common, not divided, purpose. The major theorist for the former group was Kita Ikki (1883–1937), whereas Gondō Seikei and Tachibana Kosaburō best represented all those groups that dreamed of replacing hierarchical structure with communitarian brotherhood. Nonetheless, there was considerable overlapping between these groups. In fact, some activists, notably Ōkawa Shūmei, were accomplished scholars who moved easily between the various restorationist factions as strategists and planners of coups d'état.

## *Kita Ikki*

Kita Ikki's restorationist theory of action originated in late Meiji nationalism and socialism. In Kita's first major treatise, "The Theory of National Polity and Pure Socialism" (Kokutairon oyobi junsei shakaishugi, 1906), Kita proposed an identity between ancient political society and socialism and equated the traditional absence of private property with the diminished role of state structure. To him the emperor symbolized the common ownership of property and hence a communal form of social existence. He therefore regarded the idea of the national polity (*kokutai*) as an appropriate "historical" model for the present to emulate in order to remove inequality and the sources of contemporary divisiveness; it also justified undertaking political action to install the communalistic ideal. Although Kita remained faithful to this ancient ideal of community, he modified his overall thinking significantly in the course of his career as a theorist and activist.

The crucial turning point altering Kita's angle of vision came with his involvement in Sun Yat-sen's revolutionary movement in China in 1911. Following the revolution and China's subsequent effort to construct a viable state, Kita, though refusing to surrender his earlier communalism, became convinced of the importance of the imperial figure as a unifying principle of politics. In his estimation, the Chinese revolution failed precisely because of its leadership's inability to establish a persuasive centralized political order. In the end they fell back, he observed, to relying on an illegitimate monarchy that only aggravated the problem and forestalled its resolution. While still in Shanghai, Kita began to draft his program for total political reorganization, in a tract called "An Outline Plan for the Reorganization of the Japanese State" (Nihon kokka kaizō hōan, 1919). Soon to become a major manifesto read by a wide variety of malcontents in the military and civilian populations, Kita's "Outline" explained the contemporary political malaise in Japan and the reasons that it called for radical action. He identified what many had felt uneasy about in the political environment of the 1920s but what had not yet been articulated. Implicit in Kita's treatise was a perspective on what he called the crisis of the time, a plan for resolving the domestic failure and a sanction for direct action and the seizure of power in the emperor's name.

Underlying Kita's writings is a sense of national crisis unleashed by capitalist and bureaucratic exploitation and leading to extreme inequality and misery in society that, he feared, would sap the strength and energy of the people. The existing constitutional order, he reasoned, had necessitated divisive party and interest politics (an observation shared by a number of contemporaries along the political spectrum), created new privileged classes, and separated the public realm from the general populace. Kita committed himself, therefore, to revolutionary upheaval as the surest antidote to the evils of the modern Japanese state and its mode of distributing resources. Although he never abandoned his earlier communitarian vision of socialism, derived from his reading of ancient mythohistory, he supplemented it with an organizational scheme that would replace the existing constitutional structure.

In his earlier text on the national polity, Kita had failed to raise the question of industrial production; he was satisfied to base his conception of communitarianism on an ancient agrarian model. But in his later work, he recognized the role of industrialism in modern socialism. It was this perception that prompted him to find a new organizational model to replace the established constitutional order. To achieve his revolutionary aim, Kita advocated overthrowing the prevailing leadership in a swift and conclusive coup d'état. By reconstituting the structure of authority, he believed, Japan would rid itself of Western political institutions and economic practices as a necessary condition for a final confrontation in Asia. Kita called this program a "national renovation" (*Nihon kaizō*) based on the ideal of the "people's emperor" (*kokumin tennō*).

The imperial principle was vital to Kita's overall plan for a revolutionary reorganization of the state. He saw the importance of the emperor not so much as an institution that had survived from ancient times but as a symbol of community. His view came close to the conception of the early Meiji rebels Etō Shimpei and Saigō Takamori, who demanded the installation of what they called a "people's emperor" free from the meddling mediation of bureaucrats. In Japan, Kita argued, the imperial institution had been preserved to represent the national culture, but its potential as a social monarchy had been suppressed by the rise of bourgeois and bureaucratic politics within the constitutional order. It was precisely this principle of social cohesion that made the Meiji Restoration the proper solution to Japan's domestic and foreign problems in the nineteenth century but that subsequent leaders violated by reconstructing the state and society as sanctuaries for private interests and privileges. Kita was indifferent to the idea of a divine emperor. When he was executed for his role in the mutiny of 1936, he was ordered to recant by saying "long live the emperor" as a final act of reverence and submission. He is reported to have refused by replying that he had vowed long ago never to joke about his own death.

In his "Outline" Kita proposed first to suspend the Meiji constitution in the name of the emperor, that is, the national community, in order to liberate both the monarch and the people from the constraints imposed by a bureaucratic polity.[3] Revealing his awareness of the history of modern revolutionary movements elsewhere, he envisaged a

3 Kita Ikki, "Nihon kaizō hōan taikō," in *Gendai Nihon shisō taikei*, vol. 31: *Chōkokka shugi*, ed. Hashikawa Bunzō (Tokyo: Chikuma shobō, 1964), pp. 283–347.

true Japanese revolution like the earlier upheavals in France and Russia. He was convinced that such an event would inaugurate a new era in the twentieth century. Unlike earlier revolutions that had destroyed the monarchy for purposes of political and economic renewal, Kita's theory of revolution depended on establishing the principle of a "people's emperor" as a necessary condition for the eventual implementation of a socialist order. In Asian societies such as China and Japan, he noted, the maintenance of the imperial principle of authority was vital to any radical reconstruction. Without it there would almost certainly be chaos and disorder, such as he had witnessed in China. Behind this view lay Kita's conviction that "true" revolutionary movements were shaped by the specific geographical area rather than the necessities of history. Here he undoubtedly broke with prevailing Marxist theories of revolution that were being debated by many of his contemporaries. Although Kita professed admiration for Marx and Kropotkin, praising them as pioneers in the development of socialism, he believed that his conception of revolution was, by contrast, mediated by Asian realities, to which the concept of class conflict was not appropriate. From this "new" perspective, he saw a Japanese revolution clearly marking a historical break from what came before: The new socialist order in Japan would be achieved without class warfare yet would include the new forces of industry and science. A socialist revolution in Japan, moreover, would be the first step in a chain reaction leading to the liberation of all Asian countries from Western political and economic domination. As examples, Kita cited China and India where independence movements had already begun.

Kita's plan called for dismantling the structure of privilege that had been sustained by the Meiji state. The peerage would be abolished, and universal manhood suffrage would be instituted. Surplus land would be redistributed among the landless according to size and need of each household. Although allowing for the retention of personal property, Kita recommended the confiscation of "industrial capital." As this wealth was transferred to the new state, the power of big bourgeoisie, as it had been constituted, would be effectively diminished; and through the mediation of a new order, widespread deprivation would be ended. It was Kita's purpose to relocate industrial production and its management in new state agencies. Corporate bodies would hereafter direct major enterprises such as steel and iron, banks, maritime trade, railways, and mining. Moreover, he envisaged specialized agencies to administer agriculture and labor affairs. Although he was sensitive to the needs of the countryside, he was principally concerned with reorganizing the cities in order to rationalize the mobilization and distribution of industrial resources. The destruction of privilege, the reconstitution of community, the regulation of working conditions, such as the establishment of an eight-hour workday, equality of employment for both men and women, and numerous other proposals shaped this theory of mobilization.

Throughout the "Outline" Kita revealed his concern for the plight of the general population. His remedies stemmed from an earlier socialism: worker ownership of companies, the state's responsibility for the parenting of children and schooling (tuition, books, meals, and so on), and a comprehensive social welfare program for the aged, poor, disabled, and orphaned. Included here was the vision he shared with other contemporary socialists and internationalists that a universal language be taught to all youngsters in place of national languages such as French and English ordinarily used in international communication. Kita, therefore, prescribed the teaching of Esperanto as the second language after Japanese to be taught in all of the schools and the total abolition of the use of Chinese ideographs.

The ultimate aim of socialism in Japan was to force the retreat of the West and to create a new civilization based on the revival of all of Asia. Japan was uniquely suited because it had maintained the highest principle of sovereignty – the imperial monarch – despite the incursion of Western political and social institutions and thus had withstood, as had no other Asian society, the challenge of modernism. The Japanese flag, he boasted, would one day be emblazoned on the minds of all Asian peoples. The "darkness" spread over Asia by the Versailles Treaty, especially the duplicity of the United States, he promised, would be lifted in the near future when Japan engaged the West in a conclusive naval confrontation, just as the Greeks in ancient times defeated the Persians in the battle of Salamis. Although the Greek victory represented the triumph of West over East, Japan's forthcoming success would signal the reemergence of East over West. Only through such an "ultimate war" would peace and power in Asia be secured.

Not surprisingly, Kita ended his "Outline" with a passage from the Lotus Sutra, the central text of the Buddhist Nichiren sect, calling attention to the saint's determination to lead the populace from passion and chaos to light, knowledge, and salvation. Nichiren's mission was to save Japan and all humankind, which meant Asia. Throughout much of his later career, Kita identified with the twelfth-century Buddhist reformer Nichiren and often chanted from the sacred scriptures of the Lotus Sutra. He found a source of resolve in Nichiren's hostility toward the existing political order and in his intense faith in his new power as a bodhisattva to save Japan from the Mongol invasion. Kita no doubt saw himself as a latter-day saint in a time of grave national peril, as had been the case in Nichiren's time.

### *Gondō Seikei*

Although Kita's "Outline" was the most articulate and comprehensive program for radical reorganization, it was not the only proposal for violent action against contemporary political and industrial leaders. Kita's platform gave special attention to the question of industrial capital and recommended ways to redistribute the wealth of the bourgeoisie while disenfranchising them of political power. Yet his principal aim was to reorganize the industrial workplace, usually large factories, in order to improve the lot of city workers. In a sense his national socialism represented a confirmation, rather than a rejection, of both industrialism and the cities. If by mobilizing the cities, Kita sought a solution to the conditions of urban existence, others, closer to a nativist agrarian tradition, saw both industrialism and the cities as the problem for, rather than a solution to, the countryside. And although Kita emphasized the importance of a reconstituted state structure, theorists such as Gondō Seikei (1868–1937), Inoue Nisshō (1886–1967), and Tachibana Kosaburō (1893–1974), dramatized the ideal of an Asian agrarian community independent of the state and a sacred sanctuary free from the erosions of contemporary history. Moreover, this romantic view of society was shared by many important cultural theorists in the 1920s and 1930s who increasingly saw in the promise of community the only possible alternative to the divisiveness of modern political and social relations. Where they differed from more programmatic agrarian nativists was in their refusal to translate their ideals into a theory of violent action. Yet all agrarianists, like Kita Ikki, emphasized the imperial institution as central to any conception of community and frequently referred to the polity as a popular union of the emperor and people, the *kunmin kyōchi*. The people were seen as an embodiment of a common essence that derived from the local land and the tutelary shrines that defined all within a marked-off space as "brothers" under the divine protection of spiritual entities. Far from the corrupt cities and the sites of industrial capitalism, the possibility of communal brotherhood, the agrarianists believed, continued to exist as an accessible reality, even though in recent times it had been attacked by the forces of modernity. Included in these new corrosive forces were not only interest politics and bureaucracy but also the whole panoply of Western rationalism which many vociferous agrarianists saw as deceptive and alien to a community life close to nature. In the writings of people like Gondō and Tachibana, rational instrumentality separated people from community, and thus from themselves, as interest displaced reciprocity.

Gondō's analysis of the contemporary situation stemmed less from the perception of inequality, as Kita's analysis had, than from the erosion of communal ties and agricultural work that, Gondō believed, had always been the bedrock of traditional Asian societies. He compared the societies of ancient Asia with those of the West and concluded that the former were based on agricultural cultivation by the peasantry, whereas the latter were founded on animal domestication by herders, a view that prefigured Watsuji Tetsurō's later geographical typology. In fact, Gondō was convinced that the origin of agricultural production reached back so far that its recollection had lapsed in the social memory of the people. To remind the Japanese of this forgotten agricultural endowment, Gondō turned to "reading" the nature myths and first fables from the "age of the gods" when the folk first cleared lands to grow grain and irrigate paddies to cultivate rice. Yet Gondō also argued that this agricultural act was necessitated by the recognition that because the gods blessed humans with the gift of life, they were obliged to reciprocate by making this land habitable for each successive generation.

In his principal essay, "Principles of Popular Self-Government" (Jichi minsei ri, 1936), Gondō summoned the authority of a divine ordinance attributed to the sun goddess – Amaterasu – to support his claims: "The five grains are necessary, as they give life to the people."[4] This deceptively simple phrase indicated to Gondō the natural basis underlying the construction of civilized life; to reproduce the conditions of social life as they had been imparted by the gods in each generation was to produce civilization itself. It was this lesson that subsequent generations had forgotten as they were lured to the blandishments of modernity. Indeed, it was at this point that human community had become a possibility. The supposition that humans were autonomous was erroneous, Gondō reasoned, because it disregarded the natural relationships into which all persons must enter. When people are engaged in agricultural work, they are naturally part of a set

4 Gondō Seikei, "Jichi minsei ri," in *Gendai Nihon shisō taikei,* vol. 31, pp. 239–82, esp. p. 241.

of communal relations; reciprocity renders the self into a "nonself," inasmuch as the individual becomes a part of the whole. Moreover, there are corresponding moral and legal norms that regulate the life of the community that prevent the freedom of the individual from becoming absolute. Because these norms were wedded to the natural human quest for mutual nourishment and satisfaction, they were not to be confused with large, artificial, bureaucratic organizations and overarching state structures. The moral dignity of the natural individual in a communitarian context of abundance and happiness was central to Gondō and represented what was genuinely human.

If the most basic human relationships and interactions reveal the principle of mutual assistance and relief, then the village must represent the natural basis for "self-government" among the people. The symbolic authorization for such local self-rule was the indigenous tutelary shrines that, from antiquity, sanctioned the sacred character of Japanese life. From this perspective, Gondō saw the imperial institution not as the source of constitutional authority, as many contemporaries imagined, but as the sacred symbol of the natural community. In his view the creation of the land by the imperial ancestors was identical to this principle of a sacred community. In ancient times, he wrote, "politics" was referred to as a solemn religious ceremony – *matsurigoto* – ministered by a priest-king who formed a national community from this unification of the sacred and secular. For Gondō, as well as his contemporary, the ethnographer Yanagida Kunio, Japan the imperial land was simply a large tutelary shrine.

Disclaiming that this ancient pattern was unusual to Japan, Gondō emphasized its "Asian" dimension. Ancient China had also known tutelary shrines, he argued, and they were used to mark off provincial boundaries. Yet they were also synonymous with the production of the five grains and thus symbolized community life itself. The shrines transformed the earth into something divine, and agricultural cultivation was a form of religious supplication. As a result, there was no distinction made between secular administrative duties and the management of the sacred fruits of the land. Without local management of land and its produce, societies could not have survived. Nothing in modern times could alter that basic truth regarding the continuation of human society in the future.

Gondō's thinking regarding the natural community prompted his followers to reject the modern state in Japan as an artificial bureaucratic construction imported from the West and disengaged from the realities of the agricultural experience. What troubled him the most was the imposition of an artificial, centralized administration over the tradition of local self-control. The new bureaucracy was thus oppressive and distant from the people; it had even denied the imperial institution from playing its familiar role as priest-king overseeing the people's local management of the sacred village. Without a system of local self-government steeped in peasant cultivation of the soil, the spirit of the nation, Gondō feared, would be dissipated, its continuity into the future jeopardized. And he attributed the cause of this contemporary crisis to the shortsightedness and insensitivity of the modern state, centered in Tokyo, a city he especially disliked for its impersonality and its indifference to the needs of Japan's farming population. Concerned only with industrial production, the government was removed from the sacred agrarian foundations of Japanese civilization. Gondō begged the Japanese to resist the continuing migration of farmers into the cities and called for their return to the land as the only hope for retaining genuine human community. The rural landscape, like the Egyptian pyramids, emptied of humans and hope, resembled a ruin portending the death of Japanese civilization. The depth of Gondō's pessimism and the rage it generated led him to advocate direct action. Rejecting legal reforms as inadequate to Japan's needs and unlikely to succeed, Gondō envisaged an awakening of the people's consciousness stirred spontaneously by heroic deeds to save the sacred sources of Japanese life. The "evil" manipulators of the large bureaucratic, industrial, and military complexes, he believed, must be challenged and overthrown in order to realize the aim of a true "restoration." Here it is evident that Gondō's summons to act quickly in a desperate situation attracted radical activists searching for a program and malcontents seeking ways in which to channel their resentment.

### *Tachibana Kosaburō*

The tendency in agrarian fundamentalism to elicit radical and often reckless action was best dramatized by the case of Tachibana Kosaburō. Before graduating from the First Higher School, the elite educational institution from which students embarked upon prestigious careers in the bureaucracy, Tachibana decided to return to his native province in rural Japan. Although it is difficult to plumb motives, Tachibana's own testimony explaining this decision suggests that he felt compelled to deal directly with the spiritual and material misery of the countryside. In his mind there was no real distinction between spiritual and physical malaise. A complex thinker with an enormous theoretical grasp, Tachibana acknowledged his indebtedness to the examples of Tolstoi, Gandhi, the history of Western socialism, and the early ideas of Kita Ikki. He sought to combine the various themes into a coherent synthesis of radical humanism and agrarian fundamentalism. In the late 1920s and early 1930s, Tachibana turned to the strategy of direct and violent action against the existing order, inspiring sympathetic young officers in both services to commit even greater acts of daring and terrorism, which included the assassination of Prime Minister Inukai Tsuyoshi in the so-called May 15 incident. Tachibana was also implicated in the bombing attacks on the headquarters of the Seiyūkai, one of Japan's leading political parties, and on the Mitsui Bank in central Tokyo.

The central thread of Tachibana's ideas appeared in the preamble of his summons to action, "The Basic Principles of Japanese Patriotic Reform" (Nihon aikoku kakushin hongi, 1932). In this text Tachibana announced: "There can be no people who are separated from the land. There can be no national society separated from the people."[5] Despite its circularity, the call rang resonantly throughout Japan and invoked specific associations concerning the plight of the countryside among those who, because of their own agrarian origins, were most grieved by the unrelieved rural misery. Perceiving a general national crisis, much in the same manner as did Kita and Gondō, Tachibana promised resolution through a reidentification of people with land as the source of the necessary spiritual regeneration that would culminate in a patriotic reordering of the nation itself. By this reordering he meant providing direct relief to the people in order to "save them" (*kyūkoku saimin*). To accomplish this goal, however, it was necessary to uproot Western capitalistic and materialist civilization in Japan. Tachibana referred specifically to eliminating such institutions as political parties, interest groups, and large industrial combines known as zaibatsu.

Although noted as a romantic and utopian thinker, Tachibana rejected characterizations that discounted his ideas as mere abstractions dissociated from the actualities of historical conditions. The primary aim of his program was "to liberate the people" from false and arbitrary governance. Unfortunately, most Japanese had been persuaded to see their world in terms of Western concepts and things and to think of nothing else but money. The condition of life had reached this unhappy state because the Japanese, implicated in a global market,

5 Tachibana Kosaburō, "Nihon aikoku kakushin hongi," in *Gendai Nihon shisō taikei*, vol. 31, pp. 213–38, esp. p. 213.

were compelled to sell not only goods in the conventional sense but also labor, land, women, and ultimately the nation itself. Nothing escaped the iron demands of exchange value. The villages' simplicity and undifferentiated community life were torn apart by the ravaging force of money and commodities. The privileged classes, political parties, and the industrial combines, all located in the cities, effectively robbed Japan of its basic conditions of social existence and sent the nation down the road to slavery. Convincing evidence for this conclusion was the devastating extent to which Japan already had been drawn into the corrupting network of world finance that produced the Great Depression. What men in power had failed to grasp, Tachibana observed, was the divergent historical bases accounting for the development of Asian and Western societies. Like Gondō, Tachibana believed in the agrarian and village community as the original starting point of civilization in Asia, whereas the cities constituted the substance of Western history.

Tachibana also was convinced that Western modes of thinking were totally inappropriate to Asia. Marxism and dialectical materialism, with their privileging of class struggle to resolve social contradictions, were too rigid and formalistic to be applicable to Japan and Asia. The Japanese were not inclined to "assassinate reality," as he put it, by employing such abstract and limiting logic. The historical source for Western thought was rooted in the remote experiences of the ancient Greeks, whose idea of "logos" authorizing speculation and science, had led them to believe that all things and events resulted from a dialectical process. When compared with Asian modes of thinking, the differences became readily apparent. Thus in the great Asian intellectual and religious systems such as Buddhism, Hinduism, Confucianism, and even ancient Christianity (which Tachibana considered to be an oriental religion), the dialectical differentiation between self and others, subject and object, are completely overcome. For this reason, human reciprocity, the triumph of nonself over self, was the central principle in Asian civilization. The idea of humans conquering nature was offensive and alien to Asia, even though it had been used to justify the rise of capitalism everywhere. Yet this materialistic view of life now infected Tokyo and other Asian capitals. Ornamental evidences were visible everywhere, in large department stores, banks, newspapers, and industrial factories of every conceivable variety. When this new urban landscape was juxtaposed with the rural scene of Asia, it would be impossible to avoid conclusions regarding the fate of the Japanese people. What indeed, Tachibana asked rhetorically, would become of those ideals of mutual faith and trust that have defined community life in Japan since the beginning? Japan had no alternative but to abandon the capitalism of the large cities and to return to the true spirit of Asian origins and the promise of holistic national community free from fragmentation and division.

Tachibana's assessment of contemporary realities based on a conceptual differentiation between East and West convinced him that only through direct action could Japan overcome the pernicious influence of Westernization. Such a liberation from the West would simultaneously generate similar acts of separation throughout Asia. All this should be accomplished without relying on Western assistance. In Japan, he believed, a "patriotic revolution" was possible by activating the historical union between emperor and folk. The force of this union would sweep away illegitimate rule, as the past had always shown and made manifest for all to see the spiritual light of the national essence. Tachibana even speculated that the agrarian revolution begun in Japan would spread throughout the world and rid it of individualism and materialism.

Tachibana's strategy called for the formation of a "patriotic brotherhood." All Japanese shared the idea of a communal brotherhood symbolized by the national essence itself. He also believed that the culminating event could be realized only by brothers in blood (*shishi*) who would fearlessly and unselfishly lay down their own lives to save the people in accordance with the emperor's wishes. The members of this brotherhood would be recruited from all social classes and thus would represent a more perfect whole signified by the imperial will. Clearly, Tachibana aimed at a revolutionary upheaval in which the fate of the folk would once more be redirected to the establishment of an agrarian communalism. He was not recommending a mass movement but, rather, a vanguard action initiated by blood-sworn patriots pledged to violence and terror.

## *Nakano Seigō*

Although the major theorists of the restorationist revolt often occupied positions on the margins of Japanese society, explaining both their resentment and their radical summons to return to the countryside, others closer to the mainstream were involved in similar modes of thinking concerning the problematical status of Japanese and Asian cultures. A well-known journalist and leader in the 1920s of one of Japan's major political parties, the Minseitō, Nakano Siegō is an example of one who tried to bridge the concerns of the center with those of the periphery. Noted for his fiery and moving speeches, Nakano began his career as a journalist and identified with Miyake Setsurei's influential circle of intellectuals, the Seikyōsha and the magazine *Japan and the Japanese*.[6] Nakano became the principal spokesman for the cultural program promoted by this circle. The political basis of the nation, he repeated in his speeches and writings, was the "people," a collection of spiritually idealistic individuals symbolized by the social monarchy. The emperor, therefore, was the people's emperor, a view widely held by the agrarianists; he was not the captive of elites ensconced in the constitutional and industrial order. Thus, although the Meiji Restoration had succeeded in maintaining Japan's independence against the threat of colonialism, it had also produced a system of elitism contrary to the ideal of popular national community. Indeed, the new elites had led the people astray into the path of uncritical conformism with Western ideas, manners, and things and had diverted them from their true and abiding purpose. Nakano believed the time had come to contest this deception by reidentifying with the true tradition of spiritual autonomy represented in the philosophic intuitionism (*Ōyōmeigaku*) of such heroic figures as Ōshio Heihachirō and Saigō Takamori. Given the failed expectations of the Meiji Restoration, Nakano called for a "second restoration" that would result in the "reorganization of the state" (*kokka kaizō*) and join the emperor and people into a powerful egalitarian order. He emphasized that such a reorganization would also signal Japan's leadership in the liberation of colonized countries throughout Asia to realize their own indigenous popular spirit. In Nakano's thinking, the opposition to domestic bureaucratism was closely associated with an expansive vision of Asian liberation, "Asia for Asians," a theme that was monotonously repeated by ideologues in the 1930s bent on justifying Japan's own imperialist adventures on the continent.

## *Ōkawa Shūmei*

Yet an even better example of this mode of thinking was Ōkawa Shūmei (1886–1957) who, though not a "brown shirter" like Nakano, was involved in a range of activities that bridged the world of officialdom and militant paramilitary organizations. Ōkawa was, above all

6 See Tetsuo Najita, "Nakano Seigō and the Spirit of the Meiji Restoration in Twentieth-Century Japan," in *Dilemmas of Growth in Prewar Japan*, ed. James Morley (Princeton, N.J.: Princeton University Press, 1971), pp. 375–421.

else, a scholar who brought impressive credentials and intellectual accomplishments to the vision of Japan's reconstruction and Asia's liberation. A respected scholar of Islamic studies trained at the newly established Institute for Oriental Studies (Tōyōkenkyūjo) at Tokyo Imperial University and noted for his translation of the Koran, Ōkawa was devoted to the study of Asia's major religious systems as a condition for "returning" to the sources of his own indigenous tradition.

In a reflective essay describing his own reidentification with the Japanese spirit (*Nihon seishin kenkyū*, 1939), Ōkawa acknowledged that after many years of spiritual confusion, he had rediscovered the native place of the Japanese soul (*waga tamashii no kokyō*).[7] Recognizing this return as a religious experience similar to conversion, he confessed how recovering the Japanese spirit resolved the psychological contradictions in his youthful mind that had so long afflicted him. He further analogized the return as the culmination of a long, perilous ascent up the side of a steep mountain. But Ōkawa's "mountain" was a metaphor for an uphill struggle to overcome personal cultural despair; it was not simply a specific "local place," as had been the case with Gondō and Tachibana. What Ōkawa found, therefore, was not the utopian village of romantic agrarianists but the moral tradition tempered by the major religious and philosophic systems of Buddhism and Confucianism which, he believed, had always emphasized the close relationship between proper ethical conduct (*dōgi*) and religion (*shūkyō*). This combination of morality and religion was exemplified best in the spirit of the samurai class. En route to this discovery, Ōkawa observed the spiritual confusion and agony among vast numbers of people. He grieved over what he imagined was the absence of purpose in society, which he felt was caused by the failure of the existing political order to provide clear direction. Much of the imagery he used to characterize Japan's contemporary predicament called forth spiritual malaise, isolation, and alienation. The actual world before him was devoid of both peace and compassion. In his lengthy retrospective, "The Gates of Paradise" (Anraku no mon, 1951), Ōkawa recalled that a psychological dislocation bordering on a fatal illness had spread throughout all of Asia.[8]

Ōkawa's "return" to Japan, then, included concern for the "awakening" of the Asian continent. Although he saw the importance of revolutions in the West as a model for overthrowing imperialism and

7 Ōkawa Shūmei, "Nihon seishin kenkyū," in *Gendai Nihon shisō taikei*, vol. 31, pp. 137–43.
8 Ōkawa, "Anraku no mon," in *Gendai Nihon shisō taikei*, vol. 9: *Ajia shugi*, ed. Takeuchi Yoshimi, pp. 254–321.

facilitating an Asian renaissance, he believed that Asians must liberate themselves through collective movements and common purpose. The urgency behind his view was the belief that Europe and Asia stood in a relationship of master and slave; Europe had plundered the soul of Asia and had robbed it of its dignity and creative spirit. In an essay called "Revolutionary Europe and Renascent Asia" (Kakumei Europpa to fukkō Ajia, 1922), Ōkawa meditated on the consequences of the domination of Asia by Europe and saw its solution in an Asian renaissance.[9] The Russo-Japanese War of 1905 was the turning point in the awakening of independence movements in Asia. The possibility of freedom was dramatized by Japan's victory over a Western power in this war. Ōkawa's argument also rested on an appreciation of Asia's cultural contributions to human civilizations. Many of the inventions used by the West to subjugate the East – the printing press, gun powder, and the like – had been developed in Asia. And all of the great religions, Ōkawa observed, had originated in Asia. It was for this reason that the peoples of Asia should not be cowed into accepting the status of inferiors that had been accorded them. During the past several years, he emphasized, the "yellow races" had been made to feel unworthy by being called the "white man's burden." Even though the Russo-Japanese war had sparked the first glimmerings of hope, there was still much that needed to be done to reach the goal of liberation and to create a new world history. The Asian renaissance must be based on the reconstruction of traditional societies into modern states. And an essential ingredient in this transformation was the installation of representative government. Here, he pointed to the failings of the Chinese revolution and its ill-advised reliance on Western powers; the Japanese example offered the only possible promise of a genuine independence.

For Asian independence movements to succeed, Ōkawa was convinced that each must reconstitute its society into an ideal state, an idea he derived from his interpretation of Platonic idealism. He argued that this ideal had been distorted by the Western experience, notably by Christ and Marx. Although he initially admired these two men, he acknowledged that a reading of Plato had changed his mind. In his view, Plato's state was divided into three parts, the leaders, who are endowed with "reason," the military who possess "commitment," and farmers, artisans, and merchants who provide for the needs of the "spirit." Yet Ōkawa's interpretation of Plato was closer to the ideal-

9 Ōkawa, "Kakumei Europpa to fukkō Ajia," in *Gendai Nihon shisō taikei*, vol. 9, pp. 239–53.

ized representation of the Tokugawa order or indeed even Mencius' "ethical realm" than it was to the philosopher's idealized polity. If people were helped to prosper, were protected, and were nourished, they would serve as a firm and healthy foundation in the quest for the ideal good. In the ideal state, private interests and passions, such as Ōkawa observed in the conduct of party politics, must be suppressed for the public good; the state must, at all times, avoid corruption and elitist competition over issues relating to interest. The ideal of the good must be grasped to overcome short-term gains of partisan rivalries. Here, he compared the Platonic state with the Mencian idea of kingly justice, *ōdōron,* and identified its traditional idealization of "letters," *bu,* with the Greek philosopher's concept of "philosophy" as the basis of civilized governance. Later he linked the Confucian tradition itself to the teachings of Plato. Within Japanese intellectual history, the philosophies of Kumazawa Banzan (1619–91) and Yokoi Shōnan (1809–69) disclosed to him a similar spirit consistent with this idealistic tradition.

Ōkawa's spiritual peregrinations spanned the globe, often disclosing a close kinship with the cosmopolitanism of the 1920s. Along with his discovery of Plato's political idealism, his intellectual curiosity led him to probe the recesses of Western civilization for figures who had been able to transcend the constraints of Christianity. Ōkawa believed that like-minded cultural heroes could be found in both East and West, people who reflected a cosmopolitan idea in their personal effort to overcome race and region. Leonardo da Vinci thus represented the great complexity of the human spirit devoid of Christian associations. He felt similar admiration for Dante, Spinoza, and Ralph Waldo Emerson. Ōkawa especially prized Emerson because of his discovery of individual "intuitionism," which went beyond Christianity, time, and place and reminded Ōkawa of the Tokugawa "intuitionism" that Nakano Seigō also admired. Yet it is also true that Emerson's appeal lay in the presumed relationship between New England "transcendentalism" and the Indian religions. In any case, the spiritual resources that Ōkawa sought in the West were those that were functionally equivalent to Asian religiosity. He saw in this universal spirituality the means by which Asians might throw off the yoke of Western domination, and the solution to Japan's own psychological dislocation under the impact of modernity and industrialism. Ōkawa's "cosmopolitanism" was therefore closely related to what he believed to be the general malaise of the human spirit in modern life. In it, individual self-awakening and the spiritual renaissance of Japan and Asia were really one and the same thing. Through the mediating role of the "Japanese spirit," Ōkawa believed, it would be possible to gain release from the "prison" and "hospital" of modernity and realize fully the promise of the ideal state.

Ōkawa's conception of the ideal state and its offer of deliverance from modern alienation led him to conclude that the existing order was prevented from accomplishing this task because it was dogged by corruption and partisan rivalries. Here Ōkawa used his idea of spiritual renaissance as a plea for action to purge political practice; to rid domestic life of the Western presence was the condition for expelling imperialism from Asia. As a student of Asian philosophy, Ōkawa had become interested in the fate of modern India and the imposition of British despotism in that country. The British had drained India of its spirituality. Hence, the cleansing of politics at home was directly related to the broader goal of returning Asia to Asians. The incorporation of capitalism in Japan, especially at the accelerated rate witnessed after World War I, produced conditions in Japan that had come to resemble those found in Western countries. Labor disturbances, tenant protests, conspicuous consumption by the new rich, and ruthless party politics all had worked against the spiritual needs of the people. Moreover, the Japanese were experiencing social conditions that earlier in Russia had led to revolution, in Hungary, abortive uprisings, and in Italy and Germany, fascism. What appeared on the horizon were "reconstructionist movements" (*kaizō undō*) consisting of various action-oriented groups dedicated to spiritual renaissance and political reorganization. Sometime in the late 1920s Ōkawa joined them.

It was clear to Ōkawa and others that the object of reconstruction was domestic politics. This goal must be reached by any means, which, in the early 1930s, meant violence and terror. Indeed, violence was a necessity because of its "cleansing" propensities. It was not simply expelling the Western presence from Japan and Asia but purging the spirit of putrefaction and pollution. Ablution of the personal soul (*watakushi no tamashii*) paved the way for the realization of the national spirit (*kokka no seishin*). The implicit Pan-Asianism that Ōkawa and other contemporaries advocated provided an ideological mapping for the construction of large-scale strategies to eliminate Western power from Asia in an ultimate encounter or, as it was increasingly expressed, "the war to end wars." That is to say, the spiritual reconstruction summoned by writers such as Ōkawa converged with plans to launch a war either on the Asian continent against the Soviet Union or in the Pacific against Great Britain and the United States.

Yet the reasons for an Asian renaissance and its intended meaning were not always the same as the diplomatic and political causes leading to military confrontation. But the merger of a spiritual ideology and military aggression often produced self-serving justifications of Japan's own presence in Asia and its destiny to lead the yellow races to a new order. If war were necessary for the "spiritual awakening" of Asia, peace would bring a "new order of coprosperity" under Japanese leadership. For example, in 1939, a pamphlet entitled the "Shōwa Restoration" openly declared that the "war to end wars" was a historical necessity and the agency of progress.[10] After World War I, the argument ran, the global trend was for states to reconsolidate into larger groupings. These new blocks were the Soviet Union, Europe, North and South America, and Asia. But according to the pamphlet, there were only two major spheres that required attention: Asia, which represented the just, and the West (Europe and North America), which was despotic. The inevitable clash between the forces of light and darkness would occur in the Pacific, where the two blocks converged. Such a war would inaugurate a millennium of peace and autonomy for all of Asia. It was also the destiny of the Japanese state itself, founded on the principle of "imperial justice," to achieve not only a Japanese "restoration" but one extending to Asia as well, a *Tōa ishin*, as it was called in the late 1930s.

## CULTURALISM

Despite Ōkawa Shūmei's own plunge into the stream of direct action, his thinking was linked to a deeper and more complex opposition to the West as it was being articulated in the 1930s. This resistance was the product of a widely shared intellectual shift from "cosmopolitanism" to "culturalism" (*bunkashugi*). The pattern of this movement exceeded the limited outlook of the radical right and its resentments to include many of the leading writers and critics of the day, such as Tanizaki Junichirō (1886–1965), Nishida Kitarō (1870–1945), Watsuji Tetsurō (1889–1960), Yanagida Kunio (1875–1962), and Yokomitsu Riichi (1898–1947). What linked this group of writers and thinkers was not so much a program of action, as promoted by the radical right, but, rather, their search for spiritual and critical resources in the world's civilizations. This quest made culture problematical and made defining its contours and meaning a more-than-adequate substitute for

10 Tōa remmei dōshikai, "Shōwa ishin ron," in *Gendai Nihon shisō taikei*, vol. 31, pp. 381–412.

politics and violent action. The search for value led first to an examination of Western culture which invariably sent the seekers to a "return" to the "native place of the spirit" (*Nihon kaiki*). After less than a decade, Japanese writers and intellectuals abandoned the cosmopolitan civilization for the familiarity of traditional culture. Those who had been most deeply engaged in discussions on "human cultivation" (*kyōyōshugi*) and "character" (*jinkakushugi*) as the condition for cultural renewal were often the same men who had turned to Western intellectual history to gain critical inspiration and who had been attached to one of the major philosophic movements in Europe in the 1920s, Neo-Kantianism. It is hardly surprising that the middle-class intellectuals in Japan who flocked to Neo-Kantianism saw themselves in an analogous relationship to the German bourgeoisie which had constituted its main support earlier. Here was an idealistic and humanistic system of thought that privileged the role of individual consciousness and moral awareness in perceiving the world as it is. Yet the categories with which this world is grasped, a world that never could be known in itself, determined what that world should be. It was also one of the premises emphasized by the Kantian revival that the immediate subject–object distinction was deceptive and required an act of sublation. The objective world and subjective intention were not dialectical equivalents; the objective world was "determined" by the actions stemming from subjective consciousness. Thus, Japanese Neo-Kantians recognized that because individual consciousness made the world or the categories with which to comprehend it, such activity would result in the creation of value. In other words, they believed that consciousness functioned primarily to judge value, as it could never really know the world as it is; the highest values acknowledged by a critical consciousness are the true (*shin*), the good (*zen*), and the beautiful (*bi*), and it is culture where such values are realized.

## *Miki Kiyoshi*

The philosopher Miki Kiyoshi (1897–1945), an early adherent to Neo-Kantianism, proposed that literature and philosophy, found in the ideal of self-cultivation, were essential to a science of culture, whereas physical science and technology belonged to material civilization. Clearly, "civilization" became a pejorative concept in the 1920s and came to mean material progress and human debasement, whereas culture was associated with creative self-realization. The important implication of this polarization of civilization (*bunmei*) and culture (*bunka*) was the belief that individual self-cultivation could not be reached through capitalism and technological industrialism. Another contemporary of Miki's, Kuwaki Genyaku (1874–1946), writing in the 1920s, announced that culturalism was a force that disclosed internalized human values endowed with universal meaning. Culture was understood as the product of human creation and contrasted with the natural order, which was merely mechanical and repetitive. Others argued that because culture is created by humans, it must reflect the internal spirit. Yet to equate culture with interiority was to disengage the inner self, as many writers called it, from the external world of politics and technology. Such a separation persuaded thinkers and writers, bent on a quest for self-cultivation, to remove themselves from the corruptions of the outside world and to refrain from trying to change it. The search for value in the creation of culture, signifying universalistic meaning, transcended the particular historical and existential context in which they were produced. The emphasis on the capacity of the self to create universalistic values turned writers and intellectuals away from questions of social responsibility and political action. In the final analysis, their philosophical aim was to construct a domain of pure creative spirit independent of the world of existing structures. Although the impulse toward culture as the manifestation of universal value was initially informed by cosmopolitanism, thus dramatizing the possibility of a unique Japanese contribution to a universal human culture that recognized no national boundaries, the affirmative role of a particular cultural inheritance could easily dissolve into cultural exceptionalism. The hermeneutic "horizon of prejudices," the realm of historical experience accessible to an observer, narrowed into provincial national culture. This was especially apparent during the years of domestic and diplomatic turbulence in the late 1920s and early 1930s.

During this cosmopolitan interlude, the Japanese turned to producing cultural histories and texts testifying to Japan's unique contribution to a global culture and praising its accomplishments as equivalent to Western achievements. A common theme in many of these "histories" was the concentration on Japanese culture before the modern era. Some of the better-known works in this genre were Watsuji's "Studies in the History of Japanese Spirit" (Nihon seishinshi kenkyū, 1926), the sinologist Naitō Torajirō's "Studies on the Cultural History of Japan" (Nihon bunkashi kenkyū, 1924), the humanist philosopher Abe Jirō's "Studies in Arts and Crafts of the Tokugawa Period" (Tokugawa jidai ni okeru geijutsu no kenkyū, 1928), Tsuda Sōkichi's exposition of the manifestation of popular spirit in literature, *Bungaku ni arawaretaru waga kokumin no shisō* (1921), and Kuki Shūzō's "The Structure of Tokugawa Aesthetic Style" (Iki no kōzō, 1929). All of these works positioned values and ideals such as beauty, goodness, and truth as central to Japan's creative endowment and as examples of how culture manifested the inner workings of self and spirit. Indeed, what many of these texts tried to make clear was not the history of cultural development but, rather, the journey of the spirit. Watsuji's "Studies" attempted to grasp "the existence or life of the Japanese throughout the ages in order to show how the self realized itself as it passes through a number of cultural artifacts."

The most comprehensive philosophical synthesis of the problem of culture and values was formulated by Nishida Kitarō. An entire generation of writers, intellectuals, and thinkers in the 1920s and 1930s fell under the powerful influence of Nishida, in either agreement or dissent. One of Nishida's key concepts was his theory of "place" (*basho*), which represented the existential space in which universal value is actualized. In his earlier and well-known treatise, "Studies of the Good" (Zen no kenkyū, 1911), Nishida formulated a theory of "pure religious consciousness." To conceptualize this state, he drew heavily on the philosophy of pure existence found in the tradition of Zen Buddhism. From this perspective he constructed an elaborate metaphysical framework for "place" as the locus of universal creation. Denying that it was his purpose either to revive Zen or to preach it, Nishida claimed to be looking for a philosophically stable basis of "life" that could transcend the limitations of material interest, historical change, and the Western bourgeois concept of egoism. His critics, particularly the Marxist thinker Tosaku Jun (1900–45), a former student of Nishida's, found Nishida's thinking to have confused "existence" with its "interpretation" in his search for metaphysical certainty. But Nishida continued to emphasize, without compromise, the superiority of knowledge and interpretation over historical actuality. He saw the category of the universal negative (*mu*) as the location of "place" unconstrained by history, individual ego, and Western definitions of absolutes such as the Judeo-Christian God.

The implications of Nishida's ontology were worked out by his students, many of whom were later associated with what was called collectively the "Kyoto school." The best known among them was Miki Kiyoshi, who was deeply affected by Nishida's "Study of the Good" and his study of German idealism. As a young intellectual, Miki was drawn to the humanistic ideas of twelfth-century Buddhism as formulated by Shinran, in contrast with Nishida's lifelong interest in Zen. And it is quite likely that Miki saw in Nishida's synthesis of Buddhism and German idealism a model for his own philosophic program. First as a pupil in Kyoto and then later as an exchange student in Germany for three years, Miki explored a diversity of ideas ranging from Neo-Kantianism, originally learned from Nishida, to Marxist and existentialist thought.

Yet the most philosophically distinct position for which Miki came to be known was his phenomenological and hermeneutical understanding of reality as it occurs in time.[11] Based on his studies in Germany, which included a close reading of Wilhelm Dilthey, Miki argued that without a phenomenological interpretation of events, humankind would be left with only meaningless "action." In particular, Miki emphasized events' temporal and spatial dimensions as the key to human meaning. Like many of his contemporaries in Europe and Japan, Miki was convinced that the principal temporal or historical problem of the day was capitalism and its culture. In his view, capitalism had spawned an egoistic and inequitable culture, and any assessment of meaning must include the possibility of going beyond the historical limitations imposed by capitalism. Miki was not advocating a simple restoration of feudalism and did not hint at a return to some essential spirit. Rather, he saw events as a world historical process and its dialectic. Yet this dialectic was produced by a combination of temporality and spatial specificity. Here he proposed a conception of "space" comparable to Nishida's idea of "place." By space, Miki meant the area of Asia that had been under Western domination and subject to the sway of capitalism and the ideas of "modernism" associated with historical force. Events within Asia, he argued, must contain the potential for a new meaning, such as the possibility of creating a different order that would go beyond the historical limitations set by Western capitalism. Specifically, Miki emphasized a new "cooperativism" for Asia, which would join the various societies in accordance with "Asian humanism" (*Tōyōteki hyumanisumu*), referring vaguely to Buddhist principles of compassion and mutual assistance. He also described this humanism as representing a synthesis of gemeinschaft and gesellschaft, traditional community and modern society. This new order would be an advancement over capitalism, as it would be the result of a dialectical encounter between capitalism and Asian society and thus would contain elements of both but yet be vastly different.

11 See for example, Miki Kiyoshi, "Kaishakugaku teki genshōgaku no kisogainen," in *Kindai Nihon shisō taikei*, vol. 27. *Miki Kiyoshi shū*, ed. Sumiya Kazuhiko (Tokyo: Chikuma shobō, 1975).

Miki also pointed to the importance of resolving the problem of class. He regarded "cooperativism" as the means to achieve the goal of first exposing "class" as a fixed category of social existence and then overcoming it altogether. The "public sphere" should always override the interest of classes based on narrow interests and provide the space within which new divisions of labor would be formed based on the acquisition of knowledge and skills. In his vision of cooperativism, informed by the principle of *techné,* the technocratic idea would become central to public life and replace criteria mandating the class lines developed under capitalism. Here Miki revealed a kinship with Max Weber's earlier assessment of the political effects of capitalism and his subsequent effort to formulate a new vision of governance founded on the primacy of expert knowledge rather than the maximization of profit. Miki, like Weber, envisaged a nonhereditary technocracy as a new stage of development that would abandon social divisions based on class. He also distinguished between cooperativism based on technocratic proficiency and the romantic communitarianism advanced by the extreme right. Although right-wing polemicists had offered a critique of capitalism, liberalism, and communism, they had failed to provide a critical basis for action, other than turning back the clock, and had slipped into incoherent and dangerous forms of folkism (*minzokushugi*) in their desperate attempt to distance themselves from both modernism and Marxism.

Miki turned his interpretative strategy to account for the China incident of 1937, which sparked Japan's full-scale invasion of China. He used the occasion to raise the question concerning Japan's future course. But he believed that this question could be answered only by grasping the "world historical meaning" of that decisive event. He understood the relationship between war and culture and saw the former as a causal condition in the transformation of the latter. Events in Russia and Germany after World War I provided him with ample evidence to support this conclusion. Writing shortly after the China invasion, he saw that the war there would produce far-reaching cultural consequences in both Japan and China. He compared these consequences with the revolutionary changes in Russia after 1917. In Japan, too, he believed that the status of its culture after the war could provoke a response from all sensitive and thoughtful intellectuals. War, he wrote, necessitated the establishment of control over popular thought and action and compromised creativity. Under such circumstances, poets might compose jingoistic songs but never real poetry. Systems of control, however, could never eradicate the creativity of the human spirit. Hence he was convinced that this spirit would remain active throughout wartime in order to shape the new culture that would appear with the reestablishment of peace.

Thus Miki refused to see the China incident simply as an act of naked invasion. Rather, he grasped the event as the starting point for the true unification of Asia based on a new order of cooperativism and the ideals of Asian humanism. As if he were able to speak for the "cunning of reason" itself, the Hegelian knowledge of hindsight, he believed that the event's larger meaning was to create a new spatial realm, free from the constraints of capitalism and poised to embark on a new development of world history. The promised liberation of Asia, Miki proposed, would signal an advancement to a new, yet-to-be-understood, historical stage beyond discredited forms of modernism. It was for this reason that Miki called on his society and those in power to understand the deeper historical meaning of the event. Moreover, it was his interpretation of the possible meaning of events that helps explain Miki's decision to join the Shōwa Research Society (Shōwa kenkyūkai) established in 1938 and composed of leading scholars of the time, such as Ryū Shintarō, Shimizu Ikutarō, Royama Masamichi, and Hayashi Tatsuo. These were scholars and intellectuals who, again like Weber, believed that the fundamental crisis of twentieth-century capitalism – the efficient distribution of resources and power – necessitated bureaucratic organization. Accordingly, they felt that such bureaucratic structures should be managed by scientifically trained experts, free from party and interest, who could, with the right kind of knowledge, ascertain the general interest and formulate the appropriate policies. It was in this sense that they saw their role in government and seized the opportunity to influence the course of action taken by the state, an issue that was first recognized in the 1930s but that remains a continuing legacy of this century. In particular, members of the Shōwa Research Society wished to improve upon capitalism by supplying politically rational management – planning – of the state comparable to the economic rationality of technology and industrialism. In effect, this meant finding ways to overcome conflict and its enduring threat that the state hitherto had not been able to resolve.

Miki saw his own participation in this group as an example of technocratic expertise serving public policy. He had long believed it important to recruit for managerial posts in government experts who had demonstrated their mastery of certain kinds of knowledge, and he saw his own role as an expert influencing policies in accordance with his informed cooperativist vision of a better future. Far from shaping policy and determining the course of events, as Miki and others in the Shōwa Research Society hoped, the reverse occurred: The expert intellectuals participated little or not at all in the actual decision making, and the ideas they advanced, like Miki's conception of a cooperativist Asia, were ultimately used for propaganda by the war mobilization structure (*kokka sōdōin*). Miki himself lived precariously throughout the war years and eventually was imprisoned by the very government he had earlier tried to serve. Before his death in prison, Miki wrote his last work on Shinran and seemingly returned to the point at which he had begun his intellectual odyssey as a young student and which initially had attracted him to Nishida Kitarō.

## CULTURAL PARTICULARISM

If Miki assessed the impact of war on culture negatively and yet recognized the necessity of intellectuals and writers preparing themselves for peace, the philosophers of the Kyoto school inverted this formulation to regard war as a requisite condition for determining national culture. These philosophers, students of Nishida, formed a group called the Kyoto faction and identified with the philosophy faculty of Kyoto University. The principal members were Koyama Iwao (1905– ), Kōsaka Masaaki (1900–69), Suzuki Shigetaka (1907– ), and Nishitani Keiji (1900– ). It was their purpose to make Nishida's more formal concepts more tangible so that they could direct national policy and action. These thinkers wrote a series of books and articles in the late 1930s dealing largely with the historicist implications of Nishida's ideas for the current political situation. Their statement was summarized in a symposium in 1941 entitled "The World Historical Position and Japan" (Sekaishiteki tachiba to Nihon) and later published in the widely read periodical *Chūō koron*.[12] This group's central purpose was to construct what they called a "philosophy of world history" that could both account for Japan's current position and disclose the course of future action. But a closer examination of this "philosophy of world history" reveals a thinly disguised justification, written in the language of Hegelian metaphysics, for Japanese aggression and continuing imperialism. In prewar Japan, no group helped defend the state more consistently and enthusiastically than did the philosophers of the Kyoto faction, and none came closer than they did to defining the philosophic contours of Japanese fascism.

12 Published in book form in 1943 by Chūō koron.

The Kyoto philosophers specified Nishida's ontological concept of "space" to mean the "world stage" where all human and social problems will be resolved under Japan's leadership role. History, or the world stage, consisted of the interaction of "blood" and "soil," a conclusion already reached by a number of Nazi apologists. Yet Japan was uniquely appointed to resolve the struggle of history because philosophically it had successfully synthesized Eastern humanism and Western rationalism and thus moved to a higher stage of human development. This accomplishment demanded the dismantling of Western hegemony. Thus despite their use of abstract philosophical language, the Kyoto philosophers unashamedly spoke on behalf of Japanese imperial expansion as the creative moment of a vast historical movement to a new level of human excellence. The historical present was pregnant with meaning for state and culture. In fact, the Kyoto faction rarely differentiated between these two categories, using them interchangeably. In the world, the state realized its fullest ethical potential in war. War was the central event, they believed, by which states came into existence. It would continue as the agency to forge a new order. The self-awareness of the state, as Kōsaka put it, would be sustained by war. "Only as the folk experience war do they become aware of the state and its subjective nature." "Place," then, was not the formal category that Nishida had envisaged but, rather, the "world, which served as the moral training ground of the state."[13] For Kōsaka, war was the test that validated or invalidated the state's moral status. And through war alone is the world's historical meaning made manifest. If war is waged for a proper cause, then the state will authenticate its ethical subjectivity. But if it is lost, Kōsaka cautioned, it will have been fought for unethical and uncultural reasons. Echoing Leopold Ranke, he proposed that world history would turn into world judgment.

The members of the Kyoto faction openly acknowledged their admiration for European fascism and its own struggle with the forces of modernity. They saw it as part of the larger world movement in which they had identified Japan's historical destiny. The purpose of this movement was the overthrow of communism and the establishment of a new future order. As homegrown fascist writers, Kōsaka and Koyama insisted on the necessity of strict state control of domestic society; the elimination of intellectual heterodoxy, however moderate or unpolitical; and rigid conformism in behavior and conduct. Although it is tempting to associate Miki Kiyoshi's own intellectual depen-

13 From Takeuchi Yoshitomo, *Shōwa shisō shi* (Tokyo: Minerva shobō, 1958), p. 406.

dence on Nishida, and his subsequent involvement in Konoe's "brain trust" to the fascism of the Kyoto faction, the two programs were worlds apart. Miki addressed his philosophy to a new future that would liberate the creative human spirit under conditions of peace. The Kyoto faction glorified the state as the ideal embodiment that justified Japan's leadership role in a war of revolt against the West.

Although it is often suggested that the revolt against the West was a militant and jingoistic movement populated by putschists, assassins, or "Japanese-style fascists" – such as some of the members of the Kyoto faction – such a characterization misrepresents the compelling nature of that problem broadly felt throughout much of Japanese culture. Involved was the reappraisal of the status of culture and the more pressing question concerning its Japanese form. Even the most rabid putschist and admirer of fascism agreed on the importance of this intellectual issue of reconceptualizing the nature of Japanese culture in the industrialized context of the twentieth century. In much of this, an earlier cosmopolitanism evolved into an appreciation of Japanese culture distinct from Western, capitalist, and "modern" society. Thus although such thinking did not necessarily require an overt revolt against the West, it informed a good deal of the Japanese vision of itself as an alternative model of culture superior to the achievements of the West.

### *Watsuji Tetsurō*

One of the most influential theorists of this cultural problem was the philosopher Watsuji Tetsurō, who taught at Kyoto University between 1925 and 1934 and then at Tokyo University until 1949. As a young scholar, Watsuji, like many of his contemporaries, immersed himself in the culture of cosmopolitanism exemplified by a deep fascination with Western philosophy and literature and in particular with the problem of the self in modern society. His graduate thesis focused on Nietzsche. Even though he rejected the Neo-Kantian explanation, which had tried to derive consciousness of the entire world from the immediate life experience, Watsuji was nonetheless concerned with its conception of a "philosophy of life." Nietzsche's philosophy offered Watsuji a powerful critique of capitalist civilization and concentrated on the contradiction between social constraints of inequalities and individual expressibility. He also was attracted to Nietzsche's idea of the heroic and creative individual. Watsuji promoted the superiority of spiritual over material civilization and thus prized the creative elite over the general populace, whose lives were determined by the relative abundance or deprivation of material things. It was within this frame of reference that he opposed universal manhood suffrage, the labor movement, and the social mass parties of the late 1920s. Nietzsche also made precisely the same criticism of the socialist movement in Germany in the 1880s. As applied by Watsuji, the Nietzschean thesis also denounced rationalism, technological culture, and utilitarianism, all of which were representations used to mask the materialistic and inauthentic life-style of the newly emergent industrial bourgeoisie. In much the same manner that Nietzsche had sought an authentic and creative moment in ancient Greece, untainted by modern bourgeois rationalism which had appropriated much from the Judeo-Christian heritage, Watsuji similarly sought in ancient Japan a comparable manifestation of an essential creative spirit. Watsuji's quest was reminiscent of Tachibana's search for an original utopian movement at the beginning of history. But unlike him, Watsuji was more concerned with the creative spirit than with the communal ties of brotherhood that Tachibana had emphasized. However, their search for an unalloyed existence, free from materialistic impulses, suggests a close resemblance. In the environment of the 1920s, Watsuji recommended a "spirit of opposition" that would lead individuals to free themselves from the material realities of the present. Such a liberation could be realized through an identification with the genuine creativity in the indigenous culture. Watsuji was specifically interested in showing how Buddhist art and architecture represented, after the middle ages, the purest expression of the Japanese creative spirit. In a series of works – "Pilgrimages to Ancient Temples" (Koji junrai, 1919), "The Culture of Ancient Japan" (Nihon kodai bunka, 1920), and "Studies of the Japanese Spirit" (Nihon seishinshi kenkyū, 1926) – Watsuji reminded his contemporaries of the pure expression of the Japanese creative power that was manifested in the past but neglected in the present. It should be noted that this path to a tradition of aesthetic purity had already been charted at the turn of the century by the art historian and Pan-Asianist Okakura Tenshin.

Watsuji's plea on behalf of Japan's creative past was reminiscent of Nietzsche's efforts to restore some of the great monuments of ancient Greece. His valorization of the creative spirit in ancient and medieval times was grounded in the conviction that he had discovered the essential creative form of the Japanese people. Here Watsuji idealized this creative tradition and even believed that the early Japanese Yamato court embodied it over time. In that ancient culture, the communitarian society resolved the contradictions between spirit and physicality, nature and person, sovereign and subject. Just as the spirit of ancient Greek culture was destroyed by Roman "materialism," so Watsuji feared that Western civilization, exemplified by Anglo-American self-centered individualism, now threatened to eliminate Japan's spiritual legacy. Americans, Watsuji once wrote, were especially afflicted by the plague of materialism. Relentlessly pursuing material things, they had lost their souls, discarded their philosophy, neglected their arts, and returned to the life of the "birds and beasts." Americans, he noted, had exchanged "capital" for the blood and iron of the ancient Romans. But it came to the same thing. With it, they had enslaved the world to the demands of materialistic civilization. Thus in Watsuji we see what earlier German politicians had referred to as the necessary "cultural struggle" (*Kultur Kampf*) which provided some of the ideological arguments for war stated in cultural terms. The thought of Watsuji, as it derived from Nietzsche, synthesized the idea of a "spiritual community" (*seishinteki kyōdōtai*) and the "personalism" of the philosophy of existence (*iki no tetsugaku*) and resulted in a powerful resistance to modern bourgeois culture, its rationalism, and the civilization that spawned it.

It was within this frame of reference that Watsuji embarked on a scholarly project to uncover the historical roots of Japanese ethics. In doing so, like Ōkawa, he expanded his understanding of the area of authenticity to include all of Asia. He justified this inclusion by using Buddhism as the integrative spiritual force. This "cultural struggle" also included a contest between Asian spirituality and Western materialism. The crucial element in Watsuji's grasp of Buddhism was the category of "nothingness" (*mu*), which Nishida Kitarō had already articulated in broad philosophical terms. To Watsuji, the transition from "nothingness," as the detachment from existing material conditions, to the pure life was the identification of that Buddhist category with universal "nature" itself. This elision of "nothingness" with "nature" was aimed at transcending the rationalist proposition that nature was an "object" to dominate or manipulate for human ends, however they might be defined. This ethic of nothingness thus opposed the rational characterization of the self as being "outside" nature rather than within its embrace. Watsuji sought, therefore, to clarify the source of this Asian view and the reasons for its superiority over the Western dialectic between humans and nature. To do so, he believed that it was necessary to begin by considering human society within nature and to explore its customs, habits, and mores in their essential and pure setting. Watsuji saw in the world of thought two basic but different ways of thinking, logical reasoning and intuition. Although the former obviously belonged to the traditional Western mode of thinking, and the latter to the East, it was important to explain the consequences of these two divergent epistemologies. It was this problem that prompted Watsuji to compose his well-known essay entitled "Climate and Culture" (Fūdo, 1935).

When Watsuji was a student in Germany in 1927, he had devoted much attention to Heidegger's classic work "Being and Time" (Sein und Zeit, 1926), which juxtaposed the relationship between existence and the dimension of historical time. In his own work, Watsuji clarified his relationship to Heidegger: Although "timefulness" was extremely important to Heidegger, especially in his exposition of a subjective and existential structure, Watsuji wondered why at the same time he had not seen "spacefulness" in a comparable philosophical light. The central problem for him, he admitted in the preface of "Climate and Culture," was to consider in detail the significance of climate and environment as they related to historical culture. In his words: "The activity of man's self-apprehension, man, that is, in his dual character of individual and social being, is at the same time of a historical nature. Therefore, climate does not exist apart from history, nor history apart from climate."[14] If Heidegger had seen time as distinct from nature and thus remained within the dialectic that he had inherited from Hegel, Watsuji aimed instead to introduce existentialism into nature, thus earning Tosaka Jun's criticism that he had "subjectivized" nature.

By concentrating on "climate and space," Watsuji was able to identify the essential features of the two major climatic divisions – monsoon and mediterranean – that accounted for the basic differences between Europeans and Asians. The theory resembled the prevailing geopolitical discussions on the geographical determination of culture, political relations, and racial differences. In Watsuji's analysis, the mediterranean zone was characterized as temperate, semiarid, and essentially pastoral, requiring relatively nonintensive agricultural labor. Grains could be planted with ease without the arduous construction of terraced farms to ward off severe climatic conditions. Nature, therefore, was seen in this area as benign and also subservient, as evoked in the female image of "mother nature." Nature was also predictable, geometrical, steady, and hence calculable. It represented orderliness and stood for

14 From Watsuji Tetsurō, *Climate*, translation of *Fūdo* by Geoffrey Bownas (Tokyo: Hokuseido Press, 1961), p. 8.

"reason." "In other words," Watsuji wrote, "where nature shows no violence she is manifested in logical and rational forms. . . . There is a link between lenience and the rationality of nature, for where she is lenient man readily discovers order in nature. . . . Thus Europe's natural science was clearly the product of Europe's meadow climate."[15]

In monsoon Asia, however, Watsuji saw a unique seasonal relationship between the Asian continent and the Indian Ocean. During the summer months the monsoon blew across the land from the southwest when the sun crossed the equator, and in the winter the winds reversed direction. The result was intense humidity and heat in the longer summer months, punctuated by torrential rains. In Watsuji's view, the combination of moisture and heat had produced countries that were rich in plants and an epistemology that saw the world as a place teeming with plant and animal life. "For nature is not death but life, for death stands instead by the side of man. Hence, the relation between man and his world is not that of resistance, but that of resignation."[16] Watsuji also noted that the violent rainstorms, savage winds, floods, and droughts persuaded the inhabitants of this area to abandon all resistance to the elemental forces of nature. Here, he believed, he had found the source of Asia's characteristic resignation to the inclemency of nature that was often reflected in the religions of Asia. Even more fundamental, however, nature was not bound by regularity and order but, on the contrary, was harsh and irregular, producing cultures that did not view the space around them in terms of geometric reason. Whereas the mediterannean climate encouraged the human domination of nature as a benign and passive object, thus allowing for a view of progressive and predictable historical time, the monsoon climate produced a different kind of culture. Human life was wholly engulfed by nature and hence resided outside progressive historical time, as it was not governed by logical sequence but was subordinate to nature and its eternal presence. It is important to recall that Hegel earlier had proposed, in his recounting of the migration of "liberty" from monsoon cultures to the West, that Asia did not possess "history" and thus had not developed a concept of "progressive" time. Watsuji may be seen in this regard as trying to recast the Hegelian scheme in terms of the relative strengths of East and West and as avoiding the characterization of world history according to the movement of the absolute spirit from one world area to another. To Watsuji, therefore, the Western spirit had led to an individualism that

15 Ibid., p. 74. 16 Ibid., p. 19.

separated humans not only from nature but also from the society around them. Although in Asia, nature and the community superseded the individual, in the West, humans constantly struggled to dominate nature and to claim a separate life meaning from society. Here Watsuji complemented Heidegger's conception of "human intentionality," *ex-sistere,* which is temporal and bounded by history, with his idea of "relationality," *aidagara,* which calls for humans' unique relationship to a specific "spatial" environment.

Central to Watsuji's theory of relationality was the characterization of Japan within monsoon Asia and, in turn, its position in the world. Watsuji argued that although Japan faced conditions similar to those of the great continental civilizations such as India's and China's, it also possessed features quite unlike the rest of Asia because it encountered climatic conditions that ranged from cold to temperate, marked by abrupt and predictable seasonal changes. In short, Japan was at the eastern extremity of the monsoon zone and thus had a "dual" weather system. The rhythms between monsoon and nonmonsoon, cold and temperate, produced a society in which the emotional vitality and passionate swings that followed the shifting season were distinct from those of the continental Asian cultures. This observation led to Watsuji's principal argument, that owing to its particular climatic conditions, Japan had created a distinctive culture based on spacial "relationality." In particular, Watsuji pointed to the organizational structure of the "household" (*ie*) and the emotionality fostered within that space. In the household, its several members were not merely a gathering of individuals but a cooperative group of selfless human beings engaged in fundamental roles of nourishing life. However, in the household, its members were not totally resigned to the massive and unpredictable forces of nature, as on the Asian continent, but also nurtured a tense and active relationship with nature. Watsuji commented, therefore, "that passivity in Japan indicated a distinctive form of selfless action," that disciplined action served not the advancement of self-interest but the good of others in the communal whole.[17] Though admitting that this communal conception of action was no longer as prevalent as it was in the Tokugawa era, he nonetheless was convinced that it distinguished the Japanese mode of action from the individualism shaped by Western history and especially European capitalism. Hence, Japanese capitalism resembles Western capitalism only

17 Ibid., pp. 136–7.

in external and superficial ways. It is grounded in the climatic and spatial foundations of Japanese civilization and is thus not influenced by Western individualism.

Watsuji claimed to have gained many of his insights into the uniqueness of Japan after his "return" from an extended tour of Europe. For the first time, he acknowledged, he realized the inappropriateness of Western uses of space, as manifested in imported buildings and trams in the Japanese setting. He likened the tram, for example, to a "wild boar" rampaging through the fields, out of step with traditional civilized society. Although he did not go as far as to urge the eradication of these objects from Japan, at the same time he clearly viewed them as "foreign." Watsuji thus despaired of the urban sprawl that had come to dominate the Tokyo landscape, viewing Western objects as an intrusion into the established order of things. He emphasized that the Japanese house was constructed so as to minimize privacy or to creat it with only minimal separations and without the need of locks anc bolts. Its security relied only on the language of trust. Despite his concern that Western architecture might steadily erode the value of community on which the small Japanese house was constructed, he also felt deeply that the people would neither relinquish their attachment to domestic architecture nor give up the integrity of that space, even as industrial capitalism persisted. Because of this attachment, true parliamentary democracy or proletarian movements, as had developed in the West, would not (and should not in his view) establish firm roots in Japan. Although there could be leaders of such movements in Japan, the people would remain confined to their architectural "space" and to the natural history that produced it. What Watsuji meant was that Japan, owing to its unique sense of space, was unlikely ever to assimilate the conception of the "public" that so much Western political practice required.

Although Watsuji did not advocate an open revolt against the West, as he expressed his thought in terms of an aesthetic protest, it is obvious that much of what he had to say could easily be worked into a programmatic ideology advocating a frontal rejection of the Western presence in Asia. His extended treatise on climate, in short, may be summed up as an indictment of Western individualism, materialism, and rationalism. His judgment against both parliamentary democracy and Marxist proletarian movements as inappropriate to Japan was also a principal condition for an overall rejection of Western civilization as a hegemonic force over Japan.

### *Yanagida Kunio*

Watsuji's ideas on community and aesthetic space interconnected with two other influential themes also current in his day, the ethnographic folklorism (*minzokugaku*) of the cultural anthropologist Yanagida Kunio and the aesthetic nostalgia of the novelist Tanizaki Junichirō. Compared with Watsuji, Yanagida proceeded from a deep distrust for the expansive power of the Meiji state. Reflecting his upbringing in a family of devout believers in local Shinto, as well as his scholarly training under Matsuura Shūhei, a well-known poet and scholar of national studies in the Meiji era, Yanagida was especially influenced by the critical attitude toward the bureaucracy and its ideology, such as the Confucianism of the Tokugawa era, that had been shaped in the popular national studies. It is hardly surprising that Yanagida revered Hirata Atsutane (d. 1843), one of the major thinkers of this anti-bureaucratic intellectual tradition in the Tokugawa who functioned as the unspoken inspiration for his own effort to formulate a Japanese science of folklore. Yanagida viewed with intense foreboding the bureaucratic penetration into the regional and local countryside. He feared its disruption of the Japanese communal life that was rooted in indigenous and customary beliefs.

Even before Yanagida resigned from his post in the Ministry of Agriculture in 1919, he had already been actively interested in Japanese folklore and popular customs. He published his first major collection of folktales, called "Tales of Tono" (Tōno monogatari, 1910), based on extensive travels particularly in the northwest regions of the country. In recounting these tales, Yanagida was able to show the vast disparity of customs and beliefs in these regions. More importantly, he was able to use these tales to support the idea that commoners in Japan were unimpressed with the official order or with a powerful emperor and, in turn, with the claims of state Shinto. Through this approach, Yanagida stated his opposition to the government's policy of coordinating Shinto shrines throughout the country within a unified bureaucratic system.

In turning his focus to the preservation of indigenous communal culture, Yanagida set out also to formulate a distinctive Japanese social science. Here he rejected the historical method that emphasized written documents and political events as constituting the central experience of the past. By avoiding this authoritative reconstruction of history, Yanagida envisioned the reunderstanding of the culture of the people as it was lived in villages and towns. Essential to his analysis were unwritten oral traditions, folktales, local dialects, regional religious practices, rituals and beliefs, and seasonal festivals. Although an assiduous collector of data concerning folk customs, Yanagida was not simply an antiquarian but believed that knowledge should be socially useful. This conviction stemmed from an earlier concern for agricultural economics that would enhance the well-being of the country populace in concrete ways. Therefore, the construction of a science of folk culture meant that it should help solve problems of rural poverty and distress caused by modern technology. He believed that his method promoted the cause of "social reconstruction" (*shakai kaizō*) and also that people learning about themselves without superficial adornments might lead to self-knowledge and self-renovation. A new society based on indigenous culture would thereby be created from within that culture itself, without relying on the bureaucratic and technological instruments being fashioned above by the central government. In order to achieve these goals, Yanagida revealed a pragmatic eclecticism so that the data could include a wide variety of materials and strategies. The ethnographic method of British anthropology, for example, though drawn from without, was considered appropriate to the task of organizing and ordering local data derived from the Japanese experience.

Yanagida's project was informed by an identification with the "abiding folk" (*jōmin*). Before being a functional individual of society as a farmer, laborer, or white-collar worker, all were first and foremost members of the *jōmin*. What this meant was that one of the most divisive aspects of modern Western capitalism was its relocation of the people according to a functional division of labor based on presumed rational premises that in fact had come to be manifested in contending classes. Although most evident in Western industrial society, comparable conflict could be observed in the context of industrial expansion in Japan. To call attention to the abiding folk and their customs was to also discuss the peculiar form of community to which they had given expression through a life-style actually lived in the countryside. Yanagida identified its distinctive feature as communitarianism, which referred to the horizontal social relations held together by a system of mutual assistance and confirmed by a territorial tutelary shrine deity. Moreover, he was confident that the communitarian life in the villages characterized Asian society and was in imminent danger of disintegrating before the relentless penetration of Western capitalism and central bureaucracies. Yanagida thus counterposed an Asian gemeinschaft against these modern intrusions. It was for this reason that he strongly resisted the policy of the Meiji state to organize the local shrines according to a systematic bureaucratic scheme.

Yanagida promoted the movement to preserve local folktales and beliefs as a means to oppose the reorganization, in late Meiji, of shrines throughout the country within the framework of state Shinto. He believed state Shinto to be a dishonest and artificial representation of popular religious practices. In folk Shinto, he emphasized, there were no professional priests or formalized doctrines. Its beliefs had sprung from the experiences of the collectivity and had been transmitted as an oral tradition since ancient times by ordinary laypersons. Moreover, these beliefs were centered on respect for communal deities wherever they were enshrined. These deities, accordingly, represented the spirit of human ancestors, both men and women equally. No deity was to be seen as hierarchically superior to another, as proposed in state Shinto. Also important, the collective beliefs of folk Shinto were rooted in a worship of nature in which trees, creatures, and all other natural objects were endowed with a spirit comparable to that of human beings. Finally, Yanagida repeated that the central purpose of folk beliefs was to offer respect for the spirits of the departed ancestors. Often, this form of worship was associated with fertility deities of agricultural production. In all of this he emphasized that folk Shinto exemplified the continuing reality of an agrarian community worshiping itself and celebrating its own communal unity and solidarity between human beings and nature. In place of the state that was responsible for the bureaucratization of folk Shinto, Yanagida envisaged an expanded tutelary shrine. In short, popular community would assume greater importance than the hierarchic state.

Although Yanagida was certainly not an exponent of militant revolt against the West, his emphasis on popular, agrarian community suggested a powerful alternative to the claims of the modern industrial and technological state, which he saw as a Western import. In this regard, his ideas may be seen as dovetailing with those of the more militant variety of agrarian fundamentalists. Even though Yanagida did not become involved in programmatic political action, as did some of these fundamentalists, such as Inoue and Tachibana, he did share a kinship with their ideas.

## *Tanizaki Junichirō*

Yanagida's protest against modern rationalism, based on the "natural culture" of one's native place, can also be related to a similar criticism from the point of view of indigenous aesthetic theory. In this theory, the "native place" is identified with aesthetic space. The Heideggerian perspective that Watsuji used in his essay on climate and character in which he emphasized the importance of geography and, in turn, living space, is shared by a number of writers who called attention to the determinant relationship between "geography" and indigenous "aesthetic style." Perhaps the most elegant representative of this view was the novelist Tanizaki Junichirō. In his essay "In Praise of Shadows" (In'ei raisan, 1934), Tanizaki redefined space in terms of nuances that were grounded in indigenous culture and that he as a Japanese chose not necessarily because they were superior to the aesthetics of other societies but because they were Japanese and he preferred them.[18] The trend toward Western industrialism was irreversible. At the same time, he felt that for this reason the aesthetic choice of "shadows" must be made in order to preserve Japan's distinctive creative soul. In an ironic gesture, Tanizaki explained the reason for his choice:

> But I know as well as anyone that these are the empty dreams of a novelist, and that having come this far we cannot turn back. . . . If my complaints are taken for what they are, however, there can be no harm in considering how unlucky we have been, what losses we have suffered, in comparison with the Westerner . . . we have met a superior civilization and have had to surrender to it, and we have had to leave a road we have followed for thousands of years.[19]

The importance of Western technology, which Tanizaki called "borrowed gadgets," had resulted in inconvenience for the Japanese, the worst of these being the incandescent light bulb that had invaded the world of shadows. This powerful gadget had illuminated the fine distinctions in Japanese life and had erased the blurred and shadowy lines that were central to indigenous sensibility.

Tanizaki developed his argument by referring first to an example that would strike his audience as absurd, the interior space of the Japanese toilet in comparison with the well-lit Western version and then, building outward from that reference, to more elegant and exquisite examples, both visual and spatial. Along with spaces defined by Japanese architecture reminiscent of Watsuji, Tanizaki also focused on the shadowy coloring of foods, skin complexion, lacquer ware, pottery, and the No drama. These were elements in the world of shadows on which Japanese should self-consciously "meditate," pre-

18 Junichiro Tanizaki, *In Praise of Shadows*, translation of *In'ei raisan* by Edward Seidensticker and Thomas Harper (New Haven, Conn.: Leete's Island Books, 1977), p. 42.
19 Ibid., p. 8.

cisely because of the unwanted glare of Western technology whose light demanded precision rather than subtlety. The shadows for Tanizaki signified silence and tranquility. The apparent mystery that Westerners saw in the Orient referred to the "uncanny silence of these dark places."[20] In these places were found the creative "magic" and "mystery" that had been vital to the cultural tradition of the Japanese, who had "cut off the brightness on the land from above and created a world of shadows. . . ."[21]

It is important to emphasize that for Tanizaki the world of shadows was no longer a dominant and realistic presence, as he saw the pull toward technology as relentless and unavoidable. The world of shadows was, therefore, for him an aesthetic and cultural choice that had to be articulated intellectually as an abstraction. Yet Tanizaki strained to express the ineffable, seeking to restore a tangible emotional identity that time and change threatened to banish. His melancholic meditation dramatized the contrast between Japanese and Western comprehensions of the world. Our way of thinking, he wrote, concentrates on finding "beauty not in the thing itself but in the patterns of shadows, the light and the darkness, that one thing against another creates."[22]

In the West the restless quest for light has dominated aesthetic sensitivity, as best characterized by the ever-increasing brightness exhibited in the candle, succeeded by the oil, gas, and electric lamps.

Although Tanizaki made no claim as to the superiority of Japanese aesthetics, it is also clear that his preference for it was absolute. Instead of arguing that it should be defended militantly, he asserted that perhaps through literature or the arts, something essential to the world of shadows might still be saved. "I do not ask," he concluded, "that this be done everywhere, but perhaps we may be allowed at least one mansion where we can turn off the electric lights and see what it is like without them."[23]

## *The Romanha writers*

The cultural protest against Western technology that Tanizaki encapsulated with the metaphors of the "electric light" and the "toilet" was echoed by a school of contemporary aestheticians referred to as the "Japan romantic school" (Nihon romanha). These were writers such as Yasuda Yojūrō (1910–81), the acknowledged leader of the group, Hayashi Fusao (1903–75), Kamei Katsuichirō (1907–66), Sato Haruo

20 Ibid., p. 20. 21 Ibid., p. 33. 22 Ibid., p. 30. 23 Ibid., p. 42.

(1892–1964), Hagiwara Sakutarō (1886–1942), and for brief periods in their young careers, the well-known novelists of the postwar era, Dazai Osamu (1909–48) and Mishima Yukio (1925–70), and were associated with a literary journal called *Nihon romanha*, which was first published in 1935.[24] These writers rallied around the intellectual position in a statement written by Yasuda Yojūrō that came to be seen as the "manifesto" of the entire group. This manifesto marked their collective break with Marxism and literary modernism, best summed up in Hayashi Fusao's words as a "farewell to realism."

Although the intellectuals in this group concentrated their criticism on the status of modern civilization, their opposition was expressed in a general condemnation of literary modernism. In the manifesto itself, they specifically identified naturalism and realism as the literary forms of rational Western society. They further called attention to the literature of vulgar and popular customs that depicted in exhaustive detail the petty trivia of everyday life. The purpose of the Japan romantic school, they announced, was "to wage war" with the pernicious trend of literary naturalism. They feared above all that the requirements of rational society had eroded the artistic sensibility of indigenous Japanese culture, expressed most recently by Tanizaki. Naturalism had vulgarized the "voice of the people," mechanized artistic talents, and made a fetish of the popular spirit. The creative self had lost all autonomy before the incessant demands of mass markets.

The romantics called upon their contemporaries, therefore, to return to the authentic literary tradition. It was time, they announced, to celebrate openly the Japanese songs of all the ages since the nation's ancient beginning and to call these the songs of youthfulness (*seishun*). In this context, these men outlined the creation of a new literary movement that would eliminate the influences of Western-oriented writings. Identifying their movement as the "main way" (*hondō*), they denounced the prevailing subordination among their contemporaries to what they termed vulgar and mediocre Western aesthetic forms. And again reminiscent of Tanizaki on "shadows," they described their effort to restore a native aesthetic sensibility and recommended the rejection of the present as "self-conscious irony." It was therefore their journal's stated aim to represent the condition of traditional aesthetics

24 See Takeuchi Yoshimi and Kawakami Tetsutarō, eds., *Kindai no chōkoku* (Tokyo: Fuzambō, 1979); and also Takeuchi's essay, "Kindai no chōkoku," in *Kindai Nihon shisōshi kōza*, vol. 7: *Kindaika to dentō*, ed. Kamei Katsuichirō and Takeuchi Yoshimi (Tokyo: Chikuma shobō, 1959), pp. 227–81. Also, Hiromatsu Wataru, *Kindai no chōkoku ron* (Tokyo: Asahi shuppansha, 1980).

that had been diminished by the impact of Western technology and to provide a new forum for its resuscitation.

The sense of loss that the romantics felt was often articulated with the metaphor of the "return" (*kaiki*). It was a theme already in evidence in activists such as Ōkawa Shūmei as well as in writers such as Watsuji and Tanizaki. For the romantics, the return was also accompanied by an awareness that it could not be fully realized. It was clearly expressed by writers such as Kamei Katsuichirō who thus identified the return with the "dream" (*yume*). The longing and yearning for return coupled with the acknowledgment that the journey's end would never be reached went far toward defining the special character of these writers as romantics. The idea of the return was perhaps best captured by the poet Hagiwara Sakutarō in his poem entitled "The Return to Japan" (Nihon e no kaiki, 1938).

In this poem Hagiwara lamented that although the Japanese had not been deprived of material things, they had surrendered their spiritual selves. "We have not lost things," he thus wrote, "but we have exhausted our all."[25] He admitted that he too had been attracted to Western culture at an earlier time, enjoying the creature comforts that it had provided, such as beds, sofas, and foods. Now, however, these things no longer satisfied him. He would thus seek a quiet home with a small tearoom and locate it in an out-of-the-way area of Kyoto and strum gently on the ancient *biwa* in the presence of a traditionally kimonoed Japanese woman. This extremely influential poem provided the romantics with a coherent metaphor to express their vague yearnings for a return to Japan. It also conveyed the return to a true aesthetic self, a sense of "wholeness," an attachment to the native land as a pristine manifestation of nature, and the identification with an indigenous historical time distinct from the Western chronological scheme of human history. These themes can be found in such writings as Yasuda Yojūrō's "The Japanese Bridge" (Nihon no hashi, 1936), which called for a "return" to the Japanese classics and the ancient aesthetic sensibility. The return to a concrete and familiar geographical "place" was also evident in Yokomitsu Riichi's novel, *The Lonely Journey Home* (Ryoshu, 1946). This novel describes an exchange student in Paris contemplating his slow journey across the Siberian tundra, becoming increasingly aware of the profoundness of the "return" to his spiritual home. And finally, it was at this time that Tanizaki himself translated the *Tale of Genji* (1938) into elegant modern Japanese, hoping thereby

25 Hagiwara Sakutarō, "Nihon e no kaiki."

to preserve the spirit of that ancient classic for his contemporaries who had strayed too far from the "Japanese thing" (*Nihonteki na mono*).

Even more important, the return also contained the concept of a reidentification with indigenous time. Hayashi Fusao's "farewell to realism" referred to a rejection of the Western rational description of the past and the narrative of material progress. Just as the Western portrayal of human experience in literary form was said to be inappropriate to Japan, so too was its mode of conveying the meaning of history. Rational description was seen as a facade for the presentation of the West's supremacy. Along with this, the dialectical mode of representing history was also discarded as misleading and inapplicable to any understanding of Japanese history. In its crudest ideological guise, the romantics claimed that history did not begin with the Christian era, but rather, in the case of Japan, it should be measured according to the origins of the nation, calculated as being roughly 660 B.C. The main issue, however, was not so much when the rational sequence began. For the romantics, the crucial point was to find a creative origin, or an authentic "moment" in which a whole was revealed for which Western modes of calculating time could not account. The return to an original aesthetic moment and to Japan's natural homeland also meant the avoidance of the Western evolutionary scheme of history. In short, the yearning for "wholeness," "nature," "native place," true and enduring aesthetic "spirit," and the culture of the indigenous folk all called attention to the dimension of "timelessness" which signified the abandonment of historicism and the discounting of progressive historical time itself.

The return to true origins and the belief in the timelessness of a cultural uniqueness distinct from the West also inaugurated a quest to create a new future that would go beyond the limitations of the present. Much of this assessment was already implicit in the meditations of Yasuda Yojūrō and the romantics. In an essay written in 1937 entitled "On the End of a Theory of Civilization and Enlightenment" (Bunmei kaika no ronri no shūen ni tsuite), Yasuda complained that modern literature expressed or concretized Western knowledge so that literary movements had merely become the thoughtless pursuit of rationalism. In this essay, he also anticipated the deterioration of the self without ever specifying what this actually meant. Yet it was true that for Yasuda, intelligence in modern Japan referred to a theory of civilization and enlightenment, which he identified with the new Meiji bureaucratism and the men who founded it. In its speculative form, it was transmitted downward as Marxism and proletarian literature. Despite the power of this modernist tradition, in Yasuda's view, there had been a number of courageous people who had self-consciously opposed the modern state and its ideology. Among those he favored most were Kumoi Tatsuo (d. 1869) and Saigō Takamori (1827–77). Beyond these rebels, Yasuda also cited, from the late Meiji era, the Japanist group, such as Miyake Setsurei (1860–1945) and the cultural essentialist Okakura Tenshin. In a sense, Yasuda saw the romantics as inheritors of this tradition of critical idealism directed against rationalistic modernism and the tyranny of the self. In proposing the end of a theory of civilization and enlightenment, Yasuda and the romantics were also suggesting the possibility of transcending or overcoming the modern, *kindai no chōkoku,* as this effort came to be called. "The last stage of civilization and enlightenment was the development of Marxian literature and art," Yasuda announced.[26] To him Marxism was also the last stage in the civilization and enlightenment movement that began in the early Meiji era. And he therefore saw the special mission of the Japanese romantic school as ending this last phase of history and starting a new one or, as he put it, to span "a bridge in the night reaching toward a new dawn." The metaphoric phrase "bridge in the night" was used to attract many intellectuals and writers to take part in the famous debates of July 1942 in Kyoto on the theme of overcoming modernity. All believed that the debates would mark the end of modern civilization in Japan and disclose the character of the glorious new age.[27]

## THE DEBATE ON MODERNITY

In particular, the participants in the debate on modernity represented two major intellectual groups, the literary society (*bungakukai*) and the romantic school. Included were literary and film critics, poets, novelists, composers, philosophers, scientists, psychologists, and historians. Among the better-known figures were Kobayashi Hideo, Nishitani Keiji, Kamei Katsuichirō, Hayashi Fusao, Miyoshi Tatsuji, Kawakami Tetsutarō, and Nakamura Mitsuo. The debate took place shortly after the outbreak of the Pacific War and had as its central purpose a discussion of the larger "world-historical" meaning of the event itself as it might relate to the vision of the uncertain future that these intellectuals sought to envisage. Kawakami Tetsutarō, one of the

26 Yasuda Yojūrō, "Bunmei kaika no ronri no shūen," quoted in Takeuchi and Kawakami, *Kindai no chōkoku,* p. iii. 27 Ibid., p. iv.

organizers of the sessions, best stated this overall concern in his concluding remarks. Aside from the deliberations' success or failure, he observed, it was an indisputable fact of immense importance that such intellectual debates had taken place within the first year of the outbreak of the war. Moreover, he saw the discussions as reflecting a struggle between "the blood of the Japanese that truly motivates our intellectual life" and "Western knowledge that has been superimposed on Japan in modern times." Unavoidably, therefore, the conflict must be a desperate and bloody one.

Using the analysis of Takeuchi Yoshimi (1910–77), an eminent scholar close to the antimodernist temperament of the romantic movement, the details of the discussions may be separated into the following broad themes: Takeuchi emphasized the commonly shared assumption that the outbreak of the Pacific War had convinced the participants that the conflict was both intellectual and military. The intellectual confrontation was between "Western intelligence" and the "blood of the Japanese."[28] The struggle was analogized to "war" as "peace" was to cultural submission. In Kamei's terms, "more to be feared than war was peace. . . . Rather a war among kings than the peace of slaves."[29] The idea of "overcoming" was also a criticism of evolutionary as well as dialectical historicism. According to Takeuchi, this included the denial of the Meiji movement for "civilization and enlightenment" (*bunmei kaika*), a view that had been advanced by members of the romantic school. The participants were also disappointed with the insensitivity of the population at large regarding the meaning of that confrontation, often resorting, in their view, to the mere recitation of slogans. And connected with this, the discussants expressed the hope that the symposium would help overcome the fragmentation of culture into specialized fields and eliminate the widespread feelings of alienation in society, by reconstituting a sense of cultural wholeness. All the participants felt immersed in the problem of "Japan's modern intellectual fate" (*gendai Nihon no chiteki unmei*) and the peculiar tragedy in which they were compelled to live out their lives, a view expressed most eloquently for the entire symposium by Kamei Katsuichirō in his perception of the "modern" as being an unyielding illness or malaise.

Although some used the metaphor of disease to refer specifically to the actual outbreak of the "glorious" war, Kamei used his phrases as a general proposition in the intellectual struggle against modernity. But

28 Ibid., p. 166. 29 Ibid., p. 298.

in either case, the analogy to actual events could hardly be separated from the war, suggesting therefore that the war's larger purpose was to accomplish the final conquest of the modern. In retrospect, this view cast a cloak of intellectual deception on the proceedings themselves. Takeuchi went through some pain to argue that the deliberations at the end remained entirely unresolved and to point out that this was due to the many differences in viewpoints among the participants regarding the meaning of the future order. Yet the sentiments expressed by certain intellectual luminaries such as Miyoshi Tatsuo (1902–64), Kawakami, Kamei, and others, clearly suggest an intellectual convergence beneath the metaphoric umbrella of "overcoming modernity."

Among many, the celebration of the "glorious war" contributed to their willingness to abandon all desire to "resist" the course of events that the government had taken. Although this desire had remained strong even after Japan's invasion of China, it dissipated rapidly after the outbreak of the Pacific War. In its new meaning, the war was interpreted as a revolt against the "modern" West and its hegemony over Asia, a view that was not unattractive by any means to Marxists and former Marxists as well. By contrast, the earlier attack on China was seen differently, not as the uncontrolled expansion of Japanese imperialism, but as part of the liberation of Asia, not yet under the domination of the West, and its subsequent modernization under Japanese tutelage.

For most, "modern" was invariably associated closely with rational "science." Much of the discussion concentrated, therefore, on showing how modern science had developed in a historically specific context, namely, the Renaissance and its aftermath in Western Europe. Recalling the thinking of Watsuji in his "Climate and Culture," the debaters traced the spirit of the European Renaissance to its roots in ancient Greece where the philosophy of science was first articulated. As expressed by Hayashi Fusao, the subsequent development of science in the West differed substantially from the Japanese experience. In the myths of the West, he noted, men were always in a state of "struggle" with the gods. But in Japan, gods and men did not contend with each other, as conflict occurred among the gods alone. This reference to mythology was aimed at showing that Western science was fundamentally inappropriate to the spirit of the Japanese people. Kamei went even further to argue that because the Japanese spirit had been alienated from the gods (*kami*), in overcoming modernity the Japanese must reintegrate themselves with the spirit of these *kami*.

Here, Kamei employed *kami* as a metaphor representing the spirit of the entire Japanese people. He defined the ways of achieving this reunion as the central problem of contemporary Japanese philosophy. In the end, the wish to overcome the West became a revolt against reason itself.

On closer examination, the basic culturalist premise appears to militate against the idea of a progressive "overcoming" of modernity. Kobayashi Hideo recognized best the problem it inspired and underscored most clearly the inescapable ambivalence resulting from any attempt to overcome the modern. The real enemy were ideas of change and advancement, which unfailingly mislead modern people to create false intellectual expectations. The "burden" of history had now come to presuppose the demonstration of progressive modernization. Among the accounts written by modern historians of Japan covering the various ages, Kobayashi claimed to have found all of them to be merely reviews or narrative summations of the past and hence shallow representations of human actualities. This was especially true of those discussions of aesthetic forms embedded in the past. Beauty, Kobayashi insisted, did not "evolve" in a progressive manner leading to modernity. It could not, therefore, be understood from the perspective of the modern experience. Yet to him, it was this subject of beauty in history in specific places and contexts that had to be perceived and grasped. However one understood history from the modern point of view, such a stance actually prevented the mind from encountering the structure of beauty in history because of the presupposition of historical evolution that concealed beauty as beauty. In short, beauty was closed off from the historian's view. The discerning eye, however, must disengage itself from the existentialist dimension of history and penetrate the underlying structure that goes beyond that immediate moment. Kobayashi exemplified this argument by explaining that the essence of Kamakura religious art contained a deep and abiding form that outlived its immediate history and the moment that had given expression to it. The art objects of the Kamakura period are before our eyes, he explained, but they contain a beauty that is independent and possesses an abiding "life" that transcends modern scholarly interpretations. Because such objects contain a passion and an elegance unbound by the specific constraints of the historical era, beauty may indeed be said to be universal. In the debates themselves, Kobayashi readily admitted that his view pointed to a universalistic conception of aesthetic form, which, as his critics acknowledged, indeed differed from modernistic historicism. Ironically, Kobayashi's ideas about beauty appeared to coincide with Western Platonic idealism, which the debaters were quick to point out. On this point, Kobayashi agreed that the distinction between existence and eternal form should be kept separate in order to grasp the fundamental aesthetic in history. Here, he acknowledged his sympathy for the spirit of Plato's idealism and, among recent philosophers, Henri Bergson's conception of creativity.[30]

To Kobayashi, then, "overcoming" the West meant essentially reidentifying with the Platonic idea of eternal forms of truth and beauty that had fallen beyond the purview of modern interpretations based on the idea of progressive evolution. Rejecting the use of such terms as *ancient, medieval, modern,* and the like, Kobayashi refused to see the "overcoming" of modernity as an "advancement" to a new and glorious era. Rather, he thought of it as "transcending" the limitations of Western modernism and as readdressing the question of eternal and enduring forms of beauty. Kobayashi's idea of lasting beauty, however, simultaneously coincided with prevailing opinions regarding the adverse effects of Western civilization in modern Japan and the need to be liberated from that unhappy legacy. Although the advocates of "overcoming" modernity spoke of a vague future better than the present – and Kobayashi did not indulge in such thinking, as he remained skeptical of this mode of conceptualizing time – they agreed on the imperative to reidentify with indigenous cultural ideals and to allow them enough space and time that they might serve as sources of renewal and creative inspiration within a continuing history.

What troubled Kobayashi most was the fear that Japan would become a pale replica of Western societies. He dramatized his concerns on this issue by drawing on the ironic lines from Marx's *Eighteenth Brumaire*. He thus referred to the modernization of the West as a "tragedy" and the second manifestation of it in Japan as a "comedy." The quintessential comedians in Japan, he observed, had not yet captured the stage, but they inevitably would.[31] The central issue for him was the proposition that history was constant change, whereas in his view, change in fact was basically unimportant to the creative act of producing art and literature. Convinced that aesthetic creations were "unhistorical" and eternal, as they were expressed in terms of form and order and not of history, Kobayashi was equally convinced that modern persons (including the Japanese) had abandoned the life-giving energy of art. Yet it was the engagement with this aesthetic energy, Kobayashi asserted, that generated the dynamic and balancing

30 Ibid., p. 229. 31 Ibid., p. 219.

"tension" undergirding the flow of history itself and that could not be grasped from the perspective of linear change in which one thing was shown to be different and somehow better than what came before. For this reason, then, Kobayashi expressed profound pessimism about the ideas of "change" and "progress," claiming to feel "sick" and "nauseous" about them. In expressing these views, Kobayashi had assumed a position close to one already occupied by Tanizaki.

What Kobayashi hoped to overcome was the conception of linear time that Japanese had imported from the West during the Meiji era. Many of his colleagues at the debates were also deeply concerned with the general question of evolutionary time and, more specifically, the meaning of "civilization," *bunmei,* that had captured the attention of early Meiji intellectuals. To Kamei Katsuichirō, for example, the civilization of enlightenment in Meiji Japan had introduced the Western idea of the specialization and compartmentalization of knowledge. This epistemological import, he claimed, resulted in the loss of a sense of "wholeness" in life among the Japanese. An identifiable event, the incorporation of Western ideas of functional specialization, was thus a major disruptive force in the spiritual life of Japan. Those who contested this disruptive impact sought solutions in nonconformist modes of thinking. Kamei cited as an outstanding example in this regard the Christian leader Uchimura Kanzō (1861–1930). To Kamei, Uchimura's greatness was his refusal to conform to the pattern of specialization that had increasingly come to dominate the world around him. Although an expert in marine biology, Uchimura saw his work as part of a unified system of knowledge in which all things were informed by an intrinsic and divine spirit (*kami*), and he retained his identification with this view of the universe. His "churchless Christianity" (*mukyōkai*) was nothing other than a sophisticated rendition of this deeper ontological commitment to a unified view of the universe.

The process of specialization, however, proceeded into the twentieth century. The cause of this disquieting trend was the adoption of Western utilitarianism accompanying the assimilation of the idea of progress in the Meiji enlightenment. In the process, the "philosopher of real life" (*tetsujin*) was destroyed. Central to Kamei's antimodernist vision was the restoration of the philosophy of "wholeness" and the "unity of knowledge" as it related to all beings, creatures, and things evident in the folk Shinto of these wise men. The resemblance here to the ideas of Yanagida Kunio is apparent, except that Kamei focused on literate culture rather than on country villages and oral tradition. Kamei and his colleagues had also shaped a cultural position analogous to that held by some of the political activists who had turned against Meiji history as a "betrayal" of the spirit of the Meiji Restoration, by manifestly constructing the bureaucratic and technological state. Even though Kamei was silent on the particular problem of state formation, unlike Kita Ikki and Nakano Seigō, he did see in the Meiji movement for civilization the unrelieved inundation of Western utilitarian and functional philosophies that, in the twentieth century, promised to destroy the theory of knowledge founded on the unity of all things that had informed the spirit of Japanese civilization before the modern era. In Kamei's harsh terms, Meiji civilization and enlightenment had introduced "deformed specialists" into contemporary Japanese culture.

This critique of Meiji bureaucratic culture was taken a step further by another leading participant in the debates, Hayashi Fusao, a novelist, cultural critic, and former Marxist who had turned his intellectual allegiance to the pure cultural ideals of Japan as advocated by the Romantic school. "I believe," he stated, "that civilization and enlightenment meant the adoption of European culture after the Meiji Restoration and resulted in the submission of Japan to the West." From an external perspective, the Meiji Restoration represented the last opposition of the East against the West. Although at one level it may be seen to have been a victory – as India was overwhelmed and China dismembered, and only Japan managed to withstand the Western wave – yet at another level, in order to maintain opposition to Europe, it was also necessary to incorporate Western utilitarian civilization. Civilization and enlightenment were thus a utilitarian culture devoid of fundamental substance.[32] Hayashi believed that the Japanese dissatisfaction with this utilitarian culture emerged in the late 1880s at which time a number of reflective intellectuals began to call for a return to cultural fundamentals. Among these prescient critics were again the Christian idealist Uchimura Kanzō, the art historian Okakura Tenshin, and such heroic figures as Saigō Takamori and General Nogi Maresuke (1849–1912). Hayashi also contended that all the men who drew attention to this critique of utilitarian civilization were defeated by the Westernizing trends of the time. Until recently, he concluded, the European conception of civilization had persisted as the dominant force over the skeptical view of progress found in the native tradition. It was in this context that Hayashi discussed the East Asian War as the final chance to turn back the tide of utilitarianism in Asia. Those in Japan who still held to this Western epistemology must also be de-

32 Ibid., pp. 239–40.

feated and transformed according to true native sensibilities. Hayashi believed the bureaucratic culture and elitism spawned by utilitarianism in the Meiji period had been resisted by the Movement for Popular Rights. Although some of the discussants disagreed with his view, seeing the movement as a product of the very ideals he had criticized, Hayashi clung to the belief that it was an indigenous movement directed against the acquisition of absolutist power by bureaucratic cliques bent on constructing a utilitarian state. In this manner, Hayashi reinterpreted the Meiji Restoration by denying its revolutionary impulse, rejecting the French or American models of such transformation, and emphasizing instead the emergence of the Japanese people as a "classless" community unified with the emperor.

Consistent with this position, Hayashi and his colleagues singled out "Americanism" as the primary force behind the global expansion of utilitarianism. Increasingly in the twentieth century, Europe had come to be replaced by the United States as the leader of the Western world. The debaters specifically cited the importation, following World War I, of crass, hedonistic materialism among Japan's urban youth, exemplified among faddish groups who called themselves "modern boys" (*mobo*) and "modern girls" (*moga*). American movies, especially, had spread the cult of "fast living" (*supīdo*) and "eroticism," seducing young Japanese minds and leading them away from their cultural roots. These cultural invasions were the result of the power of mass-production strategies developed in the United States. However impressive these strategies might seem in a certain quantitative sense, they also undermined Japan's cultural virtues and the society's faith in itself. They were especially visible in the marketing of a mass culture that reflected the absence of a deeply rooted sense of cultural purpose in the United States itself. Because the United States was a relatively new nation, these men reasoned, its cultural traditions in art and morals were perilously shallow. Their products, therefore, were accessible to everyone, owing to their simplicity and lack of philosophical depth. But here indeed was the deceptive nature of utilitarian mass-production culture that undermined societies with long cultural traditions. The danger of this Americanism was its capacity to spread a "universalistic" culture of simple materialism. Thus from a land of immigrants characterized as a "frontier" nation, the United States had acquired a new and negative image in world history.

Implicit in the comments on the mass production of movies and other American "gadgets" was the view that the ready acceptance of this materialistic culture by the youth of the early twentieth century was due to the insidious influences of Meiji utilitarianism. This harsh reading of Meiji intellectual and political history was closely linked to the deep concern that the twentieth century had witnessed the emergence of a consumer culture satisfied only with the possession of plenty rather than with the quality and beauty of scarcity and restraint. American democracy, therefore, had as its real substance the satisfaction of the masses with trivial goods produced in large quantities, a condition that had permeated Japanese life as well.

The repeatedly pessimistic appraisal of the Meiji enlightenment by the debaters points to a deep intellectual bifurcation in the intellectual history of the 1920s and 1930s. Their comments, though locked in the language of historical reassessment, were also directed against contemporaries who were quick to evaluate positively the Meiji movement for civilization and enlightenment as the starting point for a humane modern order. The representative figure of this position was the leading theorist of Taishō democracy, Yoshino Sakuzō. Under his direction, there was a collaborative effort to reconstruct Meiji intellectual history. The multivolume work on that subject, *Meiji bunka zenshū*, remains a monument to Yoshino's conviction that the Meiji achievement rescued Japan from a somnolent feudal order and backwardness and set society upon its civilizing course. Yoshino and his colleagues took a dim view of the bureaucratic elites that had come to dominate the Meiji state and that sought to redirect politics away from the democratic future as envisaged in the early Meiji enlightenment. But if the antimodernists and Yoshino found common cause in their condemnation of the bureaucratic order, they parted company over the more compelling question concerning the essence of modern Japanese culture. Hayashi Fusao and his group decried the emergence of utilitarian bureaucratism, functional specialization, and mass production and consumerism. To resist these forces, they demanded the restoration of "timeless" cultural values. Although the participants in the debate differed widely among themselves, they all subscribed to an "ahistorical" perception of culture and frequently expressed it in recurring criticisms of linear conceptions of time such as "progress." By contrast, Yoshino and those like him who prized the Meiji enlightenment, denied the virtue of "timeless" culture and emphasized instead the "timefulness" of historical movement and the continuous human potential for achieving new creative and moral goals in the future.

The debate on "overcoming the modern" concluded with a general consideration of the possibilities for Japan in the context of the early 1940s. The problem in the final analysis was how might Japan retain its technological achievements yet preserve those irreducible cultural elements that made the Japanese distinctive. None of the participants, when faced with the choice, contemplated the unrealistic solution of turning back the clock of industrialization. To these men, however, the "machine" must be defined unequivocally as the mere servant of humans, and the human spirit the creator of technology. Spirit, therefore, was determined to be autonomous and separate from manufactured things and unaffected by such products. They denied in this regard the Marxist theory of "alienation" in which manufactured goods were objects that "dehumanized" the spirit. The true "potential" (*kanōsei*) for modern Japan, then, was in the creation and retention of a culture in which the human spirit would remain independent by being anchored to timeless and essential values, whereas manufactured goods would function simply as external objects divorced from aesthetic considerations. It was over the question of how best to resurrect and clarify this cultural essence that they emphasized the significance of the great literary texts from ancient history. The importance of the great scholars of the "national studies" of the Tokugawa period, such as Motoori Norinaga, was that, by "rediscovering" those classics in the eighteenth century, themselves became manifestations of the spirit and highly esteemed artifacts.

The criticism of the harmful effects on Japanese culture by Meiji utilitarianism and the bureaucratic state was inseparable from the more general denunciation of the international order constructed and dominated by the Western powers. The criticism of domestic bureaucratism, therefore, also included the rejection of Western hegemony over Asia. To overcome the modern meant to many of these men the internal and external uprooting of Western materialism and power in Asia. Their reidentification with Japanese ideals thus led them to acknowledge the importance of reviving similar cultural ideas in other Asian countries and recognizing the necessity of Japan protecting them against colonialism. Liberating Japanese cultural idealism from Western materialism and separating Asia from Western hegemony were thus closely related sentiments, so much so that the attack on modernity provided the underlying intellectual justifications for the ideology enunciated by Prime Minister Konoe Fumimarō (1891–1945) in the declaration of 1938 calling for the establishment of an "East Asian Cooperative Union." It was in Konoe's conception of cultural communalism that the more pragmatic formulations of a "new order" were articulated. Japan's Asian neighbors, the declaration boasted, would live in friendship, defend the area in common, and cooperate economically. Although the Chinese in particular were invited to join with Japan in creating such a system of mutual cooperation, there was little doubt – despite language that strained to suppress Japan's own imperial ambitions – that the "new order" would in fact be directed primarily by Japan. Here, the rejection of the presence of Western bureaucratism was linked to Pan-Asianism in order to authorize Japan's own expansion as the hegemonic power in Asia and virtually paralleled the American claim to rope off the Western Hemisphere by the cordon sanitaire authorized by the Monroe Doctrine. It is inconceivable that the participants in the debates against modernity were not aware of the relationship between their criticism and the expansionist designs of those in the government. It may indeed be the case, as claimed by some later, that the debates did not produce a coherent and comprehensive ideology for the Pacific War and that it was hardly their aim to come up with one. Yet the fact remains that their negative reading of the Meiji legacy of the bureaucratic state had turned ironically to an endorsement of expansionism by that very order, or at least its successor, that they had so consistently vilified. In particular, the language demanding an East Asian war as the condition for Asia to reestablish control over its own cultural destinies indeed only underscores the unconsciously ironic deception in which the debaters were implicated.

## EPILOGUE

In the 1930s the Japanese romantic Yasuda Yojūrō called attention to Japan as irony. What he was referring to was the effort to preserve those elements in traditional life that attested to Japan's irreducible uniqueness while seeking to become a modern society. Yasuda recognized that the conditions for modernity necessitated eliminating those elements and forms from the past that he and his associates sought to preserve. What he failed to see was the possibility of other kinds of ironies that war and defeat eventually made certain. Indeed, more than one level of irony was already present in the debates against modernity and the strident call for a war against the West. The debaters could not have known that a total military defeat of Japan would, in fact, remove "war" itself as a central object in the discourse on culture that had dominated the 1930s. Without the militancy of the prewar years, however, much of the earlier discourse spilled over into the postwar period as issues of compelling and immediate concern. It was almost as if the earlier discourse had not quite yet completed an agenda that was interrupted by the war and that the cessation of hostilities then offered as an occasion to return to unfinished business. The implication was that nothing really had changed, yet the physical and social landscape everywhere announced ruin and tragedy. But just as ironic was that despite the criticism by the prewar writers and intellectuals against the modern state and its bureaucratic excesses, what would eventually emerge in the rubble was an even more rational bureaucratic arrangement of power, dedicated not to the pursuit of war but to industrial growth and supremacy. If as Yasuda noted earlier, modern Japan could be understood only as a totally ironic experience, a double irony prevailed to characterize the postwar restoration. For the arguments of cultural exceptionalism that earlier had been used to criticize modern organizational forms were later harnessed to represent the spiritual basis for the installation and success of a large-scale technological order capable of unprecedented productive power. The new Japanese order succeeded in producing, on a scale and at a level of excellence never before reached by most industrial nations, those things that earlier cultural critics had denounced as Western and dangerously disruptive of traditional Japanese life.

The overarching irony was captured by Kamei Katsuichirō, a refugee from the prewar debate on modernity, in a self-reflective and plaintive confessional essay, "The Ideal Image of Twentieth Century Japan" (Nijūseiki Nihon no risō, 1954). Even as postwar Japan prepared itself for massive industrial expansion, Kamei was calling for a return to Asia. The summons evoked the echo of earlier declarations for a Japanese return to the cultural homeland:

> One of the problems with which the Japanese have been burdened since the Meiji Era has been the necessity of examining Japan's place in Asia and our special fate as Asians. Japan, as everyone knows, was the first country in Asia to "modernize," but it is not yet clear what meaning this modernization had for Asia. It is also a question whether Asian thought, which possesses strong traditions despite repeated taste of defeat and a sense of inferiority before Western science, is doomed to perish without further struggle, or if it is capable of reviving in the twentieth century something which will enable us to surmount the present crisis. . . . [T]o study it [Asia] has become since the defeat the greatest responsibility incumbent on us.[33]

Kamei continued an earlier critique by stating his open displeasure with Meiji rationalism and enlightenment and sought to return to the

33 Ryusaku Tsunoda, Theodore de Bary, et al., *Sources of Japanese Tradition* (New York: Columbia University Press, 1958), pp. 392–3.

vision of Asian unity announced by Okakura Tenshin when he opened his *Ideals of the East* with a rousing call to brotherhood, "Asia is One!" Japan had abdicated its place in Asia, Kamei noted, by slavishly miming Western civilization, only to win for itself the status of a poor "stepchild." Worse still, it ended by using foreign technological instruments to wage war against Asian brothers. Japan must now return to Asia and, directed by a sense of genuine guilt and humility, secure its place as the "stepchild of the Eastern world." The need for cultural resistance against the West, he pleaded, was far from over and would continue throughout the rest of the twentieth century to complete the work begun by Gandhi, Tagore, Lu Hsun, and Okakura.

Kamei's reminder to "return to Asia" heightens our awareness that although the harsh language of the earlier "revolt against the West" had been removed because of the war, Japan's proper cultural place had remained as the central intellectual issue for the postwar period. Japan's real roots, in short, were to be found only in Asia, closer to the native land and not within the remote confines of Western civilization. This sense of cultural kinship by propinquity was reinforced by the elegant meditations of Takeuchi Yoshimi, a scholar of considerable stature who disclosed an affinity for leading cultural critics such as Okakura and Ōkawa Shūmei. Takeuchi, an authoritative interpreter of Chinese literature and culture, the translator of Lu Hsun's complete works, proposed to his generation the construction of a new science of knowledge which he described as "Asia as method" (*hōhō to shite no Ajia*). Acknowledging that this method, inspired by Asians' diverse experiences, had not yet been fully formulated, Takeuchi was certain that a sympathetic understanding of how Chinese, Japanese, and other Asian peoples had comprehended the challenge of modernity would offer instructive models for the task ahead.

In this essay, in which Takeuchi introduced the possibility of finding an alternative method to understanding the Asian experience, he confessed how he, as a student before the war, had studied China and Chinese literature as if neither the language nor its considerable literature any longer existed. Even more, he noted, he was not certain that China was anything more than an abstraction. "When we studied Chinese history and geography we never studied the fact that there were humans there."[34] Only on his first trip to China did he recognize how remote and abstract his training had been from the real thing and how ill prepared he was to cope with the enormity of a living experi-

34 Takeuchi Yoshimi, *Hōhō to shite no Ajia: Waga senzen senchū sengo* (Tokyo: Sōkisha, 1978).

ence. He admitted that he could not even communicate with the Chinese because his training had been principally in the classical language and had omitted the spoken tongue. It was as if, he mused, nobody really spoke Chinese. Yet Takeuchi apparently felt real empathy with the Chinese he encountered, recognizing that they, like the Koreans, were Japan's closest neighbors, indeed friends and brothers, yet made to appear remote by virtue of his education. To redress this great failing, he began a study of the spoken language and ultimately discovered a living literature embodied in the writings of Lu Hsun. This discovery that people did live in China, which hitherto had been prevented because of the dead hand of sinology, inspired Takeuchi to devote his own life to seeking the traces of what he called the "heart" (*kokoro*) of living Chinese.

The recognition of geographic immediacy and an authentic Chinese experience revealed to Takeuchi that Japan's own efforts to direct China's modernization were based on the same method that led him and his contemporaries to overlook the human presence and the possibility of vast differences. His own subsequent research showed him that the Chinese, the Koreans, the Indians, and other Asians had, owing to their own cultural experiences, forged different responses to the challenge of Western modernity. But what all Asians shared, apart from geography, was the quest to make sense of modernism without forfeiting their own cultural endowments. This, he observed, was not only the message of Tagore, as seen in his several trips to China and Japan, but also of Tenshin. Ironically, it was confirmed by Westerners like John Dewey and Bertrand Russell when they also visited Japan and China. Yet the Japanese, owing to their propensity to identify with Western techniques and methods, were blinded by their own experience of grappling with the problem and sought to impose on the rest of China a method of modernity alien to their own impulse. To return to Asia meant, therefore, to account for the diverse approaches enabled by living experiences and to develop an authentic method stressing differences, not abstract sameness. "There are severe limits to Western power," Takeuchi wrote:

I believe that Asians have always recognized them. Oriental poets have intuitively known this. Whether it is Tagore or Lu Hsun, they have accomplished the ideal of a general humanity in their own personal examples. The West has invaded the East; there has been opposition to this. Some, like Toynbee, have proposed to homogenize the world, but many contemporary Asians have not seen this as merely a Western limitation. In order to realize superior Western cultural values, the West has to be entrapped once more by Asia, as a means of revolutionizing Westerners themselves; it has to create universalism according to this cultural rewinding of values. The strength of the East is in revolutionizing the West in order to elevate the universal values that the West produced.

This, Takeuchi concluded, was the problem for the contemporary East and West and should be the "model for Japan, as well."[35]

A central corollary to this new "return to Asia" was the renewed emphasis on the communitarian ideal of folk culture that the Meiji state had unthinkingly suppressed in order to satisfy bureaucratic expediency. The older form of communalism celebrated by the ethnographer Yanagida Kunio was, in postwar Japan, the clarion cry of all those who believed that the state had intruded too far into the daily lives of ordinary people. Hence, it is not surprising that writers and movements would derive identity and forms of enablement by summoning the ideal of the *jōmin*, the abiding people, in their several efforts to contest and even reverse state intervention. In a sense Yanagida himself became something of a folk hero in the postwar era, and the so-called Yanagida boom that swept the country in the 1960s and early 1970s attests to the veracity of this alternative. Yet like its prewar progenitor, the new communalism was linked to all those sentiments that called for a return to Asia. The boom and its consequences for the restitution of folk culture did not mean simply a revival of the great anthropologist's writings nor a fad popularized by intellectuals and scholars. Rather, it was a countrywide movement to save folk arts and crafts, to emphasize the diversity and difference of regional and local culture against the inexorable demands of bureaucratic sameness. Because of Yanagida's emphasis on the structureless communitarianism of indigenous folk life, scholars, writers, and intellectuals began to explore the utility of this ideal for the new postwar social order. The appeal escalated as the rationalistic momentum of Japan's "phoenixlike" industrial recovery quickened. In the 1960s, intellectuals and activists like Yoshimoto Ryūmei (1924– ) and Irokawa Daikichi (1925– ) appropriated Yanagida to anticipate the state and became leaders of local protest movements demanding bureaucratic accountability in such vital issues as ecological pollution and the apparent elimination of regional self-governance. Yoshimoto, perhaps the most powerful theorist of this resuscitated ideal of community, hoped to transmute the state into a structureless entity occupied by a folk held together by mutual respect and affection. Yet this concentration on

35 Ibid., vol. 3, p. 420.

the community opened the way for a renewed emphasis on particularism and cultural exceptionalism. The discourse on cultural exceptionalism was transformed into a social science or "sociology" focused on explaining Japan's uniqueness. But it should be recalled that Yanagida and his generation of researchers had already called attention to the possibility of establishing a social science in Japan as the necessary methodology to grasp *difference*. Where the new interest in social science departed from this prewar precedent was in its insistence that normative conceptions and methods could be used to explain what was unique about Japan. Many of its most strident students were Japanese who had been trained in the West. Books too numerous to mention appeared in the 1960s and 1970s pledged to performing a "scientific" analysis of Japan's uniqueness, why Japan was fundamentally unlike and hence superior to other societies.

The withdrawal from a universalistic understanding of the world to the familiar confines of a culturally unique homeland was most pronounced among ultranationalistic critics such as Hayashi Fusao, another survivor of the prewar debates on modernity. His own celebration of the native land was expressed in a work called "Japan, the Green Archipelago" (Midori no Nihon rettō, 1966) and in an influential dialogue with Mishima Yukio on the meaning of Japanism. Mishima also made his own statement in the "defense of culture" (Bunka bōeiron, 1969). It is hardly surprising that both attempted to reconfirm the martial spirit of the prewar restorationist radicals who had sacrificed their own lives to dramatize the urgency of the cultural problem. Whereas Mishima extolled the revolutionary idealism of Ōshio Heihachirō, recalling the prewar idealization of this late Tokugawa radical, Hayashi provided a historical interpretation of the Pacific War. In his "Thesis Affirming the Great East Asia War" (Dai Tōa sensō kōteiron, 1964), Hayashi saw Japan's revolt against the West as the culmination of the "first one-hundred-year war in Asia" that began with the Opium War in 1840 and reached its climax with the bombing of Pearl Harbor. War was now over for Japan, but a second one-hundred-year war had already started in other places in Asia, such as Southeast Asia and the Chinese mainland. Thus Hayashi read these signs as an affirmation of Japan's own revolt against the West and a justification for its decision to go to war despite the overwhelming odds favoring defeat and destruction. And as recent events showed, he concluded, the contest was still far from over.

Both the range of articulations concerning what it means to be Japanese (*Nihonjinron*) and the concomitant impulse to "return to

Asia" were represented by the Nobel laureate Kawabata Yasunari (1899–1972). Although he reached back to the idea of enduring aesthetic forms marking Japan's exceptionalism – as proposed earlier by Tanizaki, Kobayashi, and the Romantics – in his Nobel Prize acceptance speech, "Japan, the Beautiful," Kawabata called attention to this "unique" inheritance of the beautiful that distinguished the Japanese from others. Yet some years earlier in an eloquent poetic eulogy he delivered to his departed friend Yokomitsu Riichi, he acknowledged this tradition of beauty as part of a larger Asian whole. His language applied to an entire generation of prewar and, later, postwar intellectuals and writers of whom Yokomitsu was perhaps the archetype because of his own tortuous odyssey from West to East. Kawabata lamented:

> Sufferer of the New Asia that fought the West,
> Pioneer of the New Tragedy in the Asian Tradition,
> You shouldered such a destiny.
> And you left the world sending a smile to Heaven.[36]

36 Quoted in Yuasa Yasuo, *Watsuji Tetsurō* (Tokyo: Minerva shobō, 1981), dedication page.

# WORKS CITED


Abe Isoo 安部磯雄. *Shakaishugiron* 社会主義論. Tokyo: Heiminsha, 1903.

Abe Isoo 安部磯雄. *Meiji Shakaishugiron* 明治社会主義論. Tokyo: Wabei Kyokai, *1907*.

*Abe Isoo* 安部磯雄. "Meiji sanjūnen no shakai minshutō" 明治三十年の社会民主党. In *Nihon shakai undō* 日本社会運動 in *Shakai Kagaku* 社会科学 (February 1928).

Abe Isoo 安部磯雄. "Shakaishugi shōshi" 社会主義小史. In *Shakaishugi shiron* 社会主義史論, ed. Kishimoto Eitarō 岸本英太郎. Tokyo: Aoki shoten, 1955.

Abegglen, James C. *The Japanese Factory: Aspects of Its Social Organization*. Glencoe, Ill.: Free Press, 1958.

Adachi Gan 安達巖. *Kokumin undō no saishuppatsu* 国民運動の再出発. Tokyo: Kasumigaseki shobō, 1940.

Agawa Hiroyuki 阿川弘之. *Yamamoto Isoroku* 山本五十六. Tokyo: Shinchōsha, 1965; new ed., 1969.

Akita, George. *The Foundations of Constitutional Government in Modern Japan, 1868–1900*. Cambridge, Mass.: Harvard University Press, 1967.

Akuto Hiroshi 飽戸弘, Tominaga Ken'ichi 富永健一 and Sobue Takao 祖父江孝男, eds. *Hendōki no Nihon shakai* 変動期の日本社会. Tokyo: Nihon hōsō kyōkai, 1972.

Allen, G. C. *A Short Economic History of Modern Japan*. London: Allen & Unwin, 1946.

Allinson, Gary D. *Japanese Urbanism: Industry and Politics in Kariya, 1872–1972*. Stanford, Calif.: Stanford University Press, 1975.

Amakawa Akira 天川晃. "Senryō seisaku to kanryō no taiō" 占領政策と官僚の対応. In *Kyōdō kenkyū: Nihon senryōgun: Sono hikari to kage* 共同研究: 日本占領軍その光と影, ed. Shisō no kagaku kenkyūkai 思想の科学研究会, vol. 1. Tokyo: Tokuma shoten, 1978.

Amakawa Akira 天川晃. "Chihō jichi hō no kōzō" 地方自治法の構造. In *Senryōki Nihon no keizai to seiji* 占領期日本の経済と政治, ed. Nakamura Takafusa 中村隆英. Tokyo: Tōkyō daigaku shuppankai, 1979.

Amakawa Akira 天川晃. "Dai-43-dai: Higashikuni naikaku: Miyasama naikaku no shūsen shori 第43代 東久邇内閣—宮様内閣の終戦処理. In *Nihon naikaku shi roku* 日本内閣史録. vol. 5, ed. Hayashi Shigeru and Tsuji Kiyoaki 林茂, 辻清明. Tokyo: Daiichi hōki, 1981.

Amakawa Akira 天川晃. "Dai-44-dai: Shidehara naikaku: 'Minshu' kaikaku no hajimari" 第44代 幣原内閣—「民主」改革の始まり. In *Nihon naikaku shi roku* 日本内閣史録, vol. 5, ed. Hayashi Shigeru 林茂 and Tsuji Kiyoaki 辻清明. Tokyo: Daiichi hōki, 1981.

Amakawa Akira 天川晃. "Dai-45-dai: Dai-1-ji Yoshida naikaku: Shin kenpō taisei e no ikō" 第45代 第一次吉田内閣—新憲法体制への移行. In *Nihon naikaku shi roku* 日本内閣史録, vol. 5, ed. Hayashi Shigeru 林茂 and Tsuji Kiyoaki 辻清明. Tokyo: Daiichi hōki, 1981.

Andō Yoshio 安藤良雄, ed. *Shōwa seiji keizai shi e no shōgen* 昭和政治経済史への証言, 3 vols. Tokyo: Mainichi shinbunsha, 1972.

Andō Yoshio 安藤良雄 and Yamamoto Hirofumi 山本弘文, eds. *Kōgyō iken hoka Maeda Masana kankei shiryō* 興業意見他前田正名関係資料. Tokyo: Kōseikan, 1971.

Aoki Kōji 青木虹二. *Nihon rōdō undōshi nenpyō* 日本労働運動史年表, vol. 1. Tokyo: Shinseisha, 1968.

Aoki Nobumitsu 青木信光. *Baba Eiichi den* 馬場鍈一傳. Tokyo: Ko Baba Eiichi-shi kinenkai, 1945.

Arahata Kanson 荒畑寒村. "*Kindai shisō* to *Shinshakai*" 近代思想と新社会. *Shisō* 思想 460 (October 1962): 115–25.

Arai Kurotake 新居玄武. *Taiheiyō sensōki ni okeru yūgyō jinkō no suikei* 太平洋戦争期における有業人口の推計, Nihon tōkei gakkai hōkoku 日本統計学会報告 (July 1978).

Arai Naoyuki 新井直之. "Senryō seisaku to jānarizumu." 占領政策とジャーナリズム. In *Kyōdō kenkyū: Nihon senryō* 共同研究: 日本占領, ed. Shisō no kagaku kenkyūkai 思想の科学研究会. Tokyo: Tokuma shoten, 1972.

Ari Bakuji 阿利莫二. "Chihō seido (hōtaisei hōkai-ki): Burakukai chōnaikai seido" 地方制度(法体制崩壊期): 部落会町内会制度. In *Kōza: Nihon kindaihō hattatsu shi – shihonshugi to hō no hatten*, vol. 6, ed. Fukushima Masao 福島正夫, Kawashima Takeyoshi 川島武宜, Tsuji Kiyoaki 辻清明 and Ukai Nobushige 鵜飼信成. Tokyo: Keisō shobō, 1959.

Arima Yoriyasu 有馬頼寧. *Seikai dōchūki* 政界道中記. Tokyo: Nihon shuppan kyōdō kabushiki kaisha, 1951.

Arisawa Hiromi 有沢広巳, ed. *Gendai Nihon sangyō kōza*, vol. 5: *Kikai kōgyō* (1) 現代日本産業講座 5: 機械工業(1). Tokyo: Iwanami shoten, 1960.

Asada Kyōji 浅田喬二. *Nihon teikokushugi to kyū shokuminchi no jinushisei* 日本帝国主義と旧植民地の地主制. Tokyo: Mizu shobō, 1968.

Asada, Sadao. "The Japanese Navy and the United States." In *Pearl Harbor As History: Japanese-American Relations 1931–1941*, ed. Dorothy Borg and Shumpei Okamoto. New York: Columbia University Press, 1973.

Asahi shinbunsha 朝日新聞社. *Asahi nenkan* 朝日年鑑. Tokyo: Asahi shinbunsha, annual.

Asahi shinbunsha 朝日新聞社, ed. *Yokusan senkyo taikan* 翼賛選挙大觀. Tokyo: Asahi shinbunsha, 1942.

Asahi shinbunsha 朝日新聞社. *Hyakka binran* 百科便覧 (*Asahi nenkan*, 1969, appendix) 朝日年鑑別冊. Tokyo: Asahi shinbunsha, 1969.

Asahi shinbunsha yoron chōsa shitsu 朝日新聞社世論調査室編, ed. *Asahi shinbun yoron chōsa no 30-nen: Nihonjin no seiji ishiki* 朝日新聞世論調査の30年: 日本人の政治意識. Tokyo: Asahi shinbunsha, 1976.

Baerwald, Hans H. *The Purge of Japanese Leaders Under the Occupation* (*University of California Publications in Political Science*, vol. 8). Berkeley and Los Angeles: University of California Press, 1959.

Bailey, Thomas Andrew. *A Diplomatic History of the American People*. New York: Appleton-Century-Crofts, 1950.

Barraclough, Geoffrey. *An Introduction to Contemporary History*. Harmondsworth, England: Penguin, 1967.

Beckmann, George M. *The Making of the Meiji Constitution: The Oligarchs and the Constitutional Development of Japan, 1868–1891*. Lawrence: University of Kansas Press, 1957.

Beckmann, George M., and Okubo, Genji. *The Japanese Communist Party 1922–1945*. Stanford, Calif.: Stanford University Press, 1969.

Bennett, John W., and Ishino, Iwao. *Paternalism in the Japanese Economy: Anthropological Studies of Oyabun-Kobun Patterns*. Minneapolis: University of Minnesota Press, 1963.

Berger, Gordon Mark. *Parties Out of Power in Japan, 1931–1941*. Princeton, N.J.: Prinecton University Press, 1977.

Bernstein, Gail Lee. "Women in Rural Japan." In *Women in Changing Japan*, ed. Joyce Lebra et al. Boulder, Colo.: Westview Press, 1976.

Blumenthal, Tuvia トゥヴィア・ブルメンソール. "Senkanki no Nihon keizai" 戦間期の日本経済. In *Senkaki no Nihon keizai bunseki* 戦間期の日本経済分析, ed. Nakamura Takafusa 中村隆英. Tokyo: Yamakawa shuppansha, 1981.

Board of Planning. "On the National Mobilization Law." *Tokyo Gazette* 11 (May 1938): 1–9.

Board of Planning. "Invocation of the National General Mobilization Law." *Tokyo Gazette* 2 (March 1939).

Bōeichō bōei kenshūjo senshishitsu 防衛庁防衛研修所戦史室. *Senshi sōsho* 戦史叢書, 102 vols. Tokyo: Asagumo shinbunsha, 1966–80.

Bōeichō bōei kenshūjo senshishitsu 防衛庁防衛研修所戦史室. *Daihon'ei rikugunbu* 大本營陸軍部, 2 vols. Tokyo: Asagumo shinbunsha, 1967–8.

Bōeicho bōei kenshūjo senshishitsu 防衛庁防衛研修所戦史室, ed. *Kantōgun* 関東軍, vol. 1. Tokyo: Asagumo shinbunsha, 1969.

Bōeichō bōei kenshūjo senshishitsu 防衛庁防衛研修所戦史室, ed. *Daihon'ei kaigunbu: Rengō kantai* (1) 大本営海軍部: 聯合艦隊 (1). Tokyo: Asagumo shinbunsha, 1970.

Bōeichō bōei kenshūjo senshishitsu 防衛庁防衛研修所戦史室. *Daihon'ei rikugunbu: Dai Tōa sensō kaisen keii* 大本營陸軍部: 大東亜戦争開戦経緯, vol. 1. Tokyo: Asagumo shinbunsha, 1973.

Borg, Dorothy, and Okamoto, Shumpei, eds. *Pearl Harbor As History: Japanese-American Relations 1931–1941*. New York: Columbia University Press, 1973.

Boulding, Kenneth E., and Gleason, Alan H. "War as an Investment: The Strange Case of Japan." In *Economic Imperialism*, ed. Kenneth E. Boulding and Tapan Mukerjee. Ann Arbor: University of Michigan Press, 1972.

Boyle, John H. *China and Japan at War 1937–45: The Politics of Collaboration.* Stanford, Calif.: Stanford University Press, 1972.

Brown, A. J. *The Mastery of the Far East: The Story of Korea's Transformation and Japan's Rise to Supremacy in the Orient.* New York: Scribner, 1919.

Brudnoy, David. "Japan's Experiment in Korea." *Monumenta Nipponica* 25 (1970): 155–95.

Butow, Robert J. C. *Tōjō and the Coming of the War.* Princeton, N.J.: Princeton University Press, 1961.

Chang, Han-yu, and Myers, Ramon H. "Japanese Colonial Development Policy in Taiwan, 1895–1906: A Case of Bureaucratic Entrepreneurship." *Journal of Asian Studies* 22 (August 1963): 433–49.

Chen, Ching-chin. "The Japanese Administration of the Pao-chia System in Taiwan, 1895–1945." *Journal of Asian Studies* 24 (February 1975): 391–446.

Chen, Ching-chin. "Community Control Systems and the Police in Japanese Colonies." In *The Japanese Colonial Empire, 1895–1945*, ed. Ramon H. Myers and Mark R. Peattie. Princeton, N.J.: Princeton University Press, 1984.

Chen, Edward I-te. "Japanese Colonialism in Korea and Formosa: A Comparison of the Systems of Political Control." *Harvard Journal of Asiatic Studies* 30 (1970): 126–58.

Chen, Edward I-te. "Japan's Decision to Annex Taiwan: A Study in Itō-Mutsu Diplomacy." *Journal of Asian Studies* 47 (November 1977): 61–72.

Chiang Kai-shek 蒋介石. *Shō Kai-seki hiroku – 9: Manshū jihen* 蒋介石秘録·9: 満州事変. Tokyo: Sankei shinbunsha, 1976.

Chiang Kai-shek 蒋介石. *Shō Kai-seki hiroku – 12: Nitchū zenmen sensō* 蒋介石秘録·12: 日中全面戦争. Tokyo: Sankei shinbunsha, 1976.

Chiang Kai-shek 蒋介石. *Shō Kai-seki hiroku – 13: Dai Tōa sensō* 蒋介石秘録·13: 大東亜戦争. Tokyo: Sankei shinbunsha, 1977.

Chihara Jun 茅原潤. "Gunju sangyō rōdōsha no haisen e no taiō" 軍需産業労働者の敗戦への対応. In *Kyōdō kenkyū: Nihon senryō* 共同研究: 日本占領, ed. Shisō no kagaku kenkyūkai 思想の科学研究会. Tokyo: Tokuma shoten, 1972.

Chihōshi kenkyū kyōgikai 地方史研究協議会, ed. *Nihon sangyōshi taikei* 日本産業史大系, 7 vols. Tokyo: Tōkyō daigaku shuppankai, 1960.

Chubachi, Masayoshi, and Taira, Koji. "Poverty in Modern Japan: Perceptions and Realities." In *Japanese Industrialization and Its Social Consequences*, ed. Hugh T. Patrick. Berkeley and Los Angeles: University of California Press, 1976.

Chūō bukka tōsei kyōryoku kaigi 中央物価統制協力会議. *Nihon ni okeru nōgyō keiei narabi ni tochi shoyū no hensen ni kansuru sankōshiryō* 日本に於ける農業経営ならびに土地所有の変遷に関する参考資料. Tokyo: Chūō bukka tōsei kyoryoku kaigi, 1943.

Clark, Colin. *The Condition of Economic Progress*, 2nd ed. London: Macmillan, 1951.

Cohen, Jerome B. *Japan's Economy in War and Reconstruction*. Minneapolis: University of Minnesota Press, 1949.

Cohen, Theodore. "Labor Democratization in Japan: The First Years." In *The Occupation of Japan*, ed. Laurence H. Redford. Norfolk, Va.: MacArthur Memorial, 1980.

Cole, Alan B., Totten, George O., and Uyehara, Cecil H. *Socialist Parties in Postwar Japan*. New Haven, Conn.: Yale University Press, 1966.

Cole, Robert E. *Japanese Blue Collar: The Changing Tradition*. Berkeley and Los Angeles: University of California Press, 1971.

Cole, Robert E. *Work, Mobility and Participation*. Berkeley and Los Angeles: University of California Press, 1979.

Conroy, Hilary. *The Japanese Seizure of Korea, 1868–1910*. Philadelphia: University of Pennsylvania Press, 1960.

Coox, Alvin D. *Japan: The Final Agony*. New York: Ballantine, 1970.

Coox, Alvin D. *Nomonhan: Japan Against Russia, 1939*, 2 vols. Stanford, Calif.: Stanford University Press, 1985.

Crawcour, E. Sydney. "The Tokugawa Heritage." In *The State and Economic Enterprise in Japan: Essays in the Political Economy of Growth*, ed. William W. Lockwood. Princeton, N.J.: Princeton University Press, 1965.

Crawcour, E. Sydney. "Japan, 1868–1920." In *Agricultural Development in Asia*, ed. R. T. Shand. Canberra: Australian National University Press, 1969.

Crawcour, E. Sydney. "Japanese Economic Studies in Foreign Countries in the Postwar Period." *Keizai kenkyū* 経済研究 30 (January 1979): 49–64.

Crawcour, E. Sydney, and Yamamura, Kozo. "The Tokugawa Monetary System: 1787–1868." *Economic Development and Cultural Change* 18 (July 1970): pr. 1, pp. 489–518.

Crowley, James B. *Japan's Quest for Autonomy: National Security and Foreign Policy, 1930–1938*. Princeton, N.J.: Princeton University Press, 1966.

Crump, John. *The Origins of Socialist Thought*. New York: St. Martin's Press, 1983.

Curtis, Gerald L. *Election Campaigning Japanese Style*. New York: Columbia University Press, 1971.

Dai Nihon fukugyō shōreikai 大日本副業奨励会, ed. *Nihon no fukugyō* 日本の副業. Tokyo: Dai Nihon fukugyō shōreikai, 1911.

Divine, Robert A. *Roosevelt and World War II*. Baltimore: Johns Hopkins University Press, 1969.

Donnelly, Michael W. "Setting the Price of Rice: A Study in Political Decision-making." In *Policymaking in Contemporary Japan*, ed. T. J. Pempel. Ithaca, N.Y.: Cornell University Press, 1977.

Dore, Ronald P. *Land Reform in Japan*. London: Oxford University Press, 1959.

Dore, Ronald P. "The Meiji Landlord: Good or Bad?" *Journal of Asian Studies* 18 (May 1959): 343–55.

Dore, Ronald P. "Agricultural Improvement in Japan, 1870–1890." *Economic Development and Cultural Change* 9 (October 1960): 69–91.

Dore, Ronald P., ed. *Aspects of Social Change in Modern Japan*. Princeton, N.J.: Princeton University Press, 1967.

Dore, Ronald P. *British Factory – Japanese Factory: The Origins of National Diversity in Industrial Relations*. Berkeley and Los Angeles: University of California Press; London: Allen & Unwin, 1973.

Dore, Ronald P. *Shinohata: A Portrait of a Japanese Village*. London: Lane, 1978.

Dōshisha daigaku jinbunkagaku kenkyūjō 同志社大学人文科学研究所, ed. *Rikugō zasshi* 六合雑誌 (microfilm). Tokyo: Nihon shiryō kankōkai, 1964.

Dower, John W. *Empire and Aftermath: Yoshida Shigeru and the Japanese Experience, 1878–1954*. Cambridge, Mass.: Harvard University Press, 1979.

Drea, Edward J. *The 1942 Japanese General Election: Political Mobilization in Wartime Japan* (International Studies, East Asian Series Research Publication 11). Lawrence: Center for East Asian Studies, University of Kansas, 1979.

Dull, Paul S. *A Battle History of the Imperial Japanese Navy (1941–1945)*. Annapolis, Md.: U.S. Naval Institute, 1978.

Dunn, Frederick S. *Peace-Making and the Settlement with Japan*. Princeton, N.J.: Princeton University Press, 1963.

Duus, Peter. *Party Rivalry and Political Change in Taishō Japan*. Cambridge, Mass.: Harvard University Press, 1968.

Duus, Peter. "Whig History, Japanese Style: The Min'yūsha Historians and the Meiji Restoration." *Journal of Asian Studies* 33 (May 1974): 415–36.

Duus, Peter. "Yoshino Sakuzō: The Christian as Political Critic." *Journal of Japanese Studies* 4 (Spring 1978): 301–26.

Duus, Peter. "Economic Dimensions of Meiji Imperialism: The Case of Korea, 1895–1910." In *The Japanese Colonial Empire, 1895–1945*, ed. Ramon H. Myers and Mark R. Peattie. Princeton, N.J.: Princeton University Press, 1984.

Duus, Peter. "Liberal Intellectuals and Social Conflict in Taisho Japan." In *Conflict in Modern Japanese History*, ed. Tetsuo Najita and Victor Koschmann. Princeton, N.J.: Princeton University Press, 1982.

Eguchi Eiichi 江口英一. *Gendai no "teishotokusō"* 現代の「低所得層」, 3 vols. Tokyo: Miraisha, 1979–80.

Endō Saburō 遠藤三郎. *Nitchū jūgonen sensō to watakushi*. 日中十五年戦争と私. Tokyo: Nitchū shorin, 1974.

Fei, John C. H., and Ranis, Gustav. *Development of the Labor-Surplus Economy*. Homewood, Ill.: Irwin, 1964.

Fieldhouse, David. *The Colonial Empires; a Comparative Survey from the Eighteenth Century*. New York: Delacorte, 1966.

Flanagan, Scott C. "Electoral Change in Japan: An Overview." In *Political Opposition and Local Politics in Japan*, ed. Kurt Steiner, Ellis S. Krauss, and Scott C. Flanagan. Princeton, N.J.: Princeton University Press, 1980.

Fletcher, William Miles, III. *The Search for a New Order: Intellectuals and Fascism in Prewar Japan*. Chapel Hill: University of North Carolina Press, 1983.

Fogel, Joshua A. *Politics and Sinology: The Case of Naitō Kōnan (1866–1934)*. Cambridge, Mass.: Harvard University Press, 1984.

Franck, Harry A. *Glimpses of Japan and Formosa*. New York: Century, 1924.

Frank, Charles A., and Webb, Richard, eds. *Income Distribution and Growth in the Less Developed Countries*. Washington, D.C.: Brookings Institution, 1977.

Fridell, Wilbur M. *Japanese Shrine Mergers 1906–12: State Shinto Moves to the Grassroots*. Tokyo: Sophia University Press, 1973.

Fuchida Mitsuo 淵田美津雄. *Shinjuwan sakusen no shinsō* 真珠湾作戦の真相. Tokyo: Kawade shobō, 1967.

Fujii, Shōichi. "Capitalism, International Politics, and the Emperor System." In *The Emergence of Imperial Japan: Self-Defense or Calculated Aggression?* ed. Marlene Mayo. Lexington, Mass.: Heath, 1970.

Fujimura Michio 藤村道生. "Iwayuru jūgatsu jiken no saikentō" いわゆる十月事件の再検討. *Nihon rekishi* 日本歴史, no. 393 (February 1981): 52–65.

Fujinawa Masakatsu 藤縄正勝. *Nihon no saitei chingin* 日本の最低賃金. Tokyo: Nikkan rōdō tsūshinsha, 1972.

Fujiwara Akira 藤原彰, Imai Seiichi 今井清一 and Tōyama Shigeki 遠山茂樹. *Shōwa shi* 昭和史, rev. ed. Tokyo: Iwanami shoten, 1959.

Fukai Eigo 深井英吾. *Kaiko shichijūnen* 回顧七十年. Tokyo: Iwanami shoten, 1941.

Fukawa Kiyoshi 布川清司. "Nihonjin no hi-senryō kan" 日本人の被占領観. In *Kyōdō kenkyū: Nihon senryō* 共同研究: 日本占領, ed. Shisō no kagaku kenkyūkai 思想の科学研究会. Tokyo: Tokuma shoten, 1972.

Fukudome Shigeru 福留繁. *Kaigun no hansei* 海軍の反省. Tokyo: Nihon shuppan kyōdō, 1951.

Fukudome Shigeru 福留繁. *Shikan: Shinjuwan kōgeki* 史観: 真珠湾攻撃. Tokyo: Jiyū Ajiyasha, 1955.

Fukui Haruhiro 福井治弘. *Jiyū minshutō to seisaku kettei* 自由民主党と政策決定. Tokyo: Fukumura shuppan, 1969.

Fukui, Haruhiro. *Party in Power: The Japanese Liberal-Democrats and Policy-making*. Canberra: Australian National University; Berkeley and Los Angeles: University of California Press, 1970.

Fukui, Haruhiro. "The Japanese Communist Party: The Miyamoto Line and Its Problems." In *The Many Faces of Communism*, ed. Morton A. Kaplan. New York: Free Press, 1978.

Fukushima Jūrō 福島鑄郎. "Senryōka ni okeru ken'etsu seisaku to sono jittai" 占領下における検閲政策とその実態. In *Senryōki Nihon no keizai to seiji* 占領期日本の経済と政治, ed. Nakamura Takafusa 中村隆英. Tokyo: Tōkyō daigaku shuppankai, 1979.

Fukushima Masao 福島正夫, Kawashima Takeyoshi 川島武宜, Tsuji Kiyoaki 辻清明 and Ukai Nobushige 鵜飼信成, eds. *Kōza: Nihon kindaihō hattatsu shi – shihonshugi to hō no hatten* 講座: 日本近代法発達史—資本主義と法の発展, vol. 6. Tokyo: Keisō shobō, 1959.

Fukutake, Tadashi. *Japanese Rural Society*, trans. Ronald P. Dore. New York: Oxford University Press, 1967.

Funayama Shin'ichi 船山信一. *Meiji tetsugakushi* 明治哲学史. Kyoto: Minerva shobō, 1959.

Furushima Kazuo 古島一雄. Ichi rō-seijika no kaisō 一老政治家の回想. Tokyo: Chūō kōronsha, 1951.

Furuta Hikaru 古田光. *Kawakami Hajime* 河上肇. Tokyo: Tōkyō daigaku shuppanbu, 1959.

Gaimushō 外務省, ed. *Shūsen shiroku* 終戦史録. Tokyo: Shinbun gekkansha, 1952.

Gaimushō 外務省, ed. *Nihon gaikō nenpyō narabini shuyō bunsho – jo* 日本外交年表竝主要文書·上, rev. ed. Tokyo: Hara shobō, *1965*.

Gaimushō 外務省, ed. *Nihon gaikō nenpyō narabi ni shuyō bunsho-ge* 日本外交年表竝主要文書·下. Tokyo: Hara shobō, 1966.

Gaimushō chōsabu 外務省調査部. "Nihon koyū no gaikō shidō genri kōryō" Dec. 1939. 日本固有の外交指導原理綱領. In *Gaikō shiryōkan shiryō* 外交資料館資料 (Foreign Ministry File No. A-1-0-0-6).

Galenson, Walter, and Odaka, Konosuke. "The Japanese Labor Market." In *Asia's New Giant: How the Japanese Economy Works*, ed. Hugh T. Patrick and Henry Rosovsky. Washington, D.C.: Brookings Institution, 1976.

Gayn, Mark. *Japan Diary*. Tokyo: Tuttle, 1981.

Genda Minoru 源田実. *Kaigun kōkūtai shimatsuki* 海軍航空隊始末記, 2 vols. Tokyo: Bungei shunjūsha, 1968.

*Gendaishi shiryō* 現代史資料. *Nitchū sensō* 日中戦争, vols. 8–10, 12–13, 1964–66; *Taiheiyō sensō* 太平洋戦争, vol. 34–36, 38–39, 1968–75; *Daihonei* 大本営, vol. 37, 1967. Tokyo: Misuzu shobō.

Gerschenkron, Alexander. *Economic Backwardness in Historical Perspective: A Book of Essays*. Cambridge, Mass: Belknap, 1962.

Gluck, Carol. *Japan's Modern Myths: Ideology in the Late Meiji Period.* Princeton, N.J.: Princeton University Press, 1985.

Gomikawa Junpei 五味川純平. *Gozen kaigi* 御前会議. Tokyo: Bungei shunjūsha, 1978.

Gondō Seikei 権藤成卿. "Jichi minsei ri" 自治民政理. In *Gendai Nihon shisō taikei*, vol. 31: *Chōkokkashugi* 現代日本思想大系, 31: 超国家主義, ed. Hashikawa Bunzō 橋川文三. Tokyo: Chikuma shobō, 1964.

Gordon, Andrew. *The Evolution of Labor Relations in Japan: Heavy Industry, 1853–1955*. Cambridge, Mass.: Harvard University Press, 1985.

Gotō Yasushi 後藤靖, ed. *Tennōsei to minshū* 天皇制と民衆. Tokyo: Tōkyō daigaku shuppankai, 1976.

Gouldner, Alvin. *The Two Marxisms*. New York: Oxford University Press, 1980.

Government Section, Supreme Commander for the Allied Powers. *Political Reorientation of Japan, September 1945 to September 1948*, 2 vols., Reprint ed. Grosse Pointe, Mich.: Scholarly Press, 1968.

Grajdanzev, Andrew. *Modern Korea: Her Economic and Social Development Under the Japanese*. New York: Institute of Pacific Relations, 1944.

Grajdanzev, Andrew. *Formosa Today: An Analysis of the Economic Development and Strategic Importance of Japan's Tropical Colony*. New York: Institute of Pacific Relations, 1942.

Griswold, Alfred Whitney. *The Far Eastern Policy of the United States*. New York: Harcourt, Brace, 1938.

Hadley, Eleanor. *Antitrust in Japan*. Princeton, N.J.: Princeton University Press, 1970.

Hafner, Sebastian. *Hitorā to wa nanika* ヒトラーとは何か, trans. Akabane Tatsuo 赤羽竜夫. Tokyo: Sōshisha, 1979.

Hagiwara Sakutarō 萩原朔太郎. *Nihon e no kaiki* 日本への回歸. Tokyo: Hakusuisha, 1938.

Hagiwara Susumu 萩原進. "Senji chingin tōsei no isan" 戦時賃金統制の遺産. *Chingin fōramu* 賃金フォーラム, nos. 11–20 (1977).

Hall, John Whitney. "A Monarch for Modern Japan." In *Political Development in Modern Japan*, ed. Robert E. Ward. Princeton, N.J.: Princeton University Press, 1968.

Hanzawa Hiroshi 判沢弘. *Ajia e no yume* アジアへの夢, vol. 6 of *Meiji no gunzō* 明治の群像. Tokyo: San'ichi shobō, 1970.

Hara Akinori 原晃徳. *Teikoku kaigun shireichōkan no nazo* 帝国海軍司令長官の謎. Tokyo: Tokuma shoten, 1972.

Hara Akira 原朗. "1930 nendai no Manshū keizai tōsei seisaku" 1930年代の満州経済統制政策. In *Nihon teikokushugika no Manshū* 日本帝国主義下の満州, ed. Manshū kenkyūkai 満州研究会. Tokyo: Ochanomizu shobō, 1972.

Hara Akira 原朗. " 'Manshū' ni okeru keizai tōsei seisaku no tenkai – Mantetsu kaiso to Mangyō setsuritsu o megutte" 「満州」における経済統制政策の展開—満鉄改組と満業設立をめぐって. In *Nihon keizai seisakushi ron – ge* 日本経済政策史論—下, ed. Andō Yoshio 安藤良雄. Tokyo: Tōkyō daigaku shuppankai, 1976.

Hara Shirō 原司郎. "Kinyū kikan tachinaoru" 金融機関立ち直る. In *Shōwa keizai shi* 昭和経済史, ed. Arisawa Hiromi 有沢広巳. Tokyo: Nihon keizai shinbunsha, 1976.

Hara Takashi 原敬. *Hara Takashi nikki* 原敬日記, vol. 8. Tokyo: Tōkyō kengensha, 1950.

Hara Takashi 原敬. *Hara Takashi nikki* 原敬日記, vol. 2. Tokyo: Fukumaru shuppan, 1965.

Harada Kumao 原田熊雄. *Saionji-kō to seikyoku* 西園寺公と政局 (also known as *Harada nikki* 原田日記), 9 vols., ed. Maruyama Masao 丸山眞男 and Hayashi

Shigeru 林茂. Tokyo: Iwanami shoten, 1950–6.
Harris, John R., and Todaro, Michael P. "Migration, Unemployment and Development: A Two-Sector Analysis." *American Economic Review* 60 (March 1970): 126–42.
Hashikawa Bunzō 橋川文三. "Kakushin kanryō" 革新官僚. In *Kenryoku no shisō* 権力の思想, vol. 10 of *Gendai Nihon shisō taikei* 現代日本思想大系. ed. Kamishima Jirō 神島次郎. Tokyo: Chikuma shobō, 1965.
Hata Ikuhiko 秦郁彦. *Nitchū sensō shi* 日中戦争史. Tokyo: Kawade shobō, 1961.
Hata Ikuhiko 秦郁彦. *Gun fashizumu undōshi* 軍ファシズム運動史. Tokyo: Kawade shobō shinsha, 1972.
Hata Ikuhiko 秦郁彦. *Taiheiyō kokusai kankei shi* 太平洋国際関係史. Tokyo: Fukumura shuppan, 1972.
Hata Ikuhiko 秦郁彦. *Taiheiyō sensō: Roku daikessen: Naze Nihon wa yaburetaka* 太平洋戦争: 六大決戦: なぜ日本は敗れたか. Tokyo: Yomiuri shinbunsha, 1976.
Hata Ikuhiko 秦郁彦. *Nitchū sensō shi* 日中戦争史, rev. ed. Tokyo: Hara shobō, 1979.
Hata Ikuhiko 秦郁彦. "Onnenshikan kara no dakkyaku" 怨念史観からの脱却. *Keizai ōrai* 経済往来 (February 1979).
Hata Ikuhiko 秦郁彦. "Rokōkyō daiippatsu no hannin" 蘆溝橋第一発の犯人. In *Ichiokunin no Shōwa shi 3: Nitchū sensō (2)* 一億人の昭和史 3: 日中戦争 (2). Tokyo: Mainichi shinbunsha, 1979.
Hata Ikuhiko 秦郁彦. *Gun fashizumu undōshi* 軍ファシズム運動史, rev. ed. Tokyo: Hara shobō, 1980.
Hata Ikuhiko 秦郁彦. "Ryojōkō jiken no saikentō" 柳条溝事件の再検討. *Seiji keizai shigaku* 政治経済史学, no. 183 (August 1981): 1–19.
Hatada Takashi 旗田巍. "Nihonjin no Chōsenkan" 日本人の朝鮮観. In *Nihon to Chōsen* 日本と朝鮮, vol. 3 of *Ajia-Afurika Kōza* アジア·アフリカ講座. Tokyo: Keiso shobō, 1965.
Hatai, Yoshitaka. "Business Cycles and the Outflow of Labor from the Agricultural Sector." In *The Labor Market in Japan*, ed. Shunsaku Nishikawa and trans. Ross Mouer. Tokyo: Tokyo University Press, 1980.
Hatanaka Sachiko, comp. *A Bibliography of Micronesia from Japanese Publication* [*sic*]. *Occasional Papers* no. 8, Gakushūin University, Tokyo, 1979.
Hatano Sumio 波多野澄雄. " 'Tōa shinchitsujo' to chiseigaku" 「東亜新秩序」と地政学. In *Nihon no 1930 nendai* 日本の一九三〇年代, ed. Miwa Kimitada 三輪公忠. Tokyo: Sōryūsha, 1980.
Hattori Takushirō 服部卓四郎. *Dai Tōa sensō zenshi* 大東亜戦争全史, 4 vols. Tokyo: Masu shobō, 1953.
Havens, Thomas R. H. *Farm and Nation in Modern Japan: Agrarian Nationalism, 1870–1940*. Princeton, N.J.: Princeton University Press, 1974.
Havens, Thomas R. H. *Valley of Darkness: The Japanese People and World War Two*. New York: Norton, 1978.
Hayami, Yujirō, in association with Masakatsu Akino, Masahiko Shintani, and

Saburō Yamada. *A Century of Agricultural Growth in Japan, Its Relevance to Asian Development*. Minneapolis: University of Minnesota Press; and Tokyo: Tokyo University Press, 1965.

Hayami, Yūjirō, and Yamada, Saburō. "Agricultural Productivity and the Beginning of Industrialization." In *Agriculture and Economic Growth: Japan's Experience*, ed. Kazushi Ohkawa et al. Tokyo: Tokyo University Press; and Princeton, N.J.: Princeton University Press, 1969.

Hayashi Chikio 林知己夫. "Sengo no seiji ishiki" 戦後の政治意識. *Jiyū* 自由 (January 1964): 57–65.

Hayashi Chikio 林知己夫. "Nihonjin no ishiki wa seitōshijibetsu ni dō chigau ka" 日本人の意識は政党支持別にどう違うか. *Nihonjin kenkyū* 日本人研究 No. 2 (*Tokushū: Shijiseitōbetsu nihonjin shūdan*) 特集: 支持政党別日本人集団, ed. Nihonjin kenkyūkai 日本人研究会. Tokyo: Shiseidō, 1975.

Hayashi Fusao 林房雄. *Dai Tōa sensō kōteiron* 大東亜戦争肯定論, 2 vols. Tokyo: Banchō shobō, 1964, 1966.

Hayashi Saburō 林三郎. *Taiheiyō sensō rikusen gaishi* 太平洋戦争陸戦概史. Tokyo: Iwanami shoten, 1951.

Hayashi Shigeru 林茂. *Nihon shūsenshi* 日本終戦史, 3 vols. Tokyo: Yomiuri shinbunsha, 1962.

Hayashi Shigeru 林茂, *Taiheiyō sensō* 太平洋戦争. *Nihon no rekishi* 日本の歴史, vol. 25. Tokyo: Chūō kōronsha, 1967.

Hayashi Shigeru 林茂, and Tsuji Kiyoaki 辻清明. *Nihon naikakushi roku* 日本内閣史録, 6 vols. Tokyo: Daiichi hōki, 1981.

Hayashi Shigeru 林茂 et al., eds. *Heimin shinbun ronsetsushū* 平民新聞論説集. Tokyo: Iwanami shoten, 1961.

Hayashi Takehisa 林健久. "Shaupu kankoku to zeisei kaikaku" シャウプ勧告と税制改革. In *Keizai kaikaku* 経済改革, vol. 7 of *Sengo kaikaku* 戦後改革, ed. Tōkyō daigaku shakaikagaku kenkyūjo 東京大学社会科学研究所. Tokyo: Tōkyō daigaku shuppankai, 1974–5.

Hazama Hiroshi 間宏. *Nihon rōmu kanrishi kenkyū* 日本労務管理史研究. Tokyo: Diamondosha, 1964.

Hellmann, Donald C. *Japanese Domestic Politics and Foreign Policy: The Peace Agreement with the Soviet Union*. Berkeley and Los Angeles: University of California Press, 1969.

Hellmann, Donald C. *Japan and East Asia: The New International Order*. New York: Praeger, 1972.

Henderson, Dan F., ed. *The Constitution of Japan: Its First Twenty Years, 1947–67*. Seattle: University of Washington Press, 1968.

Henderson, Gregory. *Korea: Politics of the Vortex*. Cambridge, Mass: Harvard University Press, 1966.

Higashikuni Naruhiko 東久邇稔彦. *Ichi kōzoku no sensō nikki* 一皇族の戦争日記. Tokyo: Nihon shūhōsha, 1959.

Hijikata Seibi 土方成美. "Shokugyōbetsu jinkō no hensen o tsūjite mitaru shitsugyō mondai" 職業別人口の変遷を通じて見たる失業問題. *Shakai seisaku*

*jihō* 社会政策時報 108 (September 1929).
Hirai Tomoyoshi 平井友義. "Soren no dōkō (1933 nen-1939 nen)" ソ連の動向一九三三年—一九三九年. In *Taiheiyō sensō e no michi* 太平洋戦争への道, vol. 4, ed. Nihon kokusai seiji gakkai Taiheiyō sensō gen'in kenkyūbu 日本国際政治学会太平洋戦争原因研究部. Tokyo: Asahi shinbunsha, 1963.
Hirano Ken'ichirō 平野健一郎. "Manshū jihenzen ni okeru zai-Man Nihonjin no dōkō" 満州事変前における在満日本人の動向. *Kokusai seiji* 国際政治, no. 43 (1970): 51-76.
Hirano Yoshitarō 平野義太郎, ed. *Kōtoku Shūsui senshū* 幸徳秋水選集, 3 vols. Tokyo: Sekai hyōronsha, 1948-50.
Hiratsuka Atsushi 平塚篤, ed. *Itō Hirobumi hiroku* 伊藤博文秘録. Tokyo: Bunshusha, 1929.
Hiratsuka Atsushi 平塚篤, ed. *Zoku Itō Hirobumi hiroku* 続伊藤博文秘録. Tokyo: Bunshūsha, 1930.
Hiromatsu Wataru 廣松渉. *Kindai no chōkoku ron* 近代の超克論. Tokyo: Asahi shuppansha, 1980.
Hirota Kōki denki kankōkai 広田弘毅伝記刊行会, ed. *Hirota Kōki* 広田弘毅. Tokyo: Chūō kōron jigyō shuppan, 1966.
Hirschman, Albert O. *Exit, Voice, and Loyalty*. Cambridge, Mass.: Harvard University Press, 1970.
Hirschmeier, Johannes, S. V. D. "Shibusawa Eiichi: Industrial Pioneer." In *The State and Economic Enterprise in Japan: Essays in the Political Economy of Growth*, ed. William W. Lockwood. Princeton, N.J.: Princeton University Press, 1965.
Hirschmeier, Johannes, and Yui Tsunehiko. *The Development of Japanese Business, 1600-1973*. London: Allen & Unwin, 1975.
Ho, Samuel P. S. "Agricultural Transformations Under Colonialism: The Case of Taiwan." *Journal of Economic History* 28 (September 1968): 313-40.
Ho, Samuel P. S. "The Economic Development Policy of the Japanese Colonial Government in Taiwan, 1895-1945." In *Government and Economic Development*, ed. Gustav Ranis. New Haven, Conn.: Yale University Press, 1971.
Ho, Samuel P. S. "The Economic Development of Colonial Taiwan: Evidence and Interpretations." *Journal of Asian Studies* 34 (February 1975): 417-39.
Hofstadter, Richard. *The Idea of a Party System*. Berkeley and Los Angeles: University of California Press, 1969.
Horiba Kazuo 堀場一雄. *Shina jihen sensō shidō shi* 支那事変戦争指導史. Tokyo: Jiji tsūshinsha, 1962.
Hornbeck, Stanley. Memorandum, September 5, 1941. Hornbeck papers, Box 254, Hoover Institution, Stanford University, Stanford, Calif.
Hōsei daigaku Ōhara shakai mondai kenkyūjo 法政大学大原社会問題研究所. *Taiheiyō sensōka no rōdōsha jōtai* 太平洋戦争下の労働者状態. Tokyo: Tōyō keizai shinpōsha, 1964.
Hoshino Naoki 星野直樹. *Mihatenu yume: Manshūkoku gaishi* 見果てぬ夢: 満州国外史. Tokyo: Diamondosha, 1963.

Hoshino Yasusaburō 星野安三郎. "Keisatsu seido no kaikaku" 警察制度の改革. In *Seiji katei* 政治過程, vol. 3 of *Sengo kaikaku* 戦後改革, ed. Tōkyō daigaku shakaikagaku kenkyūjo 東京大学社会科学研究所編. Tokyo: Tōkyō daigaku shuppankai, 1974–5.

Hosoi Wakizō 細井和喜蔵. *Jokō aishi* 女工哀史. Tokyo: Kaizōsha, 1925.

Hoston, Germaine A. *Marxism and the Crisis of Development in Prewar Japan*. Princeton, N.J.: Princeton University Press, 1986.

Hozumi Yatsuka 穂積八束. *Kenpō teiyō* 憲法提要. Tokyo: Yūhikaku, 1935.

Hunt, Frazier. *The Untold Story of Douglas MacArthur*. New York: Devin-Adair, 1954.

Ichihara Ryōhei 市原亮平. "Seitō rengō undō no kiban: 'Zaibatsu no tenkō' o shōten to shite" 政党連合運動の基盤:「財閥の轉向」を焦點として *Keizai ronsō* 經済論叢73 (February 1954): 106–22.

Ichihara Ryōhei 市原亮平. "Seitō rengō undō no hasan: 'Teijin jiken' o shōten to shite" 政党連合運動の破産:「帝人事件」を焦點として, *Keizai ronsō* 經済論叢73 (March 1954): 161–82.

Ide Yoshinori 井出嘉憲. "Sengo kaikaku to Nihon kanryōsei: Kōmuin seido no sōshutsu katei" 戦後改革と日本官僚制—公務員制度の創出過程. In *Seiji katei* 政治過程, vol. 3 of *Sengo kaikaku* 戦後改革, ed. Tōkyō daigaku shakaikagaku kenkyūjo 東京大学社会科学研究所編. Tokyo: Tōkyō daigaku shuppankai, 1974–5.

Ienaga Saburō 家永三郎. *Taiheiyō sensō* 太平洋戦争. Tokyo: Iwanami shoten, 1968.

Ike, Nobutaka. *Japan's Decision for War*. Stanford, Calif.: Stanford University Press, 1967.

Ike, Nobutaka. "War and Modernization." In *Political Development in Modern Japan*, ed. Robert E. Ward. Princeton, N.J.: Princeton University Press, 1968.

Ikeda Shigeaki 池田成彬. *Zaikai kaiko* 財界回顧. Tokyo: Konnichi no mondaisha, 1949.

Iki Makoto 伊木誠. "Izanagi keiki" いざなぎ景気. In *Shōwa keizai shi* 昭和経済史, ed. Arisawa Hiromi 有沢広巳. Tokyo: Nihon keizai shinbunsha, 1976.

Imada Sachiko 今田幸子. "Gakureki kōzō no suisei bunseki" 学歴構造の趨勢分析. In *Nihon no kaisō kōzō* 日本の階層構造, ed. Tominaga Ken'ichi 富永健一. Tokyo: Tōkyō daigaku shuppankai, 1979.

Imada Takatoshi 今田高俊 and Hara Junsuke 原純輔. "Shakaiteki chii no ik-kansei to hi-ikkansei" 社会的地位の一貫性と非一貫性. In *Nihon no kaisō kōzō* 日本の階層構造, ed. Tominaga Ken'ichi 富永健一. Tokyo: Tōkyō daigaku shuppankai, 1979.

Imai Seiichi 今井清一 and Itō Takashi 伊藤隆, eds. *Kokka sōdōin* 国家総動員, vol. 2 of *Gendai shi shiryō* 現代史資料. Tokyo: Misuzu shobō, 1974.

Imamura Hitoshi 今村均. *Shiki: Ichigunjin rokujūnen no aikan* 私記: 一軍人六十年の哀歓. Tokyo: Fuyō shobō, 1970.

Imanishi Kinji 今西錦司, ed. *Ponape-tō* ポナペ島. Tokyo: Shoko shoin, 1944.

Inoguchi Rikihei 猪口力平 and Nakajima Tadashi 中島正. *Kamikaze tokubetsu kōgekitai* 神風特別攻撃隊. Tokyo: Nihon shuppan kyōdōsha, 1951.

Inoki Masamichi 猪木正道. *Hyōden Yoshida Shigeru* 評伝吉田茂, 4 vols. Tokyo: Yomiuri shinbunsha, 1981.

Inoue Ichirō 井上一郎. "Senryō shoki no sozei gyōsei'in" 占領初期の租税行政院. In *Kyōdō kenkyū: Nihon senryōgun: Sono hikari to kage* 共同研究: 日本占領軍その光と影, ed. Shisō no kagaku kenkyūkai 思想の科学研究会. Tokyo: Tokuma shoten, 1978.

Inoue Kiyoshi 井上清. "Nihon teikokushugi no keisei" 日本帝国主義の形成. In *Kindai Nihon no keisei* 近代日本の形成, ed. Rekishigaku kenkyūkai 歴史学研究会. Tokyo: Iwanami shoten, 1953.

Inoue Kiyoshi 井上清 and Watanabe Tōru 渡部徹, eds. *Kome sōdō no kenkyū* 米騒動の研究, vol. 5. Tokyo: Yūhikaku, 1962.

International Military Tribunal for the Far East. "Proceedings" (mimeographed). Tokyo, 1946–9.

Inumaru Yoshikazu 犬丸義一. *Kōza: Gendai no ideorogii II, Nihon no marukusushugi, sono 2* 講座: 現代のイデオロギーII, 日本のマルクス主義, その 2, Tokyo: San'ichi shobō, 1961.

Iriye, Akira. *After Imperialism: The Search for a New Order in the Far East, 1931–1941*. Cambridge, Mass.: Harvard University Press, 1965.

Iriye Akira 入江昭. *Nichi-Bei sensō* 日米戦争. Tokyo: Chūō kōronsha, 1978.

Ishibashi Tanzan 石橋湛山. *Ishibashi Tanzan zenshū* 石橋湛山全集, 15 vols. Tokyo: Tōyō keizai shinpōsha: 1970–2.

Ishida Takeshi. "Movements to Protect Constitutional Government – A Structural Functional Analysis." In *Democracy in Prewar Japan: Groundwork or Façade?* ed. George O. Totten. Lexington, Mass.: Heath, 1965.

Ishida, Takeshi. "The Development of Interest Groups and the Pattern of Political Modernization in Japan." In *Political Development in Modern Japan*, ed. Robert E. Ward. Princeton, N.J.: Princeton University Press, 1968.

Ishida Takeshi 石田雄. "Sengo kaikaku to soshiki oyobi shōchō" 戦後改革と組織および象徴. In *Kadai to shikaku* 課題と視角, vol. 1 of *Sengo kaikaku* 戦後改革, ed. Tōkyō daigaku shakaikagaku kenkyūjo 東京大学社会科学研究所. Tokyo: Tōkyō daigaku shuppankai, 1974–5.

Ishida, Takeshi, and George, Aurelia D. "Nōkyō: The Japanese Farmers' Representative." In *Japan & Australia: Two Societies and Their Interaction*, ed. Peter Drysdale and Hironobu Kitaoji. Canberra: Australian National University Press, 1981.

Ishii Itarō 石射猪太郎. *Gaikōkan no isshō* 外交官の一生. Tokyo: Yomiuri shinbunsha, 1950.

Ishii Kin'ichirō 石井金一郎. "Nihon fuashizumu to chihō seido: 1943-nen no hōkaisei o chūshin ni" 日本ファシズムと地方制度: 1943年の法改正を中心に. In *Rekishigaku kenkyū* 歴史学研究 307 (December 1965): 1–12.

Ishikawa Shingo 石川信吾. *Shinjuwan made no keii* 真珠湾までの経緯. Tokyo: Jiji tsūshinsha, 1960.

Ishikawa Tatsuzo 石川達三. "Kokoro no naka no sensō" 心の中の戦争. *Chūō kōron* 中央公論 (March 1963): 201–7.

Ishiwara Kanji 石原莞爾. "Genzai oyobi shōrai ni okeru Nihon no kokubō" 現在及将来における日本の国防. In *Ishiwara Kanji shiryō (2): Sensō shiron* 石原莞爾資料(2): 戦争史論, ed. Tsunoda Jun 角田順. Tokyo: Hara shobō, 1967.

Ishiwara Kanji 石原莞爾. *Ishiwara Kanji shiryō (1): Kokubō ronsaku* 石原莞爾資料(1): 国防論策, ed. Tsunoda Jun 角田順. Tokyo: Hara shobō, 1971.

Ishizaki Tadao 石崎唯雄. "Sangyō kōzō to shūgyō kōzō" 産業構造と就業構造. In *Waga kuni kanzen koyō no igi to taisaku* 我国完全雇用の意義と対策, ed. Shōwa dōjinkai 昭和同人会編. Tokyo: Shōwa dōjinkai, 1957.

Ito, Daikichi. "The Bureaucracy: Its Attitudes and Behavior." *The Developing Economies* 6 (December 1968).

Ito, Hirobumi. *Commentaries on the Constitution of Empire of Japan*, trans. Miyoji Ito. Tokyo: Chūō daigaku, 1906.

Itō Mitsuharu 伊東光晴. *Hoshu to kakushin no Nihonteki kōzō* 保守と革新の日本的構造. Tokyo: Chikuma shobō, 1970.

Itō Takashi 伊藤隆. *Shōwa shoki seijishi kenkyū* 昭和初期政治史研究. Tokyo: Tōkyō daigaku shuppankai, 1969.

Ito, Takashi. "Conflicts and Coalitions in Japan, 1930: Political Groups [and] the London Naval Disarmament Conference." In *The Study of Coalition Behavior*, ed. Sven Groennings, W. W. Kelley, and Michael Leiserson. New York: Holt, Rinehart and Winston, 1970.

Itō Takashi 伊藤隆. " 'Kyokoku itchi' naikakuki no seikai saihensei mondai: Shōwa jūsan-nen Konoe shintō mondai kenkyū no tame ni" 「挙国一致」内閣期の政界再編成問題: 昭和十三年近衛新党問題研究のために. In *Shakai kagaku kenkyū* 社会科学研究 24 (1972): 56–130.

Ito, Takashi. "The Role of Right-Wing Organizations in Japan." In *Pearl Harbor As History: Japanese-American Relations 1931–1941*, ed. Dorothy Borg and Shumpei Okamoto. New York: Columbia University Press, 1973.

Itō Takashi 伊藤隆. *Taishōki "Kakushin" ha no seiritsu* 大正期「革新」派の成立, Tokyo: Hanawa shoten, 1978.

Itō Takashi 伊藤隆. "Sengo seitō no keisei katei" 戦後政党の形成過程 In *Senryōki Nihon no keizai to seiji* 占領期日本の経済と政治, ed. Nakamura Takafusa 中村隆英. Tokyo: Tōkyō daigaku shuppankai, 1979.

Itoya Toshio 糸屋寿雄. *Kōtoku shūsui kenkyū* 幸徳秋水研究. Tokyo: Aoki shoten, 1967.

Iwabuchi Tatsuo 岩淵辰雄. *Yabururu hi made* 敗る日まで. Tokyo: Nihon shūhōsha, 1946.

Iwamoto Sumiaki 岩本純明. "Senryōgun no tai-Nichi nōgyō seisaku" 占領軍の対日農業政策. In *Senryōki nihon no keizai to seiji* 占領期日本の経済と政治, ed. Nakamura Takafusa 中村隆英. Tokyo: Tōkyō daigaku shuppankai, 1979.

Iwasaki Chikatsugu 岩崎允胤. *Nihon marukusushugi tetsugakushi josetsu* 日本マルクス主義哲学史序説. Tokyo: Miraisha, 1971.

Izumiyama Sanroku 泉山三六. *Tora daijin ni naru made* トラ大臣になるまで.

Tokyo: Tōhō shoin, 1953.

Jansen, Marius B. *The Japanese and Sun Yat-sen*. Cambridge, Mass.: Harvard University Press, 1954.

Jansen, Marius B. "Modernization and Foreign Policy in Meiji Japan." In *Political Development in Modern Japan*, ed. Robert E. Ward. Princeton, N.J.: Princeton University Press, 1968.

Jay, Martin. *The Dialectical Imagination*. Boston: Little, Brown, 1973.

Jiji tsūshinsha 時事通信社. *Jiji nenkan* 時事年鑑. Tokyo: Jiji tsūshinsha, annual.

Johnson, Chalmers. "Japan: Who Governs? An Essay on Official Bureaucracy." *Journal of Japanese Studies* 2 (Autumn 1975): 1–28.

Johnson, Chalmers. *MITI and the Japanese Miracle: The Growth of Industrial Policy, 1925–1975*. Berkeley and Los Angeles: University of California Press, 1982.

Johnston, Bruce F. "The Japanese 'Model' of Agricultural Development: Its Relevance to Developing Nations." In *Agriculture and Economic Growth: Japan's Experience*, ed. Kazushi Ohkawa et al. Tokyo: Tokyo University Press; and Princeton, N.J.: Princeton University Press, 1969.

Jūyō sangyō kyōgikai 重要産業協議会. *Gunju kaishahō kaisetsu* 軍需会社法解説. Tokyo: Teikoku shuppan, 1944.

Kahn, Herman. *The Emerging Japanese Superstate: Challenge and Response*. Englewood Cliffs, N.J.: Prentice-Hall, 1970.

Kajimura Hideki 梶村秀樹. "Shokuminchi Chōsen de no Nihonjin" 植民地朝鮮での日本人. In *Chihō demokurashii to sensō* 地方デモクラシーと戦争, ed. Kimbara Samon 金原左門, vol. 9 of *Chihō bunka no Nihonshi* 地方文化の日本史. Tokyo: Bun'ichi sokai shuppan, 1978.

Kamei Katsuichirō 亀井勝一郎 and Takeuchi Yoshimi 竹内好, eds. *Kindai Nihon shisōshi kōza*, vol. 7: *Kindaika to dentō* 近代日本思想構座, 7, 近代化と伝統. Tokyo: Chikuma shobō, 1959.

Kamishima Jirō 神島二郎, ed. *Kenryoku no shisō* 権力の思想, vol. 10 of *Gendai Nihon shisō taikei* 現代日本思想大系. Tokyo: Chikuma shobō, 1965.

Kanamori Hisao 金森久雄. "Tenbō I: Kyōran doto no naka no seichō" 展望 I：狂瀾怒濤の中の成長. In *Shōwa keizai shi* 昭和経済史, ed. Arisawa Hiromi 有沢広巳. Tokyo: Nihon keizai shinbunsha, 1976.

Kaneda, Hiromitsu. "Long-Term Changes in Food Consumption Patterns in Japan." In *Agriculture and Economic Growth, Japan's Experience*, ed. Kazushi Ohkawa et al. Princeton, N.J.: Princeton University Press, 1969.

Kaneko Tamio 金子人雄. *Chūō Ajia ni haitta Nihonjin* 中央アジアに入った日本人. Tokyo: Shinjinbutsu ōraisha, 1973.

Kankyōchō 環境庁. *Kankyō hakusho* 環境白書. Tokyo: Ōkurashō insatsu kyoku, annual.

Kannappan, Subbiah, ed. *Studies of Urban Labour Market Behaviour in Developing Areas*. Geneva: International Institute for Labour Studies, 1977.

Kanō Masanao 鹿野政直. "Meiji kōki ni okeru kokumin soshikika no katei" 明治後期における国民組織化の過程. *Shikan* 史観, no. 69 (March 1964): 18–46.

Kanō Masanao 鹿野政直. *Taishō demokurashii no teiryū* 大正デモクラシーの底流. Tokyo: Nihon hōsō shuppan kyōkai, 1973.

*Kanpō gogai–Shōwa 12-nen 1-gatsu 22-nichi, Shūgiin giji sokkiroku dai 3-go.* 官報号外·昭和十二年一月二十二日, 衆議院議事速記録第三号.

*Kanpō gogai–Shōwa 14-nen 1-gatsu 22-nichi, Shūgiin giji sokkiroku dai 3-go.* 官報号外·昭和十四年一月二十二日, 衆議院議事速記録第三号.

Kaplan, Morton A., ed. *The Many Faces of Communism*. New York: Free Press, 1978.

Karita Tōru 刈田徹. *Shōwa shoki seiji–gaikō shi kenkyū* 昭和初期政治·外交史研究. Tokyo: Ningen no kagakusha, 1978.

Karube Kiyoshi 加留部清. "Nihonjin wa dono yō ni shite shijiseitō o kimeru ka" 日本人はどのようにして支持政党をきめるか. In *Tokushū: Shijiseitōbetsu Nihonjin shūdan* 特集: 支持党別日本人集団, vol. 2 of *Nihonjin kenkyū* 日本人研究, ed. Nihonjin kenkyūkai 日本人研究会. Tokyo: Shiseidō, 1975.

Kata Kōji 加太こうじ. "Gunsei jidai no fūzoku" 軍政時代の風俗. In *Kyōdō kenkyū: Nihon senryō* 共同研究: 日本占領, ed. Shisō no kagaku kenkyūkai 思想の科学研究会. Tokyo: Tokuma shoten, 1972.

Katakura Tadashi 片倉衷. *Kaisō no Manshūkoku* 回想の満州国. Tokyo: Keizai ōraisha, 1974.

Katayama Sen 片山潜. "Waga shakaishugi" 我社会主義. In *Katayama Sen, Tazoe Tetsuji shū* 片山潜·田添鉄二集, ed. Kishimoto Eitarō 岸本英太郎. Tokyo: Aoki shoten, 1955.

Katsura Tarō 桂太郎. "Katsura Tarō jiden III" 桂太郎自伝. Unpublished material in the Kokuritsu kokkai toshokan, Kensei shiryōshitsu.

Kawabe Torashirō 河辺虎四郎. *Ichigayadai kara Ichigayadai e* 市ヶ谷台から市ヶ谷台へ. Tokyo: Jiji tsūshinsha, 1962.

Kawai Ichirō 川合一郎 et al., eds. *Kōza: Nihon shihonshugi hattatsu shiron*, vol. 3: *Kyōkō kara sensō e* 講座 日本資本主義発達史論 III. 恐慌から戦争へ. Tokyo: Nihon hyōronsha, 1968.

Kawai, Kazuo. *Japan's American Interlude*. Chicago: University of Chicago Press, 1960.

Kawakami Hajime 河上肇. "Minponshugi to wa nanizoya" 民本主義とは何ぞや. *Tōhō jiron* 東方時論 (October 1917).

Kawamura Nozomu 河村望. "Kosaku sōgi ki ni okeru sonraku taisei" 小作争議期における村落体制. *Sonraku shakai kenkyū nenpō* 村落社会研究年報, no. 7 (1960): 106–50.

Kawasaki Hideji 川崎秀二. *Yūki aru seijikatachi* 勇気ある政治家たち. Tokyo: Sengoku shuppansha, 1971.

Kawashima Takeyoshi 川島武宜. "Nōson no mibunkaisōsei" 農村の身分階層制. In *Nihon shihonshugi kōza* 日本資本主義講座, vol. 8. Tokyo: Iwanami shoten, 1954.

Kazahaya Yasoji 風早八十二. *Nihon shakai seisakushi* 日本社会政策史. Tokyo: Nihon hyōronsha, 1937.

Kazama Daiji 風間大治. "Chūnensō no shijiseitōbetsu seikatsu ishiki" 中年層の

支持政党別生活意識. In *Nihonjin kenkyū* 日本人研究, no. 2 (*Tokushū: shiji seitōbetsu Nihonjin shūdan*) 特集: 支持政党別日本人集団, ed. Nihonjin kenkyūkai 日本人研究会. Tokyo: Shiseidō, 1975.

Keene, Donald. "The Sino-Japanese War of 1894–95 and Its Cultural Effects in Japan." In *Tradition and Modernization in Japanese Culture*, ed. Donald H. Shively. Princeton, N.J.: Princeton University Press, 1971.

Keizai antei honbu 経済安定本部. *Taiheiyō sensō ni yoru wagakuni no higai sōgō hōkokusho* 太平洋戦争による我国の被害総合報告書. Tokyo, 1948.

Keizai antei honbu sōsai kanbō kikakubu 経済安定本部·総裁官房企画部. *Taiheiyō sensō ni yoru waga kuni higai sōgō hōkokusho* 太平洋戦争による我国被害綜合報告書. Tokyo, 1949.

Keizai kikakuchō 経済企画庁. (1976) *Gendai Nihon keizai no tenkai* 現代日本経済の展開. Tokyo, 1976.

Keizai kikakuchō 経済企画庁, ed. *Kokumin seikatsu hakusho: Shōwa 54-nen ban* 国民生活白書 昭和54年版. Tokyo: Ōkurashō insatsu kyoku, 1979.

Keizai kikakuchō kokumin shotokuka 経済企画庁国民所得課. *Kokumin shotoku dōkō* 国民所得動向. Tokyo, 1986.

Keizai kikakuchō chōsakyoku 経済企画庁調査局, ed. *Shiryō: keizai hakusho ni-jūgo nen* 資料: 経済白書25年. Tokyo, 1972.

Keizai kikakuchō sōgō keikakukyoku 経済企画庁総合計画局. ed. *Shotoku shisan bunpai no jittai to mondaiten: Shotoku bunpai ni kansuru kenkyūkai hōkoku* 所得資産分配の実態と問題点: 所得分配に関する研究会報告 Tokyo: Ōkurashō insatsu kyoku, 1975.

Kelley, Allen C., and Williamson, Jeffrey G. *Lessons from Japanese Economic Development. An Analytical Economic History*. Chicago: University of Chicago Press, 1974.

Kenpō chōsakai 憲法調査会. *Kenpō seitei no keika ni kansuru shōiinkai hōkokusho* 憲法制定の経過に関する小委員会報告書. (*Kenpō chōsakai hōkokusho fuzoku bunsho*, no. 2) 憲法調査会報告書付属文書. Tokyo: Kenpō chōsakai, July 1964.

Keynes, John Maynard. The Economic Consequences of Mr. Churchill. London: L. and V. Woolf, 1925.

"Kimura Eiichi riji no setsumei" 木村鋭一理事の説明. *Kikan gendai shi* 季刊·現代史 (November 1972).

Kinoshita Hanji 木下半治. "Kokuminshugi undō no gendankai" 国民主義運動の現段階. *Chūō kōron* 中央公論 615 (December 1938): 216–23.

Kishimoto Eitarō 岸本英太郎 and Koyama Hirotake 小山弘健, eds. *Nihon kindai shakai shisōshi* 日本近代社会思想史. Tokyo: Aoki shoten, 1959.

Kishimoto Eitarō 岸本英太郎 and Koyama Hirotake 小山弘健. *Nihon no hi-kyōsantō marukusushugisha* 日本の非共産党マルクス主義者. Tokyo: San'ichi shobō, 1962.

Kita Ikki 北一輝. "Nihon kaizō hōan taikō" 日本改造法案大綱. In *Gendai Nihon shisō taikei* 現代日本思想大系, vol. 31: *Chōkokka shugi* 超国家主義, ed. Hashikawa Bunzō 橋川文三. Tokyo: Chikuma shobō, 1964.

Kitaoka Shin'ichi 北岡伸一. "Rikugun habatsu tairitsu (1931–35) no saikentō" 陸軍派閥対立(一九三一—三五)の再検討. In *Shōwaki no gunbu* 昭和期の軍部, ed. Kindai Nihon kenkyūkai 近代日本研究会. Tokyo: Yamakawa shuppansha, 1979.

Kiya Ikusaburō 木舎幾三郎. *Konoe-kō hibun* 近衛公秘聞. Wakayama: Kōyasan shuppansha, 1950.

Ko-Baba Eiichi-shi kinenkai 故馬場鍈一氏記念会. *Baba Eiichi den* 馬場鍈一伝. Tokyo: Ko-Baba Eiichi-shi kinenkai, 1945.

Kobayashi Hideo 小林英夫. "Manshū kin'yū kōzō no saihensei katei – 1930 nendai zenhanki o chūshin to shite" 満州金融構造の再編成過程—1930年代前半期を中心として. In *Nihon teikokushugika no Manshū* 日本帝国主義下の満州, ed. Manshū kenkyūkai 満州研究会. Tokyo: Ochanomizu shobō, 1972.

Kobayashi Yukio 小林幸男. "Tai-So seisaku no suii to Man-Mō mondai" 対ソ政策の推移と満蒙問題. In *Taiheiyō sensō e no michi* 太平洋戦争への道, ed. Nihon kokusai seiji gakkai Taiheiyō sensō gen'in kenkyūbu 日本国際政治学会太平洋戦争原因研究部. Tokyo: Asahi shinbunsha, 1962.

Koiso Kuniaki jijoden kankōkai 小磯国昭自叙伝刊行会, ed. *Katsuzan kōsō* 葛山鴻爪. Tokyo: Koiso Kuniaki jijoden kankōkai, 1963.

Kokumin seikatsu sentā 国民生活センター, ed. *Kokumin seikatsu tōkei nempō '80* 国民生活統計年報 '80. Tokyo: Shiseidō, 1980.

Kolakowski, Leszek. *Main Currents of Marxism*, vol. 2: *The Golden Age*. New York: Oxford University Press, 1978.

Komatsu Ryūji 小松隆二. *Kigyōbetsu kumiai no seisei* 企業別組合の生成. Tokyo: Ochanomizu shobō, 1971.

Komiya Ryutarō 小宮隆太郎. *Gendai Nihon keizai kenkyū* 現代日本経済研究. Tokyo: Tōkyō daigaku shuppankai, 1975.

Komiya Ryutarō 小宮隆太郎 et al., eds. *Kōdo seichō no jidai* 高度成長の時代. Tokyo: Nihon hyōronsha, 1981.

Komiya Ryutarō 小宮隆太郎 et al., eds. *Nihon no sangyō seisaku* 日本の産業政策. Tokyo: Tōkyō daigaku shuppankai, 1984.

*Konoe Fumimaro-kō no shuki: ushinawareshi seiji* 近衛文磨公の手記: 失はれし政治. Tokyo: Asahi shinbunsha, 1946.

Kōsai Yutaka 香西泰. "Iwato keiki" 岩戸景気. In *Shōwa keizai shi* 昭和経済史, ed. Arisawa Hiromi 有沢広巳. Tokyo: Nihon keizai shinbunsha, 1976.

Kosai, Yutaka, and Ogino, Yoshitaro. *The Contemporary Japanese Economy*. New York: Macmillan, 1981.

Kōtoku Shūsui 幸徳秋水. "Shakaishugi no taïsei" 社会主義のたいせい. *Nihonjin* 日本人 August 20, 1900.

Kōtoku Shūsui 幸徳秋水 *Hyōron to zuisō* 評論と随想. Tokyo: Jiyūhyōronsha, 1950.

Kōtoku Shūsui 幸徳秋水. *Teikokushugi: Nijūseiki no kaibutsu* 帝国主義: 二十世紀の怪物. Tokyo: Iwanami shoten, 1954.

Kōtoku Shūsui 幸徳秋水. *Shakaishugi shinzui* 社会主義神髄. Tokyo: Iwanami shoten, 1955.

Kovalio, Jacob. "The Personnel Policy of Army Minister Araki Sadao: The Tosa-Saga Theory Re-examined." In *Tradition and Modern Japan*, ed. P. G. O'Neill. Tenterden, Kent: Paul Norbury, 1981.

Koyama Hirotake 小川弘健. *Nihon marukusushugishi* 日本マルクス主義史. Tokyo: Aoki shoten, 1956.

Koyama Hirotake 小山弘健. "Nihon no marukusushugi no keisei" 日本のマルクス主義の形成. In *Shōwa no hantaisei shisō* 昭和の反体制思想. ed. Sumiya Etsuji 住谷悦治. Tokyo: Haga shobō, 1967.

Koyama Hirotake 小山弘健 and Koyama Hitoshi 小山仁示. "Taishō shakaishugi no shisōteki bunka" 大正社会主義の思想的分化. *Shisō* 思想 466 (April 1963): 119-30.

Koyama Hirotake 小山弘健 and Sugimori Yasuji 杉森康二. "Rōnōha marukusushugi" 労農派マルクス主義. In *Shōwa no hantaisei shisō* 昭和の反体制思想. ed. Sumiya Etsuji 住谷悦治. Tokyo: Haga shobō, 1967.

Krauss, Ellis S. "Opposition in Power: The Development and Maintenance of Leftist Government in Kyoto Prefecture." In *Political Opposition and Local Politics in Japan*, ed. Kurt Steiner, Ellis S. Krauss, and Scott C. Flanagan. Princeton, N.J.: Princeton University Press, 1980.

Krebs, Gerhard ゲルハルト・クレープス. "Doitsu kara mita Nihon no Dai Tōa seisaku" ドイツから見た日本の大東亜政策. In *Nihon no 1930 nendai* 日本の一九三〇年代, ed. Miwa Kimitada 三輪公忠. Tokyo: Sōryūsha, 1980.

Kublin, Hyman. "The Evolution of Japanese Colonialism." *Comparative Studies in Society and History* 2 (1959): 67-84.

Kublin, Hyman. *Asian Revolutionary: The Life of Sen Katayama*. Princeton, N.J.: Princeton University Press, 1964.

Kublin, Hyman. "Taiwan's Japanese Interlude, 1895-1945." In *Taiwan in Modern Times*, ed. Paul K. T. Sih. New York: St. John's University Press, 1973.

Kubota, Akira. *High Civil Servants in Postwar Japan: Their Social Origins, Educational Background, and Career Patterns*. Princeton, N.J.: Princeton University Press, 1969.

Kūki Shūzō 九鬼周造. *"Iki" no kōzō* 「いき」の構造. Tokyo: Iwanami shoten, 1967.

Kume Shigeru 久米茂. "Kokutetsu rōso to Suzuki Ichizō ni miru senryōka rōdō undō" 国鉄労組と鈴木市蔵にみる占領下労働運動. In *Kyōdō kenkyū: Nihon senryō* 共同研究: 日本占領, ed. Shisō no kagaku kenkyūkai 思想の科学研究会. Tokyo: Tokuma shoten, 1972.

Kusaka Ryūnosuke 草鹿龍之介. *Rengō kantai sanbōchō no kaisō* 連合艦隊参謀長の回想. Tokyo: Kōwadō, 1979.

Kusuda Minoru 楠田実. *Shushō hishokan* 首相秘書官. Tokyo: Bungei shunjūsha, 1975.

Kuznets, Simon. *Economic Growth of Nations: Total Output and Production Structure*. Cambridge, Mass: Harvard University Press, 1971.

Lamley, Harry J. "Assimilation in Colonial Taiwan: The Fate of the 1914

Movement." *Monumenta Serica* 29 (1970–1): 496–520.

Landes, David S. "Technological Change and Development in Western Europe, 1750–1914." In *Cambridge Economic History of Europe*, vol. 1, ed. H. J. Habakuk and M. Postan. Cambridge, England: Cambridge University Press, 1965.

Large, Stephen S. *The Rise of Labor in Japan: The Yūaikai*. Tokyo: Sophia University Press, 1972.

Large, Stephen S. "Perspectives on the Failure of the Labour Movement in Prewar Japan." *Labour History* 37 (November 1979).

Large, Stephen S. *Organized Workers and Socialist Politics in Interwar Japan*. Cambridge, England: Cambridge University Press, 1981.

Lee, Bradford. *Britain and the Sino-Japanese War 1937–39*. Stanford, Calif.: Stanford University Press, 1977.

Lee, Chong-sik. *The Politics of Korean Nationalism*. Berkeley and Los Angeles: University of California Press, 1973.

LeMay, Curtis E., with Mackinlay Kantor. *Mission with LeMay: My Story*. Garden City, N.Y.: Doubleday, 1965.

Levine, Solomon B. *Industrial Relations in Postwar Japan*. Urbana: University of Illinois Press, 1958.

Levine, Solomon B., and Kawada, Hisashi. *Human Resources in Japanese Industrial Development*. Princeton, N.J.: Princeton University Press, 1980.

Lewis, W. Arthur. "Economic Development with Unlimited Supplies of Labour." *Manchester School of Economic and Social Studies* 22 (May 1954): 139–91.

Lichtheim, George, *Marxism: An Historical and Critical Study*. London: Routledge & Kegan Paul, 1961.

Lockwood, Willam W. *The Economic Development of Japan: Growth and Structural Change, 1868–1938*. Princeton, N.J.: Princeton University Press, 1954.

Lockwood, William W. *The State and Economic Enterprise in Japan: Essays in the Political Economy of Growth*. Princeton, N.J.: Princeton University Press, 1965.

(*Long-Term Economic Statistics*) Ōkawa Kazushi 大川一司, Shinohara Miyohei 篠原三代平 and Umemura Mataji 梅村又次, eds. *Chōki keizai tōkei* 長期経済統計 (*LTES, Long-Term Economic Statistics*). Tokyo: Tōyō keizai shinpōsha, 1965– ).

(*LTES*, vol. 1) Ōkawa Kazushi 大川一司, Takamatsu Nobukiyo 高松信清 and Yamamoto Yūzō 山本有造, eds. *Kokumin shotoku* 国民所得. Tokyo: Tōyō keizai shinpōsha, 1974.

(*LTES*, vol. 3) Ōkawa Kazushi 大川一司 et al., eds. *Shihon sutokku* 資本ストック. Tokyo: Tōyō keizai shinpōsha, 1966.

(*LTES*, vol. 4) Emi Koichi 江見康一, ed. *Shihon keisei* 資本形成. Tokyo: Tōyō keizai shinpōsha, 1971.

(*LTES*, vol. 6) Shinohara Miyohei 篠原三代平, ed. *Kojin shōhi shishutsu* 個人消費支出, Tokyo: Tōyō keizai shinpōsha, 1967.

(*LTES*, vol. 7) Emi Koichi 江見康一 and Shionoya Yuichi 塩野谷祐一, eds. *Zaisei shishutsu* 財政支出, Tokyo: Tōyō keizai shinpōsha, 1966.
(*LTES*, vol. 8) Ōkawa Kazushi 大川一司等 et al., eds. *Bukka* 物価 Tokyo: Tōyō keizai shinpōsha, 1967.
(*LTES*, vol. 9) Umemura Mataji 梅村又次 et al., eds. *Nōringyō* 農林業. Tokyo: Tōyō keizai shinpōsha, 1966.
(*LTES*, vol. 10) Shinohara Miyohei 篠原三代平, ed. *Tekkōgyō* 鉄鋼業, Tokyo: Tōyō keizai shinpōsha, 1972.
(*LTES*, vol. 11) Fujino Shozaburō 藤野正三郎, Fujino Shirō 藤野志朗 and Ono Akira 小野旭, eds. *Sen'i kōgyō* 繊維工業. Tokyo: Tōyō keizai shinpōsha, 1979.
(*LTES*, vol. 12) Minami Ryōshin 南亮進, ed. *Tetsudō to denryoku* 鉄道と電力. Tokyo: Tōyō keizai shinpōsha, 1965.
(*LTES*, vol. 14) Yamazawa Ippei 山沢逸平 and Yamamoto Yūzō 山本有造, *Bōeki to kokusai shūshi* 貿易と国際収支. Tokyo: Tōyō keizai shinpōsha, 1979.
Lory, Hillis. *Japan's Military Masters: The Army in Japanese Life*. Westport, Conn.: Greenwood Press, 1943.
McCormack, Gavin. *Chang Tso-lin in Northwest China, 1911–1928: China, Japan, and the Manchurian Idea*. Stanford, Calif.: Stanford University Press, 1977.
McKean, Margaret A. "Political Socialization Through Citizen's Movement." In *Political Opposition and Local Politics in Japan*, ed. Kurt Steiner, Ellis S. Krauss, and Scott Flanagan. Princeton, N.J.: Princeton University Press, 1980.
McNair, Harley Farnsworth, and Lach, Donald F. *Modern Far Eastern International Relations*. New York: Van Nostrand, 1950.
Maddison, Angus. *Economic Growth in Japan and the USSR*. London: Allen & Unwin, 1969.
Maeda Masana 前田正名. "Kōgyō iken" 興業意見 (1885). In *Kōgyō iken hoka Maeda Masana kankei shiryō* 興業意見他前田正名関係資料, ed. Andō Yoshio 安藤良雄 and Yamamoto Hirofumi 山本弘文. Tokyo: Koseikan, 1971.
Maeda Yasuyuki 前田靖幸. *Shōkō seisakushi dai 11-kan: Sangyō tōsei* 商工政策史第11巻: 産業統制. Tokyo: Tsūshō sangyō kenkyūsha, 1964.
Magota Ryōhei 孫田良平. "Kigyōbetsu kumiai no keisei" 企業別組合の形成. *Journal of Humanities and Social Sciences*, no. 12 (May 1975): 21–38.
Makise Kikue 牧瀬菊枝. "Kichi no mawari de no kikigaki" 基地のまわりでの聞き書. In *Kyōdō kenkyū: Nihon senryō* 共同研究: 日本占領, ed. Shisō no kagaku kenkyukai 思想の科学研究会. Tokyo: Tokuma shoten, 1972.
*Man-Mō shūsenshi* 満蒙終戦史. Tokyo: Kawade shobō shinsha, 1962.
Manshūshi kenkyūkai 満州史研究会, ed. *Nihon teikokushugika no Manshū* 日本帝国主義下の満州. Tokyo: Ochanomizu shobō, 1972.
Marr, David G. *Vietnamese Tradition on Trial, 1920–1945*. Berkeley and Los Angeles: University of California Press, 1981.
Marshall, Alfred. *Principles of Economics*, 8th ed. London: Macmillan, 1949.
Marshall, Byron K. *Capitalism and Nationalism in Prewar Japan: The Ideology*

*of the Business Elite, 1868–1941*. Stanford Calif.: Stanford University Press, 1967.

Maruyama Kanji 丸山幹治. "Minshuteki keikō to seitō" 民主的傾向と政党. *Nihon oyobi Nihonjin* 日本および日本人 (January 1913).

Maruyama, Masao. "Patterns of Individuation and the Case of Japan: A Conceptual Scheme." In *Changing Japanese Attitudes Toward Modernization*, ed. Marius B. Jansen. Princeton, N.J.: Princeton University Press, 1965.

Maruyama, Masao. *Thought and Behaviour in Modern Japanese Politics*, expanded ed., ed. Ivan Morris. London: Oxford University Press, 1969.

Matsuishi Yasuji 松石安治. "Kokubō daihōshin ni kansuru iken" 国防大方針ニ関スル意見. In *Daihon'ei rikugunbu* (1) 大本営陸軍部 (1), ed. Bōeichō bōei kenshūjo senshi shitsu 防衛庁防衛研修所戦史室. Tokyo: Asagumo shinbunsha, 1967.

Matsumoto Hiroshi 松元宏. "Meiji-Taishō ki ni okeru jinushi no beikoku hanbai ni tsuite" 明治大正期における地主の米穀販売について. *Hitotsubashi ronsō* 一橋論叢 60 (November 1968): 547–65.

Matsumura Shu'itsu 松村秀逸. *Miyakezaka: Gunbatsu wa ikanishite umareta ka* 三宅坂: 軍閥は如何にして生れたか. Tokyo: Tōkō shobō, 1952.

Matsumura Shu'itsu 松村秀逸. *Sensen kara shūsen made* 宣戦から終戦まで. Tokyo: Nihon shūhōsha, 1964.

Matsuo Takayoshi 松尾尊允. *Taishō demokurashii no kenkyū* 大正デモクラシーの研究. Tokyo: Aoki shoten, 1966.

Matsuo Takayoshi 松尾尊允. "Dai'ichi taisengo no fusen undō" 第一大戦後の普選運動. In *Taishōki no seiji to shakai* 大正期の政治と社会, ed. Inoue Kiyoshi 井上清. Tokyo: Iwanami shoten, 1969.

Matsuo Takayoshi 松尾尊允. "Katayama Sen, Miura Tetsutarō, Ishibashi Tanzan" 片山潜, 三浦銕太郎, 石橋湛山. In *Kindai Nihon to Chūgoku – ge* 近代日本と中国 – 下, ed. Takeuchi Yoshimi 竹内好 and Hashikawa Bunzō 橋川文三. Tokyo: Asahi shimbunsha, 1974.

Matsuoka Yōsuke denki kankōkai 松岡洋介傳記刊行会, eds. *Matsuoka Yōsuke* 松岡洋介. Tokyo: Kōdansha, 1974.

Matsushima Keizō 松島慶三. *Higeki no Nagumo chūjō* 悲劇の南雲中将. Tokyo: Tokuma shoten, 1967.

Matsushita Keiichi 松下圭一. "Sengo kenpōgaku no riron kōsei" 戦後憲法学の理論構成. In *Seiji katei* 政治過程, vol. 3 of *Sengo kaikaku* 戦後改革, ed. Tōkyō daigaku shakaikagaku kenkyūjo 東京大学社会科学研究所. Tokyo: Tōkyō daigaku shuppankai, 1974–5.

Matsushita Yoshio 松下芳男. *Meiji Taishō hansensō undōshi* 明治大正反戦争運動史. Tokyo: Sōbisha, 1949.

Matsuzawa Hiroaki 松沢弘陽. "Meiji shakaishugi no shisō" 明治社会主義の思想. In *Nihon no shakaishugi* 日本の社会主義, ed. Nihon seiji gakkai 日本政治学会. Tokyo: Iwanami shoten, 1968.

Matsuzawa Hiroaki 松沢弘陽. *Nihon shakaishugi no shisō* 日本社会主義の思想. Tokyo: Chikuma shobō, 1973.

Mitchell, B. R. *European Historical Statistics*. New York: Macmillan, 1975.

Miki Kiyoshi 三木清. *Miki Kiyoshi Zenshū* 三木清全集. vol. 3, ed. Ōuchi Hyōe 大内兵衛. Tokyo: Iwanami shoten, 1966–8.

Miki Kiyoshi 三木清. "Kaishakugakuteki genshōgaku no kisogainen" 解釈学的現象学の基礎概念. In *Kindai Nihon shisō taikei*, vol. 27: *Miki Kiyoshi shū* 近代日本思想大系, 27: 三木清集, ed. Sumiya Kazuhiko 住谷一彦. Tokyo: Chikuma shobō, 1975.

Mikuriya Takashi 御厨貴. "Kokusaku tōgōkikan setchi mondai no shiteki tenkai" 国策統合機関設置問題の史的展開. In *Nenpō kindai Nihon kenkyū – 1; Shōwa-ki no gunbu* 年報近代日本研究・1; 昭和期の軍部. Tokyo: Yamakawa shuppansha, 1979.

Mikuriya Takashi 御厨貴. "Meiji kokka kikō sōsetsu katei ni okeru seiji shidō no kyōgō: Naikaku seido oyobi teikoku gikai sōsetsu no seiji katei" 明治国家機構創設過程における政治指導の競合—内閣制度および帝国議会創設の政治過程. *Kokka gakkai zasshi* 国家学会雑誌 92 (April 1979): 61–4, 77–9.

Miller, Frank O. *Minobe Tatsukichi, Interpreter of Constitutionalism in Japan*. Berkeley and Los Angeles: University of California Press, 1965.

Minami Manshū tetsudō kabushiki kaisha 南満州鉄道株式会社, comp. *Minami Manshū tetsudō kabushiki kaisha sanjū-nen ryakushi* 南満州鉄道株式会社三十年略史. Dairen: Minami Manshū tetsudō kabushiki kaisha, 1937.

Minami, Ryoshin. *The Turning Point in Economic Development*. Tokyo: Kinokuniya, 1973.

Minami Ryōshin 南亮進. *Dōryoku kakumei to gijutsu shimpo: Senzen-ki seizōgyō no bunseki* 動力革命と技術進歩: 戦前期製造業の分析. Tokyo: Tōyō keizai shinpōsha, 1976.

Minami, Ryoshin. "The Introduction of Electric Power and Its Impact on the Manufacturing Industries: With Special Reference to Smaller Scale Plants." In *Japanese Industrialization and Its Social Consequences*, ed. Hugh T. Patrick. Berkeley and Los Angeles: University of California Press, 1976.

Minami, Ryoshin. "Mechanical Power in the Industrialization of Japan." *Journal of Economic History* 37 (December 1977): 935–58.

Minami Ryōshin 南亮進. *Nihon no keizai hatten* 日本の経済発展. Tokyo: Tōyō keizai shinpōsha, 1981.

Minami, Ryoshin, and Ono, Akira. "Wages." In *Patterns of Japanese Economic Development: A Quantitative Appraisal*, ed. Kazushi Ohkawa and Miyohei Shinohara. New Haven, Conn.: Yale University Press, 1979.

Minobe Tatsukichi 美濃部達吉. *Kenpō satsuyō* 憲法撮要. Tokyo: Yuhikaku, 1926.

Minobe Tatsukichi 美濃部達吉. *Chikujō kenpō seigi* 逐条憲法精義. Tokyo: Yuhikaku, 1927.

Minobe Tatsukichi 美濃部達吉. "Waga gikai seido no zento" 我が議会制度の前途. *Chūō kōron* 中央公論 553 (January 1934): 2–14.

Mishima Yukio 三島由紀夫. "Bunka bōeiron" 文化防衛論. In *Mishima Yukio zenshū* 三島由紀夫全集, vol. 33, ed. Saeki Shōichi 佐伯彰一. Tokyo: Shinchōsha, 1973–76.

Mita Munesuke 見田宗介. *Gendai nihon no shinjō to ronri* 現代日本の心情と論理. Tokyo: Chikuma shobō, 1971.

Mitani Taichirō 三谷太一郎. *Nihon seitō seiji no keisei, Hara Kei no seiji shidō no tenkai* 日本政党政治の形成, 原敬の政治指導の展開. Tokyo: Tōkyō daigaku shuppankai, 1967.

Mitani Taichirō 三谷太一郎. "Taishō shakaishugisha no 'seiji' kan – 'seiji no hitei' kara 'seijiteki taikō' e" 大正社会主義者の「政治」観 –「政治の否定」から「政治的対抗」へ. In *Nihon no shakaishugi* 日本の社会主義, ed. Nihon seiji gakkai 日本政治学会. Tokyo: Iwanami shoten, 1968.

Mitani Taichirō 三谷太一郎. *Taishō demokurashiiron* 大正デモクラシー論. Tokyo: Chūō kōronsha, 1974.

Mitani Taichirō 三谷太一郎. "Seiyūkai no seiritsu" 政友会の成立. In *Iwanami kōza Nihon rekishi, Kindai 3* 岩波講座日本歴史, 近代 三. Tokyo: Iwanami shoten, 1976.

Mitani Taichirō 三谷太一郎."Nihon ni okeru baishinsei seiritsu no seijishiteki imi, Shihōbu to seitō kenryoku kankei no tenkai (1)" 日本における陪審制成立の政治的意味—司法部と政党との権力関係の展開（一）. *Kokka gakkai zasshi* 国家学会雑誌92 (March 1979).

Mitani Taichirō 三谷太一郎. "Nihon ni okeru baishinsei seiritsu no seijishiteki imi, Shihōbu to seitō kenryoku kankei no tenkai (2)" 日本における陪審制成立の政治史的意味—司法部と政党との権力関係の展開（二）. *Kokka gakkai zasshi* 国家学会雑誌92 (June 1979).

Mitani Taichirō 三谷太一郎. "Nihon ni okeru baishin sei seiritsu no seijishiteki imi, Shihōbu to seitō kenryoku kankei no tenkai (3)" 日本における陪審制成立の政治史的意味—司法部と政党との権力関係の展開（三）. *Kokka gakkai zasshi* 国家学会雑誌 92 (October 1979).

Mitani Taichirō 三谷太一郎. *Kindai Nihon no shihōken to seitō: baishinsei seiritsu no seijishi* 近代日本の司法権と政党: 陪審制成立の政治史. Tokyo: Hanawa shobō, 1980.

Mitani Taichirō 三谷太一郎. "Kokusai kin'yū shihon to Ajia no sensō" 国際金融資本とアジアの戦争. In *Kindai Nihon kenkyū – 2: Kindai Nihon to Higashi Ajia* 近代日本研究·2: 近代日本と東アジア, ed. Kindai Nihon kenkyūkai 近代日本研究会. Tokyo: Yamakawa shuppansha, 1980.

Mitchell, Richard H. *Thought Control in Prewar Japan*. Ithaca, N.Y.: Cornell University Press, 1976.

Mitsubishi Zōsen K.K., Sōmuka 三菱造船株式会社総務課, ed. "Honpō kindai zōsen hogoseisaku no enkaku" 本邦近代造船保護政策の沿革. Reprinted in *Nihon sangyō shiryō taikei* 日本産業資料大系, vol. 5. Tokyo: Chūgai shōgyō shinpōsha, 1926.

Miwa Kimitada 三輪公忠. *Matsuoka Yōsuke* 松岡洋右. Tokyo: Chūō kōronsha, 1971.

Miwa Ryōichi 三和良一. "1926-nen kanzei kaisei no rekishiteki ichi" 1926年関税改正の歴史的位置. In *Nihon shihonshugi: Tenkai to ronri* 日本資本主義: 展開と論理, ed. Sakasai Takahito 逆井孝仁 et al. Tokyo: Tōkyō daigaku shuppankai, 1978.

Miwa Ryōichi 三和良一. "Takahashi zaiseiki no keizai seisaku" 高橋財政期の経済政策. In *Senji Nihon keizai* 戦時日本経済, ed. Tōkyō daigaku shakai kagaku kenkyūjo 東京大学社会科学研究所. Tokyo: Tōkyō daigaku shuppankai, 1979.

Miyake Ichirō 三宅一郎. "Yūkensha kōzō no hendō to senkyo" 有権者構造の変動と選挙. In *Nenpō seijigaku* 年報政治学 1977 (*55-nen taisei no seiritsu to hōkai: Zoku gendai Nihon no seiji katei*) 55年体制の成立と崩壊—続現代日本の政治過程, ed. Nihon seiji gakkai 日本政治学会. Tokyo: Iwanami shoten, 1979.

Miyake Seiki 三宅晴輝. *Shinkō kontserun tokuhon* 新興コンツェルン読本. Tokyo: Shunjūsha, 1937.

Miyamoto Mataji 宮本又治. "Shōkō kumiai" 商工組合. In *Nihon keizaishi jiten* 日本経済史辞典, ed. Keizaishi kenkyūkai 経済史研究会. Tokyo: Nihon hyōronsha, 1940.

Miyashita Buhei 宮下武平. "Keisha seisan hōshiki" 傾斜生産方式. In *Shōwa keizai shi* 昭和経済史, ed, Arisawa Hiromi 有沢広巳編. Tokyo: Nihon keizai shinbunsha, 1976.

Miyazaki Giichi 宮崎義一. *Gendai Nihon no kigyō shūdan* 現代日本の企業集団. Tokyo: Tōyō keizai shinpōsha, 1976.

Miyazaki Yoshimasa 宮崎吉政. *Saishō: Satō Eisaku* 宰相佐藤栄作. Tokyo: Hara shobō, 1980.

Miyazawa Toshiyoshi 宮沢俊義. *Tennō kikansetsu jiken* 天皇機関説事件, 2 vols. Tokyo: Yūhikaku, 1970.

Miyoshi, Masao. *As We Saw Them*. Berkeley and Los Angeles: University of California Press, 1979.

Mizuguchi Norito 水口憲人. "Kamitsuchi ni okeru seiji sanka: Ōsaka daitoshi ken o rei to shite," 過密地における政治参加: 大阪大都市圏を例として. In *Nenpō seijigaku* 年報政治学 1974 (*Seiji sanka no riron to genjitsu*) 政治参加の理論と現実, ed. Nihon seiji gakkai 日本政治学会. Tokyo: Iwanami shoten, 1975.

Mochiji Rokusaburō 持地六三郎. *Taiwan shokumin seisaku* 台湾植民政策. Tokyo, Fuzanbō, 1912.

Mochikabu kaisha seiri iinkai 持株会社整理委員会, ed. *Nihon zaibatsu to sono kaitai* 日本財閥とその解体. Tokyo, 1951.

Moore, Barrington. *Social Origins of Dictatorship and Democracy: Lord and Peasant in the Making of the Modern World*. Boston: Beacon Press, 1967.

Mori Giichi 森義一. *Kosaku sōgi senjutsu* 小作争議戦術. Tokyo: Hakuyōsha, 1928.

Mori Katsumi 森克巳. *Manshū jihen no rimen shi* 満州事変の裏面史. Tokyo: Kokusho kankōkai, 1976.

Mori Takemaro 森武麿. "Nihon fuashizumu no keisei to nōson keizai kōsei undō" 日本ファシズムの形成と農村経済更生運動. *Rekishigaku kenkyū* 歴史学研究 (1971 special supplement): 135–52.

Morishima Morito 森島守人. *Imbō, ansatsu, guntō* 陰謀·暗殺·軍刀. Tokyo: Iwanami shoten, 1950.

Morita Yoshio 森田良雄. *Nihon keieisha dantai hatten shi* 日本経営者団体発展史. Tokyo: Nikkan rōdō tsūshin, 1958.

Morley, James W., ed. *Dilemmas of Growth in Prewar Japan*. Princeton, N.J.: Princeton University Press, 1971.

Morley, James W., ed. *Deterrent Diplomacy: Japan, Germany and the USSR. 1935–1940*. New York: Columbia University Press, 1976.

Morley, James W., ed. *The Fateful Choice: Japan's Advance into Southeast Asia, 1939–1941*. New York: Columbia University Press, 1980.

Morley, James W., ed. *The China Quagmire: Japan's Expansion on the Asian Continent*. New York: Columbia University Press, 1983.

Morley, James W., ed. *Japan Erupts: The London Naval Conference and the Manchurian Incident, 1928–1932*. New York: Columbia University Press, 1984.

Morris, Morris D. "The Problem of the Peasant Agriculturalist in Meiji Japan." *Far Eastern Quarterly* 15 (1956): 357–70.

Moskowitz, Karl. "The Creation of the Oriental Development Company: Japanese Illusions Meet Korean Reality." *Occasional Papers on Korea*, no. 2, Joint Committee on Korean Studies and the Social Science Research Council, March 1974, pp. 73–109.

Muramatsu, Michio, and Krauss, Ellis S. "Bureaucrats and Politicians in Policymaking: The Case of Japan" *American Political Science Review* 78 (March 1984): 126–46.

Muramatsu Takeji 村松武司. "Shokuminsha no kaisō" 植民者の回想. *Chōsen kenkyū* 朝鮮研究. (September 1967–December 1968): 1–14.

Murata, Kiyoaki. "Emotions in Dispute." *Japan Times Weekly*, August 28, 1982.

Mutō Akira 武藤章. *Hitō kara Sugamo e* 比島から巣鴨へ. Tokyo: Jitsugyō no Nipponsha, 1952.

Myers, Ramon H. "Taiwan as an Imperial Colony of Japan, 1895–1945." *Journal of the Institute of Chinese Studies* 6 (December 1973): 425–51.

Myers, Ramon H., and Ching, Adrienne. "Agricultural Development in Taiwan Under Japanese Colonial Rule." *Journal of Asian Studies* 33 (August 1964): 555–70.

Myers, Ramon H., and Peattie, Mark R., eds. *The Japanese Colonial Empire, 1895–1945*. Princeton, N.J.: Princeton University Press, 1984.

Nagai Ryūtarō 永井柳太郎. *Kaizō no risō* 改造の理想. Tokyo, 1920.

Nagai Ryūtarō hensankai 永井柳太郎 編纂会, ed. *Nagai Ryūtarō* 永井柳太郎. Tokyo: Seikōsha, 1959.

Nagaoka Shinjirō 長岡新次郎. "Nanpō shisaku no gaikōteki tenkai (1937 nen–1941 nen)" 南方施策の外交的展開（一九三七年——九四一年）. In *Taiheiyō sensō e no michi* 太平洋戦争への道, vol. 6, ed. Nihon Kokusai seiji gakkai Taiheiyō sensō gen'in kenkyūbu 日本国際政治学会太平洋戦争原因研究部. Tokyo: Asahi shimbunsha, 1963.

Nagata Tetsuzan 永田鉄山. "Kokka sōdōin junbi shisetsu to seishōnen kunren" 国家総動員準備施設と青少年訓練. In *Kokka sōdōin no igi* 国家総動員の意義, ed. Tsujimura Kusuzō 辻村楠造. Tokyo: Aoyama shoin, 1925.

Nagata Tetsuzan 永田鉄山. *Kokka sōdōin* 国家総動員. Osaka: Ōsaka mainichi shinbunsha, 1928.

Nahm, Andrew, ed. *Korea Under Japanese Colonial Rule: Studies of the Policy and Techniques of Japanese Colonialism*. Kalamazoo, Mich.: Center for Korean Studies, Institute of International and Area Studies, Western Michigan University, 1973.

*Naigai senkyo dēta* 内外選挙データ. (*'78 Mainichi nenkan bessatsu*) '78毎日年鑑別冊. Tokyo: Mainichi shinbunsha, 1978.

Naitō Norikuni 内藤則邦. "Rikugun no rōso hinin to danketsuken yōgo undō" 陸軍の労組否認と団結権擁護運動. In *Rōdō keizai to rōdō undō* 労働経済と労働運動, ed. Ōkōchi Kazuo sensei kanreki kinen ronbunshū hakkō iinkai 大河内一男先生還暦記念論文集発行委員会. Tokyo: Iwanami shoten, 1966.

Najita, Tetsuo. *Hara kei in the Politics of Compromise, 1905–1915*. Cambridge, Mass.: Harvard University Press, 1967.

Najita, Tetsuo. "Nakano Seigō and the Spirit of the Meiji Restoration in Twentieth-Century Japan." In *Dilemmas of Growth in Prewar Japan*, ed. James W. Morley. Princeton, N.J.: Princeton University Press, 1971.

Nakagawa, Keiichiro, ed. *Labor and Management: Proceedings of the Fourth Fuji Conference*. Tokyo: Tokyo University Press, 1979.

Nakagawa, Keiichirō, and Rosovsky, Henry. "The Case of the Dying Kimono: The Influence of Changing Fashions on the Development of the Japanese Woolen Industry." *Business History Review* 37 (Spring–Summer 1963): 59–80.

Nakamura Hideo 中村英郎, ed. *Saikin no shakai undō* 最近の社会運動. Tokyo: Kyōchokai, 1929.

Nakamura, James I. *Agricultural Production and the Economic Development of Japan 1873–1922*. Princeton, N.J.: Princeton University Press, 1966.

Nakamura, James I. "Incentives, Productivity Gaps, and Agricultural Growth Rates in Pre-War Japan, Taiwan and Korea." In *Japan in Crisis: Essays in Taishō Democracy*, ed. Bernard Silberman and H. D. Harootunian. Princeton, N.J.: Princeton University Press, 1974.

Nakamura Katsunori 中村勝範. "Nihon shakaitō no soshiki to undō" 日本社会党の組織と運動. *Hōgaku Kenkyū* 法学研究 33 (October 1960).

Nakamura Katsunori 中村勝範. *Meiji shakaishugi kenkyū* 明治社会主義研究. Tokyo: Sekai shoin, 1966.

Nakamura Masanori 中村正則. "Keizai kōsei undō to nōson tōgō" 経済更生運動と農村統合. In *Fuashizumuki no kokka to shakai* ファシズム期の国家と社会, vol. 1 of *Shōwa kyōkō* 昭和恐慌, ed. Tōkyō daigaku shakai kagaku kenkyūjō 東京大学社会科学研究所. Tokyo: Tōkyō daigaku shuppankai, 1978.

Nakamura Takafusa 中村隆英. "Zairai sangyō no hatten kikō – Meiji Taishō-ki no Nihon ni oite" 在来産業の発展機構—明治大正期の日本において. *Keizai hyōron* 経済評論 16 (January 1967): 134–56.

Nakamura Takafusa 中村隆英. *Senzenki Nihon keizai seichō no bunseki* 戦前期日本経済成長の分析. Tokyo: Iwanami shoten, 1971.

Nakamura Takafusa 中村隆英. "Shijō kōzō to sangyō soshiki" 市場構造と産業組織. In *Nihon keizai ron – keizai seichō 100-nen no bunseki* 日本経済論—経済

成長100年の分析, ed. Emi Kōichi 江見康一 and Shionoya Yūichi 塩野谷祐一. Tokyo: Yūhikaku, 1973.

Nakamura Takafusa 中村隆英. "Zairai sangyō no kibo to kōsei – Taishō 9-nen kokusei chōsa o chūshin ni –" 在来産業の規模と構成—大正 9 年国勢調査を中心に. In *Sūryō keizaishi ronshū I. Nihon keizai no hatten* 数量経済史論集 I. 日本経済の発展. ed. Umemura Mataji 梅村又次, Shimbo Hiroshi 新保博, Nishikawa Shunsaku 西川俊策 and Hayami Akira 速水融. Tokyo: Nihon keizai shinbunsha, 1976.

Nakamura Takafusa 中村隆英. "Sensō keizai to sono hōkai" 戦争経済とその崩壊. In *Iwanami kōza, Nihon rekishi – 21: Kindai 8* 岩波講座, 日本歴史—21: 近代 8. Tokyo: Iwanami shoten, 1977.

Nakamura Takafusa 中村隆英. *Shōwa kyōkō to keizai seisaku* 昭和恐慌と経済政策. Tokyo: Nihon keizai shinbunsha, 1978.

Nakamura Takafusa 中村隆英. "Chōki tōkei no seido ni tsuite – 19-seiki Nihon no jakkan no sūji o megutte" 長期統計の精度について—19世紀日本の若干の数字をめぐって. *Keizai kenkyū* 経済研究30 (January 1979): 1–9.

Nakamura Takafusa 中村隆英. "Zairai men orimonogyō no hatten to suitai – oboegaki" 在来綿織物業の発展と衰退—覚書き. In *Sūryō keizaishi ronshū 2. Kindai ikōki no Nihon keizai – Bakumatsu kara Meiji e* 数量経済史論集 2. 近代移行期の日本経済, ed. Shinbo Hiroshi 新保博 and Yasuba Yasukichi 安場保吉. Tokyo: Nihon keizai shinbunsha, 1979.

Nakamura Takafusa 中村隆英. "Nihon no kahoku keizai kōsaku" 日本の華北経済工作. In *Kindai Nihon kenkyū – 2: Kindai Nihon to Higashi Ajia* 近代日本研究—2: 近代日本と東アジア, ed. Kindai Nihon kenkyūkai 近代日本研究会. Tokyo: Yamakawa shuppansha, 1980.

Nakamura, Takafusa. *The Postwar Japanese Economy: Its Development and Structure*. Tokyo: Tokyo University Press, 1981.

Nakamura, Takafusa. *Economic Growth in Prewar Japan*, trans. Robert A. Feldman. New Haven, Conn.: Yale University Press, 1983.

Nakamura Takafusa 中村隆英 and Hara Akira 原朗, eds. "Kaisetsu," "Ōkyū butsudō keikaku shian," "Setsumei shiryō" "解説" "応急物動計画試案", "説明資料." In *Kokka sōdōin (1) keizai – Gendaishi shiryō 31* 国家総動員(一)経済 – 現代史資料31. Tokyo: Misuzu shobō, 1970.

Nakamura Takafusa 中村隆英 and Hara Akira 原朗. "Keizai shintaisei" 経済新体制. In *Nihon seiji gakkai nenpō 1972-nen* 日本政治学会年報 1972年. Tokyo: Iwanami shoten, 1972.

Nakane, Chie. *Kinship and Economic Organization in Rural Japan*. London: Athlone, 1967.

Nakano Tatsuo 中野達雄 and Iizuka Shigetarō 飯塚繁太郎. *Nihon o ugokasu soshiki: Shakaitō; minshatō* 日本を動かす組織: 社会党, 民社党. (*Nihon o ugokasu soshiki series*) 日本を動かす組織シリーズ. Tokyo: Sekkasha, 1968.

Nakase, Toshikazu. "The Introduction of Scientific Management in Japan and Its Characteristics – Case Studies of Companies in the Sumitomo Zaibatsu." In *Labor and Management: Proceedings of the Fourth Fuji Conference*, ed.

Keiichiro Nakagawa. Tokyo: Tokyo University Press, 1979.

Nakayama Ichirō 中山伊知郎, ed. *Nihon no kokufu kōzō* 日本の国富構造. Tokyo: Tōyō keizai shinpōsha, 1959.

Namiki Masayoshi 並木正吉. "Nōka jinkō no idō keitai to shūgyō kōzō." 農家人口の移動形体と就業構造. In *Nōgyō ni okeru senzai shitsugyō* 農業における潜在失業, ed. Tōhata Seiichi 東畑精一編. Tokyo: Nihon hyōronsha, 1956.

Namiki Masayoshi 並木正吉. "Chingin kōzō to nōka rōdōryoku" 賃金構造と農家労働力. In *Nihongata chingin kōzō no kenkyū* 日本型賃金構造の研究, ed. Shinohara Miyohei 篠原三代平 and Funahashi Naomichi 舟橋尚道. Tokyo: Rōdō hōgaku kenkyūjo, 1961.

Naoi Masaru 直井優. "Sangyōka to kaisō kōzō no hendō" 産業下と階層構造の変動. In *Hendōki no Nihon shakai* 変動期の日本社会, ed. Akuto Hiroshi 飽戸弘, Tominaga Ken'ichi 富永健一 and Sobue Takao 祖父江孝男. Tokyo: Nihon hōsō kyōkai, 1972.

Naoi Michiko 直井道子. "Kaisō ishiki to kaikyū ishiki" 階層意識と階級意識. In *Nihon no kaisō kōzō* 日本の階層構造, ed. Tominaga Ken'ichi 富永健一. Tokyo: Tōkyō daigaku shuppankai, 1979.

Nichi-Man nōsei kenkyūkai 日満農政研究会. *Saikin ni okeru jinkō idō no seikaku to nōgyō* 最近における人口移動の性格と農業. Tokyo, 1940.

*Nichi-Man zaisei keizai kenkyūkai shiryō* 日満財政経済研究会資料, 3 vols. Tokyo: Nihon kindai shiryō kenkyūkai, 1970.

Nihon gaikō gakkai 日本外交学会, ed. *Taiheiyō sensō shūketsuron* 太平洋戦争終決論. Tokyo: Tōkyō daigaku shuppankai, 1958.

Nihon ginkō chōsakyoku 日本銀行調査局. "Kantō shinsai yori Shōwa ni-nen kin'yū kyōkō ni itaru waga zaikai" 関東震災ヨリ昭和二年金融恐慌ニ至ル我財界. *Nihon kin'yūshi shiryō: Meiji Taishō hen* 日本金融史資料: 明治大正編, vol. 22. Tokyo, 1959.

Nihon ginkō chōsakyoku 日本銀行調査局. "Sekai taisen shūryōgo ni okeru hompō zaikai dōyōshi" 世界大戦終了後ニ於ケル本邦財界動揺史 *Nihon kin'yūshi shiryō: Meiji Taishō hen* 日本金融史資料: 明治大正編, vol. 22. Tokyo, 1959.

NHK hōsō yoron chōsajo 日本放送世論調査所, ed. *Gendai Nihonjin no ishiki kōzō* 現代日本人の意識構造. (*NHK Books*, 344) NHK ブックス. Tokyo: Nihon hōsō shuppankai, 1979.

Nihon kokusai seiji gakkai 日本国際政治学会. *Taiheiyō sensō e no michi* 太平洋戦争への道, 8 vols. Tokyo: Asahi shinbunsha, 1962–3.

Nihon seiji gakkai 日本政治学会, ed. *Nihon no shakaishugi* 日本の社会主義. Tokyo: Iwanami shoten, 1968.

Nihon seiji gakkai 日本政治学会, ed. "*Konoe shintaisei" no kenkyū*" 「近衛新体制」の研究. (*Nenpō seijigaku 1972*) 年報政治学 1972. Tokyo: Iwanami shoten, 1973.

Nihon tekkō renmei 日本鉄鋼連盟. *Sengo tekkō shi* 戦後鉄鋼史. Tokyo: Nihon tekkō renmei, 1959.

Nihonjin kenkyūkai 日本人研究会. ed. *Nihonjin kenkyū, 2 Tokushū: Shijiseitō betsu Nihonjin shūdan* 日本人研究, 2 特集: 支持政党別日本人集団. Tokyo: Shiseido, 1975.

Nish, Ian. *Japan's Foreign Policy, 1868–1942: Kasumigaseki to Miyakezaka*. London: Routledge & Kegan Paul, 1977.

Nishida Kitarō 西田幾多郎. *Zen no kenkyū* 善の研究. Tokyo: Iwanami shoten, 1946.

Nishida Yoshiaki 西田美昭. "Kosaku sōgi no tenkai to jisakunō sōsetsu iji seisaku" 小作争議の展開と自作農創設維持政策. *Hitotsubashi ronsō* 一橋論叢 60 (November 1968): 524–46.

Nishida Yoshiaki 西田美昭. "Shōnō keiei no hatten to kosaku sōgi" 小農経営の発展と小作争議. *Tochi seido shigaku* 土地制度史学, no. 38 (1968): 24–41.

Nishida Yoshiaki 西田美昭. "Reisai nōkōsei to jinushiteki tochi shoyū: Niigata ken ichi tezukuri jinushi no bunseki" 零細農耕制と地主的土地所有: 新潟県一手作地主の分析. *Hitotsubashi ronsō* 一橋論叢 63 (1970).

Nishida Yoshiaki 西田美昭. "Nōmin undō no hatten to jinushi sei" 農民運動の発展と地主制. *Iwanami kōza Nihon rekishi* 岩波講座 日本歴史, vol. 18, Tokyo: Iwanami shoten, 1975.

Nishida Yoshiaki 西田美昭, ed. *Shōwa kyōkōka no nōson shakai undō* 昭和恐慌下の農村社会運動. Tokyo: Ochanomizu shobō, 1978.

Nishikawa Shunsaku 西川俊作. " 'Chōki keizai tōkei' no keiryō keizaigaku – Ōkawa hoka *Kokumin shotoku* no tembō rombun"「長期経済統計」の計量経済学—大川他国民所得の展望論文. *Kikan riron keizaigaku* 季刊理論経済学 27 (August 1976): 126–34.

Nishikawa Shunsaku, ed., and Mouer, Ross, trans. *The Labor Market in Japan*. Tokyo: Tokyo University Press, 1980.

Nishimura Kumao 西村熊雄. *San Furanshisuko heiwa jōyaku* サンフランシスコ平和条約, vol. 27 of *Nihon gaiko shi* 日本外交史, ed. Kajima heiwa kenkyūjo 鹿島平和研究所. Tokyo: Kajima kenkyūjo shuppankai, 1971.

Nishio Masaru 西尾勝. "Gyōsei katei ni okeru taikō undō: Jūmin undō ni tsuite no ichikōsatsu" 行政過程における対抗運動—住民運動についての一考察. In *Nenpō seijigaku* 年報政治学 1974 (*Seiji sanka no riron to genjitsu*) 政治参加の理論と現実, ed. Nihon seiji gakkai 日本政治学会. Tokyo: Iwanami shoten, 1975.

Nishio Masaru 西尾勝. "Kaso to kamitsu no seiji gyōsei" 過疎と過密の政治行政. In *Nenpō seijigaku* 年報政治学 1977 (*55-nen taisei no keisei to hōkai: Zoku gendai Nihon no seiji katei*) 55年体制の形成と崩壊: 続現代日本の政治過程, ed. Nihon seiji gakkai 日本政治学会. Tokyo: Iwanami shoten, 1979.

Nishio Yōtarō 西尾陽太郎. *Kōtoku Shūsui* 幸徳秋水. Tokyo: Yoshikawa Kōbunkan, 1959.

Nishioka Takao 西岡孝男. *Nihon no rōdō kumiai soshiki* 日本の労働組合組織. Tokyo: Japan Institute of Labor, 1960.

Nitobe Inazō 新渡戸稲造. *Zenshū* 全集, 16 vols. Tokyo: Kyōbunkan, 1969–70.

Nōmin undōshi kenkyūkai 農民運動史研究会, ed. *Nihon nōmin undōshi* 日本農民運動史. Tokyo: Tōyō keizai shinpōsha, 1961.

Nomura Masao 野村正男. *Hōsō fūunroku - ge* 法曹風雲録—下. Tokyo; Asahi shinbunsha, 1966.

Nōsei chōsakai nōchi kaikaku kiroku iinkai 農制調査会農地改革記録委員会. "Shōwa 8-10 nen kijun seisan shisū 昭和8-10年基準生産指数. In *Dai sanjū ji Nōrinshō tōkeihyō* 第三十次農林省統計表. Tokyo, 1900.

Nōsei chōsakai nōchi kaikaku kiroku iinkai 農制調査会農地改革記録委員会. *Nōchi kaikaku tenmatsu gaiyō* 農地改革てん末概要. Tokyo, 1951.

Notehelfer, F. G. *Kōtoku Shūsui: Portrait of a Japanese Radical*. Cambridge, England: Cambridge University Press, 1971.

Oda Toshiyo 小田俊與. *Yokusan undō to Konoe-kō* 翼賛運動と近衛公. Tokyo: Shunpei shobō, 1940.

Odaka Konosuke 尾高煌之助. "Dainiji taisen zengo no kyū-Mitsubishi jūkō rōdō tōkei ni tsuite" 第二次大戦前後の旧三菱重工労働統計について. *Hitotsubashi ronsō* 一橋論叢 74 (1975): 1-16.

Odaka, Konosuke. "Historical Development in the Wage-Differential Structure." Paper presented at the Japan Economic Seminar, New York City, April 14, 1973.

Ōe Shinobu 大江志乃夫. "Shokuminchi ryōyū to gunbu" 植民地領有と軍部. *Rekishigaku kenkyū* 歴史学研究 (September 1978): 10-41.

Ogata, Sadako. *Defiance in Manchuria: The Making of Japanese Foreign Policy, 1931-1932*. Berkeley and Los Angeles: University of California Press, 1964.

Ogura Takekazu 小倉武一. *Tochi rippō no shiteki kōsatsu* 土地立法の史的考察. Tokyo: Nōrinshō nōgyō sōgō kenkyūjo, 1951.

Ogura, Takekazu, ed. *Agricultural Development in Modern Japan*. Tokyo: Fuji Publishing, 1963.

Ogura, Takekazu. *Can Japanese Agriculture Survive?* 2nd ed. Tokyo: Agricultural Policy Research Institute, 1980.

Ōhara shakai mondai kenkyūjo 大原社会問題研究所. *Nihon rōdō nenkan* 日本労働年鑑, vol. 50. Tokyo: Rōdō junpōsha, 1979.

Ōhashi Takanori 大橋隆憲. *Nihon no kaikyū kōsei* 日本の階級構成. (*Iwanami shinsho*, no. 789) 岩波新書. Tokyo: Iwanami shoten, 1971.

Ohkawa, Kazushi. *Differential Structure and Agriculture: Essays on Dualistic Growth*. Tokyo: Kinokuniya, 1972.

Ohkawa, Kazushi, and Rosovsky, Henry. "The Role of Agriculture in Modern Japanese Economic Development." *Economic Development and Cultural Change* 9 (October 1960): 43-67.

Ohkawa, Kazushi, and Rosovsky, Henry. *Japanese Economic Growth: Trend Acceleration in the Twentieth Century*. Stanford, Calif.: Stanford University Press, 1973.

Ohkawa, Kazushi, and Shinohara, Miyohei, with Meissner, Larry, eds. *Patterns of Japanese Economic Development: A Quantitative Appraisal*. New Haven, Conn.: Yale University Press, 1979.

Ohkawa, Kazushi, with Shinohara, Miyohei, Umemura, M., Ito, M., and

Noda, T. *The Growth Rate of the Japanese Economy Since 1878*. Tokyo: Kinokuniya, 1957.

Ōi Atsushi 大井篤. *Kaijō goeisen* 海上護衛戦. Tokyo: Nihon shuppan kyōdō, 1952.

Ōishi Kaichirō 大石嘉一郎. "Nōchi kaikaku no rekishiteki igi" 農地改革の歴史的意義. In *Nōchi kaikaku* 農地改革, vol. 6 of *Sengo kaikaku* 戦後改革, ed. Tōkyō daigaku shakaikagaku kenkyūjo 東京大学社会科学研究所. Tokyo: Tōkyō daigaku shuppankai, 1974–5.

Oka Toshirō 岡利郎. "Kindai Nihon ni okeru shakai seisaku shisō no keisei to tenkai" 近代日本における社会政策思想の形成と展開. *Shisō* 思想 558 (December 1970): 69–88.

Oka Yoshitake 岡義武, ed. *Gendai Nihon no seiji katei* 現代日本の政治過程. Tokyo: Iwanami shoten, 1958.

Oka, Yoshitake. "Generational Conflict after the Russo-Japanese War." In *Conflict in Modern Japanese History*, ed. Tetsuo Najita and Victor Koschmann. Princeton, N.J.: Princeton University Press, 1982.

Oka Yoshitake 岡義武 and Hayashi Shigeru 林茂, eds. *Taishō demokurashii ki no seiji, Matsumoto Gōkichi seiji nisshi* 大正モデクラシー期の政治, 松本剛吉政治日誌. Tokyo: Iwanami shoten, 1959.

Okakura, Kakuzo. *Ideals of the East, with Special Reference to the Art of Japan*. Rutland, Vt.: Tuttle, 1970.

Okamoto, Shumpei. *The Japanese Oligarchy and the Russo-Japanese War*. New York: Columbia University Press, 1970.

Ōkawa Kazushi 大川一司 et al. *Chōki keizai tōkei – 1: Kokumin shotoku* 長期経済統計・1: 国民所得. Tokyo: Tōyō keizai shinpōsha, 1974.

Ōkawa Shūmei 大川周明. "Nihon seishin kenkyu" 日本精神研究. In *Gendai Nihon shisō taikei* 現代日本思想大系, vol. 31: *Chōkokka shugi* 超国家主義, ed. Hashikawa Bunzō 橋川文三. Tokyo: Chikuma shobō, 1964.

Ōkawa Shūmei 大川周明. "Anraku no mon" 安楽の門. In *Gendai Nihon shisō taikei*, vol. 9: *Ajia Shugi* 現代日本思想大系 9: アジア主義, ed. Takeuchi Yoshimi 竹内好, Tokyo: Chikuma shobō, 1964.

Ōkawa Shūmei 大川周明. "Kakumei Europpa to fukkō Ajia" 革命ヨーロッパと復興アジア. In *Gendai Nihon shisō taikei*, vol. 9: *Ajia Shugi* 現代日本思想大系 9: アジア主義, ed. Takeuchi Yoshimi 竹内好. Tokyo: Chikuma shobō, 1964.

*Okazaki Ayakoto* 岡崎文勲. *Kihon kokuryoku dōtai sōran* 基本国力動態総覧. Tokyo: Kokumin keizai kenkyū kyōkai, 1953.

Oki Kibatarō denki hensan gakari 沖牙太郎伝記編纂係, ed. *Oki Kibatarō* 沖牙太郎. Tokyo: Oki Kibatarō denki hensan gakari, 1932.

Oki Shūji 沖修二. *Yamashita Tomoyuki* 山下奉文. Tokyo: Akita shoten, 1968.

Ōkōchi Kazuo 大河内和男. *Reimeiki no Nihon rōdō undō* 黎明期の日本労働運動. Tokyo: Iwanami shoten, 1952.

Ōkōchi Kazuo 大河内一男. *Sengo Nihon no rōdō undō* 戦後日本の労働運動, rev. ed. 改訂版. (*Iwanami shinsho*, no. 217) 岩波新書. Tokyo: Iwanami shoten, 1961.

Ōkōchi Kazuo sensei kanreki kinen ronbunshū hakkō iinkai 大河内一男先生還暦記念論文集発行委員会, ed. *Ōkōchi Kazuo sensei kanreki kinen ronbunshū, 2, Rōdō keizai to rōdō undō* 大河内一男先生還暦記念論文集, 第 2 巻 労働経済と労働運動. Tokyo, 1966.
Ōkōchi Kazuo 大河内和男. *Kurai tanima no rōdō undō* 暗い谷間の労働運動. Tokyo: Iwanami shoten, 1970.
Okuda, Kenji. "Managerial Evolution in Japan." *Management Japan*, vol. 5, nos. 3 & 4, 1971–2; vol. 6, no. 1, 1972.
Okudaira Yasuhiro 奥平康弘. "Hōsōhōsei no saihensei" 放送法制の再編成. In *Seiji katei* 政治過程, vol. 3 of *Sengo kaikaku* 戦後改革, ed. Tōkyō daigaku shakaikagaku kenkyūjo 東京大学社会科学研究所. Tokyo: Tōkyō daigaku shuppankai, 1974–5.
Okumura Kiwao 奥村喜和男. "Henkaku-ki Nihon no seiji keizai" 変革期日本の政治経済. In *Kenryoku no shisō* 権力の思想, ed. Kamishima Jirō 神島次郎, vol. 10 of *Gendai Nihon shisō taikei* 現代日本思想大系. Tokyo: Chikuma shobō, 1965. pp. 274–90.
Ōkurashō zaiseishi hensanshitsu 大蔵省財政史編纂室. *Shōwa zaiseishi dai 10-kan kin'yū jō* 昭和財政史 第10巻 金融 上. Tokyo: Tōyō keizai shinpōsha, 1955.
Ōkurashō zaiseishishitsu 大蔵省財政史室. *Shōwa zaisei shi: shūsen kara kōwa made* 昭和財政史: 終戦から講和まで, vol. 20. Tokyo: Tōyō keizai shinpōsha, 1982.
Ōmae Sakurō 大前朔郎 and Ikeda Shin 池田信. *Nihon rōdō undō shiron* 日本労働運動史論. Tokyo: Nihon hyōronsha, 1966.
Orchard, John E. *Japan's Economic Position: The Progress of Industrialization in Japan*. New York: McGraw-Hill, 1930.
Ōsawa Masamichi 大沢正道. *Ōsugi Sakae kenkyū* 大杉栄研究. Tokyo: Dōseisha, 1968.
Oshima, Harry T. "Meiji Fiscal Policy and Agricultural Progress." In *The State and Economic Enterprise in Japan: Essays in the Political Economy of Growth*, ed. William W. Lockwood. Princeton, N.J.: Princeton University Press, 1965.
Ōta Masao 太田雅夫, ed. *Taishō demokurashii ronshū* 大正デモクラシー論集, vols. 1 and 2. Tokyo: Shinsuisha, 1971.
Ōta Toshie 太田敏兄. "Kosakunō kaikyū no keizaiteki shakaiteki jōtai" 小作農階級の経済的社会的状態. *Sangyō kumiai* 産業組合 no. 261 (1927): 83–111.
Ōtani Keijirō 大谷敬二郎. *Rakujitsu no joshō* 落日の序章. Tokyo: Yagumo shoten, 1959.
Ōtani Keijirō 大谷敬二郎. *Shōwa kenpeishi* 昭和憲兵史. Tokyo: Misuzu shobō, 1966.
Otoda Masami 音田正巳. "Kōgai mondai" 公害問題. In *Shōwa keizai shi* 昭和経済史, ed. Arisawa Hiromi 有沢広巳. Tokyo: Nihon keizai shinbunsha, 1976.
Ōtsu Jun'ichirō 大津淳一郎. *Dai Nippon kensei shi* 大日本憲政史, vol. 6. Tokyo: Hōbunkan, 1927–8.

Ōtsuka Katsuo 大塚勝夫. "Seishigyō ni okeru gijutsu dōnyū" 製糸業における技術導入. In *Nihon keizai no hatten* 日本経済の発展, ed. Umemura Mataji 梅村又次 et al. Tokyo: Nihon keizai shinbunsha, 1976.

Ōtsuka, Katsuo. "Technological Choice in the Japanese Silk Industry: Implications for Development in LDCs." (Working Paper Series no. A-05, mimeographed). Tokyo: International Development Center of Japan, March 1977.

Ōuchi Tsutomu 大内力. *Nihon nōgyō no zaiseigaku* 日本農業の財政学. Tokyo: Tōkyō daigaku shuppankai, 1950.

Ōuchi Tsutomu 大内力. "Nōchi kaikaku" 農地改革. In *Shōwa keizai shi* 昭和経済史, ed. Arisawa Hiromi 有沢広巳. Tokyo: Nihon keizai shinbunsha, 1976.

Oyama Azusa 大山梓. *Nichi-Ro sensō no gunsei shiroku* 日露戦争の軍政史録. Tokyo: Fūyo shobō, 1973.

Ōyama Ikuo 大山郁夫. "Kokka seikatsu to kyōdō rigai kannen" 国家生活と共同利害観念. *Shin shosetsu* 新小説 (February 1917).

Ōyama Ikuo 大山郁夫. "Rokoku kagekiha no jisseiryoku ni taisuru kashohi to sono seiji shisō no kachi ni taisuru kadaishi" 露国過激派の実勢力に対する過小視とその政治思想の価値に対する過大視. *Chūō kōron* 中央公論 (May 1917).

Ōyama Ikuo 大山郁夫. *Ōyama Ikuo zenshū* 大山郁夫全集, vol. 1. Tokyo: Chūō kōronsha, 1947.

Ozawa Yūsaku 小沢有作. "Kyū Nihonjin jinushi no Chōsenkan" 旧日本人地主の朝鮮観. *Chōsen kenkyū* 朝鮮研究 (December 1968): 34–41.

Packard, George R., III. *Protest in Tokyo: The Security Crisis of 1960*. Princeton, N.J.: Princeton University Press, 1966.

Passin, Herbert. *Society and Education in Japan*. New York: Teachers College, Columbia University, 1965.

Patrick, Hugh T. "Japan 1868–1914." In *Banking in the Early Stages of Industrialization*, ed. Rondo Cameron et al. London: Oxford University Press, 1967.

Patrick, Hugh T. "The Economic Muddle of the 1920's." In *Dilemmas of Growth in Prewar Japan*, ed. James W. Morley. Princeton, N.J.: Princeton University Press, 1971.

Patrick, Hugh T., ed. *Japanese Industrialization and Its Social Consequences*. Berkeley and Los Angeles: University of California Press, 1976.

Patrick, Hugh T., and Rosovsky, Henry, eds. *Asia's New Giant: How the Japanese Economy Works*. Washington, D.C.: Brookings Institution, 1976.

Peattie, Mark R. *Ishiwara Kanji and Japan's Confrontation with the West*. Princeton, N.J.: Princeton University Press, 1975.

Peattie, Mark R. *Nan'yō: The Rise and Fall of the Japanese in Micronesia 1885–1945*. Honolulu: University of Hawaii Press, 1988.

Pempel, T. J., ed. *Policy Making in Contemporary Japan*. Ithaca, N.Y.: Cornell University Press, 1977.

Pempel, T. J. "Political Parties and Social Change: The Japanese Experience." In *Political Parties: Development and Decay*, ed. Louis Maizel and Joseph

Cooper. Beverly Hills, Calif: Sage, 1978.

Pempel, T. J., and Tsunekawa, K. "Corporatism without Labor? The Japanese Anomaly." In *Trends Toward Corporatist Intermediation*, ed. P. C. Schmitter and G. Lehmbruch. Beverly Hills, Calif: Sage, 1979.

Pierson, John D. *Tokutomi Sohō, 1863–1957: A Journalist for Modern Japan.* Princeton, N.J.: Princeton University Press, 1980.

Pittau, Joseph. *Political Thought in Early Meiji Japan.* Cambridge, Mass.: Harvard University Press, 1967.

Purcell, David, Jr. "Japanese Expansion in the South Pacific, 1890–1935." Ph.D. diss., University of Pennsylvania, 1967.

Pyle, Kenneth B. *The New Generation in Meiji Japan: Problems of Cultural Identity.* Stanford, Calif.: Stanford University Press, 1969.

Pyle, Kenneth B. "The Technology of Japanese Nationalism." *Journal of Asian Studies* 33 (November 1973): 51–65.

Pyle, Kenneth B. "Advantages of Followership: German Economics and Japanese Bureaucrats, 1890–1925." *Journal of Japanese Studies* 1 (Autumn 1974): 127–64.

Quigley, Harold S. *Japanese Government and Politics: An Introductory Study.* New York: Century, 1932.

Ranis, Gustav. "The Financing of Japanese Economic Development." In *Agriculture and Economic Growth: Japan's Experience*, ed. Kazushi Ohkawa et al. Tokyo: Tokyo University Press; and Princeton, N.J.: Princeton University Press, 1969.

Redford, Lawrence H., ed. *The Occupation of Japan.* Norfolk, Va.: MacArthur Memorial, 1980.

Reischauer, Edwin O. *The United States and Japan*, rev. ed. New York: Viking 1957.

Reynolds, Lloyd G., and Gregory, Peter. *Wages, Productivity and Industrialization in Puerto Rico.* Homewood, Ill.: Irwin, 1965.

Rikugunshō 陸軍省. "Jūyō sangyō gokanen keikaku jisshi ni kansuru seisaku taikō (an)" 重要産業 5 ヶ年計画実施に関する政策大綱(案). In *Gendaishi shiryō – 8: Nitchū sensō* 現代史資料 8: 日中戦争, ed. Shimada Toshihiko 島田俊彦 and Inaba Masao 稲葉正夫. Tokyo: Misuzu shobō, 1964.

Roden, Donald. "Baseball and the Quest for National Dignity in Meiji Japan." *American Historical Review* 85 (June 1980): 511–34.

Rōdō daijin kambō tōkei jōhō bu 労働大臣官房統計情報部, ed. *Nihonjin no kinrō kan* 日本人の勤労観. Tokyo: Shiseidō, 1974.

Rōdō undōshi kenkyūkai 労働運動史研究会. *Chokugen* 直言. Tokyo: Meiji bunken shiryō kankōkai, 1960.

Rōdō undōshi kenkyūkai 労働運動史研究会. *Shinkigen* 新紀元. Tokyo: Meiji bunken shiryō kankōkai, 1961.

Rōdō undō shiryō iinkai 労働運動史料委員会. *Rōdō sekai* 労働世界. Tokyo: Rōdō undō shiryō kankō iinkai, 1960.

Rōdō undō shiryō iinkai 労働運動史料委員会, ed. *Nihon rōdō undō shiryō* 日本労

働運動史料, vol. 3. Tokyo: Rōdō undō shiryō kankō iinkai, 1968.

Rōdō undō shiryō iinkai 労働運動史料委員会, ed. *Nihon rōdō undō shiryō* 日本労働運動史料, vols. 6 and 9. Tokyo: Rōdō undō shiryō kankō iinkai, 1965.

Rōdō undō shiryō iinkai 労働運動史料委員会, ed. *Nihon rōdō undō shiryō* 日本労働運動史料, vol. 10. Tokyo: Rōdō undō shiryō kankō iinkai, 1959.

Rōdōshō 労働省. *1954-nen kojinbetsu chingin chōsa* 1954年個人別賃金調査. Tokyo: Rōdōshō, 1955.

Rōdōshō 労働省. *1961-nen chinginjittai sōgō chōsa* 1961年賃金実態総合調査. Tokyo: Rōdōshō, 1962.

Rōdōshō – Daijin kanbō rōdō tōkei chōsabu 労働省·大臣官房労働統計調査部. *Chinginkōzō kihon tōkei chōsa hōkoku* 賃金構造基本統計調査報告. Tokyo: 1965– .

Rōyama Masamichi 蝋山政道. *Nichi-Man kankei no kenkyū* 日満関係の研究. Tokyo: Shibun shoin, 1933.

Sagara Shunsuke 相良俊輔. *Akai yūhi no Masunogahara ni* 赤い夕陽の満州野が原に. Tokyo: Kōjinsha, 1978.

Saigusa Hiroto 三枝博音. *Nihon no yuibutsuronsha* 日本の唯物論者. Tokyo: Eihōsha, 1956.

Saitō Takao 斎藤隆夫. *Saitō Takao seiji ronshū* 斎藤隆夫政治論集. Izushi-machi, Izushi-gun, Hyōgo-ken: Saitō Takao sensei kenshōkai, 1961.

Saitō Yoshie 斎藤良衛. *Azamukareta rekishi* 欺かれた歴史. Tokyo: Yomiuri shinbunsha, 1955.

Sakaguchi Akira 阪口昭. "Iki fukikaesu zaikai" 息吹き返す財界. In *Shōwa keizai shi* 昭和経済史, ed. Arisawa Hiromi 有沢広巳. Tokyo: Nihon keizai shinbunsha, 1976.

Sakamoto Fujiyoshi 坂本藤良. *Nihon koyōshi* 日本雇用史. Tokyo: Chūō keizaisha, 1977.

Sanbō honbu 参謀本部, ed. *Sugiyama Memo* 杉山メモ, 2 vols. Tokyo: Hara shobō, 1967.

Sanpei Takako 三瓶孝子. *Nihon mengyō hattatsu shi* 日本綿業発達史. Tokyo: Keiō shobō, 1941.

Sansom, G. B. *Japan: A Short Cultural History*. Stanford, Calif.: Stanford University Press, 1957.

Sartori, Giovanni. *Parties and Party Systems: A Framework for Analysis*. Cambridge, England: Cambridge University Press, 1976.

Sashihara Yasuzō 指原安三編. Meiji seishi 明治政史, vol. 8. Tokyo: Fuzanbō shoten, 1893.

Satō Kazuo 佐藤和夫. "Senkanki Nihon no makuro keizai to mikuro keizai" 戦間期日本のマクロ経済とミクロ経済. In *Senkanki no Nihon keizai bunseki* 戦間期の日本経済分析, ed. Nakamura Takafusa 中村隆英. Tokyo: Yamakawa shuppansha, 1981.

Satō Kenryō 佐藤賢了. *Tōjō Hideki to Taiheiyō sensō* 東条英機と太平洋戦争. Tokyo: Bungei shunjū shinsha, 1960.

Satō Kenyrō 佐藤賢了. *Dai Tōa sensō kaikoroku* 大東亜戦争回顧録. Tokyo:

Tokuma shoten, 1966.

Satō Motohide 佐藤元英. "Tōhō kaigi to shoki Tanaka gaikō" 東方会議と初期田中外交. *Kokusai seiji* 国際政治, no. 66 (1980).

Satō Susumu 佐藤進. *Nihon no zeikin* 日本の税金. Tokyo: Tōkyō daigaku shuppankai, 1979.

Satō Tatsuo 佐藤達夫. *Nihonkoku kenpō seiritsu shi* 日本国憲法成立史, 2 vols. Tokyo: Yūhikaku, 1962, 1964.

Satō Tetsutarō 佐藤鉄太郎. *Teikoku kokubō shi ronshō* 帝国国防史論抄. Tokyo: Tōkyō insatsu kabushiki gaisha, 1912.

Sawyer, M. Income Distribution in OECD Countries. Paris: Organization for Economic Cooperation and Development, 1976.

Saxonhouse, Gary S. "Country Girls and Communication Among Competitors in the Japanese Cotton-Spinning Industry." In *Japanese Industrialization and Its Social Consequences*, ed. Hugh T. Patrick. Berkeley and Los Angeles: University of California Press, 1976.

Scalapino, Robert A. *Democracy and the Party Movement in Prewar Japan: The Failure of the First Attempt.* Berkeley and Los Angeles: University of California Press, 1962.

Scalapino, Robert A. *The Japanese Communist Movement, 1920–1966*. Berkeley and Los Angeles: University of California Press, 1967.

Scalapino, Robert A. "Elections and Political Modernization in Prewar Japan." In *Political Development in Modern Japan*, ed. Robert E. Ward. Princeton, N.J.: Princeton University Press, 1968.

Scalapino, Robert A., ed. *The Foreign Policy of Modern Japan*. Berkeley and Los Angeles: University of California Press, 1977.

Scalapino, Robert A., and Masumi, Junnosuke. *Parties and Politics in Contemporary Japan.* Berkeley and Los Angeles: University of California Press, 1962.

Schaller, Michael. *The U.S. Crusade in China, 1938–1945*. New York: Columbia University Press, 1979.

Schroeder, Paul W. *The Axis Alliance and Japanese-American Relations*. Ithaca, N.Y.: Cornell University Press. 1971.

Seki Hiroharu 関寛治. "Taigai kankei no kōzōhenka to gaikō" 対外関係の構造変化と外交. In *Nenpō seijigaku* 年報政治学 1977 (*55-nen taisei no keisei to hōkai: Zoku gendai Nihon no seiji katei*) 55年体制の形成と崩壊—続現代日本の政治過程, ed. Nihon seiji gakkai 日本政治学会. Tokyo: Iwanami shoten, 1979.

Seki Kanji 関寛治. "Manshū jihen zenshi" 満州事変前史. In *Taiheiyō sensō e no michi* 太平洋戦争への道, vol. 1, ed. Nihon kokusai seiji gakkai Taiheiyō sensō gen'in kenkyūbu 日本国際政治学会太平洋戦争原因研究部. Tokyo: Asahi shimbunsha, 1962.

Semple, Elizabeth C. "Japanese Colonial Methods." *Bulletin of the American Geographical Society* (April 1913).

Shibagaki Kazuo 柴垣和夫. "Zaibatsu kaitai to shūchū haijo" 財閥解体と集中排

除. In *Keizai kaikaku* 経済改革, vol. 7 of *Sengo kaikaku* 戦後改革, ed. Tōkyō daigaku shakaikagaku kenkyūjo 東京大学社会科学研究所. Tokyo: Tōkyō daigaku shuppankai, 1974–5.

Shibusawa, Keizo, comp. and ed. *Japanese Life and Culture in the Meiji Era*, trans. Charles S. Terry. In *Japanese Culture in the Meiji Era*, vol. 5, ed. Centenary Cultural Council. Tokyo: Ōbunsha, 1958.

Shidehara heiwa zaidan 幣原平和財団, ed. *Shidehara Kijūrō* 幣原喜重郎. Tokyo: Shidehara heiwa zaidan, 1955.

Shigemitsu, Mamoru. *Japan and Her Destiny*, ed. F. S. G. Piggott and trans. Oswald White. London: Hutchinson, 1958.

Shillony, Ben-Ami. *Revolt in Japan*. Princeton, N.J.: Princeton University Press, 1973.

Shillony, Ben-Ami. *Politics and Culture in Wartime Japan*. Oxford, England: Clarendon Press, 1980.

Shima Yasuhiko 島恭彦 et al. *Chōson gappei to nōson no henbō* 町村合併と農村の変貌. Tokyo: Yūhikaku, 1958.

Shimada Toshihiko 島田俊彦. *Kantōgun* 関東軍. Tokyo: Chūō shinsō, 1965.

Shimane ken nōrinbu, nōchi kaitakuka 島根県農林部, 農地開拓課, ed. *Shimane ken nōchi kaikaku shi* 島根県農地改革誌. Hirata: Shimane ken, 1959.

Shimane Kiyoshi しまね きよし. "Tsuihō kaijo o yōsei suru ronri" 追放解除を要請する論理. In *Kyōdō kenkyū: Nihon senryō* 共同研究: 日本占領, ed. Shisō no kagaku kenkyūkai 思想の科学研究会. Tokyo: Tokuma shoten, 1972.

Shimizu Mutsumi 清水睦. "Kenpō 'kaisei' to gikai-seido kaikaku" 憲法「改正」と議会制度改革. In *Seiji katei* 政治過程, vol. 3 of *Sengo kaikaku* 戦後改革, ed. Tōkyō daigaku shakaikagaku kenkyūjo 東京大学社会科学研究所. Tokyo: Tōkyō daigaku shuppankai, 1974–5.

Shimomura Kainan 下村海南. *Shūsenki* 終戦記. Tokyo: Kamakura bunko, 1948.

Shimura Yoshikazu 志村嘉一. "Antei kyōkō" 安定恐慌. In *Shōwa keizai shi* 昭和経済史, ed. Arisawa Hiromi 有沢広巳. Tokyo: Nihon keizai shinbunsha, 1976.

Shinmyō Takeo 新名丈夫. *Kaigun sensō kentō kaigi kiroku: Taiheiyō sensō kaisen no keii* 海軍戦争検討会議記録: 太平洋戦争開戦の経緯. Tokyo: Mainichi shinbunsha, 1976.

Shinohara Hajime 篠原一. *Gendai Nihon no bunka henyō: Sono seijigakuteki kōsatsu* 現代日本の文化変容: その政治学的考察. Tokyo: Renga shobō, 1971.

Shinohara Hajime 篠原一 and Miyazaki Ryūji 宮崎隆次. "Sengo kaikaku to seiji karuchā" 戦後改革と政治カルチャー. In *Kadai to shikaku* 課題と視角, vol. 1 of *Sengo kaikaku* 戦後改革, ed. Tōkyō daigaku shakaikagaku kenkyūjo 東京大学社会科学研究所. Tokyo: Tokyo daigaku shappankai, 1974–5.

Shinohara, Miyohei. *Growth and Cycles in the Japanese Economy*. Tokyo: Kinokuniya, 1962.

Shinohara Miyohei 篠原三代平. *Chōki keizai tōkei – 10: Kōkōgyō* 長期経済統計·10: 鉱工業. Tokyo: Tōyō keizai shinpōsha, 1972.

Shinohara Miyohei 篠原三代平, and Funahashi Naomichi 舟橋尚道, eds. *Nihon-*

*gata chinginkōzō no kenkyū* 日本型賃金構造の研究. Tokyo: Rōdō hōgaku kenkyūjo, 1961.

Shiota Shōbei 塩田庄兵衛. *Sutoraiki no rekishi* ストライキの歴史. Tokyo: Shin Nihon shuppansha, 1966.

Shiraki Masayuki 白木正之. *Nihon seitō shi: Shōwa hen* 日本政党史: 昭和編. Tokyo: Chūō kōronsha, 1949.

Shisō no kagaku kenkyūkai 思想の科学研究会, ed. *Kyōdō kenkyū: Nihon senryō kenkyū jiten* 共同研究: 日本占領研究事典 (*Kyōdō kenkyū: Nihon senryōgun*, appendix) 共同研究: 日本占領軍, 別冊. Tokyo: Tokuma shoten, 1978.

Shōda Tatsuo 勝田龍夫. Jūshintachi no Shōwa shi 重臣たちの昭和史, 2 vols. Tokyo, 1981.

Shōwa dōjinkai 昭和同人会, ed. *Waga kuni kanzenkoyō no igi to taisaku* 我国完全雇用の意義と対策. Tokyo: Shōwa dōjinkai, 1957.

*Shōwa shi no tennō* 昭和史の天皇, 30 vols. Tokyo: Yomiuri shinbunsha, 1967–75.

Shūgiin 衆議院 and Sangiin 参議院編, eds. *Gikai seido shichijū-nen shi* 議会制度七十年史, 12 vols. Tokyo: Ōkurashō insatsukyoku 大蔵省印刷局. 1960–62.

Shunpōkō tsuishōkai 春畝公追頌会. Itō Hirobumi den 伊藤博文伝, vol. 2. Tokyo: Shunpōkō tsuishōkai, 1940.

Sievers, Sharon Lee. "Kōtoku Shūsui, The Essence of Socialism: A Translation and Biographical Essay." Ph.D. diss., Stanford University, 1969.

Silberman, Bernard, and Harootunian, H. D., eds. *Japan in Crisis: Essays on Taishō Democracy*. Princeton, N.J.: Princeton University Press, 1974.

Sinha, R. P. "Unresolved Issues in Japan's Early Economic Development." *Scottish Journal of Political Economy* 16 (June 1969): 141–8.

Smethurst, Richard J. "The Military Reserve Association and the Minobe Crisis in 1935." In *Crisis Politics in Prewar Japan: Institutional and Ideological Problems of the 1930s*, ed. George M. Wilson. Tokyo: Sophia University Press, 1970.

Smethurst, Richard J. *A Social Basis for Prewar Japanese Militarism: The Army and the Rural Community*. Berkeley and Los Angeles: University of California Press, 1974.

Smith, Henry D., II. *Japan's First Student Radicals*. Cambridge, Mass.: Harvard University Press, 1972.

Smith, Robert J. *Kurusu: The Price of Progress in a Japanese Village, 1951–1975*. Folkestone, Kent: Dawson, 1978.

Smith, Thomas C. *Political Change and Industrial Development in Japan: Government Enterprise 1868–1880*. Stanford, Calif.: Stanford University Press, 1955.

Soda Osamu 祖田修. *Maeda Masana* 前田正名. Tokyo: Yoshikawa kōbunkan, 1973.

Soda Osamu 祖田修. *Chihō sangyō no shisō to undō* 地方産業の思想と運動. Kyoto: Minerva shobō, 1980.

Soma Masao 杣正夫. "Senkyo seido no kaikaku" 選挙制度の改革. In *Seiji katei*

政治過程, vol. 3 of *Sengo kaikaku* 戦後改革, ed. Tōkyō daigaku shakaikagaku kenkyūjo 東京大学社会科学研究所. Tokyo: Tokyo daigaku shuppankai, 1974–5.

Sōrifu tōkeikyoku 総理府統局, ed. *Nihon no tōkei* 日本の統計. Tokyo: Ōkurashō insatsu kyoku, annual.

Spaulding, Robert M., Jr. *Imperial Japan's Higher Civil Service Examinations*. Princeton, N.J.: Princeton University Press, 1967.

Spaulding, Robert M., Jr. "Japan's 'New Bureaucrats,' 1932–1945." In *Crisis Politics in Prewar Japan: Institutional and Ideological Problems of the 1930s*, ed. George M. Wilson. Tokyo: Sophia University Press, 1970.

Spaulding, Robert M., Jr. "The Bureaucracy as a Political Force, 1920–1945." In *Dilemmas of Growth in Prewar Japan*, ed. James W. Morley. Princeton, N.J.: Princeton University Press, 1971.

Stanley, Thomas A. *Ōsugi Sakae: Anarchist in Taishō Japan*. Cambridge, Mass.: Harvard University Press, 1982.

Steiner, Kurt. *Local Government in Japan*. Stanford, Calif.: Stanford University Press, 1965.

Steiner, K., Krauss, E., and Flanagan, S. C., eds. *Political Opposition and Local Politics in Japan*. Princeton, N.J.: Princeton University Press, 1980.

Stephan, John. *Sakhalin: A History*. Oxford, England: Clarendon Press, 1971.

Steven, R. P. G. "Hybrid Constitutionalism in Prewar Japan." *Journal of Japanese Studies* 3 (Winter 1977): 183–216.

Stockwin, J. A. A. *The Japanese Socialist Party and Neutralism: A Study of a Political Party and Its Foreign Policy*. Carlton, Victoria, Australia: Melbourne University Press, 1968.

Stockwin, J. A. A. *Japan: Divided Politics in a Growth Economy*. New York: Norton, 1975.

Storry, G. Richard. *The Double Patriots: A Study of Japanese Nationalism*. Boston: Houghton Mifflin, 1957.

Storry, G. Richard. *Japan and the Decline of the West in Asia, 1894–1943*. New York: St. Martin's Press, 1979.

Sudō Shinji 須藤真志. "Tōjō naikaku to Nichi-Bei kōshō" 東条内閣と日米交渉. *Kyōto sangyō daigaku ronshū* 京都産業大学論集 10 (1980).

Suehiro Izutarō 末弘厳太郎. *Nihon rōdō kumiai undōshi* 日本労働組合運動史. Tokyo: Chūō kōronsha, 1954.

Sugihara Masami 杉原正巳. *Kokumin soshiki no seiji-ryoku* 国民組織の政治力. Tokyo: Modan Nipponsha, 1940.

Sugihara Masami 杉原正巳. *Atarashii Shōwa shi* 新しい昭和史. Tokyo: Shin kigensha, 1958.

Suh, Chang-chul. *Growth and Structural Change in the Korean Economy 1910–1940*. Cambridge, Mass: Council on East Asian Studies, Harvard University, 1978.

Sumiya Etsuji 住谷悦治. *Nihon keizaigaku shi – zōteiban* 日本経済学史·増訂版. Kyoto: Minerva shobō, 1967.

Sumiya Mikio 隅谷三喜男. *Nihon chinrōdō shiron* 日本賃労働史論. Tokyo: Tōkyō daigaku shuppankai, 1955.

Sumiya, Mikio. *Social Impact of Industrialization in Japan*. Tokyo: UNESCO, 1963.

Sumiya Mikio 隅谷三喜男. *Shōwa kyōkō* 昭和恐慌. Tokyo: Yūhikaku, 1974.

Sumiya Mikio 隅谷三喜男, ed. *Nihon rōshi kankei shiron* 日本労使関係史論. Tokyo: Tōkyō daigaku shuppankai, 1977.

Sumiya, Mikio, and Taira, Koji, eds. *An Outline of Japanese Economic History, 1603–1940*. Tokyo: Tokyo University Press, 1979.

Suzuki Masayuki 鈴木正幸. "Nichi-Ro sengo no nōson mondai no tenkai" 日露戦後の農村問題の展開. *Rekishigaku kenkyū* 歴史学研究 (1974 special issue): 150–61.

Suzuki Masayuki 鈴木正幸. "Taishōki nōmin seiji shisō no ichi sokumen – jō" 大正期農民政治思想の一側面(上). *Nihonshi kenkyū* 日本史研究, no. 173 (January 1977): 1–26.

Szal, Richard, and Robinson, Sherman. "Measuring Income Inequality." In *Income Distribution and Growth in the Less-Developed Countries*, ed. Charles R. Frank, Jr., and Richard C. Webb. Washington, D.C.: Brookings Institution, 1977.

Tachibana Kōsaburō 橘孝三郎. "Nihon aikoku kakushin hongi" 日本愛国革新本義. In *Gendai Nihon shiso taikei*, vol. 31: *Chōkokka shugi* 現代日本思想大系, 32, 超国家主義, ed. Hashikawa Bunzō 橋川文三. Tokyo: Chikuma shobō, 1964.

Tachibanaki Toshiaki 橘木俊昭. "Shūnyū bunpai to shotoku bunpai no fubyōdō" 収入分配と所得分配の不平等. *Kikan gendai keizai* 季刊現代経済, no. 28 (1977): 160–75.

Taikakai 大霞会, ed. *Naimushō shi* 内務省史, 4 vols. Tokyo: Chihō zaimu kyōkai, 1970.

Taira, Koji. "Characteristics of Japanese Labor Markets." *Economic Development and Cultural Change* 10 (January 1962): 150–68.

Taira, Koji. *Economic Development and the Labor Market in Japan.* New York: Columbia University Press, 1970.

Taira, Koji. "Education and Literacy in Meiji Japan: An Interpretation." *Explorations in Economic History* 8 (July 1971): 371–94.

*Taiyō* 太陽 16 (November 1910).

Takabatake Michitoshi 高畠通敏. "Taishū undō no tayōka to henshitsu" 大衆運動の多様化と変質. In *Nenpō seijigaku* 年報政治学 1977 (*55-nen taisei no keisei to hōkai: Zoku gendai nihon no seiji katei*) 55年体制の形成と崩壊—続現代日本の政治過程, ed. Nihon seiji gakkai 日本政治学会. Tokyo: Iwanami shoten, 1979.

Takagi Sōkichi 高木惣吉. *Taiheiyō sensō to riku-kaigun no kōsō* 太平洋戦争と陸海軍の抗争. Tokyo: Keizai Ōraisha, 1967.

Takagi Sōkichi 高木惣吉. *Shikan: Taiheiyō sensō* 私観: 太平洋戦争. Tokyo: Bungei shunjūsha, 1969.

Takahashi Hisashi 高橋久志. "Tōa kyōdōtai ron" 東亜協同体論. In *Nihon no 1930 nendai* 日本の一九三〇年代, ed. Miwa Kimitada 三輪公忠. Tokyo: Sōryūsha, 1980.

Takahashi Hiroshi 高橋紘 and Suzuki Kunihiko 鈴木邦彦. *Tennōke no misshi tachi: "Hiroku senryō" to kōshitsu* 天皇家の密使たち—「秘録」占領と皇室. Tokyo: Tokuma shoten, 1981.

Takahashi Iichirō 高橋伊一郎 and Shirakawa Kiyoshi 白川清, eds. *Nōchi kaikaku to jinushi sei* 農地改革と地主制. Tokyo: Ochanomizu shobō, 1955.

Takahashi Kamekichi 高橋亀吉. *Nihon zaibatsu no kaibō* 日本財閥の解剖. Tokyo: Chūō kōronsha, 1930.

Takahashi Kamekichi 高橋亀吉. *Taishō Shōwa zaikai hendōshi* 大正昭和財界変動史, 3 vols. Tokyo: Tōyō keizai shinpōsha, 1954.

Takahashi Korekiyo 高橋是清. *Zuisōroku* 随想録. Tokyo: Chikura shobō, 1936.

Takamura Naosuke 高村直助. *Nihon bōsekigyō shi josetsu* 日本紡績業史序説. Tokyo: Hanawa shobō, 1971.

Takasuka Yoshihiro 高須賀義博. *Gendai Nihon no bukka mondai* 現代日本の物価問題, rev. ed. Tokyo: Shinhyōron, 1975.

Takayama Shinobu 高山信武. *Sambō honbu sakusenka: sakusen ronsō no jissō to hansei* 参謀本部作戦課: 作戦論争の実相と反省. Tokyo: Fuyō shobō, 1978.

Takekoshi, Yosaburo. "Japan's Colonial Policy." In *Japan to America*, ed. Masaoka Naoichi. New York: Putnam, 1915.

Takekoshi Yosaburō 竹越與三郎, Inukai Tsuyoshi 犬養毅, et al. "Chōsen shidan zōsetsu mondai" 朝鮮師團増設問題. *Taiyō* 太陽 17 (August 1911): 81–92.

Takemae Eiji 竹前栄治. "Reddo pāji" レッドパージ. In *Kyōdō kenkyū: Nihon senryōgun: Sono hikari to kage* 共同研究: 日本占領軍: その光と影, vol. 1, ed. Shisō no kagaku kenkyūkai 思想の科学研究会. Tokyo: Tokuma shoten, 1978.

Takemae Eiji 竹前栄治. "1949-nen rōdōhō kaisei zenshi: Senryō seisaku o chūshin to shite" 1949年労働法改正前史—占領政策を中心として. In *Senryōki nihon no keizai to seiji* 占領期日本の経済と政治, ed. Nakamura Takafusa 中村隆英. Tokyo: Tōkyō daigaku shuppankai, 1979.

Takemae Eiji 竹前栄治. *Senryō sengo shi: Tai-Nichi kanri seisaku no zenyō* 占領戦後史: 対日管理政策の全容. Tokyo: Keisō shobō, 1980.

Takanaka Emiko 竹中恵美子. "Kyōkō to sensōka ni okeru rōdō shijō no henbō" 恐慌と戦争下における労働史上の変貌. *Kōza Nihon shihonshugi hattatsu shiron*, vol. 3: *Kyōkō kara sensō e* 講座 日本資本主義発達史論: III 恐慌から戦争へ, ed. Kawai Ichirō 川合一郎 et al. Tokyo: Hyōronsha, 1968.

Takeuchi Yoshimi 竹内好. *Hōhō to shite no Ajia: Waga senzen, senchū, sengo* 方法としてのアジア: わが戦前·戦中·戦後. Tokyo: Sōkisha, 1978.

Takeuchi Yoshimi 竹内好, and Kawakami Tetsutarō 河上徹太郎, eds. *Kindai no chōkoku* 近代の超克. Tokyo: Fuzambo, 1979.

Takeuchi Yoshitomo 竹内良知. *Shōwa shisōshi* 昭和思想史. Tokyo: Minerva shobō, 1958.

Takeuchi Yoshitomo 竹内良知 and Suzuki Tadashi 鈴木正. " '*Shinkō kagaku no hata no moto ni*' to '*Yuibutsuron kenkyū*' "「新興科学の旗のもとに」と「唯物論研究」. *Shisō* 思想 465 (March 1963): 108–19.

Tamura Yoshio 田村吉雄, ed. *Hiroku Daitōa sensō* 秘録大東亜戦争. Tokyo: Fuji shoen, 1952–5.

Tanaka Giichi 田中義一. "Zuikan zatsuroku" 随感雑録 (1906). In *Tanaka Giichi bunsho* 田中義一文書 in the possession of Yamaguchi ken bunsho kanzō 山口県文書館蔵.

Tanaka Manabu 田中学. "Nōchi kaikaku to nōmin undō" 農地改革と農民運動. In *Nōchi kaikaku* 農地改革, vol. 6 of *Sengo kaikaku* 戦後改革, ed. Tōkyō daigaku shakaikagaku kenkyūjo 東京大学社会科学研究所. Tokyo: Tōkyō daigaku shuppankai, 1974–5.

Tanaka Manabu 田中学. "Rōdōryoku chōtatsu kikō to rōshi kankei" 労働力調達機構と労使関係. In *Kaikakugo no Nihon keizai* 改革後の日本経済, vol. 8 of *Sengo kaikaku* 戦後改革, ed. Tōkyō daigaku shakaikagaku kenkyūjo 東京大学社会科学研究所. Tokyo: Tōkyō daigaku shuppankai, 1974–5.

Tanaka Ryūkichi 田中隆吉. *Haiin o tsuku: Gunbatsu sen'ō no jissō* 敗因を衝く：軍閥専横の実相. Tokyo: Sansuisha, 1946.

Tanaka Sōgorō 田中惣五郎, ed. *Shiryō: Taishō shakai undōshi* 史料·大正社会運動史. Tokyo: San'ichi shobō, 1970.

Tanemura Sakō 種村佐孝. *Daihonei kimitsu nisshi* 大本営機密日誌. Tokyo: Diamondosha, 1979.

Tanizaki, Junichirō. *In Praise of Shadows*, trans. Edward Seidensticker and Thomas Harper. New Haven, Conn.: Leete's Island Books, 1977.

Teishinshō 逓信省, ed. *Tetsudō kokuyū shimatsu ippan* 鐵道國有始末一斑. In *Nihon sangyō shiryō taikei* 日本産業資料大系, vol. 11, ed. Takimoto Seiichi 瀧本誠一 and Mukai Shikamatsu 向井鹿松. Tokyo: Chūgai shōgyō shinpōsha, 1927.

Tendō Akira 天藤明. *Sangokai daikaisen: Kantai jūgun hiroku* 珊瑚海大海戦：艦隊従軍秘録. Tokyo: Masu shobō, 1956.

Terasaki, Gwen. *Bridge to the Sun*. Harmondsworth, England: Penguin, 1962.

Tetsudō jihōkyoku 鐵道時報局, ed. *10-nen kinen Nihon no tetsudō ron* 10年記念日本の鐵道論. *Meiji-ki tetsudōshi shiryō* 明治期鉄道史資料, suppl. vol. 1, ed. Noda Masaho 野田正穂, Harada Katsumasa 原田勝正 and Aoki Eiichi 青木栄一. Tokyo: Nihon keizai hyōronsha, 1981.

Tetsudōin 鐵道院, ed. *Hompō tetsudō no shakai oyobi keizai ni oyoboseru eikyō* 本邦鐵道の社會及經濟に及ぼせる影響. Tokyo: Tetsudōin, 1930.

Tezuka Kazuaki 手塚和彰. "Kyū-rōdōkumiaihō no keisei to tenkai: Shoki rōdō iinkai no kinō bunseki o chūshin to shite" 旧労働組合法の形成と展開—初期労働委員会の機能分析を中心として—. In *Rōdō seisaku* 労働政策, vol. 5 *of Sengo kaikaku* 戦後改革, ed. Tōkyō daigaku shakaikagaku kenkyūjo 東京大学社会科学研究所. Tokyo: Tōkyō daigaku shuppankai, 1974–5.

Thayer, Nathaniel B. *How the Conservatives Rule Japan*. Princeton, N.J.: Princeton University Press, 1969.

Thorne, Christopher. *Allies of a Kind: The United States, Britain, and the War*

*Against Japan, 1941–1945*. New York: Oxford University Press, 1978.

Tiedemann, Arthur E. "Big Business and Politics in Prewar Japan." In *Dilemmas of Growth in Prewar Japan*, ed. James W. Morley. Princeton, N.J.: Princeton University Press, 1971.

Tōa remmei dōshikai 東亜連盟同志会. "Shōwa ishin ron" 昭和維新論. In *Gendai Nihon shisō taikei* 現代日本思想大系, vol. 31: *Chōkokka shugi* 超国家主義, ed. Hashikawa Bunzō 橋川文三. Tokyo: Chikuma shobō, 1964.

Tōbata Seiichi 東畑精一. "Jinushi no shohanchū" 地主の諸範疇. *Kokka gakkai zasshi* 国家学会雑誌 55 (June 1941): 37–56.

Tōbata Seiichi 東畑精一, ed. *Nōgyō ni okeru senzai shitsugyō* 農業における潜在失業. Tokyo: Nihon hyōronsha, 1956.

Tōbata Seiichi 東畑精一 and Ōkawa Kazushi 大川一司, eds. *Nihon no keizai to nōgyō* 日本の経済と農業, vol. 1. Tokyo: Iwanami shoten, 1956.

Tōgō Minoru 東郷實. *Nihon shokumin ron* 日本植民論. Tokyo: Bunbudo, 1906.

Tōgō, Shigenori. *The Cause of Japan*, trans. F. Tōgō and B. B. Blakeney. New York: Simon & Schuster, 1956.

Tōkyō daigaku shakaikagaku kenkyūjo 東京大学社会科学研究所, eds. *Nachisu keizai to nyuu deiiru* ナチス経済とニューディール, vol. 3 of *Fuashizumuki no kokka to shakai* ファシズム期の国家と社会. Tokyo: Tōkyō daigaku shuppankai, 1979.

Tōkyō daigaku shakaikagaku kenkyūjo 東京大学社会科学研究所, eds. *Senji Nihon no hōtaisei* 戦時日本の法体制, vol. 5 of *Fuashizumuki no kokka to shakai* ファシズム期の国家と社会. Tokyo: Tōkyō daigaku shuppankai, 1979.

Tōkyō daigaku shakaikagaku kenkyūjo 東京大学社会科学研究所, eds. *Yooropa no hōtaisei* ヨーロッパの法体制, vol. 4 of *Fuashizumuki no kokka to shakai* ファシズム期の国家と社会. Tokyo: Tōkyō daigaku shuppankai, 1979.

Tominaga Ken'ichi 富永健一. "Shakai kaisō to shakai idō no sūsei bunseki" 社会階層と社会移動の趨勢分析. In *Nihon no kaisō kōzō* 日本の階層構造, ed. Tominaga Ken'ichi 富永健一. Tokyo: Tōkyō daigaku shuppankai, 1979.

Totten, George O., III, ed. *Democracy in Prewar Japan: Groundwork of Façade?* Lexington, Mass.: Heath, 1965.

Totten, George O., III. *The Social Democratic Movement in Prewar Japan*. New Haven, Conn.: Yale University Press, 1966.

Totten, George O., III. "Collective Bargaining and Works Councils as Innovations in Industrial Relations in Japan during the 1920s." In *Aspects of Social Change in Modern Japan*, ed. Ronald P. Dore. Princeton, N.J.: Princeton University Press, 1967.

Totten, George O., III. "Japanese Industrial Relations at the Crossroads: The Great Noda Strike of 1927–1928." In *Japan in Crisis: Essays on Taishō Democracy*, ed. Bernard Silberman and H. D. Harootunian. Princeton, N.J.: Princeton University Press, 1974.

Toyama Saburō 外山三郎. *Dai Tōa sensō to senshi no kyōkun* 大東亜戦争と戦史の教訓. Tokyo: Hara shobō, 1979.

Toyama, Saburo. "Lessons from the Past." U.S. Naval Institute *Proceedings*, September 1982.

Tōyō keizai shinpōsha 東洋経済新報社, ed. *Meiji Taishō kokusei sōran* 明治大正国勢総覧. Tokyo: Tōyō keizai shinpōsha, 1927.

Tōyō keizai shinpōsha 東洋経済新報社. *Shōwa kokusei sōran* 昭和国勢総覧, 2 vols. Tokyo: Tōyō keizai Shinpōsha, 1980.

Toyoda Jō 豊田穣. *Namimakura ikutabizo* 波まくらいくたびぞ. Tokyo: Kōdansha, 1973.

Tsuchiya Takao 土屋喬雄. *Zaibatsu o kizuita hitobito* 財閥を築いた人々. Tokyo: Kōbundō, 1955.

Tsuchiya Takao 土屋喬雄. *Nihon no keieisha seishin* 日本の経営者精神. Tokyo: Keizai ōraisha, 1959.

Tsuda Sōkichi 津田左右吉. *Bungaku ni arawaretaru waga kokumin no shisō* 文学に現はれたる我が国民の思想. Tokyo: Rakuyōdō, 1918–1921.

Tsuji Kiyoaki 辻清明. "Sengo kaikaku to seiji katei" 戦後改革と政治過程. In *Seiji katei* 政治過程, vol. 3 of *Sengo kaikaku* 戦後改革, ed. Tōkyō daigaku shakaikagaku kenkyūjo 東京大学社会科学研究所. Tokyo: Tōkyō daigaku shuppankai, 1974–5.

Tsuji Masanobu 辻政信. *Guadalcanal* ガダルカナル. Tokyo: Kawade shobō, 1967.

Tsukuda Jitsuo 佃実夫. "Yokohama kara no shōgen" ヨコハマからの証言. In *Kyōdō kenkyū: Nihon senryō* 共同研究: 日本占領, ed. Shisō no kagaku kenkyūkai 思想の科学研究会, Tokyo: Tokuma shoten, 1972.

Tsukui Tatsuo 津久井龍雄, ed *Nippon seiji nenpō: Shōwa jūshichi-nen* 日本政治年報: 昭和十七年 vol. 1. Tokyo: Shōwa shobō, 1942.

Tsunoda Fusako 角田房子. *Issai yume ni gozasōrō: Honma Masaharu chūjō den* いっさい夢にござ候: 本間雅晴中将伝. Tokyo: Chūō kōronsha, 1973.

Tsunoda Jun 角田順, ed. *Ishiwara Kanji shiryō: Kokubōronsaku* 石原莞爾資料: 国防論策. Tokyo: Hara shobō, 1967.

Tsunoda, Ryusaku, de Bary, Theodore et al. *Sources of Japanese Tradition*. New York: Columbia University Press, 1958.

Tsurumi, E. Patricia. *Japanese Colonial Education in Taiwan, 1895–1945*. Cambridge, Mass.: Harvard University Press, 1977.

Tsuruta Yoshimasa 鶴田俊正. *Sengo Nihon no sangyō seisaku* 戦後日本の産業政策. Tokyo: Nihon keizai shinbunsha, 1982.

Tsurutani, Taketsugu. *Political Change in Japan*. New York: McKay, 1977.

Tsūshō sangyōshō 通商産業省. *Sangyō gorika hakusho* 産業合理化白書. Tokyo: Nikkan kōgyō shinbunsha, 1957.

Tsūshō sangyōshō 通商産業省, ed. *Shōkō seisaku shi*, vol. 15: *Sen'i kōgyō* (1) 商工政策史, 繊維工業 (1). Tokyo: Shōkō seisakushi kankōkai, 1968.

Tsūshō sangyōshō 通商産業省, ed. *Shōkō seisaku shi*, vol. 17: *Tekkō* 商工政策史, 鉄鋼. Tokyo: Shōkō seisakushi kankōkai, 1970.

Tsūshō sangyōshō jūkōgyō kyoku 通商産業省重工業局. *Tekkōgyō no gōrika to sono seika* 鉄鋼業の合理化とその成果. Tokyo: Kōgyō tosho shuppan, 1963.

Tung Hsien-kuang 董顯光. *Shō Kai-seki* 蔣介石, trans. Terashima Masashi 寺島正 and Okuno Masami 奥野正巳. Tokyo: Nihon gaisei gakkai, 1956.

Uchikawa Yoshimi 内川芳美. "Masukomi jidai no tenkai to seiji katei" マスコミ時代の展開と政治過程. In *Nenpō seijigaku* 年報政治学 1977 (*55-nen taisei no keisei to hōkai: Zoku gendai Nihon no seiji katei*) 55年体制の形成と崩壊: 続 現代日本の政治過程, ed. Nihon seiji gakkai 日本政治学会. Tokyo: Iwanami shoten, 1979.

Uehara Nobuhiro 上原信博. "Nōchi kaikaku katei to nōchi kaikaku ron" 農地改革過程と農地改革論. In *Nōchi kaikaku* 農地改革, vol. 6 of *Sengo kaikaku* 戦後改革, ed. Tōkyō daigaku shakaikagaku kenkyūjo 東京大学社会科学研究所. Tokyo: Tōkyō daigaku shuppankai, 1974–5.

Ueno Hiroya 上野裕也. *Nihon no keizai seido* 日本の経済制度. Tokyo: Nihon keizai shinbunsha, 1978.

Uesugi Shinkichi 上杉慎吉. *Teikoku kenpō chikujō kōgi* 帝国憲法逐条講義. Tokyo: Nihon hyōronsha, 1935.

Ueyama Shunpei 上山春平. *Dai Tōa sensō no imi* 大東亜戦争の意味. Tokyo: Chūō kōronsha, 1964.

Ugaki Kazushige 宇垣一成. *Ugaki Kazushige nikki* 宇垣一成日記, vol. 2. Tokyo: Misuzu shobō, 1970.

Umemura Mataji 梅村又次. *Sengo Nihon no rōdōyoku* 戦後日本の労働欲. Tokyo: Iwanami shoten, 1964.

Umemura Mataji 梅村又次. "Sangyōbetsu koyō no hendō 1880–1940 nen" 産業別雇用の変動1880–1940年. *Keizai kenkyū* 経済研究 24 (April 1973): 107–16.

Umemura, Mataji. "Population and Labor Force." In *Patterns of Japanese Economic Development: A Quantitative Appraisal*, ed. Kazushi Ohkawa, Miyohei Shinohara et al. New Haven, Conn.: Yale University Press, 1979.

Umemura Mataji 梅村又次 et al. *Chōki keizai tōkei – suikei to bunseki*, vol. 9: *Nōringyō* 長期経済統計—推計と分析 9: 農林業. Tokyo: Tōyō keizai shinpōsha, 1966.

Umihara Osamu 海原修. *Senshi ni manabu* 戦史に学ぶ. Tokyo: Asagumo shinbunsha, 1970.

Uraki Shin'ichi 浦城晋一. *Nihon nōmin no henkan katei* 日本農民の変換過程. Tokyo: Ochanomizu shobō, 1978.

U.S. Strategic Bombing Survey (Pacific), Military Analysis Division. *Japanese Air Power*. Washington, D.C.: USGPO, 1947.

U.S. Strategic Bombing Survey, Military Analysis Division. *Air Campaigns of the Pacific War*. Washington, D.C.: USGPO, 1946.

U.S. Strategic Bombing Survey (Pacific), Naval Analysis Division. *Interrogations of Japanese Officials*, 2 vols. Washington, D.C.: USGPO, 1946.

Ushiomi Toshitaka 潮見俊隆 et al. *Nihon no nōson* 日本の農村. Tokyo: Iwanami shoten, 1957.

Usui Katsumi 臼井勝美. *Nitchū sensō* 日中戦争. Tokyo: Chūō kōronsha, 1967.

Usui Katsumi 臼井勝美. *Nitchū gaikō shi: Hokubatsu no jidai* 日本外交史: 北伐の時代. Tokyo: Hanawa shobō, 1971.

Usui Katsumi 臼井勝美. *Manshū jihen* 満州事変. Tokyo: Chūō kōronsha, 1974.

Usui, Katsumi. "On the Duration of the Pacific War." *Japan Quarterly* (October–December 1981): 479–88.

Utley, Freda. *Japan's Feet of Clay*. New York: Norton, 1937.

Wada Hidekichi 和田日出吉. *Nissan kontserun tokuhon* 日産コンツェルン読本. Tokyo: Shunjūsha, 1937.

Wagner, Jeffrey Paul. "Sano Manabu and the Japanese Adaptation of Socialism." Ph. D. diss., University of Arizona, 1978.

Ward, Robert E. *Political Development in Modern Japan*. Princeton, N.J.: Princeton University Press, 1968.

Ward, Robert E. "Reflections on the Allied Occupation and Planned Political Change in Japan." In *Political Development in Modern Japan*, ed. Robert E. Ward. Princeton, N.J.: Princeton University Press, 1968.

Waswo, Ann. *Japanese Landlords: The Decline of a Rural Elite*. Berkeley and Los Angeles: University of California Press, 1977.

Waswo, Ann. "In Search of Equity: Japanese Tenant Unions in the 1920s." In *Conflict in Modern Japanese History: The Neglected Tradition*, ed. Tetsuo Najita and Victor Koschmann. Princeton, N.J.: Princeton University Press, 1982.

Watanabe, Akio. "Japanese Public Opinion and Foreign Policy, 1964–1973." In *The Foreign Policy of Modern Japan*, ed. Robert A. Scalapino. Berkeley and Los Angeles: University of California Press, 1977.

Watanabe Akio 渡辺昭夫. "Dai 61-dai: Dai 1-ji Satō naikaku: 'Kan'yō to nintai' kara 'kan'yō to chōwa' e" 第61代·第 1 次佐藤内閣「寛容と忍耐」から「寛容と調和」へ. In *Nihon naikakushi roku* 日本内閣史録. vol. 6, ed. Hayashi Shigeru 林茂. Tokyo: Daiichi hōki, 1981.

Watanabe Akio 渡辺昭夫. "Dai 62-dai: Dai 2-ji Satō naikaku: Jūjitsu shita 3-nen kan" 第62代·第 2 次佐藤内閣—充実した 3 年間. In *Nihon naikakushi roku* 日本内閣史録, vol. 6, ed. Hayashi Shigeru 林茂. Tokyo: Daiichi hōki, 1981.

Watanabe Akio 渡辺昭夫. "Dai 63-dai: Dai 3-ji Satō naikaku: Gekidō no 70-nendai e no hashi watashi" 第63代·第 3 次佐藤内閣—激動の70年代への橋渡し. In *Nihon naikakushi roku* 日本内閣史録, vol. 6, ed. Hayashi Shigeru 林茂. Tokyo: Daiichi hōki, 1981.

Watanabe Haruo 渡辺春男. *Nihon marukusushugi undō no reimei* 日本マルクス主義運動の黎明. Tokyo: Aoki shoten, 1957.

Watanabe, Hisamaru 渡辺久丸. "Shōchō tennōsei no seijiteki yakuwari" 象徴天皇制の政治的役割. In *Tennōsei to minshū* 天皇制と民衆, ed. Gotō Yasushi 後藤靖. Tokyo: Tōkyō daigaku shuppankai, 1976.

Watanabe Shin'ichi 渡辺信一. *Nihon no keiei kōzō – senzen hen* 日本の経営構造—戦前篇. Tokyo: Yushōdō, 1971.

Watanabe Toru 渡部徹. "Nihon no marukusushugi undō ron" 日本のマルクス主義運動論. In *Kōza marukusushugi* 講座 マルクス主義, vol. 12. Tokyo: Nihon hyōronsha, 1974.

Watanabe Yōzō 渡辺洋三. "Nōchi kaikaku to sengo nōchihō" 農地改革と戦後農地法. In *Nōchi kaikaku* 東京大学出版会, vol. 6 of *Sengo kaikaku* 戦後改革, ed. Tōkyō daigaku shakaikagaku kenkyūjō 東京大学社会科学研究所. Tokyo: Tōkyō daigaku shuppankai, 1974–5.

Watanabe Yōzō 渡辺洋三. "Sengo kaikaku to Nihon gendaihō" 戦後改革と日本現代法. In *Kadai to shikaku* 課題を視角, vol, 1 of *Sengo kaikaku* 戦後改革, ed. Tōkyō daigaku shakaikagaku kenkyūjo 東京大学社会科学研究所. Tokyo: Tōkyō daigaku shuppankai, 1974–5.

Watanuki Jōji 綿貫譲治. "Kōdo seichō to keizai taikokuka no seiji katei" 高度成長と経済大国化の政治過程. In *Nenpō seijigaku* 年報政治学 1977 (*55-nen taisei no keisei to hōkai: Zoku gendai nihon no seiji katei*) 55年体制の形成と崩壊—続現代日本の政治過程. Tokyo: Iwanami shoten, 1979.

Watsuji Tetsurō 和辻哲郎. *Nihon kodai bunka* 日本古代文化. Tokyo: Iwanami shoten, 1920.

Watsuji Tetsurō 和辻哲郎. *Koji junrei* 古寺巡禮. Tokyo: Iwanami shoten, 1947.

Watsuji, Tetsurō. *Climate*, trans. Geoffrey Bownas. Tokyo: Hokuseido Press, 1961.

Watsuji Tetsurō 和辻哲郎. *Nihon seishinshi kenkyū* 日本精神史研究. Tokyo: Iwanami shoten, 1970.

White, James W. *The Sōkagakkai and Mass Society*. Stanford, Calif.: Stanford University Press, 1970.

Whitney, Courtney. *MacArthur: His Rendezvous with History*. New York: Knopf, 1956.

Williams, David E. "Beyond Political Economy: A Critique of Issues Raised in Chalmers Johnson's *MITI and the Japanese Miracle*." Social and Economic Research on Modern Japan, Occasional Paper no. 35. Berlin: East Asian Institute, Free University of Berlin, 1983.

Wilson, George M. *Radical Nationalist in Japan: Kita Ikki, 1883–1937*. Cambridge, Mass.: Harvard University Press, 1969.

Wilson, George M., ed. *Crisis Politics in Prewar Japan: Institutional and Ideological Problems of the 1930s*. Tokyo: Sophia University Press, 1970.

Wray, William D. *Mitsubishi and the N.Y.K., 1870–1914: Business Strategy in the Japanese Shipping Industry*. Cambridge, Mass.: Harvard University Press, 1985.

Yabe Teiji 矢部貞治, ed. *Konoe Fumimaro* 近衛文麿, 2 vols. Tokyo: Kōbundō, 1952.

Yamabe Kentaro 山辺健太郎. "Nihon teikokushugi to shokuminchi" 日本帝国主義と植民地. In *Iwanami kōza rekishi* 岩波講座歴史, vol. 19, ed. Iwanami kōza. Tokyo: Iwanami shoten, 1963.

Yamabe Kentarō 山辺健太郎. *Nihon tōchika no Chōsen* 日本統治下の朝鮮. Tokyo: Iwanami shinso, 1975.

Yamada Junzō 山田準三. "Senjichū no rōdōsha" 戦時中の労働者. In *Gendai Nihon shihonshugi taikei IV: Rōdō* 現代日本資本主義体系 Ⅳ: 労働, ed. Aihara Shigeru 相原茂. Tokyo: Kōbundō, 1958.

Yamada Saburō 山田三郎. "Nōgyō" 農業. In *Nihon keizai ron - Keizai seichō 100-nen no bunseki* 日本経済論－経済成長百年の分析 ed. Emi Kōichi 江見康一 and Shionoya Yūichi 塩野谷祐一. Tokyo: Yūhikaku, 1973.

Yamada, Saburo, and Yujiro, Hayami. "Agriculture." In *Patterns of Japanese Economic Development: A Quantitative Appraisal*, ed. Kazushi Ohkawa and Miyohei Shinohara et al. New Haven, Conn.: Yale University Press, 1979.

Yamada Yūzō 山田雄三. *Nihon kokumin shotoku suikei shiryō* 日本国民所得推計資料, rev. ed. Tokyo: Tōyō keizai shinpōsha, 1957.

Yamaguchi Jūji 山口重次. *Manshū teikoku* 満州帝国. Tokyo: Gyōsei tsūshinsha, 1975.

Yamaji Aizan 山路愛山. "Genji no shakai mondai oyobi shakaishugisha" 現時の社会問題及び社会主義者. In *Shakaishugi shiron* 社会主義史論, ed. Kishimoto Eitarō 岸本英太郎. Tokyo: Aoki shoten, 1955.

Yamakawa Hitoshi 山川均. "Rōdō undō no shakaiteki igi" 労働運動の社会的意義. In *Yamakawa Hitoshi zenshū* 山川均全集, vol. 2, ed. Yamakawa Kikue 山川菊栄 and Yamakawa Shinsaku 山川振作. Tokyo: Keisō shobō, 1966.

Yamakawa Hitoshi 山川均. "Tami o moto to sezaru Yoshino hakase to Ōyama Ikuo shi no minponshugi" 民を本とせざる吉野博士と大山郁夫氏の民本主義. In *Yamakawa Hitoshi zenshū* 山川均全集, vol. 2, ed. Yamakawa Kikue 山川菊栄 and Yamakawa Shinsaku 山川振作. Tokyo: Keisō shobō, 1966.

Yamakawa Hitoshi 山川均. "Musan kaikyū undō no hōkō tenkan" 無産階級運動の方向転換. In *Yamakawa Hitoshi zenshū* 山川均全集, vol. 4, ed. Yamakawa Kikue 山川菊栄 and Yamakawa Shinsaku 山川振作. Tokyo: Keisō shobō, 1967.

Yamakawa Hitoshi 山川均. "Rōdō undō ni taisuru chishiki kaikyū no chii" 労働運動に対する知識階級の地位. In *Yamakawa Hitoshi zenshū* 山川均全集, vol. 3, ed. Yamakawa Kikue 山川菊栄 and Yamakawa Shinsaku 山川振作. Tokyo: Keisō shobō, *1967*.

Yamakawa Hitoshi 山川均. " 'Kaizō Nihon' to musan kaikyū undō" 「改造日本」と無産階級運動. In *Yamakawa Hitoshi zenshū* 山川均全集, vol. 5, ed. Yamakawa Kikue 山川菊栄 and Yamakawa Shinsaku 山川振作. Tokyo: Keisō shobō, 1968.

Yamamoto Kiyoshi 山本潔. "Sengo rōdō kumiai no shuppatsuten" 戦後労働組合の出発点. In *Nihon rōshi kankei shiron* 日本労使関係史論, ed. Sumiya Mikio 隅谷三喜男. Tokyo: Tōkyō daigaku shuppankai, 1977.

Yamamoto Kiyoshi 山本潔. *Sengo rōdō undō shiron* 戦後労働史論, vol. 1. Tokyo: Ochanomizu shobō, 1977.

Yamamura, Kozo. "The Founding of Mitsubishi: A Case Study in Japanese Business History." *Business History Review* 41 (1967): 141–60.

Yamamura, Kozo. "Success Illgotten? The Role of Meiji Militarism in Japan's Technical Progress." *Journal of Economic History* 37 (March 1977).

Yamamura Kōzō ヤマムラ　コーゾー. "Kikai kōgyō ni okeru seiō gijutsu no dōnyū" 機械工業における西欧技術の導入, trans. Nakamura Takafusa 中村隆

英. In *Washinton taisei to Nichibei kankei* ワシントン体制と日米関係, ed. Hosoya Chihiro 細谷千博 and Saitō Makoto 斉藤真. Tokyo: Tōkyō daigaku shuppankai, 1978.

Yamanouchi Yasushi 山之内靖. "Iwayuru shakai ishiki keitai ni tsuite" いわゆる社会意識形態について. *Shisō* 思想 568, 569 (October 1971–November 1971).

Yamazawa Ippei 山沢逸平 and Yamamoto Yūzō 山本有造. *Chōki keizai tōkei – 14: Bōeki to kokusai shūshi* 長期経済統計・14: 貿易と国際収支. Tokyo: Tōyō keizai shinpōsha, 1974.

Yamazumi, Masumi. "Textbook Revision: The Swing to the Right." *Japan Quarterly* (October–December 1981): 472–8.

Yanagida Izumi 柳田泉. *Kinoshita Naoe* 木下尚江. Tokyo: Rironsha, 1955.

Yanagida Kunio 柳田国男. *Tōno monogatari* 遠野物語. Tokyo: Kyōdo kenkyūsha, 1938.

Yanaihara Tadao 矢内原忠雄. "Sōsetsu" 総説. In *Sengo nihon shōshi* 戦後日本小史, vol. 1, ed. Yanaihara Tadao 矢内原忠雄. Tokyo: Tōkyō daigaku shuppankai, 1958.

Yano Tōru 矢野暢. *Nihon no Nan'yō shikan* 日本の南洋史観. Tokyo: Chūō shinsho, 1979.

Yano Tsuneta kinenkai 矢野恒太記念会, ed. *Nihon kokusei zue* 日本国勢図会. Tokyo: Kokuseisha, 1981.

Yasuba, Yasukichi. "The Evolution of Dualistic Wage Structure." In *Industrialization and Its Social Consequences*, ed. Hugh T. Patrick. Berkeley and Los Angeles: University of California Press, 1976.

Yasuba Yasukichi 安場保吉. "Senzen no Nihon ni okeru kōgyō tōkei no shimpyōsei ni tsuite" 戦前の日本における工業統計の信憑性について. *Ōsaka daigaku keizaigaku* 大阪大学経済学 17 (1977–8).

Yasuda Tsuneo 安田常雄. *Nihon fuashizumu to minshū undō* 日本ファシズムと民衆運動. Tokyo: Renga shobō shinsha, 1979.

Yasuda Yojūrō 保田與重郎. "Nihon no hashi" 日本の橋. *Bungakukai* 文学界 (October 1936).

Yasuda Yōjūrō 保田與重郎. "Bunmei kaika no ronri no shūen" 文明開化の論理の終焉. In *Kindai no chōkoku* 近代の超克, ed. Takeuchi Yoshimi 竹内好 and Kawakami Tetsutarō 河上徹太郎. Tokyo: Fuzanbō, 1979.

Yatsugi Kazuo 矢次一夫. *Rōdō sōgi hiroku* 労働争議秘録. Tokyo: Nihon kōgyō shinbunsha, 1979.

Yawata seitetsusho 八幡製鉄所, ed. *Yawata seitetsusho 50-nen shi* 八幡製鉄所五十年史. Tokyo: Yawata seitetsusho, 1950.

Yayama, Taro. "The Newspapers Conduct a Mad Rhapsody over the Textbook Issue." *Journal of Japanese Studies* 9 (Summer 1983): 301–16.

Yoda Seiichi 依田精一. "Sengo kazoku seido kaikaku to shinkazokukan no seiritsu" 戦後家族制度改革と新家族観の成立. In *Kadai to shikaku* 課題と視角, vol. 1 of *Sengo kaikaku* 戦後改革, ed. Tōkyō daigaku shakaikagaku kenkyūjo 東京大学社会科学研究所. Tokyo: Tōkyō daigaku shuppankai, 1974–5.

Yoda Seiichi 依田精一. "Senryō seisaku ni okeru fujin kaihō" 占領政策における婦人解放. In *Senryōki Nihon no keizai to seiji* 占領期日本の経済と政治, ed. Nakamura Takafusa 中村隆英. Tokyo: Tōkyō daigaku shuppankai, 1979.

Yokoyama Gen'nosuke 横山源之助. *Nihon no kasō shakai* 日本の下層社会. Tokyo: Kyōbunkan, 1899.

Yokoyama Keiji 横山桂次. "Toshi saikaihatsu to shimin sanka no seidoka" 都市再開発と市民参加の制度化. In *Nenpō seijigaku* 年報政治学 1974 (*Seiji sanka no riron to genjitsu*) 政治参加の理論と現実, ed. Nihon seiji gakkai 日本政治学会. Tokyo: Iwanami shoten, 1975.

*Yokusan kokumin undō shi* 翼賛国民運動史, ed. Yokusan undō shi kankōkai 翼賛運動史刊行会, Tokyo: Yokusan undō shi kankōkai, 1954.

Yoshida Katsumi 吉田克巳. "Nōchi kaikakuhō no rippō katei: Nōgyō keiei kibo mondai o chūshin to shite" 農地改革法の立法過程—農業経営規模問題を中心として. In *Nōchi kaikaku* 農地改革, vol. 6 of *Sengo kaikaku* 戦後改革, ed. Tōkyō daigaku shakaikagaku kenkyūjo 東京大学社会科学研究所. Tokyo: Tōkyō daigaku shuppankai, 1974–5.

Yoshida Kei 吉田啓. *Denryoku kanrian no sokumen shi* 電力管理案の側面史. Tokyo: Kōtsū keizaisha shuppanbu, 1938.

Yoshida Shigeru 吉田茂. *Kaisō jūnen* 回想十年 4 巻, 4 vols. Tokyo: Shinchōsha, 1957.

Yoshida, Shigeru. *The Yoshida Memoirs*. New York: Houghton Mifflin, 1962.

Yoshihara, Kunio. *Japanese Economic Development: A Short Introduction*. Tokyo: Oxford University Press, 1979.

Yoshii Hiroshi 義井博. *Shōwa gaikō shi* 昭和外交史. Tokyo: Nansōsha, 1975.

Yoshimura Michio 吉村道男. *Nihon to Roshia* 日本とロシア. Tokyo: Hara shobō, 1968.

Yoshino Sakuzō 吉野作造. "Minponshugi, shakaishugi, kagekishugi" 民本主義, 社会主義, 過激主義. *Chūō kōron* 中央公論. (June 1919).

Yoshino, Shinji. "Our Planned Economy." *Contemporary Japan* 6 (December 1937): 369–677.

Yoshino Toshihiko 吉野俊彦. *Rekidai Nihon ginkō sōsai ron* 歴代日本銀行総裁論. Tokyo: Mainichi shinbunsha, 1976.

Yuasa Yasuo 湯浅泰雄. *Watsuji Tetsurō* 和辻哲郎. Tokyo: Minerva shobō, 1981.

Yui Masaomi 由井正臣. "Gunbu to kokumin tōgō" 軍部と国民統合. In *Fuashizumuki no kokka to shakai* ファシズム期の国家と社会, vol. 1 of *Shōwa kyōkō* 昭和恐慌, ed. Tōkyō daigaku shakaikagaku kenkyūjo 東京大学社会科学研究所. Tokyo: Tōkyō daigaku shuppankai, 1978.

Yui Tsunehiko 由井常彦. *Chūshō kigyō seisaku no shiteki tenkai* 中小企業政策の史的展開. Tokyo: Tōyō keizai shinpōsha, 1964.

# GLOSSARY-INDEX

Hoshino Naoki 星野直樹 (1892– ), 333
"Hōsō tōronkai" 放送討論会 (Roundtable of the air), 168
*hōtoku* 報徳 (repayment), 573
Hōtokukai 報徳会 (repayment movement), 573
Hotta Masayasu 堀田正睦 (1810–1864), 78
House of Councilors, 162
House of Councilors Members Election Law (1946), 181
House of Peers: partisanship of appointees, 87, replaced by House of Councilors, 156
House of Representatives: enlarged in size and power, 156; new election laws for, 162; postwar power of, 31; precedence of, 86; purpose of, 30; shift of power to, 35
House of Representatives Committee on Legislative Investigation, 181
House of Representatives Election Law (1946), 181; revision of, 85
household expenses, rise in, 514
Hozumi Nobushige 穂積信重 (1856–1926), 89
Hozumi Yatsuka 穂積八束 (1860–1912), 62–3, 86, 654
Hsingchong 興中 ("Revive China" Company), 476
Hull, Cordell, nonrecognition doctrine (1941), 281; and U.S. aid to Kuomintang, 337–8
Hull note, 338
Hyakutake Haruyoshi 百武晴吉 (1888–1947), 355–6
hyperinflation (*kyōran bukka*), 511
Hypothec Bank of Japan, 392

Ichiki Kitokurō 一木喜徳郎 (1867–1944), 89
"ideals" (*risō*), 662
*ie* 家 ("household"), 748
*iegara* 家柄 (family lineage or standing), 547
Ikeda Hayato 池田勇人 (1899–1965), 187–8; and Income Doubling Plan, 523; named prime minister, 187; noncontroversial policies, 187
Ikeda Seihin, *see* Ikeda Shigeaki
Ikeda Shigeaki 池田成彬 (1867–1950), 122–4, 133, 478; and conservatives' defense of power, 133
Iki no kōzō いきの構造 ("The Structure of Tokugawa Aesthetic Style," Kuki, 1929), 737
*iki no tetsugaku* いきの哲学 (philosophy of existence), 745
*ikizumari* 息詰り ("suffocation"), 692
*ikō* 意向 (will), 677
Imamura Hitoshi 今村均 (1886–1968), 347, 357
Imperial Academy (Teikoku gakushiin), 88
Imperial Agricultural Association, 47, 573
Imperial Conference (July 2, 1941): Outline of National Policies, 327; war preparations, 327
Imperial Conference (Sept. 6, 1941), war plans, 329
Imperial Conference (Nov. 5, 1941), decision for war, 335
Imperial Conference (Dec. 1, 1941), review of diplomatic failures, 339
Imperial General Headquarters, abolished, 156
Imperial Military Reservist Association (Teikoku zaigō gunjinkai), 116, 574–5; and local mobilization, 144
Imperial Rescript on Education (1891), purpose of elementary education, 402
Imperial Rule Assistance Association (IRAA) (Taisei yokusankai), 42, 146–8, 182
Imperial Rule Assistance Young Adult Corps (Yokusan sōnendan), 150–2
Imperial Silk Filature Company (Teikoku sanshi kabushiki gaisha), 461
imperial subject concept (*kōmin*), role in assimilation, 241
Imperial Way faction (*kōdōha*), 111; revolt of (1936), 119
imperialism: "army-first," 271, 275; belief in Japan's "mission" in Asia, 221; cordon of advantage, 220; cordon of sovereignty, 220; Leninist opposition to, 8; "navy-first," 271; situational nature of, 223
imperialization (*kōminka*), 243
Important Industries Control Law, 459, 464, 474
Important Industries Council (Jūyō sangyō kyōgikai; Jūsankyō), 179
imports: administrative control of, 29; forced import substitution, 501; import plans (1937–1945), 481; major, 526; raw materials, 527;

Outer Mongolia, independence of, 279
"outer territories," 243
"Outline of Basic National Policies" (Kihon kokusaku yōkō) (1940), 143
"Outline of Measures for Solution of Manchurian Problem," 293
"Outline Plan for the Reorganization of the Japanese State, An" (Nihon kokka kaizō hōan), 718–20
"overflowing self" (*jiga no jūitsu*), 693
Owner–Farmer Establishment Special Measures Law (1945), and land reform, 171
*oyabun* 親分 ("patron"), 402, 553
*oyagokoro* 親心 (hearts of parents), 631
*oyakata* 親方 ("patron"), 402
Ōyama Ikuo 大山郁夫 (1880–1955), 676, 678–80, 682, 686; cofounder of *Warera*, 685; and theory of democratic nationalism, 680
*Ōyōmeigaku* 王陽明学 (philosophic intuitionism), 729

Pacific islands: German possessions seized, 280; retaken by U.S., 359
Pacific War: air attacks on home islands, 369–70; causes of, 310–12; conquests (1942), 485; continued overconfidence of leadership, 358; damage to national wealth, 506; diplomacy to avert, 337–40; and economic collapse (1937–1945), 451; economic mobilization neglected, 488–90; effect of wartime controls, 493; extreme hardship during, 488; Japanese shipping decimated, 487–8; Japan's surrender, 376; Koiso-Yonai phase, 364–6; losses in personnel and wealth, 492; merchant marine statistics, 486; preparations for landings on home islands, 370–2
"Pacific War" (*Taiheiyō sensō*), 381
Pan-Asianism, 7, 243, 768
*pao chia* 保甲 (*hōkō*), 251–2
Parkes, Harry, 394
parliamentary sovereignty, 60
"partisanization" (*seitōka*): of the bureaucracy, 40; of House of Peers, 84, 86
party cabinets: emergence of, 35–6, 55–96; as established rule, 101; first, 68; opposition of Meiji leaders to, 56
paternalism, and prevailing labor market conditions, 632
paternalism, corporate, 23–4; and labor market dualism, 624
Patriotic Industrial Associations (*Sangyō hōkoku kai*), 492
patriotism, inculcated in conscripts, 544
patron–client ties, 553–4
Pauley Report, 501
Pearl Harbor attack, 341–2
peasantry, *see* rural areas
Peking, occupation of, 305
Peking Conference (1900), 7
Peking Tariff Conference (1925), 9
"people" (*kokumin*), 686
people's common interests (*kokumin kyōdō no rigai*), 680
Percival, Arthur E., surrendered Singapore, 345
"period of emergency" (*hijōji*) (1932), 108
Perry, Matthew, 381
persimmon theory, 326–8
Pescadores islands: ceded to Japan, 225; strategic plan to occupy, 225
Petrochemical Industry Development Policy (1955), 521
petroleum embargo by U.S. (1941), 27, 310, 485
Phan Boi Chau, 7, 8
Philippine Sea, battle of, 362
Philippines: occupation of, 346–7; retaken, 364–5
Plan for Economic Resuscitation of Agrarian and Fishing Villages (Nōson gyoson keizai kōsei keikaku) (1932), 109
Plan for Expansion of Productivity (1942), 485
Plan for Liberalization of Foreign Trade and Foreign Exchange (1960), 522
Plan for the Reconstruction of the Japanese Archipelago (1972), 536–7
plant council (*kōjō kondankai*), 644
police: central control of, 159; jurisdiction divided, 157
Police Bureau, 181
Police Law (1947), 181
Police System Council, 181
political change, effect of, on socioeconomic changes, 155
political parties, 34–9; antiparty mood, 107; challenges to power (1929–1936), 105–18; conservative (*kisei seitō*), 97;

Seiyūkai 政友会 (political party), 35, 55, 74–82, 84–6, 91–5, 107–9, 117–18, 121, 128, 131, 135, 140, 162, 461, 592, 706, 726; confrontation with Okada government, 117; establishment of, 66–76; majority in House of Representatives, 80; organized (1900), 35; policies of, 36; positive policy, 79, 461; as progovernment party, 80; relations with Yamagata faction, 74; withdrawal from national-unity government, 114–15

*sekai no taisei* 世界の大勢 (trends in the world), 655

"self-cultivation" (*kyōyōshugi*), 710

self-determination, right of national, 8

self-reliance movement (*jiriki kōsei undō*), 470

senior ministers (*jūshin*), 31, 37, 143, 339

seniority wage system (*nenkō joretsu*), 199, 462; spread of, 492

Senji gyōsei shokken tokureihō 戦時行政職権特例法 (special wartime administrative law), 150

Senke Takanori 千家尊宣 (1899– ), 78

Senkyohō kaisei kisei zenkoku kakushi rengōkai 選挙法改正期成全国各市連合会 (Joint Committee of the National Chambers of Commerce for the Revision of the House of Representatives Election Law), 72

"sense of common interest" (*kyōdō rigai kannen*), 680

*sensei taisei* 専政太政 (authoritarian political structure), 62

"Senshū no kokkai kara" 先週の国会から (The Diet last week), 168

sericulture, 409

sex discrimination, 200

*shakai kaizō* 社会改造 ("social reconstruction"), 751

*shakai minshushugi* 社会民主主義 ("social democracy"), 684

Shakai minshutō 社会民主党 (Social Democratic Party), 659, 666

*Shakai mondai kenkyū* 社会問題研究 (*Studies in Social Problems*; journal), 685

Shakai seisaku gakkai 社会政策学会 (Social Policy Association), 658

*shakai shinka* 社会進化 (social evolution), 655

*shakai shinpo* 社会進歩 (social progress), 655

Shakai taishūtō 社会大衆党 (Social Masses Party), 114

*shakaihakaishugi* 社会破壊主義 ("social destructionism"), 673

Shakaishugi kyōkai 社会主義協会 (Socialist Society), 659

Shakaishugi shinzui 社会主義神髄 ("The quintessence of socialism," Kōtoku), 660

*shakaiteki kyōyū* 社会的共有 (public ownership of means of production), 667

Shanghai incident, 305; as diversion from Manchurian occupation, 297

Shantung peninsula: expeditions (1920s), 9; first intervention, 287; German bases seized, 279

Shibusawa Eiichi 渋沢栄一 (1840–1931), 72, 400, 425, 448

Shidehara diplomacy: ineffectiveness of, 298; principles of, 284–5, versus Tanaka diplomacy, 285–90

Shidehara Kijūrō 幣原喜重郎 (1972–1951), 105, 161; appointed head of postwar cabinet, 161; China policy and fall of Wakatsuki cabinet, 286; foreign policy, 284–6, 290, 292–3; military operations in Manchuria and, 296

Shigemitsu Mamoru 重光葵 (1887–1957), 376

*shihōkan* 司法官 (judicial service), 88

*shihonteki seiji minshushugi* 資本的政治民主主義 ("capitalist political democracy"), 684

Shimada Shigetarō 嶋田繁太郎 (1883– ), 335, 363

Shimazaki Shigekazu 嶋崎重和, 342

*shimin undō* 市民運動 (citizen's movement), 190

Shimizu Ikutarō 清水幾太郎 (1907– ), 740

Shimonoseki, Treaty of, 225

*shin* 真 (the true), 735

*Shin kigen* 新紀元 (*New era*; journal), 659

*shin no sei* 真の生 ("true existence"), 696

*Shin shakai* 新社会 (journal), 689

Shinagawa Yajirō 品川弥二郎 (1843–1900), 66

*shinchishiki* 新知識 ("new knowledge"), 655

*Shinchō* 新潮 (magazine), 167

Taoka Reiun 田岡嶺雲 (1870–1912), 665
tariffs, 461; campaigns, 46; decline of, in 1960s, 29; discriminatory, 468
"task" management, 628
Tatekawa Yoshitsugu 建川美次 (1880–1945), 295
tax breaks, 180
tax cuts, 201
taxation, 534–5
Taylorism, and prewar Japanese paternalism, 627–8
Tazoe Tetsuji 田添鉄二 (1873–1908), 671–2
Te 徳王 (Prince) (1902– ), 301
technical innovation, development of, 518–22
technocrats, government by, 103
technology, 507; adapted to local conditions, 418; easy transfer of, 29; introduction of foreign, 447, 520, 521
Teijin 帝人, 471
Teikoku gakushiin 帝国学士院 (Imperial Academy), 88
Teikoku jinken 帝国人絹 (company), 111
Teikoku sanshi kabushiki kaisha 帝国蚕株式会社 (Imperial Silk Filature Company), 461
Teikoku zaigō gunjinkai 帝国在郷軍人会 (Imperial Military Reservists Association), 116
*teki no naka no yūjin* 敵の中の友人 ("passing friends among the enemy"), 696
Tekkō kumiai 鉄工組合 (Metalworkers' Union), first trade union, 633
telegraph, 399
telephones, introduced (1890), 399
Temporary Capital Adjustment Law (1937), 481
Temporary Export and Import Commodities Law (1937), 481
Temporary Measure for Promotion of Machine Tool Industry (1956), 521
temporary workers, extensive use of, 629
tenancy: disputes, 597; increase of, after Meiji Restoration, 543
Tenancy Conciliation Law of 1924, 588
tenant farmers, 408; benefits to, from land reform, 171; and collective bargaining, 577; commercial farming by, 580; compared with factory workers, 587; direct attention to, 604; militancy of, and government measures, 588; and powers of attorney, 577; and status inequality, 586; unions, 555, 585
tenant movement, 555–6, 576–89; curtailment of, 589; demise of, 558; proximate causes of, 578–84; waning of, 584–9
*tenkō* 転向 ("conversion"), 474
*tennō kikan setsu* 天皇機関説 ("organ theory"), 675
*tennō taiken* 天皇大権 (imperial sovereign power), 59–60
*tenshoku* ("heavenly calling") 天職, 239
Terauchi Hisaichi 寺内寿一 (1879–1945), 345
Terauchi Masatake 寺内正毅 (1852–1919), 82–3, 85, 94, 227, 230, 234, 281; fall of government, 583
terrorism: antipolitical, 107; political, 558, 733; right-wing, by farmers, 596
*tetsujin* 哲人 ("philosopher of real life"), 763
textile industry, 423
textiles: duties lifted, 425; voluntary restrictions on exports of, 526
Thailand, 335; capitulated to Japanese, 345
"The Aims of Imperial National Defense" (Teikoku kokubō hōshin) (1907), 276
thermal power generation, 519
"tie-up finance," 123
tight money policy, 466, 509, 534
Tinian captured by U.S., 362
*Tōa ishin* 東亜維新 (restoration of Asia), 734
*Tōa kyōdōtai* 東亜協同体 ("East Asian Gemeinschaft"), 301
*Tōa shinchitsujo* 東亜新秩序 ("new order in East Asia"), 134, 301
*tōchi taiken* 統治大権 (right of sovereignty), 60
Tōgō Minoru 東郷實 (1881–1959), 240
Tōgō Shigenori 東郷茂徳 (1882–1950), 335, 337, 339, 368; urged emperor to accept Potsdam Declaration, 374
Tōjō Hideki 東條英機 (1884–1948), 143, 329, 347; domestic politics, 149–52; foreign policy, 332–3; formed new cabinet, 333; named prime minister, 149; as prime minister, 37; resigned as prime minister, 361–3; strategic